DR

# Primary Care
# Sports Medicine

# Primary Care Sports Medicine

**Douglas B. McKeag, M.D., M.S.**
Professor of Family Practice
Coordinator of Sports Medicine
College of Human Medicine
MSU Team Physician
Michigan State University

**David O. Hough, M.D.**
Professor of Family Practice
Director of Sports Medicine
College of Human Medicine
MSU Team Physician
Michigan State University

with
**Eric D. Zemper, Ph.D.,** President,
Exercise Research Associates of Oregon
Eugene, Oregon

Copyright © 1993, by Wm. C. Brown Communications, Inc.

ALL RIGHTS RESERVED.

No part of this publication may be reproduced, stored in a retrieval system, or transmitted, in any form or by any means, electronic, mechanical photocopying, recording, or otherwise, without the prior written permission of the publisher.

Library of Congress Cataloging in Publication Data:

McKeag, Douglas B., 1945 -
Hough, David O.
PRIMARY CARE SPORTS MEDICINE

Cover Design: Gary Schmitt
Executive Editor: I. L. Cooper
Production Manager: Joanne Cooper
Project Coordinator: Jan Edmondson

Library of Congress Catalog Card Number: 91-71471
ISBN: 0-697-14841-6

Printed in the United States of America by Brown & Benchmark, 2460 Kerper Boulevard, Dubuque, IA 52001.

10 9 8 7 6 5 4 3 2 1

# Contents

**Contributors** xi
**Dedication** xiii
**Preface** xv
**Foreword** xvii

## PART I: BASIC AND BEHAVIORAL SPORTS MEDICINE

**1. Primary Care Perspective** 3
   A. Philosophy of Primary Care Sports Medicine   3
   B. Sports Medicine and The Law   6
   C. Ethics and Medical Decision-Making   8
   Helpful Hints   9
   References   9
   Recommended Readings   9
   Appendix 1-1. MSU Sports Medicine Rotation   10

**2. Basic Science Review in Sports Medicine** 15
   Unit 1:  Basic Science Sports Medicine   15
      A. Exercise Physiology (Van Huss)   15
      B. Body Composition (Schafle)   27
      C. Fluids and Electrolytes (Schafle)   29
      D. Nutrition (Mutch)   31
      E. Pharmacology   43
      References   48
   Appendix 2B-1. Percent Fat Estimate for Women: Sum of Triceps, Abdomen and Suprailium Fatfolds   50
   Appendix 2B-2. Percent Fat Estimate for Men: Sum of Triceps, Chest and Subscapula Fatfolds   51
   Appendix 2B-3. Percent Fat Estimate for Women: Sum of Triceps, Suprailium and Thigh Fatfolds   52
   Appendix 2B-4. Percent Fat Estimate for Men: Sum of Chest, Abdomen, and Thigh Fatfolds   53
   Appendix 2B-5. Body Mass Index   54
   Appendix 2D-1. Complications of Hazardous Weight Loss Methods   55
   Appendix 2D-2. Sports Nutrition Myths   56
   Appendix 2E-1. ACSM Position on "Blood Doping as an Ergogenic Aid"   58

Unit 2: Epidemiology of Athletic Injuries   63
   Epidemiologic Rates   63
   Potential Uses of Sports Injury Rate Data   64
   Current Literature on Sports Injury Rates   66
   National Sports Injury Data Collection Systems   67
   Summary of Data from National Data Collection Systems   68
   Current Applications of National Sports Injury Data   70
   Local Sports Injury Data Collection   71
   Conclusion   72
   References   73

## 3. Sports Psychology for the Primary Care Physician   75
The Importance of Sports Psychology   75
Psychological Factors Involved in Performance   76
Psychological Factors in the Treatment of Injury and Pain   77
The Role of Sports Physician in Facilitating Performance   78
Role of the Sports Psychologist   79
Psychological Assessment   80
Future of the Sports Psychology Field   80
Psychological Aspects of the Young Athlete   80
Violence in Sports   82
Summary   82
References   82
Recommended Readings   82
Appendix 3-1. Important Points in Considering Scholastic Athletic Programs   84
Appendix 3-2. Bill of Rights for Athletes   86
Appendix 3-3. Parental Guide to Selecting Youth Sports Programs   87

# PART II: PREVENTIVE SPORTS MEDICINE

## 4. Preparticipation Screening   91
Initial Considerations   91
Essentials   91
Prospective Athlete   92
Contemplated Exercise Program   93
Motivation   93
Implementation   94
Frequency   94
Timing   96
Content   96
Assessment   103
Injury Prediction   105
Conclusion   105
References   105
Appendix 4-1. Task Force PPPE Form   106
Appendix 4-2. Initial PPPE Form   108
Appendix 4-3. Intercurrent PPPE Form   111

## 5. Conditioning and Training Programs for Athletes/Non-Athletes   113
A. General Principles   113
B. The Young Athlete   120
C. The Female Athlete   123

D. The Older Athlete   132
E. The Sedentary Adult   134
References   141
Suggested Readings   142
Appendix 5A-1. ACSM Position Statement on the Recommended Quantity and Quality of Exercise for Developing and Maintaining Fitness in Healthy Adults   143

## 6. Exercise and Chronic Illness   151
A. Diabetes Mellitus   151
B. Asthma   156
C. Chronic Obstructive Pulmonary Disease   158
D. Epilepsy   159
E. Congenital Heart Disease   161
F. Chronic Musculoskeletal Problems   162
G. Mental Retardation   164
H. Handicapped Athletes   165
References   168
Suggested Readings   169

## 7. Injury Prevention   171
Epidemiology of Injuries   173
Areas of Preventive Impact   175
Internal Factors — Athlete Responsibility   181
Rehabilitation   182
Summary   184
References   184
Appendix 7-1. ACSM Position Stand on Prevention of Thermal Injuries During Distance Running   185

## 8. Covering Athletic Competition   191
Role of the Coach or Trainer   191
Medical Equipment Necessary to Cover Competition   192
Physician's Role in Covering Competition   193
Summary   195
References   196
Recommended Readings   196
Appendix 8-1. The Sportsmedicine Physician's Bag   197
Appendix 8-2. The Trainer's Equipment   198

## PART III: CLINICAL SPORTS MEDICINE

## 9. Management of On-Site Emergencies   203
Severe Orthopedic Injuries   203
Intracranial Injury and Concussion   204
Cervical Spine Injuries   206
Emergency Management of Head and Neck Injuries   210
Respiratory Obstruction   210
Respiratory Failure   211
Cardiac Arrest   211
Heat Injuries   211
Prevention of Heat Injury   215
Hypothermia   215

Conclusion   218
References   218
Appendix 9-1. Pediatric Exercise Guidelines: Prevention of Heat Disorders   219
Appendix 9-2. Guidelines for Runners: Hot Weather Participation   221

## 10. Common Sports-Related Injuries and Illnesses — Generic Conditions   223
How to Use the Following Chapters (11-16)   223
Generic Conditions   223
Acute Infections   232
Chronic Illness   233
Allergies   234
References   235
Recommended Readings   235

## 11. Common Sports-Related Injuries and Illnesses — Head and Neck   237
A. Head Injuries   237
B. Face   245
C. Neck (Swenson)   249
D. Eye Injuries and Illnesses   256
E. Ears   264
F. Nose   267
G. Mouth Injuries in Sports   270
H. Throat Injuries and Illnesses   272
References   274
Suggested Readings   275
Appendix 11A-1. Checklist for Essential Support Facilities for the Sports Physician at Sports Events   277
Appendix 11A-2. Patient With A Head Injury   278
Appendix 11A-3. Rapid Neurologic Evaluation of Cranial Nerve Function   279

## 12. Common Sports-Related Injuries and Illnesses — The Upper Extremity   281
A. The Shoulder   281
B. Upper Arm   302
C. Elbow   303
D. Wrist, Hand, and Fingers   314
References   338
Appendix 12A-1. Muscular Function Testing of the Shoulder   340
Appendix 12D-1. Colles' Fracture Reduction   342

## 13. Common Sports-Related Injuries and Illnesses — Thorax & Abdomen   343
A. Chest   343
B. Cardiovascular   348
C. Pulmonary   362
D. Abdomen   367
E. Back Injuries in Sports   369
F. Genital-Urinary   380
References   391
Suggested Readings   393

## 14. Common Sports-Related Injuries and Illnesses — Pelvis and Lower Extremity   395
A. Hip and Pelvis   395
B. Upper Leg   403
C. Knee (Swenson)   406

    D. Lower Leg   424
    E. Ankle   433
    F. Feet and Toes   448
    References   464
    Suggested Readings   466
    Appendix 14C-1. Knee Examination   467
    Appendix 14E-1. Ankle Examination   468
    Appendix 14F-1. Foot Examination   469

**15. Common Sports-Related Injuries and Illnesses — Skin**    **471**
    Skin Problems in Athletics   471
    Abrasions and Friction Blisters   471
    Cold-Induced Injuries   472
    Heat-Induced Injuries   473
    Acne   475
    Skin Infections in Athletes   476
    Viral Infections   477
    Infestations   479
    Other Skin Problems in Athletics   479
    Insect Allergies and Sports   481
    References   481
    Additional Readings   482

**16. Common Sports-Related Injuries and Illnesses — Hematology, Endocrine, and Environment**    **483**
    A. Hematology   483
    B. Endocrine   487
    C. Environmental Induced Injury   487
    References   503
    Appendix 16C-1. Treatment of Hypothermia   504
    Appendix 16C-2. Rewarming Procedure   506
    Appendix 16C-3. Routine Frostbite Treatment   507
    Appendix 16C-4. Stay Warm . . . And Alive   508

**17. Radiology of Sports Injuries (Pera, Sierra, and Yee)**    **509**
    Plain Film X-ray   509
    Radionuclide Scanning   509
    Computed X-ray Tomography (CT)   509
    Magnetic Resonance Imaging (MRI)   510
    Ultrasound   510
    Fractures   510
    Head   512
    Face   513
    Neck   514
    Shoulder   516
    Elbow   518
    Wrist, Hand and Fingers   519
    Chest   523
    Abdomen   523
    Back   523
    Hip and Pelvis   524
    Knee   526
    Ankle   528
    Foot and Toes   528

Summary  534
References  535

## 18. Rehabilitation (Morgan) — 537
Introduction  537
Principles of Rehabilitation  538
Rehabilitation Protocols for Specific Athletic Injuries  554
Summary  570
Bibliography  570

## 19. Establishing A Local Sports Medicine Network — 573
Resources for the Primary Care Sports Medicine Practitioner  573
Suggestions for Assessing Sports Medicine Literature  578
References  585
Suggested Readings  585
Appendix 19-1. Sports Medicine-Related Organizations  586
Appendix 19-2. Sports Medicine Journals  587
Appendix 19-3. Institutions with Sports Medicine Fellowship Programs  588

## 20. Patient and Community Education on Physical Fitness — 589
Importance of Being Involved in Patient and Community Education  589
Raising Patient and Public Awareness  591
Motivating People to Act on Information  592
Importance of the Physician, Staff, and Office Environment in Promoting Healthy Lifestyles  594
References  594

**Index**  597

# Contributors

G. Thomas Morgan, M.D., Pikes Peak Physical Medicine; Assistant Clinical Professor, University of Colorado; Team Physician, Colorado College, Colorado Springs, Colorado. Former Sports Medicine Fellow, Michigan State University.

Barbara L. Mutch, M.D., Nutritionist, Program Leader, Michigan State University Extension, East Lansing, Michigan.

Abraham Pera, D.O., Staff Radiologist, The General Hospital, Eureka, California. Former Assistant Professor, Department of Radiology, Michigan State University.

Marie D. Schafle, M.D., Primary Care Sports Medicine Physician, Center for Sports Medicine, St. Francis Memorial Hospital; Physician for U.S. Volleyball Association and San Francisco Ballet, San Francisco, California. Former Sports Medicine Fellow, Michigan State University.

Arlene Sierra, B.S., Director, Clinical Services, Department of Radiology, Michigan State University.

E. James Swenson, J.R., M.D., Primary Care Sports Medicine, Assistant Professor of Department of Orthopedics, University of Rochester; Assistant Professor, Department of Family Practice, Highland Hospital, Rochester, New York. Former Sports Medicine Fellow, Michigan State University.

Wayne D. Van Huss, Ph.D., Professor Emeritus of Physical Education and Exercise Science. Former Director, Center for The Study of Human Performance, Michigan State University.

Harvey Yee, M.D., Staff Radiologist, Hurley Hospital, Flint, Michigan. Former Instructor, Department of Radiology, Michigan State University.

# Dedication

This book is dedicated to the most important people in our lives. For all the lost weekends, late nights, and frustrations endured during the preparation of this book, and for the constant support and love given us.

To: Di and Jill
Heather, Ian, Jeffrey, Kelly, and Kristin
(Yes, this is *the book*!)

# Preface

As the American Board of Medical Specialities (ABMS) moves to recognize those primary care physicians with special interests and expertise in the area of sports medicine, the authors wish to acknowledge that the organization of this book was set up to approximate the curriculum offered in Sports Medicine at Michigan State University. It is our hope that aside from serving as a reference text for practicing physicians and a learning instrument for students and future primary care physicians, this also becomes a study guide for the upcoming Certificate of Added Qualification (CAQ) offered by the American Boards of Family Practice, Pediatrics, Internal Medicine, and Emergency Medicine.

# Foreword

Alas, we finally come to the end of the academic road after pursuing this project for 12 years. In 1981, you could count on one hand the number of primary care sports medicine training programs in the country; and the other hand would represent the number of reasonable and useful reference texts in sports medicine. Things seemed to be a little bit simpler then, including our approach to the care of the competitive athlete. A dozen years have produced dozens of surprises and changes. This 12-year period of time has seen the proliferation of training and fellowship programs, the formalization of education in the area of primary care, and a true, measureable improvement in the quality of health care given to the recreational and competitive athlete. Primary care has taken a dominant role in this movement, a situation not ignored by the "medical establishment." The newly formed American Medical Society for Sports Medicine (AMSSM) has joined other organizations such as American Orthopedic Society for Sports Medicine (AOSSM) and the American College of Sports Medicine (ACSM) in addressing controversial, clinical concerns and providing practicing physicians with answers to difficult, thought provoking problems. The disciplines of Family Practice, Pediatrics, Internal Medicine, Emergency Medicine, and Physical Medicine and Rehabilitation have all begun to include, as part of training in their respective discipline, experiences in sports medicine.

How does one define "Sports Medicine"? We feel that this special interest area of medicine is nothing more than "medicine in motion." The physiologic intricacies of the human body become even more complex when this body is placed in motion. Yet, we are not stagnate animals. We move, we turn, we bend, we stoop, we run, we swim. With movement, we do what the human body was built to do. With movement, we enhance our lives. We feel good. We help our psyche, our lungs; but we also strain tendons, dislocate joints, stress hearts; and concuss brains. We have discovered that exercise is a double-edged sword.

We hope that this book will serve as a compendium of **how to do things right** in sports medicine. As primary care physicians, we have always felt that we brought a somewhat unique perspective to an area of medicine dominated by musculoskeletal injury. From our family practice training we have borrowed the concepts of **prevention** and **rehabilitation** and brought them to the forefront of treatment of sports-induced injury and illness. Hopefully, this book reflects that type of thinking. This book is not merely another reference text in sports medicine, but is an outline of a philosophy and a perspective. It was never meant to be a complete text, but one that would evolve constantly over time as principles of diagnosis and management change. It is our gift to those who come after us; those whose interest in sports and sports medicine can be met with a recommended, organized approach to learning the subject, something the authors and our colleagues never had.

After teaching over 500 residents and medical students the principles of sports medicine, and having the honor of training 14 incredibly competent primary care sports medicine fellows, we have begun to realize just how important this area truly is. We have always felt that you really didn't have to know the difference between a basketball and a baseball; your patients surely will. More and more of our general population continue interests in sports beyond youth in many forms of recreational activity. We must all become "team physicians" of sort to those recreational exercisers we call our patients.

It is important to acknowledge those who have helped and stimulated us to produce this text. First and foremost, Frederick Bakker-Arkema, Ph.D., Professor of Agricultural Engineering at Michigan State University, has remained an academic role model and source of encouragement for us. He was most responsible for planting the "seed" that became this text. Acknowledgement is necessary to our colleagues with whom we shared ideas and a strong sense of teaching each other: William Anderson, Ph.D., Ronnie Barnes, A.T., C., Henry Barry, M.D., John Bergfeld, M.D., Howard Brody, M.D., Vicky Curley, R.N., Brian Halpern, M.D., John Henderson, D.O., Warren Howe, M.D., Al Jacobs, D.O., Rob Johnson, M.D., Ed Kowaleski, M.D., James Kyle, M.D., John Lombardo, M.D., William Moats, M.D., Jeff Monroe, A.T., C., Sally Nogle, A.T., C., James O'Brien, M.D., Randy Pearson, M.D., James Potchen, M.D., James Puffer, M.D., Lee Rice, D.O., Lon Rosen, M.D., Herb Ross, D.O., Vern Seefeldt, Ph.D., and Carol Smookler, Ph.D.

We also want to take this opportunity to thank all of the residents, medical students, private physicians, and, most importantly, former sports medicine fellows who provided the stimulus to push on with this project: Tom Morgan, M.D., Marie Schafle, M.D., Jim Swenson, M.D., Chris McGrew, M.D., Wade Lillegard, M.D., Dave Petron, M.D., Jeff Kovan, D.O., Neil Spiegel, D.O., Dave Peck, M.D., Brent Rich, M.D., Phil Zaneteas, M.D., Scott Eathorne, M.D., Scott Naftulin, D.O., Margo Putukian, M.D. Some of their work is reflected in this text.

We would like to gratefully acknowledge the assistance and help of Bud Schultz, Anne Schultz, the Michigan State University Training Staff and Athletes for their assistance in the development of this book, its figures, and illustrations.

Appreciation also needs to go to Butch Cooper, executive editor, Jan Edmondson, project coordinator, and Virginia Cowart, copy editor, for lending assistance and "direction" for this long and winding road.

Lastly, we want to acknowledge the effort of Susan Curtis, M.A., who coordinated this project acting as typist, graphic artist, and manuscript editor for the entire text. Without question, this book is a testament to her hard work and dedication.

# PART I

# Basic and Behavioral Sports Medicine

# 1

# Primary Care Perspective

## SECTION A.
## PHILOSOPHY OF PRIMARY CARE SPORTS MEDICINE

### Justification

Despite the recent proliferation of sports medicine textbooks and information on this special interest area, we believe there is a need for a single source of appropriate and practical sports medicine information for the *primary care practitioner*, *resident*, and *medical student*.

Primary care physicians can find a dozen justifications for studying and practicing sports medicine:

- **Health care delivery in this country continues toward *community-oriented medicine*.** This trend places much of the burden of health care delivery, including sports medicine health care delivery on the shoulders of primary care practitioners.
- ***Most sources of information about sports medicine for the primary care physician remain poorly organized.*** Good, practical concepts for treating patients with athletic injuries occasionally appear in medical journals, but there is no organized approach to the subject in the form of a practical reference work.
- **Sports medicine is a *rapidly changing field*.** Technological advances have an impact on both treatment and rehabilitation. Changes in equipment, techniques, and training that allow athletes to perform better have made it difficult for practitioners, even those well-versed in sports medicine, to remain current.
- **There is a *lack of formal sports medicine education*.** Most physicians now practicing sports medicine received little, if any, formal sports medicine education either in medical school or at the post-graduate level. This has created inconsistencies in patient care. There are encouraging change. Several organizations — American College of Sports Medicine, American Academy of Family Physicians, and the American Orthopedic Society for Sports Medicine — are presenting quality post-graduate courses in sports medicine. The formation of the American Medical Society for Sports Medicine, as well as the anticipated arrival of Certificates of Added Qualifications (CAQs) in several primary care disciplines, will add professional definition to this important special interest area of sports medicine. The foundation for these changes was built by sports medicine teaching programs that established the curricula to teach. The legacy of these programs will be the definition of primary care sports medicine as a future discipline.
- **Injured athletes are not always treated in the same manner as injured non-athletes.** Time constraints, patient motivation, and accessibility to highly technical therapy modalities are factors that contribute to this dichotomy of injury care.
- **The number of sports-related injuries has increased.** Improved equipment and better supervision have reduced injury *rates* in certain organized sports settings, but the total number of sports injuries has been on the rise. Many fac-

tors contribute to this increase in injuries, including:

a. An *increase in participation*. With more people involved in sports, more will be injured.
b. The *disappearance of "natural selection"* — Most adults involved in recreational sports 25 years ago were individuals who had learned proper training techniques as youngsters. They had developed their exercise capacity over time. Today, many middle-age individuals are *beginning* to participate in exercise after 15 to 25 years of sedentary life. Their lack of knowledge or experience about appropriate training methods generates more injuries.
c. An *increased variety of sports* is available. The rising popularity of such sports as rugby, soccer, and gymnastics, and the advent of aerobics in various forms has generated a whole new subpopulation of recreational athletes.
d. Individuals have *increased opportunities* for participation. The "positive economy" of sport has provided more avenues for participation. The increase in recreational sports has created a demand for biking trails, jogging clubs, ski areas, tennis facilities, and fitness centers. This, in turn, makes participation in sports more accessible.
e. An *increased sophistication* has gradually developed along with increasing knowledge of the biomechanical aspects of sport. Researchers help players become more successful through better technical skills development. Greater sophistication can, however, lead to cheating, abuse, and the production of additional injuries.
f. An *increase in intensity* usually accompanies increases in level of play. It takes more effort to succeed; more commitment and practice time are required to train. Many athletes *specialize* at much younger ages. Early specialization can result in overuse injuries.
g. Coaching professionalism has not kept pace with the increased popularity of sports. Despite scientific revelations in training, *poor coaching and training methods* remain major factors in the generation of sports injuries.

- **The educational level of patients with sports injuries has risen.** The lay public obtains information about sports medicine from many sources, reliable and unreliable. Much information is contradictory and some is potentially harmful. Often, it is based upon studies of elite athlete, not the type of athlete seen by most primary care physicians.
- **Even those individuals with ill health or chronic disease can benefit from exercise as medical therapy.** The treatments of psychological disorders, chronic pulmonary disease, hypertension, obesity, and coronary artery disease all may include exercise as a powerful adjunct to conventional therapy.
- **Exercise has a positive affect on every major system of the body.** Recent studies have shown that it is not just the cardiovascular and musculoskeletal system that receive a protective benefit. Exercise holds the promise of decreased morbidity and mortality. Its health promotion potential is staggering.
- **Sports medicine principles can be used to benefit patients, active or otherwise, as they encounter maladies and injuries in any of their activities of daily living.** Active interest or knowledge of sports is not a requirement of an effective sports medicine practitioner; an understanding and appreciation of the effects of exercise on the human condition is.
- **There is a *lack of quality assurance* in sports medicine.** This is a *special interest area* and by no means a discipline. There are no universal minimum standards to achieve in order to become a "sports medicine practitioner". The difficulty in achieving such standards and the cooperation necessary to implement them should not be underestimated. Who is eligible and what must he/she know?
- **Sports medicine care can be an *excellent marketing tool*.** Accepting patients with sports injuries is an effective method for a practitioner to capture new patients.

Primary care residents may find that a general knowledge of sports medicine has additional advantages beyond those already cited:

1. Sports medicine training allows the resident to integrate a number of medical disciplines previously studied (e.g., cardiology, physiology, nutrition, orthopedics).
2. The experience of a formal sports medicine rotation gives residents an opportunity to place appropriate primary care emphasis on areas traditionally thought of as secondary or tertiary care (see Appendix 1-1). Many concepts of of-

fice orthopedics either are absent or not emphasized during general orthopedic rotations.
3. A formal background in sports medicine training can be a definite asset in gaining rapid entrance into a community.
4. New physicians with a sports medicine interest and background are perceived as more current, knowledgeable, and interested in community affairs. They may be asked to make presentations on exercise and sports to lay groups. They may be asked to serve on committees to establish guidelines for the conduct of community sports programs (see Chapter 20). The list of potential opportunities is exhaustive.

It is the authors' conclusion that medical students today realize the value of exercise in their own lives. We have discovered a profound interest in the area of sports medicine as early as the first quarter of the first year of medical school in a class we teach entitled "Introduction to Sports Medicine". Many medical students come from disciplines that have begun to embrace sports medicine (e.g., kinesiology, nutrition, psychology). It is unfortunate that medical school curricula do not change as readily as society. As has been the case with nutrition, the importance of sports medicine has been overlooked in most medical school curricula. Our experience tells us that because of its interdisciplinary nature, sports medicine offers a natural integrative bridge between disciplines. Where else can the integration of the basic sciences (e.g., physiology, pharmacology) be so naturally incorporated into such clinically related fields as cardiology and orthopedics? Furthermore, psychosocial sciences such as biomedical ethics and psychology also assimilate well. Because of its popularity and preventive medicine aspects, sports medicine becomes a natural common pathway for medical school curricular integration.

## Interdisciplinary Approach to Sports Medicine

As we have said, sports medicine draws upon and integrates a variety of disciplines. But what of the *approach* to sports medicine? It is important to state that this book deals specifically with the primary care perspective of sports medicine. In our view, the first-contact, comprehensive, continuing care given by most primary care physicians to athletes is sports medicine. The primary physician as *gatekeeper* in an ever evolving well-defined athlete health care system is a philosophy underlying the organization of this book.

Is there an overemphasis on the musculoskeletal injury in the athlete? When people think of sports medicine, do they really mean sports orthopedics? When the public thinks of a sports medicine "specialist," are they really thinking orthopedic surgeon? Orthopedic surgeons have done much to advance and upgrade the care of musculoskeletal injuries in the athlete. Their contributions include: 1) arthroscopic surgery (e.g., knee, ankle, shoulder, elbow); 2) adaptation of conservative approaches to previously operable injuries (e.g., severe ankle sprains, third degree ligament tears); 3) further definition of many subtle yet common syndromes (e.g., patellofemoral dysfunction, shoulder impingement, cervical stenosis), and 4) delineation of more appropriate diagnostic testing to examine the musculoskeletal system (e.g., Lachman's test, lateral pivotal shift). Certainly musculoskeletal injuries require a great deal of emphasis in the study of sports medicine. They account for 84% of all sports related injuries (NEISS, 1981).

However, other disciplines also have contributed. *Physical rehabilitation* and *athletic training* are areas where new modalities have been discovered and new treatment regimens generated. More sharply defined rehabilitation programs for specific injuries have evolved. The principles of biomechanics have been applied to injury definition and subsequently to the rehabilitative process. Emphasis now is on rehabilitation of specific muscles or muscle groups. This has produced specific techniques that allow athletes to return to play more quickly than ever before.

*Cardiology* has made its contributions to sports medicine. Cardiologists first recognized the importance of physical activity as therapy to improve cardiac function. What began as scientifically documented improvement after myocardial insult has evolved into sophisticated rehabilitative programs following coronary artery bypass and cardiac surgery. The need for a defined cardiac rehabilitation program first spurred the effort for exercise physiology. The guidelines of such programs have been applied with modification to the healthy population.

*Physiology* has long studied the effects of exercise on various body systems, describing what exercise can and cannot do (see Chapter 2). This basic science has defined the various types of exercise that we do, what is appropriate, in what circumstances, and what specific biologic changes take place that are exercise dependent. The definition of minimal exercise requirements has been of major importance because it gives the lay public an opportunity to use guidelines that are applicable on an everyday basis.

*Nutrition* as an applied science has contributed much to the understanding of sports and performance. These contributions include: 1) the realization that diet does affect performance; 2) the further realization that manipulation of diet can improve performance; 3) the delineation of the nutritional costs of exercise, and 4) the role of various nutrients, minerals, and fluids in exercise performance.

*Psychology* as an applied behavioral science has just begun to examine how the mind can interact with the exercising body (see Chapter 3). The realization that exercising individuals have an enhanced sense of well-being has led to the use of exercise as therapy for many psychiatric disturbances. The fascinating research on the effect of competition on an individual's mental outlook remains an area of specific interest. Future work may show that psychological well-being is a major predictor of athletic performance.

Many other disciplines are involved, including pharmacology (the appropriate and inappropriate use of drugs by athletes), optometry (the prevention of eye injuries), and podiatry (studies of the interface between foot and running surface).

Musculoskeletal injury remains the single most important type of injury to concern the sports medicine physician even though it is no longer the only system. It is safe to say that every body system can and has been affected by exercise or exercise-induced injury or illness. Each has been shown to benefit from exercise. Each can be adversely affected by it.

An important concept needs to be emphasized — the athlete is not merely a moveable bony skeleton upon which musculotendinous units are draped. Every sports injury is not an orthopedic injury. The athlete is a human being with multiple systems, each capable of reacting to movement. Precisely for this reason, the athlete or exerciser should receive the type of comprehensive care that only the primary care physician can and should give. The entire person, not just the body part or system, should be considered.

This book advocates an interdisciplinary approach to sports medicine. The authors believe strongly that a comprehensive continuing care approach to the athlete can only be directed by the primary care specialist, usually a family physician, internist, or pediatrician. The primary care practitioner should then gather a cadre of additional specialists (e.g., athletic trainer, physical therapist, nutritionist, or podiatrist) to complete creation of the sports medicine network.

## SECTION B.
## SPORTS MEDICINE AND THE LAW

As our society becomes more litigious, the medical/legal aspects of sports medicine take on increasing importance. A fair question to ask might be: Is there truly any difference in risk between serving the athletic population and the non-athletic population? The answer is yes. At this time, the risk is not significant in the context of all sports-related lawsuits. Most often local boards of education, coaches, and equipment manufacturers are the target of sports injury lawsuits. Physicians have been remarkably free of involvement in such actions but this should not lull the practitioner into a false sense of security. There is a trend in the opposite direction. As sports medicine becomes a more recognized special interest area, it is only natural that all its practitioners will be held to higher medical standards commensurate with the increased duties and responsibilities they have assumed. A summary of important areas of medical/legal interaction in sports medicine includes the following:

### Negligence

Team physicians must treat athletes the same as other patients. It is immaterial whether care is provided for a fee or for free. Furthermore, the statute of limitations is no safeguard, as a suit can be withheld until a young athlete reaches maturity. Tort liability is the prevalent concept. This is liability for personal injury that is alleged to be the result of the defendant's negligence. Because negligence is the principal charge, its definition is of interest: "failure to act as a prudent physician would under similar circumstances." Generally speaking, four elements must be present to prove negligence —

1. the physician had a duty to act to avoid unreasonable risk to others,

2. the defendant failed to observe that duty,
3. failure to observe that duty was the proximate cause of damage, and
4. actual damage or injury did occur.

The "standard of care" concept is applied to most of these situations. For a primary care practitioner, the standard of care incorporates what would normally be done by a primary care specialist in this locale, in this situation.

Legal defenses in this case usually encompass one or two strategies: *Assumption of Risk* — In other words, the athlete assumed a certain degree of risk with his or her participation in the activity, or *Contributory Negligence* — The athlete in question was participating in a reckless or negligent manner.

## Avoiding Lawsuits

The risk of litigation over medical treatment of athletes can be reduced if sports physicians are guided by the following:

1. follow established guidelines (that you may have helped formulate);
2. generate a written contract with the school or group with which you are working;
3. if at all possible, work with athletic trainers;
4. generate a thorough preparticipation sports physical examination;
5. always use sound judgement concerning return to competition;
6. institute early, proper care;
7. seek informed consent for treatment, and
8. be careful with release of information.

Make sure to follow standard procedures and established methods in the treatment of injuries. The playing field and/or lockerroom is no place for experimentation. Reserve the right to await developments before making a final judgment about any injury.

The contract with the sponsoring organization should be an agreement spelling out the responsibilities and limits of the team physician. The agreement should show that the team physician has final word in all medical decisions, including return to participation after injury or illness. Encourage communication by meeting with parents, athletes, and coaches prior to the start of each season to discuss how injuries will be handled and what the line of authority will be. At such meetings, indicate your plans for reducing the incidence of injuries.

Obtaining the services of an athletic trainer is an important step in establishing a comprehensive sports medicine network. The athletic trainer is a very important member of the community sports medicine "team" and should act as the on-site coordinator for all sports medicine activities, and as a liaison between team physician, athlete, and/or school officials. Athletic trainers should be responsible for the initial treatment and early triage of the injury. They should be responsible also for the implementation of injury prevention programs.

The importance of the preparticipation exam is underlined by its function not only as a screening examination but as a base of referral (see Chapter 4). It is important to avoid statements, either written or verbal, that say: *"It is safe for _____ to participate in _____."* More appropriate terminology might be: *"I can find no medical reason why _____ should not participate in _____."* In event of a disqualification, it is important to remember that even if parents wish to give permission for the disqualified athlete to participate, the law gives parents no authority to release future claims on behalf of the child.

It should be standard policy that all injuries are reported to the team physician and that no return to play should occur until assessment is complete (see Chapter 8). A sound judgement will incorporate both the physician's clinical impression of the seriousness of the injury and the trainer's impression of how it occurred and how well the athlete has progressed in rehabilitation.

It is important to institute early proper care (see Chapter 9). Because it is impractical for most physicians to be in attendance at practices, early institution of proper care should, by necessity, fall into the hands of the athletic trainer or other capable personnel. It is important to arrange for availability of medical coverage during practices and competition and to make sure transportation from sites of participation is practical in the event of serious injury (see Chapter 19). The physician should instruct athletic trainers and other personnel in the proper use of the stretcher or other means of emergency transport.

The principle of *informed consent* is especially important in the treatment of athletic injuries. Injuries should be explained and proposed treatment options discussed with the athlete and parents (if appropriate). Good records should be maintained as to what was said and decided. Treatment should not end prematurely because of a desire to return an athlete to play.

The doctor/patient relationship has been and continues to be a foundation for all of medicine. This is no different in treating athletes. Such a relationship should be confidential. Barring specific permission from the athlete, no part of the written medical record or verbal impressions of an injury should be disclosed to other interested parties. Of particular concern to the team physician is the relationship between himself and the athlete's primary care physician, if one has been identified. From a professional standpoint, communication and consultation should also involve this colleague.

Team physicians should provide athletic trainers with ongoing medical updates and evaluation to ensure against negligence on the part of the trainer. They also should familiarize themselves with the safety limits of equipment to be used by athletes in the sports to be covered.

## SECTION C.
## ETHICS AND MEDICAL DECISION-MAKING

Sports medicine, like any other special interest area (e.g., prison, occupational, military medicine), is subject to patient care problems that require ethical analysis for rational solution. These can be called conflict of interest or divided loyalty dilemmas (Murray, 1984). Such dilemmas result from being situated between two or more parties, each evoking a strong sense of commitment and duty from the care provider. Such conflicts may differ, depending upon the level of sport covered (professional, college, high school, or youth programs), but remain a continuing problem and major factor in medical decision-making in sports.

Just what are these conflicts? (McKeag, 1984)

1. *Role of team physician vs role of fan* — The fact remains that most sports physicians are involved because they are fans. At times this can create a conflict of interest in the treatment of injury and judgment concerning return to play. Obviously, the role of the fan/booster must be subservient to the role of team physician.
2. *Welfare of the athlete vs welfare of the team* — This is probably the most common dilemma occurring at all levels. It becomes more of a conflict as the pressure to win takes priority over medical values in a program. Established return to play criteria can help tremendously.
3. *Welfare of the athlete vs wishes of the athlete* — The principle that should prevail in confronting this problem is — "Physician, do no harm." The team physician must think about long-term harm vs short-term benefit. Is the athlete making this decision in the presence of coercion, either overt or covert? Is the athlete old enough to fully consider the ramifications of his/her actions?
4. *Welfare of the athlete vs welfare of the family* — Occasionally (though not often) the wishes of an athlete's family unit conflict with the long-term welfare of the athlete.

How does one minimize such divided loyalty dilemmas? It is important to avoid ambiguity and that can be achieved as follows:

1. Clarify the nature of the relationship between you and other parties at the outset (e.g., coaches, parents, athletes, school administrators, team owners).
2. Insist upon professional autonomy over all medical decisions.
3. Anticipate, identify, then insulate yourself formally from all possible coercive pressures to ensure such autonomy.
4. Communicate those principles and guidelines under which you intend to deliver care and make decisions *before* becoming the care provider.
5. Eliminate, or at least recognize and minimize any personal biases you may have that might adversely affect your function as team physician.

Lastly, it is important to realize that adroit initial handling of a potential problem can eliminate later, more complicated conflicts of interest. With the onset of any injury:

1. Remove the athlete from the field/court of play to a quieter environment.
2. Carry out an unhurried, thorough examination.
3. Decide whether return to play is possible, considering potential further risk of injury. If the decision concerning return to play is *no*, inform the coach of your decision. If the decision is *yes*, follow steps a-e.
   a. Discuss return to play with the athlete only, exclusive of others.
   b. In the case of the young athlete, insist on discussion to clarify the athlete's wishes, then

confer where appropriate with other family members.
c. Any doubts expressed by the athlete about return to play should strongly bias the physician toward elimination of the athlete from further play in that contest.
d. Act as the athlete advocate when dealing with the coach concerning a decision not to play.
e. Be very clear on the limits of your responsibility as team physician. If a physician concludes that an athlete can return to play, but at a diminished level of performance, it becomes the coach's decision as to whether or not the athlete is more valuable than a healthy backup.

## HELPFUL HINTS

Finally, consider the following list *prior* to becoming or agreeing to become team physician. While these are recommendations only, the authors feel they may help in putting your participation as team physician in perspective.

- Do you have current training in CPR (BCLS)?
- Do you know how to manage an acutely traumatized athlete with an injury to the head, neck or back?
- Will your malpractice insurance extend to sports medicine?
- Does the team or program sponsoring the activity you are covering have liability insurance to cover a team physician?
- Are the athletes to be covered provided with a consent form for treatment of non-emergency injuries?
- Are you comfortable with your knowledge base concerning reentry into a sporting event following injury?
- Can you recognize your own limitations and call in other specialists when necessary?

**REFERENCES**

McKeag, D.B., Brody, H., Hough, D.O. Medical Ethics in Sport. *Phys and Sportsmed* 12(8):145, 1984.
Murray, T.H. Divided loyalities in sports medicine. *Phys and Sportsmed* 12(8):134, 1984.
National Electronic Injury Surveillance System (NEISS), U.S. Consumer Product Safety Commission/EPHA, 1981.

**RECOMMENDED READINGS**

*Section B. Sports Medicine and the Law*

Hurt, W.T. Elements of tort liability as applied to athletic injuries. *JSchoolHealth* XLVI(4):200, 1976.
Lowell, C.H. Legal responsibilities and sportsmedicine. *Phys and Sportsmed* 5(7):60, 1977.
Weistant J.C., Lowell C.H.: *The Law of Sports*. Charlottesville, Virginia, Merril, 1979.
Willis, G.C. The legal responsibilities of the team physician. *J of Sports Med*:28, Sept-Oct, 1972.

*Section C. Ethics and Medical Decision-Making*

Proceedings of "Ethics in Sports Medicine" Symposium. University of Connecticut, Hartford, May 1986.
Steingard, P., Sekerak, N., Erickson, K. Legal, moral, and ethical questions in sports medicine, a round table. *Phys and Sportsmed* 3(3):71, 1975.

# Appendix 1-1.
# MSU Sports Medicine Rotation

Curricular Content of Athletic Medicine Rotation in Family Practice

SECTION I  *Philosophy of Sport — Social and Behavioral Science*
- A. History of sports medicine
- B. Sports medicine as practiced elsewhere in the world (concentration on Western and Eastern Europe)
- C. Integration of family practice philosophy into sport
- D. Ethics of primary care in sports medicine
- E. Psychology of sport
- F. Sports economics
- G. Social issues
- H. Interaction with other allied health professionals — roles on health care team
- I. Medical-legal issues

SECTION II  *Basic Science of Sport*
- A. Exercise physiology
- B. Biomechanics and kinesiology
- C. Pharmacology of sport
- D. Anatomy
- E. Nutrition

SECTION III  *Health Promotion Aspects of Sport — Preventive Sports Medicine*
- A. Preparticipation evaluation — age and sport specific
- B. Conditioning and training techniques
- C. Exercise prescription
    1. age related
    2. chronic illness
    3. handicapped
    4. cardiac rehabilitation
    5. community care
- D. Establishing a sports medicine network
- E. Injury prediction — by examination and testing
- F. Epidemiology of exercise and injury
- G. Injury prevention — pre-competition
    1. equipment
    2. taping techniques
    3. coaching techniques
    4. sport environment — facilities, rules, etc.

SECTION IV  *Clinical Science — Patient Care Aspects*
- A. Field supervision of athletes
- B. Emergency assessment and case of acutely injured athlete — including transportation of patient

C. Diagnosis and treatment — organ-system approach
D. Medical management of common sports injuries
E. Rehabilitation of ill and injured athlete
F. Exercise as treatment — physical and psychological problems
G. Medical care considerations for special athlete groups
   1. prepubescent
   2. female
   3. geriatric
   4. impaired
   5. recreational
H. Medical equipment and supplies for covering competition
I. Medical decision making for primary care physician
   1. use of consultants
   2. interaction with athlete, coach, parents, significant others

SECTION V  *Research in Sports Medicine*

A. Critical Assessment of literature
B. Research methology
C. Preparation and presentation of research by resident


MINIMAL COMPETENCIES REQUIRED FOR
SPORTS MEDICINE PRIMARY CARE RESIDENTS

SECTION I  PHILOSOPHY OF SPORT

- The resident will explain the Family Practice philosophy of sports medicine (which emphasizes prevention and rehabilitation of sports injuries) in relation to the orthopedic philosophy (which emphasizes the treatment of sports injuries).
- With regard to ethics in sport, the resident will make decisions in terms of patient or medical concerns rather than game or even related concerns.
- The resident will recognize those occasions and situations in both community and practice settings when he should refer patients to other health care professionals (trainers, nurses, consultants, others) for treatment.
- The resident will recognize those occasions and situations in both community and practice settings in which he should request information and/or assistance from other health care professionals in the overall treatment of the athlete.
- The resident will employ the "educational pathway" inherent in the Family Practice philosophy:

  —observe the athlete when healthy
  —observe the athlete being injured
  —observe the biomechanical mechanism of the injury
  —observe the role of the trainer in immediate treatment of the athlete after the injury
  —observe transportation of the acutely injured athlete
  —receive verification of diagnosis from team physician
  —discuss injury with team physicians, trainers and other residents
  —follow injured athlete through treatment and definitive procedures (eg. arthroscopy, surgery)
  —follow the patient through rehabilitation
  —determine when the athlete will return to action

- The resident will determine the psychological motivation for individual atheltes who participate in various sports (eg. weight loss, professional career, pure enjoyment, etc.)
- The resident will ask questions, take a history

and prescribe treatment appropriate to the psychological motivation of the athlete.
- The resident will counsel the athlete with regard to his/her psychological state.

SECTION II  BASIC SCIENCE OF SPORT

- The resident will list and classify the various sources (eg., texts, journals, papers, consultants) to which he should refer for any problem in sports medicine basic science.
- The resident will take an accurate and complete biomedical history of an injury.
- The resident will recall pertinent anatomical and kinesiological information (eg. muscle groups, attachments, functions, etc.) for treating a specific injury.
- With regard to medication, the resident will distinguish appropriate treatment plans for both high school and college athletes.
- With regard to a particular injury, the resident will correctly assess the value of the following drug groups:
    —NSAID
    —Analgesics
    —Cortical steroids
- The resident will determine:
    —which drug to use
    —when to use it
    —appropriate dosage
    —duration of prescription
    —side effects
- The resident will list the proper medications with which to equip his bag for on-site event coverage.
- The resident will devise appropriate treatment plans for athletes with common illnesses.
- The resident will list current dietary fads engaged in by the athlete.
- The resident will counsel athletes with regard to the dietary fads listed above.
- The resident will list and describe exercise physiology concepts and effects on the human body.

SECTION III  PREVENTIVE SPORTS MEDICINE

- The resident will conduct an appropriate age-specific but non-sports-specific pre-participation physical exam.
- The resident will discriminate between appropriate conditioning and training techniques for various sports.
- The resident will discriminate between proper *coaching* techniques and those improper techniques which can result in unnecessary injury.
- The resident will use the information from above as a diagnostic tool in explaining injuries.
- The resident will prescribe appropriate exercise for athletes according to the following:
    —age of athlete
    —presence of chronic illnesses
    —physical impairments
    —rehabilitation from illness
    —rehabilitation from injury
- The resident will design the establishment of a community-based sports medicine network. The design will include the appropriate allied health professionals.
- The resident will identify the common injuries seen in the sports being dealt with in the rotation.
- The resident will describe the appropriate treatments for the injuries identified above.
- The resident will identify the appropriate injury-preventing protective equipment for the sports being dealt with during the rotation.
- The resident will describe the proper use of the equipment listed above.
- The resident will properly apply the basket weave ankle strapping.
- As a pre-competition injury prevention technique, the resident will evaluate the sports environment to determine unnecessary potential hazards to the athlete.

SECTION IV  PATIENT CARE ASPECTS

- The resident will list his duties and responsibilities on the sidelines at on-site event coverage. At a minimum, the list will include:
    —a description of the relationship between the resident and the coach
    —what must be carried in the resident's bag
    —what must be carried on the resident's person
- As occasions arise, the resident will properly perform the following sports medicine techniques:
    —emergency care of the injured athlete
    —diagnostic screening of the athlete while s/he is on the field
    —transportation of the injured athlete
- The resident will correctly diagnose and appro-

priately treat sports injuries in the following settings:
- —acute injuries seen at the informal clinic
- —chronic injuries seen at the informal clinic
- The resident will design and prescribe an appropriate program of rehabilitation for an ill or injured athlete.
- The resident will identify and describe medical care considerations for special athlete groups.
- The resident will list the supplies and equipment that the school or community should furnish for athletic competition.
- The resident will recognize when to use and what kind of consultant to use in medical decision-making.
- The resident will determine when to interact with coaches, parents and significant others in medical decision-making.
- The resident will perform the following physical examinations and arrive at correct differential diagnoses:
    - —knee
    - —ankle
    - —shoulder
    - —neck
    - —head
- The resident will appropriately prescribe the following treatment modalities:
    - —cybex
    - —TNS units
    - —orthotron
    - —cold pressure boot
    - —paraffin baths
    - —medcason
    - —ice
    - —heat
    - —EMS units
    - —pressure wraps
    - —taping
    - —protective padding
    - —stretching (for warming up)
    - —orthoplast splints
- The resident will describe and explain the concept of the overuse syndrome.
- The resident will diagnose symptoms of the overuse syndrome for the sports being dealt with during the rotation.
- The resident will properly treat the symptoms of the overuse syndrome.

SECTION V   RESEARCH IN SPORTS MEDICINE

- The resident will identify the major sports medicine journals.
- The resident will indicate the emphasis of the major sports medicine journals.
- The resident will discriminate between opinion and fact in the sports medicine literature (journals, books, papers, etc).
- The resident will actively seek new information from journals, books, papers, etc in a sports medicine area of personal concern.
- The resident will describe strategies for researching topics of personal concern in the sports medicine literature.
- The resident will read widely to extend and enrich his/her knowledge in a sports medicine area of personal concern.
- The resident will cite the paucity/abundance of literature in a sports medicine area of personal concern.
- The resident will write a research paper or a literature review in an area of personal concern.

# 2

# Basic Science Review in Sports Medicine

## Unit 1: Basic Science Sports Medicine

### SECTION A.
### EXERCISE PHYSIOLOGY

This section is intended to provide a brief overview of exercise physiology for readers with a sound background in basic physiology. The sports medicine practitioner may wish it to serve as a partial basis for the further development of experimental models, concepts and applications. As one attempts to apply the information presented here, it is important to realize that the research base of exercise and sport training is still in its formative stages. This application is similar to other medical areas in which the research base is inadequate for simple direct applications. Successful clinical applications of exercise physiology still require art to a high degree. This section should be read in that light.

Work is classified as requiring aerobic capacity, anaerobic capacity, or some combination of the two. Aerobic capacity by definition is the maximal amount of oxygen per unit of body weight that can be consumed per minute during exercise. Several terms are synonymous with aerobic capacity, including $VO_2max$, maximal oxygen consumption, or aerobic power. The biochemistry involved in energy production from glucose, fatty acids, and amino acids can be seen in Table 2A-1 (Brooks, 1984; Newsholme, 1977; Noble, 1986). Aerobic ca-

Table 2A-1. Three Systems for Supplying Energy (ATP) to the Muscle

|  | *Immediate* (<30 sec) | — ATP-CP Stores |
|---|---|---|
| Anaerobic Energy Systems | *Short Term* (<90 sec) | — Anaerobic Glycolysis |
| Aerobic Energy Systems | *Long Term* (>3 min) | — Breakdown of Carbohydrates, Fats and Proteins through the TCA Cycle |

pacity has received a great deal of attention since it clearly relates to health and is the type of fitness required for extended work performance.

Anaerobic capacity, on the other hand, represents the maximal ability of systems to produce energy without the utilization of additional oxygen. The anaerobic systems involve: (1) the high energy phosphate bonds contained in the creatine phosphate (CP) and adenosine triphosphate (ATP) present in the muscle, and (2) the lactic acid levels resulting from anaerobic glycolysis.

An understanding of aerobic and anaerobic capacities is a reasonable starting point to understand training adaptations and techniques for acquiring specific adaptations. At the outset, it should be recognized that exercise physiology is infinitely complex.

## Specificity of Fitnesses

Sports medicine practitioners often are called upon to interpret exercise test results for athletes. The process is quite different from interpreting similar test results from a health perspective. Anyone who works with athletes recognizes that very specific fitnesses are found in different types of athletes (Van Huss, 1977).

Exercise is not a single entity but a sequence of specific adaptations, with different anatomical-physiological bases resulting in significantly different responses. Ultimately we may have an encyclopedia of exercise comparable with what the pharmacopeia is to pharmacists. Unfortunately, sufficient information to allow such a compilation is not available yet. In our work at Michigan State, we have tried to develop a model that provides greater understanding of the specific levels or types of fitness Table 2A-2 (Van Huss, 1977). We have studied the characteristics of high performance athletes at five levels of fitness that were readily identifiable from energy metabolism responses. It should be noted that there may be many additional levels or types of fitness between those levels we have identified. However, we do not have sufficient data to identify them now. Further, in this work we have confined our data to runners and swimmers because these activities are "purer". Clearly there are specific fitnesses relevant to ice hockey, basketball, handball, etc., that we are not able to quantify at this time.

Another limitation to the continuum presented is that we are not yet able to adequately quantify, evaluate, or explain the lactate levels produced during various exercise regimens. Where the measures are pure, we have attempted to list values. Where the types of fitness and the values are less pure, as in ice hockey, basketball, or soccer, for example, it is far more difficult to identify the specific fitness so as to be able to identify the specific overload(s) required to bring about the desired changes.

The data in Table 2A-2 were derived from the relevant literature and from the testing of high level performers with very specific adaptations. In Level 1, of eight seconds duration or less, the subject does not breath. The Valsalva maneuver with

**Table 2A-2. The Characteristics of Five Specific Fitnesses***

| | Level 1 | Level 2 | Level 3 | Level 4 | Level 5 |
|---|---|---|---|---|---|
| Approximate time of maximum performance (min., sec.) | 0-0:8 | 0:12-0:30 | 0:30-1:30 | 3:00-7:00 | 20:00-240:00 |
| Event | | | | | |
| Runners | 60 yards | 200 meters | 400 meters | 1,500 meters | Marathon |
| Swimmers | — | 50 meters | 100 meters | 400 meters | 10,000 meters |
| Energy metabolism | | | | | |
| Oxygen intake | None | Low | Low-moderate | High | High |
| Oxygen debt | Low | Moderate | High | High | Low |
| Arterial lactate | Low | Moderate | High | High | Low |
| Relative contribution of major energy sources for muscular contraction | | | | | |
| Endogenous ATP and CP** | High | Moderate | Moderate | Low | Very low |
| Muscle glycogen | Low | High | High | High | Low |
| Blood Glucose | None | None-very low | Low | Moderate | Moderate |
| Free fatty acids | None | None | Very low | Low-moderate | High |
| Approximate percentages of muscle fiber types | 10-25 ST** | 25 ST | 30 ST | 57 ST | 80 ST |
| | 75-90 FT** | 75 FT | 70 FT | 43 FT | 20 FT |
| Nutritional recommendations for enhanced performance | | | CHO | CHO | CHO |

*Examples drawn from the data of high-performance athletes.
**ATP = adenosine triphosphate, CP = creatine phosphate, ST = "red" slow-twitch fibers, FT = "white" fast-twitch fibers, CHO = carbohydrate.

the setting of the abdominal and thoracic musculature is a necessity for the application of maximal force and, thus, achievement of maximal performance. The oxygen debt is 2 to 3 liters at most, with little or no rise in arterial lactate. The source of energy is the high energy phosphate bonds of ATP and CP (Ceretelli, 1974). The muscle fiber type being recruited is primarily the fast twitch (white, FT).

For level 2, with performance durations of 12 to 30 seconds, the subject breathes minimally in very short gasps. Thus the oxygen intake is very low, the gross oxygen debt is moderate (6-12 L), and the lactate levels are only moderate (3-10 mMol). The energy sources include the breakdown of glycogen and the endogenous high energy phosphate bonds found in ATP and CP. It is highly unlikely that blood glucose is utilized. The muscle fiber composition of high level performers is approximately 75% fast twitch (Costill, 1976; Fink, 1977).

In level 3, greater depletion of the high energy phosphate bonds and glycogen takes place. Tolerance to a high gross oxygen debt (18-26 L) and high lactate levels (22-28 mMol) is a necessity for outstanding level 3 performance.

For outstanding level 4 performance, the athlete must have both a very high oxygen intake capacity during the work and a high oxygen debt and lactate tolerance. It is highly likely that a greater proportion of the energy is being derived from glycogen and blood glucose. The muscle fiber composition of the working muscles for this type of performance has been reported as 57% slow twitch (Costill, 1976; Fink, 1977).

Level 5 differs markedly from the other levels. Also, we know there are levels between 4 and 5 but they cannot be clearly identified at this time. Performances that last more than 20 minutes require a high steady-state oxygen intake. Most performers have relatively low oxygen-debt capacities (about 8-14 L) and show relatively low lactate levels (6-12 mMol). Energy is derived primarily from the free fatty acids, with some carbohydrate from glycogen and blood glucose. The muscle fiber composition of the working muscles of these performers is about 80% slow twitch (Costill, 1976; Fink, 1977). It is interesting that performance times are related to the pre-run muscle glycogen levels even though the primary fuel is of lipid origin. Carbohydrate stores are limited and can be depleted. When this occurs, the rate of work, and thus performance time, drops off markedly. Herein lies the basis for *carbohydrate loading*.

The exercise continuum shows the relationship between events of different durations, the energy metabolism, substrates used for energy, and muscle fiber populations. It is evident that the adaptations at each level are unique to that type of fitness.

Test interpretations related to performance may be vastly different. To emphasize this important point, two series of data are presented. The first is selected treadmill test data for three outstanding athletes tested in our laboratory, a 2:12 marathoner, a Canadian national 400-meter-run champion (<46 sec), and an outstanding intramural athlete. The athletes were tested on three different treadmill runs: (a) a six mi/hr, zero grade run for five minutes to evaluate work economy (Figure 2A-1); (b) a modified Taylor-Henschel protocol to measure the maximal oxygen consumption (Figure 2A-2)[1], and (c) an all-out run at a high intensity workload (Figure 2A-3). The pulse rates are plotted on each graph and the relevant exercise and recovery oxygen values are presented. The athletes are identified only as A, B, and C. It is an interesting exercise to attempt to identify them from their physiologic responses to the different test protocols.

Note that subject B ran most economically, had by far the highest VO$_2$max, and performed second best on the all-out run. Subject A had the second best economy, about the same VO$_2$max as subject C, but was able to work much longer than subject C on the maximal oxygen consumption test protocol. He had the poorest performance on the all-out run. Subject C ran least economically, performed poorest on the maximal oxygen consumption test, yet he performed best on the all-out run, with a recovery oxygen capacity almost double the values obtained by the other two athletes.

Differentiating the athletes is not difficult after one has knowledge of the specific fitnesses. Subject B was the marathoner, Subject C was the national champion quarter miler, and Subject A was the outstanding intramural athlete.

It should be noted that in Figure 2A-1 (the economy run), the most aerobic subject performed most economically. Often tests of standard work utilize a 30 sec pulse count as a test score to evaluate performance on that test. On the pulse rate

---

[1] In this protocol, following five minutes of warm-up, the subject runs at 7 min/hr with the treadmill grade increased 2½ percent every two minutes. The test continues to exhaustion.

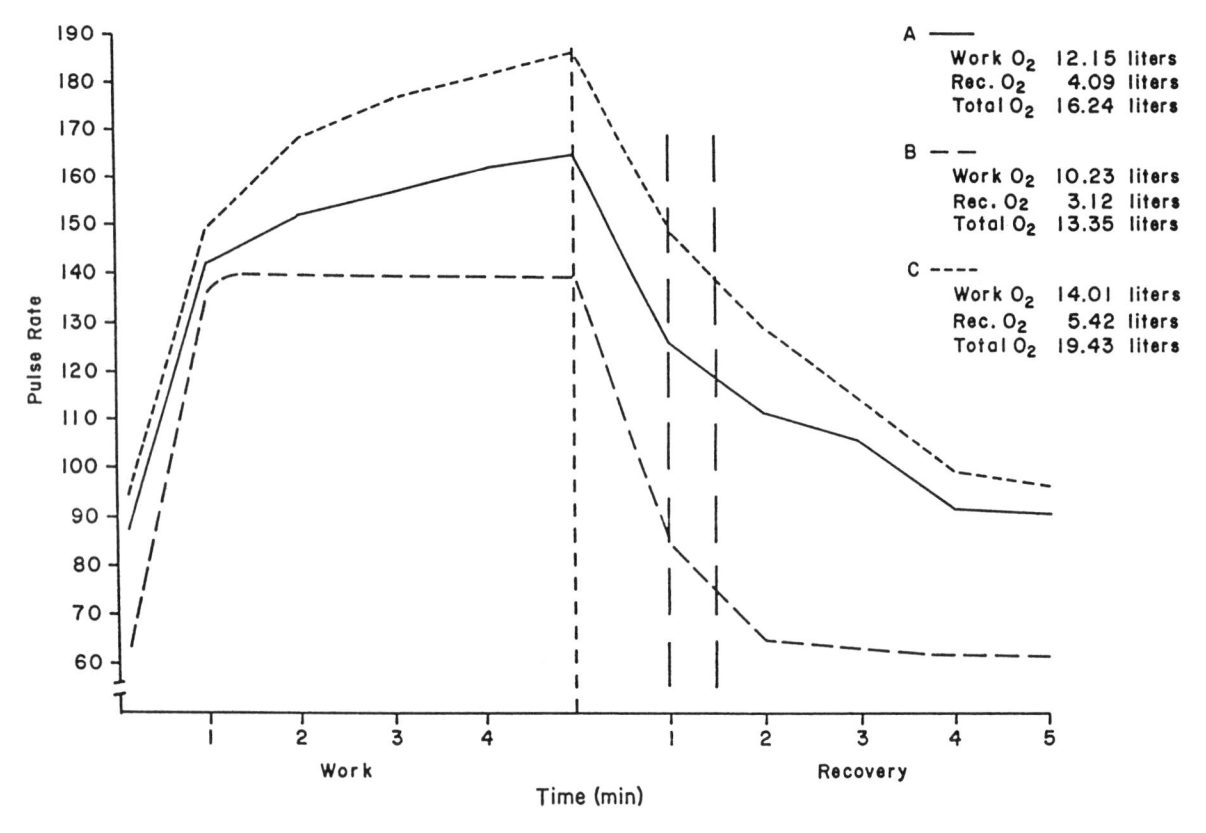

**Fig. 2A-1.** Standard Run

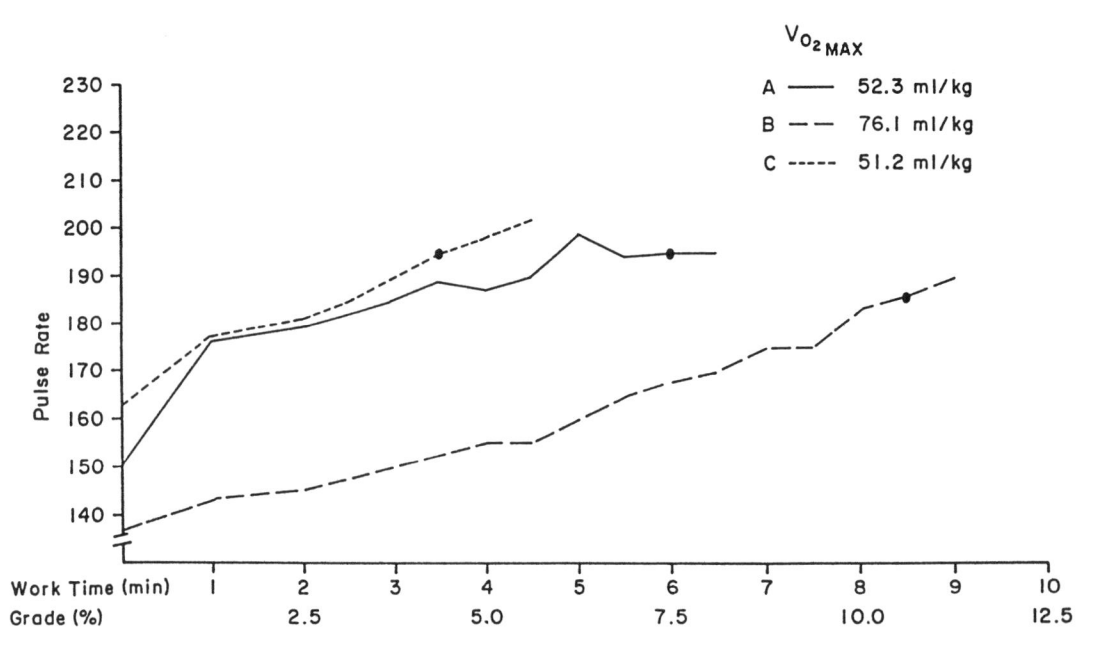

**Fig. 2A-2.** Pulse Rates

18  *BASIC AND BEHAVIORAL SPORTS MEDICINE*

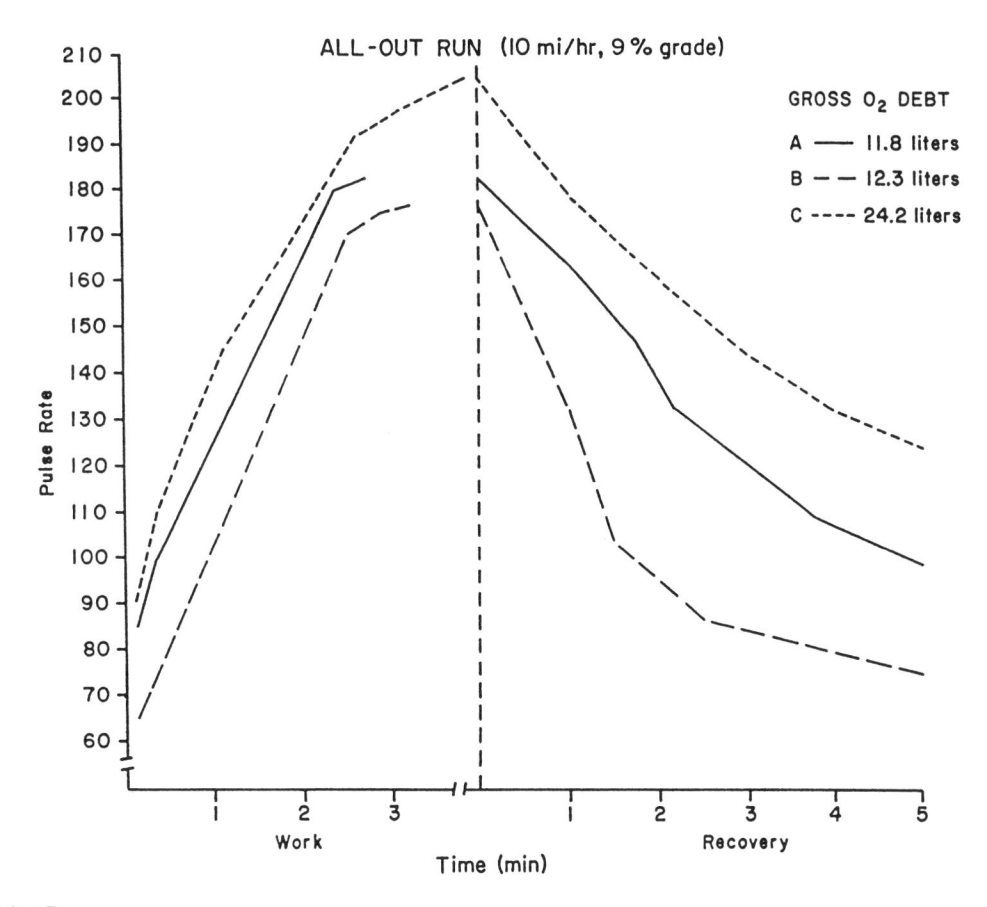

**Fig. 2A-3.** All-Out Run

recovery curve, the vertical lines delineate the most common 1:00-1:30 pulse count that is used. In this test the 1:00-1:30 pulse count clearly reflects the actual performance in the test. These results also raise the question as to how "healthy" are the general intramural level of fitness and the fitness required to excel in the 400 meter run.

Another look at specific fitnesses is provided by studying national class performers in the 100 m, 400 m, 1500 m, and 10,000 m events who ran a maximal effort 400 m (Rankin, 1983). During the run, heart and respiration rates were telemetered and recorded. Pre- and post-run serum lactate data were collected. Because psychologic results might be related to the time of the 400 m run, each subject also completed an additional run for one minute on a treadmill at a 16.1 km/hr (10 mi/hr), 9% grade work intensity. Similar data were collected for the treadmill run.

The results are rather striking. The respirations were regular and deep for the 10,000 m group, regular but less deep for the 1500 m. For the 400 m and 100 m performers, however, the respirations totaled no more than six for the entire 400 m and they came in gasps. The heart rate for the 100 m and 400 m performers was at 180-190 bts/min within 20 seconds and stayed at that level (Figure 2A-4). Increases in heart rate of the 1500 m and the 10 k performers were more progressive. The pre-post lactate differences were progressively less from the short to the longer distance performers. These responses indicate that individuals adapted to longer distances perform all out work at shorter distances more aerobically. The responses are progressively more anaerobic with the adaptation to shorter races. Maximal performance of the 400 m by the elite runners at distances from 100-10,000 m is accomplished in a significantly different manner physiologically. The types of fitness involved are specific to the training undergone.

## Training

The establishment of realistic goals is the initial step in developing an individualized program. To set the goals, the desired level of fitness should be identified, present status should be determined

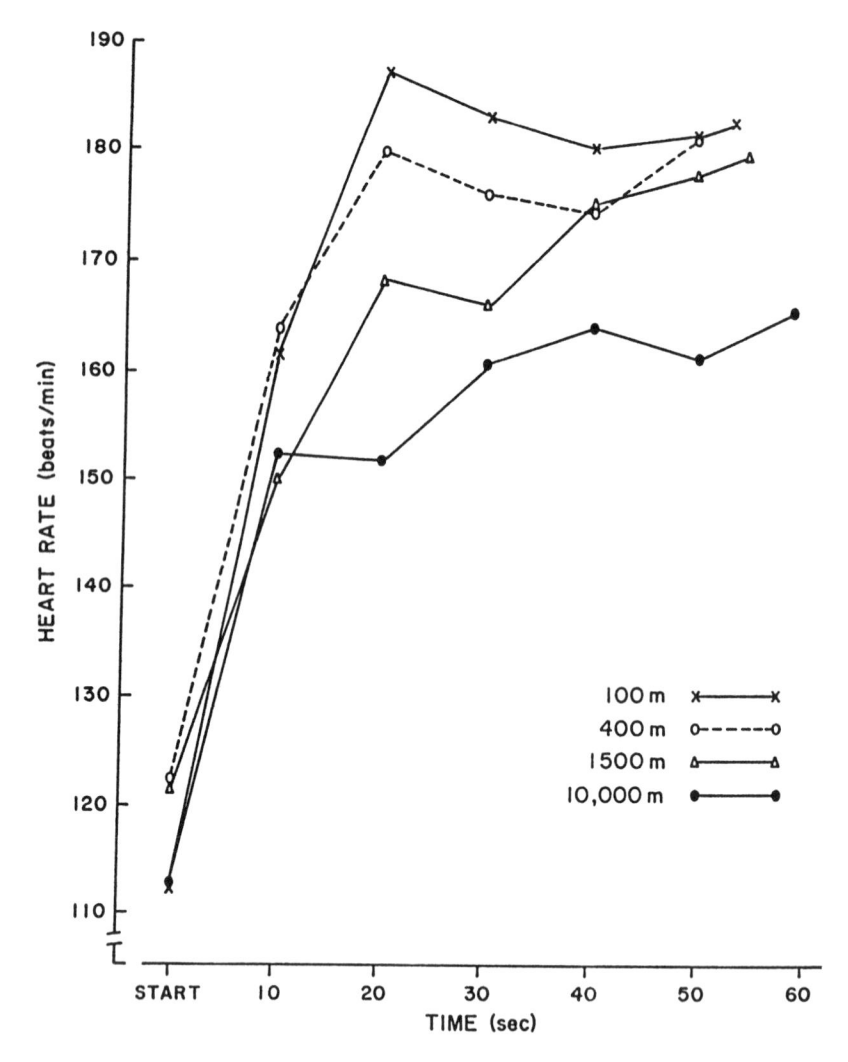

**Fig. 2A-4.** Heart Rate

(quantitatively, if possible), the specific capacities to be improved should be identified, and the specific overload to mediate the desired changes should be identified. Training becomes the implementation of controlled stress (overload) to mediate the desired changes. Overload of the specific capacity requiring improvement must be accomplished if performance is to be enhanced. The specific capacities may be such things as oxygen uptake capacity, level at which steady state can be maintained, or ability to recover from specific work.

### Principles of Training

Training follows some well tested principles:

1. The effects of training are specific to the type of training used.
2. Overload is mandatory for improved performance.
3. Retrogression in capacity may precede improvement.
4. Responses to a training program are unique to the individual.
5. Motivation is essential for effective training.
6. The body does not tolerate two heavy stressors simultaneously.

### Theoretical Basis of Training

The principles are helpful in prescribing training programs, but the theoretical basis of training as the controlled application of stress may be of more value. Selye (1971) identified the General Adaptation Syndrome (GAS) in the 1930s. The GAS provides a reasonable basis for understanding train-

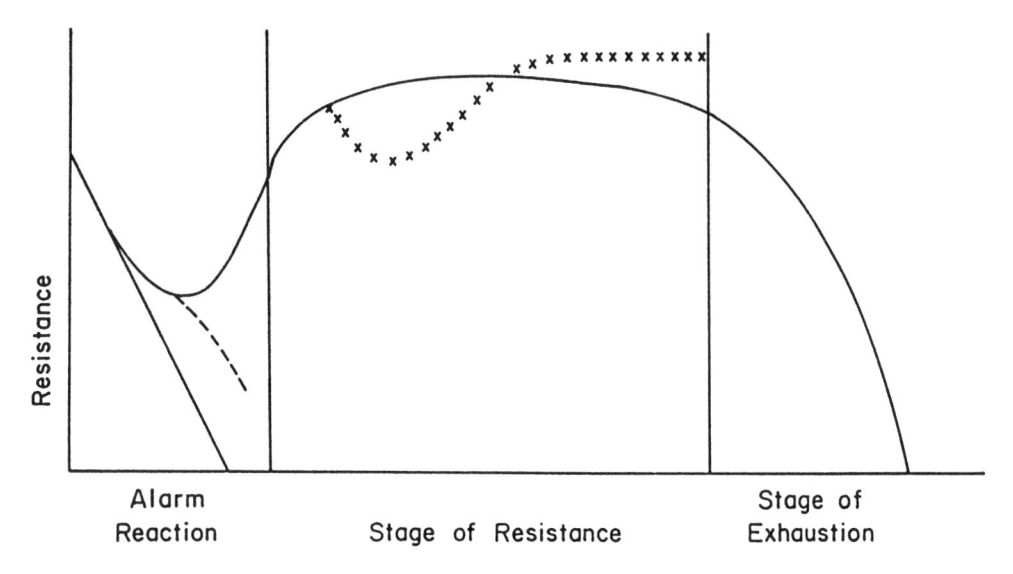

**Fig. 2A-5.** General Adaptation Scheme

ing (Figure 2A-5). The alarm reaction is related to the initiation of training. During this period the body attempts to adapt to the stress placed upon it. During this period the eosinophil count may drop (Selye, 1971), blood cell destruction has been shown to occur (Steinhaus, 1963) and, in contact sports, the incidence of injuries may be elevated. Animal experiments have shown that if the initial stress is too great during this period, the animal may die. Also, if an infection develops and the exercise load is not diminshed, the animal may die. If, however, the exercise overload is reasonable, the individual will adapt to it and move to a higher level in the stage of resistance. The level attained will be equivalent to the training overload — not greater. "Only that which is practiced will come off" is a good axiom.

Once enhanced resistance (performance) is attained, the individual and/or coach usually wishes to move to a new level of performance. It is important to remember that performance capacity may be impaired for a short period during these "mini-alarm-type" reactions before further improvement is attained (XX lines, Figure 2A-5). Particular care must be taken to not overload excessively before an important competition. Rest and tapering techniques are indicated here.

Training results in marked hormonal changes. In particular, both the adrenal cortex and medulla are hypertrophied in the resistance stage. The alarm and resistance stages form a good basis for understanding training and training responses; however, the stage of exhaustion is less clear. Whether or not it is related to "staleness" is controversial.

### Overloading and Testing the Energy Systems

The relative importance of the energy systems according to the time durations of maximal performance is portrayed in Figure 2A-6. This information supports data presented in Table 2A-2 under relative contribution of major energy sources for muscular contraction. The key to effective training is the specific overloading of the appropriate energy system. Following are some general principles and one method of overload for each energy system. There may be many methods of overloading a particular system, and there is much disagreement as to which is best. It is in the application that "art" is needed. For our purposes, identification of the specific system and one method of overloading in general terms should suffice to illustrate the idea.

The alactic portion involves utilization of endogenous CP and ATP stores in work of short duration. The intent of training is to increase the quantity of CP present in the working musculature, which should result in extending the time that the very highest intensities of work can be maintained. The overload involves very high level work of 6-8 sec with a rest interal of several minutes. Work time should be gradually increased as training progresses. Work intervals on a given day may be continued until performance time starts to deteriorate. Most individuals cannot tolerate

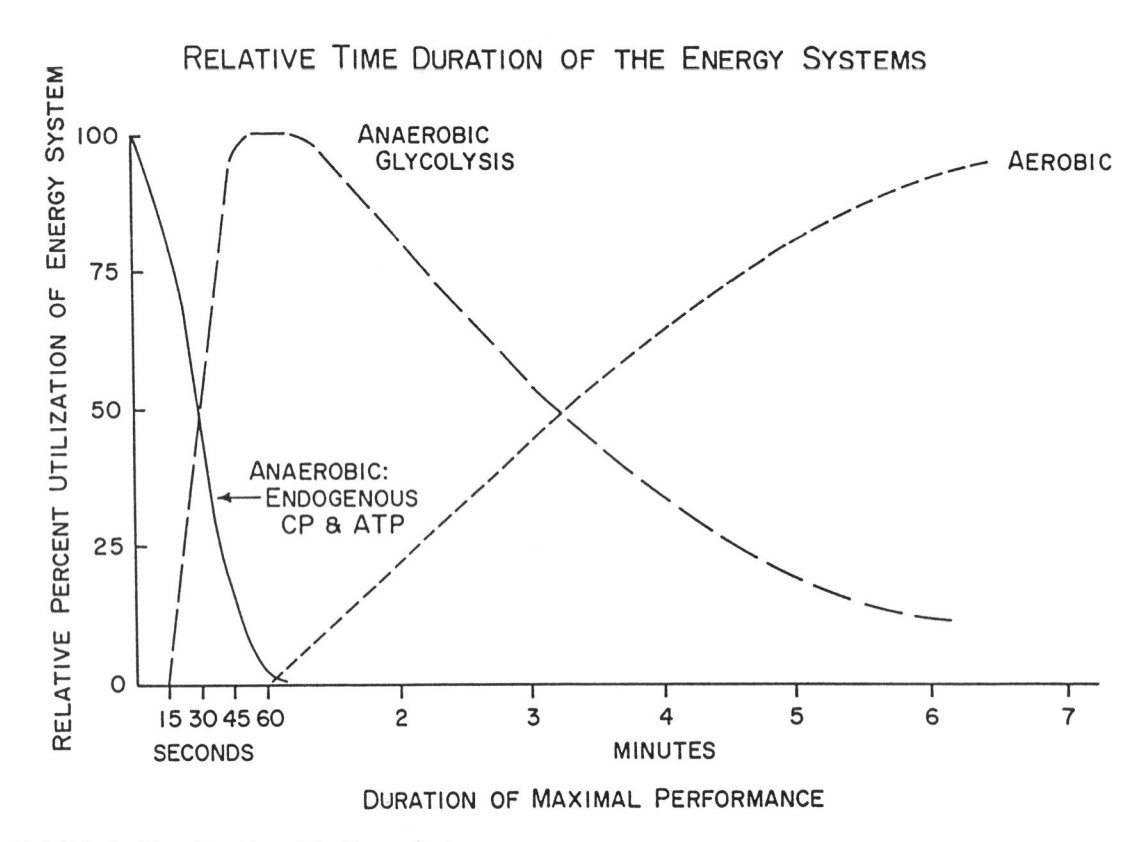

**Fig. 2A-6.** Relative Time Duration of the Energy Systems

more than three days per week of hard work. Every training session must be preceded by a warm-up and stretch. Most individuals require three to five days of rest or low intensity work before an important competition.

The lactacid portion of the anaerobic system involves anaerobic glycolysis utilizing endogenous glycogen and/or blood glucose. The body must tolerate high levels of lactic acid and oxygen debt in performances utilizing this energy system. With heavy anaerobic training, post exercise lactate values may be changed from 8-10 to 22-24 mMol lactate and the gross oxygen debts may go from 6-8 to 24-26 liters of oxygen. This can be accomplished with high intensity work intervals of 30 sec with 60 sec rest intervals. Intervals may be continued until the 30 sec performance deteriorates, but should not be continued beyond this point. Good results also may be obtained by all-out 60 sec work intervals with 15-20 min rest intervals. The training must be adapted for each individual. Some can tolerate four hard days per week, whereas others can tolerate only two hard days per week. If the individual is training too hard for this fitness level, resting blood pressures may be elevated as high as 160/110. In such situations the number of hard training sessions per week or the training intensity must be reduced. Rest or light work for several days prior to competition are required.

The training of anaerobic capacities has received little attention but there is no question that anaerobic capacities may be altered markedly by training. However, the best methods, as well as many of the physiologic adaptations that are involved, are still controversial. Maximal recruitment of motor units is necessary for maximal anaerobic performance, as well as the ability to continue working at a rate in which high levels of lactate are produced.

The testing of anaerobic capacities is neither well developed nor well understood. There are several tests of anaerobic power (see Table 2A-3). The Margaria Power Test (Kalamen, 1968; Margaria, 1966) measures the power generated sprinting up a flight of stairs; the Wingate Test (Bar-Or, 1978), uses maximal exercise for 30 sec on the bicycle ergometer. These are both general tests and not sports specific. Both are intended to estimate the potential of the CP-ATP system. The decay observed during the 30 sec duration of the Wingate test is thought to be related to the relative potential of the lactacid system utilizing anaerobic glycolysis.

The importance of the decay noted in high intensity performance of about one minute duration has been recognized but not studied intensively. In 1935, Cureton developed the 100-yd drop-off test in swimming (Cureton, 1935). The decay between the first and fourth 25-yd length was found to correlate (r = .70) with 100-yd performance times (Van Huss, 1955).

The procedures for testing anaerobic capacities is a particularly fruitful area for future research. Sport-specific tests that will identify the energy systems requiring improvement are needed. There is much room in this area for practitioner creativity.

The aerobic energy system is utilized in work of longer duration (Table 2A-2, Figure 2A-6). It involves greater economy of work and utilization primarily of free fatty acids and glucose through the aerobic pathways. The key adaptation in this fitness is the maximum level at which an individual can maintain steady state. In general, this is not the same level as the maximal oxygen consumption. Work intervals of one to three minutes with progressively shorter rest intervals will overload this mechanism. The work interval intensity should be directly related to the pace desired. No work should continue if the work interval pace cannot be maintained. The number of work intervals is dependent upon the intensity. The goal is to put together a continuous performance at the desired pace. There are many ways to do this. The goal is clear in that the individual should be able to increase the pace they can hold, that is increase the level of steady state. The strategy is to progressively increase pace and the number of intervals related to the desired performance while decreasing the rest intervals.

Aerobic capacity has been well studied and many practical applications have been derived. The tests involve applications of the relationships shown in Figure 2A-6 and Table 2A-2. For example, a graded exercise test may be continuous with progressively more intensive levels of work, each lasting for two or three minutes up to the point of exhaustion, some predetermined pulse rate level, or until specific symptoms limiting performance develop. The cardiovascular stress test protocols (Bruce, Balke, Naughton) (Ellested, 1975; Jones, 1975) and the common tests for determining $VO_2$max, such as the Taylor-Henschel protocol (Buskirk, 1957) are of this type. Pulse rate, oxygen uptake, and recovery oxygen (reflecting the increase in oxygen deficit) are essentially linear when work intensity is progressively increased to the point of maximal oxygen consumption (Figure 2A-7). The test may be continuous or intermittent, with short rests between levels. $VO_2$max also may be measured with an intermittent protocol, with the added benefit of obtaining more reliable blood pressures blood lactates, and/or cardiac output values during the rest interval. The test equipment may be a bicycle ergometer, benches of different heights or of the same height with different rates of stepping, a treadmill, a swimming flume where the rate of water flow is controlled, or a tethered swim in which the load is progressively increased. The more specific the test is to the activity of the individual being measured, the better. The $VO_2$max of swimmers, for example, is highest in the water and that of runners is highest during running (Astrand, 1977). Following these principles, tests of other activities such as cross country skiing or ice skating could be devised.

$VO_2$max is a useful measure but has not correlated as well with maximum performance as had been hoped. A variation of the $VO_2$max test, in which a ramp is used, has yielded measures that correlate highly (r = .94) with endurance running performance (Conconi, 1982; Kumagai, 1982; Rhodes, 1984). The ramp is either a slow continuous increase in load or one in which small gradations of increased workload are utilized on the bicycle ergometer or on the treadmill. With the advent of reduced time increment respiratory samples, including breath-by-breath analysis, we found there are breakpoints in some of the parameters, in particular, $V_E/VO_2$ (ventilation rate divided by the oxygen consumption rate) and the respiratory quotient ($VCO_2/VO_2$) (34). The second breakpoint was called the anaerobic threshold initially, and was defined as the highest oxygen uptake before lactate begins to accumulate in the blood, causing a metabolic acidosis. The physiologic meaning of the breakpoints is highly controversial and cannot be resolved here. The issues have been discussed

---

**Table 2A-3. Tests of Anaerobic Capacity**

**Anaerobic Power**
Margaria Power Test (Kalamen, 1968; Margaria, 1966)
Wingate Bicycle Test (Bar-Or, 1978)

**Anaerobic Decay** (Drop from initial value)
Wingate Bicycle Test (Bar-Or, 1978)
100-yd Drop-Off Test (Swimming) (Cureton, 1935)

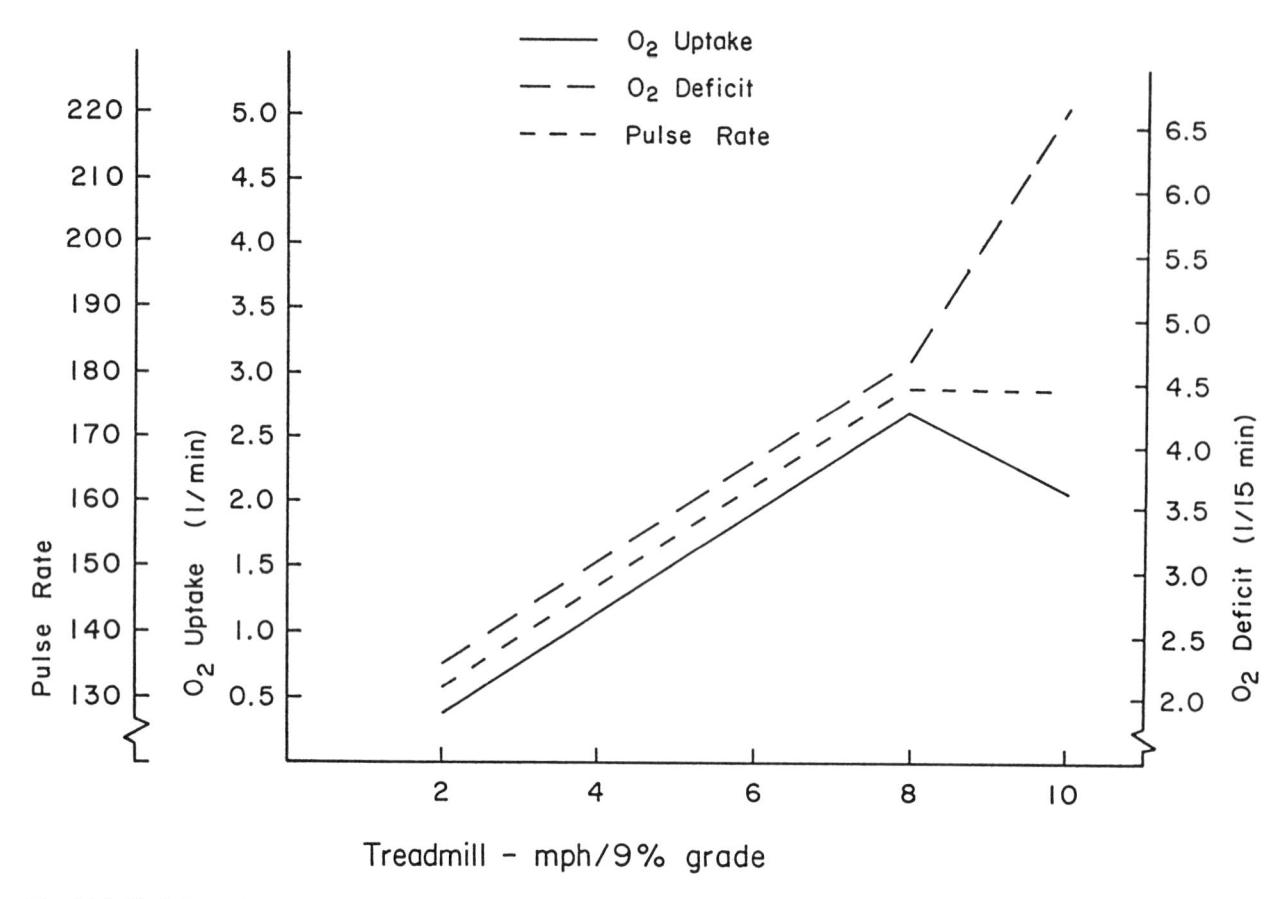

**Fig. 2A-7.** Work Intensity

in detail elsewhere (Brooks, 1985; Brooks, 1984; Davis, 1985). To avoid controversy, we prefer to label the two breakpoints as ventilatory breakpoints 1 and 2 (Vent-Brp 1 and 2).

Representative plots of the $V_E/VO_2$ vs running speed at 0 degrees on the treadmill are shown in Figure 2A-8. The effect of training is to move the slope down and the breakpoints to the right, that is, they take place at a higher velocities. Because the breakpoints are highly correlated with performance, the measures become an attractive method for coaches and athletes to evaluate current status and progress in training. With improved energy metabolism data collection procedures, it should be possible to produce a test that is useful to the practitioner. At this time, it is not clear what is occuring physiologically and test results are erratic. It appears that the measures may reflect the maximal level of steady state that can be maintained, if the measures can be refined.

The data in Figure 2A-8 show the lactate and Vent-Brps occuring at the same point. *This has not been established.* These data are presented to show that there are promising potential measures of aerobic fitness. As relatively low cost and accurate lactate analyzers are developed, there is hope for improved control of aerobic training.

The essential skill in prescribing effective training programs, as mentioned, is to identify the specific overload needed and how to achieve it so as to enhance the specific fitness required for improved performance. The application of what one considers to be the specific overload desired sometimes does not work out as expected. One example of a situation in which an unexpected reversal occurred follows. Commercial companies market weighted wristlets, anklets, and weighted belts to wear during training. An unsupported claim was made that these devices would improve rhythmical endurance (i.e., distance running) performance. The logic seemed sound, in that by using weights, greater numbers of motor units would be recruited and "trained." It was hypothesized that with fatigue, additional trained musculature could be expected to be available to maintain the work rate. The following study was designed to test the theory (Kennedy, 1974).

Six university-team distance runners were ran-

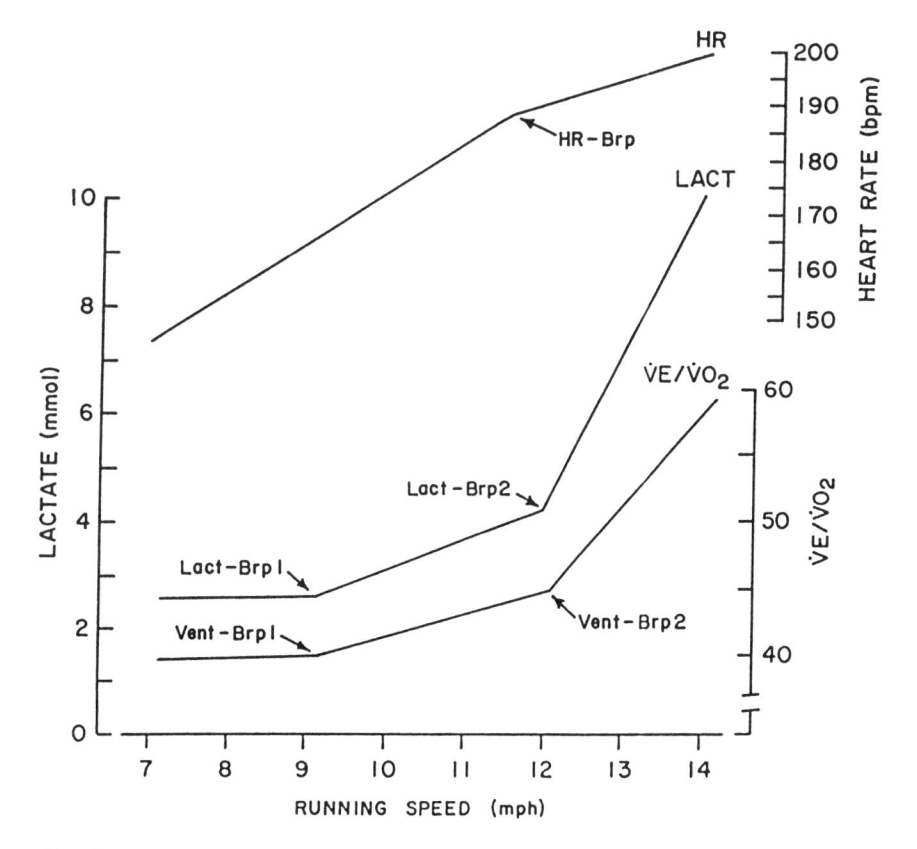

**Fig. 2A-8.** $\dot{V}E/\dot{V}O_2$ vs. Speed

domly placed into experimental and control groups. Both received identical on-track training for eight weeks, except that for three days each week the experimental subjects wore weighted wristlets, anklets, and belts. The weights were progressively increased during the experimental period (wristlets: 184-794 gm; anklets: 284-907 gm; belt: 709-2,126 gm). Pre- and post-test energy metabolism measurements were taken during and following both a low-intensity 15-minute run (9.7 km/hr, zero grade) to determine economy of running, and a high intensity run to exhaustion (16.1 km/hr, nine percent grade) to determine performance capacity in work that is predominantly anaerobic. The results are shown in Figures 2A-9 and 2A-10.

The results for the control group in the low-intensity run were as expected. They performed more economically post-training. However, the experimental subjects who trained with the weights performed *less* economically ($P < .01$).

In the exhaustive run, the results for the control group were as expected. There was a significant increase in oxygen intake and a slight increase in the recovery oxygen. The experimental subjects, on the other hand, had a *reduced* oxygen intake and a markedly increased recovery oxygen ($P < .01$). This was the reverse of the hypothesized results. Clearly the experimental group performed the high-intensity work in a significantly more anaerobic manner. The changes observed in both runs show that *the adaptations to the training with weights were not conducive to enhanced endurance performances.*

Why did this reversal occur? Our interpretation is that the load imposed by the weights caused a greater signal to be generated by the muscle spindles. We know that the motor nerves of the fast-twitch motor units at the spinal cord have larger soma and higher threshold levels (Henneman, 1965). Thus, the fast-twitch motor units likely were recruited when the weights were worn. It appears that even though the subjects were measured on the treadmill not wearing weights, they had "learned" to recruit the fast twitch, more anaerobic muscle fibers as a result of training. The response was clearly anaerobic. Whereas the more aerobic, slower twitch motor units are more desirable for endurance running.

Much can be learned about the adaptation of muscle, in particular, to different types of training.

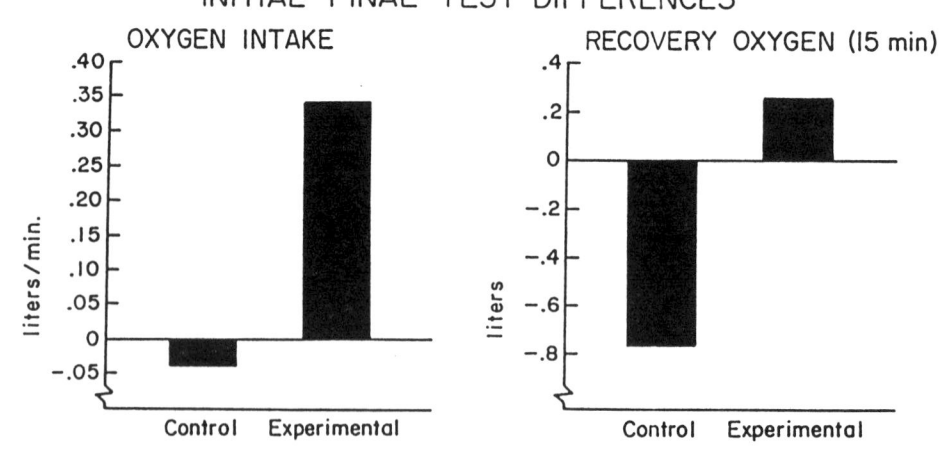

**Fig. 2A-9.** Low Intensity Run Results

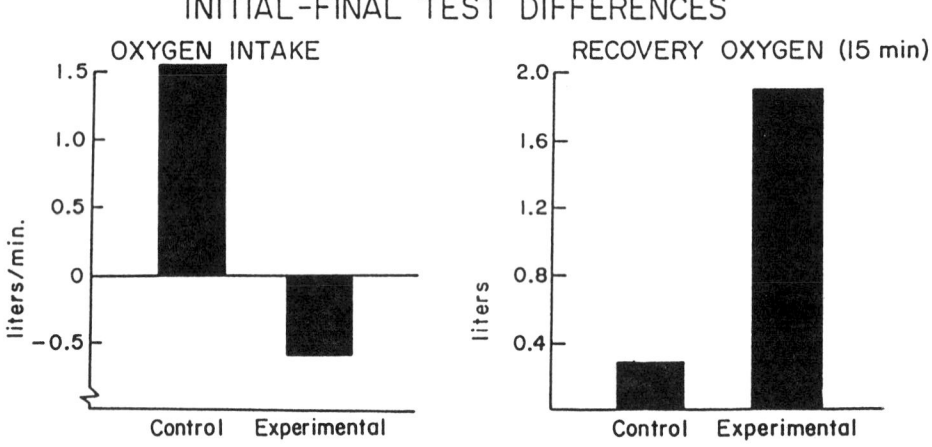

**Fig. 2A-10.** High Intensity Run Results

In Table 2A-2 of the specific fitness levels or types, we see that the muscle fiber type populations of high performance athletes are very different and are closely related to performance needs. This poses some difficult questions. Are the fiber populations established by heredity or are they mediated by as yet undefined mechanisms related to the activity. Animal data demonstrates that young animals trained on rhythmical endurance programs of relatively long duration have greater populations of slow twitch fibers, whereas animals trained on high-intensity short-duration training programs have greater populations of fast twitch fibers. Furthermore, the muscle fiber populations of adult animals have been altered by specific training programs (Prince, 1976). In particular, the Fast Glycolytic (FT) have been altered to Fast Oxidative Glycolytic (FOG) by endurance running programs and reversed by weight training programs. It also has been shown that muscle fibers subjected to exercise stress may split (Carrow, 1970). The hypothesis is that hyperplasia of muscle may result, and the Bulgarians have applied this knowledge in young power lifters with exceptional results (Buskirk, 1985).

Voluntary muscle in man is far more adaptable than previously thought. We know, for example, that motor units are considered to be homogeneous as to fiber type (Kugelberg, 1968), changes in muscle appear to be mediated by the nerve, and that muscle fiber populations may be altered (Prince, 1976). We do not know, however, how these changes are mediated, what their time course is, whether such changes are reversible, and how many of these changes can be mediated. These changes in muscle obviously are closely related to training and to performance.

We need to know more about the specific fitnesses needed for particular sports such as ice hockey, football, basketball. Ice hockey is a repeat anaerobic sport with short high intensity work shifts interspersed with longer rest periods. What training regimen will allow the athlete to achieve optimal performance that does not diminish during the final period? Should he start with an aerobic base and maintain it? The logic here is that the "trained" slow twitch and intermediate muscle fibers involved in the strong aerobic base are known to be capable of metabolizing lactate (Jones, 1975). Should conditioning programs be continued into the competitive season to prevent the known loss of fitness across a season of competition? These are just several of the questions facing the sports medicine practitioner. Specific answers in many instances are not clear. To make applications, a task analysis of the sport is advisable, that is, exactly what does the sport consist of, how long are the work periods, how intensive are the work periods, etc? The next step is to apply as much relevant scientific evidence as possible in making the decisions on how to proceed. This is the art of training, where judgments must be based on partial evidence.

## SECTION B.
## BODY COMPOSITION

Attempts to manipulate body composition for improvement of athletic performance can be affected by many variables: 1) physical training including intensity, duration and frequency; 2) presence or absence of weight bearing as a component of physical training (Ward, 1984); 3) caloric and carbohydrate intake, and 4) genetic predisposition to leanness (Bergstrom, 1967). Attempts to adjust lean:fat ratio by exercise alone have resulted in only a 1%-2% increase in lean body mass (Gollnick & Matoba, 1984). Attempts to adjust the same ratio with a diet restricted in calories alone have resulted in loss of both fat and lean body weight. Diets which restrict carbohydrate to < 100-125 grams will promote catabolism of lean tissue to provide amino acids which are converted to glucose for use by the brain and nervous system. However, when caloric restriction is combined with physical activity, fat is decreased and lean body weight stabilized. Most studies have been done with populations of non-elite athletes, which represents the majority of athletes.

Athletic performance appears to be positively affected by a low fat:lean ratio. McLeod (1983) found that performance of specific skills decreased dramatically as percent fat exceeded 10% in males and 19% in females. There is also a positive relationship between lean body mass and maximal oxygen consumption ($VO_2max$), due to the higher rate of metabolism (oxygen consumption) of lean body mass compared to fat.

Table 2B-1 provides body fat percentage estimates for elite level athletes in various sports but it is potentially harmful to expect rigid conformity to these numbers as standards in a particular sport. Therefore, it is recommended that athletes be counseled individually with regard to "optimal performance" body composition.

**Table 2B-1. Relative Body Fat Values in World-Class Athletes***

| Sport | Body Fat (%) in Males | Body Fat (%) in Females |
|---|---|---|
| Baseball/softball | 12-14 | 16-26 |
| Basketball | 7-10 | 16-27 |
| Football | 8-18 | |
| Gymnastics | 4-6 | 9-15 |
| Ice hockey | 13-15 | |
| Jockeys | 12-15 | |
| Skiing | 7-14 | 18-20 |
| Soccer | 9-12 | |
| Speed skating | 10-12 | |
| Track and field | | |
|   Sprint | 6-9 | 8-20 |
|   Middle distance running | 6-12 | 8-16 |
|   Distance running | 4-8 | 6-12 |
|   Discus | 14-18 | 16-24 |
|   Shot put | 14-18 | 20-30 |
|   Jump and hurdle | 6-9 | 8-16 |
| Tennis | 14-16 | 18-22 |
| Volleyball | 8-14 | 16-26 |
| Weightlifting | 8-16 | |
| Wrestling | 4-12 | |

*Values represent the range of means reported in various published and unpublished studies.

Athletes attempting to change body composition may follow the following formula:

(Present Weight)(present % fat) = Lean Body Mass

(Lean Body Mass)(1+desired % fat) = Desired Weight

The athlete may approach these formulas from any perspective. He/she can select any of the three variables most important to performance, then determine how to manipulate the other two to achieve a desired weight. The adolescent athlete must take care to provide enough calories for growth and activity.

Weight gain in athletes should be monitored closely. Weekly fatfold measurements are recommended for those attempting to gain or lose weight. A rapid gain or loss can result in gain of fat mass or loss in lean body mass, both of which are associated with diminished ability to perform. Attempts to decrease weight using diuretics, sweat suits, sweat boxes, laxatives, vomiting, or deliberate dehydration (wrestlers) are associated with potentially dangerous losses of body water and electrolytes, little loss of fat, and impaired performance.

## Estimating Body Composition

1. *Direct Techniques* — These techniques, although accurate, are complicated and expensive. They can measure fat-free body mass, body cell mass, fat mass, and bone and muscle mass. None of these methods is practical to situations other than research at present.
2. *Indirect Techniques* (refer to Table 2B-2)
   a. *Height and Weight Tables* — The Metropolitan Life Insurance tables (1979 Build Study, Society of Actuaries and Association of Life Insurance Medical Directors of America) are the simplest and most frequently used method of estimating recommended body weight but there are limitations. Many people are unable to use the chart correctly to determine frame size. Elbow breadth is used to determine frame size but it tends to underestimate fat in lean persons and over estimate for obese people (Whitney, 1990). The weights used to develop the charts represent weights reported at the time of purchasing life insurance (not weights at time of death). The sample (population) used to develop the charts (persons who purchase life insurance) is not representative of the general population. Body composition is not considered; the tables are not appropriate for persons (athletes) with high lean mass. The weight ranges are not standards — they are average weights associated with greatest longevity of persons who purchased life insurance.
   b. *Visual Appraisal* — A subjective assessment of body weight and/or fat distribution.
   c. *Ultrasound* — This technique is based upon the speed at which sound waves are passed through different tissue. It gives no more accurate information than fatfold measurements.
   d. *Hydrostatic Weighing* — With an error rate of 2.5% (Nash, 1985), this technique has become the research standard. It is limited by patient comfort under water, availability of a tank or pool, and ability to estimate lung volumes accurately. More recent techniques allow for the measurement of lung volumes while the subject is underwater and obviate the necessity for breath-holding. If lung vol-

Table 2B-2. Techniques for Estimating Body Fat

|  | Underwater Weighing | Fatfold Measurements | Electrical Impedance |
| --- | --- | --- | --- |
| Accuracy | Most accurate | ± error | Wide Swings in error |
| Accessibility | Relatively easy through fitness clubs | Easy | Poor at present |
| Cost | Tank & spirometer $25-30 per weight/pt | Large caliper | Portable unit 60,000 for TOBEC |
| Reproducibility | Good | Good if done by same person. Not affected by day-to-day fluctuations in hydration | Markedly affected by state of hydration |
| Training | Requires training for accuracy | Requires training for accuracy | Requires training for portable unit but not for TOBEC unit |

ume is estimated by spirometry, weighing should be done as close in time to the hydrostatic weighing as possible (Ward, 1984). For better reproducibility, food and fluid intake and other conditions (time of day, number of hours postworkout) should be closely approximated from one measurement to the next.

e. *Bioelectrical Impedance* — Electrical impedance is based upon the principle that lean tissue has a far greater electrolyte concentration than fat. However, because the water component of lean tissue is high, changes in body water vary the electrolyte concentrations (Nash, 1985). This method overestimates fat in lean persons and underestimates fat in the obese (Ward, 1984).

f. *Fatfolds* — Measurement of subcutaneous fat using calipers is the most practical, acceptable, and reproducible (Manjarez and Birrer, 1983) method of estimating body density when underwater weighing is not possible. The error rate is only 3% when trained personnel are used (Nash, 1985; Ward, 1984). Day to day changes in body water have little effect on fatfold measurements. The three limitations of fatfold assessment are inter- and intra-clinician variation, the assumption that the fat in the areas of measurement is representative of total body fat, and accurate calibration of the caliper. The recommended procedure is for the clinician to take multiple measurements at triceps, subscapular, and abdominal regions. The athlete should compare these values over time, especially when weight is lost or gained.

Over 100 equations have been used to predict the changes in body composition as a function of changes in the subcutaneous fat layer. In 1985, Jackson and Pollock devised tables which correlate the sums of fatfold measurements to age and sex. These are reproduced in Appendix 2B-1 to 2B-4. The fatfold sites should be standard:

*Chest*: A diagonal fold halfway between the anterior axillary line and the nipple for men and one third of the distance from anterior axillary line to nipple in women.

*Axilla*: A vertical fold on the midaxillary line at the level of the xyphoid process.

*Triceps*: A vertical fold, posterior midline of the upper arm halfway between the acromion and olecranon processes (over the triceps). The elbow should be relaxed and extended.

*Subscapular*: Diagonal fold on line from the vertebral border to 1-2 cm from the inferior angle of the scapula.

*Abdominal*: Vertical fold approximately 2 cm lateral to umbilicus.

*Suprailium*: Fold above the crest at the anterior axillary line on a diagonal line from above the chest to the symphysis pubis.

*Thigh*: Vertical fold on anterior thigh halfway between hip and knee.

The skinfolds should be measured with the caliper at right angles to the fold and 1 cm from the pinching thumb and forefinger. The caliper should be read to the nearest 0.5mm 1-2 seconds after the caliper grip has been released. Each site should be measured at least twice, with a third reading if there is more than 1mm variation in the first two. Measurements made immediately after exercise will be falsely high because of the shift of fluid toward the skin.

g. *Body Mass Index (BMI)* — This assessment is an index of weight in relation to height. It is calculated by dividing the weight (kg) by height squared (meters)(Bray, 1976). A BMI of > 27.8 for males or 27.3 for females indicates overweight (Whitney, 1990). This index is being used with increasing frequency to estimate body fatness. (Refer to Appendix 2B-5).

## SECTION C.
## FLUIDS AND ELECTROLYTES

### Water

The maintenance of adequate body water is perhaps the most critical factor in athletic performance. Water serves as the vehicle for nutrients and wastes to enter and leave cells. Urine production and excretion, hormone transport, energy production, temperature control, as well as other essential functions require adequate body water.

Water's most important function to the athlete is maintaining normal body temperature. Heat is produced by muscular work. To maintain a safe internal temperature during exercise, the body dissipates heat through radiation and evaporation. When radiation cannot account for enough heat loss, sweating begins. Evaporating sweat helps release heat and cools the body.

Even an untrained, unacclimatized body has a large capacity for sweat production. Sweat losses of 1 to 2 liters an hour are not uncommon during exercise in the heat. Sweat losses in trained athletes can exceed 3 liters per hour (ADA, 1986). Cold weather exercise also produces sweat, making hydration an important concern for cold weather athletes. Water loss also occurs from respiration which is increased during activity.

Dehydration occurs when fluid loss exceeds 1% of body weight. Work capacity and temperature control can be impaired with a loss of as little as 2% of body weight (Costill, 1980). When dehydration becomes sufficiently severe, sweating ceases as the body attempts to conserve water. The efficiency of sweating is decreased when humidity is high because of the increased water content of the air. Body temperature then rises quickly, dramatically increasing the chance of heat cramps, exhaustion, and stroke. Athletes and coaches/trainers should become familiar with the symptoms of heat stroke which include headache, nausea, loss of coordination, dizziness, and confusion.

**Fluid Replacement**

Adequate fluid intake before, during, and following exercise is necessary to prevent dehydration. Thirst is not a reliable gauge of fluid needs; significant dehydration can occur before the thirst mechanism is triggered. A hydration plan must be developed to assure that enough fluid is consumed during exercise to prevent heat injury and fatigue.

The critical factor in fluid replacement is how quickly the fluid leaves the stomach. Stomach emptying is affected by volume, temperature, and composition of the fluid ingested (Costill, 1974). Consuming too much liquid during exercise can cause a feeling of fullness and sluggishness. The upper limit for gastric emptying during exercise appears to be about 800 ml/hours (26 ounces) (Costill, 1974). This fact emphasizes the importance of prehydration. There must be a balance between fluid loss and intake. Both dehydration and bloating can be prevented when fluid is consumed in small amounts (3-6 ounces) at regular intervals (every 10-20 minutes) during exercise (Costill, 1984).

Cool drinks empty more rapidly from the stomach than warm fluids so that the optimum temperature is 40-50°F (5-10°C)(Hecker, 1984).

Plain water is an effective fluid replacement and it is readily available and absorbed. It should be the fluid of choice prior to exercising or competition. There are two reasons why drinks containing carbohydrates should not be consumed in the hour before activity. They promote an insulin response which can cause a hypoglycemic reaction and premature utilization of glycogen stores leading to decreased performance capacity. Also as carbohydrate content of fluids increase, gastric emptying decreases (Costill, 1974; Foster, 1979). The athlete should begin using other fluid replacement beverages (see Table 2C-1) only after the onset of exercise.

**Electrolytes**

Electrolytes (sodium, potassium, chloride, and magnesium) are lost in sweat, but the water loss is significantly greater (extracellular sodium *increases* with activity). There usually is no need to add electrolytes to a fluid replacement beverage. Electrolytes added to fluids elevate osmolality and retard gastric emptying, although recent research indicates that electrolytes increase the rate of water absorption in the intestines. The ideal drink should be hypotonic with an osmolality of about 200 millimoles per liter (Costill, 1984). Fluids should contain less than 10 mEq sodium and chloride and less than 5 m#q potassium per liter of solution (Am. Coll. Sports Med, 1975).

Electrolyte balance in exercising individuals is maintained by dietary intake and renal conservation. Electrolytes are replaced at the athlete's next meal. Electrolyte supplements are not necessary and can cause cramping, dehydration, and/or vomiting.

**Glucose**

Glucose replacement is important for the athlete who exercises more than two hours. By this time, glycogen will be depleted and performance will be impaired if a source of glucose is not provided. Although high levels of glucose will decrease fluid absorption, beverages that are up to 6% glucose have the same absorption rate as plain water

**Table 2C-1. Beverages for Rapid Fluid Replacement**

| | |
|---|---|
| Water | Use as is |
| Body Punch* | Mix 1 part Body Punch and 1 part water |
| ERG* | Mix 1 part ERG and 1 part water |
| Bike Half Time Punch* | Mix 1 part B.H.T.P and 2 parts water |
| Gatorade | Mix 1 part Gatorade and 2 1/4 parts water |
| Quick Kick* | Mix 1 part Quick Kick and 2 1/2 parts water |
| Pripps Plus* | Mix 1 part Pripps Plus and 2 1/2 parts water |
| Sportade* | Mix 1 part Sportade and 3 parts water |
| Take 5* | Mix 1 part Take 5 and 7 parts water |
| Fruit juices/fruit drinks | Mix 1 part juice/drink and 7 parts water |

**CARBONATED BEVERAGES**
Defizz carbonated beverages when using before or during exercise.

| | |
|---|---|
| Club soda | Use as is |
| Perrier | Use as is |
| Seltzer | Use as is |
| All-Sport | Use as is |
| Sugar-free soda | Mix 1 part soda and 1 part water |
| Sugar-sweetened soda | Mix 1 part soda and 3 parts water |

*Made according to manufacturer's directions.

(Davis, 1988). Some sports beverages contain fructose which causes gas, bloating, and diarrhea in some users (Whitney, 1990). Some sports beverages contain glucose polymers which have a lower osmatic effect in the intestines and taste less sweet than glucose.

## Water Intoxication

Water intoxication or hyponatremia can occur when an athlete consumes only plain water during prolonged (more than 90 minutes) activity such as a marathon, triathalon, or similar endurance event (Noakes, 1985). This type of electrolyte disturbance may cause diarrhea, exhaustion, mental confusion, syncope, pulmonary edema, and EKG alterations. Consumption of fluid replacements containing electrolytes are recommended to prevent the disorder.

## Summary Guidelines

- Adequate daily hydration with water, fruit juices, milk, etc. Tea, coffee and soft drinks contain water, but caffeine is a diuretic which can increase urine production and fluid loss. Alcohol should be avoided for that reason as well as for its negative affect on performance.
- Drink adequate fluids before exercise. Twenty ounces of fluid, preferably water, should be consumed an hour or two before exercise.
- Consume another 10-15 ounces of cool water 15 minutes before exercise.
- Drink 3 to 6 ounces of water every 10 to 20 minutes during exercise (ADA, 1986).
- Following exercise, consume 2 cups of fluid for every pound of weight lost from activity.

## SECTION D. NUTRITION

### General Nutrition

Athletes are advised to follow the same dietary guidelines that are recommended for the general public. A daily diet consisting of 12% of total energy as protein, 30% as fat, and 58% as carbohydrate (with < 10% from simple sugars) is recommended. Ample quantities of water are also required for nutrient metabolism and temperature regulation. Adherence to this type of diet will generally provide adequate amounts of vitamins and minerals. Table 2D-1, "A Pattern for Daily Food Choices" is a useful guide to help the athlete plan meals and assess nutrient adequacy.

#### Energy Needs

Calorie needs for athletes vary depending on factors such as body surface area, age, lean mass, intensity, duration, type of exercise, and a person's movement efficiency (Town and Wheeler, 1986). It is not unusual for individuals engaged in vigorous training programs to have energy needs > 5,000 kcalories per day (Katch and McArdle, 1983).

#### Energy Nutrients — Fuels for Performance

**Protein.** Protein is needed on a daily basis to maintain growth, for the repair of all body tissues to maintain fluid and pH balance, and to produce antibodies, hormones, and enzymes. The RDA for protein in adult men and women is 0.8 grams per kilogram of desirable body weight. Some groups, generally those where growth is occurring, need more protein, including children, adolescents, and pregnant or lactating women. Athletes are not in-

**Table 2D-1. A Pattern for Daily Food Choices**

**Use this guide for a varied and nutritious diet . . .**
- Choose foods daily from each of the first five major groups.
- Include different foods from within the groups. As a guide, use the subgroups listed below the major food group heading.
- Have at least the smaller number of servings suggested from each group. Limit total amount of food eaten to maintain desirable body weight.
- Most people should choose foods that are low in fat and sugars.

| Food Group | Suggested Daily Serving |
| --- | --- |
| Breads, Cereals, and Other Products<br>• Whole-grain<br>• Enriched | 6-11<br>(Include several servings a day of whole-grain products.) |
| Fruits<br>• Citrus, melon, berries<br>• Other fruits | 2 to 4 |
| Vegetables<br>• Dark-green leafy<br>• Deep-yellow<br>• Dry beans and peas (legumes)<br>• Starchy<br>• Other vegetables | 3 to 5<br>(Include all types regularly: use dark-green leafy vegetables and dry beans and peas several times a week.) |
| Meat, Poultry, Fish and Alternates<br>(Eggs, dry beans and peas, nuts and seeds) | 2 to 3<br>(total 5 to 7 ounces lean) |
| Milk, Cheese, and Yogurt | 2 (3 servings for teens and women who are pregnant or breastfeeding; 4 servings for teens who are pregnant or breastfeeding.) |
| Fats, Sweets, and Alcoholic Beverages | Avoid too many fats and sweets. If you drink alcoholic beverages, do so in moderation. |

**What Counts as a Serving?**

The Examples listed below will give you an idea of the amounts of food to count as one serving when you use the guide above.

- **Breads, cereals, and other grain products:** 1 slice of bread; 1/2 hamburger bun or english muffin; a small roll, biscuit, or muffin; 3 to 4 small or 2 large crackers; 1/2 cup cooked cereal, rice, or pasta; or 1 ounce of ready-to-eat breakfast cereal.
- **Fruits:** A piece of whole fruit such as an apple, banana, orange; a grapefruit half; a melon wedge; 3/4 cup of juice; 1/2 cup berries; or 1/2 cup cooked or canned fruit; or 1/4 cup dried fruit.
- **Vegetables:** 1/2 cup of cooked or chopped raw vegetables or 1 cup of leafy raw vegetables, such as lettuce or spinach.
- **Meat, poultry, fish, and alternates:** Serving sizes will differ. Amounts should total 5 to 7 ounces of lean meat, fish, or poultry a day. A serving of meat the size and thickness of the palm of a woman's hand is about 3 to 5 ounces and a man's, 5 to 7 ounces. Count 1 egg, 1/2 cup cooked dry beans, or 2 tablespoons of peanut butter as 1 ounce of lean meat.
- **Milk, cheese, and yogurt:** 1 cup of milk, 8 ounces of yogurt, 1-1/2 ounces natural cheese, or 2 ounces of process cheese.

cluded in this population (Food and Nutrition Board, 1980). However, recent evidence suggests that protein requirements are increased when muscle tissue growth is occurring. Some studies indicate that strength exercise may also increase protein needs (Dohm et al, 1982). Even so, this increased RDA for athletes is only 1.0 grams of protein per kilogram of desirable body weight, (American Dietetic Association, 1989). It is likely that most athletes exceed the recommendation by at least 40 grams since the average protein need for athletes is 60-70 grams protein, and the average protein intake in the U.S. is 100-120 grams/day. Probably the easiest way to insure adequate protein intake is to consume 12%-15% of total calories from protein. This should provide sufficient protein regardless of exercise level because protein consumption will increase as calorie consumption increases (Lemon, 1987). High protein intake should not be encouraged because athletes consume 2-3 times the recommended amount, and because protein is not a preferred source of fuel for activity. Among the potential disadvantages of consuming excess protein: foods high in protein tend to be high in fat (beef, pork, nuts, whole milk, cheese); foods high in protein tend to cost more than other foods; excess protein is stored as fat if positive energy balance occurs, and excess protein is deaminated and used for energy needs resulting in increased renal solute load and urinary nitrogen. Amino acid supplementation is not necessary or beneficial since dietary protein is provided beyond the amount needed for athletes.

**Fat.** Fat is the most concentrated source of energy (9 kcalories per gram). It contains more than twice as many calories per gram as either protein or carbohydrate. In addition to supplying energy, fat is the only source of linoleic acid, an essential fatty acid. Linoleic acid is present in high amounts in protein, vegetable oils, and products made from vegetable oil (mayonnaise, margarine). Dietary fat is necessary for the absorption of the fat soluble vitamins (A,D,E and K). It also is the trigger for satiety, and it provides insulation (subcutaneous fat). Some fat is necessary in the athlete's diet but a high fat diet (greater than 30% of total calories) is not recommended. The minimum fat needed is estimated to be 10%-12% kcalories. The recommendation is that no more than 30% kcalories be provided by fat and that no more than 10% kcalories come from saturated fat. Fat should not be consumed before activity/competition because it delays gastric activity.

**Carbohydrate.** Carbohydrates (sugars and starches) are the primary source of energy for the human body and the primary fuel for activity. Carbohydrates cannot be stored in large amounts except as triglycerides in adipose tissue so they are an important part of the daily diet. Foods high in complex carbohydrate, vegetables, grains, and dried beans and peas, should be emphasized to promote optimal glycogen storage (ADA, 1987). Glycogen storage in the liver is used to maintain blood glucose levels; muscle glycogen is used for muscle activity. Glycogen stores depend on carbohydrate intake and muscle activity. If a low fat diet (15%-20% kcalories) is acceptable to the athlete, carbohydrate intake can be increased to provide 60%-65% of total calories (Sherman, 1983). When inadequate carbohydrate is consumed, muscle glycogen must be used to maintain blood glucose levels, thereby decreasing the supply available to support anaerobic activity and maintain aerobic metabolism. An athlete who competes/trains for more than 90 minutes should consume a source of glucose during activity to prevent impaired performance from glycogen depletion. Simple sugars (sucrose or glucose snacks or beverages) should not be consumed within the 60 minutes preceding competition/exercise (Costill, 1990). Simple carbohydrates are rapidly digested and absorbed, resulting in increased blood glucose followed by an insulin response and a fall in blood glucose at the time exercise begins. Simple sugars can be consumed after activity to assist in glycogen replenishments.

**Carbohydrate Loading.** Carbohydrate loading (also called glycogen loading) is the process of manipulating the diet and the amount of exercise in an effort to increase glycogen stores. Increased glycogen stores enhance performance by providing greater energy reserves for muscles to draw on during long-term competition. Strenuous activity for 60 minutes decreases liver glycogen by 55% (Hultman, 1971). Muscle glycogen declines most rapidly at the onset of exercise. Glycogen depletion depends on intensity of exercise, length of activity, environmental temperature, physical conditioning, and availability of oxygen to support aerobic metabolism. When the oxygen supply is not adequate, anaerobic metabolism of carbohydrate increases. The greater the glycogen supply in muscles, the longer the athlete can continue to perform (Costill, 1990). The procedure for "classical" carbohydrate loading is glycogen depletion followed by high carbohydrate intake but it has been associated with side effects and risks. Chest pains, abnormal electrocardiograms, as well as weight gain, stiffness, loss of flexibility, cramps, and early fatigue have been reported (Stamford, 1984).

The current recommendation is for athletes to follow a high carbohydrate diet (60% kcalories) until 7 days prior to competition when carbohydrate is increased to 80% kcalories and activity is tapered. The carbohydrate depletion phase is not needed to promote glycogen storage and it may cause the side effects listed. The total grams of carbohydrate is considered the key to loading, rather than the percentage from total calories (ADA, 1987). Table 2D-2 illustrates a modified carbohydrate loading plan.

An important note is that there is no known advantage of carbohydrate loading in events lasting less than 1.5 hours of continuous, non-interrupted effort. Muscle and hepatic glycogen provide adequate glucose for activity lasting 60-90 minutes.

**Vitamins and Minerals.** Vitamins and minerals play an important role in the metabolism of nutrients, in oxidative reactions in the muscle, with oxygen transport systems, and in muscular contraction (ADA, 1987). While physical activity increases the need for some vitamins and minerals, the athlete can easily meet these needs without use of supplements by consuming a balanced diet.

The RDA (Recommended Dietary Allowances) are "levels of intake of essential nutrients considered . . . to be adequate to meet the known nutritional needs of practically all healthy person." (Food and Nutrition Board, 1980). The RDAs have been established as recommendations (not requirements) for nutrient needs based on age, gender,

Table 2D-2. Modified Carbohydrate Loading Plan

| Days Prior to the Event | Training | Diet |
|---|---|---|
| 7 | long, hard | ~350 grams complex carbohydrate |
| 6-4 | taper | continue to increase carbohydrate >350 grams but <550 grams |
| 3 & 2 | taper | diet should provide 550 grams or 60-65% complex carbohydrate, whichever is greater |
| 1 | complete rest | same as above (days 3 & 2) |
| 0 | competition | precompetition meal |

(Adapted from Sherman et al, 1983. Reprinted by permission.)

and growth status (pregnancy, breastfeeding). There is a wide margin of safety because they are set at the 97.5 percentile of mean need. Although a deficiency of one or more of the vitamins or minerals can impair physical performance, there is no conclusive evidence that performance will be enhanced by taking in nutrients in excess of the RDA (ADA, 1987). Tables 2D-3 and 2D-4 provide information on the estimated intake, sources, and function of necessary vitamins and minerals. Female athletes may have difficulty in consuming sufficient amounts of calcium and iron. This may be due to a low caloric intake, avoidance of many major dietary sources of calcium and iron due to their caloric and fat content, lactose intolerance or milk protein allergies, and personal food preferences.

**Calcium.** The RDA for calcium is 1200 milligrams for adolescent females and 800 milligrams per day for women over 25. Female athletes with normal menses will benefit from increased bone

**Table 2D-3. Vitamins**

| Vitamin | Adult RDA* | Sources | What it Does |
|---|---|---|---|
| A | 800-1,000 mcg (micrograms) | Liver, eggs, fortified milk, carrots, tomatoes, apricots, cantaloupe, fish | Promotes good vision; helps form and maintain healthy skin and mucous membranes; may protect against some cancers |
| C | 60 mg (milligrams) | Citrus fruits, strawberries, tomatoes | Promotes healthy gums, capillaries, and teeth; aids iron absorption; may block production of nitrosamines; maintains normal connective tissue; aids in healing wounds |
| D | 5-10 mcg (200-400 IU) | Fortified milk, fish; also produced by the body in response to sunlight | Promotes strong bones and teeth; necessary for absorption of calcium |
| E | 8-10 mg | Nuts, vegetable oils, whole grains, olives, asparagus, spinach | Protects tissue against oxidation; important in formation of red blood cells; helps body use vitamin K |
| K | 60-80 mg* | Body produces about half of daily needs; cauliflower, broccoli, cabbage, spinach, cereals, soybeans, beef liver | Aids in clotting of blood |
| $B_1$ (Thiamine) | 1-1.5 mg | Whole grains, dried beans, lean meats (especially pork), fish | Helps release energy from carbohydrates; necessary for healthy brain and nerve cells and for functioning of heart |
| $B_2$ (Riboflavin) | 1.2-1.7 mg | Nuts, dairy products, liver | Aids in release of energy from foods; interacts with other B vitamins |
| $B_3$ (Niacin) | 13-19 mg | Nuts, dairy products, liver | Aids in release of energy from foods; involved in synthesis of DNA; maintains normal functioning of skin, nerves, and digestive system |
| Pantothenic acid | 4-7 mg** | Whole grains, dried beans, eggs, nuts | Aids in release of energy from foods; essential for synthesis of numerous body materials |
| $B_6$ (Pyridoxine) | 1.6-2.0 mg | Whole grains, dried beans, eggs, nuts | Important in chemical reactions of proteins and amino acids; involved in normal functioning of brain and formation of red blood cells |
| $B_{12}$ | 2 mcg | Liver, beef, eggs, milk, shellfish | Necessary for development of red blood cells; maintains normal functioning of nervous system |

### Table 2D-3. Vitamins (*Continued*)

| Vitamin | Adult RDA* | Sources | What it Does |
|---|---|---|---|
| Folacin | 180-200 mcg | Liver, wheat bran, leafy green vegetables, beans, grains | Important in the synthesis of DNA; acts together with $B_{12}$ in the production of hemoglobin |
| Biotin | 30-100 mcg** | Yeast, eggs, liver, milk, widespread in foods | Important in formation of fatty acids; helps metabolize amino acids and carbohydrates |

*These figures are not applicable to pregnant women, who need additional vitamins.
**Although there is no RDA for this vitamin, the Food and Nutrition Board recommends this range of intakes.

### Table 2D-4. Minerals

| Mineral | Adult RDA or Estimated Intake | Food Sources | What it Does |
|---|---|---|---|
| Calcium | 800-1,200 mg* (1,200-1,500 mg for older women, according to an NIH consensus report) 1 quart milk = 1,250 mg | Milk and milk products, sardines and salmon eaten with bones, dark green leafy vegetables, shellfish, hard water | Builds bones and teeth and maintains bone density and strength; helps prevent osteoporosis in older population; plays a role in regulating heartbeat, blood clotting, muscle contraction, and nerve conduction; may help prevent hypertension |
| Chloride | 750 mg** | Table salt, fish, pickled and smoked foods | Maintains normal fluid shifts; balances pH of the blood: forms hydrochloric acid to aid digestion |
| Magnesium | 280 mg (women), 350 mg (men)* 1 cup spinach = 160 mg | Wheat bran, whole grains, raw leafy green vegetables, nuts (especially almonds and cashews), soybeans, bananas, apricots, hard water, spices | Aids in bone growth; aids function of nerves and muscles, including regulation of normal heart rhythm |
| Phosphorus | 800-1,200 mg, 1 cup milk = 993 mg; 1 serving chicken = 231 mg | Meats, poultry, fish, cheese, egg yolks, dried peas and beans, milk and milk products, soft drinks, nuts; present in almost all foods | Aids bone growth and strengthening of teeth; important in energy metabolism |
| Potassium | 2,000 mg**, 1 cup raisins = 524 mg; 1 banana = 400 mg; 1 small potato = 400 mg | Oranges and orange juice, bananas, dried fruits, peanut butter, dried peas and beans, potatoes, coffee, tea, cocoa, yogurt, molasses, meat | Promotes regular heartbeat; active in muscle contraction; regulates transfer of nutrients to cells: controls water balance in body tissues and cells; contributes to regulation of blood pressure |
| Sodium | 500 mg**, 1 frozen pot pie = 1,600 mg | All from salt | Helps regulate water balance in body; plays a role in maintaining blood pressure |
| Chromium | .05-.20 mg** | Meat, cheese, whole grains, dried peas and beans, peanuts, brewer's yeast | Important for glucose metabolism; may be a cofactor for insulin |
| Copper | 2.0-3.0 mg** | Shellfish (especially oysters), nuts, beef and pork liver, cocoa powder, chocolate, kidneys, dried beans, raisins, corn oil margarine | Formation of red blood cells; cofactor in absorbing iron into blood cells; assists in production of several enzymes involved in respiration; interacts with zinc |

Table 2D-4. Minerals (*Continued*)

| Mineral | Adult RDA or Estimated Intake | Food Sources | What it Does |
| --- | --- | --- | --- |
| Fluorine (fluoride) | 1.5-4.0 mg** | Fluoridated water; foods grown with or cooked in fluoridated water; fish, tea, gelatin | Contributes to solid bone and tooth formation; may help prevent osteoporosis in older people |
| Iodine | 150 mcg | Primarily from iodized salt, but also seafood, seaweed food products, vegetables grown in iodine-rich areas, vegetable oil | Necessary for normal function of the thyroid gland; essential for normal cell function; keeps skin, hair, and nails healthy; prevents goiter |
| Iron | 10 mg (male), 15 mg (female, during childbearing years, 4 oz calf's liver = 12 mg | Liver (especially pork liver), kidneys, red meats, egg yolks, peas, beans, nuts, dried fruits, green leafy vegetables, enriched grain products, blackstrap molasses | Essential to formation of hemoglobin, the oxygen-carrying factor in the blood; part of several enzymes and proteins in the body |
| Manganese | 2.5-5.0 mg**, 1/2 cup peanut butter = 2 mg | Nuts, whole grains, vegetables, fruits, instant coffee, tea, cocoa powder, beets, egg yolks | Required for normal bone growth and development, normal reproduction, and cell function |
| Molybdenum | .15-.50 mg** | Peas, beans, cereal grains, organ meats, some dark green vegetables | Important for normal cell function |
| Selenium | .55-.70 mcg, 4 oz fish = .038 mg | Fish, shellfish, red meat, egg yolks, chicken, garlic, tuna, tomatoes | Complements vitamin E to fight cell damage by oxygen |
| Zinc | 12-15 mg*, 5 oysters = 160 mg; 2 slices whole wheat bread = 2 mg | Oysters, crabmeat, beef, liver, eggs, poultry, brewer's yeast, whole wheat bread | Maintains normal taste and smell acuity, growth, sexual development; important for fetal growth and wound healing |

*These figures are not applicable to pregnant women, who need additional vitamins.
**Although there is no RDA for this vitamin, the Food and Nutrition Board recommends this range of intakes.

resorption of calcium associated with weight bearing exercise. By making proper food choices (low fat foods), they will be able to meet their calcium needs without supplements. Amenorrheic athletes may need as much as 1,500 milligrams calcium per day to achieve calcium balance due to the low estrogen levels and decreased calcium absorption that are observed with prolonged training (ADA, 1987). A calcium supplement which contains Vitamin D to enhance absorption may be necessary.

**Iron.** Iron is a component of hemoglobin and myoglobin and is needed for energy metabolism. The RDA for adult males is 10 milligrams per day and 15 milligrams per day for premenopausal females (ages 11-50). The average U.S. diet contains about 6 milligrams iron per 1000 kcalories so that many females consume less than the RDA unless they consume foods high in iron (meat) or enriched with iron (grains). An iron supplement should be considered if intake is not adequate. Female athletes who consume less than 2500 kcalories per day are at risk and should consider supplementation. Low serum ferritin and low total iron stores have been noted in endurance runners and in athletes who do not exhibit evidence of iron-deficiency anemia (Colt and Heyman, 1984). Iron loss occurs from hemolytic breakdown and/or GI loss (Loosli, 1990). The significance of this in terms of athletic performance is debated (Steinhaugh, 1984), but has been linked to post-exercise hyperlactic acidemia (Pate, 1983; Colt and Heyman, 1984; Steinbaugh, 1984). There are several ways athletes can increase absorption of dietary iron. They can eat food rich in Vitamin C along with high iron foods. They can cook in cast iron cookware several times a week — especially when preparing acidic foods (like tomato sauce). Meat (contains heme iron) is absorbed more efficiently than iron from plant foods (non-heme). They should avoid drinking tea which contains tannic acid and decreases iron absorption (Clark, 1985). With the exception of iron and calcium for female athletes, supplementation is not necessary and is not recommended because of the potential side effects:

toxicity from fat soluble vitamins; increased risk of kidney stones and gout from high levels of vitamin C; flushing/itching from niacin, and cost of the supplements. Athletes who consume less than 2000 kcalories (dancers, gymnasts) should choose foods with nutrient density to meet nutrient needs (lean meats, skin milk, fruits, vegetables, legumes, cereals, grain, and pasta).

**Water.** Water is the *limiting nutrient* for any athletic activity. A loss of 2% body weight due to water loss will result in a decreased ability to thermoregulate — even though this amount of water loss does not appear to affect performance (Hecker, 1984). A loss of 3% negatively affects endurance performance; at 4%, physical ability can be severely compromised. Six percent (6%) dehydration can be an extreme, life-threatening condition, especially when associated with maximal or near maximal exertion (Torramin et al, 1979). Thirst is an unreliable indicator of dehydration. Approximately 16 to 20 fluid ounces of water should be consumed about 2 hours before exertion. Another 16 ounces of cool water should be taken 15 to 20 minutes prior to endurance exercise. During activity, frequent small servings (4-6 ounces every 10-15 minutes) of plain cool water (40 to 50 degrees F) are recommended throughout an event to avoid gastric distress (Sports Nutrition, 1986; Slavin, 1984; Manjarez and Birrer, 1983). During hot temperatures, fluid needs increase. Athletes should weigh themselves before and after activity and drink 2 cups of water following activity for every pound of weight lost.

### Weight Loss/Gain

A weight-loss or weight-gain program weight should be part of pre-season training. Weight control should not be an issue once the competitive season has begun. Body weight should not fluctuate by more than 2 pounds per week (7000 kcalories stored as fat or metabolized from adipose) during either a weight loss or gain regimen; therefore, it is important to allow adequate time during the pre-season for weight adjustment.

**Weight Loss.** Increasing energy expenditure and decreasing caloric intake is the most effective method of weight control and maintenance. One pound of weight loss will occur each time caloric expenditure exceeds input by 3,500 kcalories. The recommended rate of weight (fat) loss is 1-2 pounds per week (a caloric deficit of 500-1,000 kcalories per day).

To lose weight an athlete should:

- restrict portion size.
- restrict high calorie, high fat foods.
- restrict frequency of eating.
- increase daily calorie output by increasing the duration and intensity of workouts.
- choose low calorie foods such as vegetables, fruits, breads, cereals, pasta, grains, legumes, skim milk products, lean meat, fish, and poultry.
- drink plenty of water.
- check weight weekly; not more or less often.
- keep a diet diary to increase awareness of when, where, and what is eaten.
- consume at least 1000 kcalories per day; 1,200 kcalories per day is preferred (NCAHF, 1987).
- increase water soluble fiber to promote a feeling of fullness (apple peels, barley, oat bran, carrots).

Sometimes athletes may attempt to lose weight in an unsafe manner. It is not unusual for wrestlers, for example, to "make weight" by employing such techniques as food restriction, fluid deprivation, and/or vomiting. The American College of Sports Medicine issued a position stand in 1976 discouraging these practices and noting the adverse effects that may be associated with unsafe weight loss practices:

- reduction of muscular strength.
- decrease in work performance times.
- lower plasma and blood volumes -reduction in cardiac functioning during maximal work conditions which are associated with higher heart rates, smaller stroke volumes, and reduced cardiac outputs.
- lower oxygen consumption, especially with food restriction.
- impairment of thermoregulatory processes.
- decrease in renal blood flow and in the volume of fluid being filtered by the kidney.
- depletion of liver glycogen stores.
- increase in the amount of electrolytes being lost from the body.

A carbohydrate restricted diet ($<$ 100 grams/day) will promote muscle breakdown to provide amino acids which can be converted to glucose to meet the energy needs of the brain. Since muscle is 75% water by weight, this diet promotes rapid weight (water) loss. Its disadvantages include decreased BMK (from decreased lean tissue), decreased muscle mass, fluid/electrolyte loss, ketoacidosis, and rebound weight gain when "normal" carbohydrate intake is resumed.

### Compulsive Dieters and Runners

A compulsive runner is a person who runs more than 25 miles a week, who runs when ill or injured, and who makes running such an important part of his life that he becomes depressed and feels guilty or irritable when he doesn't run (Knight et al, 1987).

Research has suggested that compulsive runners (also termed obligatory athletes) and compulsive dieters (individuals who display pathogenic weight control behaviors such as anorexia nervosa or bulimia) share personality traits (Yates et al, 1983). Yates says compulsive individuals are high achievers who come from the upper-middle socio-economic class and exhibit austere personality characteristics and extremely self-disciplined lifestyles.

Other studies indicate that anorectics are significantly different from compulsive runners (Knight et al, 1987). Knight believes that the runners don't display the same degree of depression as anorectics and that their body image is not as distorted. Whether or not there is an interconnection between pathogenic dieting and compulsive running, similar behaviors are demonstrated in both groups.

Pathogenic weight control methods as defined by Rosen et al (1986) include "the presence of one or more of the following behaviors . . . self-induced vomiting, use of laxatives to expel unwanted calories, or regular use of diet pills or diuretics for the purpose of weight control" (see Table 2D-5).

**Anorexia Nervosa** is characterized by fat-phobia, excessive weight loss ($\geq$ 25% appropriate weight), and distorted body image (the athlete "feels fat" despite obvious emaciation). These persons normally do not have previous psychiatric history. They exhibit personality changes concomitant with excessive weight loss, including social withdrawal (Maloney, 1983). They may exercise several times daily and are obsessively concerned with the caloric content of foods. See Appendix 2D-1 for other characteristic changes.

**Weight Gain.** Some athletes have a hard time gaining or maintaining weight due to high energy needs (3,000 to 11,000 kcalories per day) from vigorous activity performed several hours a day.

Most athletes attempting to gain weight want to increase muscle mass, not body fat. To achieve this result, the athlete needs to continue training and exercise while increasing caloric intake (Slavin, 1986).

Athletes interested in gaining weight should:

- be taught that eating habits for weight gain will not be appropriate when activity is decreased.
- use diet records to monitor food intake and nutrient adequacy.
- not increase daily calories by more than 1,000 kcal per day of fat.
- maintain exercise to promote muscle growth.
- increase frequency of eating.
- eat a varied diet, that is 10%-15% protein, 30% fat and 55%-60% carbohydrate.
- increase portion sizes of "regular" foods (meat, dairy, fruits, vegetables, grains).

**Pregame (Pre-Event) Meal.** There is no specific recommended precompetition meal. However, what an athlete eats before competition does make a physical and psychological difference (ADA, 1987). The pre-event meal should:

- prevent hunger during the competition.
- be eaten 3½ to 4 hours prior to competition to insure gastric emptying by the time of competition so as to avoid discomfort or cramping.
- range from 300 to 1,000 calories; the lighter the better.
- be primarily starch-bread, cereals, fruits, vegetables.
- not be high in fiber which promotes intestinal motility (may promote diarrhea).
- contain two to three cups of fluid.
- not be high in sugar which promotes an insulin response resulting in entry of glucose into cells from blood (Keller and Schwarzkoph, 1984).
- should not contain fat which delays gastric emptying.
- should include foods well tolerated (usually consumed).

It is important to remember that the immediate pre-competition period is not the time to attempt drastic changes in the athlete's diet.

### Nutrition Myths

Nutrition myths regarding the relationship between nutrition and sports performance proliferate as evidence accumulates suggesting that nutritional status can significantly affect an athlete's performance (Smith, 1982). Athletes or coaches

Table 2D-5. Eating Disorder Syndromes

| | History | Physical Signs | Laboratory |
|---|---|---|---|
| Pathogenic Weight Control | Concern about weight as related to athletic performance<br>Considered self obese at some time in life<br>Unaware of harmful nature of weight control practice.<br>Use of laxatives, self-induced vomiting, amphetamines.<br>Fear of losing control of eating behavior | Rectal bleeding<br>Parotid enlargement<br>Ulcerations or sores at the corners of the mouth<br>Alopecia<br>Hyperkinesis<br>Bloodshot eyes and odor of vomitus on breath | Hypokalemia<br>Hypoglycemia |
| Anorexia Nervosa | Voluntary food restriction causing weight loss of at least 25% weight.<br>Overwhelming phobia of fat and joy in weight loss<br>Distorted body image (feels fat despite emaciation)<br>Food hoarding<br>Absence of other psychiatric illness.<br>Adolescent or young adult usually female | Loss of 25% of premorbid weight<br>Amenorrhea<br>Fine lanugo hair<br>Hyperactivity/fatigue<br>Bradycardia with hypotension<br>Cold intolerance, hypothermia<br>Constipation | Hypoglycemia<br>Elevated BUN<br>Hypokalemia<br>Anemia with pancytopemia and marrow hypoplasia<br>Increased AM cortisol levels<br>Increased carotene levels<br>Prominent blue-green granules in marrow histocytes<br>Gelatinous background material in marrow |
| Bulimia | Binge-purge eating behavior<br>Depression<br>Fluctuating, near-normal weight<br>Abuse of laxatives, ipecac, illicit drugs<br>Extroverted, impulse oriented<br>Extreme feeling of guilt/shame following purges | Parotid enlargement<br>Loss of dental enamel<br>Rectal bleeding<br>Alopecia<br>± amenorrhea | Hypokalemia<br>Hypoglycemia |
| Obligatory Athlete | Often male<br>Distorted body image<br>Obsessive pursuit of *perfect* fitness<br>Self-image dependent upon athletic ability and success<br>Anxiety when deprived of exercise<br>Diet conscious | Low body fat<br>Muscular<br>Bradycardia (2% to fitness or relative starvation)<br>May develop pressure sores | Hypoglycemia<br>Elevated BUN<br>Low potassium<br>Anemia with pancytopemia and marrow hypoplasia<br>Increased AM cortisols<br>Increased carotene levels<br>Prominent blue-green granules in marrow histocytes<br>Gelatinous background material in marrow |

(Compiled from Rosen et al, 1986; Maloney, 1983; Yates, 1983; Chipman, 1983)

who misinterpret facts or who draw conclusions from poorly designed research studies, and inaccurate or misleading commercial advertising claims are chief sources of misinformation. Unfortunately, nutrition practices based on myths can impair athletic performance. Some of the common ones are listed on Appendix 2D-2.

**Ergogenic Aids**

"Ergogenic" refers to anything that helps increase work performance (Aronson, 1986). Ergogenic aids include mechanical, psychological, physiological, pharmacological, and nutritional aids. The *Journal of the American Dietetic Association*

(1987) has stated that virtually every food has at some time been promoted as an ergogenic aid. Some of the most commonly consumed substances include alcohol, amino acids, bee pollen, bicarbonate, caffeine, glandulars, minerals, protein supplements, vitamins, and wheat germ. Table 2D-6 is a list of these perceived ergogenics, their purported action, and research conclusions indicating effects and/or risks associated with their use.

Most often, ergogenics are simply foods or substances containing protein, sugar, vitamins, and minerals; but the athlete believes they will increase muscle mass, endurance, strength, or performance. With the exception of possible psychological benefits, no scientific evidence supports the physiological claims made for these substances (Williams, 1983). The practice of relying on ergogenic aids becomes a serious problem when they replace sound nutrition because the athlete's health and performance may be severely compromised (ADA, 1987).

## The Pregnant or Breastfeeding Athlete

More calories, protein, and other nutrients are needed during pregnancy and lactation. Even more may be required for increased energy expenditures related to exercise. In addition, the pregnant or breastfeeding adolescent athlete must allow higher

**Table 2D-6. Ergogenic Aids**

| Substance | Purported Action | Effects/Risks |
| --- | --- | --- |
| Alcohol | Facilitates proper hydration during prolonged exercise | Diuretic action may contribute to dehydration/heat illness |
|  | Improves psychological well-being | Deterioration of psychomotor skills<br>May decrease production and output of glucose by the liver |
| Amino Acids | More readily digested and absorbed than protein from food resulting in increased muscle growth | No evidence that more rapid absorption is beneficial |
| Arginine and ornithine | Stimulate the secretion of growth hormone resulting in increased muscle growth | No effect on growth hormone or body composition when taken orally<br>There may be as yet unidentified long-term risks |
| Beta-agonists | Increased muscle energy | Questionable cardiac risk/arrhythmias |
| Bee pollen | Increased energy | No improvement of athletic performance<br>May cause allergic reactions |
| Bicarbonate | Improved muscle endurance by raising the pH level in the muscle to rid more quickly of hydrogen ions | Induced alkalosis did not affect blood levels of lactic acid; no improvement in athletic performance observed |
| Caffeine | Improved endurance by enhancing lipolysis | Results inconsistent; no clear cut enhancement of performance or lipid metabolism; may be ergogenic for some<br>May raise blood cholesterol levels and increase the risk of heart disease<br>Tremor, hyperactivity |
| Glandulars (liver, pancreas, lungs, testicles) | Will help the function of the corresponding organ | Body handles like any other protein<br>No quality control; difficult to determine exact content; cleanliness a problem |

Table 2D-6. Ergogenic Aids (*Continued*)

| Substance | Purported Action | Effects/Risks |
| --- | --- | --- |
| Minerals | | |
|   Sodium, potassium | Sweat loss necessitates supplementation | Salt tablets irritate the gastrointestinal tract, cause dehydration and cramps |
|   Chromium | Aids carbohydrate metabolism to delay fatigue | Liver and kidney damage |
|   Selenium | Delays fatigue | Hair loss, brittle nails, skin lesions; fatigue; can be fatal in acute poisonings |
|   Zinc | Speeds wound healing, losses incurred with exercise necessitate supplementation | Anorexia; nausea; diarrhea; lethargy; dizziness; muscle pain; interferes with copper metabolism, calcium and iron absorption; may impair immune response, decrease blood levels of high-density lipoproteins, trigger bleeding of ulcers |
|   Iron | Reduces fatigue, weakness; improves performance, endurance; supplementation required by all athletes | Overdoses have caused death in children; dangerous for adults with hemochromatosis |
| Protein supplements | Enhanced performance | Excess protein is converted to fat and used for energy or stored<br>May lead to ketosis, dehydration, increased tendency towards gout, and increased loss of calcium |
| Vitamins | | |
|   Vitamin B Complex | Increases energy and endurance, enhances performance, delays fatigue | |
|     Thiamine | | Interferes with absorption of other B vitamins |
|     Riboflavin | | Relatively nontoxic |
|     Niacin | | Flushing, itchy skin, headache, diarrhea, nausea, low blood pressure, fainting, irregular heartbeat, liver damage |
|     Pyridoxine ($B_6$) | | Liver damage, nerve damage (sensory ataxia), limb impairment of vibration sense |
|     Folacin | | Gastric upset; sleep disturbances, malaise, irritability; masks certain anemias |
|     Biotin | | Depresses secretion of gastric hydrocholoric acid |
|     Pantothenic acid | | Diarrhea, water retention |
|     $B_{12}$ | | Liver damage, some allergic reactions |
|   Vitamin C | Protects against illness and infection, aids in rapid recovery from injury | Gastrointestinal upset, increases need for vitamin E, interferes with copper and iron status, may cause kidney stones and gout, interferes with pregnancy |
|   Vitamin E | Improves performance, increases endurance | Depression, fatigue; flu-like symptoms; interferes with vitamins A and K; hypertension, phlebitis, clots; gynecomastia |

Table 2D-6. Ergogenic Aids (*Continued*)

| Substance | Purported Action | Effects/Risks |
| --- | --- | --- |
| Vitamin A | Improves vision and immunity to infection | Anorexia, hair loss, increases cranial pressure, hypercalcemia, bone and kidney damage, liver damage, birth defects |
| Vitamin D | Builds stronger bones | Anorexia; weakness; hypercalcemia; deposits in soft tissue; irreversible kidney damage; damage to heart, lungs, and tissues surrounding joints |
| Vitamin K | Aids in recovery from injury | Interferes with normal clotting; liver damage |
| Wheat germ | Enhanced performance | No reproducible effects known<br>Expensive source of vitamin E and calories |

[1] Coleman, E. "Alcohol and Sports," Sports Medicine Digest, 8(2), 1986.
[2] Short, S. "College Athletes are Losing to Food Quacks," Phys. Sportsmed., 14(8), 1986.
[3] Mirkin, G. Bee Pollen: Living Up to Its Hype?:, Phys. Sportsmed., 13 (7), 1985.
[4] Anon. "Studies: Bicarbonate Doping has no Benefit," Phys. Sportsmed., 15 (12), 1987.
[6] Eichner, E. "The Caffeine Controversy: Effects on Endurance and Cholesterol," Phys. Sportsmed., 14(12), 1986.
[7] Dyment, P. "The Adolescent Athlete and Ergogenic Aids," J. Adolescent Health Care 8(1), 1987.
[8] Aronson, V. "Vitamins and Minerals as Ergogenic Aids," Phys. Sportsmed. 14(3), 1986.
[9] Dubick, M. and R. Rucker "Dietary Supplements and Health Aids—A Critical Evaluation," J. Nutr. Ed 15(3), 1983.

intakes to supply nutrients for her own growth. Nutrient dense foods must be emphasized because nutrient needs generally increase more than caloric needs. The lactating athlete must pay special attention to fluid consumption. Eighty-seven percent of the volume of breast milk is water — nearly 750 milliliters per day. Generous fluid intake is needed to prevent dehydration and decreased breastmilk production. A sedentary female needs 3 liters of fluid per day whereas a lactating athlete must provide for replacement of exercise-related water loss in addition to the 3 liters needed daily for breastmilk production.

**The Vegetarian Athlete**

Recent surveys show that more American athletes are adopting vegetarian diets, are decreasing their intake of red meat, and increasing their consumption of plant foods (Slavin et al, 1986). Vegetarian diets form a continuum ranging from strict vegetarians (vegans) who consume no animal products, to "vegetarians" who decrease frequency of consuming beef, fish, or poultry (Dwyer et al, 1973). The major risk of strict vegan diets is inadequacy of vitamin B-12, iron, zinc, calcium, protein, vitamin D, riboflavin, and total kcalories (Grandjean, 1987). As the diet becomes more restrictive in food sources, it becomes difficult to get needed nutrients in sufficient amounts. The other types of vegetarian diets are nutritionally adequate and tend to be high in carbohydrate, vitamins, minerals, adequate in protein, and low in fat.

**Conclusion**

Nutrition plays a significant role in successful training and competition. It is not possible to change an average athlete into a champion simply by altering their diet (Aronson, 1986), but a poor diet can negate much hard work on the training field (Brotherhood, 1984). The most important determinant of athletic performance is genetics, followed by training. Nutrition ranks third.

The best nutritional advice for athletes is to consume a balanced diet that is adequate in nutrients and calories for the energy demands of their specific sport. Fluid replacement is critical, especially for endurance athletes who also need a high carbohydrate (starch) intake.

In an attempt to gain the competitive edge, some athletes are willing try anything. Professionals who interact with them need to be aware of nutrition practices that impair performance or that have been shown to be dangerous to health (Town and Wheeler, 1986).

# SECTION E.
# PHARMACOLOGY

Any discussion of sports pharmacology brings with it the connotation of drug use and abuse. We do not intend to debate the issues, but rather to lay down the special concerns of medication use and drug abuse by athletes. This section is organized to help the primary care physician who deals with athletes and is not meant to be a complete compendium of commonly used medications.

Generally speaking, medications used to treat athletes and drugs used by athletes are similar to those used by nonathletes. Drug use has three indications: 1) disease; 2) deficiency, and 3) injury. This is the same whether the patient is nonexercising or a competitive athlete. Because athletics deals with performances as measured by time, distance, or quality of biomechanical movement, a fourth pseudo-indication arises: medications used for artificial enhancement of performance (ergogenic aids).

The legitimate use of medications by athletes should be similar to the use of medications by the general population, with a few important differences:

- Exercise has an effect on the pharmacokinetics of any drug; it can aid or impede its effects. When a hypertensive athlete is given a beta blocker, aerobic exercise can aid in decreasing blood pressure. Conversely, when a nonsteroidal anti-inflammatory drug (NSAID) is taken to treat soft tissue inflammation, and the athlete then exercises that injured musculotendinous unit, the effect of the NSAID is diminished when compared with the effect in a resting individual.
- Much of the medication used to treat athletes is prescribed for injuries. Exercise may reduce the prevalence of disease and deficiency in the general population but it increases the prevalence of injury. Thus, medication prescribed by the team physician will be heavily weighted toward treatment of injury.
- The population cared for by a team physician is different; athletes are younger, healthier, and more motivated to return to health. This last point is significant because athletes are more apt to comply with a reasonable treatment regimen than the general population. However, by nature, the competitive athlete can be superstitious, impressionable, faddish, gullible, and extremely susceptible to suggestion (Percy, 1978).
- Lastly, athletes may get better rehabilitation techniques and modalities than the general population. This sometimes obviates the need for intensive pharmacologic treatment.

While each physician has his own philosophy of medication use, some points can be made concerning their use in sports:

- The athlete's age is a determining factor in the use of medication. As an adjunct to rehabilitation and healing time, medicating should be less strenuously practiced in the younger and older sports population age groups. There is no need or reason to hurry up the healing process in either age groups.
- There is a strong placebo effect of medication for most athletes.
- Most medications need to be used only over a short period of time so that time-dependent side effects are not so strong a consideration. An athlete usually wants medication with a quick onset of action.
- The potential for abuse of even appropriately given medications remains high. If the athlete perceives that the medication aids performance (even if it was given for an injury), he may use it prophylactically in the future.

## Epidemiology of Drug Use in Sport

Drug use epidemiology is a perplexing area. The subject is sensitive and has many legal ramifications. Accurate data is hard to collect and harder to verify. Use patterns change constantly. Drug use permeates society and there is a good possibility that drug use in sport will increase substantially. Policing, in the form of drug testing, has been enacted at elite and amateur levels (International Olympic Committee, USOC, NCAA, various colleges and universities). Many professional sports organizations now do drug testing. Even so, drug testing technology continues its up-hill battle with the "new pharmacology" of sport (EPO, human growth hormone, "designer" steroids).

Most of the research on drug use is on the college athlete. Blyth et al (1981) conducted a study of athletes of the Big 10 conference involving over 1,000 athletes. Heitzinger (1984) surveyed 2,000 college athletes about drug use. Anderson and McKeag (1985, 1989) surveyed 2,000 college athletes in another study. In all four of these multi-institutional studies, drug use by college athletes mirrored that of non-athlete college students. Ninety percent of the athletes use alcohol, 30%-50% use marijuana, and 10%-20% use cocaine.

We also know that the following trends are present in the college-age population for socially related drugs such as alcohol, caffeine, cocaine, cigarettes, marijuana, smokeless tobacco, and psychedelics (Anderson, 1985):

1. Student-athletes use alcohol and drugs more frequently with non-athlete friends than with their teammates.
2. Major sources for obtaining illegal drugs are friends, relatives, and non-teammates.
3. With the exception of cocaine, most of student athletes began their use of alcohol and drugs in *high school* or before.
4. Student athlete use of alcohol and drugs is social and experimental.

The following trends have been seen with perceived ergogenic drugs (amphetamines, anabolic steroids, anti-inflammatories, barbiturates, tranquilizers, major pain medications, minor pain medications, and vitamins/minerals).

1. Some coaches and trainers illegally dispense ergogenic drugs.
2. The overall use of anabolic steroids is much lower than estimates given in the lay press.
3. Major sources of anabolic steroids are from non-team related sources.

High school surveys have concentrated on the athletic incidence of use of ergogenic aids. Table 2E-1 summarizes these studies and their findings. The use profile changes rapidly, with certain drugs falling out of favor as quickly as new improved chemical aids replace them. This much can be said:

1. Ergogenic drug use is initiated in high school or before at least 25% of the time.
2. Their use has spread to other less traditional power sports (other than football).
3. School/community size or level of competition is *not* a predictor of drug use.
4. Increased numbers of women athletes are using these substances.
5. A significant number of *non-athletes* use these drugs.

The problem will continue to be major. Physician responsibility in this area is paramount and involves: education of athletes, coaches, and trainers about side-effects, adverse reactions, and the dangers of indiscriminate use of medications and drugs; responsibility for early identification, counseling and treatment of those who abuse medications and drugs, and appropriate use and supervision of all medications used in sports. Does this include "monitoring" an athlete known to be abusing an illegal drug? The authors do not think so.

## Medications

Many attempts have been made to classify the pharmacology of sport into various broad catego-

Table 2E-1. Anabolic Steroids in High School Athletes

| Study | Area | Population | N | % as use |
|---|---|---|---|---|
| Buckley et. al. (1989) | Pennsylvania | M — 12 grade | 3403 | 6.6 |
| Neuman (1986) | Michigan | M — 12 grade |  | 5 |
|  |  | F — 12 grade |  | 1 |
| Terney, McLain (1988) | Illinois | Athletes |  | 5.5 |
|  |  | M — athletes |  | 6.6 |
|  |  | F — athletes |  | 3.9 |
| Johnson (1989) | Arkansas | M — 11 grade | 853 | 11.1 |
| Windsor, Domitrov (1989) | Texas | Students | 1010 | 3.0 |
|  |  | Affluent athletes |  | 4.5 |
|  |  | Less affluent athletes |  | 1.9 |
|  |  | M — athletes |  | 6.7 |
|  |  | F — athletes |  | 0.7 |
| Anderson et. al. (1990) | Washington | Students |  | 0.9 |

ries. This chapter lists drugs and medications only for easy reference. We should mention that not all drugs used in a sports medicine framework are listed; only those drugs of special sports concern.

**Adrenal corticosteroids.** These medications can be administered by three different routes:

1. *Topically* — Either alone or in combination with NSAIDs, corticosteroids have been used to decrease local superficial inflammation. Because they are known to cause skin atrophy, synthetic corticosteroids should not be applied to the face. Until a vehicle is found to carry the steroid into deeper subcutaneous tissues this means of combating soft tissue inflammation is not very effective.
2. *Orally* — A steroid "burst" (prednisone or Medrol®) followed by a taper has been advocated to treat neuropraxia. In addition, it is used to treat persistent skin rashes created by allergies to sports equipment and clothing. Using it to treat inflammation or pain of an acute or chronic injury is not a proven or valid medical indication. Please refer to Table 2E-2 for potential corticosteroid side-effects.
3. *Extra Articular Injection* — Proper indications include treatment for bursitis and tenosynovitis as well as ganglion cysts. Whenever possible, withdrawal of bursal fluid followed by injection of corticosteroids is best. The use of corticosteroids injected into soft tissues such as tendons and/or ligaments has been controversial. Kennedy and Willis (1976) found that such injections cause collagen necrosis of the surrounding soft tissue and a weakening of the tensor strength of the unit. These changes persist for as long as two weeks after a single injection. The decrease in tensor strength should preclude injection of corticosteroids into soft tissue. Steroids injected around peritenons and sheaths can achieve the desired effect of decreasing surface inflammation of tendons and tendonous attachments (hip pointers) without going into the substance of the soft tissue. Three prominent, commonly injured soft tissue structures should *never* be injected — biceps attachment at the elbow, patellar ligament at the tibial tuberosity, and the Achilles tendon attachment at the calcaneus.

**Anabolic steroids.** These naturally occurring and synthetic hormones are used in sports primarily to enhance muscle strength and power. After reviewing the contradictory and confusing literature, it appears that with high intensity weight training and proper diet, lean body mass and strength can be increased by a small but significant amount by using anabolic/androgenic steroids (Lombardo, 1985). Although there are no sports medicine-related indications for prescribing anabolic steroids, their use in sports for acquisition of strength has vastly increased. Ten percent of all college student-athlete football players (Anderson, 1990), and 6 percent of all high school football players (Buckley, 1989) use these substances. An important point is that athletes may use these medications at 5-10 times the recommended dose. Significant and common adverse effects accompany anabolic steroid use. See Table 2E-3 for a list of the more prevalent reversible and irreversible effects. There are four methods of administration:

1. Orals (e.g., Dianabol, Winstol) — taken at 5-10 times the recommended medical use dose;
2. Injectables (e.g., Durabolin, testosterone) — again taken at 5-10 times the recommended medical use dose;
3. "Stacking" multiple different drugs taken simultaneously,
4. Cycling — dosing for 6-10 weeks followed by a 4-12 week rest period.

---

**Table 2E-2. Potential Side Effects of Corticosteroids**

Hyperglycemia
Pancreatitis
Muscle atrophy
Osteoporosis and Bone fractures
Myopathy
Striae
Skin thickening
Purpura
Hirsutism
Acne
Cushingoid moon face
Distal cervical fat pads (buffalo hump)
Edema
Congestive heart failure
Hypertension
Increased susceptibility to infection
Suppression of the hypothalmic-pituitary-adrenal axis
Dyspnea
Psychosis
Cataracts
Glaucoma
Pseudorheumatism (on withdrawal)

**Table 2E-3. Major Adverse Effects — Anabolic Steroids**

A. Male Reproductive System
   1. Decreased testicular size and firmness
   2. Oligospermia
   3. Gynecomastia
B. Female Reproductive System
   1. Masculinization
      a. Increase in facial hair
      b. Increase in body hair
      c. Depening voice
      d. Increase in clitoris
   2. Oligo/amenorrhea
C. Integument
   1. Acne
   2. Temporal hair recession
   3. Alopecia
D. Liver
   1. Tumors (benign and malignant)
   2. Peliosis hepatitis
E. Cardiovascular Status
   1. Decreased HDL, increased LDL cholesterol
   2. Increased blood pressure
   3. Myocardial infarction
F. Psychological Status
   1. Increase aggression, irritability
   2. Interpersonal relationship problems
   3. Asocial behavior
G. Musculoskeletal Status
   1. Increased injury tendency

Use in the prepubertal athlete is especially troublesome because premature closure of the epiphyseal growth centers and adverse effects to hormonal feedback loops have been shown. Needless to say, this dangerous group of drugs should not be prescribed for any sports medicine related reason. See Appendix 2E-1 for the ACSM Position Statement on this subject.

**Growth hormone.** Human growth hormone (HGH, somatotropin) is a polypeptide hormone coming from either human or animal sources. Its anabolic action has an effect on protein and fat synthesis. No evidence of any sports enhancing properties has been found. Moreover, use of HGH is not without risk because it is diabetogenic and capable of stimulating natural antibody formation which could render normal endogenous HGH ineffective.

**Diuretics.** These drugs are frequently misused by wrestlers or boxers in an attempt to induce rapid weight loss through discharge of fluid in urine. Hypovolemia and even shock can result if this is done in combination with other dehydration techniques. No indications exist for use in specific sports related problems.

**Local anesthesia.** Local anesthetics often are inappropriately used to relieve pain and disability in an injured athlete prior to or during competition. Simply put, any athlete who requires local anesthesia to compete should be eliminated from competition until the injury has healed.

**Major pain medication.** These drugs may be often used to treat injury, but they have no place being used in an athlete during competition. As with the general population, drug dependence is a concern and athlete use should be well monitored. Control of such drugs and prescribing should be in the hands of the team physician. No athlete should be permitted to play who remains on any of these medications.

**Minor pain medications.** These drugs are non-narcotic and won't cause drug dependency but they still represent a special concern in sports. Many of these are commonly used over-the-counter preparations. They may be taken for their analgesic properties and to allow athletes to "play over" minor pain. This, of course, delays healing and can lead to more significant injury. We do not believe that physicians should prescribe or advocate the use of these medications during competition.

**Stimulants.** This class of drugs is used in the general population with increasing regularity. They are said to aid athletic performance but have yet to be proven to do so. Many athletes use them to enhance bursts of speed and improve ability and endurance. Athletes in such sports as long distance running, swimming, and bicycling are at risk for using this class of drugs. Football players also use stimulants to heighten aggression. It is likely that stimulants do not decrease fatigue, only mask it (Chandler and Blair, 1980). Performance enhancement is inconsistent and depends upon the status of the endogenous sympathetic nervous system. At worse, stimulant use is a dangerous manipulation of the body fatigue-alarm system.

**Sedatives, Tranquilizers, and Anti-depressants.** Occasionally, these drugs may be useful for relieving precompetition tension, anxiety, or to promote sleep. In addition, some tranquilizers are appropriately used as muscle relaxants in treating acute spasms secondary to injury. The use of these medications should be predicated on the individual not playing because their performance effect is to slow reaction time and increase the risk of injury. The abuse potential of these drugs is significant and their prescription should not be commonplace. It is important to note that all muscle relaxants have a CNS depressant effect to some degree.

**Vitamins.** This group of compounds was discussed earlier.

**Beta blockers.** These drugs are used to lower the excitability of athletes so that performance is enhanced. Activities such as pistol shooting, ski jumping, performing arts, and archery are examples where beta blockers have been used and abused. It is important to clarify therapeutic use of beta blockers in athletics. Generally speaking, these medications generate a dose-related, time-dependent side effect of premature fatigue. An athlete placed on beta-blockers for therapeutic reasons (hypertension, arrhythmias) should be warned of this initial drug effect which usually last 4-6 weeks until tolerance is achieved.

**Nonsteroidal anti-inflammatory drugs.** This expanding group of medications has a major role in treating sports injuries. The drugs in this group all have both analgesic and anti-inflammatory properties to some degree. It is important to realize this because their use will create analgesia and, in some situations, actually mask pain in an athlete. These drugs are misused when administered to reduce pain and disability so that an athlete can perform. However, they are a valuable adjunct in treating most overuse injuries, chronic soft tissue injuries, and to lessen the course of acute injury. They should not be used within 72 hours of acute trauma.

There is a wide variability of clinical response to any given NSAID. At similar serum levels and under similar conditions, one person may respond to a particular NSAID while another will not. Therefore, it is important to consider using another NSAID from a different chemical group if the initial NSAID treatment does not work.

Another Important Point — Recent research has determined that some nephrotoxicity can occur with the use of NSAIDs. Within the time frame of most sports injuries (1-2 weeks), this will not be a significant consideration unless the athlete already has renal compromise. The main effects desired of NSAID used for sports injury are: quick onset of action; absence of any dose related side-effects; strong anti-inflammatory response, and convenience.

**Dimethylsulfoxide (DMSO).** This drug is an acetone analog and a byproduct of the wood pulp industry. It has been advocated to treat acute inflammation. The topically applied agent is rapidly absorbed through the skin into the subcutaneous soft tissues. It is not approved by the FDA at present and is legal only in a few states. Its anti-inflammatory capability approximates most NSAIDs but its induced garlic taste and smell make it less attractive as an anti-inflammatory.

**Recreational drugs.** These drugs are not related specifically to sports, except that they may be used by athletes socially. Alcohol, caffeine, cocaine, cigarettes, marijuana, smokeless tobacco, and psychedelics are examples. Anderson (1985, 1989) showed that the use of these drugs in a college athletic population is no greater than it is in the non-athlete college population. Each of these drugs could affect performance, usually negatively, but none are specifically concerned with performance or treatment of injury.

## Non-Pharmacologic Performance Aids

**Physiologic Aids.** The physician also should be aware of nonchemical methods employed to improve athletic performance. Most are fads or other advocated methodologies comprising a great deal of the sports medicine "lore."

**Oxygen administration.** The effect of an athlete breathing pure oxygen is approximately 30 seconds of artificially induced oxygen saturation in the blood. It has little or no effect on performance or recovery from fatigue of performance.

**Blood doping.** Creation of a hyperconcentration of red blood cells by drawing a quantity of blood from the athlete, storing it, and then reinfusing it prior to competition to provide enhanced oxygenation capability is increasingly popular in endurance sports (cycling, long distance running). If an athlete's own blood is used, the risks are primarily from infection (including AIDs). When the infusate is not from the athlete, transfusion reaction as well as infection become a concern. Efficacy of the procedure has never been proven (see Appendix 2E-1).

Human erythropoietin (EPO), a kidney hormone that mediates red blood production in bone marrow, is now produced commercially as EPO. Clinically, it is indicated for the treatment of anemia. Evidence suggests that athletes are now using it as an alternative blood doping technique to enhance performance in endurance events (Cowart,

1989). Recent studies do show enhanced maximal aerobic power parallel to the stimulated hemoglobin increase (Ekblom, 1989). The International Olympic Committee and the NCAA have banned its use.

**High altitude training.** Athletes sometimes train at higher elevations in an attempt to increase red blood cell size (an effect of high altitude) and thus enhance their oxygen carrying capacity. Subsequent performance at lower altitudes may be improved.

**Warm-up exercises.** Warm-ups, such as those advocated in this book, should be a part of preparation for an athletic event. Such exercise can facilitate the release of oxygen at tissue level through increased enzymatic stimulation of metabolic activity of muscle (Percy, 1980). No studies to date have confirmed what appear to be sound physiologic principles in this matter.

**Nutritional Aids.** Nutrition and its impact on physical performance has been discussed earlier.

## REFERENCES

### Section A. Exercise Physiology

Astrand, P.O. and K. Rodalh. *Textbook of Work Physiology* New York: McGraw-Hill Book Co., 1977.

Bar-Or, O. A new anaerobic capacity test: Characteristics and applications. *Proceedings Twenty-First World Congress of Sports Medicine*, Brasilia, 1978.

Baldwin, K.M., A.M. Hooker and R.E. Herrick. Lactate oxidative capacity in different types of muscle. *Biochem and Biophysics Res Com* 83:1:151, 1978.

Brooks, G.H. Anaerobic threshold: review of the concept and directions for future research. *Med Sci Sports Exer* 17:22, 1985.

Brooks, G.A. and T.D. Fahey. *Exercise Physiology, Human Bioenergetics and Its Application* New York: John Wiley and Sons, 1984.

Buskirk, E. and H.L. Taylor. Maximal oxygen intake and its relation to body composition, with special reference to chronic physical activity and obesity. *J Appl Physiol* 11:72, 1957.

Buskirk, E.R. Observations of extraordinary performances in an extreme environment and in a training environment. In D.H. Clarke and H.M. Eckert, *Limits of Human Performance* The Academy Papers No. 18. Champaign: Human Kinetics, 1985.

Cureton, T.K. A test for endurance in speed swimming. *Suppl to Res Quart* V-1:8:106-112, 1935.

Carrow, R.E., R.E. Brown and W.D. Van Huss. Exercise and the incidence of muscle fiber splitting. *Proceedings 18th International Congress on Sport Sciences*, 1970.

Ceretelli, P. Exercise and endurance. In L. Larson (Ed.) *Fitness, Health and Work Capacity* New York: The Macmillan Co., 1974.

Conconi, F., M. Ferrari, P.G. Ziglio, P. Droghetti and L. Codica. Determination of the anaerobic threshold by a noninvasive field test in runners. *J Appl Physiol: Resp Environ Ex Physiol* 52:869, 1982.

Costill, D.L., W.J. Fink and M.L. Pollock. Muscle fiber composition and enzyme activities of elite distance runners. *Med Sci Sports* 8:96, 1976.

Davis, J.A. Anaerobic threshold: review of the concept and directions for future research. *Med Sci Sports Exer* 17:6, 1985.

Ellested, M.H. *Stress Testing: Principles and Practices* Philadelphia: F.A. Davis Co., 1975.

Fink, W.J., D.L. Costill and M.L. Pollock. Submaximal and maximal working capacity of elite distance runners: Part II muscle fiber composition and enzyme activities. *Ann N Y Acad Sci* 301:727, 1977.

Henneman, E., G. Somjen and D.L. Carpenter. Functional significance of cell size in spinal motoneurons. *J Neurophysiol* 28:560, 1965.

Hultman, E. Physiological role of muscle glycogen in man, with special reference to exercise. *Circulation Research*, Supplement I to Vols. XX and XXI, 99-133, 1967.

Ivy, J.L., D.L. Costill, W.J. Fink et al. Influence of caffeine and carbohydrate feedings on endurance performance. *Med Sci Sports* 11:6, 1976.

Jones, N.L., E.J. Campbell, R.H.T. Edwards and D.G. Robertson. *Clinical Exercise Testing* Philadelphia: W.B. Saunders Co., 1975.

Kalamen, J.L. *Measurement of Maximal Muscular Power in Man* Unpublished Ph.D. dissertation, The Ohio State University, 1968.

Kennedy, C., W.D. Van Huss and W. W. Heusner. Reversal of the energy metabolism responses to endurance training by weight loading. *Percept Mot Skills* 39:847, 1974.

Kugelberg, E. and L. Edstrom. Differential histochemical effects of muscular contraction on phosphorylase and glycogen in various types of fibers, relation to fatigue. *J Neurol Neurosurg Psychiatry* 31:415, 1968.

Kumagai, S., T. Tanaka, Y. Matsuura, A. Matsuzaka, K. Hirakoba and K. Asano. Relationships of the anaerobic threshold with the 5 km, 10 km, and 10 mile races. *Europ J Appl Physiol* 49:13, 1982.

Margaria, R. et al. Measurement of muscular power (anaerobic) in man. *J Appl Physiol* 21:1662, 1966.

Newsholme, E.A. The regulation of intracellular and extracellular fuel supply during sustained exercise. *Ann N Y Acad Sci* 301:81, 1977.

Noble, B.J. *Physiology of Sport and Exercise* St. Louis: Times Mirror/Mosby College Publishing, 1986.

Prince, F.P., R.S. Hikida and F.C. Hagerman. Human muscle fiber types in power lifters, distance runners, and untrained subjects. *Pflugers Arch* 363-419, 1976.

Rankin, J.M. *Specific Physiological Responses of Elite Runners: 100M-10,000M* Doctoral Dissertation: Michigan State University, 1983.

Rhodes, E.P. and D.C. McKenzie. Predicting marathon times from anaerobic threshold measurements. *Physician and Sportsmed* 12:95, 1984.

Selye, H. *Stress in Health and Disease* Boston: Butterworth, 1971.

Steinhaus, A.H. *Toward an Understanding of Physical Education.* Dubuque: W.C. Brown, 1963.

Van Huss, W.D. Specific responses to heavy exercise stress. *Osteopath Ann* 5:10:53, 1977.

Van Huss, W.D. and T.K. Cureton. Relationship of selected tests to energy metabolism and swimming performance. *Res Quart* 26:206, 1955.

Wasserman, K. and M.B. McIllroy. Detecting the threshold of anaerobic metabolism in cardiac patients during exercise. *Am J Cardiol* 14:844, 1969.

### Section B. Body Composition

Bergström, J., Hermansen, L., Hultman, E. et al. Diet, muscle glycogen and physical performance. *ACTA Physiol Scand* 17:140-150, 1967.

Bray, G.A. Evaluation of the obese patient. *JAMA* 235:1487, 1976.

Jackson, A.S. and Pollock, M.L. Practical assessment of body composition. *Phys and Sportsmed* 13(5):76-90, May 1985.

Lohman, T.G. Skinfolds and body density and their relation to fitness: a review. *Human Biology* 53:181-225, 1981.

Manjarrez, C. and Birrer, R. Nutrition and athletic performance. *American Family Practitioner* 28(5):105-115, Nov, 1983.

McKeag, D.B. Sport and the young athlete: a family practice perspective. From the symposium "Medical Care of the Pediatric Athlete", March 1980, 27th ACSM Annual Meeting, Las Vegas, NV.

McLeod, W.D, Hunter, S.C., Etchison, B. Performance measurement and percent body fat in the high school athlete. *Am J Sports Med* 11(6):390-397, 1983.

Nash, H.L. Body fat measurement: weighing the pros and cons of electrical impedance. *Phys and Sportsmed* 13(11):124-127, Nov. 1985.

Smith, N.J., Weight control in the athlete. *Clinics in Sports Medicine* 3(3):693-704, July 1984.

Ward, G.M., Johnson, J.E., Stagu, J. Body composition — methods of estimation and effect upon performance. *Clinics in Sports Medicine* 3(3):705-722, July 1984.

Whitney, E.N., Hamilton, E., and Rolfes, S. *Understanding Nutrition*, Fifth Edition. West Publishing, 1990.

Wilmore, J.H. Body composition in sports and exercise: directions for research. *Med Sci Sports Exer* No. 15, pgs. 21-31, 1983.

### Section C. Fluids and Electrolytes

American College of Sports Medicine. Position Statement: Prevention of heat injuries during distance running. *Med Sci Sports* 1:vii, 1975.

Costill, D.L. Nutrition for endurance sports: carbohydrate and fluid balance. *Int J Sports Med* 1:2, 1980.

Costill, D.L. and Satlin, B. Factors limiting gastric emptying during rest and exercise. *J Appl Physiol* 37:679, 1974.

Costill, D.L. Water and electrolyte requirements during exercise. In *Clin-*

ics in Sports Medicine, Hecker, A.L. (ed.). W.B. Saunders:Philadelphia, 1984, pp. 639-648.

Davis, J.M. Carbohydrate-electrolyte drinks: effects on endurance cycling in the heat. Am M Clin Nutr 48:1023-1030, 1988.

Foster, C. Costill, D.L. and Fink, W.J. Effects of preexercise feedings on endurance performance. Med Sci Sports 11:1, 1979.

Hecker, A.L. Nutritional conditioning in athletic competition. In Clinics in Sports Medicine, Hecker, A.L. (ed.). W.B. Saunders:Philadelphia, 1984.

Marcus, J.B. (ed.) Sports Nutrition: A Guide for the Professional Working with Active People. American Dietetic Association, 1986.

Noakes, T.D., Goodwin, N., Rayner, B.L. et al. Water intoxication: a possible complication during endurance exercise. Med Sci Sports Exer 17:370, 1985.

Vitousek, S.H. Is more better? J Nutr 14:10, 1979.

Whitney, E., Hamilton, E. and S. Folfes. Understanding Nutrition, West Publishing, 1990.

### Section D. Nutrition

ADA Reports. Nutrition for physical fitness and athletic performance for adults: technical support paper. J Am Dietetic Assoc 87(77), 1987.

American College of Sports Medicine. Position Stand on Weight Loss in Wrestlers, 1976.

Aronson, V. Protein and miscellaneous ergogenic aids. Phys and Sportsmed 14(5):199-202, May 1986.

Aronson, V. Vitamins and minerals as ergogenic aids. Phys and Sportsmed 14(3):209-212, March 1986.

Black, A.L., Henderson, S.A., McCormack, S. and Brooks, G.A. Protein catabolism during exercise in rats (Abstract). Fed Proc 44:1895, 1985.

Brotherhood, J. Nutrition and sports performance. Sports Med 1(Sept-Oct), 1984.

Clark, N. Increasing dietary iron. Phys and Sportsmed 13(1):131-132, 1985.

Colt, E. and Heyman, B. Low ferritin levels in runners. J of Sports Med 24:13-17, 1984.

Costill, D. Food Paper National Dairy Council, Rosemont, IL, 1983.

Costill, D.L. Carbohydrate for athletic training and performance. Contempory Nutrition 15:9, 1990.

Dohm, G.L., Williams, R.T., Kasperek, G.J. and vanRig. A.M. Increased excretion of urea and Nt-methylhestidine by rats after a bout of exercise. J Appl Physiol 52:27-33, 1982b.

Dwyer, J.T., Mayer, L.D., Xandel, R.F. et al. The new vegetarian. J Am Diet Assoc 62 (May), 1973.

Evans, W.J., Fisher, E.C., Hoerr, R.A. and Young, V.R. Protein metabolism and endurance exercise. Phys and Sportsmed 11:63-72, 1983.

Food and Nutritional Board. Recommended Dietary Allowances Ninth Edition. National Research Council, National Academy of Sciences, Washington, D.C. 1980.

Friedman, J.E. and Lemin, P.W.R. Effect of protein intake and endurance exercise on daily protein requirements (Abstract). Med Sci Sports Exercise 17:231-232, 1985.

Grandjean, A.C. The vegetarian athlete. Phys and Sportsmed 15(5), 1987.

Hecker, A.L. Nutritional conditioning for athletic competition. Clinics in Sports Medicine 3(#):567-582, July 1984.

Hultman, E., Nilsson, L.H. In Muscle Metabolism During Exercise. Edited by B. Pernow and B. Salton. Plenum Press, New York, NY pp. 143-151, 1971.

Katch, F. and McArdle, W. Nutrition, Weight Control and Exercise. Philadelphia, Lea & Febiger, 1983.

Keller, K., Schwarzkopf, R. Pre-exercise snacks may decrease exercise performance. Phys and Sportsmed 12(4):89-91, April 1984.

Knight, P.O., Schocken, D., Powers, P.S., et al. Gender comparison in anorexia nervosa and obligate running. Med Sci Sports Exercise 19:566, 1987.

Lemon, P. Protein and exercise: update 1987. Med Sci Sports Exercise 19(5):1987.

Loosli, A.R. Athletes, food and nutrition: sports nutrition from a sports medicine physician. Food and Nutrition News 62(3):15-18.

Manjarrez, C. and Birrer, R. Nutrition and athletic performance. American Family Practitioner 28(5):105-115, Nov. 1983.

Nash, H. Do compulsive runners and anorexic patients share common bonds. Phys and Sportsmed 15(12), 1987.

NCAHF Newsletter, National Council Against Health Fraud, March/April, 1987.

Pate, R.R. Sports anemia: a review of the current research literature. Phys and Sportsmed 11(2):115-131, February 1983.

Rosen, L.W., McKeag, D.B., Hough, D.O., Curley, V. Pathogenic weight-control behavior in female athletes. Phys and Sportsmed 14(1):79-88, Jan 1986.

Sansone, R.A. Complications of hazardous weight loss methods. American Family Practitioner 30(2):141-146, August 1984.

Sherman, W. Carbohydrate, muscle glycogen and muscle glycogen supercompensation. In Williams, M.H (ed.) Ergogenic Aids in Sport. Champaign, IL: Human Kinetic Publishers 3, 1983.

Sherman, W.M., Costill, D.L., Fink. W.J. and Miller, J.N. The effects of exercise and diet manipulation of muscle glycogen and its subsequent utilization during performance. International J of Sports Med 2:114, 198.

Slavin, J.L., McNamara, E.A., Lutter, J.M. Nutritional practices of women cyclists, including recreational riders and elite racers. In Katch F.I. (ed.) Sports, Health, and Nutrition. Champaign, IL: Human Kinetics Publishers, Inc, 1986, pp. 107-111.

Slavin, J. Calorie supplements for athletes. Phys and Sportsmed 14(11), 1986.

Slavin, J. Dietary advice for athletes. Agricultural Extension Service, University of Minnesota, St. Paul, MN, HE-FS-2340, 1984.

Smith, N.J. Nutrition and the athlete. American Journal of Sports Medicine 10(4):253-255, 1982.

Sports Nutrition: A Guide for the Professional Working with Active People. Chicago: American Dietetic Association, 1986.

Stamford, B. Does carbohydrate loading work? Phys and Sportsmed 12(9):196, 1984.

Steinbauth, M. Nutritional needs of female athletes. Clinics in Sports Medicine July 1984, pgs. 649-670.

Town, G., and Wheeler, K. Nutritional concerns for the endurance athlete. Diet Cur 13(March-April), 1986.

Williams, M.H. Nutritional Aspects of Human Physical and Athlete Performance. Springfield, IL. Charles C. Thomas, 1976.

Yates, A., Leckey, K., Shisslak, C.M. Running — an analog of anorexia? NEJM 308:251-255, 1983.

### Section E. Pharmacology

Anderson, W.A., McKeag, D.B. Substance use and abuse habits of college athletes. Phys and Sportsmed, Submitted, 1985.

Blyth, C.S., Murphy, R.J., Sherman, G.P., Schaub, N., Zemper, E.D. Student-athlete questionnaire on use of drugs in athletics. Mission, Kansas; NCAA, 1981.

Chandler, J.B and Blair, V.S. The effect of amphetamines on selected physiological components related to athletic success. Med Sci Sports Exer 12(1):65-69, 1980.

Cowart, V.S. Erythropoietin: a dangerous new form of blood doping? Phys and Sportsmed 17:115-118, 1989.

Ekblom, B. Effects of iron deficiency, variation in hemoglobin concentration and erythropoietin injections on physical performance and relevant physiological parameters. Proceedings of First I.O.C. World Congress on Sport Sciences, pp. 9-11, 1989.

Heitzinger, R.L., Heitzinger, D.L. 1981-1984 Data Collection and Analysis; High School, College, Professional Athletics Alcohol/Drug Survey. Madison, Wisconsin; Heitzinger and Assoc., 1985.

Kennedy, J.C. and Willis, R.B. The effects of local steroid injections on tendons: A biomechanical and microscopic correlative study. Am J Sports Med 4:11-21, 1976.

Lombardo, J.A. Recognizing anabolic steroid use. Patient Care, Aug 15, 1985.

Strauss, R.H. Anabolic Steroids. Chapter 5 in Drugs and Performance in Sports, RH Strauss, ed., Saunders, Philadelphia, 1987.

# Appendix 2B-1.
# Percent Fat Estimate for Women: Sum of Triceps, Abdomen and Suprailium Fatfolds

|                     | Age to Last Year |       |       |       |       |       |       |       |         |
|---------------------|------|------|------|------|------|------|------|------|---------|
| Sum of Fatfolds (mm) | 18-22 | 23-27 | 28-32 | 33-37 | 38-42 | 43-47 | 48-52 | 53-57 | Over 57 |
| 8-12    | 8.8  | 9.0  | 9.2  | 9.4  | 9.5  | 9.7  | 9.9  | 10.1 | 10.3 |
| 13-17   | 10.8 | 10.9 | 11.1 | 11.3 | 11.5 | 11.7 | 11.8 | 12.0 | 12.2 |
| 18-22   | 12.6 | 12.8 | 13.0 | 13.2 | 13.4 | 13.5 | 13.7 | 13.9 | 14.1 |
| 23-27   | 14.5 | 14.6 | 14.8 | 15.0 | 15.2 | 15.4 | 15.6 | 15.7 | 15.9 |
| 28-32   | 16.2 | 16.4 | 16.6 | 16.8 | 17.0 | 17.1 | 17.3 | 17.5 | 17.7 |
| 33-37   | 17.9 | 18.1 | 18.3 | 18.5 | 18.7 | 18.9 | 19.0 | 19.2 | 19.4 |
| 38-42   | 19.6 | 19.8 | 20.0 | 20.2 | 20.3 | 20.5 | 20.7 | 20.9 | 21.1 |
| 43-47   | 21.2 | 21.4 | 21.6 | 21.8 | 21.9 | 22.1 | 22.3 | 22.5 | 22.7 |
| 48-52   | 22.8 | 22.9 | 23.1 | 23.3 | 23.5 | 23.7 | 23.8 | 24.0 | 24.2 |
| 53-57   | 24.2 | 24.4 | 24.6 | 24.8 | 25.0 | 25.2 | 25.3 | 25.5 | 25.7 |
| 58-62   | 25.7 | 25.9 | 26.0 | 26.2 | 26.4 | 26.6 | 26.8 | 27.0 | 27.1 |
| 63-67   | 27.1 | 27.2 | 27.4 | 27.6 | 27.8 | 28.0 | 28.2 | 28.3 | 28.5 |
| 68-72   | 28.4 | 28.6 | 28.7 | 28.9 | 29.1 | 29.3 | 29.5 | 29.7 | 29.8 |
| 73-77   | 29.6 | 29.8 | 30.0 | 30.2 | 30.4 | 30.6 | 30.7 | 30.9 | 31.1 |
| 78-82   | 30.9 | 31.0 | 31.2 | 31.4 | 31.6 | 31.8 | 31.9 | 32.1 | 32.3 |
| 83-87   | 32.0 | 32.2 | 32.4 | 32.6 | 32.7 | 32.9 | 33.1 | 33.3 | 33.5 |
| 88-92   | 33.1 | 33.3 | 33.5 | 33.7 | 33.8 | 34.0 | 34.2 | 34.4 | 34.6 |
| 93-97   | 34.1 | 34.3 | 34.5 | 34.7 | 34.9 | 35.1 | 35.2 | 35.4 | 35.6 |
| 98-102  | 35.1 | 35.3 | 35.5 | 35.7 | 35.9 | 36.0 | 36.2 | 36.4 | 36.6 |
| 103-107 | 36.1 | 36.2 | 36.4 | 36.6 | 36.8 | 37.0 | 37.2 | 37.3 | 37.5 |
| 108-112 | 36.9 | 37.1 | 37.3 | 37.5 | 37.7 | 37.9 | 38.0 | 38.2 | 38.4 |
| 113-117 | 37.8 | 37.9 | 38.1 | 38.3 | 39.2 | 39.4 | 39.6 | 39.8 | 39.2 |
| 118-122 | 38.5 | 38.7 | 38.9 | 39.1 | 39.4 | 39.6 | 39.8 | 40.0 | 40.0 |
| 123-127 | 39.2 | 39.4 | 39.6 | 39.8 | 40.0 | 40.1 | 40.3 | 40.5 | 40.7 |
| 128-132 | 39.9 | 40.1 | 40.2 | 40.4 | 40.6 | 40.8 | 41.0 | 41.2 | 41.3 |
| 133-137 | 40.5 | 40.7 | 40.8 | 41.0 | 41.2 | 41.4 | 41.6 | 41.7 | 41.9 |
| 138-142 | 41.0 | 41.2 | 41.4 | 41.6 | 41.7 | 41.9 | 42.1 | 42.3 | 42.5 |
| 143-147 | 41.5 | 41.7 | 41.9 | 42.0 | 42.2 | 42.4 | 42.6 | 42.8 | 43.0 |
| 148-152 | 41.9 | 42.1 | 42.3 | 42.8 | 42.6 | 42.8 | 43.0 | 43.2 | 43.4 |
| 153-157 | 42.3 | 42.5 | 42.6 | 42.8 | 43.0 | 43.2 | 43.4 | 43.6 | 43.7 |
| 158-162 | 42.6 | 42.8 | 43.0 | 43.1 | 43.3 | 43.5 | 43.7 | 43.9 | 44.1 |
| 163-167 | 42.9 | 43.0 | 43.2 | 43.4 | 43.6 | 43.8 | 44.0 | 44.1 | 44.3 |
| 168-172 | 43.1 | 43.2 | 43.4 | 43.6 | 43.8 | 44.0 | 44.2 | 44.3 | 44.5 |
| 173-177 | 43.2 | 43.4 | 43.6 | 43.8 | 43.9 | 44.1 | 44.3 | 44.5 | 44.7 |
| 178-182 | 43.3 | 43.5 | 43.7 | 43.8 | 44.0 | 44.2 | 44.4 | 44.6 | 44.8 |

## Appendix 2B-2.
## Percent Fat Estimate for Men: Sum of Triceps, Chest and Subscapula Fatfolds

| | \multicolumn{9}{c|}{Age to Last Year} |
|---|---|---|---|---|---|---|---|---|---|
| Sum of Skinfolds (mm) | Under 22 | 23-27 | 28-32 | 33-37 | 38-42 | 43-47 | 48-52 | 53-57 | Over 57 |
| 8-10 | 1.5 | 2.0 | 2.5 | 3.1 | 3.6 | 4.1 | 4.6 | 5.1 | 5.6 |
| 11-13 | 3.0 | 3.5 | 4.0 | 4.5 | 5.1 | 5.6 | 6.1 | 6.6 | 7.1 |
| 14-16 | 4.5 | 5.0 | 5.5 | 6.0 | 6.5 | 7.0 | 7.6 | 8.1 | 8.6 |
| 17-19 | 5.9 | 6.4 | 6.9 | 7.4 | 8.0 | 8.5 | 9.0 | 9.5 | 10.0 |
| 20-22 | 7.3 | 7.8 | 8.3 | 8.8 | 9.4 | 9.9 | 10.4 | 10.9 | 11.4 |
| 23-25 | 8.6 | 9.2 | 9.7 | 10.2 | 10.7 | 11.2 | 11.8 | 12.3 | 12.8 |
| 26-28 | 10.0 | 10.5 | 11.0 | 11.5 | 12.1 | 12.6 | 13.1 | 13.6 | 14.2 |
| 29-31 | 11.2 | 11.8 | 12.3 | 12.8 | 13.4 | 13.9 | 14.4 | 14.9 | 15.5 |
| 32-34 | 12.5 | 13.0 | 13.5 | 14.1 | 14.6 | 15.1 | 15.7 | 16.2 | 16.7 |
| 35-37 | 13.7 | 14.2 | 14.8 | 15.3 | 15.8 | 16.4 | 16.9 | 17.4 | 18.0 |
| 38-40 | 14.9 | 15.4 | 15.9 | 16.5 | 17.0 | 17.6 | 18.1 | 18.6 | 19.2 |
| 41-43 | 16.0 | 16.6 | 17.1 | 17.6 | 18.2 | 18.7 | 19.3 | 19.8 | 20.3 |
| 44-46 | 17.1 | 17.7 | 18.2 | 18.7 | 19.3 | 19.8 | 20.4 | 20.9 | 21.5 |
| 47-49 | 18.2 | 18.7 | 19.3 | 19.8 | 20.4 | 20.9 | 21.4 | 22.0 | 22.5 |
| 50-52 | 19.2 | 19.7 | 20.3 | 20.8 | 21.4 | 21.9 | 22.5 | 23.0 | 23.6 |
| 53-55 | 20.2 | 20.7 | 21.3 | 21.8 | 22.4 | 22.9 | 23.5 | 24.0 | 24.6 |
| 56-58 | 21.1 | 21.7 | 22.2 | 22.8 | 23.3 | 23.9 | 24.4 | 25.0 | 25.5 |
| 59-61 | 22.0 | 22.6 | 23.1 | 23.7 | 24.2 | 24.8 | 25.3 | 25.9 | 26.5 |
| 62-64 | 22.9 | 23.4 | 24.0 | 24.5 | 25.1 | 25.7 | 26.2 | 26.8 | 27.3 |
| 65-67 | 23.7 | 24.3 | 24.8 | 25.4 | 25.9 | 26.5 | 27.1 | 27.6 | 28.2 |
| 68-70 | 24.5 | 25.0 | 25.6 | 26.2 | 26.7 | 27.3 | 27.8 | 28.4 | 29.0 |
| 71-73 | 25.2 | 25.8 | 26.3 | 26.9 | 27.5 | 28.0 | 28.6 | 29.1 | 29.7 |
| 74-76 | 25.9 | 26.5 | 27.0 | 27.6 | 28.2 | 28.7 | 29.3 | 29.9 | 30.4 |
| 77-79 | 26.6 | 27.1 | 27.7 | 28.2 | 28.8 | 29.4 | 29.9 | 30.5 | 31.1 |
| 80-82 | 27.2 | 27.7 | 28.3 | 28.9 | 29.4 | 30.0 | 30.6 | 31.1 | 31.7 |
| 83-85 | 27.7 | 28.3 | 28.8 | 29.4 | 30.0 | 30.5 | 31.1 | 31.7 | 32.3 |
| 86-88 | 28.2 | 28.8 | 29.4 | 29.9 | 30.5 | 31.1 | 31.6 | 32.2 | 32.8 |
| 89-91 | 28.7 | 29.3 | 29.8 | 30.4 | 31.0 | 31.5 | 32.1 | 32.7 | 33.3 |
| 92-94 | 29.1 | 29.7 | 30.3 | 30.8 | 31.4 | 32.0 | 32.6 | 33.1 | 33.4 |
| 95-97 | 29.5 | 30.1 | 30.6 | 31.2 | 31.8 | 32.4 | 32.9 | 33.5 | 34.1 |
| 98-100 | 29.8 | 30.4 | 31.0 | 31.6 | 32.1 | 32.7 | 33.3 | 33.9 | 34.4 |
| 101-103 | 30.1 | 30.7 | 31.3 | 31.8 | 32.4 | 33.0 | 33.6 | 34.1 | 34.7 |
| 104-106 | 30.4 | 30.9 | 31.5 | 32.1 | 32.7 | 33.2 | 33.8 | 34.4 | 35.0 |
| 107-109 | 30.6 | 31.1 | 31.7 | 32.3 | 32.9 | 33.4 | 34.0 | 34.6 | 35.2 |
| 110-112 | 30.7 | 31.3 | 31.9 | 32.4 | 33.0 | 33.6 | 34.2 | 34.7 | 35.3 |
| 113-115 | 30.8 | 31.4 | 32.0 | 32.5 | 33.1 | 33.7 | 34.3 | 34.9 | 35.4 |
| 116-118 | 30.9 | 31.5 | 32.0 | 32.6 | 33.2 | 33.8 | 34.3 | 34.9 | 35.5 |

## Appendix 2B-3.
## Percent Fat Estimate for Women: Sum of Triceps, Suprailium and Thigh Fatfolds

### Age to Last Year

| Sum of Skinfolds (mm) | Under 22 | 23-27 | 28-32 | 33-37 | 38-42 | 43-47 | 48-52 | 53-57 | Over 57 |
|---|---|---|---|---|---|---|---|---|---|
| 23-25 | 9.7 | 9.9 | 10.2 | 10.4 | 10.7 | 10.9 | 11.2 | 11.4 | 11.7 |
| 26-28 | 11.0 | 11.2 | 11.5 | 11.7 | 12.0 | 12.3 | 12.5 | 12.7 | 13.0 |
| 29-31 | 12.3 | 12.5 | 12.8 | 13.0 | 13.3 | 13.5 | 13.8 | 14.0 | 14.3 |
| 32-34 | 13.6 | 13.8 | 14.0 | 14.3 | 14.5 | 14.8 | 15.0 | 15.3 | 15.5 |
| 35-37 | 14.8 | 15.0 | 15.3 | 15.5 | 15.8 | 16.0 | 16.3 | 16.5 | 16.8 |
| 38-40 | 16.0 | 16.3 | 16.5 | 16.7 | 17.0 | 17.2 | 17.5 | 17.7 | 18.0 |
| 41-43 | 17.2 | 17.4 | 17.7 | 17.9 | 18.2 | 18.4 | 18.7 | 18.9 | 19.2 |
| 44-46 | 18.3 | 18.6 | 18.8 | 19.1 | 19.3 | 19.6 | 19.8 | 20.1 | 20.3 |
| 47-49 | 19.5 | 19.7 | 20.0 | 20.2 | 20.5 | 20.7 | 21.0 | 21.2 | 21.5 |
| 50-52 | 20.6 | 20.8 | 21.1 | 21.3 | 21.6 | 21.8 | 22.1 | 22.3 | 22.6 |
| 53-55 | 21.7 | 21.9 | 22.1 | 22.4 | 22.6 | 22.9 | 23.1 | 23.4 | 23.6 |
| 56-58 | 22.7 | 23.0 | 23.2 | 23.4 | 23.7 | 23.9 | 24.2 | 24.4 | 24.7 |
| 59-61 | 23.7 | 24.0 | 24.2 | 24.5 | 24.7 | 25.0 | 25.2 | 25.5 | 25.7 |
| 62-64 | 24.7 | 25.0 | 25.2 | 25.5 | 25.7 | 26.0 | 26.7 | 26.4 | 26.7 |
| 65-67 | 25.7 | 25.9 | 26.2 | 26.4 | 26.7 | 26.9 | 27.2 | 27.4 | 27.7 |
| 68-70 | 26.6 | 26.9 | 27.1 | 27.4 | 27.6 | 27.9 | 28.1 | 28.4 | 28.6 |
| 71-73 | 27.5 | 27.8 | 28.0 | 28.3 | 28.5 | 28.8 | 29.0 | 29.3 | 29.5 |
| 74-76 | 28.4 | 28.7 | 28.9 | 29.2 | 29.4 | 29.7 | 29.9 | 30.2 | 30.4 |
| 77-79 | 29.3 | 29.5 | 29.8 | 30.0 | 30.3 | 30.5 | 30.8 | 31.0 | 31.3 |
| 80-82 | 30.1 | 30.4 | 30.6 | 30.9 | 31.1 | 31.4 | 31.6 | 31.9 | 32.1 |
| 83-85 | 30.9 | 31.2 | 31.4 | 31.7 | 31.9 | 32.2 | 32.4 | 32.7 | 32.9 |
| 86-88 | 31.7 | 32.0 | 32.2 | 32.5 | 32.7 | 32.9 | 33.2 | 33.4 | 33.7 |
| 89-91 | 32.5 | 32.7 | 33.0 | 33.2 | 33.5 | 33.7 | 33.9 | 34.2 | 34.4 |
| 92-94 | 33.2 | 33.4 | 33.7 | 33.9 | 34.2 | 34.4 | 34.7 | 34.9 | 35.2 |
| 95-97 | 33.9 | 34.1 | 34.4 | 34.6 | 34.9 | 35.1 | 35.4 | 35.6 | 35.9 |
| 98-100 | 34.6 | 34.8 | 35.1 | 35.3 | 35.5 | 35.8 | 36.0 | 36.3 | 36.5 |
| 101-103 | 35.3 | 35.4 | 35.7 | 35.9 | 36.2 | 36.4 | 36.7 | 36.9 | 37.2 |
| 104-106 | 35.8 | 36.1 | 36.3 | 36.6 | 36.8 | 37.1 | 37.3 | 37.5 | 37.8 |
| 107-109 | 36.4 | 36.7 | 36.9 | 37.1 | 37.4 | 37.6 | 37.9 | 38.1 | 38.4 |
| 110-112 | 37.0 | 37.2 | 37.5 | 37.7 | 38.0 | 38.2 | 38.5 | 38.7 | 38.9 |
| 113-115 | 37.5 | 37.8 | 38.0 | 38.2 | 38.5 | 38.7 | 39.0 | 39.2 | 39.5 |
| 116-118 | 38.0 | 38.3 | 38.5 | 38.8 | 39.0 | 39.3 | 39.5 | 39.7 | 40.0 |
| 119-121 | 38.5 | 38.7 | 39.0 | 39.2 | 39.5 | 39.7 | 40.0 | 40.2 | 40.5 |
| 122-124 | 39.0 | 39.2 | 39.4 | 39.7 | 39.9 | 40.2 | 40.4 | 40.7 | 40.9 |
| 125-127 | 39.4 | 39.6 | 39.9 | 40.1 | 40.4 | 40.6 | 40.9 | 41.1 | 41.4 |
| 128-130 | 39.8 | 40.0 | 40.3 | 40.5 | 40.8 | 41.0 | 41.3 | 41.5 | 41.8 |

## Appendix 2B-4.
# Percent Fat Estimate for Men: Sum of Chest, Abdomen, and Thigh Fatfolds

| Sum of Skinfolds (mm) | Under 22 | 23-27 | 28-32 | 33-37 | 38-42 | 43-47 | 48-52 | 53-57 | Over 57 |
|---|---|---|---|---|---|---|---|---|---|
| 8-10 | 1.3 | 1.8 | 2.3 | 2.9 | 3.4 | 3.9 | 4.5 | 5.0 | 5.5 |
| 11-13 | 2.2 | 2.8 | 3.3 | 3.9 | 4.4 | 4.9 | 5.5 | 6.0 | 6.5 |
| 14-16 | 3.2 | 3.8 | 4.3 | 4.8 | 5.4 | 5.9 | 6.4 | 7.0 | 7.5 |
| 17-19 | 4.2 | 4.7 | 5.3 | 5.8 | 6.3 | 6.9 | 7.4 | 8.0 | 8.5 |
| 20-22 | 5.1 | 5.7 | 6.2 | 6.8 | 7.3 | 7.9 | 8.4 | 8.9 | 9.5 |
| 23-25 | 6.1 | 6.6 | 7.2 | 7.7 | 8.3 | 8.8 | 9.4 | 9.9 | 10.5 |
| 26-28 | 7.0 | 7.6 | 8.1 | 8.7 | 9.2 | 9.8 | 10.3 | 10.9 | 11.4 |
| 29-31 | 8.0 | 8.5 | 9.1 | 9.6 | 10.2 | 10.7 | 11.3 | 11.8 | 12.4 |
| 32-34 | 8.9 | 9.4 | 10.0 | 10.5 | 11.1 | 11.6 | 12.2 | 12.8 | 13.3 |
| 35-37 | 9.8 | 10.4 | 10.9 | 11.5 | 12.0 | 12.6 | 13.1 | 13.7 | 14.3 |
| 38-40 | 10.7 | 11.3 | 11.8 | 12.4 | 12.9 | 13.5 | 14.1 | 14.6 | 15.2 |
| 41-43 | 11.6 | 12.2 | 12.7 | 13.3 | 13.8 | 14.4 | 15.0 | 15.5 | 16.1 |
| 44-46 | 12.5 | 13.1 | 13.6 | 14.2 | 14.7 | 15.3 | 15.9 | 16.4 | 17.0 |
| 47-49 | 13.4 | 13.9 | 14.5 | 15.1 | 15.6 | 16.2 | 16.8 | 17.3 | 17.9 |
| 50-52 | 14.3 | 14.8 | 15.4 | 15.9 | 16.5 | 17.1 | 17.6 | 18.2 | 18.8 |
| 53-55 | 15.1 | 15.7 | 16.2 | 16.8 | 17.4 | 17.9 | 18.5 | 19.1 | 19.7 |
| 56-58 | 16.0 | 16.5 | 17.1 | 17.7 | 18.2 | 18.8 | 19.4 | 20.0 | 20.5 |
| 59-61 | 16.9 | 17.4 | 17.9 | 18.5 | 19.1 | 19.7 | 20.2 | 20.8 | 21.4 |
| 62-64 | 17.6 | 18.2 | 18.8 | 19.4 | 19.9 | 20.5 | 21.1 | 21.7 | 22.2 |
| 65-67 | 18.5 | 19.0 | 19.6 | 20.2 | 20.8 | 21.3 | 21.9 | 22.5 | 23.1 |
| 68-70 | 19.3 | 19.9 | 20.4 | 21.0 | 21.6 | 22.2 | 22.7 | 23.3 | 23.9 |
| 71-73 | 20.1 | 20.7 | 21.2 | 21.8 | 22.4 | 23.0 | 23.6 | 24.1 | 24.7 |
| 74-76 | 20.9 | 21.5 | 22.0 | 22.6 | 23.2 | 23.8 | 24.4 | 25.0 | 25.5 |
| 77-79 | 21.7 | 22.2 | 22.8 | 23.4 | 24.0 | 24.6 | 25.2 | 25.8 | 26.3 |
| 80-82 | 22.4 | 23.0 | 23.6 | 24.2 | 24.8 | 25.4 | 25.9 | 26.5 | 27.1 |
| 83-85 | 23.2 | 23.8 | 24.4 | 25.0 | 25.5 | 26.1 | 26.7 | 27.3 | 27.9 |
| 86-88 | 24.0 | 24.5 | 25.1 | 25.7 | 26.3 | 26.9 | 27.5 | 28.1 | 28.7 |
| 89-91 | 24.7 | 25.3 | 25.9 | 26.5 | 27.1 | 27.6 | 28.2 | 28.8 | 29.4 |
| 92-94 | 25.4 | 26.0 | 26.6 | 27.2 | 27.8 | 28.4 | 29.0 | 29.6 | 30.2 |
| 95-97 | 26.1 | 26.7 | 27.3 | 27.9 | 28.5 | 29.1 | 29.7 | 30.3 | 30.9 |
| 98-100 | 26.9 | 27.4 | 28.0 | 28.6 | 29.2 | 29.8 | 30.4 | 31.0 | 31.6 |
| 101-103 | 27.5 | 28.1 | 28.7 | 29.3 | 29.9 | 30.5 | 31.1 | 31.7 | 32.3 |
| 104-106 | 28.2 | 28.8 | 29.4 | 30.0 | 30.6 | 31.2 | 31.8 | 32.4 | 33.0 |
| 107-109 | 28.9 | 29.5 | 30.1 | 30.7 | 31.3 | 31.9 | 32.5 | 33.1 | 33.7 |
| 110-112 | 29.6 | 30.2 | 30.8 | 31.4 | 32.0 | 32.6 | 33.2 | 33.8 | 34.4 |
| 113-115 | 30.2 | 30.8 | 31.4 | 32.0 | 32.6 | 33.2 | 33.8 | 34.5 | 35.1 |
| 116-118 | 30.9 | 31.5 | 32.1 | 32.7 | 33.3 | 33.9 | 34.5 | 35.1 | 35.7 |
| 119-121 | 31.5 | 32.1 | 32.7 | 33.3 | 33.9 | 34.5 | 35.1 | 35.7 | 36.4 |
| 122-124 | 32.1 | 32.7 | 33.3 | 33.9 | 34.5 | 35.1 | 35.8 | 36.4 | 37.0 |
| 125-127 | 32.7 | 33.3 | 33.9 | 34.5 | 35.1 | 35.8 | 36.4 | 37.0 | 37.6 |

## Appendix 2B-5.
## Body Mass Index*†

WEIGHT kg. (lb.)

| HEIGHT Inches / Meters | 45.3 (100) | 49.90 (110) | 54.43 (120) | 58.97 (130) | 63.50 (140) | 68.04 (150) | 72.57 (160) | 77.11 (170) | 81.65 (180) | 86.18 (190) | 90.72 (200) | 95.25 (210) | 99.79 (220) | 104.33 (230) | 108.86 (240) | 113.40 (250) | 117.93 (260) | 122.47 (270) | 127.01 (280) | 131.54 (290) | 136.08 (300) |
|---|---|---|---|---|---|---|---|---|---|---|---|---|---|---|---|---|---|---|---|---|---|
| 55 / 1.397 | 23.24 | 25.56 | 27.89 | 30.21 | 32.54 | 34.86 | 37.19 | 39.51 | 41.84 | | | | | | | | | | | | |
| 56 / 1.422 | 22.43 | 24.67 | 26.92 | 29.16 | 31.40 | 33.65 | 35.89 | 38.13 | 40.37 | 42.62 | | | | | | | | | | | |
| 57 / 1.448 | 21.64 | 23.80 | 25.96 | 28.13 | 30.29 | 32.46 | 34.62 | 36.79 | 38.95 | 41.12 | 43.28 | | | | | | | | | | |
| 58 / 1.473 | 20.90 | 22.99 | 25.08 | 27.17 | 29.26 | 31.35 | 33.44 | 35.53 | 37.62 | 39.71 | 41.80 | 43.89 | | | | | | | | | |
| 59 / 1.498 | 20.20 | 22.22 | 24.24 | 26.26 | 28.28 | 30.29 | 32.32 | 34.33 | 36.35 | 38.37 | 40.39 | 42.41 | 44.43 | | | | | | | | |
| 60 / 1.524 | 19.53 | 21.48 | 23.43 | 25.39 | 27.34 | 29.29 | 31.25 | 33.20 | 35.15 | 37.11 | 39.06 | 41.01 | 42.96 | 44.92 | 46.87 | 48.82 | 50.78 | 52.73 | 54.68 | 56.65 | 58.59 |
| 61 / 1.549 | 18.89 | 20.78 | 22.67 | 24.56 | 26.45 | 28.34 | 30.23 | 32.12 | 34.01 | 35.90 | 37.79 | 39.68 | 41.57 | 43.46 | 45.35 | 47.24 | 49.13 | 51.02 | 52.90 | 54.79 | 56.68 |
| 62 / 1.575 | 18.29 | 20.12 | 21.95 | 23.78 | 25.61 | 27.44 | 29.26 | 31.09 | 32.92 | 34.75 | 36.58 | 38.41 | 40.24 | 42.07 | 43.90 | 45.72 | 47.55 | 49.38 | 51.21 | 53.04 | 54.87 |
| 63 / 1.600 | 17.71 | 19.48 | 21.26 | 23.03 | 24.80 | 26.57 | 28.34 | 30.11 | 31.88 | 33.66 | 35.43 | 37.20 | 38.97 | 40.74 | 42.51 | 44.28 | 46.06 | 47.83 | 49.60 | 51.37 | 53.14 |
| 64 / 1.626 | 17.16 | 18.88 | 20.60 | 22.31 | 24.03 | 25.75 | 27.46 | 29.18 | 30.90 | 32.61 | 34.33 | 36.05 | 37.76 | 39.48 | 41.20 | 42.91 | 44.63 | 46.34 | 48.06 | 49.78 | 51.49 |
| 65 / 1.651 | 16.64 | 18.30 | 19.97 | 21.63 | 23.30 | 24.96 | 26.62 | 28.29 | 29.95 | 31.62 | 33.28 | 34.94 | 36.61 | 38.27 | 39.94 | 41.60 | 43.26 | 44.93 | 46.59 | 48.26 | 49.92 |
| 66 / 1.676 | 16.14 | 17.75 | 19.37 | 20.98 | 22.60 | 24.21 | 25.82 | 27.44 | 29.05 | 30.67 | 32.28 | 33.89 | 35.51 | 37.12 | 38.74 | 40.35 | 41.96 | 43.58 | 45.19 | 46.81 | 48.42 |
| 67 / 1.702 | 15.66 | 17.23 | 18.79 | 20.36 | 21.93 | 23.49 | 25.06 | 26.62 | 28.19 | 29.76 | 31.32 | 32.89 | 34.46 | 36.02 | 37.59 | 39.15 | 40.72 | 42.29 | 43.85 | 45.42 | 46.99 |
| 68 / 1.727 | 15.20 | 16.72 | 18.24 | 19.77 | 21.29 | 22.81 | 24.33 | 25.85 | 27.37 | 28.89 | 30.41 | 31.93 | 33.45 | 34.97 | 36.49 | 38.01 | 39.53 | 41.05 | 42.57 | 44.09 | 45.61 |
| 69 / 1.753 | 14.77 | 16.24 | 17.72 | 19.20 | 20.67 | 22.15 | 23.63 | 25.10 | 26.58 | 28.06 | 29.53 | 31.01 | 32.49 | 33.96 | 35.44 | 36.92 | 38.39 | 39.87 | 41.35 | 42.82 | 44.30 |
| 70 / 1.778 | 14.35 | 15.78 | 17.22 | 18.65 | 20.09 | 21.52 | 22.96 | 24.39 | 25.83 | 27.26 | 28.70 | 30.13 | 31.57 | 33.00 | 34.44 | 35.87 | 37.30 | 38.74 | 40.17 | 41.61 | 43.04 |
| 71 / 1.803 | | 15.34 | 16.74 | 18.13 | 19.52 | 20.92 | 22.32 | 23.71 | 25.10 | 26.50 | 27.89 | 29.29 | 30.68 | 32.08 | 33.47 | 34.87 | 36.26 | 37.66 | 39.05 | 40.45 | 41.84 |
| 72 / 1.829 | | 14.92 | 16.27 | 17.63 | 18.99 | 20.34 | 21.70 | 23.05 | 24.41 | 25.77 | 27.12 | 28.48 | 29.84 | 31.19 | 32.55 | 33.90 | 35.26 | 36.62 | 37.97 | 39.33 | 40.69 |
| 73 / 1.854 | | 14.51 | 15.83 | 17.15 | 18.47 | 19.79 | 21.11 | 22.43 | 23.75 | 25.07 | 26.39 | 27.71 | 29.02 | 30.34 | 31.66 | 32.98 | 34.30 | 35.62 | 36.94 | 38.26 | 39.58 |
| 74 / 1.879 | | 14.12 | 15.41 | 16.69 | 17.97 | 19.26 | 20.54 | 21.83 | 23.11 | 24.39 | 25.68 | 26.96 | 28.25 | 29.53 | 30.81 | 32.10 | 33.38 | 34.66 | 35.95 | 37.23 | 38.52 |
| 75 / 1.905 | | | 14.99 | 16.25 | 17.50 | 18.75 | 20.00 | 21.25 | 22.50 | 23.75 | 25.00 | 26.25 | 27.49 | 28.75 | 30.00 | 31.25 | 32.50 | 33.75 | 35.00 | 36.25 | 37.50 |
| 76 / 1.930 | | | 14.61 | 15.82 | 17.04 | 18.26 | 19.47 | 20.69 | 21.91 | 23.13 | 24.34 | 25.56 | 26.78 | 27.99 | 29.21 | 30.43 | 31.65 | 32.86 | 34.08 | 35.30 | 36.52 |

*From Bray, G.A., et al.: Evaluation of the obese patient. I. An algorithm. JAMA, 235:1487, 1976.
†Expressed as weight (kg.)/height meters².

# Appendix 2D-1.
# Complications of Hazardous Weight Loss Methods

**Vomiting**
- Dental erosion
- Parotid and submandibular gland enlargement
- Oral and perioral trauma
- Pharyngeal and esophageal inflammation
- Aspiration
- Esophageal and gastric tears
- Fluid and electrolyte disturbances
- Specus — potentially cardiotoxic (10 bottles/wk x 6 mos) (or 3-4 bottles/d x 3 mos)
- Metabolic alkalosis in chronic abuse

**Laxative Abuse**
- GI complaints
- Cathartic colon — loss of mucosal pattern and "pseudo-structure" formation, punctate ulcers
- Melanosis coli — no functional impairment
- Fixed drug eruption (phenophthalein)
- Fluid and electrolytic disturbances (decreased K+ most frequently)
- Steatorrhea
- Protein-losing enteropathy
- Osteomalacia

**Diuretic Abuse**
- Dehydration
- Electrolyte disturbances (decreased K+ most frequently)
- Metabolic alkalosis in chronic users

(From Sansome, 1984)

# Appendix 2D-2.
# Sports Nutrition Myths

## MUSCLE BUILDING MYTHS

Myth:

1. Consuming large amounts of protein or taking protein supplements will increase muscle size and strength.

2. Vegetarian athletes cannot get enough protein to develop muscles and maintain strength.

Fact:

1. Excess protein will not increase muscle growth or muscle strength. Heavy muscular workouts stimulate the growth and, therefore, the strength of muscle. Extra protein is stored as fat or deaminated and used for energy.

2. A vegetarian athlete can obtain all the nutrients needed for top performance by eating a wide variety of foods. Meat alternates, such as dry beans and peas, nuts, soy products, eggs, and dairy supply protein and other nutrients usually supplied by meats.

## QUICK ENERGY MYTHS

Myth:

3. Eating honey, sugar, soft drinks or a candy bar is an excellent way to get quick energy just before competition or practice.

4. Tea and coffee are the best pre-competition beverages.

5. Athletes require extra vitamins and minerals and should take vitamin pills to "supercharge" their bodies.

Fact:

3. Sweets eaten or drunk an hour or less before competition can cause hypoglycemia because sugar is quickly digested and absorbed prompting an insulin response.

4. Tea and coffee contain caffeine which is a stimulant. Some researchers have found that caffeine can improve endurance performance only in events lasting longer than two hours. They found that drinking a caffeine-containing beverage about an hour before an event stimulated the use of fat as a fuel instead of carbohydrate. Therefore, less muscle glycogen was burned and an athlete could perform longer. However, since they are diuretics, caffeine-containing beverages promote dehydration so they are not recommended.

5. Vitamin and minerals don't supply energy. Taking large amounts of some vitamins (particularly A and D) can be harmful; they accumulate in the athlete's fat stores.

## PERFORMANCE MYTHS

Myth:

6. Drinking water during an event or practice causes cramps and upset stomach and slows the athlete down.

Fact:

6. Water is the most important nutrient for athletes-especially during hot weather. Even ice cold water does not cause cramps or stomach upset. However, a lack of water may

7. Eating steak and eggs before an event will improve performance.

8. Milk before an event causes cotton mouth, decreases speed, and cuts wind.

9. Salt tablets are necessary to replace that lost in sweat.

affect performance. Athletes should drink 1/2 cup of cool, plain water every 10-15 minutes during exercise to replace body fluids lost as sweat. Cramps are caused by water loss.

7. High-protein meals eaten on the day of the event contribute little to energy production and performance. High-fat foods like meat and eggs stay in the stomach a long time and can cause indigestion, nausea, or even vomiting if eaten within a few hours of competition.

8. "Cotton mouth" is a dryness and discomfort in the mouth. It appears to be due to emotional stress and fluid loss, not to drinking milk. Studies show no performance (speed or wind) decline when the diet includes milk. Even as part of the pre-competition meal, 6-10 ounces of skim milk will not interfere with performance.

9. Sweat is mostly water and contains relatively little salt. The athlete's normal diet usually supplies enough salt to replace whatever is lost as sweat. The kidneys control the amount of salt in the body and they conserve it if too little is taken in or excrete more if too much is consumed. There are many side effects from using salt tablets.

Appendix 2E-1.
# American College of Sports Medicine Position on Statement on "Blood Doping as an Ergogenic Aid"

**Summary**

Blood Doping is an ergogenic[1] procedure wherein normovolemic erythrocythemia is induced via autologous (i.e. reinfusion of athlete's own blood) or homologous (i.e. transfusion of type matched donor's blood) red blood cell (RBC) infusion (11, 27, 28, 34). The resultant hemoconcentration increases arterial oxygen content ($CaO_2$) (9, 23). During peak exercise, oxygen delivery [cardiac output ($\dot{Q}$)x$CaO_2$] to skeletal muscle is enhanced, improving maximal oxygen uptake ($\dot{V}O_2$max) and endurance capacity (9, 28, 29, 31). Such terms as blood boosting, blood packing and induced erythrocythemia are also variously used to describe this ergogenic procedure (11, 34).

It is the position of the American College of Sports Medicine that the use of blood doping as an ergogenic aid for athletic competition is unethical and unjustifiable, but that autologous RBC infusion is an acceptable procedure to induce erythrocythemia in clinically controlled conditions for the purpose of legitimate scientific inquiry.

**Applications: Experimental and Ergogenic**

Blood doping was first used as an experimental procedure to study hematological control mechanisms for systemic transport of oxygen during acute hypoxic exposure (23). Subsequent investigations have experimentally manipulated hemoglobin concentration ([Hb]) via RBC infusion to demonstrate the rate-limiting effect of peak Hb flow rate ($\dot{Q}$x[Hb]) and oxygen delivery on $\dot{V}O_2$max and endurance capacity (4, 8, 9, 13, 27, 28, 29, 31, 37). These experimental applications have shown that RBC infusion is a valuable laboratory tool when examining the effect of [Hb] on oxygen transport function during dynamic exercise under both normoxic and hypoxic conditions.

While reports of blood doping for scientific purposes appeared as early as 1947 (23), it was not until the 1976 Olympic games in Montreal that it was suggested the procedure had been used as an ergogenic aid for endurance events (11, 34). Since that time, both athletes and sports officials have publicly admitted having employed homologous RBC infusion as an ergogenic aid during international competition. These actions prompted a call for an unequivocal statement regarding the *ergogenic*, *physiological*, *medical* and *ethical* implications underlying the use of blood doping as an ergogenic aid. This position statement was prepared by the American College of Sports Medicine in response to these concerns.

**Ergogenic Effect**

The ergogenic properties of normovolemic erythroythemia have, in part, been inferred from the increase in oxygen transport capacity that attends prolonged exposure to high altitude. As both $\dot{V}O_2$max and endurance performance are improved under hypoxic conditions following long term altitude acclimatization, it was hypothesized that artificial production of a normovolemic erythrocythemia via RBC infusion might have a similar ergogenic effect. While documentation of the beneficial effect of blood doping during actual competitive conditions is lacking, a significant amount of experimental evidence supports the ergogenic properties of RBC infusion under both normoxic and hypoxic conditions.

The ergogenic effectiveness of blood doping is dependent on a significant elevation in [Hb] following RBC infusion (11, 34). When autologous blood is used, postreinfusion hemoconcentration occurs only if normocythemia has been restored prior to artificial expansion of the RBC mass. In investigations where this methodological criterion was met, the prephlebotomy to postinfusion increase in [Hb] was associated with a significantly

---

[1] An ergogenic aid is a physical, mechanical, nutritional, psychological or pharmacological substance or treatment that either directly improves physiological variables associated with exercise performance or removes subjective restraints which may limit physiological capacity (35).

higher $\dot{V}O_2$max (i.e., 3.9 to 12.8%) and/or endurance capacity (i.e., 2.5 to 35%) (4, 23, 27, 28, 29, 31, 37). Improvements in maximal aerobic power following blood doping were achieved when subjects received 2000 ml of homologous blood (23) or 900-1800 ml of freeze-preserved autologous blood (4, 27, 28, 29, 37). Infusion of smaller volumes of blood was not sufficient to elevate [Hb] or significantly improve $\dot{V}O_2$max and/or endurance capacity (7, 11, 18, 27, 36).

A number of investigations have not found a statistically significant improvement in maximal aerobic power following blood doping (10, 20, 25, 35). Some reasons for this finding include: improper experimental designs, such as the absence of placebo and control conditions; the designation of preinfusion (anemic) values rather than prephlebotomy (normocythemic) values as control levels; protocols that could have produced a training effect in the experimental subjects; and most importantly, failure to achieve a significant increase in [Hb] due to an inappropriate storage technique and/or inadequate transfusion volumes and time between phlebotomy and transfusion. Consequently, reviewers of these studies incorrectly concluded that blood doping does not alter $\dot{V}O_2$max or endurance performance (24, 33).

**Physiological Mechanism**

The physiological mechanism underlying the hemoconcentration that attends blood doping involves a shift of protein-free plasma filtrate from the intravascular to interstitial compartment; resolving the immediate postinfusion hypervolemia (16, 35). The resulting decrease in plasma volume produces a comparatively rapid restoration of normal blood volume in the presence of a greater [Hb] and $CaO_2$. Provided Hct does not exceed 50%, $\dot{Q}$ during peak exercise is not attenuated by erythrocythemia (9, 28, 29, 30). As such, the higher $CaO_2$ following blood doping increases oxygen delivery (i.e., $\dot{Q} \times CaO_2$). At peak exercise, augmented oxygen delivery increases the differences between arterial and venous oxygen content [C(a-v)$O_2$] (9, 28, 29, 31). The greater tissue respiration increases $\dot{V}O_2$max and endurance capacity. Additionally, both $CO_2$ transport and acid-base balance are favorably affected by an increase in [Hb]. Such changes in blood-buffering capacity may also contribute to the ergogenic properties of induced erythrocythemia.

Following blood doping, heart rate (4, 9, 23, 27, 28, 29), $\dot{Q}$ (28), and lactic acid concentration (4, 9, 13, 29) decrease as C(a-v)$O_2$ increases for a given submaximal oxygen uptake. At exercise intensities $\geq$40% $\dot{V}O_2$max, stroke volume is unaffected by erythrocythemia (28). Although oxygen uptake during submaximal exercise is unchanged following blood doping, the relative oxygen (%$\dot{V}O_2$max) requirement is reduced as a result of the increased $\dot{V}O_2$max.

The blood concentration of 2,3-diphosphoglycerate (4, 9, 11, 28, 37) and the oxygen partial pressure at which 50% of Hb is saturated ($P_{50}$) (28) are not affected by induced erythrocythemia. These findings indicate there is no change in the affinity of the RBC for oxygen when [Hb] is increased.

The time course of the postinfusion hematologic changes is an important consideration for the application of blood doping. Provided normocythemia has been re-established, both [Hb] and Hct are significantly elevated within 24 hours following autologous infusion of 900 ml of blood (11, 12). The erythrocythemia remains relatively constant for seven days, whereupon hematology values return gradually and linerarly, to control levels over a 15 week period. Thus, increased oxygen carrying capacity is observed not just for a brief period following the blood reinfusion, but for many weeks thereafter (4, 28). In this context, research involving induced erythrocythemia should be scheduled approximately 120 d (i.e., RBC life span) before an athletic event to insure that normocythemia is restored in experimental subjects prior to their participation in competition.

**Procedure for Blood Storage and Reinfusion**

Blood is preserved either by refrigeration at 4°C or a glycerol freezing technique (22). When blood is refrigerated, there is a progressive loss of erythrocytes with a concomitant accumulation of cellular aggregates. As such, regulatory agencies in North America have set three weeks as the maximum refrigeration storage time for blood. Of concern in an autologous blood doping protocol is that a three week storage period is normally insufficient to restore prephlebotomy [Hb] when more than one unit of blood is removed (11, 12). In addition, RBCs are also destroyed in the transfusion process or become so fragile during storage that they hemolyze shortly after they are reinfused. The net result is that only 60% of originally removed cells are viable following reinfusion. The comparatively s ort storage time and the marked hemolysis associated with storage and transfer make it very difficult to restore normocythemia prior to blood doping when a refrigeration storage procedure is used.

In contrast, when blood is stored as frozen cells, the aging process of the RBC is interrupted, allowing preservation for an indefinite period of time (32). In the context of autologous blood doping, freeze preservation makes it possible to delay reinfusion as long as necessary to insure that normocythemia has been re-established in the donor. Re-establishing normocythemia following phlebotomy is a primary requisite for postreinfusion erythrocythemia. When used in a blood doping protocol, frozen blood is thawed and reconstituted with physiologic saline to a Hct of approximately 50 percent. The reconstituted blood is usually infused within 24-48 hours prior to laboratory testing or athletic competition.

## Medical Implications

While blood doping appears to be an effective ergogenic aid, the safety of its use is suspect. Transfusion of red blood cells to the extent of raising the hematocrit over 60% may subject the individual to a hyperviscosity syndrome which includes intravascular clotting, potential heart failure and death (21). If blood transfusions are performed without adhering to standard medical procedures, severe bacterial infections, air and clot emboli, and major transfusion reactions may occur, in rare instances leading to death (1, 15, 38).

The medical risks of "blood doping" can be separated into those associated with homologous transfusions and those associated with autologous transfusions. Homologous transfusions, even under standardized medical procedures carry several risks. Despite appropriate typing and cross matching of blood there is a three to four percent incidence of minor transfusion reactions consisting of fever, chills and malaise (2, 19). Delayed reactions can cause destruction of the transfused red cells (26). Both of these reactions can occur without demonstrable incompatibility with the donor cells. Viral infections transmitted by blood also pose a serious risk with homologous transfusions. Malaria (6), hepatitis (14), acquired immune deficiency syndrome (AIDS) (5), and cytomegalovirus (18) are the most common and dangerous of these infections. Although progress has been made in detecting contaminated blood, there is still a slightly less than one percent chance of acquiring one of these diseases from transfused blood despite the use of the best detection methods (17). All of these infections can be fatal. In contrast, autologous transfusions limited to two units of packed RBC and performed under proper medical supervision carry a substantially lower medical risk (3).

## Ethical Considerations

The International Olympic Committee (IOC) defines doping as "the use of physiological substances in abnormal amounts and with abnormal methods, with the exclusive aim of attaining an artificial and unfair increase of performance in competition" (7). Based on this definition, the IOC has banned blood doping as an ergogenic aid. However, techniques to detect an artificially induced erythrocythemia are not available. In addition, if such detection techniques were available, their validity would be confounded by altitude acclimatization, hydration status and normally occurring individual differences in Hct.

## Conclusion

A position statement on the use of blood doping must distinguish between scientific and sport applications of the procedure. *Autologous* RBC infusion is considered a scientifically valid and acceptable laboratory procedure to induce erythrocythemia for legitimate scientific inquiry under clinically controlled conditions. However, because RBC infusion (i.e., autologous and homologous) has attendant medical risks and violates doping control regulations, it is the position of the American College of Sports Medicine that the use of blood doping as an ergogenic aid during athletic competition is unethical and unjustifiable.

**REFERENCES**

1. Braude, A.I. Transfusion reactions from contaminated blood: their recognition and treatment. *N. Eng. J. Med.* 258:1289-1293, 1958.
2. Brittingham, T.E. and H. Chaplin. Febrile transfusion reactions caused by sensitivity to donor leukocytes and platelets. *JAMA* 165:819-825, 1957.
3. Brzica, S.M., A.A. Pineda, and H.F. Taswell. Autologous blood transfusion. *Mayo Clin. Proc.* 51:723-737, 1976.
4. Buick, F.J., N. Gledhill, A.B. Froese, L. Spriet, and E.C. Meyers. Effect of induced erythrocythemia on aerobic work capacity. *J. of Appl. Physiol.: Respirat. Environ. Exercise Physiology.* 48:636-642, 1980.
5. Curran, J.W., D.N. Lawrence, H. Jaffe, J.E. Kaplan, L.D. Zyla, M. Chamerland, R. Weinstein, K-J Lui, L.B. Schonberger, T.J. Spira, W.J. Alexander, G. Swinger, A. Ammann, S. Solomon, D. Auerbach, D. Mildvan, R. Stoneburner, J. Jason, H.W. Haverkos, and B.L. Evatt. Acquired immune-deficiency syndrome (AIDS) associated with transfusion. *N. Eng. J. Med.* 310:69-75, 1984.
6. Dover, A.S. and W.G. Schultz. Transfusion-induced malaria. *Transfusion* 11(6):353-357, 1971.
7. Dugal, R. and M. Bertrand. Doping. In: *IOC Medical Commission Booklet*. Montreal: *Comite' Orginisateur des Jeux Olympiques* 1976, p. 1-31.
8. Ekblom, B., A.N. Goldbarg, and B. Gullbring. Response to exercise after blood loss and reinfusion. *J. Appl. Physiol.* 40:379-383, 1972.
9. Ekblom, B., G. Wilson, and P.O. Astrand. Central circulation during

exercise after venesection and reinfusion of red blood cells. *J. Appl. Physiol.* 40:379-383, 1976.

10. Frye, A., and R. Ruhling. RBC infusion, exercise, hemoconcentration, and $VO_2$ (Abstract). *Med. Sci. Sports.* 9:69, 1977.

11. Gledhill, N. Blood doping and related issues: a brief review. *Med. Sci. Sports Exerc.* 14:193-189, 1982.

12. Gledhill, N., F.J. Buick, A.B. Froese, L. Spriet, and E.C. Meyers. An optimal method of storing blood for blood boosting. *Med. Sci. Sports* (abstract) 10:40, 1978.

13. Gledhill, N., L.L. Spriet, A.B. Froese, D.L. Wilkes, and E.C. Meyers. Acid-base status with induced erythrocythemia and its influence on arterial oxygenation during heavy exercise. *Med. Sci. Sports Exercise* 12:122, 1980. (abstract).

14. Grady, G.F., and T.C. Chalmers. Risk of post-transfusion viral hepatitis. *New Eng. J. Med.* 271:337, 1964.

15. Greenwalt, T.J. (ed.): *General Principles of Blood Transfusion.* American Medical Association, Chicago, 1977, p. 65-74.

16. Gregersen, M., and S. Chien. Blood volume. In: *Medical Physiology* V.B. Mountcastle (ed.). St. Louis, MO: Mosby, 1968, p. 244-283.

17. Harrison, T.R. *Harrison's Principles of Internal Medicine.* G.W. Thorn, R.D. Adams, E. Braunwald, K.J. Isselbacher and R.G. Petersdorf (ed.), New York: McGraw Hill, 1977, p. 1703-1706.

18. Henle, W., G. Henle, M. Scriba, C.R. Joyner, F.S. Harrison, Jr. R. von Essen, J. Paloheimo, and E. Klemola. Antibody responses to the Epstein-Barr virus and cytomegaloviruses after open heart surgery. *New Eng. J. Med.* 282(14):1068-1074, 1970.

19. Honig, C.L. and J.R. Bove. Transfusion: associated fatalities: review of Bureau of Biologies reports 1976-1978. *Transfusion* 20(6):653-661, 1980.

20. Kots, Y.M., M.M. Shcherba, Y.S. Kolner, V.D. Gorodetskii, and L.D. Sin. Experimental study of the relationship between the blood hemoglobin and physical aerobic working capacity. *Fiziologiya Cheloveka* 4(1):53-60, 1978.

21. McGrath, M.A. and R. Penny. Paraproteinuria: Blood hyperviscosity and clinical manifestations. *J. Clin. Invest.* 58:1155-1162, 1976.

22. Merryman, H.T., and T. Hornblower. A method for freezing and washing red blood cells using a high glycerol concentration. *Transfusion* 12:145-156, 1972.

23. Pace, N., E.L. Lozner, W.V. Consolazio, G.C. Pitts, and J.L. Pecora. The increase in hypoxia tolerance of normal men accompanying the polycythemia induced by transfusion of erythrocytes. *Am. J. Physiol.* 148:152-163, 1947.

24. Pate, R. Does the sport need new blood? *Runner's World Magazine* Nov.: 25-27, 1976.

25. Pate, R., J. McFarland, J.V. Wyck, and A. Okocha. Effect of blood reinfusion on endurance performance in female distance runners. *Med. Sci. Sports* 11:97, 1979 (abstract).

26. Pineda, A.A., H.F. Taswell, and S.M. Brzica, Jr. Delayed hemolytic transfusion reaction: An immunologic hazard of blood transfusion. *Transfusion* 18(1):1-7, 1978.

27. Robertson, R.J., R. Gilcher, K.F. Metz, G.S. Skrinar, T.G. Allison, H.T. Bahnson, R.A. LAbbott, R. Becker, and J.E. Falkel. Effect of induced erythrocythemia on hypoxia tolerance during physical exercise. *J. Appl. Physiol.: Respirat. Environ. Exercise Physiol.* 53:490-495, 1982.

28. Robertson, R.J., R. Gilcher, K.F. Metz, C.J. Casperson, T.G. Allison, R.A. Abbott, G.S. Skrinar, J.R. Krause, and P.A. Nixon. Hemoglobin concentration and aerobic work capacity in women following induced erythrocythemia. *J. Appl. Physiol.: Respirat. Environ. Exercise Physiol.* 57(2):568-575, 1984.

29. Spriet, L.L., N. Gledhill, A.B. Froese, and D.L. Wilkes. Effect of graded erythrocythemia on cardiovascular and metabolic responses to exercise. *J. Appl. Physiol.* 61(5):1942-1948, 1986.

30. Stone, H.O., H.K. Thompson, and K. Schmidt-Nielson. Influence of erythrocytes on blood viscosity. *Am. J. Physiol.* 214:913-918, 1968.

31. Thompson, J.M., J.A. Stone, A.D. Ginsberg, and P. Hamilton. $O_2$ transport during exercise following blood reinfusion. *J. Appl. Physiol.: Respirat. Environ. Exercise Physiol.* 53(5):1213-1219, 1982.

32. Valeri, C.R. *Blood Banking and the Use of Frozen Blood Products.* Cleveland: CRC Press, 1976, p. 9-174.

33. Williams, M.H. Blood doping in sports. *J. Drug Issues* 3:331-340, 1980.

34. Williams, M.H. (ed.). Blood Doping. *Ergogenic Aids in Sport.* Champaign, Illinois: Human Kinetics, 1983, pp. 202-217.

35. Williams, M.H., A.R. Goodwin, R. Perkins, and J. Bocrie. Effect of blood reinjection upon endurance capacity and heart rate. *Med. Sci. Sports* 5:181-186, 1973.

36. Williams, M.H., M. Lindheim, and R. Schuster. Effect of blood infusion upon endurance capacity and ratings of perceived exertion. *Med. Sci. Sports* 10:113-118. 1978.

37. Williams, M.H., S. Wesseldine, T. Somma, and R. Schuster. The effect of induced erythrocythemia upon 5-mile treadmill run time. *Med. Sci. Sports Exercise* 13:169-175, 1981.

38. Williams, W.J., E. Beutler, A.J. Ersley and R.W. Rundles. *Hematology*, New York: McGraw-Hill, 1977, p. 1540-1547.

# Unit 2: Epidemiology of Athletic Injuries

This unit will introduce some fundamental concepts of epidemiology, the basic science of preventive medicine, and its application to sports medicine, specifically the epidemiology of athletic injuries. The word "epidemiology" is comprised of three Greek root terms: epi (meaning "upon"), demos ("people"), and logos ("study"). Therefore, epidemiology is the study of what is upon, or befalls, a people or population. A more formal definition is that provided by Duncan (12):

> "Epidemiology is the study of the distribution and determinants of the varying rates of diseases, injuries, or other health states in human populations."

The basic method of studying and determining these distributions and determinants is comparing groups within a population (the sick and the well; the injured and the non-injured). Doing an epidemiological study is a lot like being a detective, using logic to discover cause and effect relationships for illnesses or other medical conditions in a population. In many ways it is similar to diagnosing an illness, but it is done with a large population rather than with an individual patient.

The initial development of the theory and methods of epidemiology focused on applications to communicable diseases. However, in recent years epidemiologic theory and methodologies have been applied to a broader range of subject areas, including athletic injuries.

Duncan (12) lists seven major uses for epidemiological data:

- Identifying the causes of disease.
- Completing the clinical picture of a disease.
- Allowing identification of syndromes.
- Determining the effectiveness of therapeutic and preventive measures.
- Providing the means to monitor the health of a community or region; i.e., input for rational health planning.
- Quantifying risks (health hazard appraisals).
- Providing an overview of long-term disease trends.

For our purposes in athletic medicine, epidemiological data can be used to:

- Identify causes of injuries.
- Provide a more accurate picture of clinical reality. Clusters of injuries (and the resulting media attention they often generate) give a distorted view of reality; on the other hand, data may reveal a previously unsuspected injury problem.
- Determine the effectiveness of preventive measures (on a local or national scale), whether they are rule changes, new or modified equipment, or modifications of training techniques.
- Monitor the health of athletes, which will assist in rational medical planning.
- Quantify the risks of various types, frequencies, and intensities of exercise activities.
- Provide an overview of long-term injury trends in specific sports.

## EPIDEMIOLOGIC RATES

The basic tool of epidemiology is the calculation of rates of occurrence of medical cases of interest in a given population. The two most commonly used rates are incidence and prevalence. The prevalence rate includes all cases of the medical condition of interest that exist at the beginning of the study period and all new cases that develop during the study period. Incidence rates include only the newly developed cases. In sports medicine, the incidence rate is predominantly used to study athletic injuries, since it is assumed that all athletes are uninjured at the beginning of the season and it is the incidence of new injuries during the season that is of interest. Therefore, we will deal only with incidence rates here.

The incidence rate is a measure of the rate at which new events (illnesses, injuries, etc.) occur during a specified time in a defined population:

$$\text{Incidence Rate} = \frac{\text{\# new events (during specified time period)}}{\text{\# in the population at risk}} \times k$$

The numerator is simply a count of the number of new cases that occur during the study period.

The denominator is the total number of people in the population under study who are "at risk" or exposed to the possibility of infection, injury, etc. To provide reasonable numbers that are neither extremely large nor extremely small, and to make comparisons easier, this ratio is transformed to a common metric by multiplying by a convenient multiple of 10 (represented by the constant k in the above equation). If k=1,000 the result would be a rate per 1,000 in the population; if k=100,000 the result would be a rate per 100,000. For example, suppose 24 cases of measles were reported on a college campus of 34,000 students. A moment's thought will show that stating a rate of 24/34,000 is not the most informative way of presenting this information. The probability of an individual having the disease is not readily apparent, and it is not easy to compare the rate with the five cases that occurred in the population of 630 student-athletes on that campus. The base ratio of 24/34,000 is 0.000706, which is the probability that any one individual has measles. But obviously this is not an easy number to work with. Using k=100,000 we transform this rate to 70.6 cases per 100,000, which is a little more manageable. If we make the same calculation for student-athletes, we get a case rate of 793.7 cases per 100,000. Now it is easier to see that student-athletes had a much higher rate of measles, so immediate preventive measures might be in order for this special population.

Determining the numerator of the case rate equation is usually relatively easy. The most critical part of the calculation is determining the denominator, or the "population at risk." This should include everyone in the population who could be affected by the disease or condition of interest, and should exclude those who could not be affected or are not really a member of the population of interest. For instance, in calculating a case rate for pregnancy, males, females past menopause, and females who have not reached menarche should not be used in the denominator. In calculating a case rate for football injuries during games, only those who actually played and were exposed to the possibility of injury, not the whole team, should be included in the denominator.

In sports medicine, case rates generally are used to present epidemiological information about athletic injuries. These rates are presented most often as injuries per 100 athletes, which is analogous to the rate per 100,000 population used for reporting disease rates. However, there is a difference between the continuous exposure of a population to a disease and the discrete exposure of an athlete to injury, which occurs only during practices or games. The number of practices and games varies considerably from one sport to another, and often varies from one team to another, or even from one year to another in a given sport. In addition, not every player participates in every practice and every game, and the number of participants on a team may change considerably as the season progresses. Thus, the common practice of reporting athletic injuries as a rate per 100 participants can lead to questionable conclusions, particularly when results from different sports, or even from different studies of the same sport, are compared. A more precise method is to report case rates per 1,000 athlete-exposures. An athlete-exposure is defined as one athlete participating in one practice or game where there is the possibility of sustaining an athletic injury. If a football team of 100 players has five practices during the week, there are 500 athlete-exposures to the possibility of being injured in practice during that week. If 40 players get into the game on Saturday, the team has 40 athlete-exposures in the game, and the weekly total is 540 athlete-exposures to the possibility of being injured.

Using athlete-exposures as the denominator allows more accurate and precise comparisons of injury rates between sports and in different years. Case rates per 1,000 athlete-exposures was used by the National Athletic Injury/Illness Reporting System (NAIRS) (1) and was adopted and is currently used by the NCAA Injury Surveillance System (31) and the Athletic Injury Monitoring System (32). An even more precise approach would base the exposure rate on the amount of time actually spent in practices or games. This might be possible in small local studies but, in most cases, the amount of record keeping required for a national-scale surveillance system would be prohibitive and impractical for those doing the on-site data recording. Case rates per 1,000 athlete-exposures is believed to be a reasonable compromise that gives a more accurate picture of the epidemiology of athletic injuries than the use of simple rates per 100 athletes.

## POTENTIAL USES OF SPORTS INJURY RATE DATA

It has become evident over the past twenty years that there is a need for data on injury rates for various sports and athletic activities. The research literature on the epidemiology of athletic injuries has been growing slowly but steadily as individuals and groups have gathered data on the risks of participating in sports. Most are short-term observations of single sports involving relatively small numbers of individuals or teams in a school or college setting. In a presentation to the American Orthopaedic Society for Sports Medicine in July 1975, Professor Kenneth S. Clarke noted the lack of meaningful and dependable data on athletic injuries (5). Ten years later, in 1985, at a workshop on Epidemiologic and Public Health Aspects of Physical Activity and Exercise, Jeffrey P. Koplan, M.D., made the same observation about the lack of data on athletic injuries and on regular physical activity in general (14). With the increase in participation in organized sports and in fitness activities, participation that is encouraged by the medical community as a public health intervention, people often do not realize that there still is little or no dependable risk data available. Effort is focused on defining the benefits of participation, but little is done to assess risk. This information is needed to make informed decisions about the value of taking part in a particular activity, and to provide information on how injury rates can be reduced.

Among the groups and organizations that need data on athletic injury rates are national sports governing bodies such as the National Federation of State High School Associations (NFSHSA), the National Collegiate Athletic Association (NCAA), the National Association for Intercollegiate Athletics (NAIA) and the National Junior College Athletic Association (NJCAA). They are responsible for segments of the school-college athletic community where a great deal of sports activity takes place. Through their rules committees, they are directly or indirectly responsible for the safety and well-being of athletes under their jurisdiction. Accurate and reliable injury rate data would indicate the types of injuries or situations where injuries occur that could be positively affected by appropriate rule changes, equipment changes, or suggested changes in coaching technique. These groups now make safety-related changes based primarily on impressions or anecdotal data from coaches, trainers, and others. Obviously, it would be more desirable to have safety-related rule changes based on documented data. It also would be useful to have data showing why a suggested rule change was not adopted; for instance, whether the numbers of a particular type of injury are not as high as was believed, or the injury does not occur during the situations affected by a suggested rule change. (Often, public perception of the extent or seriousness of a problem is greatly inflated by selective attention by the media to a few cases. Responding to resultant public pressures is difficult without data on the actual extent of the problem.) The actions of rule-making committees of major national organizations like the NCAA and the NFSHSA also have an impact on sports at other levels.

Accurate injury data could be used by manufacturers of sporting goods to target areas where new protective equipment could reduce injury rates, where design changes might be needed in existing equipment, or where a particular brand or model is not meeting expectations. In a similar vein, standard-setting groups such as the National Operating Committee on Standards for Athletic Equipment or the American Society for Testing and Materials could use injury rate data to pinpoint areas where implementation of new standards could help in reducing injury rates, or where modification of an existing standard is needed to further cut down equipment-related injuries. All of these organizations would find that data on rates and situations related to specific types of injuries is valuable in preparing legal arguments in athletic injury-related court cases. These lawsuits have become more common, but little reliable national data is available to either party or the court.

There also is a need for national athletic injury data within the sports medicine community for theoretical purposes, such as providing a data base for epidemiological research. It also is needed for practical purposes like providing physicians, athletic trainers, and administrators with information on the types of injuries that are most likely to occur in given settings and situations. Educators need this data to train coaches, physical educators, physicians, and other medical personnel. Primary care physicians need data on the risks of various types, frequencies, and intensities of exercise when advising patients about the adoption of a more active lifestyle (see Chapter 20).

While all these groups and organizations are interested in reducing the number and severity of sports-related injuries, only rarely has it been possible for them to directly monitor the impact of their efforts to reduce injury rates. The only practical way to do this is through a continuing national data collection system that provides data over a period of years. Data for only one or two years is not sufficient because it provides no basis for making reasonable comparisons (before and after implementation of a change). Sometimes it may take more than one year for a rule or equipment change to produce a noticeable impact on injury rates because there may be local or regional differences in using a piece of equipment or in adopting, interpreting or enforcing a rule change.

Another reason for a national injury data collection system to operate continuously over time is because there are yearly fluctuations in injury rates. Using only one or two years of data can lead to invalid conclusions and faulty decisions. An illustration of this type of problem is found in fatality data among high school pole vaulters collected by Carl Blyth, Ph.D., and Fred Mueller, Ph.D., at the University of North Carolina (17). During the first year they began collecting fatality and catastrophic injury data (a catastrophic injury being defined as a cervical spine injury resulting in permanent paralysis) for youth, high school, college, and professional sports, they recorded four fatalities among high school pole vaulters. Few high school athletes compete in this track and field event, so this data caused considerable concern about safety at the high school level. However, there was no way to know whether these four deaths represented an average year or were an unusually high or low number because there was no previous data for comparison. (Note also that if Blyth and Mueller had not started collecting national fatality data, nobody would have been aware of the problem.) If these four deaths represented a statistical aberration resulting in a much higher number of fatalities than normal, then the need for immediate major action was not so great. The next year no deaths among high school pole vaulters were recorded, much to everyone's relief. But even this second year of data collection did not settle the question of the normal fatality rate. Which year's data, four deaths or no deaths, was more representative? That question cannot be answered until data is collected for several more years. Meanwhile, the realization that there is a potentially major problem with pole vaulting resulted in a closer look at the design and performance characteristics of landing pits and renewed emphasis on proper coaching techniques, particularly how to "bail out" of a bad vault. The mere fact that national fatality and catastrophic injury data collection was begun has had a positive impact on the safety of that one sport.

While fatalities are rare, and yearly fluctuations in the numbers are therefore relatively more noticeable, the same principle applies to common non-fatal injuries. With a representative national sample, injury rates for some types of injuries will tend to be fairly stable from year to year, but there will be enough statistical fluctuation in the rates for many types of injuries to require data collection over several years to establish stable patterns. Decisions on measures to reduce injury rates should be based only on stable long-term data. Besides the expected yearly fluctuations in specific injury rates, there also are potential differences in injury rates at different levels of a given sport (youth sports, high school, college, professional, elite, masters and recreational levels). Therefore, it is desirable to collect data at each of these levels. Unfortunately, little or no data is available at this time for any level other than college and high school.

## CURRENT LITERATURE ON SPORTS INJURY RATES

A major weakness in much of the published literature on athletic injury rates is that the denominator data for the incidence rate equation is poorly defined or has not been determined. This reduces these articles to simple case series reports that have little or no epidemiological value (29). Unless the calculation of rates is based on the population at risk, it is impossible to generalize the results beyond the specific population used in the study. This highlights a major problem in current research literature on athletic injury rates: most authors have little or no training in epidemiology, so these articles often are not of any great use on a broader scale in that the information cannot be generalized to other places and situations. For example, Powell et al. (20) did a thorough review of the literature on running injuries through 1985 and found only two published articles and one meeting presentation that met minimal criteria for factors such as definition of injury, selection of subjects, and use of proper denominator data ("population at risk") in calculating injury rates.

Twenty years ago the research literature on the epidemiology of athletic injuries was very sparse; the only continuing study was the yearly football fatality study begun in 1931 and currently conducted by Blyth and Mueller at the University of North Carolina and Dick Schindler of the NFSHSA

(18). Since the mid 1960s there has been a slow growth in sports injury rate research as the need for this type of data has become more apparent. Even so, most studies cover only one year (or season), occasionally two (21, 22), and most cover only one sport (16). Nearly all studies have limitations imposed by sample size, covering one school or one city or one geographic area (21, 22, 24). Some studies (6, 11, 17, 25) are limited to injuries of one anatomical site, such as the knee, or one type of injury, such as fatalities or ankle sprains. Getting a clear national perspective by combining results from different studies are greatly hindered by differences in methodologies, such as different definitions of a reportable injury or means of collecting and reporting data. Combining study results would be ill-advised anyway because of the lack of representativeness of the combined data sources.

Still another problem with many studies is the source used to obtain injury data. Some rely on insurance claim forms (9, 10, 13), which has the disadvantage of not representing the true injury rate since not all athletic injuries result in insurance claims. Also, these records seldom contain much detail on the circumstances and mechanisms of injury. Some studies rely on a coach's assessment or recognition of an injury even though we know that, unless coaches have received specific training, they do a poor job of recognizing most treatable injuries (23). Studies that depend on recall of injuries at the end of a season have the obvious problems of inaccuracy and incompleteness of recall.

One ongoing attempt to collect national injury data is the National Electronic Injury Surveillance System conducted by the Consumer Product Safety Commission. This system collects data on product-related injuries from approximately 60 hospital emergency rooms around the country. Athletic injury records are one part of this project (26). However, athletic injury rates based on this data are questionable because not all athletic injuries are treated in an emergency room. Also, those that are treated in the ER would not be recorded if they were not product-related. Injuries from activities like running or swimming probably would go unrecorded because they do not involve a product. There is also a question of defining the population at risk, because we would not know exactly how large a population each emergency room covers. At best, this data tells us the relative proportions of the more serious types of injuries in certain activities.

## NATIONAL SPORTS INJURY DATA COLLECTION SYSTEMS

There are three exceptions to this general picture of a lack of adequate national athletic injury data: the National Athletic Injury/Illness Reporting System (NAIRS) designed by Kenneth S. Clarke, Ph.D., while at Pennsylvania State University; the NCAA Injury Surveillance System (ISS), designed and implemented by Eric D. Zemper, Ph.D., while a member of the NCAA staff; and most recently the Athletic Injury Monitoring System (AIMS), also designed and implemented by Zemper while at the University of Oregon.

NAIRS was intended to be a continuing data collection effort that would provide a rich source of data for epidemiological research on athletic injuries. It incorporated many important features such as longitudinal data collection from a much larger sample than previously had been attempted, standardized definitions and procedures, and the use of case rates per 1,000 athlete-exposures. However, there were concerns about the number and complexity of the data collection forms and the lack of a truly representative national sample. NAIRS stopped collecting high school and college data in 1983 because of chronic funding problems, but it produced by far the best and most comprehensive sports injury data available up to that time and resulted in a number of valuable pieces of research literature (e.g., 1, 2, 3, 7, 8).

In 1982, the NCAA began its own sports injury data collection system (ISS), similar in many ways to NAIRS but using only two basic data collection forms and with a representative national sample of NCAA member schools (19, 31). However, ISS covers only selected NCAA sponsored sports at member schools and there has been no broad dissemination of results. AIMS was begun in 1986 with the intent of covering a wider variety of sports at all levels of participation (32-43).

There are a few specialized data collection systems that focus on fatalities or on specific types of injuries like paralytic or major head and neck injuries (17), but the NCAA's Injury Surveillance System and the Athletic Injury Monitoring System are the only two currently operating national-scale data collection systems dealing with general sports injuries. With the exception of the brief presence of NAIRS and the recent start-ups of ISS and AIMS, both of which are just beginning to publish results in the sports medicine literature, the overall data lack has changed little since Clarke made his observation more than fifteen years ago (5).

## SUMMARY OF DATA FROM NATIONAL DATA COLLECTION SYSTEMS

Since NAIRS, ISS and AIMS are basically similar in format and use the same definition of a reportable injury (one occurring in a practice or contest that prevents an athlete from participating for one day or more), with data provided by on-site athletic trainers, and injury rates reported as cases per 1,000 athlete-exposures, it is possible to summarize and compare data from these three collection systems. The one sport for which data is available from all three systems is college football. Table 1 summarizes the overall football injury rates over a total of 13 seasons. The cumulative injury rates for ISS and AIMS are essentially the same, whereas that for the earlier NAIRS rate is higher. There are several possible explanations for this difference. As noted earlier, the NAIRS sample was not as representative as the ISS and AIMS samples. Except for two seasons (1988 and 1989), it appears there has been a general downward trend in college football injury rates over the years. This may be due to the major rule changes in the mid to late 1970s that were aimed at reducing the risk of major head and neck injuries (a direct result of data from the annual Blyth and Mueller football fatality studies showing an increase in major injuries during the 1960s). Along with the rule changes came shifts in coaching philosophy and technique, which have had a positive impact on injury risk, as have continuing improvements in protective equipment. Any or all of these factors may have contributed to this difference between the NAIRS data from the 1970s and the ISS/AIMS data from the 1980s.

**Table 1. Injury Rates in College Football From Three National Data Collection Systems**

| System | Injury Rate per 1,000 athlete-exposures | Seasons |
|---|---|---|
| NAIRS | 10.1 | 1977-81 |
| ISS | 6.6 | 1982-89 |
| AIMS | 6.6 | 1986-89 |

Sources: Buckley (1982); NCAA (1990); Zemper (1989a,d); Zemper (unpublished data).

Based on these data showing 6.6 injuries per 1,000 athlete-exposures for college football, the average college team of 100 players can expect about two time-loss injuries every three times they take the field for a practice or game. (As we will show later, there can be major differences in injury rates between practices and games, particularly for football.) As would be expected, the body parts injured most often in football are the knees, ankles, and shoulder, in that order. The most common types of injuries are ligament sprains, muscle strains, and contusions.

NAIRS and ISS have data from other college sports, and AIMS has data from other levels of participation besides college. Table 2 summarizes the male and female injury rates for sports covered by these systems. The data in this table cover from one to eight seasons, at least two or three seasons in most cases. Since these are reported in the common metric of rate per 1,000 athlete-exposures, direct comparisons are possible between sports, males and females, and different levels of a sport. The exceptions in this table are injury rates for taekwondo (a Korean full-contact martial art form), which are competition data only, unlike the other sports which show injury rates for practice and competition combined.

**Table 2. Injury Rates for Various Sports From Three National Data Collection Systems**

| Sport | NAIRS | ISS | AIMS |
|---|---|---|---|
| *College* | | | |
| Baseball | 01.9 | 3.3 | |
| Basketball — Men's | 7.0 | 5.1 | |
| Basketball — Women's | 7.3 | 5.0 | |
| Cross Country — Men's | 1.6 | | |
| Cross Country — Women's | 6.7 | | |
| Field Hockey | 5.4 | 4.9 | |
| Football | 10.1 | 6.6 | 6.6 |
| Gymnastics — Men's | 4.3 | 5.1 | |
| Gymnastics — Women's | 7.0 | 8.0 | |
| Ice Hockey | 9.1 | 5.7 | |
| Lacrosse — Men's | 5.7 | 6.2 | |
| Lacrosse — Women's | 4.2 | 4.1 | |
| Soccer — Men's | 9.8 | 7.7 | |
| Soccer — Women's | | 8.0 | |
| Softball | 1.7 | 4.0 | |
| Swimming-Diving — Men's | 0.9 | | |
| Swimming-Diving — Women's | 0.6 | | |
| Tennis — Men's | 1.3 | | |
| Tennis — Women's | 3.3 | | |
| Track & Field — Men's | 3.4 | | |

Table 2. Injury Rates for Various Sports (*Continued*)

| Sport | Injury rate/1,000 athlete-exposures | | |
|---|---|---|---|
| | NAIRS | ISS | AIMS |
| Track & Field — Women's | 4.1 | | |
| Ultimate Frisbee — Men's | | | 5.0 |
| Ultimate Frisbee — Women's | | | 3.7 |
| Volleyball — Men's | 2.4 | | |
| Volleyball — Women's | 4.8 | | |
| Wrestling | 7.7 | 9.6 | |
| *Elite* | | | |
| Gymnastics — Women's | | | 3.7 |
| Taekwondo — Men's (competition only) | | | 27.2 |
| Taekwondo — Women's (competition only) | | | 22.2 |
| *Youth* (6-17 years old) | | | |
| Soccer — Boy's | | | 2.7 |
| Soccer — Girl's | | | 2.1 |
| Taekwondo — Boy's (competition only) | | | 25.5 |
| Taekwondo — Girl's (competition only) | | | 28.6 |
| *Recreational* (45-70 years old) | | | |
| Running — Men's | | | 11.1 |
| Running — Women's | | | 12.3 |
| Walking — Men's | | | 12.7 |
| Weightlifting — Men's | | | 7.0 |

Sources: Buckley (1982); Caine et al. (1989); NAIRS (unpublished data); NCAA (1990); Watkins (1990); Zemper (1991); Zemper (unpublished data).

From Table 2, we can see that participants in men's wrestling, soccer, football and lacrosse, and women's gymnastics and soccer have the highest overall injury rates. The injury rates for corresponding men's and women's sports generally are similar, the exceptions being the higher rates in cross country and gymnastics for women. Younger female gymnasts in a full-time elite training program are less likely to be injured than older collegiate gymnasts. The injury rates for youth soccer players were considerably lower than at the collegiate level. Injury rates for middle-aged and older recreational athletes were noticeably higher (although the older athlete presumably does not have as much pressure to participate, and may be more willing to take a few days off when injured). Data for the non-collegiate levels must be considered preliminary because these databases are relatively small in comparison with the amount of collegiate data available, but they do indicate the possibility of some interesting trends.

Data across all the sports show the most frequently injured body part is the ankle, followed by the knee and then the shoulder. All are major joints that undergo considerable stress in most sports. Sprains, strains, and contusions are the most frequent types of injuries. Overall, ankle sprains are the most frequently occurring injuries in most sports.

An interesting point that becomes apparent when data are reported in rates per 1,000 athlete-exposures, that is not evident when rates are reported per 100 participants, is the difference in injury risk between practices and competitions. Table 3 breaks down the injury rates for 17 collegiate sports into practice and competition rates, along with their relative rankings within each column. The competition injury rate for Senior (18-30 years old) taekwondo athletes is included for comparison. Also included in the right-hand col-

Table 3. Injury Rates in Practices vs Competition in Seventeen College Sports

| Sport | Injury Rate/1,000 athlete-exposures (Column Rank) | | Relative Risk* |
|---|---|---|---|
| | Practice | Competition | |
| Baseball | 2.0 (16) | 5.7 (14) | 2.9 |
| Basketball (M) | 4.1 (8) | 8.9 (9) | 2.2 |
| Basketball (W) | 4.2 (7) | 8.1 (11) | 1.9 |
| Field Hockey | 3.8 (11) | 8.4 (10) | 2.2 |
| Football | 4.1 (8) | 35.6 (1) | 8.7 |
| Gymnastics (M) | 4.4 (6) | 16.5 (6) | 3.8 |
| Gymnastics (W) | 7.2 (1) | 21.5 (3) | 3.0 |
| Ice Hockey | 2.5 (15) | 16.2 (8) | 6.5 |
| Lacrosse (M) | 4.1 (8) | 16.4 (7) | 4.0 |
| Lacrosse (W) | 3.4 (13) | 6.3 (13) | 1.9 |
| Soccer (M) | 4.5 (5) | 19.2 (4) | 4.3 |
| Soccer (W) | 5.1 (3) | 17.0 (5) | 3.3 |
| Softball | 3.4 (13) | 5.1 (17) | 1.5 |
| Ultimate Frisbee (M) | 3.5 (12) | 7.0 (12) | 2.0 |
| Ultimate Frisbee (W) | 2.0 (16) | 5.6 (15) | 2.8 |
| Volleyball (W) | 4.6 (4) | 5.3 (16) | 1.2 |
| Wrestling | 7.1 (2) | 30.8 (2) | 4.3 |
| Taekwondo (M) | | 27.2 | |
| Taekwondo (W) | | 22.2 | |

*Relative Risk = higher rate divided by lower rate

Example: Men's lacrosse — 16.4 injuries/1,000 athlete-exposures in games divided by 4.1 injuries/1,000 athlete-exposures in practices equals a relative risk of 4.0; i.e., a men's lacrosse player participating in a game is 4 times as likely to be injured as he would be if he were participating in a practice session.

Sources: NCAA (1990); Watkins (1990); Zemper (unpublished data).

umn of the Table is an indication of the relative risk of injury in practice and in competition; in each case injury risk is higher in competition.

It often is reported that most injuries occur in practices, giving the impression that practices are at least as risky as competitions. Most injuries in a given sport usually do occur during practices, but the actual risk of an individual athlete being injured is much higher in competition. As an example, in college football nearly 60% of the recorded injuries occur in practice (32). However, while the total number of injuries in college football over a season may be higher in practices, the rate of injuries is considerably higher in games, in this case 8.7 times higher (Table 3). In other words, a college football player is nearly nine times as likely to be injured in a game as he is in a practice session. Bear in mind that there are at least five to six times as many practices as games in a football season, and not every player who participates in practice will participate in a game. The most obvious explanation for the difference in risk between practices and games is the continuously higher intensity of play during games.

Football represents the upper extreme in the difference between practice and competition injury rates. At the other end of the spectrum is women's volleyball, where the risk of injury in games is only slightly higher than in practices (Table 3). This is only reasonable considering that, at the collegiate level, volleyball practices often are as intense as the games. The data presented in Table 3 show that most sports at the collegiate level have a competition injury rate about two to four times higher than for practice.

## CURRENT APPLICATIONS OF NATIONAL SPORTS INJURY DATA

National data collection systems such as ISS and AIMS gather information not just on the number and type of injuries, but also on the circumstances. These data therefore can be used to develop specific recommendations for rule changes, equipment modifications, or changes in training techniques, all aimed at reducing the number and severity of injuries. For example, AIMS has been collecting injury data at national taekwondo competitions for the U.S. Olympic Committee and the U.S. Taekwondo Union, the national governing body for this sport (39-43). One result has been to draw immediate attention and concern to the high rate of cerebral concussions recorded during taekwondo competitions (41-43). The cerebral concussion rate over a two year period for taekwondo compared with AIMS data for college football showed that the rate for taekwondo competition (5.45 cerebral concussions per 1,000 athlete-exposures) is 3.2 times as high as the rate seen in college football games (1.69 cerebral concussions per 1,000 athlete-exposures). Based on time of exposure, taekwondo (1.2 per 1,000 minutes of exposure) has a cerebral concussion rate 9.2 times that of college football games (0.13 per 1,000 minutes of exposure). These rates are essentially the same for Junior (6-17 years old) and Senior (18 and older) taekwondo competitors. Football has one of the higher cerebral concussion rates of any American sport, so these results should immediately raise a red flag indicating a need for measures to reduce the risk of head injuries in taekwondo.

Now that these data have uncovered a previously unsuspected problem with head injuries in taekwondo, the AIMS staff is working with the national governing body to develop recommendations. The primary suggestions include working with the manufacturers of the helmet used in taekwondo to develop a more protective product; changing the rules to require mouthguards, rather than just recommending their use as is currently the case (the data showed that the more severe the cerebral concussion, the less likely the competitor was wearing a mouthguard); establishing and enforcing standards for competition mats (several third degree concussions were observed when competitors fell back and hit their heads on obviously inadequately padded floor mats); and adopting rules similar to those of amateur boxing which require a minimum time period before an athlete is allowed to return to participation after a loss of consciousness from a blow during a bout. That period varies according to age, severity of concussion, and previous history of concussion.

Epidemiological studies of sports injuries may be used to evaluate new protective equipment or monitor the performance of existing equipment, if the study is properly designed to collect the necessary data. An example of this use is an ongoing study of preventive knee braces in college football being conducted by AIMS (34, 36) as a part of general data collection on football injuries. Braces designed to prevent medial collateral ligament injuries from lateral blows to the knee came into widespread use in the 1980s before any studies were performed to see if they actually worked. All we had were anecdotes and a few one- or two-season, one-team studies. There are many variables that could have an impact on the results of any study like this, such things as brand or type of brace, position played, proper placement of brace, whether it was actually being worn at the time of injury, previous history of knee injury, intensity of practices, condition of playing surface, or weather, to name a few.

From an epidemiological perspective, the only way to "control" these numerous variables is to do a large-scale, long-term study with as many teams as possible so that the impact of the uncontrollable and essentially unrecordable variables (proper brace placement, practice intensity, condition of playing surface, weather) will "wash out" in the data collection process. At the same time, the more easily recordable variables (position played, whether the brace was worn at the time of injury, brand or type of brace, previous history) will be recorded in sufficient numbers to provide more reliable results than could ever be possible with a study of a single team or a small number of teams. The results of earlier, small-scale studies were mixed, with some showing that braces reduced the number of MCL injuries and others showing they did not, but the more recent large-scale studies, such as those of Teitz (28) and Zemper (34, 36) show that wearing preventive knee braces appears to have no effect on reducing the number or severity of MCL injuries, or on the time lost due to injury.

A well-controlled smaller-scale study done at the U.S. Military Academy (27) does show some positive effect in reducing MCL injuries by wearing preventive knee braces, but only with defensive players. This indicates that position played may be an important factor. There was no effect on the severity of knee injuries. However, the subjects were cadets playing intramural football rather than larger and heavier intercollegiate players, so the study may indicate a possible size/weight and, therefore, a force threshold involvement. Obviously, much more data must be collected from large-scale epidemiologic studies, as well as biomechanical studies, before complex issues such as this can be resolved.

## LOCAL SPORTS INJURY DATA COLLECTION

Although the importance of longitudinal, national-scale epidemiologic data collection to adequately address major sports injury issues has been emphasized here, the small-scale local data collection effort also has a place in sports medicine. A primary care physician who is responsible for medical care of a high school or other local sports program, or who is part of a local sports medicine network (see Chapter 19), is in a good position to track local injury patterns. At a minimum this will require some form of centralized records of all sports injuries treated. Forms like those suggested in Chapter 19 for the records of a local sports medicine network would serve this purpose very well.

An alternative to normal patient files, which would make data compilation much easier, is a brief check-off form describing the athlete, injury, and circumstances. This would be similar to those used by larger data collection systems. These forms could be filled out by the physician, nurse, or athletic trainer at the high school for every sports injury treated, and kept in a single file. As we mentioned earlier, this data is only a case series and cannot be used to make comparisons across sports or with data from other sources. However, they might alert the physician if an unexpected number of injuries of a certain type or ones that happen under specific circumstances are noted.

If comparisons are desired, some form of exposure or "denominator" data is required to calculate injury rates, as discussed earlier. The simplest denominator data to obtain are the number of athletes on the team, so injury rates per 100 athletes can be calculated. The fact that many teams have more athletes at the beginning of the season than at the end presents a problem. The most reasonable solution is to use an average number of athletes if the rate of attrition is fairly stable over the season, or use the number of athletes on the team during the majority of the season if the dropouts tend to occur at the beginning of the season and then the numbers stabilize as the season progresses.

For reasons presented previously, rates per 100 athletes are not the most accurate way to calculate sports injury rates. With some extra effort and on-site assistance from a student athletic trainer or coach, it is feasible to get data at the local level on the number of athletes participating in practices and competitions, or possibly even the amount of time of participation, so that rates per 1,000 athlete-exposures or rates per 100 hours or 1,000 minutes can be calculated.

In some team sports, the time of exposure in

games is relatively easy to estimate, because the games last a specified length of time and involve a specified number of players at any one time. A high school football game will involve four quarters of twelve minutes each, and eleven players from a team are on the field at any given time. Therefore, the amount of exposure time for a single team in a single game will be 528 player-minutes per game (4 quarters/game x 12 minutes/quarter x 11 players). It is more difficult to get data on time of exposure in practices, but it basically means keeping track of the number of players participating in each practice and the length of the practices. When collecting athlete-exposure data, the time element is ignored, and data are recorded only on the number of players at each practice and the number who actually get into the games and are exposed, however briefly, to the possibility of injury (not the number who dress for the game).

Once appropriate denominator data on the population at risk are available, the rate equation presented earlier can be used to calculate injury rates that can be used in comparisons across local sports teams or with data from other sources that are calculated in a similar manner. When comparing local data with injury data from other sources (or for that matter when comparing injury data from any sources), always note any differences in methodologies used (data sources and collection procedures, definition of an injury, type of rate calculated, etc.). If there are any major differences, conclusions drawn from the comparisons may not be valid. Of particular importance are the type of rate calculated and the definition of an injury. Obviously, trying to compare injury rates per 100 athletes with rates per 1,000 athlete-exposures would be meaningless. Less obvious is the need to ensure that the same definition of a reportable injury is being used. If one set of data includes everything seen by the medical staff and another includes only injuries that cause three or more days of time lost from participation, comparisons would be meaningless. The most commonly used definition of a reportable injury is based on time-loss:

> A reportable injury is any injury a) occurring in a scheduled practice or competition, b) requiring medical attention, and c) resulting in the athlete being restricted from further normal participation for the remainder of that practice or competition or for the following day or more.

This is the basic definition of a reportable injury used by NAIRS, ISS, and AIMS, and we recommend its use in local data collection systems. By basing the definition on time-loss of one day or more before a return to unrestricted participation, all minor scrapes, bumps, and bruises that do not cause time-loss are eliminated, so they do not overburden the data collection system. (The only exception to this in AIMS is that any mild concussion is reported, even though it may not cause time-loss.).

Rates for specific types of injuries or body parts also can be calculated for local injury data. For example, the total number of knee injuries could be the numerator rather than the total number of all injuries. If game and practice exposure data are available, separate game and practice injury rates can be calculated. Make sure the appropriate denominator is matched with the numerator. If a game injury rate is being calculated, be sure to divide the number of game injuries by the number of game exposures. As with large-scale sports injury data collection systems, the more local data collected over time, the more useful and valuable the information becomes.

## CONCLUSION

Applying the principles of epidemiology to sports injuries is a relatively recent development, and dependable epidemiologic data for sports injuries are still quite scarce, particularly for levels other than high school and college sports (5, 14, 15). In addition, the quality and usefulness of a great deal of the available literature leaves much to be desired, for reasons outlined earlier, and as demonstrated by Powell et al. (20). National-scale data collection systems such as NAIRS, ISS, and AIMS are beginning to make important contributions, and must be a primary focus of activity in the future. However, there will be ample opportunity for contributions from others, such as a primary care physician working with a local sports program. Understanding the basic principles of epidemiology presented in this chapter will allow the primary care physician to be more discriminating in reading the literature, but also will be useful in setting up a system for keeping track of local injury patterns. These efforts may play a role in reducing the number and severity of sports injuries in the local community.

# REFERENCES

1. Alles, W.F., Powell, J.W., Buckley, W., and Hunt, E.E. The National Athletic Injury/Illness Reporting System 3-Year Findings of High School and College Football Injuries. *J Orthop Sp Phys Therapy* 1(2):103-108, 1979.
2. Alles, W.F., Powell, J.W., Buckley, W., and Hunt, E.E. Three Year Summary of NAIRS Football Data. *Athletic Training* Summer 1980:98-100, 1980.
3. Buckley, W.E. Five Year Overview of Sport Injuries: The NAIRS Model. *JOPERD* June 1982:36-40, 1982.
4. Caine, D., Cochrane, B, Caine, C., and Zemper, E. An Epidemiologic Investigation of Injuries Affecting Young Competitive Female Gymnasts. *Am J Sp Med* 17(6):811-820, 1989.
5. Clarke, K.S. Premises and Pitfalls of Athletic Injury Surveillance. *J Sp Med* 3(6):292-295, 1976.
6. Clarke, K.S. A Survey of Sports-Related Spinal Cord Injuries in Schools and Colleges, 1973-1975. *J Safety Res* 9:140, 1977.
7. Clarke, K.S., and Buckley, W.E. Women's Injuries in Collegiate Sports. *Am J Sp Med* 8(3):187-191,1980.
8. Clarke, K.S., and Powell, J.W. Football Helmets and Neurotrauma — An Epidemiological Overview of Three Seasons. *Med Sci Sports* 11(2):138-145, 1979.
9. Cleavinger, J.D. The Incidence of Injuries to Football Players in Kansas Junior High Schools. Thesis, Univ. of Kansas, 1974.
10. Conant, R.D. The Nature and Frequency of Injuries Occurring to High School Athletes Insured Through the Oregon School Activities Association Mutual Benefit Plan From 1965 to 1968. Dissertation, Univ. of Oregon, 1969.
11. Downs, J.R. Incidence of Facial Trauma in Intercollegiate and Junior Hockey. *Phys Sportsmed* 7(2):88-92, 1979.
12. Duncan, D.F. *Epidemiology: Basis for Disease Prevention and Health Promotion*, New York: Macmillan Publ. Co., 1988.
13. Hansen, V.A. The Nature and Incidence of Injuries to Students in Physical Education Classes in Oregon Secondary Schools During the Period From 1964-65 to 1968-69. Dissertation, Univ. of Oregon, 1971.
14. Koplan, J.P., Siscovick, D.S., and Goldbaum, G.M. The Risks of Exercise: A Public Health View of Injuries and Hazards. *Public Health Reports* 100:189-195, 1985.
15. Kraus, J.F., and Conroy, C. Mortality and Morbidity From Injuries in Sports and Recreation. *Ann Rev Publ Health* 5:163-192, 1984.
16. Martin, G. L., Costello, D.F., and Fuenning, S.I. The 1970 Intercollegiate Tackle Football Injury Surveillance Report. Report prepared for the Joint Commission on Competitive Safeguards and Medical Aspects of Sports, 1971.
17. Mueller, F.O., and Blyth, C.S. National Center for Catastrophic Sports Injury Research — Second Annual Report 1982-1984. Univ. of North Carolina, 1985.
18. Mueller, F.O., and Schindler, R.D. Annual Survey of Football Injury Research 1931-1990. Univ. of North Carolina, 1991.
19. National Collegiate Athletic Association. NCAA Injury Surveillance System Reports. Overland Park, KS. 1990.
20. Powell, K.E., Kohl, H.W., Casperson, C.J., and Blair, S.N. An Epidemiological Perspective on the Causes of Running Injuries. *Phys Sportsmed* 14(6):100-114, 1986.
21. Requa, R.K., and Garrick, J.G. Injuries in Interscholastic Track and Field. *Phys Sportsmed* 9(3):42-49, 1981.
22. Requa, R.K., and Garrick, J.G. Injuries in Interscholastic Wrestling. *Phys Sportsmed* 9(4):44-51, 1981.
23. Rice, S.G., Schlotfeldt, J.D., and Foley, W.E. The Athletic Health Care and Training Program. *West J Med* 142:352, 1985.
24. Robey, J.M., Blyth, C.S., and Mueller, F.O. Athletic Injuries: Application of Epidemiologic Methods. *JAMA* 217(2):184-189, 1971.
25. Rovere, G.D., and Nichols, A.W. Frequency, Associated Factors, and Treatment of Breastroker's Knee in Competitive Swimmers. *Am J Sp Med* 13(2):99-104, 1985.
26. Rutherford, G.W., Miles, R.B., Brown, V.R., and McDonald, B. Overview of Sports-Related Injuries to Persons 5-14 Years of Age. U.S. Consumer Products Safety Commission, 1981.
27. Stitler, M., Ryan, J., Hopkinson, W., Wheeler, J., Santomier, J., Kolb, R., and Polley, D. The Efficacy of a Prophylactic Knee Brace to Reduce Knee Injuries in Football. *Am J Sp Med* 18(3):310-315, 1990.
28. Teitz, C.C., Hermanson, B.K., Krommal, R.A., and Diehr, P.H. Evaluation of the Use of Braces to Prevent Injury to the Knee in Collegiate Football Players. *J Bone Joint Surg* 69A(1):3-9, 1987.
29. Walter, S.D., Sutton, J.R., McIntosh, J.M., and Connolly, C. The Aetiology of Sports Injuries: A Review of Methodologies. *Sp Med* 2:47-58, 1985.
30. Watkins, R.J. An Epidemiological Study: Injury Rates Among Collegiate Ultimate Frisbee Players in the Western United States. Thesis, Univ. of Oregon, 1990.
31. Zemper, E.D. NCAA Injury Surveillance System: Initial Results. Paper presented at the 1984 Olympic Scientific Congress, July 19-26, Univ. of Oregon, Eugene, OR, 1984.
32. Zemper, E.D. Injury Rates in a National Sample of College Football Teams: A Two-Year Prospective Study. *Phys Sportsmed* 17(11):100-113, 1989a.
33. Zemper, E.D. Cerebral Concussion Rates in Various Brands of Football Helmets. *Athletic Training* 24(2): 133-137, 1989b.
34. Zemper, E.D. A Prospective Study of Prophylactic Knee Braces in a National Sample of American College Football Players. *Proceedings of the First International Olympic Committee World Congress on Sport Sciences*, U.S. Olympic Committee, Colorado Springs, pp.202-203, 1989c.
35. Zemper, E.D. A Prospective Study of Injury Rates in a National Sample of American College Football Teams. *Proceedings of the First International Olympic Committee World Congress on Sport Sciences*, U.S. Olympic Committee, Colorado Springs, pp.194-195, 1989d.
36. Zemper, E.D. A Two-Year Study of Prophylactic Knee Braces in a National Sample of College Football Players. *Sports Training, Medicine and Rehabilitation* 1:287-296, 1990.
37. Zemper, E.D. Four-Year Study of Weightroom Injuries in a National Sample of College Football Teams. *National Strength and Conditioning Association Journal* 12(3):32-34, 1990.
38. Zemper, E.D. Exercise and Injury Patterns in a Sample of Active Middle-Aged Adults. International Congress and Exposition on Sport Medicine and Human Performance, Vancouver, B.C., April 1991. Programme/Abstracts: p. 98, 1991.
39. Zemper, E.D., and Pieter, W. Injury Rates at the 1988 U.S. Olympic Team Trials for Taekwondo. *Br J Sp Med* 23(3):161164, 1989.
40. Zemper, E.D., and Pieter, W. Injury Rates in Junior and Senior National Taekwondo Competition. *Proceedings of the First International Olympic Committee World Congress on Sport Sciences*, U.S. Olympic Committee, Colorado Springs. pp. 219-220, 1989.
41. Zemper, E.D., and Pieter, W. The Oregon Taekwondo Research Project — Part II: Preliminary Injury Research Results. *Taekwondo USA* Winter 1990.
42. Zemper, E.D., and Pieter, W. Cerebral Concussion Rates in Taekwondo Competition. *Med Sci Sp Exerc* 22(2-Supplement): S130, 1990.
43. Zemper, E.D., and Pieter, W. Two-Year Prospective Study of Injury Rates in National Taekwondo Competition. International Congress and Exposition on Sport Medicine and Human Performance, Vancouver, B.C., April 1991. Programme/Abstracts: p. 99, 1991.

# 3

# Sports Psychology for the Primary Care Physician

Few people would argue the fact that athletics occupies a position of major significance and influence in American society. The coverage given to sports by the media, the sporting interests of well-known political figures, the number of fans attending events of all types, and the high salaries of professional athletes all exemplify the priority given athletics. This emphasis is especially visible at the high school and college level. However, athletic ability is extremely important to younger school age children and may even encourage the development of favorable personality traits.

Opinions about the psychological effects of exercise have appeared in the literature for more than 2,000 years, often without supporting scientific evidence. The ancient Greek civilization had a significant sports culture, along with some understanding of the close interrelationship between mind and body. Athletes have always known that a significant part of performance and rehabilitation from injury is mental in nature. Empirical research began to appear in the late 1920s and early 1930s, but not until the last two decades has published research in the field of sports psychology increased in quantity and quality. The research conclusions are often confusing and there are few clear-cut relationships between physical and psychological variables.

The field of sports psychology has an extensive history, development, and utilization in Russia and the Eastern European countries, but it has had a modest impact in the United States.

## THE IMPORTANCE OF SPORTS PSYCHOLOGY

Interest in sports participation and the related field of sports psychology has been rising and can be attributed to several factors:

Sport has become big business at political, economic, and social levels. In addition to more participants and better training programs, a higher level of competitiveness has been achieved, whether the athlete is involved in recreational activities or performing at the elite level.

Psychological factors have a profound effect on athletic achievement. Athletes really do need to control both mind and body to perform optimally. Research on the interrelationships between performance, physiologic arousal, and attentional processes provide considerable support for the concept that psychological or mental factors directly affect an athlete's ability to perform.

Our information about sports psychology is still relatively limited. The services of sports psychologists usually is restricted to college level athletes and a small number of elite athletes, although that may be changing to include even recreational athletes. Consequently, primary care physicians working in sports medicine can promote awareness of relevant sports psychology principles and applications. For these reasons, primary physicians should have some knowledge of the definition, structure, and practice of sports psychology.

Three content areas deserve special mention. The first is understanding the developmental aspect of sport. It is important to recognize, emphasize, and teach that the primary motivation of children who engage in sport is to have fun. Children's issues such as why they participate or quit, what children like or do not like in sports, motivating young athletes, communicating with them, overcoming fear, promoting sportsmanship, and the effects of award ceremonies on participants are some examples of topic areas that should be understood by the primary physician involved in sports medicine.

Developmental issues are also important for older athletes. Attention should be given to skill development in sports other than those performed by college-age athletes. The older athlete can obviously participate in a wide variety of exercise activities. The sports physician and trainer should recognize that only about 2% of the athletes recruited at the college level are actually able to play professional sports. Therefore, most older athletes should be given advice on how to deal with participation in sports over time and also to prepare them for the termination of sports participation, whether through injury, illness, aging, or choice.

Proper management of sports injury and, even more importantly, its prevention is the main emphasis of sports medicine. Psychological factors also play an important role in the occurrence of injuries and in the athlete's response to them and to recovery. The athlete-doctor relationship is crucial to providing optimal health care in the sports setting and also is an important aspect of sports psychology that should be understood by the primary care physician.

Finally, the sports physician should understand the behavioral components of programs they may prescribe for noncompetitive athletes and patients in exercise programs for chronic diseases and cardiac rehabilitation. Behavioral contracting and self-monitoring are interventions known to significantly increase compliance in prescribed exercise programs like cardiac rehabilitation. Other behavior modification techniques are known to increase compliance in general exercise programs. The practicing sports physician needs to learn these techniques, because only through an open-minded approach can the physician apply practical suggestions from sports medicine to the sports participant.

## PSYCHOLOGICAL FACTORS INVOLVED IN PERFORMANCE

The sports physician should understand the normal responses of arousal, concentration, and performance. An athlete's psychological profile is used to identify strengths, weaknesses, and dominant personality characteristics. These might include an athlete's need to be in control, his or her level of confidence or self-esteem, speed of decision-making, extroversion vs. introversion, interpersonal expressiveness, or recognizing what causes personal stress. This information is invaluable in treating an injured athlete.

Motivation is what keeps an athlete working; however, goals must be realistic, challenging, and attainable. They must be clearly related to the athlete's skill level. If they are set too high, failure will ensue and generate anxiety, decrease motivation, and destroy feelings of self-worth, leading to decreased performance. The process can develop into a downward spiral that coaches refer to as "choking" and means a pattern of negative reinforcement and decreased performance.

Arousal is an important psychological factor (see Figure 3-1). In general, increased arousal affects performance because it improves concentration (less boredom and distraction) and quickens reaction times. However, if arousal rises too high it interferes, especially in sports like diving and gymnastics where fine muscle coordination and timing are involved (see Table 3-1). If the pressure of competition continues to increase, the athlete's

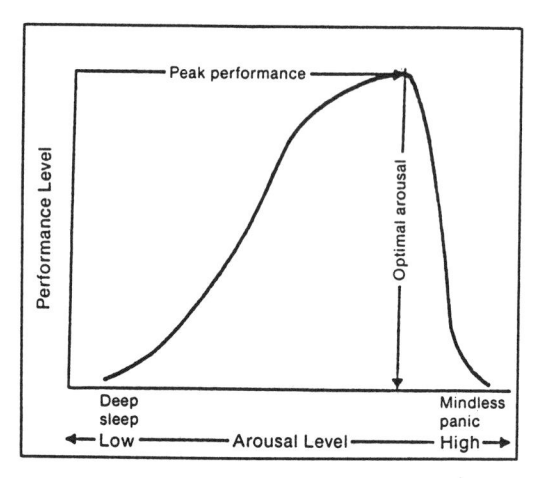

**Fig. 3-1.** The inverted-U hypothesis demonstrates the relationship between performance and emotional arousal. The vertical line indicates the predicted optimal arousal level for a tennis player. (From Finn, J.A. Competitive excellence: It's a matter of mind and body. *Phys Sportsmed* 13(2):63, Feb 1985)

Table 3-1. Psychological Changes Experienced by Athletes in a Stress State

| | |
|---|---|
| ↑Heart rate | ↑Breathing rate |
| ↑Blood pressure | ↑Blood flow |
| ↑Sweating | ↑Muscle tension |
| ↑RBC count | ↑Adrenaline levels |
| ↑Brain wave activity | ↑Oxygen uptake and transfer |
| ↑Carbon dioxide production | ↑Blood sugar levels |
| Pupil dilation | Cessation of digestion |

(Adapted from Finn, J.A. Competitive excellence: It's a matter of mind and body. *Phys Sportsmed* 13(2):63, Feb 1985)

ability to shift his focus of attention begins breaking down. Performance usually decreases and the possibility of injury rises. As mistakes are made and as arousal, frustration, anger, and worry increase, the athlete's attention narrows involuntarily. The athlete becomes more distracted by his own thoughts and feelings, which adversely affects muscle tension and concentration (see Table 3-2). The result can be an unending cycle of increasing disturbances resulting in more performance errors that make the problem worse (see Table 3-3).

Control of arousal refers to the ability to change the intensity of a certain behavior. The athlete must: 1) be educated about the nature of arousal and its effect on performance; 2) be taught the tools necessary to control both affective and cognitive power, and 3) practice what he has learned. It generally takes years of practice to perfect a physical skill and an equal amount of time to practice new behavioral skills. One approach to help athletes who are experiencing excessive arousal and stress is to teach them how to exert control over their performance, to reduce distractions, and to improve task-relevant concentration.

Table 3-2. Common Stress-Associated Behaviors

| | |
|---|---|
| Nail biting | Eye blinking |
| Foot tapping | Knuckle cracking |
| Muscle twitching | Yawning |
| Loud talking | Excessive conversing |
| Scowling | Rapid gum chewing |
| Repeated bathroom use | Shivering |

(From Finn, J.A. Competitive excellence: It's a matter of mind and body. *Phys Sportsmed* 13(2):66, Feb 1985)

Table 3-3. Aspects of Competition That Worry Athletes

| Category | Cause for Concern |
|---|---|
| Feelings of inadequacy | Getting tired<br>Physical appearance<br>Being afraid<br>Inability to concentrate<br>Feeling silly |
| Loss of control | Behavior or spectators<br>Bad luck<br>Temperature<br>Condition of playing surface<br>Injuries |
| Fear of failure | Performing up to ability level<br>Losing<br>Choking up<br>Making foolish mistakes<br>Letting people down |
| Guilt | Making opponent look foolish<br>Swearing too much<br>Losing temper<br>Sportsmanship<br>Spectators' disapproval |
| Somatic complaints | Upset stomach<br>Urge to urinate<br>Muscle tightness<br>Sweating too much<br>Awareness of heart beat |

(From Finn, J.A. Competitive excellence: It's a matter of mind and body. *Phys Sportsmed* 13(2):66, Feb 1985)

## PSYCHOLOGICAL FACTORS IN THE TREATMENT OF INJURY AND PAIN

The relationship between arousal, muscle tension, and concentration provides a practical base for integrating psychological factors into preventing and treating injury. Pain has a definite physiologic etiology, but psychological factors greatly affect an athlete's perception of pain. Whether due to injury or fatigue, pain is a stressor. It can become a physically and emotionally arousing stimulus because it signals that something is wrong. Injury may mean that an athlete will lose valuable time from training and future competition. The onset of pain and its ramifications can have severe economic implications for a professional athlete. Mental perception of pain can result in aggravation of injuries, increase the likelihood of further trauma as a result of reduced flexibility, and ultimately cause deterioration of performance. Self-doubt can also cause excessive muscle tension, reduced flexibility, and the potential for increased musculoskeletal injury. These factors have a bearing on the relationship between the physical and psychological balance that the physician must consider in treating pain and injury.

An athlete typically undergoes a sequence of psychological reactions to injury, including: 1) disbelief, denial, and isolation; 2) anger; 3) bargaining; 4) depression, and 5) acceptance and resignation although hope remains (Normand, 1985). It is important that an injured athlete accept or cope with his injury while remaining positive and enthusiastic about recovery before a physical rehabilitation program starts. This is more difficult if the injury is serious and potentially career-ending.

All personnel involved in rehabilitation need to be supportive and reassuring, and they must encourage the athlete to maintain a rational, self-enhancing outlook. It is appropriate for an athlete to feel irritated, frustrated, and sad, but unreasonable to view the situation as totally hopeless (Normand, 1985). Honest and accurate information that eliminates uncertainty or misconceptions about the diagnosis and prognosis should be provided. Setting realistic short-term goals for rehabilitation will give the athlete a focus. Injured athletes should be encouraged to be active in their rehabilitation, and they should be allowed to participate in any physical activities, including aerobic fitness and strength training, which do not interfere with treatment.

The sports psychologist may keep an injured athlete active and interested in rehabilitation by using visual-motor behavior rehearsal (VMBR) training (Suinn, 1972). This technique has been widely advocated but no controlled studies have assessed its effectiveness. Inactivity often subjects athletes to doubts about the strength of the injured part and about loss of coordination and timing from lack of practice. VMBR allows the athlete to mentally practice the skills he cannot performed physically. VMBR involves training deep muscle relaxation along with the use of imagery. Relaxation enhances the ability to use imagery. All muscle groups involved in a particular physical skill can be used.

Biofeedback is another technique that can aid in healing of certain injuries although it is an expensive procedure that may not be used frequently enough to warrant the purchase of necessary equipment. Through the use of electromyography (EMG), athletes learn to reduce the strain that excessive muscle tension places on the injury (Nideffer, 1981).

Even when an athlete is physically recovered from an injury, emotional recovery may not have proceeded far enough that the athlete can be an effective competitor. Anxiety about returning to competition and a lack of confidence could cause an athlete to have irrational thoughts that would interfere with performance. A football player who has been out of competition for a long time with a knee injury may have severe doubts about his ability to perform up to his previous level. His anxiety could cause poor performance. This is a common sports scenario.

When a trainer, physician, or sports psychologist suspects that an athlete has a fear of re-injury or performance anxiety, such techniques as desensitization, hypnosis, VMBR, and other stress reduction techniques may be employed. Although these techniques have not been well documented with properly designed scientific studies, they seem to have a place in the management of physical and psychological injuries to athletes (Feltz, 1984).

The techniques for psychological rehabilitation of an injured athlete are considered clinical in nature and should be carried out under the direction of a qualified counselor or sports psychologist. The therapist should maintain close contact with the team physician and/or trainer during the treatment period. Cooperation among the sports psychologist, physician, trainer, and coach is essential if full benefit of these techniques is to be realized. In summary, the psychological state of an athlete has a bearing on the chances of sustaining a sports injury and it can influence the rehabilitation process once injury has occurred. The team physician should be aware of the factors that influence injury and rehabilitation.

## THE ROLE OF THE SPORTS PHYSICIAN IN FACILITATING PERFORMANCE

Only a few teams in the United States travel with a team psychologist so the team physician is in the best position to assist athletes to perform at optimal levels. The physician must help the athlete control physiologic arousal and concentration and to work with the coach, teammates, athletic trainer, and family members. The team physician must also be able to assess an athlete's level of physiologic tension to determine whether there are internal distractions such as negative thoughts or self-doubt.

An injured athlete often doubts the advice of the trainer or physician because of his lack of knowledge or confidence in the medical staff. To counteract this, the team physician can give the athlete a rational explanation of his injury and reassure him about recovery. This helps lessen the athlete's self doubts and often improves the athlete's chance for an earlier return to participation. Optimal athletic performance requires a coordination of both mental and physical energy and can be accomplished only when an athlete has faith and confidence in his ability. From an athlete's perspective, the physician's credibility is critical to improving his chance for recovery.

When fatigue or self doubt interfere with performance, the physician can also assist the athlete. Team physicians may see performance deteriorate because of frustration, fear, or increasing levels of tension. Although the physician must be careful not to interfere with the relationship between the athlete and coach, he can assist if he knows enough about the technical aspects of the sport to help direct the athlete's attention to tasks that will improve performance. Distracting the athlete from negative thoughts also will help, but afterwards, attention must be refocused on tasks relevant to the sport.

Simple breathing techniques, tension/redirection strategies (distraction, tension-control training), and direct instructions to relax specific muscle groups can have an immediate and dramatic effect on excessive physiologic arousal and self-doubt. A physician might teach progressive relaxation and self-hypnosis to help an athlete lower arousal, increase confidence, and sleep well prior to competition. Physicians who use these techniques must be well trained in this type of medical care (Nideffer, 1984).

Sports physicians need to understand sport and performance from both the healthy and abnormal perspective. The team physician must understand the role that individual differences in personality and perceptual processes play in affecting performance. They should be sensitive to situational, interpersonal, and intrapersonal factors when they attempt to understand, predict, and control behavior. Although physicians may be able to accomplish a great deal by assisting athletes to integrate physical and psychological functions, their role does have limitations. The amount of technical training needed in psychology, psychiatry, and the biomechanics of specific sports may further limit their use of psychological techniques. Applied sports psychology is becoming a highly developed discipline with a sophisticated body of knowledge and many theoretical approaches.

## ROLE OF THE SPORTS PSYCHOLOGIST

In reality, the only individuals qualified to call themselves sports psychologists are licensed psychologists. Prior to 1981, subspecialty training as a sports psychologist was nonexistent and, even now, most sports psychology programs are academic or research-oriented and focus primarily on motor learning and development. There are certification procedures for sports psychologists.

The clinical role of a qualified sports psychologist may involve treating neurotic or psychotic problems. When clinical problems arise with an athlete, it is best to refer to a clinically trained therapist who specializes in sports. Sports psychology practitioners often function in other roles and may face a conflict of interest if they attempt to meet the needs of the sports organization and team as well as the needs of an individual athlete with severe psychological problems. Some of the severe problems include anorexia nervosa, bulimia, and a variety of hysterical and psychological complaints, all of which typically require the intervention of a skilled clinician for resolution.

In addition, the sports psychologist may deal with dependency problems which are prevalent in women's sports and in younger athletes, and with alcohol and drugs dependency. The high salaries, travel, and media exposure associated with sports can cause additional problems or lead some athletes to long-term drug addictions. A need for excitement and risk-taking is common among athletes, especially in the professional ranks. Their athletic success leads some to the delusion that they can maintain control of their lives despite their use of drugs. All sports physicians are well aware of the physical and emotional cost of acute and chronic alcohol and drug use. Early detection is critical and organizational pressure may be needed to motivate an athlete to seek professional help.

Sports psychologists are useful in improving

communication between the athlete and his coach or teammates. Effective communication skills are extremely important. In highly stressful situations, athletes, like other individuals, rely heavily on their dominant needs or interpersonal style. The consultant's job in this situation is to help sports participants recognize when they are under pressure and see how it affects their interactions with others. This often is done by the coach, but in situations where communication is poor and out of the control of the coach, a sports psychologist can be involved. Most consultants are trained as researchers and may be able to apply their theoretical knowledge in the practical setting.

## PSYCHOLOGICAL ASSESSMENT

Psychological assessment involves using a wide variety of instruments and procedures, including systematic behavioral observations, personality tasks, projective tasks, objective measures of various tensional abilities and skills, and psychophysiologic measurements. Through the assessment process, the consultant identifies the performance-relevant personality characteristics, situations, or interactions that must be changed to improve performance. There is little data at present to suggest that psychological tests predict performance well enough to justify their use in the selection and screening of athletes. Because there are many inaccuracies, these tests should only be used as one part of a total assessment procedure by a sports psychologist, team physician, and coach.

## FUTURE OF THE SPORTS PSYCHOLOGY FIELD

Sports psychology is an emerging field with applications for sports medicine. Professional organizations now are attempting to establish ethical standards, role definitions, and training recommendations. This discipline is not yet well understood or accepted by team physicians and coaches. Application of sports psychology theory should be based on properly designed studies. It may be that the application of premises of sports psychology will help improve the performance of athletes in this country in the future. A number of other references are available in the recommended readings for the physician who wishes to learn more about sports psychology.

## PSYCHOLOGICAL ASPECTS OF THE YOUNG ATHLETE

American society supports a very active organized sports program beginning in the early childhood years and continuing at various levels of competition through the adolescent years. There is organized activity for hockey, soccer, swimming, figure skating, gymnastics, football, baseball, basketball, martial arts, distance running, and wrestling, with local, regional, and national championships. The American public apparently assumes that organized sports are a valuable adjunct to growing up as both emotional and financial support for athletic teams, has been increasing without limit.

The possibility of both physical and psychological trauma figures prominently in the arguments of those who condemn programs that introduce youngsters to the stress of competition. However, the few studies available on juvenile sports fail to indicate higher injury rates in young athletes who participate in competitive sports, as compared with noncompetitive activities. Although the risk of injury is not great, the participation of preadolescent youth in highly organized sports programs does raise several points. Urban society provides limited opportunity for spontaneous play and demands that healthy, energy-expending activity be experienced through organized sports. It is regrettable that organized programs for the very young are patterned after varsity or professional sports and are supervised most often by enthusiastic but untrained adult volunteers (see Appendix 3-1). Present knowledge does suggest that certain youths are highly vulnerable to psychological trauma — those individuals who for various reasons will invariably experience failure in sports competition. It is important to be able to recognize the vulnerable young participant in sports.

Before doing this, we must have some understanding of normal preadolescent development. Children vary substantially in physical and psychological maturation. The evidence suggests that matching children in the competitive setting on the basis of physical and psychological maturity is preferable to the use of chronological age alone. Parents and coaches probably are the most able to assess the psychological maturity of their children and this, along with physical maturation, should be considered when counseling youngsters about appropriate sports. Children develop considerable interest in competition — comparing their skills with other children — at about age six (chronological age). From 6-12 years has been labelled the "social comparison stage of child development," because youngsters are greatly interested in discovering how their abilities and skills compare with those of others.

Children who are late-maturers, either physically or psychologically, should be advised to delay entry into competitive sports unless the program has the potential to help the child mature. Programs that place the major emphasis on the child's development, rather than winning, will be most beneficial for the late-maturer. Children just beginning to participate should start in low level programs where the intensity of competition increases only as the child's skill level and interest increase. Competitive programs at young ages probably should not consume all of a youngster's time. Young children should have the opportunity to learn other sports skills and to participate in unorganized leisure activities.

Participation in competitive sports should teach youngsters how to win and lose and deal with others with respect, honesty, and cooperation (see Appendix 3-2). What values are actually taught are determined by the behavior and attitude of coaches and parents. The team physician should be concerned when a training schedule is developed that stresses the preadolescent both physically and psychologically.

Sports competition has the potential to produce severe stress and anxiety. This phenomenon has been well-documented in the literature. Yet, competitive stress can be beneficial for youngsters in certain sports situations. Commonly, children's sports are more stressful for the adults involved (see Appendix 3-3).

Those who support children's sports have argued that stress in sports will help children prepare for stressful situations as adults. Data in this area is relatively limited. A major question is: If some stress is beneficial, how much is good and how much is too much? When the primary emphasis of children's sports activities is aimed at healthy physical and psychological development, and toward having fun rather than just winning, children generally will not be overly stressed. Children can grow from the stress of sports if they know that their family, peers, and coaches see them as worthy persons regardless of the outcome of their performance in the game.

It is extremely important to identify the youngster who might suffer the psychological trauma of high levels of anxiety or repeated failure in athletic competition. Two groups of individuals at risk have been identified:

Group 1: those who demonstrate a low level of confidence relative to their age/peer group, which may be due to late maturation, inexperience, or lack of innate ability.

Group 2: those who perceive that they are not meeting the expectations of their age/peer group, coach, or parent (high competitive trait anxiety).

Children in group 1 respond well to proper coaching, which is influenced by their physical, psychological, and intellectual potential. The child's anxiety level can be reduced by appropriate training and/or switching to a sports activity more appropriate to the child's ability.

Children in group 2 are in a more complex situation. They are often involved in highly competitive sports and participate in "win-at-any-cost" environments. The child not only carries the burden of a personal need to succeed, but also the needs of his peers, coaches, parents, and community members who want to be vicarious winners. Some athletes are successful in this environment, but many suffer psychological trauma when they cannot deal with the demands placed on them. It is appropriate and important to identify the failure-prone youngster and guide him/her into activities that are challenging and rewarding.

Youth coaches often have difficulty in detecting a child's level of competitive anxiety. They must be taught to recognize individual differences in children's anxiety levels and how to respond appropriately for each youngster. The low self-esteem child and the child with a high level of competitive anxiety need different coaching approaches. When children learn effective coping skills to deal with stressful events within the framework of sports, they may be better able to deal with other stressful situations in their adolescent and young adulthood years.

To guard against emotional injury in youth sports, several prevention techniques have been developed. They are organized into three general categories: 1) modifying features of the athletic environment; 2) training coaches to relate more effectively to their players, and 3) counseling and stress management. Most often in youth sports, stress can be handled by modifying the environment and through effective training of coaches (Smith, 1982).

Examples of modifying the competitive setting to reduce stress are: Rules can be changed to permit greater success; game scores, league standings, or individual performance statistics can be eliminated to reduce the emphasis on evaluation and on winning; coaches can provide a supportive rather than punitive environment which will lessen the fear of failure, and parents can reduce the fear of failure by encouraging and supporting their children.

## VIOLENCE IN SPORTS

Acts of violence and hostility are more prevalent in sports today than at any time in the past. The problem of violence in sports has become a major concern. Football and hockey have been most often criticized for violence; however, it takes very little study to see that violence is not limited to any particular sport or just to the players. Violent action becomes part of a pattern, of the players and the fans who may vent their emotions on the players, officials, coaches, and security forces. Health professionals and others involved in youth sports should examine the conduct of sporting activities. The team physician, coach, and parents should be on the alert for violent tendencies in youngsters and be ready to help them cope more effectively with competitive stress. The team physician also should consider the possible use of street drugs, anabolic steroids, or alcohol when violent acts occur.

## SUMMARY

Regular exercise programs are essential for the normal development of youngsters and can encourage involvement in physical fitness and activity programs into adulthood. Children should be counseled about appropriate sport-related activities as an integral part of family life, not just sent to highly organized team sports that may not be appropriate. The physical and psychological safety of organized leagues should be determined before a child participates.

Some questions parents should ask about an organized sport in which their child plans to participate are (see Appendix 3-3):

- What are the goals of the program?
- Who runs the program?
- Are the coaches and supervising staff qualified and well-trained?
- Why does the child want to participate?
- Are the time commitments and sacrifices of the child and family understood?
- What would be the effect on the child and parent if the young athlete becomes a "bench warmer"?
- Is the child ready to compete? Can losing be tolerated? How does he handle stress and anxiety?
- Does the child know about getting hurt?
- If the child wants to quit, what happens?

A highly competitive parent may need further guidance and counseling in order to protect the health and safety of a child athlete. Occasionally, the primary care physician is the child's only advocate when the interests of the athlete's coach, peers, and parents become too overwhelming. Children need to be successful in their early endeavors with exercise and sport so that lifelong positive attitudes toward physical activity are fostered along with the development of motor skills and fitness. The sports physician can and should be involved in deciding which sports activities are in the best interest of the young athlete.

### REFERENCES

Feltz, D.L. The psychology of sports injuries. In Vinger, P.E. and Horner, E.F. (Eds) *Sports Injuries: the Unthwarted Epidemic* (2nd ed). Boston: John Wright, P.S.G., 1984.
Nideffer, R.M. Applied Sports Psychology. In Strauss, R.H. (ed): *Sports Medicine* Philadelphia: W.B. Saunders Co, pgs. 501-510, 1984.
Nideffer, R.M. *The Ethics and Practice of Applied Sports Psychology*, New York: Random House, 1981.
Normand, P. Controlling performance anxiety. *Drug Therapy* pgs. 33-40, May 1985.
Smith, R.E., Smoll, S.L. Psychological stress: a conceptual model and some intervention strategies in youth sports. In Magill, R.A., Ash, M.J., Smoll, S.L. (eds) *Children in Sports*, Champaign, IL: Human Kinetics, pgs. 153-177, 1982.
Suinn, R. Removing emotional obstacles to learning and performance by visual motor behavior rehearsal. *Behavior Therapy* 3:308, 1972.

### RECOMMENDED READINGS

Asken, M.J. A curriculum in sports psychology in a family medicine residency program. *Family Medicine* 18(1):23-24, 1986.
Begel, D.M. Concepts of sports psychology. *Annals of Sports Medicine* 2(3):133-135, 1985.
Biesser, A. *The Madness in Sports: Psychosocial Observations*. New York: Appleton-Century-Crofts, 1967.
Feltz, D.L., Ewing, M.E. Psychological characteristics of elite young athletes. *Med Sci Sports Exer* 19(5):S98-S105, 1987.
Feigley, D.A. Psychological burnout in high level athletes. *Phys Sportsmed* 12(10):109-119, October 1984.
Finn, J.A. Competitive excellence: it's a matter of mind and body. *Phys Sportsmed* 13:61, 1985.
Gould, D. Sports psychology in the 1980's: status, direction and challenge in youth sports research. *J Sports Psychology* 4:203, 1982.
Kennedy, S., Kiecolt-Glaser, J.K, and Glaser, R. Immunologic consequences of acute and chronic stressors: Mediating role of interpersonal relationships. *British Journal of Medical Psychology* 61:77-85, 1988.
Kozar, B. and Lord, R.N. Overuse injuries in the young athlete: reasons for concern. *Phys Sportsmed* 11:116, 1983.
Lanning, W. The privileged few: special counseling needs of athletes. *J Sport Psych* 4:19-23, 1982.

Legwold, G. Adolescent athletes face emotional and physical abuse. *Phys Sportsmed* 11:57-58, March 1983.

Leonard, G. *The Ultimate Athlete: Re-visioning Sports, Physical Education and the Body*. New York: The Viking Press, 1975.

Locke, E.A. and Latham, G.P. The application of goal setting to sports. *J Sport Psych* 7:205-222, 1985.

Magill, R., Ash, M.J., Smoll, F.L. (Eds.) *Children in Sports*. Champaign, IL: Human Kinetics Publishers, Inc. 1978.

Mahoney, M.J., Gabriel, T.J. and Perkins, T.S. Psychological skills and exceptional athletic performance. *Sport Psychologist* 1:181-199, 1987.

Martens, R. ed. *Joy and Sadness in Children's Sports*. Champaign, IL: Human Kinetics Publishers, Inc., 1978.

McCauley, E. Sport psychology in the eighties: some current developments. *Med Sci Sports Exer*. 19(5):S95-S97, 1987.

McNair, D., Lorr, M. and Droppleman, L. *Profile of Mood States manual*. San Diego: Educational and Testing Service, 1971.

May, J.R. and Asken, M.J. *Sport Psychology: The Psychological Health of the Athlete*. New York: PMA Publishing Corporation, 1987.

Morgan, W.P., Brown, D.R., Raglin, J.S., O'Connor, P.J. and Ellickson, K.A. Psychological monitoring of overtraining and staleness. *British Journal of Sports Medicine* 21:107-114, 1987.

Murray, T.H. Divided loyalties in sports medicine. *Phys Sportsmed* 12:124, 1984.

Nideffer, R.M., Sharpe, R.C. *Attention Control Training*, San Diego, CA: Enhanced Performance Assoc, 1978.

Orlick, T. and Partington, J. Mental links to excellence. *Sports Psychologist* 2:105-130, 1988.

Orlick, T. *In Pursuit of Excellence*. Ottawa, Ontario: Coaching Association of Canada, 1980.

*Orthopedic Clinics of North America* 14(2):373-385, April 1983, The injured athlete: psychological factors in treatment.

Rotella, R.J. Psychological care of the injured athlete. In D.N. Kulund (Ed.). *The Injured Athlete*. Philadelphia: J.B. Lippincott, 1982.

Rowland, T.W. Motivational factors in exercise training programs for children. *Phys Sportsmed* 14:122, 1986.

Rushall, B. *Psyching in Sports*. London, England: Pelham, 1980.

Ryan, A.J. (Ed.) Overtraining of athletes — a roundtable. *Phys Sportsmed* 11(6):93-110, June 1983.

Scanlan, T.K., Passer, M.W. Factors related to competitive stress among male youth sports participants. *Medicine and Science in Sports and Exercise* 10(2):103-108, 1973.

Shields, C.E. Physical activity in the young. *American Family Physician* 33:155, 1986.

Silva, J.M. III and Weinberg, R.S. (Eds.). *Psychological Foundations of Sport*. Champaign, IL: Human Kinetics, 1984.

Singer, R.N. Sports psychology. *American Corrective Therapy Journal* 29(4):115-120 July 1975.

Straub, W.F. and Williams, J.M. (Eds.). *Cognitive Sport Psychology*. Lansing, NY: Sport Science Associates, 1984.

Suinn, R. (Ed.). *Psychology in Sports: Methods and Applications*. Minnesota: Burgess Press, 1980.

Tutko, T. and Tosi, U. *Sports Psyching*. Los Angeles: J.P. Tarcher, 1976.

Wiese, D.M. and Weiss, M.R. Psychological rehabilitation and physical injury: implications for the sportsmedicine team. *Sport Psychologist* 1:318-330, 1987.

Williams, J.M. (Ed.). *Applied Sports Psychology: Personal Growth to Peak Performance*. Palo Alto, CA: Mayfield Publishing Co., 1986.

Yukelson, D. Psychology of sport and the injured athlete. In D.B. Bernhart (ed.), *Clinics in Physical Therapy* (pp. 175-195). New York: Churchill Livingston, 1986.

# Appendix 3-1.
## Important Points In Considering Scholastic Athletic Programs
### (Adapted from American Academy of Pediatrics)

### I. Philosophy and Principles

1. There is a written statement expressing the philosophy, principles, and objectives of the athletic department.
2. The stated philosophy expresses the need for physicians with interest and competence in sports medicine to be available to staff and athletes.
3. The statement reflects the roles and responsibilities in the sports medicine program for coaches, parents, athletes, athletic trainers and physicians.
4. The school administration communicates this philosophy to all parents and athletes to help insure a clear understanding of policies.
5. The statement is required reading for parents, coaches and athletes.
6. Sports medicine is regarded as an essential part of the total athletic program, not just as game or event coverage.
7. The organization and function of the school's sports medicine program is under direction of a licensed physician.
8. School personnel support recommendations of the sports medicine staff regarding treatment, rehabilitation, and the necessity to exclude certain athletes from participation for medical reasons.
9. Parents' or guardians' consent for emergency medical treatment is on file with sports medicine personnel.

### II. Organization and Administration

1. At least one athletic trainer, certified by the National Athletic Trainer's Association, is on the sports medicine staff.
2. The director of the sports medicine staff is responsible to the school administration for conducting a program to minimize sports injuries.
3. The athletic trainer is employed to treat and reduce the risks of sports injuries and is not involved in coaching.
4. A job description outlining duties and responsibilities of the sports medicine staff is available in writing.
5. There is an accessible file of individual health examination reports.
6. There is a method for maintaining records of weight, injuries, illnesses, and other pertinent information about the athletes.
7. There is a comprehensive insurance program for the medical care of injured athletes.
8. The director of the sports medicine program is a paid member of the staff.
9. The administration of the sports medicine program is delegated to a licensed physician whose responsibilities include planning, scheduling, organizing, supervising, and evaluating the total sports medicine program.
10. Equal opportunity is given to programs for both sexes in matters of policy, budget, use of facilities, equipment, scheduling, and the extent of participation.
11. A staffing pattern or chart is developed which specifies relationships among staff in the school sports program.
12. A systematic evaluation is used to maintain the effectiveness of the total program.

### III. The Staff

1. The athletic director has professional preparation and experience necessary for planning and directing an interscholastic athletic program in a broad range of sports activities.
2. The athletic director is involved in the selection of the athletic department staff, including sports medicine personnel.
3. The athletic director encourages the sports medicine staff to attend professional meetings and educational programs in sports medicine.
4. Coaches are knowledgeable in medical aspects

of sports, including conditioning, care of the injured athlete, principles of rehabilitation and carry current certification in first aid and CPR.
5. Coaches put the safety and health of the athlete as the highest priority.
6. The sports medicine physicians are licensed to practice in the state.
7. The physicians in the sports medicine program are involved in protecting the health of all athletes, are on call during practices, and attend all sports events that have high injury rates.
8. The school has a National Athletic Trainers Association certified athletic trainer on the sports medicine staff.
9. Aides to the certified staff personnel in the sports program have had training in first aid, basic life support, and CPR.
10. The athletic director, coaches, athletic trainers and team physicians recognize that they are responsible as individuals, and also a team, for providing consistent, high standards in health care for young athletes.

## IV. Event Coverage

1. All coaches and sports medicine personnel are certified in CPR and trained in emergency management of life-threatening injuries.
2. Effective telephone access to a medical emergency unit is available.
3. A suitable vehicle is available for immediate transportation of the injured athlete to a designated medical resource which has been alerted.
4. Competent adult supervision of the crowd is provided.
5. The playing area is surveyed before each event to identify injury hazards on or near the field or court.
6. A physician member of the sports medicine staff attends high risk sports events such as football, wrestling, hockey and gymnastics and events with a large spectator attendance.
7. Emergency first aid supplies and equipment are readily available to all competing teams.
8. Visiting teams have ready access to facilities for care of an injured athlete.
9. Environmental conditions are monitored by sling psychrometer or other means during hot, humid weather and strenuous activity is modified as needed.
10. Abundant supplies of drinking water and ice are available at all times.

## V. Facilities and Equipment

1. Adequate funds are allocated to the sports medicine program for:
   a. expendable supplies
   b. capital improvements
   c. continuing education
   d. repairs and maintenance
2. There is adequate space to handle the flow of routine care of the athletic population:
   a. conditioning & reconditioning programs
   b. prophylactic taping, wrapping & padding
   c. privacy for physical examinations
   d. office space or station for record-keeping
3. There is an adequate supply of emergency equipment readily available, i.e.:
   a. slings
   b. knee immobilizers
   c. crutches
   d. splints
   e. cervical collar
   f. stretcher
   g. spine board
   h. sand bags
   i. equipment for maintaining an airway
   j. icepacks
4. An adequate supply of first aid supplies is readily available.
5. There is an adequate and readily available communication system between the athletic participation areas and medical or para-medical assistance.
   a. emergency situation
   b. non-emergency situation
7. There are adequate provisions for heating or cooling body areas.
8. Sanitation and safety of players and staff are assured by written policies and proper facilities.
9. All electrical supply in the sports medicine area is controlled by ground fault interrupters at the outlet or control panel.
10. Adequate sports medicine facilities are available to all competing teams.

## VI. Education

1. The sports medicine staff conducts educational sessions for all athletes, covering the following:

a. heat illness
  b. nutrition
  c. harmful effects of drugs, alcohol and tobacco
  d. general hygiene for the athlete
  e. rehabilitation
2. The school makes available, for selected students, an elective course for athletic trainer aides.

# Appendix 3-2.
# Bill of Rights for Athletes

I. Right to participate in sports
II. Right to participate at a level commensurate with each child's maturity and ability
III. Right to have qualified adult leadership
IV. Right to play as a child and not as an adult
V. Right of children to share in the leadership and decision-making of their sport participation
VI. Right to participate in safe and healthy environments
VII. Right to proper preparation for participation in sports
VIII. Right to an equal opportunity to strive for success
IX. Right to be treated with dignity
X. Right to have fun in sports

(From R. Martens and V. Seefeldt (Eds.). *Guidelines for Children's Sports*, Washington, D.C. American Alliance for Health, Physical Education, Recreation and Dance, 1979.)

# Appendix 3-3.
# Parental Guide to Selecting Youth Sports Programs

Answers to questions such as the following will usually prompt the appropriate decision as to whether youth sport competition is something parents wish to be involved in.

1. Who really wants our son or daughter involved in the sport program? Is it the parent, the coach, or the program organizers? Or is it the child?
2. Is this a "good" sport for a child of the maturity level of our son or daughter?
3. What will our children receive as benefit from participation in the program? Will they have fun? Learn skills? Get some needed exercise and fitness benefit? Learn about teamwork and cooperation?
4. Does your child appreciate the time commitment that is to be involved and the time taken away from other forms of play and recreation?
5. What will becoming a member of this team mean to family life such as mealtimes, vacation, and weekend activities?
6. What do we know about the goals and objectives of the program and the qualifications of the people in charge?
7. Are the practices and games conducted in a safe and well-supervised manner? Are there well-planned arrangements for dealing with sport injuries?
8. How are competitors matched and assigned to compete?
9. Do all the children get to play in the games?
10. Is our child ready to accept instruction and criticism from a coach?
11. What are the time and financial commitments of the parents? Are there uniforms to be purchased? Travel funds to be provided? Practice lights to be paid for? Do all parents have to attend practices and games? Do parents provide weekend transportation to matches and games?
12. Is our child emotionally ready to deal with winning and losing?
13. Are we prepared to be the parents of a winner or a loser? Are we ready to be parents of a bench-warmer?
14. What do we do if our child wants to quit?
15. How will we get out of the program if we want to? How do we get out if our child does not want to?

Youth sport programs can be organized on a very low-key recreational basis emphasizing fun, skills, and health-promoting exercise and fitness. Parent involvement can be kept to a minimum, and the program actually be designed to give first priority to the enjoyment and benefit of the child participants.

(From *Children and Parents: Growth, Development, and Sports*, pg. 213-214, 1986)

# PART II
# Preventive Sports Medicine

# 4

# Preparticipation Screening

## INITIAL CONSIDERATIONS

Performing preparticipation physical examinations (PPPE) has been part of the primary care physician's armamentarium for years. As more people participate in exercise and conditioning programs, the consistent advice from the medical establishment is: "confirm your state of physical fitness prior to beginning an exercise program." That advice carries with it an unspoken implication that the pre-exercise evaluation obtained should at least assess risk of injury or harm from anticipated exercise. Some say these evaluations are merely a specialized health screening and argue about what should constitute the preparticipation examination. We believe consistency is of utmost importance. At a minimum, the examination should assess risk factors and detect disease/injury that might cause problems during subsequent physical activity. Once past this generalized goal, disagreement arises from the different philosophical and medical viewpoints. The purpose of this chapter is to outline what should be determined and assessed, and how, when, and where such an exam should be conducted. It will not address the question of whether preparticipation physicals are worthwhile. A strong argument can be made for the development of a standardized examination form and protocol designed to identify potential risk factors in a *consistent* manner. Just such a form — the result of a task force initiative — is featured in Appendix 4-1. (Lombardo and Smith, personal communications).

## ESSENTIALS

By nature, any exercise evaluation of an individual should involve an awareness of the stress the exercise places upon three major body systems — musculoskeletal, cardiovascular, and psychological. It is logical to emphasize these areas in the pre-exercise evaluation. The major question is: Will this individual be at any greater risk of injury or illness given the anticipated exercise program? Any evaluation should include clearly defined objectives and various objectives have been suggested by various authors (Table 4-1). Some objectives (1-5, 8, 11 and 12) are germane for any athlete; others may be more specific. Failure to meet these objectives will do both the athlete and the physician a disservice. A final note: the number of pre-evaluation screenings must not compromise the principles of efficacy and cost effectiveness.

Different situations and settings call for different types of evaluation. Flexibility in changing the PPPE is implicit in any of the subsequent recommendations in this chapter. The PPPE also should meet community and individual needs (McKeag, 1989). While there is no "right" way to perform the preparticipation physical examination, the physician should look at who are the prospec-

**Table 4-1. Objectives of Preparticipation Screening**

1. To determine the general health.
2. To disclose defects that could limit participation.
3. To discover conditions predisposing the athlete to injury.
4. To advise the athlete concerning optimal performance.
5. To classify the athlete according to his individual qualifications.
6. To fulfill legal and insurance requirements for organized athletic programs.
7. To evaluate the size and maturation level of young athletes.
8. To improve fitness and performance.
9. To provide opportunities for students to compete who have either physiological or pathological health conditions that might preclude "blanket" approval.
10. To counsel youth and answer personal health questions.
11. To establish an initial doctor/patient relationship.
12. To initiate medicolegal documentation of pre-exercise examination.

(Compiled from Allman, 1983; Lombardo, 1984; Goldberg & Boiardo, 1984; Linder, 1981; Schaffer, 1983 and McKeag, 1985.)

tive athletes, what is the contemplated exercise program, and what is the motivation to participate.

## PROSPECTIVE ATHLETE

Understanding the characteristics of the target population is essential in determining what is assessed. One way to develop an appropriate examination is to look at prospective athletes by maturational age.

### Prepubescent Athlete (approximate age range: 6-10 years)

Youngsters have always been involved in spontaneous play but there is a current trend toward increased organization. One consideration with this age group is the manifestation of previously undiagnosed congenital abnormalities. Physicians should be well acquainted with all the common abnormalities of the age group. The psychological make-up of young athletes is also important. At this age, the philosophy of the program the candidate is anticipating joining can be a major factor in predicting the possibility of a poor outcome.

The most common reasons for youth non-participation in sports (including those who started and stopped, as well as those who never began) in order of prevalence are: a) not getting to play; b) negative reinforcement; c) mismatching; d) psychological stress; e) failure, and f) over-organization (Martens, 1980). When asked about sports participation, 95% of youngsters felt the most important thing about sports was having fun, not winning, and 75% said they would rather play on a losing team than sit on the bench on a winning team (Henschen and Griffin, 1977). Generally this population is very healthy. The physician can exert a great deal of influence in the patient education aspects because habits have not been established. For instance, after correct methods of warm-up and cool-down are explained, a high degree of compliance can be expected.

### Pubescent (11-15 years)

These athletes are undergoing rapid body growth and change with the advent of physical, psychological, and sexual maturation (Caine, 1987; McKeag, 1986). This group will have many non-exercise-related concerns (sexual activity, drugs). Given the appropriate examination format (see "Implementation" in this chapter), most of their questions can be addressed. If ever there were a time to expand a focused screening examination, it would be in this age group. Most participating athletes at this age are involved in organized sports activities. The effect of exercise on human maturation directly relates to them.

### Post-pubescent/young adult (16-30 years)

This group include athletes with many reasons for exercising. Most elite athletes in the country are in this age group, and it also is the age where most recreational athletes continue to compete. The PPPE needs to take into account the athlete's skill level. Most of these athletes begin in organized sports and then become more involved in recreational and individual sports as they grow older. Important points to take into account when formulating the PPPE for this age group include the past medical history (especially as it concerns previous injuries), and the need to make the examination sport-specific (see Table 4-2).

Table 4-2. Physical-Examination Emphasis

| Sport | Area to Check |
|---|---|
| Baseball | Shoulder, elbow, arm |
| Basketball | Ankle |
| Football | Neck, head, knee |
| Gymnastics | Wrist, shoulder |
| Handball | Wrist, hands |
| Running | Back, hip, knee, ankle, foot |
| Soccer | Hip, pelvis, foot |
| Swimming | Ears, nose, throat, shoulder |
| Wrestling | Body fat (%), shoulders, skin |

### Adults (30-65 years)

Most adults participate primarily in informal recreational sports. They may be categorized into roughly two types, the sporadic athlete and the regularly exercising one. Participation of the first type is organized around team-oriented sports (softball, basketball) that play or practice one or two times a week. Such an individual is prone to acute injury and should be informed of the importance of warm-up and flexibility exercise prior to participation. The regularly exercising athlete may participate in an individual or paired sport such as running, swimming, cycling, or racket sports. These individuals are more apt to suffer overuse syndromes and need to have the necessity for true exercise prescription stressed to them. This group of athletes rarely participates in any type of pre-exercise evaluation and usually surface only after an injury has occurred. Yet, from a motivational standpoint, they are the most adamant about their athletic participation resulting in prevention or illness of disease.

### Elderly (66 years and over)

Many elderly individuals enter exercise programs as a result of the well-recognized rehabilitation potential of exercise after a serious injury or illness. Exercise is now a major part of the therapeutic regimen for many injuries and illnesses such as myocardial infarction, coronary artery bypass, diabetes mellitus, asthma, and depression. These individuals often wish to continue exercising after their rehabilitation has ended. In most cases, the PPPE should merely be a part of the comprehensive health appraisal called for in this age group.

## CONTEMPLATED EXERCISE PROGRAM

Not all exercise is the same. Depending upon what kind of exercise is anticipated or wanted and what is discovered on the PPPE, several assessment options can be considered. There are three major types of exercise, aerobic, anaerobic and combined. Aerobic exercise is characterized by continuous, long-duration, low-power movements involving aerobic generation of energy through oxidative phosphorylation. Examples include repetitive endurance type sports such as swimming, running, or biking. Anaerobic exercise is characterized by short-duration, high-power energy bursts requiring generation of energy from glycolysis or muscle stores of adenosine triphosphate (ATP) and phosphocreatine. Examples include sprinting and weight-lifting. Most exercise tends to combine aerobic/anaerobic systems. Examples are soccer and basketball. Figure 5A-1 in Chapter 5 portrays various activities and the relative contribution of the aerobic and anaerobic systems to each.

## MOTIVATION

Performing a pre-exercise evaluation on a prospective athlete warrants asking this question: Why do you want to exercise? Assessment of motivation is an extremely important part of the physical examination. In a prepubescent athlete, the answer may determine what comprises the remainder of the exam. In an adult athlete, over-motivation may predispose and predirect future overuse problems. There are four major reasons (McKeag, 1989) commonly given by recreational athletes for wishing to exercise:

- Becoming healthy and gaining a feeling of self-satisfaction.
- Fear of dying.
- For the social components of exercise.
- As a part of a therapeutic regimen for illness or injury.

Adjusting the evaluation to take into account the characteristics of the patient population, type of exercise contemplated, and reasons why it is desired becomes not only a recommended but essential means of achieving the objectives of the preparticipation physical examination. The PPPE is thus "matched" to the potential athlete.

## IMPLEMENTATION

Formal, organized programs at any age (usually high school or college) involve enough athletes to warrant screenings. Conversely, physicians dealing with the informal recreational athlete should do so on an individual basis only. However, the objectives of the evaluations are similar, if not the same.

Implementation of the examination can involve any of three different approaches:

a. *Individual examination* — to be carried out by the athlete's primary care physician. Advantages of this type of examination include:
   1. past medical history is already known
   2. motivation can be better assessed
   3. relationship between doctor and patient is usually already established, which facilitates the discussion of sensitive issues
   4. greater continuity of care in the event of injury
   5. if required, medical consultation can be quick, with follow-up more complete.

   Disadvantages of the individual exam include:
   1. lack of consistency among physicians leading to inconsistency in judgments concerning qualification issues
   2. the process is not cost effective
   3. lack of time to address issues that are important to the patient but which may be overlooked by the busy practitioner
   4. inconsistent knowledge base of practitioners concerning the medical aspects of sports
   5. lack of familiarity with the demands of specific sports leading to either too conservative or too liberal judgments, causing unfairness to the athlete
   6. individual examinations lack appropriate comparative data for the physician to use.

b. *Locker Room Technique* — This is the least satisfactory of the three processes. One physician does all aspects of each physical examination, usually in cramped quarters. He examines an entire group so there is no privacy for the individual athlete. It is done under rushed and noisy conditions and usually fails to address important questions.

c. *Station Technique* — This is directed by a primary care physician and uses a team approach with volunteers from the school system including school nurses, athletic trainers, physician's assistants, coaches, interested teachers, and administrators. If it is correctly set up, it offers some accommodations for privacy and becomes a relatively cost-effective way of performing mass screening examinations. Table 4-3 illustrates an outline of a station technique.

The PPPE format determinants are summarized in Table 4-4. The standard to be achieved, regardless of the method used, is certification from a knowledgeable primary care physician, who has expertise in the medical aspects of the sports for which the screening is done.

## FREQUENCY

Many clinicians advocate the traditional yearly sports examination. Some consider evaluation necessary prior to each sport season (Micheli, 1984). Realistically, most sports medicine physicians favor doing an examination prior to the beginning of any new level of competition in an athlete's career. For youngsters, this usually corresponds to school levels (grade school, junior high, high school, and

**Table 4-3. Station Technique**

| Station | Task | Responsibility of: |
|---|---|---|
| 1. | Registration and fill out history | Teacher, administrator |
| 2. | Vital signs are gathered | Teacher, coach, trainer |
| 3. | Blood pressure and pulse | Nurse, coach, trainer |
| 4. | Urine sample gathered | Nurse, coach, trainer |
| 5. | Visual acuity — Snellen chart | Nurse, coach, trainer |
| 6. | Hearing acuity | Nurse, coach, trainer |
| 7. | General medical exam and Tanner staging | Physician |
| 8. | Student athlete exits examination area; examine materials for completeness | Teacher, administrator |

Table 4-4. PPPE Format Determinants

| Life Cycle | Problems | Importance of Exercise Type | Motivation | Site | Plan |
|---|---|---|---|---|---|
| Prepubescent 6-10 Years | Poorly thought out organized sports program | ++ | ++++ | Office | Begin correct athlete education |
| | Congenital abnormalities | | | | |
| Pubescent 11-15 Years | Non-sports related concerns (sex, drugs) | + | + | Station | (Re)establishment of a doctor-patient relationship |
| | Effect of exercise on growth. | | | | |
| Post-pubescent/ Young Adult | Wide range of skill levels (elite to recreational) | + | ++ | Office | Sports-specific PPPE PMH of past injuries |
| Adult | Sporadic athlete— acute injury | +++ | +++ | Office | Stress warm up, flexibility |
| | Regular athlete— overuse injury | | | | Stress exercise prescription. |
| Elderly | Multiple problems affecting different exercise modalities | ++++ | ++ | Office | PPPE should merely be part of CPE |

college). We advocate the use of an intercurrent (or interval) review prior to the start of each sport season, following the initial full scale examination at the entrance to the particular level of participation. This intercurrent review would allow for follow-up on rehabilitation of injuries incurred during the previous season or previous sport. The examination itself could be brief and directed at the injury. Examples of the self-administered forms used for both the preparticipation physical examination and the intercurrent examination can be found in Appendices 4-2 and 4-3 respectively.

It would be well to keep in mind two very important factors, the age of the athlete in question, and the goals of the examination. Recommendations for each age group follow:

1. *Prepubescent* — As indicated in Table 4-4, the initial examination should be done by the practitioner in the office setting. This first sports physical is the most important because it may represent the first interaction the child has had with the health care system for perhaps 8-10 years. Follow-up intercurrent examinations should be held on a yearly basis with attention to vital signs, injuries incurred since the last examination, maturation and development, and the wearing of any new appliances (glasses, contact lenses, bridges).

2. *Pubescent/Post-pubescent* — The initial preparticipation examination can be done with either technique. One screening exam for junior high school, high school, and college should be done. Intercurrent examinations should focus on vital signs, completion of physical development, recent injury, and nonsports-related health concerns (drug use, eating habits, sexual history).

3. *Adult (recreational)* — Any adult 40 years of age or under should consider having a comprehensive physical examination (*not* a PPPE) before beginning any exercise program. Afterward,

PREPARTICIPATION SCREENING

a yearly assessment of physical fitness by means of a limited but directed physical exam should suffice (see Figure 4-1A) (Taylor, 1983).
4. *Older Adults (recreational)* — Any adult 41 years or older with health problems or risk factors should have a comprehensive yearly physical examination. This advice is independent of whether the person is an athlete or not. If the older athlete has no health problems or risk factors, a limited yearly physical exam, plus any needed testing is sufficient. (See Figure 4-1B).

## TIMING

Only one principle should dictate the timing of the preparticipation physical examination. Examinations should occur prior to a particular sport season to allow adequate time for rehabilitation of injury, muscle imbalances, and other correctable problems, but not so far ahead as to make the passage of time an important factor in the development of new problems. McKeag (1985) recommends 4-6 weeks prior to a sport season as reasonable. If a longer time is taken, especially with the younger athlete, such factors as maturation and new injuries can decrease the comprehensiveness and effectiveness of the examination and decrease its preventive aspects.

## CONTENT

**History.** A thorough history is the cornerstone of all medical evaluations (Lombardo, 1984). Risser (1985) advocates consideration of the history as the principle screening tool. It is clearly the most sensitive and specific part of the process.

### THE OFFICE WORKUP

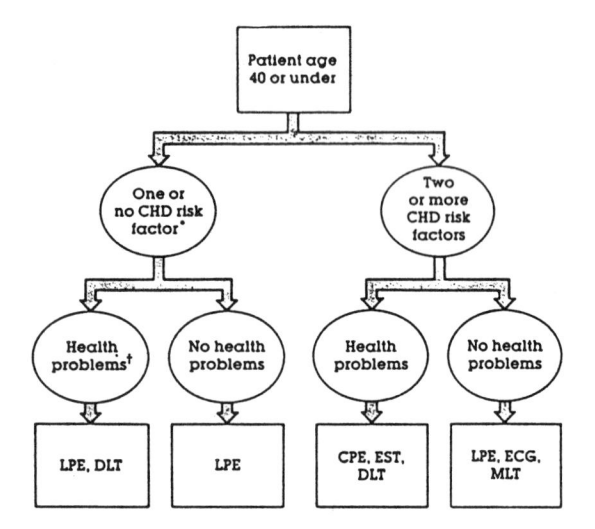

*Risk factors for coronary heart disease (CHD)*

- Cigarette smoking
- Hyperlipidemia
- Hypertension
- Hyperglycemia or diabetes mellitus
- Hyperuricemia or gout
- Obesity

†Health problems

- Hematologic
- Cardiopulmonary
- Neurologic
- Endocrine
- Musculoskeletal
- Psychiatric
- Renal or hepatic

**Fig. 4-1A.** The Adult PPPE Work-up

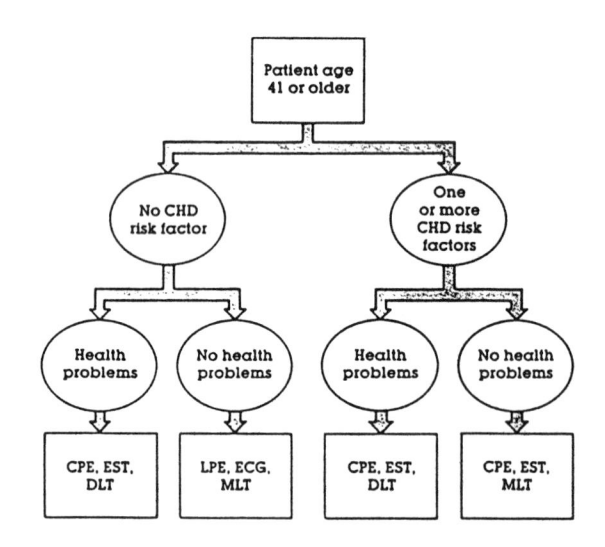

**Recommended evaluation**

LPE: Limited physical exam
CPE: Comprehensive physical exam
ECG: Resting electrocardiogram
EST: Exercise stress test (if patient has cardiopulmonary disease)
MLT: Minimal laboratory testing
DLT: Diagnostic laboratory testing (if CHD risk factors include hyperlipidemia, hyperglycemia, or hyperuricemia)

**Fig. 4-1B.**

96  *PREVENTIVE SPORTS MEDICINE*

Forms are preferable for a PPPE to insure that all essential information has been captured across various examiners. No one form could or should be advocated as being totally appropriate for a particular sports medicine program. However, recommended characteristics of that form can be found in Appendices 4-1, 4-2, and 4-3. Any form should be easy to complete, short, limited to one side of a piece of paper, self-administered, time efficient, and contain lay language easily understood by the athlete. Important highlights of any history include:

1. *Exercise-Induced Syncope* — Used to rule out life threatening cardiac abnormalities (IHSS, aberrant coronary arteries, arrhythmias) and seizures. A history of occasional exertional dyspnea, light-headedness or non-specific chest discomfort, may be of little value in athletes (Epstein, 1986). Table 4-5 lists the causes of sudden death in young athletes. If an athlete has a history of exercise-induced syncope, two further questions should be asked. Is there a family history of cardiomyopathy or of premature sudden death (less than 40 years of age) in a first degree or other close relative?
2. *Family History of Myocardial Infarction Before 50* — Used to rule out familial risk factors that could be aggravated by exercise. An informal cardiac risk assessment to identify a child/adolescent at risk for coronary disease. We pay special attention to adults with positive risk factors such as family history, obesity, or hypertension.
3. *Loss of Consciousness/Concussions As A Result of Exercise* — A complete history of head trauma resulting from athletic competition is important to have when qualifying a potential athlete for a contact sport. It is important to note and monitor cumulative, subtle, neurologic loss of function. This additional information acts as a check on the previously mentioned exercise-induced syncope.
4. *Past Medical History* — This should elicit information about injuries, illnesses, and past surgeries and will shed light on the general health and well-being of the individual. It may also explain functional abnormalities such as muscle imbalance, decreased respiratory volume, or below-normal exercise tolerance.
5. *Medications/Drugs* — The effect of medications and drugs on the exercising body can be serious. It is vital knowledge if an individual is injured or rendered unconscious. Otherwise, appropriate steps to treat an injured or ill athlete cannot be taken.
6. *Allergies* — Common occurrences, such as allergies to beestings (especially on artificial turf), and medications need to be known so that prophylactic measures can be taken in case of exposure.
7. *Appliance Use* — Information about mouth, eye, or ear appliances should be known in case an athlete is injured or unconscious. Such appliances can hinder resuscitation.
8. *Last Tetanus Vaccination* — An up-to-date tetanus vaccination is necessary because of the possibility of lacerations from unclean metal surfaces. Guideline: a booster within the last 10 years imparts sufficient immunity from secondary infection from major or minor trauma.
9. *Review of Systems* — A review of systems is often overlooked but lets a prospective athlete write down any current problem or injury. Inclusion of this on a PPPE form allows the individual to indicate any concerns about any particular body system.
10. *Additional Historic Information* — The authors would urge anyone setting up a sports medicine network to include specific and/or particular historical question. This might be used for community epidemiology, or spring from a particular community concern. Such information should be included at the discretion of the community and agreed upon by all concerned.

**Table 4-5. Causes of Sudden Death in Young Athletes ($\leq 35$ years old)**

Most common causes:
  Hypertrophic cardiomyopathy
  Idiopathic left ventricular hypertrophy*
  Aortic rupture (due to "cystic medial necrosis")
  Coronary artery disease
  Congenital coronary abnormalities

Less common causes:
  Valvular aortic stenosis
  Prolonged QT syndrome
  Primary cardiac electrophysiologic abnormalities
  Cardiac sarcoidosis
  Myocarditis

*May be a variant of hypertrophic cardiomyopathy.

**Physical Examination.** Whenever possible, a sport-specific physical examination, emphasizing those areas where injury and/or illness have the greatest epidemiologic occurrence, is a primary goal (McKeag, 1985). Any examination assessing a sports candidate without an awareness of the demands of their specific sport suffers a major weakness (see Table 4-2). Evaluation of a potential swimmer *should* be different from that of a football player.

Regardless of age, sex, or situation, three areas of the PPPE should always be emphasized:

- Cardiovascular system (including blood pressure determination);
- Musculoskeletal system (including range of motion and strength assessment);
- Psychological assessment (including motivation for exercise).

Because the prevalence of disqualifying conditions is low among athletes and because few of these patients produce significant physical findings, the yield from the physical exam is very low (Runyan, 1983). The existing community sports medicine network, and specifically the office based sports medicine practitioner, should take the time to study what is needed in the local environment.

Content highlights of the "generic" physical examination include:

1. *Vital Signs* — Blood pressure monitored with the proper size cuff, remembering the variance in upper limits by age (Figure 4-2). Sustained isometric activity (improper weight lifting) causes a marked and sometimes prolonged elevation in blood pressure and should be discouraged in athletes with borderline high blood pressure. Remember that weight training is often part of the preseason conditioning for many sports so that athletes already preparing for their competitive season may exhibit increased blood pressure at the PPPE.
2. *Height and Weight* — Unusual variance in either of these vital signs should signal further investigation. Aside from some rare endocrine disorders, four common problems are:
   a. *Eating Disorders* — Abnormal eating or weight loss patterns are often seen in sports requiring strict adherence or emphasis on body weight such as wrestling, women's gymnastics, and cross-country or distance running (Rosen, 1986) — See Chapter 2.

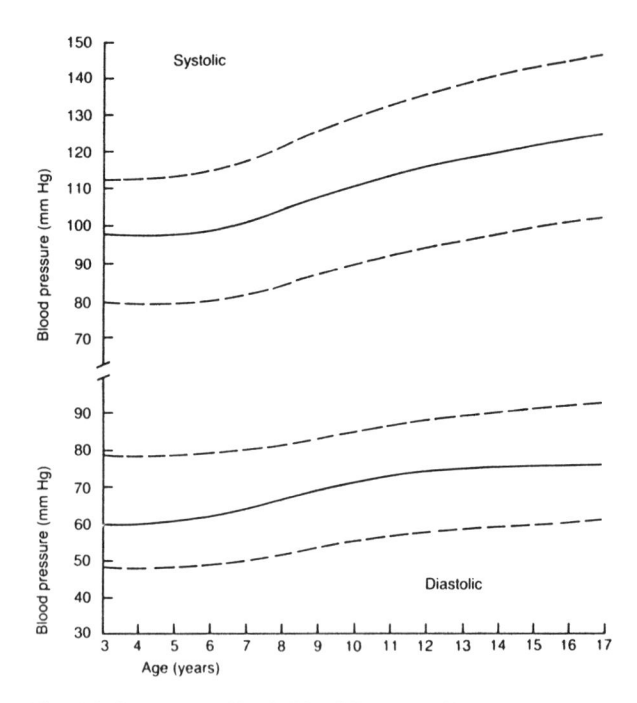

**Fig. 4-2.** Continuous Youth Blood Pressure Chart

   b. *Exogenous Hormone Consumption* — Ingestion/injection of ergogenic aids for increased strength and power or suppression of puberty is unfortunately not an uncommon occurrence — See Chapter 2.
   c. *Obesity* — An athlete greater than 20% overweight for height, age, and stature has a relative cardiac and health risk. Referral for dietary counseling is advised.
   d. *Late Maturation* — Occurring naturally or secondary to poor nutrition, delayed maturation can affect both height and weight measurements in the potential athlete. It should not be a major cause of concern unless the delay is long enough that another diagnosis (beyond that of constitutional delay of puberty) should be considered. It also should be remembered that strenuous exercise prior to puberty can delay the process.
3. *Visual Acuity* — The Snellen eye chart can be used to test correctable vision to better than 20/200. Such emphasis is necessary for detection of legal blindness, a major basis for disqualification, and impaired vision, a major factor in poor performance.
4. *Cardiovascular Examination* — Major emphasis in this area is necessary in any athletic screening examination. When the musculoskeletal system provides motion, making exer-

cise possible, the cardiovascular system responds. Sudden death in healthy athletes is uncommon, but it does occur and the primary mechanism usually involves the cardiovascular system. The catastrophe is almost always totally unexpected, all the more tragic and alarming. Most young athletes suffering sudden death have underlying cardiovascular disease (Maron, 1986). The potential efficacy of screening studies to uncover this cardiovascular physiology is also summarized (see Table 4-6). The following important points should be remembered:

a. *Murmurs*
1. A normal "functional" heart murmur may be audible in every child sometime during development.
2. Murmur intensity does not correlate with the significance of the problem.
3. The differential diagnosis of normal murmurs in young athletes, as outlined by Strong and Steed (1984), should be familiar to the examiner (see Table 4-7).

Guidelines when listening to heart murmurs in perspective athletes are helpful:
a. If the first sound can be heard easily the murmur is not holosystolic — therefore VSD and mitral insufficiency can be ruled out.
b. If $S_2$ is normal — Tetralogy of Fallot, ASD, and pulmonary hypertension are ruled out.
c. If there is no ejection click — aortic and pulmonary stenosis can be excluded.
d. If a continuous diastolic murmur is

Table 4-6. Major Causes of Sudden Death in Athletes and Potential Efficacy of Screening Studies

| CAUSES | SCREENING PROCEDURES | SENSITIVITY | PREDICTIVE VALUE |
| --- | --- | --- | --- |
| Hypertrophic cardiomyopathy | History* | Poor | Poor |
|  | Chest x-ray film | Fair | Poor |
|  | Auscultation | Fair | Excellent |
|  | Echocardiogram | Excellent | Excellent‖ |
|  | 12-lead EKG | Good† | Poor |
| Cystic medial necrosis (Marfan's) | History | Poor | Poor |
|  | Chest x-ray film | Fair | Excellent |
|  | Auscultation | Poor | Fair |
|  | Echocardiogram | Excellent | Excellent |
|  | 12-lead EKG | — | — |
| Congenital coronary abnormalities | History | Poor | Poor |
|  | Chest x-ray film | Poor | Fair¶ |
|  | Auscultation | — | — |
|  | 12-lead EKG | Fair-good | Poor |
|  | Exercise EKG | Excellent | Poor‡ |
|  | Radionuclide studies |  | Poor‡ |
| Aortic valve stenosis | History | — | — |
|  | Chest x-ray film | Poor | Poor |
|  | Auscultation | Excellent | Good§ |
|  | 12-lead EKG | Fair | Poor |
|  | Echocardiogram | Poor | Poor |

*Specifically, a history of syncope or sudden premature death in a close family member.
†Both in making the diagnosis of hypertrophic cardiomyopathy and in identifying patients at risk of sudden death.
‡Of increasing value in subjects older than 40 years of age when the prevalence of coronary artery disease increases; however, most abnormal responses will still be falsely positive.
§The predictive value of auscultation depends on intensity of murmur; the high prevalence of softer innocent murmurs will necessitate a more sophisticated and expensive evaluation in many individuals.
‖Predictive value is critically dependent on the magnitude of ventricular septal thickness (septal thickness > 20 mm would be highly indicative of hypertrophic cardiomyopathy; septal thickness of 13 to 14 mm, as an isolated clinical finding, would provide only suggestive evidence of disease).
¶Only if coronary calcifications are detected by fluoroscopy; poor if fluoroscopy is not carried out. The rating system is based on the following sequence; excellent > good > fair > poor.
(*Adapted from* Maron BJ, Epstein SE, Roberts WC: Causes of sudden death in competitive athletes. *J Am Coll Cardiol* 7:204-214, 1986; with permission.)

#### Table 4-7. Murmurs in Young Athletes

Normal

Aortic stenosis (congenital or hypertrophic obstructive cardiomyopathy)

Pulmonary stenosis

Coarctation of the aorta

Atrial septal defect

Ventricular septal defect

Patent ductus arteriosus

Mitral insufficiency (rheumatic or prolapse)

Aortic insufficiency

---

absent — patent ductus arteriosus is not present.
e. If no early diastolic decrescendo murmur exists — aortic insufficiency can be ruled out.
f. If normal femoral pulses exist — coarctation of the aorta is not present.

A cardiologist should be consulted by an athlete with a significant murmur, and certification should be postponed until that murmur has been evaluated sufficiently. Generally speaking, mild defects do not prevent participation in normal competition or activity. Athlete with moderate defects that produce signs or symptomatology such as cardiomegaly, shortness or breath, or abnormal electrocardiograms should be screened with a graded exercise test. For the most part, these individuals need be eliminated only from strenuous competitive athletics. Finally, severe defects causing significant symptomatology should render an individual ineligible for any competitive athletics. A summary of common innocent murmurs found in adolescents can be found in Table 4-8.

b. *Arrhythmias* — Isolated premature ventricular contractions (PVCs) represent the single most common arrhythmia encountered in the PPPE. Occurring in youngsters, they are rarely of consequence, but numerous factors come into play with the older individual. Caffeine, tobacco, and alcohol ingestion, as well as bronchodilator therapy, can result in PVCs. Three major characteristics make most arrhythmias benign: 1) unifocal in origin; 2) disappearance with exercise; 3) no history of syncope with exercise. Coupling of PVCs or bigeminy may indicate myocarditis and should temporary disqualify an athlete. A finding of paroxysmal superventricular tachycardia should initiate a search for the cause but, once controlled with medication, should

#### Table 4-8. Common Innocent Murmurs in Children

| Type | Characteristic | Etiology | Differential Diagnosis | Notes |
|---|---|---|---|---|
| Pulmonary Flow Murmur | Grade 1/6 to 3/6 ejection murmur; left upper sternal border | Flow across *normal* pulmonic valve | A.S.D. (Valvular P.S.) | Most common innocent murmur |
| Still's Murmur | Grade 1/6 to 3/6 vibratory systolic murmur; halfway between lower left sternal border and Apex | Vibrations under aortic valve | Small V.S.D. Subvalvar A.S. Mitral regurgitation | Very characteristic sound, sometimes musical |
| Venous Hum | Grade 1/6 to 3/6 continuous murmur through the 2nd sound; one or both upper sternal borders | Turbulent flow at confluence of veins; disappears when neck is turned or patient supine | P.D.A. | Maneuvers mentioned make diagnosis easy |
| Carotid Bruit | Grade 1/6 to 3/6 ejection murmur; in the neck | Turbulence in carotid blood flow; murmur fainter as approach upper sternal borders | Valvular stenosis | |

not be a reason for disqualification. Controlled Wolfe-Parkinson-White syndrome should not be reason for disqualification. It is important to remember that bradycardia and some irregular rhythms are more common among conditioned athletes than among the general population (Salem, 1980). Other observed athletic irregularities include first or second degree heart block, Wenckebach phenomena, and junctional rhythms.

5. *Skin* — Contagious cutaneous infections (herpes, impetigo, or louse infestation) should be screened. Such conditions are promoted by skin-to-skin contact in sports such as wrestling. Participation should be allowed only after the problem is controlled.

6. *Abdomen* — Any significant organomegaly needs further investigation, with participation qualification delayed.

7. *Genito-urinary* — A maturational index should be determined for all developing prepubertal and pubertal athletes. Guidelines for such secondary characteristic staging are reliable, proven, and practical to use (see Figure 4-3). Recent prospective studies (McKeag, 1991) indicate that inappropriate maturational matching of athletes is a major injury-risk factor in youth contact sports. In addition, late maturers can be detected by staging. Male examination should include a testicular exam (to detect absent or undescended testicle in youngsters; in older individuals to detect scrotal masses, sexually transmitted diseases, or hernias). A history of menstrual abnormality, early sexual activity, or lack of recent PAP smear in a female athlete usually indicates a need for further historical information and possibly a pelvic exam.

8. *Musculoskeletal* — Full attention should be given to the range-of-motion of major joints and the relative strength of opposing muscle groups,

**BOYS**

| STAGE | PUBIC HAIR | PENIS | TESTIS |
|---|---|---|---|
| 1 | None | Preadolescent | |
| 2 | Slight, long, slight pigmentation | Slight enlargement | Enlarged scrotum, pink slight ruga |
| 3 | Darker, starts to curl small amount | Longer | Larger |
| 4 | Coarse, curly, adult type but less quantity | Increase in glans size and breadth of penis | Larger, scrotum darker |
| 5 | Adult - spread to inner thighs | Adult | Adult |

**GIRLS**

| STAGE | PUBIC HAIR | BREASTS |
|---|---|---|
| 1 | Preadolescent (none) | Preadolescent (no germinal button) |
| 2 | Sparse, lightly pigmented, straight medial border of labia | Breast and papilla elevated as small mound; areolar diameter increased |
| 3 | Darker, beginning to curl increased | Breast and areola enlarged; no contour separation |
| 4 | Coarse, curly, abundant, but less than adult | Areola and papilla form secondary mound |
| 5 | Adult female triangle and spread to medial surface | Mature, nipple projects, areola part of general breast contour |

**Fig. 4-3.** Tanner Staging

comparing gross strength bilaterally. Table 4-9 summarizes one recommended approach to the musculoskeletal exam, (Lombardo, 1984), as well as a shortened version. Always examine the site of any old injury to determine the presence of any residual effects.

**Laboratory.** A dip stick urinalysis for protein and glucose usually has been advocated for the young sports candidate. Several authors (Lombardo, 1984; Goldberg, 1980) have questioned the advisability of routine urine screenings as part of athletic screening exams. Proteinuria in childhood is a benign event in all but .08 percent of cases (Peggs, 1986). Our feeling is that the prevalence of benign proteinuria in adolescents makes the cost benefit ratio of this test inappropriate. In the absence of a positive history, hemoglobin analysis is also unlikely to reveal any significant anemia that is likely to have an adverse impact on health or performance. Any additional laboratory testing in this age group should be based upon special circumstances. For the older recreational athlete, consult the flow chart by Taylor (1983) (see Figure 4-1B).

**Additional Screening Procedures.** Any additional tests need to have adequate sensitivity, specificity, and predictive value to justify inclusion in a routine PPPE. Though not complete, a list of additional screening procedures follows. Any of these *may* be deemed necessary given the sport, age group or level of competition:

1. *Audiometry/Tympanometry* — The natural extension of a positive finding on ear examination.
2. *Body Composition Testing* — Information on percent body fat and ideal body weight can be helpful and important in weight control sports such as wrestling. The most accurate means of such measurement is underwater immersion; however skin fold measurements with calipers, using numerous regression equations to determine percent body fat, is a cheaper, if less accurate, method (see Chapter 2).
3. *Endurance and Flexibility Testing* — Although poor predictors of future injury, these tests can be included, especially in the older adult and elderly athlete. Any unilateral laxity needs to be considered in light of the paired extremity, the age of the athlete, and the activity. This testing can be extremely useful in establishing a baseline for future monitoring of the effects of exercise, especially in the old athlete. Endurance testing using a run/walk for 12-15 min-

Table 4-9. Musculoskeletal Physical Examination

| Athletic Activity (instructions) | Observations |
| --- | --- |
| 1. Stand facing examiner | AC joints, general habitus |
| 2. Look: at ceiling, floor, over both shoulders, touch ears to shoulders | Cervical spine motion |
| 3. Shrug shoulders (examiner resists) | Trapezius strength |
| 4. Abduct shoulders 90°(examiner resists at 90° | Deltoid strength |
| 5. Full external rotation or arms | Shoulder motion |
| 6. Flex and extend elbows | Elbow motion |
| 7. Arms at sides, elbows at 90° flexed; pronate and supinate wrists | Elbow and wrist motion |
| 8. Spread fingers; make fist | Hand/finger motion and deformities |
| 9. Tighten (contract) quadriceps; relax quadriceps | Symmetry and knee effusion, ankle effusion |
| 10. "Duck walk" 4 steps (away from examiner) | Hip, knee and ankle motion |
| 11. Back to examiner | Shoulder symmetry; scoliosis |
| 12. Knees straight, touch toes | Scoliosis, hip motion, hamstring tightness |
| 13. Raise up on toes, heels | Calf symmetry, leg strength |

OR
(shortened version)

1. *Nod* your head *yes*.......................*shake* your head *no*.
2. Hands behind your head..................hand behind your back.
3. Slowly bend forward and touch your toes.
4. Stand up straight...jump on your left foot, now on your right foot.
5. Squat like a baseball player.
6. Walk toward me like a duck.

utes can uncover such conditions as exercise-induced asthma or bronchospasm. If suggested by the history or physical exam, such testing can be done under more controlled circumstances with the exercise challenge in the form of graded exercise testing. This can be of immeasurable benefit to the individual especially the post-cardiac athlete.

4. *Hemoglobin/hematocrit* — This becomes important when the nutrition of a candidate is suspect.
5. *Lipoprotein Studies* (Fasting HDL, cholesterol, triglyceride levels) — These studies are especially important for older athletes to detect possible hyperlipoproteinemias. These also should be done as an extension and further delineation of the cardiac risk index if the family history or other risk factors are positive.
6. *Drug Testing* — Most colleges and Olympic levels of sport participation conduct random or reasonable suspicion drug testing, usually on an institutional basis. Such screening may encompass both erogenic and recreational drugs. If a screening is done, counseling and rehabilitation programs are a necessary follow-up for any positive test.
7. *Electrocardiogram* — Routine EKG testing in athletes is unwarranted because of the low prevalence of cardiac disease in young age groups and the relative lack of specificity of the test. It is, however, appropriate as a natural extension if any cardiac abnormality is detected.
8. *Marfan Syndrome* — Screening may be done where it seems appropriate in unusually tall men and women. A suggested screening format for this syndrome is given (see Table 4-10).

## ASSESSMENT

Assessment represents a clinical impression and conclusion, and is made after review of the medical history, the physical examination, and any necessary laboratory testing. The decision to be given concerns the athlete's type and level of sports involvement, not just a blanket approval to participate in any activity. Hirsch (1981) proposes a workable yet specific classification of sports injuries (Table 4-11).

The options available to the physician at the end of the preparticipation physical examination are as follows:

---

**Table 4-10. Suggested Screening Format for Marfan's Syndrome**

Screen all men over 6 feet and all women over 5 feet 10 inches in height with electrocardiogram and slit lamp examination when any two of the following are found:

1. Family history of Marfan's syndrome*
2. Cardiac murmur or midsystolic click
3. Kyphoscoliosis
4. Anterior thoracic deformity
5. Arm span greater than height
6. Upper to lower body ratio more than one standard deviation below the mean
7. Myopia
8. Ectopic lens

*This finding *alone* should prompt further investigation.

---

**Table 4-11. Classification of Sports**

STRENUOUS — CONTACT
  Football
  Ice hockey
  Lacrosse (boys)
  Rugby
  Wrestling

STRENUOUS — LIMITED CONTACT
  Basketball
  Field Hockey
  Lacrosse (girls)
  Soccer
  Volleyball

STRENUOUS — NONCONTACT
  Crew
  Cross-country
  Fencing
  Gymnastics
  Skiing
  Swimming
  Tennis
  Track and Field
  Water polo

MODERATELY STRENUOUS
  Badminton
  Baseball (limited contact)
  Curling
  Golf
  Table Tennis

NONSTRENUOUS
  Archer
  Bowling
  Riflery

- *Clearance without limitation* for sport and level desired.
- *Clearance deferred* pending consultation, special treatments, special equipment fitting, or rehabilitation. This option implies that clearance must be obtained after the remedial steps have been taken.
- *Clearance with limitation* includes medical recommendations for a sport or position.
- *Disqualification* — This option implies that the athlete has a condition that contraindicates his/her participation in any sport.

Decisions that involve options 3 and 4 should involve not only the physician, but the athlete, parents, and coach(es), as well as a representative of the organization or school system.

Any tables such as that reproduced as Table 4-12 should be considered only as guidelines for disqualifying conditions. All disqualifications or limitations in participation should be dealt with on an individual basis. Conditions that constitute absolute or relative contraindications for specific sports activity fall into six major categories: 1) neurologic; 2) defects in paired organ systems; 3) organ enlargement; 4) active infection; 5) vertebral/pelvic defect, and 6) cardiopulmonary disorders. Once again, it is imperative to always weigh each case on its merits. Dogma has no place in the total disqualification of a potential athlete regardless of age. Any athlete who comes to a physician for a PPPE should leave with an appropriate idea of what he/she can or cannot do.

Five (5) copies should be made of the prepar-

**Table 4-12. Disqualifying Conditions**

| | Absolute Contraindications | | Relative Contraindications | |
|---|---|---|---|---|
| | Contact | Noncontact | Contact | Noncontact |
| Seizure within past year | X | X[1] | | X |
| Concussions with consciousness loss | X | | | |
| Large post-surgical cranial defect | X | | | X |
| Solitary functioning eye | X | | | |
| Retinal detachment history | X | X | | |
| Congenital glaucoma | X | X | | |
| Pulmonary infection, including tuberculosis | X | X | | |
| Pyelonephritis | X | X | | |
| Bone infection | X | X | | |
| Systemic infection | X | X | | |
| Cardiomegaly | X | | | X |
| Aortic or mitral stenosis | X | | | X |
| Cyanotic heart disease | X | | | X |
| Active myocarditis/pericarditis | X | | | X |
| Major visceromegaly (liver, kidneys, spleen) | X | | | X |
| Solitary functional kidney | X | | | X |
| Testis overlying pubic ramus | X | | | |
| Unhealed fracture | X | | | X |
| Spondyolisthesis with back pain | X | X | | |
| Painful hip disease | X | X | | |
| Spinal epiphysitis | X | X | | |
| Blood coagulation defect | X | | | X |
| Uncontrolled asthma | | | X | X |
| Skin infection, including herpes | X[a] | | X | X |
| Active otitis media | | X[2] | | |
| Uncontrolled diabetes mellitus | | | X | X |
| Recurrent shoulder subluxation | | | X | X |
| Uncontrolled hypertension | | | X | X |

1 = diving, swimming, high bar and rings
2 = swimming and diving
a = herpes simplex in wrestlers
(Adapted from Hara, 1988)

ticipation sports physical and distributed to the school nurse, parents, primary care physician, team physician (if different), and a copy to be carried with the team to all practices and competitions so it is available in event of injury or illness. The last copy set should be kept by a responsible individual under confidential conditions for the duration of the season.

## INJURY PREDICTION

For years, investigators have been attempting to identify conditions and factors that might predict injury in athletes. Most of the following have some proven value for this purpose. They are given here so the reader may further evaluate the literature as to the importance of each factor.

1. *Maturity Staging* — Unbalanced competition between late and early maturing adolescents in contact sports such as football is a major factor in some serious injuries. This predictor is useful only with junior high school and early high school age athletes. Maturational staging is directly related to strength, power, and flexibility (Wilmore, 1979), but, by itself, is not a strong enough predictor of injury to qualify or disqualify any individual from competition. However, it is strong enough to base a recommendation for a delay in some types of sports participation.
2. *Flexibility* — The lack of body flexibility or (conversely) ligamentous laxity seen in many young athletes has been advocated as a predictor of future injury (Nicholas, 1977; Nicholas, 1980). Neither of these conditions has proven to be an effective predictor and may simply represent a state of normalcy in the developing athlete (Godshall, 1975; Grana, 1978).
3. *Family Functioning* — An inadequate or poorly functioning family unit or acute crisis situations in the family do result in increased rate of injury (Coddington, 1980).
4. *Cardiovascular Fitness* — The unconditioned athlete is seen more often at the beginning of a season. A common assumption is that an individual should be conditioned for his or her sport prior to training; however, this is not the case most of the time. Cardiovascular unfitness leads to fatigue, which in turn leads to increased injury.
5. *Lean Body Mass* — There is a misconception that the leaner the body, the better the performance. This has lead to unrealistic weight loss goals set by coaches in various sports. While obesity does slow down reaction time and decrease cardiovascular efficiency, extreme weight loss also results in major fatigue, loss of strength, and eventual injury (Rosen, 1986; Rarick, 1974).
6. *Muscular Strength* — The detection of unilateral weakness in a muscle or a muscle group is a powerful indicator of future injury (Nicholas, 1977; Garrick, 1977; Cahill, 1978). All paired muscles should be tested, comparing sides as well as agonist-antagonist muscle groups. If questionable results are seen in the clinical screening exam, isokinetic testing should be done.

## CONCLUSION

The PPPE for sports candidates of all ages represents one of several places where the office based physician can prevent injury. Although such an examination is not cost effective, it can be justified if it is molded to the characteristics of the athlete and made as specific as possible. The PPPE should be a medical "chameleon," taking different forms as the need arises. Future PPPEs should have a higher level of sophistication that will include predictive factors in sport specific examinations so as to lessen the number of injuries as well as assess general health.

**REFERENCES**

Allman, F.L., McKeag, D.B., Bodner, L.M. Prevention and emergency care of sports injuries. *Fam Pract Recert* 5:4, April, 1983.
American Medical Association. *Medical Evaluation of the Athlete: A Guide.* Pamphlet #OP 209 Sports, Chicago, Ill. 1979.
Delman, A., Waugh, T. School screening for scoliosis. *J Fam Med*, pp. 6-12, August, 1983.
Goldberg, B., Boiardo, R. Profiling children for sports participation. *Clinics in Sports Med* 3:1, pp. 153-169, Jan., 1984.
Hara, J.H., Puffer, J.C. The preparticipation physical examination. In Mellion MB, ed., *Office Management of Sports Injuries and Athletic Problems.* Philadelphia, Harley and Belfus, Chap. 1, 1988.
Henschen, K., Griffin, L. quoted in "Parent egos take the fun out of Little League." *Psych Today*, p. 18-22, Sept., 1977.
Lombardo, J., Smith, D. Personal Communications, 1992.
Martens, R. The uniqueness of the young athlete: psychologic considerations. *Am J SportsMed* 8(5):382, 385, 1980.
McKeag, D.B. Preparticipation screening of the potential athlete. *Clinics in Sports Med* 8(3):373-397, 1989.
Micheli, L.J., Stone K.R. The pre-sports physical: only the first step. *J of Musculoskeletal Med*, pp. 56-60, May, 1984.
Shaffer, T.E. The adolescent athlete. *Ped Clinic of NA* 28:4, Nov., 1983.
Shaffer, T.E. The health examination for participation in sports. *Ped Annuals* 7:10, pp. 27-40, October, 1978.
Tanner, J.M. *Growth at Adolescence* 2nd ed. Blackwell, Oxford, England, pp. 28-39, 1962.
Taylor, R.B. Pre-exercise evaluation: which procedures are really needed? *Consultant*, pp. 94-101, April, 1983.

Appendix 4-1.
## Task Force PPPE Form
# History Form

Name _____ Date of Birth _____ Sex _____
Grade _____ Sports _____ _____ _____
Personal Physician _____ Physician's phone number _____

|  | YES | NO |
|---|---|---|
| *Fill in details of "YES" answers in space below: | | |
| 1. Have you ever been hospitalized? | ___ | ___ |
| Have you ever had surgery? | ___ | ___ |
| 2. Are you presently taking any medication or pills? | ___ | ___ |
| 3. Do you have any allergies (medicine, bees, other stinging insects)? | ___ | ___ |
| 4. Have you ever passed out during or after exercise? | ___ | ___ |
| Have you ever been dizzy during or after exercise? | ___ | ___ |
| Have you ever had chest pain during or after exercise? | ___ | ___ |
| Do you tire more quickly than your friends during exercise? | ___ | ___ |
| Have you ever had high blood pressure? | ___ | ___ |
| Have you ever been told you have a heart murmur? | ___ | ___ |
| Have you ever had racing of your heart or skipped beats? | ___ | ___ |
| Has anyone in your family died of heart problems or a sudden death before age 50? | ___ | ___ |
| 5. Do you have any skin problems? (itching, rash, acne) | ___ | ___ |
| 6. Have you ever had a head injury? | ___ | ___ |
| Have you ever been knocked out or unconscious? | ___ | ___ |
| Have you ever had a seizure? | ___ | ___ |
| Have you ever had a stinger, burner, or pinched nerve? | ___ | ___ |
| 7. Have you ever had heat cramps? | ___ | ___ |
| Have you ever been dizzy or passed out in the heat? | ___ | ___ |
| 8. Do you have trouble breathing or cough during or after exercise? | ___ | ___ |
| 9. Do you use special equipment, pads, braces, mouth or eyeguards? | ___ | ___ |
| 10. Have you had problems with your eyes or vision? | ___ | ___ |
| Do you wear glasses, contacts or protective eyewear? | ___ | ___ |

11. Have you ever sprained/strained, dislocated, fractured/broken, or had repeated swelling or other injuries of any of your bones or joints?
    ___ Head    ___ Neck    ___ Chest    ___ Back    ___ Hip
    ___ Shoulder ___ Elbow   ___ Forearm  ___ Wrist   ___ Hand
    ___ Thigh   ___ Knee    ___ Shin/Calf ___ Ankle   ___ Foot
12. Have you ever had any other medical problems such as:
    ___ Mononucleosis  ___ Diabetes           ___ Asthma
    ___ Hepatitis      ___ Headaches (frequent) ___ Tuberculosis
    ___ Eye injuries   ___ Stomach ulcer      ___ Other

13. Have you had a medical problem or injury since last exam? _____
14. When was your last tetanus shot? _____
    When was your last measles immunization? _____
15. When was your first menstrual period? _____
    When was your last menstrual period? _____
    What was the longest time between periods last year? _____

Explain "YES" answers here:
_____
_____
_____

*PREVENTIVE SPORTS MEDICINE*

# Physical Examination Form

```
C  L   Height _____  Weight _____  BP ___/___  Pulse _____
O  I   Visual acuity  R____/20   L____/20   Corrected Y N   Pupils _____
M  M
P  I                          Normal            Abnormal
L  T   Cardiopulmonary
E  E       Pulses             _____           _____
T  D       Heart              _____           _____
E          Lungs              _____           _____
       Tanner                 I   II   III      IV   V
       Skin                   _____           _____
       Abdominal              _____           _____
       Genitalia              _____           _____
       Musculoskeletal
           Neck               _____           _____
           Shoulder           _____           _____
           Elbow              _____           _____
           Wrist              _____           _____
           Hand               _____           _____
           Back               _____           _____
           Knee               _____           _____
           Ankle              _____           _____
           Foot               _____           _____
```

## Clearance/Recommendations

Clearance:
- A. Cleared
- B. Cleared after completing evaluation/rehabilitation for: _____

- C. *NOT* cleared for:  _____ Collision
  - _____ Contact
  - _____ Non-contact
    - _____ Strenuous
    - _____ Moderately strenuous
    - _____ Non-strenuous

Due to: _____

Recommendation: _____

Examined by:

Physician Name: _____  Date: _____
Address: _____  Phone: (___) ___

## Appendix 4-2.
## Initial PPPE Form

To be completed by athlete or parent:

NAME _____ SPORT/Position _____
        Last    First    Middle
SCHOOL YEAR _____
ADDRESS _____
_____
CITY/STATE _____ PHONE # _____
BIRTHDATE _____ AGE _____ CLASS _____ STUDENT ID # _____
PARENT'S NAME _____
ADDRESS _____
_____
PHONE # _____
Person to contact in case of emergency _____
PHONE # _____
Family Doctor _____ CITY/STATE _____
PHONE # _____

**PAST MEDICAL HISTORY:**  YES  NO  If yes, please explain (what, where, when)

1. Presently taking medication (including birth control/pills) ___ ___
2. Allergic to medicine, foods, bee-stings? ___ ___
3. Wears any appliances - glasses, contact lenses? ___ ___
4. History of braces, chipped teeth, bridges? ___ ___
5. Has ongoing medical problem. ___ ___
6. Had serious or significant illness in past ___ ___
7. Any past surgical operations, accidents, non-sports or related injuries? ___ ___
8. Any past injuries directly related to sports? ___ ___
9. Any hospitalization not explained above? ___ ___
10. Any known deformities (such as curvature of back, heart problems, one kidney, blindness in one eye, one testicle, etc.)? ___ ___
11. Any serious family illness (such as diabetes, bleeding disorders, heart attack before age 50, etc.)? ___ ___
12. Any fainting or dizziness while exercising? ___ ___
13. Any loss of consciousness, concussion, or head injury? ___ ___

**DATE**

14. a. Last tetanus shot _____
    b. Last dental exam _____
    c. Last eye exam _____
    d. Last menstrual period (if female) _____

**PERSONAL HABITS:** Please indicate use of any of the following:
1. Smoking                                     _____
2. Smokeless tobacco                           _____
3. Alcohol                                     _____
4. Recreational drugs:
   marijuana, cocaine, etc.                    _____
5. Steroids                                    _____

**REVIEW OF SYSTEMS:** Please check if you have any problems with any of the following areas of your body:

| | | |
|---|---|---|
| \_\_\_\_\_Skin | \_\_\_\_\_Neck | \_\_\_\_\_Genital (including menstrual for females) |
| \_\_\_\_\_Head | \_\_\_\_\_Lungs | |
| \_\_\_\_\_Eyes | \_\_\_\_\_Heart | \_\_\_\_\_Shoulders, arms, hands |
| \_\_\_\_\_Ears | \_\_\_\_\_Abdomen | \_\_\_\_\_Hips, legs, feet |
| \_\_\_\_\_Nose | \_\_\_\_\_Back | \_\_\_\_\_Muscles-strength, feeling |
| \_\_\_\_\_Mouth/throat | \_\_\_\_\_Urination, bowel control | \_\_\_\_\_Mental, emotional |
| \_\_\_\_\_Nutrition, weight control | | \_\_\_\_\_Fatigue |
| | | \_\_\_\_\_Other: what? |

I certify that the above information is correct to the best of my knowledge.

Student/parent Signature _____

**PHYSICAL EXAMINATION:**

Height _____  Weight _____  Blood Pressure: _____
Pulse:   resting _____
Visual Acuity:   Eyes (R) 20/_____ w/o glasses   (L) 20/_____ w/glasses _____

**Other Testing:**

|  | NORMAL | ABNORMAL FINDINGS |
|---|---|---|
| 1. General | _____ | |
| 2. Skin | _____ | |
| 3. HEENT | _____ | |
| 4. Teeth (Dental exam) | _____ | |
| 5. Neck | _____ | |
| 6. Lungs | _____ | |
| 7. Heart | _____ | |
| 8. Breasts | _____ | |
| 9. Abdomen | _____ | |
| 10. Genitalia (hernia) | _____ | |
| Tanner Stage _____ | | |
| 11. Back | _____ | |
| 12. Musculoskeletal | _____ | |
| 13. Peripheral pulses | _____ | |
| 14. Neurological | _____ | |
| 15. Mental status | _____ | |

**OTHER TESTS:**

   Auditory _____         U/A _____         EKG _____
   % Body fat _____     Drug Screen _____     Chest x-ray _____
   HgH/Hcb _____         SMAC _____        Marfan's Screen _____

**ASSESSMENT:**
1. Clearance without limitation  _____
                          Sports _____
2. Clearance deferred            _____
                          Reason _____
3. Clearance with limitation     _____
                      Limitation _____
4. Disqualification              _____
                          Reason _____

Exam Date _____  Physician's Signature _____

# Appendix 4-3.
## Intercurrent PPPE Form

**Master Problem List**                                **Date Identified**          **Date Resolved**

1.

2.

3.

4.

Date of Entrance Physical Examination: _____

**Past Medical History:** Since your initial preparticipation physical examination have you had any of the following? (If yes, please explain what, where and when)

|  | Yes | No | Explanation |
|---|---|---|---|
| 1. Presently taking medication (including birth control pills)? | | | |
| 2. Allergic to medicine, foot, bee-sting? | | | |
| 3. Wearing any new appliances—glasses, contact lenses, dentures or hearing aids? | | | |
| 4. History of braces, chipped teeth, bridges? | | | |
| 5. New medical problem requiring treatment or medication? | | | |
| 6. Surgical operations or accidents requiring medical help? | | | |
| 7. Injuries directly related to sports participation? (If so, explain nature of injury) | | | |
| 8. Recent fainting or dizziness while exercising? | | | |
| 9. Recent head injury or loss of consciousness? | | | |
| 10. (For women) Date of last menstrual period? | | | |

**REVIEW OF SYSTEMS:** Please check if you have developed any new problem to the following areas of your body since your last physical exam.

_____ Skin                _____ Neck               _____ Genital (including menstrual for females)
_____ Head                _____ Lungs              _____ Knees
_____ Eyes                _____ Heart              _____ Shoulders, arms, hands

_____ Mouth/throat          _____ Abdomen              _____ Hips, legs, feet
_____ Nutrition, weight control   _____ Urination, bowel   _____ Muscle strength, feeling
                             _____ Blood                _____ Mental, emotional

I would like to meet with the team physician _____
I certify that the above information is correct to the best of my knowledge.

      Student/parent Signature _____

## VITAL SIGNS:

Height _____     Weight _____
Vision Screening (optional)   (R) 20/ _____   (L) 20/ _____ w/o Glasses
                              (R) 20/ _____   (L) 20/ _____ with Glasses

Blood Pressure _____
Pulse _____
Other testing:

## REVIEW BY MEDICAL STAFF:

Approved for participation _____   Other disposition _____
Must see physician _____
Team physician Signature _____ Date _____

# 5

# Conditioning and Training Programs for Athletes/Non-Athletes

## SECTION A.
## GENERAL PRINCIPLES

The information outlined in this chapter comes from scientific application of theories and principles of exercise physiology, using both animal and human studies. The organization begins with the adult male competitor, the type of participant used most often in studies of training and conditioning.

### Metabolic Specificity

To maximize its beneficial effect, any training program must develop the specific physiologic capabilities required to perform a given sport or activity (see Chapter 2). This concept is absolutely necessary to keep in mind when advising an athlete concerning his/her conditioning or training program. From the conditioning standpoint, the most important physiologic capability to be enhanced is the ability to supply energy [adenosine triphosphate (ATP) and the substrate phosphocreatine (PC)] to working muscles. ATP can be supplied in any of three ways to the muscles.

1. Phosphagen stores → skeletal muscle (ATP-PC)
2. Anaerobic glycolysis → lactic acid (LA)
3. Aerobic → oxygen via oxidative phosphorylation ($O_2$)

As illustrated in Table 5A-1, the capacity and the rate at which energy (ATP) can be supplied by these three systems in the body differ. The *rate* of supply can be referred to as "power." The predominant energy source will be a function of the total amount and rate of energy demanded by that exercise (see Table 5A-2). When a training/conditioning program is constructed, such a regimen logically should specifically increase the capacity of the energy system used most often in that particular sport. For instance, a sprinter needs a program to enhance the anaerobic generation of energy; a runner never wants to exceed the capacity of his aerobic energy supply.

Table 5A-1. Capacity and Power of Three Energy Systems in Untrained Male Subjects

| Energy system | ATP production Capacity (total moles) | Power (moles/minute) |
|---|---|---|
| ATP-PC | 0.6 | 3.6 |
| LA | 1.2 | 1.6 |
| $O_2$ | | 1.0 |

(ATP — adenosine triphosphate; PC — phosphocreatine; LA — lactic acid; $O_2$ — oxygen)
(Fox, E.L. Physical Training: methods and effects. *Orthopedic Clinics of North America* 8:533-548, 1977.)

Table 5A-2. Performance Time and Energy Systems

| Performance Time | Predominant Energy System(s) |
|---|---|
| 30 sec | ATP-PC |
| 30 sec-1 1/2 min | ATP-PC and LA |
| 1 1/2-3 min | LA and $O_2$ |
| 3 min | $O_2$ |

(ATP — adenosine triphosphate; PC — phosphocreatine; LA — lactic acid; $O_2$ — oxygen)

Many activities require efficient working of all three systems. Refer to Figure 5A-1 for the contributions of each energy system to various sports and activities. Other factors to consider to achieve maximal benefits from a training program include:

- The mode of exercise used during training should be the mode used in the performance of the sports skill. For example — unless he is injured, an athlete should not train for running by swimming. Training effects induced by running, although still specific, are more general than those of other activities such as cycling. There do appear to be beneficial cross-over effects for other sports from conditioning based upon running.

- Training effects tend to be specific to muscle groups. The major objective of physical training is to cause specific and efficient biological adaptation to improve performance in specific events.

Four major principles should be applied to any training/conditioning program:

- *Specificity* — Specific training elicits specific adaptations, enhancing specific actions.
- *Overload* — Overload refers to exercising at above normal levels, and is achieved by manipulating combinations of training frequency, intensity, duration, and type of activity.
- *Individual Differences* — People respond and perform differently to similar stimuli. Individual variations should be taken into account in the construction of any training program. A specific training program that works for one athlete will not for another.
- *Reversibility* — This refers to the principle of de-training. Unfortunately, the beneficial conditioning effects of exercise training are transient and reversible so that conditioning should be continuous in nature. A swift and significant de-training effect may be seen when a person stops exercising. After only two weeks of inactivity, significant reductions in work capacity can be measured. There apparently is about a 1% decrease in physiologic functioning for each day of inactivity in trained subjects.

Necessary steps in the construction of a training program should include the following:

- Consider the predominant energy system used (Table 5A-2 and Figure 5A-1).
- Select an appropriate training regimen (Table 5A-3). While Fox (1977) has used running as his example for both Tables 5A-2 and 5A-3, any mode of exercise could be used (with corresponding distance and time changes; that is, 440 yds of swimming (approximates) = 1 mile of running (approximates) = 2.25 miles of cycling.
- Any training prescription and its content should include movement patterns specific to the sport and/or position to enhance motor unit recruitment patterns. Repetitive motor skill work will augment neuromuscular skills and enhance subsequent performance.
- To prevent boredom, introduce variability into the training program. Overuse injury is a significant result of lack of training variability.

### Aerobic — Anaerobic

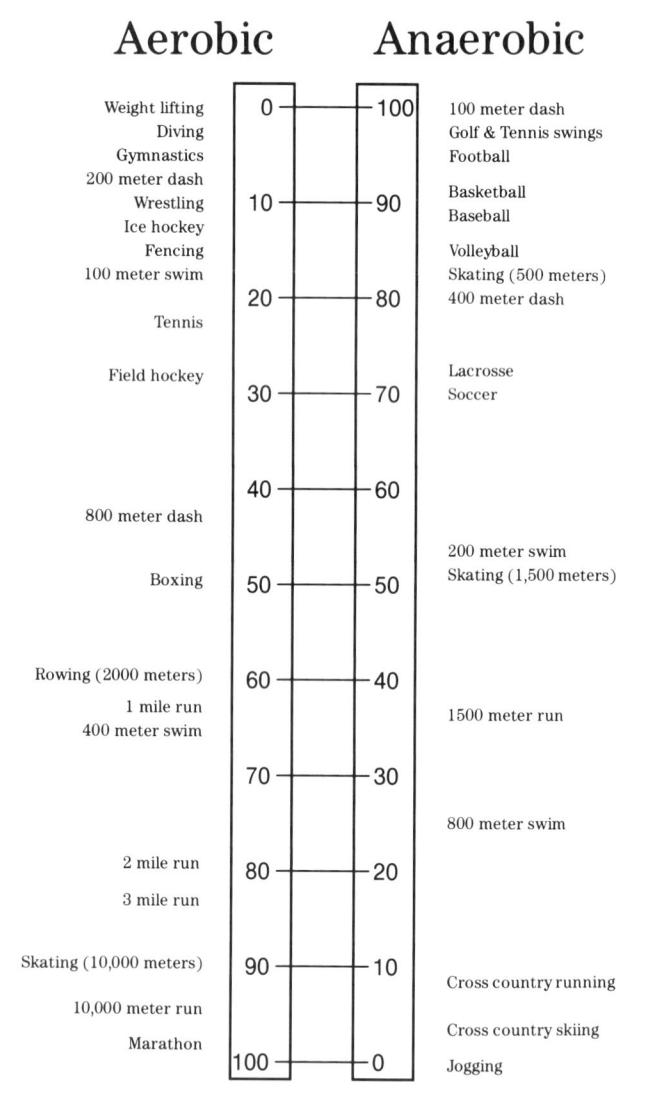

| Aerobic | % | % | Anaerobic |
|---|---|---|---|
| Weight lifting, Diving, Gymnastics, 200 meter dash | 0 | 100 | 100 meter dash, Golf & Tennis swings, Football |
| Wrestling, Ice hockey, Fencing, 100 meter swim | 10 | 90 | Basketball, Baseball |
|  | 20 | 80 | Volleyball, Skating (500 meters), 400 meter dash |
| Tennis |  |  |  |
| Field hockey | 30 | 70 | Lacrosse, Soccer |
|  | 40 | 60 |  |
| 800 meter dash |  |  |  |
| Boxing | 50 | 50 | 200 meter swim, Skating (1,500 meters) |
| Rowing (2000 meters), 1 mile run, 400 meter swim | 60 | 40 | 1500 meter run |
|  | 70 | 30 | 800 meter swim |
| 2 mile run, 3 mile run | 80 | 20 |  |
| Skating (10,000 meters), 10,000 meter run, Marathon | 90 | 10 | Cross country running, Cross country skiing |
|  | 100 | 0 | Jogging |

**Fig. 5A-1.** A Comparison of Aerobic and Anaerobic Contributions of ATP During the Performance of Various Sports

Table 5A-3. Definitions of Various Training Methods and Development of the Energy Systems

| Training Method | Definition | ATP-PC | LA and $O_2$ | $O_2$ |
|---|---|---|---|---|
| Acceleration sprints | Gradual increases in running speed from jogging to striding to sprinting in 50-yd to 120-yd segments | 90 | | 5 |
| Continuous fast running | Long-distance running (or swimming) at a fast pace | 2 | 8 | 90 |
| Continuous slow running | Long-distance running (or swimming) at a slow pace | 2 | 5 | 93 |
| Hollow sprints | Two sprints interrupted by periods of jogging or walking | 20 | 10 | 5 |
| Interval sprinting | Alternate sprints of 50 yd and jogs of 60 yd for distances of up to 3 miles | 20 | 10 | 70 |
| Jogging | Continuous walking or running at a slow pace over a moderate distance (e.g., 2 miles) | 10-30 | 30-50 | 20-60 |
| Repetition running | Similar to interval training buunger work and relief intervals | 10 | 50 | 40 |
| Speed play (fartlek) | Alternating fast and slow running over natural terrain | 20 | 40 | 40 |
| Sprint training | Repeated sprints at maximal speed with complete recovery between repeats | 90 | 6 | 4 |

Abbreviations: ATP-PC = adenosine triphosphate phosphocreatine; LA = lactic acid
(From: Fox, E.L. Physical training: methods and effects. *Orthopedic Clinics of North America* 8:533-548, 1977)

## Exercise Prescription

For an in-depth justification of the recommendations given here, please refer to the ACSM statement on quality and quantity of exercise (Appendix 5A-1). As mentioned earlier, the four major training components of conditioning are frequency, intensity, duration, and mode of activity.

### Frequency

Training should occur three to five times per week. In a primary care setting, the practitioner must clearly ask a patient to set aside time for training before any exercise program is begun. This time must be sufficient for the complete workout and it should have a high priority on the individual's daily schedule.

### Intensity

Intensity is the factor that varies the most when individuals first begin an exercise program. Consider the following when making recommendations about intensity of exercise:

1. Determine either the maximum aerobic capacity ($VO_2$max) or maximum heart rate (beats per minute). Maximum heart rate (MHR) levels adjusted to age and fitness have been estimated using graded exercise testing (see Table 5A-4). Another convenient, reasonably accurate method is MHR = 220 minus the age of the patient.
2. An appropriate training level should be established within these ranges:
   a. $VO_2$max — Range — 50% (beginners) to 85% (elite athletes).
   b. Maximum Heart Rate — Range — 60% (beginners) to 90% (elite athletes); Average — 70%.
3. Fine adjustments need to be made considering:
   a. Motivation.
   b. Musculoskeletal limiting factors.
   c. The body habitus — The more obese the individual is, the less intense and weight-bearing a training program should be at the beginning.
4. Advise the patient to monitor pulse rate every ten to fifteen minutes through the course of activity. This can be done by educating the patient to take either carotid or radial pulse.

### Duration

Fifteen to sixty minutes of continuous aerobic activity is recommended. The frequency of exercise is a factor with a wide and flexible range. An individual who exercises only three times a week

CONDITIONING AND TRAINING PROGRAMS 115

Table 5A-4. Age-fitness Adjusted Predicted MHR for Three Levels of Fitness

| Age | Predicted MHR, bpm Below Average | Average | Above Average | Age | Predicted MHR, bpm Below Average | Average | Above Average |
|---|---|---|---|---|---|---|---|
| 20 | 201 | 201 | 196 | 45 | 174 | 183 | 183 |
| 21 | 199 | 200 | 196 | 46 | 173 | 182 | 183 |
| 22 | 198 | 199 | 195 | 47 | 172 | 181 | 182 |
| 23 | 197 | 198 | 195 | 48 | 171 | 181 | 182 |
| 24 | 196 | 198 | 194 | 49 | 170 | 180 | 181 |
| 25 | 195 | 197 | 194 | 50 | 168 | 179 | 180 |
| 26 | 194 | 196 | 193 | 51 | 167 | 179 | 180 |
| 27 | 193 | 196 | 193 | 52 | 166 | 178 | 179 |
| 28 | 192 | 195 | 192 | 53 | 165 | 177 | 179 |
| 29 | 191 | 193 | 192 | 54 | 164 | 176 | 178 |
| 30 | 190 | 193 | 191 | 55 | 163 | 176 | 178 |
| 31 | 189 | 193 | 191 | 56 | 162 | 175 | 177 |
| 32 | 188 | 192 | 190 | 57 | 161 | 174 | 177 |
| 33 | 187 | 191 | 189 | 58 | 160 | 174 | 176 |
| 34 | 186 | 191 | 189 | 59 | 159 | 173 | 176 |
| 35 | 184 | 190 | 188 | 60 | 158 | 172 | 175 |
| 36 | 183 | 189 | 188 | 61 | 157 | 172 | 175 |
| 37 | 182 | 189 | 187 | 62 | 156 | 171 | 174 |
| 38 | 181 | 188 | 187 | 63 | 155 | 170 | 174 |
| 39 | 180 | 187 | 186 | 64 | 154 | 169 | 173 |
| 40 | 179 | 186 | 186 | 65 | 152 | 169 | 173 |
| 41 | 178 | 186 | 185 | 66 | 151 | 168 | 172 |
| 42 | 177 | 185 | 185 | 67 | 150 | 167 | 171 |
| 43 | 176 | 184 | 184 | 68 | 149 | 167 | 171 |
| 44 | 177 | 184 | 184 | 69 | 148 | 166 | 170 |
|  |  |  |  | 70 | 147 | 165 | 170 |

needs a longer exercise period (usually 45 to 60 minutes) than someone does who exercises five to six times a week, and who may only need 15 to 30 minutes of exercise. Consider the "F × I × D" product, Frequency times Intensity times Duration, to get a rough idea of work done over a period of time. A desirable exercise program for the recreational non-competitive adults will be of longer duration with low to moderate intensity because of better compliance and less chance of injury.

### Mode of Activity

Generally speaking, the training effect achieved is independent of the specific aerobic activity performed. Improving aerobic capacity requires the use of large muscle groups, continuous exercise, rhythmic repetitive movement, and stimulation of the aerobic energy system. It should be mentioned that anaerobic exercise is usually static, very intense in nature, and only results in a beneficial effect on the cardiovascular system. Anaerobic exercise will increase muscular strength and endurance. This type of exercise is generally contraindicated for patients with heart disease and/or hypertension (Table 5A-5). Consult Tables 5E-4 and 5E-5 for approximate sport specific energy expenditures.

### Progression — Part 1

The progression of any individual exercise program is, at best, an inexact art. Individuals are different in their response to exercise and other stimuli. The best advice a physician can give a patient is to "listen to his/her body" and use common sense. Figure 5A-2 illustrates in schematic fashion the progression of an exercise regimen over time as the body adapts to the stimulus. There is controversy about the definition of upper limits of exercise and it involves all four of the previously dis-

**Table 5A-5. Diseases That Contraindicate Anaerobic Exercising For Recreational Athletes**

| Cardiac | Vascular and Circulatory |
|---|---|
| Angina pectoris, uncontrolled of unstable | Anemia, severe or of unknown cause |
| Aortic stenosis, severe | Aneurysm, large or dissecting |
| Cardiac arrhythmia, uncontrolled | Cerebrovascular accident, acute |
| Congestive heart failure, uncontrolled (Class III or IV) | Embolism, pulmonary or systemic, acute |
| Myocardial infarction, acute | Hypertension, uncontrolled |
| Myocarditis or cardiomyopathy | Thrombophlebitis, acute |
| Valvular heart disease, severe | Transient ischemic attack, recent |

(Adapted from Taylor, 1983)

cussed determinants. The main question is: How much exercise is really necessary?

1. *Frequency* — In the beginning, it is important to incorporate "rest" days between exercise episodes to give the body an opportunity to accommodate to the additional stimulus. As exercise progresses, it may become a daily habit. If more than one mode of exercise is involved, this is probably a reasonable and healthy approach. The authors prefer that individuals take at least one day of rest from exercise each week.
2. *Intensity* — The daily exerciser who performs at 70-80% of his/her maximal heart rate will get enough effective stimulus and gain in functional capacity. Exercising at a greater intensity causes the risk benefit ratio to invert so that there is more risk of cardiovascular complications for a relatively small amount of improvement in functional capacity.
3. *Duration* — The length of time of any exercise regime is one of the most flexible parts of the exercise prescription. As little as 12 minutes of regular aerobic exercise has resulted in significant improvement in functional capacity. The optimal range of an exercise episode is probably in the 20-30 minute range. Exercise that continues much past 45 minutes brings about an adverse risk benefit ratio. Duration should be increased if the exercise is scheduled on an every other day plan.
4. *Mode of Activity* — From a preventive medicine and health care standpoint, any exercise program needs to contain first and foremost aerobic exercise. However, it is important to understand that other components are involved in physical fitness, some are more important than others. These components include flexibility, muscular strength and endurance, cardiorespiratory endurance, and body composition. All of these can be developed through an exercise program. Flexibility can be incorporated into warm-up and cool-down exercises (discussed later in this chapter). Some muscular strength and endurance exercises can be incorporated, into the warm-up or cool-down or they can be worked on separately during "off" days. Improved cardiorespiratory endurance and a leaner body composition are a result of the actual exercise phase. All of these activities should be incorporated into a schedule which is convenient and interesting.

**Additional Concepts**

The primary care physician should also take into account the following considerations in prescribing an exercise program. They are not part of the five major factors normally considered in an exercise program, but they represent important additional information.

1. *Detraining* — Detraining (loss of functional capacity) can occur as quickly in two weeks. A total loss of conditioning following rest or inactivity takes place between 10 to 34 weeks after training ceases. Stopping may be voluntary

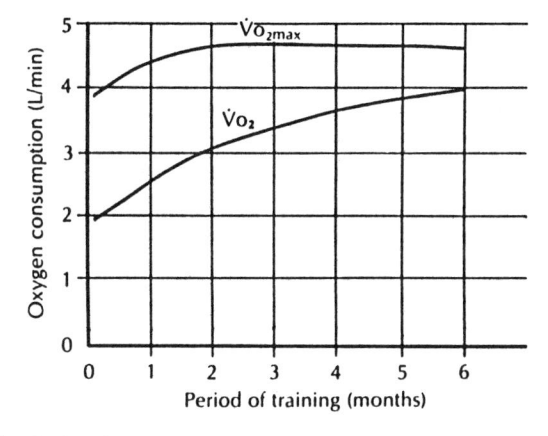

**Fig. 5A-2.** Adaptation of Body to Training over Time

(vacations, other obligations) or involuntary (illness, injury).
2. *Epidemiologic Studies* — It appears that more injuries occur in weight bearing activities than in non-weight bearing ones. The only consistent biological characteristic associated with non-compliance or dropout from an exercise program is obesity (Dishman, 1981). For this reason, we suggest foregoing most weight-bearing exercise until later in the program.
3. *Energy Equivalents* — These rough equivalents can give the prescribing physician some idea of possible "cross-over" training activities that can be used in the event of injury. The approximate formula is: 9 units biking = 4 units running = 1 unit swimming. This formula is very useful for determining relative rest when treating overuse injuries.
4. Age should not be a deterrent to training. The major consideration of age is a need for a longer period of adaptation. Natural decreases in functional status that occur with age can be delayed or even reversed. Those decreases are outlined in Table 5A-6. The effect of a chronic disease such as osteoarthritis may be reversed by the application of the right amount of exercise and movement for the affected joints.
5. A program that occurs less than three days a week, represents less than 50% $VO_2$max levels in intensity, and has a duration of less than 10 minutes a day is inadequate to achieve a training effect.

## Major Components of a Good Training Program

### Preconditioning

Preconditioning is absolutely imperative at the *beginning* of exercise. Preconditioning gives the body time to adjust and provide a safer, more measured response to exercise. It is less taxing on the cardiovascular system and causes fewer injuries. Ten to fourteen days at intensity levels lower than normal is advocated. For example, the use of the run-walk (run until tired, then walk, then run again) is appropriate as a preconditioning program for jogging. Another example is the use of low gear biking on level ground prior to adjusting to high gear cycling on hills.

### Warm-Up

A warm-up lasting between 5 and 10 minutes should precede the beginning of every exercise program. The two components to any warm-up program are low intensity activity and stretching. The order is important. Warm-up should begin with 5 minutes of low intensity activity, preferably the same type that will be done during exercise, although jogging is a good all-purpose warm-up activity. The purpose of warm-up is to increase blood flow to major muscle groups, gradually increase the heart rate, reduce muscle stiffness, facilitate enzymatic activity, and ready the body for more

Table 5A-6. Age-Related Decreases in Functional Status

| | | |
|---|---|---|
| Cardiovascular System | ↓Maximum Heart Rate | 10 beats/minute/decade |
| | ↓Resting Stroke Volume | 30% by 85 years of age |
| | ↓Maximum Cardiac Output | 20-30% by 65 years of age |
| | ↓Vessel Compliance | ↑blood pressure 10-40 mmHg |
| Respiratory System | ↑Residual Volume | 30-50% by 70 years of age |
| | ↓Vital Capacity | 40-50% by 70 years of age |
| Nervous System | ↓Nerve conduction | 10-15% by 60 years of age |
| | ↓Proprioception and balance | 35-40% ↑ in falls by 60 years of age |
| Metabolism | ↓Maximum $O_2$ uptake | 9%/decade |
| Musculoskeletal System | ↑Bone loss — ♀ >35 | 1%/year |
| | ♂ >55 | |
| | ↓Muscle strength | 20% by 65 years of age |
| | ↓Flexibility | Degenerative disease or inactivity |

(Compiled from data: Fitzgerald, 1985)

strenuous effort. This should be followed by about 5 minutes of slow, gentle stretching (no bouncing) of major muscle groups, particularly those that will be heavily used during exercise. The warm-up period is not benign. Overstretching, "ballistic," or improper stretching have caused many acute soft tissue injuries. The period can be expanded to include 5-10 minutes of muscular strength and endurance exercises (push-ups, pull-ups, sit-ups, etc.). Less time is spent in warm-up as the program progresses (presumably because muscles should now be more flexible). However, the warm-up phase should *never* be eliminated.

### Exercise Period

Discussed earlier in this chapter.

### Cool-Down

This is another transition period and should consist of low intensity activity such as jogging and some light stretching. This important component should last 3-5 minutes. It covers an extremely dangerous physiologic time in the course of a work-out session. Just as the warm-up physiologically prepares an individual for the exercise stimulus, the cool-down allows for proper recovery from exercise. During the cool-down, there are rapid changes in peripheral vascular resistance and venous return so that the induction of life-threatening cardiac arrhythmias is most likely to occur. This part of the training program allows the body (specifically the cardiovascular system) to accommodate and adjust to the non-exercise mode.

### Progression — Part 2

- If an increase is contemplated in an exercise program, it should be accomplished slowly over a period of time. There should be no pain or history of recent injury before an increase is undertaken.
- Never increase two of the three components of a training program simultaneously (frequency, intensity and duration). Only one at a time should ever be increased, and that on a gradual basis. For example, a patient on a jogging program should be advised to add no more than 10-15% at a time to the distance or time being run, with the increases coming no more often than every two weeks while the same frequency and intensity are maintained.

### Return From Injury

- Relative rest vs absolute rest — *Relative rest* refers to decreasing the training regimen but allowing an athlete to train at a lower level. *Absolute rest* pulls an athlete completely off training. From a primary care perspective, we feel that patient compliance is easier to achieve and there is less muscle atrophy and detraining if the relative rest concept is advocated for most patients.
- Alternative activity — There are many times in the treatment of injuries when a particular mode of activity is contraindicated. An alternative activity is an option for some patients. The basic premise is to decrease the force load placed upon the body by the activity in question (Table 5A-7).

### Light Intensity Training (LIT) Program

The objective of LIT is to steer away from dogma concerning a return to activity after injury, and allow an individual some self-determination in how quickly the return is accomplished. This program can be instituted when the individual is able to ambulate or perform "activities of daily living" without symptoms (pain, swelling). A specific activity is begun on an every other day basis and at a very low level without regard for duration or intensity. The three options to be considered during and after this trial return to activity are:

- If pain and/or swelling develops *during* the activity → stop all activity and *decrease* the following day's activity by 25% (at the start, less as distance or duration of activity increases).
- If pain and/or swelling develop *after* exercise is completed → continue the following day at the same level but do *not* increase the level of activity.
- If pain and/or swelling are not present during or after activity → *increase* activity slightly (up to 25% at the start, less later).

---

Table 5A-7. Equivalent Force Loads

| | |
|---|---|
| Jumping | 10-14 x body weight |
| Running | 4-7 x body weight |
| Walking | 1 x body weight |
| Biking | .25-.50 x body weight |
| Swimming | 0 x body weight |

This program allows an orderly stepwise return to a previous training regimen and incorporates the cooperation and help of the patient.

## SECTION B.
## THE YOUNG ATHLETE

This section presents those aspects of conditioning/training programs for young athletes that might differ from what already has been discussed.

It is appropriate to discuss the role of exercise in adolescents and younger children. The leadership of a knowledgeable primary care physician who can lend assistance to a community organizing a youth sports program can be powerful and invaluable. It may well represent one of the most effective preventive medicine interventions a physician can undertake in his community. Childhood and adolescence are the most active periods of life, and interest in exercise and sports are at their peak. Unfortunately, medical science has yet to quantify, or even describe with any degree of accuracy, the major characteristics of growth and exercise and how they relate to each other. The effect of both long and short term exercise on physical training of youth remains a matter of speculation. It should come as no surprise that medical science has difficulty setting fitness guidelines for preadolescents and adolescents. Nevertheless, a summary of exercise prescription in youth is useful even if difficult to do. We will not debate such points as the physical fitness levels of existing youth population groups in this country here.

Some food for thought — more than 7 million boys and girls are involved in a wide variety of high school sports. At least 20 million boys and girls aged 8-16 years are involved in non-school community-sponsored athletic programs; another 20 million youngsters engage in recreational activities without supervision or structure. It is estimated that half of all adolescent boys and a quarter of all adolescent girls are seen as patients because of their involvement in competitive sports (Schafer, 1980).

### The Prepubescent Athlete

Unique physiological characteristics of the young athlete include:

- *Physical growth* — Of the three growth spurts occurring in humans, the first (inuteral) is nutritionally and genetically determined, and the second (occurring at approximately 54-60 months of age) takes place before major athletic involvement begins. However, the third (rapid growth associated with puberty) is affected by the amount of exercise.
- *Exploration of new areas of interest* — Inquisitive youngsters often look upon sports activity as a new experience.
- *Maturation* — With the initiation of maturational changes during puberty, there is an augmentation of strength, endurance, and neuromuscular skills.
- *Body proportion changes* — During the adolescent growth spurt, approximately 15% of the adult height and 40% of the skeletal mass are achieved.
- *Body composition alterations* — Prepubertal boys and girls have approximately the same percent body fat but, during pubertal growth, male body fat decreases whereas female body fat increases. In addition, muscular body strength in the male increases more than in the female.
- *Other considerations* — In addition to the physical changes, massive psychologic and sociologic changes occur simultaneously, affecting to a great extent the developing child and his/her relationship with athletic activities.

A summary of pertinent questions that might be asked of a physician about prepubescent training regimens includes:

1. *Is such training dangerous to the preadolescent epiphysis?* No. In a large study of athletes suffering epiphyseal injuries, 98% resulted in uneventful recovery with no major medical intervention needed once proper diagnosis was made (Larson, 1966).
2. *Are there any special nutritional or thermoregulatory considerations for children in training?* No. The nutritional requirements of this group vary little from those of nonathletes of the same age group. Heavy growth demands dictates the rate of nutritional uptake. Little in the way of special diet or supplements are needed for young athletes as long as they eat a normal, well balanced diet (Harvey, 1984; Marino, 1980). The only special consideration would be replacing those calories used in train-

ing with pure complex carbohydrates. The thermoregulatory mechanism of the young athlete is extremely efficient, even though the amount of sweating is less than in an adult. The capacity to thermoregulate remains higher and more efficient in the prepubescent child (Lamb, 1985).

3. *Do growth and development benefit from training or are they impeded by exercise?* There appears to be no data to accurately answer this question but several studies have indicated that a "normal" amount of exercise is beneficial for growth and development. *Excesses* in exercise can have a harmful dampening effect on growth and development.

4. *Are there psychological effects or ramifications of participation at a young age?* People exercise for many reasons and children are no different. The major motivation to participate in exercise or enter competitive sports is a desire to have fun. Indeed, the pressure to win appears to be an adult creation. One study has shown that 95% of children polled believed that having fun while participating in a sport was more important than winning; 75% would rather play on a loosing team than "sit" on a winning team (Henschen). Sports competition can produce severe stress and anxiety, and psychological trauma can occur when children are subjected to repeated episodes of failure in competition. Two groups of vulnerable children have been identified: those with a low level of athletic competence due to late maturation, inexperience, or genetic lack of ability, and those who perceive they are not meeting the expectations of their age/peer group, coach, or (or most importantly) parents. Seefeldt (1980) offers the following "Bill of Rights" for young athletes:
   1. The right to participate in sports.
   2. The right to participate at a level commensurate with maturity and ability.
   3. The right to have qualified adult leadership.
   4. The right to play as a child and not as an adult.
   5. The right to share in the leadership and decision-making of their particular sport.
   6. The right to participate in a safe and healthy environment.
   7. The right to proper preparation for participation in sport.
   8. The right to an equal opportunity to strive for success.
   9. The right to be treated with dignity.
   10. The right to have fun in sports.

5. *What are children's norms, and how far can they drive themselves or be driven by others?* This represents one of the least known and most potentially dangerous areas of sports medicine. It is an important question to ask even if it is unanswerable at present.

6. *Can children achieve a training effect?* To answer this question, we must look closely at the growth and maturation processes taking place in the pubescent individual. The "trigger hypothesis" has been used to explain specific changes and lack of changes in the physical conditioning of children. This hypothesis states that there is one critical time period in a child's development (termed the "trigger point"), usually coinciding with puberty, *before* which the effects of physical conditioning from any mode are minimal if they occur at all. It is felt that this phenomenon is the result of the modulating effects of hormones, the same hormones that initiate puberty and influence the functional development and subsequent organic adaptations seen in the mature adult. We must be careful not to imply that prepubertal changes in conditioning do not occur. On the contrary, functional changes and adaptations are apparently a normal consequence of the growth-maturation process (Hamilton, 1976; McKeag, 1988). Figure 5B-1 illustrates a schematic drawing compiling data on $VO_2$max levels of various age groups.

It has long been suspected that the ultimate limit for physiologic performance is set by genetic makeup. The contribution of genetic potential to the adaptation to conditioning is major. Heredity has been shown to account for anywhere between 81%-93% of the observed differences in cardiorespiratory endurance. Researchers who have studied the phenomenon of puberty state that, for puberty to occur, certain yet-to-be-known organic adaptations involving endocrine functions must be present. The trigger hypothesis represents a parallel assumption that, for organic adaptations for training and conditioning to occur, certain necessary conditions must precede those adaptations. An increase in lean to fat body ratio, maturation of the neuromuscular system, and levels of endocrine function must precede any significant training effect in children (Gilliam, 1980).

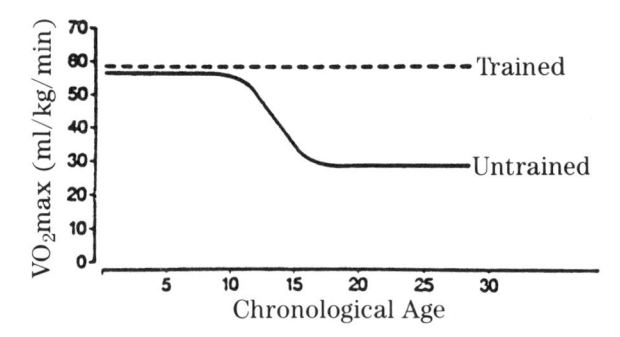

(A) *Cardiorespiratory performance during childhood and adolescent years.* Trained *refers to individuals maximally trained by aerobic means, regardless of age or sex.* Untrained *refers to individuals whose exercise is limited to activities of daily living.*

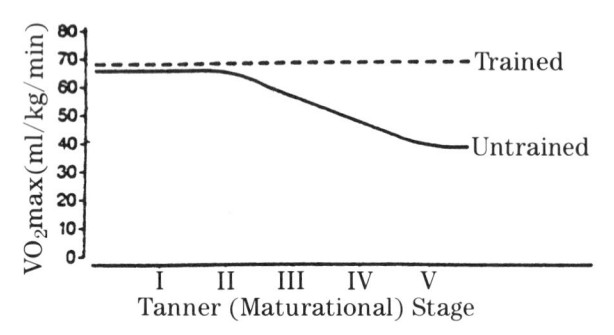

(B) *Cardiorespiratory performance related to maturational stage.* Trained *refers to individuals maximally trained by aerobic means, regardless of age or sex.* Untrained *refers to individuals whose exercise is limited to activities of daily living.*

**Fig. 5B-1.** Trigger Hypothesis

Both androgen and growth hormone are thought to play a part in the development of functional capacity in the pubescent individual. Androgen levels determine muscular response to resistance exercise. That response is minimal in a prepubertal youngster (Vrigens, 1978). Should a 9-year-old boy weight train? The risk (injury) —benefit (minimal muscle growth) ratio would say "No." Because of its many functions throughout the body, growth hormone is believed to be the prime agent working in the presence of physical conditioning to induce organic adaptations. Prepubertal athletes and nonathletes differ little in their metabolic adaptation processes, yet they can be markedly different in athletic performance. It appears that *athletic performance in this age group is more dependent upon the level of skill development than on physiologic conditioning.* This principle should guide the practitioner in advising prepubertal athletes on constructing an athletic training program. Additionally, the primary care physician should be well versed in the clinical use of physical maturity staging to allow for accurate assessment of the stage of puberty prior to formulating any exercise program (see Chapter 4, Figure 4-3).

**Post-Pubescent Athlete**

Post-pubertal children require physiologic conditioning along with skill training for optimal athletic performance. There does not appear to be a definitive answer about whether conditioned prepubertal children will demonstrate greater physiologic changes after puberty, but there is evidence to suggest that prepubertal conditioning may prime the body to accept changes occurring in the post-pubertal individual as a result of training. Any post-pubertal individual follows predictable adult patterns concerning exercise-induced adaptations from training and conditioning.

When working with a post-pubertal individual, the concept of initial level of fitness at the beginning exercise is important. An individual who starts at a low level of functioning should have room for considerable improvement. For many children who are beginning their first serious exercise training, the previous consideration is important. Aerobic fitness improvements of 5%-25% can be expected from systematic training by post-pubertal individuals. In strength training, it is not unusual to see 100%-200% improvement during the adolescent years. Physiologic adaptations to exercise in the post-pubescent period may be dependent upon initial levels of strength and endurance, but they can be demonstrated within one to two weeks after starting a conditioning program if the intensity is sufficient. Optimal physical conditioning in the post-pubescent individual also depends upon the frequency, intensity, and duration of exercise just as it does with adults. Most changes seen in this group result from the *intensity* of the training overload. Wilmore (1979) indicates that the greater the relative training intensity, the greater the training adaptation. There probably is a "minimal" threshold intensity below which training effects will not occur, as well as a possible "ceiling" threshold above which there are no further gains in adaptation. Studies of the frequency of activity in the post-pubertal individual have shown that training more than 3-4 days a week yields very little additional change in physiologic function. It appears that rest between exercise sessions is an important component in producing biologic adaptations in this age group. The duration of exercise needed to build endurance requires a minimum of 25-30 minutes and an approximate 300 kcal expenditure for adaptations to take place. Strength training workouts need not exceed 40 minutes at maximum intensity levels.

## SECTION C.
## THE FEMALE ATHLETE

There has been a dramatic increase in the participation of women in physical activity in the past decade. More women of all ages are exercising and training intensively for endurance events. More women of all ages are participating in a variety of sports in the competitive and recreational setting. This surge has raised a number of issues that pertain to the female athlete. Many relate to the female reproductive/endocrine function. Puberty may be delayed in young women involved in intensive training programs, and menstrual cycle abnormalities resulting from endurance training have been increasingly reported. These include shortened luteal phases, oligomenorrhea, amenorrhea, and anovulation. Concerns about future infertility and accelerated osteoporosis, in addition to the effects of active exercise programs on pregnancy, fetal growth retardation, and birth complications must be addressed.

It is important to look at the physical and mental makeup of the female athlete involved in exercise and sport. There are obvious physical differences between male and female athletes (Table 5C-1) that may affect their potential for sports participation (Drinkwater, 1986). However, the female can and should enjoy all the benefits of sports, exercise, and better health through active participation in a regular program.

The change in society's attitudes toward athletic participation by women during the early 1970s, along with opportunity for older women to become actively involved in exercising, has led more female athletes to seek advice about exercise. The physical skills and knowledge about sports by women born after 1960 is vastly different than for older women who are entering the sports world as novices. The older woman may be enthusiastic in pursuing a regular exercise program, but she lacks the rudimentary knowledge of conditioning techniques, how to select appropriate equipment and clothing, and how to protect herself from overuse and acute injuries. Before we consider some of the issues that confront the modern female athlete, we will look at the differences between male and female athletes and the effect of aging.

### Aerobic Power

Habitual level of activity, not gender or age, is the primary determinant of an individual's cardiovascular fitness. Male and female athletes who participate in the same sport are more similar in aerobic power ($VO_2$max), than athletes of the same sex in different sports. The elite male athlete has a higher $VO_2$max than the elite female athlete. The lower oxygen carrying capacity of a woman, a reflection of lower hemoglobin levels, is probably the major factor in this difference. Absolute levels of $VO_2$max usually are higher for men since males have a larger body mass than females and $VO_2$max is directly related to body size. This presents a problem for women only in sports or activities where both sexes must perform at the same absolute work rate.

One of the most important concepts in all descriptive research studies is the fact that female athletes can obtain higher levels of cardiovascular fitness. They are physiologically capable of undergoing the physical stress of endurance sports and they do not, as many texts imply, reach their peak fitness levels at age 15 (Drinkwater, 1986). Older female athletes generally possess cardiovascular fitness levels equivalent to those of sedentary women a decade younger, while older women trained specifically for endurance events, gain two decades or more in fitness levels. Women who were inactive during their early adult years but now are actively engaged in physical fitness programs show significant training effects which may improve longevity and general fitness.

Male and female athletes of all ages can increase cardiovascular fitness and enjoy all the benefits of exercise mentioned in this book. Gender per se is not the factor that must be considered when prescribing exercise for women. The female's initial level of fitness, her previous exercise experience, and her level of knowledge and skill are more important. The younger female with no previous experience in sports who wants to be in a regular exercise program will require much more guidance than a woman with prior competitive experience. The basic principles of exercise pre-

Table 5C-1. Physiologic Differences Between Men and Women and Their Effects on Athletic Performance

| Body System | Men | Women |
| --- | --- | --- |
| **Musculoskeletal** | | |
| Ligaments | Joints are more taut; stronger ligamentous structure | Joints are usually more lax; more delicate ligamentous structure |
| Bones | Larger, longer bones; greater articular surface and larger structure produce a mechanical advantage; greater lever arm and more force in kicking, sticking and hitting | Smaller, shorter, less dense bones; more susceptible to stress fractures |
| Pelvis | Narrower; must widen stance to achieve a woman's degree of balance | Wider; lower center of gravity produces excellent balance; increase valgus angulation at hip; greater incidence of inflammatory hip disorders, iliotibial tendinitis, and trochanteric bursitis |
| Knee | Less acute angle of femoral articulation; smaller valgus attitude (5°-7°); fewer knee injuries | Increased angle between the femur and tibia; wider pelvis and weaker quadriceps allow the patella to move laterally, leading to patella subluxation and chondromalacia; greater valgus attitude (9° to 10°); vastus medialis is usually undeveloped; improper patella tracking |
| Foot | Less foot pronation; less likely to suffer lower leg injuries | More foot pronation; more likely to have shin splints and chondromalacia develop |
| Muscle Mass | Approximately 40% of total body weight; more power and speed | Approximately 23% of total body weight; less power and speed; more difficulty with lifting, throwing and sprinting |
| **Metabolic** | | |
| Body Fat | Approximately 14% of total body weight; less efficient in energy utilization | Approximately 22% to 25% of total body weight; better energy utilization |
| Endurance | Less efficient use of glycogen storage; more calories needed to sustain the same amount of muscular activity; often "hit the wall" (depletion of glycogen stores) | More efficient use of glycogen storage; equal or greater endurance; excel in long- distance sports; rarely "hit the wall" |
| **Hematopoietic** | | |
| Blood | Greater iron supply and less depletion; less chance of having anemia and the resulting fatigue develop | Greater depletion of iron supply; more prone to iron deficiency anemia |
| $VO_2max$ | Greater; higher oxygen capacity; more hemoglobin; can reach maximum training peak earlier | Smaller; begin training with lower oxygen capacity and lower arterial oxygen; less hemoglobin; must train longer to reach maximum training peak |

scription outlined in this chapter apply equally to men and women. It is likely, however, that there will be greater variation in the background and experience of women seeking advice regarding exercise.

## Strength

The potential of female athletes to develop strength has been greatly underestimated. Women benefit from strength training and demonstrate improved athletic performance and prevention of injury. The female can obtain approximately the same kind of increase in strength as men with only a fraction of the male's increase in bulk. Increased muscle mass in men gives the male athletes a strength advantage that most women are unlikely to overcome. The anabolic properties of testosterone account for the major difference in muscle size between the sexes. In general, the overall strength of women is approximately 67% that of men. Upper body strength of the female averages approximately 65% of the males, while leg strength is almost identical when expressed relative to body mass. Strength training will not close the gap, and it is unlikely that men and women can ever compete equally in events where success is determined primarily by strength and power. The major gender differences lie in the size of the muscle fiber. While fiber area can be increased with strength training, men still maintain an advantage in fiber size as a result of biological differences between the sexes.

Female athletes should not be discouraged from developing the muscular strength to meet the demands of their sport. Development of upper and lower body strength should be a priority for most female athletes. Female athletes should be encouraged to strengthen their quadricep and hamstring muscles to prevent knee injuries.

## Body Composition

Generally, female athletes have a higher percent body fat than do male athletes. Endurance athletes like runners and cross country skiers may average 12%-18% body fat, whereas some marathon runners will have 6%-8% body fat. Female athletes in team sports like basketball, lacrosse, volleyball, swimming, and tennis average 18%-24% body fat. These are average figures and there are wide variations. Also, they are estimates that are only one aspect of an athlete's physiological profile. Excessive body fat percentage which is determined by appropriate techniques may require dietary and exercise interventions to promote weight reduction. Education about nutrition is mandatory for all female athletes. Improper interpretation of body fat percentage may lead some female athletes toward pathologic weight reduction techniques. The physician should be cautious when using body fat data alone to counsel athletes to lose weight. An older female athlete is likely to have 10%-15% less body fat than sedentary women of the same age. An increase in percent body fat is not an inevitable consequence of aging in active women.

## Heat Intolerance

When men and women are matched for exercise at the same percentage of $VO_2$max, there are no differences in their ability to work in the heat. High intensity exercise, in combination with high ambient heat, is a dangerous combination no matter how well trained the athlete. Men and women matched for cardiovascular fitness, body surface area, and surface area to mass will acclimatize to the heat equally well. An erroneous past belief held that women sweat less than men and have difficulty coping with heat stress.

The sweating response is related to a need for heat loss through evaporation of sweat and is related to absolute, not relative, work load. Even though a heavier male and lighter female run at the same percentage of $VO_2$max, the male will produce more heat. Also, regardless of gender, the person who is acclimatized to heat and well-conditioned will sweat sooner and in greater quantity than the untrained person. In summary, numerous studies have failed to find any evidence that gender per se affects thermoregulatory response or that women are at greater risk of developing heat stress injury. Females who are beginning to exercise after years of sedentary living or who are obese should be warned of the potential hazards of exercising strenuously in hot weather. Beyond this, the same precautions for hot weather exercising apply equally to male and female athletes (Drinkwater, 1986).

## Effects on Menstrual Cycle

An increased incidence of menstrual abnormalities is associated with increased participation of women in regular exercise programs. Exercise-related menstrual problems are well recognized in women in endurance sports or professional dance. Studies have shown that exercise-induced menstrual dysfunction is difficult to bring about with exercise alone. There are multiple risk factors, including low body weight, changes in nutrition, eating disorders, weight and body fat loss, history of late menarche, and previous menstrual irregularity (Brooks-Gunn, 1987; Duester, 1986). Compared with an incidence of 3%-5% in the general population, 15%-20% of exercising women and upwards of 50% of endurance female athletes experience menstrual abnormalities. Exercise alone does not delay the onset of puberty or affect future pregnancies. In fact, regular exercise can decrease dysmenorrhea and may help certain women attain more regularity in their menstrual cycle (Shangold, 1986).

Amenorrhea is defined as follows: *primary* — no menses by age 18; *secondary* — no menses for six or more months after the initial onset of menarche. The average age of menarche in the United States is 12.5-13.0 years; however, a higher age for menarche is seen in ballerinas and gymnasts. Generally, linear growth is not affected during periods of amenorrhea but it may be compromised if an eating disorder is present as well.

Alterations in certain reproductive hormones do occur with exercise and training. Even after an assessment of the literature, an accurate characterization of the acute hormonal response to exercise is difficult. The mechanisms responsible for amenorrhea and developmental delay in female athletes have yet to be elucidated, but several hypotheses have been offered. All the theories postulate interference in some way with the delicate mechanisms that control interactions along the hypothalamic-pituitary-ovarian axis. Inhibition of gonadotropin-releasing hormone by the hypothalamus apparently prevents the pituitary from being normally stimulated to produce age appropriate pulses of luteinizing hormone (LH) and follicle stimulating hormone (FSH). The direct result is estrogen deficiency and anovulation. Consequently, there is a deficiency in progesterone production and inhibition of negative feedback between the ovary and hypothalamus (Bonen, 1984; Killinger, 1986; Lutter, 1982; Shangold, 1985; Cummings, 1985).

Vigorous exercise is believed to interfere with normal menstrual function by reducing body weight and/or body fat or by causing excessive stress (Frisch, 1974). Many of the hypotheses about hormones and menstrual cycles have yet to be proven. Factors most often associated with alterations in menstrual function include training intensity, relative leanness, and variables relating to reproductive immaturity. It is important to note that longitudinal studies have shown a return of normal menstrual function in women who continue to train but gain body mass, and in those who decrease training intensity while maintaining low body fat (DeSouza, 1987; Sanborn, 1987).

Any female athlete presenting with amenorrhea or changes in her menstrual cycle should be medically evaluated. Exercising females are susceptible to the same problems as other women who present with infertility or menstrual problems. The physician should determine that the athlete's menstrual abnormality is related to her sports participation and not due to other pathologic etiologies.

A thorough history should be taken for each female with amenorrhea, followed by a physical and the following laboratory tests: CBC, iron/total iron binding capacity (TIBC), sedimentation rate, T4 index, TSH, prolactin level, urinalysis, pregnancy test, and serum estradiol. Any female who has menstrual cycles should undergo documentation of basal body temperature for at least a one month period (Shangold, 1986).

After the history, physical and lab tests have been performed, a progesterone challenge is administered. If it is negative, FSH, LH, testosterone, and dehydroepiandrosterone sulfate (DHEA-S) levels should be measured. An increase in DHEA-S suggests an adrenal source of excess androgen production, whereas an elevated level of testosterone suggests ovarian origin. Plasma LH and FSH levels help rule out primary ovarian failure. An abnormal LH to FSH ratio supports the diagnosis of polycystic ovarian disease. Where there are these additional findings, it is very difficult to predict when the next ovulation will occur. Consequently, oral contraceptives are probably contraindicated and a barrier method of contraception should be used. If the estradiol level is normal, and there is a normal E1/E2 ratio <1, and withdrawal bleeding following a progesterone challenge, the physician should consider cycling the athlete with progesterone every 3-6 months to prevent endometrial hyperplasia.

Oral contraceptives carry a risk of cerebral vascular accident, especially in patients who smoke or who have a history of migraine headaches. The risk of thromboembolic complications is related to estrogen dosage and is less significant with current low dose contraceptives. Oral contraceptives can be considered in a female athlete under age 30 who does not smoke or have hypertension or migraines. A history of fractures may also influence the decision to provide replacement hormones.

Although not proven, exercise-associated menstrual dysfunction is probably reversible. This theory is supported by findings of resumed menses after training is interrupted or decreased in amount or intensity. However, it is important not to assume the female athlete has amenorrhea due to strenuous athletic activity (see Figure 5C-1). Other causes of amenorrhea include pregnancy, anorexia nervosa, chronic illness, and CNS neoplasms and should be considered and ruled out by history, physical examination, laboratory testing, CT scan, or MRI. If amenorrhea is the result of strenuous athletic activity, the athlete should be advised to decrease her activity and perhaps seek nutritional counseling. Hormone replacement should be considered as an alternative.

Since anovulation and the resulting progesterone deficiency appear responsible for most com-

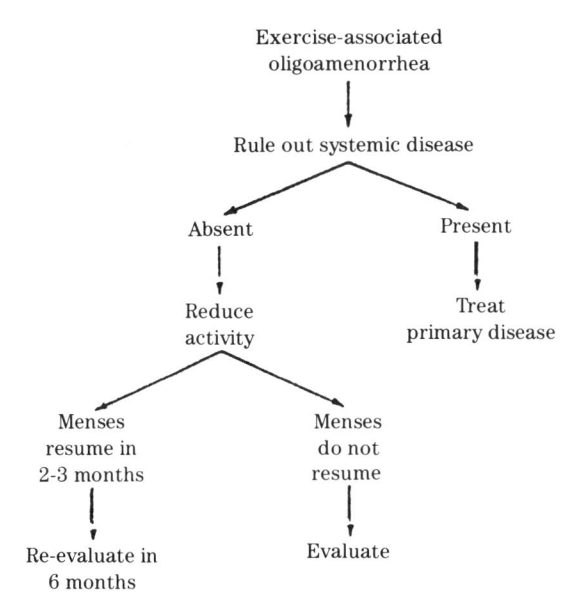

```
    Exercise-associated
      oligoamenorrhea
              │
              ▼
      Rule out systemic disease
         ╱           ╲
      Absent       Present
        │             │
        ▼             ▼
     Reduce        Treat
     activity    primary disease
       ╱    ╲
   Menses    Menses
  resume in   do not
  2-3 months  resume
      │         │
      ▼         ▼
 Re-evaluate  Evaluate
  in 6 months
```

**Fig. 5C-1.** Evaluation of Exercise-Associated Oligoamenorrhea

plications of athletic amenorrhea (osteoporosis, cancer of the ovary and endometrium), administration of progesterone is appropriate. This is usually accomplished with Provera[R] 10 mg a day for 10 days monthly, corresponding to days 16-25 of normal menstrual cycle. The sexually active female athlete can be placed on an oral contraceptive if appropriate, even though "postpill amenorrhea" occurs with higher frequency in the female athlete with secondary amenorrhea. Adequate calcium intake (1-2 grams per day) is recommended through the use of calcium carbonate (Tums 500 mg) or 4-8 daily servings of dairy products.

The most effective physiologic approach to amenorrhea is the encouragement of time off from intensive training. Two months appears to be enough for this purpose in most cases. An alternative action may be a 10% reduction in exercise frequency and intensity. This technique has been shown to be effective in restoring normal ovulatory function in adult athletes with amenorrhea (Killinger, 1986; Lutter, 1982; and Shangold, 1986).

## Osteoporosis

Athletes of both sexes undergo bone mass decreases with aging, beginning at age 30-35 in women and approximately age 50 in men. The loss in women occurs three times faster than in men. The perimenopausal female is at even higher risk of accelerated bone loss for a five year period around the time of menopause (Cann, 1984; Cummings, 1986; Drinkwater, 1984; Gonzales, 1982; Markus, 1985).

Most women have a slightly negative calcium balance and require adequate dietary calcium. Recommended calcium intake is 1 gram daily for premenopausal women and 1.5-2 grams daily for the post-menopausal female. Estrogen also is important in controlling bone resorption, and a decreased serum estrogen level is responsible for accelerated bone loss after menopause.

Recommendations for the prevention of early osteoporosis in the actively exercising female include an adequate calcium intake. The use of estrogen replacement remains controversial. Oral contraceptives can be used in the young female with no contraindications. Otherwise, low dose estrogen in the form of Premarin[R] or estradiol preparations are suggested. These often are used in combination with progesterone (Provera[R], 5-10 mg daily for 10 days per month) to guard against endometrial hyperplasia. The use of estrogen is not universally accepted, and careful attention to dietary calcium intake may be sufficient to prevent accelerated osteoporosis in the exercising female athlete.

When cyclic estrogen is indicated, a dose of 0.625 mg Premarin or its equivalent for 25 days is usually sufficient, with the addition of Provera 10 mg on days 17 to 25. This dose is thought to be protective for the bones. The patient may or may not have cyclic bleeding. If periods are desirable, 1.25 to 2.5 mg of Premarin daily may be needed. Exercise also is recommended to preserve or increase bone mass, especially for the postmenopausal patient. Weight-bearing exercise and strength training will be the most beneficial.

## Exercise in Pregnancy

Many patients remain active during pregnancy and there are physical and psychological benefits from exercise at that time. However, there are few adequately controlled studies in animal and human subjects so that the information about the effects of exercise on maternal and fetal well-being during pregnancy is incomplete. Multiple physiological changes occur during pregnancy to accommodate fetal development (Clapp, 1989). Many women are concerned that exercise could lead to premature labor and delivery, miscarriage, or poor fetal outcome, so they ask their physicians for guidelines on exercise.

### Physiological Changes in Pregnancy

Normal physiological changes of pregnancy may affect the total exercise capacity of the female athlete. Some of the common effects of pregnancy are a 40%-50% increase in plasma volume with a 30%-50% increase in cardiac output, decreased hematocrit and hemoglobin concentration, increased respiratory rate, increased lumbar lordosis, and softening of the joints by the hormone relaxin.

#### Cardiovascular

Pregnancy causes an increase in maternal blood volume, heart rate, cardiac stroke volume, and consequently, cardiac output. Blood volume and associated cardiac output start to rise at 6-8 weeks gestation and reach a peak increase of 40%-50% by the middle of the second trimester (Romen, 1986). Stroke volume and heart rate rise early in pregnancy and peak by mid-pregnancy, with stroke volume increasing by as much as 30% and heart rate by 15-20 beats per minute. The rise in cardiac output creates a marked cardiovascular reserve in early pregnancy when exercise is well tolerated by most patients. Some women reported an improved exercise tolerance then as compared with prepregnancy levels. Cardiovascular reserve generally decreases after 28 to 32 weeks gestation.

The increase in blood volume is important because many complications of pregnancy such as premature labor, hypertension, and growth retardation are associated with maternal hypovolemia or failure of plasma volume expansion. Anemia is common in the second and third trimester of pregnancy and may be significant, but it most often reflects an expansion of plasma volume that exceeds increases in red cell mass. It is important to help women understand that if they begin exercising before conception, it might improve their cardiac reserve and prevent complications from hypovolemia.

#### Respiratory

As pregnancy progresses, effective maternal vertical chest height decreases by approximately 4 cm as the enlarging uterus pushes on the diaphragm. Chest diameter increases in a compensatory mechanism by as much as 10 cm. Consequently, vital capacity remains essentially unchanged, but functional residual volume is markedly reduced in late pregnancy, causing a decrease in oxygen reserve (Goodlin, 1984).

#### Weight Gain

The female athlete must overcome the added discomfort and increased work load that results from weight gain as the pregnancy progresses. Most women gain an average of 10-12 kg (22-26 lbs) secondary to increased body fluid, increased uterine weight and contents, and breast enlargement. The increase in body mass has little effect on the performance of non-weight bearing activities (swimming, cycling), but it significantly increases the energy costs and physical discomforts associated with weight-bearing activities (jogging, aerobics, tennis).

#### Musculoskeletal Changes

Increased estrogen and relaxin levels cause softening of connective tissue in addition to relaxation of ligaments and joints. These changes may cause pain that interferes with movement and decreases the exercise tolerance. Specific joints, especially the interspinous and sacroiliac joints, pubic symphysis, and knees and ankles, become less stable and may be more prone to sprains. The expanding uterus moves the center of gravity more anteriorly, resulting in progressive lumbar lordosis, alterations in balance, and the potential for low back pain. Due to these normal changes in pregnancy, the female athlete may need to vary or modify athletic activities later in the course of pregnancy.

#### Energy and Metabolism

The base line increase in energy expenditure due to pregnancy is estimated to be about 150 kilocalories a day during the first trimester and 350 kilocalories a day during the second and third trimesters. The World Health Organization advises that an average addition of 285 kilocalories per day over baseline requirements is adequate to meet the needs of most pregnant women (WHO, 1985, Clapp, 1989). As the pregnancy progresses, the increased plasma insulin and fetal use of glucose predispose women to symptomatic hypoglycemia which may be worsened by exercise (Goodlin, 1984).

### Potential Risk of Exercise

Concerns about potential effects of exercise during pregnancy center on several major areas, fetal hypoxia, hyperthermia, miscarriage or premature delivery, decreased fetal weight, and maternal musculoskeletal injuries. Many of these concerns developed from animal research data which differs from results obtained in recent human studies. Pregnancy is a normal occurrence, and both fetal and maternal outcome studies on athletes have shown good results for most women. In fact, labors are shorter with fewer complications, less medication is used, and there is a quicker return to activity. Most animal studies used untrained pregnant animals which were exercised to exhaustion. Most of the human studies were on physically fit women exercising at more moderate levels.

### Fetal Hypoxia

Concerns for the fetus center around appropriate fetal oxygenation and the effects of exercise. One issue is whether exercise-induced blood flow to the working muscles might lower placental blood flow. Human studies have reported fetal bradycardia when the mothers do moderate to strenuous exercise (Dale, 1982). Many researchers believe that the bradycardia is normal and that there is a return to baseline fetal heart rates within 10-15 minutes after exercise ceases. Prolonged fetal bradycardia and tachycardia are also believed to be signs of fetal hypoxia or stress. Studies have shown no effect on fetal heart rate when healthy women exercise at 70%-80% of their maximal heart rate; in fact, pregnant women who do exercise at these levels have had normal neonatal outcomes (Beller, 1987; Collings, 1985). Most relines for exercise during pregnancy use 140-160 beats per minute as a safe target range for the maternal heart rate. This approximates 70%-80% of the maximal heart rate for the average pregnant woman and is a relatively safe level of exercise during pregnancy.

### Hyperthermia

Hyperthermia has been reported to cause fetal damage and abortion in several animal species when maternal core temperatures reached or exceeded 102° during early gestation (Henswall, 1984). Recent studies have shown that thermal balance is maintained during exercise by several thermoregulatory adaptive mechanisms that are present during pregnancy (Clapp, 1987). Pregnant women should be advised to avoid hot environments, to control the intensity and duration of exercise, and to remain well hydrated in order to limit core temperature increases.

### Premature Delivery and Miscarriage

Despite early animal studies that showed fetal mortality when mothers exercised to exhaustion, human studies show that moderate exercise does not appear to increase the risk of fetal mortality where there is no history of premature delivery or miscarriage (Clapp, 1989; Hall, 1987). A pregnant woman with an incompetent cervix or history or more than one premature delivery or miscarriage may be at greater risk for a recurrence of fetal death and should avoid exercise during pregnancy.

### Decreased Fetal Weight

Many studies in the literature have shown that exercise during pregnancy does not decrease fetal weight or increase the rate of neonatal complications (Kolpa, 1987; Hall, 1987; Curet, 1985).

## Recommendations for the Pregnant Female Athlete

In general, recommendations for exercise training during pregnancy should be individualized (Dale, 1986; Gauthier, 1986). Pregnancy is not the time to begin a new sport or conditioning program. It is important to know the pre-pregnancy fitness and activity levels. There are some relative contraindications to increased exercise during pregnancy, including diabetes, hypertension, anemia, infection, vaginal bleeding, any contractions that persist more than one hour after exercise, phlebitis, extreme fatigue, leaking amniotic fluid, or toxemia (see Table 5C-2).

The sedentary pregnant female who wants to start exercising should begin with a gentle walking or swimming program. Easy-going muscle strengthening and pelvic floor strengthening exercises in prenatal classes are recommended. Water skiing, horseback riding, ice skating, weight-lifting, anaerobic exercises, and strenuous racquet sports that increase core temperature, along with scuba diving (possible decompression sickness of the fetus), should be avoided by all pregnant female athletes.

Non-weight bearing exercises such as biking or swimming are generally preferable. The pregnant woman should allow for changes in balance and timing over time. Body temperature should be monitored frequently during exercise and kept below 101°F maximum. Overheating should be avoided and the pregnant female athlete should keep her maximum heart rate between 140-160

**Table 5C-2. Contraindications to Exercise During Pregnancy**

**General Contraindications**
- Hemodynamically significant heart disease
- Recurrent cervical incompetence
- Current uterine bleeding
- Current ruptured membranes
- Intrauterine growth retardation
- Fetal distress
- Previous miscarriage (more than one)
- Previous premature labor (more than one)
- Uncontrolled hypertension
- Uncontrolled diabetes mellitus
- Uncontrolled renal disease
- Hemodynamically significant anemia

**Relative contraindications**
- Essential hypertension
- Controlled diabetes mellitus
- Excessive obesity
- Malnutrition
- Multiple gestations
- Thyroid disease
- Anemia

beats/min (<85% of maximum heart rate) during exercise. She should consume adequate calories, calcium and iron, and maintain proper hydration. Exercise should be done three times a week at a moderate level of intensity and with adequate emphasis on flexibility.

General and relative contraindications to exercise during pregnancy are represented in Table 5C-2. Pregnant patients with heart disease may experience a marked decrease in cardiac output even in the early stages. They should see a cardiologist to determine the appropriate activity levels. Relative contraindications to exercise during pregnancy exist but an exercise program can be designed which considers the specific needs of the patient.

General guidelines for exercise in the pregnant female should taken into account her level of aerobic training prior to conception. Well trained patients will handle the additional demands of exercise better during pregnancy than will the untrained patient. Sedentary women can begin some type of physical activity during pregnancy so long as they begin at low intensity and increase exercise gradually. The American College of Obstetricians and Gynecologists (ACOG) has developed a set of guidelines for safe exercise during pregnancy that applies to most women. These guidelines have been well received by the public and by physicians and have become the legal standard in some states.

However, these guidelines have also generated controversy. One complaint is that the guidelines are not based on hard data and that they are far too general and conservative.

The ACOG guidelines do not apply to high performance athletes who become pregnant (Gauthier, 1986). They should be considered as a framemark that is modified by the physician according to his/her knowledge of the patient. Signals to stop exercising are shown in Table 5C-3 (Paisley, 1988). The American College of Sports Medicine guidelines on the frequency, intensity, and duration of exercise can be very useful in developing an exercise program for gestational women even though the guidelines were not developed specifically for pregnant women. Most pregnant patients can start exercising up to 75% of predicted maximal heart rate and increase their exercise intensity gradually. Women who have exercised before pregnancy can exercise up to 85% of the predicted maximal heart rate. Most authorities agree that the pregnant patient may easily exercise 3-5 exercise sessions per week as long as the patient continues to gain weight adequately and increases caloric intake to account for the calories used during exercise. Weight-bearing activities may be alternated with non-weight-bearing activities to control any musculoskeletal symptoms that may occur during the exercise cycle.

The following recommendations can be made for the three trimesters of pregnancy. Hot baths, whirlpools, and saunas should be avoided during the first trimester. A strenuous exercise program should not be started by a female athlete who knows she is pregnant. However, it is not necessary to make major changes in an ongoing exer-

**Table 5C-3. Signals to Stop Exercising**

- Breathlessness
- Dizziness
- Headache
- Muscle weakness
- Nausea
- Chest pain or tightness
- Back pain
- Hip or pubic pain
- Difficulty walking
- Generalized edema
- Decreased fetal activity
- Uterine contractions
- Vaginal bleeding
- Amniotic fluid leakage

cise program. During the second trimester, female athletes should not resort to special diets except when hypertension or diabetes mellitus complicate the pregnancy. Foods high in energy content and low in nutritional value should be avoided. A well balanced diet should be prescribed and followed. Exercise during pregnancy is not intended to control body mass but rather to control body tone. Strong muscles may shorten the labor period, make delivery easier for both mother and baby, and hasten the post partum return to optimal fitness.

During the third trimester, exercises that compromise blood flow to the mother's vital organs and the fetus should be avoided. Long periods of standing or lifting heavy objects also should be avoided. Individuals vary considerably in their exercise tolerance during the final trimester and the exercise program may need to be restricted. If training is continued, it should be under close supervision by the physician. Safe exercise during pregnancy which can normalize or improve fetal and maternal outcomes are possible by adhering to these general guidelines and the specific recommendations that follow.

### Specific Recommendations

**Jogging.** Women should not start jogging during pregnancy if they have not been running before. If jogging is begun during pregnancy, it should be at low intensity and frequency levels, with monitoring for symptoms listed in Table 5C-3. As the pregnancy progresses, speed and distance are gradually reduced so that the perceived level of exertion remains the same throughout the program.

**Cycling.** Cycling can be started during pregnancy; a stationary bike is generally safer than a standard bicycle. The serious cyclist may switch from a racing or touring bicycle to an upright model during the last trimester.

**Aerobics.** Generally, low to moderate impact aerobics should be well tolerated by pregnant women up through the third trimester. The ACOG guidelines which restrict the use of the supine position and as bouncing movements after the fourth month of gestation are highly restrictive. These guidelines are controversial and not supported by all authorities.

**Swimming.** Swimming is an excellent aerobic exercise that can be safely initiated during pregnancy. Swimming in excessively cold or hot water should be avoided to minimize the potential effects of hypo- or hyperthermia on the fetus (St John Repovich, 1986).

**Weight-Lifting.** Many pregnant females lift light weights throughout their pregnancy to maintain strength. Proper breathing techniques should be maintained throughout the lifting cycle. Lifting heavy weights, especially by patients with low back problems, or doing exercises that strain the lower back should be avoided.

**Contact Sports.** Because of potential trauma to the abdomen and fetus, pregnant women should avoid collision sports and contact sports such as football, field hockey, basketball, volleyball, gymnastics, and horseback riding. Racquet sports like tennis, racquetball, and squash are believed to be fairly safe. As the pregnancy progresses, the intensity of participation should be reduced to prevent injuries. Waterskiing should be avoided because of the possibility of high speed falls and the potential for forceful entry of water into the uterus and subsequent miscarriage (Mullinax, 1986).

**Scuba Diving.** Inexperienced divers should avoid scuba diving during pregnancy because of the potential for decompression sickness, maternal acidbase and nitrogen imbalances, and intravascular air embolism in the fetus. Some researchers say that experienced pregnant divers may continue on a conservative basis, with dives not exceeding 33 feet in depth or lasting longer than 30 minutes (Bergfeld, 1987).

**Downhill and Cross Country Skiing.** The experienced pregnant patient can continue to ski cautiously during pregnancy. Downhill skiing may present a significant danger during the later stages of pregnancy, especially if the skier is inexperienced. Healthy women have been known to cross country ski up to the day of delivery without problems.

**Ice Skating.** Ice skating is likely to be more dangerous than snow skiing because of its potential for falls on hard ice. Skating should be pursued only with extreme caution and only by very experienced skaters (St John Repovich, 1986).

There are many benefits to exercise and pregnancy and the present standard guidelines are considered conservative (Leaf, 1989). Exercise during pregnancy leads to shorter labors, easier deliveries, and increased self-esteem. Following a vaginal delivery, exercise may be started within 1 week and water sports can begin when all bleeding stops (Leaf, 1989). After a Cesarian section the general recommendation is to have 6-10 weeks of an exercise free period. The scar following a Cesarian section is maximally strong 21 days post-surgery, but should not be stressed prior to that time. After a dilation and curettage, weight training and aerobic exercise can be started within 2 days and water sports within 1 week.

## Post-Partum Exercises

Depending on the type of delivery and its progress, exercise programs should be resumed as soon as possible within the comfort range of the patient. Even before leaving the hospital, the mother can begin restoring muscular tone to the abdomen and pelvis to reduce the likelihood of urinary incontinence or a prolapsed uterus. During the post-partum period Kegel exercises to strengthen the muscles of the pelvic floor are recommended. Multiple exercises and stretching programs are outlined in other textbooks. Exercise promotes improved blood flow and may prevent the complications of varicose veins, cramps, edema, and thrombophlebitis.

## Summary of Exercise Prescription for the Female Athlete

Exercise can be prescribed for females of all ages if the requirements for a properly designed program are followed. Specific information relative to the exercise needs and concerns of the female athlete have been outlined here and should be considered when a physician designs an exercise program. A properly designed program will prevent undue injury and lead to more successful, long-term, enjoyable exercise for female athletes (Warren, 1991).

## SECTION D.
## THE OLDER ATHLETE

The number of older adults in America has increased markedly over the past 15 years. More than 10% of the U.S. population is now 65 years of age or older, as compared with less than 5% at the turn of the century. The U.S. Census Bureau predicts that by 2030, approximately 20%-21% of the population will be aged 65 and older.

The aging process represents a gradual decline in the ability of an individual to adapt to environmental changes. As the U.S. population ages, health care providers will be challenged to meet their special needs, especially helping them to remain functional. One way this goal may be met is through programs of regular exercise. Physical activity has more potential for promoting healthy aging than anything science or medicine has to offer today (Shepard, 1989). Early retirement, more leisure time, and an increased awareness of the benefits of exercise have prompted many older people to increase their activities. The upsurge has meant an increased number of acute and chronic injuries in this age group.

Some physicians tell their older patients with exercised-induced symptoms to stop their activity altogether but this is not warranted. We will examine the importance and benefits of exercise in older people and evaluate the most common types of injuries. There is little evidence that the elderly are less physically active than younger people; in fact, exercise may increase longevity. The growing number of older people and their role in society makes it imperative that health professionals understand their needs and problems.

Before instituting an exercise program in an older person, consider the exercise goals of the patient, the availability of equipment and facilities, and cost of the program. Do a thorough assessment of the patient's health, reviewing: (a) appropriate history and physical, (b) assessment of nutritional status, present activity level, smoking habits, alcohol use, and weight, (c) diseases that lead to decreased exercise tolerance, (d) orthopedic problems and disabilities that produce physical limitations, (e) any prior injuries and rehabilitation, (f) the patient's current physical condition and training status, and (g) medications that may interfere with or alter the exercise response.

Physical changes that occur during aging include decreased cardiac output (decreased stroke volume, decreased heart rate); decreased ventilatory capacity, decreased pulmonary blood flow, decreased aerobic power, and decreased physical work capacity; decreased body muscle mass and strength, decreased nerve conduction, decreased elasticity of tissue, and progressive bone loss; hypertension (blood pressure greater than 150/95) in 50% of patients over age 80, and increased potential for developing heat stress (see Table 5D-1) (Clarke, 1983).

Gerontologists distinguish three categories of senior citizens: "old-old" persons over 75 years of age, "young-old" persons under 75 years of age, and "athletic-old" persons who have maintained fitness throughout their lives. These older patients

Table 5D-1. Biological Functional Changes Between the Ages of 30 and 70

| Biological Function | Change |
|---|---|
| Work capacity (%) | ↓25-30 |
| Cardiac output | ↓30 |
| Maximum heart rate (beats·min$^{-1}$) | ↓24 |
| Blood pressure (mm Hg) | |
|   Systolic | ↑10-40 |
|   Diastolic | ↑5-10 |
| Respiration (%) | |
|   Vital capacity | ↓40-50 |
|   Residual volume | ↑30-50 |
| Basal metabolic rate (%) | ↓8-12 |
| Musculature (%) | |
|   Muscle mass | ↓25-30 |
|   Hand grip strength | ↓25-30 |
| Nerve conduction velocity (%) | ↓10-15 |
| Flexibility (%) | ↓20-30 |
| Bone (%) | |
|   Women | ↓25-30 |
|   Men | ↓15-20 |
| Renal function (%) | ↓30-50 |

(From *Phys Sportsmed* 11(8):92, August 1983)

should be considered when looking at maximal oxygen uptake. Old-old persons can reach a maximal oxygen uptake of 2.4 METS (7-14 ml oxygen uptake per kg/body weight). Young-old persons can attain maximum oxygen uptake of 5.7 METS (17.5-24.5 ml/kg). The athletic-old can achieve maximal oxygen uptake greater than 10 METS (Fitzgerald, 1985).

Among the benefits of exercise for older adults are improved muscle tone, range of motion, posture, coordination and physical work capacity; increased VO$_2$max, decreased blood pressure; improved weight control and body image; a reduction in the amount of low back pain; an improvement in accident prevention; improved social contacts and sleep patterns and a decreased incidence of depression; and improved functional ability and independence (Williams, 1982).

Recent studies have demonstrated that elderly participants in regular exercise programs will show a gradual training effect, although the elderly need more time to adapt (Fiatarone, 1990). The benefits of physical conditioning on cardiovascular systems in older patients are similar to those observed in younger patients even though the initial baseline in older patients is lower (Ninimaa, 1978). Respiratory fitness does not appear to limit exercise capacity in normal individuals of any age. The ventilation changes that occur with aging do not preclude significant improvement in aerobic capacity with training (Fitzgerald, 1985). An active life style appears to delay the natural lengthening of neurovascular reaction times that comes with aging but there is little evidence that sedentary elders enjoy the positive effect on reaction time.

Much of the early gains in strength elderly people achieve on a training program are due to increased neuronal activation rather than muscle hypertrophy (Elia, 1991). The expected improvement in strength from resistance training is difficult to assess, because strength increases are affected by the participant's initial level of strength and his potential for improvement which is, in turn, affected by the presence of chronic disease. Elderly patients with arthritis can increase VO$_2$max, flexibility, and muscle strength with low intensity exercise programs with no adverse effects on joints (Ike, 1989; Minor, 1989). Mean bone mineral content can increase 20% over controls with high intensity training. Studies also confirm that exercise is beneficial in increasing mineral content in the elderly with senile osteoporosis (Aloia, 1978). Many of the benefits of exercise have been well documented in other textbooks.

The goals of the exercise evaluation are: 1) to determine the appropriate exercise (type, frequency, intensity, and duration) for the patient; 2) to evaluate any chronic health problems that may compromise physical capacity; 3) to become aware of medical conditions that preclude vigorous activity; 4) to instruct the patient how to start his exercise gradually and increase the activity level appropriately; 5) to understand the absolute contraindications for exercise participation; 6) to perform a thorough history, physical examination, and appropriate lab tests, urinalysis, EKG and graded exercise test (GXT). The elderly may be at more risk from the GXT than the increased incidence of coronary artery disease. After age 65, 30% of patients develop myocardial ischemia during exercise so that the use of a modified GXT protocol is imperative (ACSM, 1988; Barry, 1986; Elkowitz, 1986; Laslett, 1980; Mean, 1981).

Patient education regarding exercise for the older adult should include: 1) specificity about the exercise prescribed; 2) instructions to exercise three to four times a week with proper warmup and cool down, and not at all during hot/humid weather; 3) information on how to gradually increase activity from week to week; 4) acquainting the patient with the significance of muscles or joint pain and instructing them to heed the warning signs of fatigue and localized muscle or joint pain (Elkowitz & Elkowitz, 1986; Hanson, Giese, 1980; Smith, 1983).

The goals of an exercise program for elders should include increasing cardiovascular fitness, endurance, flexibility, balance, and strength through walking, jogging, swimming, or biking; avoiding running, jumping rope, and heavy weight lifting; avoiding isometric exercise in hypertensive patients; staying within the aerobic limits established by the GXT or alternative evaluation; establishing a target heart rate of 60%-75% of maximum heart rate; and making patients with decreased visual or hearing acuity aware of the dangers of exercising without special precautions.

Some of the common injuries in the elderly include: 1) strains and sprains which are often secondary to hearing or visual loss or unsteady gait; 2) degenerative joint disease which may affect as many as 50% of those aged 50 years and 85% of those aged 70 years; 3) fractures, especially of the femur, wrist, and vertebrae (femoral neck fractures are 2.5 times more frequent in females over age 50); 4) rheumatoid arthritis which affects 15% of females and 5% of males over age 65; 5) an increased incidence of gout over age 60, and 6) other musculoskeletal problems which account for the largest number of visits to physicians — low back injuries, acute cervical strains, bursitis and tendinitis of the shoulder, patellofemoral dysfunction, and chronic ankle injuries. Hypothermia and hyperthermia also are common in older people group and preventative measures should be discussed.

Principles of injury treatment in the elderly athlete include proper analysis of the specific movement or activity producing the injury and then modifying it, provision of an appropriate and aggressive rehabilitation program, and instruction in the maintenance of strength and as much normal muscle and tendon range of motion as possible through an appropriate flexibility program.

With these guidelines in mind, a safe and effective exercise program can be developed for the older patient who is interested in sports and exercise. The more competitive adult will pursue an active program with an increased focus on flexibility, strength training, agility and neuromuscular skill attainment as well as to a high level of cardiorespiratory fitness (Simons-Morton et al, 1988).

## SECTION E.
## THE SEDENTARY ADULT

In the past 30 years, there have been more than 40 published studies on the effect of regular physical activity. Most sought to learn whether people who are active are healthier than less active or sedentary people (Laporte & Blair, 1985). Not all studies support the hypothesis that active people are healthier, but most demonstrate that active individuals fare better, particularly with regard to chronic disease. Coronary artery disease is the major one for which we have evidence that active people are healthier. They have substantially lower mortality rates.

Studies from the past 10 years have demonstrated other potential benefits of regular activity. Paffenbarger (1986) did a study of Harvard alumni that demonstrated a lower total mortality rate in active people. Such disorders as obesity, osteoporosis, and hypertension were less prevalent in the active group. The amount and type of activity that is beneficial seems to be well within the capacity of most adults. The risk for these diseases can be lowered by activities like walking, stair climbing, hiking, even the routine activities of everyday life. Healthy people should try to reduce other risk factors for heart disease by lowering dietary cholesterol, avoiding cigarettes, and treating hypertension if it is present. This is routine advice for patients likely to develop heart disease. A comprehensive approach that includes these behavioral modifications, treatment techniques, and a regular exercise program can significantly change the long term health of active individuals (Simons-Morton et al., 1988).

Before giving an exercise prescription to a sedentary adult, the physician should begin with a thorough history, and physical, and appropriate laboratory testing. Some type of stress test should be performed in patients with multiple primary risk factors and/or symptoms of coronary heart disease. Testing protocols that use constant treadmill speeds with gradual work increments and increases in grade are available and are suitable for the elderly (Ciscovick, 1984; Smith, 1983). The goal of the exercise treadmill test should be to express the patient's full range of exercise performance over a reasonable period of time. A bicycle ergometer is another useful method of exercise testing in the elderly population. Grossly overweight patients and those in the coronary-prone age (males aged 40-49) should to undergo stress testing (Goodman, 1985). We strongly recommend that healthy patients undergo some form of submaximal exercise test to determine functional capacity in conjunction with a general fitness assessment.

Absolute contraindications for exercise training and testing have already been presented. Exercise testing is useful in those patients where the closer monitoring of the exercise programs may be needed. These patients should undergo a medically supervised test for functional capacity. Patients with the following conditions require supervised stress testing (Smith, 1988):

- recent myocardial infarction or post-coronary artery bypass surgery;
- presence of a pace maker — fixed rate or demand;
- use of chronotropic or inotropic cardiac medications;
- presence of morbid obesity combined with multiple coronary risk factors;
- occurrence of ST-segment depression at rest;
- severe hypertension,
- intermittent claudication.

Both medical and environmental conditions that require moderation of activity or caution in prescribing exercise are listed in Tables 5E-1 and 5E-2. All exercise programs for sedentary adults or beginning exercisers should follow the requirements of proper exercise prescription described earlier. A simple check list such as a Physical Activity Readiness Questionnaire (PARQ) along with an updated version of the Cornell Medical Index can help identify individuals who need detailed clinical examination before a training program is initiated (Shepard, 1986). Peripheral neuropathy, gait disturbance, impaired equilibrium, or orthostatic hypertension, or degenerative joint disease should alert the physician to the increased risk of falls or other injury. Joint stability and range of motion must be assessed before exercise so that activities can be adjusted if that is needed (Fitzgerald, 1985). All exercise programs should include warm-up and flexibility and strength training exercises.

## Intensity of Exercise

The most important variable in any exercise prescription is *intensity*, but it is the most difficult factor to determine. Intensity is expressed as a percentage of maximum heart rate (MHR), heart rate reserve (maximum HR- resting HR), or functional capacity ($VO_2$max or METs). The intensity rate for training depends on the initial fitness level of the adult. Unconditioned individuals have a low threshold for improving functional capacity, whereas conditioned patients require a greater intensity level to increase their aerobic fitness.

### Determining Intensity by Heart Rate

Maximum heart rate is determined through a linear relationship between the heart rate and $VO_2$max. Intensity is expressed as a percentage of maximum heart rate ($HR_{max}$), where $HR_{max}$ = 220 HR-age. Intensity levels of 60%-80% of maximal heart rate can induce training. These values correspond to approximately 60%-80% of functional capacity. The predicted maximal heart rate in the above formula deviates by ± 15 beats/min from the actual value using standard deviation tests.

The Karvonen method of prescribing exercise intensity is based on the following formula using heart rate reserve (HRR): HRR = ($HR_{max}$ - $HR_{rest}$).

The training heart rate (THR) is calculated as follows:

$$THR = [(.60 \text{ to } .85) \times (HR_{max} - HR_{rest})] + HR_{rest}$$

where (.60 to .85) represents a potential range of training intensities from 60%-85% of maximal heart

---

**Table 5E-1. Conditions Requiring Caution in Exercise Prescription**

1. Viral infection or cold
2. Chest pain
3. Irregular heart beat
4. Exercise-Induced Asthma
5. Prolonged, unaccustomed physical activity
6. Conduction disturbances (LBBB, complete AV block, or bifascicular block with or without first degree block)

**Table 5E-2. Conditions Requiring Moderation of Activity**

1. Extreme heat and high relative humidity
2. Extreme cold, especially when strong winds are present
3. Following heavy meals
4. Exposure to high altitudes (greater than 1700 meters)
5. Significant musculoskeletal injuries

rate. Intensity should begin at low levels and increases gradually as fitness improves. This method has an advantage over simple measures of maximal heart rate because variability in the athlete's resting heart rate is accounted for in the formula (Goodman, 1985). Table 5E-3 shows average maximum heart rates and THR for various age groups.

### Exercise Prescription Using METS

Intensity of exercise may be prescribed in MET units (1 MET = $O_2$ consumption of 3.5 ml/kg/min/m$^2$) once the functional capacity has been determined. This method allows prescription of activity only where documented metabolic costs are available (Table 5E-4). A range of 60%-85% of maximum METs (MMET) corresponds to low and peak conditioning intensity levels. An average training intensity (TMET) is calculated as follows:

$$TMET = [(MMET \times 60) + MMET]/100.$$

Concurrent measurements of heart rate and metabolic rate (METs) during a graded exercise test allows for interpretation of functional capacity at any heart rate. Since 1 MET = 4.2 kilojoules/kg/hr/m$^2$, energy expenditure per session also can be determined (1 kcal=4.18 kjoule).

## Duration

The exercise must last long enough to increase energy expenditure by at least 12,000 kilojoules or 287 calories. Short periods of exercise (5-10 minutes) can induce cardiovascular training if performed at high intensity levels (90%-95% of functional capacity). The ideal duration of exercise for most athletes is 20-60 minutes of continuous aerobic activity performed at moderate intensity. Exercise sessions should be extended gradually from the initial 15-20 minutes as cardiovascular endurance improves. High intensity programs have poor compliance and account for a high incidence of musculoskeletal injuries. Because fat utilization increases significantly after approximately 20 minutes of light to moderate exercise, body fat reduction will be better during longer periods of aerobic exercise.

## Frequency

The threshold for improvement of aerobic power seems to be two sessions of exercise per week, but intensity must be relatively high if gains are to occur. The minimum exercise frequency recommended for adults is 3 sessions a week. This is an optimal frequency for people who are beginning exercise programs and allows for sufficient rest to prevent musculoskeletal overuse syndromes. Obese adults or those with low functional capability (< 3 METs) may do better with a program of repeated exercise sessions of five minutes each several times a day. When functional capacity improves, one or two longer daily sessions may be undertaken.

As functional capacity improves, exercise sessions usually can be increased to three or more a week. The program should include easier days when both the duration and intensity of exercise are reduced. Five days of exercise per week is sufficient to obtain optimal fitness levels. Progression from three to five days a week should occur gradually over a four week period, and include no more than three intense sessions weekly. Exercising seven days a week does not further improve aerobic power and causes overuse problems. The exception to this general rule is the obese adult who can profit from daily low intensity sessions aimed at making the energy expenditure necessary to reduce body fat.

Isotonic resistance training or other strength training methods should be incorporated into a regular aerobic program no more than two or three days a week. A minimum of 8 to 10 exercises involving the major muscle groups should be performed, with 8 to 12 repetitions to near fatigue for each exercise. A need for longer recuperative

Table 5E-3. Average Maximum Heart Rates by Age and Recommended Target Heart Rates (THR) for Normal Asymptomatic Participants During Exercise*

| Age (Yrs) | 20-29 | 30-39 | 40-49 | 50-59 | 60-69 |
| --- | --- | --- | --- | --- | --- |
| HR$_{max}$ | 190 | 185 | 180 | 170 | 160 |
| Peak THR 0.9 (HR$_{max}$-75)+75 | 179 | 174 | 170 | 161 | 152 |
| Lowest THR 0.6 (HR$_{max}$-75)+75 | 144 | 141 | 138 | 132 | 126 |
| Average THR 0.7 (HR$_{max}$-75)+75 | 155 | 152 | 149 | 141 | 135 |

*Modified from the American College of Sports Medicine: *Guidelines for Graded Exercise Testing and Exercise Prescription*, 2nd ed. Philadelphia, Lea & Febiger, 1980. Reprinted from Fox, E. *The Physiological Basis of Physical Education and Athletics* 3rd ed. Philadelphia, Saunders College Publishing, 1981, p. 412.

periods after performing heavy resistance work makes the rest period necessary.

## Exercise Mode

The focus of any exercise program should be on components such as cardiorespiratory endurance, body composition, flexibility, muscular strength, and endurance. Reduced joint mobility is often secondary to arthritis and is a disabling condition for many elderly patients. An exercise program should be designed to maintain adequate levels of strength and dynamic flexibility in the major joints. Accidents are a major cause of injury and death in the elderly and many of them can be

**Table 5E-4. Approximate Metabolic Cost of Activities***

| Intensity (70-kg Person) | Endurance Promoting | Occupational | Recreational |
|---|---|---|---|
| 1 1/2-2 mets<br>4-7 ml·kg$^{-1}$<br>2-2 1/2 kcal·min$^{-1}$ | Too low in energy level | Desk work, driving auto, electric calculating machine operation, light housework-polishing furniture or washing clothes | Standing, strolling (1 mph), flying, motorcycling, playing cards, sewing, knitting |
| 2-3 mets<br>7-11 ml·kg$^{-1}$·min$^{-1}$<br>2 1/2-4 kcal·min$^{-1}$ | Too low in energy level unless capacity is very low | Auto repair, radio and television repair, janitorial work, bartending, riding lawn mower, light woodworking | Level walking (2 mph), level bicycling (5 mph), billiards, bowling, skeet shooting, shuffleboard, powerboat driving, golfing with power cart, canoeing, horseback riding at a walk |
| 3-4 mets<br>11-14 ml·kg$^{-1}$·min$^{-1}$<br>4-5 kcal·min$^{-1}$ | Yes, if continuous and if target heart rate is reached | Brick laying, plastering, wheelbarrow (100 lb load), machine assembly, welding (moderate load), cleaning windows, mopping floors, vacuuming, pushing light power mower | Walking (3 mph), bicycling (6 mph), horseshoe pitching, volleyball (6 person, noncompetitive), golfing (pulling bag cart), archery, sailing (handling small boat), fly fishing (standing in waders), horseback riding (trotting), badmitton (social doubles) |
| 4-5 mets<br>14-18 ml·kg$^{-1}$·min$^{-1}$<br>5-6 kcal·min$^{-1}$ | Recreational activities promote endurance. Occupational activities must be continuous, lasting longer than two minutes | Painting, masonry, paperhanging, light carpentry, scrubbing floors, raking leaves, hoeing | Walking (3 1/2 mph), bicycling (8 mph), table tennis, golfing (carrying clubs), dancing (foxtrot), badminton (singles), tennis (doubles), many calisthenics, ballet |
| 5-6 mets<br>18-21 ml·kg$^{-1}$·min$^{-1}$<br>6-7 kcal·min$^{-1}$ | Yes | Digging garden, shoveling light earth | Walking (4 mph), bicycling (10 mph), canoeing (4 mph), horseback riding (posting to trotting), stream fishing (walking in light current in waders), ice or roller skating (9 mph) |
| 6-7 mets<br>21-25 ml·kg$^{-1}$·min$^{-1}$<br>7-8 kcal·min$^{-1}$ | Yes | Shoveling 10 times/min (4 1/2 kg or 10 lb), splitting wood, snow shoveling, hand lawn mowing | Walking (5 mph), bicycling (11 mph), competitive badminton, tennis (singles), folk and square dancing, light downhill skiing, ski touring (2 1/2 mph), water skiing, swimming (20 yards·min$^{-1}$) |

*Energy range will vary depending on skill of exerciser, pattern of rest pauses, environmental temperature, etc. Caloric values depend on body size (more for larger person). Table provides reasonable relative strenuousness values, however.

Table 5E-4. Approximate Metabolic Cost of Activities* (*Continued*)

| Intensity (70-kg Person) | Endurance Promoting | Occupational | Recreational |
|---|---|---|---|
| 7-8 mets<br>25-28 ml·kg$^{-1}$·min$^{-1}$<br>8-10 kcal·min$^{-1}$ | Yes | Digging ditches, carrying 36 kg or 80 lb, sawing hardwood | Jogging (5 mph), bicycling (12 mph), horseback riding (gallop), vigorous downhill skiing, basketball, mountain climbing, ice hockey, canoeing (5 mph), touch football, paddleball |
| 8-9 mets<br>28-32 ml·kg$^{-1}$·min$^{-1}$<br>10-11 kcal·min$^{-1}$ | Yes | Shoveling 10 times/min (5 1/2 kg or 14 lb) | Running (5 1/2 mph), bicycling (13 mph), ski touring (4 mph), squash (social), handball (social), fencing, basketball (vigorous), swimming (30 yards·min$^{-1}$), rope skipping |
| 10+ mets<br>32+ ml·kg$^{-1}$·min$^{-1}$<br>11+ kcal·min$^{-1}$ | Yes | Shoveling 10 times (7 1/2 kg or 16 lb) | Running (6 mph = 10 mets, 7 mph = 11 1/2 mets, 8 mph = 13 1/2 mets, 9 mph = 15 mets, 10 mph = 17 mets), ski touring (5+ mph), handball (competitive), squash competitive), swimming (greater than 40 yards·min$^{-1}$) |

*Energy range will vary depending on skill of exerciser, pattern of rest pauses, environmental temperature, etc. Caloric values depend on body size (more for larger person). Table provides reasonable relative strenuousness values, however.

linked to inadequate muscle strength. Strength deficits impair a person's ability to control body weight, or handle external objects, or perform activities of daily living. Properly designed and graded resistance exercises promote maintenance of acceptable levels of muscle strength.

The most critical factor in an older person's ability to function independently is his/her ability to move without assistance. Those who maintain adequate levels of cardiorespiratory fitness and acceptable body composition are more apt to retain that ability longer than those who become obese or allow their muscular and cardiorespiratory systems to deteriorate. The preferred types of aerobic exercise are exercises that use large muscle groups in a rhythmic and continuous manner. Different activities affect the heart rate differently so that strict attention should be paid to the energy requirements for each specific exercise or sport (Table 5E-4).

Similar cardiovascular training can be generated by jogging/running, swimming, bicycling, or cross country skiing programs. Less intense activities such as golf, bowling, and archery offer little training stimulus because heart rates rarely exceed 100 beats/min. Rope skipping has become popular but it can produce excessively high heart rates and should be avoided by people with restricted exercise intensity levels. Tennis and squash are adequate training stimuli if the skill level is high enough. Squash does involve rapid starting and stopping and it increases systolic blood pressure and myocardial oxygen demands. For those reasons, it should be prescribed only for healthy, risk-free patients.

Sustained isometric activities against heavy resistance are strongly discouraged in unconditioned, hypertensive, and coronary-prone patients. These activities provide little or no improvement in VO$_2$max. Weight training programs should have enough intensity to elicit a strength training effect while minimizing the risk of musculoskeletal injury or an elevation in blood pressure. The exercise should be enjoyable and the patient should be able to see improvement. This increases motivation and compliance.

### Aerobic Activities

Continuous and intermittent (interval) exercise can elicit a training response (Shepard, 1989). Interval training (high intensity, short duration, with rest periods) is widely recognized and is a form of training practiced by most endurance athletes. High intensity exercise may be performed without significant accumulations of lactic acid. The high speed training should result in faster performance times. A sedentary adult can accomplish more total work with less physiologic stress by doing interval training.

We recommend prescribing exercise on a run-walk basis initially. As functional capacity improves, a higher energy output may be performed more continuously (see Table 5E-5). Activities that yield a constant heart rate response (walking/jogging, jogging/running, cross-country skiing, swimming, cycling) are preferred, as close control of both duration and intensity of exercise is desired. More intense interval activities are recommended only after an adequate period of continuous training (usually six to ten weeks).

Flexibility exercises and calisthenics should be performed during the warm-up and cool-down periods. They should be done slowly, utilizing static stretching techniques (reach and hold). Bounce-stretching beyond the normal range of motion of the muscle is ill-advised and may lead to acute soft tissue injury. Attempting to build muscular strength through dynamic, high resistance, low repetition exercises should be strongly discouraged in patients who are poorly conditioned, hypertensive, or at risk of cardiovascular disease. Dynamic and static strength exercises, especially when combined with a valsalva maneuver, may cause an excessive rise in systemic blood pressure, reduce venous return, and increase the after-load of the heart. Low resistance, high repetition strength exercises without breath holding are a better alternative.

Floor/surfaces should be evaluated and the patient's shoes should have firm, gripping soles that give good traction. Reduced muscle strength and degenerative changes in bones and joints as a result of aging may produce higher injury rates in certain activities. Non-weight-bearing activities such as swimming and cycling have many advantages for sustaining aerobic activity while decreasing the effects of gravity on the joints of the lower extremity. Road hazards and falls on the pool deck are the potential sources of injury for these activities. Stationary cycling is recommended for the less healthy adult. Cross country skiing on flat, well groomed trails is an excellent athletic activity for the elderly. Impaired coordination and osteoporosis increase the risk of injury, and alternate forms of exercise should be considered in icy conditions. Rhythmic calisthenics and low impact aerobics can provide both sustained activity and opportunities for gentle warm-up and cool-down periods.

Proper counseling is essential to avoid overuse or sudden twisting injuries. Access to aerobic machines such as Nordic Track,® Stair Climber,® and Concept Rowing® may add to the aerobic fitness potential for the elderly. However, lack of access to these machines may limit continued participation. The exercise potential in daily living should

Table 5E-5. Average Work Intensities for Activities Suitable For Exercise Prescription*

| Activity | Average Work Intensity | |
|---|---|---|
| | METs | Kcal/hr (75 kg) |
| Walking, 0% grade | | |
| 2.5 mph | 3.0 | 225 |
| 3.0 | 3.3 | 240 |
| 3.5 | 3.5 | 262 |
| 4.0 | 4.6 | 345 |
| Jogging-running | | |
| 4.5 mph | 5.7** | 375-490 |
| 5.0 | 8.4 | 630 |
| 6.0 | 10.0 | 750 |
| 7.0 | 11.4 | 855 |
| 8.0 | 12.8 | 960 |
| Cycling (ergometer) | | |
| 300 kpm | 3.7 | 278 |
| 450 | 5.0 | 375 |
| 600 | 6.0 | 450 |
| 750 | 7.0 | 525 |
| 900 | 8.5 | 630 |
| 1050 | 10.0 | 750 |
| 1200 | 11.0 | 825 |
| 1500 | 13.5 | 1010 |
| Swimming, crawl*** | | |
| 20 yr/min | 6.0 | 420 |
| 30 | 9.0 | 675 |
| 40 | 12.0 | 900 |
| Games (average intensity) | | |
| Basketball | 7-15 | 525-1125 |
| Volleyball | 5-12 | 375-900 |
| Soccer | 7-15 | 525-1125 |
| Handball | 8-12 | 600-900 |
| Tennis | 6-10 | 450-750 |

*From Hanson, P.G., Giese, M.D. and Corliss, R.J. Clinical guidelines for exercise training. *Postgrad Med* 67:120, 1980.
**Metabolic cost of jogging at 4 to 5 mph is variable owing to the transition between fast walk and slow jog.
***Metabolic cost of swimming is highly variable owing to efficiency, buoyancy, and technique; values may vary by 25 per cent.

be used to supplement formal exercise. Walking to the store, hedge trimming, painting, and gardening assist in improving fitness. Many stairways are available and can provide valuable sources for physical training if the individual's vision and balance are good.

All exercise sessions should include a warm-up period, the endurance phase, and a cool-down period. The warm-up period should last 5-10 minutes and consists of calisthenics, stretching exercises, and slow jogging or walking. The endurance phase involves exercising at the prescribed duration and intensity level. A gradual cool-down phase lasts 5-10 minutes and consists of exercises similar to those used during warm-up. Abrupt cessation of exercise, especially in warm, humid temperatures may cause venous pooling, circulatory collapse with syncope, vertigo, nausea, and possibly myocardial ischemia. Hot showers, saunas, and whirlpools should be avoided until well after the cool-down period and they are contraindicated in patients with coronary heart disease.

## Monitoring Exercise

Palpation of the carotid or radial pulse is the easiest method to monitor intensity and progression of exercise. This method can be as accurate as telemetry. Wrist palpation avoids the possibility of reflex hypotension that can occur with overly vigorous carotid massage. During the first sessions of exercise, patients should stop after three to five minutes of exercise and locate the radial pulse. The pulse is counted for six seconds and this number is multiplied by 10 to yield a per minute rate. Pulse counting should begin immediately because the heart rate decreases rapidly after exercise ends.

## Progression of the Exercise Program

Increases in intensity, frequency, and duration of exercise can be made as the athlete becomes more cardiovascularly fit. The rate of progression is difficult to predict because it depends on the individual athlete and his exercise goals, and upon the training environment. The American College of Sports Medicine recommends a three phase exercise progression that will allow an individual to attain optimal fitness without undue risk of musculoskeletal injuries. The program can be obtained from the ACSM.

The initial stage of exercise includes the first five weeks of the program. Stretching, light calisthenics, and low intensity aerobics are introduced so as to avoid undue discomfort that might be discouraging. The aerobic phase should be started at a lower intensity level than what it will be over time. The athlete is ready to progress when there is a 3-8 beat/min decrease in heart rate during the aerobic exercise phase, voluntary adoption of a slightly faster jogging/walking pace, and an improvement in functional capacity demonstrated by exercise testing.

Objective measurements can provide useful indications for exercise progression, as can the athlete's level of fatigue, facial expression, breathing pattern, perceived exertion, and movement patterns.

When the program first begins, the aerobic sessions should last 12-15 minutes. The athlete should attempt to expend 800 kilojoules per session (approximately 200 kcal) during the first week of training, and try to reach the recommended 1200 kilojoules (approximately 300 kcal) per session by the end of the first phase. The second phase of the program commonly lasts from week 6 to week 27. Exercise duration is extended and intensity is gradually raised from 60% to 70%-90%. If the patient's functional capacity is low, the transition from walking to jogging is best accomplished by first using a discontinuous walk/run pattern and gradually progressing to a more steady and continuous pattern.

The third or maintenance phase of exercise is reached after six months of regular activity. At this point, the athlete is exercising at 70%-90% of estimated functional capacity for at least 45-60 minutes, four to five times per week. Compliance is important as are the exercise goals of the athlete if the program is to continue to satisfy the participant's needs over long periods. Other aerobic activities should be introduced during this period, not only for variety but also to avoid overtraining of selected muscles and to diminish the potential for overuse injuries.

## Summary

It is important to encourage sedentary adults to enter regular exercise programs. Individual patients/athletes respond in different ways to any exercise program so that the exercise prescription should be set up with a specific individual in mind. The program should appeal to the patient and conform to family leisure and business schedules. Availability of equipment and costs of the program should be considered. The use of training diaries and follow-up tests to monitor progress provides external feedback along with the usual rewards of improved well-being and vigor experienced by the athlete. Physician support and encouragement improves compliance and helps determine the effectiveness of the program.

Older athletes should be told that the early stages of exercise are most uncomfortable, that initial improvements in fitness levels are rapid, but that further improvements occur much more slowly. The athlete should be well aware of the potential problems associated with increasing any of the variables of intensity, duration, or frequency too rapidly. The concept of maintaining optimal fitness should be stressed. Most adult athletes will find it difficult to show continued improvement in fitness as they did during the early stages of their exercise program. The musculoskeletal system is prone to overuse injuries when training progresses too fast. Adequate rest periods between exercise bouts should be stressed to avoid overuse injuries caused by errors in the training regimen.

Appropriate exercise prescription for the sedentary adult is easy to provide. The primary care physician can use the principles outlined here and encourage safe and effective exercise for all adult patients.

**REFERENCES**

*Section A. General Principles*

Dishman, R.K. Biologic influences on exercise adherence. *Res. Quart. for Ex. and Sport* 52, 143-159, 1981.
Fitzgerald, P.L. Exercise for the elderly. *Med Clinics of North Am* 69(1):189, 1985.
Fox, E.L. Physical training: methods and effects. *Orthop. Clin. North Am.* 8:533-548, 1977.
Taylor, R.B. Pre-exercise evaluation: which procedures are really needed? *Consultant*, April:94-101, 1983.

*Section B. The Young Athlete*

Gilliam, T.B., Freedson, P.S. Effects of a 12-week school fitness program on peak $VO_2$ body composition, and blood lipids in 7 to 9 year old children. *In J Sports Med* 1:73-8, 1980.
Hamilton, P., Andrew, G.M. Influence of growth and athletic training on heart and lung functions. *Eur J Appl Physiol* 36:27- 38, 1976.
Harvey, J.S. Nutritional management of the adolescent athlete. *Clin Sports Med* 3:671-78, 1984.
Lamb, D.R. Proper nutrition and hydration in athletics. Read before the 1985 Sports Medicine Congress/Exposition, Indianapolis, Ind., July 1985.
Larson, R.L., McMahan, R.O. The epiphyses and the childhood athlete. *JAMA* 196:607-612, 1966.
Marino, D.D., King, J.C. Nutritional concerns during adolescence. *Pediatr Clin North Am*, 27:125-39, 1980.
McKeag, D.B., Fuller, R., Bakker-Arkema, F.W. Serial treadmill testing in children and adolescent competitive swimmers — a demographic study. *Med Sci Sports* 9:53-4, 1977.

McKeag, D.B. Adolescents and exercise. *J of Adol Health Care* 7:121s, 1986.
Seefeldt, V. Physical fitness guidelines for preschool children. Proceedings of the National Conference on Physical Fitness and Sports for All. Washington, DC, February 1980.
Vrijens, J. Muscle strength development in the pre- and post-pubescent age. *Medicine and Sport* 11:152-8, 1978.
Wilmore, J.H. Physical conditioning of the young athlete. In: Smith, N.J., ed. *Sports Medicine for Children and Youth*. Columbus, Ohio, 10th Ross Roundtable, p. 63, 1979.

*Section C. The Female Athlete*

Beller, J.M., Dolmy, E.G. Effect of an aerobic endurance exercise program on maternal and fetal heart rate during the second and third trimester. *Med Science Sports and Exercise* 19:S5, 1987.
Bergfeld, J.A., Martin, M.C., Shangold, M.M., Warren, M.P. Women in athletics: five management problems. *Patient Care* 21:60-64, 73- 74, 76-80, 82, 1987.
Bonen, A., Keizer, H.A. Athletic menstrual cycle irregularity: endocrine response to exercise and training. *Phys Sportsmed* 12(8):78-94, 1984.
Brooks-Gunn, J., Warren, M.P., Hamilton, H. The relationship of eating disorders to amenorrhea in ballet dancers. *Med Sci Sports Exercise* 19(1):41, 1987.
Cann, C.E., Martin, M.C., Genant, H.K., et al. Decreased spinal mineral content in ammenorrhic women. *JAMA*, 251:626, 1984.
Clapp, J.F., Bathay, E.R., Wesley M, Slemaker, R.H. Thermoregulatory and metabolic responses to jogging prior to and during pregnancy. *Medical Science in Sports and Exercise* 19:124-130, 1987.
Clapp, J. Oxygen consumption during treadmill exercise, before, during and after pregnancy. *Am J Obstetrics and Gyn* 161:1458, 1989.
Collings, C., Curet, L.B. Fetal heart rate response to maternal exercise. *Am J Obstertrics and Gyn* 151:495-501, 1985.
Cummings, D.C., Vickovic, M.D., Wall, S.R., et al. The effect of acute exercise on pulsatile release of luteinizing hormone in women runners. *Am J Obstet Gynecol* 153:482, 1985.
Cummings, S.R., Black, D. Should perimenopausal women be screened for osteoporosis. *Annals Int Med* 104:817-823, 1986.
Curet, L.B. Fetal heart rate response to maternal exercise *Am J OBGYN* 151:498-501, 1985.
Dale, E., Maharam, L.G. Exercise and pregnancy. In Welsh/ Shephard (eds) *Current Therapy Sports Medicine* 1985-86, pgs. 122-125, 1986.
Dale, E., Mullinex, K.M., Bryan, D.H. Exercise during pregnancy: effects on the fetus. *Canadian J of Sports Science* 7:98, 1982.
DeSouza, M.J., Maresh, C.M., Abraham, A., et al. Body compositions of eumenorrheic, oligomenorrheic and amenorrheic runners. *J Appl Sport Sci Res* 2(1):13, 1987.
Drinkwater, B.L. Physiological characteristics of women athletes. In Welsh/Shephard (eds) *Current Therapy Sports Medicine*, pgs. 130-134.
Drinkwater, B.D., Nilson, K.L., Chesnut, C.S. III. Bone mineral content of ammenorrheic and eumenorrhoic athletes. *NEJM* 311:277, 1984.
Duester, P.A., Kyle, S.B., Moser, P.B., et al. Nutritional intakes and status of highly trained amenorrheic and eumenorrheic women runners. *Fertil Steril* 46:636, 1986.
Frisch, R.E., McArthur, J.W. Menstrual cycles: fatness as a determinant of minimum weight for height necessary for their maintenance or onset. *Science* 185(4155):949-51, 1974.
Gauthier, M.M. Guidelines for exercise during pregnancy: too little or too much? *Phys Sportsmed* 14(4):162-169, 1986.
Gonzales, E.R. Premature bone loss found in some non-menstruating sportswomen. *JAMA*, 248:513, 1982.
Goodlin R.C., Buckley K.K. Maternal exercise. *Clinics in Sports Med* 3:881-94, 1984.
Hall, D.C., Kaufmann, D.A. Effects of aerobic and strength conditioning on pregnancy outcomes. *Am J Obstetrical and Gyn* 157:1199-203, 1987.
Henswal and Scientific Affairs. *AMA* Effects of physical forces in the reproductive cycle. *JAMA* 251:247-51, 1984.
Joint FHO/WHO/UNU expert consultation. Energy and protein requirements. Albany, New York. World Health Organization, 1985.
Killinger, D.W. Athletes with menstrual irregularities. In Welsh/ Shephard (eds) *Current Therapy Sports Medicine* pgs. 121-122, 1985-86.
Kolpa, P.H., White, B.M. Visscher, R. Aerobic exercise in pregnancy. *Am J OBGYN* 156:1395-403, 1987.
Leaf, D.A. Exercise during pregnancy: guidelines and controversies. *Post-Grad Med* 85:233, 1989.
Lutter, J.M., Cushman, S. Menstrual patterns in female runners. *Phys Sportsmed* 10(9):60-72, 1982.
Markus, R., Cann, C., Madvig, P. et al. Menstrual function and bone mass

in elite women distance runners: endocrine and metabolic features. *Annals Int Med* 102(2):158-63, 1985.

Mullinax, K.M., Dale, E. Some considerations of exercise during pregnancy. *Clinicals in Sports Med* 5:559-570, 1986.

Paisley, J.E., Mellion, M.B. Exercise during pregnancy. *Am Family Phys* 38(5)143-150, 1988.

Romen, Y, Hartel, R. Physiologic and endocrine adjustments to pregnancy. In: Hartel R, Siswell RA, editors *Exercise in Pregnancy.* Baltimore, Williams and Wilkins, 59-82, 1986.

Sanborn, C.F., Albrecht, B.H., Wagner Jr., W. Athletic amenorrhea: lack of association with body fat. *Med Sci Sports Exerc* 19(3):207, 1987.

Shangold, M.M. Causes, evaluation, and management of athletic oligoammenorrhea. *Med Clinics North Am* 69(1):83-95, 1985.

Shangold, M.M. How I manage exercise-related menstrual disturbances. *Phys Sportsmed* 14(3):113-120, 1986.

St John Repovich, W.E., Wiswell, R.A., Artal, R. Sports activies and aerobic exercise during pregnancy. In Artal R, Wiswell RA (eds) *Exercise and Pregnancy*, Baltimore: Williams and Wilkins, 205- 214, 1986.

Warren, M.P. Exercise in women — effects on reproductive system and pregnancy. In DiNubile, N.A. (ed). *Clinics in Sports Medicine*. W.B. Saunders Co., Philadelphia, PA. 131, 1991.

### Section D. The Older Athlete

Aloia, J.F., Cohn, S.H., Ostuni, J.D., et al. Prevention of involutional bone loss by exercise. *Annals of Internal Med* 89:356, 1978.

American College of Sports Medicine. *Guidelines for Graded Exercise Testing and Exercise Prescription* (2nd ed.), Philadelphia: Lea & Febiger, 1980.

Barry, H.C. Exercise Prescriptions for the Elderly. *Am Fam Phys* 34(3):155-162, 1986.

Clarke, H.H. (Ed.) Exercise and Aging. *Physical Fitness Research Digest*, President's Council on Physical Fitness and Sports. 7(2):1-27, 1977.

Elia, E.A. Exercise in the elderly. In DiNubile MA (ed) *Clinics in Sports Medicine*, Philadelphia PA, W.B. Saunders Company, 10(1):141, January 1991.

Elkowitz, E.B., Elkowitz, A. Prescribing Exercise for the Elderly. *J Fam Prac Recert* 8(1):117-130, 1986.

Fiatarone, M.A., Marks, E.C., Ryan, N.D., et al. High intensity strength training in non nonagenariams. *JAMA* 263:3029, 1990.

Hanson, P.G., Giese, M.D., Corliss, R.J. CLinical Guidelines for Exercise Training. *Postgrad Med* 67:120-138, 1980.

Ike, R.W., Lambman, R.M., Castor, C.W. Arthritis and aerobic exercise. *Phys Sportsmed* 17:128, 1989.

Laslett, L.J., Amsterdam, E.A., Mason, D.T. Exercise Testing in the Geriatric Patient. *Annals of Internal Med* 112:56, 1980.

Mean, W.F., Hartwig, R. Fitness Evaluation and Exercise Prescription. *J FamPract* 13:1039-1050, 1981.

Minor, M.A., Hewett, J.E., Webel, R.R., et al. Efficacy of physical condition exercise in patients with rheumatoid arthritis and osteoarthritis. *Arthritis Rheumatology* 32:1396, 1989.

Ninimaa, V., Shepard, R.J. Training and oxygen condutance in the elderly: the cardiovascular system. *J of Gerontology* 33:362, 1978.

Shephard, R.J. Physical training for the elderly. *Clin Sports Med* 5:515, 1986.

Shephard, R.J. *Prescribing Exercise for the Senior Citizen: Some Simple Guidelines*. Chicago Year Book, 1989.

Smith, D.M., Khairri, M.R., Norton, J. Age and activity effects on bone and mineral loss. *J of Clinical Investigations* 58:716, 1976.

Smith, E.L. and Gilligan, C. Physical Activity Prescription for the Older Adult. *Phys Sportsmed* 11:91, 1983.

Williams, R.S. How Beneficial is regular exercise? *J Cardiovascular Med* 119:1112-1120, 1982.

### Section E. The Sedentary Athlete

Ciscovick DS, Weiss MS, Fletcher RH, et al. The incidence of primary cardiac arrest during vigorous exercise. *NEJM* 311:874, 1984.

Goodman, J.M., Goodman, L.S. Exercise prescription for the sedentary adult. In *Current Therapy in Sports Medicine*. Welsh, R.P., Shephard, R.J. (Eds) Toronto: P.C. Decker Inc., pgs. 17-24, 1985.

Laporte, R.E., Blair, S.N. Physical activity or cardiovascular fitness: which is more important for health? A pro and con. *Phys Sportsmed* 13:145-157, March 1985.

Paffenbarger, R.S., Hyde, R.T., Wing, A.L., et al. Physical activity — all cause mortality and longevity of college alumni. *NEJM* 314:605-613, 1986.

Simons-Morton, B.G., Pate, R.R., Simons-Morton, D.S. Prescribing physical activitiy to prevent disease. *Postgrad Med* 83(1):165, 1988.

Smith, E.L., Gilligan, C. Physical activity prescription for the older adult. *Phys Sportsmed* 11:91, 1983.

Smith, L.K. Medical clearance for vigorous exercise. *Postgrad Med* 83(1):146, 1988.

## SUGGESTED READINGS

### Section A

Fox, E.L. Methods and effects of physical training. *Pediatric Annuals* 7(10):690, 1978.

Fox, E.L. Training of youth for sport. In: Kelley V.C., ed. *Practice of Pediatrics*. Philadelphia, Harper and Row, 1984, Vol. 10, Chapter 74.

McKeag, D.B. Adolescents and exercise. *J of Adol Health Care* 7:121s, 1986.

### Section C

American College of Sports Medicine. Official position: the female athlete in long-distance running. *Phys Sportsmed* 8:135-136, 1980.

Bonen, H., Haynes, F.I., Watson-Wright, W. et al. Effects of menstrual cycle on metabolic responses to exercise. *J Appl Physiol* 55:1506-1513, 1983.

Bullen, B.A., Fkrinar, G.S., Beitins, I.Z. et al. Induction of menstrual disorders by strenuous exercise in untrained women. *NEJM* 312(21):1349-53, 1985.

Collings, Curet, Murlin. Maternal and fetal responses to a maternal aerobic exercise program. *Am J of Obstertrics and Gynecology* 145:702-707, March 1983.

Drinkwater, B.D., Nilson, K.L. Chesnut, C.W. III. Bone mineral content of amenorrheic and eumenorrheic athletes. *New Engl J Med* 311:277-228, August 2, 1984.

Gehlsen, G. and Albohm, M. Evaluation of sports bras. *Phys Sportsmed* 8:89, 1980.

Hale, R.W. Exercise, sports and menstrual dysfunction. *Clin Obstet Gynecol* 26:728-735, 1983.

Hall, J.E. Females and Physical Activity. In Welsh/Shephard (eds) *Current Therapy Sports Medicine 1985-86*. Pgs. 116-121.

Haycock, C. Breast support and protection in the female athlete. *AAHPER Research Consortium Symposium Papers* I:2, 1978.

Haycock, C. The female athlete and sports medicine in the 70's. *J Florida MA* 67:411, 1980.

Levit, F. Jogger's Nipple. *JAMA* 297:1127, 1977.

Litt, I.F. Ammenorrhea in the adolescent athlete. *Postgrad Med* 80(5):245-253, 1986.

Monahan, T. Should women go easy on exercise? *Phys Sportsmed* 14(12):188-197, 1986.

O'Donoghue, D.H. *Treatment of Athletic Injuries* (3rd Ed). Philadelphia: W.B. Saunders & Co., pgs. 381-385., 1976.

Schuster, K. Equipment update: jogging bras hit the streets. *Phys Sportsmed* 7:125, 1979.

Spiroff, L., Redwine, D.B. Exercise and menstrual function. *Phys Sportsmed* 8(5):42-52, 1980.

Thomas, C. Factors important to women participants in vigorous athletics. *Sports Medicine Physiology* Philadelphia: W.B. Saunders & Co., 1979.

### Section D and E

Delisa, J.A., DeLateur, D.J. Therapeutic Exercises: Types and Indications. *Am Fam Phys* 28(4):227-233, 1983.

DeVries, H.A. Physical fitness for the elderly. *Medical Times* 111:70, 1983.

Erickson, D.J. Exercise for the Older Adult. *Phys Sportsmed* 6:99-107, 1978.

Hogan, D.B. Exercise in the Elderly. *Geriatric Medicine Today* 3:47, 1984.

Kamenetz, H.L. History of exercises for the elderly. In Harris, R., Frankel, L. (eds) *Guide to Fitness After Fifty.* New York City: Plenum Pr, 1977, p. 13-31.

Piscopo, J. Aging and human performance. In Burke, E.J. (ed) *Exercise, Science and Fitness* Ithaca, New York: Mouvement Publications, 1980, pp 98-120.

Sager, K. Senior Fitness For the Health Of It. *Phys Sportsmed* 11:31, 1983.

Smith, E.L. Exercise for prevention of osteoporosis: a review. *Phys Sportsmed* 19:72-83, March 1982.

Appendix 5A-1.

American College of Sports Medicine 1990
Position Statement on
The Recommended Quantity and Quality of Exercise
for Developing and Maintaining Cardiorespiratory
and Muscular Fitness in Healthy Adults

Increasing numbers of persons are becoming involved in endurance training activities and thus, the need for guidelines for exercise prescription is apparent. Based on the existing evidence concerning exercise prescription for healthy adults and the need for guidelines, the American College of Sports Medicine (ACSM) makes the following recommendations for the quantity and quality of training for developing and maintaining cardiorespiratory fitness, body composition, and muscular strength and endurance in the healthy adult:

1. Frequency of training: 3-5 d · wk$^{-1}$.
2. Intensity of training: 60-90% of maximum heart rate (HR$_{max}$), or 50-85% of maximum oxygen uptake ($\dot{V}O_2$max) or HR$_{max}$ reserve.[1]
3. Duration of training: 20-60 minutes of continuous aerobic activity. Duration is dependent on the intensity of the activity, thus lower intensity activity should be conducted over a longer period of time. Because of the importance of the "total fitness" effect and the fact that it is more readily attained in longer duration programs, and because of the potential hazards and compliance problems associated with high intensity activity, lower to moderate intensity activity of longer duration is recommended for the nonathletic adult.
4. Mode of activity: any activity that uses large muscle groups, can be maintained continuously, and is rhythmical and aerobic in nature, e.g., walking-hiking, running-jogging, cycling-bicycling, cross-country skiing, dancing, rope skipping, rowing, stair climbing, swimming, skating, and various endurance game activities.

5. Resistance training: Strength training of a moderate intensity, sufficient to develop and maintain fat-free weight (FFW), should be an integral part of an adult fitness program. One set of 8-12 repetitions of eight to ten exercises that condition the major muscle groups at least 2 d · wk$^{-1}$ is the recommended minimum.

## RATIONALE AND RESEARCH BACKGROUND

### Introduction

The questions, "How much exercise is enough," and "What type of exercise is best for developing and maintaining fitness?" are frequently asked. It is recognized that the term "physical fitness" is composed of a wide variety of characteristics in the broad categories of cardiovascular-respiratory fitness, body composition, muscular strength and endurance, and flexibility. In this context fitness is defined as the ability to perform moderate to vigorous levels of physical activity without undue fatigue and the capability of maintaining such ability throughout life (167). It is also recognized that the adaptive response to training is complex and includes peripheral, central, structural, and functional factors (5,172). Although many such variables and their adaptive response to training have been documented, the lack of sufficient in-depth and comparative data relative to frequency, intensity, and duration of training makes them inadequate to use as comparative models. Thus, in respect to the above questions, fitness is limited mainly to changes in $\dot{V}O_2$max, muscular strength and endurance, and body composition, which includes total body mass, fat weight (FW), and FFW. Further, the rationale and research background used for this position stand will be divided into

---

[1]Maximum heart rate reserve is calculated from the difference between resting and maximum heart rate. To estimate training intensity, a percentage of this value is added to the resting heart rate and is expressed as a percentage of HRmax reserve (85).

programs for cardiorespiratory fitness and weight control and programs for muscular strength and endurance.

**Fitness versus health benefits of exercise.** Since the original position statement was published in 1978, an important distinction has been made between physical activity as it relates to health versus fitness. It has been pointed out that the quantity and quality of exercise needed to attain health-related benefits may differ from what is recommended for fitness benefits. It is now clear that lower levels of physical activity than recommended by this position statement may reduce the risk for certain chronic degenerative diseases and yet may not be of sufficient quantity or quality to improve $\dot{V}O_2$max (71, 72, 98, 167). ACSM recognizes the potential health benefits of regular exercise performed more frequently and for a longer duration, but at lower intensities than prescribed in this position statement (13A, 71, 100, 120, 160). ACSM will address the issue concerning the proper amount of physical activity necessary to derive health benefits in another statement.

**Need for standardization of procedures and reporting results.** Despite an abundance of information available concerning the training of the human organism, the lack of standardization of testing protocols and procedures, of methodology in relation to training procedures and experimental design, and of a preciseness in the documentation and reporting of the quantity and quality of training prescribed make interpretation difficult (123, 133, 139, 164, 167). Interpretation and comparison of results are also dependent on the initial level of fitness (42, 43, 58, 114, 148, 151, 156), length of time of the training experiment (17, 45, 125, 128, 139, 145, 150), and specificity of the testing and training (5, 43, 130, 139, 145A, 172). For example, data from training studies using subjects with varied levels of $\dot{V}O_2$max, total body mass, and FW have found changes to occur in relation to their initial values (14, 33, 109, 112, 113, 148, 151); i.e., the lower the initial $\dot{V}O_2$max the larger the percentage of improvement found, and the higher the FW the greater the reduction. Also, data evaluating trainability with age, comparison of the different magnitudes and quantities of effort, and comparison of the trainability of men and women may have been influenced by the initial fitness levels.

In view of the fact that improvement in the fitness variables discussed in this position statement continues over many months of training (27, 86, 139, 145, 150), it is reasonable to believe that short-term studies conducted over a few weeks have certain limitations. Middle-aged sedentary and older participants may take several weeks to adapt to the initial rigors of training, and thus need a longer adaptation period to get the full benefit from a program. For example, Seals et al. (150) exercise trained 60-69-yr-olds for 12 months. Their subjects showed a 12% improvement in $\dot{V}O_2$max after 6 months of moderate intensity walking training. A further 18% increase in $\dot{V}O_2$max occurred during the next 6 months of training when jogging was introduced. How long a training experiment should be conducted is difficult to determine, but 15-20 wk may be a good minimum standard. Although it is difficult to control exercise training experiments for more than 1 yr, there is a need to study this effect. As stated earlier, lower doses of exercise may improve $\dot{V}O_2$max and control or maintain body composition, but at a slower rate.

Although most of the information concerning training described in this position statement has been conducted on men, the available evidence indicates that women tend to adapt to endurance training in the same manner as men (19, 38, 46, 47, 49, 62, 65, 68, 90, 92, 122, 166).

## Exercise Prescription for Cardiorespiratory Fitness and Weight Control

Exercise prescription is based upon the frequency, intensity, and duration of training, the mode of activity (aerobic in nature, e.g., listed under No. 4 above), and the initial level of fitness. In evaluating these factors, the following observations have been derived from studies conducted for up to 6-12 months with endurance training programs.

Improvement in $\dot{V}O_2$max is directly related to frequency (3, 6, 50, 75-77, 125, 126, 152, 154, 164), intensity (3, 6, 26, 29, 58, 61, 75-77, 80, 85, 93, 118, 152, 164), and duration (3, 29, 60, 61, 70, 75-77, 101, 109, 118, 152, 162, 164, 168) of training. Depending upon the quantity and quality of training, improvement in $\dot{V}O_2$max ranges from 5 to 30% (8, 29, 30, 48, 59, 61, 65, 67, 69, 75-77, 82, 84, 96, 99, 101, 102, 111, 115, 119, 123, 127, 139, 141, 143, 149, 150, 152, 153, 158, 164, 168, 173). These studies show that a minimum increase in $\dot{V}O_2$max of 15% is generally attained in programs that meet the above stated guidelines. Although changes in

$\dot{V}O_2$max greater than 30% have been shown, they are usually associated with large total body mass and FW loss, in cardiac patients, or in persons with a very low initial level of fitness. Also, as a result of leg fatigue or a lack of motivation, persons with low initial fitness may have spuriously low initial $\dot{V}O_2$max values. Klissouras (94A) and Bouchard (16A) have shown that human variation in the trainability of $\dot{V}O_2$max is important and related to current phenotype level. That is, there is a genetically determined pre-training status of the trait and capacity to adapt to physical training. Thus, physiological results should be interpreted with respect to both genetic variation and the quality and quantity of training performed.

**Intensity-duration.** Intensity and duration of training are interrelated, with total amount of work accomplished being an important factor in improvement in fitness (12, 20, 27, 48, 90, 92, 123, 127, 128, 136, 149, 151, 164). Although more comprehensive inquiry is necessary, present evidence suggests that, when exercise is performed above the minimum intensity threshold, the total amount of work accomplished is an important factor in fitness development (19, 27, 126, 127, 149, 151) and maintenance (134). That is, improvement will be similar for activities performed at a lower intensity-longer duration compared to higher intensity-shorter duration if the total energy costs of the activities are equal. Higher intensity exercise is associated with greater cardiovascular risk (156A), orthopedic injury (124, 139) and lower compliance to training than lower intensity exercise (36, 105, 124, 146). Therefore, programs emphasizing low to moderate intensity training with longer duration are recommended for most adults.

The minimal training intensity threshold for improvement in $\dot{V}O_2$max is approximately 60% of the HRmax (50% of $\dot{V}O_2$max or HRmax reserve) (80, 85). The 50% of HRmax reserve represents a heart rate of approximately 130-135 beats·min$^{-1}$ for young persons. As a result of the age-related change in maximum heart rate, the absolute heart rate to achieve this threshold is inversely related to age and can be as low as 105-115 beats·min$^{-1}$ for older persons (35, 65, 150). Patients who are taking beta-adrenergic blocking drugs may have significantly lower heart rate values (171). Initial level of fitness is another important consideration in prescribing exercise (26, 90, 104, 148, 151). The person with a low fitness level can achieve a significant training effect with a sustained training heart rate as low as 40-50% of HRmax reserve, while persons with higher fitness levels require a higher training stimulus (35, 58, 152, 164).

**Classification of exercise intensity.** The classification of exercise intensity and its standardization for exercise prescription based on a 20-60 min training session has been confusing, misinterpreted, and often taken out of context. The most quoted exercise classification system is based on the energy expenditure (kcal·min$^{-1}$·kg$^{-1}$) of industrial tasks (40, 89). The original data for this classification system were published by Christensen (24) in 1953 and were based on the energy expenditure of working in the steel mill for an 8-h day. The classification of industrial and leisure-time tasks by using absolute values of energy expenditure have been valuable for use in the occupational and nutritional setting. Although this classification system has broad application in medicine and, in particular, making recommendations for weight control and job placement, it has little or no meaning for preventive and rehabilitation exercise training programs. To extrapolate absolute values of energy expenditure for completing an industrial task based on an 8-h work day to 20-60 min regimens of exercise training does not make sense. For example, walking and jogging/running can be accomplished at a wide range of speeds; thus, the relative intensity becomes important under these conditions. Because the endurance training regimens recommended by ACSM for nonathletic adults are geared for 60 min or less of physical activity, the system of classification of exercise training intensity shown in Table 1 is recommended (139). The use of a realistic time period for training and an in-

Table 1. Classification of intensity of exercise based on 20-60 min of endurance training.

| Relative Intensity (%) | | Rating of Perceived Exertion | Classification of Intensity |
|---|---|---|---|
| HRmax* | $\dot{V}O_2$max* or HRmax reserve | | |
| <35% | <30% | <10 | Very light |
| 35-59% | 30-49% | 10-11 | Light |
| 60-79% | 50-74% | 12-13 | Moderate (somewhat hard) |
| 80-89% | 75-84% | 14-16 | Heavy |
| ≥90% | ≥85% | >16 | Very heavy |

*HRmax = maximum heart rate; $\dot{V}O_2$max = maximum oxygen uptake.

(Table from Pollock, M.L. and J.H. Wilmore. *Exercise in Health and Disease: Evaluation and Prescription for Prevention and Rehabilitation*, 2nd Ed. Philadelphia: W.B. Saunders, 1990. Published with permission.)

dividual's relative exercise intensity makes this system amenable to young, middle-aged, and elderly participants, as well as patients with a limited exercise capacity (3, 137, 139).

Table 1 also describes the relationship between relative intensity based on percent HRmax, percentage of HRmax reserve or percentage of $\dot{V}O_2$max, and the rating of perceived exertion (RPE) (15, 16, 137). The use of heart rate as an estimate of intensity of training is the common standard (3, 139).

The use of RPE has become a valid tool in the monitoring of intensity in exercise training programs (11, 37, 137, 139). It is generally considered an adjunct to heart rate in monitoring relative exercise intensity, but once the relationship between heart rate and RPE is known, RPE can be used in place of heart rate (23, 139). This would not be the case in certain patient populations where a more precise knowledge of heart rate may be critical to the safety of the program.

**Frequency.** The amount of improvement in $\dot{V}O_2$max tends to plateau when frequency of training is increased above 3 d·wk$^{-1}$ (50, 123, 139). The value of the added improvement found with training more than 5 d·wk$^{-1}$ is small to not apparent in regard to improvement in $\dot{V}O_2$max (75-77, 106, 123). Training of less than 2 d·wk$^{-1}$ does not generally show a meaningful change in $\dot{V}O_2$max (29, 50, 118, 123, 152, 164).

**Mode.** If frequency, intensity, and duration of training are similar (total kcal expenditure), the training adaptations appear to be independent of the mode of aerobic activity (101A, 118, 130). Therefore, a variety of endurance activities, e.g., those listed above, may be used to derive the same training effect.

Endurance activities that require running and jumping are considered high impact types of activity and generally cause significantly more debilitating injuries to beginning as well as long-term exercisers than do low impact and non-weight bearing type activities (13, 93, 117, 124, 127, 135, 140, 142). This is particularly evident in the elderly (139). Beginning joggers have increased foot, leg, and knee injuries when training is performed more than 3 d·wk$^{-1}$ and longer than 30 min duration per exercise session (135). High intensity interval training (run-walk) compared to continuous jogging training was also associated with a higher incidence of injury (124, 136). Thus, caution should be taken when recommending the type of activity and exercise prescription for the beginning exerciser.

Orthopedic injuries as related to overuse increase linearly in runners/joggers when performing these activities (13, 140). Thus, there is a need for more inquiry into the effect that different types of activities and the quantity and quality of training has on injuries over short-term and long-term participation.

An activity such as weight training should not be considered as a means of training for developing $\dot{V}O_2$max, but it has significant value for increasing muscular strength and endurance and FFW (32, 54, 107, 110, 165). Studies evaluating circuit weight training (weight training conducted almost continuously with moderate weights, using 10-15 repetitions per exercise session with 15-30 s rest between bouts of activity) show an average improvement in $\dot{V}O_2$max of 6% (1, 51-54, 83, 94, 108, 170). Thus, circuit weight training is not recommended as the only activity used in exercise programs for developing $\dot{V}O_2$max.

**Age.** Age in itself does not appear to be a deterrent to endurance training. Although some earlier studies showed a lower training effect with middle-aged or elderly participants (9, 34, 79, 157, 168), more recent studies show the relative change in $\dot{V}O_2$max to be similar to younger age groups (7, 8, 65, 132, 150, 161, 163). Although more investigation is necessary concerning the rate of improvement in $\dot{V}O_2$max with training at various ages, at present it appears that elderly participants need longer periods of time to adapt (34, 132, 150). Earlier studies showing moderate to no improvement in $\dot{V}O_2$max were conducted over a short time span (9), or exercise was conducted at a moderate to low intensity (34), thus making the interpretation of the results difficult.

Although $\dot{V}O_2$max decreases with age and total body mass and FW increase with age, evidence suggests that this trend can be altered with endurance training (22, 27, 86-88, 139). A 9% reduction in $\dot{V}O_2$max per decade for sedentary adults after age 25 has been shown (31, 73), but for active individuals the reduction may be less than 5% per decade (21, 31, 39, 73). Ten or more yr follow-up studies where participants continued training at a similar level showed maintenance of cardiorespiratory fitness (4, 87, 88, 138). A cross-sectional study of older competitive runners showed progressively lower values in $\dot{V}O_2$max from the fourth to seventh decades of life, but also showed less training in the older groups (129). More recent 10-yr follow-up data on these same athletes (50-82 yr of age) showed $\dot{V}O_2$max to be unchanged when training quantity and quality remained unchanged (138). Thus, lifestyle plays a significant role in the maintenance of fitness. More inquiry into the relationship of long-term training (quantity and quality), for both competitors and noncompetitors, and physiological function with increasing age is necessary before more definitive statements can be made.

**Maintenance of training effect.** In order to maintain the training effect, exercise must be continued on a regular basis (18, 25, 28, 47, 97, 111, 144, 147). A significant reduction in cardiorespiratory fitness occurs after 2 wk of detraining (25, 144), with participants returning to near pretraining levels of fitness after 10 wk (47) to 8 months of detraining (97). A loss of 50% of their initial improvement in $\dot{V}O_2$max has been shown after 4-12 wk of detraining (47, 91, 144). Those individuals who have undergone years of continuous training maintain some benefits for longer periods of detraining than subjects from short-term training studies (25). While stopping training shows dramatic reductions in $\dot{V}O_2$max, reduced training shows modest to no reductions for periods of 5-15 wk (18, 75-77, 144). Hickson et al., in a series of experiments where frequency (75), duration (76), or intensity (77) of training were manipulated, found that, if intensity of training remained unchanged, $\dot{V}O_2$max was maintained for up to 15 wk when frequency and duration of training were reduced by as much as $^2/_3$. When frequency and duration of training remained constant and intensity of training was reduced by $^1/_3$ or $^2/_3$, $\dot{V}O_2$max was significantly reduced. Similar findings were found in regards to reduced strength training exercise. When strength training exercise was reduced from 3 or 2 d·wk$^{-1}$ to at least 1 d·wk$^{-1}$, strength was maintained for 12 wk of reduced training (62). Thus, it appears that missing an exercise session periodically or reducing training for up to 15 wk will not adversely effect $\dot{V}O_2$max or muscular strength and endurance as long as training intensity is maintained.

Even though many new studies have given added insight into the proper amount of exercise, investigation is necessary to evaluate the rate of increase and decrease of fitness when varying training loads and reduction in training in relation to level of fitness, age, and length of time in training. Also, more information is needed to better identify the minimal level of exercise necessary to maintain fitness.

**Weight control and body composition.** Although there is variability in human response to body composition change with exercise, total body mass and FW are generally reduced with endurance training programs (133, 139, 171A), while FFW remains constant (123, 133, 139, 169) or increases slightly (116, 174). For example, Wilmore (171A) reported the results of 32 studies that met the criteria for developing cardiorespiratory fitness that are outlined in this position stand and found an average loss in total body mass of 1.5 kg and percent fat of 2.2%. Weight loss programs using dietary manipulation that result in a more dramatic decrease in total body mass show reductions in both FW and FFW (2, 78, 174). When these programs are conducted in conjunction with exercise training, FFW loss is more modest than in programs using diet alone (78, 121). Programs that are conducted at least 3 d·wk$^{-1}$ (123, 125, 126, 128, 169), of at least 20 min duration (109, 123, 169), and of sufficient intensity to expend approximately 300 kcal per exercise session (75 kg person)[2] are suggested as a threshold level for total body mass of FW loss (27, 64, 77, 123, 133, 139). An expenditure of 200 kcal per session has also been shown to be useful in weight reduction if the exercise frequency is at least 4 d·wk$^{-1}$ (155). If the primary purpose of the training program is for weight loss, then regimens of greater frequency and duration of training and low to moderate intensity are recommended (2, 139). Programs with less participation generally show little or no change in body composition (44, 57, 93, 123, 133, 159, 162, 169). Significant increases in $\dot{V}O_2$max have been shown with 10-15 min of high intensity training (6, 79, 109, 118, 123, 152, 153); thus, if total body mass and FW reduction are not considerations, then shorter duration, higher intensity programs may be recommended for healthy individuals at low risk for cardiovascular disease and orthopedic injury.

## Exercise Prescription for Muscular Strength and Endurance

The addition of resistance/strength training to the position statement results from the need for a well-rounded program that exercises all the major muscle groups of the body. Thus, the inclusion of resistance training in adult fitness pro-

---

[2]Haskell and Haskell et al. (71, 72) have suggested the use of 4 kcal·kg$^{-1}$ of body weight of energy expenditure per day for a minimum standard for use in exercise programs.

grams should be effective in the development and maintenance of FFW. The effect of exercise training is specific to the area of the body being trained (5, 43, 145A, 172). For example, training the legs will have little or no effect on the arms, shoulders, and trunk muscles. A 10-yr follow-up of master runners who continued their training regimen, but did no upper body exercise, showed maintenance of $\dot{V}O_2$max and a 2-kg reduction in FFW (138). Their leg circumference remained unchanged, but arm circumference was significantly lower. These data indicate a loss of muscle mass in the untrained areas. Three of the athletes who practiced weight training exercise for the upper body and trunk muscles maintained their FFW. A comprehensive review by Sale (145A) carefully documents available information on specificity of training.

Specificity of training was further addressed by Graves et al. (63). Using a bilateral knee extension exercise, they trained four groups: group A, first ½ of the range of motion; group B, second ½ of the range of motion; group AB, full range of motion; and a control group that did not train. The results clearly showed that the training result was specific to the range of motion trained, with group AB getting the best full range effect. Thus, resistance training should be performed through a full range of motion for maximum benefit (63, 95).

Muscular strength and endurance are developed by the overload principle, i.e., by increasing more than normal the resistance to movement or frequency and duration of activity (32, 41, 43, 74, 145). Muscular strength is best developed by using heavy weights (that require maximum or nearly maximum tension development) with few repetitions, and muscular endurance is best developed by using lighter weights with a greater number of repetitions (10, 41, 43, 145). To some extent, both muscular strength and endurance are developed under each condition, but each system favors a more specific type of development (43, 145). Thus, to elicit improvement in both muscular strength and endurance, most experts recommend 8-12 repetitions per bout of exercise.

Any magnitude of overload will result in strength development, but higher intensity effort at or near maximal effort will give a significantly greater effect (43, 74, 101B, 103, 145, 172). The intensity of resistance training can be manipulated by varying the weight load, repetitions, rest interval between exercises, and number of sets completed (43). Caution is advised for training that emphasizes lengthening (eccentric) contractions, compared to shortening (concentric) or isometric contractions, as the potential for skeletal muscle soreness and injury is accentuated (3A, 84A).

Muscular strength and endurance can be developed by means of static (isometric) or dynamic (isotonic or isokinetic) exercises. Although each type of training has its favorable and weak points, for healthy adults, dynamic resistance exercises are recommended. Resistance training for the average participant should be rhythmical, performed at a moderate to slow speed, move through a full range of motion, and not impede normal forced breathing. Heavy resistance exercise can cause a dramatic acute increase in both systolic and diastolic blood pressure (100A, 101C).

The expected improvement in strength from resistance training is difficult to assess because increases in strength are affected by the participants' initial level of strength and their potential for improvement (43, 66, 74, 114, 172). For example, Mueller and Rohmert (114) found increases in strength ranging from 2 to 9% per week depending on initial strength levels. Although the literature reflects a wide range of improvement in strength with resistance training programs, the average improvement for sedentary young and middle-aged men and women for up to 6 months of training is 25-30%. Fleck and Kraemer (43), in a review of 13 studies representing various forms of isotonic training, showed an average improvement in bench press strength of 23.3% when subjects were tested on the equipment with which they were trained and 16.5% when tested on special isotonic or isokinetic ergometers (six studies). Fleck and Kraemer (43) also reported an average tested with the equipment that they trained on (six studies) and 21.2% when tested with special isotonic or isokinetic ergometers (five studies). Results of improvement in strength resulting from isometric training have been of the same magnitude as found with isotonic training (17, 43, 62, 63).

In light of the information reported above, the following guidelines for resistance training are recommended for the average healthy adult. A minimum of 8-10 exercises involving the major muscle groups should be performed a minimum of two times per week. A minimum of one set of 8-12 repetitions to near fatigue should be completed. These minimal standards for resistance training are based on two factors. First, the time it takes to complete a comprehensive, well-rounded exercise program is important. Programs lasting more than 60 min per session are associated with higher dropout rates (124). Second, although greater frequencies of training (17, 43, 56) and additional sets or combinations of sets and repetitions elicit larger strength gains (10, 32, 43, 74, 145, 172), the magnitude of difference is usually small. For example, Braith et al. (17) compared training 2 d·wk$^{-1}$ with 3 d·wk$^{-1}$ for 18 wk. The subjects performed one set of 7-10 repetitions to fatigue. The 2 d·wk$^{-1}$ group showed a 21% increase in strength compared to 28% in the 3 d·wk$^{-1}$ group. In other words, 75% of what could be attained in a 3 d·wk$^{-1}$ program was attained in 2 d·wk$^{-1}$. Also, the 21% improvement in strength found by the 2 d·wk$^{-1}$ regimen is 70-80% of the improvement reported by other programs using additional frequencies of training and combinations of sets and repetitions (43). Graves et al. (62, 63), Gettman et al. (55), Hurley et al. (83) and Braith et al. (17) found that programs using one set to fatigue showed a greater than 25% increase in strength. Although resistance training equipment may provide a better graduated and quantitative stimulus for overload than traditional calisthenic exercises, calisthenics and other resistance types of exercise can still be effective in improving and maintaining strength.

## SUMMARY

The combination of frequency, intensity, and duration of chronic exercise has been found to be effective for producing a training effect. The interaction of these factors provide the overload stimulus. In general, the lower the stimulus the lower the training effect, and the greater the stimulus the greater the effect. As a result of specificity of training and the need for maintaining muscular strength and endurance, and flexibility of the major muscle groups, a well-rounded training program including resistance training and flexibility exercises is recommended. Although age in itself is not a limiting factor to exercise training, a more gradual approach in applying the prescription at older ages seems prudent. It has also been shown that endurance training of fewer than 2 d·wk$^{-1}$, at less than 50% of maximum oxygen uptake and for less than 10 min·d$^{-1}$, is inadequate for developing and maintaining fitness for healthy adults.

In the interpretation of this position statement, it must be recognized that the recommendations should be used in the context of participants' needs, goals, and initial abilities. In this regard, a sliding scale as to the amount of time allotted and intensity of effort should be carefully gauged for both the cardiorespiratory and muscular strength and endurance components of the program. An appropriate warm-up and cool-down, which would include flexibility exercises, is also recommended. The important factor is to design a program for the individual to provide the proper amount of physical activity to attain maximal benefit at the lowest risk. Emphasis should be placed on factors that result in permanent lifestyle change and encourage a lifetime of physical activity.

References available upon request from ACSM. (*Med. Sci. Sports Exec.* 22:2, pp. 265-274, 1990)

# 6

# Exercise and Chronic Illness

## SECTION A.
## DIABETES MELLITUS

Diabetes currently affects 5% of the U.S. population, and well over half of them are still undiagnosed or improperly treated. Classification systems and terminology used to describe diabetes mellitus has changed dramatically during the last 10 years. Approximately 20% of all persons with diabetes mellitus take insulin. Within this number are three distinct groups:

*Group 1* — Type I or insulin dependent diabetes mellitus (IDDM) - insulin deficient patients who developed diabetes prior to age 30 and who represent 10% of the diabetes population (Brink, 1991).

*Group 2* — Type II or non-insulin dependent diabetes mellitus (NIDDM) — the largest group of patients taking insulin that normally would not need it if their weight were normal. Seventy-five percent of patients are obese, over age 40, and have inadequate insulin stores.

*Group 3* — This least common group consists of insulin deficient persons who experience later onset of diabetes and are totally dependent on insulin as in Type I diabetics.

A discussion of the differences between Type I and Type II diabetes mellitus is beyond the scope of this book and is available in many textbooks. The three groups described above have diverse genetic, autoimmune, and environmental etiologies and clinical manifestations. The end result is abnormal glucose metabolism and a host of potential longterm complications. There is a close relationship between obesity and overnutrition with Type II diabetes. Weight control may to modify the severity and influence the time of onset of this form of diabetes. Treatment of diabetes mellitus has changed little since the introduction of insulin in 1922. Joslin introduced his famous triad of exercise, diet, and insulin as the cornerstone of diabetic treatment and his method is in almost all textbooks on diabetes. Treatment currently focuses on diet and weight control, home glucose monitoring of diabetic status, insulin therapy, oral hyperglycemic agents, various behavioral modification techniques, and exercise.

Exercise as a tool for improving diabetic control is controversial and is the least understood and most imprecisely used tool for improving glycemic control. Reports of the last few years show that exercise is not a universal remedy for diabetes (Brink, 1991). It is important to understand the effects of physical exercise, especially the Type I diabetic, who will want to know whether he or she can participate in sports or exercise programs without restrictions. An important issue for patients with Type II diabetes is whether physical exercise can improve glucose tolerance or delay the onset of diabetes in older individuals.

A review of the literature shows that exercise can help both diabetic and nondiabetic individuals reduce their risk of cardiovascular disease (see Table 6A-1) (Robbins, 1989). The positive effects of exercise are more dramatic in patients with non-insulin dependent diabetes than they are in those with insulin dependent diabetes (Robbins, 1989). It is unclear whether exercise increases insulin sensitivity in both Type I & II diabetes (Peder-

**Table 6A-1. Potential Beneficial Effects of Long-Term Exercise in Diabetes**

Enhanced sense of physical well-being
Modestly improved glucose tolerance (some Type II diabetics)
Reduced cardiovascular disease risk factors
　↓VLDL-triglyceride
　↓LDL-cholesterol
　↑HDL-cholesterol
　↓Risk of hypertension
Increased myocardial reserve

son, 1980). Certain Type II diabetics can increase glucose tolerance by restricting caloric intake and performing regular exercise. The combination of exercise and moderate caloric restrictions creates a negative energy balance and leads to weight loss, increased insulin sensitivity, decreased fasting blood glucose, and beneficial changes in blood lipids. The overall effects of regular exercise in diabetics appear to be moderate at best. Some diabetics incorporate an aerobic exercise program in their daily activities on their own, but most look to their physicians for accurate and up-to-date advice.

## Response to Exercise

The metabolic effects of acute exercise in normal men and women is summarized in Figure 6A-1. The diabetic patient's response to exercise is mediated in part by the type of diabetes and also by the level of metabolic control at the time of exercise. No two patients respond the same. Therefore, management of an athlete's diabetes always is a collaborative effort between patient and physician.

## Type I Diabetes

For purposes of discussion, it is useful to look at two different groups (see Figure 6A-2). Type I diabetics with blood glucose levels < 240 mg% usually have excessive insulin availability. Since injected insulin absorbs at a fixed rate from its depot site, the normal suppression of insulin that occurs during exercise cannot take place, and the result is an inappropriately high insulin level. Enhanced absorption of insulin from the injection site in an extremity being exercised may add to this phenomenon. This will cause a marked increase in glycogenolysis and gluconeogenesis observed in the liver during exercise. The result will be a below normal increase in hepatic glucose production which, in the face of increased muscle glucose utilization, leads to a fallen blood glucose level.

In contrast, the Type I diabetic in poor metabolic control (blood glucose > 240 mg%) has inadequate insulin during exercise. This prevents the normal process of accelerated glucose utilization by muscle from occurring and results in a paradoxical rise in blood glucose with exercise. Hepatic

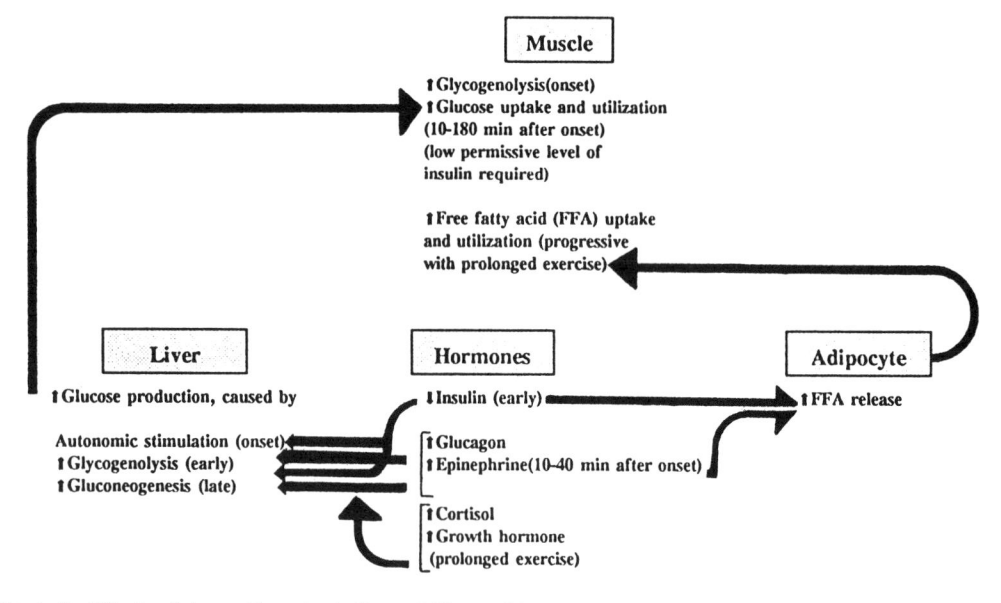

**Fig. 6A-1.** Metabolic Effects of Acute Exercise in Normal Men and Women

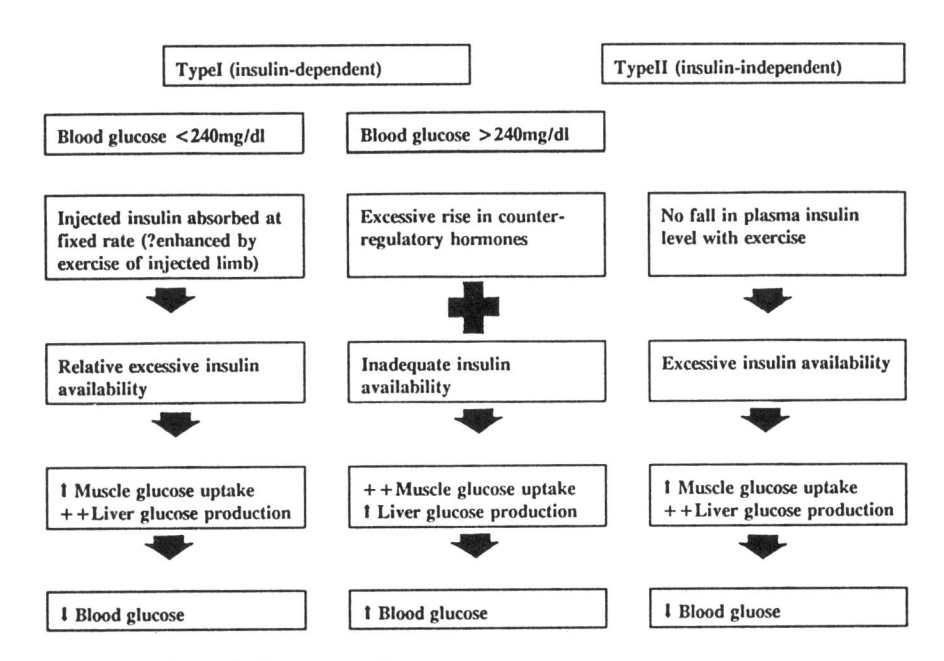

```
                    ┌─────────────────────────┐           ┌──────────────────────────┐
                    │ Type I (insulin-dependent)│           │ Type II (insulin-independent)│
                    └─────────────────────────┘           └──────────────────────────┘

      ┌──────────────────────┐   ┌──────────────────────┐
      │ Blood glucose <240mg/dl│   │ Blood glucose >240mg/dl│
      └──────────────────────┘   └──────────────────────┘

   ┌─────────────────────┐   ┌─────────────────────┐   ┌─────────────────────┐
   │ Injected insulin    │   │ Excessive rise in   │   │ No fall in plasma   │
   │ absorbed at fixed   │   │ counter-regulatory  │   │ insulin level with  │
   │ rate (?enhanced by  │   │ hormones            │   │ exercise            │
   │ exercise of injected│   │                     │   │                     │
   │ limb)               │   │                     │   │                     │
   └─────────────────────┘   └─────────────────────┘   └─────────────────────┘
            ▼                         +                          ▼
   ┌─────────────────────┐   ┌─────────────────────┐   ┌─────────────────────┐
   │ Relative excessive  │   │ Inadequate insulin  │   │ Excessive insulin   │
   │ insulin availability│   │ availability        │   │ availability        │
   └─────────────────────┘   └─────────────────────┘   └─────────────────────┘
            ▼                         ▼                          ▼
   ┌─────────────────────┐   ┌─────────────────────┐   ┌─────────────────────┐
   │ ↑ Muscle glucose    │   │ ++ Muscle glucose   │   │ ↑ Muscle glucose    │
   │   uptake            │   │    uptake           │   │   uptake            │
   │ ++ Liver glucose    │   │ ↑ Liver glucose     │   │ ++ Liver glucose    │
   │    production       │   │   production        │   │    production       │
   └─────────────────────┘   └─────────────────────┘   └─────────────────────┘
            ▼                         ▼                          ▼
   ┌─────────────────────┐   ┌─────────────────────┐   ┌─────────────────────┐
   │ ↓ Blood glucose     │   │ ↑ Blood glucose     │   │ ↓ Blood gluose      │
   └─────────────────────┘   └─────────────────────┘   └─────────────────────┘
```

**Fig. 6A-2.** Effects of Diabetes on Metabolic Response to Exercise

blood glucose production is unrestrained due to the low insulin levels that usually are present. Excessive increases in the counterregulatory hormones (catecholamines) and glucagon that are usually present in the inadequately controlled diabetic also may increase glucose production in the liver.

A third possible situation is a diabetic patient who starts exercising with below normal glucose levels and elevated levels of plasma insulin. Here, glucose production is inhibited while muscle glucose utilization is increased. This may lead to severe hypoglycemia during or after exercise.

For practical purposes, the patient in good diabetic control who starts exercising usually maintains safe and adequate blood glucose levels throughout and after the exercise period. If the intensity and duration of exercise vary from day to day, control may be more difficult. The most appropriate exercises for diabetic patients involve highly predictable levels of activity on a routine basis (Nathan, 1985). Insulin reduction alone may be the best strategy for an obese diabetic patient who wishes to exercise. In this way the energy expended during exercise induces a physiologic caloric deficit, leading in time to weight loss. At the beginning of an exercise program, the obese patient might withhold more insulin than necessary and end up with post-exercise blood glucose elevations. If that happens, the patient should withhold less insulin or exercise for longer periods to correct the situation.

A number of variables affect the hypoglycemic effects of exercise in the diabetic. These include:

- Exercise intensity — glucose utilization by muscle increases in normal persons and in adequately controlled diabetics as the intensity of exercise increases. In a well controlled diabetic, hypoglycemia is more likely to occur when exercise is intense.
- Duration of exercise — when exercise is prolonged, symptomatic hypoglycemia is more likely to occur in type I diabetics as hepatic glycogen stores become depleted as the duration of exercise increases.
- Timing of meals and snacks — significant hypoglycemia is less likely to occur in individuals who have eaten a meal or carbohydrate snack prior to exercise. Carbohydrate ingestion is useful for preventing hypoglycemia during exercise in Type I diabetics.
- Time and absorption of insulin injection — exercise may cause inappropriately high plasma insulin levels by increasing the absorption of insulin from its injection site, especially if injected into an exercising limb.
- Training status — trained diabetic patients use fat more efficiently as do normal individuals. This phenomenon may protect the diabetic from

significant hypoglycemia, but it remains to be proven in research studies.

- Metabolic status — decreases in blood glucose during and following exercise are less in Type I diabetics with high circulating levels of prefatty acids and ketone bodies. These high levels apparently diminish the utilization of glucose by muscle.

## Type II Diabetes

Inappropriately high levels of insulin are present in Type II diabetics, resulting in a lower level of blood glucose by the same mechanism discussed in Type I patients. It is unclear why plasma insulin levels do not fall appropriately with exercise in these patients is unclear. Exercise produces markedly decreased blood plasma glucose levels in Type II diabetics who are on a dietary regimen alone or in those taking an oral hypoglycemic agent. The long term effects of maintaining normoglycemia in Type II diabetics is disappointing at best. Increased glucose tolerance has not been shown to be of long duration. Exercise alone does not appear to be an appropriate treatment for elevated blood glucose levels and must be combined with a weight loss program and appropriate use of insulin or oral hypoglycemic agents (Brink, 1991).

### Initial Evaluation

Because there is a high incidence of accelerated atherosclerosis in diabetics, it is imperative that silent coronary artery disease be ruled out in diabetic patients over 40 years of age or those who have had diabetes more than 25 years. Graded exercise stress testing should be performed before prescribing an exercise regimen. The physician also should look for evidence of peripheral sensory neuropathy or vascular deficiency since minor trauma to the extremities (especially the feet) can lead to increased morbidity. Patients with proliferative diabetic retinopathy should avoid strenuous exercise because it could induce a vitreous hemorrhage. Diabetics with very poor metabolic control should not engage in strenuous exercise programs due to the paradoxical rise in blood glucose.

All diabetic patients should have a thorough history, physical, and appropriate laboratory screening before beginning any exercise program. The physician should review the program and then review it for intercurrent problems four to six weeks after the initial evaluation. This provides an opportunity to evaluate the patient's level of compliance and to make any appropriate changes in the therapeutic regimen.

Less well controlled diabetics and those with autonomic neuropathy are prone to severe dehydration, particularly on warm days. The untrained diabetic also may experience post-exercise hypotension after prolonged intense exercise. Proteinuria may increase transiently following exercise in many diabetics; however, the prognostic significance of this is not known. The potential complications of exercise in diabetics is summarized in Table 6A-2.

### Exercise as a Tool for Improving Control

Multiple factors influence the glycemic response to exercise. Some reports in the literature indicate that Type I diabetes control is not improved with exercise despite a decreased requirement in daily insulin dosage (Brink, 1991; Robbins, 1989). Exercise is definitely an adjunct to therapy, especially when it is correlated with meals. Most patients do not exercise on a regular basis and are not consistent in their timing of exercise sessions after meals. Home glucose monitoring will help patients predict their response to exercise performed at different times of the day, or exercise of varying intensity and duration. Physical training will usually increase the sensitivity of insulin and the circulation, but the overall effect is modest at best. Diabetics should be encouraged to exercise because of the measurable benefits mentioned. The physician can influence improved metabolic control by prescribing appropriate exercise programs for his diabetic patients.

---

Table 6A-2. Potential Complications of Exercise in Diabetics

Hypoglycemia
Hyperglycemia and ketosis
Retinal hemorrhage
Increased proteinuria
Dehydration and hypotension
Foot ulcers
Orthopedic injury
Acceleration of degenerative arthritis
Sequelae of occult ischemic heart disease, e.g., arrhythmias, angina

(From *Hospital Practice* May 30, 1986, pg. 51)

### Prevention of Hypoglycemia

Prevention of hypoglycemia is an important therapeutic goal in diabetic patients who exercise. This is best accomplished by utilizing the following guidelines.

- Ingesting additional carbohydrates before exercise — approximately 15 grams of carbohydrate or one bread exchange for each 30 minutes of moderate to vigorous exercise. Variations in carbohydrate amounts are dependent upon the size of the patient and the level of metabolic control before exercise. Pre-and post-exercise meals (known as "sandwiching") should consist of complex carbohydrates so that there is a steady, gentle rise in blood glucose levels (Nathan, 1985).
- Insulin should be injected into a non-exercising site such as the abdomen to reduce inappropriately high blood levels of insulin. If hypoglycemia occurs repeatedly during exercise, the appropriate insulin component should be gradually decreased. Some patients may require a 20%-50% unit reduction in the total daily dose. Only the insulin dose that reaches peak activity during training or competition may have to be modified (Robbins, 1989).
- Regularity of exercise is an important principle and should be stressed, especially to the Type I patient. This allows consistent adjustments in diet and insulin therapy to be made and minimizes instability and wide swings in glycemic control.
- Because of the dangers of hypoglycemia, the diabetic patient should wear a medical identification at all times.
- Certain sports involving prolonged vigorous exercise such as swimming, scuba diving, or marathon running should be done with another individual who knows about the patient's condition and who can treat hypoglycemia appropriately. All diabetics should be cautioned about using alcohol and beta-blockers, both of which may contribute to exercise-related hypoglycemia.

### Conclusions

Exercise may have therapeutic benefits for diabetics as well as enhance their quality of life. While physical training is not without undesirable side effects, with proper supervision and adequate patient education, almost all diabetics can enjoy the benefits of exercise.

On the basis of available information, it is reasonable to encourage well controlled diabetics to engage in rigorous exercise as part of their overall therapeutic regimen. A well designed program of monitored exercise of graded intensity is the most prudent course for the diabetic just beginning an exercise program. The exercise should be aerobic and involve repetitive, submaximal contractions of large muscles. Swimming, cycling, jogging, or racquetball are examples. Exercise sessions should last 30 minutes, be performed 3-5 times per week, and include a warm-up and cool-down period. Patients should be taught to monitor their pulse, using a training heart rate between 60%-75% of their maximal heart rate or $VO_2$max. Gradual weight loss should be encouraged in overweight diabetic patients.

The following guidelines should be helpful in describing the physician's approach to diabetes and exercise.

- Exercise is beneficial to both normal and diabetic populations.
- Exercise should be performed regularly so as to gain the maximal benefits and predict appropriate dietary and insulin needs.
- Exercise helps promote weight loss and should be used as an adjunct to therapy, especially in Type II diabetics.
- The patient's clinical status should be carefully evaluated before beginning an exercise program, with special attention to all systems potentially affected by the long-term complications of diabetes.
- Proper training and conditioning techniques should be encouraged by the physician to reduce the occurrence of overuse problems and the high exercise dropout rate commonly seen.
- An adequate level of diabetic management should be achieved before starting an exercise program. Is the patient's diet appropriate and is there compliance with it? How does the patient monitor his/her diabetes? These facts must be known to ensure that the diabetes is managed properly and to avoid episodes of hypoglycemia and deterioration of glycemic control.
- Detailed records should be kept by the patient, particularly when unstable glycemic control is evident. Without accurate records, it is difficult to make appropriate changes in either caloric intake, insulin dosages, or both.
- Be prepared to change the diet. The child who

exercises vigorously will need increased high carbohydrate snacks during the day. Brief episodes of vigorous exercise are best handled by dietary manipulation. Activity that is rigorous and of long duration will require increased caloric intake and/or a decrease in insulin dosage. Most diabetic patients will not require dietary change because their exercise is of moderate intensity and usually not after meals.

- Be prepared to revise the insulin dosage. Approximately one third of all active runners require a change in insulin. Children who exercise vigorously may need a 15%-25% reduction in their daily insulin dose, whereas some adults require up to a 50% reduction.
- Prevent hypoglycemia — all patients who exercise should have ready access to easily absorbed carbohydrate during activity and follow all precautions mentioned in the text.

Extremes in weather can affect the insulin-carbohydrate-exercise balance. Cold weather may slow insulin absorption while very warm weather may increase it. A patient exercising in weather extremes must expend extra energy to maintain body temperature; therefore, additional calories may be needed before winter workouts. Cross-country skiers must distinguish between the sweating and shaking that are signs of hypoglycemia and normal perspiration and weakness resulting from strenuous exercise. Scuba diving poses a similar problem because perspiration and clammy skin are difficult to detect underwater and in a wet suit.

Sports involving unpredictable levels of activity are another area of potential problems. Team sports commonly involve participation for limited periods. It may be hard to maintain blood glucose control. The diabetic in this situation should have access to rapid-acting carbohydrates which can be taken before and after being sent onto the field of play. Even when blood glucose levels returned to normal, physical performance and judgment may still be impaired. Attention to these clinical considerations should minimize any adverse effects of exercise on diabetic patients and maximize the beneficial effects of long term exercise. A clear understanding of the effects of exercise on glycemic control in the diabetic population will enable the team physician to care for the patient appropriately.

The first step in managing an older diabetic patient who is beginning a program is to take into account the relationship between exercise, insulin, proper nutrition, and blood glucose levels already discussed. If the patient fears exercise or is at high cardiovascular risk he/she may benefit from consulting an exercise physiologist or sports medicine physician. Fear of having a coronary event or fall during exercise must be dealt with sympathetically and realistically. Older people frequently live in neighborhoods that are unsafe and the patient may fear walking alone. Mall walking or specially arranged classes should be recommended.

Older diabetic patients should exercise with another person as a safeguard if possible. If an exercise companion is not available, someone should know where the diabetic person is exercising and when the period will end. Older diabetic patients in nursing homes usually have limited mobility and will need specific exercise training instructions from their physician. The exercise regimen should be easy to perform, enjoyable, and should not put the patient at risk for hypoglycemia or injury. Family members may be asked for support when exercise is recommended for the older person with diabetes. All health professionals should encourage the older diabetic patient to exercise (MacDonald, 1987; Rogers, 1988; Staten, 1991).

## SECTION B.
## ASTHMA

Vigorous physical activity often leads to acute exacerbation of asthmatic symptoms. The degree of bronchoconstriction during exercise correlates highly with the severity of frank asthma. Exercise is the only stimulus that promotes asthma in some asthmatic athletes, but this is a rare phenomenon. Historically, asthma patients have avoided or been excluded from exercise. However, this practice is unwarranted and detrimental. A full discussion of exercise-induced asthma (EIA) is presented in Chapter 13-C.

Exercise-induced asthma occurs in about 80% of asthmatics (Katz, 1983). The clinical manifestations often occur within 5-10 minutes of beginning strenuous exercise. Common symptoms include shortness of breath, coughing, wheezing, chest tightness, and sometimes headache and abdominal pain with nausea and vomiting. Exercise is generally the triggering mechanism for EIA, just as many viruses, danders, dust, mold, pollens, pollutants, and emotional disorders trigger asthma and other reactive airway disorders. EIA can occur at any age but is more common in younger athletes (McCarthy, 1989). Most EIA symptoms resolve within 45-60 minutes although some patients experience a late response about 4-6 hours after exercise (Voy, 1984; Bar-Or, 1977, Mink, 1991).

Increases in both the duration and intensity of exercise can cause EIA, with maximal symptoms reached at approximately 85% of maximal work capacity. The type of exercise is a factor; running causes more EIA than cycling at the same intensity. Walking and swimming are less likely to provoke EIA. EIA is more severe where the air is dry and cold than when it is humidified. Nasal breathing virtually eliminates post-exercise bronchial obstruction because of the increased humidification and heating of air inhaled through the nose (Bar-Or, 1977) but nasal breathing is impractical in many competitive sports.

Guidelines for prescribing exercise for asthmatics contain the following components (Morton, 1981):

**Warm-Up.** The patient should warm up before doing vigorous activity. This should consist of walking, progressing to jogging and other low-level activity, flexibility exercises, and some light mobilizing and strengthening activities. The warm-up should aim to increase the body temperature until mild sweating occurs.

**Cool-Down.** The patient should cool down at the end of each exercise session. Vigorous work should not stop abruptly; rather, a low level of activity (such as walking) should be maintained for about five minutes or until the heart rate returns to within 20 beats minute of the resting level.

**Duration.** Sessions should last 30 to 40 minutes. (A very unfit subject may need to begin with 15-minute sessions.)

**Frequency.** Four to five times a week.

**Intensity.** Exercise should start at a low level of intensity and gradually increase as fitness level improves. If interval training is used, the work interval should be at an intensity that produces an initial heart rate of 70% of the maximum, gradually progressing to 85%. The rest interval should be long enough to reduce the heart rate to 50% to 60% of maximum. If continuous training techniques are used, the work intensity should progress slowly to 85% of the maximum heart rate.

**Age.** Regular exercise should be continued throughout life.

**Mode.** Activities and games of the patient's choice should be prescribed. If possible, the asthmatic should be involved in swim training at some time (preferably during developmental years). Regardless of the activity selected, the program must aim at increasing the person's aerobic power. Sports participation in dry, cold environments places the patient at risk for EIA. Hence, swimming is an excellent sport at all ages.

**Exercise Loading.** Programs should begin with walking. A subject who is experiencing EIA regularly should progress to low-level interval training, with work intervals of 10 to 30 seconds followed by rest periods of 30 to 90 seconds. Next, the patient goes to high-intensity interval training. If an asthmatic is able to "run through" asthma or use suitable preexercise medication, long-distance continuous activity may be pursued with benefit despite its greater asthmogenicity. With suitable medication, either continuous or interval training is well tolerated by most asthmatics.

**Preexercise Medications.** Proper medication taken before exercising allows most asthmatic children to participate in nearly all sports. Good protection usually is seen after inhalation of cromolyn but it will not stop symptoms once they begin. Beta sympathetic agonists are highly effective in most patients when given as aerosols (albuterol and terbutaline) and are the drugs of choice. Oral preparations of beta sympathetic agents have variable effects and should not be used (Mink, 1991). Oral or inhaled corticosteroids have little immediate value in treating EIA but may be needed for serious asthmatics. Calcium blockers have only a slight protective effect. A serum level of 10 grams per liter of xanthine derivatives such as aminophylline or theophylline generally offers protection. There are drugs that cannot be used if the athlete is subject to drug testing and the physician should be aware of them. Treatment of allergic syndromes and respiratory infection prior to exercise training and competition is imperative in an athlete with EIA.

The therapeutic effectiveness of anti-asthma drugs can be summarized as follows: beta sympathetic agonists are the most effective and parasympathetic antagonists are least effective. Disodium cromoglycate (cromolyn) has minimal side effects and is an important drug for the prevention of EIA during sports. It should be used before activity and may need to be repeated after one or more hours. If this medication does not offer sufficient protection, inhalation of beta-sympathetic agonists may be considered, but too frequent usage may cause tremor or tachycardia.

Regular exercise can benefit children with EIA. Physical training programs should be tailored to their individual needs so that they may realize their potential regardless of their initial physical condition. Physical training will improve the cardiovascular/respiratory fitness as well as the psychological outlook of asthmatic athletes. Full levels of activity can be performed without respiratory distress, and less medication may be need to control EIA. Many patients with asthma can avoid EIA and undertake a training program by following the regimen subscribed above (Morton, 1981; Mink, 1991).

## SECTION C.
## CHRONIC OBSTRUCTIVE PULMONARY DISEASE

Patients with airflow obstruction complain of breathlessness with exertion and they have limited exercise capacity. In chronic obstructive pulmonary disease (COPD), the abnormalities of lung mechanics prevent ventilation from meeting the metabolic demand. Airway obstruction does not develop during exercise as it does in the asthmatic but airflow limitation increases. During exercise, patients with COPD are more dyspneic than the normal subject at comparable levels of ventilation. The emphysematous patient, with an $FEV_1$ equal to that of a chronic bronchitic, will invariably experience more dyspnea than the latter. A bronchitic patient is likely to improve gas exchange and be able to increase tidal volume more readily than the patient with COPD. Shortness of breath and effort intolerance are major symptoms in patients with COPD, regardless of whether they are classified as Type A ("fighters" or pink-puffers) or Type B (chronic bronchitic "blue bloaters"). In the latter, exercise capacity is limited primarily by an inability to increase ventilation in proportion to metabolic demand.

Patients with COPD have altered mechanics that reduce maximal static recoil pressure, obstruct the airway and increase intrathoracic pressure and reduce $VO_2max$, ventilatory capacity, minute ventilation, and maximal voluntary ventilation. A typical COPD patient has a tidal volume during maximal exercise that does not exceed 55% of vital capacity. Patients with COPD use 35%-40% percent of their total oxygen uptake for restoration of the respiratory muscles during exercise, compared with 10%-15% in normal individuals (Shayevitz, 1986). Consequently, there are high oxygen costs that significantly limit exercise performance by the COPD patient. In addition, significant deficiencies in diffusion and perfusion limit $VO_2max$. $VO_2max$ can be reduced by as much as 50% in COPD patients as compared with that of normal men of the same age (Mink, 1991).

There is agreement that exercise conditioning produces no improvement in pulmonary mechanics and probably does not alter the rate of decline in lung function that is commonly seen in these patients. Nevertheless, exercise conditioning allows them to exercise with a lower heart rate, respiratory rate, and minute ventilation than they had before conditioning. Exercise tolerance usually is improved after exercise training. It is well known that inspiratory muscle training can improve the exercise tolerance of COPD patients. However, there is no evidence that exercise will alter the long-term prognosis for COPD patients, although it may improve the level of function and decrease the number of hospitalizations (Mink, 1991).

### Medical Treatment of COPD Patients

Exercise training should begin when COPD patients are clinically stable or have recovered from an acute exacerbation. Pulmonary mechanics in COPD patients should be optimized with available medical therapy. The most important first line of therapy is smoking cessation. Beta-2 selective agonists are useful as bronchodilators and should be administered by the aerosol method to minimize side effects. Beta-2 agonists may be replaced by newer anticholinergic agents such as ipratropium bromide, which are effective bronchodilators in COPD and free of cardiovascular and systemic side effects. Theophylline should be administered twice daily in sustained release formulations, and it is a useful adjunct to the aerosolized bronchodilators. Pulmonary function testing should be performed to determine the most effective bronchodilator for the COPD patient. The role of corticosteroids in COPD is not well established and presents potential serious side effects. They should not be prescribed in the absence of objective improvement in pulmonary function. Frequent usage of broad spectrum oral antibiotics at the onset of any exacerbation of infection should be encouraged.

### Testing Protocols for COPD Patients

No consensus exists regarding the best exercise testing protocol for COPD patients. Initial assessment should include electrocardiographic monitoring to detect significant cardiac arrhythmias or ECG signs of ischemic heart disease which are common. Arterial oxygen saturation or ear oximetry should be continuously monitored during exercise testing. A practical approach to evaluating the COPD patient is the 12-minute walk in which a patient is asked to cover as much distance as possible within 12 minutes of walking at a comfortable pace. The result gives a comprehensible yardstick (Mink, 1991).

### Training Protocols

The most helpful form of training for COPD patients is treadmill exercises. Walking is an important activity of everyday living and can be easily prescribed to maintain fitness gains following completion of a formal training program. A cycle ergometer or stationary bicycle for home use in inclement weather is very helpful. Swimming has not been extensively evaluated in this group but may be useful for selected patients with disorders of weight bearing joints or other complications that prevent walking or cycling.

A reasonable goal for moderate to severe COPD patients is to exercise at or near their symptom-limited maximum work level for 20-30 minutes per session. Initial training periods of 10-20 minutes at low work rates are advisable. The work rate and duration can be increased gradually during exercise sessions, three times per week. A realistic program of one to two months duration, followed by a home prescription to maintain conditioning is advised. COPD patients should be reevaluated at three to six month intervals, using either normal treadmill protocols or the 12-minute walk test.

### Adjuncts to Training

Pursed-lip breathing is commonly adopted by most emphysematous patients and is taught as part of the pulmonary rehabilitation program. This may provide mild relief during episodes of dyspnea and during exercise. Proper dietary intake is advisable for COPD patients. The use of other medications such as inotropic agents (digoxin) or afterload reducing agents (hydralazine) provide little benefit unless there are coexisting left ventricular function abnormalities. Oxygen administration during exercise may relieve dyspnea and improve the exercise tolerance of many patients. Oxygen should be administered by face mask or nasal prongs and will be helpful in hypoxemic patients with COPD.

In summary, it is reasonable to attempt to improve the physiologic functioning of the potential athlete with COPD. The main therapy for the patients is a comprehensive program of respiratory rehabilitation that includes mild to moderate exercise protocols.

## SECTION D.
## EPILEPSY

Years ago epileptics were cautioned to restrict their physical activity but this practice has changed and epilepsy alone is not a barrier to athletic participation. There is very little information in the literature for sports physicians to use in advising epileptic patients and their families. The fundamental issue is whether physical activity will precipitate the seizure disorder. An equally important issue is whether a seizure during sporting activity exposes the athlete or others to unnecessary harm.

Only one rare type of seizure disorder has been shown to be induced by activity per se. These are tonic seizures, a type of reflex epilepsy and they are induced by movement. Fortunately, they are very responsive to anti-convulsant therapy. There is no well-defined relationship to exercise in all other types of seizure disorders. Physiological changes induced by exercise may precipitate a seizure. Hyperventilation associated with exertion is a cause for concern as it is a known stimulus for activation of epilepsy. The conclusion from research data is that physical exercise can raise the patient's seizure threshold (Naken, 1990).

The team physician will be concerned about possibility of seizure disorders following head trauma sustained during contact sports. There are may opinions on this subject, including those who state there are no studies to prove that seizures can be caused by repeated head trauma in a person with epilepsy. Many studies have shown that accident rates in convulsive and nonconvulsive children are virtually identical, and that seizures are not common events precipitated by or associated with physical activity. However, the research also notes that epileptics may be at greater risk for epileptic activity following exercise periods (Gates, 1991).

Despite a lack of objective criteria, experience reported by neurologists is that seizures are infrequent during physical exertion. Even in contact sports, there is little evidence to support limiting the participation of epileptics. The risk from exercise is small and can be completely avoided by taking simple precautions. Common sense and good judgment are the key. A reasonable degree of seizure control can be achieved, with maintenance of adequate blood levels of anti-convulsants an essential (Mendel, 1985). Certain activities such as scuba diving and climbing are high risk sports that epileptic patients may wish to eliminate. Patients who experience frequent seizures have an increased risk of falling and should choose activities that minimize the risk. Epileptics are likely to have fewer seizures when they are actively occupied than when they are bored or inattentive. Moreover, precautionary measures that go beyond what is reasonable and necessary may result in altered self-image and feelings of being different or inferior.

Epilepsy is a brain disorder characterized by a tendency to have recurrent seizures. Although 10% of the population will have a seizure at some time in their lives, only 2% of the population will develop epilepsy (Hauser, 1975). During a seizure there may be disturbances of movement and altered sensations, perceptions, behavior, mood, or level of consciousness. Epilepsy may be produced by conditions which irritate or damage neurons, including head injury, brain infection, exposure to toxic substances, tumor, or stroke. Head injuries are the leading cause of epilepsy. However, no clear cause can be identified in more than half of all cases, especially in younger patients (Arid, 1984).

There are three major types of seizures:

- Generalized tonic-clonic seizures (grand mal seizure). This type begins without warning and is characterized by irregular breathing, peripheral cyanosis, and a pronounced ictal phase. In the post-ictal state the patient is usually tired and may have a headache and wish to rest. The seizure lasts approximately $70 \pm 20$ seconds (Gates, 1985).
- Absence attacks (petit mal seizure). This seizure is characterized by blank staring and fluttering of the eyelids. Absence attacks are usually brief, lasting an average of 3-10 seconds. A patient may experience numerous absence spells in rapid succession.
- Complex Partial Seizures (temporal lobe or psychomotor seizures). This seizure is characterized by loss of awareness of the environment, a blank facial expression, semi-purposeful movements such as lip smacking, picking at clothing, or walking without purpose. This seizure usually lasts 1-5 minutes and the individual may be momentarily confused when it is over. This type of seizure is marked by an "aura" or subjective sensation lasting for a few seconds.

It is important that the type of epilepsy is diagnosed after a minimum of two documented seizures. A thorough history and physical examination, appropriate laboratory tests, EEG, and other brain imaging such as MRI or CT evaluation should be performed. Epilepsy treatment includes medications, proper nutrition, and adequate sleep and rest. Surgery is rarely needed to correct seizure disorders. Half of all patients on anti-epileptic medications have complete recovery and do not need to make lifestyle changes. Another 30% rarely have seizures so that their lifestyle is not limited. Others have seizures often enough to be greatly incapacitated (Gates, 1991). The most common anti- epileptic medications include phenytoin (Dilantin), phenobarbital (Luminal), ethosuximide (Zarontin), primidone (Mysoline), carbamazepine (Tegretol), valproic acid (Depakane), and clonazepam (Klonopin). Tegretol is becoming the drug of choice in the U.S. Dilantin has many side effects, including coarsing of features and hirsutism. This is unacceptable to most women. The bone marrow toxicity seen with Tegretol can be avoided by close monitoring of serum drug levels. Phenobarbital is no longer used as initial therapy because of its sedative and cognitive side effects. These medications cause many patients to feel fatigued, have difficulty in concentrating, experience impaired coordination, or have diplopia. Any of these side effects should be reported to the physician.

Patients who are planning to undertake new physical activities should be cautioned about the side effects of anti-epileptic medications. Significant weight loss or gain can affect dosage of medications so that adjustments may be necessary. Dosing changes should be made by a physician. Most individuals with epilepsy should be able to participate fully in sports.

About 4 million Americans have some form of epilepsy according to the Epilepsy Foundation of

America. Most cases are diagnosed before adulthood so that exercise patterns formed in childhood are critical in determining adult life-style. Unhealthful life patterns can be set when young children with epilepsy are denied the opportunity to acquire skills and have the experiences that are vital to becoming successful adults. The responsibility for decisions about sports participation for them should be shared by the parents, physician, and patient. Additional readings on epilepsy and exercise are found in the selected readings section of this chapter.

## SECTION E.
## CONGENITAL HEART DISEASE

The increased emphasis on exercise, recreation, and physical fitness has shown potential benefits for children with chronic health problems, including cardiac disease. Physical exercise for a child with heart disease must be structured within the limits of the patient's cardiac problem.

About 85% of young athletes have ejection-type murmurs. This challenges the team physician to identify the small number of significant hemodynamic abnormalities among them (see Table 4-7). Where there is doubt, a cardiologist should be consulted. Full, active interscholastic competition is possible — and often desirable — for youngsters with rheumatic and/or congenital heart defects that have not caused hemodynamic impairment.

### Arrhythmias

Most arrhythmias in children or adolescents arise as atopic beats from atrial, ventricular, or junctional origin. Sinus arrhythmia, wandering pace maker, and intermittent junctional rhythms usually are normal and due to increased vasoactivity or related to the stress of athletic conditioning, asthma, or abdominal distension. Less commonly, arrhythmias may be due to paroxysmal superventricular tachycardia and atrial ventricular block. Atopic beats that are ventricular or superventricular in origin usually are benign. If they are unifocal and disappear with exercise, there should be no cause for concern. This does not apply to PVCs, where low grade exercise may increase them in some individuals and decrease them in others. Myocarditis should be considered whenever an atopic arrhythmia appears in a child who has previously been well.

Children with paroxysmal superventricular tachycardia can participate fully in sports if the arrhythmia is controlled. An exercise ECG to evaluate the cardiac rhythm during intense exercise is necessary. Children with congenital complete heart block usually can participate in normal activities. Consultation with a cardiologist is desirable and necessary where rhythm disorders are complex. As a general recommendation, we believe children or adolescents should be allowed to participate in athletic activities rather than imposing restrictions that may lead to long term psychological barriers. A more complete description of arrhythmias is elsewhere in this text.

### Cardiac Defects

Heart disease covers many anatomic defects, with over a third requiring surgery within the first year of life. The incidence of congenital heart disease is 8:1000 live births. Surgical intervention and drug therapy have improved mortality and morbidity rates significantly. The exercise tolerance of children with significant hemodynamic lesions generally is abnormal in the preoperative state (Goldberg, 1990). This usually is due to intrinsic cardiac defects, lack of exercise activities, or is a function of restrictions placed on the child's activity. Post-operative exercise-testing also shows lower than normal maximal work capacity and oxygen consumption despite excellent hemodynamic responses.

Children with heart disease do face hazards from participating in intense physical activity but they may benefit from specific training programs. A child with congenital heart disease should receive a complete cardiopulmonary assessment before beginning any training program. Past surgical improvement in exercise tolerance has been demonstrated in patients with aortic stenosis or ventricular septal defect. Further studies are needed to define the exercise potential of children with congenital heart diseases. Physical training programs for children with congenital heart disease should be considered so they can reach their maximum functional potential. Aerobic training at 60%-75% of maximal heart rate for 10-20 minutes three times a week should be emphasized. Activities that improve flexibility, muscular strength, and body composition are important. The physician should carefully outline what a child should not do and what the child can do for physical exercise.

Children with surgically corrected cardiac defects should be able to take part in all school sports even though their performance may be below the level of their healthy peers. This should not be a deterrent to participation by children with correctable heart defects.

## SECTION F.
## CHRONIC MUSCULOSKELETAL PROBLEMS

### Rheumatoid Arthritis

Rheumatoid arthritis is a chronic disease affecting individuals between the ages of 25 and 60 years, with a female preponderance of 3:1. The inflammatory process progresses slowly with periods of exacerbation and remission, and it involves all joints. Gradual destruction of the joint surface, joint capsule, and ligaments often occurs. Tendons and skeletal muscles also can be affected. These changes can affect the RA patient's ability to do physical exercise. The general functional capacity and physical performance of each RA patient is categorized as follows by the American Rheumatology Association:

- Class 1 — complete ability to carry out all duties.
- Class 2 — adequate ability to carry out normal activities despite some handicap, discomfort, or limitation of motion.
- Class 3 — limited ability to carry out usual occupation or self-care.
- Class 4 — incapacitated, largely or totally.

Patients in Class 1 generally can perform any type of physical exercise. Exceptions may be hard physical exercise, running, and individual racquet sports that place excessive stress on the knees and feet. Bicycle or cycle ergometer exercise is nearly always possible. Patients in Class 2 and a few in Class 3 can perform most types of physical exercise, especially bicycling, walking, even light jogging, during low activity phases of the disease. When the disease is highly active, they can exercise only in a low or very low mode format because of the inflammatory process in their joints, muscles, and tendons. Recommended is exercise on a cycle ergometer set at low watt values. After the acute phase of the disease passes, the patient usually has a relatively quick return to functional status.

Most patients in Class 3 can swim and exercise on a bicycle provided the type of exercise, intensity, and range of movement are modified for their needs. Polyneuritis and peripheral arteritis are common and may alter the ability to exercise.

Most patients in Class 4 are unable to carry out complicated movements. However, many can exercise while suspended in water with a life vest.

The state and activity of the disease must be known before prescribing a training program for RA patients. During exacerbations, low intensity exercise — "no load" pedaling on a bicycle or swimming in warm water — can be performed. Mobility training to avoid contractures is recommended. After the exacerbation of the disease is over, most patients in functional Class 1, 2 and a few in Class 3 can perform walking and bicycle training to develop cardiovascular fitness and increase muscle strength and endurance.

### Physical Training

Training sessions should begin with long warm-ups of 10-15 minutes at low intensity and gradually increase to interval or continuous high intensity training. Group training after acute exacerbations is recommended to avoid the high drop-out rates often seen in exercise programs for patients with RA. Swimming, rowing, and bicycling are probably the best modes of exercise in RA, because minimal loading of the joints of the lower limb is possible. An active program of range of motion exercises and exercise combined with rest periods is highly recommended. Long term physical training restores most measurable physiologic variables to the normal or above range for corresponding age groups in patients without RA. Physical training is one of the few ways in which an RA patient can influence the outcome of his disease.

### Rehabilitation Therapy

To properly treat arthritis, the physician must have a good understanding of the structure, function, and metabolism of the connective tissues. Knowledge of joint biology, the role of the inflammatory process, and how hematologic mechanisms impact on rheumatic diseases is also helpful. The epidemiology and classification of rheumatic diseases is well described in the literature. There have been dramatic changes in recent years as new pathophysiologic mechanisms were discovered that explain clinical observations dating back centuries. A correct diagnosis of the patient's joint complaints must be ascertained. Careful evaluation of the synovial fluid is an important step in making a proper differential diagnosis. Laboratory, radiographic studies, scintigraphy, computed tomography, and arthroscopy are useful diagnostic procedures. Prior to instituting any therapy, the physician should obtain a detailed history and do a thorough physical. Systematic joint examination is invaluable in determining the extent of damage, the overall activity of arthritis, and the patient's response to treatment. The functional status of all joints should be ascertained, including an assessment of muscle strength and gait.

Physical therapy for arthritis should be balanced with the use of properly selected anti-rheumatic drugs, immunosuppressive agents, corticosteroids, or intraarticular injections. Surgical management may be necessary. Comprehensive treatment will require a health care team.

The goal of therapeutic programs should be to restore patients to their highest level of social and vocational function. Ideally, this means restoration to full employment and social participation or, less ideally, to enhanced independence and self-care for the severely afflicted arthritic. Relief of pain and maintenance of joint function are extremely important in the therapy program. Medical management or surgical intervention are combined with a wide range of supporting services. Every therapy program should include the patient's family and available community resources.

Appropriate periods of rest and exercise must be balanced in the arthritic patient. Splinting, temporary joint rest, proper posture and positioning of joints, and the use of exercise to prevent muscle atrophy and loss of range of motion are cornerstones of therapy. Passive and/or active range of motion exercises have been designed so as to maximize any possible joint motion. The Arthritis Foundation has published recommended range of motion exercises for arthritis patients and these publications are available through local chapters. Also, consultation with a physical therapist may be useful. Currently, physical therapy programs include increasing or maintaining range of motion to prevent deformity, and increasing or maintaining strength to avoid atrophy and improve independence. Most physical therapy programs encourage recreational activities that help the arthritic child remain active (Goldberg, 1990).

Children with rheumatoid arthritis have commonalities with other children who have chronic medical problems. They need frequent medical attention, must comply with prescribed therapy and prescriptions, and must adapt to the functional limitations imposed by their disease. Psychosocial problems of the child with rheumatoid arthritis are well described. Physicians cannot assume that schools will provide either physical therapy or physically stimulating activities for children with rheumatoid arthritis. Consequently, it is up to the physician to educate parents regarding the rights of children with chronic diseases to attain their full educational rights.

It is important to keep the fundamentals in mind in order to provide a safe and effective exercise program for patients with arthritis. Future research is expected to further define proper exercise parameters.

## Scoliosis

Curvature of the spine in the coronal plane is not normal. An estimated 5%-6% of North American children have curvature of the spine in excess of 10°. Annual school screenings performed between the ages of 10-14 have been successful in detecting most scoliosis curvatures. Children with curves below the range of 20° as measured by the Cobb technique are generally followed and supplemental exercises may be needed. A variety of exercises may be used to correct spinal imbalances or weaknesses. Curvature of more than 20° requires consideration of spinal bracing with either the Milwaukee or Boston brace systems. Full time bracing is no longer believed to be necessary. Most physicians require the patient to undergo bracing at least 18 hours/day in addition to doing exercises to correct spinal curvature or muscle weaknesses.

The child with scoliosis is at no increased risk of injury with moderate curves, up to the range of 45°. Regular exercise will help maintain the functional curve of the spine. Children and adolescents with no progressive curvature despite bracing, or when the curvature has already progressed into the 45-50° range may require spinal fusion. It usually takes 9 to 12 months after surgery to obtain satisfactory spinal stability. The child may participate in progressive exercises including walking, jogging, or swimming as early as 6 months after fusion surgery.

Most surgeons believe that contact sports are contraindicated after spinal fusion. There usually is an increased rate of degeneration at spinal levels immediately above and below the fused area. Specific advice from an orthopedic surgeon with experience in managing spinal deformities should be sought after a young athlete has spinal fusion surgery. Most patients may still be able to participate in vigorous light contact or non-contact sports (Lonstein, 1988; Bunnel, 1986; Renshaw, 1988, 1985, 1991; Weinstein, 1983).

Children with severe scoliosis do not participate in physical exercise programs as often as they should because of unattractive appearance, exercise dyspnea, or the influence of an overprotective family or physician. It is true that reduced ventilation and dyspnea may become significant problems in those with severe scoliosis. Some authors believe that physical training plays a significant role in retarding the progression of spinal curvature and in improving pulmonary function and work capacity. In large studies, many patients with big curvatures of the spine do not improve with training. Moderate training cannot help patients who have severe limitations of $VO_2$max because of the persistent hyperventilated or underused areas of the lungs. Additional research is required to clarify the clinical picture of moderate to severe scoliosis. Other references in the literature should be helpful in discussing this issue with the patient and his or her family.

Patients with mild scoliosis (30° or less) who are asymptomatic can participate in weight-lifting during their out of brace time. Other sports such as swimming during out of brace time will help the youngster maintain good conditioning while treatment is proceeding. Weight-lifting for a skeletally immature child with a spinal problem should consist of multiple repetitions with weights of 10-14 lbs or less. Any strengthening exercises or exercise machine that produces a vertical or rotatory loading of the spine should limit the amount of weight lifted to no more than 10%-15% of the child's body weight. Bench pressing is allowed up to 50% of the child's body weight. Once skeletal maturity is attained, lifting can become more vigorous within the limits of individual capacity. Excessive weight-lifting has caused spinal deformity (spondylolysis and hyperkyphosis) in these individuals.

## Congenital Subluxation of the Hip, Legg Calve'-Perthes Disease, Slipped Capital Femoral Epiphysis

Recommendations for exercise in children with these problems are essentially the same. Mild deformity of the femoral neck permits mild to moderate athletic activity. A moderate deformity allows mild to moderate activity, and a severe deformity only mild or no activity. The compensation by the acetabulum and the amount of motion in the hip are important considerations in prescribing exercise for youngsters with these problems. With mild limitation of hip motion but adequate joint space and strong muscle function about the hip, a child should be able to compete through high school without difficulty. Moderate limitation of hip motion means the youngster should not play collision sports such as football and wrestling, and probably is not a candidate for basketball. Overactivity in a child with this deformity will cause recurring hip pain to develop. Keeping the activity at a level where there is no hip pain or muscle spasm is required. Swimming and non-weightbearing activities are more easily tolerated by children with these conditions. Slipped capital femoral epiphysis (SCFE) is common in adolescents and should be considered in a patient with groin, thigh, or knee pain. Advanced cases of SCFE will present with an external rotation contracture at the hip. These cases require orthopedic surgery evaluation and appropriate treatment.

## SECTION G.
## MENTAL RETARDATION

Physicians who make recommendations about athletic activities for mentally retarded children or adults should consider the differences in the patient's body size, level of coordination, degree of physical fitness, and general physical health. The stage of maturation, level of mental development, and emotional stability of the child also are very important. Special types of recreational and athletic activities for children with average mental development is not necessary. Children should be able to safely participate in athletic activities that are properly supervised.

Some parents of mentally retarded children restrict their youngster's physical activities, while others may push them at a rapid pace. Proper guidance by the physician about appropriateness of activities is very important.

Mentally retarded children usually are more successful in individual and dual sports rather than in team sports. Activities requiring gross rather than fine motor coordination should be stressed. Competition is highly motivating in itself and may provide a means of promoting self-confidence, self-esteem, and self-satisfaction during the development of gross motor coordination. The Special Olympics have shown how mentally retarded children can compete successfully in a happy and safe environment (Stein, 1991).

Where joint activities with normal and retarded children are planned, it should be remembered that there is some correlation between developmental levels and persistence, attention span, emotional control, and understanding the rules of the game. Mentally retarded children usually perform best and enjoy themselves most when children of the same developmental level rather than chronological age are competing together.

All retarded children need physical training consisting of regular exercise and supervised athletic activities. Many activities are available for the retarded youngster that can promote a sense of participation and provide social contacts and physical exercise in a healthy environment. The Department of Education, Division of Innovation and Development, 400 Maryland Ave. SW, Donohoe Bldg, Room 3159, Washington, DC, 20202 is a rich source of information about physical education and recreational activities for the mentally retarded. In general, every effort should be made to include the mentally retarded child in all appropriate recreational activities.

## Down Syndrome

Some 17% of people with Down Syndrome have atlantoaxial instability. Serious injury may result if the neck is flexed forcibly, allowing the vertebrae to shift or squeeze the spinal cord. Half of moderately or severely mentally retarded people have Down syndrome. Although many Down athletes compete in the Special Olympics, none has suffered serious injury during training or competition to date (Stein, 1991). Despite this relative freedom from serious injury, the following guidelines have been proposed to protect athletes with Down syndrome.

1. Participation in gymnastics, diving, swimming the butterfly stroke, high jump, pentathlon, soccer, and any warm-up exercise placing excessive pressure on the head or neck muscles is prohibited until the examining physician has tested the athlete for atlantoaxial stability. X-rays of the head and neck should be performed (Cooke, 1984).
2. In the presence of atlantoaxial instability, the activities mentioned are not allowed in competition. Only those without atlantoaxial instability will be allowed to participate.
3. Every parent, coach, and trainer should require medical clearance for Down syndrome athletes to ensure that their sports activity is safe and enjoyable.

## SECTION H.
## HANDICAPPED ATHLETES

### Paraplegic/Wheelchair Athletes

Special Olympics and may other organizations offer the disabled patient opportunities to compete against other individuals with similar degrees of disability. These competitive events have been helpful to the participants and successful in promoting increased morale and providing a stimulus to maximize individual function. We will give a brief reference to the available testing and training methods, a functional classification system, and discuss potential sports involvement for the disabled athlete, especially the paraplegic.

The demanding nature of sports in disabled athletes causes certain risks. The medical complications of the athlete do not outweigh the physical or psychological benefits of sports participation, but they can delay training, impede competition, or even interfere with the daily functioning of the disabled athlete. Information about disabled athletes is relatively sparse and it is clear that more is needed about the benefits of exercise and the nature of injury in this population. In the Curtis and Dillon study, 72% of wheelchair athletes suffered at least one sports-related injury after they began athletic participation. The most common injuries were soft tissue damage, blisters, and lacerations. Pressure ulcers, fractures, weakness and numbness of the hand, and disorders of temperature regulation were less common. High risk sports include track, basketball, and road racing, followed by tennis and field events. Injuries were uncommon in pool, bowling, archery, slalom, and table tennis (Curtis, 1986; DeLisa, 1988). Other texts have dealt with injuries and their prevention in wheelchair athletes.

## Testing Programs

**Arm Ergometry.** Aerobic power and fitness can be assessed with a forearm-crank ergometer while the patient is sitting in a wheelchair. Conditions can be held constant from one person to another. The major disadvantage is that the muscles used in operating the crank are not identical to those used in propelling a wheelchair. Because the muscles involved are small, the rate of rotation (80 rpm) is higher than that for normal cycle ergometry. However, in all other respects, this exercise testing protocol is much the same as cycle ergometer measurements of aerobic power. Submaximal tests can be performed but it is hard to extrapolate findings to a predicted maximum.

**Wheelchair Tests.** The simplest test available is to measure the distance covered in a wheelchair over a 12 minute time period. With standardization of testing conditions, this procedure provides some indication of the condition of the athlete although scores are susceptible to ground surface changes, the mass of the wheelchair, and skill of the operator. Another option with a wheelchair is to have the patient propel the wheelchair up a specially made treadmill. This is a more realistic task and tests the muscles that are important in day-to-day performance. Scores are influenced by wheelchair design and experience of the users (Hoffman, 1986).

**Muscle Strength.** Isometric dynamometer and tensiometer measurements, with a machine such as a Cybex II, are helpful in measuring arm muscle strength. There appears to be a close relationship between isometric and isokinetic scores, with both having an important influence on aerobic power and endurance performance.

**Body Fat.** The average wheelchair patient does not get adequate exercise and tends to accumulate body fat, especially if the patient uses a motorized wheelchair. Skin fold thicknesses are measured as in normal individuals. However, it is not possible to predict body fat or lean body mass using standard equations because muscle wasting and atrophy of the lower body are often present.

**Potential Condition of the Athlete.** Well trained wheelchair athletes can develop remarkable anaerobic power (3.5-4.0 liters per minute). Marked muscle hypertrophy often is present. It is difficult to predict maximum scores regarding aerobic power, especially in female wheelchair athletes, since few well-designed studies of aerobic power have been pursued (Hoffman, 1986).

## Training Programs

There have been only a few systematic studies of exercise training by wheelchair patients (Stein 1991). Intensity, frequency, and duration of conditioning all influence the training response just as they do in normal athletes. The athletes increases his aerobic power and gains muscle strength at high speeds of movement (180° per second). It is common to see increases in stroke volume and cardiac output at high work rates. In general, the optimal exercise prescription is comparable to that of a normal athlete: 30 minutes of continuous exercise at 60%-70% of maximum oxygen intake performed three to four times a week.

## Functional Classification

The optimal method of classifying paraplegic patients is a matter of increasing debate. The most widely used format was developed by the International Stoke Mandeville Games Federation (ISMGF) and can be found in many texts dealing with disabled athletes. The advantage of the ISMGF scheme is that it combines information on the patient's anatomical lesion with an assessment of the quality and quantity of functioning musculature (Table 6H-1).

## Characteristics of Participation

There are many activities available for wheelchair athletes and they are promoted by the ISMGF. This organization espouses the principle that minimal rule changes are all that is necessary for the various categories of disabled individuals to participate successfully in recreational and competitive events (Bloomquist, 1986). Wheelchair races from 40-1500 meters and unofficial marathons are held. Field events include all the usual throwing competitions performed from an anchored chair. Other individual sports include swimming, table tennis, fencing, weight lifting, archery, rifle shoot-

Table 6H-1. Classification for National Wheelchair Athletic Association Competitions

| Class | Equivalent Spinal Cord Level | Function Present | Function Absent |
|---|---|---|---|
| IA | C-6 or higher | Wrist extensor | No better than fair triceps; nothing distally; no balance or lower extremity function |
| IB | C-7 | Good or normal triceps | No finger flexors of extensors; no balance or lower extremity function |
| IC | C-8 | Finger flexors and extensors | No intrinsics; no balance or lower extremity function |
| II | T-1→T-5 | Normal upper extremity function | No better than poor abdominal muscles; no useful balance or lower extremity function |
| III | T-6→T-10 | Upper abdominal muscles | Some balance but not normal; no lower extremity function |
| IV | T-11→L-2 | Normal abdominal strength | No better than poor quadriceps; nothing distally |
| V | L-3→S-5 | Fair or better quadriceps | Lower extremity weakness "significant and permanent" |
| VI | | (Swimming only; ability to push off a wall with lower extremities L-5→S-5) | |

ing, bowling, and snooker. Wheelchair basketball is the most popular of all sports. Recreational sports opportunities include riding, sailing, gliding, and five pin bowling.

Disabled athletes in training for major competitions are no more likely to be injured than their "normal" counterparts. The five highest-risk sports (in decreasing order) are track, basketball, road racing, tennis, and field events. The medical staff should be prepared to treat the usual injuries and other problems found in international competition. Common injuries in wheelchair sports are soft-tissue injuries, blisters, abrasions, pressure sores, carpal tunnel syndrome, and muscle soreness. Shoulder and elbow injuries are more prevalent in wheelchair athletes over age 40 (Bloomquist, 1986).

Prevention of injury includes routine static stretching, warm-up and cool-down periods, slow progression of training programs, padding of wheelchair push rims, preventive taping, splinting, and wearing gloves. Athletes involved in Special Olympics and the National Cerebral Palsy/Les Autres Games may have a wide variety of medical conditions, but they are generally are well selected before they get to higher competition so that there are few health related problems (Mangus, 1987).

Hypothermia could become a critical problem for a wheelchair athlete (Curtis, 1986). Because their lack of muscle mass doesn't allow the athlete to shiver or generate heat, it is important to wrap a wheelchair marathoner in plastic, remove wet clothing and replace it with dry, or have him/her take a warm shower immediately after the event. While warming body parts below a spinal injury, care should be taken not to apply enough heat to cause burns. Providing adequate hydration is extremely important for hypothermic wheelchair athletes.

Hyperthermia presents a greater danger to the disabled athlete because sweating may be deficient below the level of the spinal cord injury. Most wheelchair athletes rely on evaporative heat loss from the arms and trunk alone. An additional common problem for the paraplegic is vasomotor paralysis of the lower extremity and the absence of normally active muscles that help pump blood to the heart. Dehydration is even more damaging to a handicapped athlete's performance. He/she already may be hypovolemic because of pooling of blood in the buttocks, posterior thighs, and ankles. Wheelchair athletes should be encouraged to drink water on a regular basis and acclimatize properly to heat.

The benefits of sports participation for the disabled are immense. Arm strength can be increased through exercise training and has a direct carryover to everyday life. More sports participants return to the labor force than do those who are sedentary or bedridden. They also have a lower rate of absenteeism and higher wage earning. Physiologic gains are remarkable and top competitors are capable of developing greater aerobic power and muscle strength than nondisabled athletes. Physicians should support and advise the disabled athlete who is interested in sports participation.

## Sensory Handicapped

Deaf and blind individuals and others with sensory deficits now are being encouraged to participate in safe, well-organized physical education programs, general exercises, and sports. Many world organizations are available to help deaf, blind, and other sensory disabled groups participate at all levels. Many qualified health professionals work with the disabled and are aware of early signs of sensory disability. The sooner a young child with a sensory disability is treated, the earlier appropriate exercise opportunities can be made available. This can lead to development of better exercise skills which benefits the general well-being of the patient.

Physical education programs for the sensory disabled are offered at schools where classes are taught in much the same way as for the nondisabled. Warmup exercises of at least 15 minutes that include strength and aerobic components should be emphasized. Various sports skills should be taught, followed by games that use them. A cool down period should follow all exercise sessions. The exercise program itself should incorporate fun activities with music where appropriate. Specialized equipment including electronic beeper balls, balls with bells inside, and other specialized audio or visual equipment, are available and can be used successfully if they are safe, colorful, and easily handled. Balls and bats may be made of sponge, plastic, foam, vinyl, or leather. Talking directly to the deaf athlete who reads lips is important for good communication.

## Sport and Exercise Opportunities

Exercise opportunities for these individuals have been available for years, and a classification system has been developed for each group. All competitors should be tested by an audiologist, ophthalmologist, or other specialist before taking part in any organized competition. Most of the rules for athletic events for the sensory disabled are the same or very similar to nondisabled sports. When rule changes are necessary, it is usually for fairness or availability of equipment.

Equipment is rarely changed but may be adapted for the sensory disabled athlete. Specialized equipment, whether stationary or electronic, often has been eliminated due to improved training techniques. Competitive sites, including running tracks, swimming pools, and other competitive areas should be well maintained. The metal curve on the inner lane of running tracks should be removed when blind athletes are competing, and a very small pylon or plastic disk should be substituted against the inner perimeter. Housing for athletes with sensory disabilities should be safe and of good quality but seldom are more than a few modifications required. Arrangements for guide dogs and normal medical backup of physicians, physical therapists, athletic trainers, and medical supplies should be available at all games and sites.

## Training

Individuals with sensory disabilities are more apt to be at a disadvantage in attaining maximal cardiovascular fitness because of a lack of childhood development. Frequently, children have subnormal maximal oxygen intake and have not developed a normal working heart rate. This is due to lack of training and general exercise opportunities. Muscle fatigue is a common limiting factor regardless of the exercise modalities. However, when the sensory disabled athlete becomes trained, his/her fitness levels approach those of other trained athletes. With sensible training programs, many aspiring athletes with sensory disabilities can attempt high level competition with good success.

**REFERENCES**

Aird, R.B., Maslend, R.I., Woodbury, D.M. *The Epilepsies: A Critical Review*, New York, New York. Raven Press, 1984.
Bar-Or, O., Neuman, I., Doton, R. Effects of dry air in humid climates on exercise-induced asthma in children and pre-adolescents. *J Allergy and Clinical Immunology* 60:163-168, 1977.
Bloomquist, L.E. Injuries to athletes with physical disabilities: prevention implications. *Phys and Sportsmed* 14(9):97-105, 1986.
Brink, S.J., Eisenbarth, G.S., Rubenstein, A.H. Type I Diabetes: Metabolic control and more. *Patient Care* pgs. 49, February 28, 1991.
Bunnel, W.P. The natural history of idiopathic scoliosis before skeletal maturity. *Spine* 11:773, 1986.
Cooke, R.E. Atlantoaxial instability in individuals with Down Syndrome. *Adapted Physical Activity Quarterly* 1(3):194-195, 1984.
Curtis, K., Dillon, D. Survey of wheelchair athletic injuries — common patterns and prevention. *Sport and the Disabled Athlete* 9:211-219, 1986.
DeLisa, J. *Rehabilitation medicine, principles and practice.* J.P. Lippincott and Company, Philadelphia, PA. 1988.
Gates, J.R., Ramani, V., Whalen, S. et al Characteristics of pseudoseizures. *Archives in Rheumatology* 1985 42(12):1183-1187.

Gates, J.R. Epilepsy in sports participation. *Phys and Sportsmed* 19(3):98-104, 1991.
Goldberg, B. Children, sports and chronic disease. *Phys and Sportsmed* 18(10):45, 1990.
Hauser, W., A., Kurland, L.T. The epidemiology of epilepsy in Rochester, Minneosta 1935-1967. *Epilepsia* 16(1):1-66, 1975.
Katz, R.M. Asthma in sports. *Annals of Allergy* 51:153-163, 1983.
Lonstein, J.E. Natural history in school screening for scoliosis. *Orth Clin of NA* 19:227, 1988.
MacDonald, M.J. Post-exercise late-onset hypoglycemia and insulin-dependent diabetic patients. *Diabetes Care*, 10(5):584-588, 1987.
McCarthy, P. Wheezing or breathing through exercise-induced asthma. *Phys and Sportsmed* 125-130, 1989.
Mendel, J.R. The nervous system. In Strauss, R.H. (ed) *Sports Medicine* Philadelphia: W.B. Saunders Co. 155-157, 1985.
Mink, B. D. Pulmonary concerns in the exercise prescription. In DiNubile, N.A. *Clinics in Sports Medicine*, Philadelphia, PA, W.B. Saunders Company, 10(1):111-112, 1991.
Monahan, T. Wheelchair athletes need special treatment- but only for injuries. *Phys and Sportsmed* 14:121, 1986.
Morton, A.R., Fitch, K.D. and Hahn, A.G. Physical activity in the asthmatic. *Phys and Sportsmed* 9(3):51-60, March 1981.
Nathan, D.M., Madnek, S.F., Delahamty, L. Programming pre-exercise snacks to prevent post-exercise hyperglycemia in intensively treated insulin-dependent diabetics. *Annals of Internal Med* 102(4):483-486, 1985.
Pederson, O., Beck-Nielsen, H., Hebing, L. Increasing swimmer's glucose tolerance after exercise in patients with insulin-dependent diabetes mellitus. *NEJM* 302(16)886-892, 1980.
Renshaw, T.S. Screening school children for scoliosis. *Clinical Orthopedics* 229:226, 1988.
Renshaw, T.S. Orthotic treatment of idiopathic scoliosis and kyphosis. *AAOS Instructions Course Lectures* 34:110, 1985.
Renshaw, T.S. Diagnosis and management of idiopathic scoliosis. *Fam Practice Recertification* 13(1):46, 1991.
Robbins, D.C., Carleton, S. Managing the diabetic athlete. *Phys and Sportsmed* 17(12):45, 1989.
Rogers, M.A., Yamamoto, K., King, D.S. et al. Improvement in glucose tolerance after one week of exercise in patients with mild NIDDM. *Diabetes Care* 11(8):613-618, 1988.
Shayevitz, M., Shayevitz, B.D. Athletic training in chronic obstructive pulmonary disease. *Clinics in Sports Med* 5:471-491, 1986.
Staten, M.A. Diabetes and older adults. *Phys and Sportsmed* 19(3):66, 1991.
Stein, J.U. Physical activity from rehabilitation to independent community function: the rate of physical activity in handicapping conditions. In:Dinubile, M.A. (ed) *Clinics in Sports Medicine — Exercise Prescription*, W.B. Saunders Company, Philadelphia, PA, 10(1):211-221, 1991.
Naken, J. *Epilepsia* 31(1):88-94, 1990.
Voy, R. The U.S. Olympic experience with exercise-induced bronchospasm. *Medical Sci Sports Exercise* 18:328-330, 1984.
Weinstein, S.L., Ponds, P.O. in Setti, I.B. Curve prevention in idiopathic scoliosis. *J Bone Joint Surgery* 65A:447, 1983.

**SUGGESTED READINGS**

*Section A*

Berger, M., et al. Metabolic and hormonal effects of exercise in diabetic patients. In Brownley, M. (ed) *Diabetes Mellitus: Intermediary Metabolism and Its Regulation*. New York: Garland S.T.P.M. Press Vol. 3, 273-305, 1981.
Brownley, M. and Valssara, H. Exercise and the diabetic patient. *Drug Therapy* pgs 66-72, March 1982.
Caron, D., et al. Effects of post-prandial exercise on meal-related glucose intolerance in insulin-dependent diabetic individuals. *Diabetes Care* 5:364-369, 1982.
Devlin, J.T. and Horton, E.S. Diet and exercise: important therapeutic tools. *Drug Therapy* pp. 109-115, March 1984.
Duckworth, W.C. and Swanson, S.K. Insulin therapy in type II diabetes — pros and cons. *Drug Therapy* pgs 111-117, May 1983.
Felig, P. Exercise and diabetes. In Peterson, C.M. (ed) *Diabetes Management in the 1980's* New York: Praeger, pp 118-124, 1982.
Flood, T.M. Ten steps to a successful exercise program. *Medical Times* 108:69-76, 1980.
Genuth, S.M. Why the response to insulin is impaired. *Drug Therapy* ppg. 64-80, March 1984.
Kemmer, F.W. and Berger, M. Exercise and diabetes: physical activity as part of daily life and its role in the treatment of diabetic patients. *International Journal of Sports Medicine* 4:77, 1983.
Nelson, J.D. et al. Metabolic response of normal man and insulin-infused diabetics to post-prandial exercise. *Am J of Physiology* 24:E209-E316, 1982.
Painter, P., Blackburn, G. Exercise for patients with chronic disease. *Postgrad Med* 83(1):185, 1988.
Prosser, P.R. and Anding, R. Diet therapy for patients who take insulin. *Consultant* pp. 29-36, Dec. 1983.
Richter, E.A., Ruderman, N.B. and Schneider, S.H. Diabetes and exercise. *AmJMed* 70:201-209, 1981.
Rowland, T.W., Swadba, L.A. et al. Glycemic control of physical training in insulin dependent diabetes mellitus. *Am J Diabetics* Care Vol. 139, 307-310, March 1985.
Ruderman, M.B., Young, J.C. and Schneider, S.H. Exercise as a therapeutic tool in the type I diabetic. *Practical Cardiology* 10:143-153, 1984.
Schneider, S.H. and Ruderman, N. Exercise and diabetes. In *Diabetes Mellitus and Obesity* Baltimore: Williams & Wilkins, 185-191, 1982.
Stephens, P., Hoffman, W.H., et al. Exercise for children with chronic disease: What is allowable? *J Musculoskeletal Med* 5(2):13-29, 1988.
Tamborlane, W.V. et al. Reduction to normal plasma glucose in juvenile diabetes by subcutaneous administration with a portable insulin infusion pump. *New Engl J of Med* 300:573, 1979.
Unger, R.H. The Berson Memorial Lecture: Insulin-Glucagon relationships in the defense against hypoglycemia. *Diabetes* 32:575-583, 1983.
Vranic, M. and Berger, M. Exercise and diabetes mellitus. *Diabetes* 28:147, 1979.
Zinman, B. Exercise and diabetes treatment. *Clinical Diabetes* 1:18-21, 1983.

*Section B*

Kennell, J.H. Sports participation for the child with a chronic health problem. In Strauss, R.H. (ed) *Sports Medicine* Philadelphia: W.B. Saunders Co, 218-236, 1984.
Neijens, H.J., Duiverman, E.J., Kerrebijn, K.F. Exercise-induced bronchial obstruction. In *Current Therapy in Sports Medicine*. Welsh, R.P., Shephard, R.J. (eds). Toronto: P.C. Decker, Inc., pgs. 95-98, 1985.

*Section C*

Rebuck, A.S., E'Urzo, A.D., Chapman, K.R. Exercise and chronic obstructive lung disease. In *Current Therapy in Sports Medicine*. Welsh, R.P., Shephard, R.J. (eds). Toronto: P.C. Decker, Inc., pgs. 101-105, 11985.

*Section D*

Committee on Children with Handicaps and Committee on Sports Medicine: American Academy of Pediatrics position statement on sports and the child with epilepsy. *Pediatrics* 73(December):884-885, 1983.
Cowart, V.S. Should epileptics exercise? *Phys and Sportsmed* 14:183, 1986.
Ellenberg, J.H., Hirtz, D.G., Nelson, K.B. Do seizures in children cause intellectual deterioration? *N Engl J Med* 314:1085-1088, 1986.
Greensher, J. Challenge for the 80s. Presented at the Pediatric Patient Education Symposium, Dallas, Nov 29-30, 1983.
Middleton, A.H., Attwell, A.T., Walsh, G.D. *Epilepsy.* Boston:Little Brown & Company, p. 45, 1981.
Orlowski, J.P., Rothner, A.D., Lueders, H. Submersion accidents in children with epilepsy. *Am J Dis Child* 136(Sept):777-780, 1982.
Pearn, J. Drowning risk to epileptic children: a study from Hawaii. *Br J Med* 6147(Nov4):1284-1285, 1978.
Should epileptics be barred from contact sports? The AMA changes position. *Medical World News* 15:62, 1974.
Temkin, N.R., Davis, G.R. Stress as risk factor for seizures among adults with epilepsy. *Epilepsia* 25(Aug 25):450-456, 1984.

*Section F*

Ekblom, B.T. Exercise and rheumatoid arthritis. In *Current Therapy in Sports Medicine*. Welsh, R.P., Shephard, R.J. (eds). Toronto: P.C. Decker, Inc., pgs. 108-110, 1985.

*Section H*

Birrer, R.B. The Special Olympics: an injury overview. *Phys and Sportsmed* 12:95-97, 1985.

Cantu, R. Sports and handicapped children. In Micheli, L. (ed) *Pediatrics and Adolescent Sports Medicine.* Boston: Little, Brown and Company, pgs. 179-193, 1984.

Curtis, K.A. Injuries of wheelchair athletes. Sports and recreation for the child and young adult with physical disability, in *Proceedings of the Winter Park Seminar.*

Shepard, R.J. Exercise for the disabled: the paraplegic. In *Current Therapy in Sports Medicine.* Welsh, R.P., Shephard, R.J. (eds). Toronto: P.C. Decker, Inc., pgs. 110-111, 1985.

Curtis, K.A. Wheelchair sportsmedicine, part 4: athletic injuries. *Sports N' Spokes* 7:20-24, 1982.

Hoffman, M. Cardiorespiratory fitness and training of quadriplegics and paraplegics. *Sports Medicine* 3:312-330, 1986.

Mangus, B. Sports injuries, the disabled athlete and the athletic trainer. *Athletic Training* 22(4):305-310, 1987.

Nelsen, R., Nygaard, P. et al. Complications that may occur in those with spinal cord injuries who could participate in sports. *Paraplegic* 23:152-158, 1985.

# 7
# Injury Prevention

Can a team physician prevent athletic injuries? For that matter, can any member of a sports medicine network effectively prevent injury? The answer to both questions is an unequivocal yes. Consider Cahill's (1978) work on knee injuries in a community high school football system. When a preseason leg strengthening program was established, the incidence of knee injuries was cut in half (50%). Although this study looked at only a small portion of what could be done to prevent injury, there still was a major impact on the epidemiology of sports injuries in that system. The sports medicine doctor, more specifically the primary care sports physician, is best suited to direct a preventive conditioning program that includes cardiovascular, heat acclimation, weight training, flexibility, and agility elements.

The concept of injury prevention in sports is relatively new and mostly unproven. Sports medicine researchers have yet to turn their attention to preventive medicine in any substantial way. Instead of reacting to injury when it occurs, our philosophy is to make every attempt to prevent it. Evidence suggests that conditioning involving flexibility, cardiovascular status, and resistance training contributes to the structural integrity of major joints as well as muscle-tendon units (Feiring, 1989). The preparticipation physical exam (PPPE) as a screening device should provide the team physician with an accurate assessment of an athlete's level of conditioning. Based upon the strength and weaknesses identified with this evaluation, an appropriate preseason conditioning program could be developed. Such a specific program could make a significant contribution to the prevention of injuries.

We see the primary care team physician having three different priorities in the course of fulfilling his/her duties:

- Before competition → prevention
- During competition → triage
- After competition → rehabilitation

In this chapter, we will discuss the identification of generic factors to be addressed in any community sports system regardless of size, community interest, or economic resources. An active sports medicine network can make sports participation safer. Schematically, this point can be illustrated in Figures 7-1 to 7-3. A dissection of this schematic portrayal in a fictional community system (Figure 7-1) serves as a framework.

Realistically, many of the athletes in this system are recreational and never come in contact with the health care system until *after* an injury occurs. Not much can be done to induce change except improve the lay athlete's education about sports injury prevention and training. However, an athlete who is involved in formal programs (school sports, organized amateur programs, etc.) can be reached and influenced about injury prevention. Two areas of preventive impact (Figure 7-2) exist in this hypothetical scheme:

- *Preparticipation physical examination* — discussed and outlined in Chapter 4.
- *Control of the sports environment*

Interacting at these two points in the community sports medicine network can reap large dividends. Regardless of how aggressively a community

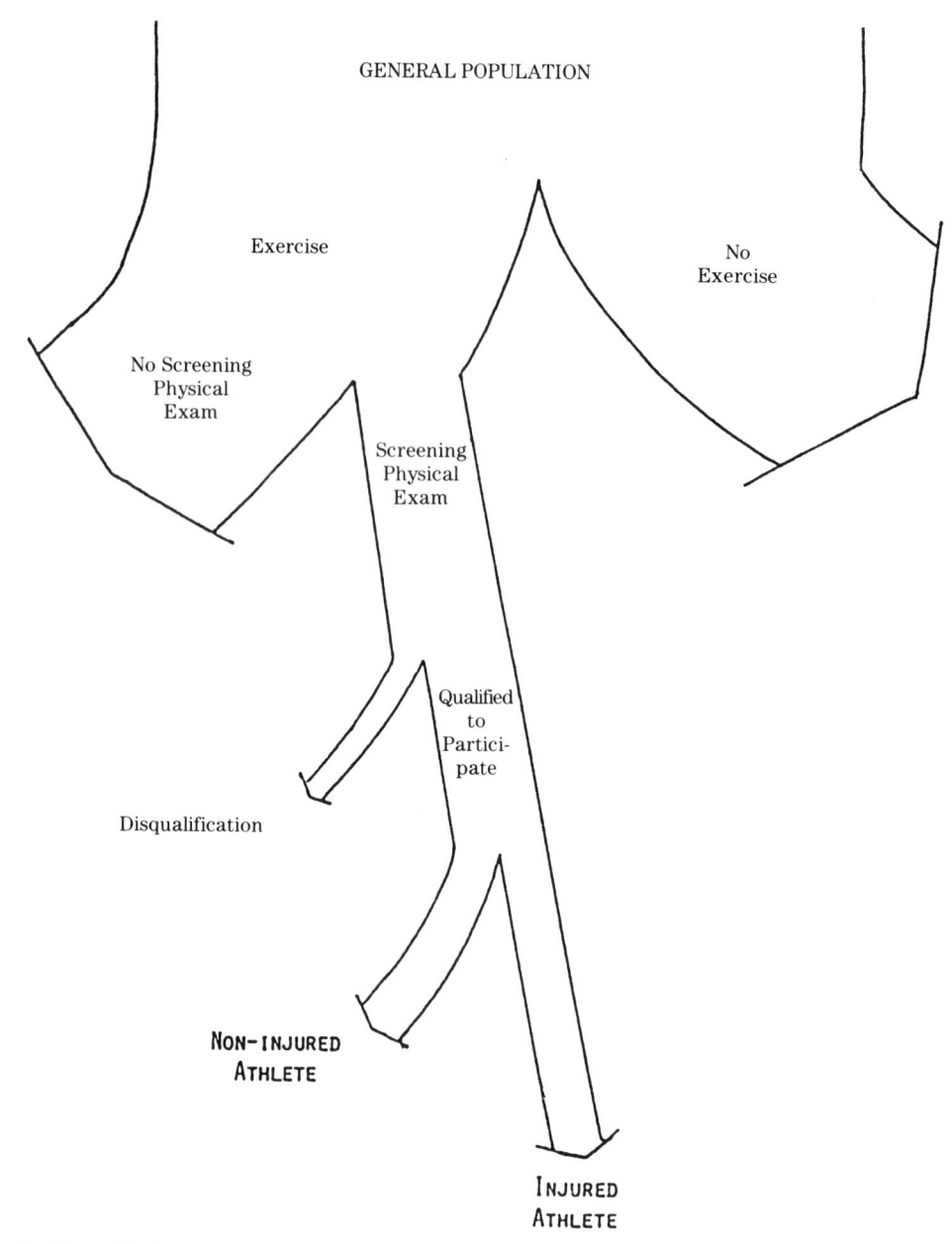

**Fig. 7-1.** Community Sports Medicine — Schematic

chooses to pursue these areas of impact, there will always remain the "inevitable injury" (Figure 7-3).

As we outline many of the important aspects of injury prevention in this chapter, examples of prominent factors to be considered by the community sports medicine physician are given. The emphasis is on practical and important principles instead of on vague philosophical thought. For easy reference the chapter is organized as follows:

- Epidemiology of Injuries
- Areas of Preventive Impact
  a. Preparticipation evaluation
  b. External factors — the sports medicine environment
     a. equipment
     b. playing conditions
     c. rule enforcement
     d. balanced competition
     e. coaching techniques
- Internal Factors — the athlete
  a. Proper conditioning
  b. Health care maintenance
  c. Athlete education

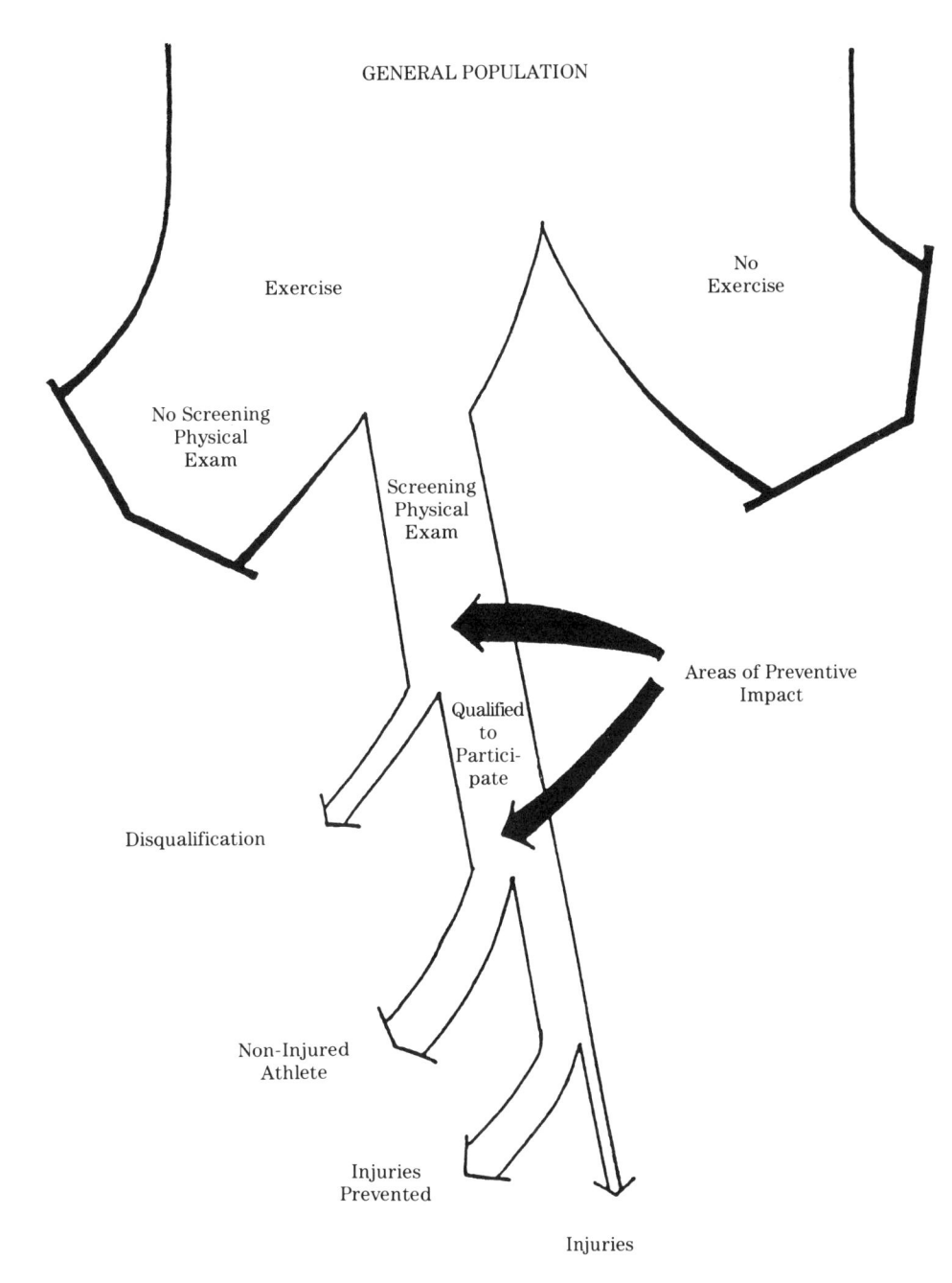

**Fig. 7-2.** Community Sports Medicine — Areas of Impact

## EPIDEMIOLOGY OF INJURIES

The top ten sports that are most likely to produce injury-related visits to the sports medicine physician are:

- Running/jogging
- Racket sports
- Basketball
- Ballet/dancing/aerobics
- Football
- Skiing
- Weightlifting
- Baseball/softball
- Soccer
- Martial arts

Numerous studies have analyzed different athletic populations seeking to identify the most common injuries. In a classic study, Garrick and Requa

*INJURY PREVENTION* 173

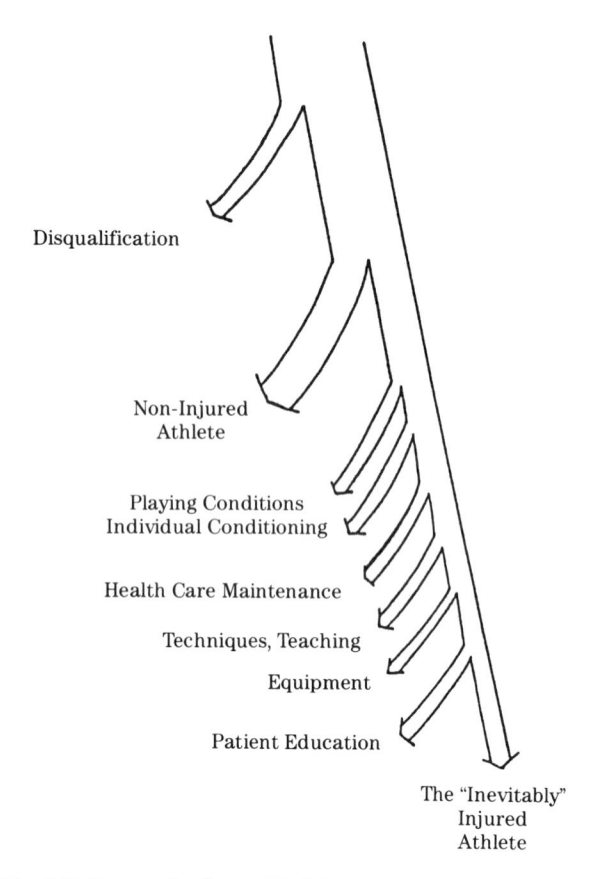

**Fig. 7-3.** Community Sports Medicine — Factors in Injury Prevention

**Table 7-1. Anatomic Sites of High-School Sports Injuries**

|  | No. | % |
| --- | --- | --- |
| Head | 60 | 5.1 |
| Spine | 111 | 9.4 |
| Shoulder | 50 | 4.2 |
| Hand, wrist, fingers | 102 | 8.6 |
| Other upper extremities | 66 | 5.6 |
| Back/trunk | 66 | 5.6 |
| Thigh | 173 | 14.6 |
| Knee | 175 | 14.8 |
| Ankle | 164 | 13.9 |
| Other lower extremities | 214 | 18.1 |
| Total | 1181 |  |

(From Garrick J.G., Requa R.: Medical care and injury surveillance in the high school setting. *Phys Sportsmed* 9:115, 1981)

**Table 7-2. Types of High-School Injuries**

|  | No. | % |
| --- | --- | --- |
| Fractures | 63 | 5.5 |
| Sprains | 349 | 29.5 |
| Strains | 366 | 31.0 |
| Lacerations | 21 | 1.8 |
| Contusions | 162 | 13.7 |
| Inflammations | 70 | 5.9 |
| Other | 150 | 12.7 |
| Total | 1181 |  |

(From Garrick J.G., Requa R.: Medical care and injury surveillance in the high school setting. *Phys Sportsmed* 9:115, 1981)

**Table 7-3. Percentage of Emergency Room-Treated Injuries Associated With Sports Activities by Body Part Injured and Age Group of Victim**

| Body Part | Total | 5-14 Years | 15+ Years |
| --- | --- | --- | --- |
| Hand and Finger | 20% | 28% | 17% |
| Elbow and Wrist | 7% | 10% | 6% |
| Arm | 3% | 4% | 2% |
| Leg | 4% | 3% | 5% |
| Knee and Ankle | 28% | 18% | 33% |
| Foot and Toe | 7% | 6% | 7% |
| Head and Face | 19% | 21% | 17% |
| Shoulder and Trunk | 12% | 10% | 13% |

Sports included in study are: football, baseball, basketball, gymnastics, soccer, wrestling, volleyball, ice hockey, track and field, racquet sports, golf, trampoline, tetherball, lacrosse, and ball sports not otherwise specified.

(Source: National Electronic Injury Surveillance System (NEISS) U.S. Consumer Product Safety Commission/EPHA, Dec., 1981.)

(1981) reported on a high school population (Tables 7-1 and 7-2). The National Electronic Injury Surveillance System (NEISS, 1981) monitored 1.8 million emergency room-treated injuries associated with sports activities for all ages. Breakdown by body part can be found on Table 7-3.

Any individual responsible for the care of athletes in a particular sport needs to know what to expect. What is the frequency and severity of injuries in that sport at that level in that community? Clinical epidemiology can supply some answers about the most common injuries. Others come from having a good knowledge of community-dependent variables, coaches, players, philosophies, conditions, etc. Epidemiologic studies help the primary care physician because they use what *has* happened to gauge what *will* happen.

Table 7-4 provides recent data on NCAA college sports injury rates (NCAA, 1987). As important as national data is, it is more important for the physician to actively seek out information on the community sports injury incidence. School officials, other physicians in the community, recollection of past coverage, and emergency room visits

Table 7-4. College Sports Injury Rates (Injuries/1000 Athlete Exposures)

| Year | Football | Wrestling | Ice Hockey | Men's Soccer | Women's Soccer | Men's Gymnastics | Women's Gymnastics | Baseball | Softball | Men's Lacrosse | Women's Lacrosse | Women's Volleyball | Field Hockey |
|---|---|---|---|---|---|---|---|---|---|---|---|---|---|
| 1982 | 7.17 | — | — | — | — | — | — | — | — | — | — | — | — |
| 1983 | 7.33 | 10.25 | — | — | — | — | — | 10.23 | 3.29 | — | 8.12 | 3.69 | 5.30 | — |
| 1984 | 7.22 | 10.36 | — | — | — | — | — | 7.94 | 4.06 | — | 7.96 | 3.73 | 5.47 | — |
| 1985 | 6.81 | 10.84 | — | — | — | — | — | 9.38 | 3.37 | — | 5.82 | 3.37 | 5.44 | — |
| 1986 | 6.02 | 8.30 | 5.38 | 8.35 | 7.55 | 5.67 | 6.29 | 3.20 | 4.90 | * | 4.91 | 3.71 | 4.43 |
| 1987 | 5.43 | 10.21 | 6.14 | 7.33 | 8.44 | 6.00 | 6.05 | 3.07 | 4.06 | 5.07 | 4.04 | 4.62 | 5.17 |
| 1988 | 6.68 | 8.20 | 5.80 | 7.22 | 8.28 | 3.70 | 6.50 | 3.30 | 2.90 | 6.80 | 3.50 | 4.46 | 5.80 |

*Data not available

all serve as sources for this type of information. If the picture still is not clear, such injury data should be collected. To emphasize again, the possession of this information is not a *luxury*; it is a *necessity* for well-prepared sports coverage.

## AREAS OF PREVENTIVE IMPACT

### Preparticipation Evaluation

This subject is discussed elsewhere (see Chapter 4) and we will only summarize the role of the preparticipation exam here. Any preparticipation screening should answer these questions:

- Is this candidate *mature enough* to compete in the sport or sports for which screening is being done?
- Is this person in adequate *physical condition* to compete in sports?
- Does this candidate have any *increased potential* for injury?
- Does this person have *medical problems* that may disqualify him/her from competition?

The team physician is doing him/herself and the athlete an injustice if all these questions cannot be answered after the exam.

### External Factors — Controlling the Sports Environment

An important question team physicians often ask is: Can I have an impact upon the sports environment? Will the "system" allow adequate medical input at the appropriate time? The answer to this question must be "yes" if there is to be any effective change in any system for the purpose of preventing sports injuries. There is no literature to consult on this subject. We believe that the ability to have an impact on the system is *not* present in 20% to 30% of the sports medicine community networks across this country. Prevention requires the establishment of protocol and procedures and is a virtual impossibility without the cooperation of school/program administrators, officials, coaches, athletes, parents, and the community in general.

1. **Equipment.** Clothing should be considered equipment and vital to good performance in sports like running (see Figures 7-4 and 7-5). This is the single most important factor in the generation of injuries in some sports (running, skateboarding). A study of skateboard injuries (Kemon, 1978) cited the use of protective clothing and equipment such as helmet, elbow pads, and knee pads as the single most important factor in preventing injuries. Most equipment is purchased by athletes or their parents. Three factors commonly influence the selection of the equipment: safety or protection, cost, and influence or perceived influence on performance or the prevailing peer attitude (Finke, 1982). There is no question that poor equipment causes a substantial number of injuries. In some sports, there is standardization of equipment based upon appropriate testing and certification (NOCSAE — football helmets). Still, far too much equipment is offered and/or modified without safety in mind. A community should have a representative who is knowledgeable in sports equipment to act as a resource to advise parents and athletes. The practice of handing down equipment originally purchased for older, more developed,

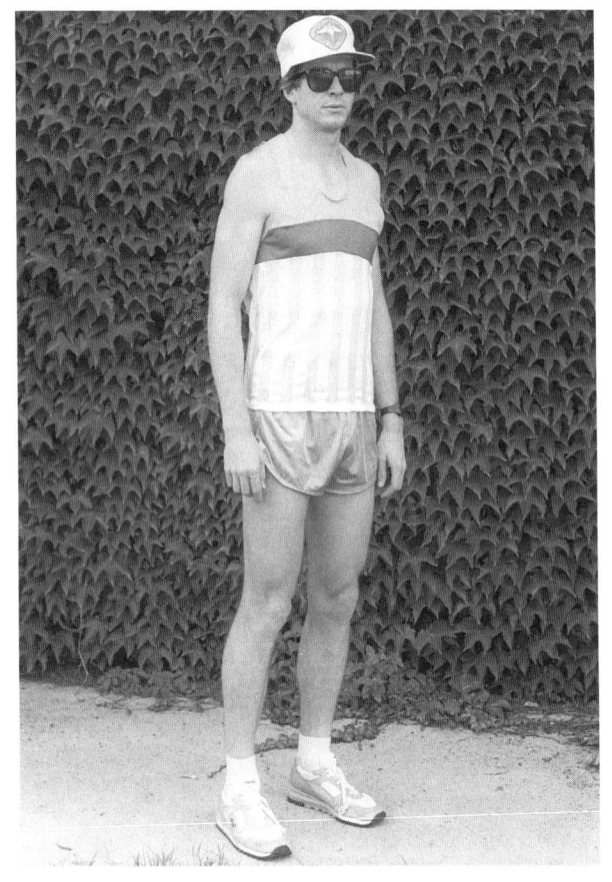

1. Hat with visor to shade eyes from bright sunlight
2. Sunglasses for additional eye protection
3. Low cut jersey (neck and arms) for freedom of movement and prevention of skin abrasions
4. Smooth bright reflective chest band for visibility day or night
5. White mesh for maximum cooling
6. Lightweight chronograph and watch for training
7. Inside pocket to secure keys, identification
8. Slit side for maximum freedom of leg movement (inside brief for convenience)
9. Short sock with "wicking" action to keep feet dry (should fit snugly to prevent sliding into shoe)
10. Reflective material for visibility in the dark
11. Mesh on top of shoe for foot ventilation
12. Thick sole to insulate feet from road heat

**Fig. 7-4.** Running in the Heat

1. Hood to protect neck and head
2. Cotton stocking cap for scalp warmth
3. Lightweight reflective fabric resistant to water but allowing evaporation of perspiration (allowing good visibility)
4. Layered clothing (lightweight) for maximum warmth; turtle neck shirt to keep wind off neck
5. Long jacket to cover lower back for warmth; midbody vents for maximum ventilation
6. Adjustable arm straps to decrease or increase heat loss
7. Reflective mittens (not gloves) to protect fingers from cold injury and for visibility
8. Storm flap over zipper to prevent water soaking
9. Adequate inner lower body and extremity protection (underwear) for "wicking" action and warmth
10. Reflective strip for visibility
11. Leg zippers to adjust ventilation and to enable removal of pants without shoe removal
12. Water-resistant shoes to keep feet dry

**Fig. 7-5.** Running in the Rain

or bigger athletes to be used by younger, less mature ones should be condemned, even if it can be understood. This is a common practice in economically- depressed school systems, especially in the sport of football. Football helmets and shoulder pads bought for 18-year-olds may be used by 14-year-olds once they become out of date and worn. The practice leads to an unacceptable risk of injury to the younger, immature athlete.

Poor equipment fit is a common etiologic agent in other areas as well:
- Lack of hand pads for bicycling leads to an increased incidence of radioneuropathy.
- A football helmet that is too loose can result in head injury.
- Shoulder pads that are too small causes an increase in acromio-clavicular shoulder injuries.

- Worn running shoes decrease the effect of cushioning and cause an increase in overuse injuries to the lower feet.

Improper equipment also affects the biomechanics of a sport.

- Tennis rackets that are too heavy or have a handle grip that is too thick can create overuse problems in the elbow.
- Running shoes that are too big or broken down are ineffective in pronation control and can cause ankle joint injuries.
- Hand paddles worn to give a swimmer sensory feedback about his/her arm pull underwater can overwhelm the shoulder with stress forces.
- Downhill skis that are too heavy, too long, or too short can affect the ability to turn and create the potential for injury, either externally from obstacles or internally from the mechanics of turning.
- Knee braces worn on the lateral side across the knee joint to protect the medial side from injury have been implicated in creating more knee and/or ankle injuries because the biomechanical forces were altered.

Unauthorized "equipment" worn for convenience or perceived support can generate injury.

- Basketball players who wear rings can get them caught on the rim or in the net, creating massive damage to digits.
- Necklaces can become caught or entangled in other players' hands, clothes, or equipment and cause neck injury.
- Improperly made eyeglasses can shatter on impact and create massive damage to and around the face.

Other equipment that has the potential of becoming a source of injury:

- Poorly fitted equipment
- Equipment that gives the athlete a false sense of security.
- Equipment that is so sturdy that the athlete causes injury to an opponent with it.

The purpose of equipment is to protect an athlete from potential injury (shoulder pads), protect an existing injury (protective padding), or permit participation by correcting biomechanics (patellar braces). It should never be used as a weapon. Occasionally equipment can be made to serve its purpose better by adding support to or around the joint (prophylactic ankle taping, knee braces).

Table 7-5 summarizes the important NCAA rules (listed by sport) regarding equipment at the collegiate level. Consult other rulebooks concerning other levels of competition and other sports.

2. **Playing Conditions.**

**Heat.** The potential for heat injury can be measured fairly accurately with a sling psychrometer. Both heat and ambient temperature are important when considering heat effect on playing conditions. Consult Table 7-6 and the ACSM position stand (Appendix 7-1) for guidelines on athletic activity in the heat. The major factors to consider (refer to Chapter 16 for further explanation) are actual environmental temperature, acclimization, clothing, and water/electrolyte loss. Ask how accessible drinking water is to athletes during team practice. Many soccer, football, and baseball fields (especially at newly-built schools) are far away from running water. Documented elsewhere (Chapter 16) is the existence of a special population at risk for heat injury — malignant hyperthermia.

**Cold.** Hypothermia can also generate injury (refer to Chapter 16). The potential for frostbite and other cold injury can be related directly to the wind chill index (see Table 7-7). Proper clothing is the most important factor in preventing this type of injury.

**Area of Play, Practice, Competition.** The team physician should inspect the areas of play in any sport covered. Injury can be caused by running into equipment on the sidelines (scorers' table, band instruments, etc.) or as a result of equipment used (javelin, hurdle, etc.). Always inspect the area of play and adjacent out-of-bounds areas for possible injury-producing sites. Prior to a competition, the pool, field, court, arena, or rink should be inspected and all potential injury-producing construction points protected or removed. Some of the possible hazards to be considered are: Holes or irregularities in fields — soccer, football; Water on a court — basketball; Unlatched doors — hockey; Large gravel stones on basepaths — baseball, softball, unprotected fence tops-baseball, softball; Changes in running surfaces or unbanked tracks — running. In addition to the area of competition, it has been suggested that a buffer zone of 18 feet surrounding the field of play be cleared of all obstacles including fences, scorers tables, etc. (Garrick, 1977).

**Spectator Initiated Obstacles.** Game officials

**Table 7-5. NCAA Playing Rules Governing Protective Equipment**

| Sport | Mandatory Equipment |
|---|---|
| Baseball | 1. NOCSAE-certified, double-ear flap protective helmet while batting and running bases.<br>2. All catchers must have a built-in or attachable throat guard on masks.<br><br>*Other Protective Equipment Rules*<br>None<br><br>*Approval Authority*<br>Institutions must be able to verify, through the date of manufacturer stamp, that helmet was manufactured after July 22, 1982. Umpire-in-chief duties include checking equipment for legality and safety. |
| Basketball — Men's | *Mandatory Equipment*<br>None<br><br>*Other Protective Equipment Rules*<br>Elbow, hand, finger, wrist or forearm guards, and casts or braces made of leather, plaster, pliable (soft) plastic, metal or any other hard substance, even though covered with soft padding always shall be declared illegal.<br><br>*Approval Authority*<br>The referee shall not permit any player to wear equipment that, in his judgment, is dangerous to other players. |
| Basketball — Women's | Same as Men's |
| Men's and Women's Fencing | *Mandatory Equipment*<br>1. Masks with mesh cover.<br>2. Gloves.<br>3. Jacket of double thickness.<br>4. Ladies chest protectors.<br><br>*Other Protective Equipment Rules*<br>None<br><br>*Approval Authority*<br>Equipment and clothing are inspected one hour before competition and must bear an inspection stamp at the time of competition. |
| Football | *Mandatory Equipment*<br>1. Four-point chin strap with all snaps secured.<br>2. Soft knee pads at least one-half inch thick worn over the knees.<br>3. An intraoral moutpiece that covers all upper jaw teeth.<br>4. Hip pads must have a tail bone protector.<br>5. Helmet that is NOCSAE approved.<br>6. Shoulder pads, thigh guards.<br><br>*Other Protective Equipment Rules*<br>1. All casts and splints are permissible only to protect an injury and must be properly padded on all sides.<br>2. Therapeutic or preventative knee braces are permitted if covered from direct external exposure.<br><br>*Approval Authority*<br>The head coach or his designated representative shall certify to the umpire prior to the game that all players are equipped in compliance with NCAA football rules and:<br>1. Have been informed what equipment is mandatory by rule and what constitutes illegal equipment.<br>2. Have been provided the equipment mandated by rule.<br>3. Have been instructed what to wear and how to wear mandatory equipment during the game.<br>4. Have been instructed to notify the coaching staff when equipment becomes illegal through rule change. |

**Table 7-5. NCAA Playing Rules Governing Protective Equipment (*Continued*)**

| Sport | Mandatory Equipment |
|---|---|
| Gymnastics | None |
| Ice Hockey | *Mandatory Equipment*<br>1. Helmets with chin straps securely fastened.<br>2. Face masks that have met the standards established by the HELL-ASTM F13-77 eye and face protective equipment for hockey players standard.<br>3. An intra-oral mouthpiece that covers all the remaining teeth of one jaw.<br><br>*Other Protective Equipment Rules*<br>1. The use of pads or protectors made of metal or of other material likely to cause injury to another player is prohibited.<br>2. Any protective equipment is not injurious to the player wearing it or other players is recommended.<br><br>*Approval Authority*<br>When a referree becomes aware of any lack of conformity to the regulation on equipment, it shall be his duty to see that the required equipment is used. |
| Men's Lacrosse | *Mandatory Equipment*<br>1. Protective helmet equipment with face mask and chin pad, with a cupped four-point chin strap (high point hook-up). Throat and chest protector for goalie.<br>2. Intraoral mouthpiece that covers all upper jaw teeth.<br>3. Protective gloves.<br><br>*Other Protective Equipment Rules*<br>None.<br><br>*Approval Authority*<br>Players "should" use helmets and face guards that met NOCSAE standards. Play is stopped if a piece of protective equipment is lost. |
| Rifle | None. |
| Men's Soccer | *Mandatory Equipment*<br>None.<br><br>*Other Protective Equipment Rules*<br>1. A player shall not wear anything that is dangerous to another player.<br>2. Casts are permissible if covered and not considered dangerous.<br>3. Use of any hard or dangerous head, face or body protective equipment is illegal.<br><br>*Approval Authority*<br>The referee prior to each game must examine the equipment of each player to see that it complies. A player wearing equipment not in compliance shall be sent from the field temporarily. |
| Men's and Women's Swimming | None. |
| Men's and Women's Track | *Mandatory Equipment*<br>None.<br><br>*Other Protective Equipment Rules*<br>No taping of any part of the hands or fingers will be permitted in the hammer, discus, javelin, and 35-pound weight throw unless there is an injury, cut, or wound that will be protected by tape.<br><br>*Approval Authority*<br>Referee must approve taping. |
| Water Polo | None. |

Table 7-5. NCAA Playing Rules Governing Protective Equipment (*Continued*)

| Sport | Mandatory Equipment |
|---|---|
| Wrestling | *Mandatory Equipment*<br>Protective ear guards.<br><br>*Other Protective Equipment Rules*<br>1. Mechanical devices must allow normal movements of joints and must not prevent an opponent from applying normal holds.<br>2. A hard and abrasive legal device must be covered and padded.<br><br>*Approval Authority*<br>The legality of any equipment shall be decided by the referee. |

Table 7-6. This heat/humidity risk scale for exercise is based on analysis of heatstroke cases among football players and Marines.

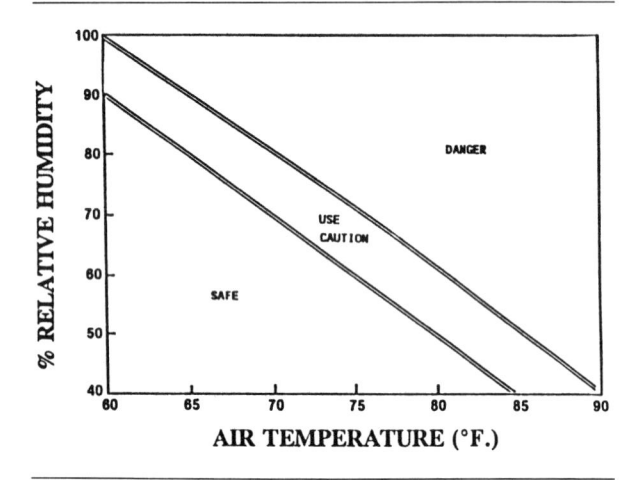

should be the monitors for spectator-initiated obstacles either thrown or left on the field of play. This can happen in practically any sport and should result in cessation of play until the area is totally clear.

3. **Rule Enforcement/Officiating.** Game officials are responsible for exercising direct control of contests through proper enforcement of rules. The physician also should be familiar with the rules. Injuries can result from improper rule enforcement in such sports as football — spearing; hockey — slashing; basketball — charging; wrestling — illegal holds; baseball — interference on base paths, and diving — coming too close to the board. The physician should acquaint himself with the rules while observing and monitoring the contest. It may even be necessary to report improper enforcement of the rules or to perhaps advocate rule change where appropriate.

4. **Balancing Competition.** The concept of balancing competition is especially important in the early adolescent age group. Differences in size, maturity, and skill level can be great even when the chronologic age is the same. The result of "imbalanced" competition can be summarized as follows:
   - physical impact — the rate of physical injuries to smaller, less mature athletes increases.
   - psychological impact — two groups of vulnerable, sometimes overwhelmed athletes who may have problems are those who are immature, lack training, conditioning, or neuromuscular skill, and those who perceive they are not meeting the expectations of peer group, coach, or parents in a win-at-all-cost environment.

5. **Coaching Techniques.** We believe that coaching techniques may represent the single most important factor in preventing injury. The coach's knowledge of the sport and his understanding of the physical and psychological ramifications of program design are directly responsible for the evolution or prevention of many injuries.
   - *Incorrect Technique* — poor coaching includes teaching incorrect technique which often leads to both musculoskeletal and psychological overuse syndromes. Improper coaching can cause sudden changes in the workout schedule as it relates to the mode of activity, frequency, intensity, or duration.
   - *Dangerous Practices* — Teaching dangerous practices such as spearing or cutting in football can lead to acute injury. Sometimes the

Table 7-7. Cold Chart — Windchill

### Windchill factors

Wind can chill exposed skin, making a cold temperature feel even colder and increasing the risk of frostbite. To find out how cold the windchill factor makes it seem outside, find today's temperature at the left and read across to the column for today's wind speed. In that box, you'll find the windchill temperature in degrees Fahrenheit (and, in parentheses, degrees Celsius).

| Actual temperature | \multicolumn{9}{c}{Estimated wind speed in mph (and kph)} | Danger of frostbite |
|---|---|---|---|---|---|---|---|---|---|---|
| | calm | 5 (8) | 10 (16) | 15 (24) | 20 (32) | 25 (40) | 30 (48) | 35 (56) | 40 (64) | |
| 50°F (10°C) | 50 (10) | 48 (8.9) | 40 (4.4) | 36 (2.2) | 32 (0) | 30 (−1.1) | 28 (−2.2) | 27 (−2.8) | 26 (−3.3) | LITTLE DANGER (for properly clothed person) Maximum danger from false sense of security |
| 40°F (4.4°C) | 40 (4.4) | 37 (2.8) | 28 (−2.2) | 22 (−5.6) | 18 (−7.8) | 16 (−8.9) | 13 (−10.6) | 11 (−11.7) | 10 (−12.2) | |
| 30°F (−1.1°C) | 30 (−1.1) | 27 (−2.8) | 16 (−8.9) | 9 (−12.8) | 4 (−15.5) | 0 (−17.8) | −2 (−18.9) | −4 (−20) | −6 (−21.1) | |
| 20°F (−6.7°C) | 20 (−6.7) | 16 (−8.9) | 4 (−15.5) | −5 (−20.5) | −10 (−23.3) | −15 (−26.1) | −18 (−27.8) | −20 (−28.9) | −21 (−29.4) | |
| 10°F (−12.2°C) | 10 (−12.2) | 6 (−14.4) | −9 (−22.8) | −18 (−27.8) | −25 (−31.6) | −29 (−33.9) | −33 (−36.1) | −35 (−37.2) | −37 (−38.3) | INCREASING DANGER from freezing of exposed flesh |
| 0°F (−17.8°C) | 0 (−17.8) | −5 (−20.5) | −24 (−31.1) | −32 (−35.5) | −39 (−39.4) | −44 (−42.2) | −48 (−44.4) | −51 (−46.1) | −53 (−47.2) | |
| −10°F (−23.3°C) | −10 (−23.3) | −15 (−26.1) | −33 (−36.1) | −45 (−42.7) | −53 (−47.2) | −59 (−50.5) | −63 (−52.7) | −67 (−55) | −69 (−56.1) | |
| −20°F (−28.9°C) | −20 (−28.9) | −26 (−32.2) | −46 (−43.3) | −58 (−50) | −67 (−55) | −74 (−58.8) | −79 (−61.6) | −82 (−63.3) | −85 (−65) | GREAT DANGER |
| −30°F (−34.4°C) | −30 (−34.4) | −36 (−37.7) | −58 (−50) | −72 (−57.7) | −82 (−63.3) | −88 (−66.6) | −94 (−70) | −98 (−72.2) | −100 (−73.3) | |

teaching can be unintentional or represent hidden encouragement on the part of the coach to obtain an advantage over an opponent by any means possible, including cheating, use of drugs (ergogenic aids), or practices such as rapid weight loss (seen in wrestling).

## INTERNAL FACTORS — ATHLETE RESPONSIBILITY

Certain factors that have a bearing on injury rates are the direct responsibility of the athlete. These are internal factors that can be a positive or negative influence and they include:

1. **Proper Conditioning**

   The athlete has a responsibility to be physically fit to *begin* competition/training (see Chapter 4). Being "in condition" means the athlete is equal to the neuromuscular demands and has the necessary strength and stamina for his sport (Hirata, 1974). The following pre-participation testing is one way athletes can measure conditioning prior to competition/training.
   - *Cybex Testing* — Isokinetic testing of muscle groups surrounding the knee and shoulder joints can detect and quantify muscle weakness or imbalance (predisposing injury factor). Even if these expensive isokinetic testing devices are unavailable, gross muscle testing

can be incorporated into the preparticipation physical examination or any other deemed appropriate.

- *Body Composition* — Percent body fat and lean body mass can be determined any number of ways (see Chapter 2B) and this figure should be used to guide weight loss practices. The states of Iowa and Wisconsin, with the guidance of sports medicine professionals, have adopted strict new guidelines to control weight loss practices in high school wrestling.

Any training program should be specific to a particular sport or event. It should take into account the demands of the sport and tailor conditioning regimens accordingly — aerobic or anaerobic exercise (or a mixture of both). Please refer to Figure 5A-1 (Chapter 5) for an explanation of energy demands by sport. The goals of an appropriate conditioning program should include:

- Improvement of the neuromuscular skills demanded by the sport in question — overuse syndromes can result from improper biomechanics.
- Improve muscular strength — hypertension or various musculoskeletal strains can result from improper technique.
- Increased muscular and cardiorespiratory endurance — premature fatigue and overuse leading to injury are the most likely sequellae of improper conditioning.
- Increased flexibility — any conditioning program should include proper warm-up, cool-down, and flexibility exercises. It should *not* include activities such as ballistic stretching or bouncing. Stretches have been implicated in numerous training injuries. Eight of these have been identified and are summarized and illustrated on Figure 7-6 (a-h) (Dominquez, 1982). Stretching can produce injury as well as prevent it. Athletes must also understand that once an injury occurs — *the longer the delay in seeking medical help and proper treatment, the longer the recovery of time.*

2. **Health Care Maintenance**

Team physicians are obligated to consider the whole individual. A lack of psychological well-being in the form of increased stress, a family crisis, or other personal problems, can be a factor in increasing the injury rate (Coddington, 1980; Passer, 1983). "Minor" viral infections can lead to major cardiopulmonary compromise (myocarditis) or even death. A physician who is dedicated to giving complete health care can deal with more than just musculoskeletal aches and pains. Drug use is easier to detect and can be dealt with better by physicians who know the athlete and are sensitive to his/her behavior. Such a physician can prevent minor problems from becoming major ones, such as an ignored, infected boil that becomes thrombophlebitis in the lower extremity, or the "cold" that becomes pneumonia. Another possibility to which the physician must be sensitive is that an athlete may have hidden problems undiscovered on the preparticipation physical that will be exacerbated by training. These can be significant.

Health care maintenance also involves the nutritional aspects of training. The team physician should help prevent inappropriate weight loss whether by starvation, drug use, or dehydration. This can decrease performance and increase susceptibility to disease. He/she should be able to spot pathologic eating disorders such as anorexia, bulimia, or the use of medications to gain and/or lose weight (see Chapter 2). The physician should be able to serve as a resource about new fads in performance enhancement so as to decrease the likelihood of increased injury or illness secondary to fads.

3. **Athlete (Patient) Education**

As is true with all patients, the more knowledgeable the athlete, the less likely he/she will become injured or ill. Patient education is a guard against most of the injury factors we have discussed (over-conditioning, poor technique, improper environment, inappropriate use of equipment).

## REHABILITATION

Rehabilitation is covered in detail in Chapter 18 and is mentioned here only as the most important factor in the return of an athlete to activity following injury. Reinjury can be minimized if the resumption of activity is closely monitored by a team physician who is familiar with the injury and the demands of the sport and position. Moving too slowly can result in an unnecessary loss of conditioning whereas progressing too quickly may prevent proper healing. Full competitive activity must not be resumed until the athlete has met the following criteria (Finke, 1981):

a. *Yoga Plow*
   — interruption of circulation to the vertebral artery
   — ↑ pressure to intervertebral discs in neck and lower back
   — stretching of sciatic nerve

b. *Hurdler's Stretch*
   — overstretching of groin muscles and ligaments
   — meniscal injury
   — medial collateral ligament injury
   — sciatic nerve stretch

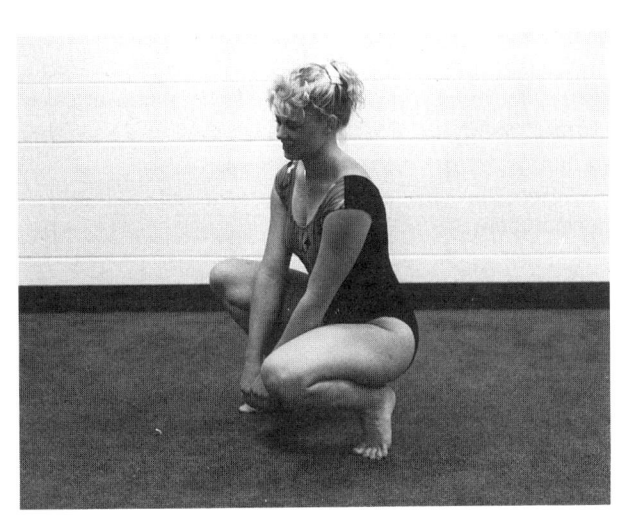

c. *Duck Walk and Deep Knee Bend*
   — lateral meniscal damage (can be done briefly during a pre-participation musculoskeletal exam

d. *Stiff Leg Raises* — Overstretching sciatic nerve

e. *Toe Touching*
   — posterior longitudinal ligament involvement
   — sciatic nerve damage

**Fig. 7-6.** Inappropriate Stretches and Their Possible Injuries

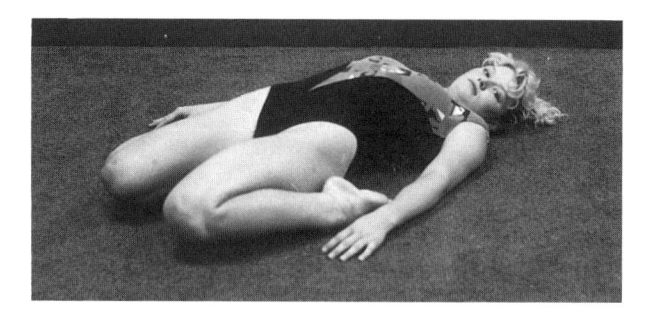

f. *Knee Stretch*
   — Involvement of patellar ligament, quadriceps tendon and both collateral knee ligaments

g. *Ballet Stretches*
   — overstretching the sciatic nerve
   — low back ligaments
   — intervertebral discs

h. *Full Sit-Ups*
   — greater than 30° hip flexion does not affect abdominal muscles
   — overstretching of the lower back

**Fig. 7-6.** *(Continued)*

- No pain with activity
- Full strength of the injured area
- Full range of motion
- Proper mental attitude

This last requirement recognizes that people respond differently to injury. Attention to all these criteria will give the best results.

## SUMMARY

Pain need not be accepted as part of athletic participation. Injuries are inevitable, but the causes of all injuries should be analyzed with the goal of elimination of the cause. All injury prevention techniques should be used to attain the safest and best sports environment. This should be a primary care team physician's most important goal and the first to be addressed.

### REFERENCES

Cahill, B.R., Griffith, E.H. Effect of preseason conditioning on the incidence and severity of high school knee injuries. *AJSM* 6:180-184, 1978.

Coddington, R. and Troxell, J. The effects of emotional factors on football injury rates — a pilot study. *J. Human Stress* 6(4):3-5, 1980.

Dominquez, R.H. *Total Body Training.* Charles Scribner's Sons, New York, 1982.

Feiring, D.C, Derscheid, G.L. The role of preseason conditioning in preventing athletic injuries. *Clinics in Sports Med* 8(3):361-372, 1989.

Finke, R.C. Principles: prevention, rehabilitation, protection. *Sideline View* 3(4):1, 1981.

Garrick, J.G., Collins, G.S. and Requa, R.K. Out of bounds in football: player exposure to probability of collision injury. *J of Safety Research* 9(1):34, 1977.

Garrick, J.G., Requa, R. Medical care and injury surveillance in the high school setting. *Phys Sportsmed* 8(2):115, 1981.

Hirata, Isao. *The Doctor and the Athlete.* J.B. Lippincott, Philadelphia, 1974.

Kemon, I. Skateboard injuries. *Br Med J* :894, 1978.

NEISS, Division of Hazard Analysis and Human Factors: Overview of Sports related injures is persons 5-14 years of age. U.S. Consumer Products Safety Commissions Report, Washington, D.C., December 1987.

Passer, M.W. and Seese, M.D. Life stress and athletic injury: examination of positive versus negative events and three moderator variables. *J of Human Stress* 9(2):11-16, 1983.

Zemper, E. and Walsh, U. NCAA Injury Surveillance System. National Collegiate Athletic Association, Mission, KS, 1987.

# Appendix 7-1.
# American College of Sports Medicine Position Stand on Prevention of Thermal Injuries During Distance Running

**Purpose of the Position Stand**

1. To alert sponsors of distance-running events to potentially serious health hazards during distance running — especially thermal injury.
2. To advise sponsors to consult local weather history and plan events at times when the environmental heat stress would most likely be acceptable.
3. To encourage sponsors to identify the environmental heat stress existing on the day of a race and communicate this to the participants.
4. To educate participants regarding thermal injury susceptibility and prevention.
5. To inform sponsors of preventive actions which may reduce the frequency and severity of this type of injury.

This position stand replaces that of "*Prevention of Heat Injury During Distance Running,*" published by the American College of Sports Medicine in 1975. It has been expanded to consider thermal problems which may affect the general community of joggers, fun runners, and elite athletes who participate in distance-running events. Although hyperthermia is still the most common serious problem encountered in North American fun runs and races, hypothermia can be a problem for slow runners in long races such as the marathon, in cold and/or wet environmental conditions or following races when blood glucose is low and the body's temperature regulatory mechanism is impaired.

Because the physiological responses to exercise and environmental stress vary among participants, strict compliance with the recommendations, while helpful, will not guarantee complete protection from thermal illness. The general guidelines in this position stand do not constitute definitive medical advice, which should be sought from a physician for specific cases. Nevertheless, adherence to these recommendations should help to minimize the incidence of thermal injury.

**Position Stand**

It is the position of the American College of Sports Medicine that the following RECOMMENDATIONS be employed by directors of distance runs or community fun runs.

1. **Medical Director**

    A medical director knowledgeable in exercise physiology and sports medicine should coordinate the preventive and therapeutic aspects of the running event and work closely with the race director.

2. **Race Organization**

    a. Races should be organized to avoid the hottest summer months and the hottest part of the day. As there are great regional variations in environmental conditions, the local weather history will be most helpful in scheduling an event to avoid times when an unacceptable level of heat stress is likely to prevail. Organizers should be cautious of unseasonably hot days in the early spring, as entrants will almost certainly not be heat acclimatized.

    b. The environmental heat stress prediction for the day should be obtained from the meteorological service. It can be measured as wet bulb globe temperature (WBGT) (see Appendix I), which is a temperature/humidity/radiation index (1). If WBGT is above 28°C (82°F), consideration should be given to rescheduling or delaying the race until safer conditions prevail. If below 28°C, participants may be alerted to the degree of heat stress by using color-coded flags at the start of the race and at key positions along the course (Appendix II; 26).

    c. All summer events should be scheduled for the early morning, ideally before 8:00 a.m., or in the evening after 6:00 p.m., to minimize solar radiation.

d. An adequate supply of water should be available before the race and every 2-3 km during the race. Runners should be encouraged to consume 100-200 ml at each station.
e. Race officials should be educated as to the warning signs of an impending collapse. Each official should wear an identifiable arm band or badge and should warn runners to stop if they appear to be in difficulty.
f. Adequate traffic and crowd control must be maintained at all times.
g. There should be a ready source of radio communications from various points on the course to a central organizing point to coordinate responses to emergencies.

3. **Medical Support**
   a. **Medical Organization and Responsibility:** The Medical Director should alert local hospitals and ambulance services to the event and should make prior arrangements with medical personnel for the care of casualties, especially those suffering from heat injury. The mere fact that an entrant signs a waiver in no way absolves the organizers of moral and/or legal responsibility. Medical personnel supervising races should have the authority to evaluate, examine, and/or stop a runner who displays the symptoms and signs of impending heat injury, or who appears to be mentally and/or physically out of control for any other reason.
   b. **Medical Facilities:**
      i. Medical support staff and facilities should be available at the race site.
      ii. The facilities should be staffed with personnel capable of instituting immediate and appropriate resuscitation measures. Apart from the routine resuscitation equipment, ice packs and fans for cooling are required.
      iii. Persons trained in first aid, appropriately identified with an arm band, badge, etc., should be stationed along the course to warn runners to stop if they exhibit signs of impending heat injury.
      iv. Ambulances or vans with accompanying medical personnel should be available along the course.
      v. Although the emphasis in this stand has been on the management of hyperthermia, on cold, wet, and windy days, athletes may be chilled and require "space blankets," blankets, and warm drinks at the finish to prevent or treat hypothermia (23, 45).

4. **Competitor Education**

   The education of fun runners has increased greatly in recent years, but race organizers must not assume that all participants are well informed or prepared. Distributing guidelines at the pre-registration, publicity in the press and holding clinics/seminars before runs are valuable.

   The following persons are particularly prone to heat illness: the obese (3, 17, 43), unfit (13, 29, 39, 43), dehydrated (6, 14, 31, 37, 38, 47), those unacclimatized to the heat (20, 43), those with a previous history of heat stroke (36, 43), and anyone who runs while ill (41). Children perspire less than adults and have a lower heat tolerance (2). Based on the above information, all participants should be advised of the following.
   a. Adequate training and fitness are important for full enjoyment of the run and also to prevent heat-related injuries (13, 28, 29, 39).
   b. Prior training in the heat will promote heat acclimatization and thereby reduce the risk of heat injury. It is wise to do as much training as possible at the time of day at which the race will be held (20).
   c. Fluid consumption before and during the race will reduce the risk of heat injury, particularly in longer runs such as the marathon (6, 14, 47).
   d. Illness prior to or at the time of the event should preclude competition (41).
   e. Participants should be advised of the early symptoms of heat injury. These include clumsiness, stumbling, excessive sweating (and also cessation of sweating), headache, nausea, dizziness, apathy, and any gradual impairment of consciousness (42).
   f. Participants should be advised to choose a comfortable speed and not to run faster than conditions warrant (18, 33).
   g. Participants are advised to run with a partner, each being responsible for the other's well-being (33).

## Background for Position Stand

There has been an exponential rise in the number of fun runs and races in recent years and, as would be expected, a similar increase in the number of running-related injuries. Minor injuries such as bruises, blisters and musculoskeletal injuries are most common (41, 45). Myocardial infarction or cardiac arrest is, fortunately, very rare and occurs almost exclusively in patients with symptomatic heart disease (44). Hypoglycemia may be seen occasionally in normal runners (11) and has been observed following marathons (21) and shorter fun runs (41).

The most serious injuries in fun runs and races are related to problems of thermoregulation. In the shorter races, 10 km (6.2 miles) or less, hyperthermia with the attendant problems of heat exhaustion and heat syncope dominates, even on relatively cool days (4, 5, 10, 15, 16, 18, 27, 41). In longer races, heat problems are common on warm or hot days (31), but on moderate to cold days, hypothermia may be a real risk to some participants (23).

**Thermoregulation and hyperthermia.** Fun runners may experience hyperthermia or hypothermia, depending on the environmental conditions and clothing worn. The adequately clothed runner is capable of withstanding a wide range of environmental temperatures. Hyperthermia is the potential problem in warm and hot weather, when the body's rate of heat production is greater than its ability to dissipate this heat (1). In cold weather, scanty clothing may provide inadequate protection from the environment and hypothermia may develop, particularly towards the end of a long race when running speed and, therefore, heat production, are reduced.

During intense exercise, heat production in contracting muscles is 15-20 times that of basal metabolism and is sufficient to raise body core temperature in an average size individual by 1°C every 5 min if no temperature-regulating mechanisms were activated (25). With increased heat production, thermal receptors in the hypothalamus sense the increased body temperature and respond with an increased cutaneous circulation; thus, the excess heat is transferred to the skin surface to be dissipated by physical means, primarily the evaporation of sweat (9). The precise quantitative relationships in heat transfer are beyond the scope of this position stand, but are well reviewed elsewhere (24, 25).

When the rate of heat production exceeds that of heat loss for a sufficient period of time, thermal injury will occur. In long races, sweat loss can be significant and result in a total body water deficit of 6-10% of body weight (47). Such dehydration will subsequently reduce sweating and predispose the runner to hyperthermia, heat stroke, heat exhaustion, and muscle cramps (47). For a given level of dehydration, children have a greater increase in core temperature than do adults (2). Rectal temperatures have been reported above 40.6°C after races and fun runs (7, 22, 31, 35) and as high as 42-43°C in fun run participants who have collapsed (32, 34, 41, 42).

Fluid ingestion before and during prolonged running will minimize dehydration (and reduce the rate of increase in body core temperature) (7, 14). However, in fun runs of less than 10 km, hyperthermia may occur in the absence of significant dehydration (41). Runners should avoid consuming large quantities of highly concentrated sugar solution during runs, as this may result in a decrease in gastric emptying (8, 12).

**Thermoregulation and hypothermia.** Heat can be lost readily from the body when the rate of heat production is exceeded by heat loss (46). Even on moderately cool days, if the pace slows and/or if weather conditions become cooler en route, hypothermia may ensue (23). Several deaths have been reported from hypothermia during fun runs in mountain environments (30, 40). Hypothermia is common in inexperienced marathon runners who frequently run the second half of the race much more slowly than the first half. Such runners may be able to maintain core temperature initially, but with the slow pace of the second half, especially on cool, wet, or windy days, hypothermia can develop (23).

Early symptoms and signs of hypothermia include shivering, euphoria, and an appearance of intoxication. As core temperature continues to fall, shivering may stop, lethargy and muscular weakness may occur with disorientation, hallucinations, and often a combative nature. If core temperature falls below 30°C, the victim may lose consciousness.

Organizers of distance races and fun runs and their medical support staff should anticipate the medical problems and be capable of responding to significant numbers of hyperthermic and/or hypothermic runners. Thermal injury can be minimized with appropriate education of participants and with adequate facilities, supplies, and support staff.

# Appendix I
## Measurement of Environmental Heat Stress

Ambient temperature is only one component of environmental heat stress; others are humidity, wind velocity, and radiant heat. Therefore, measurement of ambient temperature, dry bulb alone, is inadequate. The most useful and widely applied approach is wet bulb globe temperature (WBGT).

$$WBGT = (0.7\ T_{wb}) + (0.2\ T_g) + (0.1)\ T_{db},$$

where $T_{wb}$ = temperature (wet bulb thermometer), $T_g$ = temperature (black globe thermometer), and $T_{db}$ = temperature (dry bulb thermometer).

The importance of wet bulb temperature can be readily appreciated, as it accounts for 70% of the index, whereas dry bulb temperature accounts for only 10%. A simple portable heat stress monitor which gives direct WBGT in degrees C or degrees F to monitor conditions during fun runs has proven useful (19).

Alternatively, if a means for readily assessing WBGT is not available from wet bulb, globe, and dry bulb temperatures, one can use the following equation (48).

$$WBGT = (0.567\ T_{db}) + (0.393\ P_a) + 3.94,$$

where $T_{db}$ = temperature (dry bulb thermometer) and $P_a$ = environmental water vapor pressure. These environmental variables should be readily available from local weather or radio stations.

Instruments to measure WBGT are available commercially. Additional information may be obtained from the American College of Sports Medicine.

## Appendix II
### Use of Color-Coded Flags to Indicate the Risk of Thermal Stress*

1. A RED FLAG: High Risk: When WBGT is 23-28°C (73-82°F).
   This signal would indicate that all runners should be aware that heat injury is possible and any person particularly sensitive to heat or humidity should probably not run.
2. AN AMBER FLAG: Moderate Risk: When WBGT is 18-23°C (65-73°F).
   It should be remembered that the air temperature, probably humidity, and almost certainly the radiant heat at the beginning of the race will increase during the course of the race if conducted in the morning or early afternoon.
3. A GREEN FLAG: Low Risk: When WBGT is below 18°C (65°F).
   This in no way guarantees that heat injury will not occur, but indicates only that the risk is low.
4. A WHITE FLAG: Low Risk for hyperthermia, but possible risk for hypothermia: when WBGT is below 10°C (50°F).
   Hypothermia may occur, especially in slow runners in long races, and in wet and windy conditions.

* This scale is determined for runners clad in running shorts, shoes and a T-shirt. In warmer weather, the less clothing the better. For males, wearing no shirt or a mesh top is better than wearing a T-shirt because the surface for evaporation is increased. However, in areas where radiant heat is excessive, a light top may be helpful.

## Appendix III
### Road Race Checklist

**Medical Personnel**

1. Have aid personnel available if the race is 10 km (6.2 miles) or longer, and run in warm or cold weather.
2. Recruit back-up personnel from existing emergency medical services (police, fire rescue, emergency medical service).
3. Notify local hospitals of the time and place of the road race.

**Aid Stations**

1. Provide major aid station at the finish point which is cordoned off from public access.
2. Equip the major aid station with the following supplies:
   — tent
   — cots
   — bath towels
   — water in large containers
   — ice in bag or ice chest or quick-cold packs
   — hose with spray nozzle
   — tables for medical supplies and equipment
   — stethoscopes
   — blood pressure cuffs
   — rectal thermometers or meters (range up to 43°C)
   — dressings
   — blankets
   — aluminum thermal sheets ("space blankets")
   — elastic bandages
   — splints
   — skin disinfectants

— intravenous fluids (supervision by a physician is required).
3. Position aid stations along the route at 4 km (2.5 mile) intervals for races over 10 km and at the halfway point for shorter races.
4. Stock each aid station with enough fluid (cool water is the optimum) for each runner to have 300-360 ml (10-12 ounces) at each aid station. A margin of 25% additional cups should be available to account for spillage and double usage.

## Communications/Surveillance

1. Set up communication between the medical personnel and the major aid station.
2. Arrange for a radio-equipped car or van to follow the race course, and provide radio contact with director.

## Instructions To Runners

1. Apprise the race participants of potential medical problems in advance of the race so precautions may be followed.
2. Advise the race director to announce the following information by loudspeaker immediately prior to the race:
   — the flag color: the risks for hyperthermia and/or hypothermia
   — location of aid stations and type of fluid available
   — reinforcement of warm weather or cold weather self-care.
3. Advise the race participants to print their names, addresses, and any medical problems on the back of the registration number.

## Appendix IV
## Medical Stations
## General Guidelines

### Staff for Large Races

1. Physician, podiatrist, nurse or EMT, a team of 3 per 1000 runners. Double or triple this number at the finish area.
2. One ambulance per 3000 runners at finish area; one cruising vehicle.
3. One physician to act as triage officer at finish.

### Water

Estimate 1 liter (0.26 gallon) per runner per 16 km (10 miles), or roughly, per 60-90 min running time, and depending on number of stations. For 10 km, the above rule is still recommended.

Cups = (number of entrants × number of stations) + 25% additional per station.
= (2 × number of entrants) extra at finish area.
Double this total if the course is out and back.

In cold weather, an equivalent amount of warm drinks should be available.

Table 1. Equipment needed at aid stations and the field hospital (per 1000 runners).

Aid Stations

| No. | Item |
|---|---|
|  | ice in small plastic bags or quick-cold packs |
| 5 | stretchers (10 at 10 km and beyond) |
| 5 | blankets (10 at 10 km and beyond) |
| 6 each | 6 inch and 4 inch elastic bandages |
| ½ case | 4 × 4 inch gauze pads |
| ½ case | 1½ inch tape |
| ½ case | surgical soap |
|  | small instrument kits |
|  | adhesive strips |
|  | moleskin |
| ½ case | petroleum jelly |
| 2 each | inflatable arm and leg splints |
|  | athletic trainer's kit |

Field Hospital

| No. | Item |
|---|---|
| 10 | stretchers |
| 4 | sawhorses |
| 10-20 | blankets (depending on environmental conditions) |
| 10 | intravenous set-ups |
| 2 each | inflatable arm and leg splints |
| 2 cases | 1½ inch tape |
| 2 cases each | elastic bandages (2, 4, and 6 inches) |
| 2 cases | sheet wadding underwrap |
| 2 cases | 4 × 4 inch gauze pads adhesive strips moleskin |
| ½ case | surgical soap |
| 2 | oxygen tanks with regulators and masks |
| 2 | ECG monitors with defibrillators |
|  | ice in small plastic bags |
|  | small instrument kits |

Adapted from reference 26.

REFERENCES available upon request from ACSM.

# 8

# Covering Athletic Competition

No athletic event is free from the possibility of a catastrophic injury. Early recognition and proper treatment of injuries are the keys to providing quality care. Besides evaluating injuries occurring on the field and providing initial treatment, the team physician must often make other decisions, such as deciding how to transport an injured athlete and how follow-up care should proceed. The athlete's safety should always be the primary consideration in making these decisions.

Designing a plan to deal with emergency situations before the beginning of the sports season can minimize later problems and affect the outcome of all serious injuries (DiNubile, 1985). One person should make the arrangements for emergency care, whether at home or away. Emergency equipment that should be available at or adjacent to the site of play, includes a spine board, sandbags, stretcher, slings, equipment for cardiopulmonary resuscitation (CPR), splinting materials, and a fully equipped trainer's bag. A detailed list of equipment is included in this text (see Appendices 8-1 and 8-2).

Arrangements should be made for ambulance back-up, and the nearest hospital emergency room should be notified of upcoming sports events. Ambulance and hospital telephone numbers and change for pay phone calls should be at hand and the location of the nearest phone should be posted so it is readily accessible.

## ROLE OF THE COACH OR TRAINER

Anyone who has critiqued the handling of a serious injury at a sporting event knows that some things are readily apparent. First, most catastrophic injuries that occur in sports do so when the doctor is not present. About two-thirds of all athletic injuries occur in practice. Second, coaches are not equipped to handle catastrophic injuries. Most coaches who have first-aid training usually practiced it in college and have not upgraded their skills since graduation. Third, emergency equipment is either inadequate or unavailable. Fourth, there often is no protocol for obtaining an ambulance to transport a critically injured or ill athlete. The key to upgrading any community athletic medicine program lies in three areas — education, equipment standardization, and an improved communication system.

Although the physician should be present at the event site whenever athletes are participating, he/she may not be routinely available when injuries occur. Consequently, the coach is the primary person who responds to injuries. This means that the first task of the team physician is to upgrade the coach's ability to handle injuries, especially those that are potentially catastrophic. It should be mandatory that all coaches know CPR and a proper method for handling a severe head or neck injury.

It is important that the team physician give educational seminars for the coaching staff and discuss management of an injured athlete. Instruction and hands-on experience in recognizing common sports-related injuries and performing basic first aid measures should be discussed by the physician. The seminar setting also is the place to discuss current concepts of conditioning, prevention of heat injuries, and how to deal with common extremity injuries. A program of this nature can be offered with minimal effort and is very effective in helping the coach or trainer evaluate injuries and care for their athletes.

The team physician should work with school officials and parents to formulate policies that will result in optimal event coverage (DiNubile, 1985; McKeag, 1985; Ryan, 1975). These include:

- Making sure that players, coaches, managers, athletic directors, and parents know that the physician is in charge when an injury occurs and his/her decision must prevail.
- Ensuring the presence of emergency transportation and trained personnel at the game site.
- Ensuring that a working communication system (telephone) is available at the game site for summoning emergency transportation if it cannot be at the scene.
- Reviewing all pertinent aspects of legal liability involving the school, athlete, and physician.
- Making sure that parents understand that the team physician is not the athlete's primary physician and that referral to the personal/primary physician remains at the discretion of the parents.
- Seeing that all recommendations of the team physician are in writing so as to avoid misunderstanding.
- Providing for a well documented medical record.

If there is an athletic trainer at the school, the team physician should attempt to develop a relationship with him/her also. Realistically, financial limitations make this prospect unlikely for most high schools. Schools that do not have a certified athletic trainer should appoint a coach or faculty member who is qualified in first-aid to serve as the trainer. The physician should encourage students interested in athletic training to enroll in workshops in their area offered by the National Association of Athletic Trainers (NATA).

In order to provide optimal care to the athlete, the team physician should perform the following functions when working with an athletic trainer:

- Serve as supervisor and advisor to the athletic trainer.
- Act as instructor to the trainer for therapeutic procedures. The trainer should have a clear understanding of how to handle triage procedures when an athlete is injured. The trainer should know how to reach the team physician during practices or competitions.
- Recommend only those therapeutic techniques for which a trainer is qualified.
- Communicate with the trainer as to when an athlete may be cleared for return to competition.
- Provide supportive guidance to facilitate effective communication among the school, coach, athlete, and parents.

## MEDICAL EQUIPMENT NECESSARY TO COVER COMPETITION

When covering athletic events, the team physician should carry appropriate medical equipment to deal with most emergency situations, including CPR. There are many variations on "appropriate" equipment to be carried in the medical bag or maintained at the event site. Appendices 8-1 and 8-2 include what is necessary for the team physician's bag, trainer's field kit, and what equipment should be provided by the sponsoring sports organization.

Finding an appropriate bag in which to carry the equipment may be a problem for the physician. One of the most useful solutions is a large plastic fishing tackle box that is sturdy, lockable, and big enough to carry everything that is necessary, including intravenous solutions and plaster bandages. It is compartmented with a large, deep bottom container and foldout, sliding drawers. The contents of the bag should not be a substitute for standard medical supplies which the high school, college, or organized sports club should keep in an emergency bag or storage closet. If these supplies are not currently available, the physician may supply the more portable items such as gauze pads, elastic bandages, and slings.

Team physicians should know that new standards have been developed for advanced cardiac life support (ACLS) using different techniques and drug protocols for various life-threatening situations. Even though few athletes will need cardiac resuscitation, spectators and officials, many of them middle-age and older, may be prone to cardiac problems. The equipment in Appendix 8-1 is designed to manage the most commonly encountered cardiac conditions. However, in most emergency situations where only one physician is present, basic CPR is all that can be initiated. Drugs used in CPR are standardized and carried by most paramedics.

Any physician covering an athletic event should practice ACLS techniques, endotracheal intubation, and the use of oral airways and airbags. There is no substitute for basic CPR and maintaining an adequate airway. Cricothyrectomy, with a large-gauge needle or cutting instrument seems inadequate for providing normal ventilation in adults and may cause fibrosis below the vocal cords. A tracheotomy is a very difficult procedure under field conditions and probably should be reserved for the hospital setting. No medication or treatment given on the field or game site, regardless of the urgency or effectiveness is a substitute for rapid, safe transportation to a hospital. Medical treatment on the field should be given as time permits and where the physician feels he or she is qualified to administer it. Other physicians with special competencies may be available at many sporting events and these individuals should be identified in advance in case their services are needed.

The team physician should consider using a portable two-way radio/telephone communication system to talk with ambulances and hospitals in more remote areas that are not served well by telephone. Most sports sites will have a telephone.

## PHYSICIAN'S ROLE IN COVERING COMPETITION

One of the most uncomfortable and disquieting moments faced by team physicians is making sideline decisions under the close scrutiny of thousands of spectators. There is nothing like the feeling of opening up your entire decision-making process to community view. Actually, it is this type of challenge that draws many primary physicians to the field of sports medicine (McKeag, 1985).

### Field Protocol

The team physician should arrive 15-30 minutes before an athletic event begins to make sure that appropriate medical supplies are available. At the same time, he/she can check the location of a telephone, see if emergency transportation services are available, and survey the site for safety hazards. The home team physician frequently provides medical supervision for visiting players as well as the home team, so it is important that the team physician be introduced to both coaches. This gives the physician an opportunity to check the medical status of both teams and review any problems that require closer supervision.

The physician should also introduce him/herself to the referees and other game officials and tell them where he/she will be located during the competition since the physician should not go onto the field until play has been properly stopped by the officials and medical assistance has been requested. The physician should station himself where the competition can be observed properly. The physician should also have easy, rapid access to the playing field, ideally at the field side rather than in the pressbox or stands. Anticipation of injury is a valuable habit, and a clear view of the event often provides considerable diagnostic information about any injury that occurs. A primary responsibility of the team physician is to determine the extent of any injury or illness occurring during a game and to determine the player's specific medical needs. The physician must also decide if or when the athlete can return to play. If the athlete cannot return immediately, a decision must be made about how the athlete should be transported and what the initial treatment should be. Again, because most injuries occur when physicians are not present, specific protocols for triage of injured athletes should be established, and coaches, trainers, or other responsible paramedical personnel should be taught how to evaluate the injury and give initial treatment.

Also as noted earlier, the physician, coach, and trainer should have an agreement that the physician will be completely independent and that he does not have to consult the coach about medical decisions regarding an injured player (DiNubile, 1985; Lucas, 1977; Tucker, 1986). This frees the physician from pressures to return a player to the game. One of the major responsibilities of the physician is to prevent further injury. Sometimes he/she cannot determine if the player risks reinjury and the coach must understand if a player cannot return to the game. Decisions made on the field by the team physician can and should be discussed after the game.

Many times it is difficult to perform an appropriate on-the-field assessment and the player must be transported by stretcher to a better examining site. Coaches, athletes, and parents should be told that the use of the stretcher does not mean the athlete's career is over but that it is used primarily for safety reasons. The athlete may need to be examined in a quiet, secluded place where clothing and equipment can be removed.

The major decision by the physician must make at this point is if the athlete can return to play. A decision to allow the athlete to resume play following an injury should be made only when these conditions have been met:

- A definite diagnosis has been established.
- Continued play will not worsen the injury and the athlete will not be at greater risk of further injury.
- The person will be able to compete fairly and the injury will not render the athlete incapable of protecting him/herself.

Table 8-1 lists medical situations that preclude further participation by an injured athlete.

The approach to evaluating acute athletic injuries should be neither excessively conservative nor liberal. Athletes of any age deserve a fair, unbiased decision about their ability to continue playing. The team physician who successfully and consistently follows the guidelines given here will find decision-making rewarding, and he/she will be respected by the coach, athlete, parent, and school administrators.

## Management of Acute Injuries at the Event Site

All acute injuries sustained during competition should follow the triage pathway outlined in Figure 8-1 (McKeag, 1985). Once an acute injury occurs, immediate assessment is mandatory to evaluate the significance and look for signs of catastrophic injury. One of the first components of the process is to observe the position of the athlete and the injured part in relation to the rest of the body. Obtain a history of how the injury occurred, and talk with others who may have seen the injury occur (trainer, coach or official). Any appropriate past medical history should be obtained. The third component of the initial assessment is a focused assessment of the injury, concentrating on muscular function, neurological, and vascular integrity.

The next step is to address two major issues: appropriate transportation of the injured athlete and determining the initial treatment. The physician must decide if the athlete can walk safely and, if not, what mode of transportation to use. Transportation options include the upright support of others, a stretcher, motorized cart, or ambulance. The athlete will be taken to the sidelines, room, or directly to the hospital, depending on the severity of his injury.

If the physician decides that the athlete may no longer participate but is allowed on the sidelines, the player should be checked periodically before a final assessment and treatment plan are made. The period between assessments depends upon the severity of the injury and how rapidly symptoms are evolving. If there are rapid changes in signs and symptoms, reevaluations must be frequent and the athlete should not be left alone. If the athlete is in the locker room, he/she should be watched carefully by people who are aware of the significance of changing symptoms. Subsequent assessments at the sideline or in the locker room will build on the findings of the original assessment.

If the athlete is allowed to return to participation and is reinjured, he/she should be withdrawn from play for the remainder of the contest. Even when a decision is made to allow full participation, periodic reassessment of the athlete should

---

**Table 8-1. Guidelines for Disallowing Continued Participation by an Injured Athlete**

The following is a list of situations generally precluding further athletic participation:

1. Unconsciousness, however brief.
2. Dazed appearance or inappropriate responses lasting more than 10 seconds as a result of head trauma.
3. Any focal neurologic complaint or deficit such as numbness or tingling.
4. Obvious swelling, with the possible exception of the digits.
5. Limited range of motion, either passive or active, when compared to opposite side.
6. Pain within the normal range of motion.
7. Decreased strength through the normal range of motion.
8. Obvious significant bleeding.
9. Any injury the examiner cannot diagnose or properly manage.
10. Obvious loss of normal functions (sight, ability to move extremity).
11. Any injury that requires assistance for the athlete to get off the field, mat, or court.
12. Anytime an athlete says he or she is injured and cannot participate (regardless of what the examiner thinks of the injury).

(Adapted from Garrick, J.G. *Sports medicine.* Pediatric Clinics of North America. 24:737-747, 1977.)

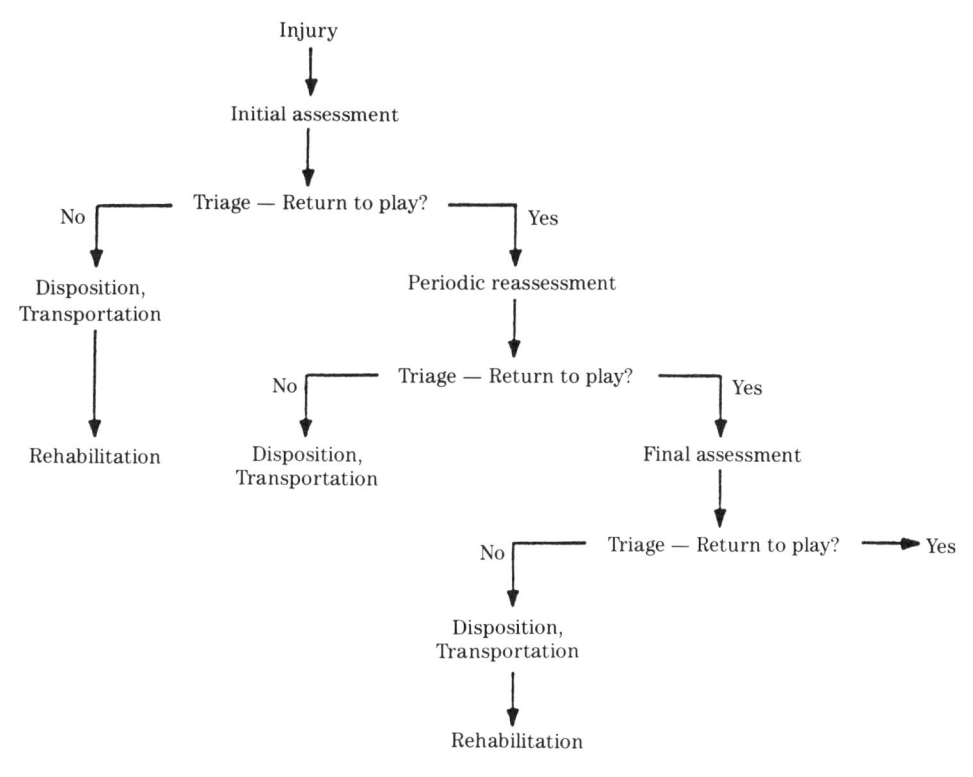

**Fig. 8-1.** Injury Assessment Pathway

continue during the practice or competition. Once the event ends, the physician can reevaluate the athlete and give appropriate treatment. The athlete should be seen again at a specific time after the injury so that the team physician can plan further rehabilitation or return the athlete to full practice status.

## SUMMARY

In summary, the primary care physician who acts as a team doctor should understand the following principles of covering athletic competition:

- He or she should possess a thorough knowledge of the frequency and severity of the types of injuries most often seen in the sport being covered.
- All medical policies and protocols should be under the absolute authority of the physician.
- The team physician should have the complete support of the school administrators and coaches. Total responsibility and authority to handle all athletic injuries should be given to the medical staff.
- A teaching program for ancillary personnel (coaches and trainers) is mandatory in order to implement a proper injury triage policy.
- The team physician should insist that the coaching staff be instructed in CPR training and subscribe to the triage system outlined by the physician. The coaching staff should maintain appropriate standards of conditioning and training, and report all injuries to ancillary or responsible medical personnel.
- Proper equipment for on-site care of the injured athlete should be provided by the supporting organization. Although the team physician will carry appropriate medical equipment and supplies. Arrangements for proper and orderly transportation of acutely injured athletes should be made before all events.
- The team physician should appoint appropriate ancillary personnel to triage injuries at all practices and games.
- Appropriate medical records should be kept on all injured athletes.
- Referrals to consulting physicians initiated by the team physician should be made in coordination with the athlete's primary care physician. A consultation list should be established to provide medical and surgical referral sources for

the medical problems common to sports participation.
- The team physician will assist in the rehabilitation of all athletic injuries along with the appropriate physical therapist or athletic trainer.

If these guidelines are followed, the team physician will be able to provide quality medical care in an organized manner at athletic events. A team physician might be required to manage an injury that could be crippling or fatal; in that event, proper medical care is a matter of sound judgement and basic knowledge of emergency techniques. Specific techniques for handling on-field emergencies will be discussed in Chapter IX. The tables and appendices are designed to provide information about the medical equipment needed to deal with emergency situations at athletic events. (Also see Appendix 7-1 on covering marathon events).

### REFERENCES

DiNubile, N. Emergency care on the field: the physician's role. *Drug Therapy*, p. 41-55, September 1985.

Lehman, R.C, Vegso, J.J. and Torge, J.S. Life-threatening injuries incurred by athletes. *J Musculoskel Med* 3(10):14-24, 1986.

Lucas, C.E. Early care of critically injured patients. *Hospital Medicine*, p. 31-45, August 1977.

McKeag, D.B. On-site care of the injured youth. In Kelly, V.C. et al (Eds.) *Brennemann's Practice of Pediatrics* Vol 10, New York: Harper & Row, p. 1-23, 1985.

Ryan, A.J. (moderator). Guidelines to help you in giving on-field care. *Phys and Sportsmed* 3(9):50-63, 1975.

Tucker, J.B., Marron, J.T. Field-site management of athletic injuries. *Am Fam Phys* 14(3):137-142, 1986.

### RECOMMENDED READINGS

Standards and Guidelines for Cardiopulmonary Resuscitation (CPR) and Emergency Cardiac Care (ECC). *JAMA* 255:2905-2989, 1986.

Torg, J.E. (Ed). *Athletic Injuries to the Head, Neck and Face*. Philadelphia: Lea & Febiger, 1982.

# Appendix 8-1.
# The Sportsmedicine Physician's Bag

(Adapted From: *Phys and Sportsmed* 9(5):86-87, 1981)

**The Sportsmedicine Bag**

1. Padded tongue blade for convulsions
2. Diazepam (10 mg in prefilled syringe for convulsion)
3. Dexamethasone (Decadron) 24 mg/ml, 5-ml vial for spinal cord injury
4. Alupent inhaler for asthmatic or allergic attack
5. Ophthalmological irrigating solution and eye cup
6. Fluor-I-Strip (3) for staining cornea
7. Tetracaine, 0.5%, 2-ml ampule
8. Small eye spud
9. Sodium Sulamyd eye drop or ointment
10. Sterile suture set (1)
11. Plastic suture material 5-9, 6-0 (2 each) with swaged PRE-2 needles
12. Ster-I-Strip, 1/4 in. and 1/2 in. (2 packages each)
13. Tape adherent, 1 can
14. Sterile gloves (2 pairs)
15. Sterile gauze pads, 2x2 in., 3x3 in., 4x4 in. (3 each)
16. Povidone-iodine (Betadine) solution
17. ABD pads (2)
18. Medicine cups (2)
19. Q-tips (1 package)
20. Betadine ointment
21. 8-in. heavy-duty bandage scissors
22. Swiss army knife with as many gadgets as possible
23. Disposable flashlight (1)
24. Elastic bandages, 3 in., 4 in., 6 in., (1 each)
25. Prewrap foam bandage 3 in. (1)
26. Elastic tape, 1 in., 3 in. (2 each)
27. Cotton web roll 4 in. (2)
28. Tufskin (Cramer), 1 can
29. Skin lube (Cramer), 1 tube
30. Plastic foam sheet, 3/8-in. thick
31. Felt padding, 3/8 in. (4x4 in. sheet)
32. Super glue (1)
33. Stethoscope
34. Aneroid manometer
35. Ophthalmoscope-otoscope
36. Thermometer
37. Orthoplast sheet (6x6 in.) for splinting fingers
38. Bandaids, all sizes
39. Moleskin (6x6 in.)
40. Reflex hammer
41. Safety pins
42. Tongue blades
43. Tape measure
44. Latex exam gloves

## Cardiopulmonary Equipment and Drugs

**Cardiopulmonary Resuscitation Equipment**

1. Oral airways, small, medium, and large
2. Ambu bag with face mask and adapter for endotracheal tubes
3. Endotracheal tubes, cuffed, small, medium, and large
4. Disposable laryngoscope with light source
5. Cricothyrectomy kit
6. Syringe (50 ml) and large catheter for suction

**Cardiopulmonary Medications**

1. Atropine sulfate 1.0 mg in prefilled syringe (10ml)
2. Epinephrine 1:10,000 in prefilled syringe (10ml)
3. Lidocaine hydrochloride 100 mg in prefilled syringe (5 ml)
4. Sodium bicarbonate 50 mEq in prefilled syringe (50ml)
5. Lactated Ringer's 500 ml with tubing and needles
6. Nitrostat 0.4 mg sublingual tablets
7. Morphine sulfate 15 mg Tubex with syringe
8. Demerol 100 mg in 2-ml ampule
9. Lasix 40 mg IU ampule

# Appendix 8-2.
# The Trainer's Equipment

**Basic Training Room Equipment**

Examination tables
Refrigerator
Sink
Whirlpool
Infrared heat lamp or hydrocollator
Scales
Weight charts
Stethoscope and blood pressure cuff
Locked cabinet for medications
Bulletin board (for emergency telephone numbers)

**Trainer's Side Table (out of the way)**

Gauze pads (4in x 4in and 2in x 2in)
Band-Aids
Tongue depressors
Cotton buds (Q-tips)
Buffered salt tablets
AlCl$_2$ solution (30%) (aluminum chloride)
Petrolatum
Analgesic cream (gold)
(Heavy) skin lubricant (green)
Foam pads for tapings
Tape remover
Bandage scissors
Callus file
Electric hair clipper

**Trainer's Kit**

Oral screw
Tongue forceps
Airways
Tourniquet
Tongue depressors
Paper bag (hyperventilation)
Contact lens case, contact lens solution, contact lens extractor
Eye cup
Eye wash
Toothache kit
Oral thermometer
Flashlight

Scalpel
Bandage scissors
Surgical scissors
Hemostat
Forceps
Hand mirror
Safety pins
Surgical Razor with blades
Nail clippers
Callus file
Sling
Finger splints
Transcutaneous electrical nerve stimulator (TENS) unit and cream
Plastic ice bags
1-oz cups
Tape measure
Marking pen, paper, pencils
Shoe horn
Coins for pay phone
Nonadhering sterile pads
Gelfoam
Band-aids
Butterfly closures & Steri-Strips
Roll of cotton & cotton balls
3in x 3in sterile gauze
2in x 2in nonsterile gauze
3-in roller gauze
Felt horseshoe
Tape adherent
Skin lubricant
Foam heel and lace pads
Underwrap
1/2-in adhesive tape
1-in adhesive tape
1 1/2-in adhesive tape
3-inch elastic tape
Elasticon tape
Conform tape
Waterproof tape
Tape cutter
Tape remover
2-in elastic wrap
3-in elastic wrap

4-in elastic wrap
Ankle wrap
Ear drops
Nose drops
Throat lozenges
Cough syrup
Cold tablets
Aspirin
Motion sickness tablets
Antacid tablets
Salt tablets
Sun lotion
Envelopes for pills
First aid spray
Ointment for minor skin irritations
Zinc oxide ointment
Betadine
Liquid soap
Tinactin
Ethyl chloride
Ammonia capsules
Flexible collodian
Petrolatum
Saline in plastic squeeze bottle
Alcohol
Alcohol prep sponges
Cotton buds
First aid manual

**Travel Trunk**

Dental kit
Tongue depressors
Mouthpieces
Cotton buds
Examination gloves
Towels
Plastic ice bags
Drinking cups
Calamine lotion
Talcum powder
Analgesic balm

Telfa pads
Nonsterile gauze pads
Roller gauze
Assorted pieces of foam rubber
Orthopedic felt
Felt horseshoes
Tape adherent
Skin lubricant
Adhesive tape (1in and 1 1/2in)
Elastic tape (3in)
Elastic wraps (2in, 3in, 4in and 6in)
Tape remover
Moleskin
Stockinette (3in and 6in)
Rolls of plaster (3in, 4in and 6in)
Neck collars
Thomas collars
Assorted protective pads
Acromioclavicular pads
Sternum pad
Thigh caps
Heel cups
Ensolite (1/4in, 3/8in, 1/2in)
Orthoplast
Slings
Rib belts
Knee immobilizer
Air splints
High-intensity lamp
Equipment hardware
Spare parts
   Chinstraps
   Shoulder pad straps
   Clips
   Screws
Pliers
Screwdrivers
Collapsible cane
Shoe horn
Coat hanger
Umbrella

**Equipment Schools and Clubs Should Provide**

| No. | Item | Comments |
| --- | --- | --- |
| 1 | Double-action bolt cutter | This may be used to remove a face mask quickly to establish an airway without removing the helmet. |
| 1 | Stretcher | The folding Army-type field stretcher is satisfactory. A metal rescue stretcher that can be assembled under the victim without lifting him is even better. |

**Equipment Schools and Clubs Should Provide** *(Continued)*

| No. | Item | Comments |
|---|---|---|
| 1 | Backboard | This may be in one or two pieces and should have strap restraints attached. |
| 2 | Blankets | The regular Army blanket is desirable. |
| 4 | Sandbags | The 5-lb size is very helpful to immobilize the player during transportation. |
| 2 pairs | Crutches, adjustable lengths | These are handy for moving the player off the field and from bench to dressing or training room. |
| 3 | Slings | Large muslin triangles are satisfactory, but these require two large safety pins each. |
| 2 each | Splints, upper and lower extremity | Plastic air splints or the cardboard splints of the National Ski Patrol are both satisfactory. The former are expensive and tend to disappear, the latter are cheap and disposable. Rolls or muslin in 3-in. widths need to be supplied with the cardboard splints. |
| 1 | A sling psychrometer or a device to measure wet bulb, globe and dry air temperatures | On hot humid days the heat stress index should be determined before and sometimes during football games or other outdoor sports events. |
| 12 each | Rubberized elastic bandages, 3 in., 4 in., and 6 in. | |
| | Ice with small plastic bags to contain it | This is invaluable for cooling off players and injured body parts and is cheaper and far more practical than the chemically activated cold packs. |

# PART III
# Clinical Sports Medicine

# 9

# Management of On-Site Emergencies

The number of individuals participating in athletics has increased dramatically in recent decades. As a result, a proportionate increase in athletic injuries and related problems also has been observed. Team physicians covering sports events could be responsible for the management of an injury that could be crippling or fatal. Life-threatening situations in competitive and recreational athletics are by no means epidemic but they do occur. For example, the actual mortality rate for tackle football in this country is on the order of 2 deaths per 100,000 participants (DiNubile, 1985). Mortality rates for other athletic activities are also available. The team physician, trainer, and coach must deal with the possibility of death as a result of an athletic contest, even though the probability is low.

A life-threatening condition becomes a very significant episode in the life of a team physician. Therefore, anyone who is responsible for the medical care of athletes should be able to recognize and deal effectively with the most common life-threatening conditions that occur in sports events. Proper medical care in a crisis is a matter of sound judgment and basic knowledge of emergency techniques.

In this chapter, we will discuss seven situations that can immediately threaten the life of an athlete: orthopedic injuries, head and neck injuries, respiratory obstruction, respiratory failure, cardiac arrest, heat injury, and hypothermia. Each topic will be discussed in detail in other chapters.

Cardiac arrest, airway and breathing difficulty, uncontrolled bleeding, severe head and neck injuries, shock, and open chest or abdominal wounds have top priority when managing on-site injuries. Unreduced joint dislocations should have second priority. Uncomplicated fractures, sprains, strains, subluxations, dislocations with spontaneous reduction, and contusions should have a lower priority when emergency treatment is necessary.

## SEVERE ORTHOPEDIC INJURIES

A thorough discussion of orthopedic injuries that occur frequently during athletic events is outlined in Chapters 10-14. The following rules apply to the management of on-site orthopedic emergencies.

Athletes with probable fractures, dislocations, subluxations, or unstable joints will be out of competition. Warning signs of serious injury include acute ecchymosis or swelling, limited passive or active range of motion, and decreased ability to bear weight on or resist force against the affected joint. Joint pain that persists for 15-25 minutes after injury, even if warning signs of more serious injury are not present, should stop further competition.

General management principles for joint trauma apply to the on-site management of orthopedic emergencies. If a bony or supporting soft-tissue injury is suspected, the area should be stabilized and immobilized and cryotherapy instituted. The use of an elastic wrap, sling, or air cast to diminish pain and potential swelling is helpful. This equipment should be available at all event sites. Moving a patient quickly so play can resume or aggressively attempting to reduce a deformity without adequate planning could bring about problems far worse than the initial injury. The physician should be thorough in his initial evaluation and look for obvious deformity, lacerations, puncture wounds, or neurovascular compromise.

If there is a gross malalignment or deformity, it is reasonable to attempt gentle traction in line with the limb without manipulation. After evaluation and treatment at the playing site, the limb should be properly splinted and the athlete transported to a local emergency facility. Clinical examination will often detect potential fractures but it is never possible to completely define the extent of injury without radiographic evaluations.

## INTRACRANIAL INJURY AND CONCUSSION

Intracranial injuries are a frequent occurrence in contact sports and include concussion, skull fracture, subdural and epidural hematoma, and intracerebral hemorrhage. It is important for the team physician to understand the natural course of these potentially serious injuries to avoid the collapse and death of the athlete.

Brain injuries sustained in sports competition may be focal or diffuse. The athlete may be conscious, unconscious, ambulatory, or nonambulatory, and it is important to remember that the patient's initial presentation does not reliably indicate the pathological diagnosis or severity of the injury. Appropriate initial evaluation and periodic reassessment of all intracranial injuries is mandatory. The field examination of the athlete with a head injury includes evaluating the patient's facial expression, orientation to time, place, and person, post-traumatic amnesia, retrograde amnesia, and gait (Bruno, et al., 1985; Lehman et al, 1986; Torg & Vegso, 1985). Table 9-1 provides simple guidelines that show when an athlete with a head injury should be referred for additional treatment. Table 9-2 compares three systems for classifying concussions. For purposes of the following discussion, the Torg method is used.

### Grade 1 Concussion

The athlete is confused, has a dazed expression, and complains of dizziness, tinnitus, and has an unsteady gait. Loss of consciousness rarely occurs and there is no evidence of post-traumatic or retrograde amnesia. The symptom complex is short; most athletes are free of all symptoms within 10-15 minutes. The athlete may return to competi-

**Table 9-1. Referral of Athletes with Head Injuries**

**Refer to Local Hospital for Evaluation and Observation**
- Unresolved concussions
- Drowsy victims without focal signs but with possible complicating factors (medications, alcohol, intoxication, etc.)
- Preschool children, even with a normal neurological examination

**Refer to Neurosurgical Center**
- Penetrating cranial injuries
- Deteriorating level of consciousness
- Lateral deficit
- Prolonged unconsciousness (> 5 minutes)
- Head injuries associated with painful injuries requiring narcotic analgesics
- CSF leak
- Post-traumatic seizures
- Preschool children with skull fractures

(From "Memory jogger: guidelines for managing head injuries at sports events", *Phys Sportsmed* 11(6), June 1986)

tion under close supervision but should be reassessed every 5-10 minutes. Symptoms that preclude further competition are vertigo, headache, photophobia, and labile emotions.

### Grade 2 Concussion

Athletes with a Grade 2 concussion have symptoms similar to those of Grade 1 with the addition of post-traumatic amnesia (unable to recall events since the time of injury). The athlete should not compete further and should be watched closely for postconcussion syndrome, persistent headache, inability to concentrate, and irritability. If these symptoms occur, the athlete should be reevaluated and consultation with a neurosurgeon should be considered.

### Grade 3 Concussions

Signs and symptoms are similar to Grade 2 concussion with the addition of retrograde amnesia (inability to remember events prior to injury). These athletes should not be allowed to return to competition and they may need a period of hospital observation. Traumatic injuries that cause epidural or subdural hematomas may result in gradually increasing intracranial pressure and collapse of a seemingly normal athlete. This is a medical

Table 9-2. Comparison of Classifications of Concussion

| Torg | Kuland | Nelson |
|---|---|---|
| GRADE 1<br>'Bell rung'<br>Short-term confusion<br>Unsteady gait<br>Dazed appearance<br>Loss of consciousness (LOC) | MILD<br>Stunned, dazed<br>No confusion, dizziness<br>No nausea, visual disturbance<br>Feels well after 1 or 2 minutes | GRADE 0<br>Head struck or moved rapidly<br>Not stunned or dazed initially<br>Subsequently complains of headache and difficulty in concentrating |
| GRADE 2<br>Post-traumatic amnesia<br>Vertigo | MODERATE<br>LOC<br>Mental confusion<br>Retrograde amnesia<br>Tinnitus, dizziness<br>Skill recovery may be rapid | GRADE 1<br>Stunned or dazed initially<br>No LOC or amnesia<br>'Bell rung'<br>Sensorium quickly clears (less than 1 minute) |
| GRADE 3<br>Post-traumatic amnesia<br>Retrograde amnesia<br>Vertigo | SEVERE<br>Longer LOC<br>Headache, confusion<br>Post-traumatic amnesia<br>Retrograde amnesia | GRADE 2<br>Headache, cloudy sensorium > 1 min<br>No LOC<br>May have tinnitus, amnesia<br>May be irritable, hyperexcitable, confused, dizzy |
| GRADE 4<br>Post-traumatic amnesia<br>Immediate, transient LOC | | GRADE 3<br>LOC < 1 min<br>Not comatose (Arousable with noxious stimuli)<br>Demonstrate grade 2 symptoms during recovery |
| GRADE 5<br>Paralytic coma<br>Cardiorespiratory arrest | | GRADE 4<br>LOC > 1 min<br>Not comatose<br>Demonstrate grade 2 symptoms during recovery |
| GRADE 6<br>Death | | |

emergency that requires hospitalization and neurosurgical consultation. A suggested treatment protocol is listed in Table 9-3. Guidelines for return to play after concussion are outlined in Table 9-4.

## Grade 4 Concussions

Athletes with Grade 4 concussions are usually in a paralytic coma but recover within seconds to minutes. They emerge from coma in a stuporous and confused state, pass through a lucid period, and then become fully alert. Post-traumatic and retrograde amnesia is almost always present. These athletes should be transported by stretcher with precautions taken to protect the cervical spine. The athlete should be moved on a spine board to the nearest hospital for overnight observation (see Figure 9-1 to 9-3b). Any athlete who

Table 9-3. Treatment Protocol for Head Injury

*First Aid:* Hyperventilation

*Diagnosis:* CT Scan

*Surgery:* For epidural hematoma, large subdural hematoma or large intracerebral hematoma

*No Surgery:* For small subdural hematoma, confusion, diffuse injury, most intracerebral hematomas

*ICP Monitoring and Treatment*
Goal: Keep ICP less than 15 mm Hg
*Modalities*
- Hyperventilation (PCO$_2$) 22 to 30 mm Hg
- Corticosteroids (1mg/kg)
- Mannitol (1 g/kg, serum osmolality 330 to 320 mOsm/L)
- Barbiturates (30 mg/kg loading and 0.5 to 3 mg/kg/h maintenance)

(From *Current Therapy in Sports Medicine*, 1985-1986, p. 138)

Table 9-4. Guidelines for Return to Play After Concussion

|  | 1st Concussion | 2nd Concussion | 3rd Concussion |
| --- | --- | --- | --- |
| Grade 1 (mild) | May return to play if asymptomatic* for 2-3 days | Return to play in 2 weeks if asymptomatic* at that time for 1 week | Terminate season; may return to play next season if asymptomatic* |
| Grade 2 (moderate) | Return to play after asymptomatic for 1 week | Minimum of 2-3 weeks; may return to play then if asymptomatic for 1 week; consider terminating season | Terminate season; may return to play next season if asymptomatic |
| Grade 3 (severe) | Minimum of 2-3 weeks; may then return to play if asymptomatic for 1 week | Terminate season; may return to play next season if asymptomatic |  |

*No headache, dizziness, or impaired orientation, or memory during rest of exertion.
(From *Phys Sportsmed* 14(10):79, 1986 with permission of McGraw-Hill, Inc.)

has been unconscious during an athletic event should not return to competition that day even if they later become mentally clear.

Any athlete with an unsteady gait or stuporous condition should be transported from the field by stretcher. Avoid manipulating the head and cervical spine and perform basic CPR if necessary. The athlete should be properly transported to the nearest hospital for definitive care.

## Grade 5 Concussions

Characteristically, this condition is accompanied by prolonged coma and often is associated with secondary cardiorespiratory collapse. CPR should be instituted immediately and the athlete transported to the hospital.

Symptoms and signs that demand emergency action after a head injury include increasing headache, nausea and vomiting, inequality of pupil size, disorientation, progressive or sudden impairment of consciousness, gradual rise in blood pressure, and a decrease in pulse rate. These signs are evidence of increasing intercranial pressure which requires immediate intervention by a neurosurgeon (Torg et al., 1975; Torg & Vegso, 1985; Tucker & Marron, 1986). An initial treatment protocol for severe head injury is listed in Table 9-3.

## Subdural Hematoma

Subdural hematomas are a result of injury to the subdural veins that lie between the brain and the cavernous sinus. Because of the slow bleeding, symptoms are not appreciated until 24-48 hours post-injury. Low pressure bleeding leads to a gradual increase in intracranial pressure and to the potentially dangerous signs already mentioned. The presence of any of these signs or symptoms requires immediate transportation of the athlete to the hospital for definitive neurosurgical care.

## Epidural Hematoma

Laceration of the middle meningeal artery occurs when there is a direct blow to the side of the head and results in rapid bleeding and increased intracranial pressure within 20-30 minutes. The athlete may be lucid initially but his condition will deteriorate rapidly after several hours. The signs will become apparent and the athlete should be transferred immediately to the nearest medical facility. Table 9-3 should be consulted for initial management of increased intracranial pressure symptoms.

## CERVICAL SPINE INJURIES

Fracture dislocation of the cervical spine is one of the most catastrophic injuries associated with contact sports. Technological improvements in equipment have reduced the incidence of cervical spine injuries in football and other sports but the team physician must still be prepared to manage them. Injury to the cervical spine should al-

**Fig. 9-1.** When an athlete has a suspected injury to the cervical spine, maintain the position of the head while checking for breathing.

**Fig. 9-2.** With assistance, place arms and legs in axial alignment with the torso, then "logroll" the athlete onto a spineboard. The leader is *always* responsible for protecting the head and neck during transfer taking care to prevent head movement not relative to the torso. The leader also is responsible for all movement commands of the injured athlete by the rescue team.

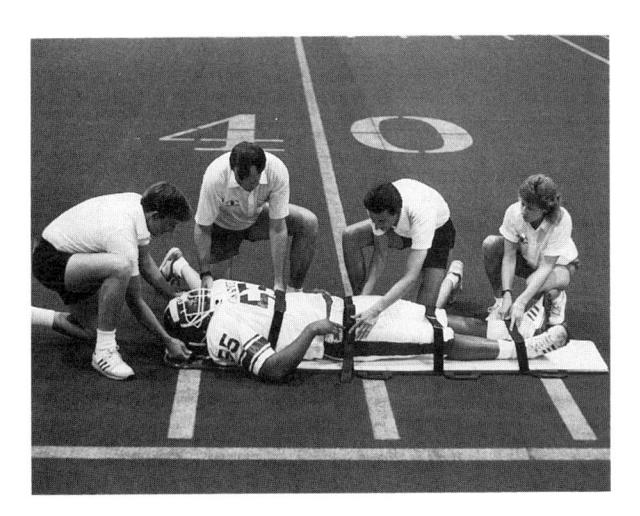

**Fig. 9-3a.** Once the athlete is on the spineboard, the head and neck continue to be protected until immobilization via straps is satisfactorily achieved. The leader remains at the athlete's head until transfer to emergency vehicle is complete.

**Fig. 9-3b.** If breathing is compromised, the football face mask is attached to the helmet so that it can be removed easily with the use of a sharp pocket knife cutting plastic support clips. A respiratory airway then can be achieved without any need to remove the helmet.

ways be suspected in an unconscious athlete and handled judiciously.

Management of injuries to the cervical spine requires an understanding of normal anatomical structures as well as how to determine the severity of injury (see Figure 9-4). Fortunately, only a small percentage of neck injuries result in permanent neurological damage. However, improper han-

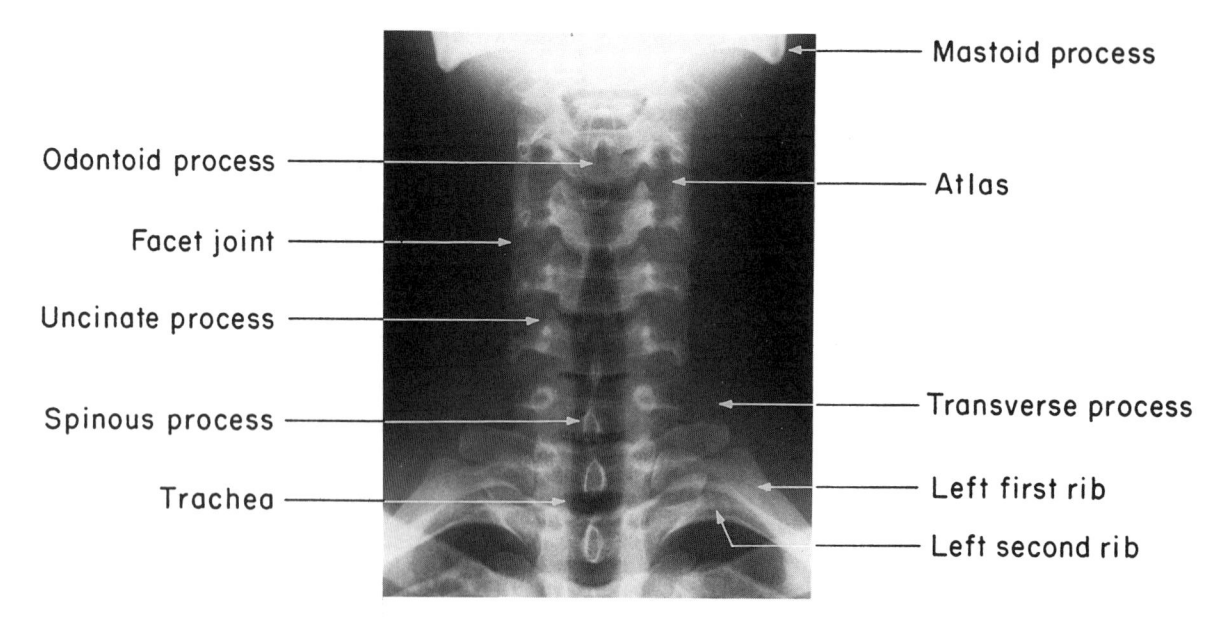

Fig. 9-4. Normal Bony Anatomy of the Cervical Spine

dling of an unstable cervical spine without neurological deficit can very easily result in a neurological deficit (Bruno, 1985; Lehman, 1986; Tucker & Marron, 1986).

Serious injury to the cervical spine should be evaluated by performing a thorough neurological exam at the event site (see Table 9-5). The range of motion of the cervical spine should be determined. If the athlete is unable or unwilling to perform range of motion activities of the cervical spine while standing erect, the examination should stop and the athlete taken to the hospital for roentgenographic evaluation. Any athlete who complains of persistent limb paraesthesia, extremity weakness, or painful movement of the cervical spine should be excluded from further activity and properly evaluated.

**Table 9-5. Brief Neurological Examination**

| VERBAL | MOTOR |
|---|---|
| In response to command and/or pain | Posture of each limb |
| Presence | Spontaneous and voluntary movement of each limb |
| Content | Response of each limb to pain |
| Quality of speech | |
| EYES | SENSORY |
| Position | Touch or pinch proprioception in each limb if conscious |
| Movement | |
| Pupil size (mm) | Response to pain in each limb if impaired consciousness |
| Pupil reaction | |
| REFLEX | |
| Tendon reflexes at elbows and knees | |
| Plantar responses | |

(From "Memory jogger: Guidelines for managing head injuries at sports events. *Phys Sportsmed* 11(6), June 1986)

### Neurapraxia ("Burner")

Nerve root and brachial plexis neurapraxia ("burner") are the most common cervical injuries in athletes (Clancy et al, 1977). The neurapraxia is short and is associated with a full, pain-free range of cervical motion. Typically, an athlete who is hit on the head or shoulder experiences a sharp, burning pain in the neck that radiates into the shoulder, arm, and hand. The athlete may experience associated weakness and paraesthesia of the involved arm that lasts for several seconds to minutes. An athlete whose paraesthesia disappears completely, who demonstrates full strength of the intrinsic muscles of the shoulder and upper extremities, and who has a full, pain-free range of cervical motion may return to sports activities. Motor and sensory testing of the major peripheral nerves can be found in Table 9-6.

Recurrent episodes of brachial plexis neurapraxia require cervical spine roentenograms and

Table 9-6. Testing the Major Peripheral Nerves of the Brachial Plexus

| Nerve | Motor Test | Sensation Test |
|---|---|---|
| Radial Nerve | Wrist Extension | Dorsal web space between thumb and index finger |
| Ulnar Nerve | Abduction, little finger | Distal ulnar aspects, little finger |
| Median Nerve | Thumb pinch<br>Opposition of thumb<br>Abduction of thumb | Distal radial aspect, index finger |
| Axillary Nerve | Deltoid | Lateral arm, deltoid patch on upper arm |
| Musculocutaneous Nerve | Biceps | Lateral Forearm |

electromyographic (EMG) studies. If these studies are within normal limits, an intensive isotonic neck muscle strengthening program is begun; several months of training are required before benefits can be noticed. Any athlete susceptible to neurapraxia should continue with a cervical strengthening program year-round and wear a neck roll when participating in contact sports such as football. If the EMG demonstrates involvement of the deltoid, infraspinatus, supraspinatus, and biceps muscles, the lesion should be considered an axonotmesis and appropriate neurological consultation is indicated.

If paraesthesia, weakness, or limited cervical motion persists, further contact sports should be discontinued and individuals should undergo a complete neurologic, EMG, and x-ray evaluation. A full muscle strengthening program should be started and a repeat EMG performed within four to six weeks. Repeat EMGs may be abnormal for many months post-injury. When full muscle strength is achieved, the athlete is allowed to return to contact sports (Clancy et al, 1977; Torg, 1982).

## Cervical Fractures and Dislocations: General Principles

Fractures or dislocations of the cervical spine may be stable or unstable and some are associated with neurological deficits. Whenever a fracture or disruption of the soft-tissue supporting structures violates or threatens to violate the integrity of the spinal cord, certain management and treatment principles must be implemented.

The first goal of treatment is to protect the spinal cord and nerve roots from injuries and mismanagement (Lucas, 1977; McKeag, 1985; Tucker & Marron, 1986). Second, the malaligned cervical spine should be reduced as quickly and gently as possible to effectively decompress the spinal cord (Torg et al, 1975; Torg & Vegso, 1985). Obviously, the athlete in this situation should be moved to the nearest emergency facility capable of handling this problem. The third goal in managing fractures and dislocations of the cervical spine is to effect stability of the cervical spine in the most time efficient manner. Prevention of residual deformity and cervical spine instability with its associated pain and the possibility of further trauma to the spinal cord is a major goal of the examining physician. Patients with stable compression fractures of the vertebral body, undisplaced fractures of the lamina or lateral mass, or soft tissue injuries without neurologic deficit can be treated adequately with traction. A cervical brace will provide protection while healing occurs. Both surgical and nonsurgical methods have been used to treat unstable cervical spine fractures or fracture/dislocations without neurologic deficit. A neurosurgeon should be consulted.

Athletes who have been treated for cervical sprains, intervertebral disk injuries without neurologic involvement, and stable wedge compression fractures may return to all sporting activities when their symptoms cease (Bruno et al, 1985; Torg & Vegso, 1985). The athlete must have a full range of cervical motion, full muscle strength, and stability of the cervical spine as demonstrated by flexion and extension radiographic films. Athletes with subluxation of the cervical spine without fracture should be excluded from further participation in contact sports even when stability of the cervical spine can be demonstrated by lateral flexion/extension films. Athletes who have undergone successful cervical fusion for a herniated disk or anterior instability may return to all activities once they have full range of motion and normal strength of the cervical spine. However, the possibility of intervertebral disk herniation at an adjacent level is always present. Athletes who require more than one level of anterior or posterior fusion following a cervical spine injury should be evaluated on an individual basis with regard to noncontact sports.

## EMERGENCY MANAGEMENT OF HEAD AND NECK INJURIES

Treatment of the unconscious athlete or one with cervical spine injuries must never be carried out in a haphazard manner. Prior preparation is mandatory in order to prevent actions that might convert a stable injury into a disaster. To ensure the best possible care, make sure that all emergency equipment is readily available at the event site, including a spine board, stretcher, and CPR equipment (refer to Chapter 8).

In order to prevent further injury to the athlete, immediately immobilize the patient's head and neck by holding them in a neutral position. Check quickly for the presence of breathing and pulse. If the athlete is breathing, remove the face mask and maintain the airway. Removing the face mask is necessary only if respiration is threatened or unstable or if the athlete remains unconscious for a prolonged period. Keeping the chin strap in place on the helmet maintains the stability of the head inside the helmet. If there is no breathing, or the patient has a respiratory arrest, the airway must be reestablished.

If the patient is lying on his abdomen or face down, you must turn him over and "log rolling" is the safest and easiest method. Examples of the log rolling technique are provided in Figure 9-1 to 9-3b. The medical team usually consists of five members. It is important that the leader of the five man group keep the head properly immobilized. This is accomplished by applying slight traction with the hands and using a crossover technique that allows the arms to unwind during the log-roll. If CPR is required, the face mask must be removed from the helmet with a bolt cutter or sharp knife, depending on the type of face mask attachment.

The cervical spine can be immobilized by several methods. The Purdue University fracture board is outfitted with an outrigger and buckles for a four-tailed chin strap. Where such equipment is unavailable, the head and neck may be supported with sandbags, wet towels, adhesive tape, or by simply holding on to the head and neck and keeping it in a neutral position. During any of the immobilization or transportation procedures, frequent rechecks of breathing and pulse, and evaluation of the athlete's neurologic status are necessary. Basic CPR should be maintained until an ambulance arrives. The athlete should be taken to the most appropriate medical facility for care by a neurosurgeon and/or orthopedic surgeon.

## RESPIRATORY OBSTRUCTION

### Trauma-induced Occlusion of the Airway

The first concern of the team physician in dealing with a traumatized athlete is ensuring that the airway is patent. An athlete who has been rendered unconscious during play may fall supine, causing the relaxed oropharyngeal muscles to fall posteriorly and block the airway. The airway must be established immediately by supporting the neck with one hand and tilting the head back with the other, allowing the retropharyngeal musculature to fall forward in the airway. If this maneuver is unsuccessful, try to grasp the mandible and pull it forward while the head is tilted backwards. One caution — if a cervical spine injury is suspected, the jaw thrust maneuver should be performed without tilting the head backwards.

### Aspiration

Foreign body aspiration is possible during athletic competition, with the foreign body becoming lodged in the trachea and obstructing the airway. The Heimlich maneuver should be performed immediately. If this is unsuccessful, emergency tracheostomy techniques may have to be instituted.

### Laryngeal Fracture

Neck trauma can result in a fracture of the larynx that produces a deformation that obstructs the airway. This injury usually causes localized edema, disarticulation of one or both vocal cords, and/or hemorrhage. Common symptoms are localized pain, dyspnea, and hoarseness or loss of voice, with increased discomfort when the patient leans forward. Hemorrhage or edema may cause the symptoms to progress rapidly. Any athlete with this complication needs an immediate tracheostomy with a cricothyroid cannula (Torg, 1982). This is a difficult procedure at best and should be performed by an experienced individual. The athlete should be transported to the nearest hospital as quickly as possible. Even if the situation appears stable, the physician should accompany the athlete to the hospital because of the risk of rapid hemorrhage and airway obstruction. Other causes of respiratory failure should be considered once the physician has determined that the airway is patent.

## RESPIRATORY FAILURE

### Syncope

The most common type of acute respiratory failure in athletes is simple syncopal apnea. Syncope occurs in many athletes when they face a diagnostic or therapeutic procedure such as an arthrocentesis or injection. The athlete has a psychophysiologic episode that results in vasovagal stimulation that is associated with hypotension, loss of consciousness and, rarely, seizures. Transient apnea may follow but there are usually no sequelae. Breathing usually begins spontaneously but CPR should be initiated if it doesn't. Transportation to an emergency facility may be necessary.

### Respiratory Arrest

Initial management of acute respiratory arrest is the same as for airway obstruction. Make sure that the airway is patent and, if spontaneous breathing is not resumed, start initial CPR procedures with mouth-to-mouth resuscitation. Emergency equipment at the event site should include a plastic or pharyngeal airway to maintain airway patency in an unconscious patient once breathing has been established. The use of an Ambu bag for prolonged respiratory support is highly recommended. Transportation by ambulance to an emergency facility and definitive care is mandatory for a favorable outcome.

### Pneumothorax

Pneumothorax during competition may occur either spontaneously or secondary to chest trauma (Figure 9-5a). The classic presentation involves acute unilateral chest pain with dyspnea and the presence of tachypnea. Usually, the findings of hyperresonance and diminished or absent breath sounds on the affected side of the chest are diagnostic. The athlete should not compete further or engage in any endeavor that increases intrathoracic pressure.

If the respiratory rate is >30 per minute or the athlete shows signs of cyanosis or severe pain, immediate transportation to the hospital is indicated. Tension pneumothorax is a potential complication and may result in vascular compromise and hypotension (Figure 9-5b). If this occurs, insertion of a large bore needle into the intercostal space may be life-saving.

## CARDIAC ARREST

Cardiac arrest is unusual in young athletes but it has been the cause of sudden unexplained deaths during competition. Cardiac arrest usually occurs after cardiovascular collapse following ventricular fibrillation or standstill. If cardiac arrest occurs, lifesaving measures should be instituted immediately. In the absence of a carotid pulse, an airway is established and the patient placed on the ground or backboard and CPR initiated. With appropriate medical equipment and medications, advanced cardiac life support could be initiated at the event site if the physician is experienced. New standards for basic CPR and ACLS have been implemented and are available through the American Heart Association, 44 E. 23rd Street, New York, New York 10010. Physicians involved in the care of athletes at events should be ACLS certified.

## HEAT INJURIES

Climate plays a major and often crucial role in both the performance and well-being of the exercising individual. Many athletes are at risk for problems caused by excessive heat under certain climatic conditions. The common features of heat related injuries are summarized in Table 9-7.

### Heat Cramps

Heat cramps are a short-term heat disorder that occurs commonly in highly conditioned indi-

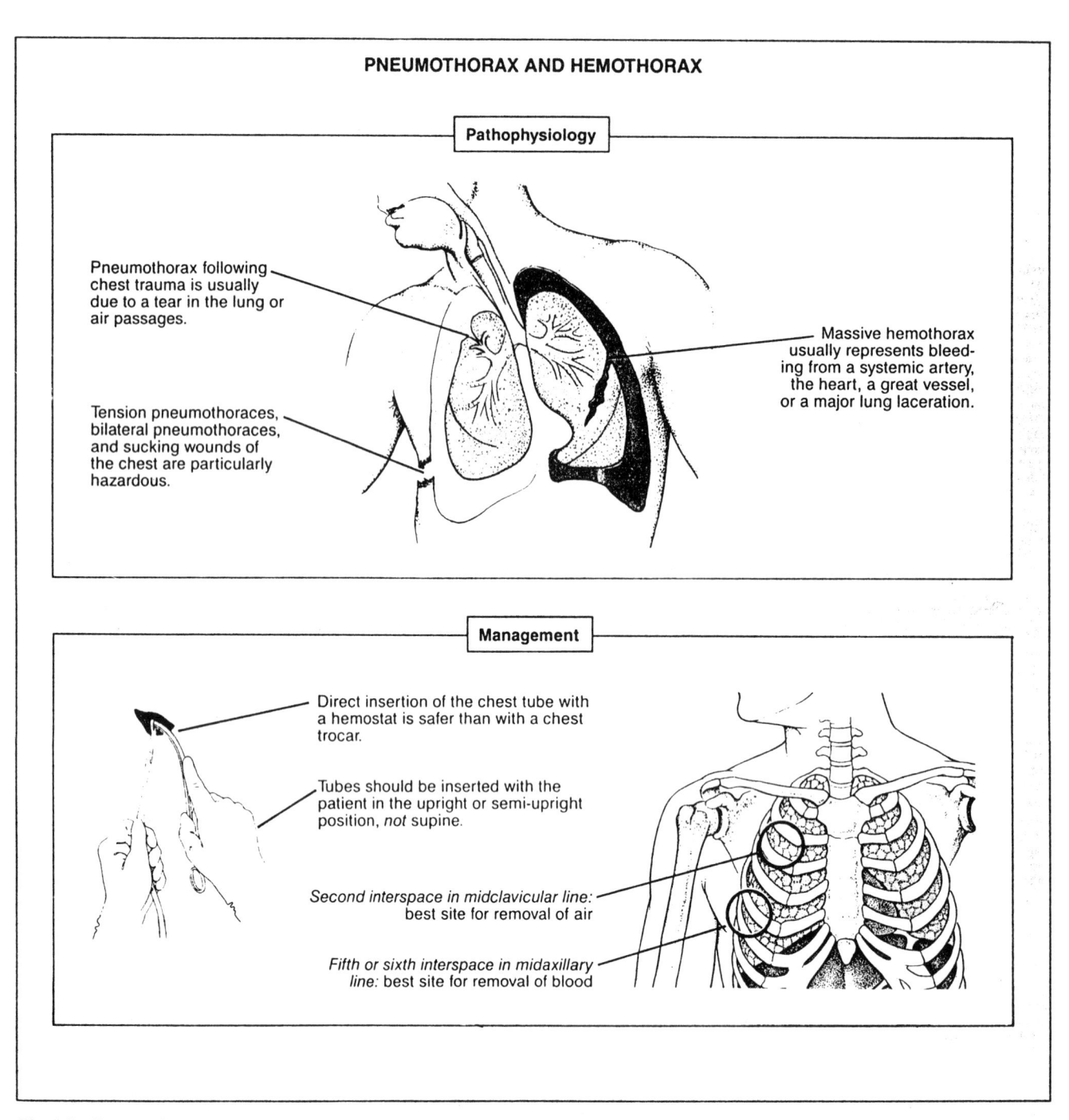

**Fig. 9-5a.** Pneumothorax and Hemothorax (From Campbell, G.S. Thoracic injuries: practical points of ERCare. *Hosp. Med.* p. 18, 3/85, with permission of Cahners Publishing Co.)

viduals who train in extremely hot weather. Excessive loss of fluid, salts, and possibly other minerals is due to the failure of the athlete to replace water losses incurred through sweating. Cramping of actively exercising muscles, associated with muscle spasm and an inability to use the affected extremity, is common and lasts several minutes.

Emergency management consists of replacing fluids and electrolytes, stretching the involved muscles, and rest. Massage may help. Ice cold water is the fluid replacement of choice, and the athlete should drink liberally while practicing and competing in hot, humid weather. Intravenous administration of saline may be required in more difficult cases.

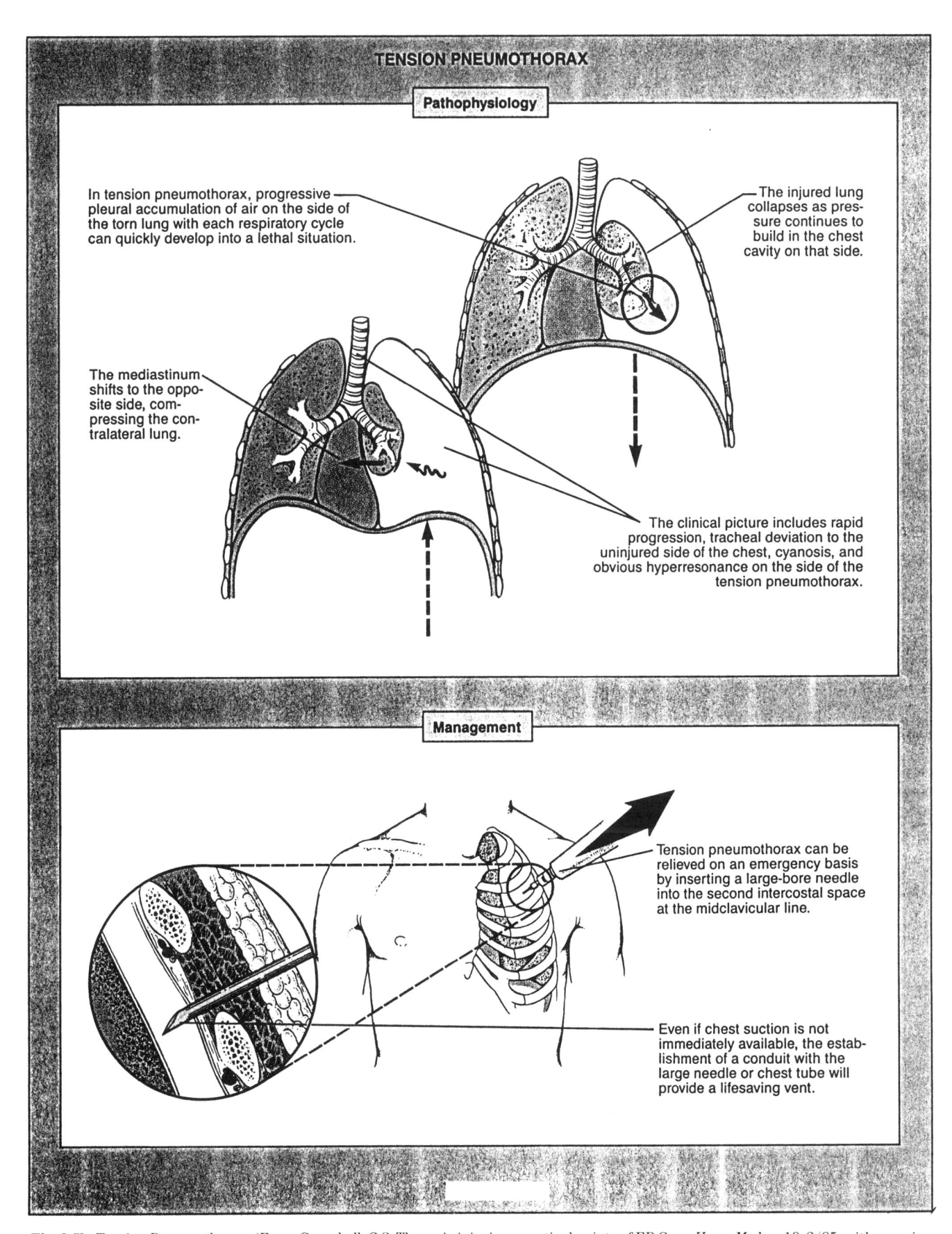

**Fig. 9-5b.** Tension Pneumothorax (From Campbell, G.S. Thoracic injuries: practical points of ER Care. *Hosp. Med.* p. 19, 3/85, with permission of Cahners Publishing Co.)

Table 9-7. Heat Injury Management in Athletes

|  | Hyperthermia-Heat Stroke | Hypovolemia-Heat Exhaustion | Other "Exertional Syncope" |
|---|---|---|---|
| Clinical Findings | Initial temp > 41°C (rectal) (May fall during transport) Impaired consciousness-variable (Initial unconsciousness or severe disorientation) Active sweating (may be found initially) Cutaneous vasodilation (unless shock) C-V:HR 120-160 BP wide pulse pressure 140-120/0 (shock may ensue) | Initial temp 39-40°C (or less) Mild disorientation Active sweating Cutaneous vasoconstriction, piloerection C-V:HR 120-140 BC 100-80/60-40 supine Orthostatic ↓ prominent | Brief syncope or collapse associated with prolonged or intense exercise. May occur in cool weather (Usually "under-conditioned" person) Temp <39°C C-V:HR 120 BP normal with mild orthostatic drop |
| Initial Management | TREAT AS TRAUMA CASE Establish IV line Use ECG monitor, Foley Cath Do lab studies-STAT CBC, Lytes, LFTS, PT, PTT, Glucose, ABG, U/A BUN/Cr Initiate cooling with ice on wet towels Continue active cooling to 39°C (rectal) Give IV:1/2 NS/D5W to replete ECF vol. Do not overload Give mannitol 12.5 GM IV Maintain urine output and C-V status. Use Swan-Gantz to direct fluid therapy if shock develops Avoid vasopressors | Establish IV line Do labs-STAT Lytes, Glucose, U/A (expect ↑ WBC. RBC in runners) Cool if temp = 40°C Give IV: 1/2 NS D5W Give 1 liter 30 min Continue volume repletion based on urine output and V.S. Add K if depleted | Determine volume status (Orthostatic >'s) Check Glucose, Lytes, U/A, ECG Treat as heat exhaustion |
| Complications | HOSPITALIZE FOR 48-72 HRS Watch urine (hematuria, myoglobinuria)(Except WBC, RBC in runners) Expect hepatocellular damage Max 48-72 hrs Expect PT, PTT and platelets Max 48-72 hrs DIC-may develop Watch for occult sepsis | Discharge if condition is uncomplicated Warn patient to watch for urine changes in subsequent 48 hrs | Watch for other cause of syncope in exercise: Hypertrophic cardiomyopathy Mitral valve prolapse Dysrhythmia Myocarditis-myocardial infarction Drug abuse |

## Heat Syncope

This heat disorder is caused by poor blood distribution to the affected extremity and is relatively harmless. The blood volume is distributed to peripheral vessels, especially in the lower extremities, after prolonged standing and/or an exercise period that is halted abruptly. This causes a decrease in blood pressure and inadequate oxygen supply to the brain. Major symptoms of heat syncope include profuse sweating and an abnormally high pulse rate. The affected individual should lie in a horizontal position with the legs elevated, and drink ice cold water as a fluid replacement (O'Donnel, 1980; Reed & Anderson, 1986).

## Heat Exhaustion

The signs and symptoms of heat exhaustion and heat stroke should be familiar to team physicians. Heat exhaustion is a severe disorder that develops slowly over several days and may lead to heat stroke if not treated. Body temperature usually is 38-40°C and the athlete has profuse sweating with higher than normal respiratory and pulse rates. Other features include nausea, headache, fatigue, confusion, drowsiness, giddiness, scant urine production, frequent vomiting, and diarrhea. Emergency treatment involves keeping the patient supine in a cool, shaded area. Clothing should be removed and replacement fluids (ice cold water) given by mouth or intravenously. Hospitalization may be indicated if symptoms persist.

## Heat Stroke

Heat stroke is the most serious heat disorder and can be fatal. It may develop gradually over several days as the result of heat exhaustion or appear suddenly when heavy exercise is performed in a hot, humid environment. Symptoms include high body temperature (41-43°C) and *dry* skin. Weakness, dizziness, confusion, rapid breathing, convulsions, and even coma may be present. Medical management calls for immediate cooling of the body by removing clothing and placing the patient in the shade in a supine position. The athlete may be placed in an ice bath or sponged with cool water while blowing warm air over the body (to evaporate the water and simulate sweating). Treatment is continued until the rectal temperature drops to 38°C (Inbar, 1985). Intravenous fluids must be used to restore blood pressure and acid/base balance. Immediate diagnosis and proper treatment greatly reduce the chances of a fatal outcome. Convulsions often occur during the cooling period and increase the patient's heat production. Seizure activity must be suppressed with short-acting anticonvulsants (diazepam).

## PREVENTION OF HEAT INJURY

The physiologic mechanisms that can lead to heat injuries are outlined in Figure 9-6. Many of the acute effects can be avoided by simple preventative measures:

- All athletes doing physical exercise in the heat should have an acclimation period. This is particularly true for those moving from a cold or temperate climate to a warm, hot, or humid region. A minimum of 6 days of exposure, with at least 2 hours of physical exercise in the heat is often necessary. The work rate should be progressively increased, but final heart rate and rectal temperatures should never exceed 180 beats per minute and 39.2°C, respectively.
- Workouts should be done in the early morning or late afternoon, not at mid-day. Light practice clothing that allows moisture to evaporate from the body is preferable. Exercise intensity should be reduced on hot days until the athlete is comfortable with the work rate. Age, sex, level of acclimation, physical fitness, clothing, and current health are factors that affect the amount and duration of allowable exercise in the heat. Use of wet-bulb temperature charts to dictate timing of practice is preferable (Table 9-8).
- Body weight should be recorded daily (or twice daily) when training and working in extreme heat. If the cumulative weight loss is greater than 3% of initial body mass, a schedule of forced water replacement should be implemented. Athletes should drink fluids freely, as much as they want before, during, and after athletic participation.
- The use of salt tablets is unnecessary. Liberal use of table salt at meals will replace lost sodium. Liberal use of salt tablets could result in an excessive solute load in the stomach, causing an increase in intravascular volume loss, vomiting, and worsening of dehydration.
- Refer to ACSM Position Statement on Thermal Injuries (Appendix 7-1).

## HYPOTHERMIA

Hypothermia is defined as a condition of cold injury with rectal temperature of 34.4°C (94°F) or lower. Hypothermia is caused when the body loses more heat to the environment than it produces and it can occur at ambient temperatures well above freezing. Acute hypothermia may occur after a rapid loss of body heat during sudden immersion in cold water. The thermoregulatory system response is inadequate and the body does not get an increase in metabolic and heart rates (see Figure 9-7).

```
                    Athlete
                Normal temperature
                Normal blood volume
                        │
                        ▼
                  Exercise (work)
                        │
          ┌─────────────┴─────────────┐
          ▼                           ▼
Environmental (exogenous) factors   Internal (endogenous) factors
Temperature                         Degree of acclimatization
Humidity                            Body build
Cloud cover                         Cardiopulmonary status
Wind velocity                       Age
Clothing                            State of health
Activity surface                    Medications
Peer pressure and stress            Psychological state
                                    Sex
                                    Heat-producing foods
          │                           │
          ▼                           ▼
Sweat (water) and electrolyte loss ──×── Radiant heat and metabolic calories
          │                           │
          ▼                           ▼
Hypovolemia (decreased blood volume)  +  Hyperthermia (increased core body
Electrolyte imbalances                    temperature)
          │                                     │
  ┌───────┴───────┐                    ┌────────┴────────┐
  ▼               ▼                    ▼                 ▼
Heat cramps                                      Failure of heat regulators
  │               │                                      │
  ▼               ▼                    ▼                 ▼
Heat exhaustion   Mixed heat injury                Heat stroke
Fluid and         Varying combinations of fluid    Metabolic and radiation
electrolyte       depletion and hyperthermia       heat problems
problems
```

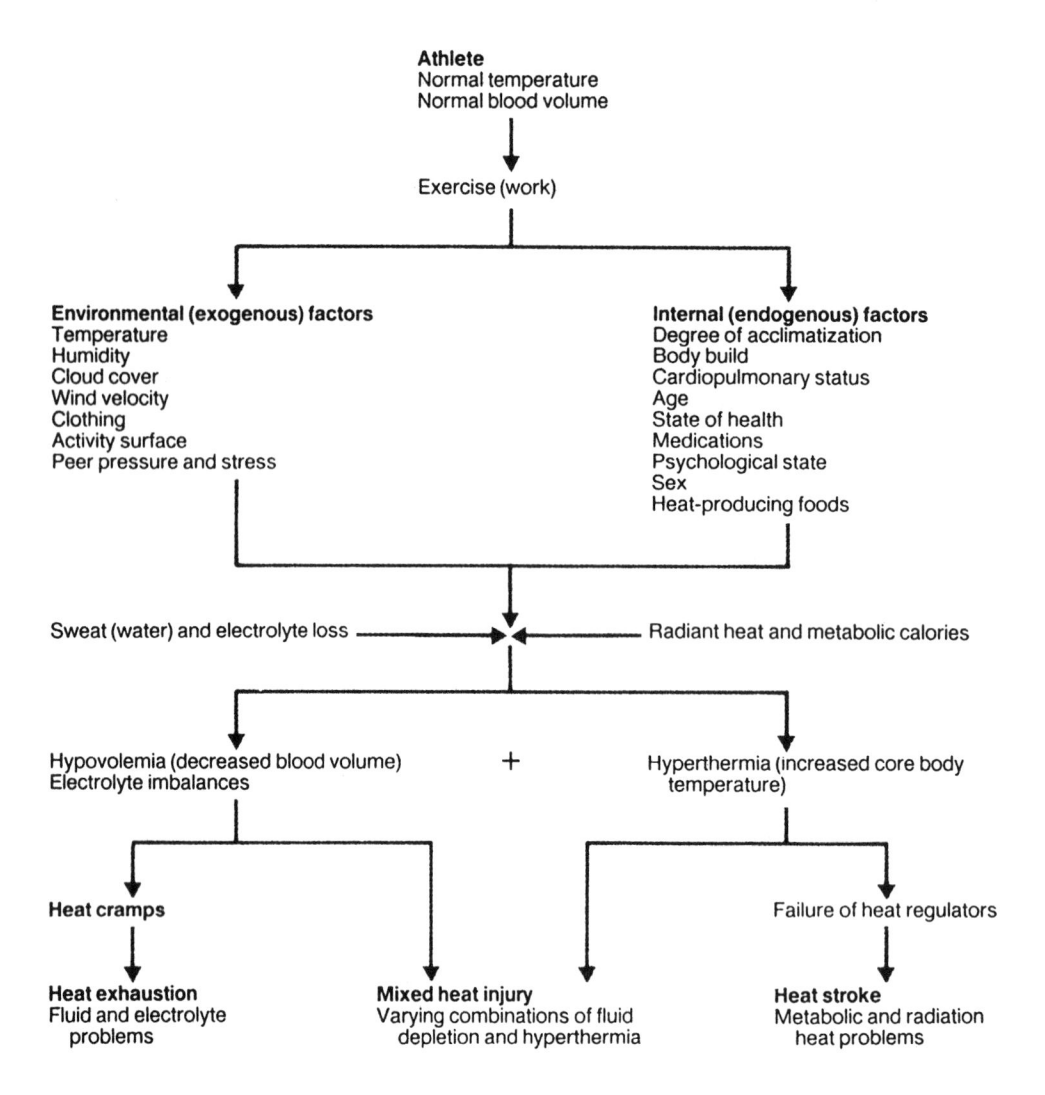

**Fig. 9-6.** Evolution of Heat Injury in the Athlete (From: Sinclair, R.E. Be serious about siriasis. *Postgrad Med.*, 77 (5), 263, 1985.)

Chronic hypothermia is the result of slow body cooling and is commonly encountered where there is prolonged exposure to cold, wet conditions. In this situation, the thermoregulatory system has had ample time to increase the athlete's metabolic and heart rates. Vasal constriction shifts blood from the periphery to the core of the body, causing increased diuresis. Consequently, athletes with chronic hypothermia are often volume depleted and respond to cooling with intense shivering, decreased heart and respiratory rate, decreased oxygenation, and decreased blood supply to actively exercising muscles. Increased lactic acid production causes metabolic acidosis so that there are fluid and electrolyte imbalances that become serious concerns during rewarming and treatment.

## Treatment

Profound hypothermia (unconsciousness and core temperature < 30°C) should be treated in a hospital (Shepherd, 1985). Field treatment other than preventing additional heat loss is not recommended if a hospital is nearby. Gentle handling of the athlete is of utmost importance in preventing ventricular fibrillation.

The first step in treating hypothermia is to

Table 9-8. Wet-Bulb Temperature Table

| Wet-Bulb Temperature* | Precautions |
|---|---|
| Under 66°F | No precautions are necessary except close observation of the most heat-susceptible squad members (those who lose over 3% of their body weight as determined from the weight chart). |
| 67-77°F | Insist that unlimited amounts of water be given on the field. Iced water is preferable. If desired, other dilute solutions very low in salt content (electrolyte solutions) may be substituted. |
| Over 78°F | Alter practice schedule to provide a lighter practice routine or conduct sessions in shorts. Withhold susceptible players from participation. |

*If the relative humidity is over 95 percent, the precautions listed for temperature over 78°F should be observed regardless of the wet-bulb reading.

(From Johnson, L.W. Preventing Heat Stroke. *AFP.*, p. 139, July, 1982.)

prevent additional heat loss by putting the patient in a shelter or wrapping him in blankets or plastic sheets. A second priority is to establish an airway; artificial respiration may be necessary to encourage the patient to breathe. In the hospital setting, endotracheal intubation may be preferable, but ventricular fibrillation is highly likely (Boswick et al, 1986; Shepherd, 1985).

An athlete with hypothermia has a vastly reduced metabolic demand so that a brief additional time in this condition adds little further injury. Consequently, if warming is started at the event site, it must be continued aggressively until the patient is rewarmed and safely moved to the hospital. If a hospital can be reached in 30 minutes, the athlete should be moved there as soon as possible. Rapid rewarming in a bath at 40°C is recommended if the core temperature is below 32°C. If the core temperature is lower than that, the extremities should not be immersed because it will induce extensive vasodilation and raise the possibility of ventricular fibrillation. Giving warm fluids or having the patient sit near a fire could reduce

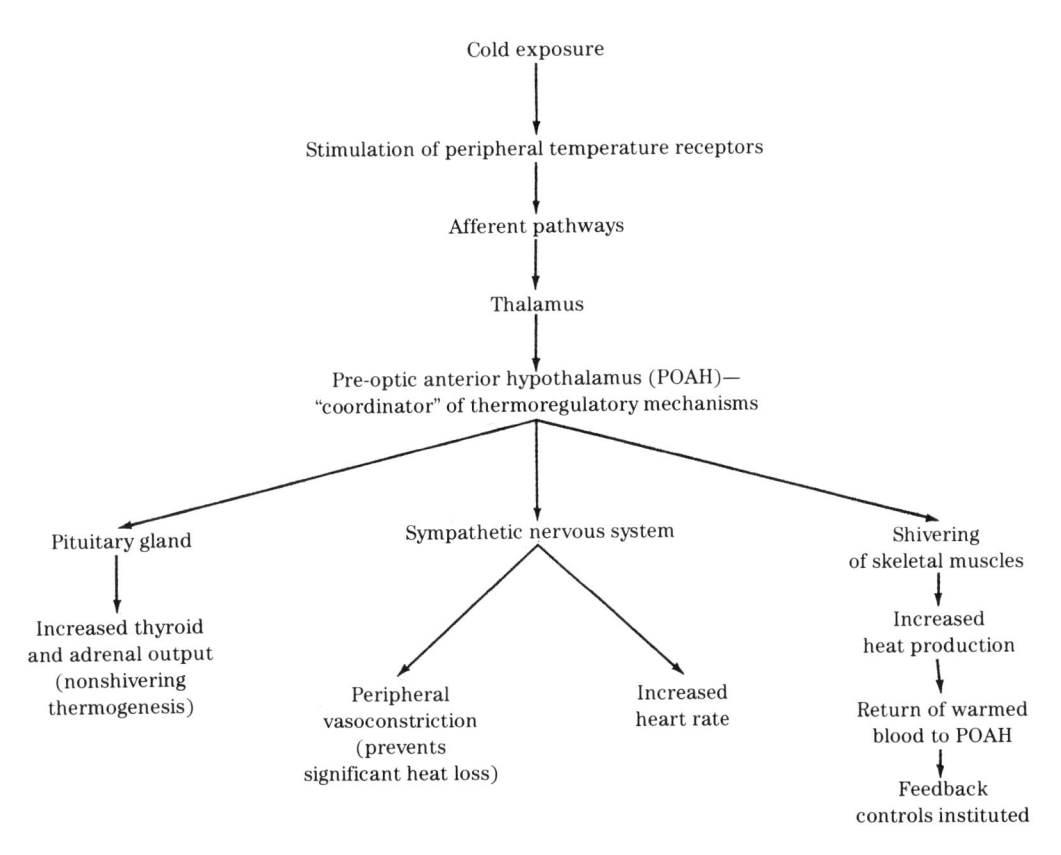

Fig. 9-7. Basic Thermoregulatory Mechanisms in Response to Cold Exposure. (From Dembert, M.L. Medical problems from cold exposure. *AFP*, p. 103, Jan. 1982.)

the body's sensation of cold and lessen the beneficial effects of shivering.

Respiratory support and correction of body fluid abnormalities should be continued during rewarming. Temperature, blood pressure, blood gases, PH, and electrolytes must be monitored frequently and the EKG watched constantly. Atrial arrhythmias and fibrillation often occur with hypothermia but correct themselves as rewarming takes place. Drugs that are used to treat these symptoms are ineffective in a cold body.

The patient should be monitored for several days after recovery. The most frequent complications are pneumonia, renal failure, pancreatitis, and frostbite. The thermoregulatory system also may be impaired for a time and cold environments should be avoided.

### Prevention

Hypothermia can be prevented by using appropriate clothing that protects against cold, wind, and moisture. Several layers of loose clothing, topped by a windproof, water-repellent shell is effective. Clothing like this may be incompatible with athletic activity. Many winter sports have evolved highly specialized styles of dress but some of this specialized clothing can lead to cold injury if used inappropriately.

Hypothermia usually results from unforeseen circumstances (getting lost, becoming injured, falling in water). If that happens, the first priority is to find shelter from the elements, especially the wind. Wet clothing should be changed if possible. Wrapping the person in plastic sheets reduces convective and other heat losses. Additional external heat sources such as a fire, contact with a warm body, or warm fluids can further reduce cooling but should be used with caution (Shepherd, 1985).

Further injury may be prevented by recognizing the early symptoms of hypothermia. The body shows increased shivering initially but after the core drops below 35°C, metabolism declines and shivering intensity is reduced markedly. Heat production drops substantially with a core body temperature below 35° and the rate of cooling increases. Symptoms such as mental confusion, disorientation, and poor coordination are accompanied by mood changes like as depression and introversion. Simple tasks become difficult or impossible to perform. At core temperatures approximating 32°C, cardiac arrhythmias appear and the athlete may lose consciousness and have fixed dilated pupils and no tendon reflexes.

In general, a person who is shivering violently but who is alert may become hypothermic. When the shivering response is weak or stops and mental confusion is present, the athlete is hypothermic and potentially in serious danger.

## CONCLUSION

Medical decisions at the event site often are difficult to make and the problem can be compounded by coaches, players, and parents who voice opinions. The team physician must resist the temptation to deviate from a sound, rational approach to treating sports injuries. He must exercise good medical judgment so as to give optimal care. Refer to the following appendices for further information regarding topics in this chapter:

Appendix 9-1: Pediatric Exercise Guidelines: Prevention of Heat Disorders

Appendix 9-2: Guidelines for Runners: Hot Weather Participation

See Appendix 7-1: ACSM Position Statement on Prevention of Thermal Injuries During Distance Running

### REFERENCES

Boswick, J.A., Martyn, J.W., Schultz, A.L. Hypothermia: not just a winter problem. *Patient Care* pgs. 84-116, November 15, 1986.

Bruno, L.A., Gennarelli, E.A., Torg, J.S. Head injuries in athletes. *Current Therapy in Sports Medicine*, 1985-86. In Welsh, R.P., Shephard, R.J. (Ed) St. Louis, MO:C.V. Mosby Co., 134-140, 1985.

Clancy, W., Bland R., Bergfeld, J. Upper trunk brachial plexus injuries in contact sports. *Am J Sports Med* 5:209, 1977.

DiNubile, N. Emergency care on the field: the physician's role. *Drug Therapy* p. 41-55, September 1985.

Inbar, O. Exercise in the heat. In Welsh, R.P., Shephard, R.J. (Eds), *Current Therapy in Sports Medicine* 1985-86. St. Louis, MO:C.V. Mosby Co., 45-49, 1985.

Lehman, R.C., Vegso, J.J. and Torge, J.S. Life-threatening injuries incurred by athletes. *J. Musculoskel. Med.* 3(10):14-24, 1986.

Lucas, C.E. Early care of critically injured patients. *Hospital Medicine* p. 31-45, August 1977.

McKeag, D.B. On-site care of the injured youth. In Kelly, V.C. et al (eds) *Brennemann's Practice of Pediatrics* Vol. 10, New York: Harper & Row, 1-23, 1985.

O'Donnell, T.F. Management of heat stress injuries in the athlete. *Orthop Clinics of North Am* 11(4):841-855, 1980.

Reed, G., Anderson, R.J. Emergency: heat stroke. *Hospital Medicine* pgs. 19-36, August 1986.

Shepherd, R.J. Hazards of cold water. In Welsh, R.P., Shephard, R.J. (Eds), *Current Therapy in Sports Medicine* St. Louis, MO: C.V. Mosvby Co., 39-45, 1985.

Torg, J.S. *Athletic Injuries to the Head, Neck and Face* Philadelphia, Lea & Febiger, 1982.

Torg, J.S., Quedenfeld, T.C., Newell, W. When the athlete's life is threatened. *Phys Sportsmed* p. 54-60, March 1975.

Torg, J.S. and Vegso, J.J. Athletic Injuries to the Cervical Spine. In Welsh, R.P., Shephard, R.J. (Eds), *Current Therapy in Sports Medicine* St. Louis, MO:C.V. Mosvby Co., 155-158, 1985.

Tucker, J.B., Marron, J.T. Field-site management of athletic injuries. *Am Fam Phys* pgs. 137-142, August 1986.

Appendix 9-1.
# Pediatric Exercise Guidelines: Prevention of Heat Disorders

## Guidelines for Thermoregulation in the Conduct of Athletic Events

Because physicians are credited with considerable prestige and trust, they should assume responsibility for educating young athletes, parents, coaches, and organizers about the health aspects of thermoregulation in athletics. The following guidelines for preventing harmful effects of heat are intended for all physicians and others working with athletes or helping to plan athletic events:

1. Ensure acclimatization to exercise in heat. Before this stage is reached, control the intensity and duration of activities. Remember that children acclimate slowly, and most adverse reactions to heat happen during the first few days of the training season.
2. Schedule activities to the prevailing climate. Remember that humidity, solar radiation, and air velocity are factors to be considered in addition to environmental temperature (see chart for climate-related changes in allowable activities).
3. Schedule periodic rest periods in the shade during a practice; this is important for dissipation of heat previously accumulated.
4. Identify and screen for close observation and attention those athletes at high risk because of obesity, poor conditioning, excessive weight loss during exercise, or health problems. A preparticipation health history and evaluation is recommended.
5. Secure full hydration prior to any practice or competition.
6. Keep fluids (preferably chilled water) at the site of practice or competition.
7. Identify athletes who lose more than 3% of body weight during practice.
8. Enforce periodic drinking above and beyond the amounts required by thirst, with special attention to the athletes who have lost excessive weight.
9. Never use water restriction as a disciplinary measure.
10. Discourage deliberate dehydration in young athletes. Help enforce regulations to reduce the temptation for this practice.
11. Avoid excessive clothing, taping, or padding in hot or humid climates. Ensure optimum evaporation from the skin by use of porous clothing and frequent changes from sweat-saturated to dry garments. Avoid prolonged exposure of skin to direct solar radiation. A hat and clothing of light color are recommended whenever feasible.
12. Adjust the timing of practice and competition (hour of day, time of year) as needed. Extremes of hot, humid weather are a bona fide reason for cancellation of a scheduled competition.

(From Committee on Sports Medicine: Climatic heat stress and the exercising child. *Pediatrics* 69:808, 1982)

### Climate-Related Changes in Athletics Activities (Wet Bulb)

| Wet-Bulb Temperature* | Safety Level | Field Precautions |
|---|---|---|
| <19°C(66°F) | Safe | No precautions necessary, except close observation of the squad members most susceptible to heat (those who lose more than 3% of their body weight as determined from before and after practice weight chart). |

*If relative humidity is more than 95%, danger-level procedures should be observed, regardless of the wet bulb reading.

**Climate-Related Changes in Athletics Activities (*continued*)**
**(Wet Bulb)**

| Wet-Bulb Temperature* | Safety Level | Field Precautions |
|---|---|---|
| 19°-25°C (66°-78°F) | Caution | Insist that unlimited amounts of water be given on the field. Iced water is preferable. If desired, other dilute solutions low in salt may be used (the electrolyte solutions). |
| >25.5°C (78°F) | Danger Level | Alter practice schedule to provide a lighter practice routine, or conduct sessions in shorts. Mandatory "water breaks." withhold susceptible players (>3% weight losers) from participation. |

*If relative humidity is more than 95%, danger-level procedures should be observed, regardless of the wet bulb reading.

# Appendix 9-2.
# Guidelines for Runners: Hot Weather Participation

**Acclimatization.** A minimum of four to five days of physical training in a new stressful environment is required for heat acclimatization. Intensity of training should be reduced initially and increased only as the participant adapts to the new conditions. Careful maintenance of adequate fluid intake before, during, and after exertion, and a balanced diet are strongly advised. The major adaptations that occur with heat acclimatization are an earlier onset of sweating, greater sweat rate, lower skin and rectal temperatures, and a reduced heart rate.

**Susceptibility to Heat.** Factors that predispose a person to exertional heat injury include lack of acclimatization, poor fitness, voluntary dehydration, previous fever or illness, or inappropriate running pace for environmental conditions. A small segment of the population, including previous heat stroke victims, might be intolerant to the heat in spite of attempts to acclimatize.

### Prevention of Physical Problems

1. Runners attempting to participate in a race should have trained adequately. This should include at least two long-distance runs within the previous month that are at least two-thirds the length of this race.
2. Avoid running to exhaustion within the week preceding the race.
3. Remember, you will be running on yesterday's meals. We suggest a light meal no less than two hours before the race. Avoid fatty foods on race day. Emphasize carbohydrate intake the day before the race.
4. Maintenance of adequate hydration is the most important preventive measure. If you become thirsty, you are behind in fluids. Drink two 8-oz. glasses of fluid (preferably water) within 10 to 15 minutes of race time. Drink continuously throughout the run. Unless you are totally committed to time, stop to drink; finishing is the goal. There will be water stations at the start as well as along the course.
5. Prerun warm-up must include stretching exercises of the calf, hamstring, quadriceps, groin, and trunk muscles. If you begin to feel muscle tightness or cramps, stop and stretch.
6. Blisters can be prevented by wearing well-fitted, broken-in shoes and soft lightweight socks. Powder in shoes and socks will reduce friction. Remove pebbles immediately. Nails should be trimmed. If you feel a hot spot developing, stop at an aid station for care. They will be positioned ever 2.5 miles.
7. Chafing occurs where clothing rubs against the skin. It can be prevented by wearing loose fitting clothing and applying petroleum jelly or protective bandaging in susceptible areas such as nipples, armpits, neckline, and groin.
8. You will be one of many runners, so run defensively. Stay to the right. Watch out for other runners and yield if necessary.
9. Pace yourself. Don't burn yourself out by starting too quickly. Common sense is the key.

### Recognition of Physical Problems

While every runner will experience varying degrees of discomfort, significant changes in physical status should be recognized. If in doubt, stop to ask for advice. Medical personnel, identifiable by red caps, will be positioned at all aid stations.

1. Symptoms of overexertion: nausea, vomiting, extreme breathlessness, dizziness, unusual fatigue, headache.
2. Symptoms of heat injury: piloerection (hair on end or gooseflesh) on the chest or upper arms, chilling, headache or throbbing pressure, unsteadiness, vomiting or nausea, labored breathing, faintness, muscle cramps. Continuing the race with these symptoms may result in collapse or unconsciousness. Stop. Get help.
3. Not only can blisters be painful, but infection can result and be literally life-threatening. Have them treated at an aid station.

4. If stretching does not relieve cramps, stop at an aid station.
5. Abrasions (skin scrapes, "strawberries") may become infected. Have them treated.

Report significant injuries or downed runners to medical personnel. A field hospital will be established at the finish line. Injured runners will be transported there.

# 10

# Common Sports-Related Injuries and Illnesses — Generic Conditions

**HOW TO USE THE FOLLOWING CHAPTERS (11-16):**

The following seven chapters are an organ/system/anatomic area approach to the treatment of most common sports injuries. They are divided into 31 subheadings, designed to be used for reference, and organized in easy to use fashion. Under each of these subheadings are listed *major, common* injuries seen in sports medicine. Other more esoteric injuries may be listed and referenced to other texts but not discussed. Each injury is cross-referenced by sport in the index. This will allow the reader/physician to refer to the material in three ways: specific injury, organ/system/anatomic area involved, or sport or activity.

To facilitate reading and information gathering, each area will be presented in this outline:

1. Epidemiology
2. Pertinent Anatomy
3. Biomechanics
4. Initial Assessment/Description of Injury including important differential diagnosis considerations
5. Diagnostic Aids Used
6. Immediate/Initial Treatment — including medications, physical therapy modalities, and patient education
7. Rehabilitation — and use of protective devices
8. Special Considerations — including equipment needed
9. Return to Activity Considerations
10. Specific Points to Remember

Many injuries involve similar treatment plans and some of these protocols are outlined below. Where there is controversy about definitive therapy, the differences of opinion will be noted and the authors' primary care perspective (or bias) discussed.

## GENERIC CONDITIONS

The philosophies of care given here serve as "ground rules" for the following chapters. We will refer to these protocols in discussing specific injuries. The general conditions covered are:

- Acute injury
- Chronic injury (with emphasis on overuse syndromes)
- Acute infectious conditions (with specific exercise considerations)
- Chronic disease (affected by exercise and sports participation)
- Allergy

### Acute Injury

Acute injury is the most common sports medicine condition; unfortunately, it also is the one most likely to be ignored. Injuries that require attention on the playing field are rare in comparison to the number of acute injuries incurred in less formal contests. Beyond the initial involuntary rest (usually temporary, whether symptoms have disappeared or not), the only other attention which might be given an acute injury is the application of a pressure dressing (elastic bandage) and/or hot/

cold therapy. Little else is done and rarely is medical attention sought. Most athletic injuries do not occur in competition but in practice or unobserved, unsupervised surroundings. Granted that most acute injuries are not true medical emergencies, but they can be treated easily if proper diagnosis is made. The untoward effects of any athletic injury can be minimized by proper care, especially in the first 24 hour post-injury period.

*Coverage* of athletic competition and/or practice is discussed in Chapter 8, but the following guidelines apply to the care of any acute injury.

Become familiar with the frequency level of common injuries for the sport you are covering and for the *community* you live in. Of the multiple factors that determine injury frequency, the two with the greatest effect are the local community environment and the specific position played by an athlete. Sport and exercise produce more than a fair share of "zebras", but for the most part we still see and care for mostly "horses". *Learn to take care of them and expect them.*

There is no one true philosophy of primary care sports medicine, only guidelines. Those guidelines should reflect individual community situations. The following mind-set for covering a sports event works well in any community regardless of the situation, geography, or personnel involved:

*before* competition → prevention
*during* competition → triage
*after* competition → rehabilitation

Someone who understands and accepts this philosophy is the best person to be responsible for the care of competitors in a sports event in your community. Contrary to what some may think, this does *not* require compromising *any* principles of medicine. Athletes are no different from non-athletes where health care is concerned. Where the groups diverge is with respect to exercise-induced injury. Athletes are in an environment that exposes them to acute *macrotrauma* as well as chronic *microtrauma*. In that environment, they will suffer more injury than the non-athlete.

**Before competition.** Active intervention in the pre-competitive aspects of any community sports system offer the greatest opportunity for significant injury prevention. The preparticipation screening and assessment of the sports environment are two major areas of preventive impact and are discussed in Chapter 7.

**During competition.** One of the most uncomfortable and disquieting moments a team physician can have is when he must make sideline decisions while under the close scrutiny of many spectators. However, 67% of all injuries occur during practices or training, a time when the physician is unlikely to be present. The situations are different but they are the norm in covering athletic teams and they underline the need to have established protocols for triage in place. Coaches, trainers, and other responsible parties need to learn appropriate triage techniques for the more common injuries. Even when the physician is present, his or her major responsibility is the *triage* of the acutely injured athlete.

A decision on whether or not to allow the participant to resume play should be made only when: 1) a definite diagnosis has been made; 2) the injury will not worsen with continued play so that the athlete is at *no greater risk* of further injury, and 3) the athlete can still compete fairly and is not incapable of protecting him/herself because of the injury. Consult Table 10-1 for a list of injuries that preclude further participation. This table may seem conservative at first; please *reread* it. It is less conservative than most lists and can be helpful in assessing most common athletic injuries of youngsters. With college age or professional athletes, this apparent conservatism can be addressed on an individual basis if the physician finds it nec-

---

**Table 10-1. Situations Precluding Return to Participation in Competitive Sports Following an Injury**

1. Unconsciousness (however brief). See subsection on head injuries.
2. Dazed or inappropriate responses for longer than 10 seconds as a result of a blow to the head.
3. Any complaint of neurologic abnormalities such as numbness or tingling.
4. Obvious swelling, with the possible exception of the digits.
5. Limited range of motion.
6. Decreased strength through normal range of motion.
7. Obvious bleeding.
8. An injury that the examiner is unsure of or does not know how to handle.
9. Obvious loss of some normal function.
10. An injury that requires the athlete to need assistance getting on or off the field, mat, or court.
11. Whenever an athlete says he or she cannot continued to participate (regardless of what the examiner thinks of the injury).

Source: Garrick, J.G. *Pediatric Clinics of North America* 24:737-747, 1977.

essary to move outside these vaguely defined boundaries. The best philosophy for evaluating acute athletic injuries on site should be neither excessively conservative nor dangerously liberal. The final decision on return to competition always belongs to the physician.

Generally speaking, the evaluation of all acute injuries that occur in competition should follow the same steps (Figure 10-1). Immediate initial assessment is mandatory and will help elicit signs and symptoms before the inevitable secondary reactions (pain, swelling, inflammation, spasm, decreased range of motion, and guarding). First, observe the position of the athlete and the injured part in relation to the rest of the body. Begin the history with the patient's account of how the injury occurred and amplify it with the physician's assessment of the biomechanics of the situation, as well as that of others who may have seen the injury occur (trainer, coach, teammate, or official). Determine any positive past medical history from available records if they exist. Next comes a focused clinical appraisal of the injury; that is, an examination emphasizing function, range of motion, and the neurologic and vascular integrity of the injured area.

With serious injury, a protocol is implemented that addresses whether to treat the injured player at the site or take him/her to a medical facility. If he/she is unable to walk safely, then a decision must be made on how to transport the athlete.

With less serious injuries, the first decision is whether to allow the athlete to continue play. Even if the decision is affirmative, he/she should be *periodically* rechecked. The interval between checks depends upon the severity and rapidity of evolving symptoms. **Any athlete with an evolving injury where signs and symptoms are changing must be watched and not left alone.** If an athlete leaves the sideline, he/she should be accompanied by someone who is aware of the significance of the changing symptoms. Subsequent assessment on the sidelines or in the locker room should include the same components: observation, history, and reexamination. Clothing and equipment should be removed whenever possible. The later examination should focus not only on the injured area but also above and below it. An appraisal of how signs and symptoms have progressed since the first exam also should be made.

If an athlete is allowed to return to play and sustains a recurrence or exacerbation of the in-

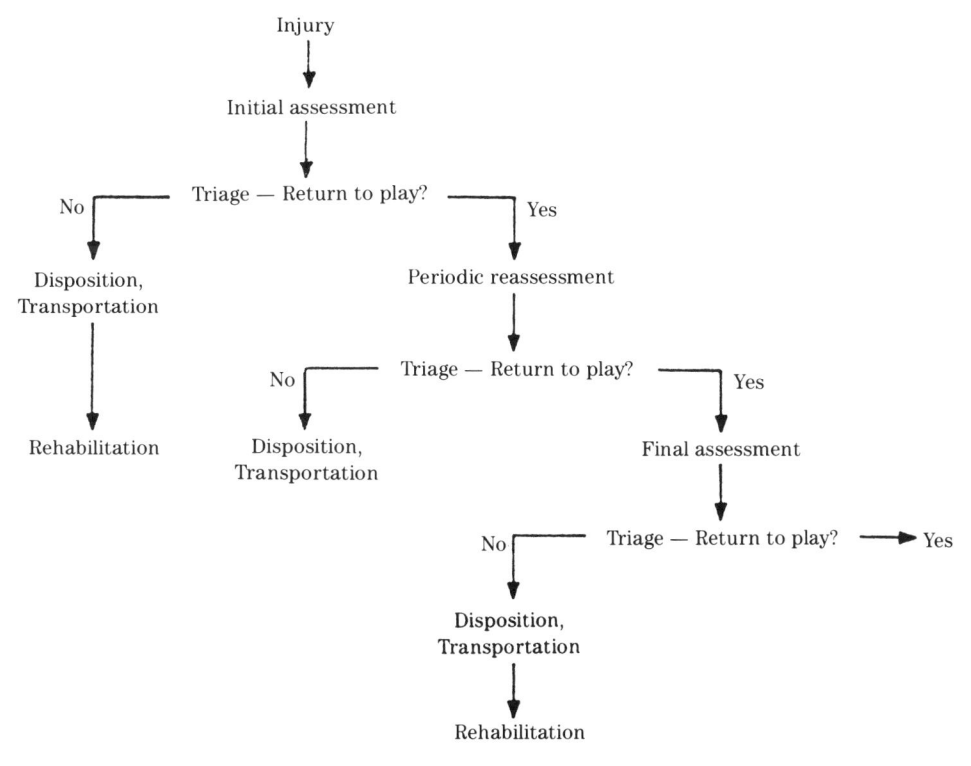

**Fig. 10-1.** Steps Used to Evaluate all Acute Injuries that Occur in Competition

jury, he/she must be withdrawn from play for the remainder of the contest. If the athlete is not allowed to return, periodic assessments should continue and initial treatment and/or transportation begun.

**After competition.** After a diagnosis is established and appropriate treatment given, rehabilitation can be considered and a multidisciplinary team approach involving the team physician, athlete's personal physician, other consultants (if necessary), trainer, and coach should be initiated. In reality, such a coordinated effort rarely happens. Statistics in West Virginia (Bowers, 1974) revealed that only 13.5% of acute injuries from a high school system were seen by a physician within 24 hours, the period when evaluation and treatment are the most productive. Even so, proper rehabilitation is the most important factor in the rapid return of an injured athlete to participation sports (see Chapter 18).

**Common acute injuries by type.** One of the best and most useful surveys on sports injuries was conducted by Garrick and Requa (1981). While it dealt only with the high school level, it broke down sports injuries by type and provides a guideline on what to expect for the common acute sports injury. The numbers in parenthesis are from Garrick and Requa's study.

1. *Sprains and Strains* (60.5%) — There are two ways most sprains and strains develop. The common etiology is a sudden, abrupt, violent extension or contraction on an overloaded, unprepared, or undeveloped ligament or musculotendinous unit. There can be varying degrees of severity from the over-stretching of a few myofibrils to complete unit rupture. A second, less common, mechanism involves chronic stress placed upon the unit over time, in association with poor technique, overuse, or deformity. Strains are stretch injuries to the *musculotendinous unit*; sprains involve similar injury to *ligamentous structures*. A grading system is used to assess these injuries:

   *First Degree/Grade 1* — There is little tissue injury and no increase in laxity. There usually is little immediate swelling because the tissues have not been stretched enough to produce instantaneous hemorrhage. With strains, there is usually no significant damage to the muscle or tendon and only a brief period of pain and disability if it is properly treated. Secondary tissue edema and inflammation develop within hours, restricting range of motion and resulting in minimal loss of function. Pathologically, less than 25% of the tendinous or ligamentous fibers are involved in a first degree sprain or strain.

   *Second Degree/Grade 2* — These injuries are the result of tears and disruptions of ligament or tendons. The partial tearing ranges from 25% to 75% of the fibers and there is demonstrable laxity and loss of function. There is immediate swelling and function is significantly reduced. Signs and symptoms increase until bleeding is controlled and the injury immobilized.

   *Third Degree/Grade 3* — Complete disruption of the ligament or tendon usually exists with immediate pain, disability, and loss of function. However, some third degree sprains may actually be less painful than second degree sprains. Once a ligament is torn, there is no further stretch to cause pain sensation. Third degree strains usually have diffuse bleeding and continuous pain.

   The treatment of a third degree injury (ligament or tendon rupture) continues to undergo change. With proper immediate care, including immobilization, these injuries can be treated conservatively without surgical intervention. Common examples of this type of injury include the medial collateral ligament in the knee, the lateral supporting structures of the ankle, and clavicular ligaments of the shoulder. Ligaments or tendons that normally are under a high amount of natural stress (Achilles tendon, biceps tendon, and the patellar ligament), as well as tendons that have retracted or ruptured, require prompt surgical intervention. Occasionally, when the tear is at the musculotendinous junction (such as an Achilles liggament rupture), the preferred treatment is immobilization. Bear in mind that severe strains and sprains may cause fewer symptoms and signs than more moderate ones. Many young athletes have natural ligamentous laxity. Always examine and compare the injured and uninjured sides to help resolve those cases where the findings appear equivocal.

   Frequent sprains sites are ankles (anterior talofibular ligament), knee (medial collateral ligament), and fingers (intrinsic collateral, interphalangeal ligaments). Frequent sites of strains are upper leg (hamstring muscles and adductors), back (paraspinal muscles), and the shoulder (rotator cuff tendons).

The following modalities are useful in treating strains and sprains:

**R** — rest the injured part to allow healing to begin and prevent further injury.
**I** — apply ice to the injured part to reduce of swelling and extravasation of blood into the tissue (the ice should be applied directly to the skin as a massage unit at frequent intervals, but not to exceed 10-15 minutes per session).
**C** — compression with an elastic bandage, air splint, etc., to prevent movement and further swelling.
**E** — elevate the injured area whenever possible to prevent pooling of blood and control swelling.

When you know that an athlete cannot return to practice or competition, it often is beneficial to start nonsteroidal anti-inflammatory drugs (NSAIDs) to combat the inevitable soft tissue inflammatory response. Do not use these medications if the injury is minor or if continued observation of the athlete is not possible. Some physicians now caution against early initial use of aspirin and related compounds (including NSAIDs) because they may possibly promote bleeding secondary to inhibition of platelet function.

2. *Contusions* (13.7%) — A contusion is bruising of the skin and/or underlying dermal tissues caused by direct trauma. Capillaries and other small vessels rupture causing extravasation of blood and effusion, followed by swelling and inflammation to soft tissues of the surrounding areas. The secondary swelling is usually superficial and local, but occasionally may be deep if something like a hockey puck strikes an unprotected thigh. Because extravasation of blood into soft tissue can cause extreme inflammation, marked decreases in function may occur. Use the RICE regimen for treatment. It is important to immobilize a contusion because more bleeding may occur if the injured area is moved. An individual should not return to play until there is painless full range of motion. Complications of contusions include deep vein thrombosis and thrombophlebitis within the injured muscle mass. A more common long-term sequela of repeated contusions in the same area is *myositis ossificans*, a condition where there is deposition of bone substance into the soft tissue areas. Thorough treatment and rehabilitation should be initiated promptly and full rehabilitation accomplished before the athlete returns to activity. The injured area should be protected from repeated trauma. The most common etiology of contusions is blunt trauma caused by an object hitting a muscle group in an extremity (a helmet against the anterior thigh of a player, a field hockey stick hitting an opponent's forearm). The most frequent sites of contusions are the lateral upper arm and anterior thigh.

3. *Inflammation* (5.9%) — Inflammation is almost a universal sequela of acute injury and can be controlled with the RICE regimen and appropriate use of nonsteroidal anti-inflammatory medications (NSAIDs). Inflammation (in this situation) usually is *not* the result of *infection*, but a sign of minor injury.

4. *Fractures* (5.5%) — A fracture is a break in the continuity of bone. The major mechanism for sports injuries is a direct blow and it is reasonable to expect a significant number of fractures in any epidemiologic survey of sports injuries. The onsite care of all suspected fractures is the same. Immobilize the injured area, including the proximal and distal joint, and then transport the person to a hospital or office to obtain x-rays and definitive care. Fractures can happen at any site and range from relatively insignificant breaks of the distal phalanx of the toe to life threatening skull or neck fractures. Because of the possibility of further injury to the neurovascular bundle, manipulation of a fracture prior to radiographic examination is contraindicated. However, if the blood supply appears to be compromised, manipulation to re-establish vascularity may be necessary in this rare orthopedic emergency. Under ordinary circumstances, immobilize the fracture, place ice and slight compression around it, and transport immediately.

5. *Lacerations* (1.8%) — Lacerations are no different in sports than in any other area of medicine. Most are superficial, caused by trauma to an unprotected portion of skin. Occasionally, equipment used in the game, such as basketball hoops or high jump standards, or worn by the athlete (braces) have been responsible. Rapid

disinfection, then debridement followed by primary closure (where appropriate), produces an uneventful recovery. Neuromuscular function and vascular status of underlying tissues should be tested before anesthesia is given. If there is any possibility of a foreign body in the wound, an x-ray should be taken to identify the location before extraction. X-rays may help when there is a non-radio-opaque foreign body by showing pockets of subcutaneous air caused by the path of the object. Most athletes will want to play with repaired lacerations so the wound must be protected and thoroughly disinfected before and after each participation. It is wise to cover and protect a wound longer than would be done for a non-athlete because the skin is continually exposed to trauma and there is a significant possibility of wound dehiscence. A check of medical records from the preparticipation screening will indicate whether the athlete needs a tetanus toxoid injection.

6. *Other* (12.7%) — While the musculoskeletal and skin systems account for most of the acute injuries to athletes, other systems (internal organ trauma, thermal injury) also are involved. This highlights the need for the physician to have a primary care perspective.

**Chronic Injury**

Less dramatic but only slightly less prevalent are chronic injuries, most of them overuse syndromes. Significant medical intervention often is lacking with these injuries, perhaps because of the lack of intensity of the symptoms or signs. Many athletes self-treat these injuries and take the advice of fellow athletes, partly because of the inconsistencies of medical treatment regimens that may be given. The frequency and prevalence of chronic and overuse injuries should not be understated; they parallel the increase of exercise participation more than acute injuries do. About 71% of the patients seen in our primary care oriented sports medicine clinic present with complaints of overuse, overtraining, or overconditioning (McKeag, 1991). In a survey of over 16,000 recreational runners, more than 1800 overuse injuries were identified in a two year span (Clement et al., 1981). From the primary care perspective, the overuse syndrome, regardless of how it is defined, will account for many of the problems seen by the physician in the *recreational*, non-organized athletic population.

The individual most likely to suffer from overuse is the regular daily exerciser. The sporadic "weekend" athlete is prone to acute injuries as described earlier. Overuse is a process, not an event. It is directly related to the amount, intensity, and frequency of exercise. The biomechanics of the sport or activity involved dictate the geographic body area affected. The overuse process causes breakdown and fatigue of body structures, usually resulting in inflammation followed by swelling. Tenosynovitis, tendonitis, fasciitis, compartment syndromes, and stress fractures are common examples of overuse syndromes. Most of these terms imply inflammation of specific types of structures, with most classified as soft-tissues. These structures are the first to show the impact of exertional over-indulgence. If exercise continues and warning signals (in the form of perceived pain) are ignored, the process continues and begins to involve hard tissue such as bone. In these cases, *abnormal stress* will result in damage to *normal tissue*.

The concept of normal tissue being injured by abnormal stress is entirely consistent with the opinion held by most pathophysiologists that mechanical stress is the most important cause of overuse syndromes. We occasionally see an athlete suffering the result of another phenomenon, *normal stress* on *abnormal tissue*. Congenital defects and abnormalities, post injury weakness or imbalance, and other types of structural malalignment may cause a predisposition to overuse problems.

Because overtraining and overconditioning happen so often and are becoming so prevalent in primary care practices, the entire concept of overuse has caused a great deal of frustration for physicians who are attempting to learn all the various treatment regimens advocated for specific areas and parts of the body. McKeag (1984) contends that most overuse injuries could and should be treated in one common "generic" way. The practical guidelines (Table 10 2) of overuse as a spectrum of injury is a concept which assures the athlete of receiving consistent treatment regardless of the specific physician seen or the malady suffered. This protocol is based upon clinical experience, taking into consideration the history, physical examination, an understanding of the pathophysiology behind a specific overuse syndrome, and the appropriateness of various diagnostic aids. Others (Blazena, 1974; Jackson, 1978) have advocated using similar guidelines to treat more specific injuries. These clinical guidelines cover all musculoskeletal injuries caused by overuse, with the understanding that incorrect biomechanics and athlete lack of knowledge must be corrected at the same time if the condition is to be treated successfully. The protocol is designed to cover most overuse injuries encountered in primary care settings. Overuse injuries are divided into four grades across an injury continuum. One word of caution: the clinical protocol is not intended to be used in a dogmatic way. Individual injuries may overlap grades and inconsistencies will exist. However, *most* injuries will approximate one of the clinical pictures outlined.

**Continuum of Injuries.** The following is a general description of the four grades of chronic injuries used in Table 10-2.

*Grade 1.* Patients presenting with Grade 1 injuries give a vague history of transient pain, usually occuring many hours after injury. It may be perceived as soreness, is commonly present in the beginning athlete attempting to "get into shape," and is accompanied by generalized tenderness. The cause of postexercise muscle soreness has been studied by various researchers (Schwane et al, 1987; Tiidus, 1983). Increased levels of lactic acid, muscle breakdown, or minor inflammation have been advanced as possible explanations. There are no diagnostic aids for the physician and the only treatment is reassurance and occasional use of ice. However, the physician has an excellent opportunity to intercede in the prevention of further injury at this point by appropriate athlete education and advocacy of established exercise guidelines (see Chapter 5).

*Grade 2 Injuries.* Grade 2 describes pain of approximately two to three weeks duration that typically occurs late in activity or immediately following it. Physical examination reveals more localized pain but no true point tenderness. The signs and symptoms may suggest mild musculoskeletal inflammation, but useful diagnostic aids are absent. Treatment consists of repeated applications of ice directly to the affected area for 10-15 minutes at a time. In addition, relative rest is achieved by decreasing the training regimen by 10%-25%. The physician should look at such environmental factors as use of improper or worn out equipment, or at poor technique or intrinsic biomechanical abnormalities. Grade 2 is the most common presenting clinical picture of overuse.

*Grade 3 Injuries.* Pain usually occurs in the middle of activity and, over time, moves nearer to the start of activity. Physical examination demonstrates point tenderness and other signs. A bone scan at this point may be positive but the finding adds little to the clinical diagnosis or treatment plan. Treatment includes using ice and decreasing the exercise regimen between 25%-75%. In addition, we have found that a five to seven day period of complete rest with concurrent NSAIDs medication is helpful in arresting the initial inflammation, and allows the individual to return to higher levels of activity quicker.

*Grade 4 Injuries.* Grade 4 is the most serious injury in the continuum and has a pain pattern similar to Grade 3. Pain prevents further activity and affects performance. If swelling is a major finding, especially in the lower extremity, compartment syndrome should be considered. A positive bone scan indicating the extent of a stress fracture(s) may be helpful in obtaining better patient compliance. Treatment of Grade 4 injury consists of ice, *complete rest*, and treatment with NSAIDs. Some physicians believe that stress fractures in certain areas of the body, such as the proximal tibia, require immobilization with a cast or brace. However, this is not generally recognized as present standard of care.

The following points about Table 10-2 should be kept in mind:

- The onset of pain as a symptom will occur closer to the beginning of exercise as the severity of the grade increases. Figure 10-2 illustrates the interrelationship between the injury (pain) continuum and the physiologic continuum.
- Tenderness changes from vague to specific as the process increases in severity.
- The duration and intensity of signs and symptoms increases with each grade.
- The findings on physical examination involves increasingly more functions as one moves through the continuum.
- The underlying pathophysiology can be subdivided: Grades 1 and 2 affect only soft tissue, and 3 and 4 affect both soft and hard tissue.
- By using this table, a costly test like a bone scan can sometimes be avoided. A bone scan should be ordered to confirm an already suspected stress fracture, rule out multiple sites, and improve treatment compliance.

Consistency in the treatment of overuse injuries is a desired result of widespread use of a clinical protocol such as this. A major factor contributing to patient compliance is faith in the regimen. If the regimen is consistent and the patient can be

Table 10-2. Musculoskeletal Overuse Injuries: A Clinical Guide

| | History | Physical Exam | Pathophysiology | Diagnostic Aids | Treatment | Comments |
|---|---|---|---|---|---|---|
| GRADE 1 | Transient pain *after* activity — usually hrs. "Soreness" (HX < 2 weeks) | Generalized tenderness | + Lactic acid Muscle breakdown Minor inflammation | None | ± Ice | Look at training regimen "Non" athlete "Getting in shape" |
| GRADE 2 | Longer standing pain — *late* in activity or immediately *after* activity | Localized pain, but not discrete point tenderness | Mid musculotendinous (soft tissue) inflammation | None | Ice ↓ regimen 10-25% | True overuse Wrong environment Wrong equipment Poor technique |
| GRADE 3 | Pain in *early* or *middle* of activity (getting closer to beginning of activity) | Point tenderness Percussion tenderness Pressure elsewhere produces pain at point Other evidence of inflammation (heat, erythema, swelling, crepitation) | Major musculotendinous Inflammation Periostitis Bone Microtrauma | X-ray ± Bone scan + 40% | Ice ↓ regimen 25-75% Initial 5-7 day rest period with concurrent NSAID course | "Pre-stress" fracture syndrome |
| GRADE 4 | Pain *before* or *early* in exercise preventing or affecting performance (HX > 4 weeks) | All of the Grade 3 signs plus: —disturbance in function —↓ ROM —muscle atrophy | Breakdown in soft tissue Stress fracture Compartment syndrome (especially if swelling is major finding) | X-ray ± Bone scan + 95% | Ice Rest from exercise NSAID | Immobilization? —Usually not |

Source: McKeag, D.B. *Primary Care* 11 (1): 43-59, 1984

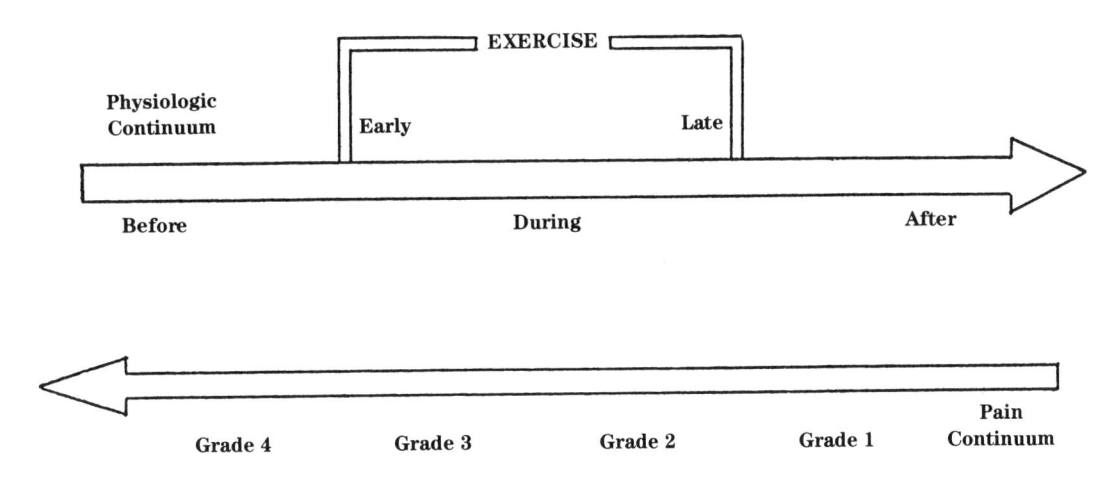

**Fig. 10-2.** Relationship of Pain Continuum to Physiologic Continuum (McKeag, 1984)

assured that the physician has not unduly restricted exercise, compliance usually will follow.

Important points to be emphasized in treating overuse syndromes:

- The use of heat in any form in the treatment of overuse injuries is *not* indicated.
- Decreasing the training regimen (relative rest) should be based not only on the grade of injury but also on factors known to the physician about the individual (lifestyle, motivation, and ability to comply).
- Long-term complete rest is not well accepted by most athletes as a legitimate treatment but they will comply with five to seven days of complete rest and treatment with NSAIDs. In Grade 3 injuries, this is very effective in initially controlling inflammation and allowing a better pharmacologic effect. The rest period is followed by light intensity training (LIT).
- The application of ice should come after exercise in Grade 2-4 injuries. Ice should be applied frequently, directly on the skin whenever possible for 10-15 minutes at a time. An ice allergy may develop, but this is rare and can be controlled by stopping the ice therapy. An easy preparation of ice for therapy is to fill small paper cups with water and freeze it for use in ice massage.
- NSAIDs should not be used if the history reveals any previous allergies or hypersensitivity reactions to those drugs.

**Return to activity.** After rest, ice, and medications have been used, a return to activity is the next problem. Using the following protocol for Light Intensity Training (LIT) allows the patient to dictate his/her own pace of return to activity and, thus, to maintain some control over the process. LIT involves the following principles:

- Training should restart only when the individual is able to function in daily activity without pain. Once this has been achieved, exercise begins at a very low level of intensity and duration (1/2 mile jog, 100 yard swim, 1 mile low gear biking).
- At the conclusion of this daily activity, the athlete then has three options:
  a. If the athlete experiences pain and/or swelling during the exercise, stop immediately and decrease duration by 25% the next day.
  b. If the athlete experiences pain after exercise, ice the area and continue at this level of exercise the next day.
  c. If the individual experiences neither pain nor swelling during or after exercise, the program may be increased by up to 25%.

Five major points that need to be examined during the treatment of overuse injuries to try and prevent recurrence include:

- The athlete's philosophy about exercise should be considered.
- A brief but knowledgeable look at the training regimen may show the possibility of beneficial alterations.
- A systematic appraisal of the exercise environment of the athlete should be made, with an idea of making needed changes.

- Congenital or injury-induced biomechanical problems, including muscle imbalance (inherent or the result of previous injury), leg length discrepancy, or self-treatment with orthotics, should be addressed.
- The athlete should be educated in the concept of pain so he/she knows when to stop exercising and when to resume.

**Treatment Modalities**

Five basic modalities are used to treat most chronic injuries. Three are used in combination, occasionally with some form of electrical impulse therapy (the fourth modality), before resorting to surgery, the fifth modality.

**Ice.** Ice is the foundation treatment for all overuse injuries. It is the most effective intervention currently available.

**Rest.** Absolute rest from exercise has advantages and disadvantages. The ability to allow healing to progress unimpeded is one advantage. Minor reinjury, caused by using an injured part, will slow the healing process. Rest combined with medication enhances the effect of the medication. The disadvantages include noncompliance and dissatisfaction on the part of the athlete. Also, rest can cause muscle atrophy, deconditioning, and loss of fine motor skills which then may predispose an individual to further injury once activity is resumed. Relative rest is a reasonable compromise.

**Anti-inflammatory Medications.** Anti-inflammatory medications that are applied topically, taken orally, or injected can be used to treat overuse injuries. Topical medications have yet to come into widespread use. Dimethyl sulfoxide (DMSO), while not a federally approved medication, may be used in some self-treatment of overuse injuries.

Oral NSAIDs are used frequently to treat overuse syndromes and there are many different NSAIDS. All have a dual action: anti-inflammation and analgesia. They do tend to mask pain, an important consideration in caring for an athlete with a serious overuse injury. Do not prescribe an NSAID initially unless the patient is willing to rest completely and allow the medication to work.

The use of corticosteroid medication, either alone or in combination with an anesthetic, should be reserved for such conditions as bursitis or tenosynovitis. Injections into tendons or ligamentous structures can significantly weaken these structures for up to 14 days afterward (Kennedy and Willis, 1976; Gottlieb and Riskin, 1980). Repeated injections can cause biomechanical disruption of soft tissue and lead directly to collagen necrosis. The possibility of tendon or ligamentous rupture is a signficant side-effect of such therapy and should be avoided.

**Electrical Impulse Therapy.** The use of low grade electrical circuits set up over an injured muscle or ligamentous unit have successfully aided healing. Transcutaneous nerve stimulation not only eliminates pain feedback to the brain via the "gate theory" (Ersek, 1978), but it also stimulates the healing process peripherally and allows the soft tissue unit to relax. Similar types of therapy include galvanic stimulation, electromyostimulation, and the use of surface electrodes for serious injuries like slow healing stress fractures. The latter treatment usually is reserved for the most serious of overuse injuries.

**Surgery.** The use of surgery to treat overuse injuries, including superspinatus tendonitis, plantar fasciitis, Achilles tendonitis, and compartment syndromes is appropriate, but only after medical measures have proven ineffective. Most clinicans argue that surgery, especially where an athlete is attempting to function at high performance levels, should be avoided at all costs.

## ACUTE INFECTIONS

Acute infections in athletes call for little in the way of special consideration. Most acquired infections in athletes seem to emanate from factors other than exercise. The epidemiology of infection is the same for athletes and nonathletes, with several possible exceptions.

- **Myocarditis** caused by viral infections can result in cardiac arrhythmia during *strenuous* exercise. It is believed that this condition has accounted for several sudden deaths among athletes. Several days of rest from strenuous activity (the higher and longer the fever — the more time for rest) is advisable. More specific, if less scientific, is the old rule of thumb: Rest two days for every day of fever over 100°F.
- **Mononucleosis**, a common viral infection, can cause two potentially serious complications: First, splenomegaly means the enlarged organ is no longer protected by the rib cage and other abdominal organs and can become the object of blunt trauma. Splenic hemorrhage is a life threat-

ening situation. Athletes with splenomegaly should not participate in contact sports. Secondly, hepatitis is associated with mononucleosis; strenuous exercise can exacerbate this problem (Knidernecht, 1989).
- **Wounds** sustained during exercise can become contaminated. Adequate protection from tetanus is emphasized for any participating athlete.
- **Non-traumatic skin infections** such as herpes simplex and staphylococcus aureus are directly associated with exercise. Herpes simplex (a.k.a. herpes gladiatorum (wrestling), herpes rugbeiorum) are significant acute infections transmitted through athletic participation. The chance of a wrestler contracting herpes from an opponent is two times the normal risk resulting from skin to skin contact (Belongia, 1990). The "scrum" in rugby where there is very close skin-to-skin contact also promotes transmission of herpes simplex (White, 1984). An outbreak of s. aureus among river rafting guides proved to be the result of minor skin wounds (secondary to rafting) combined with prolonged close contact with other humans (Decker, 1986).
- **Aseptic menningitis** caused by enteroviruses has been described in high school football players, perhaps as a result of both physical contact and the sharing of water bottles (Moore, 1983).
- **Measles**, once considered a disease of young children, has had significant impact in high school and college athletics. Constant traveling and exposure to close knit cosmopolitan groups of young adults presents a particularly high communicable disease risk to young athletes. It is now the recommendation of CDC that an athlete given a first measles vaccination before 15 months of age should have a second measles vaccination prior to entering college.
- **Winter flu** (flu-like illness), especially if it is respiratory in nature, will prevent athletes from participating during the late fall and winter months. Athletes in winter sports especially prone to intense training and close proximity to teammates and opponents should probably be immunized with the most recent trivalent flu vaccine in the late fall.
- **Blood borne viruses** (HIV, hepatitis B) can be a concern where lacerations or sores may expose one participant to the blood of another. The risk of such contact during athletic participation is small, but prevention by using universal precautions (MMWR, 1987) on the part of athletes and physicians is highly recommended.

The issue of **immunology** of exercise has been addressed by Simon (1984). Habitual exercise may protect athletes against infection. A transient increase in various host-defense factors is thought to be caused by exercise hyperthermia. Other evidence regarding immune function suggests exactly the opposite. The rigorous training programs of some aerobic sports (swimming, long distance running, bicycling) can result in anorexia and poor nutrition. While not proven, many team physicians believe that such training regimens actually decrease an athlete's resistance to endemic infections. Practices like losing a large amount of weight (wrestling, gymnastics) may put the body in a state of vulnerability. Also, many athletes, especially at the collegiate level, live in close proximity, a setting that lends itself to the spread of minor illness among team members.

It seems unlikely that exercise produces substantial functional changes in immunoglobins or complement. A number of studies (among them Schouten, 1988) have found that an increased level of habitual physical activity in a young, normal population does not result in fewer upper respiratory symptoms or shorter duration. In addition, maximal aerobic power as a measure of cardiovascular fitness is not related to the incidence or duration of upper respiratory symptoms. We can conclude that there is no clinical evidence that exercise alters the frequency or severity of human infections.

As primary care team physicians, the authors bias is that high intensity training done in the winter months or in close proximity to large groups does constitute at least a minor risk factor for developing acute contagious infections. Whenever possible, the team physician should try to aid athletes by pre-outbreak immunization or emphasizing good eating and sleeping habits.

## CHRONIC ILLNESS

A cluster of common chronic conditions that are affected (both positively and negatively) by exercise and/or injury include:

- Asthma, chronic pulmonary diseases
- Exercise-induced asthma, bronchospasm, or histamine release
- Diabetes Mellitus
- Epilepsy, seizure disorder
- Chronic musculoskeletal syndromes

- Cystic Fibrosis
- Hypertension
- Heart Disease
- Mental retardation

It is important to realize that sports participation means a great deal to athletes with these conditions and constitutes major therapy for them. The benefits of exercise (physical development of strength, coordination, and cardiovascular conditioning, and the psychological development of behavior and sense of accomplishment) are just as important in people suffering chronic disease as they are in those with no handicaps. Perhaps they are more important. Accomplished appropriately, exercise can enhance blood glucose control in diabetes, decrease seizure incidence in epilepsy, improve respiratory status in most asthma patients, and increase cardiac function in heart disease. It offers children with chronic disorders a chance to be normal. Properly guided participation becomes a therapeutic essential in the management of chronically ill youngsters. A short discussion of specific problems follows.

**Diabetes Mellitus.** Watch for the onset of a hypoglycemic episode caused by exercise participation. The individual in charge should always keep a concentrated sugar source (orange juice, candy) on hand. The athlete should be advised on the timing of specific dietary intake, including preceding exercise with a snack and avoiding exercise at bedtime. Guidelines for adjustment of insulin dosage for exercise can be found in Chapter 6.

Much less common is the condition of hyperglycemia and/or ketoacidosis. On rare occasions, an athlete might feel sick and choose not to take insulin, or he/she might exercise strenuously and develop hyperglycemia. For this reason, a physician covering an event involving a diabetic should always have regular insulin present.

**Epilepsy.** Epileptic seizures vary dramatically in both cause and manifestation. Sports that pose a serious risk as a result of sudden unconsciousness (diving, gymnastics) should be actively discouraged. Risks should always be weighed in these cases. However, in other sports, no special injuries should be expected from athletic participation by epileptic individuals.

**Asthma.** Asthma can be either extrinsic (usually with an allergic etiology) or recurrent intrinsic asthma. Both benefit from sports participation. The major goal in taking care of an asthmatic athlete is to protect against infections (see earlier section on acute infections). Prompt attention is necessary when there is an infection. Many asthmatics have problems with atmospheric pollutants in places where competition and practices are held. Pollutants can include dust, molds, tobacco smoke, cold air, and generic industrial air pollution.

A special problem for the non-asthmatic athlete is exercise-induced respiratory problems (exercise-induced asthma, bronchospasm, or histamine release). These individuals are asymptomatic at the onset of exercise but develop respiratory distress shortly thereafter. Fortunately, control can be achieved rather easily with prophylactic use of cromolyn sodium or albuterol dose inhalers.

**Cystic Fibrosis.** Recent controlled experiments indicate that the management of cystic fibrosis can be aided by regular exercise. Clearing respiratory secretions is an inherent problem in the control of this chronic disease and exercise can aid in keeping the lungs clear and free of such secretions.

**Hypertension.** Mild blood pressure elevation warrants no limitation in participation. However, isometric activity (such as that seen in weight lifting) causes marked and sometimes prolonged elevations in blood pressure and should be discouraged in individuals with hypertension. Consult the appropriate blood pressure charts (Chapter 5) for guidelines on blood pressure readings, especially as they apply to children.

**Heart Disease.** Consult the cardiovascular subsection in Chapter 13.

**Mental Retardation.** Mental retardation poses no serious problems from the standpoint of sports participation. The benefit derived from participation by these individuals is so great as to preclude any discussion of possible risks on their part.

**Musculoskeletal Disorders.** These disorders include Osgood-Schlatter's Disease (knee), spondylolisthesis (back), Legg-Calve-Perthes Disease (hip), and dermatomyositis.

## ALLERGIES

Allergies can cause everything from chronic symptoms of the upper respiratory tract to decreased performance secondary to respiratory inefficiency. Following is a list of allergies that can be factors in athletic performance:

1. *Ice* — Ice allergies are relatively rare, affecting no more than 1%-2%. The allergy is generally seen following ice treatment for soft tissue injury. Symptoms include the development of wheals and urticaria to the area surrounding the skin where ice was applied. Treatment is removal of the ice. Rarely, an antihistamine such as Benadryl® may be necessary.
2. *Equipment* — Equipment that has been washed and cleaned in certain types of detergent can result in allergic dermatitis. Consider this in an individual with an unexplained skin rash.
3. *Medications* — Always a possible problem. This can be avoided by obtaining a history of allergies before placing an athlete on any medications.
4. *Airborne Dust and Molds* — Competing indoors in large arenas, athletes may be susceptible to problems caused by dust and molds that collect in the rafters or are circulated by ventilation systems.
5. *Chlorine* — Some swimmers have an unfortunate allergy to the chlorine or bromide used to disinfect pools. This results in a contact dermatitis and should be treated as such.
6. *Personal Contact* — On occasion, participants will spray or apply substances on their skin to which they or their opponents are allergic. During contact, an allergic reaction to the substance develops. Examples of substances include tape, rubber, and Vaseline®.

**REFERENCES**

Baron, R.C. et al. Aseptic meningitis among members of high school football teams, *JAMA* 248(14), October 8, 1982.

Blazena, D.E., Fox, J.S., Caron, S.J. Basketball injuries. *Medical Aspects of Sports*, AMA, Vol. 15, 1974.

Bowers, K.D. Disposition of high school athletic injuries. *West Virginia Medical Journal*, 73:88-89, 1974.

Clement, D.B., Taunton, J.E., Smart, G.W., McNichol, K.L. A survey of overuse running injuries. *Phys and Sportsmed* 9(5):47-58, 1981.

Ersek, R.A. Transcutaneous electrical neurostimulation: a new therapeutic modality for controlling pain. *Clinical Ortho and Related Research* 128:314-324, 1978.

Garrick, J.G., Requa, R. Medical care and injury surveillance in a high school setting. *Phys Sportsmed* 9(2):115-120, 1981.

Garrick, J.G. Sports medicine. *Pediatric Clinics of North America* 24(4), November 1977.

Gottlieb, N.L., Riskin, W.G. Complications of local corticosteroid injections. *JAMA* 243(15):1547-1548, 1980.

Jackson, D.W. Shinsplints: an update. *Phys and Sportsmed* 6(10):51-62, 1978.

Kennedy, J.C., Willis, R.B. The effects of local steroid injections on tendons: a biomechanical and microscopic correlative study. *Am J Sports Med* 4(1):11-21, 1976.

McKeag, D.B. and Kinderknecht, J. Infectious mononucleosis. Chapter in *Common Problems in Pediatric Sports Medicine*, N. Smith, ed., Year Book Publishers, Chicago, IL, 1989.

McKeag, D.B. The concept of overuse: the primary care aspects of overuse syndromes in sports. *Primary Care* 11(1):43-59, 1984.

Schwane, J.A., Williams, J.S., Sloan, J.H. Effects of training on delayed muscle soreness and serum creatine kinase activity after running. *Med Sci Sports Exerc* 19:584-590, 1987.

Simon, H.B. The immunology of exercise. *JAMA* 252(19):2735-2738, 1984.

Tiidus, P.M., Ianuzzo, C.D. Effects of intensity and duration of muscular exercise on delayed soreness and serum enzyme activities. *Med Sci Sports Exerc* 15:461-465, 1983.

**RECOMMENDED READINGS**

Andrews, J.R. Overuse syndromes of the lower extremity. *Clinics in Sports Med* 2(1):137-148, 1983.

Harvey, J.S. Overuse syndromes in young athletes. *Ped Clin North America* 29(6):1369-1381, 1982.

Ryan, A.J., Brown, R.L. et al. Overtraining of athletes. A Round Table. *Phys and Sportsmed* 11(6):93-108, 1983.

Sandish, W.D. Overuse injuries in athletes: a perspective. *Med Sci Sports Exerc* 16(1):1-7, 1984.

# 11

# Common Sports-Related Injuries and Illnesses—Head and Neck

## SECTION A.
## HEAD INJURIES

Head injuries, or the fear of them, remain one of the most powerful motivating forces for change in sports. Advances in the technology of protective equipment have transformed the athlete into a modern-day gladiator. Death rates secondary to football head and neck injuries have gradually decreased (see Figure 11A-1). The main reason for this decrease is improved helmet design and enforcement of rule changes regarding "spearing". Non-fatal head injuries accounted for 19% of all football injuries in a Minnesota study (Gerberich, 1983). At the high school level, the incidence of head injury drops to an average of 4.5% for all sports injuries (Garrick, 1981). Significant head injuries usually fall into one of four types — concussion, contusion, intracranial hemorrhage, and skull fracture.

**Anatomy**

Head injury includes trauma to the scalp, skull, or brain. The scalp itself has five distinct layers:

- Epidermis/dermis — common site of lacerations
- Superficial fascia — contains the major extracranial blood supply from the external carotid artery. There are no peripheral blood vessels from the bone to nourish the scalp. The venous system parallels that of the arterial, except for communication with the cavernous, superior sagittal, and lateral sinuses. Secondary scalp infections (as a result of laceration) can potentially spread intracranially via these veins.

| YEAR | HIGH SCHOOL | COLLEGE |
|---|---|---|
| 1977 | 0.77 | 2.67 |
| 1978 | 0.92 | 0.00 |
| 1979 | 0.62 | 4.00 |
| 1980 | 0.84 | 2.67 |
| 1981 | 0.46 | 2.67 |
| 1982 | 0.54 | 2.67 |
| 1983 | 0.84 | 1.33 |
| 1984 | 0.38 | 0.00 |
| 1985 | 0.38 | 2.67 |
| 1986 | 0.23 | 0.00 |

*Based on 1,300,000 High School - Junior High School Players and 75,000 College Players

**Fig. 11A-1.** Incidence per 100,000 Participants 1977-1986* (Adapted from Mueller and Blyth, 1987A)

- Galea aponeurotica — a tough, dense layer of fibrous tissue.
- Subaponeurotic layer.
- Pericranium — the periosteum or glia of the skull.

The skull consists of a bony vault made up of 8 tightly joined bones — parietal (2), temporal (2), occipital, frontal, ethmoid, and sphenoid. Three distinct tissue layers lie between the skull and the brain:

- Dura Mater — contains venous sinuses, meningeal arteries, and veins. Laceration of the middle meningeal artery, the terminal branch of the external carotid, is the most frequent cause of epidural hematoma.
- Arachnoid — a thin layer containing the spinal fluid of the brain. Subdural hematomas appear between the dura and the arachnoid as a result of intracranial venous laceration.
- Pia Mater — layer closely adherent to the cerebral cortex.

The brain is unique because it has a fixed volume enclosed in a non-expandable vault (the skull and dura mater). A significant increase in volume creates an increase in intracranial pressure, which leads to more serious progressive brain injury.

## Biomechanics

The location and degree of head injury depends upon the magnitude and direction of impact, the structural features and physical reactions of the skull, and the state of the head at the moment of impact. It is the response to a force rather then just the force itself that causes these injuries (Reid, 1974). Consult Figure 11A-2 for a delineation of the types of primary head injuries.

Any blow to the head can cause injury. Concussion and minor contusion have been associated with sudden head movement and shifting of the brain with contact. Minor impacts can cause tearing of small vessels and petecchaie formation (Ommaya and Gennarelli, 1974). A concussion may not necessarily be the result of a single blow, but can reflect the cumulative effect of a series of past blows. Following a concussion, there is a reduction in the ability to process information. This deficiency is of much greater magnitude and longer duration if the individual has experienced a previous concussion (Gronwall, 1974). Also, fatal head injuries are frequently associated with prior concussions (Schneider, 1972).

## Mechanisms of Injury to the Head

### Direct Injuries

- Moving object striking the head (boxing, baseball, field hockey, ice hockey)
- Moving head striking a fixed or slow moving object (contrecoup injuries opposite the impact site — football and horseback riding)

### Indirect Injuries

Trauma impact on another body part can be transferred to the cranium (Guardian, 1980). For example, a fall on the coccyx while ice skating can lead to an injury at the base of the brain.

## Scalp Injuries

### Lacerations

Lacerations should be treated as outlined earlier (see Chapter 10). The increased vascularity and other properties of the superficial layer of the scalp make these lacerations prone to continued bleeding, in many cases hampering appropriate wound closure. Repair should be done under as sterile conditions as possible, shaving where necessary to clear the field.

### Subglial Hematoma

A blunt injury quite commonly causes blood to collect between the glia and the skull. Early treatment involves the application of ice as well as a skull x-ray to rule out fracture. If there is no skull fracture, pressure to the area minimizes the size of the hematoma. Careful follow-up should take place to detect any infection secondary to the injury.

## Skull Fractures

Skull fractures may be open or closed. Because the force of the blow may actually be absorbed during the skull fracturing process, the resulting intracranial damage may actually be less. Fracture lines crossing the grooves of meningeal arteries, especially middle meningeal arteries, are a cause

**Primary injury**

*Contusions, lacerations, shearing injuries, hemorrhage, and swelling can occur at the time of impact and cannot be reversed by treatment.*

**Contusions** typically occur over the frontal and temporal poles of the brain regardless of the cranial impact site.

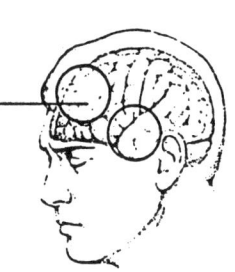

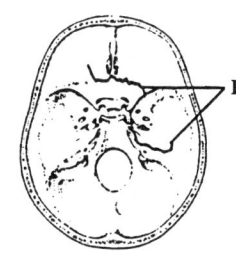

**Lacerations,** with or without associated fractures, are usually located near the midline, adjacent to the floor of the anterior or middle cranial fossa, and often involve the corpus callosum or pontomedullary junction.

**Shearing injuries** occur when the impact is accompanied by sudden angular rotation of the skull.

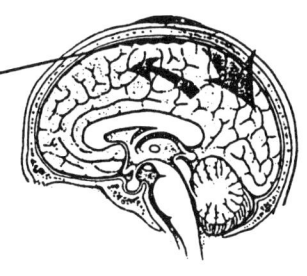

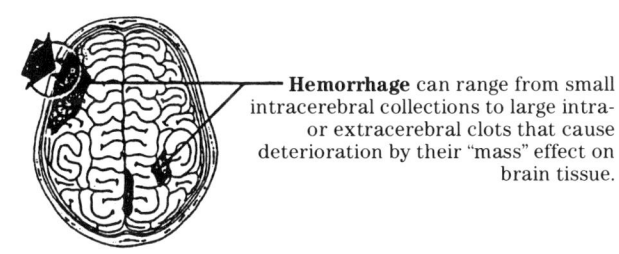

**Hemorrhage** can range from small intracerebral collections to large intra- or extracerebral clots that cause deterioration by their "mass" effect on brain tissue.

**Fig. 11A-2.** Types of Primary Head Injuries

for concern. Battle's sign (ecchymosis behind the ear secondary to skull fracture) may represent a basilar skull fracture.

### Skull Fracture Classification

- Linear — hairline separation with loss of curvature of the skull produced by blunt impact. They represent 70% of all skull fractures.
- Comminuted — small impact area causing indentation and fragmentation.
- Depressed — skull fragment is displaced inwardly, depression increasing with the pointedness of the object (baseball vs. javelin). Major problems will arise if fracture has entrapped brain or meninges.
- Blow-out fracture of orbit — caused by direct blunt impact to the orbit involving fracture of the floor of the orbit. This may involve inferior oblique muscle.
- Blow-in fracture of orbit — caused by shearing forces during initial impact of the orbit roof.

Below are suggested criteria to aid the physician in deciding which athletes should have skull x-rays. The presence of one or more of these signs indicates the need for radiologic exam (Quick, 1985):

- Unconsciousness at the time of examination
- History of focal trauma capable of producing a depressed skull fracture
- Penetrating injury to the head
- Compromised athlete unable to give a good history
- Prolonged post-traumatic syndrome (headache, dizziness, vomiting)
- CSF rhinorrhea or otorrhea
- Certain neurologic findings — anisocoria, hemiparesis, unilateral Babinski's sign
- Battle's sign

### Brain Injury

The best way to prevent the sequelae of serious head injury is to be prepared for it and diagnosis it rapidly. The team physician should carry the necessary supplies or have them at the event site. Consult Appendix 11A-1 for this check list. In determining the seriousness of the injury, a brief neurological examination and a tentative diagnosis should be made. That neurologic exam should include an assessment as outlined in Table 9-5 (Chapter 9) as well as Appendix 11A-3. With the information from this examination, a score on the Glasgow Coma Scale can be reached. Consult Table 11A-1 for determining the proper score. Depending upon the situation, the physician may need to start treatment for increased intracranial pressure. The initial head injury management and treatment protocol is listed in Table 11A-2.

Table 11A-1. Glasgow Coma Scale

| Eye Opening | Spontaneous | E4 |
|---|---|---|
| | To Speech | 3 |
| | To pain | 2 |
| | Nil | 1 |
| **Best Motor Response** | Obeys | M6 |
| | Localizes* | 5 |
| | Withdraws | 4 |
| | Abnormal flexion⁺ | 3 |
| | Extends° | 2 |
| | Nil | 1 |
| **Verbal Response**# | Oriented | V5 |
| | Confused conversation | 4 |
| | Inappropriate words | 3 |
| | Incomprehensible sounds | 2 |
| | Nil | 1 |

*Response to painful stimulus; apply knuckles to sternum; observe arms
⁺Indicating decardicate rigidity
°Indicating decerebrate rigidity
#Arouse with painful stimulus if necessary

## Concussion

Concussion is defined as a clinical syndrome characterized by immediate and transient impairment of neural function such as alteration of consciousness, disturbance of vision and equilibrium, due to mechanical forces (Congress of Neurological Surgeons, 1966). A concussion involves a change in mental behavior with or without loss of consciousness. It is the most common head injury in contact sports. Of the 250,000 concussions that occur annually in football alone, 90% are mild or first degree (Cantu, 1988).

The "traditional" graded breakdown is based on subjective and objective findings in the athlete:

1. *Mild concussion* (Grade 1)

    Symptoms can include headache, tinnitus, lack of motor coordination, mental confusion, and short-term memory impairment.

    Signs involve unsteadiness of gait and occasional post-traumatic amnesia 10-20 minutes after the injury, but no loss of consciousness. Recovery is rapid.

    The period following a mild concussion should be monitored for post-concussion syndrome, vulnerability to subsequent and successive head trauma, and insidious intracranial hemorrhage. The chance of incurring a second concussion is more than four times greater than it is for a player without a previous concussion. A return to contact sports while a player is still symptomatic can result in "second impact syndrome," in which catastrophic brain edema occurs after minor head contact in someone who still has symptoms from a prior concussion.

    Treatment is removal from competition with periodic examination to monitor neurologic status (see Chapter 10, Figure 10-1). No athlete should return to competition until the symptoms have disappeared, motor activity is normal, and the athlete can give appropriate answers to questions about the pre-traumatic period. No return to competition should be allowed if any of the following findings are present:

    - unconsciousness
    - seeing "stars" — (indicates a precortical blow)
    - localized paresthesia
    - dizziness
    - severe headache
    - abnormal or unequal pupils
    - amnesia
    - disorientation
    - lethargy
    - hyperirritability

    An athlete who sustains three or more mild concussions in the same year should be disqualified from contact sports and evaluated by a neurologist and/or neurosurgeon.

2. *Moderate concussion* (Grade 2)

    Symptoms expand to include visual disturbances (blurred vision, double vision), auditory hallucinations, drowsiness, and nausea.

    Loss of consciousness lasts less than five minutes and is usually accompanied by retrograde amnesia. PTA is usually longer than 30 minutes and less than 24 hours. Recovery is rapid. Treatment is removal from competition with no possibility of reentry. A complete neurological exam should be followed by close observation for changes in neurological status. If any neurologic abnormality persists, the athlete should be hospitalized. No athlete sustaining a 2nd degree concussion should return to play until cleared by a physician after a minimum of 72 hours out of participation. An athlete who sustains two moderate concussions in the same year should be evaluated by a neurologist and/

**Table 11A-2. Acute Care of the Head Injured Patient at the Site of Injury**

1. Check for Responsiveness
    - Conscious: $R_x$-100% $O_2$ (10 breaths/min) via reservoir mask
    - Unconscious: $R_x$-oral airway — bag mask ventilation (24 breaths/min, 100% $O_2$)

2. Check for Breathing Difficulty
    - Conscious: $R_x$-bag mask ventilation (24 breaths/min, 100% $O_2$) without oral airway
    - Unconscious: $R_x$-bag mask ventilation (24 breaths/min, 100% $O_2$) with oral airway

3. Establish Circulation
    - Absent Carotid Pulses: $R_x$-Advanced Life Support under medical control
    - Hypotension: $R_x$ — elevate foot of backboard
        — establish I.V. line with #18 percutaneous plastic catheter using 5% dextrose in Ringer's lactate

4. Get History and Do Physical Exam
    - Establish level of consciousness (Glasgow Coma Scale)
    - Check for change in level of consciousness since injury
    - Check for pupil size, position, equality and reaction to light
    - Evaluate length of unconsciousness

5. Prevent Aspiration Pneumonia In Unconscious Patients
    - Minimal oral secretion: $R_x$-periodic nasopharyngeal suctioning
    - Excessive oral secretions: $R_x$-esophageal airway

6. Reduce Intracerebral Edema
   $R_x$-methylprednisolone (Solumedrol)
   15 years and older — 2 grams I.V.
   5-15 years — 1 gram I.V.
   <5 years — 0.5 grams I.V.

7. Transport Patient to Hospital Base Station with Advanced Life Support Capability
    - Monitor vital signs every 15 minutes
    - Contact Hospital Base Station
      Communicate:
      | | |
      |---|---|
      | Patient's age | Neurological exam |
      | Patient's sex | Glasgow Coma Scale score |
      | Mechanism of injury | Pupillary response |
      | Vital signs | Other injuries |
      | Brief history | Treatment |
    - Continue communication with hospital base station

(Adapted from: Rimel et al., 1978)

---

or neurosurgeon and excluded from play for the remainder of the season.

3. *Severe concussion* (Grade 3)

Loss of consciousness for longer than five minutes is most worrisome. Eye movements are usually wandering. There may be little or no response to pain. Retrograde amnesia may be prolonged and PTA continues for more than 24 hours. Convulsions may ensue and prophylaxis should be available. An airway may be needed.

Immediate transportation (see Chapter 9, Figure 9-1 to 9-3), hospitalization, and neurosurgical consultation is indicated.

*Important* — in the case of an unconscious patient with an unavailable history, care must be taken to avoid further injury. *Head* and *neck* injuries often occur together (Schneider, 1985). Any individual rendered unconscious during competition should be treated as if a cervical spine injury has occurred.

Two alternate classifications of concussion have been proposed. Torg's classification (1982) consists of six grades of cerebral concussion and involves the assessment of post-traumatic amnesia as well as retrograde amnesia (see Figure 11A-3).

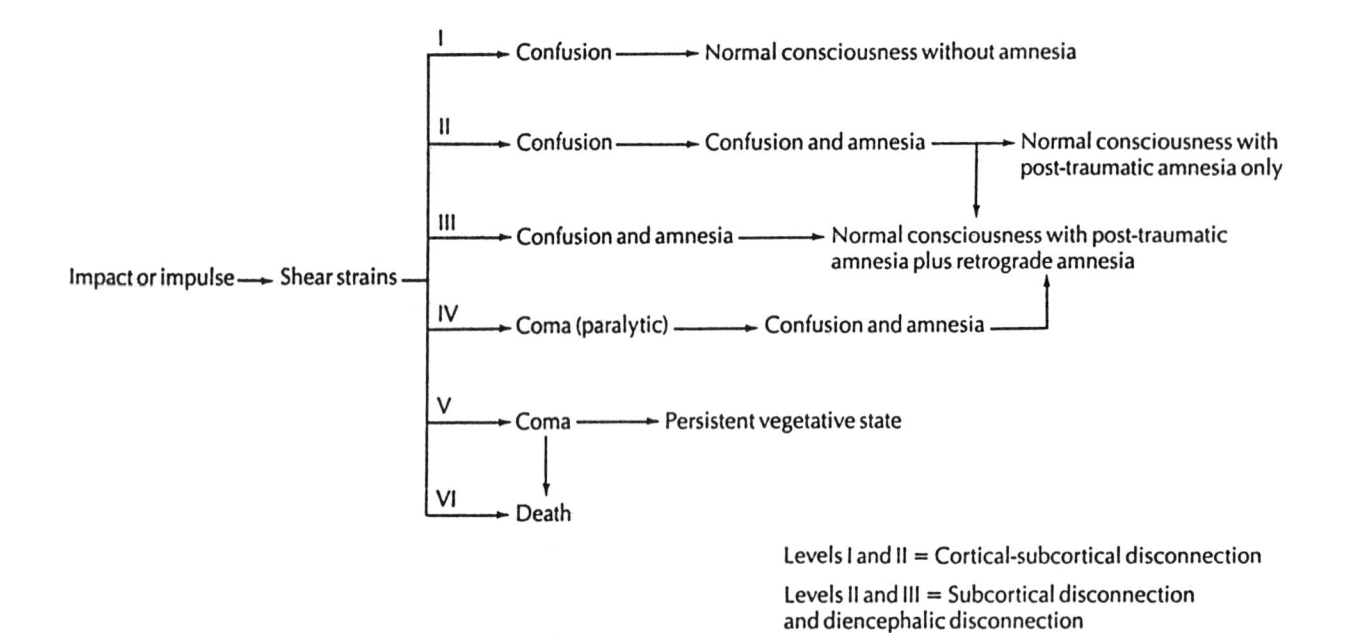

**Fig. 11A-3.** Levels of Severity of Head Injury (Source: Torg, 1982)

Levels I and II = Cortical-subcortical disconnection
Levels II and III = Subcortical disconnection and diencephalic disconnection
Levels IV to VI = Diencephalic disconnection and mesencephalic disconnection

The authors think the classification advocated by Nelson (1984) is the most appropriate and useful yet for the primary care physician who is evaluating an injury on the sidelines. It classifies minor head injury better and is much more useful than the traditional classification of head injuries. Below are common conditions to consider in evaluating a head injury. Figure 11A-4 outlines the major points of the classification and suggested management.

### Differential Diagnosis

*Vasovagal Syncope* — This fainting episode is often the result of a significant blow to the body but not necessarily the head. The vagus nerve is stimulated, causing decreased pulse, hypotension, lightheadedness, or perhaps unconsciousness. There is no associated amnesia but respiratory difficulty can occur.

*Migraine Seizures* — Rarely, cerebral vasospasm caused by trauma has resulted in a migraine-type clinical picture. Albright (1984) and Bennett (1980) suggest that the symptoms do not occur at the time of impact but shortly afterward. Prodromal, visual, motor, or sensory symptoms are noted by the player. These can be confused with seizures and more serious neurologic conditions.

*Contusions* — Contusions are created by mass movement of brain tissue that cause tears of connecting blood vessels between the brain and meninges. Such "bruising" can be widespread or localized, depending on etiology. Symptoms include weakness, loss of memory, loss of speech, and depression. A decreasing level of consciousness is the single most important sign for determining severity, as well as subsequent development of hematoma and possible need for surgical intervention.

A brain CT scan is recommended because it can differentiate between a brain contusion (area or areas of high-density blood intermixed with normal-density parenchyma) and concussion (normal).

### Intracranial Lesions

Intracranial hemorrhage is responsible for most injury-related deaths, but it also is the most amenable to surgery. Bleeding may be arterial, most commonly the middle meningeal artery, or venous, most commonly the longitudinal sinus or bridging cerebral veins. A generic treatment protocol is

| GRADE | SIGNS & SYMPTOMS | MANAGEMENT |
|---|---|---|
| 0 | -Head struck or moved rapidly<br>-Not stunned or dazed initially<br>-Subsequently complains of headache and difficulty in concentrating | -Return to play when sensorium clears<br>-Ask about symptoms periodically during remainder of activity<br>-Remove from activity if symptoms redevelop |
| 1 | -Stunned or dazed initially<br>-No loss of consciousness or amnesia<br>-"Bell rung". Sensorium quickly clears (less than 1 minute) | -Same as for Grade 0 |
| 2 | -Headache, cloudy sensorium (greater than 1 minute) | -Remove from practice or game<br>-Do not return until asymptomatic<br>-If symptoms increase or do not clear within 2 days, refer to neurosurgeon |
| 3 | -LOC (less than 1 minute)<br>-Not comatose (arousable with noxious stimuli)<br>-Demonstrates Grade 2 symptoms during recovery | -Remove from activity<br>-Do not return to sports until cleared by neurosurgeon<br>-If symptoms increase, urgent consultation is indicated |
| 4 | -LOC (greater than 1 minute)<br>-Not comatose<br>-Demonstrates Grade 2 symptoms during recovery | -Transport to neurologic trauma center for evaluation and treatment |

**Fig. 11A-4.** Classification of Concussion (Based upon Nelson et al., 1984)

outlined in Table 11A-3, placing emphasis on the level of consciousness over time.

**Classification**

1. *Epidural hemorrhage* — Fortunately, these injuries, usually the result of head-on collisions, are rare in sports. *Arterial* hemorrhaging occurs between the skull and the fibrous dura. Because the dura is so closely attached to the skull, the lesion usually forms a localized bulge. These hemorrhages represent only 1%-3% of all head injuries. The mortality rate is high (8%-50%) considering that it is a highly treatable lesion that may occur with a relatively mild blow (Schneider, 1985). Clinical signs include:
    a. Dilation and fixation of ipsilateral pupil (mortality approaches 90% if both pupils are affected)
    b. Contralateral weakness or paralysis and attenuated deep tendon reflexes (DTRs)
    c. Natural history — short period of initial unconsciousness following the injury → lucid interval → drowsiness, headache, and vomiting 1-2 hours → later progressive loss of consciousness → impaired respiration → arrest.
2. *Chronic epidermal hemorrhage* — Source of the hemorrhage is *venous* and will result in vague neurologic symptoms taking two to seven days to appear.
3. *Subdural hemorrhage/hematoma* — Subdural hemorrhage is arbitrarily classified as acute, subacute, or chronic.

*Acute:* Acute subdural hematoma is the most

Table 11A-3. Head Injury: Trend of Consciousness, Diagnostic Procedure and Treatment

| Trend of Consciousness | Diagnostic Procedure | Treatment |
| --- | --- | --- |
| No LOC* | C-spine and skull x-rays as indicated | Pain relief for headache if indicated |
| Transient LOC and improving | C-spine and skull x-rays | Consider admission to hospital if clinical or patient support system not satisfactory |
| Transient LOC and deteriorating (lucid intervals) | C-spine and skull x-rays (epidural hematoma); emergency CT scan | Admit; hyperventilate; furosemide 20-80 mg IV; mannitol if condition deteriorates |
| Prolonged unconsciousness with signs of brain herniation | C-spine and skull x-rays; emergency CT scan | Admit; hyperventilate; furosemide 40-80 mg IV; early ICP monitoring; manitol if needed to lower ICP |
| Rapidly deteriorating consciousness with signs of herniation | C-spine and skull x-rays; emergency craniotomy after CT scan if there is surgical lesion | Admit; hyperventilate; furosemide 40-80 mg IV; mannitol 1 g/kg; consider emergency burr hole |

*LOC = Loss of Consciousness

frequent cause of death in athletic head injuries, accounting for nearly 75% of all vascular complications encountered in sports. It can be associated with skull fractures. Hemorrhage occurs in the subdural space between the dura mater and the arachnoid membrane after an injury to the cerebral veins communicating with the cerebral cortex through the arachnoid. A common cause is a cerebral contusion that tears the cortical surface vessels. It usually is a *contrecoup* injury involving vessels opposite the area of impact. Hemorrhage spreads widely and thinly over the brain, with acute symptoms appearing immediately or up to 24 hours post-injury.

In most cases, the patient is rendered unconscious by the cerebral contusion, secondary to the initial impact which overshadows many of the symptoms of the expanding hemorrhage. Unconsciousness usually continues from the time of the injury and may become associated with progressive neurologic deterioration. The prognosis is favorable in those less common circumstances where there is not a concomitant brain contusion in addition to the hemorrhage (Albright, 1984). The treatment is surgical removal of the hemorrhage via craniotomy.
*Subacute:* A subacute subdural hematoma occurs when the symptoms and signs appear two to ten days after the injury. The presentation is similar to an acute hematoma once neurologic deterioration begins. For several days after the injury, the patient usually is drowsy and disoriented. Treatment is the same as that for an acute hematoma.
*Chronic:* Chronic subdural hematomas produce signs and symptoms two weeks or more after the initial injury. The symptoms are usually subtle and may include persistent headaches, personality changes, or other signs of cerebral irritation. These hematomas tend to enlarge as a result of bleeding from more fragile vessels in the subdural space. This type of injury results in a slow increase in pressure as a result of venous bleeding. This rare, insidious injury points to the necessity for close follow-up of any head injury.

*Any* head injury in sports should be treated with periodic follow-up, and patient education instructions should be given to families or roommates (see Appendix 11A-2).

## Post-Traumatic Problems

### Post-Concussion Syndrome

Athletes who sustain a concussion may later develop a constellation of symptoms termed post-concussion syndrome (PCS) that includes persistent headaches, inability to concentrate, irritability, or fatigue. These symptoms can last for several weeks. Athletes should not return to participation as long as symptoms are present. They should rest and be treated symptomatically until symptoms resolve. For as long as a year following a head injury, 20% of athletes will have at least one symptom of PCS; 5% will have five or more symptoms (Auerbach, 1987).

### Post-Traumatic Seizures

Albright (1984) states that the incidence of seizures associated with closed head injury is from 2 1/2% — 10%. Severe head injury where there is dural laceration, focal cortical damage, or post-traumatic amnesia that lasts more than 24 hours is associated with epileptic seizures in 30%-60% of cases (Wohns and Wyler, 1979). Less severe forms of head injury usually do not result in post-traumatic seizures. Epilepsy could develop up to two years (rare) after a significant head injury.

Anti-epileptic drugs are used to prevent seizures that may follow head trauma. Phenytoin (Dilantin) is the most commonly prescribed drug in this group. Temkin (1990) concluded that the beneficial protective effect of Phenytoin in reducing seizures lasts only for the first week after a severe head injury.

### Long-Term Minor Head Disability

Neuropsychological assessment of patients with minor head injuries indicated that over half were experiencing difficulties three months or more after their initial injury (Rimel, 1981, 1982). This demonstrated that "minor" head injuries incurred in sports were actually much more significant than once was assumed. Athletes who have head injuries are sustaining organic brain damage that causes problems in attention, concentration, memory, and judgment. This can cause significant performance problems for an athlete attending school at any level. Long-term minor head disability is another important reason why follow-up of all sports related head injuries is indicated, even after the more obvious symptomatology disappears.

The Glasgow Coma Scale (GCS) defines the severity of head injuries well; the GCS score at the time of the injury correlates quite well with the degree or severity. Athletes scoring 13-15 on this scale are defined by Rimel (1982) as having minor head injuries. Those scoring 9-12 have a moderate head injury and those who score from 3-8 are in the severe category (see Table 11A-1). Evidence suggests that brain damage increases linearly in the descending GCS scale from 12 to 6. The most severe head injuries fall into the 3-5 GCS category and there is little hope for these patients because most have suffered irreversible brain injury prior to admission to the hospital.

## SECTION B.
## FACE

### Introduction/Epidemiology

Injuries to the maxillofacial area of the body represent 2%- 3% of all sports injuries.

- Sports activities account for 12% of all maxillofacial injuries.
- Despite the use of face guards, masks, and other protective equipment, facial trauma continues to present significant problems for primary care sports phyicians. Most injuries occur in one of two ways:
  a. direct blow — from fists, elbows, or objects such as pucks, baseballs, tennis balls, hockey sticks
  b. direct contact with a playing surface — ice rink, basketball court, turf

### General Principles

There are several common factors common in the management of maxillofacial injuries:

- Be aware of associated injuries. Additional, sometimes hidden, trauma may be present in an athlete with maxillofacial injury and these non-facial problems often should take precedence.
- Infection must be prevented. The risk of possible contamination of the wound by intra-oral flora or extrinsic agents is high. Consider antibiotics on a prophylactic basis.
- Tetanus toxoid should be given if previous immunization was more than 10 years ago (5 years if the wound is deep and/or contaminated).
- Dental occlusion should be assessed in evaluating jaw fractures and dislocations. Normally, the anterior upper teeth are slightly in front of the lower teeth (Figure 11B-1). Deviation in occlusion may indicate malalignment (malocculsion) secondary to jaw fracture or pterygoid muscle spasm.
- Significant maxillofacial trauma may interfere with either oral or nasotracheal airway maintenance. The following airway equipment is sug-

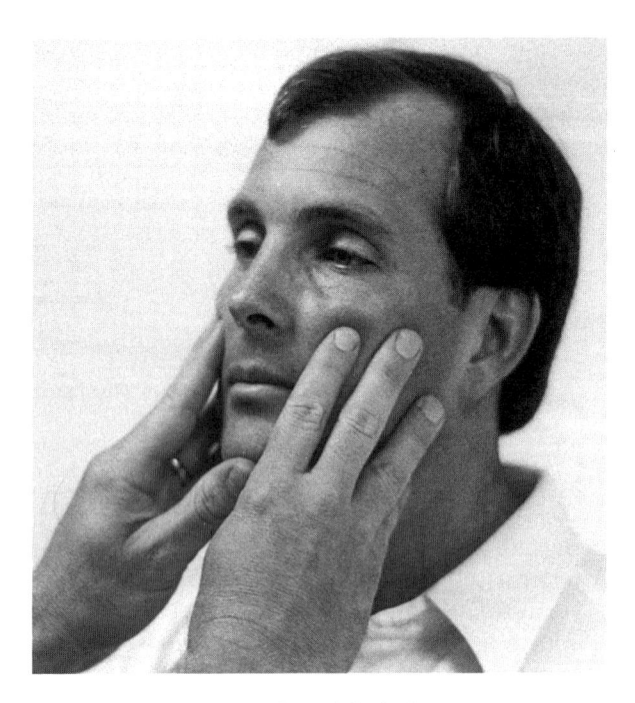

**Fig. 11B-1.** Assessment of Dental Occlusion

gested by Solon (1984): Ambu-bag and mask, oral airway, laryngoscope, endotrachial tube, suction tip. This equipment should be available for use on-site at competition and practice.

## Contusions/Abrasions

Soft tissue facial injuries constitutes the majority. Contusions usually resolve spontaneously but they must be differentiated from facial edema associated with underlying fractures (see Figure 11B-2).

Abrasions must be cleansed and small foreign bodies removed to prevent permanent tatooing. A surgical scrub brush is helpful. Grease or oil can be dissolved and removed with small amounts of acetone (Handler, 1982) or xylol.

## Lacerations

Treating facial lacerations is complicated by the increased *vascularity* of the face, and the necessity for acceptable cosmetic results.

The absence or presence of underlying damage to neural, vascular, muscular, and bony structures should be determined prior to closure of any wound. If there is damage, referral (without wound closure) to a surgeon is appropriate. The wound should be covered with sterile gauze and any avulsed or predicated tissue preserved for possible inclusion in the final repair.

Strive for cleanliness in repair to eliminate the possibility of cellulitis. Skin approximation can be accomplished with steri-strips if the laceration is small, superficial, or non-complicated. Skin on either side of the laceration is prepared with tincture of benzoin to promote tape adherence. More extensive lacerations require the use of 5-0 or 6-0 non-absorbable suture (PDS suture is recommended because there is less foreign-body inflammation from the suture material) after local anesthesia with 1% xylocaine with epinephrine (to control bleeding) is given. If the wound is deep, a two-layer closure is necessary, using absorbable sutures to approximate deep structures prior to final closure. Cartilage must be very carefully approximated. Insertion of a rubber drain may be necessary to prevent hematoma formation in large, deep wounds. Hematoma of the pinna resulting in "Cauliflower ear" is discussed in this chapter in the section entitled Ear. If there are jagged edges in cut skin, they should be trimmed to leave an uninterrupted linear surface. The suture process should be removal of every other suture 3-4 days post injury with the remainder at 6-7 days. Avoid premature removal of sutures and possible wound separation. This is especially important if an individual is returning to a contact sport where there will be pressure or stress on the area.

Facial lacerations can present special problems and the following points made by Schultz and deCamara (1984) should be considered:

- Eyebrows should not be shaved.
- Eyebrow shape and direction are important landmarks for repair.
- Eyelids should be closed in layers.
- Facial muscles should be repaired at the time of initial injury.
- Deep cheek lacerations can involve either the parotid gland or the branches of the facial nerve.
- Interoral and tongue lacerations should be loosely closed first, followed by antibiotic prophylatic therapy.

## Fractures

These are not usually medical emergencies but prompt recognition is necessary to provide the

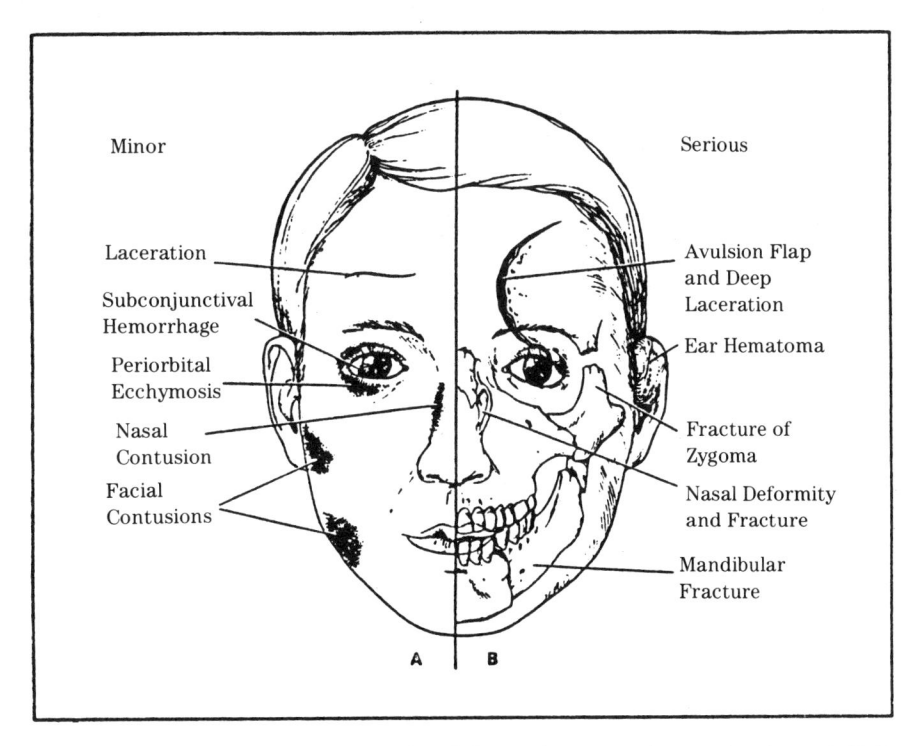

**Fig. 11B-2.** Comparison of minor vs serious facial injuries. A, Simple lacerations, contusions, and ecchymosis. B, Complex lacerations, facial asymmetry, deformity, and malocclusion with underlying facial bone fractures. (Schultz, 1984)

necessary repositioning to restore form and function. Nasal fractures are the most frequent facial bone fracture and are discussed in the section of this chapter entitled Nose.

### Maxillary Trauma

*Zygoma* — Fractures of the zygomatic arch account for 10% of the sport-related maxillary fractures (Handler, 1982). They usually are caused by blunt trauma to the cheek bone. Deformity of the zygoma can be detected by looking at both cheeks from the top of the patient's head as one is palpating to determine the presence and degree of depression (Figure 11B-1). A "step-off" deformity can be palpated at any one of three attachments (maxilla, frontal bone, temporal bone). All three attachments should always be palpated if the physician suspects a zygomatic fracture. The degree of displacement can be determined best with the use of a Water's view. The maxillary sinus on the affected side is opacified with blood when the orbital floor has been fractured.

Complications include restriction and entrapment of extraocular muscles. Fractures involving the attachment to the maxilla can result in hyperesthesia of the infraorbital branch to the facial nerve.

Immediate examination and treatment of these injuries should include a thorough examination of the affected eye and all eye movements (ophthalmologic consultation may be necessary if extraocular movements are restricted), and prophylactic antibiotics. Exploration of the fracture is necessary in the presence of cosmetic deformity of the malar eminence >1 cm, enophthalmas, or restricted ocular mobility.

If only the zygomatic arch is fractured at midpoint, it is usually inward and can impinge upon mandibular function, specifically jaw opening (trismus). In addition to the Water's view, the submental-vertex view (see Chapter 17, Figure 17-11) is helpful. Reduction by a maxillofacial surgeon may be necessary.

**Orbital Blowout Fracture.** Direct trauma to the eye can transmit a force that fractures the bony orbit. The fracture usually occurs in the orbital floor or, less commonly, the medial wall. Enophthalmos, diplopia, and extraoccular muscle restriction are common findings. Sports where this injury is likely to be seen include racket sports, handball, and baseball. For further information, see this chapter, section entitled Eye.

**LeFort Fractures.** High velocity impact to the mid-face can cause fractures of the maxilla that result in varying degrees of deformity. LeFort fractures I-III are gradations of severity based upon the pathological mobility of the maxilla. Malaocclusion, massive tissue edema, intraoral bleeding (causing respiratory distress), and CSF rhinorrhea are common findings in this rare injury. Fortunately, these injuries are uncommon in sports since the force needed to generate them is rarely found in competitive situations.

**Sinus Fractures.** Fractures of facial bones can be associated with extension into paranasal sinuses. Specifically, a maxillary sinus fracture may occur where there is a zygomatic arch or blowout fracture. Fractures of the maxillary sinus are best seen on Water's view or lateral views of the face. Sinus opacification secondary to filling of blood will be the major finding (refer to Chapter 17, Figure 17-10). Air sometimes can be seen in the soft tissues of the cheek or orbit in these fractures. Treatment includes antibiotics to prevent infection in the blood filled sinus and close observation for signs of further swelling that could indicate development of a facial abcess. Athletes normally can resume activities within a week. Long-term complications rarely include chronic sinusitis or osteomylitis of the maxilla.

Frontal sinus fracture secondary to forehead trauma can present significant problems. There will be pain and swelling of the forehead and the depression normally seen with such fractures may be masked by immediate post-injury swelling. Epistaxis as well as CSF rhinorrhea (secondary to disruption of the cribiform plate) frequently accompany such fractures. A fracture to the posterior wall of the frontal sinus should be treated as a compound skull fracture since there is communication between the sinus and anterior cranial fossa. Treatment includes hospitalization and prophylactic antibiotics. Close observation for developing meningitis should be maintained.

Ethmoid sinuses sometimes can be involved, not as a result of direct trauma, but by forces transmitted through exposed structures such as the orbit and nasal bones. Presenting signs include swelling and palpable crepitus along the medial orbit. Treatment includes antibiotics, observation for infection, and restricted nose blowing for 5-7 days. Sports participation should be restricted 7-10 days.

**Mandibular Fractures**

Mandibular fractures account for approximately 10% of maxillofacial fractures seen in sports (Schultz, 1977). Biomechanically, the mandible becomes involved when the athlete falls and strikes it against a hard playing surface, or when contact is made with another player or piece of equipment.

Most of these fractures extend through the intraoral mucosa and cause bleeding from the mouth. There is malocclusion of bite and abnormal mobility of the mandible. Drooling, caused by the athlete's inability to move his mandible without pain, can be present. Palpation shows irregularity in both the open and closed position of the jaw. The most frequently fractured parts of the mandible are shown in Figure 11B-3.

Because of the semicircular structure of the mandible, fractures often occur at two sites (Fig-

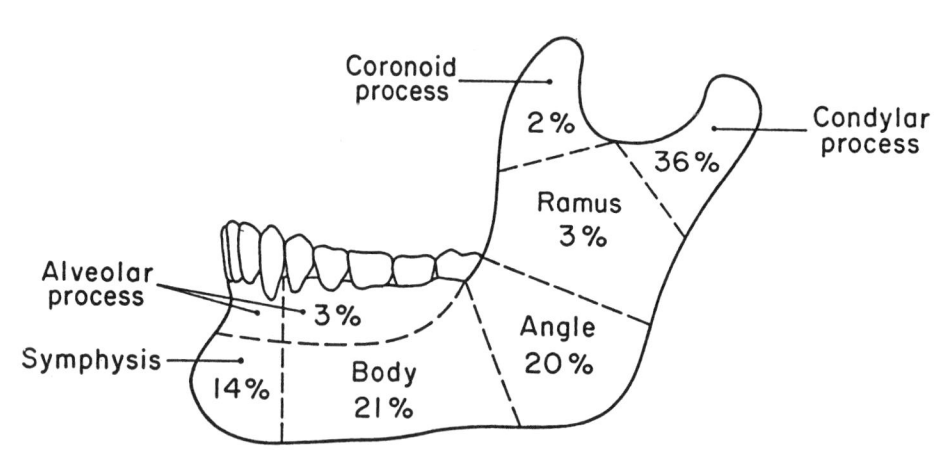

**Fig. 11B-3.** Regions of the Mandible with Relative Incidence of Fractures

ure 11B-4). It is important to look for a second fracture site after the initial fracture has been identified. Treatment includes immobilization of the jaw with a Barton or barrel bandage and radiographic films. Mandibular trauma can transmit significant forces that may involve the external auditory canal so that a careful examination will include the ears.

If no compression exists in the airway, treatment consists of a liquid and then soft diet for six weeks until jaw can be moved without pain, prophylactic antibiotics if the oral mucosa or facial skin is broken, and reduction and immobilization of fracture fragments for six weeks. If there is a malocclusion, surgical referral is indicated.

**Mandibular Dislocation.** Biomechanically, if the lower jaw is suddenly depressed during sports activity, dislocation of the mandible can occur. The mandibular condyle simply moves anterior to the temporal mandibular joint. The chin deviates to the side opposite the dislocation and the patient is unable to close his/her mouth (open-bite deformity). Reduction of the dislocation should occur as soon as possible. The thumbs are placed supporting each side of the mandible as the hands pull in a downward and backward fashion.

## Prevention

Today's athletes are wearing better protective equipment and this has had a significant impact on the prevention of facial injuries. Many factors influence the occurence of facial injuries including the attitude, experience, and competence of coaches, players, and officials (see Chapter 7). In addition, however, the player's personal equipment, the playing surface, court, or field, and structures on or nearby the playing surface must be considered. The prevention of facial injuries means a different set of circumstances in each sport.

The football face mask provides varying degrees of protection. The full cage face mask linemen wear protects them from most injuries including finger-induced facial lacerations. The half face mask used by backs and receivers will not prevent fractures of the cheek or nose or lacerations of the upper portion of the face. The mouthguard protects against facial injuries by acting as a cushion against blows to the lower jaw.

One form of protection in baseball and softball is the catcher's face mask. However, the mask does not protect against possible injury to the throat (larynx and trachea). Various sport governing bodies recently have begun recommending or requiring the use of throat guards by catchers and hockey goalies to remedy this situation.

Hockey has adopted the concept of full facial protection in recent years. Clear plastic masks, as well as cage-type helmets and face masks have signficantly reduced the incidence of facial injuries in non-goalie hockey players. Before this rule change, approximately 60% of all facial injuries in hockey resulted from contact with the stick in non-goalie players (Wilson, 1977).

The hockey goalie remains at significant risk for facial and throat injuries. Most hockey goalies now use a helmet with a wire face mask or a form-fitting mask to keep the puck from making contact with facial bones. A throat protector that hangs below the face mask is sporadically used at present.

Racket sports (squash, handball, paddleball, racket ball, tennis, and variations) pose the most significant risk of eye injury for the recreational athlete. Lightweight eye guards have been developed to prevent or cushion a racket blow, or prevent a ball from entering the orbit. Recreational athletes who are involved in these sports should be encouraged to wear some type of guard specifically protecting the eye. Further information about protective equipment in sports can be found in Chapter 7. A summary of required protective equipment in college sports can be found in Table 7-5.

## SECTION C.
## NECK

The neck is not injured as often as some joints but neck injuries can be catastrophic and result in

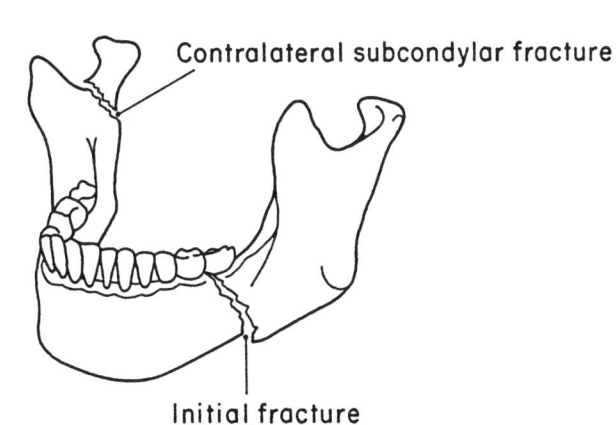

**Fig. 11B-4.** Mandibular Injuries

permanent paralysis. Neck injuries represent less than 1% of the total injuries seen in a larger sports medicine population (DeHaven, 1986). Water sports and football were the activities most often resulting in catastrophic neck injury in a series of 152 sports related cases in Southern California. Estimates indicate that between 1:7000 and 1:58,000 players sustain a severe cervical spine injury at the high school level (Fourie, 1991). Ice hockey, rugby, wrestling, gymnastics, and competitive swimming also expose athletes to significant cervical spine injuries. The frequency of these injuries appears to be inversely proportionate to their severity.

Until recently there were almost no comprehensive guidelines that set appropriate criteria for a safe return to contact sports after an injury to the cervical spine. The most recent guidelines have been outlined by Torg and Glasgow (1991). In this section, we will present brief descriptions of catastrophic neck injuries, including the mechanism of injury, role of equipment, impact of rule changes, and the possibility of injury prevention in various sports.

## Epidemiology

### Football

The development of better protective helmets, including the addition of the facemask, led to a decrease in serious facial and intracranial injuries. This false security, however, led to "spearing" (the act of punishing an opponent by ramming him with the top of the helmet) and to the practice of making initial tackling contact with the crown of the helmet. That led directly to an increase in serious neck injuries. The most common mode of injury is when a defensive back makes a tackle with the crown of his helmet as the initial point of contact. Rule changes were made in 1976 outlawing "spearing," and there was a change in the method of teaching tackling technique. This decreased the injury rate in the years following (see Table 11C-1) (Torg, Vegso, et. al., 1990).

### Rugby

Serious cervical injuries result from hyperflexion sustained during the collapse of the scrum, the tackle, rucks, or mauls. For details on the common mechanisms of injury and recommendations for prevention, see the article by Scher (1987).

### Ice Hockey

Serious cervical injuries were not reported before 1966 but, since 1976, there has been a dramatic increase (see Table 11C-2). All injuries involved axial loading, and fracture dislocation of $C_5$-$C_6$ was the most common site of injury. Of the first 42 cervical spine injuries, 17 athletes were rendered quadriplegic and 10 had an incomplete paralysis. The majority (37) of the 42 were wearing helmets with a facemask at the time of injury. The most common mechanism of injury was a push

Table 11C-1. Serious Cervical Spine Injuries in Football (Torg and Vegso, 1987)

|  | 1959-63 | 1971-75 | '76* | '77 | '78 | '79 | '80 | '81 | '82 | '83 | '84 |
|---|---|---|---|---|---|---|---|---|---|---|---|
| C-Spine Fracture, Dislocation, Subluxation | 56 (1.36) | 259 (4.14) | 110 | 96 | 51 | 51 | 62 | 57 | 57 | 69 | 42 |
| Permanent Guard | 30 (.73) | 99 (1.58) | 34 | 18 | 16 | 3 | 16 | 11 | 10 | 11 | 5 |

( ) = rate per 100,000 participants
* = rate change penalizing spearing 1976

Table 11C-2. Serious Cervical Spine Injuries in Hockey (Tator, 1987)

|  | 1966 | 1975 | 1976-79 | 1980 | 1981 | 1982 | 1983 | 1984 |
|---|---|---|---|---|---|---|---|---|
| Cervical spine dislocation, fracture with and without spinal cord injury | 1 | 1 | 10 | 7 | 12 | 14 | 16 | 15 |

or check from behind so that the player struck the boards with the crown of his helmet (Tator, 1987).

### Wrestling

In reviewing wrestling injuries from 1976-84, Wroble and Albright (1986) found 12% of injuries involved the neck. Sprains/strain and brachial plexus injuries were by far the most common (87% of the total). This study showed that a wrestler had a 20% chance of neck injury in a given year if he had no prior neck injury, compared with 50% chance of reinjury with a history of previous injury. Similar statistics seem to exist for other sports. No single mechanism for catastrophic injury has been established. The most likely mechanism in wrestling is throwing an opponent to the mat on the crown of the head from the fireman's carry position (Wroble & Albright, 1986).

### Water Sports

Diving into shallow water (axial compression) is the most common mechanism of neck injury in water sports. Alcohol intake is often a factor. Specific preventive measures include: 1) do not dive into water that is shallower than twice your height; 2) do not dive into unfamiliar water; 3) do not assume that the water is deep enough because even familiar swimming holes change levels; 4) do not dive near dredging or construction work; 5) do not dive until the area is clear of other swimmers; 6) do not drink and dive, and 7) do not dive into the ocean surf or from lakefront beaches (Torg, 1985; Torg, 1990).

### Gymnastics

Catastrophic neck injuries have occurred in both novice and experienced gymnasts while using the trampoline and during dismounts. Although controversial, it seems appropriate to ban trampoline use in recreational, educational, or competitive gymnastics.

Methods that may aid in the prevention of catastrophic neck injuries are presented in Table 11C-3.

### Anatomy

The cervical spine has two main functions: supporting the head and soft tissue structures while allowing a wide range of motion, and protecting the spinal cord and cervical nerve roots.

Table 11C-3. Prevention of Catastrophic Neck Injuries in Athletics

*Coaches/Players*
1. Awareness of the possibility of injury and avoidance of axial loading.
2. Year round neck conditioning program.
3. Properly fitted equipment.
4. Coaches teaching proper tackling techniques.

*Sport Leagues*
1. Enforcement of current rules.
2. Introduction of new rules as needed.
3. Avoid small rinks (hockey).

*Sportsmedicine Staff*
1. Promote reporting system for injuries.
2. Research into mechanism of injury.

The first two cervical vertebrae have a unique structure designed to allow both rotational and flexion/extension movements. The anatomy of the cervical vertebra, discs, nerve roots, significant ligaments, and muscles is reviewed in Figure 11C-1. The brachial plexus anatomy and common injuries to this structure are discussed in Chapter 12-A.

### History and Physical Exam

The proper diagnosis and management of neck injuries calls for knowledge of the mechanism of injury and appropriate questioning and physical exam skills. The common mechanism of serious injury that involves axial loading has been discussed in the section on epidemiology.

When dealing with a potentially serious cervical injury such as a fracture or dislocation, with or without spinal cord involvement, every precaution should be taken to prevent further injury during the initial evaluation and transportation of the athlete. If the athlete is unconscious, assume a serious neck injury has occurred (Table 11C-4). If not, proceed with appropriate questioning and perform the examination outlined in Table 11C-5. A more complete evaluation can be completed on the sideline, in the training room or clinic (Table 11C-6).

### Neck Strengthening Program

All athletes competing in high risk sports should be involved in a year-round neck strengthening program. However, neck exercises should not

Fig. 11C-1. Typical Cervical Vertebra C-C₇

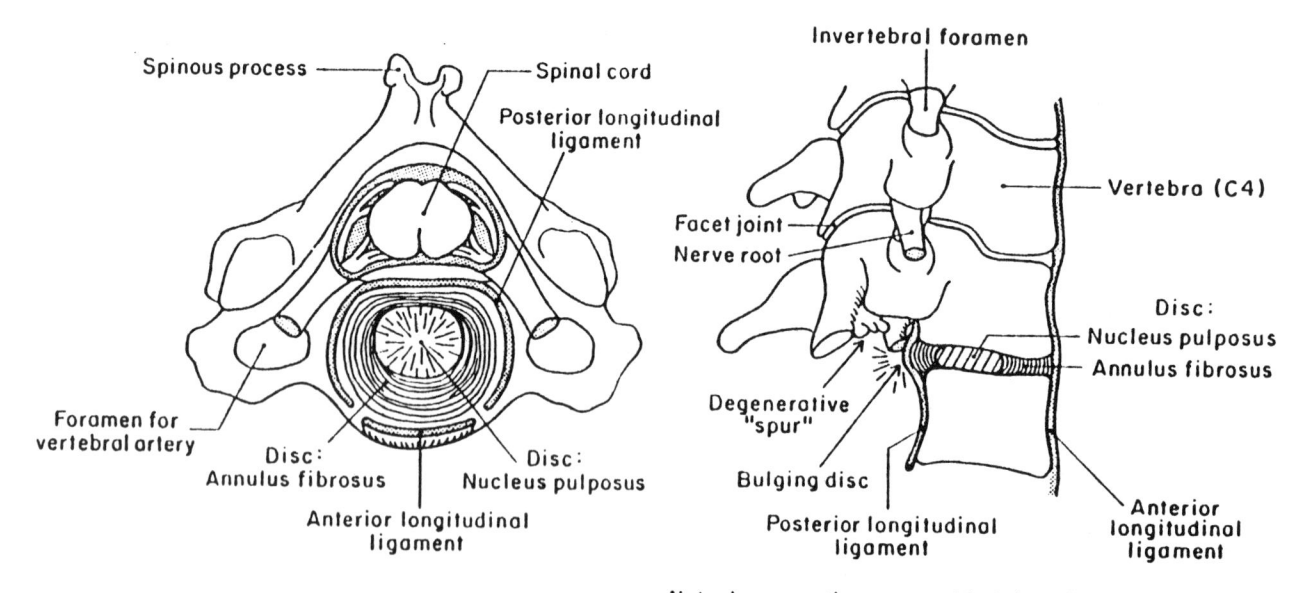

Note degenerative spur and bulging disc as potential sources of nerve root impingement.

Table 11C-4. Assessment of the Unconscious Athlete

1. Evaluate airway and, if impaired, stabilize the head and neck and establish the airway by removing the face mask without removing the helmet.
2. Check pulses and, if absent, begin CPR. Check blood pressure and pupillary reflexes.
3. Athlete should be removed from field on a spine board using appropriate transportation techniques that stabilize the head and neck. Appropriate radiographs must then be taken.

Table 11C-5. Assessment of the Conscious Athlete

1. Determine the mechanism of injury.
2. Ask about neck pain; tingling, burning or numbness going down the arms or legs; or problems moving the arms or legs.
3. Physical exam should include:
    a. A-B-C (Basic CPR evaluation)
    b. Palpation of c-spine for tenderness
    c. Perform brief neurologic exam of all extremities.
    d. Ask player to perform active range of motion of cervical spine if steps (a-c) are negative
4. If above history and physical are negative, the player can be allowed to walk off the field of play to complete a more detailed exam.
5. If any parts of the history and physical exam are positive, the player should not be allowed to move until the exam is completed. Transport the athlete using appropriate precautions to stabilize head and neck.

Table 11C-6. Assessment of the Cervical Spine in Clinic or Training Room

1. Ask about neck pain; radiation, exacerbating factors.
2. Ask about tingling, numbness or weakness of the extremities.
3. Palpate directly over c-spine, then along paracervical musculature.
4. Ask athlete to perform active range of motion including flexion, extension, lateral flexion and rotation. Repeat above against resistance. Brachial plexus symptoms may be elicited by either extreme passive lateral flexion to contralateral side or by active lateral flexion against resistance to ipsilateral side.
5. Spurling's test should be performed by placing the chin in the supraclavicular fossa and applying axial compression. A positive test results when pain radiates to the shoulder or arm, suggestive of nerve root impingement. Varying degrees of neck extension or flexion, while maintaining the chin in the supraclavicular fossa and applying axial compression, will increase the true positive result. In the presence of radicular pain, a distraction test is performed with the patient in the supine position and the examiner placing his hands on the occipital region and under the mandible. If the pain is diminished or relieved by applying traction, the test is positive and reinforces the probability of nerve root impingement.

be performed before practice, a game, or a match to avoid excessive muscle fatigue that may lead to injury.

Isotonic exercises with variable resistance in all directions (flexion, extension, lateral flexion) of motion are necessary. Optimal results can be achieved by using a buddy system with constant communication. General instructions include:

- Begin each session with the exerciser relaxed and the spotter gently applying resistance to prestretch the muscles involved.
- Allow the exerciser to warm up the neck muscles by not applying maximum resistance for the first few repetitions.
- Then perform 10 repetitions against near-maximal resistance. Each repetition should be performed for 6-8 seconds, with 3-4 seconds for the concentric contraction through the full ROM, a 1 second hold, and then a 3-4 second eccentric contraction (lengthening) while returning to the starting position. At the start of the eccentric phase, the spotter should increase resistance slightly because more weight can be handled in the eccentric phase. As the exerciser approaches the starting position, resistance must be gradually decreased.

## Common Cervical Spine Injuries

In an effort to characterize spine injuries, Bailes has defined the following classifications: Type I injury which involves the spinal cord, Type II injury involving cord type symptoms, and Type III injury involving radiographic abnormalities without neurological signs or symptoms.

Type I injuries damage the spinal cord. Symptoms may resolve or be minor in nature but a spinal cord injury may be demonstrated by MRI. Once the spinal cord injury is radiographically demonstrated, the athlete should not be allowed to return to contact sports.

Type II injuries cause neurologic symptoms and findings referable to the spinal cord. These patients are commonly referred to as having cord neuropraxia or brachialplexis neuropraxia. In the absence of a neurologic deficit or a congenital cervical spine abnormality, the athlete may return to full participation in contact sports. An athlete with repeated injuries or multiple episodes of spinal cord symptoms has a higher risk of catastrophic injury, and discontinuation of further participation should be considered (Torg, 1991).

Type III injuries are patients with radiographic abnormalities. Those with unstable fractures or fracture dislocations requiring stabilization are restricted from further participation. Bony injuries that are stable on flexion/extension and stable under stress may be candidates for further participation. Little experimental or clinical data exists to assess the stability of a healed fracture or ligamentous injury of the cervical spine when it undergoes extreme stress (Bailes). In the absence of clinical data, further sports participation is not indicated unless the injury was healed or an isolated minor vertebral body, lamina, or spinous process fracture (Torg, 1991).

MRI evidence of cord contusion (swelling) or of spinal motion on dynamic radiographs (implying ligamentous injury) require neurosurgical consultation and surgery. They preclude further participation in contact sports (Torg, 1991). The criteria for unstable cervical spine conditions can be found in the Torg (1991) reference.

### Contusion

A contusion is caused by direct trauma to the cervical spine. It may result in a muscular contusion, swelling, fracture of spinous process, injury to the spinal accessory nerve, or injury to the long thoracic nerve.

The mechanism of injury for the direct trauma could include a "karate chop" with the hand, an errant elbow while rebounding, a knee during a wrestling match, or a blow from a recklessly handled hockey stick or racquet. The athlete may complain of localized neck pain (may be severe) and have restricted range of motion and weakness. Physical findings may include localized tenderness, swelling, ecchymosis, restricted range of motion, pain with forward flexion (fractured spinous process), or weakness on shoulder deviation (injury to spinal accessory nerve), winging of scapula (injury to long thoracic nerve).

Treatment for these conditions includes:

- Muscle contusion — ice, protection, stretching, and strengthening.
- Fracture — x-ray identification followed by orthopedic referral.
- Injury to the spinal accessory nerve — heat, superficial massage. Recovery occurs in days to weeks.
- Injury to long thoracic nerve — consider re-

striction of activity for the first 2-3 weeks. The prognosis is variable; orthopedic referral may be necessary.

**Laryngeal Injury Compromising the Airway**

See Chapter 11-H.

**First and Second Degree Sprains and Strains**

First and second degree cervical sprains (ligament) and strains (muscle-tendon) are the most common neck injuries. Complete third degree ruptures are rare. Injury occcurs with and without brachial plexus involvement.

A strain results when a force exceeds the strength of the muscles involved. The most common muscles involved are the trapezius, sternocleidomastoid, erector spinae, scalenus, levator scapulae, and the rhomboids. Hyperextension, hyperflexion, rotation, and ipsilateral side-bending are common mechanisms of injury.

A sprain can result from a hyperextension injury, with the sprain occuring to the ligaments and capsule of the facet joints on the compressed side of the neck, or with hyperflexion injury involving the interspinous/ supraspinous ligaments.

**Common Sports.** Wrestling, hockey, football.

**Physical Complaints.** Neck pain and limited range of motion. The appearance of symptoms may be delayed in mild to moderate strains, but even from the outset there will be weakness when resistance is applied against the movement of that muscle. The degree of pain and limitation of range of motion at 24-48 hours seems to be a reliable indication of the severity of injury.

**Physical Exam.** Point tenderness to palpation along the involved muscle or ligament, limited range of motion, negative neurological findings except for pain and negative axial compression. Pain often is produced by movement toward the contralateral direction or when the muscle or ligament is stretched. Pain upon movement toward the ipsilateral direction occurs with active contraction against resistance of the strained muscle.

**X-rays.** Torg (1987) suggests getting a lateral view in flexion and extension to demonstrate a cervical fracture or instability in an athlete who has less than a complete pain-free range of motion or persistent paresthesia or weakness. MRI should be performed to rule out cervical cord contusion and ligamentous instability.

**Treatment**

- Brief immobilization with a soft collar as needed
- NSAID or analgesic as needed
- Proprioceptive neuromuscular facilitation (strain)
- Cold (spasm or sprain); heat (strain)
- Isometric exercises as tolerated
- Severe sprain/strain may necessitate hospitalization with halter traction or halo brace.

The risk of reinjury is high if the athlete returns to play too early. When the athlete returns with no symptoms or radiographic changes, there is no apparent increased risk of reinjury. Consult Torg (1991) reference for criteria to use to return the athlete to participation.

**Cervical Vertebra Subluxation Without Fracture**

**Mechanism of Injury.** Axial compression or flexion injuries.

**Presenting Complaint.** Neck pain or limited range of motion; often associated with a sprain/strain.

**Physical Findings.** Localized tenderness, limited range of motion, no neurologic deficit, and axial compression test is negative.

**X-ray.** Flexion-extension views demonstrate instability, anterior intervertebral disc space narrowing, anterior angulation, and displacement of the vertebral body. MRI may show cervical spine motion on dynamic testing.

**Treatment.** Soft tissue disruption without fracture will likely cause instability. Anterior subluxation greater than 20% of the vertebral body is due to a disruption of the posterior longitudinal ligament and a posterior cervical fusion is recommended.

**Brachial Plexus Syndrome**

See Chapter 12-A.

**Brachial Plexus vs Nerve Root Impingement**

*Mechanism of Injury*

**Brachial Plexus.** May involve a stretch injury as in football player making a tackle with the shoulder and having his neck drawn to the contralateral side, or a compression injury as in a takedown by a wrestler whose neck is moving in lateral flexion on toward the ipsilateral side.

**Nerve Root Impingement.** Axial loading may result in acute cervical disc bulging or herniation (rare) or chronic axial loading and hyperflexion; hyperextension stress may cause degenerative changes such as joint space narrowing or osteophyte formation.

### Presenting Complaint

**Brachial Plexus.** Transient numbness, tingling, or weakness of entire upper extremity. Symptoms of upper trunk ($C_5$-$C_6$) may persist for days to weeks.

**Nerve Root Impingement.** Numbness, tingling, and weakness of specific nerve roots rather than entire extremity.

**Physical Findings Brachial Plexus.** Reproducible symptoms with contralateral stretching or ipsilateral compression, paresthesis, reflex changes; weakness of upper trunk ($C_5$-$C_6$) may persist, and axial compression testing is negative.

**Nerve Root Impingement.** Paresthesia, reflex changes, or weakness confined to a single dermatome; axial compression and distraction tests are positive (see Table 11C-7a-b).

**X-ray.** Rule out degenerative changes or narrowing of nerve root outlet. MRI to rule out more significant injury.

### Treatment

### Brachial Plexus

- Restrict activity until full range of motion against resistance occurs
- NSAID or oral corticosteroids
- Monitor neurological changes on a weekly basis

Table 11C-7(a). **Summary of Neurological Evaluation of Cervical Nerves by Nerve Root**

| Disc | Root | Reflex | Muscles | Sensation |
|---|---|---|---|---|
| C4-C5 | C5 | Biceps Reflex | Deltoid Biceps | Lateral Arm<br>Axillary Nerve |
| C5-C6 | C6 | Brachioradialis Reflex | Wrist Extension Biceps | Lateral Forearm<br>Musculocutaneous Nerve |
| C6-C7 | C7 | Triceps Reflex | Wrist Flexors Triceps | Middle Finger<br>Median Nerve |
| C7-T1 | C8 | — | Hand Intrinsics | Medial Forearm<br>Med. Ant. Brach.<br>Cutaneous Nerve |
| T1-T2 | T1 | — | Hand Intrinsics | Medial Arm<br>Med. Brach.<br>Cutaneous Nerve |

Table 11C-7(b). **Summary of Neurological Evaluation of Cervical Nerves by Peripheral Nerve**

| Nerve | Motor Test | Sensation Test |
|---|---|---|
| Radial Nerve | Wrist Extension | Dorsal web space between thumb and index finger |
| Ulnar Nerve | Adduction, Abduction of fingers (Interosseous muscles) | Distal ulnar aspect-little finger |
| Median Nerve | Thumb pinch | Distal radial aspect-index finger |
| Axillary Nerve | Abduction | Lateral Arm-Deltoid patch on upper arm |
| Musculocutaneous Nerve | Elbow Flexion | Lateral Forearm |

- Consider EMG if neurological deficit continues longer than three weeks

### Nerve Root Impingement

- Restrict activity
- Refer to neurosurgeon for possible surgical intervention

### Cervical Spinal Cord Neurapraxia With Transient Quadriplegia

**Incidence.** 6/10,000 (Torg and Pavlov, 1987)

**Mechanism of Injury.** Forced hyperextension, hyperflexion, or axial loading of cervical spine in a susceptible patient with a decreased A-P diameter of the cervical cord (cervical stenosis). This results in mechanical compression of the cord which causes transient but completely reversible motor or sensory changes. The presence of developmental narrowing of the cervical spine (canal/body ratio 0.8 or less) does not predispose the athlete to permanent neurologic injury (Torg, 1991).

**Clinical Presentation.** The athlete may experience burning pain, numbness, tingling or loss of sensation, weakness, or complete paralysis. Episodes are transient and usually last 10-15 minutes, and rarely up to 36-48 hours. There is no neck pain at the time of injury. After resolution, there is full, pain-free range of motion and normal motor-sensory function. X-rays and MRI of the cervical spine are negative.

**Recommendations.** There is no apparent risk of permanent spinal cord injury. The risk of recurrence among football players with cervical stenosis who returned to play was 50%. Those with C-spine instability or acute or chronic degenerative changes in the spine should not be allowed to participate in contact sports. Athletes who have cervical stenosis alone should be evaluated on an individual basis. Patients with a ratio of 0.8 or less who experience either motor or sensory symptoms have a relative contraindication for return to contact sports.

Absolute contraindications to continued participation apply to the following situations after a documented episode of neuropraxia (Torg, 1991):

- Ligamentous instability
- Intervertebral disc disease
- Degenerative changes
- MRI evidence of defects or swelling
- Positive neurologic findings lasting > 36 hours
- More than one occurrence

### Cervical Spine Fracture, Dislocation or Fracture/Dislocation

**Mechanism of Injury.** Axial compression in flexion or extension of the spine.

**Presenting Complaint.** Neck pain, tingling, weakness or numbness of the extremities.

**Physical Findings.** C-spine tenderness with or without neurologic deficits. Do not perform range of motion if a severe injury is possible.

**Treatment.** Remove the athlete from the playing area using a spine board and correct technique to prevent futher injury until necessary x-rays can be taken (see History and Physical Exam section).

A detailed discussion of possible cervical spine fractures, dislocations, and fracture/dislocations, and cervical stenosis and its management is beyond the scope of this chapter. When faced with these injuries, immediate referral to a neurosurgeon or orthopedic surgeon is appropriate. Proper transportation of the athlete with a cervical spine injury is described in Chapter 9 and in the Fouire (1991) article.

## SECTION D. EYE INJURIES AND ILLNESSES

### Perspective

Sports injuries to the eye are a major source of blindness or visual impairment. Proper eye protection, formulation of regulations to limit dangerous exposure during athletic activity, and education in safe techniques could prevent as many as 150,000 eye injuries a year, and is a major goal of sports-eye care (LaForge, 1990). The National Society for the Prevention of Blindness estimates that more than 111,000 school age children suffer sports related eye injuries each year. That is in addition to approximately 100,000 eye injuries in older athletes. About 25% of persons with eye injuries develop serious complications and some lose their vision completely (Rutherford, 1981; Pine, 1991). Fortunately, 90% of all sports injuries are preventable with proper eye safety measures and protective eyewear (Pine, 1991).

The role of eye protection in sports and the appropriate management of sports injuries needs to be understood better by the sports physician. Sports eye care involves more than on-the-field diagnosis and treatment of eye injuries. The physician who cares for either recreational or competitive athletes must be able to anticipate vision hazards and provide special help for athletes who wear contact lenses or glasses. The physician must also recognize when referral to an ophthalmologist is required.

## Anatomy

The physician must understand the anatomical features of the eye to properly diagnose and manage common problems in sports. The orbit forms a complete bony socket made up of five or six different bones that is open only anteriorly and posteriorly (Figure 11D-1). It is designed to protect the eye in the recess formed by the superior orbital ridge above, the infraorbital margins below, the malar bone on the temporal side, and the nasal bone on the medial side.

## Epidemiology of Eye Injuries in Sports

Studies of eye injuries and eye protection are mostly about ice hockey and the racket sports. Several studies of ice hockey injuries have demonstrated significant reductions (greater than 95%) in eye injuries when face masks are used (Caprillo, 1977; Marton, Wilson & McKeag, 1987; Vinger, 1978). Overall, the incidence of eye injuries during athletic activity is rising steadily as more Americans engage in sports. Almost 20% of ocular trauma is sports-related and nearly 50% of the injuries occur in children under the age of 15 years; 65% occur in individuals under the age of 31 years. More ocular injury takes place in recreational sites than in the work place (Pine, 1991).

In sports where eye protection is not widespread (baseball, basketball, and football), the number of eye injuries continues to rise. This unfortunate fact contrasts sharply with hockey where the widespread use of facemasks has prevented an estimated 70,000 eye and face injuries in recent years. Eye injuries in hockey were prevalent until the mandatory requirements for facial protection (especially among younger players) by hockey associations in the United States and Canada (Pashbyt, 1979). It also helped that there were improvements in face protection design and rule changes such as the prohibition of high sticking.

Baseball and basketball are the sports with the highest number of eye injuries in the high school and college age group. The racket sports have the

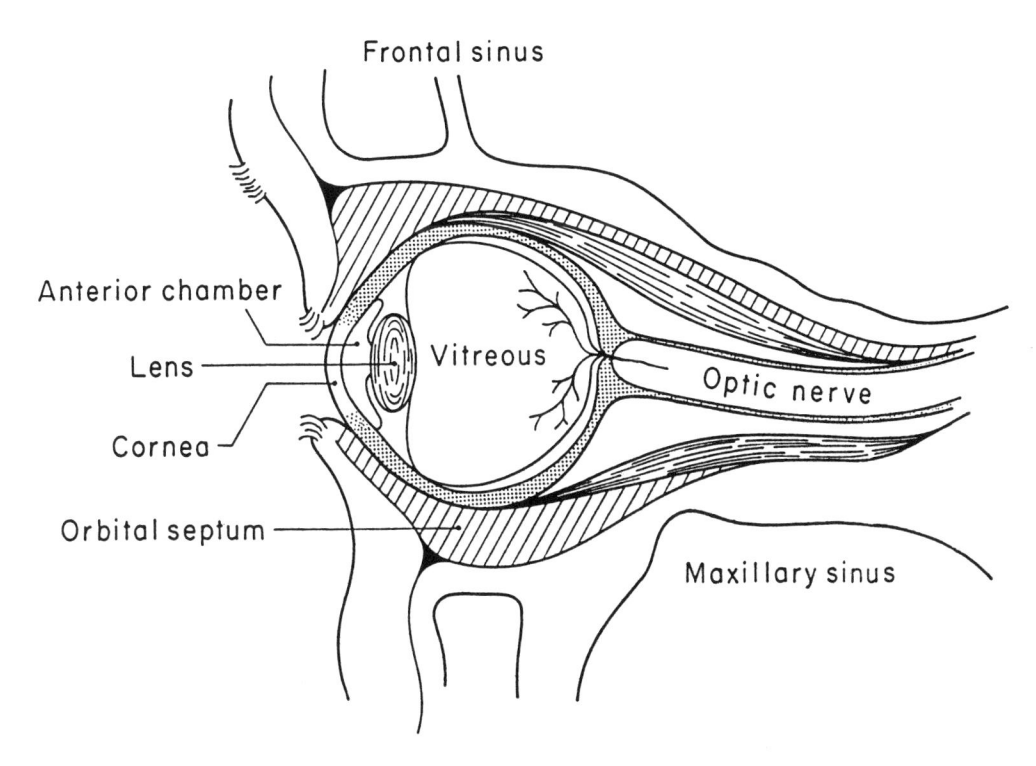

**Fig. 11D-1.** Orbital Anatomy

highest number of ocular injuries in the 25-60 year old age group. The six sport activities where ocular injuries are most common (in decreasing order) are: baseball, basketball, tennis, football, biking, and soccer. Sports that involve a ball, stick, collisions, or contact pose significant risks for serious eye injury according to research data.

Participation in racket sports has increased rapidly and much of it is informal so that it has been difficult to determine the extent to which eye protection is used. We do know that eye protection is not a universal practice so that the incidence of injury continues to rise, and the nature of racket sports increases the risk.

## Etiology

The eye and its surrounding structures are vulnerable to direct blows from objects less than or equal to 4 inches in diameter. With anything larger, the orbital rim absorbs much of the energy so that injury to the eyeball itself is less likely. Approximately 200 g's of force is required to cause an orbital rim fracture.

Injury to the eye may occur from:

- sharp objects — darts.
- small objects — fingers, BBs, hockey sticks, golf balls.
- large objects greater than 5 cm — softball and baseball. The force field of the object acts as a piston, pushing the eye tissue posteriorly and blowing out the floor of the orbit.
- contact with other players or fixed structures around the playing area, or from foreign objects thrown by spectators.

The facial structures on the side of the head offer much less protection to blows coming from the side, especially if the globe protrudes past the surrounding bone. The ideal protective device would offer protection from blows coming both from the front and the side by transferring the energy of a blow to the frontal bones. The ultimate goal of protection is to safeguard the eye without transferring the energy to the brain.

Serious injuries occurring from blows to the eye that can lead to permanent loss of vision include hyphemas, corneal lacerations, retinal detachments, macular scarring, and secondary hemorrhages. Glaucoma and cataracts are two complications of eye injuries that develop much later and which also may lead to permanent vision loss.

## Examination

The physician's task in examining an injured eye is to rule out severe intraocular trauma. Find out how the injury occurred before evaluating the injury. Check the patient history for prior injury or diminished visual acuity. On examination, establish the state of visual acuity immediately, then systematically examine the eye and its surrounding structures (see Table 11D-1).

All contusions or blows to the face that produce eye findings also may cause a concussion. The athlete should be carefully monitored for signs of concussion and treated appropriately. Separate the eyelids after instilling an anesthetic solution as necessary. Check the extra ocular movements (EOMs) and peripheral vision and completely view the conjunctiva and sclera. Restriction of EOM may be secondary to a blowout fracture of the orbit or neuromuscular damage. If it is found, the patient should be referred to an ophthalmologist. Examine the lid for lacerations and foreign bodies and check the conjunctiva and anterior chamber for clarity; also look at pupil size, reaction and shape.

Finally, thoroughly evaluate the lens and retina, using a slit-lamp microscope, if available. X-rays, including tomograms of the facial bones, should be taken to rule out fracture. Routine x-rays, however, often do not show orbital blow-out fractures. If there is any doubt about the function of the eye or seriousness of the injury, referral is indicated.

Serious eye trauma does not necessarily result in pain or visual disturbance at the time of injury. It is important that the examiner is familiar

---

**Table 11D-1. Ophthalmic Examination**

Thorough evaluation of sport-related eye injuries involves the following areas:
1. Visual Acuity
2. External lids, conjunctiva
3. Pupils
4. EOM's
5. Confrontation fields
6. Anterior segment
7. Fundus

*Equipment Needed:*
Acuity chart
Penlight or flashlight
Proparacaine
Fluorescein strips
Ophthalmoscope

with the signs and symptoms of serious trauma. The following symptoms should raise the suspicion that the eye has been seriously injured: blurred vision that does not clear with blinking, loss of all or part of visual field of an eye, steady or deep throbbing pain, or double vision after the injury. Additional signs that require transferring the player to a facility where a more detailed evaluation and treatment are available are listed in Table 11D-2.

## Common Eye Injuries and Illnesses

See Table 11D-3.

### Eyelid Lacerations

Lacerations of the eyebrow are common and require careful repair. Severing of the supraorbital nerve can occur from a contusion over the ridge of the eyebrow and, if present, accurate repair will be required. Eyelid lacerations require accurate closure, especially where they cross skin creases. An irregular scar may result if they are not carefully repaired. Lacerations of the medial canthus may involve the lacrimal system and those must be repaired microscopically with intubation. Evidence of prolapsed fat associated with a lid laceration may indicate a fracture of the orbital roof or involvement of the globe and should be evaluated by an ophthalmologist. Eyelid lacerations resulting in avulsion of tissue can be repaired by saving the avulsed portion prior to repair.

### Orbital Injury

A direct blow to the anterior orbit may produce rapid passage of serum and blood into the

Table 11D-2. Possible Signs of Serious Eye Injuries in Sports

1. Black Eye
2. Red eye
3. A foreign object on the cornea
4. An eye that does not move as completely as the opposite eye
5. One eye protruding compared with the opposite eye
6. Abnormal pupil size or shape compared with the opposite eye
7. A layer of blood between the cornea and iris
8. A cut or penetration of the eyelid or eyeball
9. A darkened subconjunctival mass that may indicate scleral rupture
10. Photophobia or "flashing lights"

Table 11D-3. Common Eye Injuries In Sports

| Problem | Usual Characteristics | Treatment |
| --- | --- | --- |
| Blow-out fracture of orbit | 1. Restricted ability to elevate the eye | 1. Consultation with an ophthalmologist |
| | 2. Hypesthesia-lower lid and cheek-due to damage to infra-orbital nerve | |
| | 3. X-ray-cloudy antrum with tissue herniation into maxillary sinus; laminogram may demonstrate break | |
| Orbital Hemorrhage | 1. Proptosis-forward bulging of eye | 1. Cold compresses |
| | 2. Hematoma | 2. Watch for signs of corneal exposure or retinal vascular compromise |
| Ptosis | 1. Droopy upper eyelid due to trauma of levator palpebral superiorus muscle or its nerve | 1. Consultation with an ophthalmologist |
| Lid Laceration | 1. Lacerations requiring special consideration: Through and through lacerations involving the lid margin | 1. For fear of lid margin notching, unless you are familiar with special techniques, seek ophthalmic consultation |
| | 2. Lacrimal canalicular, ligament, or complete severance of the levator palpebral superiorus | 2. Ophthalmic consultation |
| | 3. All other lacerations | 3. As with all peri-orbital lacerations examine the globe for injury |
| | | 4. The usual surgical repair is with 5-0 or 6-0 suture removed in 3 days |

**Table 11D-3. Common Eye Injuries In Sports (*Continued*)**

| Problem | Usual Characteristics | Treatment |
|---|---|---|
| Laceration or Penetrating Ocular Injury | 1. Seen by inspection<br>2. Anterior chamber shallower or deeper than fellow eye depending on site of entry<br>3. Pupil misshapen if iris is caught in wound | 1. Apply loose binocular eye patches<br>2. May need to sedate<br>3. Warn not to squeeze lids<br>4. Refer to ophthalmologist |
| Foreign Body Under Eyelid | 1. Pain with blinking<br>2. Vertical linear corneal abrasions<br>3. Foreign body noted after lid eversion | 1. Apply topical antibiotic<br>2. Removal of foreign body with moistened cotton swab or spud<br>3. May require 24-48 hour pressure patch if cornea scratched |
| Corneal Foreign Bodies | 1. Superficial, not involving the visual axis | 1. Apply topical anesthetic<br>2. Remove foreign body with moistened cotton swab or corneal spud<br>3. May remove some foreign body or rust ring with a spud 2-3 days post injury after the surrounding cornea softens<br>4. Apply antibiotic and pressure patch |
|  | 1. Deeply embedded corneal foreign body<br>2. Fear of anterior chamber penetration<br>3. Involving visual axis | 1. Ophthalmic consultation |
| Sub-Conjunctival Hemorrhage | 1. Non-painful<br>2. Blood under conjunctiva | 1. Reassurance<br>2. Rule out other ocular injuries<br>3. If recurrent, hematologic or migraine evaluation |
| Chemical Injury | 1. History of chemical contact<br>2. Injection and edema of ocular and periorbital tissues | 1. Copious prolonged irrigation after topical anesthetic<br>2. If opacity of the cornea or blanching of conjunctiva seek ophthalmic consultation |
| Corneal Abrasion | 1. Ocular pain, worse with blinking<br>2. Loss of epithelium demonstrated by fluorescein stain | 1. Apply topical antibiotic<br>2. Pressure patch<br>3. May need systemic analgesics |
| Traumatic Iritis | 1. Photophobia<br>2. Ciliary flush<br>3. Miosis | 1. Cycloplegic drugs<br>2. Topical steroids |
| Traumatic Hyphema | 1. Blood in anterior chamber<br>2. May have other ocular injuries | 1. Bed rest with head elevated 30°<br>2. Sedation<br>3. Binocular dressing-depending on patient<br>4. Ophthalmic consultation |
| Traumatic Cataract | 1. Lens opacity<br>2. May be from penetrating or blunt trauma<br>3. Lens may swell causing glaucoma | 1. Ophthalmic consultation |
| Vitreous Hemorrhage | 1. Decreased vision may be present<br>2. Vitreous hemorrhage seen with ophthalmoscope<br>3. Rule out underlying retinal detachment | 1. Ophthalmic consultation |
| Retinal Detachment | 1. Veils, sparks or curtain-like visual sensations may be noted by patient<br>2. Retina may be wrinkled and ballooned forward into the vitreous | 1. Ophthalmic consultation |

soft tissue of the lid, causing closure of the lid or a "black-eye". A swollen eye should not be dismissed as a minor contusion because the blow may dislocate the lens or produce a hyphema, retinal edema, retinal hemorrhage, vitreous hemorrhage, retinal tear, or retinal detachment. If the lids are swollen shut or the eye is difficult to examine, consult an ophthalmologist and do not force the lids open. The use of ice to reduce swelling is indicated.

Swelling from a black-eye usually is self-limited and ice compresses should help during the first 24-48 hours. Do not use instant cold packs because they may rupture and cause caustic burns to the eye and surrounding structures. Hemorrhage occurs more posteriorly in the orbit and, can produce significant proptosis and ophthalmoplegia (dilated, fixed pupil with paralysis of accommodation). Look for anesthesia above the orbital ridge if the underlying nerves are contused near the facial bone. Subcutaneous or subconjunctival emphysema can result from a sinus fracture, and may lead to chronic osteomyelitis of the facial bones.

### Globe Injury

#### Corneal Abrasion

The cornea is the most exposed part of the eye and its most common injury is an abrasion (Vinger, 1986) (see Figure 11D-1). The patient has significant pain and the sensation of a foreign body in the eye.

**Treatment.** Use an anesthetic solution and examine the cornea with a bright light obliquely. If there is no foreign body, evert the upper lid and look for a foreign body in the tarsal conjunctiva which can be easily removed. Use fluorescein stain on the cornea to document the extent of the abrasion. Treatment includes the use of an antibiotic solution, mydriatic drops, and eye patching for three to four days. Ophthalmological follow-up should be sought if there is no improvement.

A rupture or laceration of the cornea or sclera requires immediate ophthalmological evaluation. When this occurs, patch the eye and have the patient lie down until further evaluation can be done. If visual acuity is less than 20/30, suspect an intraocular foreign body. Never instill ointments where there is a full thickness corneal laceration. Treatment is the same as for a corneal abrasion.

Some patients with corneal abrasions may get a recurrent "erosion syndrome" where the basement membrane of the cornea is repeatedly torn away every several days, causing recurrent abrasion symptoms. Treatment involves the use of eye emollients; occasionally referral to an ophthalmologist is indicated. Full or partial corneal lacerations may result in a "tear-drop" appearance of the iris. There, the eye should be shielded and referral to the ophthalmologist is mandatory.

### Hyphema

Hyphema is a very common ocular injury and results from damage to the small vessels of the ciliary body which hemorrhage into the anterior chamber.

This injury often is associated with other severe intraocular injuries and requires immediate referral and hospitalization. Blunt trauma to the eye usually is followed by inflammation of the iris and ciliary body, producing dilation or constriction of the pupil that may persist for days to weeks. There may be increased tearing, blurred vision, photophobia, and severe eye pain. A fluid level often is visible in the anterior chamber. Immediate treatment requires shielding the eye, bed rest, and evaluation by an ophthalmologist. It may be several days before the retina can be viewed by an ophthalmologist, and the patient must continue bed rest during this period. Typically, there is a 75% chance of a good visual outcome in patients with hyphema. Long-term complications include a rebleed (results in more blood than initial injury), glaucoma, and the development of white cells and protein in the anterior chamber (hypopyon).

### Snow Blindness

Excessive ultraviolet light exposure may produce "snow blindness" or blindness related to water sports such as water skiing. This is prevalent in those who do not wear protective sun glasses or in those contact lens wearers who do not blink frequently. Treatment includes the use of cold compresses and pain medications.

### Intraocular Foreign Bodies

Foreign bodies should be identified and localized as soon as possible. Copper or iron foreign bodies may produce degenerative changes and scarring in the eye. An orbital x-ray may be necessary to localize the foreign body. Prompt referral and removal of the foreign body is necessary. Gentle removal with a topical anesthetic and moistened sterile Q-Tip® with lavage may be attempted.

### Penetrating Eye Injuries

Always refer patients with penetrating wounds of the eye to an ophthalmologist for evaluation and treatment. Proper tetanus prophylaxis should be given.

### Traumatic Cataract

Traumatic cataracts are a common secondary result of a metallic intraocular foreign body hitting the lens. The lens turns white soon after entry of the foreign body due to the lens capsule being torn and allowing aqueous or vitreous humor into the lens. Posterior subcapsular cataracts are common in boxers who have sustained repeated trauma. Symptoms of a traumatic cataract include blurred vision, red eye, opaque lens, and intraocular hemorrhage. Complications include infection, uveitis, retinal detachment, and glaucoma. Traumatic cataracts are treated with the use of antibiotics and corticosteroids, both systemically and locally, to decrease infection and the development of uveitis. Atropine sulfate 2%, two drops T.I.D., should be used to keep the pupil dilated until the injury is seen by an ophthalmologist. The cataract usually is removed after the inflammation decreases. However, if the patient is under the age of 20 years, the lens material often absorbs on its own without surgery. Have all traumatic cataracts evaluated by an ophthalmologist.

### Retinal Detachment

Retinal detachment can occur after a blow to the eye, especially in athletes with a predisposing family history. Detachment is most likely in individuals with retinal degenerative lesions such as myopia. For this reason, some ophthalmologists caution myopic people, especially those with previous retinal detachment, against vigorous athletic activity. Retinal detachment may occur weeks or months after an injury. An ophthalmologist should be consulted for full assessment and appropriate treatment. Retinal edema by itself will resolve without problems unless it is located in the area of the macula.

### Traumatic Optic Neuritis

This usually is a late development of traumatic eye injuries. A normal eye exam except for decreased visual acuity is common. However, a pale optic nerve develops much later. Treatment includes systemic steroids and ophthalmological consultation. Disc edema usually results in some degree of optic nerve atrophy.

### Blow-Out Fracture of the Orbit

Blunt trauma to the orbit may increase intraorbital hydrostatic pressure and fracture the weak bone of the orbital floor. The force of the blow may cause herniation of the orbital contents into the maxillary sinus with entrapment of the inferior rectus or inferior oblique muscle of the eye. An athlete with a blow-out fracture will have severe pain in the eye, periorbital edema and hemorrhage, nausea, limited movement of the eye, and diplopia while attempting to look up or down. The infraorbital rim may feel abnormal on palpation. This is a difficult diagnosis and requires multiple x-ray views, either Waters view or Caldwell view. CT scanning often is required to make the diagnosis. Immediate surgery will be needed if there is a large fracture or severe muscle imbalance. Surgery may be delayed 10-14 days for less serious conditions (Larrison, 1990). The eye should always be shielded and immediately evaluated by an ophthalmologist.

### Conjunctivitis

Dust and dirt from playing surfaces may irritate an athlete's eyes. If the conjunctiva becomes inflamed, the physician should look for a corneal abrasion or conjunctivitis. Conjunctivitis may be caused by bacterial (most common), viral, or trachoma infections. Allergic conjunctivitis and chemical irritations from smog, hairsprays, and deodorants should be considered in the differential diagnosis. Antibiotic drops should be administered only when the diagnosis is known or after slit-lamp examination. Use of ophthalmic steroid solutions should be reserved for chemical or allergic conjunctivitis.

All cases of conjunctivitis should be carefully examined and followed by the team physician or ophthalmologist. Chronic infection of the conjunctiva or cornea, and irritation from chemicals such as chlorine, may lead to chronic keratitis of the cornea and should be evaluated by an ophthalmologist. Edematous conjunctiva which protrude through the closed lid can be treated with Saran® wrap that covers the eye around the orbital rib and is taped in place. This gives an improvement in moisture and may take the place of ointments (Strahlman, 1988).

## Evaluation of Sports Vision

The athlete's visual needs should be properly evaluated before the beginning of the season. A complete examination includes evaluation of near and distance acuity, depth perception, spatial and peripheral awareness, stereoptic vision, night vision, and evaluation of astigmatism.

The potential benefits of visual perceptual training on athletic performance recently have been introduced by interested sports medicine professionals (Ball, Irion, & Zacks, 1983). Various testing devices have been introduced at several training centers in the United States. Information is available in numerous texts on eye care and athletics (Stern, 1983). Also see Table 11D-4.

## Contact Lenses and Glasses

Many athletes wear contact lenses or glasses during athletic competition. Glasses provide some protection from eye injury, but because there are no safety standards in the United States, the lens may shatter and cause further eye injury. There are many disadvantages to glasses which usually have heavy frames, fog-up easily, and require the use of cages, protective masks, or elastic straps for protection. Glasses can be knocked off or the lens pushed into the orbit.

**Table 11D-4. How to Sharpen Vision**

The American Optometric Association, which has been working with athletes at the U.S. Olympic training center in Boulder, Colo., offers these tips.

1. To sharpen peripheral awareness, fix your eyes on a spot on a wall, throw a tennis ball at the wall and try to catch it without moving your eyes.
2. Wear sunglasses for outdoor sports. Squinting can cause muscle fatigue and that affects timing.
3. Wear goggles to cover contact lenses when swimming or competing in other water sports. Chemicals can cause eye irritation.
4. Body movements tune into what your eyes concentrate on, so think about where you want to place a tennis or golf ball rather than on potential errors.
5. Wear impact-resistant lenses when playing racket sports even if you don't need corrective glasses. The lenses should be in a one-piece, wrap-around, plastic frame.
6. Bifocal wearers might need special glasses for sports.
7. Always have an extra pair of glasses or contact lenses.
8. Have your eyes checked regularly.

Hard contact lenses provide no protection from injury but do have the following advantages: (1) there are no frames; (2) a panoramic view is possible, especially if the athlete has a high refractive error; (3) they are not subject to environmental elements like fog or rain, and (4) they are more stable, even though they can slide or be knocked off or pop out. The disadvantages of contact lenses are (1) no protection; (2) vision is not as good, especially if there is astigmatism; (3) if a lens is lost, an extra pair must be available, and (4) they cannot be worn underwater in swimming or scuba diving without problems. Swimmers who wear soft contact lenses in chlorinated pools may suffer corneal abrasions if they attempt to remove the lens too soon after getting out of the water. This is due to an osmotic effect that makes the lens adhere to the cornea more tightly. The condition usually resolves within 30 minutes after leaving the pool. Those participants wearing eye glasses are at greater risk of eye injury because both glass and plastic lenses can break under enough force.

Wind and dust particles may slide under the contact lens and cause corneal abrasions. Soft contact lenses generally are more comfortable than hard contact lenses but they require more care than hard lenses and are far more expensive. Proper care of soft lenses requires the use of distilled water, saline solution, special lens cases, and a heating unit. The team physician and trainer should know which athletes are wearing contact lenses and have replacement sets available.

## Prevention — Eye Protectors

Because of the potential for damage when objects strike the eye at more than 100 mph, eye guards should be mandatory in sports where eye injury is likely. For optimal protection, the lens center of a spectacle should be at least 3 mm thick and made of CR39 resin or polycarbonate plastic and meet the standards of the American Society for Testing and Materials (Pine, 1991).

The polycarbonates have a higher impact-resistance and are much harder. Frames on all lenses should consist of closed-cell foam material and be soft and flexible without metal parts. The lenses should be mounted in a sports frame made of nylon with a deep posterior lip. This requires that the lenses be placed into the frame from the front so that they cannot be pushed posteriorly into the orbit. Orbit guards should be incorporated into the frame. Metal frames should not be used because they can cut the face or easily damage the eye. It is preferable to have an experienced optician fit sport goggles. Children need special attention because of their small facial features.

A variety of open eye guards are available but they do not provide adequate protection. Even so, an open eye guard is better than no eye guard at all because it will prevent slashes from rackets and damage from all center hits to the eye. Eye guards should buttress the facial bone securely. Sports involving high speed collision with other players, sticks, or mobile objects (football, hockey, lacrosse, and field hockey) require total head protection so that forces to the head are transmitted through the face mask, preventing further injury.

Streetwear spectacles with plastic lenses offer adequate protection for tennis and badminton but not squash or racketball (Vine, 1991). Industrial standards are required. Divers should have their prescription lenses bonded to the inner surface of their mask as contact lenses are not recommended for divers. Most authorities recommend that contact lens wearers use the same level of eye protection as those who require no correction (Vinger, 1988). Sturdy goggles are recommended for skiers as inexpensive plastic goggles may shatter and cause significant eye injury.

Sports-related eye injuries represent a significant public health problem and prevention is the only effective therapy. Effective eye protection is available for athletes and their use should be encouraged by all health professionals (see Table 11D-5). Reducing the incidence of sports-related eye injuries will require the cooperation of health professionals, athletes, coaches, and others. Compliance issues for the use of protective eyewear are discussed by Vine (1991).

## SECTION E.
## EARS

### Injuries/Illnesses of the External Ear

#### Contusion (Wrestler's Ear)

This injury is not seen in many athletes except boxers, rugby players, and wrestlers. The ear usually is protected in football and wrestling, but many wrestlers suffer ear contusions that can lead to chronic fibrous thickening called cauliflower ear (Figure 11E-1). It usually is caused by repeated rubbing of the athlete's ear (friction) or by absorbing repetitive blows that cause leakage of blood between the skin and perichondrium. The ear initially becomes swollen and painful, and a well-defined hematoma within the helix fossa develops within hours. If not treated carefully, chronic scarring may occur in several weeks and then the ear develops the classic deformed, cauliflower-like appearance (Figure 11E-2).

Initial treatment consists of applying ice to the ear. Any hemorrhage present between the perichondrium and cartilage should be aspirated under sterile technique. Otherwise, infection could lead to chronic chondritis and death of the cartilage. After aspiration, the ear is compressed with a collodion pack, plaster of paris cast, or silicone mold. The authors favor the collodion pack (Cooper, 1976) which is made by placing cotton balls or strips of gauze soaked in flexible collodion in layers over the affected ear and wrapping with sterile gauze.

The ear is checked after 24 hours for reaccumulation of fluid (which may require additional aspiration) and then it is repacked. This treatment is continued as long as necessary (usually three days). Another useful technique is forming a silicone mold around the end of an applicator stick. Use of the stick forms an opening which allows the athlete to equalize pressure in the inner ear (Gross, 1978). Other methods using a tie-through technique with sterile buttons or plastic surgery are also successful (Dimeff, 1989).

To prevent an ear contusion and its complications, all wrestlers, rugby players, and amateur boxers should wear ear protectors, especially during practice. The headgear must be properly fitted or it may rub against the ears, causing further damage and potential adverse longterm changes in the ear (Figure 11E-3).

#### Ear Laceration

An ear laceration is usually secondary to an injury from a sharp instrument. Partial avulsion or tearing away of the pinna is more common. Lacerations occur when the ear is forcibly pulled forward and the skinfold between the ear and the scalp is split. The laceration could be missed when the ear falls back into its normal position unless the examination is careful. This could lead to contamination and infection of the wound. Treatment consists of careful cleansing and suturing, paying attention to pertinent anatomical landmarks, especially if the auricular cartilage is torn.

Table 11D-5. Eye Guards that Meet Canadian and American Standards

| Model/Cost (US) | Manufacturer/Distributor | Address (Canada) | Address (US) |
|---|---|---|---|
| Action Eyes (A) $25.00 | Viking Sports | Black Knight Enterprises<br>3792 Commercial St.<br>Vancouver, BC<br>V5N 4G2<br>604/872-3123 | Viking Sports<br>5355 Sierra Rd.<br>San Jose, CA 95132<br>408/923-7777 |
| Albany (CA) $20.00 | Leader | International Forums Inc.<br>(Leader Sports)<br>1150 Marie Victoria<br>Longuevil, PQ<br>J4G 1A1<br>514/651-2300 | LST Leader Sports<br>Products Inc.<br>PO Box 271<br>Main St., Route 22<br>Essex, NY 12936<br>518/963-4268 |
| CRS 300 (C) $25.00 | CRS Sports | CRS Sports International<br>10021 169th St.<br>Edmonton, AB<br>T5P 4M9<br>403/483-5149 | Same as Canadian |
| Defender 600 (C) $22.50 | Peepers | Peepers Inc.<br>PO Box 951<br>Station A 150 Chatham St.<br>Hamilton, ON<br>L8N 3P9<br>416/525-3369 | Peepers International<br>417 Fifth Ave.<br>New York, NY 10016<br>212/696-9797 |
| New Yorker (CA) $25.00 | Leader | International Forums<br>Inc. (Leader Sports)<br>1150 Marie Victoria<br>Longuevil, PQ<br>J4G 1A1<br>514/651-2300 | LST Leader Sports<br>Products Inc.<br>PO Box 271<br>Main St., Route 22<br>Essex, NY 12936<br>518/693-4268 |
| Safe-T Eye-Guard (C) $25.00 | Imperial Optical | Imperial Optical Canada<br>21 Dundas Square<br>Toronto, ON<br>M5B 1B7<br>416/595-1010 | Embassy Creations<br>PO Box 143<br>234 Holmes Rd.<br>Holmes, PA 19043<br>215/586-9640 |
| Sports Scanner (C) $25.00 | American Optical | AOCO Limited<br>80 Centurian Dr.<br>Markham, ON<br>L3R 5Y5<br>416/479-4545 | American Optical<br>14 Mechanic St.<br>Southbridge, MA 01550<br>617/765-9711 |

(C) — Certified by the Canadian Standards Association
(A) — Meets the 1985 and/or 1986 standards of the American Society for Testing and Materials
(From *Phys and Sportsmed* 15(6):184, June 1987)

## Otitis Externa (Swimmer's Ear)

By definition, otitis externa is an acute bacterial infection of the auditory canal caused predominantly by *Pseudomonas aeruginosa* and occasionally *E. coli, Proteus* or fungi *(Candida* or *Aspergillus)* (Eichel, 1974). When the ear canal is exposed to water over time, the protective effect of the cerumen that normally is present is removed. The skin becomes irritated and itchy. If the athlete scratches, the canal's epithelium is disrupted. The normal epithelium produces protective substances

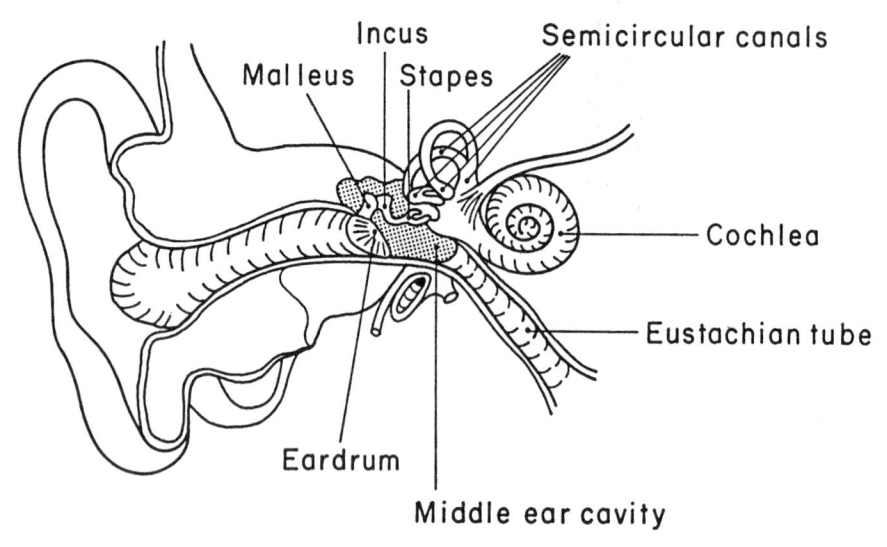

Fig. 11E-1. External Ear

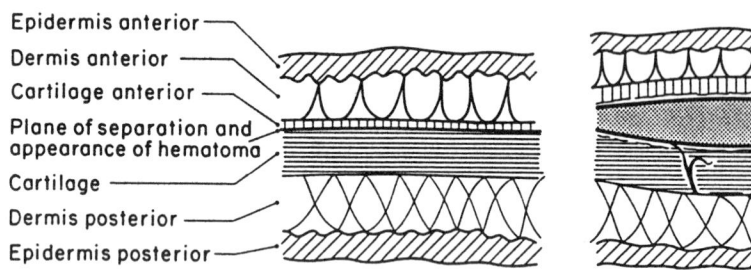

Fig. 11E-2. Cross-section of External Ear

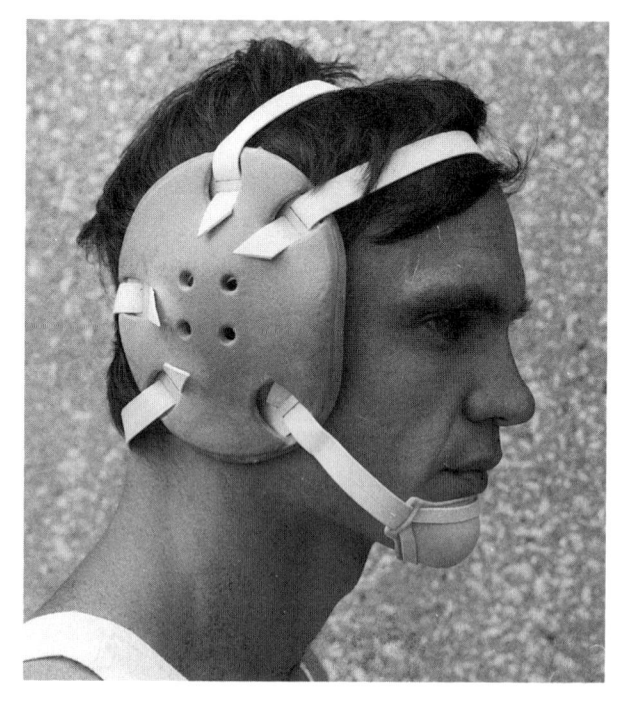

Fig. 11E-3. Ear Protector

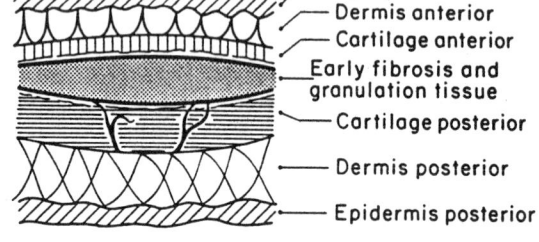

capable of inhibiting bacterial growth. When it is damaged, infection can occur and may spread to the middle ear, mastoid, or brain if not properly treated. The external canal is swollen and tender and usually has a visible discharge. Cultures of the discharge should be obtained to ensure proper treatment.

Treatment of otitis externa involves reacidifying the ear with an acetic solution (1 tbl vinegar in 1 pint water). Antibiotic and cortisone combinations are useful after all debris is removed from the canal. An ear wick soaked in Burrow's solution (aluminum acetate) can be applied every two hours. Otitis externa can be prevented if the swimmer removes trapped water by vigorously shaking the head while it is tilted to one side. Dry the ears by fanning or blowing dry with a hair dryer. Instill four drops of an acetic or boric acid solution before and after swimming to dry the canals. The use of pure vinegar, cotton tip applicators, and ear plugs should be discouraged as they may aggravate the situation (Strauss, 1979). Otitis externa cases which are resistant to conservative measures will require the use of topical and/or oral antibiotics and possibly an otolaryngological consultation.

## Injuries/Illnesses of the Middle Ear

### Tympanic Membrane Rupture

Tympanic membrane rupture is caused by a blow to the ear or a fall and is common in surfing, water skiing, scuba diving, and water polo (Eichel, 1974; Farmer & Thomas, 1976). The athlete will notice a "pop," decreased hearing acuity, and perhaps nausea and dizziness secondary to the caloric effect of cold water on the labyrinth. Fracture of the ossicular chain can occur in severe water skiing accidents and will require evaluation and possible surgical repair by an otolaryngologist.

The usual treatment of a ruptured tympanic membrane is conservative, looking for the development of an infection daily until the rupture heals. If an infection occurs, antibiotic therapy is instituted. Some otolaryngologists recommend prophylactic antibiotics and surgical repair of the rupture but this usually is not necessary. This injury can be prevented by using appropriate protective headgear and proper diving techniques.

### Barotrauma

Divers may encounter serious problems such as air embolism, pneumothorax, or the "bends". Significant trauma to the air-filled middle ear and sinus cavities and especially middle ear barotrauma is more common. Barotrauma results from inadequate pressure equalization between the middle ear or sinus and the external environment. During compression when the diver descends, continuous swallowing is necessary to keep the eustachian tube open.

Ear or sinus squeeze develops as pressure differentials cause localized inflammation and swelling and prevents further air pressure equalization. Eventually, bleeding may occur in the middle ear from blood vessel rupture of the tympanic membrane or round window rupture. The diver notices the sensation of ear blockage; then as the descent continues, ear pain, conductive hearing loss, tinnitus, vertigo, and sometimes blood-tinged sputum develop.

Inexperienced divers may not be able to equalize pressure easily, especially if they are still learning appropriate techniques. Barotrauma can occur in shallow water because the greatest pressure changes occur within the first 15 feet below the surface. Respiratory allergies, infection, rhinitis, large adenoids, or congenital obstruction of the eustachian tube may hamper a diver's ability to equalize pressure easily.

Treatment of barotrauma without perforation of the eardrum includes the use of systemic and nasal decongestants, avoidance of further diving, systemic antibiotics, and analgesics when necessary. Cases where the eardrum is perforated may require referral to an otolaryngologist.

Prevention of ear squeeze and perforation is accomplished by: (1) removing impacted cerumen; (2) using air-pressure equalization techniques frequently on descent; (3) avoiding ear plugs, and (4) not diving with sinusitis or a seasonal allergy flare-up. Divers should be cautioned about using antihistamines which can cause drowsiness.

### Otosclerosis (Hearing Loss from Firearms)

Otosclerosis is common in marksmen or sports officials who use starting guns. Repetitive noise from firearm explosion usually is worse in the ear closest to the gun (most often the ear on the same side as the handedness of the individual). The noise level that is damaging is 150 db or more. Most weapons easily exceed this limit. The patient usually presents with a neural hearing loss demonstrated on an audiogram. Prevention of otosclerosis involves modification of the gun barrel, shooting on open terrain, and wearing protective ear muffs (Odess, 1974; Taylor, 1966).

### Otitis Media and Its Complications

Otitis media and its complications are handled as usual, with the normal differential diagnosis and potential complications considered and treated.

## SECTION F.
## NOSE

### Contusions and Abrasions

Hematomas must be distinguished from simple ecchymosis and swelling which may mask more serious injury. Hematomas can cause adjacent tissue necrosis, scarring, and potential airway obstruction if they are not properly treated, especially septal hematomas. Immediate decompression will prevent collapse of the nasal dorsum and a "saddle-nose" deformity. Nasal splints and packing can be used for decompression without obstructing the nasal cavity.

Most abrasions are superficial, result from friction, and are easily treated by cleansing with soap and water and using topical antibiotic ointments. Full thickness skin loss will require skin grafting with post-auricular skin. Cleanse all foreign material from the skin, removing loose foreign bodies with a brush. Athletes may resume normal activities after an abrasion injury is appropriately dressed. Any secondary bacterial infection should be treated aggressively.

## Lacerations

Lacerations are the most common facial injury (Schendel, 1990). Most can be cleansed and repaired with plastic surgery principles within 24 hours. Lacerations that extend to or through the nasal cartilage require proper closure, and skin grafting may be necessary. All upper-or lower-lateral cartilage should be meticulously reapproximated.

## Nasal Fracture

Nasal fracture is the most frequent injury to the face (Douglas, 1985; Schendel, 1990; Maisel, 1981). A study by Illum (1986) showed that 15% of nasal fractures were repetitive. Diagnosis is made by a careful history and examination of the nose and usually is not difficult. However, nasal fractures often do not receive proper attention (Illum, 1986). This injury usually presents with epistaxis, which often is profuse, and a deformity that is obvious to the patient and examiner. The patient may hear or feel a crack in the nose at the time of injury.

The nose should be examined as soon after injury as possible, before major swelling develops. The examiner should palpate the nasal area between the fingers while looking for crepitation, which indicates a recent fracture. Look for depression of the nasal dorsum and deviation of the nasal septum. Tenderness and ecchymosis without crepitation suggests a soft tissue injury without fracture. The nose should be examined internally with a good light after clots are removed by suctioning. It may be helpful to use a vasoconstrictor medication to visualize the nasal passage.

The examiner should also check for evidence of significant head trauma or leakage of cerebrospinal fluid. Examine the nasal septum closely for development of a hematoma, which may cause obstruction. A septal hematoma produces a characteristic bluish bulge on the septum. If it is present, incision and drainage and nasal packing should be performed without delay. The mucoperichondrium may be dissected off the underlying cartilaginous septum by the hematoma and lead to resorption of the cartilage and loss of tip support. In some cases, cartilage is laid down as in a cauliflower ear, producing a mass that obstructs the airway. Formation of a septal abscess also is possible. It is very important to recognize septal hematomas, especially in children where the loss of cartilaginous tip support in a growing nose could cause a severe snub nose deformity.

Lateral and oblique radiographs of the nasal bones are indicated to confirm a fracture and will show if other facial bones are fractured. These radiographs are falsely negative 60% of the time (Schendel, 1990). An exaggerated Water's view is necessary to properly identify the nasal arch. A CT scan or a polytomogram may be needed for complex fractures. The type and extent of fracture is dependent on the force and direction of the blow. Frontal, lateral, nasal lacrimal, and globe injuries should be considered. Septal-ethmoidal fractures are typically difficult to treat (Schendel, 1990).

Timing of the reduction of nasal fractures, when necessary, is controversial. It can be done under local or general anesthesia after the swelling has subsided, usually within four days for children and 10-12 days for adults (Martinez, 1987). Intranasal packing and plaster splinting usually are necessary for complex injuries involving comminuted fractures or septal hematomas but simpler fractures may be treated without them. If there is displacement of the nose but minimal swelling, the injury may be splinted and referred to an ENT specialist for closed reduction. Where the swelling is severe, ice should be applied to the nose frequently and the injury reevaluated in two to three days, at which time definitive treatment usually is given. Delaying diagnosis of a nasal fracture over two weeks may make a closed reduction impossible (McGrail, 1985; Schendel, 1990). All nasal fractures should be managed to restore normal appearance and prevent problems associated with a deviated nasal septum or obstructed eustachian tube.

An athlete should not participate in contact sports for at least one week after a nasal fracture of any consequence. Before he/she returns, check that no significant swelling or bleeding will recur and that the fracture is stable and does not require external support. The athlete can be fitted with a protective device over the nose so that sports can be continued while the injury heals completely. The device usually is required for at least four weeks after the fracture. Hockey helmets can have a face guard attached; in football they are already worn. Chronic problems secondary to nasal fracture may require evaluation and reconstruction by a otolaryngologist.

## Epistaxis

Bleeding from the nose is a common accompaniment of traumatic injuries to the face owing to the excellent blood supply to nasal mucosa (Baker, 1979; Eichel, 1984; Schendel, 1990). Fortunately, most instances of bleeding are readily controlled. Epistaxis occurs in Kiesselbach's plexus on the anterior nasal septum in 90% of cases. In the remaining 10% of cases, bleeding originates in the posterior nose. Generally, the younger the patient, the more anterior the bleeding site. Posterior epistaxis is rare in children and usually is an ENT emergency. Epistaxis commonly presents as nasal hemorrhage alone, but if it is severe and uncontrolled, could lead to syncope, anemia, and death.

Management of epistaxis depends on the type of injury, the sport involved, and whether bleeding occurs spontaneously or after physical contact. Prophylaxis is the best approach. Athletes who have recurrent nasal hemorrhage should coat each side of the Kiesselbach area with petrolatum at least once or twice a day. These precautions are appropriate for skiers at high altitudes and for boxers or hockey players before practice or competition. The physician may use electrical or chemical cautery of the bleeding areas to help control epistaxis. Cautery should be applied conservatively to avoid perforating the septum, especially if the procedure is performed several times.

If epistaxis occurs suddenly during an athletic event, the player should sit forward with his head down and gently blow one nostril at a time. This helps remove clots and allow the vessels to contract, retract, and stop the nose bleed. Then the nose should be gently pinched and the nose bleed usually will stop quickly. The player or athlete can return to activity without problems if there is no further bleeding.

When there is an associated fracture that prevents the patient from applying pressure to the nose, ice applied to the back of the neck will cause reflex vasoconstriction. Packing both sides of the nose also helps. When an associated fracture is present, the athlete should be sent to a hospital where reduction of the fracture can be done. The reduction can be within 24 hours or within the next 7-10 days, depending on the degree of edema and bleeding.

If these simple measures are unsuccessful in controlling nose bleeds, the athlete should be seen at a medical office or hospital where the nose can be properly evaluated and packed if necessary. The type of nasal packing will depend upon the bleeding site.

Anterior packs made of Iodoform® or thrombin soaked gauze should be layered into the nose in an accordion-fashion, using 12-20 feet of gauze. Anterior-posterior nasal packs are used for severe epistaxis. This pack consists of a conventional tampon or the less reliable balloon or Foley catheter (Gottschalk, 1976; Schendel, 1990). The athlete should be hospitalized and consultation with an otolaryngologist obtained. A tampon must be cut to fit the nose properly because the material will expand inside. With this procedure, the tampon cannot be inhaled.

Patients with anterior nose bleeds that are controlled by the above procedures may return to activity if there is no further bleeding. Nasal packing should not be left in place for long periods of time since infection may be forced through the cribiform plate, with the potential to cause meningitis. All nasal packs should be removed carefully and prophylactic oral antibiotics given. Athletes should be instructed to avoid chronic use of nasal decongestants which cause to dryness and rebound swelling of the nasal mucosa and increase the potential for epistaxis.

Most nose bleeds come from septal blood vessels, but a significant nose bleed can be caused by injury to the anterior ethmoidal artery. It may occur when there is blunt injury to the root of the nose and the medial temporal area of the eye. This can cause brisk hemorrhaging which needs careful and thorough packing of the roof of the nose as described above. Even so, this type of bleeding tends to persist even after packing. Some cases may require a surgical approach through an external incision in order to clip the ethmoidal vessel. Surgery for preventing or treating epistaxis in athletes is very rare with the exception or injuries that sever the anterior or posterior ethmoidal arteries. The key diagnostic feature of this injury is lack of a bleeding focus in Kiesselbach's area and bleeding from high up in the nose. Anterior packing of the affected area often can control the bleeding and obviate the need for surgery.

## SECTION G.
## MOUTH INJURIES IN SPORTS

### Perspective

Injuries to the mouth usually are considered less serious than those to other parts of the body but this may not be the case. Before face and mouth guards were introduced, oral injuries constituted 50% of all football injuries; each player had a 10% chance of sustaining an injury during any playing season (Heintz, 1979). The tremendous increase in participation by youth and women in sports has made them vulnerable to oral injury. The frequency of dental injury is not well documented in most sports. Most statistics come from ice hockey and football.

A review of studies from 1941-1978 showed the highest frequency of mouth injuries in sports where no mouth protection was used (between 10%-20%). The injury rate for basketball, without mouth guards, is equal to the rate in football with mouthguard protection. Data on mouth injuries collected from 1975-1980 shows that the 5 to 14 year age group suffered the highest incidence of oral injuries in baseball (8.7%), followed by ice hockey (5.7%), basketball (4.6%), and football (1.5%) (Rutherford, 1981). Many sports still do not mandate the use of mouth protectors.

### Teeth Injuries

A fractured tooth is a common sport injury and often has less chance of healing normally than almost any other injury (Vinger, 1981). Most physicians see little importance in evaluating an injured baby tooth because it will be replaced by a permanent tooth. However, the roots of the front teeth (most often injured) are not completely formed until age 12. An injury prior to this age can damage the root and prevent normal root and permanent tooth development.

The examiner should try to see how the athlete was injured and look for a foreign body, especially if there is a laceration of the mouth or lips. Irrigate with warm saline, using sterile swabs soaked in a solution of 2% iodine or benzalkonium chloride (Zephiran®) 1:10,000 to debride the injured lip.

A broken tooth may or may not need emergency treatment. If it is cracked and the pulp is bleeding, the nerve may be exposed so that immediate dental evaluation is necessary. Avoid extremes of temperature (no hot or cold drinks) and biting. Make a temporary filling by covering the fractured tooth with calcium hydroxide [$Ca(OH)_2$] or Ravit® a temporary filling material. Early treatment of a pulp injury is preferable, especially in children. Apply ice packs to control swelling and reduce bleeding. Always check the teeth when a patient has a cut lip. All imbedded teeth require referral to a dentist or oral surgeon. Do not attempt to bring the tooth down into place. The tooth socket usually has been spread out during injury and grasping the imbedded tooth will dislodge it completely.

Eighty-five to ninety percent of loose teeth can be saved with proper treatment that repositions the tooth correctly. There is a 35%-40% chance of saving a tooth that is knocked out (Andreason, 1981). Pick it up by the crown only, place it in warm saline and have the patient see a dentist immediately. Oil of Clove (Eugenol®) may provide initial pain relief while in transit. Apply an ice pack to the face and have the athlete hold the tooth in its socket with his fingers or by closing his mouth. The athlete should have x-rays to rule out a mandibular or alveolar fracture after a severe mouth injuries. Fracture of the mandibular condyle can affect the growth center in children. Obviously, all dental cavities and loose fillings require the timely attention of a dentist.

### Laceration of the Tongue

All tongue lacerations require proper evaluation and examination for foreign bodies that may be embedded in the tissues. Copious lavage with benzalkonium is suggested. Many tongue lacerations do not require repair if they are not deeper than 0.5 cm. Since the tissue of the tongue is very soft, it is necessary to take a bigger bite when suturing and leave the sutures in place for two or three days.

A severely bleeding tongue should be sutured after blocking the lingual nerve distal to the second or third molar, injecting 1/2" above the plane of the molar. Use crushed ice and a solution of one part hydrogen peroxide ($H_2O_2$) to three parts water or Amosan® for 48 hours after repair. The repair of all "through and through" lacerations should be left to an oral surgeon. All lip lacerations should be carefully repaired, paying close attention to the proper alignment of the frenulum and underlying muscles.

## Jaw and Temporo-Mandibular Joint Problems

A TMJ injury or fracture/dislocation to the jaw may occur with any serious mouth injury. Refer these injuries to an oral surgeon. Taking office x-rays prior to referral is unnecessary and time consuming. The clinical diagnosis is straightforward; ask the patient if he can open and close his jaw and if his teeth meet the way they did before injury. If not, you can be almost certain that the jaw is fractured or dislocated (especially if the jaw is painful and cannot be closed) in 95% of cases. A fractured tooth often is associated with a TMJ dislocation. If the athlete has swelling of the cheek but no malocclusion, check for a fracture of the zygomatic arch. Check for numbness of the skin around the mouth which would indicate injury to the infraorbital nerve.

TMJ sprains should be differentiated from a mandibular fracture as the symptoms are similar. X-ray all TMJ joints to rule out a mandibular fracture. TMJ dysfunction is found by placing the index and middle fingers over the TMJ and feeling for irregular movement or subluxation while the patient opens and closes his mouth. Then listen with a stethoscope for clicking or crepitation in the TMJ. Also, test for spasm of the pterygoid muscles by palpating posterior to the affected side. This will produce exquisite pain if spasm is present. Arthrography, CT scan, or MRI of the TMJ may aid in the diagnosis (Volger & Helms, 1984). If the patient has TMJ dysfunction, prompt dental-medical consultation is necessary. Bear in mind that there are many critics of the significance and treatment of TMJ problems (Moore, 1981).

## Common Oral Conditions

### Abscessed Tooth

A periapical abscess usually presents with sensitivity to hot liquids or precussion. Analgesics such as aspirin, acetaminophen, or codeine may be necessary for adequate pain relief. Place the athlete on antibiotics for five to six days using penicillin or erythromycin, 250 mg QID. Oral gargles of a hydrogen peroxide solution (one part $H_2O_2$ to three parts $H_2O$) may be helpful. Referral to an oral surgeon usually is necessary.

### Wisdom Tooth

Treatment consists of using hydrogen peroxide solution (one part $H_2O_2$ to three parts $H_2O$) every two hours. If pain lasts more than 24 hours, place the athlete on antibiotics as above. Dental referral may be necessary in more difficult cases.

### Vincent's Stomatitis

This condition presents as red, painful gums with hemorrhage. Use of the hydrogen peroxide solution and vitamin B complex appears helpful. Slowly increase the athlete's intraoral care (teeth brushing, flossing), and if there is no improvement within 24 hours, start antibiotics as indicated above.

## Prevention: Mouth Protectors

Faceguards were first adopted for football during the early 1950s, with mouthguard use becoming mandatory in 1962 at the high school level and in 1973 for college athletes. Face masks and mouthguards have eliminated most serious injuries. Mouthguards were mandated for use in amateur ice hockey during the 1977-78 season but the rule is not uniformly enforced. In the U.S., children under age 13 are not required to wear mouthguards, although there is a requirement for face masks.

Mouthguards not only reduce the incidence of injury to the mouth, teeth, and lips but they also help decrease concussions by absorbing the forces of a blow to the chin. Studies indicate a decrease in both neck injuries and concussions when mouthguards are used (Vinger, 1981). All athletes, especially youngsters and women, should wear acceptable mouthguards. This is very important during informal sporting activities which is where most injuries occur in contact/collision sports.

Three types of mouth protectors are available: custom-made, mouth-formed, and stock-type. The order of preference among athletes is the same order as above. Custom-made mouthguards require a dental impression and are more expensive (Figure 11G-1). The stock-type rubber mouthguard fits poorly and it is not as effective.

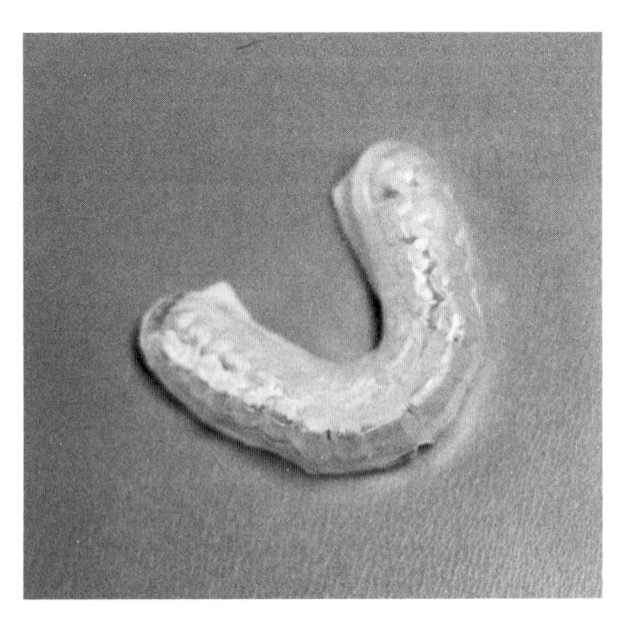

**Fig. 11G-1.** Latex Mouthguard

A properly fitted mouthguard is comfortable and does not interfere with breathing or speech. All mouthguards should be checked periodically for wear and replaced if necessary.

# SECTION H.
# THROAT INJURIES AND ILLNESSES

## Epidemiology

Injuries to the larynx can be caused by a direct blow in football or other contact sports (boxing, karate, basketball) or from objects (ice hockey, baseball, lacrosse, and field hockey). Occasionally, trail bike riders or snowmobilers strike wires, ropes, or chains and sustain laryngeal injury (McCutcheon & Anderson, 1985). Any blow to the anterior neck can cause significant airway obstruction due to glottic edema, vocal cord disarticulation, hemorrhage, laryngospasm, or a crushed larynx or trachea (Storey, 1989).

## Recurrent Uri/Tonsillitis

Upper respiratory infections and their complications are the most common illness in athletes of all ages. Proper evaluation should be performed, along with screening for Group A beta-hemolytic streptococcus. Athletes with recurrent episodes of tonsillitis or otitis media should be referred to an otolaryngologist for possible tonsillectomy. Use of appropriate antibiotics for bacterial tonsillitis is advisable.

## Laryngeo-Tracheal Injury

A blow to the anterior neck may be severe and potentially life-threatening. The athlete usually protects this area by dropping his chin before an impending blow. The structures most likely to be damaged are the larynx and trachea. Extreme agitation, dyspnea, and possible respiratory failure are common after laryngeal injury. Injuries to the cartilaginous structures, connecting muscle and soft tissue, or the supporting nervous and vascular system may occur individually or in combination.

Cartilaginous fracture most often occurs to the thyroid and cricoid cartilages (Figure 11H-1). While hyoid, epiglottic, and tracheal rings can break, it is unlikely because these structures are mobile. Cartilagineous fracture may result in a visible or palpable flattening of the laryngeal contour (Adam's apple). Thyroid cartilage fracture often occurs in the region of the attachment of the two vocal cords. Dislocation of the arytenoids or corniculates may result in hoarseness or aphonia.

The athlete is initially speechless, struggles to breathe, and has a feeling of impending doom. Acute injury may cause swelling and spasm of the larynx, and the thyroid cartilage, hyoid bone, or trachea may be contused or fractured. Laryngeal spasm usually resolves quickly and the athlete can breathe easier. The athlete may have stridorous breathing, dyspnea, and cyanosis if the airway is threatened. Crepitation may be noted on palpation of the anterior neck. Cough, hemoptysis, or hematemesis may occur where there is a mucosal tear of the larynx.

More severe cases present with hematoma either intrinsic to the larynx or in the muscles of the neck. This may lead to severe respiratory stridor or complete airway obstruction and presents an obvious medical emergency. The possibility of a concomitant vertebral fracture must always be kept in mind with severe neck injuries. Fortunately, sports-related anterior neck injuries involve less force and cause cervical vertebral fractures less often than those from automobile crashes. If the athlete is unconscious, the neck injury should be managed as if a fracture is suspected. Maintenance of gentle, stabilizing traction to the head during transportation is vital. The airway should be main-

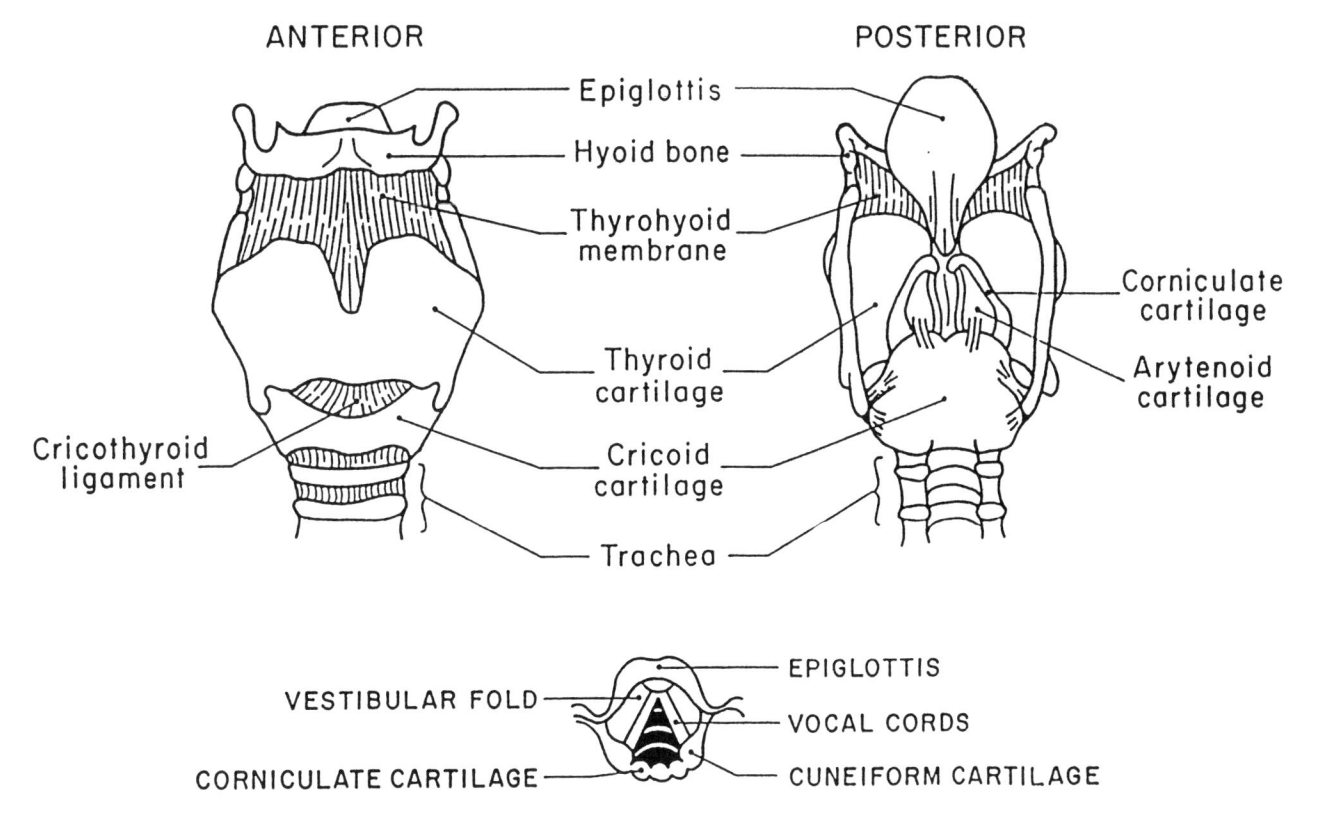

**Fig. 11H-1.** Anatomy of the Laryngeal Area

tained with as little extension of the neck as possible.

Laryngeal trauma is not always obvious in the patient who has an uncompromised airway. Physical signs and symptoms are not highly correlated with the ultimate severity of the injury. An extensive injury may have little initial evidence of airway obstruction but can produce significant airway compromise as edema and hematoma formation progress. Consequently, indirect laryngoscopy and CT scanning should be performed on every patient with anterior neck trauma and ENT consultation (McCutcheon, 1985; Storey, 1989).

The first consideration of treatment is ensuring the adequacy of the airway. If the patient does not have obvious signs of cartilaginous fracture, discontinuity of the airway, or cervical/vertebral fracture, reassure the patient and position the head in a chin-up position to straighten the airway. If the athlete's breathing is noisy but he can inflate his chest well, there is time to get the player to a hospital for proper examination and treatment.

If the athlete's breathing is ineffective or if increasing subcutaneous emphysema confirms discontinuity of the airway, CPR is instituted and an artificial airway must be established immediately. Oral airways and oral screws are useless since the obstruction is below the oral cavity. An inexperienced examiner should not attempt to intubate an agitated athlete lying on the ice or playing field. An orderly tracheostomy, usually lower than the second tracheal ring, is most desirable. Fortunately, most laryngeal fractures involve the thyroid cartilage so that placing an airway into the cricothyroid membrane alleviates most of the obstruction. Criothyreotomy is a simpler, safer, and faster alternative for the team physician at the scene of the injury. It can be performed before a more permanent tracheostomy is done in the operating room or emergency room. The cricothyroid airway should be properly secured and the patient moved to the emergency room. Supplemental oxygen and assisted ventilation may be needed.

A player with a neck injury and any degree of airway obstruction should be sent to the nearest hospital for indirect laryngoscopy as soon as possible. The most common finding on laryngoscopy is some degree of laryngeal edema, with or without submucosal hemorrhage. Because the edema is likely to progress for 12-24 hours, the athlete should be kept under close observation in the hospital until the airway returns to normal. Most injuries do not require surgical intervention and subside with rest, steam, and reassurance. Sedatives are contraindicated because of their respiratory depressant action. Most athletes can leave the hospital within three to four days.

The threat of a severe anterior neck injury is highest to baseball catchers and hockey goalies. Prevention is best accomplished by using protective head gear with a throat flap. An inexpensive flap can be made by attaching the spine pad from a football girdle to the catcher's mask with leather lacing (Middleton, 1980). Many commercially available throat protectors also are available for a wide variety of sports.

## Laryngospasm

Laryngeal spasm is another type of upper airway obstruction resulting from anterior neck trauma. Closure of the larynx is caused by a spasm of the adductor muscle of the true vocal cords and pressing of the pre-epiglottic muscles against the upper surface of the false vocal cords. The athlete becomes agitated, often panic stricken, and may become cyanotic. Persistent laryngospasm may cause loss of consciousness. The athlete usually is aphonic and unable to cough. Contours of the thyroid and cricoid cartilages are normal and there is no palpable subcutaneous emphysema.

To treat laryngospasm, move the chin forward and place strong pressure behind the angle of the jaw. This forward movement is transmitted to the hyoid bone, hypoepiglottis, and periglottis, which pulls these structures from the false cords and reopens the laryngeal passage. Spasm will begin to decrease within 45-60 seconds and a loud inspiratory crowing sound will be heard. Give the patient oxygen by venti-mask. Suctioning of the oropharynx should be avoided to prevent further laryngeal spasm.

After recovery, the athlete should be referred for immediate laryngoscopy to rule out other unsuspected injuries. Observation for the development of subsequent edema or hematoma formation may be indicated. If dyspnea persists, voice rest and thorough evaluation of the neck and larynx by a specialist is indicated. The anterior neck should be radiographed, with soft tissue and lateral views of the neck. If severe injury is suspected, hospitalize the patient for immediate laryngoscopy.

Following injury to the neck, the athlete with laryngospasm should be placed at bed rest with local ice application to the neck. Recovery may be complete in minutes but the athlete should be reevaluated frequently. If injury is more severe, observe the athlete for subsequent development of a hematoma. Appropriate treatment should be managed by the otolaryngologist.

## REFERENCES

### Section A. Head

Albright, J.P., VanGilder, J., El-khoury, G., et al. Head and neck injuries in sports. In Scott, N.W., Nisonson, B., Nicholas, J.A. (eds). *Principles of Sports Medicine.* Baltimore, Williams and Wilkins, 1984.

Auerbach, S.H. The post-concussive syndrome: formulating the problems. *Hospital Practice,* 9-12, 1987.

Bennett, D.R., Fueming, S.I., Sullivan, G. et al. Migraine precipitated by head trauma in athletes. *Am J Sports Med* 202-205, 1980.

Cantu, R.D. When to return to contact sports after a cerebral concussion. *Sports Med Digest* 19:11, 1-2, 1988.

Committee on Head Injury Nomenclature of the Congress of Neurological Surgeons: Glossary of head injury. *Clinical Neurosurg* 12:388, 1966.

Garrick, J.G., Requa, R.K. Medical care and injury surveillance in the high school setting. *Phys Sportsmed* 9:115, 1981.

Gerberich, S.G., Priest, J.D., Boen, J.R., et al. Concussion incidence and severity in secondary school varsity football players. *Am J Publ Health* 73(12):1370-1375, 1983.

Gronwall, D., Wrightson, P. Delayes recovery of intellectual function after minor head injury. *Lancet* 2:605-609, 1974.

Guardian, E.S. Acute head injury: a review. *Surg Annual* 12:225, 1980.

Mueller, F.O., Blyth, C.S. Fatalities from head and cervical spine injuries occurring in tackle football: 40 years' experience. *Clinics in Sports Med* 6(1):185-196, 1987.

Mueller, F.O., Schindler, R.D. Annual survey of football injury research 1931-1986. *American Football Coaches Association,* Orlando, 1987.

Nelson, W.E., Jane, J.A. and Grick, J.H. Minor head injury in sports: a new system of classification and management. *Phys and Sportsmed* 12(3):103, 1984.

Ommaya, A.K., Gennarelli, T.A. Cerebral concussion and traumatic unconsciousness. Correlation of experimental and clinical observations on blunt head injuries. *Brain* 97:633, 1974.

Quick, G. Head injuries — the first 60 minutes. *Emergency Revisions* 10:11-29, 1985.

Reid, S.E., Brain trauma inside a football helmet. *Phys Sportsmed* 8:32, 1974.

Rimel, R.W., Giordani, B., Barth, J.T., Boll, T.J., Jane, T.A. Disability caused by minor head injury. *Neurosurgery* 9(3):221-228, 1981.

Rimel, R.W., Giordoni, B., Barth, J.T., Jane, J.A. Moderate head injury: completing the clinical spectrum of brain trauma. *Neurosurgery* 112(3):344-351, 1982.

Rimel, R.W., Edlich, R.F., Winn, H.R., Butler, A.B., Jane, J.A. *Acute Care of the Head and Spinal Cord Injured Patient at the Site of Injury.* University of Virginia, Charlottesville, Virginia, 1978.

Schneider, R.C., Peterson, T.R., and Anderson, R.E. Football (Chapter 1). In *Sports Injuries: Mechanisms, Prevention and Treatment,* Schneider, R.C., Kennedy, J.C., and Plant, M.L., editors. Baltimore, Williams and Wilkins, 1985.

Schneider, R.C. *Head and Neck Injuries in Football. Mechanism, Treatment, and Prevention.* Baltimore, Williams and Wilkins, 1972.

Temkin, N.R., Dikem, S.S., Wilensky, A.J., Keihm, J., Chabal, S, and Winn, H.R. A randomized, double-blind study of phenytoin for the prevention of post-traumatic seizures. *NEJM* 323:497-502, 1990.

Torg, J.S. *Athletic Injuries to the Head, Neck and Face.* Philadelphia, Lea and Febiger, 1982, p. 40.

Wohns, R.N.W., Wyler, A.R. Prophylactic phenytoin in severe head injuries. *J Neurosurg* 51:507-509, 1979.

### Section B. Face

Dingman, R.O, Nating, P. Surgery of Facial Fractures. W.B. Saunders, Philadelphia, p. 144, 1964.

Handler, S.D. Diagnosis and Management of Maxillofacial Injuries. In *Athletic Injuries to the Head, Neck, and Face,* J.S. Torg, ed., Lea and Febiger, Philadelphia, p. 223-244, 1982.

Salon, R.C. Maxillofacial Trauma. In *Principles of Sports Medicine*, W.N. Scott, B. Nisonson, J.A. Nicholas, ed., Williams and Wilkins, Baltimore, MD, p. 97-109, 1984.

Schultz, R.C. *Facial Injuries*. 2nd Ed., Yearbook Medical Publisher, Chicago, 1977.

Schultz, R.C., de Camara, D.L. Athletic facial injuries. *JAMA* 252(24):3395-3398, 1984.

Wilson, K., Cam, B., Rontal, E. Rontal, M. Facial Injuries in Hockey Players. Minnesota Medicine, 60(1):13-19, 1977.

### Section C. Neck

Bailes, J.E., Hadley, M.M., Quigley, M.R. Management of athletic cervical spine and spinal cord injuries. *J Neurosurgery* (In Press).

DeHaven, K.E., Lintner, D.M. Athletic injuries: comparison by age, sport and gender. *AJSM* 14(3):218-224, 1986.

Fourie, M. On-site management of cervical spine injuries. *Phys and Sportsmed* 19(4):53, 1991.

Scher, A.T. Rugby injuries of the spine and spinal cord. *Clinics in Sports Medicine* 6(1):87-100, January 1987.

Tator, C.M. Neck injuries in ice hockey: a recent, unsolved problem with many contributing factors. *Clinics in Sports Medicine* 6(1):101-114, January 1987.

Torg, J.S., Vegso, J.J., O'Neill, M.J., Sennett, B. The epidemiologic, pathologic, biomechanical, and cinematographic analysis of football-induced cervical spine trauma. *Am J Sports Med* 18(1):56, 1990.

Torg, J.S., Pavlov, H. Cervical spinal stenosis with cord neuropraxia and transient quadriplegia. *Clinics in Sports Medicine* 6(1):115-134, January 1987.

Torg, J.S. Management guidelines for athletic injuries to the cervical spine. *Clinics in Sports Medicine* 6(1):53-60, January 1987.

Torg, J.S., Glasgow, S.G. Criteria for return to contact activities following cervical spine injury. *Clinical J of Sports Med* 1(1):12-26, 1991.

Torg, J.S. Epidemiology, pathomechanics and prevention of athletic injuries to the cervical spine. *Medicine and Science in Sports and Exercise* 17(3):295-303, 1985.

Wroble, R.R., Albright, J.P. Neck and low back injuries in wrestling. *Clinics in Sports Medicine* 5(2):295-326, April 1986.

### Section D. Eyes

Ball, R.J., Irion, P.E. and Zacks, J.L. A proposal for a visual perceptual training program for MSU athletes. Presented to the Division of Sports Medicine, Michigan State University, 1983.

Capillo, J.C. Hockey masks go on, face injuries go down. *Phys and Sportsmed* 5:77, 1977.

LaForge, R. Preventing eye injuries. *Executive Health Report* 3(26):7, 1990.

Larrison, W.I., Hersh, P.S., Kunzwerler, T., Shingleton, B.J. Sports-related ocular trauma. *Ophthalmol* 97(10:1265-1269, 1990.

Marton, K., Wilson, D., McKeag, D.B. Ocular trauma in college varsity sports. *Med and Science in Sports and Exercise* 19(2)Supp:553, April 1987.

Pashbyt, T. Eye injuries in Canadian hockey: Phase III. *Canadian Medical Assoc Journal* 121:643, 1979.

Pine, D. Preventing sports-related eye injuries. *Phys and Sportsmed* 19(2):129m, 1991.

Rutherford, G.W. and Miles, R.B. Overview of sports related injuries to persons 5-14 years of age. Report of U.S. Consumer Product Safety Commission, pgs. 17-20, 1981.

Stern, N.S. Sports vision bibliography. *J of Optimetric Vision Development* 14(4):16-19, December 1983.

Strahlman, E., Sommer, A. The epidemiology of sports-related ocular trauma. *Int Ophthamol Clin* 28:199-202, 1988.

Vinger, P.F. The eye and sports medicine. In: Duane, T.D., Jaeger, F.A. (eds.) *Clinical Opthalmology*. Philadelphia, PA: J.B. Lippincott Company, Vol. 15, Chapter 45.

Vinger, P.F. How I manage corneal abrasions and lacerations. *Phys and Sportsmed* 14(5):170, 1986.

Vinger, P.F. Racket sports:an occular hazard. *JAMA* 239:2475, 1978.

### Section E. Ears

Cooper, D.L., Fair, J. Treating "cauliflower ear". *Phys and Sportsmed* 4:103, 1976.

Dimeff, R.J., Hough, D.O. Preventing cauliflower ear with a Modified tie-through technique. *Phys and Sportsmed* 17(3):169, 1989.

Eichel, B.S. Otologic hazards in water sports. *Phys and Sportsmed* 2:43, 1974.

Farmer, J.C., Thomas, W.G. Ear and sinus problems in diving. In R.H. Strauss (Ed.), *Diving Medicine*. New York: Grune & Stratton, 1976.

Gross, C.G. Treating "cauliflower ear" with silicone mold. *Am J Sports Med* 6:4,1978.

Odess, J.S. The hearing hazard of firearms. *Phys and Sportsmed* 2:65, 1974.

Strauss, M.B. et. al. Swimmer's ear. *Phys and Sportsmed* 7:101, 1979.

Taylor, G.D., Williams, E. Acoustic trauma in the sports hunter. *Laryngoscope* 76:863, 1966.

### Section F. Nose

Baker, T.E. A quick and easy method for controlling nosebleeds. *First Aider Cramer* 48:14, 1979.

Douglas, L.G. Facial Injuries in Welsh, R.P. and Shephard, R.J. (Eds.) *Current Therapy in Sports Medicine*. St. Louis: C.V. Mosby, 151-152, 1985.

Eichel, B.S., Kaplan, H.J. How I manage nosebleeds in athletes. *Phys and Sportsmed* 12(4):67, 1984.

Gottschalk, G.H. Epistaxis and the nasostat. *JACEP* 5:793, 1976.

Illum, P. Long-term results after treatment of nasal fractures. *J Laryngol Otol* 100(3):273-277, 1986.

Maisel, R.H. Management of the broken nose. *Consultant*, p. 74, May 1981.

Martinez, S.A. Nasal fractures: what to do for a successful outcome. *Postgrad Med* 82(8):71-77, 1987.

McGrail, J.S. Ear, Nose and Throat Injuries in Welsh, R.P. and Shephard, R.J. (eds). *Current Therapy in Sports Medicine* 1985-86, St. Louis: C.V. Mosby, pgs. 147-149, 1985.

Schendel, S.A. Sports-related nasal injuries. *Phys and Sportsmed* 18(10):59-74, 1990.

### Section G. Mouth

Andreason, J.O. *Traumatic Injuries of the Teeth* (2nd Ed). Philadelphia: W.B. Saunders Co., 419-432, 1981.

Heintz, W.D. Mouth protectors: a progress report. *JADA* 77:632, 1968.

Moore, M. Corrective mouthguards: performance aids or expensive placebos? *Phys and Sportsmed* 9:127, 1981.

Rutherford, G.W., Miles, R.B. Overview of Sports-related Injuries in Persons 5-14 Years of Age. U.S. Consumer Product Safety Commission Report, 20-23, 1981.

Vinger, D.F., Hoerner, E.F. (Eds.) *Sports Injuries: The Unthwarted Epidemic* Littleton, Massachusetts: PSG Publishing Co. Inc., 1981.

Volger, J.B., Helms, C.A. Arthrography of the temporal mandibular joint. *Female Patient* 9:27, 1984.

### Section H. Throat

McCutcheon, M.L., Anderson, J.L. How I manage sports injuries to the larynx. *Phys amd Sportsmed* 13(4):100, April 1985.

Middleton, J. Football spine pad protection for baseball catchers. *Athletic Training* 15:82, 1980.

Storey, M.D., Schatz, C.F., Brown, K.W. Anterior neck trauma. *Phys and Sportsmed* 17(9):85-96, 1989.

## SUGGESTED READINGS

### Section C

Shields, C.L., Fox, J.M., Stauffer, E.S. Cervical cord injuries in sports. *Phys and Sportsmed*, 12(2):71-90, 1978.

Teitz, C.C., Cook, D.M. Rehabilitation of neck and low back injuries. *Clinics in Sports Medicine* 4(3):455-475, 1985.

Torg, J.S., Vegso, J.J., Sennett, B. The national head and neck registry: 14-year report on cervical quadriplegia (1971-84) *Clinics in Sports Medicine* 6(1):61-72, 1987.

Vegso, J.J., Lehman, R.C. Field evaluation and management of head and neck injuries. *Clinics in Sports Medicine* 6(1):1-16, 1987.

Vegso, J.J., Torg, E., Torg, J.S. Rehabilitation of cervical spine, brachial Serplexus, and peripheral nerve injuries. *Clinics in Sports Medicine* 6(1):135-158, 1987.

Watkins, R.G. Neck injuries in football players. *Clinics in Sports Medicine* 5(2):373-386, 1986.

### Section D

Doxanas, M. Racketball as an occular hazard. *Archives of Opthalmology* 98:1965, 1980.

Easterbrook, M. Eye injuries in racket sports: a continuing problem. *Phys and Sportsmed* 9:91, 1981.

Garner, A.I. An overlooked problem: athlete's visual needs. *Phys and Sportsmed* 75-82, 1977.

Hale, L.M. Emergency eye care. *Am Family Phys* 6:103, 1972.

Holt, J.E. Prevention and management of sports-related injuries. *Consultant* 117:26, July 1983.

Keeney, A. Estimating the incidence of spectacle lens trauma. *American Journal of Opthalmology* 73:289, 1972.

Morin, J. Primary management of occular trauma. *Canadian Medical Association Journal* 118:305, 1978.

Rose, C.P. and Morse, J.O. Racketball injuries. *Phys and Sportsmed* 7:73, 1978.

Ryan, A.J., Berman, P., et al. Vision, eyecare, and the athlete. *Phys and Sportsmed* 13(6):132-151, 1985.

Sanke, R.F. Blunt occular trauma. *AmFamPhys* 29:159, 1984.

Stine, C.D., Arterburn, M.R., Stern, N.S. Vision and sports: a review of the literature. *J American Optometric Association* 53(8):627-633, 1982.

### Section E

Klafs, C.E., Arnheim, D.D. *Modern Principles of Athletic Training* (4th Ed.), St. Louis: C.V. Mosby Co., 415-417, 1977.

Kulund, D.N. *The Injured Athlete.* Philadelphia: J.B. Lippincott Co, 236-248, 1982.

O'Donghue, D.H. *Treatment of Injuries to the Athletes* (3rd Ed.), Philadelphia: W.B. Saunders, 130; 1976.

Turcotte, H. Scuba divers answer the challenge of the sea. *Phys and Sportsmed* 5:67, 1977.

### Section F

Ballanger, J.J. *Diseases of the Throat & Ear* (12th Ed). Philadelphia: Lea & Febiger, 1977.

English, G.M. *Otolaryngology-A Textbook* Hargerstown, Maryland: Harper & Row, 1976.

O'Donoghue, D.H. *Treatment of Injuries to Athletes* (3rd Ed). Philadelphia: W.B. Saunders & Co. 1976:132-134.

### Section G

Collins, E.M., Kaplan, R.I. and Katz, S.R. When you see a dental problem first. *Patient Care* 106, 11/15/74.

Heintz, W.D. The case for manditory mouth protectors. *Sports Med* 3:61, 1975. Heintz, W.D. Mouth protection in sports. *Phys and Sportsmed* 7:45, 1979.

Hickley, J.C., et al. The relation of mouth protectors to cranial pressure and deformation. *JAmDentAssoc* 74:735, 1967.

Nicholas, N.K. Mouth protection in contact sports. *NZ Dent J* 65:14, 1969.

Schwartz, D.B., Novich, M.M. The athlete's mouthpiece. *AmJSportsMed* 8:357, 1980.

Smith, S.D. Sports dentistry, protection and performance from mouthguards and bite splints. *Athletic Training* 16:100, 1981.

Stenger, J.M. et al. Mouthguards: protection against shock to head, neck and teeth. *JAMA* 69:1964.

### Section H

O'Donoghue, D.H. *Treatment of Injuries to Athletes* (3rd Ed.). Philadelphia:W.B. Saunders & Co., 420-421, 1976.

# Appendix 11A-1.
# Checklist for Essential Support Facilities for the Sports Physician at Sports Events

**BASIC MEDICAL KIT FOR HEAD INJURIES**
Airways
Injectable sedative for seizure
 (phenobarbital)
Cervical collar
Ringer's solution
20% mannitol
Intravenous tubing and cannula

**NAME, LOCATION, TRANSIT TIME TO**
Nearest hospital
Neurosurgical center

**FACILITIES AND PERSONNEL**
On-site first-aid personnel
Intermediate transport (stretchers,
 ski patrol, etc)
Medical first-aid station
Ambulance transport

**TWO-WAY COMMUNICATION BETWEEN**
Site of injury
Intermediate transport team
Organizers of the event
Police and/or coroner
Ambulance
Relatives
Press

# Appendix 11A-2.
# Patient With A Head Injury

**General Observations at Home:**
1. Check on patient about every hour while he is awake.
   Signs of danger:
   a. Patient acts very "dopey" and responds progressively less to questions and stimulation.
   b. Very unsteady - poor coordination of arms and legs.
   c. Marked difference in size of pupils.

2. During the first night patient should be awakened three times to be certain that he is in natural sleep and responds normally to the waking state.

**Additional General Signs of Danger:**
1. Increasingly severe or persistent headache or vomiting. (Patient may normally have a mild headache or an upset stomach after minor concussion.)

2. Development of weakness in arms or legs.

3. Convulsive movement of limbs or face.

**Summary**
If the patient's alertness and appetite return quickly to normal, treatment may be limited to above observations and gradual increase in activity.

If *any* of the above signs appear - contact your physician *immediately*.

CALL YOUR PHYSICIAN IF YOU HAVE ANY CONCERN REGARDING THE PATIENT'S CONDITION BUT, IN ANY EVENT, REPORT TO YOUR PHYSICIAN ON THE NEXT DAY.

# Appendix 11A-3.
# Rapid Neurologic Evaluation of Cranial Nerve Function

| Nerve | Frequency | Sites of Involvement | Tests | Abnormal Findings |
|---|---|---|---|---|
| I OLFACTORY | Uncommon | Fracture of cribriform plate or in ethmoid area | Apply simple odors such as peppermint to one nostril at a time | Anosmia |
| II OPTIC | Common | Direct trauma to orbit or globe, or fracture involving optic foramen | Light flashed in affected eye | Loss of both direct and consensual pupillary constriction |
| | | | Light flashed in normal eye | Direct and consensual pupillary constriction |
| | Common | Pressure on geniculocalcarine tract. Laceration or intracerebral clot in temporal, parietal, or ocipital lobes (rarely from subdural clot) | Bring hand suddenly toward eye from the side | Absence of the blink reflex indicates a visual field defect (always homonymous) |
| III OCULOMOTOR | Very frequent | Pressure of herniating uncus on nerve just before it enters cavernous sinus or fracture involving cavernous sinus | Light flashed in affected eye | Dilated pupil, ptosis, eye turns down and out<br><br>Direct pupil reflex absent. Consensual reflex present |
| | | | Light flashed in normal eye | Direct pupil reflex present. Consensual reflex absent |
| IV TROCHLEAR | Infrequent | Course of nerve around brain stem or fracture of orbit | Isolated involvement requires special equipment | Eye fails to move down and out |
| V TRIGEMINAL | Uncommon | Direct injury to terminal branches, particularly 2nd division in roof of maxillary sinus | Sensation:<br>1st division: Above eye and cornea<br>2nd division: Upper lip<br>3rd division: Lower lip and chin | Loss of sensation of pain and touch.<br>Paresthesias |
| | | | Motor Function:<br>"Bite down" or "Chew" | Palpated masseter and temporalis fail to contract |
| VI ABDUCENS | Quite frequent | Base of brain as nerve enters clivus. Fracture involving cavernous sinus or orbit | "Look to the right — Look to the left" | Affected eye fails to move laterally.<br>Diplopia on lateral gaze |

# Appendix 11A-3.
# Rapid Neurologic Evaluation of Cranial Nerve Function (*Continued*)

| Nerve | Frequency | Sites of Involvement | Tests | Abnormal Findings |
|---|---|---|---|---|
| VII FACIAL | Frequent | Peripheral: Laceration or contusion in parotid region | | Paralysis of facial muscles. Eye remains open. Angle of mouth droops. Forehead fails to wrinkle |
| | | Peripheral: Fracture of temporal bone | | As above plus associated involvement of acoustic nerve (see below) and chorda tympani (dry cornea and loss of taste on ipsilateral $2/3$ of tongue) |
| | Frequent | Supranuclear: Intracerebral clot | "Wrinkle your forehead" | Forehead wrinkles because of bilateral innervation of frontalis. Otherwise paralysis of facial muscles as above |
| VIII ACOUSTIC | Common | Fractures of petrous portion of temporal bone. Seventh nerve also often involved | In children and uncooperative patients, slap hands close to ear | Startle reflex |
| | | | Weber Test: Tuning fork middle of forehead | Sound not heard by involved ear |
| IX GLOSSO-PHARYNGEAL | Rare | Brain stem or deep laceration of neck | Motor power of stylopharyngeus — impractical to test | Loss of taste posterior one-third of tongue |
| | | | Cotton applicator to soft palate | Loss of sensation on affected side of soft palate |
| X VAGUS | Rare | Brain stem or deep laceration of neck | Inspection of soft palate. Laryngoscopy | Sagging of soft palate; deviation of uvula to normal side. Hoarseness from paralysis of vocal cord |
| XI SPINAL ACCESSORY | Rare | Laceration of neck | Hand on side of chin: "Push your chin against my hand" | Palpated sternocleidomastoid fails to contract |
| | | | "Shrug your shoulders" | Palpated upper fibers of trapezius fail to contract |
| | | | "Stretch out your hands toward me" | Affected arm seems longer (scapula not "anchored") |
| XII HYPOGLOSSAL | Rare | Neck laceration usually associated with major vessel damage | "Stick your tongue out" | Tongue protrudes toward affected side. Dysarthria |

# 12

# Common Sports-Related Injuries and Illnesses — The Upper Extremity

## SECTION A.
## THE SHOULDER

The shoulder is man's most vulnerable joint. It also is one of the most complicated anatomical and biomechanical joints in the body. Sports medicine specialists have begun to redirect their attention from the problems of the knee to the complexities of the shoulder. Advances in arthroscopy have changed treatment protocols and extended the competitive lives of athletes, especially throwing athletes. The shoulder is a major injury site in competitive sports and is involved 8%-13% of the sports injuries (Thorndike, 1956).

### Epidemiology

As could be expected with a complex joint that has a wide range of motion, significant shoulder injury can occur in nearly any sport. A look at some representative sports indicates the ways shoulder injuries occur.

**Baseball.** Yocum (1982) indicates an 11% significant injury rate at the professional level, with 92% of the individuals being pitchers and 90% of the injuries being muscle strains.

**Swimming.** The most common competitive problem in swimming is shoulder pain usually brought on by overuse. Kennedy (1974) found a 15% incidence of injury in shoulder pain in Canadian swimmers. The incidence of shoulder pain increases dramatically with age. It is rare in swimmers under 10 years of age, but Dominquez (1978) found the incidence to be 50% in high school swimmers and Richardson (1980) found an incidence of 57% in male college swimmers. Breaststrokes seemed least affected; 92% of those reporting shoulder injuries swam freestyle, butterfly, or backstroke. Sprinters or middle distance swimmers accounted for 74% of the total.

**Football.** Dagiau (1980) reports that the shoulder accounts for 8% of all game injuries and 14% of all practice injuries in football. Acromioclavicular separation, glenohumeral dislocation, and shoulder muscle strains each account for approximately one third of the injuries.

**Wrestling.** The shoulder is the most common injury site in wrestling, accounting for 16.7% of injuries (Garrick, 1978). On the collegiate level, the shoulder causes 18% of all wrestling injuries, with most being acromioclavicular strains of varying severity or glenohumeral strains (Snook, 1982).

**Tennis.** Priest (1976) found half of elite tennis players complained of shoulder symptoms, primarily in the area of the anterior rotator cuff.

**Volleyball, Javelin.** Yohoe (1959) found shoulder involvement in 44% of volleyball players and 29% in javelin throwers. Inflammation of the bicipital tendon was seen in 90% of these injuries, secondary to the explosive hitting/throwing motion of the upper extremity.

**Skiing, Basketball.** By comparison, these sports seldom cause shoulder injuries. A survey of skiing injuries by Carr (1981) reveal that the shoulder was involved only 6.9% of the time. Likewise, very low shoulder injury rates have been reported for basketball.

### Anatomy/Biomechanics

To put the anatomy of the shoulder in perspective, consider evolution. As we evolved from a quadruped to a biped, we ceased to use our upper extremity for weight-bearing. The shoulder remains a ball and socket joint but the borders of the socket have fallen back to allow man to achieve the greatest range of motion of any body joint in the upper extremity (see Figure 12A-1). The hip joint maintains much of its stability within the bony skeleton of a deep ball and socket joint but the shoulder must achieve its stability with the musculature of the rotator cuff (see Figure 12A-2). What the shoulder has given up in stability, it gains in range of motion. There is a delicate balance between mobility and stability (Jobe, 1989).

There are three planes of motion:

- sagittal — flexion, extension, and elevation;
- coronal — adduction and abduction;
- medial — internal and external rotation.

The functional anatomy of the shoulder includes five articulations (see Figure 12A-3). From distal to proximal on the body they are:

1. *Glenohumeral* — "The" shoulder joint and major articulation of the upper extremity. This joint can be described as an incongruent joint that uses a gliding motion about a non-fixed axis of rotation. It is made up of the concave surface of the glenoid fossa and the more circular convex surface of the humeral head. During motion, only a small portion of the humeral head is in contact with the fossa at any one time. Supporting soft tissue structures intimate to the joint include the glenoid labrum, joint capsule, and the anterior placed glenohumeral ligament. The joint capsule is normally loose, becoming taut only in extreme movements (the external rotation and abduction of throwing) beyond the normal range of motion of the joint. Movement between the shoulder and elbow is coordinated by the long head of the biceps muscle, its proximal tendon running intracapsularly but extrasynovially through the glenohumeral joint.
2. *Suprahumeral* — Not a true joint but a physiologic one. This protective articulation is between the humeral head and the coracoacromial ligament. It allows the greater tuberosity of the humerus to pass under the coracoacromial ligament without compression during abduction.
3. *Scapulothoracic* — Another physiologic joint. The motion of the scapula is to glide along the posterior thoracic wall when there is motion and rotation of the clavicle. This movement is produced by the coordinated movement of two muscles — the trapezius and serratus anterior muscles.
4. *Acromioclavicular* — A plane joint containing a meniscoid structure. This meniscoid structure rapidly degenerates and disappears by the fourth

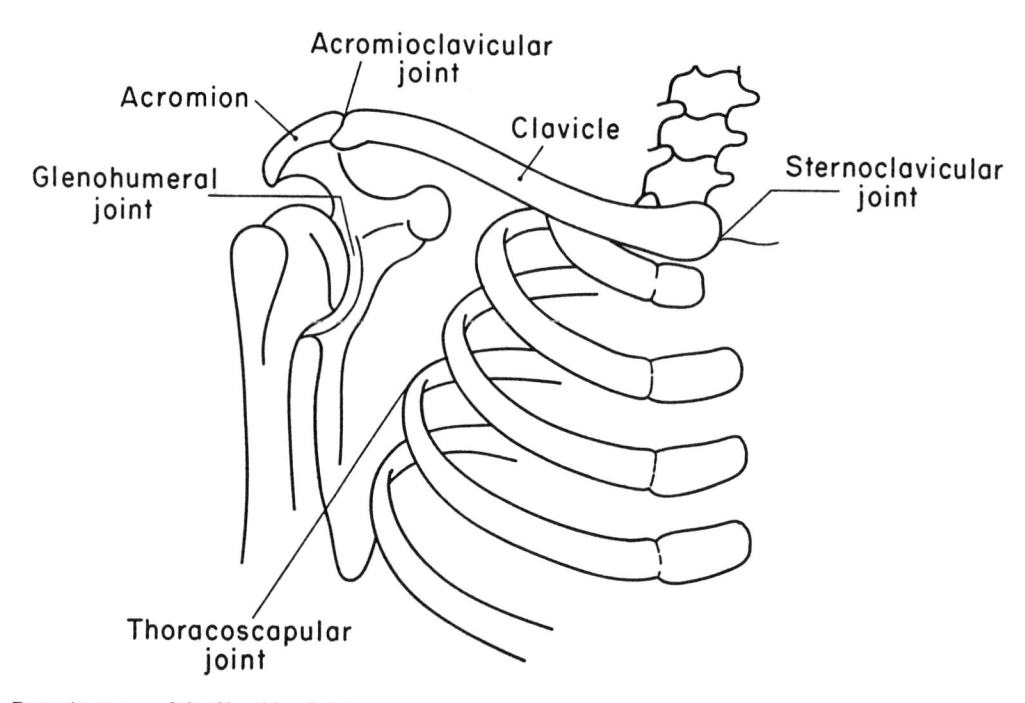

**Fig. 12A-1.** Bony Anatomy of the Shoulder Joint

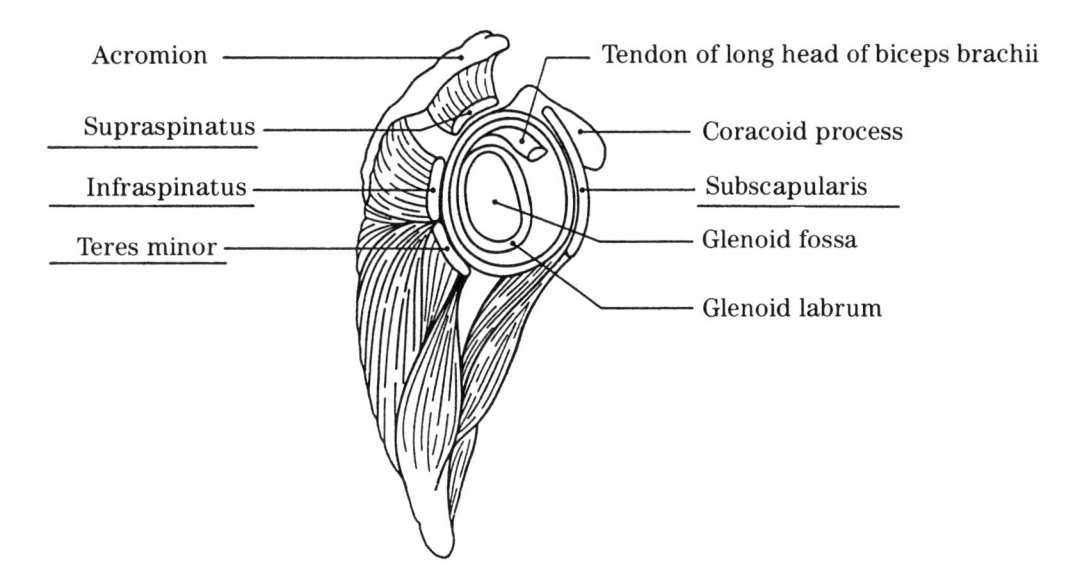

**Fig. 12A-2.** Anatomic Relationships of the Rotator Cuff

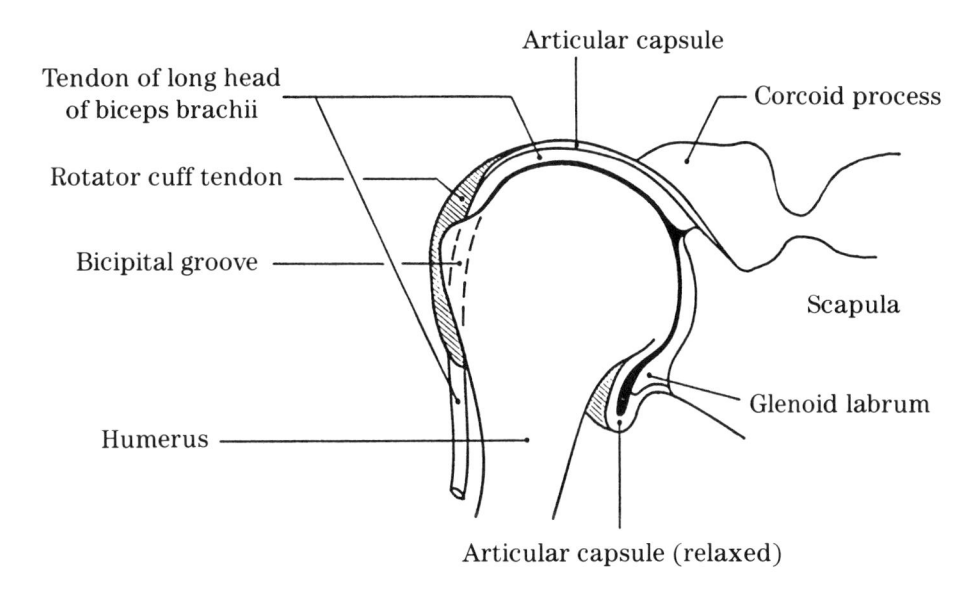

**Fig. 12A-3.** Basic Anatomy of the Shoulder

decade of life. The acromioclavicular joint is stabilized by the coracoclavicular ligament. The physiologic movement of the clavicle is by rotation when the arm is adducted or elevated.

5. *Sternoclavicular* — A plane joint that acts as a ball and socket joint. The anterior and posterior sternoclavicular ligament reinforce a loose fibrous capsule making up the joint. Stability is aided by the costoclavicular and infraclavicular ligaments.

**Bursae.** There are usually a total of eight bursae present around the shoulder joint. Only the large subacromial (subdeltoid) bursae is significant.

**Important Muscles**

**Deltoid.** Acts as an independent elevator of the arm. This is a very superficial muscle that normally contributes the round, contoured look to the anterior profile of the shoulder.

**Supraspinatus** initiates arm elevation and acts to abduct the shoulder. It passes under the acromion and coracoacromial ligament and can easily be "pinched" between these structures and a moving humeral head.

**Subscapularis, infraspinatus, teres minor** act to compress the joint and displace the upper extremity downward: a) *subscapularis* — responsible for internal rotation; b) *infraspinatus and teres minor* — responsible for external rotation.

Note: The latter four muscle attachments to the humerus make up the rotator cuff of the shoulder.

## Generic Examination

Because of the complexity of the shoulder, we will discuss the important subjective and objective aspects without relation to any specific shoulder diagnosis.

### History

When confronted with an undiagnosed shoulder injury, the primary care physician must elucidate the exact mechanism of injury and position of the shoulder at the time of injury. The history should include the following:

- *Handedness* — A key element in the historical review. A conditioned athlete using his arm in his sport (pitcher) will often have restriction in the range of motion in his dominant as compared to his non-dominant arm. The examiner should not attribute such alterations to a pathologic state.
- *Occupation/Position* — Certain positions played in sports lend themselves to certain injury. A baseball catcher throwing overhand may be at more risk than a shortstop for an overuse and impingement syndrome.
- *Review of Symptoms* — Specific inquiry should be made for history of rheumatoid arthritis, diabetes mellitus, gout, or other systemic disease. Also, the physician needs to know about previous surgery or trauma to the area.
- *Medication Use* — A history of both oral and injected medications is useful.
- *Previous Treatment for Injury* — this should include modality and frequency and will help explain why an injury may have recurred.
- *Age* — While not as important as once believed, it remains a good indicator of the propensity of the athlete for specific types of injury —Rotator cuff tears are more likely to occur in individuals over the age of 45 (Ireland, 1988).
- *Inherent Ligamentous Laxity* — Some individuals and some sports may possess generalized joint laxity (swimming). Do "loose joints" run in the family?
- *Pain* — The characterization of pain, onset, and specific biomechanical actions generating the pain are obviously important. Training habits in relationship to pain should be asked. The specific character of the pain can vary:
  a. *dull* pain may indicate a rotator cuff tear
  b. *burning* pain may indicate calcific tendinitis or neuroproxia
  c. an audible *snap* may indicate subluxation of the gleno-humeral joint or biceps tendon
  d. *crepitation* with passive motion may indicate a passive bursitis
- *Referred Pain* — Shoulder pain can be the result of referred pain. Some diagnostic possibilities include:
  a. Neoplastic disease — Pancoast's tumor secondary to metastatic lung cancer
  b. Pulmonary apical pathology — tuberculosis
  c. Diaphragmatic irritation from a gall bladder or hepatic disorder stimulating the phrenic nerve
  d. Abdominal disease — gastric or hepatic pathology is frequently referred to the interscapular region
  e. Tension myalgia — localizing in the trapezius muscle
  f. Cervical radiculitis — the result of brachial plexus lesion
  g. Cardiac disease — the classic left shoulder pain presentation should not be forgotten

### Physical Examination

Specific and unique aspects of examination of the shoulder include the following:

- Inspection — Both shoulders should be exposed to allow comparison and to detect any signs of asymmetry. The authors recommend Y-style tank tops for female patients whenever possible. Also, an examining room mirror allows the physician to face the patient and still observe the posterior motion of the scapula on abduction and range of motion testing. Look from both sides, back, and front specifically noting muscle atrophy, erythema, swelling, or deformity.
- Palpation — The primary care physician needs to think of the topographic anatomy and, whenever possible, palpate both shoulders at the same time while the patient describes differences in sensation or tenderness. Feel for crepitation and

spasm. The order of examination from proximal to distal on the upper extremity should be sternum, sternoclavicular joint, clavicle, acromioclavicular joint, coracoacromial ligament, coracoid process, glenohumeral joint (passively abducting the upper extremity), biceps tendon and groove (passively performing external rotation), and scapula.

The presence of pain, swelling, crepitation, muscle spasm, tenderness, or warmth may indicate underlying pathology:

| Anatomic Area | Possible Pathology |
| --- | --- |
| Sternoclavicular joint | Strain, dislocation |
| Clavicle | Fracture |
| Acromioclavicular joint | Separation, contusion |
| Anterior shoulder with arm at side | |
| a. anterior deltoid | Strain |
| b. anterior capsule | Subluxation |
| c. bicipital groove | Tendinitis |
| Anterior shoulder with arm held in full extension | |
| a. subdeltoid bursa | Bursitis |
| b. rotator cuff | Tendinitis, tear |
| Lateral shoulder with arm at side | |
| a. middle deltoid | Strain, tear, supraspinatus tendinitis |
| b. subdeltoid bursae | Bursitis |
| Posterior shoulder with arm at side | |
| a. posterior deltoid | Strain |
| b. posterior capsule | Anterior subluxation/dislocation |
| Scapulae | Neurapraxia, strain |

- Neurovascular exam — This should include palpation of the pulses and a determination of the sensory and motor functioning, as well as of the deep tendon reflexes of the upper extremity.
- Neck — Range of motion should be examined for any shoulder pain and for alignment of cervical vertebrae. Note any pain or tenderness over the paracervical muscles or spinous process. Abnormal movement patterns of the head and neck should be examined closely.
- Active range of shoulder motion — Look at: a) abduction — determined by raising the outstretched arm laterally over head while observing from behind; b) flexion — assessed by having the patient raise the arms forward until they touch overhead; c) internal rotation — the patient places the thumb as high as possible on the opposite scapula; d) external rotation — the patient places his/her hand on the same shoulder; e) acromioclavicular and sternoclavicular joints — the patient places the hands across the chest on the opposite shoulder; f) horizontal extension with the arm in adduction; g) horizontal flexion with the arm in abduction — ask the athlete to place his/her arm on the opposite shoulder; h) protraction and retraction; i) shrug the shoulders — testing the 11th cranial nerve innervating the trapezius; j) ask the athlete to perform movements that cause pain or that are believed to be associated with the condition (tennis serve or baseball pitch).
- Passive range of shoulder motion — If the patient has difficulty performing any of the tests mentioned in the active range of motion segment above, passively repeat each of the movements on the patient yourself.
- Test for deep tendon reflexes and sensory perception
    a. axillary nerve — loss of sensation over the lateral aspects of the upper arm
    b. long thoracic nerve — winging of the scapula (serratus anterior muscle dysfunction).
- Muscle testing (see Appendix 12A-1a-h)
    a. supraspinatus — resistance to initiation of adduction. The athlete's arm should be placed at 90° adduction, 60° of horizontal flexion, and full internal rotation. The examiner directs the force downward with *two fingers*, not the whole hand.
    b. external rotators (infraspinatus and teres minor muscles act as unit) — arm should be adducted to the side, elbow at 90° with the patient externally rotating against resistance.
    c. internal rotator (subscapularis) — with arm still abducted to the side, the elbow at 90°, and the forearm externally rotated, ask the patient to internally rotate against resistance.
    d. palpate the long head of the biceps in the groove — external rotation is necessary to find the groove.
    e. deltoid — resistance/tenderness to abduction past 30°
- Tests
    a. apprehension — to test for the stability of the glenohumeral joint, the arm is externally rotated while an anterior placed force is ap-

plied to the posterior aspect of the humeral head.
b. Impingement — the arm should be brought into extreme forward elevation (flexion) with the humerus in external rotation.
c. Speed's Test — for bicipital tendinitis — flex the arm forward against resistance with the elbow extended and the forearm supinated. A positive test produces tenderness in the bicipital groove.
d. Hyperabduction — a test for thoracic outlet syndrome.

For a summary of mechanical movement related to major muscles involved, please consult Table 12A-1. Table 12A-2 reviews the generic on-field examination of acute shoulder injuries.

### Diagnostic Injections

Occasionally, injection of an anesthetic agent (xylocaine) into a painful area can be diagnostic. It may be possible to determine if the pain origin is the glenohumeral or AC joint, subacromial bursae, long head of the biceps tendon, or the result of the biomechanics of an impingement syndrome (Barth, 1989). This is certainly a procedure that can be done by a primary care physician who is comfortable with the anatomy of the shoulder and who has the experience.

### Radiographic Studies

Standard x-ray studies should include:

- Anterior/posterior views — one in internal rotation and one in external rotation
- Lateral view — preferably in either a trans-scapular lateral or axillary view. The Hill/Sachs lesion is a radiographically demonstrable erosion on the posterior humeral head, secondary to recurrent anterior instability (Glousman, 1990).

- West Point view — the patient is in a supine position and the machine angle is at 45° to the shoulder. The anterior/inferior glenoid rim is better visualized on this view (Rowe, 1988).

### Other Diagnostic Tests

Other diagnostic tests can be done for specific indications and they include:

1. Arthrogram — usually to show bony or full thickness rotator cuff tears
2. CT arthrography — the procedure of choice to complement standard radiographs in evaluating an unstable shoulder (Rafii, 1988). A glenoid labrums tear or a labro capsular detachment will be detected.
3. Ultrasound — notably helpful for partial thickness rotator cuff tears. This test requires an experienced radiologist for interpretation.
4. Magnetic Resonance Imaging (MRI) — in general, MRIs interpreted by experienced personnel will be the secondary procedure of choice for most shoulder injuries (see Chapter 17).

### Specific Injuries

#### Sternoclavicular Injuries

Sternoclavicular injuries are relatively rare in athletes and are 4-10 times less evident than acromioclavicular injuries. Two common conditions in the athletic population are acute traumatic dislocation (which can become chronic), and atraumatic dislocation (usually spontaneous). The sports most likely to be involved are hockey and football. Anterior dislocation is more common. It is caused by forces that depress the shoulder using the clavicle as a lever on the first rib. Symptoms include pain and deformity along the SC joint. A less common posterior dislocation can be caused by a direct blow or a force acting on the posterior lateral aspect of the shoulder. A likely cause is a direct side blow that drives the body into a unyielding wall or surface that transmits impact along the clavicle to the sternoclavicular joint. These biomechanics are seen in hockey when there is a "check" along the boards. Exquisite pain is the presenting symptom of the more common anterior dislocation. The rarer posterior dislocation is a more dangerous injury because it can be accompanied by cardiopulmonary collapse and mechanical occlusion of major structures beneath the anterior chest wall, including the trachea. X-ray examination can be difficult to read. Treatment must reduce the dislocation. With an anterior dislocation, local anesthesia and passive hyperextension of abducted arms with direct pressure over the medial clavicle usually results in reduction. A Figure 8 bandage is applied to hold the reduction. Even if the reduction is lost, many patients remain asymptomatic. Surgery is indicated if they do not. Reducing a posterior dislocation may be a medical emergency if major structures are mechanically involved. Consult Figure 12A-4 for the conservative reduction

Table 12A-1. Main Action of Muscles Around the Shoulder Girdle

| Movement | Main Muscles Involved |
|---|---|
| Flexion | Deltoid (anterior portion)<br>Coracobrachialis<br>Pectoralis major (clavicular portion) |
| Extension | Latissimus dorsi<br>Teres major<br>Deltoid (posterior portion) |
| Abduction | Deltoid (middle portion)<br>Supraspinatus<br>Serratus anterior (helps steady scapula; allows deltoid to function) |
| Adduction | Pectoralis major<br>Latissimus dorsi |
| External rotators | Infraspinatus<br>Teres minor<br>(Deltoid-posterior portion) |
| Internal rotators | Subscapularis<br>Pectoralis major<br>Latissimus dorsi<br>Teres major<br>(Deltoid-anterior portion) |
| Depresses raised arm against resistance | Pectoralis major<br>Latissimus dorsi<br>Teres major |
| Arm abducted with the head of the humerus prevented from moving upwards by: | Subscapularis<br>Infraspinatus<br>Teres minor<br>Biceps-long head |
| Scapula stabilization | Trapezius<br>Serratus anterior<br>Rhomboids |
| Scapula protraction (reaching and punching) | Trapezius<br>Serratus anterior<br>Rhomboids |
| Scapula retraction (pulling scapulae toward each other) | Rhomboid major<br>Rhomboid minor |
| Elevation of scapulae (shoulder shrugs) | Trapezius<br>Levator scapulae |

techniques of sternoclavicular dislocations. However, if these techniques fail, using a towel clip (clamp) to pull the clavicle anteriorly may be necessary, and a clamp should be part of the team physicians bag (see Chapter 9).

**Clavicular Fractures**

Fractures of the clavicle are most common fractures across all age groups. They usually result from direct trauma, but can (rarely) be a secondary result of a fall on an outstretched hand that transmits force to the clavicle. Generally speaking, fractures in adolescents are the green stick variety, whereas those in adults are complete and sometimes overriding. Most fractures are mid-shaft. Treatment includes ice, a Figure 8 splint, and a sling for comfort. Healing takes six to eight weeks, depending on the age of the patient and the degree of comminution. Open reduction and internal

**Table 12A-2. On-Field Examination of Acute Shoulder Injuries**

| Examination Procedure | Possibilities Examiner Should Consider |
|---|---|
| I. Symptoms<br>  1. Pain and/or burning around shoulder area, initially diffuse.<br>  2. Weakness of arm and shoulder girdle.<br>  3. Arm just hangs down, or is supported with opposite arm. | Acromioclavicular joint separation<br>Shoulder dislocation<br>Fractured clavicle<br>Brachial plexus lesion<br>Rotator-cuff tear<br>Biceps subluxation<br>Fractured humerus |
| II. Ask athlete to point out tender area (this is often very difficult for the athlete to do initially. | |
| III. Observe and then palpate gently:<br>  1. Sternoclavicular joint<br>  2. Clavicle, midshaft<br>  3. Clavicle, outer end<br>  4. Acromioclavicular joint<br>  5. Contour of shoulder<br>  6. Rest of shoulder and upper arm | Sprain/dislocation<br>Fracture<br>Pointer or acromioclavicular separation<br>Acromioclavicular separation<br>Shoulder subluxation or dislocation<br>Fractured humerus |
| IV. If all above are negative, palpate more firmly over:<br>  1. Anterior capsule<br>  2. Biceps<br>  3. Lateral to and under acromion process<br>  4. Posterior capsule<br>  5. Greater and lesser tuberosities of humerus | Shoulder subluxation<br>Subluxation of long head of biceps<br>Supraspinatus (rotator-cuff) tear<br>Posterior dislocation or anterior subluxation<br>Avulsion fracture; greater tuberosity (supraspinatus insertion) or lesser tuberosity (subscapularis insertion) |
| V. Range of Motion<br>Check shoulder through full range of active motion. Then test range of motion against resistance. | If athlete can't bring arm across chest (adduction and internal rotation) an anterior dislocation is probably present. If athlete can't abduct and externally rotate, a rotator-cuff (and deltoid) injury or posterior dislocation is probably present. Weakness of flexion and abduction may mean:<br>  1. Muscle strain, e.g., supraspinatus strain<br>  2. Brachial plexus lesion<br>  3. Localized nerve lesion, e.g., axillary nerve<br>  4. Inhibition due to pain |
| VI. Check sensation over neck, shoulder, and arm. | Possible neck injury. |
| VII. If all above are negative, examine for tenderness over brachial plexus, neck musculature, and posterior spinous process of cervical vertebrae. | |
| VIII. If all the above are negative:<br>  1. Test for subluxation of shoulder-apprehension sign.<br>  2. Put neck through full range of motion, then full range of motion against resistance; also, compression test.<br>  3. Test power of each muscle group of the arm. | |

fixation are rarely indicated and should be discouraged because fixative devices may migrate into the chest cavity, heart, or spinal canal (Allman, 1967).

Fractures that involve the inner or proximal third of the clavicle may cause epiphyseal injury at the SC joint, as well as possible SC joint subluxation. The use of a supporting sling is the only treatment. Fractures that involve the outer or distal one-third of the clavicle are subdivided into three types:

  a. Undisplaced fractures (Type I)
  b. Displaced fractures (Type II)
  c. Articular fractures (Type III)

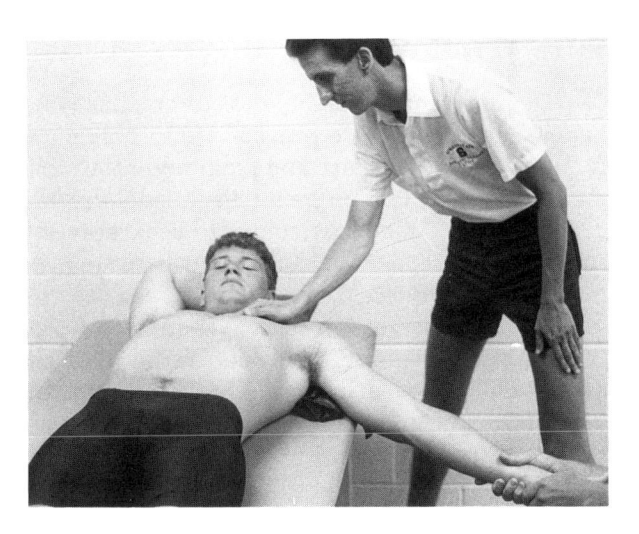

**Fig. 12A-4.** Reduction Technique of Sternoclavicular Dislocations. Appropriate elevation of the clavicle for posterior displacement and depression of the clavicle for anterior displacement.

Type I stable fractures are treated symptomatically with a sling. Unstable Type II fractures are treated with a Kenny-Howard splint or a simple sling alone. A Figure 8 should not be used. Type III fractures can use a sling, but these patients may require a surgical intervention referred to as the Mumford procedure.

### Acromioclavicular Separation

An AC separation accounts for 12% of all shoulder dislocations (Wickiewicz, 1983). An intra-articular meniscoid fibril cartilaginous disc is unique to the anatomy of this small joint. This disc may be absent in as many as half of all shoulders but it seems to be present in most children and young adults. The joint is stabilized by surrounding ligamentous and muscular structures, including the acromioclavicular ligament and the deltoid and trapezius muscles. The mechanism of injury in most AC separations is a fall on the top of the shoulder or a direct blow to it. This is the etiology common in wrestling and football. The relatively weak acromioclavicular ligaments rupture first, followed by the coracoclavicular ligaments. There are three grades of acromioclavicular sprains.

**Grade I** is by far the most common. There is no laxity of the AC joint nor any gross deformity, with the possible exception of swelling over the joint. Physical examination reveals tenderness to palpation of the joint and pain on motion, especially abduction of the shoulder. Ice should be applied acutely and a sling worn for 7-10 days as needed. When there is no pain at rest, strength and range of motion exercises (especially of the deltoid and trapezius muscles) should be begun and continued to the point pain begins. Ice should be applied after exercise. Return to competition is allowed when there is normal flexibility function and lack of symptoms. Most individuals do well after a Grade I injury but 8%-9% have persistent symptoms (Bergfeld, 1978; Cox, 1981). Bergfeld postulates that there may be a higher incidence of symptoms among patients who were treated with corticosteroid injections to hasten their return to sports.

**Grade II** injuries involve rupture of the acromioclavicular ligament and capsule, and possible tearing of the coracoclavicular ligament. A gross defect may be present. Some cases may have little or no involvement of the coracoclavicular ligament but this is unusual. Special care should be taken to palpate for posterior displacement of the clavicle. The physical exam generally reveals small gross deformity, swelling, tenderness to palpation, significant pain on motion, and joint instability elicited by distal pull on the arm at the wrist. The x-ray evaluation should include an AP standing film of both shoulders with and without weights (10 lbs.) suspended from wrists (not held in hands). This may be unreliable in heavily muscled athletes. Elevation and displacement of the distal clavicle of less than the width of the clavicle in comparison with the unaffected side is indicative of a Grade II injury.

Treatment of Grade II is similar to Grade I injuries. Wearing a sling for 10-14 days until symptoms subside is usually sufficient, although Cox (1981) feels that treatment with a Kenny-Howard splint may be more help (Figure 12A-5). If the splint is used, frequent adjustments must be made to ensure maintenance of that reduction. The physician should allow for a slight overreduction since some loss in position will occur after the splint is removed. A word of caution — the Kenny-Howard is not a comfortable brace to wear and is not tolerated well by patients. Sufficient immobilization (sling), with or without the Kenny-Howard splint, will allow normal healing and return of function. Cosmetic concern over a "bump" over the AC joint should not be a signal for surgical intervention. The rest of the treatment is identical to that of a Grade I injury.

**Grade III (Dislocation)** injuries involve complete rupture of both the acromioclavicular and

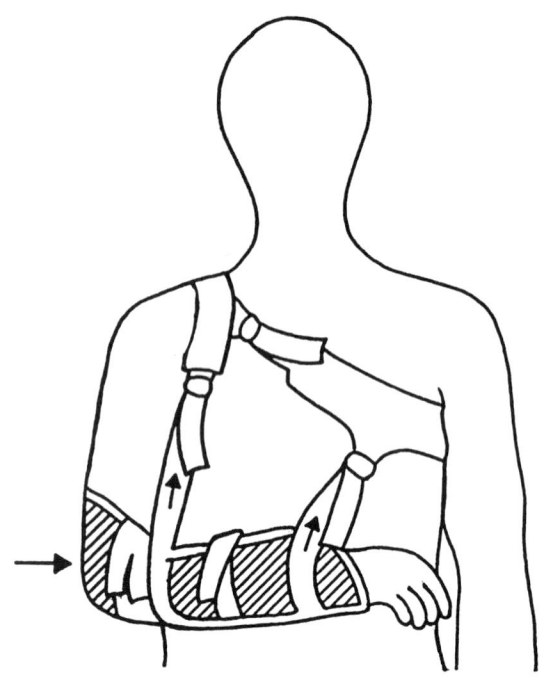

**Fig. 12A-5.** Acromioclavicular Immobilizer (Kenny-Howard Splint)

coracoclavicular ligaments. Physical examination reveals a gross deformity with distal clavicular elevation that usually creates a visual and palpable "shelf" or step-off deformity. The x-ray film shows the distal clavicle above the superior surface of the acromium. Grade III injuries can be divided into two groups: 1) marked prominence of the clavicle on examination indicates there is probable penetration of the overlying deltoid muscle, and 2) clavicular prominence demonstrated only by distal pull or weights is associated with spontaneous partial reduction.

Treatment has long been controversial. From a primary care perspective, the second group of Grade III injuries can be treated conservatively and symptomatically by using a Kenny-Howard sling for 14 days, followed by range of motion exercises that do not go above 90° abduction for four weeks. It is the first group of Grade III injuries that have caused controversy. If there is an assumption that the deltoid muscle has been penetrated, open reduction and internal fixation are recommended. This means that rehabilitation takes slightly longer, with athletics resumed at about four months (Witkowitz, 1983). Taft (1987) showed that operative management of any Grade III AC dislocation results in more complications despite comparable outcomes with conservative, non-operative treatment.

## Glenohumeral Subluxation/Dislocation

The inherent instability of the shoulder joint appears to be far more prevalent than was once thought. The very nature and anatomy of the joint makes it a candidate for instability. Glenohumeral dislocation is defined as complete separation of the articular surfaces without immediate spontaneous reduction. This injury is relatively easy to diagnose given signs, symptoms, and loss of function. However, glenohumeral subluxation, defined as transient displacement of the joint, is much more difficult. About 95% of all glenohumeral dislocations are anterior; only 1%-4.3% are posterior (Samilson, 1983). Fronek (1989) however, contends that posterior dislocations are more common than once thought.

To classify shoulder instability, Warren (1983) advocates the following system that considers etiology, direction, and type of shoulder instability (see Table 12A-3).

### Etiology

Dislocation/subluxation in sports usually is caused by trauma. With a classical anterior dislocation, there is a sudden violent overload. An arm tackle in football, with the arm at 90° abduction in forced external rotation, and with extension of the arm is an example. The humeral head, unstable in its normal relationship to the glenohumeral fossa, is held into the shoulder joint only by the anterior soft tissue supporting structures. When these are overwhelmed, the shoulder is dislocated, or at least subluxed.

**Table 12A-3. Classification of Shoulder Instability**

| Type | Direction | Etiology |
|---|---|---|
| Dislocation | Anterior | Traumatic |
| Subluxation | Posterior | Atraumatic Involuntary Voluntary |
| Dislocation/ Subluxation | Multi-directional anterior/posterior posterior/anterior anterior/inferior/ posterior | Congenital |
| | | Neuromuscular (seizure, cerebral palsy) |

Posterior dislocation usually is associated with severe trauma to the back of the shoulder. Motor vehicle accidents, seizures, and electroconvulsive therapy are the types of trauma most likely to cause posterior instability. Alcohol-associated accidents like a fall on an outstretched hand with the shoulder adducted, internally rotated, and the elbow extended will transmit stress to the posterior capsule. Athletic activities capable of producing posterior dislocation include throwing, football, and skiing.

Instabilities resulting from chronic stress on the shoulder joint occur in different sports. In the first phase of throwing, adduction and external rotation stress the anterior and inferior structures. In the follow-through (third) phase, stress is on the posterior and inferior shoulder capsule. Similarly, swimming stresses the anterior structures in backstroke and the posterior structures in freestyle. Tennis stresses the anterior structures during serving and the posterior structures in backhand strokes. Chronic instability as a result of previous dislocation, subluxation, or overuse is considered to be more disabling than periodic recurrent dislocation.

### Symptoms

It would help the primary care physician to think of shoulder instability as a continuum, with dislocation at one end of the scale and minimal subluxation (slippage) at the other. The mechanisms and pathophysiology remain the same. Pain will be the only complaint in many patients, which makes diagnosis extremely difficult. Subluxation may start suddenly or have a gradual onset. With dislocations, obviously there is almost always acute onset of pain and a lack of function which makes diagnosis easier. Where there is a gradual onset of subluxation, patients often complain of pain on the side of the shoulder that is opposite to the instability. In other words, a patient with anterior subluxation may complain of posterior pain. The physician must understand the patient's sport and know the biomechanical factors involved. It also is important to have the patient say which arm position produces pain. Many times, athletes with subluxation present with only apprehension or fear of shoulder instability.

### Signs

Accurate shoulder evaluation should include assessment of shoulder strength and stability. The position of the shoulder will be in moderate abduction with an anterior dislocation. The contour of the shoulder is flattened and the humeral head is usually palpable below the coracoid process. With a subluxation, the athlete will react when the arm is placed in certain positions. Apprehension suggests instability in that direction. Inferior subluxation can be tested by placing traction on the wrist and examining the laxity of the glenohumeral joint beneath the acromion. This type of laxity often exists in patients with multidirectional instability. Anterior instabilities are tested by having the physician stabilize the scapula and acromion while the arm is abducted and externally rotated. As the examiner pushes the humeral head anteriorly, pain, crepitation, and apprehension are elicited. To detect a posterior instability, the physicians pushes the humeral head in a posterior direction while the humerus is adducted and internally rotated and pain and apprehension will be elicited.

### Radiologic Evaluation

X-rays are necessary to diagnose any dislocation/subluxation. An AP and lateral shoulder view, plus an axillary view, are essential to confirm the position of the humerus in acute dislocation. The axillary view helps to rule out a fracture of the humeral head or glenoid labrum.

Please consult earlier portions of this chapter for a further description of diagnostic imaging techniques.

### Types of Anterior Dislocations

There are basically three types of anterior dislocation: subcoracoid (anterior) — most common; subglenoid (inferior) — relatively common, and subclavicular (anteriomedial) — rare.

### Treatment

**Reduction.** Acute dislocations of the glenohumeral joint should be reduced as quickly and gently as possible (Matsen, 1983). Early reduction minimizes stretching neuromuscular structures, decreases muscle spasm, and stops further damage to the humeral articular surface. Reduction should be attempted only after assessment of the neurovascular function of the affected extremity. Many reductions can be effected without anesthesia if performed shortly after the injury. The extent of anesthesia required for a gentle reduction depends upon severity of the trauma that produced the dislocation, the number of previous dislocations, the extent of muscle spasm, and the presence of "locking" in the dislocation.

Reduction of an anterior dislocation is usually done by applying traction to the abducted, externally-rotated, flexed arm along the line of the arm. The patient should be prone or supine with the body fixed. Slight counter traction by an assistant can be helpful. A rocking of the humerus from internal to external rotation can help unlock most dislocations and stretch out the anterior capsule to facilitate the reduction. If spontaneous reduction doesn't occur when the dislocation is unlocked, the physician internally rotates and adducts the arm. This is basically the modified Kocher method.

There are two other methods of anterior glenohumeral dislocation reduction. In the Simpson method, the patient lies on a table with a weight or tension on the arm. If done gradually, gravity and/or the tension/weight with some muscle relaxation will spontaneously reduce the humerus. In the Milch method, the physician externally rotates and abducts the arm overhead, unlocking the head of the humerus, then pushes the humeral head posteriorly back into place and returns the arm to a normal relaxed position.

After any reduction, the physician should re-access neurovascular status and the integrity of the rotator cuff.

Reduction of the rare posterior dislocation are performed in the exact opposite manner, placing the arm in adduction and doing internal rotation as traction is applied.

**Rehabilitation.** The goal of rehabilitation for shoulder dislocation/subluxation is to optimize shoulder stability. Immobilization for one or two weeks in adduction and internal rotation with the use of a shoulder immobilizer is usually more than adequate for a subluxation. Three weeks of immobilization is necessary for a frank dislocation. Curiously, Hovelius (1987) found no difference in the rate of recurrence of shoulder dislocations between shoulders that were immobilized after injury for up to 3 weeks and those where free movement was allowed. Rehabilitation is begun following the immobilization period, emphasizing the muscles of internal rotation and adduction. Progressive isometric exercises should target the subscapular and infraspinatus muscles. Mild resistance exercises with rubber tubing can be used along with the free weights. For the first two or three weeks of active rehabilitation, the athlete should use the sling during the day to rest the shoulder muscles and avoid overstress. After four to five weeks, the patient will progress to complete shoulder rehabilitation exercises on all aspects.

**Return to Competition.** Aronen (1984) found that an aggressive rehabilitation program as given above decreases the incidence of anterior shoulder dislocation recurrence, and that an average length of time for full return to unrestricted activity was three months. Full range of motion should be achieved before a return to competition. Also, the athlete should be able to perform internal and external rotation against resistance equal to his/her body weight.

### Associated Injuries

The following injuries are commonly associated with dislocation/subluxation of the glenohumeral joint and the physician should have a high index of suspicion for them during his examination.

- Joint Capsule Injury
  a. Glenoid apophyseal avulsions in the young athlete
  b. Capsular tear in older patients
- Fractures
  a. Greater tuberosity of the humerus — most common (but results in no chronic instability).
  b. Glenoid rim (labrum) — Chronic instability results particularly if more than 25% of the rim is involved in the fracture.
- Neurovascular
  a. Axillary nerve — involved in 5%-33% of the first time dislocations (Rowe, 1978).
  b. Axillary artery
- Rotator cuff tears — especially in athletes over 40

Keep in mind that recurrent glenohumeral instability may have many causes. There is no essential pathologic lesion. Correct diagnosis is necessary for appropriate treatment.

### Overuse Injuries of the Shoulder

Syndromes resulting from repeated use of the shoulder can be categorized according to the phase of motion during which symptoms appear. Overuse syndromes are a result of micro rather than macrotrauma. Throwing is a central part of most sports and the shoulder is the center of action for many of them. Overuse problems are the most common group of injuries affecting the athlete in sports such as baseball, tennis, swimming, and gymnastics (Richardson, 1983).

Throwing is the most common shoulder action in sports and there are three phases: 1) cocking — with the shoulder in adduction and external rotation; 2) acceleration forward through the action or stroke — the shoulder is rapidly internally rotated (time lapse - 0.5 seconds), and 3) follow-through — there is deceleration of the upper extremity with a slowing of internal rotation (time lapse - 0.1-0.2 seconds). Depending upon the sport, certain phases of shoulder motion obviously will be more forceful or faster than others.

### Cocking or Recovery Phase

Anterior shoulder pain can be caused by chronic inflammation of the anterior rotator cuff, including the subscapularis and supraspinatus muscles. Symptoms also may occur at the insertion of the pectoralis major, the origin of the anterior deltoid, or over the long head of the biceps (Albright, 1978). The latissimus dorsi can be involved. Generally speaking, anterior shoulder pain encountered in the cocking or recovery phase is due to a problem of eccentric muscle loading.

### Acceleration Phase

Richardson (1983) has categorized injuries in the acceleration phase as those of friction or muscle fatigue.

*Friction Injuries* — The prototypical friction injury is impingement syndrome. Many inflammations of bursae surrounding the shoulder, specifically the medial scapular bursae, fall into the category of friction injuries in the acceleration phase.

*Fatigue Injuries* — The maximum muscle power of an athlete's throw, stroke, lift, or pull takes place in this phase so that muscles subjected to repeated heavy loading can fatigue. Stress fractures at muscle insertions or origins are the result.

Since a great amount of torque is developed about the humerus during the acceleration phase, it is not surprising that stress fractures or even complete fractures of the proximal humerus have been seen (Tullos, 1972). These are sometimes referred to as spontaneous ball-throwing fractures of the humerus. The muscles involved depend upon the sport and include:

a. insertion of the pectoralis muscle — ringman's shoulder (gymnastics)
b. subscapularis, coracobrachialis/short head of the biceps at the attachment on the elbow (swimming, gymnastics)
c. triceps and teres minor originating on the lateral border of the scapula (swimming)

### Follow-Through Phase

Characteristically the follow-through phase involves deceleration. Injuries in this phase are largely the result of the eccentric load placed on the posterior structures of the shoulder. Posterior lesions occur in throwing athletes as a result of rapid deceleration. The posterior rotator cuff may have varying degrees of inflammation in muscle insertions and the shoulder capsule. The rhomboid muscles also can be injured during this phase as acceleration is completed, with the scapula rotating laterally and the rhomboids, levator scapulae, and inferior trapezius muscles acting to reverse that lateral rotation. Inflammation and tendinitis are the most common types of injury. Tendinitis of the rhomboid and levator scapulae muscles must be differentiated from the medial scapular bursitis often seen as a result of friction in the acceleration phase.

### Treatment

For treatment of these injuries, the reader is referred to the section on overuse injuries in Chapter 10.

### Rotator Cuff Injuries

Rotator cuff injuries refer to diagnoses specific to the tendinous attachments that make up the muscles of the rotator cuff. These injuries can be caused either by chronic repetitive microtrauma (just discussed), acute macrotrauma, or a combination of both. Rotator cuff injuries are the most common sports shoulder injury. This is because throwing is the most required biomechanical movement in exercise (Nicholas, 1977). The shoulder plays a major role in virtually all sports but those activities that involve repetitive use of the arm above the horizontal level of the shoulder create some of the most damaging injuries. Specifically, they can lead to impingement of any of the rotator cuff tendons. Below are some sports in this category:

a. baseball (pitching)
b. football (quarterback)
c. tennis and other racquet sports (the serve and overhand)
d. swimming (freestyle and butterfly strokes involve the anterior rotator cuff tendons)
e. swimming (backstroke involves the posterior and superior rotator cuff tendons)

### Functional Anatomy

Four muscles form an inverted U-shaped reinforcement of the glenohumeral joint. They act in common, drawing the humeral head into the shallow glenoid fossa. These muscles, taken in order of attachment to the humeral head from anterior to superior to posterior aspect, are:

**Subscapularis** the major attachment of the rotator cuff responsible for internal rotation of the humerus and downward rotation of the humeral head into the glenohumeral joint.

**Supraspinatus** forming the major superior attachment of the rotator cuff and lying underneath the coracoacromial ligament. This muscle and its tendinous attachment is responsible for elevation and abduction of the humerus and for upward traction of the humeral head into the glenohumeral joint. It is the major muscle affected in impingement syndrome.

**Infraspinatus** forms the posterior-superior attachment of the rotator cuff and is responsible for external rotation of the humerus and downward traction of the humeral head into the glenohumeral joint.

**Teres Minor** forms the posterior-inferior attachment of the rotator cuff. It is responsible for external rotation of the humerus in concert with the infraspinatus muscle and downward traction into the glenohumeral joint.

All four tendons pass approximately beneath the coracoacromial arch which is made up of the anterior acromion and the coracoacromion ligament. The space through which they pass is very limited and that predisposes these tendons to mechanical impingement if any are injured or swollen. The biceps tendon also passes within this space.

### Impingement

Neer and Welsh (1977) have postulated the basis for impingement injury to be the result of one of two mechanisms:

- The volume of the structures passing beneath the arch increases as a result of:
  a. muscle hypertrophy
  b. repetitive microtrauma resulting in local inflammation secondary to overuse. The resulting tendinitis can and usually does generate edema.
  c. acute macrotrauma resulting in a strained tendon — an example might be a forced or interrupted throw as a result of restraining contact.
- A decrease in available space, usually seen with advancing age and rotator cuff degeneration
  a. chronic fibrositis
  b. chronic inflammation with edema and osteophyte formation
  c. acute macrotrauma of a less compliant cuff, resulting in frank tears

### History and Physical Exam

The clinical picture of an athlete with rotator cuff problems can include a wide variability in signs and symptoms. These can range from minimal pain with activity but without weakness or restricted range of motion, to marked tendinitis accompanied by significant pain and decreased range of motion, and/or pain with significant weakness that may signal a tear. Rotator cuff injuries have been categorized on the basis of the clinical picture presented (Hawkins, 1980). A categorization of rotator cuff injuries based upon pathologic findings has also been done by Jobe (1982). Table 12A-4 describes the four stage clinical picture.

Classically, diagnosis of Stage III and IV rotator cuff lesions involve arthrograms. Shoulder arthroscopy has recently become a more definitive procedure in the workup. Differential diagnosis of rotator cuff pathology should include:

- acute bursitis
- chronic shoulder instabilities
- primary acromioclavicular pathology

Table 12A-4. Classification of Rotator Cuff Injury

| Stage | Symptoms | Signs | State of Fibers | Tear | Pathophysiology | Treatment | Notes |
|---|---|---|---|---|---|---|---|
| I | "toothache like" discomfort after eating | Tenderness over greater tuberosity of humerus, anterior acromion, biceps tendon; painful abduction maximizing at 90°; pain on resisted forward flexion — "impingement" sign | Swelling, edema | None | Temporary thickening of the bursae | Exercise/rehabilitation; reversible lesion | Most common |
| II | Pain worse at night; ↓ ROM | Similar to Stage I but "stiffer"; painful catching sensation as arm returns from abduction | Disassociated | None | Permanent thickening of bursae & cuff with scar formation and fibrosis | Exercise/possible decompression | Usually seen in elderly or young athletes involved in intense repetitive overhead activity |
| III | Pain more severe than Stage II | All Stage II signs plus weakness | Separated | <1 cm | Permanent thickening of bursae and cuff with scar formation | Surgery* | None |
| IV | Long history of shoulder pain | Inability to elevate with superior rotator cuff muscle wasting; ↓ active ROM, but complete passive ROM; x-ray-sclerosis, osteophyte formation on greater humeral tuberosity, acromion | Separated | 1 cm | Permanent thickening of bursae and rotator | Surgery | None |

*Some surgeons at the present time feel that conservative therapy using exercise rehabilitation especially in the elderly with no significant limitation of motion or pain on motion may be more appropriate than surgery.

- frozen shoulder syndrome (adhesive capsulitis)
- cervical rediculapathy

The philosophy of treating rotator cuff injuries should be conservative, avoiding surgery whenever possible. However, Stage IV injuries and most Stage III injuries (once diagnosed) should have diagnostic arthroscopic surgery to categorize the degree of injury. Impingement syndromes involving the supraspinatus and biceps tendons are by far the most common cause of Stage I, II, and III injuries. Conservative medical management of lesser rotator cuff injuries involves:

- *Strengthening* — all shoulder muscles should be strengthened in general, especially external and internal rotators. The exercises should be pain free and use progressive resistance (PRE)(see Appendix 12A-1 for stretching and strengthening exercises specific to the rotator cuff)
- *Biomechanic and Training Changes* — as with any overuse injury, decreasing or changing the practice regimen is imperative. In swimming, this means decreasing yardage, changing the biomechanics of the stroke, and paying specific attention to careful warm-up exercises. It may be necessary to temporarily change a swimmer from long distance training to sprinting to decrease the repetitive microtrauma. In baseball, it usually is necessary to change the throwing technique and perhaps the type of pitch. It is also important to decrease the number of pitches. With tennis, the stroke may need to be changed, with special emphasis on changing the position of the body or attempts to put "spin" on the ball. Decreasing the intensity of the serve is also important.
- *Ice* — ice should be applied directly to the area after all exercise for 10-15 minutes (see Chapter 10).
- *Heat and Deep Muscle Massage* — such therapy is impractical to increase the blood supply. However, it should be done prior to exercise if it is used.
- *Electrical Stimulation* — temporary relief of pain can be achieved by using a muscle or nerve stimulator. Electrogalvanic stimulation is used where swelling is evident.
- *Medications* — nonsteroidal anti-inflammatory medications (NSAIDs) can be used but only after an accurate clinical diagnosis has been made and masking of the pain in the individual is not a significant factor.
- *Corticosteroid Injection* — with the exception of treating the inflammation of bursae and tendon sheaths, these injections generally should be avoided in the shoulder area.
- *Rest* — relative rest should be imposed. The activity producing the pain should be decreased and maintenance of cardiovascular fitness should be accomplished either with decreased regimen or by alternative exercise.
- *Prevention* — Jobe (1982) has stated that stretching and strengthening exercises as well as warm-up are important in prevention.

## Biceps Tendon Injury

Biceps tendon injuries are common. This musculoskeletal soft tissue unit is anatomically and pathophysiologically involved with the shoulder but is unrelated to glenohumeral or "true" shoulder movement. The biceps brachii has two heads but only one common tendon insertion on the tuberosity of the radius. The short medial head originates from the coracoid process whereas the long head comes from the superior lip of the glenoid fossa traveling through the bicipital groove in the humeral head. This bicipital groove is covered by a transverse humeral ligament "roof." The biomechanical action of the biceps tendon is primarily supination of the forearm and elbow flexion. It should be pointed out that the biceps tendon does not move within the groove without movement of the glenohumeral joint.

There are three types of injuries to the biceps tendon: biceps tendinitis, dislocation of biceps tendon, biceps tendon rupture. Many biceps injuries are associated with rotator cuff Stage II and impingement injuries. One third of all rotator cuff tears in older patients also involve the biceps. The etiology, biomechanics, presentation, and treatment of accompanied biceps tendon injuries is very similar to that of impingement syndromes.

### Biceps Tendinitis

Inflammation of the biceps tendon involves one or two mechanisms:

a. Trauma to the tendon is secondary to repetitive use or overuse, usually throwing or overhead occupational work, such as baseball or overhead carpentry. Pain and varying degrees of inflammation and edema are seen.
b. Sudden violent extension of the elbow can pro-

duce bicipital trauma and pain, especially in the younger athlete. Activities where this may occur are basketball, bowling, or powerlifting.

Examination reveals tenderness of the tendon when palpated in the groove, sometimes accompanied by crepitation and/or a snapping sensation on flexion of the elbow. Yeargason's test (requesting the patient to flex the elbow to 90° before the examiner extends the elbow while externally rotating the glenohumeral joint) will produce tenderness here.

Treatment that is compatible with the foregoing soft-tissue and overuse guidelines should be started once the diagnosis is made. A word of caution about injecting corticosteroids into the bicipital tendon: they can contribute to further weakening of the tendon and increase the possibility of subsequent rupture, especially if they are repeated. They should be discouraged.

### Dislocation of Biceps Tendon

Rarely, the biceps tendon can become dislocated if a tear occurs in the transverse humeral ligament or roof of the bicipital groove. The biomechanics include three types of injuries causing actions:

a. Sudden interrupting force while the arm is abducted and externally rotated (football quarterback hit on his throwing arm while in the act of throwing).
b. Chronic degradation of the soft-tissue tendon from repetitive throwing or overhead use.
c. A congenital, shallow medial wall of the bicipital groove can predispose the transverse humeral ligament to significant stress that causes subsequent rupture and dislocation. Surgery is rarely indicated in this situation.

### Bicipital Tendon Rupture

Violent trauma may rarely result in the complete interruption and tear of the biceps tendon, usually at the musculotendinous junction. This usually is seen in younger athletes. A similar type injury in the older athlete may result from chronic impingement that causes a complete tear. Physical examination reveals classic contraction of the distal muscle unit with a balling up of the muscle at the attachment site (Popeye deformity). Surgical consultation is required, although surgical reattachment and complete repair is not usually considered until after a trial of conservative treatment. The major disadvantages of conservative treatment include a 10%-15% loss of strength and a cosmetic deformity.

### Adhesive Capsulitis (Frozen Shoulder)

This usually occurs in middle age and is more common in women and diabetics. It is not a direct result of sports participation but exercise can unmask the problem. Onset often follows a period of prolonged shoulder immobilization and results in decreased range of motion, leading to marked fibrosis and lesions surrounding the shoulder articulation. Another mechanism is that supraspinatus tendinitis spreads to the subacromial bursae causing subsequent bursitis. As the inflammation continues, fibrosis involves the soft tissue tendons, bursae and glenohumeral capsule, and synovium causing subacute decreased range of motion. The syndrome may go through three distinct stages: 1) significant pain on movement of the glenohumeral joint; 2) severe limitation of both active and passive motion (frozen), and 3) spontaneous recovery. In addition to a painful, stiff shoulder, there may be nocturnal pain, often poorly localized, which frequently extends down the arm. Unique to this condition is a palpable mechanical block to motion that is not pain related. A decrease in volume about the glenohumeral joint is usually seen on x-rays and arthrograms. There is no need for further diagnostic studies.

Treatment is analgesics and NSAIDS, immobilization, and rest with a sling, and daily increasing range of motion exercises. Occasionally, manipulation of the shoulder under general anesthesia followed immediately by physical therapy has proven effective. Rarely, surgical intervention is necessary to do an open release of adhesions.

### Epiphyseal Injury

The pre-adolescent and adolescent shoulder contains so many epiphyseal plates (Figure 12A-6) that the shoulder injury pattern in young athletes is different. Ligamentous tissue surrounding the glenohumeral joint has two to five times the strength of the epiphyseal plate (Larson, 1966). Thus, an injury that might cause the sprain of a ligament in an adult might fracture a growth plate in an adolescent.

Tibone (1983) nicely summarizes four adolescent shoulder injuries:

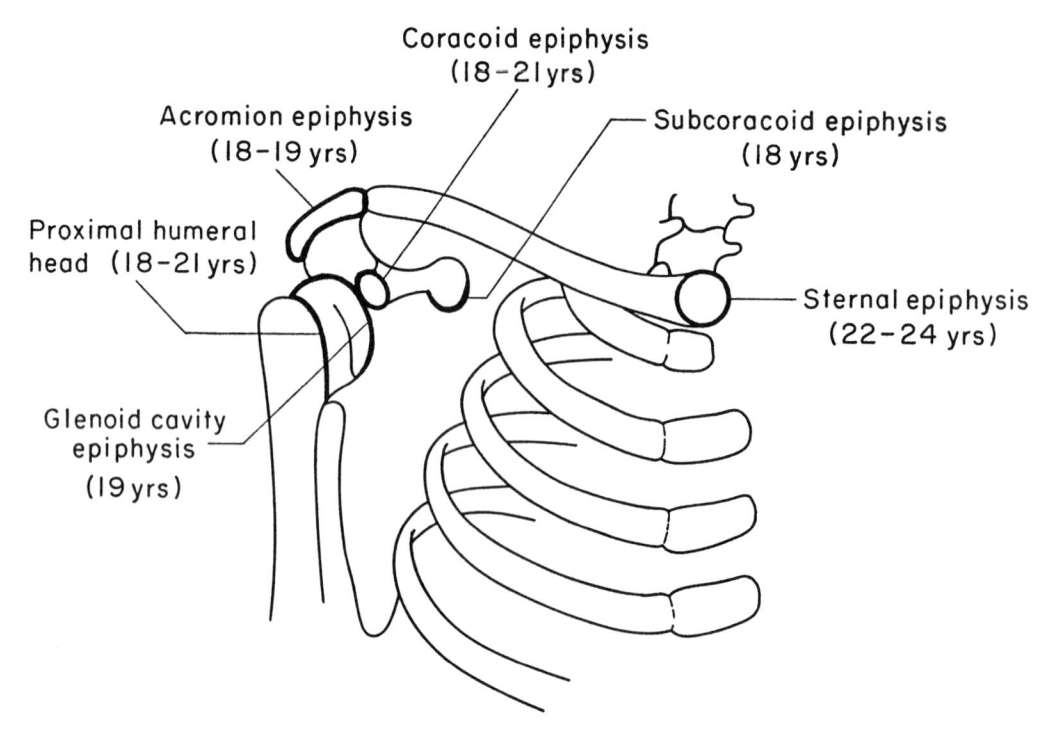

**Fig. 12A-6.** Epiphyseal Closure — Shoulder Girdle

- *Little League Shoulder* — This is believed to be the result of a proximal humeral epiphyseal separation secondary to the considerable stresses placed upon the shoulder by throwing or pitching. This repetitive stress can lead to a fracture at the epiphysis of the proximal humerus. Treatment is obvious — total cessation of pitching and throwing. There should be no long-term sequelae if the athlete complies. If an appropriate preseason conditioning and strengthening program is followed, the athlete should be able to return the following season.
- *Acromioclavicular Dislocation (Grade III Separation)* — Unlike the adult pattern of AC dislocation, injuries under the age of 13 years are rare. Children most often suffer a fracture of the distal clavicle with rupture of the coracoclavicular ligament. Surgery is not recommended.
  - *Glenohumeral Shoulder Dislocation* — Adolescents have a high incidence of glenohumeral dislocation. There is also a high incidence of recurrent shoulder dislocation in patients under the age of 20 years. It is believed that surgical repair is not appropriate in the average adolescent athlete, but that aggressive therapy should be advocated to decrease the incidence of recurrence.
- *Sternoclavicular Dislocation* — In a SC dislocation, adolescents usually suffer from fractures of the epiphyseal plate of the proximal clavicle. These fractures heal and remodel well and treatment is conservative.

### Brachial Plexus Injuries

While bony and musculotendinous injuries account for most shoulder injuries in athletes, neurologic injury can be one of the most serious and permanent injuries encountered. Shoulder trauma can produce a variety of nerve injuries. There is disagreement in the literature about the nomenclature for them. Bergfeld (1981) differentiates the various types of neurologic injuries in the shoulder as follows:

**Neck Sprain.** A mechanically-induced injury to the neck which produces local pain and stiffness but is not accompanied by neurologic symptoms or deficit. There is no fracture or dislocation.

**Burner or Stinger Phenomenon** (Cervical Nerve Pinch Syndrome, Pinched Nerve) — a neurologic injury accompanied by burning paresthesia and transient neurologic deficit probably due to instantaneous stress on a portion of the brachial plexus.

**Brachial Plexus Injury** symptoms similar to

a burner but with persistent neurologic deficit. Clancy (1977) further grades this injury (Table 12A-5).

Most neuraproxia seen in the upper extremity falls into the category of cervical pinched nerve or burner syndrome, but 5%-10% suffer the long-term neurologic deficits of brachial plexus injuries (Archambault, 1983). Contact sports like football, hockey, wrestling, and the riding sports account for most of the injuries seen in competition.

The brachial plexus is a collection of the ventral rami of spinal nerves C5-T1 (see Figure 12A-7). Injury to the brachial plexus can occur at any one of three anatomical levels:

- Cervical nerve root trunk
  a. upper (superior) trunk — ventral rami of C5 and C6
  b. middle — ventral ramus of C7
  c. lower (inferior) — ventral rami of C8 and T1
- Nerve Cords — portions of each nerve trunk divide and reform into three nerve cords named according to their relationship to the axillary artery:
  a. lateral — comes off the lateral root to the medial nerve and then becomes the musculocutaneous nerve
  b. medial cord — gives off the medial root to the medial nerve and then continues as the ulnar nerve
  c. posterior cord — terminates by dividing into the axillary and radial nerves
- Peripheral Nerves — lesions proximal to the plexus occur either in the spinal cord or spinal nerve root and cause sensory and motor deficits on a segmental basis, similar to a cervical disc

Table 12A-5. Clinical Classification of Brachial Plexus Injuries

| Grade | Findings |
|-------|----------|
| I | Transitory motor/sensory loss; may last minutes to hours; complete recovery within 2 weeks. |
| II | Significant motor weakness/sensory loss; neurologic examination abnormal at least 2 weeks. |
| III | Motor and sensory loss at least 1 year's duration. |

(From Clancy W.G., Brand R.L. and Bergfeld J.A. *Am J Sports Med* 5:209, 1977.)

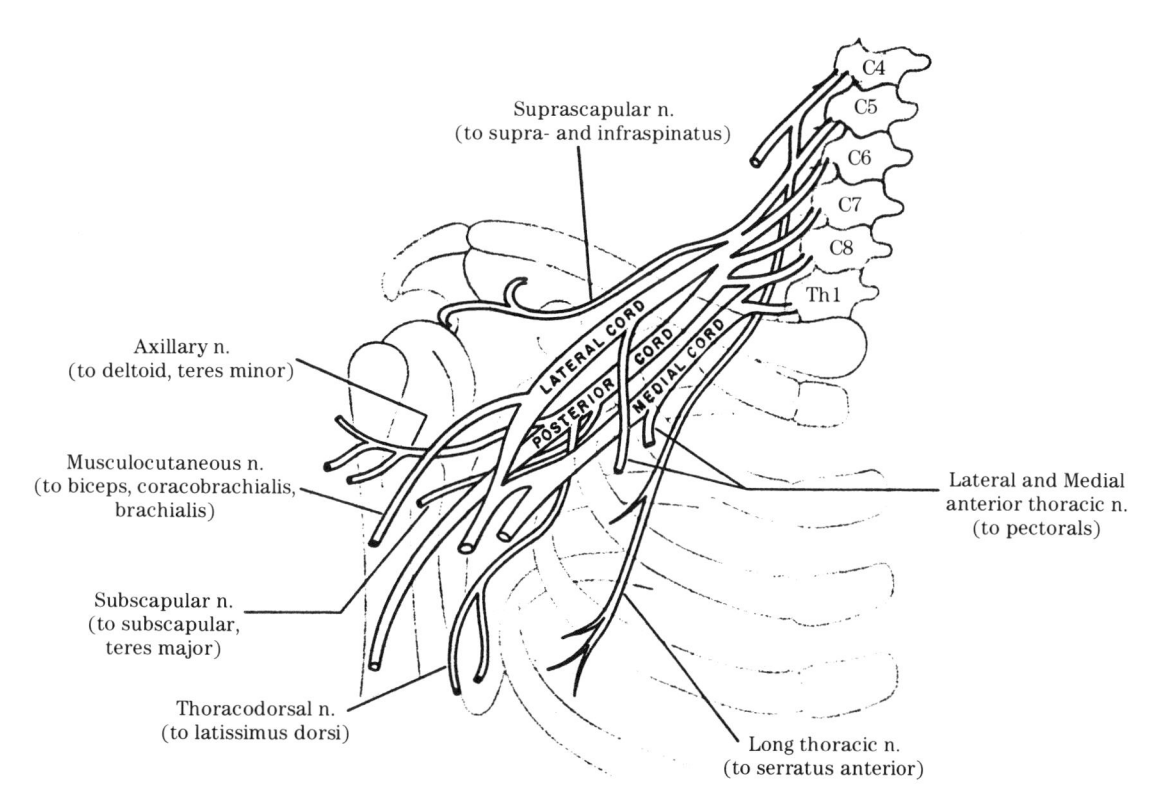

**Fig. 12A-7.** Peripheral Nerve Supply to the Shoulder Joint

protrusion. The sensory deficit follows this dermatome distribution of the upper extremity:

- C4 — shoulder pad area
- C5 — lateral aspect of the arm
- C6 — lateral aspect of forearm, hand, and radial two digits
- C7 — middle finger
- C8 — ulnar two digits and medial aspects of the hand and wrist
- T1 — middle aspect of forearm
- T2 — medial aspect of arm

Lesions may involve the plexus itself. The plexus can be damaged by forcible adduction of the arm or any type of traction trauma of the upper extremity. Various segmental deficits may occur, depending upon whether rami trunks, cords, or peripheral nerves are involved.

Injuries may be distal to the brachial plexus and involve one or more peripheral nerves somewhere along their course. Most peripheral nerve injuries are in the superclavicular portion of the brachial plexus near the actual anatomical origin of the nerve (see Table 12A-6; Figure 12A-7). The injuries are sustained either from direct trauma or from traction of the head to the opposite shoulder while the injured shoulder is depressed. This creates a bowstring effect that increases the tightness of the nerve and plexus and predisposes the nerve to a stretch injury. Infraclavicular branches plexus can be involved if the shoulder girdle is elevated so that the axilla is injured.

### Specific Injuries

**Superscapular Nerve.** The superscapular nerve emerges from the upper trunk and innervates the superspinatus and infraspinatus muscle. It is usually injured by direct trauma which causes weakness in both muscles. There will be a loss of external rotation of the scapula. It must be differentiated from a rotator cuff tear in older athletes. Because of its high position in the plexus, it is usually the first to receive the brunt of a severe impact.

**Musculocutaneous Nerve.** This nerve is often injured by direct frontal trauma and is occasionally involved in shoulder dislocations. Weakness in the biceps and a decrease in sensation over the dorsal and lateral aspect of the forearm will be noticed. Fracture of the coracoid process with displacement can also infringe upon this nerve.

**Axillary Nerve.** Axillary nerve injury may occur from direct trauma or from shoulder dislocation. There will be a loss of deltoid musculature and ability to abduct the shoulder. The pocket sign (inability to place hand in pocket) is positive.

**Long Thoracic Nerve.** The long thoracic nerve innervates the serratus anterior. Isolated paralysis of this muscle has been reported in weight lifting injuries when traction of the scalenus medius muscle entraps the nerve.

**Spinal Accessory Nerve.** This nerve does not directly originate from the cervical nerve roots (it is actually the eleventh cranial nerve) but its anatomical course makes it vulnerable when there is trauma to the upper anterior border of the trapezius at the clavicle. This type of injury most often comes from stick contact to the body (field hockey, hockey, lacrosse). Paralysis of the trapezius may result with subsequent rotatory winging of the scapula.

Sturm (1987) has correlated a significant number of vascular and thoracic injuries in patients with brachial neuropathies. We recommend that the upper thorax as well as major vessels involving the upper extremity be examined also when there is a suspected brachial plexus injury.

Table 12A-6. Brachial Plexus Muscle Innervation

| Nerve | Muscle Innervated |
|---|---|
| *Supraclavicular Branches* | |
| Dorsal Scapular | Rhomboids |
|  | Levator Scapulae |
| Long Thoracic | Serratus Anterior |
| Nerve to Subclavius | Subclavius |
| Suprascapular | Supraspinatus |
|  | Infraspinatus |
| *Infraclavicular Branches* | |
| Lateral Pectoral | Pectoralis Major and Minor |
| Median | Flexor muscles of the forearm and 5 hand muscles |
| Medial Pectoral | Pectoralis Major and Minor |
| Ulnar | 1 1/2 forearm muscles and most of the hand muscles |
| Upper Subscapular | Subscapularis |
| Thoracodorsal | Latissimus Dorsi |
| Lower Subscapular | Subscapularis |
|  | Teres Major |
| Axillary | Teres Minor |
|  | Deltoid |
| Radial | Triceps |
|  | Brachioradialis |
|  | Extensor muscles of forearm |
| Musculocutaneous | Biceps |
|  | Brachialis |

Initial treatment consists of rest and protection of the injury site while maintaining range of motion to the affected joint. Careful repeated monitoring is important because brachial plexus injuries in initial stages can be dynamic, with the full extent of neurologic loss not fully appreciated for up to two weeks after the initial trauma. Concurrent fractures (including the cervical spine) should be ruled out. If a brachial plexus injury is still a problem after two or three weeks, an electromyleogram may help demonstrate the extent of the injury. Controversy continues about using electrical stimulation to maintain muscle tone and about the use of oral corticosteroids. A program to maintain cardiovascular fitness is indicated but it should not involve major use of the affected upper extremity.

Return to play should occur only after the individual has fully recovered at least 90% of his neurologic status. Repeated examination will be necessary to fully appreciate post-injury muscle weakness. Too early a return to competition places the athlete at much greater risk for reinjury. Obtaining baseline measurements before the start of the season to see how much strength has been lost or gained will be useful.

Several important considerations for the prevention of these injuries include:

- Preseason isometric neck exercises.
- Proper coaching technique for blocking and tackling.
- Appropriate protective equipment such as properly fitted shoulder pads.
- Additional protective equipment such as cervical collars for those individuals predisposed to this type of injury (usually past victims of neuroproxia).

### Hyperabduction (Wright's Syndrome)

Compression of the brachial plexus and vessels at the thoracic outlet by the pectoralis minor and the coracoid process can result in neurocirculatory signs and symptoms when the arm is hyperabducted. During abduction, the brachial plexus and axillary vessels are pulled around the pectoralis tendon and coracoid process (Figure 12A-8). Compression of the neurocirculatory structures (brachial plexus and axillary artery) results in the axillary pulse being dampened or obliterated. The

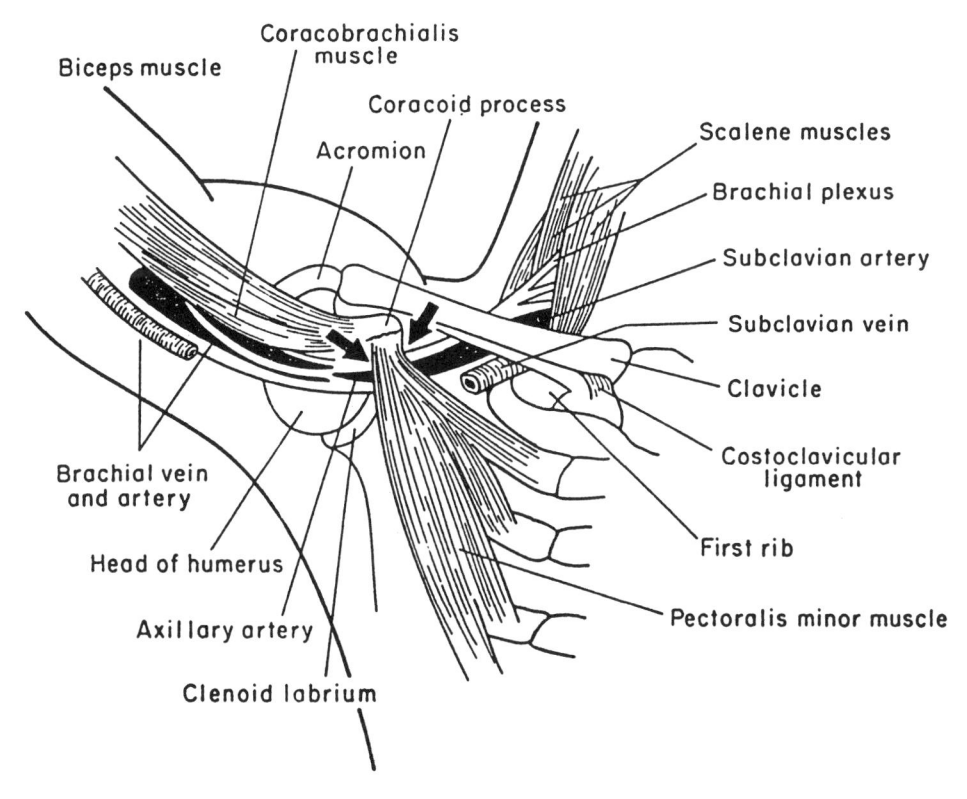

**Fig. 12A-8.** Hyperabduction Syndrome (Wright's Syndrome)

symptoms can be reproduced on examination. Wright's criteria (1945) are as follows:

- Presence of neurovascular symptoms in one upper extremity
- Reproducible obliteration of pulse with abduction of upper extremity (or exaggeration of symptoms)
- Confirmation of occupation or habit patterns involving hyperabduction (overhead work, exercise, sleep position)
- Relief through avoidance of hyperabduction

## SECTION B.
## UPPER ARM

Upper arm structures are continually exposed to athletic trauma. In football, blocking is taught with the elbows protruding and the forearms and hands held protected close to the body. This technique often results in upper arm soft tissue injury. It can include the following forms (listed in increasing severity):

**Contusion.** This is the result of a direct blow to the upper arm that causes bruising of the skin, soft tissue edema, and inflammation. Treatment consists of application of ice, compression, rest, and protection from further injury via the use of donut padding.

**Hematoma.** A deeper contusion that injures blood vessels within the musculature causes hematoma formations in relatively small, restricted areas. Physical exam will often reveal fluctuance in the area. Treatment of a first time hematoma consists of ice, compression, and protection from further injury. Aspiration of a hematoma is controversial at present. We do not advise it because no useful purpose seems to be served.

**Myositis Ossificans.** This results from ossification of encapsulated blood secondary to hematoma formation. It usually is the result of chronic, repeated trauma to the same lateral area of the forearm. A history often reveals continued use of the injured area without protection and a gradual loss of function of the underlying musculature (Huss, 1980). Physical examination will show a firm, mobile mass within the musculature, an increased forearm girth, and loss of range of motion. Pain may not be present when the forearm is moved but it is present on palpation of the mass. Diagnostic x-rays will show heterotrophic calcification within the localized muscle area if there has been chronic trauma. Ossification is a time-related, severity-related process, so the x-ray may not be positive. Treatment is ice and protection. Surgery may be necessary if the mass interferes with normal functioning of the upper arm. Early removal may provoke a recurrence of even greater growth of unwanted bone (Kuland, 1982).

**Blocker's (Tackler's) Exostosis.** This lesion is very similar in pathophysiology to myositis ossificans. It is usually present in the upper extremity, most often in the biceps muscle area and comes from repeated damage at the insertion of the deltoid or biceps brachialis muscles. Heterotrophic new bone forms after tearing of the periosteum of the bone secondary to trauma. Physical exam is similar to that in myositis ossificans. Confirmation by x-ray is possible two to three weeks post-injury. Remember, this exostosis is attached to normal bone. Treatment is as follows:

- Early recognition and follow-up;
- Ice, compression, rest;
- If the arm is seen two weeks post-injury and new bone formation is noted, the arm should be rested in a splint due to the possibility of spontaneous resorption of the heterotrophic bone formation;
- If tenderness continues with disturbance in function and no resorption of the mass, surgical excision may be necessary.

**Differential Diagnosis.** While the differential diagnosis between myositis ossificans and "Blocker's exostosis is an academic exercise, it is important to rule out osteosarcoma in the upper arm from any heterotrophic bone formation. Consult Table 12B-1 for guidelines.

Table 12B-1. Differential Diagnosis

|  | Myositis Ossificans | Osteosarcoma |
|---|---|---|
| Pain with activity | + | + |
| Pain at night | − | + |
| Population most commonly affected | <30 | 30> |
| Usual location | anterior/lateral | posterior |
| Alkaline phosphatase | normal* | ↑ |
| Size | stable | expansion |

*Normally increased in adolescents

## SECTION C.
## ELBOW

Elbow injury in athletes often causes a significant decrease in performance, especially in racquet and throwing sports which generate significant stress on the elbow. However, the overall incidence, on an age-related basis, is relatively uncommon in the young athlete. Only 2% of all adolescent sports injuries seen in one sports medicine clinic (Lombardo, 1983) involved the elbow. The NEISS survey of sport-related injuries (1981) showed that 7% of all injuries reported independent of age involved the elbow. Table 12C-1 summarizes the common elbow injuries and their relation to some specific sports.

### Anatomy

Functionally speaking, the elbow is a modified hinge joint whose primary action is flexion of the forearm (Figure 12C-1). Secondarily, the elbow permits pronation and supination of the hand as a result of the rotation of the proximal radius about the ulna. In addition, the bony prominence of the distal humerus and proximal radius and ulna serve as the origin of the flexors and extensors of the hand.

The range of motion of the elbow joint is as follows:

1. Hinge Function
   a. flexion — 135° or greater. This motion is naturally limited by the muscle mass of anterior arm. Flexion may decrease in a well-muscled athlete.
   b. extension — 0° in males and 0-5° in females. Extension may actually be less in athletes with a tight biceps mechanism.
2. Rotation of the Hand
   a. Supination — 90°
   b. Pronation — 90°
   c. Both supination and pronation of the hand can be enhanced by rotation of the humerus at the shoulder. A larger arc of up to 270° can be described with the simultaneous use of both rotational mechanisms.

The physical examination of the elbow should be approached with these points in mind:

- Observation for any variations from the norm should be done with full understanding that the dominant arm in a throwing athlete may well demonstrate hypertrophy.
- "Carrying" angle should be accessed using both elbows (a normal angle averages 10-15° valgus (Yocum, 1989)).
- Document any flexion contracture (usually in the throwing arm)
- Range of motion should cover flexion, extension,

Table 12C-1. Sports Commonly Producing Elbow Injuries*

| Sport | Common Elbow Injuries |
|---|---|
| Racquet sports | Lateral epicondylitis with backhand |
| Golf | Medial epicondylitis on downswing (trailing arm) |
|  | Lateral epicondylitis at impact (leading arm) |
| Basketball | Posterior compartment problems with follow-through on jump shot |
| Waterskiing | Valgus extension overload of posterior compartment with trick skiing |
| Bowling | Flexor-pronator soreness |
| Baseball | Valgus stress of pitching yields: medial traction lateral compression, posterior abutment |
| Volleyball | Valgus stress at instant of spiking |
| Football | Valgus stress when passing |
|  | Hyperextension and dislocation with direct trauma |
| Weight training | Ulnar collateral ligament sprain, ulnar nerve irritation |
| Canoeing, kayaking | Distal bicipital tendinitis |
| Archery | Extensor muscle fatigue, lateral epicondylitis of bow arm |

*From Whiteside, 1989

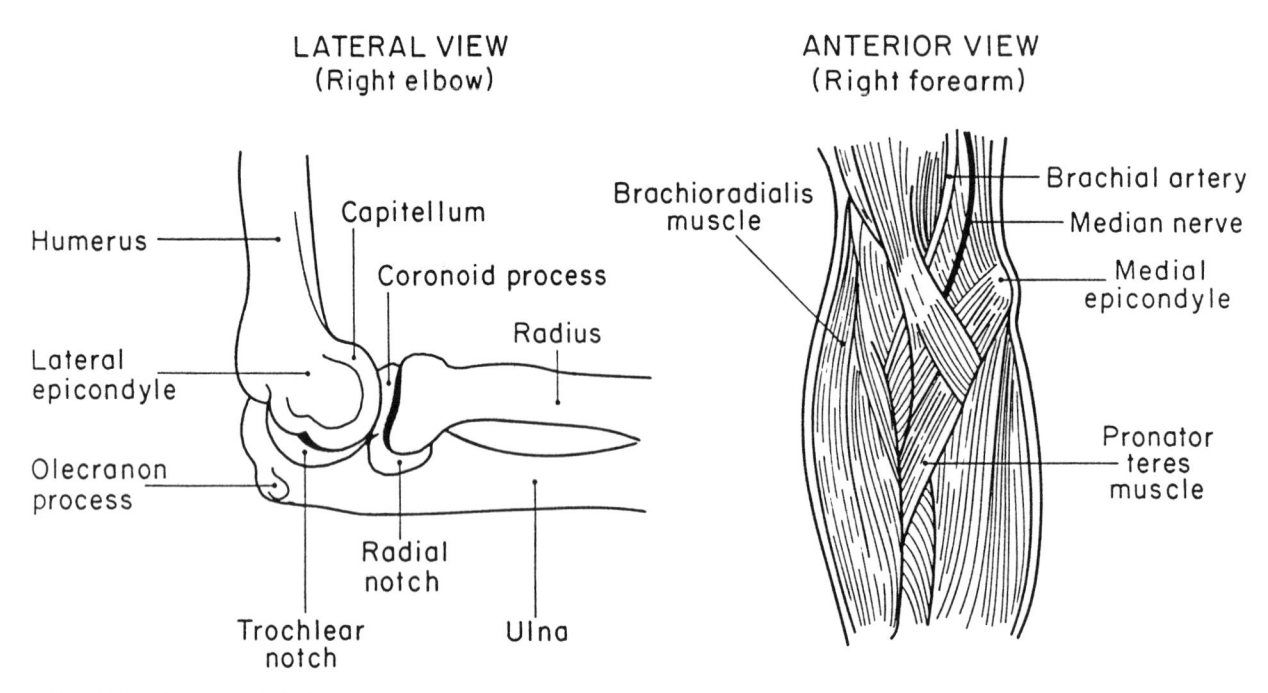

**Fig. 12C-1.** Anatomy of the Elbow

pronation, and supination comparing involved versus uninvolved joints.
- Palpation — bony prominences including the medial and lateral epicondyles and the olecranon, radial head, and olecranon fossa.
- Medial palpation will reveal the condition of the ulnar nerve. Lateral palpation just above the radial head may reveal interarticular effusion.
- Stress testing of the elbow is performed with the arm externally rotated. Instability often is reflected in very subtle changes.

Routine x-ray views for the elbow include AP and lateral views. An additional view, the reverse axial, is obtained to demonstrate the condition of articular cartilage, the bony contour of the olecranon, and the trochlear groove and is especially important in older athletes. Early osteophyte formation often can be seen along the posterior medial edge of the olecranon. Loose bodies may also be in evidence (Ireland, 1988) and may be shown well on additional oblique views.

### Throwing Injuries

Throwing injuries are a major problem in sports, and the elbow is a significant factor in the biomechanical act of throwing, so that throwing injuries should be discussed further.

### Biomechanics of Throwing

Injuries to the elbow are the most common form of discomfort in the throwing athlete (see Figure 12C-2). They occur during the last two phases of the throwing motion (see shoulder section for a detailed discussion) when forces are generated by the musculature of the shoulder girdle and upper arm in an attempt to accelerate the upper arm and the object being thrown. During acceleration and follow through, tremendous stress develops specifically at the medial aspect of the elbow, accompanied by compression and rotational forces traveling to the lateral aspect. Muscle and ligamentous structures must contend with stresses on the medial compartment; the articular surfaces of the radius and capitellum must absorb the lateral and rotational forces. In addition, during follow through, the triceps mechanism triggers rapid elbow extension, placing a great deal of force on the anterior structures of the elbow unless deceleration is timed accurately and instantaneously. Following is a general classification of elbow throwing injuries.

**Medial tendon overload.** Repeated stress to the soft tissues of the medial compartment (Figure 12C-3) results in overuse. Injuries of the medial flexor/pronator muscle group are the most common form of discomfort in the overhand thrower. Classically it causes an inability to fully extend

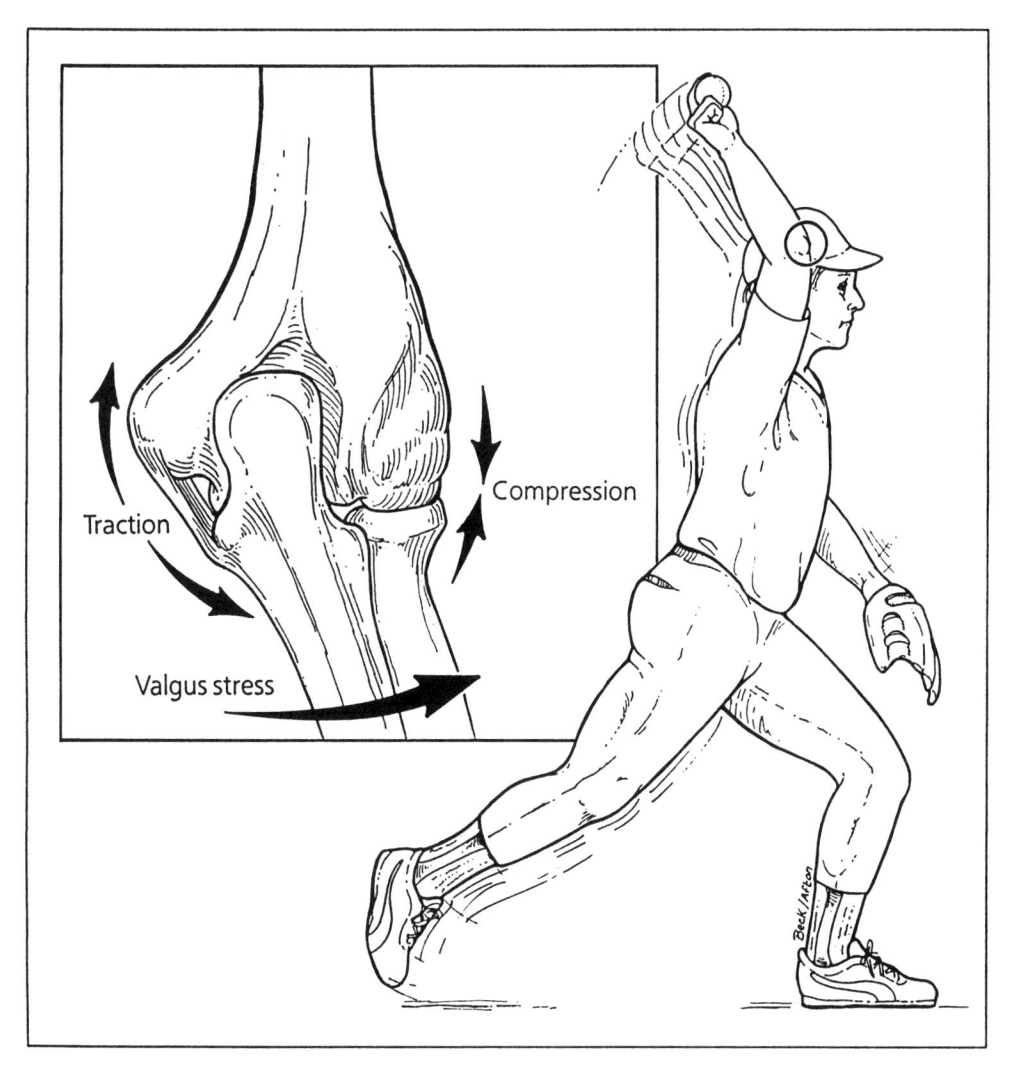

**Fig. 12C-2.** In the acceleration phase of pitching, the humerus is whipped forward with the elbow bent, placing great valgus stress on the trailing elbow. This produces strong medial traction and concurrent lateral compression, as shown in this posterior view of the right elbow (inset). (Used with permission of Joan Beck, artist.)

the elbow secondary to the pain of stretching the injured mechanism. Generally, it should be treated by following the overuse guidelines mentioned earlier (Chapter 10). Chronic manifestations of this type of stress injury can lead to the formation of:

- bone spurs; loose, intrasynovial bodies.
- premature joint degeneration (in older athletes) — frequently traced to the early onset of elbow overuse during adolescence (See "Little League Elbow").

**Lateral Compression Injury.** Injuries to the lateral side are more serious and could lead to permanent loss of elbow motion. Such entities as osteochondritis desiccans of the capitellum or osteochondrosis of the radial head frequently are associated with lateral compression and result in significant pain and limitation of motion. X-rays are useful to determine the extent and severity of lateral compression injuries, as well as for early recognition of the previously stated two serious sequellae of lateral compression injuries. Development of either osteochondritis dessicans or osteochondrosis in an adolescent athlete should call for complete restriction of throwing for up to one year, with a return to competition only when there is full range of motion and roentgenographic evidence of healing. If the symptoms of lateral compression do not disappear with rest, or interarticular loose bodies appear, referral for probable surgical intervention should be made.

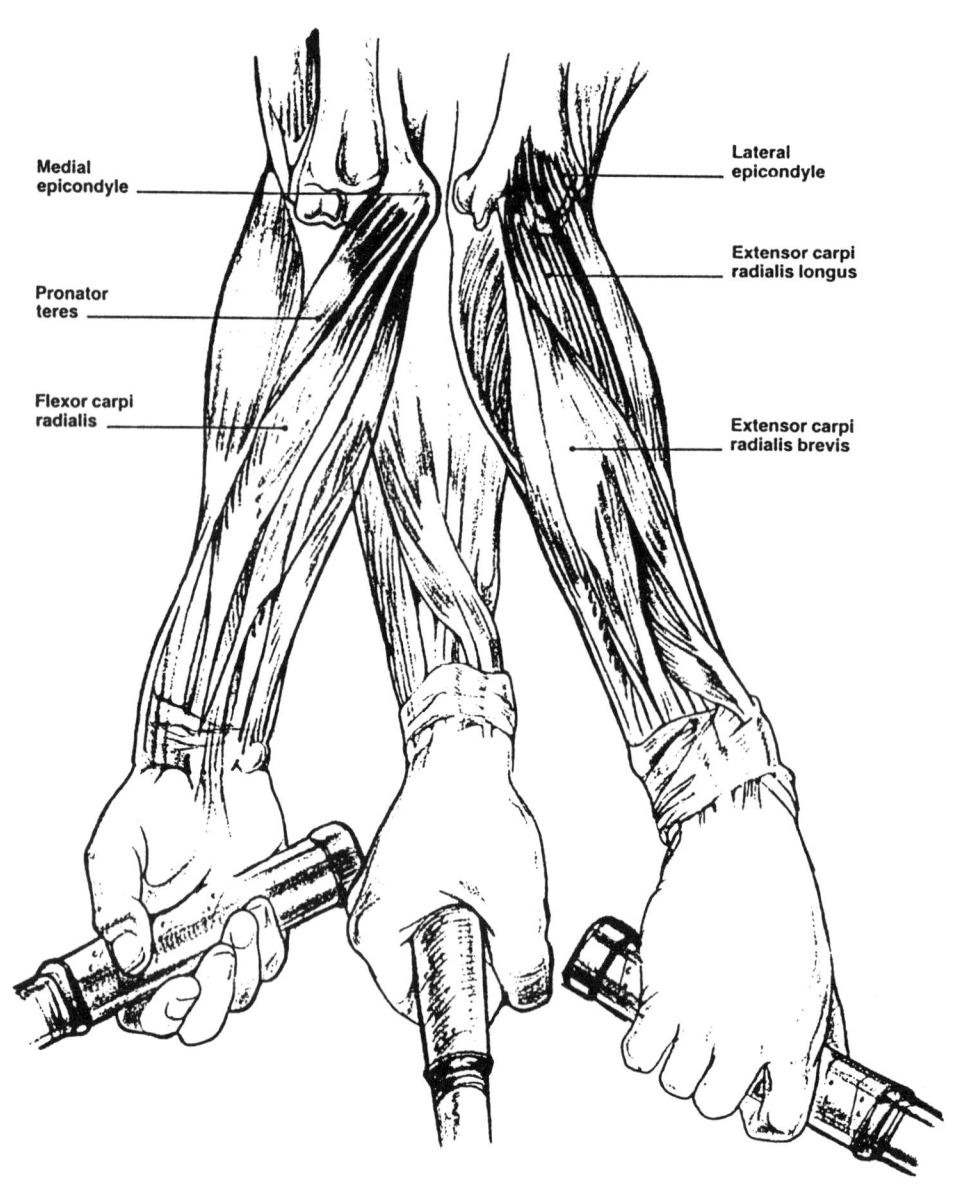

**Fig. 12C-3.** Tennis Elbow

**Extensor Overload.** In phase three of the throwing mechanism, extensors of the elbow can become repetitively stressed and overloaded if instantaneous deceleration does not occur. Acute strain of the triceps muscle at the level of its musculotendinous insertion is a common outcome. Stress fractures of the olecranon have been described as a sequela. Chronic changes associated with extensor overload include:

- bony hypertrophy with decreased range of motion.
- interarticular loose bodies.
- degenerative posterior joint changes.

### Lateral Epicondylitis (Tennis Elbow)

The most common elbow soft tissue malady is lateral tennis elbow, characterized by pain at or near the lateral epicondyle (Figure 12C-3). Various authors have looked at different classes of tennis players and they all say the incidence is between 40%-50% (Priest et al., 1980a,b; Nirschl, 1973). Tennis elbow is a significant and important sports medicine injury because tennis has become the most popular racquet sport in the United States, and the elbow is the most frequently injured joint. Elbow problems also occur in players of other racquet sports, carpenters, and anyone involved in activities that require repetitive movements of the forearm and wrist under resistance. The factors that cause injury are fairly well delineated. Lateral epicondylitis normally affects amateur players (poor biomechanics), and may reflect equipment as well as overuse problems (correct grip, proper handle thickness, proper racquet weight). Two important causes of tennis elbow in most people are ordinary overuse and faulty handstroke.

The average patient is between 35 and 55 years old. Ten percent of patients will have pain in other areas too (both lateral elbows, medial and lateral compartments of the same elbow, shoulder). Physical examination, including stress testing of the extensor supinator muscles, elicits symptoms. Localized tenderness predominantly at the origin of the extensor brevis muscle distal to the lateral epicondyle is pathognomonic.

The RICE regimen is appropriate treatment. Follow the guidelines for overuse syndromes to stage and treat. Corticosteroid injection is not advisable here because of secondary collagen necrosis. The effectiveness of elastic straps to control and diminish pain is inconclusive. A great deal depends on the design of the brace. Nirschl (1986) does indicate that counterforce bracing alters angular acceleration and may diminish the force and pain of lateral tennis elbow (Figure 12C-4). Rehabilitation should include strengthening of the forearm flexors and extensors. Rehabilitation strengthening exercises should begin after inflammation and acute pain have been controlled. Technique changes often decrease pain in the injured area. Specific attention should be placed on the backhand stroke with lateral epicondylitis. Muscle activity should be shifted away from the wrist extensors and supinators.

Proper equipment is important in injury prevention. In racquet sports, the weight and length of the racquet should be considered and handle size should be determined by grip size measurements (Figure 12C-5). String tension should be decreased two or three pounds under the manufacturers recommendation.

### Medial Epicondylitis

Medial epicondylitis is more a throwing injury, specifically pitching, than it is of racquet sports. The incidence of medial tennis elbow is one-fifth that of lateral. This injury usually is found in veteran and professional tennis players who overuse the medial compartment by intense hitting, but who have good stroke biomechanics. Studies support the contention that heavy pitching as a youth can lead to significant elbow injury. Gugenheim et al. (1976) found that 17% of Little League pitchers studied had elbow symptoms and 12% had limitation of elbow extension. Larson et al. (1976) found similar results: 23% had elbow symptoms and 10% had limitation of elbow extension. Long-term chronic changes frequently are seen in veteran athletes who throw overhand for years (baseball elbow). The long-term effects of throwing hard are:

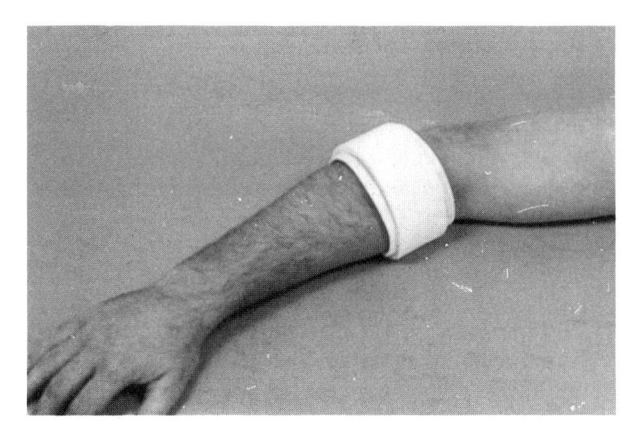

**Fig. 12C-4.** Tennis Elbow Brace

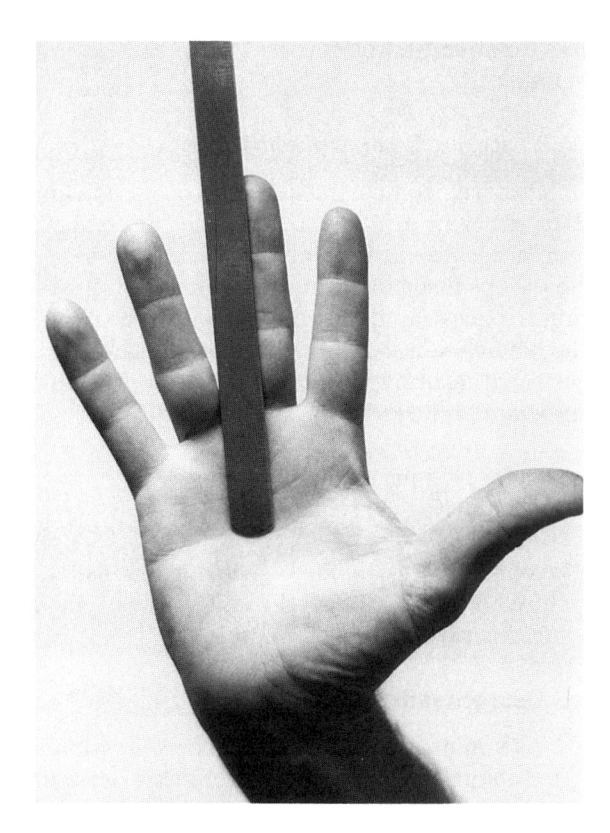

**Fig. 12C-5.** Grip Size Measurement

- Flexion contracture — anterior capsule and biceps brachii tendon are involved, secondary to build-up of bone on the coronoid process.
- Medial collateral ligament contractures and/or ruptures secondary to chronic valgus overload — bone spurs can break off and entrap the ulnar nerve.
- Ulnar neuritis — subluxation of the ulnar nerve associated with tingling pain of the fourth and fifth fingers. Rupture can result but is rare.
- Articular cartilage degeneration of the radiohumeral joint.
- Posterior compartment lesions — the olecranon process can jam into the fossa and create bony microtrauma that results in bony overgrowth or bone chips and interarticular lose bodies.

Specific changes in the young athlete with an open medial epicondylar apophysis are irritation of the apophysis (apophysitis) or, more severely, separation and fragmentation of the apophysis (Little Leaguer's Elbow) (Figure 12C-6).

Treatment includes early recognition, complete rest, ice, and NSAID. Corticosteroids should be discouraged because of tissue necrosis. If ulnar neuritis is present, an elbow pad should be used to protect the nerve during further exercise. Guidelines for all soft-tissue overuse (Chapter 10) should be followed.

**Posterior Compartment Injuries**

Posterior compartment lesions occur as a long-term effect in athletes in throwing and racquet sports. Localized tenderness is usually present at the triceps insertion or directly on the olecranon. Pain is exaggerated on stress testing of the triceps. The biomechanics of posterior compartment injuries is extensor overload, as discussed previously. Associated injuries in this area include:

- posterior tennis elbow.
- bony spurring (baseball elbow).
- bone chips.
- javelin throwers elbow — violent extension of the elbow on the follow-through phase of throwing, fracturing the olecranon tip.

**Osteochondritis Dessicans**

As a major sequela of lateral compression injuries about the elbow, osteochondritis dessicans represents a significant injury. The prepubescent

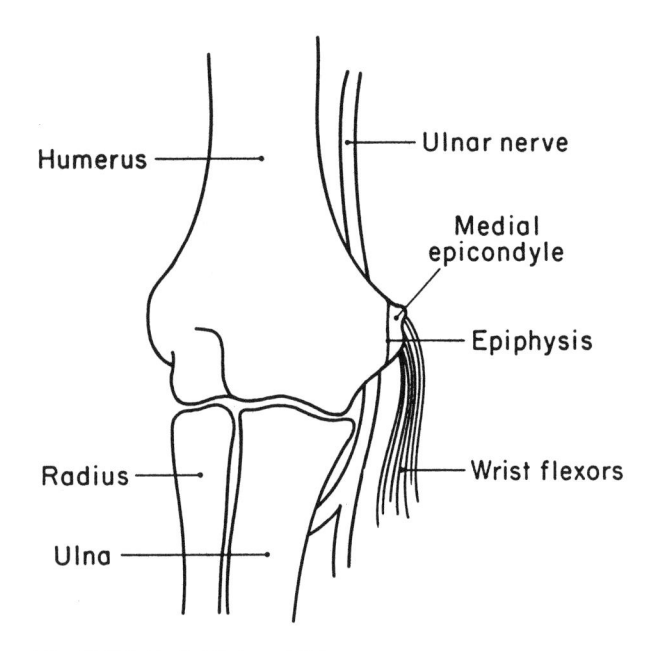

**Fig. 12C-6.** Medial Epicondylitis

athlete may have a condition known as osteochondrosis, whereas the pubescent individual will suffer from osteochondritis dessicans (Yocum, 1989). The etiology of osteochondritis includes:

- avascular necrosis of the capitellum secondary to disruption of epiphyseal blood flow.
- shearing injury that fractures through the cartilage to the bone below, resulting in the defect.

This condition is seen with increasing frequency in gymnasts who use their elbow as a weight-bearing joint (Singer, 1984). Initial treatment is conservative, consisting of refraining from activities that exacerbate the condition, and symptomatic relief. If the fragment loosens, surgery may be necessary.

**Hyperextension**

Elbow hyperextension usually occurs when an abnormal, usually violent, stress is placed upon the elbow and forces it past the normal range of motion. Treatment consists of ice, rest (usually with the elbow flexed at 90° and placed in a sling), and prevention of hyperextension upon return to play.

**Olecranon Bursitis**

Olecranon bursitis develops secondary to a direct blow to the elbow, and is the most common acute soft-tissue injury. The large olecranon bursa overlies the olecranon prominence and is predisposed to acute swelling and inflammation after any fall on a flexed, unprotected elbow (Figure 12C-7). Diagnosis is relatively easy once a history of a direct blow or fall is obtained. The athlete complains of pain, localized swelling, and erythema. If swelling is significant, there will be decreased flexion secondary to the stretching of the inflamed bursa. There is no disturbance to underlying bone.

### Treatment

**Acute.** Aspiration of the bursa followed by application of a compression dressing for 24-48 hours. Complete rest of the elbow joint without movement will decrease the likelihood of a recurrence of bursal fluid buildup. Some physicians recommend injecting a small amount of corticosteroid following the aspiration to promote quicker healing and closure of the potential space.

**Chronic.** Aspiration should be followed by injection of 1-2 cc of corticosteroid. A compression dressing should be applied for up to 72 hours. If repeated aspirations are unsuccessful or calcific bursitis evolves, surgical excision is warranted.

Prevention of chronic olecranon bursitis should be aimed at eliminating repeated trauma from pads, foam, or other equipment. It is imperative that the sterile technique be followed during aspiration to prevent a secondary infection.

Generally speaking, aspiration should occur as soon as possible after injury to decrease the limitation of range of motion by swelling and/or inflammation. An early return to activity can be accomplished by keeping the swelling and/or inflammation to a minimum. The athlete can return to activity when he has full range of motion. Ice, used prophylactically after activity for one or two weeks, will help discourage recurrence.

It is important that the primary care practitioner rule out a fracture via x-ray before a diagnosis of olecranon bursitis *alone* is made. In addition to an obvious fracture, x-ray signs to watch for include a positive anterior and/or posterior "fat pad" sign.

### Subluxation/Dislocation

Unlike the shoulder, elbows rarely sublux but they will dislocate and remain so until proper procedures are taken to reduce the joint. The elbow is more frequently dislocated in children and young adults. The reason is thought to be the incomplete development of the coronoid and olecranon processes. The most frequent dislocation is the posterior or posterio-lateral resulting from a fall on the outstretched supinated hand with the forearm in complete extension (Figure 12C-8). Hyperextension carries the joint through to dislocation.

Next in frequency is lateral dislocation of the radial head. Other dislocations of the elbow are very rare, and include:

- Anterior — usually complicated by fracture of the olecranon.
- Medial — resulting from direct severe trauma or wrenching of the forearm. This has been seen in wrestlers following maneuvers that slam their opponents to the mat.
- Lateral.
- Divergent — The radius and ulna are separated and split by the humerus.
- Posterior Ulnar — Rare because of the firm attachment of the radius to the ulna by the annular ligament.

### Initial Assessment

Posterior dislocation may be incomplete (with the coronoid process of the ulnar resting on the trochlea) or complete (with the coronoid process locked in the olecranon fossa). There may be involvement of the biceps and brachialis tendons or, more seriously, the neurovascular bundle. Symptoms will indicate impairment of the ulnar radial and/or medial nerves or brachial blood vessels. The arm or forearm usually is carried in moderate flexion. A variable degree of swelling will be seen on examination. Viewed from the side, the forearm looks shortened with an unusually prominent

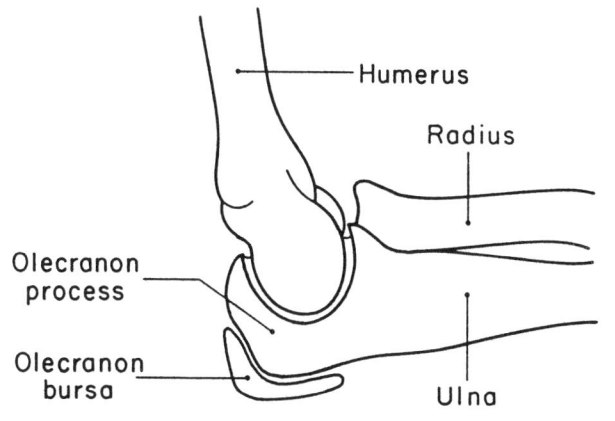

**Fig. 12C-7.** Olecranon Bursitis

## POSTERIOR DISLOCATION of the ELBOW

## FRACTURE of CORONOID PROCESS

**Fig. 12C-8.** Posterior Dislocation of the Elbow and Fracture of Coronoid Process

olecranon. Palpation of bony landmarks will show two abnormalities:

- At 90° flexion, the olecranon sits posterior to a line between the two epicondyles.
- The radial head can be palpated behind the lateral epicondyle (unless fractured).

### Diagnostic Aids

X-ray assessment is mandatory to rule out accompanying fractures, especially of the coronoid process. Occasionally a posterior dislocation will cause a fracture of the head of the radius or lateral epicondyle.

### Treatment

Dislocations should be reduced quickly before muscle spasms set in or neurovascular compromise occurs. The competency of the neurovascular bundle should be assessed before reduction. Anesthesia may be necessary, particularly for heavily muscled individuals. There are three major means of reduction (Conwell, 1969)(Figure 12C-9a-c):

- Gradual reduction — The safest and easiest method. The athlete lies face down on the table with the arm hanging over the side. After relaxation of the muscle and gradual downward traction, reduction will occur spontaneously.
- Hyperextension and traction (in children) — When the coronoid process is small and tissues are relatively lax, reduction can be effected by slight hyperextension of the joint with downward traction and counter traction followed by gradual flexion.
- Manipulation — Under general anesthesia, the athlete's hand is fully supinated and the forearm extended as far as muscular resistance will permit. Then downward traction on the upper forearm will reduce the injury.

Regardless of the method, an x-ray should be taken immediately after reduction and again in one week to rule out redislocation. After reduc-

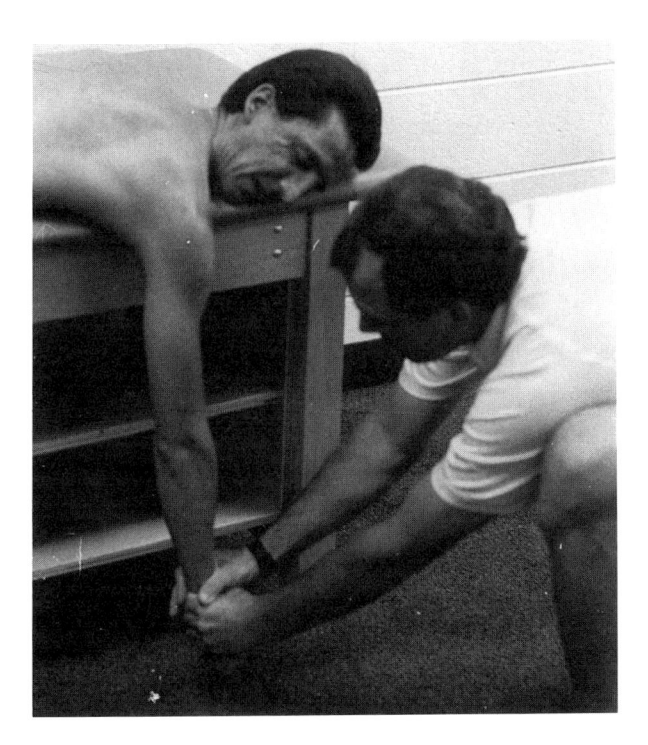

**Fig. 12C-9a.** Reduction by Gradual Traction

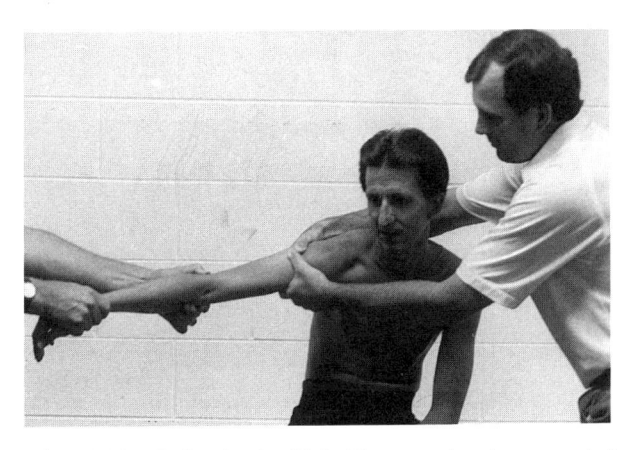

**Fig. 12C-9b.** Reduction by Slight Hypertension Accompanied by Traction and Countertraction Followed by Gradual Flexion **(c)** below

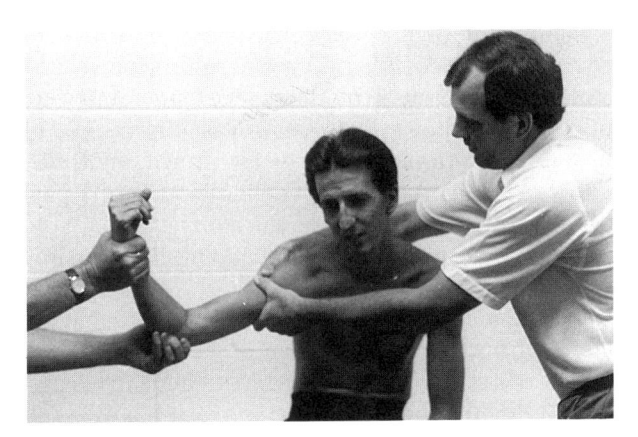

tion, the elbow should be flexed at 90-100° and immobilized in a long arm cast for four to six weeks.

Rehabilitation after the immobilization period includes active range of motion exercises. Passive motion or forced extension should be discouraged because it can promote elbow stiffness or myositis ossificans of the surrounding soft tissue.

Prevention of redislocation can be effected with adequate muscle strengthening exercises of the surrounding extensors and flexors of the joint. The elbow should be taped in slight flexion to prevent hyperextension on when the athlete returns to activity. That should be considered only after return of full range of motion, and muscle group testing shows no inherent weakness.

**Things to Remember.** The elbow should not be flexed before reduction to prevent possible damage to the brachial artery.

### Radial Head Dislocation

Radial head dislocation may occur as an isolated injury or in combination with fracture of the humerus, radius, or ulna near the elbow. Dislocation in the forward direction is the most common form of this injury (Figure 12C-10). The radial nerve may be stretched or even torn. In young children (usually between the ages of two and four, this injury is referred to as "pulled elbow" and happens when parents violently pull their children or pick them up by one arm. Biomechanically, it is the result of sudden traction on the forearm.

#### Initial assessment

The forearm usually is carried in a position of pronation and slight flexion. The radial head can be easily identified in an abnormal position by palpation. The function of the radial nerve should be evaluated prior to any treatment. This can be done by asking the athlete to extend the wrist, thumb and fingers, and by examining sensation on the dorsum of the hand and wrist.

#### Treatment

Treatment calls for reduction, accomplished with downward traction applied to the pronated forearm while pressure is applied over the radial head. The forearm is rotated 90° in supination and the elbow is flexed, maintaining pressure on the radial head (Figure 12C-11). In older children and adults, the arm must be immobilized in full supination and flexion for three weeks with a posterior

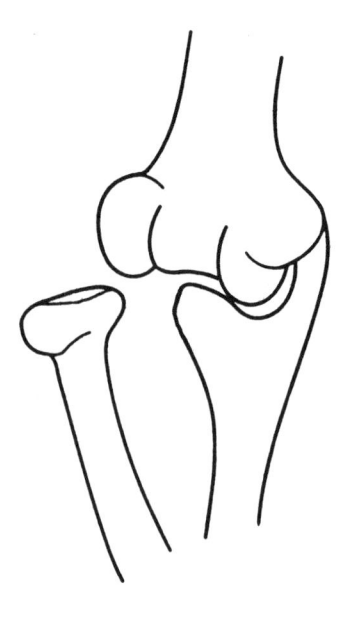

Fig. 12C-10. Dislocation of Radius at Elbow

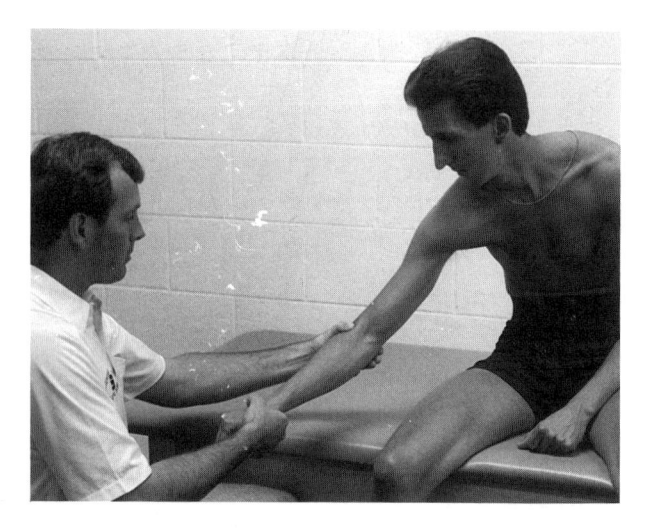

Fig. 12C-11a. Traction Applied with Pressure to Radial Head as Forearm is Supinated

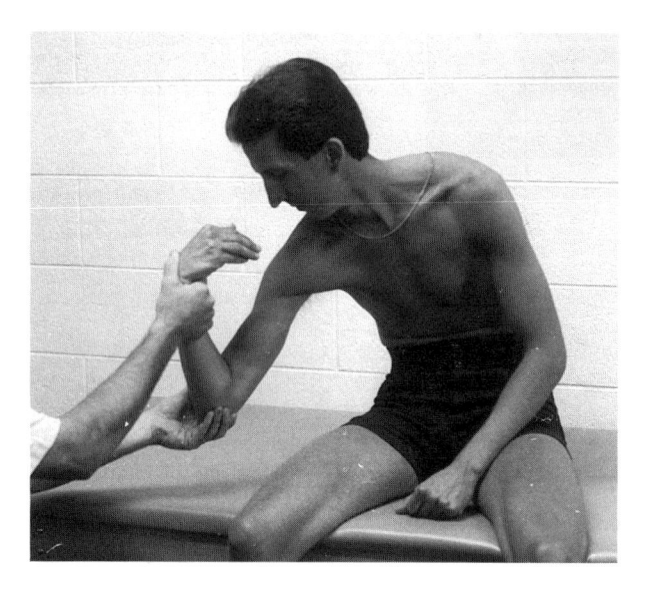

Fig. 12C-11b. Forearm is Flexed Maintaining Supination of Radial Head Pressure

plastic splint. No medical aftercare or protection is required in young children with "pulled elbow." However, education for the parents and screening for possible child abuse should be considered. The prognosis for an elbow dislocation without fracture is good if managed conservatively (Josefsson et al., 1984).

## Fractures

### Supracondylar

The most frequent fracture of the elbow is supracondylar, caused by falls on the outstretched hand with the elbow in flexion or forced hyperextension (Figure 12C-12). Once broken, the distal humeral fragment is pushed upward and backward by the force and held there by subsequent spasm of the triceps muscle. Sixty percent of all elbow fractures are of this variety. The injury is more common in adults.

**Biomechanics.** Forward and downward displacement of the distal humerus produces this injury and occasionally injures the neurovascular bundle lying in the antecubital space.

**Signs and Symptoms.** This fracture presents with a history similar to a posterior elbow dislocation; on inspection only moderate swelling of the joint is present. The epicondyle and olecranon maintain a normal relationship, with point tenderness elicited above the condyle. The arm may appear shortened. The joint capsule is torn and there is significant hemorrhage into the joint and surrounding tissues. Sometimes there may be severe swelling that renders the elbow very tender and void of bony landmarks. If the neurovascular bundle is mechanically impinged by the resulting hematoma and swelling, Volkmann's ischemic contracture can occur. As with any fracture, the neurovascular status should be evaluated before and after reduction of the supercondylar fracture.

**Diagnostic Aids.** An x-ray is mandatory, with views of both elbows for comparison before and after reduction is attempted. An occult fracture can be highly suspected if there is a positive fat

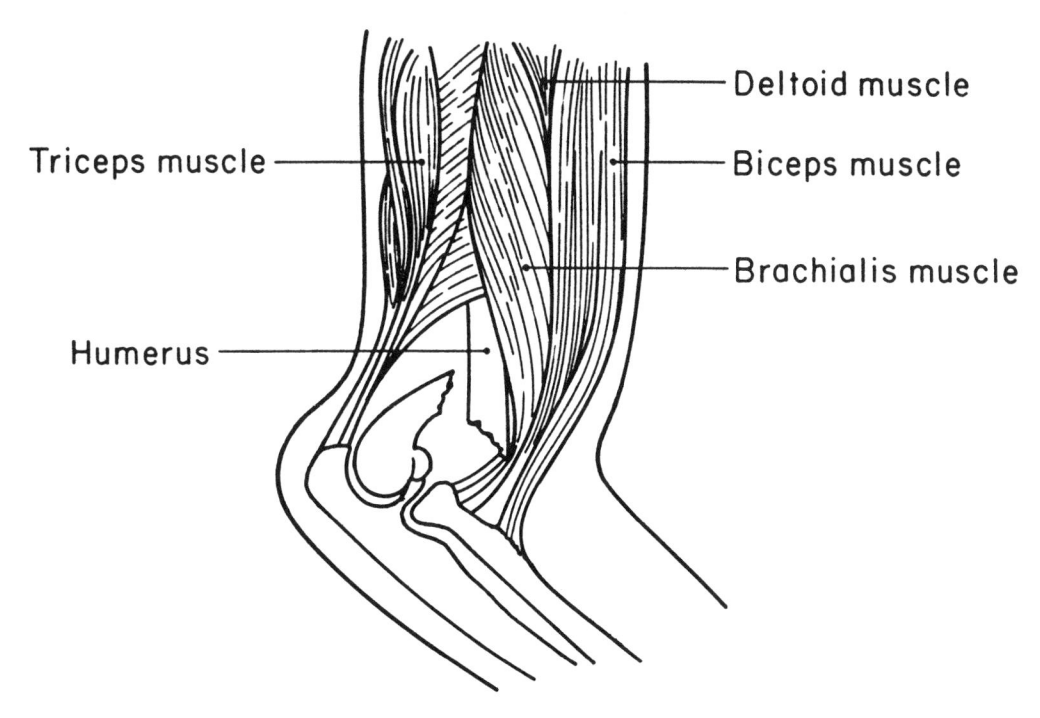

**Fig. 12C-12.** Supracondylar Fracture

pad sign on a lateral film of 90° flexed elbow (refer to Chapter 17, Figure 17-18).

**Treatment.** There are two methods of reduction:

- *Manipulative* — this usually is done under axillary block or general anesthesia, with the upper arm firmly fixed while the forearm is put in moderate downward traction followed by flexion of the elbow.
- *Suspension Traction* — the usual method for severe supracondylar fractures in young children where manipulation might be dangerous. It involves suspension of the arm with the patient lying in bed.

The method of immobilization after reduction will depend upon the position of the arm when first seen. The following signs obligate the physician to immobilize the arm in traction:

- Significant swelling.
- Decreased or absence of radial pulse or venus return.
- Difficulty extending fingers.
- Evidence of nerve involvement.

If neurovascular compromise continues despite traction, surgery to explore the brachial artery must be considered. However, if circulation improves as swelling gradually decreases, the arm may be immobilized with a cast and/or posterior splint. If the fracture is without displacement and there is no evidence of neurovascular compromise, immobilization with the elbow in acute flexion for three to six weeks is adequate.

**Return to competition** is allowed only after full range of motion is achieved and muscle weakness is corrected by muscle strengthening exercises begun after removal of the cast.

**Things to Remember.** Volkmann's ischemia contracture is the most serious complication of fracture dislocation of the elbow. It is produced by hemorrhage beneath the deep fascia of the elbow joint and can lead to permanent flexion contractures of the wrist and fingers. Close monitoring of the neurovascular status is imperative in the early stages for the treatment of this injury.

### Lateral Condyle of the Humerus

A lateral condyle fracture of the humerus is less severe than a supracondylar fracture. It is produced by hyperextension plus angulation. The fractures usually are intra-articular and have a tendency toward slow healing and nonunion. X-ray examination is important initially, and later as a monitoring device to detect a possible rotation of the fracture fragment to rotate so that its upper end tilts forward.

**Treatment.** Immobilization of the forearm in acute flexion with a posterior splint and sling.

### Medial Epicondyle

Fracture of the medial epicondyle is basically a throwing injury. The stabilizing medial ligament of the elbow as well as the flexion muscles originate from the medial epicondyle. Elbow instability may result from malalignment or nonunion of a displaced medial epicondylar fracture. Rotation of the fractured condyle downward and forward by the pull of the superficial flexors of the forearm is the main cause of nonunion. Occasionally an avulsed fragment can be displaced into the elbow joint where it decreases the range of motion. The ulnar nerve, which passes through a groove behind the medial epicondyle, is rarely involved. Physical examination reveals weakness of pronation and flexion of the wrist and fingers. Point tenderness is present over the bony prominence of the medial epicondyle.

**Assessment.** Three types of fractures have been described (Woods and Tullos, 1977);

Type 1 — Avulsion of the entire apophysis (young athlete).
Type II — Fracture through the closed epiphysis, with maintenance of the medial collateral ligament of the elbow intact.
Type III — Small chip fracture and/or avulsion involving a tear of the medial collateral ligament.

**Diagnostic Tests.** The gravity stress test is used to diagnose acute medial instability of the elbow.

**Treatment.** Displacement of the medial epicondyle by more than 1 cm is considered positive. Surgical referral is indicated in a throwing athlete with a positive gravity stress test.

**Rehabilitation.** Usual rehabilitation measures include strengthening of the involved muscle groups after immobilization.

### Other Less Common Fractures

- *Head and Neck of the Radius* — This fracture often is not visible on normal AP or lateral films of the elbow. Sometimes it can be seen only on oblique views. These fractures can interfere with the rotational component of the forearm. They usually are handled conservatively, with immobilization of the elbow for several weeks at 90° flexion and rotation at mid-neutral position.
- *Coronoid Process* — As discussed earlier, this usually occurs as a complication of a posterior elbow dislocation.
- *Olecranon* — Rare in children, this fracture is relatively common in adults and results from direct trauma such as a fall on the flexed and supinated forearm.
- *Intracondylar or T-fracture* — Again, rare in children, more prevalent in adults. This fracture is the result of more severe trauma than we have previously discussed or that is usually is present in sports.

## SECTION D.
## WRIST, HAND, AND FINGERS

### Epidemiology

Hands and fingers are the most commonly injured body parts in the 5 to 15 year-old age group and the second most frequently injured body part overall, regardless of age. Twenty-eight percent of all treated sports-related injuries involve the hand and fingers (NEISS, 1981). This may be because the hands are out in front where they receive initial contact.

There is a tendency to minimize hand/finger injuries because the hand is non-weight bearing, hand injuries rarely are debilitating initially, and because pain is more transient.

With no other injury is the potential for poor sequellae more hidden than with finger injuries. Muscles, ligaments, and bones are small and recognition of the subtleties of pathology is a challenge for any physician. Proper diagnosis and appropriate return to play are important concepts to master in treating finger injuries. Life-long dysfunction can result from improperly diagnosed and treated injuries.

Injury to the wrist, hand, or finger often is the second place "poor cousin" to the more common, better known and recognized injury of a particular sport (Table 12D-1). This may explain the relative lack of knowledge concerning these injuries among sport medicine care providers.

**Table 12D-1. Sport by Sport Profile of the Incidence of Wrist, Hand and Finger Injuries (NEISS, 1981)**

|  | All ages % | Rank | 5-14 Years % | Rank | 15 and Over % | Rank |
|---|---|---|---|---|---|---|
| Football | 35 | (1) | 44 | (1) | 29 | (2) |
| Baseball | 31 | (2) | 37 | (2) | 30 | (2) |
| Basketball | 28 | (2) | 50 | (1) | 22 | (2) |
| Gymnastics | 34 | (2) | 40 | (1) | 26 | (2) |
| Soccer | 21 | (2) | 31 | (2) | 14 | (2) |
| Wrestling | 30 | (1) | 37 | (1) | 27 | (2) |
| Volleyball | 41 | (2) | 60 | (1) | 37 | (2) |
| Ice Hockey | 23 | (2) | 28 | (2) | 21 | (3) |
| Track & Field | 13 | (2) | 16 | (2) | 13 | (2) |
| Racket Sports | 12 | (3) | 27 | (2) | 11 | (4) |

## Anatomy

The hand is the most active and least protected part of the upper extremity, an extremely vulnerable portion of the human body. It also is very complicated anatomically. Consult Figures 12D-1 to 12D-3 for normal hard and soft tissue anatomy.

The functional anatomy of the "wrist" is really a study of the radiocarpal joint. Biomechanical interplay with the distal ulna is minimal. Distal to this joint are two rows of four carpal bones each. The pisiform bone is essentionally a sesmoid bone. The proximal row of carpal bones are considered individual elements acting as intercalated segments between the distal row of carpals and the radio-ulnar articulation. Thus, the wrist joint contains three longitudinal chains:

- Central chain — capitate-lunate-radius
- Radial chain — trapezium-trapezoid-scaphoid radius
- Ulnar chain — hamate-triquetrum-ulna

In this arrangement, each proximal carpal (scaphoid, lunate, triquetrum) moves at two levels (Kauer, 1987). Wrist stability is achieved by ligaments. Major ligaments of the wrist are intracapsular, with the volar ligaments being more substantial than the dorsal. Biomechanically, the wrist not only is set up in columns as explained above, but the carpal bones also act by rows when you consider the stabilizing ligaments. With dorsiflexion (extension) and ulnar deviation of the wrists, the proximal carpal row dorsiflexes and translates radially. With flexion and radial deviation of the wrist, the prox-

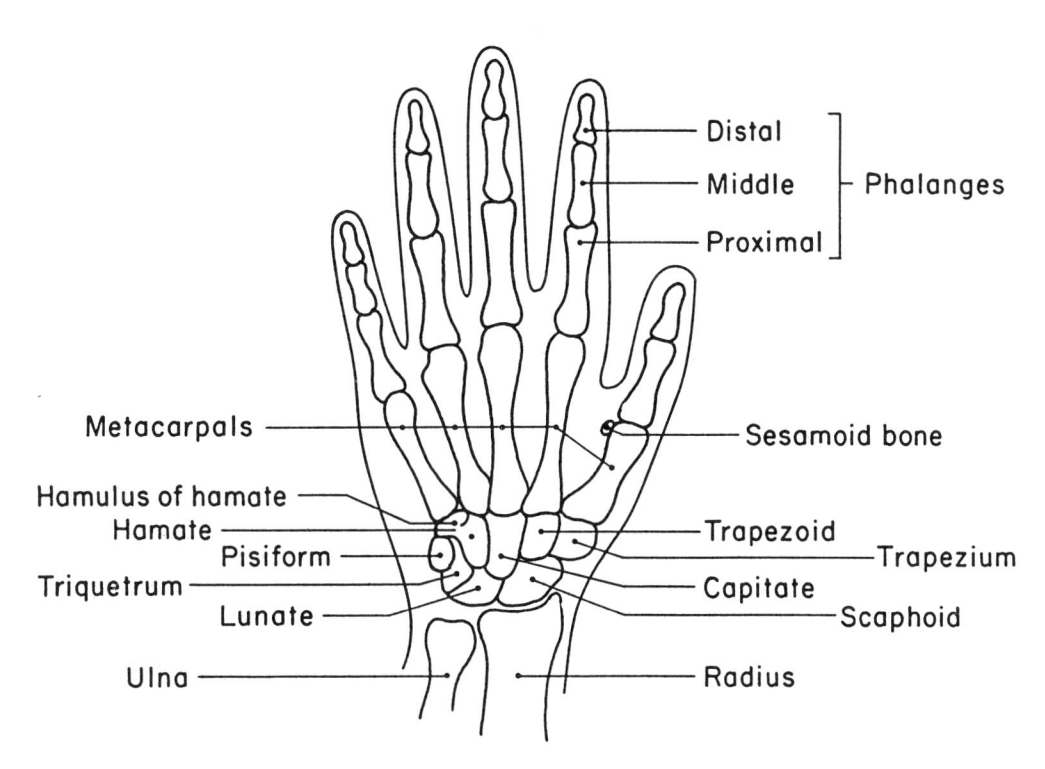

**Fig. 12D-1.** Bones of the Hand and Wrist

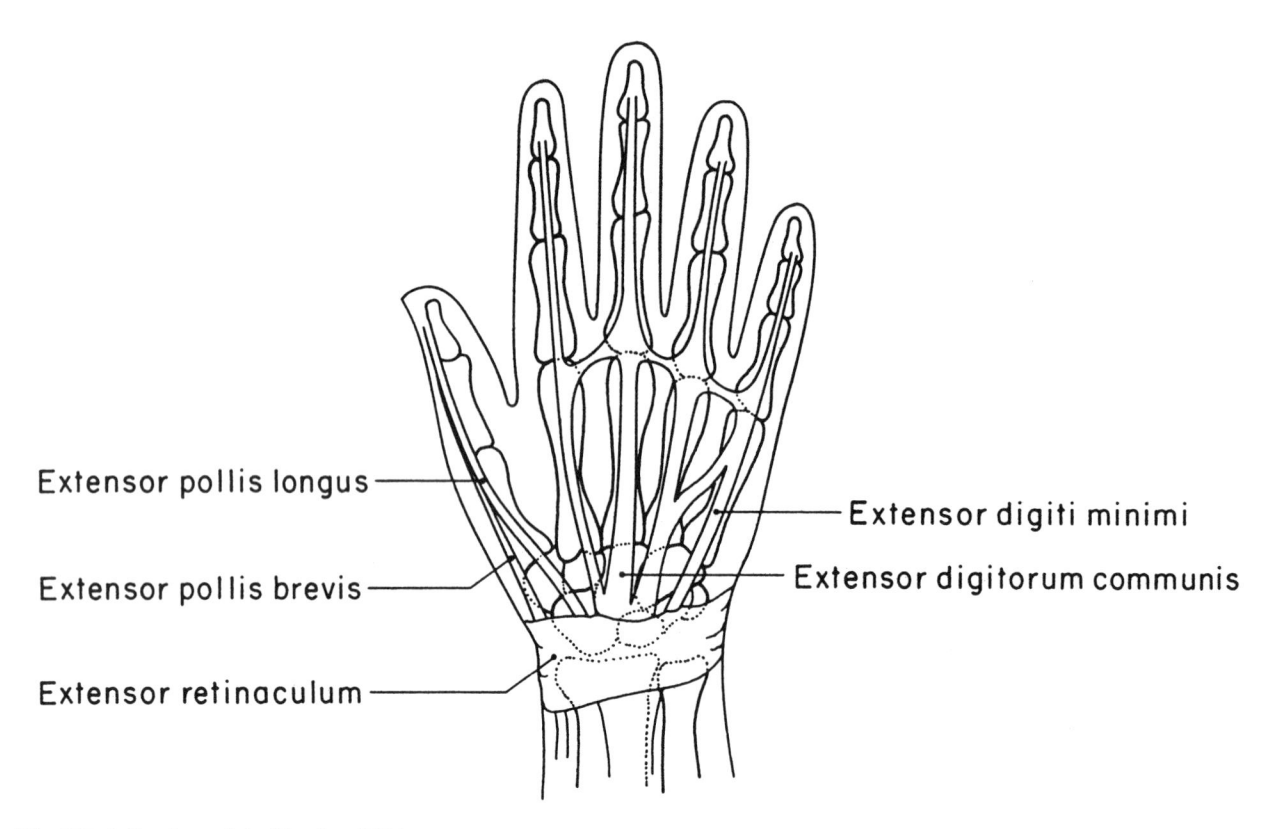

**Fig. 12D-2.** Tendons of the Hand and Wrist

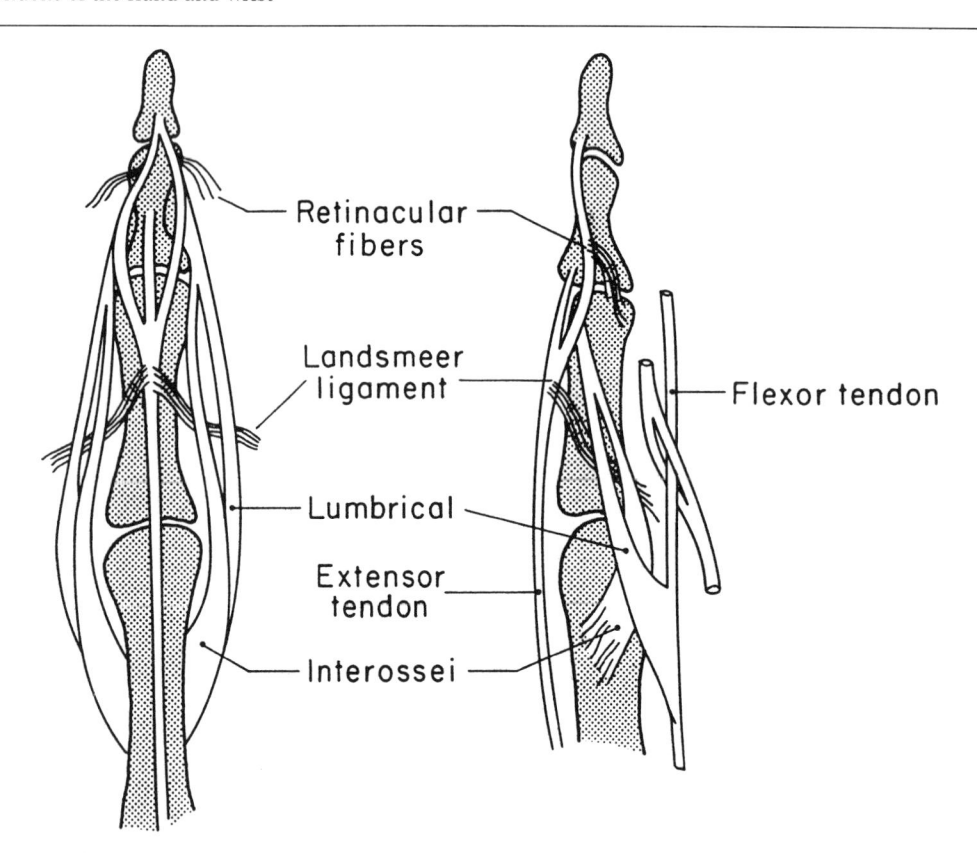

**Fig. 12D-3a.** Digital Extensor Mechanism

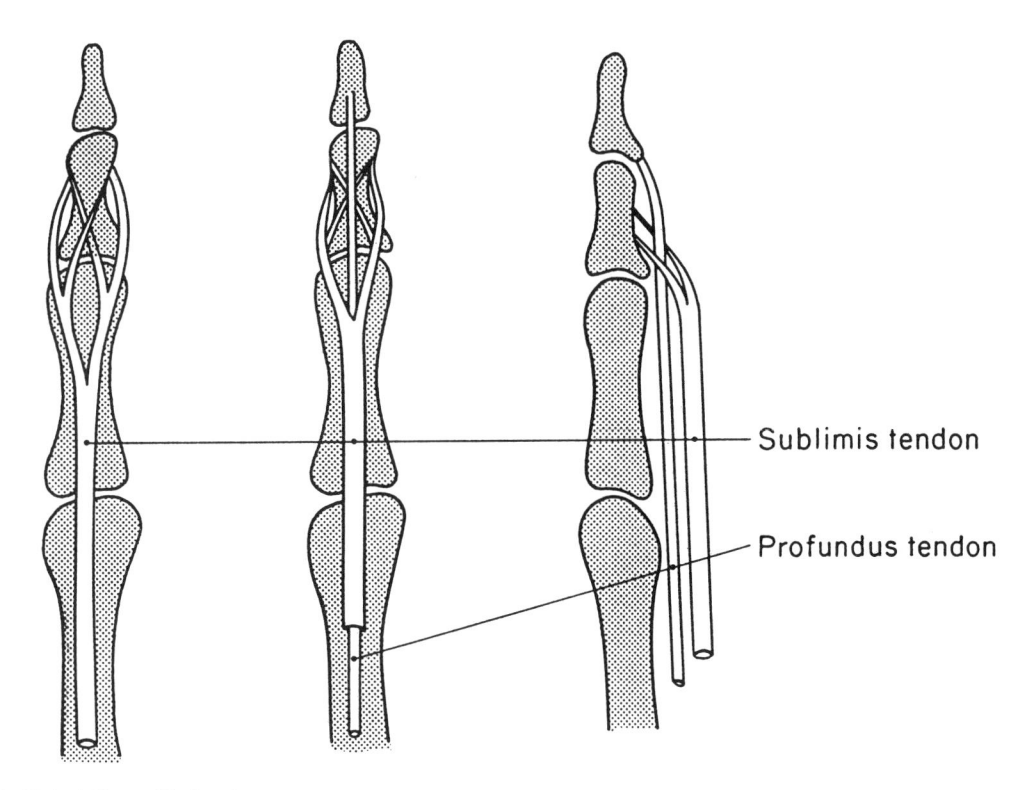

**Fig. 12D-3b.** Digital Flexor Mechanism

imal carpal rows flexes and translates ulnarally. These motions are sometimes referred to as carpal glide.

The anatomy of the hand and digits becomes much more straightforward as we move distally through a system of "pulleys and levers". There are 5 metacarpals and 14 phalanx. Some important anatomical concepts to remember:

- Scaphoid bone has a tenuous blood supply.
- The lunate is the wedge-shaped center bone of the central longitudinal chain (see above). It is prone to anterior dislocation because, anatomically, it is narrow dorsally.
- The fourth and fifth metacarpals share articulation with the hamate bone.
- The shape of the metacarpal head results in collateral ligaments surrounding the MCP joints becoming tighter in flexion versus extension.

## Generic Physical Examination

### Inspection

- Attitude — natural position of the wrist, hand, and fingers.
  a. Wrist dorsiflexed (extended) 20°.
  b. Digits flexed in parallel — 20-30° at C-MC, MCP, PIP, and DIP joints.
  c. Second-third digit tips opposed to thumb or thumb abducted — 20°.
- Thenar and hypothenar eminences (intrinsic muscle masses).
- Dorsal surface — prone to effusion (of large confluent dorsal bursa).
- Knuckle profile of clenched fist — loss of metacarpal length (secondary to fracture).

### Palpation — Wrist

- Radial styloid is more distal than ulnar styloid.
- Anatomic "snuffbox" — bordered by abductor pollicis longus and extensor pollicis brevis tendons; navicular bone constitutes the floor of the snuffbox.
- Lister's tubercle — just lateral to radial styloid prominence palpated better with wrist flexion. Distal to this is the lunate bone.
- 2nd and 3rd Metacarpals — most subcutaneous, easily palpated and immobile; 4th and 5th metacarpal — most mobile.

### Tests — Wrists

- Finkelstein's — forced ulnar deviation of clenched fist and tucked thumb positive in tenosynovitis

of snuffbox tendons (abductor pollicis longus, extensor pollicis brevis).
- Ulnar Deviation — snap and dislocation of extensor carpi ulnaris (seen in backhand stroke of racket sports). We find this test is more sensitive if wrist flexion is combined with ulnar deviation.
- Phalen's — maximal wrist flexion using both wrists — reproduces symptoms of carpal tunnel syndrome (Figure 12D-4).
- Tinel Sign — tapping over volar carpal ligament — positive for pain in carpal tunnel syndrome (Figure 12D-5). To increase the sensitivity of this test, percuss the carpal ligament with the broad-based edge of the standard reflex hammer (Mossman, 1987).

### Palpation — Hand

- Thenar Eminence — three muscles
  a. abductor pollicis brevis-superficial;
  b. opponens pollicis-middle layer;
  c. flexor pollicis brevis-deep layer (Figure 12D-6)

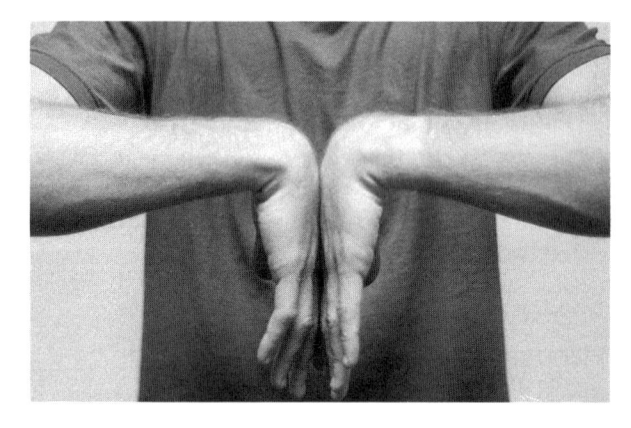

**Fig. 12D-4.** Phalen's Test

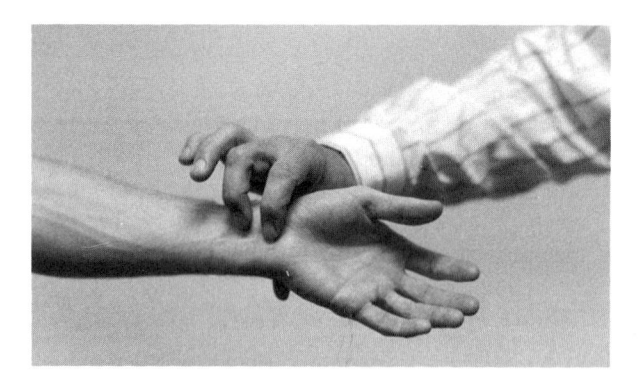

**Fig. 12D-5.** Tinel Sign

- Hypothenar Eminence — actually three muscles but working as one — abductor digiti quinti, opponens digiti, flexor digiti quinti.
- Palm
  a. Palmar aponeurosis (fascia) — probed for discrete nodules usually present on ulnar side; Dupuytren's contracture- causing flexion deformity.
  b. Flexor tendons of fingers — usually deep to palmar fascia and unable to be palpated. The "trigger finger"-nodule within a flexor tendon causes a click or snap as it enters or exits the narrower annular tendon sheath of a finger.
- Dorsum — extensor tendons-superficial.

### Palpation — Digits

The fingers contain no muscle bellies, only flexor and extensor tendons.

- Boutonniere Deformity — avulsion of central slip insertion of the common digital extensor into the PIP.
- Mallet Finger — avulsion of the distal insertion of the common digital extensor; x-ray often shows accompanying avulsion of bone fragment.
- Felon — localized infection of the distal finger tip or tuft which can spread proximally in the finger along tendon sheaths or by lymph vessels.
- Paronychia (Hangnail) — starts at side of fingernail.

### Range of Motion

Bilateral comparisons are essential when assessing the wrist and hand. Any athlete should be able to complete active range of motion testing without symptoms. If there is difficulty, passive range of motion testing should be done.

*Wrist*

flexion — 80°
extension — 70°
radial deviation — 20°
ulnar deviation — 30°
supination of forearm — 90°
pronation of forearm — 90°

*Digits*

1. Flexion at MCP joint — 90°. No lateral movement of finger with MCP joint in flexion.
2. Extension at MCP joint — 30-45°. The MCP joint

HYPOTHENAR                                                THENAR

Abductor digiti minimi
Flexor digiti minimi
Opponens digiti minimi

Flexor pollicis brevis
Opponens pollicis
Abductor pollicis brevis

Transverse carpal ligament

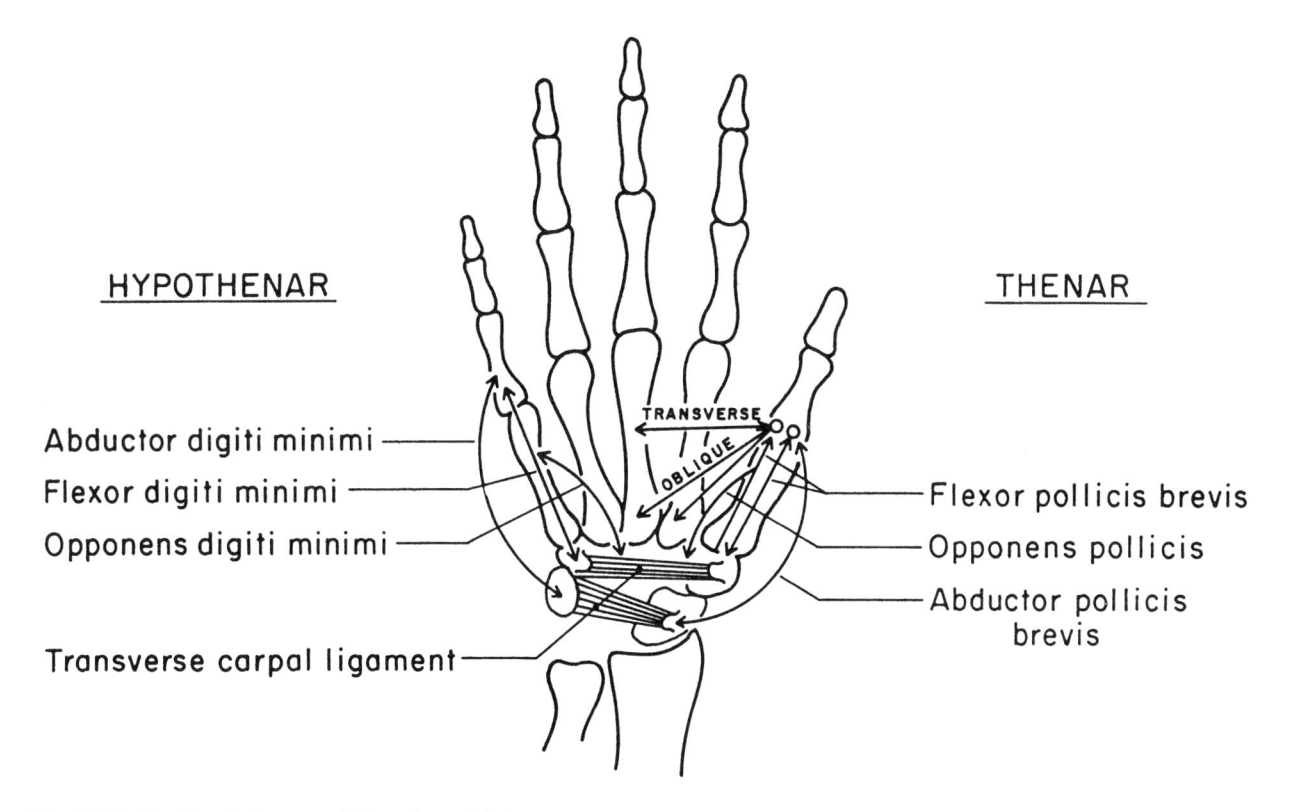

**Fig. 12D-6.** Muscles of Thenar and Hypothenar Eminences

can be moved laterally in extension because of laxity of the MCP collateral ligament.
3. Flexion at PIP — 0-100° range.
4. Flexion at DIP — 0-90° range.
5. Abduction/adduction at MCP — 20° between any 2 digits
6. Thumb flexion/extension at MCP — 0-50° range.
7. Thumb flexion/extension at IP — 20-90° range.
8. Palmar abduction/adduction of thumb — 0-70° range.
9. Opposition — ability to touch thumb to each fingertip.

### Neurologic Testing

Since there are no distinguishable deep tendon reflexes in wrist, hand or fingers, the neurologic examination concentrates on motor assessment and sensory testing (consult Table 12D-2).

### Sensory Testing

- Radial nerve — dorsum of hand from 3rd digit to thumb — *purest innervation-dorsal space between thumb and index finger (Figure 12D-7)
- Median nerve — palmar aspect of hand from 3rd digit to thumb — *purest innervation — palmar tip of index finger (Figure 12D-8).
- Ulnar nerve — palmar and dorsal aspects of 4th and 5th digits — *purest innervation — palmar tip of little finger (Figure 12D-8).

Dermatones (Figure 12D-9) — C6 — thumb and index finger, digits 1 and 2
 C7 — middle finger — digit 3
 C8 — ring and little fingers — digits 4 and 5

### Special Tests

- Superficial Digital Flexor — hold non-tested fingers in extension while athlete flexes remaining finger (Figure 12D-10).
- Deep Digital Flexor — stabilize the MCP and PIP joints of finger in extension and then ask athlete to flex finger tip (Figure 12D-11).
- Digital Extensor — stabilize PIP joint of finger in extension then ask athlete to extend finger tip.
- Allen Test — evaluates blood supply to hand (radial and ulnar arteries); a modified version can be done for each digit by compressing of the side of the base of the finger. This test method is:
  a. Ask the athlete to maximally flex the hand and digits (in effect squeezing out the blood supply).

UPPER EXTREMITY INJURIES/ILLNESSES

**Table 12D-2. Motor Testing of Distal Upper Extremity**

*Wrist* — Muscle testing (by active or passive resistance)
1. Extensors — extensor carpi radialis longus and brevis
    extensor carpi ulnaris — radial nerve
2. Flexors — flexor carpi radialis — median nerve
    flexor carpi ulnaris — ulnar nerve

*Digit*
1. Extensors — extensor digitorum communis
    extensor digiti minimi — radial nerve
2. Flexors — DIP — deep digital flexor — ulnar nerve
    PIP — supervicial digital flexor — medial nerve
    MCP — lumbricals 2 and 3 — ulnar nerve
        lumbricals 4 and 5 — median nerve
3. Abduction — dorsal interossi
    abductor digiti minimi — ulnar nerve
4. Adduction — palmar interossi — ulnar nerve (test using piece of paper grasped between two fingers)
5. Thumb extension — IP — extensor pollicis longus — radial nerve
    MCP — extensor pollicis brevis — radial nerve
6. Thumb flexion — transpalmar abduction
    IP flexor pollicis longus — median nerve
    MCP flexor pollicis brevis — ulnar and median nerve
7. Thumb abduction — abductor pollicis longus — radial nerve
    abductor pollicis brevis — median nerve
8. Thumb adduction — adductor pollicis — ulnar nerve
9. Pinch test — joining thumb and each finger

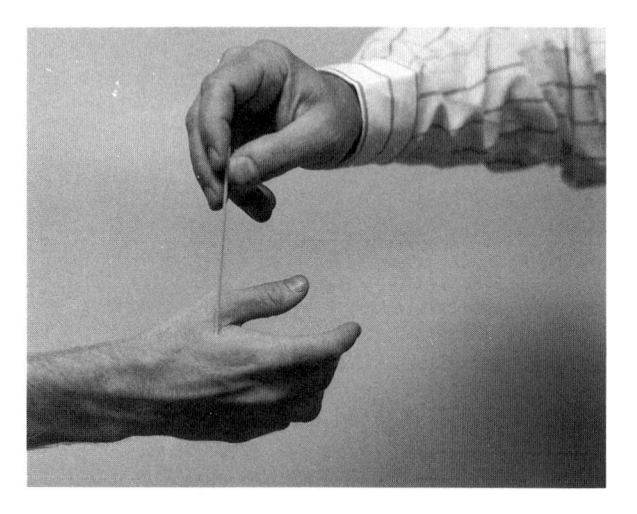

**Fig. 12D-7.** Radial Nerve Testing

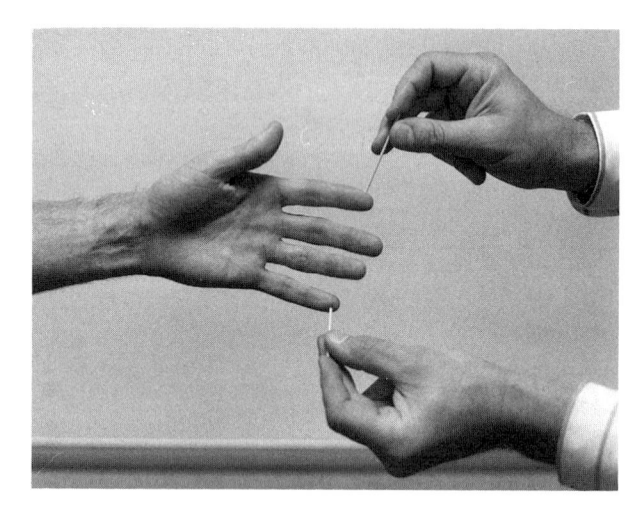

**Fig. 12D-8.** Medial and Ulnar Nerve Testing

b. The examiner places pressure over the radial and ulnar arteries to occlude them.
c. The athlete extends his hand and digits.
d. The examiner releases pressure from either the radial or ulnar artery and watches for filling in the distal hand while maintaining pressure on the occluded side.
e. This process is repeated for the opposite artery.

The Allen Test is excellent for determining the patency of a dual blood supply to the hands or any specific digit.

### Diagnostic Imaging

Routine x-ray studies of distal upper extremity injury includes the true AP, lateral, and oblique. Other specialized views or techniques may be

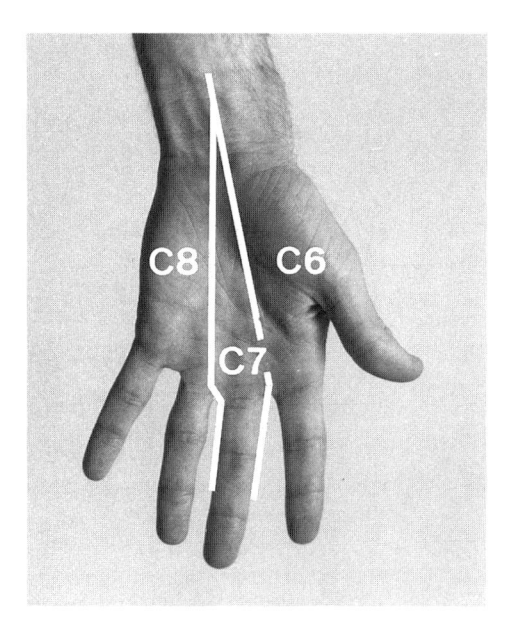

**Fig. 12D-9.** Dermatomes of the Hand

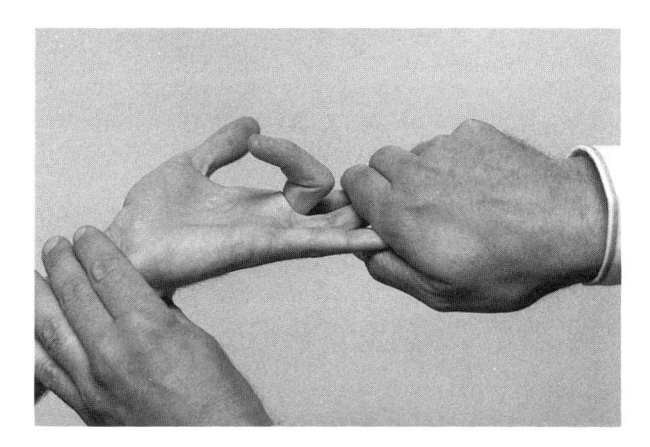

**Fig. 12D-10.** Superficial Digital Flexor Testing

**Fig. 12D-11.** Deep Digital Flexor Testing

required depending upon the suspected injury (Simmons, 1988):

1. Scaphoid navicular pathology including assessment of navicular fat stripe sign.
2. Carpal tunnel view — carpal tunnel pathology.
3. AP clenched fist view — to assess the alignment of the proximal carpal bones.
4. Hook-of-the-Hamate — Assess hamate pathology — particulary a fracture of the hook-of-the-hamate.
5. Tomography — to pick up occult fractures especially in the dorsal radial ulnar articulation.
6. Bone Scan — to detect synovitis or reflec sympathetic dystrophy.
7. MRI — to detect avascular necrosis, specifically of the lunate bone (Kienbock's Disease).
8. Arthrography — to detect ligament tears.

Make sure to order both hand and wrist x-rays if there is any concern about multiple injury.

## Common Injuries of the Hand, Wrist and Fingers

The following is an outline of the most common wrist, hand, and finger injuries encountered in sports. Because of the number, the discussion of each will be brief.

### Perspective

Most injuries in the athlete's hand are closed injuries (Burton, 1973). We will discuss tendon systems, ligamentous injuries surrounding joints, and fractures. Open hand injuries like lacerations of nerves and tendons will not be covered.

A word about fractures — some general principles about hand injuries should be emphasized:

- Tendons running through the hand and into the fingers can cause deformity once a fracture has occurred.
- Immobilization of a fracture should be done with consideration of adjacent joints and the serious consequences of prolonged immobilization. Immobilization should be in the position of function (Figure 12D-12), whenever possible:
  a. Wrist dorsiflexed 20°
  b. MCP joints flexed 45-60° (index to 5th finger)
  c. Interphalangeal joints flexed several degrees (Swanson, 1970)

*UPPER EXTREMITY INJURIES/ILLNESSES* 321

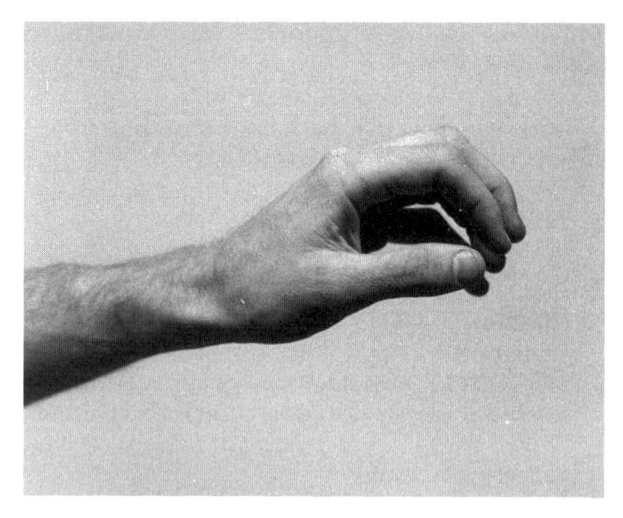

**Fig. 12D-12.** Position of Function

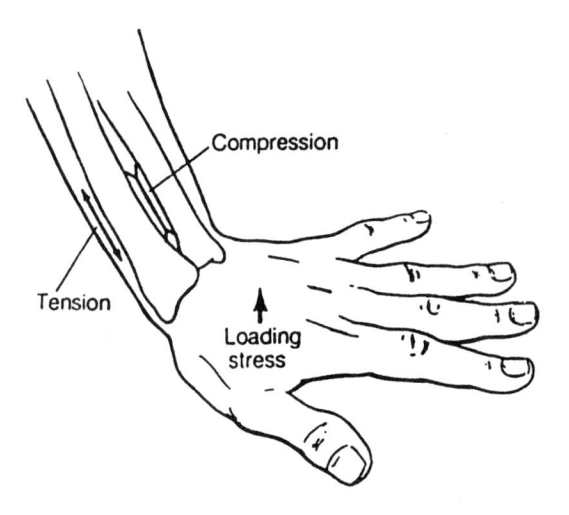

**Fig. 12D-13.** Colles' Fracture: Biomechanics

d. Thumb should be in the "Fifth" position and 20° radial abduction and 30° palmar abduction (Eaton and Littler, 1969)
- An unstable hand fracture often can be stabilized with percutaneous wires, eliminating the need for extreme positions of immobilization. This is an example of the benefits of surgery outweighting the risks.
- Normal tendon excursion over a healed bone is mandatory if satisfactory function is to return after fracture. Scarring and/or adhesions of either flexor or extensor tendons are serious complications of phalangeal fractures.
- X-rays are absolutely mandatory in evaluating these fractures (Mosher, 1985) and a true lateral and PA projection both before and after reduction are needed. We recommend that serial x-rays be taken early in the healing period to be certain that reduction has been maintained.

## Distal Forearm

The major injuries athletes sustain to the distal ulna and radius are fractures. The most frequent fractures are extension-compression fractures of the lower end of the radius (Figure 12D-13). There are two reasons for their frequency and propensity in athletes. First is the instinctive reaction to thrust out the hand during a fall so that the fall on an "outstretched hand" serves as the initial impact. Second, the lower radius is composed of cancellous bone surrounded by a mere rim of hard cortex, making it the weakest area between the point of impact and the weight of body (Conwell, 1970). These injuries are so frequent that whenever there is a history of a fall on an outstretched hand, with tenderness over the lower end of the radius, and impaired function of the hand, fracture of the radius should be the diagnosis until proven otherwise. A child may have an incomplete fracture with buckling of the thin posterior cortex and, usually, no displacement of bone (green-stick fracture). Complete fractures without displacement occur more often in the elderly.

### Colles' Fracture (Extension-Compression)

There is "dinner-fork" deformity with radial deviation secondary to the radius becoming shortened. The hand is held in pronation with slight flexion; supination is impossible (Figure 12D-14). Limitation to active movement of the hand and fingers is present. In the normal wrist, the tip of the radial styloid is slightly lower than the tip of the ulnar styloid but with a Colles' fracture, the radial styloid is displaced upward and backward. Palpation should include the ulnar styloid.

**X-Ray Findings.** Prior to treatment, there are three important things to check on the wrist x-ray (Weber, 1987):

- On the lateral film, look first for the relationship of the distal radial fragment to the proximal fragment. The true Colles' Fracture will show the distal fragment displaced dorsally. A Smith's Fracture is essentially a reversed Colles' Fracture and will have the distal fragment angling in a palmar direction.
- Examine whether extension of the fracture has gone into the distal radio-ulnar joint or radio-carpal joint. Also, look closely at the lunate bone.

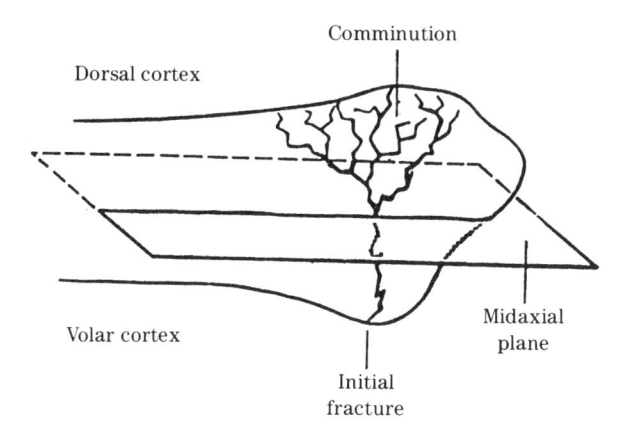

Fig. 12D-14. Colles' Fracture

Fractures of the lunate are the result of extension of fractures into the joints mentioned above.
- Examine the fracture depth, usually best appreciated on the lateral view. If the comminution extends more than halfway into the thickness of the radius, strict immobilization may fail.

**Treatment.** Reduction should be done as early as possible before swelling develops. With a typical deformity, three steps are necessary for a good reduction. The distal fragment of the radius must be pulled down until the radial styloid sits normally, pushed toward the volar surface to correct the posterior displacement, and forced into flexion to correct for backward tilting of the fragment. The method of reduction is outlined in Appendix 12D-1, including the criteria for complete reduction. The wrist should be fixed in full pronation, ulnar deviation and moderate flexion. Full flexion may lead to permanent stiffness. Casting should incorporate the elbow and lower half of the upper arm to prevent supination and pronation of the wrist. Unless the fracture is severe, the cast can be modified into a short arm type after two or three weeks. Cardiovascular and nerve functions should be checked. X-rays should be taken after reduction and again 10 days later to determine if there has been slippage.

**Complications:**

Immediate — slippage can occur within several hours causing loss of approximation of fracture.
Intermediate — Sudeck's atrophy should be suspected if pain persists unduly after reduction and immobilization.

Late complication — carpal tunnel syndrome involving the medial nerve.

### Distal Radial Epiphyseal Separation/Fracture

This epiphysis fuses between the ages of 15 to 18 years. Disruption at the epiphyseal line may take place either with pure separation of the epiphysis, or in conjunction with displacement of cortical bone. Repeated manipulations should be discouraged because of possible injury to the epiphyseal cartilage.

### Radial Styloid Fracture

This injury usually is produced by a force directed upward and outward on the adducted hand, fracturing the tip of the styloid process about 1½ cm from its end (Figure 12D-15).

### Barton's Fracture

This is basically a fracture dislocation of the wrist with evulsing of fragments from the posterior articular margin of the radial carpal joint (Figure 12D-16).

### Flexion-Compression Fractures of the Distal Radius

**Smith's Fracture.** Basically the reverse of a Colles' fracture, it is caused by a blow to or fall on

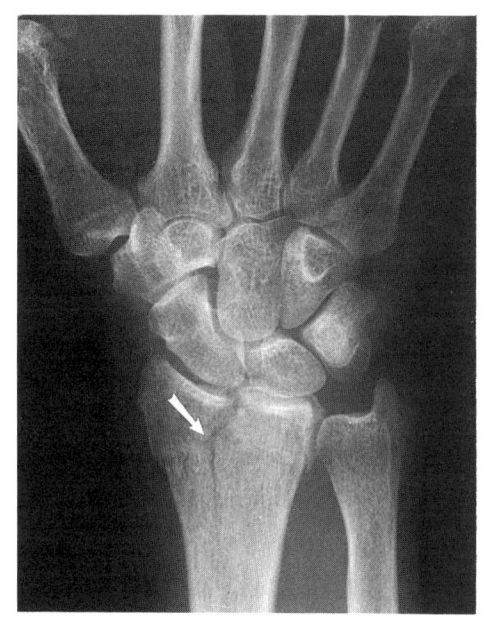

Fig. 12D-15. Radial Styloid Fracture

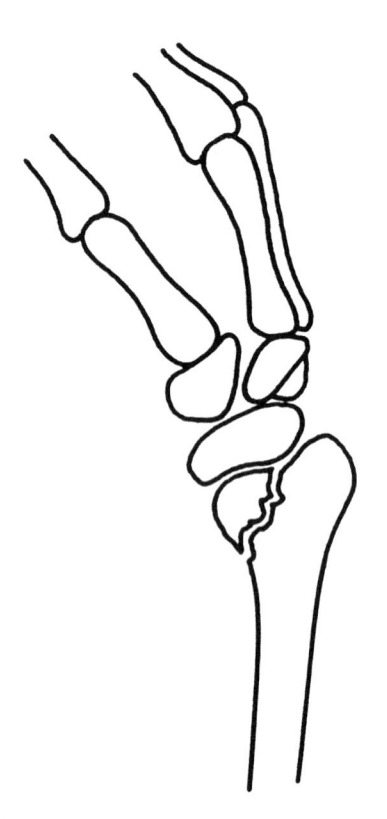

**Fig. 12D-16.** Bartan's Fracture

the dorsum of the flexed hand. The distal fragment of the radius is forced forward dorsally instead of backward and in a volar fashion. The wrist has the opposite appearance of a Colles' fracture and is referred to as a "garden spade deformity" (Figure 12D-17) Reduction is accomplished in the opposite manner of a Colles' fracture, with backward pressure on the distal fragment and forward pressure on the proximal fractured radius. Immobilization is done with the elbow flexed, forearm supinated, hand adducted, and moderately extended with the thumb widely abducted. Again, a long arm cast is used.

**Ulnar Styloid Fracture.** Caused by a fall on the ulnar side of an abducted hand. Immobilization and ulnar deviation for three to four weeks or longer is the treatment. Occasionally there is nonunion and the loose fragment must be removed.

### The Wrist

The area is defined as extending from the radio-carpal and ulno-carpal joint to the carpal meta-carpal joints.

#### Sprains

Injuries to the ligamentous wrist structures are responsible for a significant percentage of all cases of trauma affecting the hand. Many are never seen by a physician. They vary from minimal tearing (1st degree) to complete disruption of the ligament (3rd degree). Sprains should be assessed by taking a thorough history with emphasis on the biomechanics of the injury, and a physical examination and x-ray. Continued activity in the presence of 2nd and especially 3rd degree sprains can lead to chronic joint instability. Additionally, exposing an incomplete rupture of a wrist ligament to further trauma can lead to complete disruption. Incomplete tears of ligament systems should be splinted for 10 to 14 days if there is laxity. Minor "wrist sprains" not appropriately assessed or treated may heal with excessive scar tissue or may result in chronic pain, joint laxity, swelling, limited motion, or premature osteoarthritis.

#### Dislocations

In most instances, the dislocation of a joint causes complete disruption of the ligament between those joints.

**Distal Radio-Ulnar Joint.** The result of excessive pronation. When the patient attempts to pronate or supinate the forearm at physical ex-

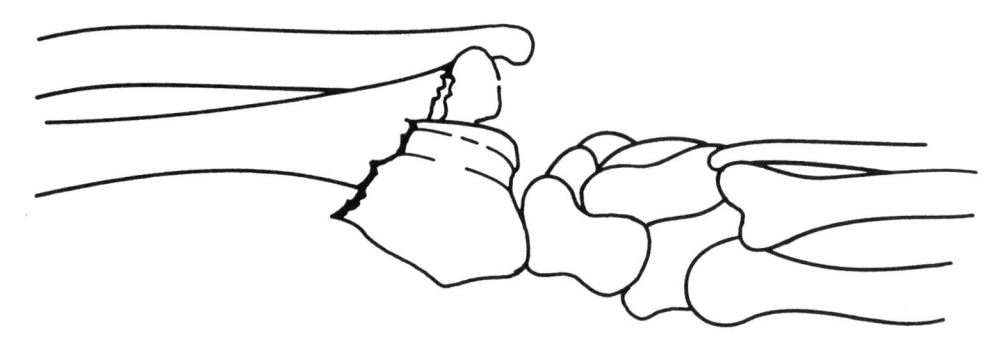

**Fig. 12D-17.** Smith's Fracture

amination, there may be a painful click caused by the motion of the radius on the ulnar. This is caused by a rupture of the radio-ulnar ligament.

**Treatment.** Immoblization in supination in a long arm cast for six weeks. This treatment can be attempted up to three weeks post-injury (Ruby, 1980).

**Carpal Bones**

**a. Lunate dislocation.** The most common carpal bone dislocation. Some believe that to have this dislocation you must also have a perilunate dislocation (McCue, 1979). There may be impingement of the medial nerve. Diagnosis can be made easily with lateral x-rays of the wrist.

*Treatment* — Reduction can be accomplished with longitudinal traction and extension of the wrist followed by pressure on the volar situated lunate, which is pushed dorsally to reduce it. Immobilization must take place with the wrist in slight flexion in a short arm cast for four weeks.

*Complications*

- A unrecognized lunate dislocation may require open reduction.
- Medial nerve palsy and flexor tendon constriction are often seen.
- A common problem is late rotatory instability of the scaphoid (McCue, 1979).
- Avascular necrosis of the lunate (Kiebock's Disease) is a rare complication.

**b. Scaphoid Dislocation** (scapholunate instability is a more common and less severe form) — Complete rupture of the scaphoid lunate ligament probably does not occur as an isolated lesion but is associated with more disruption of other ligaments surrounding the lunate bone (Zemel, 1986).

*Etiology* — Dorsiflexion of the wrist from a fall on an outstretched hand.
*Physical Exam* — Painful click may be palpated at the scapholunate joint.
*Diagnosis* — AP x-rays show a gap of greater than 2 mm with increased overlap of the capitate and lunate. This injury can occur after reduction of the lunate dislocation.
*Special Notes* — In addition to the standard x-ray views of the wrist, a closed fist view in supination should be obtained. The AP view frequently shows a gap between the scaphoid and lunate. Normal is 1-2 mm. Three millimeters or greater is considered abnormal.
*Treatment* — Open repair.

**Fractures**

**Scaphoid (Navicular).** The most common of all carpal bone fractures, this injury accounts for 8% of all fractures in organized sports (Eaton, 1971). The scaphoid spans the proximal and distal carpal rows. The distal portion of the bone has multiple soft tissue attachments and the waist portion is directly adjacent to the radial styloid.

*Biomechanics* — The most common mechanism of injury is a fall on an outstretched hand or from an impact that forces the scaphoid into the radial styloid process.
*Subjective Signs* — There usually is pain on hand grip and tenderness over the anatomical snuffbox.
*Diagnosis* — Initial x-rays should be obtained but frequently are negative. Clinicians continue to see patients with subjective signs of a scaphoid navicular fracture but negative x-rays. Terry (1975) called attention to the navicular fat stripe (NFS) as a potentially useful x-ray finding in evaluating patients with recent wrist trauma. The validity and reliability of the NFS as a screening test for fractures in the navicular area was studied by Kirk (1990). His conclusion was that an abnormal NFS is a poor predictor of a navicular fracture, but a normal NFS is a good predictor of no navicular fracture (see Figure 12D-18).
*Treatment* — If the x-ray is negative, a navicular cast or brace that incorporates the proximal phalanx of the thumb should be applied and the athlete should be reexamined clinically and radiographically every two weeks. If a fracture is present, a full shortarm cast beginning three quarters of the way up the forearm to the IP joint of the thumb should be applied, with careful molding around the base of the thumb. Immobilization usually is 8-12 weeks.
*Special Note* — Three quarters of all fractures of the scaphoid occur through its narrow waist (see Chapter 17, Figure 17-21). Next most common is a fracture through the proximal pole.
*Complications* — Fractures of the proximal pole may require more prolonged immobilization. Avascular necrosis occurs in 13%-40% of all scaphoid fractures (Szabo, 1988). The inci-

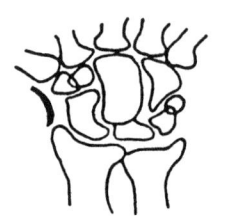

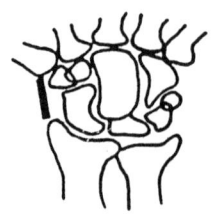

Convex Fat Stripe: Normal   Straight Fat Stripe: Indeterminate   Concave (or Absent) Fat Stripe Abnormal

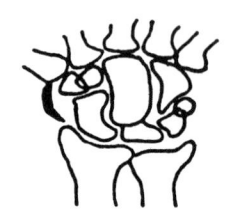

Fig. 12D-18. Normal, Indeterminate, and Abnormal Navicular Fat Strip Signs

dence of necrosis and non-union is high with injuries to this area because of an unusual retrograde blood supply. These fractures often are inaccurately diagnosed as sprains, and the subsequent inadequate treatment results in an increased incidence of non-union (McCue, 1979). Fractures of the distal pole present much less of a problem since blood supply is adequate for rapid healing. Bone grafting or replacement must be considered with non-union.

*Return to Competition* — Because of the prolonged healing time required, an asymptomatic athlete may resume competition with a silicone-type cast.

**Hook of the Hamate and Pisiform.** Both of these represent small prominences on the palmar surface of the hand with direct trauma the most common etiology. The hook of the hamate can fracture in athletes who swing a racquet, paddle, baseball bat, or golf club and who lose control of the butt-end of the handle of the instrument allowing it to strike the area and fracture the hook prominence of the hamate (Parker, 1986) (Figure 12D-19).

*Subjective Findings* — Wrist pain, decreased grip.
*Objective Findings* — Examination will show tenderness to deep pressure over the hamate hook and palmar aspect of the hand opposite the fourth or fifth finger. If the pain is distal, consider involvement of the hamate bone. If pain is more proximal, consider involvement of the pisiform.
*Diagnosis* — Can be confirmed by oblique and carpal tunnel x-ray views obtained with the wrist in maximum dorsal flexion, in addition to the standard views of the wrist.
*Complications* — Proximity of the ulnar nerve and deep digital flexor of the small finger can involve either one or both of those structures and cause symptoms of ulnar nerve impingment or tendonitis of the flexor tendon of the fifth finger.
*Treatment* — Gauntlet cast.
*Return to Competition* — Athlete may be allowed to play to pain tolerance with a gauntlet cast applied. Non-union of the fracture can occur.

### Nerve Injury/Vascular Compromise

Neurovascular injuries resulting from athletic participation are being described more frequently. These injuries are related to a particular motion

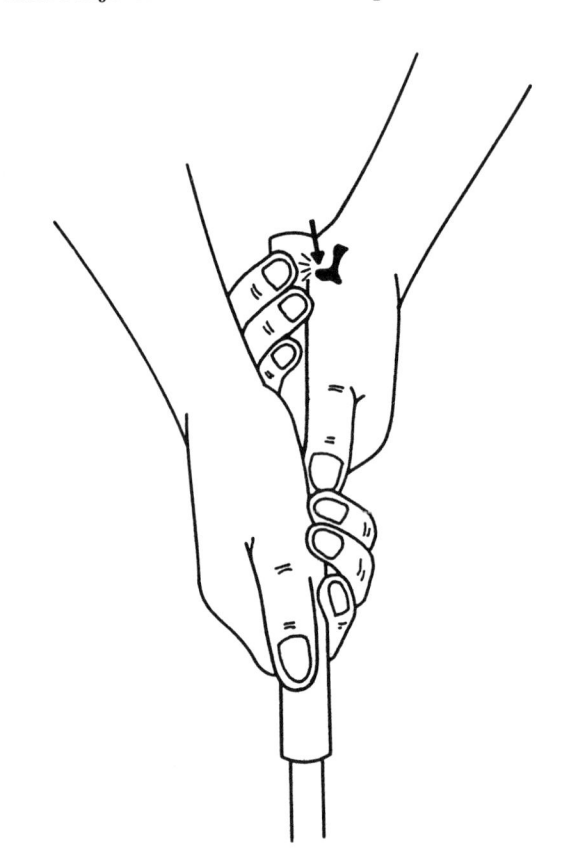

Fig. 12D-19. Fracture — Hook of the Hamate

that impinges upon the neurovascular structure involved. Treatment usually involves cessation of the movements that cause the problems and, in the case of neuropathy, a work-up for diabetes or collagen disease. Additionally, examination of the unaffected wrist is imperative.

### Ulnar Nerve

**Bowler's Thumb.** A perineural fibrosis of the ulnar digital nerve of the thumb.

*Etiology* — bowling
*Biomechanics* — Constant trauma from the edge of the hole where the thumb enters the ball.
*Treatment* — Decrease bowling, redrill the thumb hole, and pad the thumb.

**Handlebar Palsy.** Frequently seen in cyclists who develop numbness of the little finger and ulnar half of the ring finger, as well as intrinsic muscle weakness.

*Biomechanics* — The result of gripping handlebars, with constant pressure on the ulnar nerve as it comes through the canal of Guyons.
*Treatment* — Padding the handlebar and hand (special padded gloves for cyclists are made for this purpose)

**Blunt Trauma to the Ulnar Nerve.** Varying causes, from catching a thrown ball to constant use of the hypothenar eminence (weightlifting) (Dangles and Bilos, 1980) resulting in scarring and ulnar nerve compression (Figure 12D-20).

### Median Nerve

Carpal tunnel syndrome has been reported after racquet ball (Layfer and Jones, 1977) as well as from other sports requiring strenuous wrist flexion.

*Etiology and Biomechanics* — Repeated wrist flexion and stress on the flexor tendons results in tenosynovitis with median nerve compression (Figure 12D-21). Consider other more generalized conditions that may produce carpal tunnel syndrome (Table 12D-3). Pregnancy also can be a predisposing factor.
*Treatment* — Rest, one local steroid injection into tendon sheaths, and splinting of the affected wrist in a neutral position normally is enough.

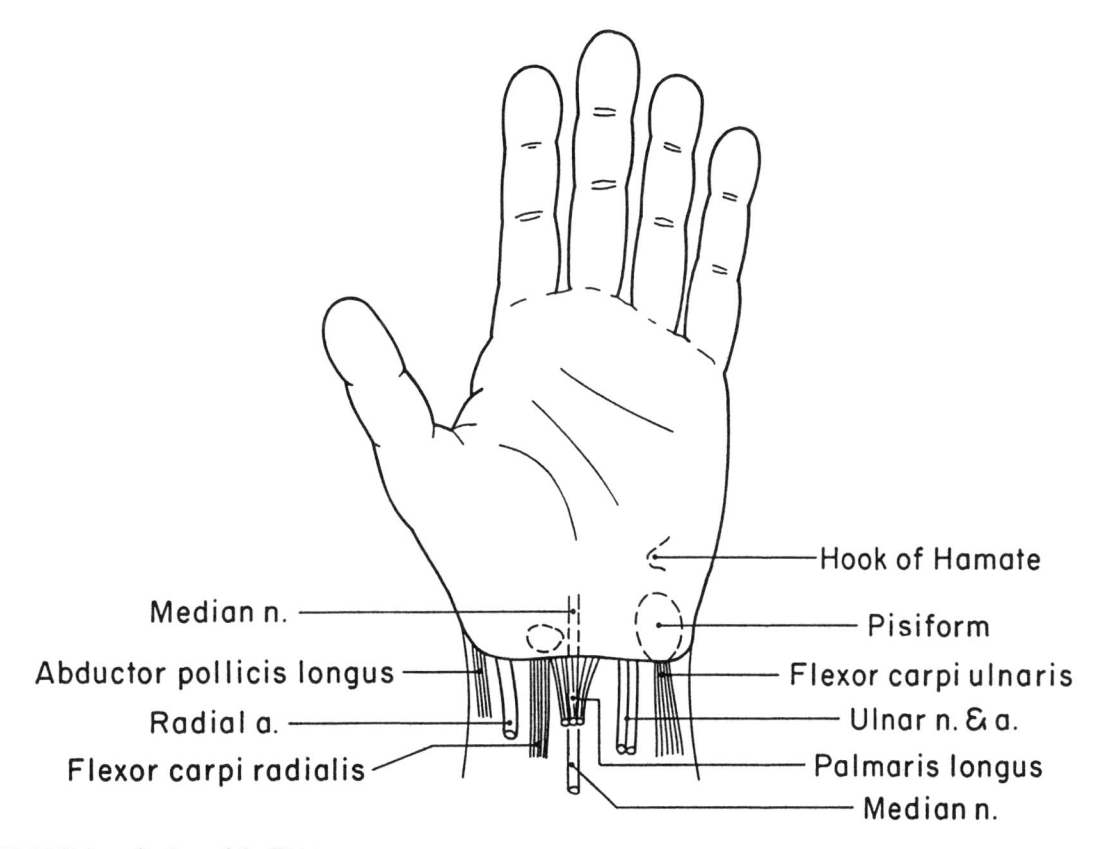

**Fig. 12D-20.** Palmar Surface of the Wrist

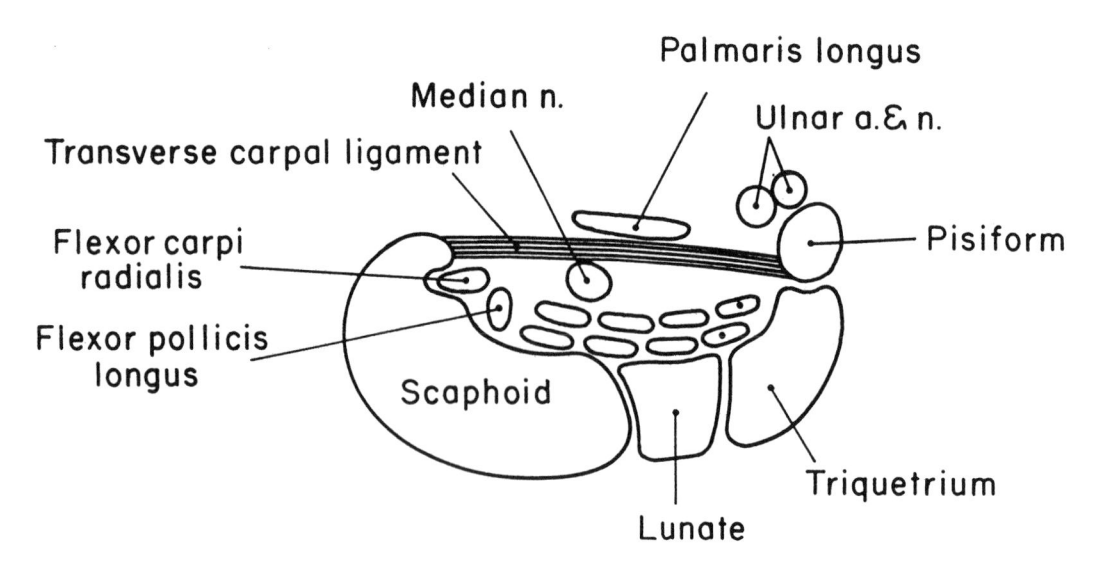

**Fig. 12D-21.** Contents of Carpal Tunnel

**Table 12D-3. Generalized Conditions That May Produce Carpal Tunnel Syndrome**

| | |
|---|---|
| Metabolic abnormalities | Alcoholism |
| | Gout |
| Endocrine abnormalities | Diabetes mellitus |
| | Hypothyroidism |
| | Acromegaly |
| Dietary abnormalities | Thiamine (vitamin $B_1$) |
| | Niacin (nicotinic acid) deficiency |
| | Malabsorption syndrome |
| Neoplasms | Multiple myeloma |
| | Lymphoma |
| | Metastatic malignancy |
| Hematologic abnormalities | Hemophilia |
| | Anticoagulatin therapy-induced abnormalities |
| Exogenous substances | Drugs: nitrofurantoin, isoniazid, vincristine, immune serums, oral contraceptives |
| | Industrial compounds: trichlorethylene, carbon monoxide, methyl alcohol, benzene, insecticides |
| | Metals: lead, mercury, copper |
| | Elements: arsenic, bismuth, phosphorus |
| Vascular disease | Atherosclerosis |
| | Periarteritis nodosa |
| Diffuse inflammatory disease | Acute febrile polyneuritis |
| | Polymyositis |
| | Polyneuropathy complicating diphtheria |
| | Infectious mononucleosis |
| | Sarcoidosis |
| Diseases of unknown etiology | Rheumatoid arthritis |
| | Primary amyloidosis |
| | Systemic lupus erythematosus |
| | Leri's plenosteosis |

*Special Note* — Carpal tunnel syndrome can be caused by direct trauma from any sport involvement.

### Decreased Vascular Perfusion to Fingers

This can occur in baseball catchers from repeated blunt trauma to the palm of the mitt hand (Lowrey and Chadwick, 1976) and in handball players (Buckhout and Warner, 1980).

## Hand

Because of its vulnerable anatomic position and wide range of functions, the hand can be exposed to a tremendous amount of trauma. Mild injuries like contusions, abrasions, and lacerations occur most frequently over the dorsum of the hand and usually result from direct trauma (thrown object or collision with another player). Swelling and ecchymosis develop rapidly due to the looseness of the dorsal skin. Immediate application of ice and elevation is indicated. As with all hand injuries, an x-ray examination is essential to eliminate the possibility of a concomitant fracture or dislocation. Superficial lacerations occur less frequently and normally are caused by bad or improperly pretested equipment. Examples include the screws stabilizing facemasks in football, a broken bat in baseball, or the sharp edge of a backboard in basketball. Fortunately, severance of tendons and nerves is uncommon. Prevention of serious lacerations requires that no rings are worn during competition or practices because they can and do get caught in equipment and may result in serious skin evulsions and deep injuries to fingers.

The "hand" area is defined as the metacarpal bones and the soft tissue structures that overlie the area between the proximal and distal ends of the metacarpal bones.

### Strains

Common Digital Extensor (CDE) at Metacarpal Phalangeal (MCP) Joint

*Etiology* — Sudden twisting of a finger or a direct blow over the MCP joint can result in a tear of the dorsal hood of the tendon and its subluxation.

*Diagnosis* — Functionally disabling and painful snapping of the tendon. Tendon usually subluxes ulnarly into the valley between the metacarpal heads. This type of an injury may limit the ability of throwing athletes to grip.

*Treatment* — Occasionally when a large amount of granulation tissue has been formed, removal and repair of the tendon hood via surgery is indicated.

### Sprains

Injuries to the ligamentous structures of the hand and metacarpal area usually involve the ligaments of the MCP joints.

**Thumb.** The most common ligamentous injury to the thumb occurs with trauma to the ulnar collateral ligament. Rupture of this ligament happens far more oten than that of the radial collateral ligament because valgus stress is more common on the joint.

*Epidemiology* — Any sport that exposes the thumb to forced abduction (football, skiing, wrestling, or baseball) will have about the same incidence of trauma to this ligament.

*Biomechanics* — Forced abduction such as catching the thumb on an opposing player or piece of equipment, or by forces generated from holding a ski pole (Figure 12D-22).

*Diagnosis* — Signs and symptoms include pain on the ulnar aspects of the base of the thumb, inability to use the thumb-index pinch, and localized swelling of the area. X-ray films should

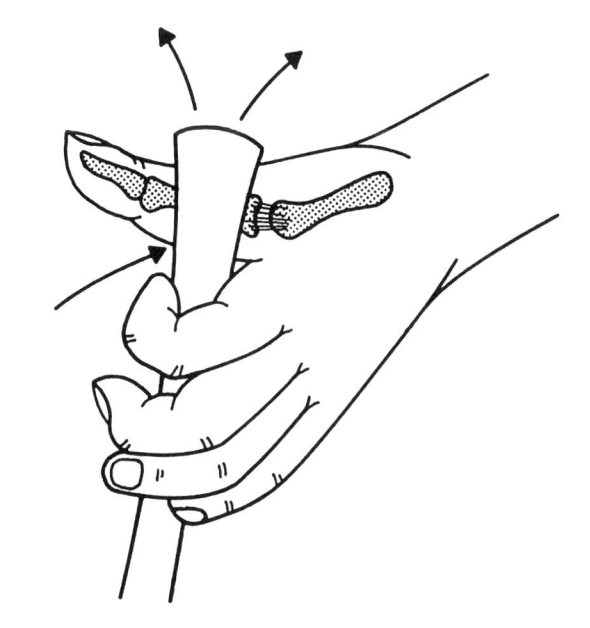

**Fig. 12D-22.** UCL Sprain Mechanism

be obtained before any stress is applied to the joint, since evulsion fractures of the proximal phalangeal attachment to the distal end of the ligament are common. If that is the case, no x-ray stress views are needed. However, if no bony fragment is present, stress films should be taken for comparison views of the normal and affected thumb. Radial deviation of the joint to more than 45° as compared with the normal side is evidence of complete tear of the ligament (Smith, 1977) (Figure 12D-23).

*Treatment* — If stress views show deviation radially of less than 45°, treatment should consist of a short arm cast with thumb immobilization for four weeks, followed by splinting for two or three weeks. If joint deviation is greater than 45°, assume there is a complete tear of the ligament. Surgery is essential. If surgery is not performed, chronic instability characterized by pain and weakness of grasp as well as non-healing of the ligament may occur (Browne et al., 1976).

*Special Note* — In 64% of the cases involving complete ulnar collateral ligament tears, an intrinsic aponeurosis becomes interposed between the torn ends of the ulnar collateral ligament, effectively preventing healing (Stener, 1962).

*Return to Competition* — After four weeks of immobilization, taping will allow the athlete to continue participation (Figure 12D-24). Taping involves placing the thumb in adduction next to the index finger. A form-fitted plastic splint also can be used. Injuries to the radial collateral ligament of the thumb are treated identically to those of the ulnar collateral ligament. Collateral ligament injuries to the second through fifth metacarpal bones are relatively uncommon.

### Dislocations

**Carpal/Metacarpal Joint.** The most common of the five C-MC joint dislocations seen is that of the base of the thumb (1st C-MC joint). These dis-

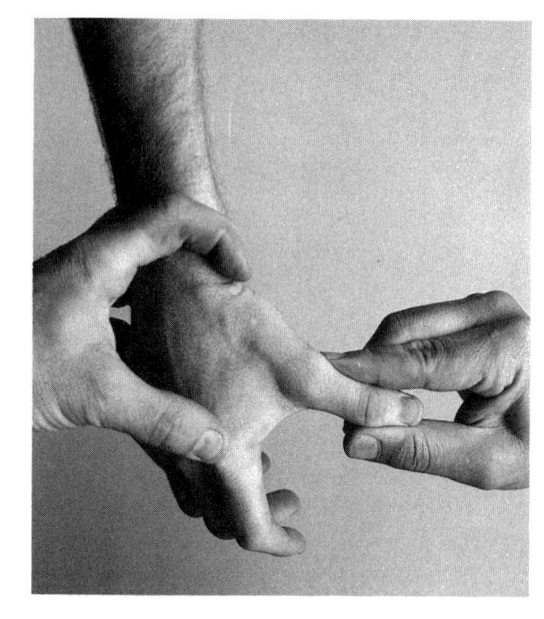

**Fig. 12D-23.** UCL Stress Test

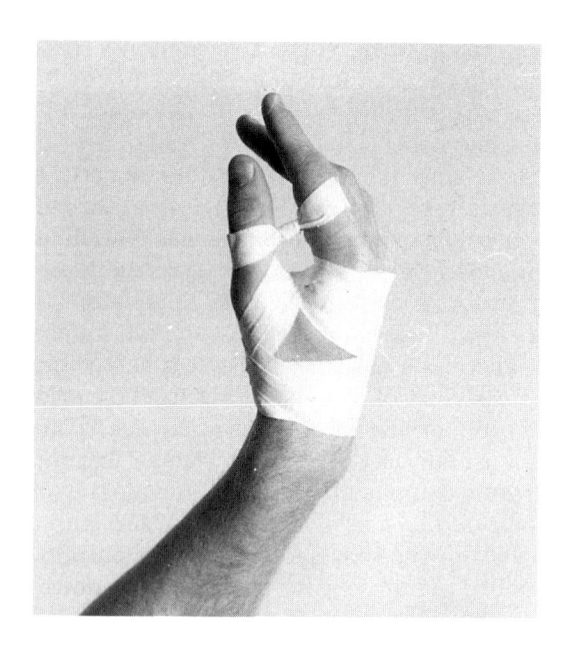

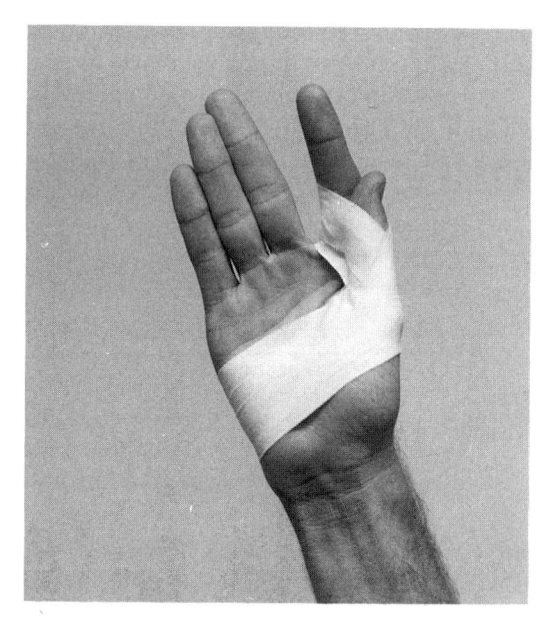

**Fig. 12D-24a, b.** Thumb Splinting

330   *CLINICAL SPORTS MEDICINE*

locations usually occur in association with a fracture (Bennett's).

*Treatment* — Reduction usually is simple, but there may be later instability. Pure dislocations may be treated with immobilization for eight weeks. Chronic instability requires the reconstruction of volar ligamentous tissue.

**MCP Joint.** The most common injury of the MCP joint is dorsal dislocation of the proximal phalanx.

*Epidemiology* — Seen most often in index finger (2nd), and then in the little finger (5th). Occasionally more than one digit will be involved. Dorsal dislocation of the thumb (1st) MCP joint is most frequent in children (Gerber, 1986).

*Anatomy* — Anatomically, the metacarpal head dislocates volarly between the lumbrical tendon and the long digital flexors through the volar plate. This creates a buttonhole deformity that causes in a constriction around the wider metacarpal neck (Figure 12D-25). This anatomical situation frequently is not condusive to reduction.

*Diagnosis* — A lump palpated in the palm will represent the volarly dislocated head of the metacarpal.

*Treatment* — Acutely, reduction can be attempted by increasing the deformity and slowly returning the proximal phalanx through the tear in the volar plate. However, after swelling occurs, dislocations become fairly irreducible, and open reduction is necessary.

**Fractures**

**Thumb**

a. **Bennett's Fracture**

*Biomechanics* — Axial compression with a force driving down at the base of the thumb, shearing off the head of the metacarpal (Figure 12D-26). Usually a small medial fragment of the proximal metacarpal stays with the joint, as the remaining portion of the metacarpal subluxes radially, secondary to the unopposed pull of the abductor pollicis longus tendon.

*Treatment* — Although reduction is easy (with thumb immobilized in full opposition), maintenance of the position usually is difficult. Therapy for this fracture is an enigma. Recent literature suggests that Bennett's fractures may be overtreated. At the present time, closed manipulation and cast immobilization (described above) is likley to be unsatisfactory (Burkhalter, 1990). Open reduction or percu-

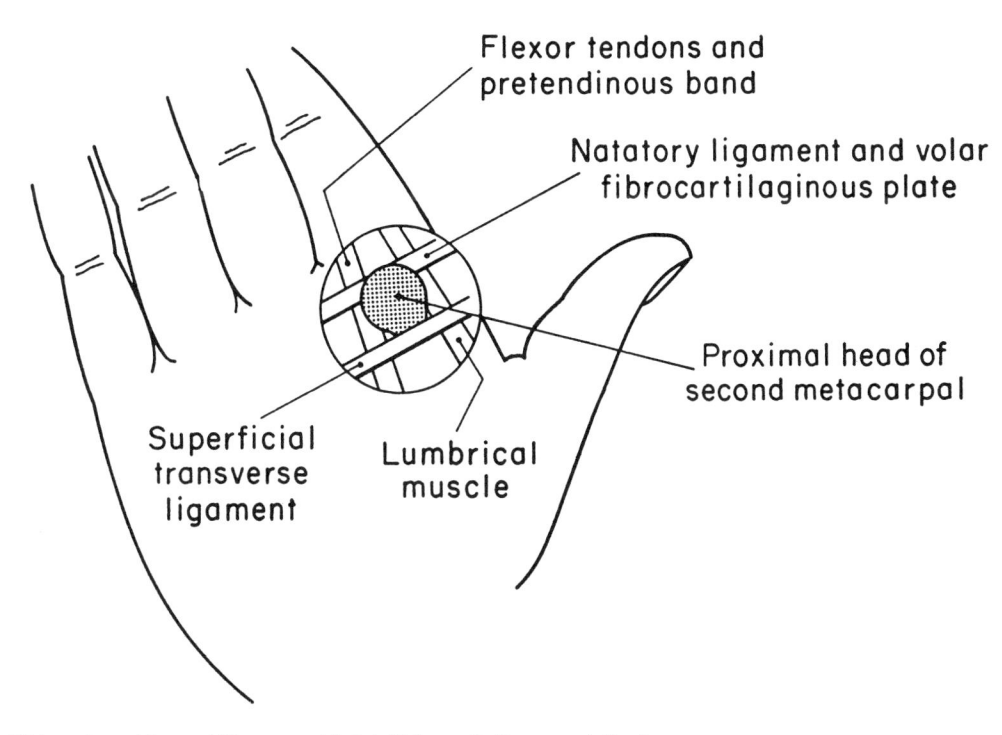

**Fig. 12D-25.** Dislocation of Second Metacarpal Joint (Schematic Representation)

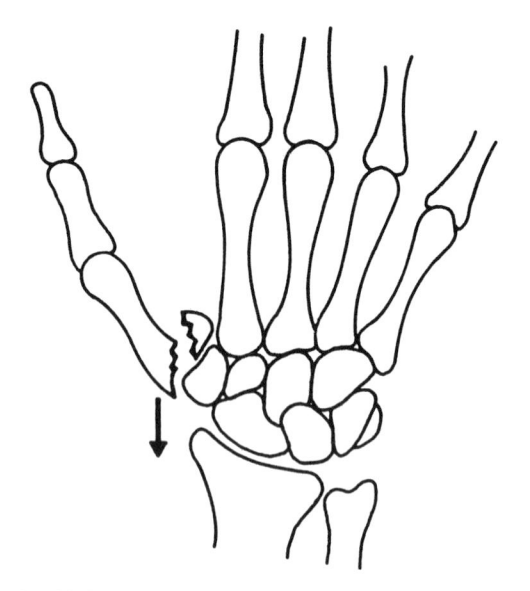

**Fig. 12D-26.** Bennett's Fracture

taneous K-wire fixation is usually required eventually. Immobilization for four to six weeks is the rule.

b. **Rolando's Fracture.** Interarticular T-shaped fracture. Such a fracture necessitates the need for surgical reduction and internal fixation.

**Injury to the Shaft or Proximal End of the Metacarpals 1-5.** Generally speaking, fractures of the proximal metacarpals do not involve articular surfaces of the MCP joint.

*Epidemiology* — Most commonly involved metacarpals are the first and fifth. The "boxer's fracture" refers to a complete fracture through the neck or shaft of the fifth metacarpal (Figure 12D-27).

*Anatomy* — Fractures in this area are common and either are compacted through the neck, oblique fractures through the shaft, or spiral fractures.

*Diagnosis* — Observation of the knuckle profile of the injured athlete as compared to his "normal" unaffected hand may show a "lost" knuckle, indicating the specific metacarpal fracture (Figure 12D-28).

*Treatment* — The digit involved should be immobilized, the metacarpal joint flexed at 60° with the interphalangeal joints free. Three to four weeks of immobilization are necessary. The degree of acceptable volar angulation of the metacarpal depends on the specific metacarpal injured.

a. The second and third metacarpal constitutes the stable longitudinal arch of the hand. If the metacarpal head is flexed more than 10° to 15°, grips will be interferred with.

b. The fourth and fifth metacarpals are much more mobile. Correction of angulation is not as essential. Angulation up to 40° for fractures of the fifth metacarpal are accepted because no significant disability is produced (Burton and Eaton, 1973). To control rotation, include the adjacent digit in the cast extension.

c. Rotational alignment must be checked carefully. In fractures where there is significant shortening or rotational deformity, internal fixation is indicated. These generally are oblique or spiral fractures.

*Complications* — Most common are: (1) malunion and malrotation; (2) interosseous muscle fibrosis; (3) extrinsic extensor tightness resulting in loss of flexion, and (4) localized Volkmann's ischemic contracture.

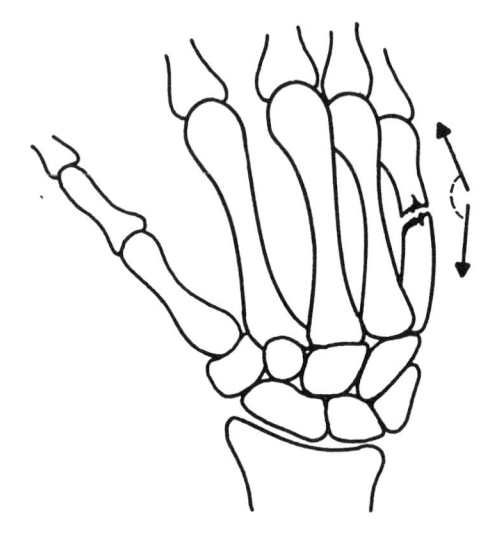

**Fig. 12D-27.** Boxer's Fracture

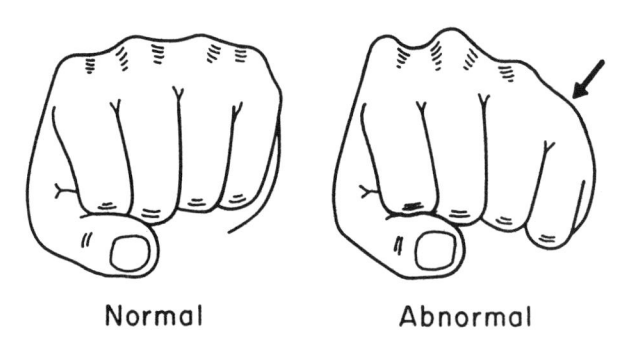

**Fig. 12D-28.** "Knuckle" Profile

## Fingers

### Proximal Phalanx

The periosteum of the proximal phalanx is directy in contact with the tendons (extensors and flexors) running dorsally and the lateral bands of the fingers. Because of this close proximity, these tendons often become involved in the injury response. When this occurs, tethering of the involved tendons limits the active and passive motion of the joints distally (McCue, 1979). Fractures in this area are potentially the most disabling in the hand. Unless there is anatomical reduction and proper immobilization, the entire unit of the finger may be permanently compromised. The proximal phalanx enters into critical proximal and distal articulations. Restrictive movement of either is serious; restriction of both is a disaster.

*Signs* — With the finger tips in flexion, all four should be pointing toward the navicular prominence at the wrist. Malrotation can be appreciated by observing the position of the injured finger in relation to the other fingers during active flexion (Figure 12D-29).

*Treatment* — Most cases fall into the category of stable fractures that can be controlled by closed splinting. Fractures that involve either proximal or distal articular surfaces of the proximal phalanx must be anatomically reduced and held. Closed reduction is easier if it is done with the fingers in flexion. Flexion decreases the deforming force of the intrinsic muscles as well as the extrinsic flexors. Injury to the proximal phalangeal epiphysis can be treated by closed means. Significant complications can occur with this fracture, making it advisable to consult an orthopedic surgeon.

*Complications* — Malrotation, tethering of the extensor mechanism, and non-union.

### Proximal Interphalangeal Joint (PIP)

Important points:

- very vulnerable joint because of its long lever arms;
- no appreciable lateral mobility;
- any fixed deformity (flexion or extension) is functionally disabling;
- small non-weight bearing joint.

In many cases, athletes return to competition before healing occurs, resulting in deformities such as the "coaches finger" (McCue, 1979) (see Table 12D-4).

*Anatomy* — The joint consists of a concave proximal end of the middle phalanx and a convex

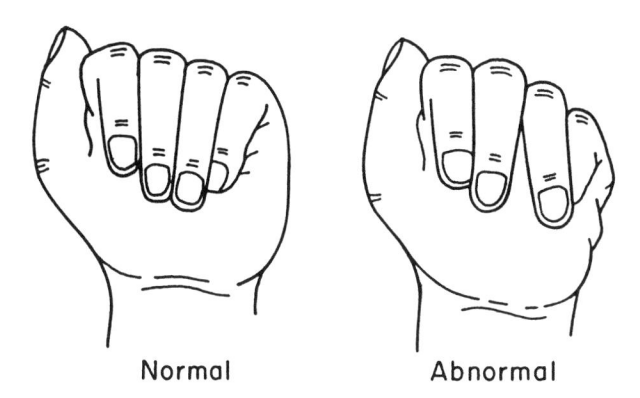

**Fig. 12D-29.** Position of Fingers in Flexion (Malrotation Test)

**Table 12D-4. Position Guidelines for PIP Joint Injuries**

| Injury | Joint Position | Splint Surface |
| --- | --- | --- |
| Articular fractures | 30° flexion | Volar |
| Fracture-dislocations | Block at 25° flexion; allow full flexion | Dorsal |
| Bountonniere deformity | Full extension | Volar |
| Pseudoboutonniere deformity | Full extension | Volar |
| Collateral ligament injuries | | |
|    Mild strain | Functional position | Volar |
|    Incomplete tear | 30° flexion | Volar |
| Volar plate injuries | 25-30° flexion | Volar or dorsal |

distal end of the proximal phalanx, fitted together to form a hinge joint with a range of motion of 0° to 100° flexion. Stability is achieved by the interdigitation of the phalangeal bones and also by the strong thick fibrocartilaginous volar plate reinforced on both sides of the finger by the collateral ligaments. This creates a three-sided box that resists all motion except extension and flexion. To displace this joint in any abnormal direction, at least two sides of this "box" must be torn. Additional stability is provided by the central slip of the extensor tendon as well as by the flexor tendons.

### Sprains, Strains and Ligament Injuries

### Collateral Ligament Injuries

*Epidemiology* — Most common on the radial side.
*Biomechanics* — History of hyperextension, creating the force that injured the collateral ligament. These injuries are associated with partial or complete rupture of the volar plate.
*Objective Findings* — Palpation of the four sides of the joints usually will localize the lesion to either the radial or ulnar collateral ligament, volar plate, or extensor tendon.
*Treatment* — 1) Partial tear, 1st and 2nd degree sprains - splinting at 30° flexion. 2) Complete tears (3rd degree) of the collateral ligament — much controversy on this subject. Most feel the conservative treatment outlined above is appropriate. Some feel surgical repair of the torn ligament is needed.
*Rehabilitation* — Active range of motion exercises should be started at 10 to 14 days with and protective splinting (buddy taping) (Figure 12D-30) for at least three weeks.

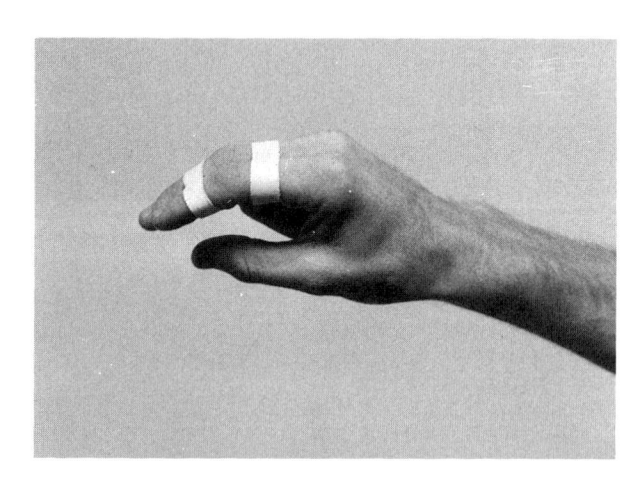

**Fig. 12D-30.** "Buddy" Taping

**Boutonniere Deformity.** This injury, while truly acute, does not manifest itself with significant symptomatology at the time of injury. It results from a tear of the central slip of the digital extensor tendon as it proceeds over the PIP joint (Figure 12D-31). It is the second most common closed tendon injury in the athlete (McCue, 1989).

*History* — Difficult to diagnose.
*Physical or Objective Signs* — There may be an inability to extend the PIP joint. The patient may be able to extend fully because of intact lateral bands, but as time passes a tendon imbalance develops and the the deformities that can be seen are hyperextension of the MCP joint, flexion of the PIP joint, and/or hyperextension of the DIP joint. Additional physical examination reveals tenderness directly over the middle phalanx dorsally and an inability to extend the PIP joint past 30° flexion.
*Treatment* — This injury is often treated as a collateral ligament sprain (see above), with splinting in 30° flexion. This position, however, lends itself to continued separation of the disrupted ends of the central slip and may prevent healing, thus leading to muscle imbalance and deformity. The deformity is caused by the unopposed pull of the superficial digital flexor. The digit must be splinted in *full* extension for six to eight weeks (Figure 12D-32). Then protective splinting (buddy taping) for an additional 6 to 8 weeks during competition. Immobilization should not extend to the MCP or DIP joints.

**Pseudo-Boutonniere Deformity.** Again a late finding resembling a Boutonniere deformity, but no disruption of the central slip is present. Instead there is a flexion contracture of the proximal membranous portion of the volar plate secondary to injury, resulting in scarring, thickening, and contracture at the PIP (Figure 12D-33).

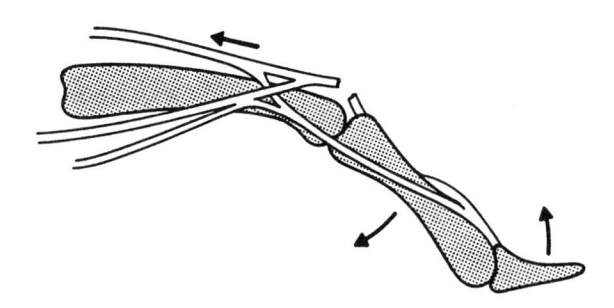

**Fig. 12D-31.** Boutonniere Deformity

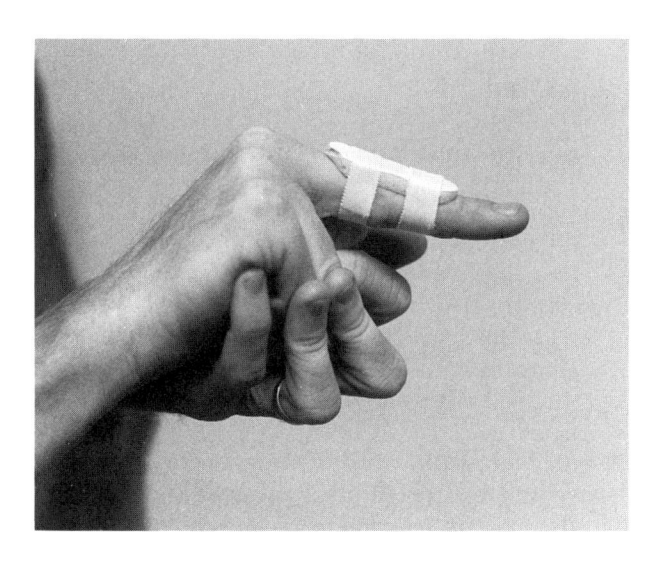

**Fig. 12D-32.** Boutonniere Splint

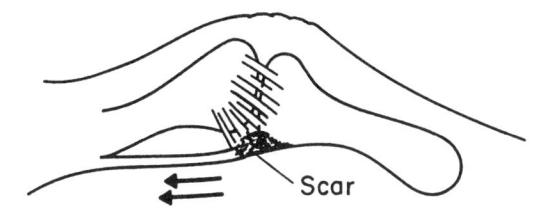

PSEUDOBOUTONNIERE DEFORMITY

VOLAR PLATE AVULSION FRACTURE

**Fig. 12D-33.** Pseudoboutonniere Deformity and Volar Plate Avulsion Fracture

**Volar Plate Injury.** Injury often occurs when there is forced hyperextension of the digit. It is an injury commonly associated with avulsing a chip of the base of the middle phalanax (Figure 12D-33). Complete disruption of the volar plate can also present with dislocation.

*Treatment* — Acutely, splinting in 20° flexion of the PIP joint for three weeks followed by protective splinting for another three to six weeks. Return to play at three weeks with buddy taping is appropriate. If the joint remains functionally unstable or dislocates spontaneously with movement at the end of three weeks, surgical open repair is indicated. Surgery is also indicated if there is an irreducible dislocation in an acute injury, or for a joint that can be hyperextended and is associated with "triggering" or "snapping."

*Complications* — Disruption of the volar plate distally results in swan neck deformity (minimal flexion of the DIP joint and hyperextension of the PIP joint). Flexion deformity secondary to volar plate injury results in the pseudo-Boutonniere deformity. Surgery in the latter is indicated if flexion is greater than 40° or, subjectively, if it represents a problem to the patient.

### Dislocations and Fractures

**Articular Fractures.** Usually involves one condyle of the distal head of the proximal phalanx.

*Treatment* — Splint with a gutter splint flexed at 30° for three weeks. Early protective flexion can begin as soon as acute swelling and pain subsides. Splints may be either dorsal or volar.

*Indications for surgery* — Displaced articular fractures involving more than 25% of the surface and dorsally displaced avulsion fractures involving insertion of the central slip.

**Fracture Dislocations.** Dorsal dislocation of the middle phalanx with volar plate fracture is most common.

*Treatment* — Splinted as indicated above.

### Dislocations

*Biomechanics* — Hyperextension is most common and usually involves injury to the volar plate. Collateral ligament system usually is intact.

*Treatment* — Reduction is quite simple. Splinting at 20-30° flexion for three weeks followed by active exercise and range of motion. Buddy taping should be done for two additional weeks until the injury is asymptomatic during competition.

*Types of Dislocations* — Dorsal is the most common but there can be collateral and volar plate involvement or volar dislocation, where the phalangeal head is "buttonholed" between central slip and lateral band. Open reduction is required for the last.

### Middle Phalanx

Fractures of the middle phalanx usually are transverse or oblique. Spiral fractures seldom occur. If fractures do not involve the articular surface as mentioned above, open reduction is not necessary. Because the two slips of the superficial digital flexor insert on the volar surface of the shaft and the central slip of the common digital extensor at the base of the middle phalanx dorsally, there usually is a characteristic deformity seen in this fracture involving volar flexion of the proximal fragment. Treatment stability can be achieved with longitudinal traction and flexion of the distal fragment so that it aligns with the proximal fragment. The use of a short arm plaster splint dorsally to hold the fracture with the joints in 20-30° flexion is necessary (Figure 12D-34).

### Distal Interphalangeal Joint (DIP)

### Dislocation

*Biomechanics* — Usually caused by a blow to the tip of the finger and is associated with a compound dislocation. The most frequent type of dislocation is dorsally.

*Treatment* — Reduction is easily accomplished by traction. Once that is obtained, the function and stability of the joint should be ascertained, especially to make sure there is no interposed volar plate within the joint. Occasionally when reduction is hard or impossible, it is secondary to volar plate entrapment (which requires open reduction). Neither the flexor nor the extensor mechanisms are disrupted in this injury. The joint should be immobilized for three weeks and protected during competition for an additional three weeks. Where there is a compound dislocation, the wound should be cleansed with appropriate antibiotics to prevent infection.

### Avulsion of the Deep Digital Flexor (DDF)

*Epidemiology* — Most commonly seen on the ring finger. Frequently, this injury is misdiagnosed as a sprain or jammed finger.

*Biomechanics* — "Sweater finger" usually occurs when player attempts to grasp an opponent's jersey and pulls the flexor tendon from its insertion causing a pop with immediate onset of acute pain.

*Physical Examination* — The degree of soft tissue reaction to this injury is variable. Occasionally the palpated distal end of the tendon appears as a tender mass in the proximal finger or palm because of tendon retraction. Weakness of hand grip and limitation of DIP joint motion will be present.

*Treatment* — Open repair with reattachment if retraction of avulsed tendon has occured or the bony fragment constitutes more than 25% of the DIP articular surface (Hoffman, 1991).

### Common Digital Extensor (CDE) Avulsion.
"Mallet" or drop finger deformity, baseball finger.

*Epidemiology* — One of the most common hand injuries sustained by the athlete. Sports involved include baseball (catcher), football (wide receiver), and basketball.

*Biomechanics* — Longitudinal force to the tip of the finger with forced flexion and disruption of the extensor mechanism. Usually this involves avulsion of the tendon insertion or fracture of the dorsal base of the distal phalanx.

*Objective Signs* — A swan neck deformity may occur with retraction of the extensor mechanism. Ability to extend the distal phalanx is lost. The following five patterns have been described for this injury complex (McCue et al.,1979) (Figure 12D-35).
  a. stretching of fibers of the extensor mechanism only
  b. avulsion of only tendon without bony involvement
  c. avulsion of tendon with small fragment of bone, usually not involving articular surface
  d. fracture with significant involvement of articular surface
  e. fracture dislocation of the epiphyseal plate (seen only in children)

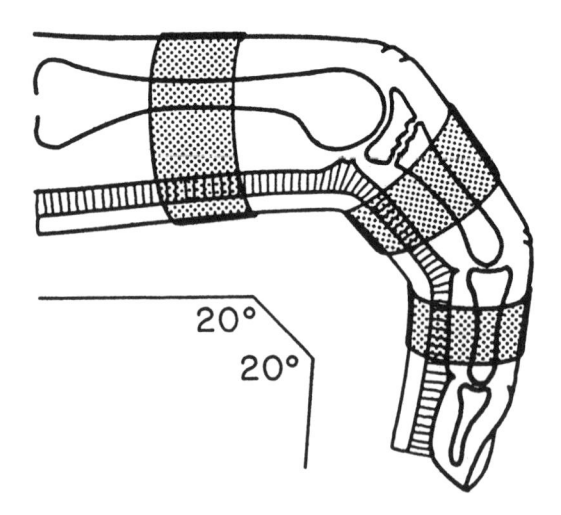

**Fig. 12D-34.** Proximal Phalanx Fracture Splinting

## MALLET FINGER PATHOLOGY

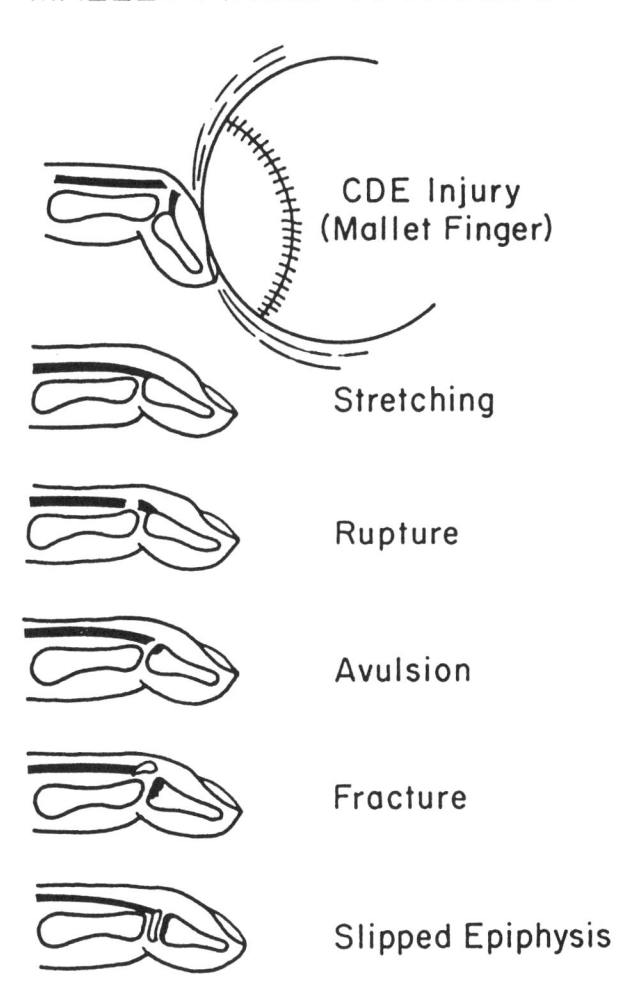

- CDE Injury (Mallet Finger)
- Stretching
- Rupture
- Avulsion
- Fracture
- Slipped Epiphysis

**Fig. 12D-35.** Mallet Finger Pathology

- Mallet Finger Splint
- Stack Finger Splint

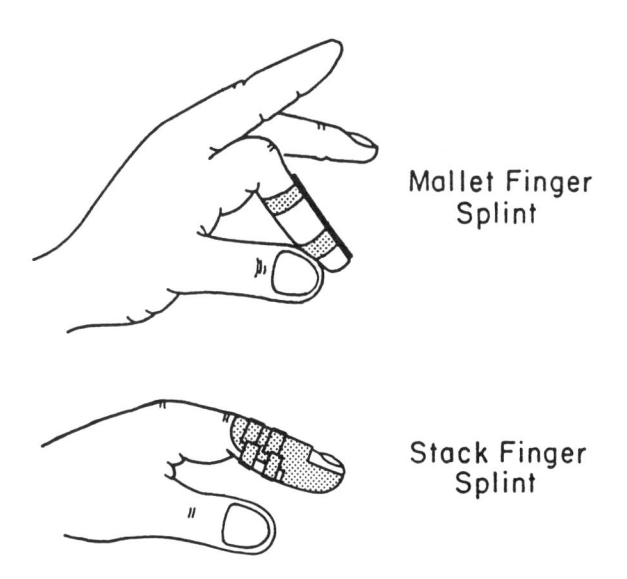

**Fig. 12D-36.** Mallet Finger Splint and Stack Finger Splint

*Treatment* — X-ray should be obtained of both the DIP joint and PIP joints. Treatment in the first three types calls for splinting the DIP in full extension or hyperextension for six to eight weeks (Figure 12D-36), plus protective splinting for an additional six to eight weeks during athletics. Splint may be either volar or dorsal; a dorsal splint allows maintenance of fingertip touch, quite useful in athletes catching balls. If fingertip touch is not important, the stack finger splint is ideal for treatment of this injury (Figure 12D-36). In type four, surgery with anatomical reduction is necessary. Type five calls for reduction of the dislocation followed by external splinting. However, Wehbe and Schneider (1984) found, that for most patients with mallet fractures, joint subluxation and the size and amount of bone fragment displacement can be disregarded and treatment can be conservative.

**Distal Phalanx**

**Fracture**

*Etiology* — Most often caused by a direct crushing injury resulting in a non-displaced fracture.

*Anatomy* — The bone is bordered dorsally by the nail bed, which rests on the periosteum of the distal phalanx, and volarly by the fingertip pulp. Since there are no musculotendinous forces present in the distal phalanx, displacement of fragments rarely occurs.

*Treatment* — L-shaped padded aluminum splint placed on the volar aspect. Tight, circumferential taping should be avoided because of increasing discomfort and risk of vascular compromise (Hoffman, 1991).

*Complications* — If the nail matrix is displaced by the crush injury or interposed between the fractured fragments of the bone, nonunion can occur. Infection can result from the nail acting as a foreign body. Some advocate approximation of such fragments with absorbable suture. We disagree.

**Subungual Hematoma.** May result from a crush injury to the finger.

*Treatment* — Evacuation of blood may be necessary by means of a small hole drilled or burnt through the nail (hot paper clip)

*Complications* — Split nail deformity.

UPPER EXTREMITY INJURIES/ILLNESSES

## Infections

**Paronychia** infection about the nail bed, with Staphylococcus aureus usually the responsible agent.

*Treatment* — Hot soaks and debridement are usually all that is necessary. Rarely, antibiotics may be needed.

**Felon.** Deep localized infection in the substance of the fingertip, usually incorporating several septae.

*Complications* — include secondary osetomyelitis and tenosynovitis of the flexor tendon.

*Treatment* — Drainage through a dorsal midlateral incision. Coverage with antibiotics is necessary. X-rays should be ordered to rule out osteomyelitis.

**Tendon Sheath Tenosynovitis Infection.** A result of infection from hematologic spread or inocculation.

*Treatment* — Immobilization for eight to ten hours. Oral antibiotic therapy. Drainage of abcesses, especially when it develops in the thenar or hypothenar region.

**Human Bites.** Infection is very prevalent in skin lacerations caused by human bites. Watch for portions of teeth remaining imbedded and hidden within the wound.

*Treatment* — Surgical debridement and antibiotics. Immobilization if the wound involves a tendon or joint. Anaerobic and aerobic cultures may be necessary; the most frequent offending agent is streptococcus.

### REFERENCES

*Section A. Shoulder*

Albright, J.A., Jokl, P., Shaw, R., et al. Clinical study of baseball pitchers: correlation of injury to the throwing arm with method of delivery. *Am J Sports Med* 6:15-21, 1978.

Allman, F.L. Fractures and ligamentous injury of the clavicle and its articulation. *J Bone Joint Surg* 49A:774-784, 1967.

Archambault, J.A. Brachial plexus stretch injury. *J Am Coll Health* 31:256-260, 1983.

Aronen, J.G., Regan, K. Decreasing the incidence of recurrence of first time anterior shoulder dislocations with rehabilitation. *Am J Sports Med* 12(4):283-291, 1984.

Barth, E., Berg, E. Practical pointers for common shoulder complaints. *J of Musculoskel Med* 6(6):38-49, 1989.

Bergfeld, J.A., Andrish, J.T., Clancy, W.G. Evaluation of the acromioclavicular joint following first and second degree sprains. *Am J Sports Med* 6:153, 1978.

Bergfeld, J.A. Brachial plexus injuries. Practical Approach to Sports Medicine Conference, East Lansing, MI, 1981.

Carr, D., Johnson, R.J., Pope, M.H. Upper extremity injuries in skiing. *Am J Sports Med* 9:378-383, 1981.

Clancy, W.G., Brand, R.L., Bengfeld, J.A. Upper trunk brachial plexus injuries in contact sports. *Am J Sports Med* 5(5):209-216, 1977.

Cox, J.S. The fate of the acromioclavicular joint in athletic injuries. *Am J Sports Med* 9:50, 1981.

Dagian, R.F., Dillman, C.J., Milner, E.K. Relationship between exposure time and injury in football. *Am J Sports Med* 8:257-260, 1980.

Dominquez, R.H. Shoulder pain in age group swimmers. In *Swimming Medicine IV*,

Eriksson, B., Furberg, B., eds. University Park Press, Baltimore, 1978, pp. 105-109.

Franek, J., Warren, R.F., Bowen, M. Posterior subluxation of the glenohumeral joint. *J Bone Joint Surg* 71A:205, 1989.

Garrick, J.G., Requa, R.K. Injuries in high school sports. *Pediatrics* 61:465-469, 1978.

Glousman, R.E., Jobe, F.W. How to detect and manage the unstable shoulder. *J Musculoskel Med* 7(3):93-110, 1990.

Hawkins, R.J., Kennedy, J.C. Impingement syndrome in athletes. *Am J Sports Med* 8:57, 1980.

Hovelius, L. Anterior dislocation of the shoulder in teenagers and young adults. *J Bone Joint Surg* 69A:393-399, 1987.

Ireland, M.L., Andrews, J.R. Shoulder and elbow injuries in the young athlete. *Clinics in SM* 7(3):474-494, 1988.

Jobe, F.W., Moynes, D.R. Delineation of diagnostic criteria and a rehabilitation program for rotator cuff injuries. *Am J Sports Med* 10:336-339, 1982.

Kennedy J.C. Hawkins, R.J. Swimmer's shoulder. *Phys Sportsmed* 2(2):35-38, 1974.

Larson, R.L, McMahon, R.O. The epiphysis and the childhood athlete. *JAMA* 196:607, 1966.

Matsen, F.A., Zuckerman, J.A. Anterior glenohumeral instability. *Clinics in Sports Med* 2(2):319-338, 1983.

Neer, C.S., Welsh, R.P. The shoulder in sports. *Ortho Clin North Am* 8:583, 1977.

Nicholas, J.A., Grossman, R.B., Hershman, E.B. The importance of a simplified classification of motion in sports in relation to performance. *Orthop Clin North Am* 8:499-532, 1977.

Priest, J.D., Nogel, D.A. Tennis shoulder. *Am J Sports Med* 4:28- 42, 1976.

Rafii, M., Minkoff, J., Bonamo, J., et al. Computed tomography (CT) arthrogram of shoulder instabilities in athletes. *Am J Sports Med* 16:352-361, 1988.

Richardson, A.B., Jobe, F.W., Collins, H.R. The shoulder in competitive swimming. *Am J Sports Med* 8:159-163, 1980.

Richardson, A.B., Overuse syndromes in baseball, tennis, gymnastics, and swimming. *Clinics in Sports Med* 2(2):379-389, 1983.

Rowe, C.R., Patil, D., Southmoyd, W.W., The Bankart procedure, a long-term end-result study. *J Bone Joint Surg* 60A:1, 1978.

Rowe, C.R. Evaluation of the shoulder. In Rowe, C.R. *The Shoulder*, Churchill-Livingston, New York, 1988.

Samilson, R.L., Prieto, V. Posterior dislocation of the shoulder in athletes. *Clinics in Sports Med* 2(2):369-378, 1983.

Snook, G.A. Injuries in intercollegiate wrestling — a 5 year study. *Am J Sports Med* 10:142-144, 1982.

Sturm, J.T., Peary, J.F. Brachial plexus injuries from blunt trauma — a harbinger of vascular and thoracic injury. *Ann Emerg Med* 16:404-406, 1987.

Taft, T.N., Wilson, F.C., Ogleby, J.W. Dislocation of the acromioclavicular joint. *J Bone Joint Surg* 69A(7):1045-1052, 1987.

Thorndike, A. *Athletic Injuries*, 4th ed. Philadelphia, Lea and Febiger, 1956.

Tibone, J.E. Shoulder problems in adolescents. *Clinics in Sports Med* 2(2):423-427, 1983.

Tullos, H.S., King, J.W. Lesions of the pitching arm in adolescents. *JAMA* 220:264, 1972.

Warren, R.F. Subluxation of the shoulder in athletes. *Clinics in Sports Med* 2(2): 339-354, 1983.

Wickiewicz, T.L. Acromioclavicular and sternoclavicular joint injuries. *Clinics in Sports Med* 2(2):429-438, 1983.

Wright, I.S. Neurovascular syndrome produced by hyperabduction of the arm. *Am Heart J* 29:1, 1945.

Yocum, L.A. Reporting athletic injuries. Presented at 81st Meeting of Major League Physicians and Trainers, Honolulu, Hawaii, December 1982.

Yohoe, K., Nanajima, H., Yamazki, Y. Injuries of the shoulder in volleyball players and javelin throwers. *Orthop Trauma Surg* 22:351-359, 1959.

### Section B. Upper Arm

Huss, C.D., Puhl, J.J. Myositis ossificans of the upper arm. *Am J Sports Med* 8(6):419-424, 1980.

Kuland, D.B. *The Injured Athlete*. J.B. Lippincott, Philadelphia, 1982, p. 450.

### Section C. Elbow

Conwell, H.E. Injuires to the elbow. *Clinical Symposia*, Ciba, 1969.

Gugenheim, J.J., Stanley, R.F., Woods G.W., et al. Little league survey: the Houston study. *Am J Sports Med* 4:189-199, 1976.

Josefsson, P.O., Johnell, O., Gentz, C.F. Long-term sequelae of simple dislocation of the elbow. *J Bone Joint Surg.* 66-a:927-930, 1984.

Ireland, M.L., Andrews, J.R. Shoulder and elbow injuries in the young athlete. *Clinics in Sports Med* 7(3):474-494, 1988.

Larson, R.L., Singer, K.M., Bergstrom, R., Thomas, S. Little league survey: the Eugene study. *Am J Sports Med* 4:204-209, 1976.

Lombardo, J.L. Shoulder, arm, elbow and forearm injuries in the athlete. Practical Approach to Sports Medicine Symposium, American Academy of Family Physicians, East Lansing, MI 1983.

National Electronic Injury Surveillance System, U.S. Consumer Product Safety Commission, Washington, D.C., 1981.

Nirschl, R.P. Tennis elbow. *Ortho Clin North Am* 4(3):787, 1973.

Nirschl, R.P. Soft-tissue injuries about the elbow. *Clinics in SM* 5(4):637-652, 1986.

Priest, J.D., Broden, V., Gerberich, J.G. The elbow and tennis - Part I. *Phys and Sports Med* 8(1):77, 1980a.

Priest, J.D., Broden, V., Gerberich, J.G. The elbow and tennis - Part II. *Phys and Sports Med* 8(4):80, 1980b.

Singer, K.M., Ray, S.P. Osteochondrosis of the humeral capitellum. *Am J Sports Med* 12(5):351-360, 1984.

Whiteside, J.A. Andrews, J.R. Common elbow problems in the recreational athlete. *J Musculoskel Med* 6(2):17-34, 1989.

Woods and Tullos. Elbow instability and medial epicondyle fracture. *Am J Sports Med* 5:23-30, 1977.

Yocum, L.A. The diagnosis and nonoperative treatment of elbow problems in the athlete. *Clinics in Sports Med* 8(3):439-459, 1989.

### Section D. Wrist, Hand and Fingers

Browne, E.Z. Jr., Dunn, H.K., Snyder, C.C. Ski pole thumb injury. *Plastic and Reconstructive Surg* 58(1):19-23, 1976.

Buckhout, B.C., Warner, M.A. Digital perfusion of handball players. *Am J Sports Med* 8(3):206-207, 1980.

Burkhalter, W.E. Bennett's fracture repair: is open-reduction best? *J Musucloskel Med* 13(8):10-12, 1990.

Burton, R.K., Eaton, R.G. Common hand injuries in the athlete. *Ortho Clinics of North America* 4(3):809-838, 1973.

Conwell, H.E. Injuries to the wrist. *Clinical Symposia*, Ciba, 1970.

Dangles, C.J., Bilos, Z.J. Ulnar nerve neuritis in a world champion weightlifter. *Am J of Sports Med* 8(6):443-445, 1980.

Eaton, R.G. *Joint Injuries of the Hand*. Springfield, Ill, Charles C. Thomas, 1971.

Eaton, R.G., Littler, J.W. A study of the basal joint of the thumb. *J Bone Joint Surg* 51A:661-668, 1969.

Gerber, S.D., Griffin, P.P., Simmons, B.P. Break dancer's wrist. *J Pediatr Orthop* 6:98-99, 1986.

Hoffman, D.F., Schaffer, T.C. Management of common finger injuries. *Amer Fam Phys* 43(5):1594-1609, 1991.

Kauer, J.M.G., deLange, A. The carpal joint. *Hand Clinics* 3(1):23-29, 1987.

Kirk, M., Orlinsky, M., Goldberg, R., Brotman, P. The validity and reliability of the navicular fat stripe as a screening test for detection of navicular fractures. *Ann Emerg Med* 19(12):1371-1376, 1990.

Layfer, L.F., Jones, J.V. Hand parasthesias after racquetball. *Illinois Med J* 190-191, 1977.

Lowrey, C.W., Chadwick, R.O. Digital vessel trauma from repetitive impact in baseball catchers, *J Hand Surg* 1:236-238, 1976.

McCue, F.C., Mayer, V. Rehabilitation of common athletic injuries of the hand and wrist. *Clinics in Sports Med* 8(4):731-776, 1989.

McCue, F.C., Baugher, W.H., Kulund, D.N., Gieck, J.H. Hand and wrist injuries in the athlete. *Am J of Sports Med* 7(5):275-286, 1979.

Mosher, J.F. Current concepts in the diagnosis and treatment of hand and wrist injuries in sports. *Med Sci Sports Exer* 17(1):48- 55, 1985.

Mossman, S.S., Blau, J.N. Tinel's sign and the carpal tunnel syndrome. *Br Med J* 294:680, 1987.

National Electronic Injury Surveillance Survey, U.S. Consumer Products Safety Commission, 1981.

Parker, R.D., Berkowitz, M.S., Brahms, M.A., Bohl, W.R. Hook of the hamate fractures in athlete. *Am J of Sports Med* 14(6):517-523, 1986.

Ruby, L.K. Common hand injuries in the athlete. *Ortho Clinics of North Am* 11(4):819-839, 1980.

Simmons, B.P., Lovallo, J.L. Hand and wrist injuries in children. *Clinics in Sports Med* 7(3):495-512, 1988.

Smith, R.J. Post-traumatic instability of the metacarpophalangeal joint of the thumb. *J Bone Joint Surg* 59:14-21, 1977.

Stener, B. Displacement of the ruptured ulnar collateral ligament of the metacarpal phalangeal joint of the thumb. *J Bone Joint Surg* 44B:869-879, 1962.

Swanson, A.B. Fractures involving the digits of the hand. *Ortho Clinics of North Am* 1:261-274, 1970.

Szabo, R.M., Manske, O. Displaced fractures of the scaphoid. *Clin Ortho and Rel Research* 230(5):30-38, 1988.

Terry, G.W., Ramin, J.E. The navicular fat stripe: a useful roentgen feature for evaluating wrist trauma. *A J Radiol* 124:25-28, 1975.

Weber, E.R. A rational approach for the recognition and treatment of Coles' fracture. *Hand Clinics* 3(1):13-21, 1987.

Wehbe, M.A., Schneider, L.H. Mallet fractures. *J Bone Joint Surg* 66-A: 658-669, 1984.

Zemel, N.P., Stark, H.H. Fractures and dislocations of the carpal bones. *Clinics in Sports Med* 5(4):709-724, 1986.

# Appendix 12A-1.
# Muscular Function Testing of the Shoulder

**a.** General Strength, Deltoid Muscle

**b.** Supraspinatus Muscle

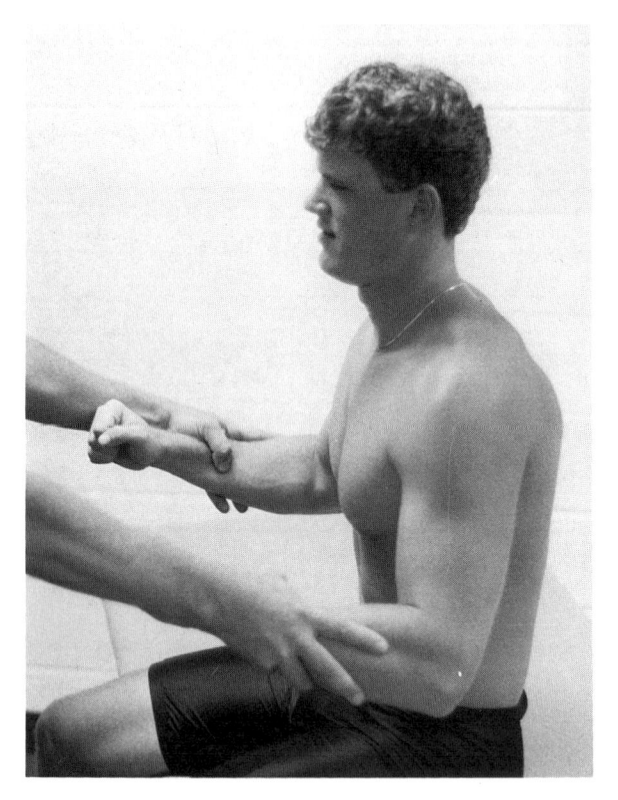

**c.** Abductors

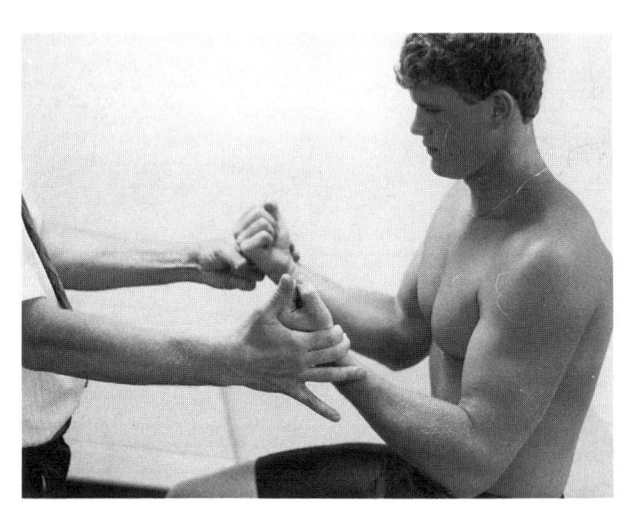

**d.** Biceps

Appendix 12A-1 (*continued*)

**e.** Biceps Tendon (long head)

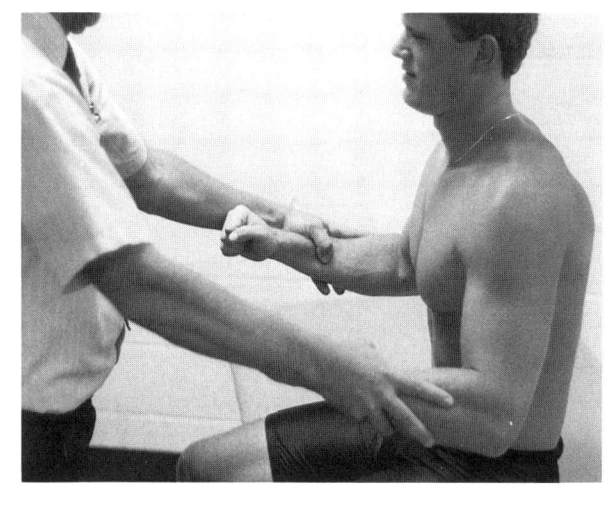

**f.** External Rotators

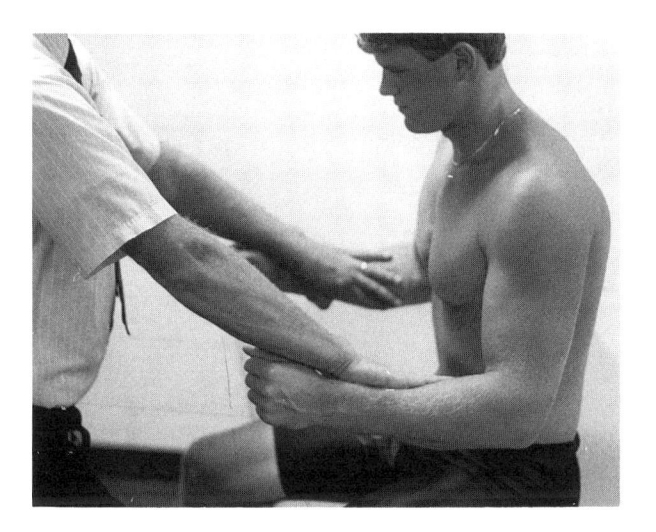

**g.** Internal Rotators

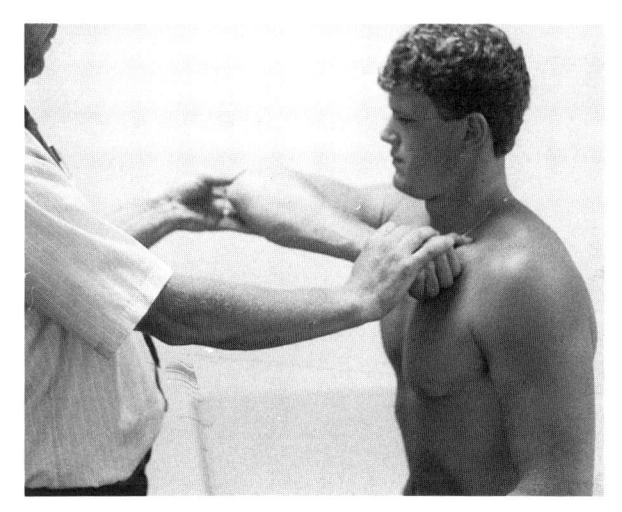

**h.** Impingement of Greater Tuberosity Under Coraco-acromial Arch

# Appendix 12D-1.
# Colles' Fracture Reduction

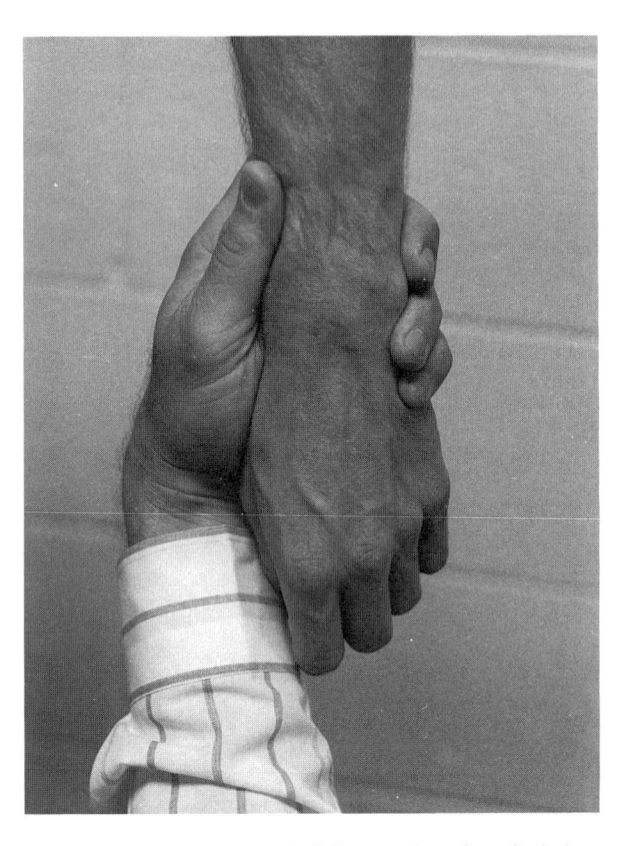

**a.** A proper position — wrist in full pronation, ulnar deviation, and moderate flexion.

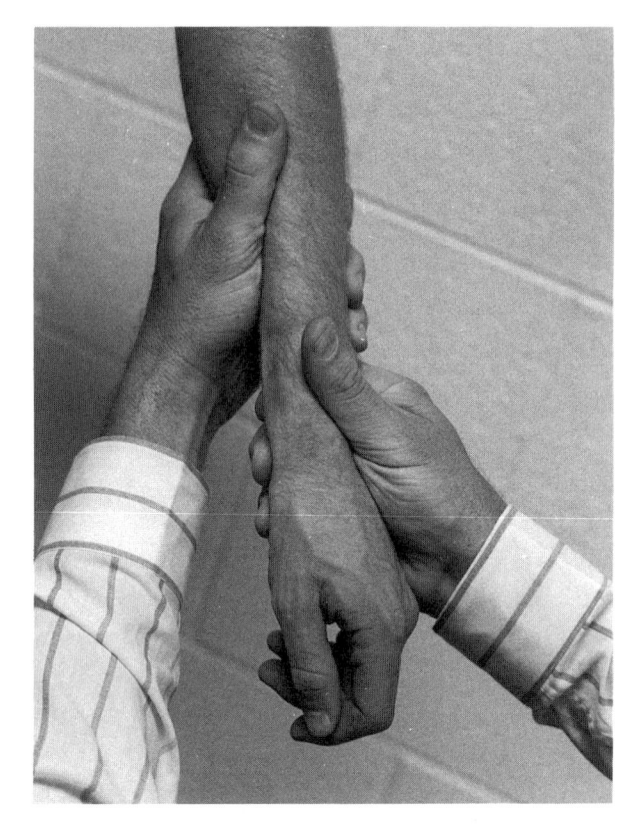

**b.** Countertraction being applied to induce reduction.

# 13

# Common Sports-Related Injuries and Illnesses — Thorax & Abdomen

## SECTION A: CHEST

Common sports-related chest injuries are usually caused by acute deceleration of the player's body or by a sudden impact as in football, baseball, diving, gymnastics, lacrosse, hockey, and skateboarding.

The thorax is a very rigid structure with strong ligamentous support between the ribs, sternum and vertebrae. The oval of the chest is smaller at the top and enlarges progressively below. The upper 7 ribs are directly attached to the sternum by costocartilage. Ribs 8 to 10 attach to the rib above through costocartilage, not directly to the sternum. The tips of the 11th and 12th ribs usually are free. The sternum consists of three parts — manubrium, body, and xiphoid. Attachments of the intercostal and accessory muscles to the ribs help elevate or depress the rib cage. The ribs are usually more elastic in childhood and become more brittle with age.

Because the intercostal nerves and vessels pass in a groove under the rib, the overlying intercostal muscle affords protection from external blows, but an injury to the rib above may damage the neurovascular supply. Finally, the abdominal muscles attach to the lower ribs anteriorly and provide support to the bony thorax from the pelvis.

## Chest Contusion

The most common chest injury is a severe blow which may result in the athlete's "breath being knocked out," with subsequent muscle spasm and severe dyspnea that usually clears rapidly. The physician should look for palpable tenderness over the chest wall or ribs. If a rib is extremely tender to palpation, and movement or breathing causes increased pain with crepitation, a fracture should be suspected. Auscultate the lungs for evidence of myocardial or pericardial damage, as a severe blow could damage the heart and even lead to sudden death. Obtain radiographic confirmation of a fracture or hemo- or pneumothorax.

Treatment of minor chest contusions involves resting the athlete and using ice and an ace wrap around the thorax. If a hematoma develops, incision and drainage may be required. Most contusions heal after several days of conservative treatment but analgesic and anti-inflammatory agents are required occasionally. Protection of the rib cage can be provided by taping a pad over the contused area or by using specially designed protectors (Figure 13A-1). Myositis ossificans, a frequent complication of many muscle contusions, is not common in chest wall injuries.

## Injuries to the Breast

### Runner's Nipple

The nipple can be irritated by friction from a runner's clothes, causing pain and bleeding (Levit, 1977). It can be prevented by using a band-aid or tape over the nipples and wearing non-abrasive clothing. This is usually less of a problem for female athletes who use the newer designs of sports bras.

### Breast Contusion

Breast contusion in males may cause localized irritation, with redness, heat, tenderness, and a

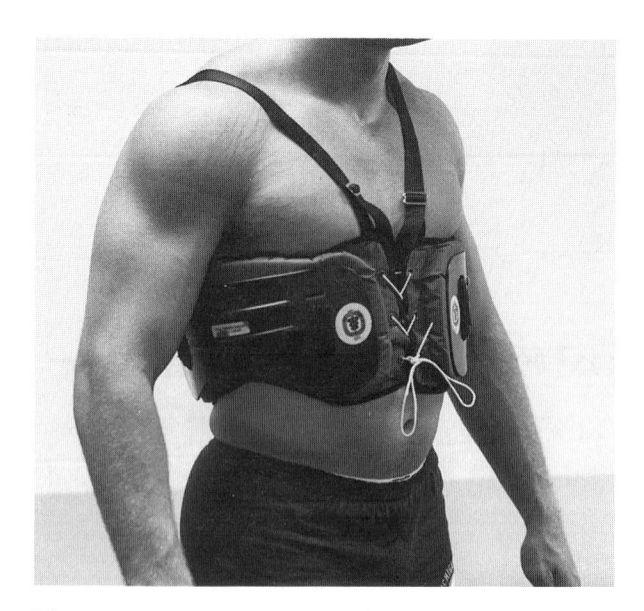

**Fig. 13A-1.** Flak Vest

palpable mass around the areola. Treatment with moist heat, anti-inflammatory agents, and protection of the breast during future participation is recommended. Occasionally, a painful fibrous nodule may develop that requires excision.

### Breast Injuries In Women

Until recently, there was little interest in the injury potential for the female breast during strenuous activity. Significant injury to the breast is rare in recreational and competitive sports and there is no association between a sports-incurred breast injury and later development of malignancy. Haycock (1980) found that up to 72% of female athletes have sore breasts after vigorous exercise.

Common breast injuries include chafing of the skin and nipples and discomfort caused by lateral and vertical displacement of the breasts during running. Without good support, the breast can slap against the chest with up to 70 foot-pounds of force, especially in large-breasted women. Pregnant women and those with fibrocystic disease suffer more exercise-related breast injuries (Eichelberger, 1981).

Breast supports for women date to Greek and Roman times. More recent studies (Gehlson, 1980; Haycock, 1978; DeHaven, 1986; Shangold, 1988; Otis, 1986) indicate that a sports brassiere should provide firm support, prevent breast motion, be constructed of an elastic, non-abrasive, sturdy material, be fitted as part of the athlete's protective equipment, and allow for the insertion of padding for extra protection if it is needed. The brassiere should contain at least 50% cotton for absorbency and have minimal elasticity so the athlete can breathe easily. It should have wide, non-elastic straps and all hooks and seams should be properly designed. An elastic wrap (4 inches wide) over the brassiere can provide extra support and reduce breast motion by 50%, but it should not be so tight it interferes with breathing (ACSM, 1979; Thomas, 1979). Newer sports bras have eliminated many earlier problems.

### Strains

Muscular strains of the chest wall are caused by overstretching or forceful exertion and they involve the muscles of the posterior thorax, intercostal muscles, or the abdominal wall muscles that attach to the ribs (Figure 13A-2). Complete muscle ruptures are rare in the thoracic region. The intercostal muscles usually are well protected and are seldom injured. Chest wall strains are usually more painful than disabling, but there may be significant spasm that can interfere with deep breathing.

Initial treatment consists of ice application. Heat and ultrasound may be used two or three

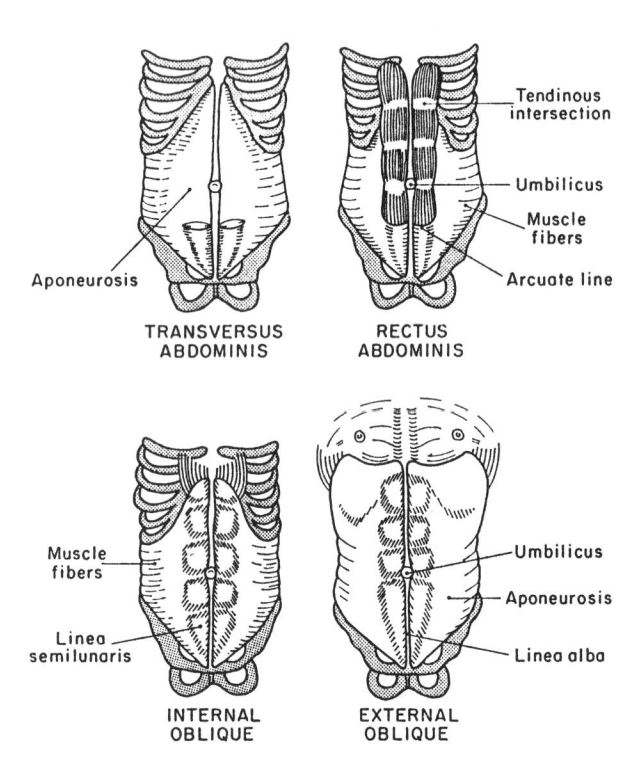

**Fig. 13A-2.** Abdominal Anatomy

days after injury, and NSAID agents may be helpful. Restriction of some activities and supportive strapping are other options. Proper rehabilitation of the injured chest wall muscles will be necessary. In some cases, trigger points (areas of acute inflammation) may respond to injection of a local anesthetic and corticosteroid use. A thorough evaluation of rib motion should be made. Abnormal movement patterns may be assisted by various manipulation techniques and massage.

**Rupture of the Pectoralis Major**

The pectoralis major is a large, fan-shaped, dually innervated muscle arising from the medial part of the clavicle, the sternum, the first six ribs, and the aponeurosis of the external oblique. Its tendon inserts into the humerus and the pectoralis major adducts, flexes, and internally rotates the shoulder. Rupture of this muscle can occur in power lifting, wrestling, and weight-training (bench press), but is most likely to happen during the bench press. Sudden overload of the muscle causes a partial or complete rupture at the musculotendinous junction. Avulsion of the attaching tendon from its bony attachment may occur. Rupture of the pectoralis major muscle was believed to be a rare injury but it is becoming more common or has been underreported and/or under recognized in the literature (Cauther, 1990; Richardson, 1990; Kretzler, 1989; Reet, 1991). Perhaps because more individuals are involved in weight-training, weight-lifting and fitness activities, we are now seeing more pectoralis major ruptures.

Muscle fatigue is a common cause of ruptures, but they also can occur during weight-lifting activities when an athlete tries to perform a maximal effort by "throwing" his/her body into the lifting procedure. Ruptures occur more often during concentric muscle contraction in the initiation phase of the exercise although some athletes believe that injuries are more likely to happen during the eccentric phase of lifting (Reet, 1989). McMaster (1933) has shown that normal tendons do not rupture unless they are injured and that the tendon insertion or musculotendinous junction, rather than the tendon itself, may rupture in response to heavy loads, particularly in younger individuals. Older athletes may have degenerative changes and are more likely to have ruptures within the tendon itself.

The injury is associated with anterior shoulder pain and a sensation of tearing in the shoulder. The athlete complains of a sudden "pop" followed by sharp pain in the upper arm or chest and acute swelling) and ecchymosis. The muscle bulges on the chest with resisted adduction. Tendon avulsion causes a palpable defect in the anterior axillary fold of the muscle. Chest x-ray often reveals an absent pectoralis shadow. A large hematoma will usually be noted on acute evaluation, accompanied by limited range of motion and weakness on muscle testing of resistance to adduction or internal rotation.

Richardson (1990) describes a "clap-test" in which the patient places the hands together in a sustained clapping position at chest level. With the elbows bent, a palpable gap is noted as the pectoralis major muscle retracts following rupture. Although a palpable defect is often seen on physical examination, soft tissue swelling may obscure it. A patient with complete rupture may not have a palpable defect when the superficial fascia is intact (Zeman, 1979). Other diagnostic tests may be useful. Ultrasonography has been helpful but MRI is preferable and may be better in locating the site of injury (tendon, musculotendinous junction, muscle) and determining the extent (partial vs. complete rupture) (Richardson, 1990).

Caughei (1990) classifies pectoralis major ruptures as Type I (contusion or strain), Type II (partial rupture), and Type III (complete rupture). Most pectoralis muscle injuries are partial (Type II).

Initial treatment consists of ice, use of a sling, and referral to an orthopedic surgeon. Surgery to reattach the tendon to the bone is recommended for serious competitive athletes (Berson, 1979; Zeman, 1979; Reet, 1991). The literature supports complete repair for athletes who are involved in strength, endurance, or power activities of the shoulder girdle. Richardson (1990) believes that surgical repair is warranted in chronic cases. The torn ends of the tendons are usually sutured to one another or directly to bone. Surgical results are excellent, with 80%-100% of patients getting good to excellent results and a return to full strength (Park, 1970; Kretzler, 1989). Significant strength deficits associated with fatigue and loss of power and endurance will occur with an unrepaired complete rupture of the pectoralis major.

The athlete usually must wear a shoulder harness for three to four weeks before gradually increasing range of motion and progressive resistance exercises (P.R.E.). Power lifting or heavy weight training routines must be avoided for three to six months after surgery but most athletes can return to competition. Proper weight training techniques (especially bench press) can help prevent this injury.

## Costochondral Separation

Costochondral separation is common in wrestling, rugby, and football. It is caused by a severe blow to the chest which results in a separation of the costocartilage from the rib. Injury to the upper seven ribs may cause a complete or partial dislocation of the affected rib from the sternum. There will be tenderness at the costochondral junction and pain on deep breathing or with direct pressure. Complete dislocation produces overriding of the rib, which then rests in front of the costocartilage. A palpable deformity or click may be felt. Radiographic studies are needed to rule out a concurrent fracture but costocartilage problems obviously will not be visualized.

If no displacement or click is noticed, the ligaments likely are intact. The athlete's chest should be strapped by placing a felt pad 1½" x 2¾" over the inner end of the rib without overlapping the affected cartilage. The injury usually heals within six to eight weeks. Most complete rib dislocations reduce spontaneously. Injection of a local anesthetic may be needed for pain control. A 10-day course of anti-inflammatory agents usually is helpful. The athlete can return to sports when he/she is fully functional, usually one to two weeks after injury. Progressive ROM exercises are used in rehabilitation.

Costochondral separation should be differentiated from costochondritis (Tietze's syndrome), an inflammatory reaction of the costochondral joint that produces tenderness, swelling, and pain with motion of the rib cage. Oral anti-inflammatory agents and frequent icing provide some relief. Injection of 1% Lidocaine and a long-acting corticosteroid can be effective in refractory cases.

## Rib Fractures

Rib fractures are common. They occur in any sport where the athlete may be hit by another player or be struck by a blunt object (e.g., football, hockey, lacrosse, field hockey, biking, baseball, golf). The athlete usually feels pain with deep inspiration and may have an associated muscle spasm that splints the chest. Respirations may be rapid and shallow. Tenderness is localized directly over the rib(s) and may be associated with crepitation or subcutaneous emphysema over the fracture site. Compression of the chest causes pain. Look for a palpable defect in the rib. Contusion of the ribs usually does not cause pain on rib motion. Obtain a rib-detail chest x-ray; however, a negative x-ray does not always rule out a rib fracture because it may be difficult to visualize. Always look for more severe pulmonary injuries (pneumothorax and pneumomediastinum) when dealing with rib fractures. Emergency medicine texts give the proper treatment of these injuries.

Spontaneous pneumopericardium is rare in the pediatric and other age groups but may occur in athletic adolescents with no history of trauma or severe pulmonary disease after weight-lifting. Symptoms of pneumopericardium include syncope, upper abdominal pain, and shock, in addition to throbbing, pressure-like substernal pain which worsens with deep inspiration or bending forward. The patient may also report dyspnea at rest. Physical findings include hyperresonance over the precordium, diminished intensity of heart sounds, hypertension with tamponade, jugular venous distension, tachycardia, and subcutaneous emphysema.

Characteristic radiographic findings of pneumopericardium include a radiolucent band along the heart defining the pericardial membrane. This band can be seen in both the lateral and posterior-anterior projections. It may also outline the great vessels on the radiograph. An EKG may be normal or show ST segment elevations, T-wave inversion, or decreased voltage. If properly diagnosed, most of these injuries have a favorable outcomes. When pneumopericardium progresses to pericardial tamponade, evacuation of air and accompanying fluid is mandatory to properly treat this emergency situation (Casamassima, 1991).

## First Rib Fractures

The first rib is usually well protected by the shoulder girdle but severe direct trauma can cause a fracture. It could happen to somone throwing or serving a tennis ball (overload of scalenus inferior muscle) or to weight lifters doing overhead presses (overloads the serratus anterior muscle). The athlete usually feels immediate sharp pain whereas a stress fracture often presents with little pain. Radiographs taken through the subclavian groove often are helpful in diagnosing a fracture. Treatment involves using a sling and gradual P.R.E. exercises.

This fracture is not an emergency unless the subclavian artery is lacerated. The major importance of finding a first rib fracture is that it often is associated with more severe and complicated trauma.

### Fractures of Other Ribs

A rib detail radiograph may not reveal a fracture at first. Tomograms should be obtained and the possibility of future pneumothorax or associated lung damage considered. An uncomplicated rib fracture can be treated by using supportive strapping (rib belt) of the chest to prevent motion and rib expansion. Strapping should never be applied higher than the xiphoid process to avoid restriction of breathing. The procedure works equally well for female athletes. Continue strapping as long as discomfort continues. Relief of pain with analgesics may be necessary.

Pain relief may be obtained by injecting 4-5 cc of a long-acting local anesthetic (Marcaine[R]). Infiltration of the intercostal nerve directly under the rib and about four inches proximal to the fracture site (toward spine) works well. We do not recommend using injection of intercostal nerves to permit sports participation.

Injury to the upper two or three ribs may be secondary to shoulder movement. Strapping to minimize shoulder elevation or use of a sling to restrict motion should be considered. Nonunion and malunion of rib fractures are rare and of little clinical importance. Most athletes can return to competition in four to six weeks when rib x-rays show healing of the fracture, tenderness to palpation and compression is minimal, analgesics are not needed, and there is a return to full range of motion. Adequate protective equipment will be required (see Figure 13A-1).

### Treatment of Complicated Rib Fractures

Comminuted fractures (splintering) of the ribs are rare in young athletes (Galladay, 1981; Smyth, 1982). Rib splinters may penetrate the internal mammary artery or lung and cause pneumothorax or hemothorax (Chetty, 1975). This development is a medical emergency. If an athlete becomes cyanotic or severely dyspneic after a chest injury, consider the possibility of a more serious internal injury. Stabilize the patient and transport to a hospital. Subcutaneous emphysema following a chest injury, with leakage of air into the soft tissues, may cause diffuse swelling under the skin and characteristic crepitation. This may extend to the level of the jaw but it rarely requires specific treatment. There should be x-rays to rule out the presence of a pneumo-or hemothorax and a surgical consultation scheduled if it is present.

## Severe Blunt Trauma to the Chest

A thrown object such as a baseball hitting an unprotected chest can cause major trauma to the sternum and underlying myocardium (Mattox, 1976). Sternum fractures can lacerate the aorta or cause a hemopericardium, possibly causing cardiac arrest and death (Ryan, 1962). An immature child is more at risk for serious chest trauma than an adult because the elastic thorax is easily compressed, increasing the potential for cardiac injury. Internal thoracic injuries can occur with no evidence of external injury or rib fractures (Smyth, 1982). Most cardiac contusions are difficult to diagnose in children.

From 1973-1980, 22 deaths were reported in children aged 5 to 14 years from direct blows to the chest in baseball, football, and basketball. Most (17/22) died secondary to cardiac arrhythmias or cardiac arrest. Data on other age groups reveals only a small number of deaths secondary to blunt chest trauma (Rutherford, 1981). Management of these injuries is beyond the scope of this text but common guidelines are outlined in available emergency medicine textbooks. Proper chest protection is just as indicated as proper playing techniques. It is likely that many of these serious injuries were unavoidable but every attempt at prevention should be made.

## Protective Equipment

A variety of chest protectors are available and should be mandatory for baseball catchers or field hockey, lacrosse, and hockey goalies. Shoulder pads for football incorporate some upper rib protection but leave the lower chest open to trauma. A flack jacket or vest can be fabricated or purchased to afford more protection to these exposed areas (see Figure 13A-1). Taping or strapping that incorporates a protective pad may be used for athletes with rib fractures, and this helps reduce chest motion while supporting the injured rib segment. Be sure not to restrict the athlete's breathing with taping, especially if they have obstructive lung disease or asthma.

# SECTION B. CARDIOVASCULAR

## The Athlete's Heart

A number of normal physiological changes occur in athletes who do endurance training (Ryan, 1980; Teare, 1958; Virmani, 1985). Common cardiovascular findings are listed in Table 13B-1. Ascultation of the heart often will reveal third or fourth heart sounds that may be interpreted incorrectly if cardiomegaly is present on the chest x-ray. Many adolescents, young adults, and endurance trained athletes have third or fourth heart sounds that may be accompanied by faint physiological murmurs. These findings are completely within normal limits. Four-chamber cardiac enlargement on chest x-ray or echocardiogram may be found (VanCamp, 1988).

As many as 30% of endurance trained athletes have evidence of cardiomegaly on chest x-ray (Huston, 1985). This is due to an increase in the end diastolic volume of the endurance trained heart. Many studies using M-mode electrocardiography have shown that the endurance trained athlete's heart may simulate the volume overloaded heart.

---

**Table 13B-1. Common Findings in Endurance-Trained Athletes**

**Auscultation**
$S_3$ (third heart sound)
$S_4$ (fourth heart sound)
Systolic murmurs (grade I or II)

**Chest x-ray**
"Cardiomegaly"

**Electrocardiogram**
"Left ventricular hypertrophy" (prominent voltage, usually not meeting Estes criterion)
T-wave inversion (inferiorly)
ST-T-wave evaluation (juvenile repolarization pattern)
Incomplete (or complete) right bundle branch block

**Rhythm**
Bradycardia (sinus)
Sinus arrhythmia
First-degree heart block (Wenckebach)
Functional bradycardia
Premature atrial contractions
Premature ventricular contractions

(From Kuland, D.N. *The Injured Athlete*. Philadelphia, PA: J.P. Lippincott Co., 1982:120)

---

The effects of endurance training on the heart are seen in two phases. In the early phase, as soon as one week after training begins, there is an increase in left ventricular volume. Myocardial wall thickening develops after approximately five weeks of endurance training.

## EKG Findings in the Athlete's Heart

Electrocardiographic findings suggestive of left ventricular hypertrophy will be seen in 60%-70% of endurance trained athletes (Amsterdam, Wilmore and Demaria, 1977; Froelicher and McHenry, 1981). Some form of T-wave abnormality, such as T-wave inversions, is often seen in the inferior leads. The EKGs of endurance-trained athletes may show ST segment or J-point elevation or evidence of abnormal ST-T segment response to exercise (VanCamp, 1988). These findings should not be interpreted as myocardial ischemia or pericarditis unless there are other historical or physical findings.

Because endurance training causes an increase in vagal tone of the heart, the athlete will have a slower resting heart rate and may have multiple sinus arrhythmias. These arrhythmias consist of first degree heart block, second degree AV heart block of the Wenkebach type, P-wave changes of right and/or left atrial enlargement, or increased QRS voltage. Incomplete right bundle branch block patterns and premature atrial or premature ventricular beats also may be encountered (VanCamp, 1988). Failure to consider these changes as normal findings in athletes may result in incorrect identification of a healthy individual as one with a cardiovascular defect.

## Valvular Heart Disease

Acquired and congenital valvular heart disease may become clinically significant at any age. Athletes with valvular abnormalities should have a thorough evaluation by the primary care physician and also by a cardiologist. There is no evidence to suggest that exercise improves the function of diseased heart valves. Some valvular abnormalities are more compatible with exercise than others; in some cases, an exercise program may actually assist the heart in adapting to the mechanical limitations posed by the valvular lesion. This often is true in athletes with rheumatic mitral stenosis, where slowing of the heart rate at submaximal levels of exercise allows for more efficient filling of the left ventricle. This more efficient LV filling may improve total cardiac output at rest and at submaximal exercise levels.

An individual with severe mitral stenosis often is unable to train because of marked dyspnea. This condition often is associated with tachycardia and reduced cardiac output during exercise, which may lead to pulmonary hypertension. Athletes with severe mitral stenosis should refrain from exercise training and testing.

Other valvular abnormalities that might contraindicate exercise testing or training include moderate to severe aortic stenosis, infravalvular aortic stenosis (hypertrophic cardiomyopathy) (Arbogast and White, 1981). Severe aortic stenosis could lead to sudden death during exertion and commonly is associated with syncope, chest pain, dyspnea, and congestive heart failure with extreme exercise. Patients with moderate to severe aortic stenosis should not undergo vigorous training or testing. On the other hand, patients with isolated aortic insufficiency appear to tolerate exercise testing and training more easily (VanCamp, 1988).

Any athlete with a known valvular heart defect who develops symptoms should be evaluated by a cardiologist knowledgeable about exercise and heart disease. A thorough evaluation is indicated for the symptomatic patient with aortic insufficiency who is beginning an exercise program or who is having problems.

Patients with Marfan's syndrome, a genetically inherited abnormality of the connective tissues, have an increased incidence of dilatation of the aorta and often develop an aortic aneurysm or rupture. They also have associated abnormalities of the aortic value that may lead to aortic insufficiency, and Marfan patients may develop mitral valve prolapse. Patients with Marfan's syndrome should be thoroughly evaluated by a cardiologist before beginning any exercise program. These patients require careful clinical assessment, including an exercise EKG, before they are given an individual exercise prescription.

The aorta must be evaluated echocardiographically for dilation. If it is present, the individual must not participate in vigorous activities. The 16th Bethesda Conference recommendations are that persons with Marfan's syndrome with aortic root dilation or mitral regurgitation should not participate in body contact sports. They may participate in low intensity sports and in those with high dynamic and low static demands (distance running, swimming, tennis) in selected cases. These individuals require careful evaluation and follow-up by experienced clinicians (VanCamp, 1988; ACSM, 1986; Duren, 1988; Bethesda Conference, 1985). Beta-blockers have been used with limited success in some of these patients to reduce the force of ventricular contraction.

Mitral valve prolapse (MVP) probably is the most common cardiac valve disorder occuring in the athletic population. The prevalence of this syndrome is about 5% of the general population (Jeresaty, 1986; Marron, 1985). It is more common in females and is manifested by prolapse of one or both of the mitral valve leaflets into the left atrium during systole. This may be associated with a regurgitation of blood from the left ventricle to the left atrium.

Patients with MVP often complain of chest pain and may have atrial or ventricular ectopic beats. An occasional patient will have a significant ventricular arrhythmia that would necessitate medication. MVP is considered a benign cardiac abnormality but complications sometimes occur. These include transient ischemic attacks, progression to mitral regurgitation, infective endocarditis, and sudden death (VanCamp, 1988, Duren, 1988). Because of the prevalence of MVP and its potential complications, the sports physician likely will be consulted about whether an athlete with MVP should participate in sports.

Patients with MVP may have a mid-systolic click or an isolated murmur on physical examination. Two-mode echocardiography has been useful in making the diagnosis. Most patients with mitral valve prolapse do not have marked mitral regurgitation. The consensus of many investigators is that patients with minimal symptoms or findings of MVP should be allowed to participate at any level of physical activity they desire (VanCamp, 1988, Bethesda Conf, 1985). Patients with marked mitral regurgitation and chamber enlargement should not play vigorous sports unless cleared by the physician. Athletes with frequent atrial ventricular arrhythmias should be evaluated carefully for MVP. Occasionally, a stress test may be indicated to document arrhythmias or significant clinical findings. If no arrhythmias develop during stress testing, the athlete should be allowed to participate in all exercise activities without restrictions. If arrhythmias occur, they often are treated satisfactorily with selective beta-blocking agents. The following conditions should disqualify athletes with MVP from sports participation or strenuous activities: 1) a history of syncope; 2) disabling chest pain worsened by exercise; 3) moderate to marked cardiomegaly; 5) prolonged QT interval; 6) Marfan's syndrome and MVP, and 7) family history of sudden death due to MVP (Jeresaty, 1986).

MVP patients who have undergone valve replacement should be enrolled in a supervised cardiac rehabilitation program after surgery. Exercise testing after the post-operative recovery phase may be indicated and should be performed by a cardiologist before any exercise training program is contemplated.

### Septal Defects

Patients with ASD or VSD may successfully undergo exercise training and testing if they have normal pulmonary artery pressure and resistance. Abnormalities that may be dangerous during exercise testing or training include coarctation of the aorta, severe aortic or pulmonic valvular stenosis, and certain stenotic abnormalities such as Ebstein's anomaly or Tetralogy of Fallot (VanCamp, 1988). Young patients with these abnormalities should be evaluated and have appropriate chest films, echocardiography, an EKG, exercise testing to determine their physical capacity before they begin any exercise training program.

### Hypertension and Exercise

Hypertension is a known primary risk factor for the development of coronary heart disease, even with mild elevation of diastolic pressure (90-105mm Hg). The risk of stroke, renal insufficiency, heart failure, and the social consequences of hypertension also are of concern to the patient and physician. Drug therapy is the main treatment for hypertension but the cost is considerable and side effects are common. Consequently, exercise programs have been considered as alternate therapy or an adjunct to drugs. In addition, many hypertensive patients are regularly involved in exercise programs, and the physician must understand the effects of dynamic exercise on blood pressure.

The effectiveness of exercise in reducing high blood pressure is uncertain, despite some favorable evidence. Boyer and Kasch (1970) demonstrated a reduction in mean systolic and diastolic pressures in 23 hypertensive men aged 35-61 years. Blackburn (1978) reviewed several studies of exercise training regimens in which blood pressure was not significantly reduced. He concluded that rigorous exercise therapy in the hypertensive patient is feasible. Moderate exercise such as brisk walking is a useful adjunct to drug therapy and may help facilitate weight control and prevent hypertension.

Some investigators have reported that exercise reduces both resting and exercise blood pressures but others have reported contrary findings. The consensus seems to be that exercise programs of adequate intensity, frequency, and duration often are effective in lowering resting blood pressure by 10-14 mm Hg, in addition to lowering blood pressures during submaximal work (Ressel, 1977). This conflicting data often confuses the physician who is considering the usefulness of exercise as a treatment or adjunctive therapy in managing essential hypertension. Most investigators do agree that exercise facilitates weight loss, long-term weight control, and stress reduction, while increasing the subjective well being of the individual involved in a regular exercise program.

The mechanism by which exercise directly lowers blood pressure in hypertensive patients is not completely understood (Blackburn, 1978) but there are several possibilities. Exercise training lowers the resting heart rate and increases the stroke volume with no apparent change in resting cardiac output. Training also decreases resting plasma catecholamine release, which in turn decreases peripheral vascular resistance. Since BP = CO X PVR, the listed effects of regular exercise training may suggest a relationship between exercise and blood pressure reduction. Reduction in blood pressure with exercise is most often demonstrable in patients with borderline or labile hypertension (Boyer, 1970; Choquette, 1973). However, it may be difficult to persuade people to participate in regular exercise programs long enough to derive a training effect. Blackburn (1978) reports that "the decision to use an intensive exercise program rests on the desires of the individual and the interest and competence of the physician prescribing such activity."

Consequently, to promote blood pressure reduction in hypertensive patients who exercise, the prudent physician should use carefully selected drug therapy in addition to a regular exercise program. Patients with uncontrolled hypertension should not participate in exercise testing or training until it is under proper control. Hypertension is easy to diagnose, requiring only a blood pressure cuff. The physician must be careful in making this diagnosis, especially in a young athlete whose anxiety about the examination may cause an increase in blood pressure. A large sized cuff may be necessary for a muscular or obese athlete to prevent false readings of elevated blood pressure. A large leg cuff should be used to avoid the possibility of a false reading. Normal blood pressure values by age group are given in the accompanying table (Table 13B-2).

Any athlete with elevated blood pressure at the preparticipation evaluation should have it checked with a properly sized cuff and confirmed by three separate readings on three separate days. History, physical examination, and laboratory data to rule out evidence of secondary hypertension are indicated. The athlete may practice or participate in sports unless readings are in the severe hypertension range. The history, physical examination, work-up, and treatment of hypertension are discussed in other texts. A thorough laboratory evaluation includes a CBC, urinalysis, BUN, creatinine, electrolytes, glucose, uric acid, lipid profile, serum calcium, EKG, or x-ray, and an echocardiogram if the EKG or chest x-ray is abnormal.

Athletes with severe hypertension should receive antihypertension drug therapy following standard protocols and should not participate in strenuous activities until blood pressure is controlled. When it is adequately controlled, an exercise stress test should be considered if management of the patient's exercise program is in doubt. The exercise stress test for severe hypertension should be done only on properly selected patients. The patient is cleared for activity if there are no ST segment changes consistent with ischemia, significant arrhythmias, or repeat exercise systolic blood pressure greater than 230 mm/Hg. Exercise therapy may be used as a therapeutic trial with borderline or mildly hypertensive patients. Exercise therapy is used most often in conjunction with drug therapy in patients with moderate hypertension. The aerobic exercise prescription should include parameters for intensity, duration, and frequency. An exercise stress test should be done for patients over 40 years of age or in younger patients with coronary artery disease risk factors.

Drug treatment for athletes with elevated blood pressure should involve a modified step care approach and the use of drugs that affect blood pressure but do not alter performance or training. Drugs of choice include the ace inhibitors, calcium channel blockers, and Prazosin. These drugs have shown fewer side effects than other agents. Diuretics can cause hypovolemia and hypokalemia and should be avoided as there is a potential for increased arrhythmias. Other treatment guidelines for the hypertensive patient should include a low sodium diet, weight reduction, a thorough aerobic exercise program, and drug treatment if the diastolic blood pressure is greater than 100 mm/Hg or in patients with pre-existing cardiovascular disease. Drug therapy should also be initiated if the systolic blood pressure is greater than 160 mm/Hg (Halpern, 1988).

Because of the higher resting heart rate and total peripheral resistance, the hypertensive patient will experience a greater rise in blood pressure at all levels of work compared to the normotensive individual. The response to isometric exercise in the hypertensive patient is markedly different from the response to dynamic exercise. Isometric exercise (weight-lifting) is associated with a greater increase in heart rate and both systolic and diastolic blood pressure than at comparable levels of dynamic leg exercise (Fraser, 1985; Storer and Ruhing, 1981; Zabetakis, 1984). Hypertensive patients are urged to avoid heavy resistance forms of exercise.

Regular exercise appears to reduce blood pressure and decrease the myocardial workload in patients with mild hypertension. When the patient stops exercising, blood pressure eventually returns to pre-exercise levels. Anti-hypertensive medication may have to be reinstituted in patients who do not need medication during exercise training. Exercise training at a modest intensity level, combined with a loss of body fat and restriction of excessive so-

Table 13B-2. Blood Pressure Values in Athletes by Age

**Normal Blood Pressure Age (mm/Hg)**

| | |
|---|---|
| 6 years | <110/75 |
| 6-10 | <120/80 |
| 10-14 | <125/85 |
| 14-18 | <135/90 |
| >18 | <140/90 |

**Systolic Blood Pressure**

| | |
|---|---|
| Normal | <140 |
| Isolated systolic hypertension | 140-159 |
| Isolated systolic hypertension | >160 |

**Diastolic**

| | |
|---|---|
| Normal | <90 |
| Mild hypertension | 90-104 |
| Moderate hypertension | 105-114 |
| Severe hypertension | <115 |

dium intake, may be beneficial in the management of essential hypertension.

## Use of Beta-Blocking Drugs and Sports

Treatment of hypertension, angina, and certain cardiac arrhythmias is common in the exercising population. Most studies in the literature state that patients with uncomplicated hypertension may achieve a training effect while on beta-blockers but the effect is likely to be modest (Powles, 1981; Wolfel, 1986) (see Table 13B-3). Patients with coronary artery disease may show an initial increase in exercise capacity because of the anti-anginal properties of beta-blockers. A severely deconditioned patient often will respond well to exercise programs that improve skeletal muscle function. Subsequent gains due to improved cardiovascular function may be small and obtained only after at least eight weeks of training.

In summary, the combination of endurance training and beta-blockers appears to have an immediate beneficial effect on the exercise capacity and conditioning level of severely deconditioned patients with angina. However, once peripheral conditioning is optimal, further gains may be difficult to achieve (Allen et al, 1984; Laslett et al, 1983).

Many patients on beta-blockers complain of tiring easily. Work capacity and oxygen consumption are significantly affected. The exercise prescription can help minimize this complaint. Exercise sessions should be relatively short (<30 minutes) but frequent enough that the total exercise time is sufficient to achieve a training effect. Available studies indicate that exercise should last at least 150 minutes a week for 8 weeks at an intensity greater than 60% of the patient's demonstrated $VO_2$max. Some patients may still complain of fatigue, but they should be strongly encouraged to continue exercising. In time, there is an adaptation to the drug and fatigue lessens. Beta blockers are not usually a first line choice for treating the hypertensive athlete and should be especially avoided in the Afro-American population.

Exercise intensity can be prescribed in terms of a target heart rate or its metabolic (MET) equivalent but perceived exertion no longer correlates well with heart rate in patients taking beta-blockers. It also may be difficult to measure the heart rate precisely enough to allow accurate monitoring of exercise intensity. Patients on high doses of beta-blockers should use the MET equivalent for a more nearly accurate determination of exercise intensity. The warm-up and cool-down period should be heavily emphasized for patients on beta-blockers. The rate of adaptation to a change in exercise intensity is slowed by beta-blockade so that a slow warm-up period will minimize anaerobic metabolism and allow time for lipolysis to increase. The slow cool-down period helps reduce the light-headedness or faintness that may occur with post-exercise hypotension.

$Alpha_1$-adrenergic blocking agents can be used alone or in combination with other medications to manage hypertension. They are safe and well tolerated and have unique advantages. Their mechanism of action involves reduction of elevated peripheral resistance which is a principal abnormality in essential hypertension. The $Alpha_1$ blockers maintain cardiac output and blood flow to vital organs and do not affect renin release. These agents have beneficial lipid and metabolic effects and can improve left ventricular hypertrophy. The only major drug interaction identified with $Alpha_1$ blockers is an increased hypertensive effect when they are combined with other anti-hypertensive drugs. It does not appear that these agents aggravate existing problems like diabetes or benign prostatic hypertrophy or hyperplasia, and they are compatible with other medications for common diseases such as arthritis and pulmonary disease (Itskovitz, 1989).

## Hypertension and the Active Child

A hypertensive child should not be restricted from physical activity and may, in fact, be adversely affected without a properly designed exercise program. Remember that hypertension, anxiety, and stress may cause transient elevations of blood pressure during physical examination. The inci-

---

**Table 13B-3. Effects of Beta-Blockade During Exercise***

Reduction in cardiac output
Elevation of peripheral resistance (except drugs with intrinsic sympathomimetic activity)
Reduction of $FEV_1$
Muscle fatigue
Reduction of lipolysis and free fatty acid release
Possible hypoglycemia with prolonged exercise
Possible hyperkalemia

*(From Tifft, C.P. *Phys and Sportsmed* 13(5):106, May 1985)

dence of hypertension in pre-adults ranges from 0.6% to 11.0% depending on the age-group and the criteria used (Rocchini, 1984; Zimmer, 1975). A child's blood pressure is considered normal if the systolic and the diastolic pressures are less than the 90th percentile for his/her age-group and sex. Readings are considered high normal if the pressures are between the 90-95th percentile, and high if they are greater than the 95th percentile on at least three occasions. Factors such as body size, height, and weight play an important role in assessing blood pressure levels. Obese children have higher blood pressures than heavier, tall children, and higher blood pressures than smaller children of the same age. A child may actually have a normal blood pressure when height and weight are taken into account. Normograms or age-specific blood pressure curves are useful in proper blood pressure determination.

Because hypertensive children frequently have no symptoms, the blood pressure should be checked routinely at each physical examination. The causes of secondary hypertension should be aggressively evaluated in childhood. Diagnostic tests that may be needed (in addition to those mentioned earlier in this section) include intravenous pyelography, renal ultrasound, renal radionuclide studies, renal angiography, renal vein renin levels, digital subtraction angiography, and CT of the kidneys or abdomen (Podalsky, 1989).

A young child with moderate hypertension may benefit from exercise and have short- or long-term reductions in blood pressure (NHLBI, 1987). Spontaneous, unsupervised play is permissible because youngsters will stop when they feel tired or uncomfortable. Systolic pressures in a hypertensive adolescent may reach 250 mm/Hg or more during exercise. It is possible to provide an adequate exercise prescription by monitoring blood pressure while the patient engages in incrementally increased activity, training, or competitive athletics. Weight and strength training programs designed to increase strength and muscle bulk may lessen the degree of hypertension in a child. Youngsters with mild elevations of blood pressure may perform weight-training safely. Physicians should warn young adolescents that intensive aerobic exercises that cause a rise in systolic pressure may not be safe (Orenstein, 1985). Many other activities involving continuous, rhythmic, and repetitive use of large muscle groups should be safe for most individuals with mild to moderate hypertension.

A proper exercise program for the young patient with hypertension can be designed by accurately measuring blood pressure and assessing the results while looking for possible causes of high blood pressure. Physicians and trainers should be comfortable about allowing young athletes with well controlled hypertension to participate in all forms of sports and exercise when the necessary restrictions are kept in mind (Podolsky, 1989).

**Coronary Artery Disease**

The factors that predispose development of coronary artery disease (CAD) have been covered extensively in the literature (Blackburn, 1977 & 1986; Kannel, 1979; Kannel, 1984; Kuller, 1966). Analysis from 43 studies shows that inactive individuals are 1.9 times more likely to develop coronary artery disease than active individuals, independent of other major risk factors. Inactivity carries a risk almost as high as the relative risk of smoking a pack of cigarettes daily (Kepowell, 1987). The changes associated with exercise that may favorably affect coronary artery disease are decreased blood pressure (Blackburn, 1986; Seals, 1984; Martin, 1990), decreased obesity (MacMahon, 1986), increased high density lipoprotein cholesterol (Goldberg, 1987), increased fibrinolytic activity and response to thrombotic stimuli (Williams, 1980), and increased insulin sensitivity (Jennings, 1986). Exercise also may promote changes in smoking and diet that lessen obesity, cholesterol levels, and hypertension (Blair, 1985; Goldfin, 1991). Risk factors and the role exercise may play in intervention will be discussed in the chapter on injury prevention (see Table 13B-4). The establishment of cardiac rehabilitation programs throughout the United States has greatly aided patients with coronary artery disease. Specific recommendations for these patients include:

- The patient with CAD should attempt to modify as many risk factors as possible, including the cessation of smoking, decreasing elevated blood pressure if present, and obtaining an optimal level of total cholesterol and high density (HDL) cholesterol. Men who do regular exercise training exhibit a modest increase in HDL-C (Coberg, 1987).
- It may be necessary to exceed the threshold of eight to ten miles of walking a week before the beneficial effects of exercise on decreasing cholesterol are seen. Up to nine months of regular

**Table 13B-4. Beneficial Effects and Potential Hazards of Endurance Exercise as a Defense Against CAD**

**BENEFITS**

Enhanced physical work capacity, hemodynamic function, hematologic action, and cardiovascular fitness
Improved profiles of plasma lipid, lipoprotein, and glucose
Increased maximum breathing capacity and oxygen utilization
Improved individual lifestyle (prudent diet, cigarette abstention, body mass control, coping with stress)
Enhanced mood, thought, and psychologic behavior
Reduced physiologic precursors of cardiovascular disease (obesity, hypertension, and electrocardiographic abnormalities)
Decreased risks of atherosclerotic, hypertensive, and ancillary diseases (angina pectoris, coronary insufficiency, myocardial infarction, stroke, peripheral vascular, renal, and diabetes mellitus), together with their consequences

**HAZARDS**

Increased risk of sudden death in susceptible (untrained and overstressed) individuals
Contraindicated for subjects with acute myocardial infarction, acute coronary occlusion, myocarditis, marked aortic stenosis, uncontrolled hypertension
Exercise-induced asthma and anaphylaxis
Sports anemia
Induced electrolyte and temperature imbalances
Exercise addiction and anxiety

(From *Current Therapy in Sports 1985-1986*, pg. 78)

---

aerobic exercise may be required before changes in HDL-cholesterol concentration can be documented (Coberg, 1987; Goldfin, 1991).

- Lack of exercise appears to shorten life and predispose an individual to lethal coronary events. However, it does not seem that exercise programs alone make as great an impact on the incidence of cardiac disease as does the control of major risk factors. Epidemiologic studies indicate that light to moderate exercise (walking, climbing stairs, gardening) is associated with a lower risk for CAD. The Harvard Alumni Study of 17,000 men showed reduced risk of CAD with as little as 500 kcal/week expended during exercise (Paffenbarger, 1986). Blair's (1989) recent follow-up of more than 13,000 healthy men and women showed a strong, graded, and consistent inverse relationship between physical fitness and mortality that was independent of age and other risk factors. This effect is due primarily to a reduction in cardiovascular disease-related deaths among the fitter subjects. It appears that moderate levels of physical exercise and fitness which are attainable by many adults appear to protect against early death.

- According to the Framingham Study, active people live longer and suffer less cardiovascular mortality than sedentary people. In men, this association of exercise and longevity persisted after adjustment for coexisting risk factors. In women, physical activity was so closely related to age that it is not possible to evaluate other coronary risk factors separately (Paffenbarger, 1986).

- Unsupervised vigorous physical activity in a middle-aged, unfit, and unconditioned coronary candidate presents a definite hazard to that individual (Paffenbarger, 1986).

- Recommendations for exercise in patients with coronary artery disease should come after a thorough history, physical examination, and appropriate laboratory testing. The exercise prescription should be based on accurate data from treadmill testing whenever possible.

- Patients with coronary artery disease who have been cleared for exercise by their physicians should give serious consideration to a vigorous walking program when jogging or another exercise option might be unwise. Achievement of fitness generally requires a level of physical exertion that maintains a heart rate of approximately 75% of the maximal heart rate for the age. A target heart rate should be prescribed for a patient with cardiovascular disease, and then a level of exercise that maintains that rate for 20-60 minutes three to five times a week (Med Sci Sports, 1990) should be sought.

- The dropout rate from active exercise programs or regular exercise programs appears to be relatively high in this patient population. An exercise program that emphasizes the goals and needs of the patients and maximizes compliance should be established.

- Weight-training has shown remarkable gains in popularity but its health benefits have not been well studied. The isometric components of weight-training causes the blood pressure to increase greatly during acute isometric exercise (O'Hare, 1981). Consequently, physicians have been reluctant to prescribe weight-training for risk factor modification as a part of cardiac rehabilitation. Newer evidence seems to prove that weight training can be beneficial and safe in programs involving moderate resistance and relatively high repetition rates. Patients with coronary artery disease who trained 30 minutes a day three times a week at 80% of maximum voluntary contraction showed no signs or symptoms of ischemia or abnormal blood pressure responses in studies (Ghilarducci, 1989). Resistance training has been shown to increase HDL-C, lower supine diastolic blood pressure, and increase insulin sensitivity (Herley, 1988; Herley, 1987).

In summary, it appears that exercise programs alone cannot have as great an impact on cardiovascular health as control of the major cardiovascular risk factors, hypertension, hyperlipidemia and cigarette smoking. Physical activity should be viewed as one component of a comprehensive cardiovascular risk reduction program, and not relied upon as the sole factor for protection against cardiovascular disease (see Table 13B-5). Most patients with CAD can participate safely in exercise training programs that help increase VO$_2$max, decrease heart rate, and increase stroke volume (Goldfin, 1991). Changes in physical status may help these patients achieve a higher functional performance level. Patients with angina pectoris can attain higher work loads at the same BP x HR product following exercise training, and this usually causes a decrease in symptoms (Bruce, 1982; Shepard, 1982).

## Management of Arrhythmias in Athletes

Disturbances of cardiac rhythm and conduction are frequently observed during exercise. It is important to understand the significance of cardiac arrhythmias and conduction disturbances when prescribing exercise programs or performing exercise testing (Amsterdam, Wilmore and Demaria, 1977).

Exercise causes many alterations in the heart's electrical activity and arrhythmias may be due to increased sympathetic drive, increased myocardial oxygen demand, or a combination of these factors. Certain arrhythmias may be diminished by exercise, particularly ventricular arrhythmias. This may be related to withdrawal of vagal stimulation and/or increased sympathetic tone as a consequence of exercise.

It is important to determine the presence and/or nature of cardiac arrhythmias when evaluating athletes. Many conduction disturbances are asymptomatic and require no treatment. However serious arrhythmias can cause hemodynamic compromise and sudden death. Arrhythmias occur at unpredictable times and may be hard to reproduce. Patients with no structural heart disease have the

**Table 13B-5. Biologic Mechanisms by Which Exercise May Contribute to the Primary or Secondary Prevention of Coronary Heart Disease**

**Maintain or increase myocardial oxygen supply**
Delay progression of coronary atherosclerosis (possible)
  Improve lipoprotein profile (increase HDL-C/LDL-C ratio) (probable)
  Improve carbohydrate metabolism (increase insulin sensitivity) (probable)
  Decrease platelet aggregation and increase fibrinolysis (probable)
  Decrease adiposity (usually)
Increase coronary collateral vascularization (unlikely)
Increase coronary blood flow (myocardial perfusion) or distribution (unlikely)

**Decrease myocardial work and oxygen demand**
Decrease heart rate at rest and submaximal exercise (usually)
Decrease systolic and mean systemic arterial pressure during submaximal exercise (usually) and at rest (possible)
Decrease cardiac output during submaximal exercise (probable)
Decrease circulating plasma catecholamine levels (decrease sympathetic tone) at rest (probable) and at submaximal exercise (usually)

**Increase myocardial function**
Increase stroke volume at rest and in submaximal and maximal exercise (likely)
Increase ejection fraction at rest and in exercise (possible)
Increase intrinsic myocardial contractility (unlikely)
Increase myocardial function resulting from decreased "afterload" (probable)
Increase myocardial hypertrophy (probable); but this may not reduce CHD risk

**Increase electrical stability of myocardium**
Decrease regional ischemia at rest or at submaximal exercise (possible)
Decrease catecholamines in myocardium at rest and at submaximal exercise (probable)
Increase ventricular fibrillation threshold due to reduction of cyclic AMP (possible)

least likelihood of sudden cardiac death. It is important to evaluate athletes with arrhythmias for heart conditions such as coronary artery disease, hypertrophic cardiomyopathy, aortic stenosis, and congenital heart disease.

Athletes with symptoms related to cardiac arrhythmias commonly complain of palpitations, tachycardia, presyncope, or syncope. These symptoms should be carefully evaluated before the athlete is allowed to participate participation in competitive sports. The evaluation should include a thorough history, physical examination, EKG, chest x-ray, echocardiogram, exercise treadmill test, long-term ambulatory electrocardiogram (Holter Monitor), and appropriate lab studies. It is important to document the arrhythmia by EKG or Holter monitor to properly characterize the arrhythmia and prescribe appropriate therapy.

Three general types of exercise-induced alterations in cardiac rhythm or conduction are commonly found:

*Supraventricular Arrhythmias*

Exercise is often associated with premature atrial contractions, wandering of an ectopic atrial pacemaker, or sinus arrhythmias. Sustained supraventricular arrhythmias (PAT) are unusual. PAT usually is due to an ectopic focus and is the most common arrhythmia in athletes. It usually is not life-threatening and is more of a nuisance. However, persistence of PAT may limit maximal performance.

Supraventricular arrhythmias like atrial fibrillation and flutter are rare in the healthy athletes but may occur from using various stimulants or alcohol. Patients over 40 years of age with these arrhythmias should be screened for underlying heart disease and an appropriate diagnostic workup instituted. Sinoatrial block or sinus arrest may occur during exercise testing, especially with maximal vagal stimulation that occurs during the post exercise phase.

*Conduction Defects*

Bundle branch blocks (left bundle branch block) frequently are noted during exercise. They are benign and require no therapy but are often mistaken for ventricular arrhythmias. This finding may cause unnecessary termination of an exercise test. A-V nodal conduction is enhanced by exercise, and A-V block that occurs during exercise is always abnormal and indicative of intrinsic conduction abnormalities.

Always look for the possibility of a pre-excitation syndrome (Wolff-Parkinson White). WPW may occur during exercise testing and cause an abnormal EKG that may be misinterpreted as to its significance. Sudden unexplained death in athletes may be due to WPW, especially when it is associated with atrial flutter or fibrillation. Patients with WPW and PAT, however, are not usually restricted from sports participation.

*Ventricular Arrhythmias*

PVCs during exercise are common and may be present in 10%-40% of patients, depending on the age group. Ectopic ventricular activity is most common in the post-exercise period; worsening of PVCs during exercise is unusual. The most serious arrhythmias in patients with coronary artery disease occur within four minutes after completion of an exercise test. Ventricular ectopic beats that degenerate into ventricular tachycardia and fibrillation may occur.

Premature ventricular contractions increase with age — 80% of all 65 year-olds will have PVCs. The types of PVCs that the physician should consider significant include: (1) greater than 60 per minute; (2) coupled PVCs or those in salvos; (3) multifocal, and (4) those associated with the R on T phenomenon. Other causes of exercise-induced ventricular arrhythmias are listed in Table 13B-6.

## Significance of Exercise-Induced Ventricular Arrhythmias

Exercise-induced ventricular arrhythmias are not always associated with organic heart disease and may occur in the normal population. However, high grade ventricular arrhythmias such as tachycardia are more likely in patients with cardiac disease, and they often occur at lower work levels and slower heart rates during the exercise program. In general, the more significant the organic heart disease, the more malignant the arrhythmias, especially in patients with ventricular dysfunction. The presence of PVCs on a resting EKG or during exercise activity has an associated increased risk

Table 13B-6. Causes of Exercise-Induced Ventricular Arrhythmias

| | |
|---|---|
| Coronary artery disease | Drug toxicity |
| | Digitalis preparations |
| Left ventricular failure | Type I antiarrhythmic agents |
| | Psychotropic agents |
| Valvular heart disease | |
| Mitral valve prolapse | Thyrotoxicosis |
| Aortic stenosis | |
| | Long QT-inverval syndromes |
| Cardiomyopathy | |
| Congestive | Hypoxia (pulmonary disease) |
| Obstructive | |
| Electrolyte disturbance | |
| Hypokalemia | |
| Hypomagnesemia | |

(From *Primary Cardiology*, pg. 143, March 1986. Reprinted with permission from Physicians World Communications Group.)

of sudden death, especially in those with organic heart disease.

Holter monitoring is more valuable than exercise testing in determining the prognosis for these arrhythmias and it may be necessary to do both tests to evaluate the significance of a ventricular arrhythmia. The presence of multifocal PVCs or ventricular tachycardia has a more ominous prognostic significance. Patients who develop significant ventricular arrhythmias at low work levels and low heart rates are at a greater risk of developing a serious arrhythmia during exercise testing or training. EKG monitoring should be maintained at least five to six minutes after exercise has stopped in these patients.

Below are more specific descriptions of arrhythmias commonly seen in athletes, along with recommendations for therapy and sports participation.

### Disturbances of Sinus Node Function

Abnormalities of sinus node function include sinus bradycardia (< 60/minute), sinus tachycardia (>100/minute), sinus arrhythmia, sinus arrest, or sick sinus syndrome. Asymptomatic patients need no treatment. Slow heart rates that cause symptoms may require a permanent pacemaker, in which case the athlete should not engage in competitive sports involving the possibility of body collision. Patients with premature atrial complexes (PAC) where premature P-waves are followed by a narrow or wide QRS complex may participate in all competitive sports.

### Atrial Flutter

Atrial flutter is regular flutter waves at 250-350 bpm with a ventricular rate 1/3 to 1/2 of the atrial rate. Atrial flutter is an unusual chronic arrhythmia seen in athletes and structural heart disease should always be ruled out. If a ventricular rate is controlled with drug therapy like digitalis or calcium channel blockers, participation in low intensity sports is permissible. The addition of other agents such as Quinidine, Procainamide, or Flecainide may convert the atrial flutter to a normal sinus rhythm and prevent recurrence, in which case full activities would be allowed after six months of therapy.

### Atrial Fibrillation

Atrial fibrillation is an irregular QRS pattern with a rapid but variable atrial rate. This arrythmia may occur in the absence of organic heart disease and the physician should investigate the use of alcohol or drugs (especially cocaine) as a cause. The recommendations for treatment are the same as those for atrial flutter. Flecainide is an excellent agent for conversion of this arrhythmia to normal sinus rhythm in a patient with a normal heart.

### Supraventricular Tachycardia

Supraventricular tachycardia involves a rapid atrial rate from 150-250 bpm with 1:1 conduction and narrow QRS complexes. There are four types of supraventricular tachycardia: a) involves AV nodal re-entrant (most common); b) concealed bypass track; c) automatic focus; and d) sinus nodal re-entrant. It is important to establish the proper diagnosis, and esophagal electrodes or electrophysiological studies may be required to make it.

Episodes of arrhythmias can be prevented by drug therapy and full activities are allowed. Many drug options are available, including digitalis, calcium channel blockers (especially Verapamil), beta blockers (caution in athletes), Quinidine, Procainamide, and Flecainide. The use of adenosine has been found to be safer and faster acting in treating SVT (Rankin, 1991). Patients with structural heart disease and presyncope or syncope should not participate in competitive sports and may require other treatment such as surgery or an automatic implantable cardioverter-defibrillator (AICD) (Dibianco, 1991).

Drug treatment is complicated by an inability to predict the efficacy of any particular anti-arrhythmic agent in an individual patient and the equally unpredictable occurrence of drug-induced, sometimes fatal, arrhythmias in up to 20% of patients receiving anti-arrhythmic agents. Placement of an AICD device or surgery is often a first consideration, especially in patients for whom no tolerable or effective drug has been found for electrophysiologic testing, and in those patients with life-threatening ventricular arrhythmias (Dibianco, 1991).

### Ventricular Pre-Excitation

Wolff-Parkinson White Syndrome (WPW) involves a PR interval of less than 120 mm/sec with a delta wave and a wide QRS complex. Most patients are asymptomatic and intermittent WPW has a good prognosis in the active individual. The most dangerous arrhythmia is due to atrial flutter or fibrillation which can lead to a rapid ventricular response.

Recommendations for therapy include full participation in all competitive sports for the older athlete who has no symptoms or structural heart disease. An extensive work-up, including electrophysiologic studies, is required for a patient with a history of atrial flutter or fibrillation. Surgery to cut the bypass tract may be achieved. Patients with supraventricular tachycardia that is controlled by drug therapy may participate in all sport activities. Drug therapy for WPW includes Flecainide, Encainide, and Amiodarone, and has been very effective. Digitalis or Verapamil are not advisable for patients with WPW and atrial fibrillation or flutter because they may cause rapid ventricular rates.

**Premature Ventricular Complexes (PVC)**

PVCs involve wide premature QRS complexes which are 120 mm/sec in duration and have no preceding P-waves. This is a common arrhythmia and may be aggravated by stress, sleep deprivation, caffeinated or alcoholic beverages, and oral decongestants. Full activities are allowed if there is no structural heart disease and rare symptoms are detected. A patient with structural heart disease and PVCs that worsen with exercise should be excluded from moderate to high intensity competitive sports. Individuals with PVCs and prolonged QT intervals should not participate in competitive sports. Exercise-induced ventricular tachycardia without heart disease responds well to drug therapy, especially calcium channel blockers and beta blockers. Again, beta blockers should be used with caution in athletes. If the ejection fraction is <40%, the patient is at increased risk for sudden death and should not participate in competitive athletics.

**Ventricular Tachycardia**

Ventricular tachycardia involves three or more PVCs in a row with a rate of over 100 bpm. The decision to treat ventricular arrhythmias depends on several factors, including the risk of sudden death, the natural history of the underlying disease, and the availability of an effective, well tolerated, and safe treatment program (Wood, 1990). Cardiac catherization and electrophysiologic testing may be required before an athlete can participate in sports activities.

Athletes without symptoms, no structural heart disease, and ventricular rates under 150 bpm can participate in competitive sports but they require continuing reevaluation. Individuals with structural heart disease who are symptomatic and have ventricular rates over 150 bpm cannot play competitive sports. If drug therapy controls the arrhythmia for six months and there is no significant organic heart disease, athletic participation can be allowed. The use of AICD is recommended for patients with life-threatening ventricular arrhythmias in whom no effective drug therapy can be found on electrophysiolgic testing, or in those patients who have no contraindications for surgery and who are capable of withstanding the procedure (Fisher, 1988; Dibianco, 1991).

**Heart Blocks (1st Degree and 2nd Degree)**

First degree AV block involves a PR interval of over 200 mm/sec. Type I second degree (Wenckebach) AV block involves progressively prolonged PR intervals with a dropped P-wave. The asymptomatic athlete without heart disease can participate fully.

**Heart Block (2nd Degree and 3rd Degree)**

Type II second degree (Mobitz) AV block involves a fixed PR interval with a conducted P-wave (2:1 or 3:1). Complete (3rd degree) AV block has no P-waves which are conducted to the ventricle. Third degree block can be either acquired (often with a wide QRS complex) or congenital (usually narrow QRS complex) forms. The asymptomatic patient with heart rates in the 40-80 bpm range can participate in all levels of sports activities. A symptomatic athlete will require a permanent pacemaker and must avoid contact sports. A patient with a heart rate less than 30-40 bpm at rest who can't increase the heart rate with exercise, cannot participate in sports activities until placement of a permanent pacemaker.

**Congenital Long QT Syndrome**

Congenital long QT syndrome involves a corrected QT interval greater than 450-500 mm/sec which is not due to drug therapy or electrolyte disturbance. Athletes with prolonged QT are at risk for sudden death and are restricted from all competitive sports.

## Sudden Cardiac Death in Athletes

One of the earliest deaths secondary to exercise is recorded in 490 B.C. when the Athenians chased the Persians across the plain of Marathon and drove them back to their ships. As the fleet sailed across the bay, General Miltaides feared the

Prussians would approach Athens by sea and the city might surrender prematurely. He sent his messenger Pheidippides to carry the news of the victory to Athens. Pheidippides raced 26 miles to Athens, and upon reaching the city gasped, "rejoice we conquer," and fell to the ground dead (Virmani, 1982).

Sudden unexpected death (SUD) has been defined in numerous ways; there is no universally accepted definition. However, most investigators define it as unanticipated, nontraumatic deaths occurring without symptoms or with symptoms of less than one hour duration. We favor the definition of SUD as terminal events that occur within one hour after the onset of symptoms. The timing of the death is unexpected.

SUD is the leading cause of death in the U.S., claiming 400,000-500,000 victims annually or 1,100 lives daily. Approximately 25% of victims have no prior symptoms of heart disease and SUD often is the first indication of clinical heart disease (Graboys, 1982; Daniels, 1984; and Malacoff, 1984). Tunstall-Pedoe (1979) has looked at the problem of determining the risk of SUD with exercise. To determine that SUD is directly related to an activity, data on the amount of time spent on that activity must be compared with the overall sudden death rates associated with that activity, or that is not related to activity in the population at risk (Tunstall-Pedoe, 1979). This information is not available for general populations so most studies have been in specific groups such as the armed forces or small athlete populations:

- Gibbons (1980) found a small risk. Their data showed that adults without major cardiac disease who exercised 30 minutes, three times weekly, had a maximum risk incidence estimated at 0.002 per year.
- Thompson et al. (1982) reviewed the incidence of death during jogging in Rhode Island from 1975-1980. Their data showed the incidence of death during jogging among men aged 30-64 was seven times the estimated death rate during more sedentary activities.
- Siscovick et al. (1982 & 1984) reported that subjects aged 25-75 who were involved in high-intensity, leisure time activity (requiring $\geq 60\%$ $VO_2max$) had a 55%-65% lower rate of sudden death.

**Etiology of SUD**

There is a major difference in the cause of SUD in older and younger athletes. Figure 13B-1 is a comparison of the cause of death in joggers, marathon runners, and young athletes.

Most SUD in older athletes (more than 30 years old) is caused by coronary heart disease (Virmani, 1982, Waller, 1980). Kuller (1966) defined SUD as death within 24 hours after the onset of symptoms and said it could be attributed to coronary heart disease in 60% of the cases. Spain (1960) reported that sudden death (occurring within an hour of the onset of symptoms) can be ascribed to coronary heart disease in 91% of cases. These studies are evidence that persons with CAD have a greater

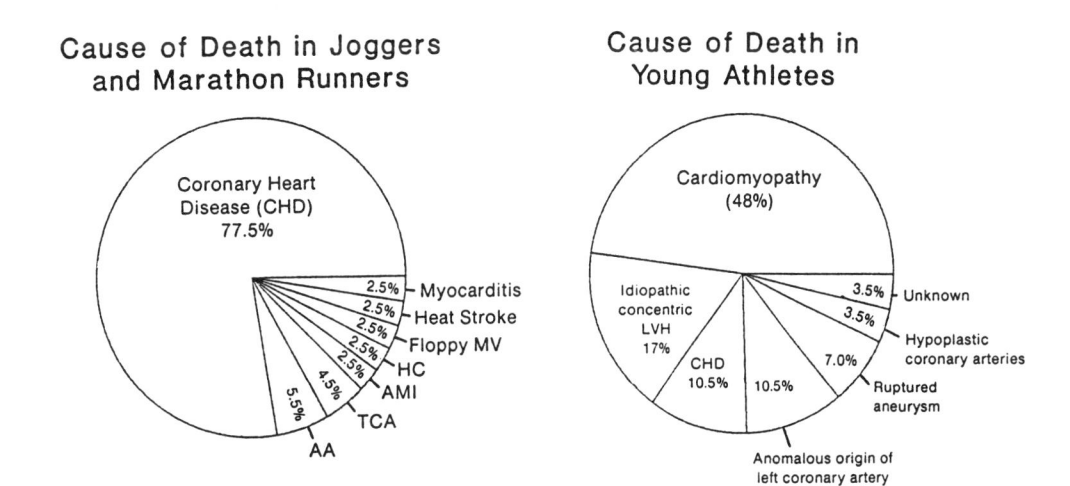

**Fig. 13B-1.** Comparison of the cause of death in joggers, marathon runners, and young athletes. AA = automobile accident; AMI = acute myocardial infarction; HC = hypertrophic cardiomyopathy; LVH = left ventricular hypertrophy; MV = mitral valve; TCA = tunnel coronary artery. (Adapted from Virmani, R. Jogging, marathon running, and death. *Primary Cardiology*, April 1982, p. 98.)

risk for sudden death while exercising, even though chronic exercise appears to lower the overall risk of cardiac arrest (Siscovick, 1984; Thompson, 1979; Thompson, 1982). It is important to detect individuals with significant CAD through screening so they can be provided with proper exercise recommendations. Those who are free of CAD should be encouraged to be physically active.

Coronary heart disease plays a limited role in younger athletes. Marron (1980) looked at the causes of sudden death in 29 highly conditioned, highly competitive athletes aged 13-30 years. Structural cardiovascular abnormalities were identified at autopsy in 28 of 29 athletes (97%). The most common cause of death in this series was hypertrophic cardiomyopathy which was present in 14 athletes (50%). Other cardiovascular abnormalities also were identified in this study. Many studies have found structural, usually congenital, cardiovascular disease in young victims of exercise-related sudden death. These diseases may be classified as myocardial, coronary arterial, aortic, valvular, and cardiac conduction system disorders (Waller, 1985; Virmani, 1982; Thompson, 1982).

Most investigators agree that malignant arrhythmias are the silent common pathway in sudden death. Hinkle (1982) reports that over 92% of sudden death cases occurring within one hour are due to arrhythmias. Unusual causes of SUD are more prevalent in the young and are listed in Table 13B-7 (Daniels, 1984; Van Camp, 1988).

It is unfortunate that individuals involved in exercise may suffer SUD. Many of the listed causes cannot be suitably screened during the preparticipation physical examination. This does not preclude a thorough examination for heart disease in any individual planning an exercise program. The physician should be aware of the possibility of SUD and try to detect any underlying etiology whenever possible.

## Cardiomyopathies

A variety of cardiomyopathies preclude further involvement in athletics after their discovery. One of the more common etiologies in young athletes is viral or rheumatic myocarditis (Neuspiel, 1985). Individuals with active myocarditis should not participate in exercise during the active inflammation period because of the possibility of ventricular arrhythmias that could lead to SUD. Typically, a young patient with myocarditis develops fever and sudden, unexplained tachycardia at rest, especially during the season for viral infections and colds. Within several weeks, there will be a noticeable decrease in exercise tolerance. The symptoms often are mistaken for viral flu and the true etiology is missed. Patients who have had myocarditis should be restricted from further participation in sports until all symptoms have cleared. Consultation with a cardiologist may be necessary in more difficult cases.

Hypertrophic cardiomyopathy (HCM) is one of the more common causes of sudden death in young athletes. This pathological entity is defined as a hypertrophied, nondilated left ventricle without any other cardiac or systemic disease that could produce ventricular hypertrophy. HCM is believed to be a familial illness. It is genetically transmitted as an autosomal dominant trait, or it may occur as an expression of cardiomyopathy, or secondary to left ventricular overload states such as hypertension. HCM is characterized by hypertrophy of the muscle cells of the ventricular septum and free wall.

Additional findings include marked myocardial cellular disarray and abnormal intramural coronary arteries with narrow lumens due to thickened arterial walls. Hypertrophy can cause obstruction of the left ventricular outflow tract during systole (see Figure 13B-2). In addition, the mitral valve often lies anteriorly and abnormally close to the septum during systole. There is inadequate filling of the left ventricle during diastole due to the loss of the compliance of the left ventricular wall. The patient may suffer dyspnea, syncope, angina, or supraventricular or ventricular tachyarrhythmias that could lead to sudden death.

---

**Table 13B-7. Causes of Possible Sudden Unexplained Death**

1. Cardiomyopathy — hypertrophic, obstructed, unobstructed or dilated
2. Mitral valve prolapse
3. Anomalous origin of the coronary arteries
4. Myocarditis
5. Sarcoidosis
6. Arrhythmogenic right ventricular dysplasia
7. Coronary arteritis
8. Delayed repolarization syndrome
9. Pre-excitation syndrome (WPW)
10. Aortic rupture
11. Massive pulmonary embolism

(From *Primary Cardiology*, pgs. 75-84, July 1984. Reprinted with permission from Physicians World Communications Group.)

PHYSICAL FINDINGS

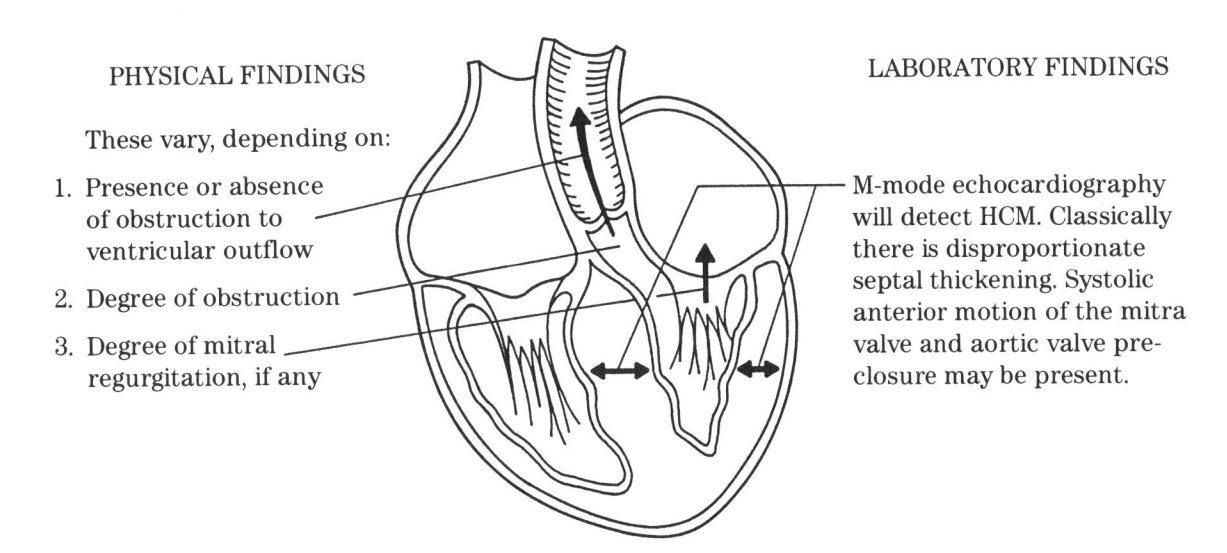

These vary, depending on:

1. Presence or absence of obstruction to ventricular outflow
2. Degree of obstruction
3. Degree of mitral regurgitation, if any

LABORATORY FINDINGS

M-mode echocardiography will detect HCM. Classically there is disproportionate septal thickening. Systolic anterior motion of the mitra valve and aortic valve pre-closure may be present.

**Fig. 13B-2.** Physical Findings of Hypertrophic Cardiomyopathy

It usually is possible to detect an increase in presystolic cardiac impulse by palpation during the physical examination. A fourth heart sound and the classic murmur of HCM (a harsh crescendo-decrescendo systolic murmur that begins well after the first heart sound) is heard best at the left sternal border. Techniques that increase contractility or decrease preload and afterload may accentuate the murmur and include Valsalva maneuvers, exercise, or the use of nitrites. By using these techniques, the clinician generally can distinguish between the murmur of HCM and that of fixed valvular disease (see Table 13B-8). Seventy-five percent of patients with HCM have an abnormal EKG (LVH by voltage and wide, deep R-wave in leads II, III and AVF or in the lateral leads) (Van-Camp, 1988). An echocardiogram is a helpful non-invasive test for diagnosing IHSS. Cardiac catherization can be used to confirm the diagnosis.

A condition related to HCM that appears to be a cause of some exercise-related sudden death is idiopathic concentric left ventricular hypertrophy. It is similar to HCM in that unexplained ventricular hypertrophy occurs but differs in that it involves the ventricle concentrically. Also, there is no bizarre cellular disarray or abnormal intramural coronary arteries, nor evidence of genetic transmission in first-degree relatives (Marron, 1980). Other myocardial disorders reported to cause exercise-related sudden death include sarcoidosis and right ventricular cardiomyopathy (Theine, 1988).

**Treatment of Cardiomyopathies**

There is a risk of a sudden major cardiac arrhythmia in patients of any age that could lead to sudden death. Patients should be followed carefully and instructed to report any new or unusual cardiac symptoms. Patients should avoid strenuous exercise as well as the use of digitalis or excessive diuretics which may increase the obstruction. They should not undergo exercise testing without prior consultation with a cardiologist. Principal drugs used to manage HCM are beta-adrenergic blockers and the newer calcium channel antagonists. Surgical intervention is an option for suitable patients with HCM who do not respond to medical management.

Uncontrolled congestive cardiomyopathies are an absolute contraindication to exercise training or testing. These patients have a large dilated left ventricle that is commonly associated with severe impairment of left ventricular function, and a very low ejection fraction. A cardiology consultation should be obtained by any patient suspected of

**Table 13B-8. Differentiating the HCM Murmur from "Physiologic" Murmurs**

|  | Intensity of Innocent Murmur | Intensity of HCM Murmur |
| --- | --- | --- |
| Valsalva maneuver | Decreased | Increased |
| Standing | Decreased | Increased |
| Squatting | Increased | Decreased |
| Sustained hand grip | No change | Decreased |

having congestive heart failure or cardiomyopathy before exercise testing or training (Teare, 1958; Roeske, 1976; Arbogast, 1981).

**Other Causes of Sudden Unexplained Death**

Multiple congenital artery anomalies may be a cause of exercise-related sudden deaths. These abnormalities include the anomalous origin of the left coronary from the right sinus of Valsalva, the anomalous origin of the right coronary artery from the right sinus of Valsalva, a single coronary artery, the origin of a coronary artery from a pulmonary artery, and coronary artery hypoplasia (VanCamp, 1988). Aortic disorders like thoracic aortic dilation may develop in athletes with Marfan's Syndrome. This dilation is due to cystic medial necrosis and is secondary to a decreased number of medial elastic fibers.

Valvular disorders like congenital aortic stenosis and mitral/valve prolapse have been found at autopsy in sudden death victims (Topaz, 1985; VanCamp, 1988). Cardiac conduction system disorders also have been isolated as potential causes (Marron, 1980). Sickle cell trait has been proposed as a potential cause of sudden unexplained death (Kark, 1987, Topaz, 1985). Eichner (1987) suggests that it may not be the sickle cell trait that increases the risk. Because of related renal abnormalities, the patient may have difficulty with a sudden load of myoglobin and potassium from severe rhabdomyolysis and risk developing a fatal hyperkalemic anemia. Table 13B-9 lists recommendations for strenuous sports participation by patients with various heart diseases.

Table 13B-9. Recommendations for Participation in Strenuous Sports by Disease Type

| Disease | Recommendation |
|---|---|
| Arrhythmias | |
|   Wolff-Parkinson-White | Yes, if no PAT* |
|   Paroxysmal atrial tachycardia | No |
|   Premature ventricular beats | Qualified yes |
|   Premature atrial beats | Qualified yes |
|   Atrial fibrillation | No |
|   Heart block | |
|     1st degree | Qualified yes |
|     2nd degree | Qualified no |
|     3rd degree | No |
| Congenital anomalies | |
|   IA septal defect | Qualified yes |
|   IV septal defect | Qualified yes |
|   Pulmonary stenosis | No |
|   Coarctation of aorta | No |
|   Persistent ductus arteriosus | No |
|   Anomalous SA/AV node artery | No |
|   Aortic stenosis | No |
|   Ebstein's anomaly | No |
| Inflammatory and degenerative | |
|   Myocarditis (active) | No |
|   Coronary artery disease | No |
|   Active rheumatic heart | No |
|   Stable rheumatic valvulitis | Qualified yes |
|   Myocardiopathy | No |
|   Hypertension | Qualified yes |
|   Coagulopathy | No |
| Physiological | |
|   Hypokalemia (overtraining) | Qualified yes |
|   Endocrine imbalances | Qualified yes |
|   "Heart strain" (undertraining) | Qualified yes |

*Paroxysmal atrial tachycardia

# SECTION C.
# PULMONARY

## Hyperventilation Syndrome

An injured athlete or one who is experiencing severe anxiety or stress may begin breathing rapidly and develop hyperventilation syndrome. The effects of prolonged hyperventilation include a decreased pCO2 and an increase in arterial pH (respiratory alkalosis). The patient usually becomes panic-stricken while gasping for breath, and may suffer carpopedal spasm or frank tetany. Less severe complaints include dyspnea, faintness, confusion, numbness of the extremities, and paraesthesia. Syncope without loss of consciousness may occur (Karofsky, 1987; Lewis, 1983).

On examination, there are no rales, wheezes, or other chest findings to account for the dyspnea. Chvostek's sign may be elicited. Carefully evaluate the patient for findings that might suggest severe underlying cardiopulmonary disease. Laboratory tests are of little assistance except to rule out more serious diseases. The EKG is usually normal. Measurements of arterial pCO2 and pH generally are unrewarding but pulmonary function tests may be helpful. Look for other causes of hyperventilation since this syndrome can be the first symptom of a multitude of other diseases (Anderson, 1985). However, hyperventilation in athletes often is a response to stress.

Reassure the athlete that there is no serious disease and advise him to breathe slowly or rebreathe into a paper bag for a few minutes in order to raise the alveolar air CO2 content. This is the treatment of choice. Once the athlete is breathing more normally, he/she may return to sports participation. An effort should be made to see that the proper diagnosis has been made and to look more carefully at the psychological aspects of the individual.

## Pneumothorax

Pneumothorax may occur during strenuous activity or at rest without direct trauma to the chest. It is a common condition in young individuals and is most often associated with a ruptured pleural lining or alveolar bleb (Pfeiffer and Young, 1980). Most patients are healthy and, in these circumstances, are designated as having primary spontaneous pneumothorax. The condition is rarely fatal except for tension or bilateral pneumothorax. Emergency management includes prompt reexpansion of the lung and reestablishment of normal ventilatory physiology.

The onset of symptoms often is insidious, presenting with a constant sharp pain and dyspnea. Cough, hemoptysis, and syncope are rare. Significant lung collapse is associated with shifting of the mediastinum away from the side of the lesion. Hyperresonance, decreased vocal fremitus, and diminished breath sounds over the affected side may be observed. Severe tension pneumothorax causes significant impairment of circulatory and ventilatory capacity.

The severity of pneumothorax can be defined by a chest x-ray. Obtain a posterior/anterior view, or lateral decubitus view with the suspected side of the chest uppermost for proper identification. A small pneumothorax will be seen as an arch of lucency peripheral to the lung margin, while a more extensive pneumothorax will cause partial collapse of the lungs or a mediastinal shift.

Conservative management is indicated for patients with a small, stable pneumothorax. Patients should avoid unnecessary physical activity and any progression of symptoms should be reevaluated. Serial chest films are advised and should show that as free air is absorbed, the lung expands. Athletes with greater than 30% collapse of one lung should be admitted to the hospital for tube thoracostomy. This will allow proper reexpansion of the lungs as most leaks seal spontaneously after 24 hours. The athlete is restricted from sports participation for two to four weeks after discharge from the hospital to allow for complete healing. Recurrence is possible and some thoracic surgeons believe that surgical intervention is indicated after the third occurrence of spontaneous pneumothorax.

## Foreign Body Aspiration

Aspiration of a foreign body during sports participation happens to both children and adults. It can include the accidental inhalation of dental appliances, food substances, gum, or chewing tobacco. If the object is located between the larynx and carina, acute symptoms of cough, wheezing, stridor, hoarseness, and dyspnea are present. The athlete may display marked retraction of the chest with use of the accessory muscles of respiration. If the obstruction is below the carina, only one lung or a portion of one lung may be affected so that the symptoms are not as dramatic or immediately life threatening. Early symptoms include cough, malaise, fever, and wheezing and can be mistaken for infection, asthma, or other respiratory diseases.

Indirect laryngoscopy should be performed where possible to look for evidence of a foreign body. Auscultation of the chest may reveal localized wheezing. A posterior/anterior and lateral x-ray of the neck and chest will reveal evidence of an opaque object. When aspiration is suspected, a Heimlich maneuver should be performed immediately. If it is unsuccessful in relieving the acute respiratory distress, a tracheostomy should be done unless the obstruction is located below the tracheostomy site. Tracheostomy is seldom needed for objects at or below the carina. Patients should be seen by an ENT specialist for endoscopic extraction of the foreign body.

Complications following foreign body aspiration may come from perforations of the respiratory tree by the aspirated object or from incidental trauma involved in extracting it. In order to prevent accidental aspiration, athletes should be instructed not to have objects in their mouths (except for mouthguards) when playing sports.

## Exercise-Induced Asthma (EIA)

EIA is a manifestation of bronchial hyperreactivity and poses a special problem for the asthmatic engaged in competitive or recreational sports. EIA is a diffuse bronchospastic response of both large and small airways in response to strenuous exercise and it causes a fall of $FEV_1$ or PEFR of 10% or more of the preexercise level (Anderson, 1986; McFadden and Ingram, 1979; Prenner, 1986). Patients typically have no immediate change in vital capacity with exercise, but develop measurable bronchospasm three to five minutes after vigorous exercise that lasts approximately 10-15 minutes at 85% or greater of $VO_2$max (Mink, 1991) (Figure 13C-1). Spontaneous resolution usually occurs in 45-60 minutes, but occasionally can last four to six hours.

EIA may be the only manifestation of asthma in an otherwise asymptomatic individual, usually a child or young adult with no prior history of asthma. Exercise may provoke EIA in 60%-90% of asthmatic children and in 40% of atopic children with no history of asthma (Anderson, 1986; McFadden, 1979; Mink, 1991). A smaller number of asthmatic adults have EIA. Certain types of exercises are more likely to precipitate EIA despite similar workloads. In decreasing order of probability, the most common sports involved are running, treadmill running, treadmill walking against a grade, bicycling, downhill skiing, swimming, walking, and kayaking.

The existence of EIA has been known for several hundred years but how exercise induces EIA is not completely understood. Many theories exist but the heat-flux hypothesis seen to provide the best explanation to date (Anderson, 1986; Anderson, 1985; McFadden and Ingram, 1979; Smith and Anderson, 1986). Many investigators now believe that exercise-induced asthma is related to exchange of heat and water across the airways. During inspiration, air is warmed to body temperature and fully saturated with moisture. This involves a transfer of heat and water from the oral pharynx and tracheal-bronchial tree to the inspired air and it has been shown that this transfer may initiate bronchospasm in some asthmatics (McFadden, 1979).

However, it now seems that the temperature of the inspired air is not as critical to the bronchospasm response as was originally thought. Enhancement of EIA in cold inspired air is not a universal finding. Furthermore, EIA also occurs when hot, dry air is inspired during exercise and when the expired air temperature is higher than that normally measured at rest in the laboratory. It has been postulated that an increase in the osmolarity of the fluid that lines the respiratory tract occurs as a result of the high rate of evaporative water loss from the airways during exercise. This phenomenon acts independently of heat loss and may cause EIA (Smith, 1986). This concept is the newest in defining the mechanism of EIA. This proposal does not detract from the theory that cooling also can produce EIA under some conditions. When cold air is inspired, both heat and water are lost; therefore, both cooling and an increase in osmolarity occur. When hot, dry air is inhaled, and the expired air temperature is higher, water loss and the hyperosmolarity induced by it are acting alone to provoke EIA.

Other investigators have found direct evidence that $Alpha_1$ adrenergic receptor-blocking agents can inhibit EIA, raising the likelihood that circulating epinephrine might stimulate mast cells to facilitate release of mediators that induce bronchospasm (Barnes, 1981). Calcium channel blockers can also prevent EIA, possibly by blocking mast cell release of mediators or through their effect on smooth muscle relaxation (Barnes, 1981). Cromolyn inhalation prevents EIA and its action is to prevent mediator release of histamine by mast cells along the tracheal bronchial tree. Cromolyn also is associated with the inhibition of neutrochemotactic factor which may be involved in the bronchoconstricting properties of EIA (Lee, 1983).

EIA should be considered when a patient complains of undue shortness of breath that develops

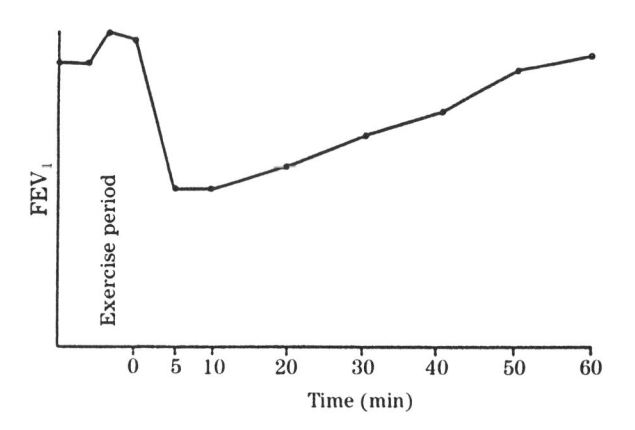

**Fig. 13C-1.** Bronchoconstriction follows a short period of bronchodilation. It is usually most severe 5 or 10 minutes after the completion of exercise. (Source: Sly, RM: Management of exercise-induced asthma. *Drug Therapy*. March 1982.)

during or after exercise. Chest tightness, paroxysmal coughing, wheezing, and sometimes headache, abdominal pain, nausea, and vomiting may be present (Mink, 1991). Some children may completely deny post-exercise dyspnea (Gropp, 1975). The diagnosis is best established in the laboratory with the simple and easily reproducible tests of PEFR and FEV1. These tests confirm the diagnosis and can be used to evaluate the effectiveness of treatment. The patient is asked to run in a dry environment for six to eight minutes at a pace that corresponds to approximately 85%-90% of the patient's maximal aerobic work capacity ($VO_2$max). A relatively fit athlete can do this on a treadmill. A decrease of 20% in PEFR or $FEV_1$ is considered a positive test.

Indications for exercise testing for EIA include: 1) the asymptomatic patient with a history suggestive of asthma; 2) evaluation of patients who develop asthma-like symptoms *only* after exercise; 3) evaluation of the severity of EIA, and 4) evaluation of the effectiveness of various medications in preventing, decreasing, or correcting the symptoms of EIA. Other tests have been used to make the diagnosis, including the cold air stimulation test in which an athlete is subjected to cold air causing increased ventilation while pulmonary function is measured.

In general, treadmill testing seems to precipitate bronchospasm more reliably than testing on a bicycle ergometer. Adequate cardiovascular monitoring is essential for the patient with possible pulmonary disease. It is important to remember that the type of exercise required to elicit wheezing often is very specific. A patient may tolerate maximal exercise on a treadmill, yet complain of wheezing after playing tennis or skiing. In these cases, a clinical trial of a bronchodilator or cromolyn therapy before exercise may be valuable in making the proper diagnosis.

## Treatment of EIA

Treatment for EIA should include alterations in the training program, environmental modifications, and pharmacologic intervention. EIA athletes should warm-up for prolonged periods. Nasal breathing will prevent exercise-induced asthma but this is an unrealistic goal for most competitive athletes. Participation in cold, dry climates places the athlete at increased risk, and a cold weather mask might be necessary to help prevent problems. The concomitant treatment of allergic rhinitis and attention to environmental pollutants is imperative for the athlete with EIA.

Drug therapy plays an important role but be sure to check doping regulations before placing the athlete on pharmacological agents prior to competition (see Table 13C-1). There are two approaches to EIA management; treating when symptoms occur or preventing the attack by administering drugs prophylactically. Please see the accompanying chart that lists the available agents for EIA treatment (Table 13C-2).

The airway obstruction in patients with mild to moderate EIA usually can be reversed by giving a beta-agonist aerosol (albuterol or terbutaline) 10 minutes before exercise. At least two metered dosages of aerosol should be taken within three to five minutes. Because brief exercise may induce bronchodilation, recovery from EIA often can be aided by doing a minute of exercise before using the aerosol. This technique is most effective in reversing EIA of mild to moderate severity. EIA is not reversed by the normal dose of a beta-agonist aerosol in approximately 10% of patients. For these

**Table 13C-1. Medications That Have Been Approved by the International Olympic Committee for Managing EIA***

|  | When to Take | Duration of Effect |
|---|---|---|
| **Inhaled beta-adrenergic agents** (cannot be used in oral form) |  |  |
| Albuterol | 10-20 min before exercise | 4-6 hr |
| Terbutaline, metaproterenol | 5-10 min before exercise | 2-4 hr |
| **Cromolyn sodium** (Spinhaler or metered dose inhaler) | 20 min before exercise | 1-2 hr |
| **Theophylline** |  |  |
| Short-acting | 30 min before exercise | 2-4 hr |
| Long-acting | 1-2 hr before exercise | 4-6 hr |

*The IOC has not approved the following medications for EIA: inhaled epinephrine (Primatene Mist), isoproterenol, isoetharine, decongestants (ephedrine, pseudoephedrine, phenylephrine, phenylpropanolamine).
(From *Phys and Sportsmed* 15(7):104, July 1987 with permission of McGraw-Hill, Inc.)

**Table 13C-2. Pharmacologic Agents in the Treatment of Exercise-Induced Asthma**

| Drug | Effectiveness | Comment |
| --- | --- | --- |
| Theophylline | + | Attack may occur despite adequate blood level. Can be used prophylactically |
| Beta-agonists (eg, isoproterenol, metaproterenol, terbutaline) | + | Act rapidly. May be used prophylactically and following onset of attack |
| Cromolyn sodium | + | Useful only prophylactically. Additional dose may be taken prior to exercise |
| Anticholinergic agents (atropine, ipratropium bromide*) | ± | Not currently approved for use in asthma, but may be effective in some patients |
| Corticosteroids | - | Generally not effective by either oral or inhaled route |

*Not commercially available in United States
(From *Postgraduate Medicine* 67(3):98, March 1980)

patients, an additional dose is administered by nebulization and oxygen is given simultaneously. Many young asthmatic patients are embarrassed when sports cause an onset of breathlessness. Also, the athlete cannot always carry an aerosol inhaler. The potential hazards of an attack of EIA while swimming or surfing are obvious; consequently, the use of prophylactic aerosols is highly recommended.

EIA is markedly inhibited and totally prevented in 90% of patients when the clinically recommended dose of a beta-agonist aerosol is given immediately before exercise. Patients who have airway obstruction at the time they wish to exercise should also use these agents to reverse their asthma. The effectiveness of these agents generally is less than two hours, even with the newer beta2-selective agents (DiPalma, 1986). Ideally, sympathomimetic aerosol therapy should be administered immediately before exercise.

Cromolyn sodium is effective in blocking the onset of EIA in 70% of patients (Mink, 1991). It has no bronchodilating effect but acts by inhibiting the release of the chemical mediators of bronchoconstriction (mast cell release). It appears that cromolyn also has other modes of action, including its effect on post-ganglionic cholinergic fibers. Cromolyn prevents EIA in non-atopic persons, and also prevents increased airway resistance induced by cold air in normal persons.

Cromolyn not only prevents the immediate asthmatic response to exercise, but also the late response which occurs within six to eight hours. The late response is associated with the release of chemical mediators known to induce inflammation, and their presence is believed to increase bronchial hyper-responsiveness in asthmatic patients. Few side effects are seen with aerosolized cromolyn. This is particularly true with the new metered-dose inhaler that uses 10%-20% of the dose used in the turbo-inhaler. The athlete should inhale cromolyn four times daily, with an additional dose immediately before each session of exercise.

Ten percent of asthmatic patients with severe EIA may require the recommended dosage of cromolyn and the addition of a beta-agonist (Anderson, 1986). The sympathomimetic aerosol usually is administered first and then the cromolyn after a five to ten minute interval. Patients who still have EIA with this regimen may benefit from the addition of 80 micrograms of ipratropium (AtroventR) to the regimen. The clinical affects of cromolyn sodium are brief so that repeated doses are necessary every three to four hours.

Oral beta-sympathomimetic preparations or theophylline play an important role and will abort EIA. However, EIA may still occur even when there is a therapeutic blood level of theophylline. Patients may take supplementary doses one hour before exercise but should be warned about the possibility of toxic reactions. Theophylline is not specifically recommended to treat EIA because of its slow onset of action and the need for high dosages.

Beta-agonist agents are valuable in inhibiting EIA, including terbutaline, solbutamol, metaproterenol, and isoproterenol. The longer acting agents in this category are the most useful. There is a danger of excessive use of these agents in the presence of endogenous catecholamines during exertion which lead to cardiovascular collapse and death. The use of AlbuteralR 10-30 minutes before exercise has been found to be 90% effective in treating EIA (Mink, 1991). One or two doses prior to exercise usually is effective and may last for as much as two hours. Anticholingeric agents are not recommended for treating asthma. Oral corticosteroids may be effective for episodic control in severe asthmatics, but aerosol preparations have little beneficial effect on the management of EIA.

## Advice to Parents Regarding EIA

Many asthmatics avoid athletic activities because they fear being at a competitive disadvantage because of EIA. Proper counseling and therapeutic intervention will help them. Do not prevent these young athletes from leading normal lives whenever possible. Participation in games and sports should be encouraged but with less emphasis on running sports. Sports like baseball or golf, which require brief bursts of activity, are better than endurance sports like as soccer and basketball. Swimming is the optimal exercise.

EIA may still occur despite precompetition medication. Consequently, the athlete should have a beta-agonist available to use at the first sign of wheezing. All medications should be taken as prescribed by the physician, but young athletes with EIA or asthma should be allowed to medicate themselves. Strenuous exercise may precipitate an attack, especially if there is no warm-up period preceding an athletic event. Also exercise performed in successive periods is more likely provoke an acute asthmatic response. The athlete should be encouraged to start exercising before the competitive event to decrease that likelihood.

Guidelines for prescribing exercise to patients with asthma or EIA can also be found in Chapter 6-B.

## SECTION D. ABDOMEN

The abdominal muscles crisscross in several layers from the back to the abdomen (see Figure 13A-3). Superiorly, the lower ribs protect the upper part of the abdominal cavity and overlie a major portion of the liver, pancreas, and spleen. Inferiorly, the abdominal cavity joins the pelvic cavity, which has a strong bony structure for protection. Anteriorly, the two rectus abdominous muscles pass from the lower ribs to the pubis, providing support to the trunk and maintaining erect posture. All muscles work together to permit movement in any direction, while providing protection to the abdominal contents.

## Perspective

There really are only two types of abdominal injuries — those to the abdominal wall or to abdominal contents. Abdominal wall injuries are common in athletes who need these strong muscles for their sports, hurdlers, ice skaters, rowers, wrestlers, gymnasts, and divers. Although rare, sports that cause rapid deceleration can cause injuries of the abdominal contents. The organs at greatest risk are the spleen, pancreas, and kidney. Injuries to the stomach, small bowel, bladder, and pelvic organs are very rare but not impossible. Solid organs are injured before hollow viscus structures. All these injuries are surgical emergencies when they occur. Penetrating injuries in sports rarely occur but require immediate evaluation by a thoracic/abdominal surgeon in the hospital setting. X-ray, isotope or CT scanning, or MRI plus abdominal peritoneal lavage will aid in the diagnosis (Soballe, 1983).

The abdomen is not covered by protective gear so the possibility of abdominal injury should be suspected in certain instances. Severe intra-abdominal injuries may present insidiously. Examine for tenderness, guarding, rigidity, rectal bleeding, and an absence of bowel sounds. The apparently rapid recovery of an athlete does not rule out serious intra-abdominal injury. A four-quadrant peritoneal tap or peritoneal lavage with sterile technique may be required to aid in the diagnosis (Bergqvist, 1982). Blood that does not clot is indicative of intra-abdominal bleeding. Isotope scans, angiography, CT scan, or MRI are diagnostic aids for these injuries. Early diagnosis and proper surgical evaluation reduces the morbidity and mortality of potentially serious intra-abdominal injuries.

## Injuries to the Abdominal Wall

**Strain of the rectus muscle** may lead to hematoma formation that presents as right lower quadrant pain. It may mimic acute appendicitis. An infrequent complication is laceration of the inferior epigastric artery which produces rapid expansion of the hematoma. This must be surgically ligated. Treatment of rectus muscle strains includes rest, ice, oral anti-inflammatory agents, and a gradual return to activity with a progressive stretching, strengthening, and running program. Once the athlete has full use of abdominal muscles, initiate strength training and return to more competitive athletics.

**Contusion of the abdominal muscles** causes localized tenderness, limited motion, and an inability to participate. Treat with ice and adequate protective padding. Return to activity depends on the severity of the injury.

**Rupture of the iliopsoas muscle** occurs in divers and gymnasts, and requires surgical evacuation of the retroperitoneal hematoma and hemostasis control. An injury of this nature usually means a slow return to athletics. Full functional status of this muscle group must be regained before competing again.

The **"hip pointer"** is a contusion along the upper or lower margin of the iliac crest where abdominal and lower extremity musculatures attach. Bony avulsion is rare but it can occur in young athletes before there is epiphyseal closure. Look for complete rupture of muscles reflecting over the iliac crest. Palpation produces tenderness over the iliac crest and lateral side bending causes localized pain. Obtain an x-ray to rule out fracture or epiphyseal separation. Immediately after injury, treat with ice and inject a local anesthetic (1% Lidocaine + 0.25% Marcaine) and long-acting corticosteroid into the site that is most tender over the iliac crest. This technique safely reduces the time away from activity. Protect with a customized hip pad to prevent recurrence. The athlete can return to competition when he/she is able to run and cut without pain. A full flexibility and strengthening program should be initiated.

A **hernia** may bulge and become painful with increased intra-abdominal pressure. It is associated with many sports and with weight training. Athletes experience all forms of hernias — direct and indirect inguinal, femoral, ventral, epigastric, and Spigelian. Hernias presenting with a narrow neck can be associated with strangulation and incarceration of the bowel. All hernias should be surgically evaluated and repaired prior to incarceration.

**Blows to the solar plexus** cause athletes to feel like their wind is knocked out. The likely cause is a blow to the upper abdomen from another player or object that causes a temporary loss of voluntary muscle function for breathing. Initially, the athlete may be unable to catch his breath. Make sure the airway is patent and not blocked by the tongue, mouthpiece, or turf. Loosen the belt if it is tight and reassure the athlete. After recovery, do repeat examinations to rule out intra-abdominal trauma. Peritoneal lavage or laparotomy may be indicated if recovery is slow or if there is persistent pain or shock.

A **muscle cramp** or "stitch" refers to a sharp pain in the side of an athlete, often an untrained runner. The causes remain unclear but may include diaphragmatic spasm, gas in the colon, or stretching of the liver capsule. The athlete may run through the pain but if it is persistent, he or she may be more comfortable lying on the back with arms above the head. The athlete may return to activity after pain resolves. Training improvements seem to lessen the frequency of the stitch. Most side stitches in runners can be avoided by "belly breathing" or breathing by expanding the abdominal muscles rather than the chest wall. This permits easier downward expansion of the diaphragm upon expansion of the lungs and prevents diaphragmatic irritation.

## Injuries to the Intra-Abdominal Organs

### Spleen

Splenic rupture should be considered in any rib fracture of the lower posterior thorax or blow to the left upper quadrant of the abdomen. A high percentage of injuries to the spleen (41% in one study) are associated with infectious mononucleosis (Frelinger, 1978). Diagnosis can be difficult as the onset of systemic symptoms and shock may be insidious and occur hours after the athlete leaves the competition. Radioisotope and CT scanning, ultrasonography, and peritoneal lavage facilitate the diagnosis (Fischer, 1978). Surgical treatment may be conservative if the athlete's cardiovascular status is stable. Unstable patients may require a partial or total splenectomy, depending on the surgeon's approach. All splenectomized patients should receive pneumococcal vaccination and penicillin prophylaxis. Patients with infectious mononucleosis should not be permitted to participate in contact sports. Their return to athletic activity is dictated by the absence of systemic signs, elevated liver function tests, and hepatosplenomegaly. A return to normal strength and a sense of well-being usually is present before the athlete can participate in sports (often three to six weeks after onset).

### Pancreas

Suspect pancreatic injury if the pain is epigastric in origin and radiates to the back. Midline tenderness over the spine, reflex ileus of the bowel, and abdominal distension usually are present. Serum amylase and lipase and the amylase/creatinine ratio may be elevated. Ultrasonography, CT scanning, and MRI aid in making the diagnosis. Trauma may cause acute pancreatitis or development of a pseudocyst. The patient should be seen by medical/surgical specialists in a hospital setting where emergency treatment can be provided.

### Liver

Contusions of the liver can produce subcapsular hemorrhage and cause pain and tenderness to palpation in the right upper quadrant. Peritoneal lavage for blood usually is negative. Liver lacerations seldom occur in sports and rarely are fatal (Cantwell, 1973). Severe liver injury will require surgical evaluation, and removal of the affected lobe often is required to control bleeding.

### Mesentery

Blunt trauma may cause hemorrhage into the mesentery, resulting in severe abdominal pain. This injury must be distinguished from other serious intra-abdominal injuries. Peritoneal lavage usually is clear but small amounts of blood may be present. These injuries often resolve spontaneously after careful observation. If symptoms persist or worsen, laparotomy is required.

### Kidney

The kidney is protected by the posterior abdominal wall muscles and surrounding fat but renal injuries are the most common intra-abdominal injury in sport. Abdominal and flank tenderness with micro/macroscopic bleeding often is present. Plain abdominal x-rays may reveal an enlarged renal shadow with loss of the margin of the psoas muscle. Ultrasonography, CT scanning, MRI, IVP, or angiography may prove helpful in properly diagnosing the problem. Urinalysis should be done after the injury and repeated often to examine for hematuria.

Renal contusion and capsular injury result in extravasation of blood into the urine. They usually are treated with bed rest, adequate hydration, and prophylactic antibiotics. More serious injuries require surgical intervention. Return to athletics is dependent on complete resolution of symptoms and absence of hematuria and often takes six to twelve weeks. Kidney protection should be used either with appropriate custom-made padding or a flak-jacket.

### Ruptured Hollow Viscus

Although uncommon, rupture of a hollow viscus organ is a medical emergency. It is most likely in sports where the abdomen is unprotected, soccer, karate kicks, gymnast doing free hip circles or striking the abdomen on the uneven parallel bars, and falls in equestrian events. Severe abdominal pain with guarding, rigidity, absent bowel sounds, and signs of shock are common. The presence of subdiaphragmatic blood or bowel contents may cause reflex pain to the shoulder.

Symptoms may take hours or days to develop. Check the stool for occult blood. Upright or left lateral decubitus x-ray views to examine for free-air under the diaphragm should be ordered. Ultrasonography, CT scanning, MRI, or peritoneal lavage may be required to make the diagnosis (Soballe, 1983). The duodenum is vulnerable to injury where it crosses the spine, and may produce retroperitoneal hemorrhage and irritation secondary to the release of its contents. Serious injuries to a hollow viscus should be suspected in blunt trauma to the abdomen, and will require surgical exploration and appropriate treatment.

## SECTION E.
## BACK INJURIES IN SPORTS

Back pain is one of the most common complaints of recreational and competitive athletes of all ages. Most back complaints are self-limited and the individual returns to athletics within two or three weeks so the true incidence of back problems is not known. Most athletes seek medical care only when they have a persistent and debilitating problem. It is estimated that 80% of all U.S. adults have had low back pain, mostly work-related (Frymoyer, 1983, 1988). Low back pain (LBP) is a symptom, not a diagnosis. The differential diagnosis is challenging because the cause of pain can be biomechanical, neoplastic, infectious, developmental, metabolic, inflammatory, emotional, or traumatic (Jacobs, 1982; Stanitski, 1982)(see Table 13E-1).

Knowledge of these various causes is required, as well as an understanding of the role of exercise in treating these problems. The physician must be able to use accurate and reliable tests of functional capacity in order to identify the patient's specific exercise needs. Follow-up is needed to evaluate the effectiveness of exercise programs for low back pain and determine if a patient is fit to return to

Table 13E-1. Major Disorders Associated with Low Back Pain

| Mechanical and Structural | Metabolic Bone Disease |
|---|---|
| *Congenital and developmental* | Osteoporosis |
| Scoliosis | Osteomalacia |
| Facet tropism | |
| Transitional vertebrae | **Infection** |
| Spondylolisthesis | Osteomyelitis |
| *Degenerative disk disease* | Discitis |
| *Injury* | Epidural abscess |
| Fracture | |
| Soft Tissue | **Neoplasia** |
| | Benign |
| **Spondylarthropathy** | Malignant |
| Ankylosing spondylitis | |
| Reiter's syndrome | **Referred Pain** |
| Psoriatic arthritis | Most commonly from the |
| Enteropathic arthropathies | pelvis, abdomen, GU tract, aorta, kidneys, pancreas or lymph nodes |

work or sport. Unfortunately, there are few controlled studies with objective evaluation of specific exercise programs for LBP. Consequently, the selection of an exercise program to treat and prevent LBP is often performed on the basis of empirical knowledge (Poster, 1991).

The medical history is the key factor in determining the cause of pain, and it should include the relationship of pain to activity. The pattern and site of injury tend to be sport specific. Increased pain with activity implies a biomechanical cause, whereas night pain may be due to neoplasm, infection, or an inflammatory cause. A history of trauma or pain radiation is helpful in determining the exact cause and extent of low back pain. Physical examination should include an assessment of gait. Look for differences in and asymmetry of thigh and calf girth. Check for structural deformities such as scoliosis, kyphosis, or lordosis, and evaluate the patient's flexibility. Look at chest expansion, hip range of motion, hamstring flexibility, and bilateral straight leg raising. Check for CVA tenderness which could indicate renal problems, and evaluate all muscle insertions over the iliac crest. Complete the evaluation with a thorough neurological exam that tests for inequality of motor, strength, sensory responses, and deep tendon reflexes.

Other tests may be required to diagnose back problems in athletes. These may include:

- Routine AP and lateral x-rays of the thoracolumbar spine and oblique views (5 view) of the lumbar spine to rule out a possible pars/interarticularis defect. X-ray the sacroiliac joint in symptomatic athletes. The $L_5$-$S_1$, disc space is best evaluated on the spot view. Flexion, extension, and lateral view and postural studies are helpful.
- Bone scans help detect overuse injuries such as pars interarticular fractures because the bone scan often is abnormal earlier than routine x-rays.
- Myelography can rule out neurological defects caused by a herniated disc. MRI and CT scanning has limited the need for myelography, especially as dynamic MRI becomes more available (Gibson, 1987).
- Tomography, CT scanning, and magnetic resonance imaging may help define lesions, especially those in the soft tissues and spine (tumor, infection, ruptured disc). A word of caution — 20% of asymptomatic patients under age 40 have evidence of disc protrusion on CT (Gibson, 1987).
- CBC, peripheral smear, sedimentation rate, serum uric acid, and RA titers help differentiate inflammatory and infectious disorders.
- Histocompatibility antigen (HL-A) typing may aid the diagnosis of ankylosing spondylitis common to the young athlete (HLA-B-27).
- A needle biopsy for tumors or infection may be required.
- EMG provides a physiologic evaluation of nerve roots, peripheral nerves, and musculature. EMG can document ongoing as well as recovering nerve injury.

A systematic approach to the diagnosis of low back injuries and illnesses is necessary. Below are the most common problems in sports.

### Anatomical Considerations

Familiarity with the essential anatomy of the lumbosacral spine permits greater accuracy in diagnosis and rehabilitation. The dorsal vertebrae have inherent stability and the lumbar spine, with its large vertebrae, is designed to permit flexion, extension, and stability (Figure 13E-1). There is little rotatory motion in the lumbar spine. The transverse and spinous processes are intricately designed to connect the vertebrae through their articulations and strong ligamentous attachments. Posteriorly, massive muscles arise from the pelvis to attach to the spinous processes and vertebral bodies, stabilize the trunk over the pelvis, and protect the abdominal contents. The abdominal mus-

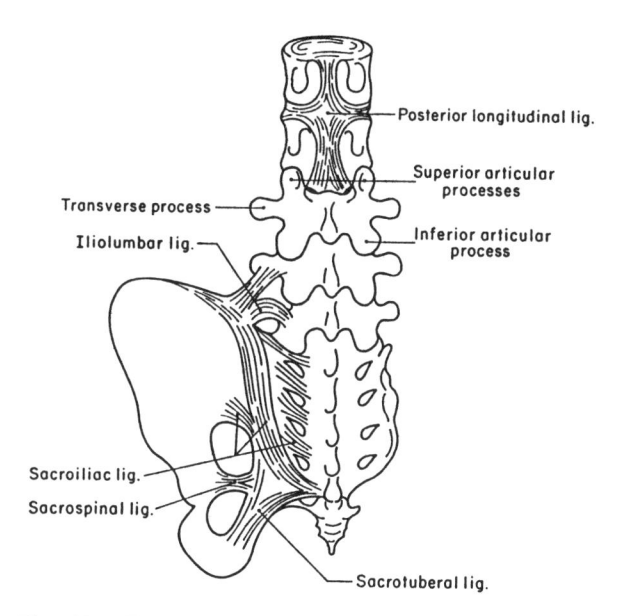

**Fig. 13E-1.** The Lumbosacral Spine

cles stabilize the trunk anteriorly and provide active forward flexion of the spine while preventing hyperextension.

The latissimus dorsi inserts onto the posterior iliac crest via the superficial thoraco-lumbar fascia. Deep in this muscle area, the long spinal extensors have a more oblique orientation to the vertebral bodies. Their distal fibers insert into the deeper layer of the thoraco-lumbar fascia. Deepest extensor muscles are the short rotators such as the multifidi. These structures are segmentally innervated and obliquely oriented. Another important posterior muscle group is the hip extensors. The gluteal muscles and the hamstrings are often involved in lumbosacral spine problems. The oblique abdominal musculature is located anteriorally. The external oblique is the most superficial of these muscles with its attachment to the ribs. [Deep to this muscle, the internal oblique blends into the thoraco-lumbar fascia as does the transverse abdominous muscle which lies below the internal oblique muscle.]

The ligaments of the lumbar spine provide stability. These structures are richly innervated and provide affective feedback. Their strong anterior longitudinal segment, posterior longitudinal segment, interspinous ligament, and supraspinous ligament help maintain the orientation of the vertebral bodies. The iliolumbar ligament, sacroiliac ligament, sacrotuberous ligament, and sacrospinal ligaments all help anchor the lumbosacral spine and pelvis. The capsular structures like the facet joint capsules also are important stabilizers and are also richly innervated.

The bony anatomy of the lumbar spine is oriented to provide significant stability. The facet joints are much more vertical in orientation than in the cervical spine. The three-joint complex of each vertebral level (disc space and two facet joints) provides a triangular base of support. The weight borne at each lumbar level is divided equally between the disc and the vertebral joint anteriorly, and the two facet joints posteriorly.

**Perspective**

Low back pain (LBP) in athletes is caused most often by a strain, sprain, or contusion with associated muscle spasm. Runners often develop pain running downhill when their lumbar spines are forced into hyperextension while their pelvises are tilted posteriorly. Running uphill reverses the process and puts increased stress on the low back muscles. Multiple forces are applied to the sacroiliac joint during the distance phase of running, especially in people with significant unilateral leg length differences (> ¼"), and this may cause problems.

Accurate identification and quantification of the many types of recreational activities contributing to LBP has been difficult. Some sports activities and the risk of LBP are:

- Golf and tennis players may suffer LBP because of the twisting of the back during execution of the sport.
- Football linemen, female gymnasts, javelin throwers, back-packers, oarsmen, and athletes in martial arts are at risk of developing spondylolysis and spondylolisthesis via a fatigue fracture of the pars interarticularis.
- Jogging and cross-country skiing sometimes are associated with disabling LBP.
- Squash and racquetball seldom produce LBP.
- Weight-lifting programs may cause LBP, occasionally because of spondylolysis, but more often due to an acute muscle strain.

Spondylolisthesis is more common in children and adolescents but may occur in older individuals. It usually is worse in girls than boys. It has both hereditary and physical stress etiologies. The pars interarticularis of the third through fifth lumbar vertebrae have the highest incidence of defects between 5½-6½ years of age, which seems to indicate that these defects develop at this time (Halpern, 1991). Trauma-induced instability of the spinal column is rare but can be caused by swimming pool and surfing accidents (Babcock, 1975). Fractures of the spinous or transverse process occur both in youth and adults as do compression fractures of the vertebrae.

Adolescents undergoing rapid growth spurts may have low back problems secondary to the effects of increased stress and muscle imbalance on the spinal column. There are two common findings in the adolescent spine: 1) Schmorl's nodes — an incidental x-ray finding in asymptomatic young adults, and 2) Scheuermann's disease — usually seen in males (especially swimmers) that involves the end-plates (epiphysitis) of the vertebrae at the thoracolumbar junction ($T_{11}$-$L_2$). Wedging of the vertebrae and progressive thoracic kyphosis occurs and may result in a rigid, round-back deformity of the spine (Stanitski, 1982).

Symptomatic lumbar disc disease is rare in youngsters but occurs with more regularity in high school and college-age athletes (DeOrio and Bianco, 1982; Gelabert, 1986; Jackson and Wiltse, 1981; Jackson and Wiltse, 1974). Ankylosing spondylitis, an inflammatory disease, usually begins before age 30 and affects 1% of the population, males more than females. However, it is being seen with more regularity in high-school athletes of both sexes (Calin, 1979). Scoliosis may add to the incidence of low back complaints in athletes. It appears in 5% of the general population between the ages of 10 and 14 and affects more girls. Approximately 50% of those with scoliosis will have chronic low back problems that require treatment.

**Low Back Pain in Athletics**

The differential diagnosis of back pain also includes disc space infection, gynecological or kidney problems, rectal tumors, and multiple myeloma in older athletes. Some common low back problems in athletes are outlined with suggestions for management.

Attempt to rule out an underlying gynecological or renal cause for back pain, especially ovarian cyst, tumor, or pyelonephritis. Older athletes may have disc degeneration, osteoarthritis, or myeloma. A rectal exam should be performed to rule out a rectal or prostatic tumor. Scoliosis may contribute to low back complaints in young adolescents so all youngsters should be screened from behind as they flex forward. Look for the typical asymmetry of the back and shoulders. X-ray and appropriate orthopedic referral may halt this process.

**Scheuermann's Disease**

Scheuermann's disease refers to the finding of epiphysitis of the vertebral end plates in the thoracic region. This condition affects young males aged 10 to 25 years and often is found in swimmers after prolonged training in the butterfly stroke. Progressive development of thoracic hypokyphosis and hypolordosis of the lumbar spine (usually $T_{11}$-$L_2$) due to anterior wedging of one or more vertebrae may be seen on x-ray (Ippolito & Ponseti, 1981). This cause of back pain presents after prolonged sitting and lying down; the low back pain may actually decrease during sports. Chronic back pain develops more commonly in the presence of kyphosis and increasing thoracic deformity.

Treatment consists of limiting the activity that accentuates the patient's kyphosis, especially the butterfly stroke, bench press, and dumbbell flies. Treat with extension exercises and rest along with a "warm-n-form" brace. Relief of pain and prevention of further kyphotic deformity may be required, using a hyperlordotic Boston-type brace (30 degrees B.O.B.) if the deformity is greater than 40 degrees (Borenstein, 1989). The brace is worn throughout the day. When it is not worn, the athlete may resume athletic activities except as noted above. Appropriate psychological and emotional support should be offered to the patient along with information on exercises and sports (Wilson & Lindseth, 1982).

**Vertebral Fractures**

Vertebral compression fractures occur rarely in gymnastics, diving, and tobogganing. The fracture is associated with paraspinous muscle spasm, limited range of motion, and pain over the spinous process of the affected vertebrae. These fractures often are unrecognized because x-rays usually are not taken and pain may not present until later in adult life.

Most vertebral fractures heal without complications. However, there can be genitourinary problems and pain due to vertebral instability and this may lead to a more permanent disability. Genitourinary dysfunction (residual volume > 60 cc after voiding) may be present despite a normal urological exam (Keene, 1980). A urologist should be consulted if this complication occurs. Paralytic ileus can follow a vertebral fracture and should be treated appropriately.

The focus of initial treatment is on strengthening the paraspinous musculature with hyperextension exercises. The athlete may require a back brace fitted by an orthopedic surgeon or a posterior spinal fusion if pain is unresolved after several months of therapy.

Acute or chronic trauma may cause to a fracture of the articular, transverse, or spinous process. The injury usually is the result of a direct blow and is associated with soft-tissue swelling and ecchymosis. Fractures heal within 8 to 12 weeks and require restricted activity only initially. Flexibility and P.R.E. exercises, and occasionally bracing, are used later. The athlete may return to activity when local tenderness resolves and x-rays reveal consolidation of the fracture site (usually three to six weeks, depending on severity).

### Intervertebral Disc Injuries

Disc herniation may produce selective motor/sensory deficits in the lower extremities of athletes over age 30 but only low back pain in younger patients. The symptoms of disc herniation in young athletes are those of muscle strain: spasm, limited range of motion, and midline pain, usually without sciatica. Pain may not be a significant presenting feature and true sciatica may not develop until years later. An x-ray to rule out a vertebral fracture (AP, lateral, and oblique views) should be obtained, although the affected disk will not be visualized.

Low back pain from this cause resolves in most young athletes after two to three weeks of bed rest. If the pain persists, consider electromyelography (EMG), nerve conduction studies (NCS), CT scanning, or MRI to document the lesion. EMG can detect paravertebral muscle denervation and lumbar nerve root changes approximately three weeks after injury. CT scanning or magnetic resonance imaging (MRI) can accurately document a disc herniation (Rosenthal, 1984).

A ruptured intervertebral disc produces nerve root pressure that presents as radicular pain radiating from the buttock to the ankle and is associated with paraesthesia and possible impairment of nerve root conduction (see Table 13E-2). This lesion is a frequent complication of a sport-related injury. Note that a patient suffering a low back strain may have back pain that is referred down the leg over the distribution of the sciatic nerve.

**Table 13E-2. Criteria for Diagnosis of Herniated Intervertebral Disc**

Leg pain is a more dominant symptom than back pain. It affects one leg only and follows a typical sciatic (or femoral) nerve distribution.

Paresthesiae are localized to a dermatomal distribution.

Straight-leg raising is reduced by 50% of normal, and/or pain crosses over to the symptomatic leg when the unaffected leg is elevated, and/or pain radiates proximally or distally with digital pressure on the tibial nerve in the popliteal fossa.

Two of the four neurologic signs are present (wasting, motor weakness, diminished sensory appreciation, or diminution of reflex activity).

A contrast study or CT scan is positive and corresponds to the clinical level.

This referred pain rarely goes below the knee and is not associated with paraesthesia or other signs of nerve root compression. Generally, reflex activity, sensory appreciation, and motor strength are unaffected in this situation.

The patient with a prolapsed disc commonly has low back pain and an inability to move. The lumbar spine is rigidly splinted and the patient moves only with difficulty, clutching his back and walking with his trunk leaning forward, while keeping the hips and knees slightly bent. Examination reveals limited range of motion and the clinical findings mentioned above. There are positive straight leg raising signs, occasionally a loss of deep tendon reflexes, and normal motor sensory testing. These latter signs usually occur later in the course of the disease.

Local ice application during the first 48 hours is helpful in relieving the pain of a prolapsed disc. The ice provides an analgesic effect that allows the patient to perform passive and active stretching of the affected muscles. Muscle relaxants and analgesics are used frequently in this situation but should be given only for a limited time. The patient may prefer to rest on the floor with the hip and knee flexed at 90° and the feet supported on a chair or bed.

If there is no evidence of nerve compression or impairment of nerve root conduction, the resolution of symptoms may be speeded by gentle manipulation techniques. The patient lies on his or her back and the physician raises the patient's legs while maintaining the knees in flexion (Figure 13E-2A). By applying gentle pressure on the heels,

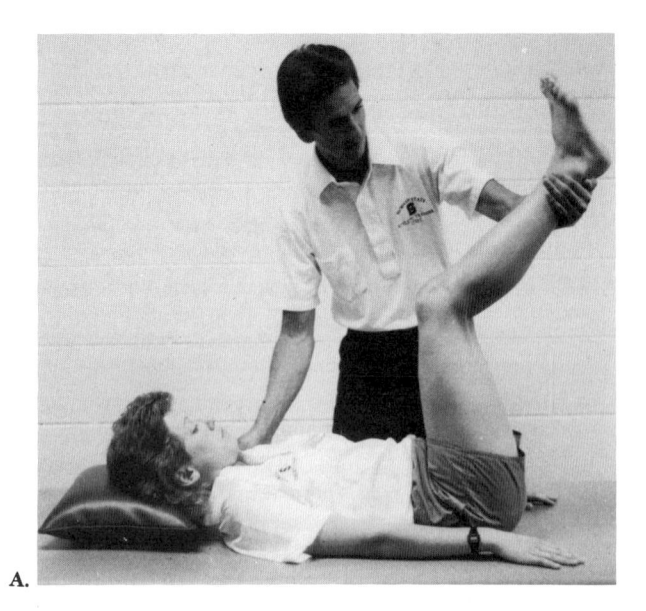

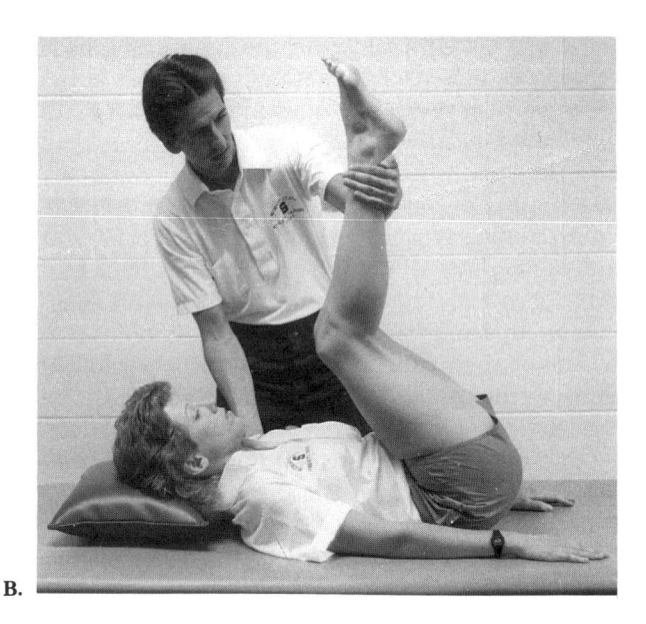

**Fig. 13E-2.** Flexion manipulation by the physician. A. The physician raises the patient's legs maintaining the knees in flexion. B. By applying pressure to the heels the physician then pushes the patient's knees towards the shoulders.

the physician then pushes the patient's knees toward the shoulders (Figure 13E-2B). This movement is done very slowly and the degree of flexion obtained is determined by the discomfort the patient experiences. This movement is repeated slowly and rhythmically over a period of five minutes. In most instances, the range of motion that can be achieved by this passive manipulation technique gradually increases. At the conclusion of the exercise, the patient is instructed to flex the knees fully and allow the feet to come down to the bed (VanHoesen, 1986).

A series of passive flexion manipulations of the spine can be carried out in this manner several times daily. The patient can do this by lying on his or her back and pulling the knees fully up to the chest (Figure 13E-3 A to D). This position should be maintained for five minutes. In acute attacks that are associated with severe pain, patients may find it easier to assume this position while lying on their side. By the second day, patients should be able to carry out the flexion manipulations of the back by themselves. Once the acute back pain attack is over, the patient must develop enough trunk muscle strength to prevent repeated attacks. The tone and strength of the abdominal muscles are vitally important in protecting the spine against weight-bearing and extension strains (Foster, 1991). The exercise program should start with pelvic tilting (see Figure 13E-3D), carried out with the patient lying supine on a firm surface with the hips and knees flexed and keeping the soles of both feet flat on the bed or floor. The patient then presses the lower back down flat against the floor so the lumbar lordosis is obliterated. This movement is achieved by contracting both the abdominal and gluteus muscles.

Once the lumbar spine is pressing against the floor, the pelvis is rotated by raising the buttock from the floor. The lower back must not be permitted to leave the floor as the buttock is raised. Raising the buttock away from the floor reverses the lumbar lordosis. Patients may find it easier if they put one hand on the symphysis pubis and the other on the xiphoid process and then try to bring their hands together while doing the exercises. This exercise should be done rhythmically, first with the hips and knees flexed before and then with the knees extended. The exercise also can be attempted with the patient standing with his/her back against a wall.

When flexion exercises are started, the patient should be on the back with hips and knees bent and the feet supported. Flexion exercises should never be performed with the patient holding the knees fully extended. This avoids hyperextension of the lumbar spine which could lead to further injury. The physician should emphasize the importance of flexibility of the hamstrings and Achilles tendons.

As with all therapeutic exercises, a few are directed toward the lesion being treated. Once the patient's discomfort subsides, it is important to

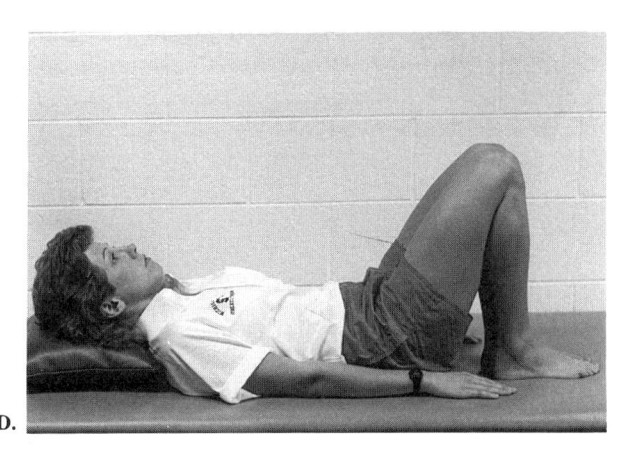

**Fig. 13E-3.** Flexion exercise-manipulation of the lumbar spine. The patient lies on the bed with the head supported by a pillow. A. The hips are flexed to 90° and the knees slightly flexed. B. The patient now attempts to kick the feet over the head, raising the buttocks approximately 6 inches off the bed. C. After each "kick-up" the patient returns to the starting position. D. After five kick-ups, the patient rests by lowering his legs with the knees fully flexed, thereby putting his feet on the bed, soles first. It is very important that he should not lower the legs with the knees fully extended because this places a painful hyperextension strain on the spine.

engage in a general, controlled physical exercise program that is supervised by the physician. Almost 90% of patients with sciatica and early intervertebral disc rupture respond to conservative treatment that combines proper diagnostic testing, appropriate physical therapy modalities, exercises, and time. The patient's exercise activity should be closely monitored. Many exercise programs for lumbar problems are available and can be referenced through additional readings supplied in this text.

### Ankylosing Spondylitis

Older adolescents and young adults with low back pain should be screened for this systemic inflammatory disease. Symptoms of ankylosing spondylitis are more pronounced in the morning and improve with exercise during the day, or they may be present at night. Pain may be localized to the low back, dorsal spine, or sacroiliac joints, with or without sciatica. Forcibly abducting both hips may produce severe pain. Forward flexion of the spine is limited in more severe cases of ankylosing spondylitis.

Oblique x-rays of the S-I joints, looking for sacroiliitis are helpful (Libson, 1984). This condition is recognized as blurring of the joint margin, joint space narrowing, erosion, sclerosis, or fusion (late finding). HLA testing (HLA B-27) is positive in 90% of patients with ankylosing spondylitis, but is also present in 5% to 10% of the normal population. An elevated erythrocyte sedimentation rate suggests inflammation but the diagnosis is confirmed by the x-ray findings and clinical signs mentioned above.

Remedial exercises are of paramount importance. Encourage the individual to participate in regular exercise, emphasizing daily flexibility activities and proper posture (Pacelli, 1991). Exercise usually does not have to be discontinued. Anti-inflammatory agents are helpful, especially indomethacin (Indocin[R]), 25 mg tid or phenylbutazone (Butazolidin[R]) 100 mg three or four times daily. The newer NSAID agents are not as helpful in treating this disease but may be tried.

**Treatment of Low Back Pain**

The focus in the initial phase of treatment of lumbosacral problems is controlling acute pain and discomfort. Appropriate use of anti-inflammatory medications and judicious use of pain medications on a dose schedule vs a PRN basis can be initiated. Medications in combination with appropriately prescribed physical therapy will help limit the disability. Large doses of pain medication and prolonged bed rest may lead to additional deconditioning and a protracted course of the disease process. A competent physical therapy program is mandatory in the rehabilitation of lumbosacral spine problems. Ice, heat, and electrical stimulation may be combined with myofascial techniques, mobilization, and an initial exercise prescription to serve as the first phase in the rehabilitation process.

The first ice application to the back should be for 20-30 minutes to relieve muscle spasm, repeated four to six times during the first 72 hours after injury. Cryotherapy works better than muscle relaxants for pain relief, muscle relaxation, and decreased swelling. Athletes with severe spasm may require analgesics (aspirin, acetaminophen, or codeine) or benefit from a NSAID agent. Strapping of the back can provide external support and aid mobility.

After 72 hours, progress to gentle flexibility exercises after applying heat to the back. Using heating pads, ultrasound, diathermy, or whirlpool may facilitate the penetration of heat into the soft tissues. The main reason for using heat is to promote flexibility. After finishing each therapy session, the athlete should again apply ice to the back to prevent swelling. Electrical nerve stimulation has been a popular method of modulating low back pain and manipulation therapy may be helpful in later stages of treatment (Sheehan, 1984).

During the acute phase of treatment, instruct the athlete not to work the abdominal muscles. Exercises of the buttock and abdominal muscles are initiated when pain and spasm decrease (Sheehan, 1984). Flexibility should begin with static exercises using the following progression: (Kulund, 1982) 1) lateral stretches of the lumbodorsal fascia; 2) anterior hip stretches in a lunging position to stretch the rectus femoris, tensor fascia lata, and iliofemoral ligament; 3) flex the trunk forward while sitting on a stool and attempt to touch the folded elbows to the floor, and 4) while lying on the back, bring the knees to the chest and hold. All stretches should be held for six to eight seconds. Three sets of 10 repetitions of each exercise should be performed daily.

When able, the athlete is started on a strengthening program that initially emphasizes isometric exercises. Start with single leg lifts, flexing one knee onto the chest, holding it, and then doing the other leg. Repeat three sets of 10 repetitions. Next, add head and shoulder curls while keeping the small of the back rounded and in contact with the ground. After successful completion of these, the athlete may advance to full sit-ups, side sit-ups, abdominal hangs, and back extensions. Once flexibility and strength return to normal, the athlete without LBP may begin a running or swimming program. The completely functional athlete may return to practice and competition.

The McKenzie Program has gained popular acceptance and is oriented to better treat a discogenic etiology of lumbosacral pain. McKenzie (1985) techniques aim to correct any lumbar shift, followed by extension type exercises. The extension position allows the nucleus pulposis to migrate anteriorally and decreases the posterior disc bulge and production of radicular symptoms. More active extension exercises follow with the assistance of a physical therapist. Gravity assisted lumbar traction may provide vertebral distraction and help with disc protrusion. Careful patient selection is obviously necessary.

Symptoms of lumbosacral spine which appear to be mostly facet or posterior element in nature require a flexion type program in the physical therapy sessions. Flexion activities increase intradiscal pressure but do not decompress the posterior elements. The use of modalities and proper selection of flexion vs extension exercises is combined with myofascial release or mobilization techniques. These techniques permit better soft tissue flexibility and help reestablish normal segmental mobility and function in the lumbosacral spine and pelvis. Education about posture and proper low back mechanics is important (Pacelli, 1991). A thorough, long-term rehabilitation program helps decrease the incidence of recurrent episodes of back pain.

Proper weight training techniques must be emphasized to the athlete in order to prevent low back injuries. All athletes should be instructed to do flexibility exercises during the warm-up and cool-down period to avoid acute back strains. They should pay attention to posture and to proper techniques when lifting heavy objects. Protective equipment/padding may be necessary when the athlete returns to certain competitive sports.

### Mechanical Back Pain

Mechanical back pain is often a diagnosis of exclusion. The most common situation involves problems with posture, prolonged standing or sitting, and complaints of relatively mild pain of the upper back and back of the neck. Children with this condition are usually hyperlordotic and have tight quadriceps and hamstrings and flexion contractures of the hip. Obtain standing PA and lateral x-rays of the lumbosacral spine which include the thoraco-lumbar junction and supine oblique lumbarsacral spine. If the child is hyperlordotic on standing x-rays, a series of supervised exercises is indicated to reduce the lordosis, strengthen the abdominals, and increase the flexibility of the lower extremity musculature. Many of these patients require postural work (Pacelli, 1991). The small number of patients who have mechanical back pain and hypolordosis ("flat back" syndrome) should do extension exercise with the back in less than 10° extension. These patient should be followed for 10-12 weeks. Bracing is rarely required to relieve pain.

### Spondylolysis

Spondylolysis is a common cause of back pain in young athletes and is due to a fracture of the pars interarticularis (Figure 13E-4). This condition probably is caused by a genetic predisposition and repetitive physical stress rather than an acute injury (Ciullo, 1985; Fredrickson, 1983; Halpern, 1991). Spondylolysis occurs more often in sports

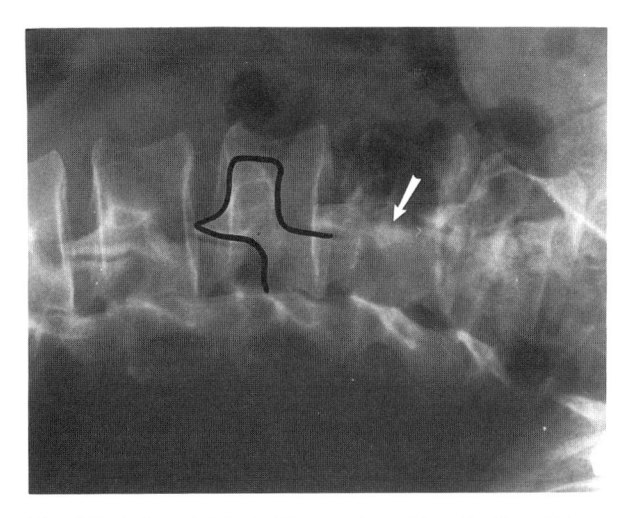

**Fig. 13E-4.** Spondylolysis ("Scotty dog with collar") and Spondylolisthesis ("Scotty dog decapitated")

that involve highly competitive and strenuous training programs (gymnastics, football lineman). Spondylosis is common in the lower lumbar spine where tension, as in the gymnast who performs front and back walkovers, vaults, and dismounts (see Figure 13E-5).

The incidence of fatigue fracture of the pars interarticularis is high among young athletes with

**Fig. 13E-5.** Hyperextension of the Spine

lumbar pain and muscle spasm. Other etiologies of LBP also should be considered. Jackson and Wiltse (1981) noted that 40% of athletes with LBP had a pars defect. Other studies by Ferguson, et al. (1974) showed a high incidence of spondylolytic changes on x-ray in athletes with LBP. Defects in the pars interarticularis occur in approximately 6% of the Caucasian population by age six, but 11% of female gymnasts in one study had the defect (Jackson, 1974). Hyperextension of the lumbar spine occurs during the volleyball and tennis serve, hurdling, pole vaulting, high jumping, hiking, and sailing.

An athlete with spondylolysis complains of low back pain usually, but not always, on one side at the belt level which is aggravated by twisting or hyperextension and relieved by rest. Physical exam reveals tight hamstrings, tenderness of the paravertebral muscles, a normal neurological exam and a positive "one-leg hyperextension" test. (Standing on one leg with the lumbar spine hyperextended causes lumbar pain (Keene, 1983). Occasionally, sciatica symptoms with a positive bone scan may be found due to irritation of the $L_5$ nerve root at the foramen. A cold bone scan does not necessarily mean that the pars interarticular defect has healed. It may simply mean that the defect has returned to a baseline status where a stress reaction is no longer active (Halpern, 1991).

Obtain x-rays of the lumbar spine, including AP, lateral, and oblique views. Oblique views visualize the pars defect best (Libson, 1984). Initial x-rays often are normal in an early pars defect, necessitating the use of a Tc99 bone scan which may help confirm the diagnosis earlier. The newer SPEC (computerized) bone scan is very sensitive in finding the pars lesion. CT scanning does not increase diagnostic yield. Repeat bone scan testing may show when spondylolysis activity is waning. However, the athlete often returns to competition before having a completely negative bone scan.

Treatment consists of restricting activities that aggravate the pain, primarily hyperextension. Flexibility exercises to stretch the hamstrings and gentle hyperextension exercises to strengthen the paraspinal muscles should be started as soon as possible. A prefabricated thermoplastic antilordotic brace (0%) worn for six months may allow the athlete to participate in sports (Micheli, 1980). Rules of participation with protective equipment may bear on the use of the brace. Modification of sports activities may be necessary (while the brace is worn) (gymnasts cannot vault easily) but many athletes return to sports such as football, basketball, or hockey without compromising their activity or causing a recurrence of symptoms (Fredickson, 1984).

If pain persists or there is evidence of spondylolythesis, a posterior spinal fusion may be indicated. In that case, a return to participation in contact sports should be restricted. The treatment of recurrent symptoms of spondylolysis by surgery remains controversial (Nicol, 1986). Consultation with an orthopedic surgeon knowledgeable about spondylolysis and spondylolisthesis in competitive athletes will be helpful (Borenstein, 1989).

**Spondylolisthesis**

Spondylolisthesis is a frequent sequela of spondylolysis and represents slippage of one vertebrae upon another. It can occur anywhere along the lumbar spine (see Figure 13E-4). The L5 vertebra is affected in 90% of cases. This condition affects all age groups but is most common in the 9 to 14 age group. The incidence of pars defect in five-year-olds is virtually zero. Wiltse (1984 and 1975) noted that 4.4% of Caucasian children have a pars defect by the first grade and another 1.3% will have the defect by age 20. High-grade slippage is four to six times more common in girls with spondylolisthesis than boys, although pars defects are more likely in young male athletes. Spondylolisthesis is more common in contact sports (football, martial arts) and in those that involve twisting and hyperextension of the spine (gymnastics or jogging).

Classification of spondylolisthesis divides the condition into five groups. In the pediatric age group, nearly all lesions occur at the $L_5/S_1$ level. In adult patients they are distributed more frequently at different levels, but are still most common at the lumbosacral junction. Most childhood cases of spondylolisthesis are of the dysplastic or isthmthic type. A related lesion (pars stress lesion) may occur in young athletes and, if recognized, may not progress to spondylolysis or spondylolisthesis. The pars stress lesion is a microfracture. Fatigue fractures of the pars interarticularis differ from stress fractures elsewhere in the body in that they do not show periosteal new bone formation and there is a high potential for fibrous union.

Two principal methods of measuring the degree of slippage have been used to grade spondylolisthesis. A more popular and precise method expresses the degree of vertebral slippage as a percentage of the A-P diameter of the top of the first sacral vertebra. The amount of slippage is graded as follows:

Grade 1 — vertebra slips 25% over the body of the vertebra below
Grade 2 — vertebra slips 25%-50% over the body of the vertebra below
Grade 3 — vertebra slips 50%-75% over the body of the vertebra below
Grade 4 — vertebra slips greater than 75% over the body of the vertebra below

The typical young athlete with the pars stress reaction has an aching low back that is unilateral and exacerbated by such motions as twisting and hyperextension. The pain is on one side along the belt line. Low back pain usually is present with daily activities, but becomes more pronounced when the patient competes and performs maneuvers involving extremes of lumbar motion, especially hyperextension. The most common aggravating activities for gymnasts include walk-overs, dismounts, vaults, and flips. Aggravating activities for other athletes include the standing overhead press, pole-vaulting, diving, sailing, hurdling, and pitching in baseball. The complaint of low back pain often is associated with radiation of pain into one or both buttocks and is insidious in onset. It usually is relieved by supine positioning.

Physical complaints of spondylolisthesis involve tight hamstrings and low back pain. Physical education teachers may notice a deformity of the athlete's low back that consists of a very short waist with a flat buttock and some lordosis. The mere presence of spondylolysis does not produce any symptoms nor does it impose any functional impairment. Pain in the low back occurs frequently in spondylolisthesis (70%), whereas sciatica is infrequent (Cailliet, 1977).

On physical examination, the pain of the pars stress reaction and spondylolisthesis is accentuated when the patient stands on one leg and then the other while hyperextending the back. If the lesion is unilateral, the test will be distinctly more positive when this maneuver is performed on the ipsilateral lower extremity. A gymnast with spondylolisthesis may demonstrate pain while rising to an upright position against resistance, and there may be some loss of hamstring flexibility. A child with spondylolisthesis may show the shortened trunk, tight hamstrings, vertical sacrum and, in severe cases, a reversal of the pelvic tilt. A step-off of the spinous processes is palpable with Grade 1 or higher spondylothesis.

**Radiological Methods of Evaluation**

Persistent lumbar pain in a young child that interferes with performance and is not associated with nerve root impingement signs should raise the suspicion of a stress fracture in the pars interarticularis. Oblique lumbar radiographs usually show the bony lesion but the diagnosis can be confirmed only by a positive Technesium 99 or SPEC (computerized) bone scan. If a pars interarticulars defect appears on initial radiographs, the physician should decide whether it represents an acute or chronic condition. Look closely at the defect for rounding and reabsorption and determine if one side is more prominent than the other. A positive bone scan indicates a lesion of recent duration; however, a chronic lesion often continues to show signs of osteoblastic activity on bone scan for up to nine months.

Detection of spondylolysis is made difficult by the potential for a high false negative rate if only A-P and lateral x-ray views are taken. A diagnosis of spondylolysis is of particular importance in childhood and adolescence as most cases in this age group progress to spondylolisthesis. If you must take only one x-ray view, it is best to order a spot-lateral x-ray of the L4-S1 vertebrae with the patient standing. Other helpful views include a large A-P view, both obliques, and a Ferguson view or a 45° lateral-oblique, which will best demonstrate slippage. If these x-ray views are normal but the athlete has persistent pain, obtain a Technesium 99 or SPEC bone scan, which may reveal a hot-spot over the pars interarticularis.

**Treatment**

All preadolescent or adolescent athletes with low back pain and slippage must be are restricted from vigorous activity until the spasm and pain are relieved. Only then are sports resumed, with continuation dependent on the absence of symptoms. Rest, heat, elevation of the legs with the knees and hips flexed, and back bracing are recommended by some orthopedists (Wiltse, 1984). Immobilization with a rigid polypropylene lumbosacral brace or elastic support around the lower back may be necessary for up to 8 to 12 months. Repeat evaluations and bone scans at three-month intervals may be necessary for proper follow-up and exercise recommendations.

Athletically incurred spondylolysis is a significant problem. Parents should be counseled that the lesion does not usually result in spinal instability, but that it has the potential of limiting activity in a young athlete or adult. If the lesion does not heal but the patient remains asymptomatic, the child likely can still safely participate in vigorous sports activities.

If a young gymnast presents with vertebral slippage and low back pain, restriction from further vigorous activity is mandatory until the pain or muscle spasm has subsided completely. Young gymnasts with asymptomatic spondylolisthesis are permitted to participate. Spondylolysis and spondylolisthesis have been seen in ballet dancers. Proper treatment consists of rest in the early stages of the disease. Prophylactic considerations and revision of dance techniques to avoid problems of low back pain are of primary importance. If the pain goes away, the young athlete is allowed to resume all sports, including football. If pain and symptoms are exacerbated after a return to competition, the activity must be stopped and consideration given to surgical fusion. As a general rule, if the slippage has progressed 25% or more or if the pain keeps the youngster from his or her normal activities, surgery probably is indicated.

Patients with Grade 2 spondylolisthesis should not participate in sports that place increased stress on the lumbar spine such as football, wrestling, gymnastics, weight lifting, and horseback riding.

Spinal fusion may be indicated in those young athletes having: (1) greater than a Grade 2 slippage; (2) severe, persistent pain over six months that is unresolved by conservative treatment methods; (3) a progression in slippage of 25% or more, or (4) progressive nerve root irritation. The athlete will be in a cast and/or brace from 9 to 12 months after surgery. Contact and collision sports, gymnastics, and skiing are not permitted during this period (Kirkaldy-Willis, 1988). Consultation with an orthopedic surgeon regarding the use of lumbar facet block techniques and facet rhizotomy for patients with chronic low back pain secondary to spondylolysis and spondylolisthesis may be considered (Destouet, 1985; Bundenf, 1985; Cousins, 1988; Oudenhove, 1979).

College-age and older athletes usually will not experience further slippage and may engage in contact sports, provided there is no evidence of nerve root irritation. These athletes may experience more chronic pain and disability in later life. A carefully designed program of back rehabilitation should be instituted for all patients with spondylolithesis.

### Prevention of Low Back Pain

Prevention of significant back problems in athletics should be the goal of all coaches and trainers. Flexibility, muscle strengthening, and agility/coordination training should be included in the year-round conditioning program that is developed to meet the specific needs of athletes in a particular sport.

Injured athletes should be correctly diagnosed and started on a rehabilitation program while modifying their sports activity until their back injury heals. Swimming may be used to maintain cardiovascular fitness. After symptoms subside, initiate a gradual return to full activity so as to prevent a recurrence. Protective equipment must fit properly. The youngest athletes often have the poorest equipment which may even be ineffective and lead to injury. Most low back problems are related to overuse and can be resolved with rest, heat, anti-inflammatory agents, non-aggravating activity, proper physical therapy techniques, and time. If pain persists, further medical attention is required.

The rapidly growing adolescent spine is a dynamic structure. Flexibility and strength training often are overlooked in preventing back problems in this age group. A program that focuses on reversing the lumbar curve, strengthening abdominal muscles and increasing hamstring flexibility should be used (Foster, 1991). Keeping these principles in mind may help reduce the tremendous morbidity associated with low back problems in athletics and in the work and school environment.

## SECTION F. GENITAL-URINARY

### Perspective

The genitourinary system is comprised of the internal and the external organs that make up the urinary system (kidney, ureter, urinary bladder, urethra) and the genital organs. Both systems are located in the lower abdomen and pelvic area. Injuries to the kidney, ureter, and bladder are the most frequent abdominal injuries in athletics. The most common symptom reported in genitourinary system injuries is hematuria.

## Anatomy

For the most part, the organs of both the genital and urinary systems are well protected. The kidneys are located in the retroperitoneal upper lumbar area of the abdomen, with the upper third of the right kidney and the upper half of the left kidney located underneath the 12th rib. The remaining parts of the kidneys are protected anteriorly by three layers of abdominal muscles, as well as the large intestine and other internal organs. Posteriorly, the kidney is protected by the psoas, paravertebral, and latissimus dorsi muscles. The kidneys themselves rest in a bed of pericapsular fat.

The ureters run their course along the posterior peritoneal wall and are primarily protected by the vertebrae and muscles of the posterior abdominal wall. The ureters are vulnerable only where they course over the pelvic rim and into the bladder. The bladder lies within the pelvis except when it is full and rises above the pelvic rim. The bladder is thinnest and most vulnerable when full. The entire female reproductive system is situated within the pelvis as are the prostate and internal portion of the male urethra. The external male genitalia (penis, scrotum, and testes) are, obviously, most vulnerable in the male. During sports these organs are protected and held close to the body by an athletic supporter.

## Kidney Injuries

Injury to the kidney can result from direct trauma, repetitive jarring, decreased renal blood flow, and medication side-effects.

### Traumatic Injuries

The kidney can be injured by a direct blow to the exposed flank area or abdomen such as happens when a football player reaches up to catch a pass and is tackled. The kidney also is subject to a contrecoup type of injury after a high speed collision. The following kidney injuries are common in sports: contusion, intra- and extra-capsular injury, capsular tear or rupture, renal parenchymal tear or rupture, and tear of the renal pedicle.

Any injury to the kidney is accompanied by pain, tenderness, ecchymosis and hematuria. In rare instances, renal colic can occur from blockage of the renal pelvis by blood clots. Hypovolemic shock may be a result of extensive bleeding. There is a weak correlation between the degree of hematuria and the degree of kidney injury. Occasionally, there will be no blood in the urine if the renal collecting system is spared. An indication of significant bleeding is the loss of renal outline and psoas muscle shadow on plain KUB films of the abdomen. Associated rib fractures, renal capsular and renal cortex tears, or bleeding may be detected on plain x-rays or IVP.

If an athlete has flank pain following an injury but the urinalysis is normal, successive urine studies should be done to ensure that the urine remains clear. If the team physician doubts the presence of a kidney injury, the urinalysis and plain films of the abdomen usually are negative. Further diagnostic tests are unnecessary and observation is all that is required to manage this situation. If an injury to a kidney is strongly suspected, an intervenous pyelogram should be obtained.

The incidence of renal trauma in sports is unknown. Kidneys that are large, malformed, or have tumors are more prone to injury. There are five classes of injury as follows:

- Class I — Contusion — This represents the majority of sports related injuries to the kidney. There is usually a history of trauma but signs of trauma may or may not be present. Hematuria is usually present and the IVP is negative. Treatment of most contusions involves observation, bed rest, and repeat urinalysis.
- Class II — Cortical Laceration — Cortical laceration is usually related to trauma and has similar findings to a contusion. On a plane radiograph, the psoas shadow may be lost and an IVP will show extravasation of dye. Again, observation, bed rest, and a repeat urinalysis are indicated.
- Class III — Caliceal Laceration — Caliceal laceration involves the same findings as in the previous two classes, but the IVP will show an intact capsule in combination with intrarenal extravasation of dye and a disruption of the pelvicaliceal system. Treatment involves observation and surgery for more serious cases.
- Class IV — Complete Renal Fracture — This is a rare sports injury and the patient usually presents in shock. The IVP shows separation of the pelviccaliceal system from the capsule with in-

trarenal and extrarenal dye extravasation. Immediate surgery is indicated.
- Class V — Vascular Pedicle Injury — This injury is also rare in sports and the patient presents in hypovolemic shock. Hematuria may or may not be present and the kidneys usually are not visualized on IVP. A selective renal arteriogram shows renal vascular damage. Treatment always involves surgery.

Most kidney trauma are intracapsular or contusion injuries and heal without sequelae or complications. The athlete should be at complete bed rest until the urine is completely free of hematuria. Any athlete who develops hematuria after a blow to the flank or abdomen should be examined with an IVP. Extracapsular kidney injuries respond well to bed rest and close follow-up by the team physician in 50% of cases. The other 50% of cases may have continued bleeding (Mandell, 1982). If the IVP shows a non-functioning kidney or major injury with extracapsular extravasation, a renal angiogram should be performed. The angiogram is useful in elucidating the exact lesion. Referral to a urologist and appropriate treatment, including bed rest and/or surgery, is preferable in managing this situation.

The examining physician should check for injury to other intra-abdominal organs whenever a serious kidney injury is suspected. The athlete should not exercise further but must be examined in a hospital setting. Surgery usually is indicated for pedicle tears, kidney lacerations, and massive hemorrhaging of the kidney.

Prevention of severe kidney injuries usually is aided by strengthening the athlete's lumbar and flank muscles. Hip pads do not extend high enough to protect the kidneys, but kidney pads can be hung by straps from the shoulders. The use of a flak jacket also provides excellent kidney protection in most cases. Proper coaching techniques and adherence to regulations about protective equipment can reduce the incidence of severe kidney injuries.

**Kidney Injuries from Prolonged Heavy Exercise**

Renal function during prolonged exercise has been outlined in a number of texts (Castenfors, 1967; Castenfors, 1978). Renal blood flow decreases in response to exercise as blood is shunted to exercising muscles. Renal blood flow decreases more in exercising dehydrated or hypovolemic patients, but renal blood flow generally will return to pre-exercise levels within approximately 60 minutes. The mechanism for decreased renal blood flow is related to sympathetic nervous system induced constriction of afferent and efferent arteries and increased levels of epinephrine and norepinephrine. Dramatic decreases in renal blood flow up to 50% may result in ischemia of the kidney and hematuria.

The following changes in renal physiology have been observed during exercise: 1) a drop in renal blood flow is proportionate to the severity of the exercise performed; 2) glomerular filtration rate usually is well maintained but may decrease; 3) free water clearance decreases during even short exercise periods in well-hydrated subjects; 4) transient proteinuria may develop; 5) significant reduction in sodium excretion is observed due to increased tubular reabsorption; 6) ADH may increase threefold with heavy exercise, and urinary water excretion is usually decreased as there is a decrease in urine flow during exercise, and 7) an increased excretion of WBC and RBC in addition to increased urinary excretion of casts (hyalin and granular) occurs.

These renal changes are transient and disappear after exercise. After short periods of heavy exercise, these parameters are normalized within 10 to 36 hours; with prolonged exercise, they normalize within 10 hours. Damage to renal parenchyma does not occur during heavy exercise. All renal changes noted above are attributed to constriction of the renal vasculature. It has been postulated that an increase in core body temperature will increase permeability and also lead to some of the renal changes noted during exercise. Acute renal failure may be seen with renal ischemia during heat injury or severe dehydration. Severe muscle damage will produce myoglobinemia. The physician should be aware that nephrotroxins are usually excreted in this situation. Treatment of acute renal failure should follow normal guidelines for this diagnosis. The prevention of this problem is related to proper hydration of the athlete before and during competition and exercise activities.

## Injury to the Ureter and Bladder

### Ureters

Injury to the ureter is commonly associated with severe renal damage. Fractures of the pelvis and lower lumbar vertebrae should be considered when assessing this type of injury. Traumatic injuries to the ureter are rare and should be referred to a urologist.

### Bladder

An empty bladder rarely is damaged by trauma. Traumatic bladder injuries do occur in the martial arts. The most common type of bladder injury is a contusion; complete rupture of the bladder is rare. Most bladder injuries are related to blunt trauma on a distended bladder. Bladder trauma is present in 10% to 15% of patients with a fractured pelvis. Repetitive jarring of the bladder in long distance racing may cause transient bladder contusions. The patient presents with a history of trauma, suprapubic pain, and guarding. Urinalysis (use a Foley catheter if necessary), cystogram, and retrograde pyelogram should be obtained to establish the diagnosis. Athletes with bladder trauma can pass small blood clots and often report dysuria and a hematuria.

Two types of bladder injury are common. The first is a contusion where the degree of hematuria does not correlate well with the severity of the injury. Patients with a contusion are treated with bed rest and observation. Severe contusions require the use of an indwelling catheter for 7-10 days and antibiotic treatment. The second type of injury involves a bladder rupture which can be intra- or extra peritoneal or a combination of both. These injuries are usually associated with a pelvic fracture and require immediate surgery.

Treatment should be dictated by the urologist. Follow-up with frequent urinalysis examinations will be necessary. The athlete may return to competition when symptom-free and all evidence of hematuria has cleared. Prevention of most bladder injuries is accomplished by having the athlete to completely empty the bladder prior to competition.

### Biker's Bladder

A possible complication of aggressive bicycling is the development of "biker's bladder." The athlete usually has an abrupt onset of urinary frequency, diminished urinary stream, nocturia, and terminal dribbling. This symptom complex may be confused with proctitis and is seen in avid bicyclists (O'Brien, 1981). It is best managed by a urologist. It may be avoided by frequent emptying of the bladder during long bicycle rides and the use of a soft bicycle seat.

### Urinary Incontinence

Stress incontinence has an unknown relationship to exercise. Athletes may notice symptoms sooner than their non-athletic peers. Treatment is the same. A referral to a urologist or gynecologist may be required for female athletes to treat severe cases of urinary incontinence that interfere with daily activities and exercise.

### Hematuria

Hematuria is the most common urinary symptom seen after vigorous athletic activity (Goldszer, Parsee and Siegel, 1984). This symptom has been found in most sports participants in lacrosse, running, football, and rowing. Distance swimmers and runners usually have the greatest incidence of exercise-induced hematuria. Most studies in the literature report clearing of hematuria within 48 hours after vigorous exercise. Hematuria also may be caused by direct kidney injury, renal vein kinking, bladder contusion, or preexisting renal pathology. The problem for the team physician is to distinguish significant organic disease from transient, benign conditions that cause hematuria.

Gardner (1956) was the first to use the term "athletic pseudonephritis" when he described hematuria and proteinuria in 45% of football players examined. Microscopic hematuria is very common in the general population. In a population-based study at the Mayo clinic, 13% of adult men and postmenopausal women had asymptomatic microscopic hematuria (Mohr, 1986). A study at Kaiser Medical Center in Honolulu on patients undergoing multiphasic screening revealed a 15% incidence of microhematuria (Mariani, 1989). Microscopic hematuria is also common in younger patients. In a survey of 8,954 Finnish school children, microscopic hematuria was found in one or more specimens in 4% of the children (Vehaskari, 1979). The lower urinary tract is regarded as the most common source of hematuria after prolonged and exhaustive exertion. The existence of renal stones, urinary tract infection, or exercise-induced irritation of the urethral meatus from contusion or cold exposure should be eliminated in the differential diagnosis of hematuria.

No consensus exists on the upper limit of normal for urinary RBC. Urinary RBC count may rise after events such as mild trauma, exercise, or sex (Eichner, 1990). A 1990 review says the most commonly accepted upper limit of normal is 3 RBC's/HPF or 1,000 RBC's/ml of urine (Sutton, 1990). False negatives may occur from contamination of the urine by menses in the female or by masturbation in the male. Any black athlete with hematuria should be checked for sickle cell disease/trait. A history of drug and medication use should be obtained. The timing of hematuria is important to note: 1) initial hematuria is most likely urethral in origin; 2) terminal hematuria is most likely bladder or posterior urethral in origin, and 3) continuous hematuria most likely originates from the upper urinary tract (kidney, ureter, or bladder). Urinalysis can provide some understanding of the location of the bleeding site. Dark brown urine probably is caused by upper tract bleeding whereas salmon pink or pink/red coloration most often results from lower tract bleeding.

The presence of casts in a post-exercise urinalysis also have been described. The incidence and significance of casts in this setting is unclear. Casts generally signify renal disease, and athletes with this finding should receive a meticulous evaluation of additional urine samples.

Proof of reversion to a normal urine after exercise-related hematuria is important in order to exclude such diseases as nephritis, nephrolithiasis, or tumors occurring in the urinary tract (Hoover and Cromie, 1981). Papillary necrosis, infection, and vascular diseases should be considered if hematuria persists. In younger athletes (<40 years old) with asymptomatic hematuria following exercise, a repeat urinalysis should be performed at 24 and 48 hours (see Figure 13F-1). A clean catch urine should be cultured if cystitis or infection is suspected. No further testing is indicated if repeated urinalyses are negative. If hematuria persists, is recurrent, or is associated with continued

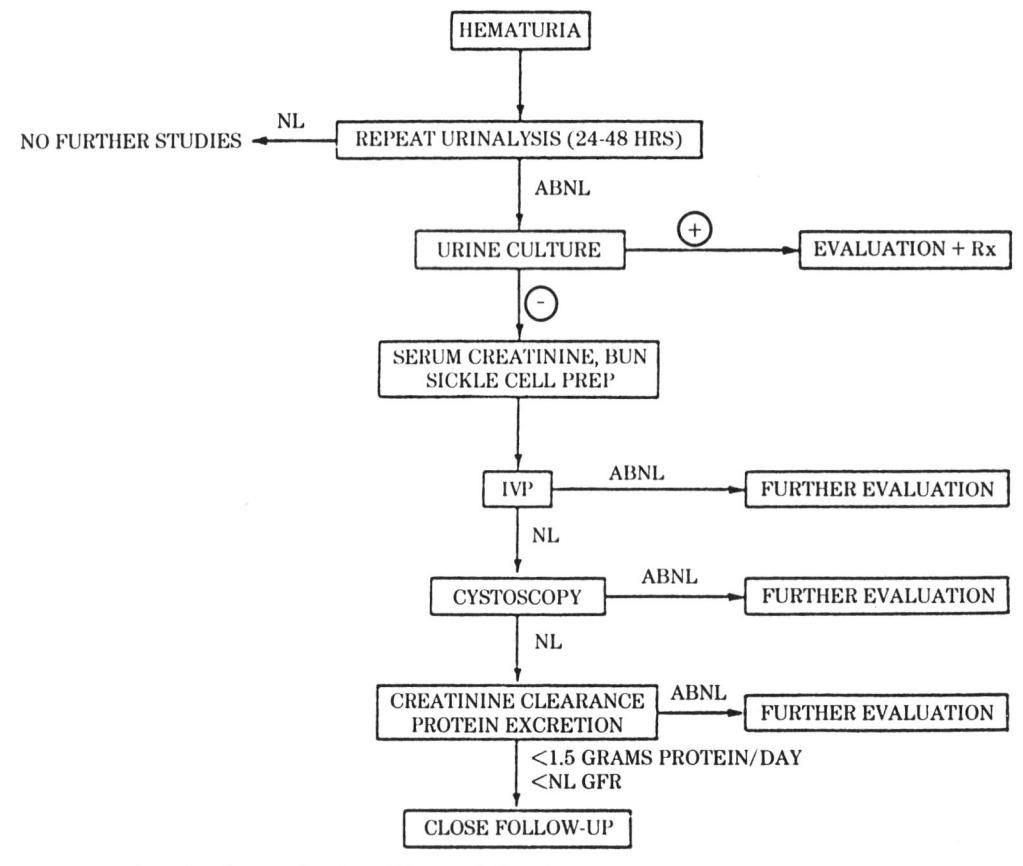

*Retrograde ureterogram, angiography, ultrasound, and renal biopsy as indicated.

**Fig. 13F-1.** Evaluation of the Patient with Hematuria. NL = Normal; ABNL = Abornal (Adapted from Goldszer, R.C., Siegel, A.J. Renal abnormalities during exercise. In Strauss, R.H. (ed.) *Sports Medicine*. Philadelphia: W.B. Saunders, 1984:133.)

symptoms such as pain, dysuria, or fever, further investigation is indicated. Renal abnormalities requiring further evaluation are listed in Table 13F-1.

Figure 13F-1 illustrates a useful approach to the diagnostic evaluation of hematuria in the nonexercising adult as well as the athlete with persistent hematuria. The follow-up urinalysis is a critical branching point and indicates the need for medical evaluation if gross or microscopic hematuria persists. In the presence of normal renal function, measurement of serum creatinine and an intravenous pyelogram are appropriate tests. If these tests are negative, an excretory urogram should be followed by cystography to exclude bladder lesions, especially if the patient is over age 40 (Hoover and Cromie, 1981).

A negative work-up at this point should not be repeated after subsequent episodes of exercise-related hematuria that clears with rest. Abnormalities on IVP or cystography are pursued in a conventional manner as shown in the diagram. Athletes with negative tests but persistent hematuria should undergo additional investigation for causes of intrinsic renal disease (Table 13F-1). The IVP confers a risk of osmotic injury to the kidney and some experts argue that a renal ultrasound could replace IVP with a minimal decrease in diagnostic yield and a substantial decrease in risk (Sutton, 1990). The CT scan can best detect small or peripheral renal lesions and may outperform MRI. Retrograde pyelography is done if the IVP completely illuminates the lower urinary tract (Sutton, 1990; Resteop, 1989). Cystoscopy is the next step, and it may provide the best initial results in an actively bleeding patient. Cystoscopy is the best method for studying the bladder and entire male urethra and can provide cytological materials (Finney, 1989). The indications for renal angiography and renal biopsy are controversial. Discussions of the pros and cons are available as are diagnostic algorithms (Sutton, 1990; Finney, 1989; Resteop, 1989; Siegel, 1987). Therapy should be based on a specific diagnosis and be performed by a nephrologist. Athletes with benign hematuria secondary to exercise may continue to be active but they should be encouraged to drink quantities of fluids before exercise and to avoid dehydration.

In summary, pseudonephritis is more common than nephritis. Asymptomatic microhematuria, especially if it occurs only once or twice and is transient, is probably best followed without an invasive work-up. However, persistent or recurrent microhematuria can signal disease, and gross hematuria can foretell bladder cancer, even in young adults (Eichner, 1990). An athlete with intermittent or persistent hematuria, but never more than 2 RBCs/HPF, might be evaluated more completely in the presence of isomorphic RBCs and if other risk factors for bladder cancer such as tobacco use, phenacetin abuse, or exposure to aniline dyes are present (Sutton, 1990; Raghavan, 1990).

A repeat urinalysis at 24-48 hours after the initial observation of microhematuria should always be performed. If the repeat urinalysis is abnormal, a urine culture should be obtained and the urinary infection treated appropriately. Abnormal serum creatinine, BUN, sickle cell prep, and/or IVP will require further evaluation by a urologist. A creatinine clearance and measurement of protein excretion should be performed. Abnormal findings will require further evaluation by a nephrologist. Therapy for athletes and non-athletes with hematuria is mostly dependent upon making an accurate diagnosis.

Physicians can help prevent hematuria by educating athletes. Hematuria from bladder contusions can be prevented by better hydration and not voiding just before running (Blacklock, 1977). Bicycle-hematuria can be prevented by lowering the nose of the saddle, using a special seat cover, and rising off the saddle for bumps. Athletes with sickle-cell trait and infrequent episodes of gross hematuria can continue to participate in sports and exercise.

## Proteinuria

Proteinuria occurs in many types of exercise such as rowing, football, track, long-distance running, swimming, and calisthenics. Its happens more often with severe, strenuous, or prolonged exer-

---

Table 13F-1. Renal Abnormalities in Athletes Requiring Further Evaluation

1. Progressive symptoms: Colic or flank pain.
2. Persistence of hematuria or proteinuria beyond 48 hours after exercise.
3. Urinary casts: Red or white blood cell; pigmented.
4. Positive urine culture for bacterial infection.
5. Oliguria after prolonged, strenuous exercise.

(From Goldszer, Parsee, Siegel. Renal abnormalities during exercise. In Strauss, R.H. (ed) *Sports Medicine* Philadelphia: W.B. Saunders, 130-139, 1984.)

tion. Normal protein excretion is 30-45 mg per day. The degree of exertional proteinuria usually is 2+ — 3+ by dip stick determination, and always transient if due to exercise alone. Quantitative measurements of proteinuria range from 100-300 mg or less in a 24 hour period.

Alterations in renal hemodynamics associated with vigorous exercise are responsible for the proteinuria. A decrease in intravascular volume from acute dehydration may be responsible for proteinuria in athletes undertaking severe exercise. The most commonly observed pattern of renal function in athletes reveals an acute decrease in renal blood flow with maintenance of normal glomerular filtration rate (GFR). Alterations in renal hemodynamics are caused by elevations of renin, angiotensin II, and ADH following sustained, vigorous exercise. Most exercise-induced proteinuria occurs within 30 minute of exercise and clears from the urine within 24-48 hours. When proteinuria is due to exercise alone, most athletes have no long-term sequelae (West, 1981; Peggs, 1986).

Proteinuria initially observed after exertion may be independent of exercise or be secondary to underlying renal disease (Goldszer, 1981). There is a direct relationship between the intensity of exercise and the amount of proteinuria. Figure 13F-2 illustrates an approach to the diagnostic evaluation of proteinuria in the non-exercising and exercising adult. If the urine does not clear within 24-48 hours after exercise, further investigation is indicated. A personal or family history of renal disease, or the presence of hypertension, edema, or anemia suggests a need for further diagnostic testing. Proteinuria that persists for 24-hours after resting should be evaluated by collecting an overnight or supine and upright urine sample to exclude benign orthostatic proteinuria. If proteinuria persists while in the supine position, serum tests for renal function and a 24 hour urine collec-

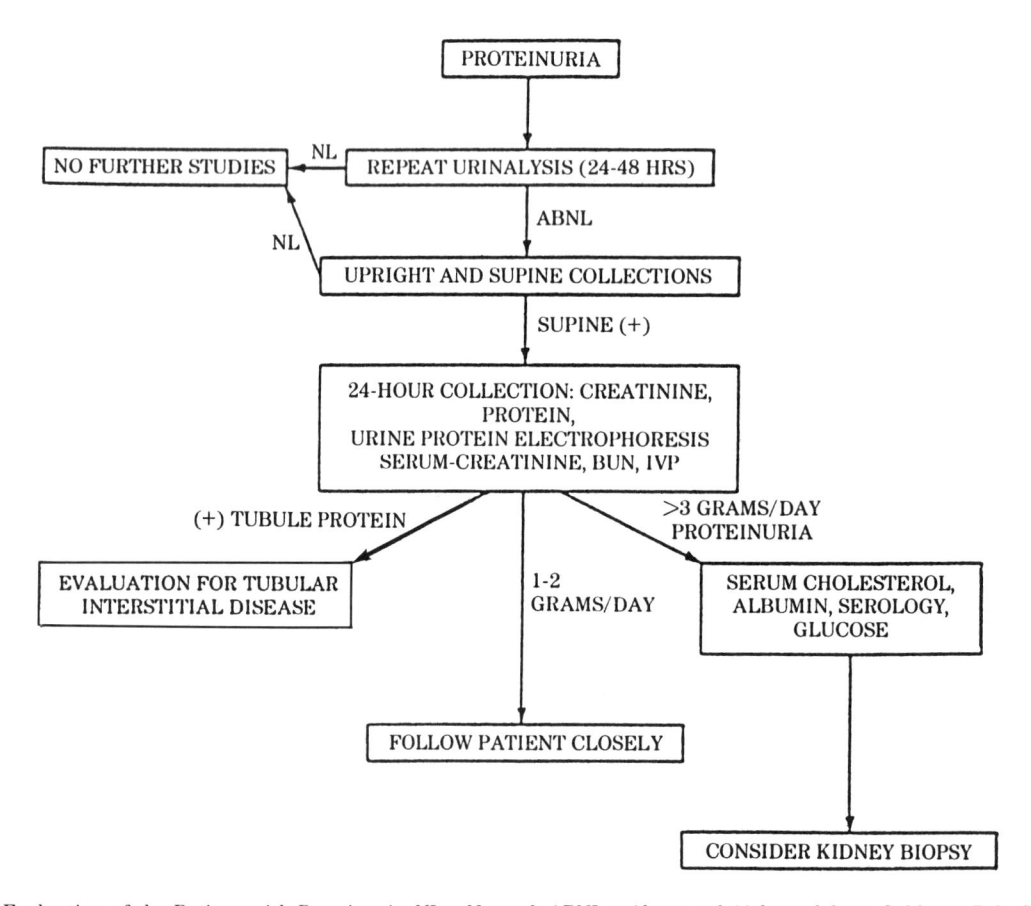

**Fig. 13F-2.** Evaluation of the Patient with Proteinuria. NL = Normal; ABNL = Abnormal (Adapted from Goldszer, R.C., Siegel, A.J. Renal abnormalities during exercise. In Strauss, R.H. (ed.) *Sports Medicine*. Philadelphia: W.B. Saunders, 1984:134.)

tion for creatinine and total protein are useful. The physician also should determine the serum creatinine and blood urea nitrogen levels and obtain a fasting blood glucose and complete blood count.

Urinary protein electrophoresis, creatinine clearance levels and IVP testing should be performed on patients with proteinuria while the patient is in a supine, resting position. Athletes with greater than 1 gram of albumin in a 24 hour urine collection should be referred to a nephrologist for consultation and possible renal biopsy, looking for renal tubular interstitial disease. In general, exercise-induced proteinuria is likely to be recurrent in athletes after physical exertion. There is no evidence to support an increased risk for chronic renal disease or reason to limit physical activity in such individuals. All athletes with proteinuria should have a medical check-up and urinalysis for protein on a yearly basis. No further evaluation is necessary unless other abnormalities are present.

## Hemoglobinuria

Runners may pass a dark red urine that contains hemoglobin pigment. This condition also is found in individuals who do karate. It is secondary to mechanical damage of red blood cells in the soles of the runner's feet or the hands of karate participants. The presence of dark red urine after these activities should indicate the possibility of hemoglobinuria. The condition can be eliminated by running on softer surfaces or padding the hand during karate. This condition usually clears on its own but may require referral to a nephrologist in more complex cases.

## Myoglobinuria

Myoglobinuria may mimic the presence of hematuria. Myoglobin may appear in the urine of runners and wrestlers, and is secondary to hemolysis of extravasated red blood cells from muscle necrosis. Urinalysis frequently shows the presence of myoglobin, hemoglobin, albumin, erythrocytes, and erythrocyte casts in combination with a dark brown urine.

Acute tubular necrosis may follow rhabdomyolysis, the breakdown of muscle. Acute renal failure associated with myoglobinuria is often associated with dehydration. This condition usually should be evaluated by a nephrologist. Myoglobinuria can be prevented by proper conditioning techniques and by avoiding dehydration. Exercise programs that gradually increase in intensity levels will help prevent this syndrome.

## Non-Steroidal Anti-Inflammatory Drug (NSAID) Associated Nephrotoxicity

The widespread use and availability of NSAIDs, and their use by athletes for prophylaxis of minor soft tissue injuries, presents a potentially serious cause of glomerular damage that manifests as proteinuria. Extensive review of the literature supports the view that combinations of antipyretic analgesics taken in large doses over long periods of time can cause kidney disease and chronic renal failure (Johnson, 1984; Kraus, 1984). No evidence has been presented to indicate that the use of single NSAIDs taken in small dosages will cause chronic renal disease. NSAID-associated nephrotoxicity accounts for approximately 2% of end-stage renal disease. The prophylactic use of multiple NSAIDs by some athletes to prevent soft tissue inflammation may lead to long term renal disease and its complications. The practice of using these medications in this manner should be discouraged by the team physician.

## Genital Injuries

A variety of genitourinary injuries may occur in sports, especially gymnastics, cycling, and the martial arts. Trauma to the unprotected perineal area of either sex can result in hematoma formation. In the female, the vulva is highly vascular and hematoma formation may result from a water skiing accident or a fall onto the balance beam in gymnastics. The male scrotum is highly vascular and prone to hematoma or hematocele formation. This can be a result of a kick to the groin or from trauma that traps the testicle and scrotum against the thigh or bony pubis (long-distance cycling). Ice application and rest are the treatment of choice. More difficult cases should be referred to the urologist.

## Injury to the Testicles

The testicles are generally well protected in the male athlete. These paired structures develop in the retroperitomeum adjacent to the fetal kidney and descend into the scrotum during the eighth fetal month. Most male athletes use an athletic supporter to elevate the testicles and decrease the discomfort caused by freely hanging organs.

The testes are prone to the development of contusion, epididymitis, or torsion. Direct trauma to the scrotum may cause testicular contusion. The athlete presents with severe pain, nausea, palor, and anxiety. Place the athlete on his back and flex the thighs to his chest to release the spasm of the cremasteric muscle. Ice to control bleeding and swelling, and elevation for 12 to 24 hours is indicated. If pain and nausea persist, torsion of the testicle must be ruled out and the athlete should be referred to a urologist. All significant testicular injuries should be seen by the team physician as soon as possible. If there is an expanding mass that cannot be transilluminated, or if the epididymis cannot be separated from the testicle, a diagnosis of fracture of the testicle or epididymis should be considered.

Scrotal ultrasound may show disruption of the tunica albuginea or epididymis and may be falsely negative. Radionuclide testicular scan is not very helpful except in delayed evaluation when the viability of the testicle is being considered. Testicular ultrasound should be done quickly to decide whether surgery is needed. If it is, it should be accomplished rapidly with a generous scrotal incision. An orchiectomy is performed in most cases (York, 1990).

Pre-existing scrotal abnormalities may predispose the testicle to increased injury. Consequently, the pre-participation physical examination should carefully evaluate for the presence of undescended testicles which may be due to anorchia, retractile testes, or undescended testes. Unilateral anorchia is found in 5% of boys presenting for surgical exploration. This is most often due to torsion of the testicle and infarction prior to birth and not to hormonal or fertility abnormalities (York, 1990). Most commonly, the undescended testicles reside permanently within the inguinal canal or just inside the internal inguinal ring and cannot be pulled into the scrotum. These testicles require surgical repair. Patients with undescended testicles are at increased risk for developing testicular cancer and they have decreased fertility.

**Torsion of the Spermatic Cord**

A single ligament normally prevents mobility of the testis by attaching the lower end of the spermatic cord and epididymis to the scrotum. If the tunica vaginalis is loosely attached to the scrotal lining, extravaginal torsion may occur as the spermatic cord rotates above the testis. Intravaginal torsion occurs when the tunica vaginalis is attached unusually high on the spermatic cord and allows motion of the testis below the deformity. Contraction of the athlete's cremasteric muscle draws the testis up over the pubis and twists it clear of the cord. Torsion of the spermatic cord is less likely to occur if the athlete wears an athletic supporter.

Diagnosis of torsion of the spermatic cord should be kept in mind whenever an athlete has scrotal pain or swelling. It usually occurs in young athletes who develop increasing abdominal or groin pain. The athlete often suffers abrupt, excruciating testicular pain, vomiting and eventual collapse. A history of a mobile testis should be ascertained. The patient may also present with an abnormal position of the epididymis, induration of the overlying scrotal skin, a high-riding testicle, or possible obliteration of the space between the epididymis and the cord. All of these conditions should alert the physician to the possibility of testicular cord torsion. Testicular cord torsion is a true emergency and warrants prompt urological evaluation. The torsion is commonly related to vigorous activity, but it is also unlikely that activity is responsible for the torsion (Skoglund, 1970).

The physician normally will find localized tenderness, edema, and hyperemia of the scrotal skin, with the scrotal contents adherent to the skin. The vas deferens is inseparable from the swollen, twisted cord. Epididymitis is a common problem to be differentiated from a torsion of the spermatic cord. Elevation of the scrotum usually relieves the pain caused by epididymitis. By contrast, a twisted spermatic cord will cause an increase in testicular and abdominal pain when the scrotum is manually elevated.

If the patient presents within 4-6 hours after cord torsion occurs, cooling of the scrotal skin, xylocaine cord block, and manual derotation may be accomplished and should not delay surgical exploration and repair. Radionucleid scanning may help distinguish torsion from epididymitis; however clinical suspicion should override a negative scan. Also, surgical intervention should not be delayed in order to obtain a scan. Testicular torsion usually can be reduced by external manipulation, and orchiopexy performed by a urologist at a later date. An unreducable torsion of the spermatic cord should undergo operative exploration to prevent infarction of the testis which can occur within hours after the onset of torsion. At surgery, the testis is fixed to the scrotum, a procedure that usually prevents further difficulty. Recent data, however, indicate that if the testis is left in place, an ischemic testicle may cause future infertility secondary to a testicular defect on the contralateral side (York, 1985).

## Scrotal Masses

Evaluation of scrotal masses is common in male athletes. Testicular cancer is the most common malignancy in 16-35 year-old male and an early urologic consultation should be obtained. The presence of a mass in the testicle which is separate from the cord and epididymis is probably due to a malignancy and demands prompt exploration. A mass separate from the testicle should be evaluated by transillumination with a bright light. Masses that cannot be transilluminated should be evaluated by ultrasound and possibly surgical exploration.

Varicocoeles are present in 9%-19% of all men (York, 1990). Varicocoeles are varicosities of the internal spermatic veins and may be described as "a bag of worms" adjacent to the testicle. Seventy percent of varicocoeles are found on the left side, 20% are bilateral, and 10% are on the right side. Surgical correction of these lesions may be indicated for pain control, diminished ipsilateral testicular size, or infertility. Cystic masses within the epididymis or adjacent to the testicle are probably spermatoceles, caused by extravasation of sperm from the epididymis following trauma or infection. They require no treatment unless they are extremely large or painful (York, 1990). A cystic mass which surrounds the testicle and epididymis is usually a hydrocele which is caused by decreased absorption of the normal tunica vaginalis secretions due to trauma, infection, or tumors. An acute hydrocele may contain an underlying malignancy and should be investigated by ultrasound or possibly surgical exploration. Traumatic or infectious hydrocele may become large enough to cause significant pain and surgical correction is usually required.

## Epididymitis

Testicular pain in male athletes commonly involves a differential diagnosis of spermatic cord torsion or epididymitis. A tender, indurated epididymis may be felt in early epididymitis. Later, the area will become hard and fixed to the skin and the spermatic cord will be swollen and indurated. The patient may develop a fever and an elevated white blood cell count. Urinalysis is usually positive for leucocytes. Treatment consists of bed rest, Sitz baths, and scrotal support on towels. The etiologic agent in men under age 35 is usually chlamydia, and E. coli over age 35. Cultures should be obtained for gonococcal infections. If gonococcal organisms are not found on culture, treatment with Doxycycline 100mg BID or tetracycline 500 mg QID is required for 10-14 days (York, 1990).

## Penile and Urethral Injuries

The penis is seldom injured in sports because most athletes wear an athletic supporter that holds the penis firmly against the body. Traumatic irritation of the pudendal nerve in bicycle racers or touring cyclists may cause priapism or ischemic neuropathy of the penis. These symptoms usually resolve when the bicycle race is over. Cyclists should be advised to use a furrowed saddle and not squeeze the saddle on uphill climbs.

The erect penis is susceptible to acute trauma and acute fractures of the tunica albuginea. The area of fracture is swollen and ecchymotic and the penis is bent to the affected side. This injury is a true urologic emergency necessitating evacuation of the hematoma and repair of the tunica tear. The patient usually neglects to mention his sexual activity that caused the fracture and ascribes the injury to work or sport-related trauma. Direct blows to the flaccid penis or perineum may lead to vascular injuries and potential impotency. These injuries are caused by straddle-type injuries or direct blows to the pubis such as spearing with football helmets. Similar mechanisms could lead to total disruption of the male urethra although this has not been described during sports activities. In the presence of these injuries, a retrograde urethrogram should be performed. Primary repair may be an option, but recent reports indicate that insertion of a transcutaneous suprapubic catheter leads to resolution of the urethral tear in approximately 20% of cases (Morehouse, 1988). Penile frostbite has been described in runners who wear inadequate clothing in very cold weather. Obviously, adequate protection of the penis and perineum in extremely cold weather is mandatory.

Partial or complete rupture of the athlete's urethra may occur when the athlete falls astride a fixed object. Immediate pain, swelling, and perineal ecchymosis usually results. Early passage of a Foley catheter into the bladder may obscure a complete rupture of the urethra after urethral injury and convert a partial urethral rupture into a complete one. A diagnostic retrograde urethrogram should be performed before urethral catheterization. A Foley catheter may be inserted if there is minor injury to the urethra. A completely ruptured urethra should be operatively repaired. The urologist likely will insert a suprapubic cystotomy to divert the urinary stream.

## Injuries to the Female Genitalia

Blunt trauma can damage the distal urethra of the female but this is rare as it is well protected. A forced water douche resulting from a fall during water skiing may cause an incomplete, spontaneous abortion as well as salpingitis. Such a douche can inject water past the vulva into the vagina and oviducts. To avoid this type of injury, female water skiers should wear rubber pants while skiing. Application of ice packs is useful in treating most vulvar hematomas and other common injuries to the external female genitalia.

## Genitourinary Infections

### Urethritis

Sexually transmitted diseases are the most common urologic problem of the athlete. Nongonococcal urethritis (NGU) is the most common disorder found in the athletic population. Patients present with dysuria and a urethral discharge. The workup should include serologic testing for syphilis and culturing for gonococcus. A blood agar medium and a non-cotton urethral swab should be used to test for chlamydia and Ureaplasma. Chlamydia infections respond to a 7 day course of tetracycline 500 mg QID or Doxycycline 100 mg BID for 10-14 days. A complete sexual history should be obtained as these infections may be reportable, depending on state law. Sexual partners should be appropriately treated and the patient should be cautioned either to abstain from sexual activity or use a condom during treatment until follow-up cultures are negative.

Gonococcal urethritis involves a history of dysuria, penile discharge 2-8 days post-exposure, and the presence of a positive gonococcal culture. Concomitant chylamydial infection is found in 25%-45% of cases (York, 1990). Due to the prevalence of penicillinase producing Neisseria and tetracycline resistant strains, the patient should be treated with intramuscular Ceftriaxome 250 mg followed by Doxycycline orally 100 mg BID for 10 days. All sexual contacts should be appropriately cultured and treated. Tests for syphilis and HIV should be offered to the patient.

### Prostatitis

Prostatitis involves a history of lower abdominal pain, urethral discharge, and dysuria. The prostate is usually swollen on physical examination but not always. A urinalysis which will show increased numbers of leukocytes in the urine. Treatment for prostatitis involves tetracycline 500 mg QID or Doxycycline 100 mg BID or Bactrium DS BID for 10-14 days.

### Venereal Warts

Condyloma acuminatum is a commonly seen sexually transmitted disease. An increased finding of abnormal cervical pap smears due to the papilloma virus has made it important that venereal warts are appropriately diagnosed and treated. These warts appear as papillary growths on the shelf of the penis, perineum, scrotum, and anal areas. If no lesions are visible, the affected areas are wrapped with a 2% acetic acid — soaked gauze pad for 10 minutes and then examined under magnification. Areas of papilloma virus will appear in a bright light.

Treatment of venereal warts involves freezing, electrical cautery, laser ablation, or local application of 10%-25% podophyllin in benzoin. Recurrence rates for venereal warts is up to 80% regardless of the treatment. The use of carbon dioxide laser at 1-2 watts seems to lead to fewer recurrences with minimal ulceration and scar formation. The use of condoms for three months with frequent examinations during that time is indicated. Intraurethral lesions should be treated with urethroscopy and laser ablation or daily intraurethral installation of 5-fluorouracil (5%) for a month.

### Herpes Simplex

Herpes progenitalis is a chronic disease with no known cure and presents as an edematous wheal with small vesicles that resolve in 7-10 days. These lesions are painful and become secondarily infected. Topical application of Acyclovir ointment or cream is used to decrease pain and works best when the first prodromal symptoms occur. Oral Acyclovir, 200 mg 5xdaily for 7-10 days may decrease pain or shorten the active period of these lesions. The virus will reside continually in the nerve ganglia so that no form of therapy completely resolves the problem. Daily suppression with Acyclovir in patients with multiple recurrences of herpes simplex has resulted in 75% of cases showing significant reduction in recurrence rates (Medical Letter, 1988). Due to the extreme contagiousness of herpes simplex, patients should abstain from sexual activity during the infectious stage.

**REFERENCES**

*Section A. Chest*

American College of Sports Medicine Committee Guidelines for Athletic Bras, 1979.
Berson, B. Surgical repair of pectoralis major rupture in an athlete. *Am J Sports Med* 7:348, 1979.
Casamassima, A.C., Sternberg, T., Weiss, F.H. Spontaneous pneumopericardium. *Phys and SportsMed* 19(6):107-110, 1991.
Cauther, M.A., Welsh, M.B. Muscle rupture affecting the shoulder girdle, In Rockwood, C.A. Jr., Matsen, F.A. (Eds): *The Shoulder*. Philadelphia, PA, W.B. Saunders Company, pgs. 864-866, 1990.
Chetty, K.G. and Davidson, P.T. A guide to the management of hemothorax. *Hospital Medicine* 25:6, 1975.
DeHaven, K. Chest injuries: comparison by age, sport, and gender. *Am J Sports Med* 14(3):218, 1986.
Eichelberger, M.R. Torso injuries in athletes. *Phys and Sportsmed* 9:87, 1981.
Galladay, E.S., Donahoo, J.S., and Haller, J.A. Special problems of cardiac injuries in infants and children. *J of Trauma* 19:526, 1981.
Gehlsen, G. and Albohm, M. Evaluation of sports bras. *Phys and Sportsmed* 8:89, 1980.
Haycock, C. The female athlete and sports medicine in the 70's. *J Florida MA* 67:411, 1980.
Haycock, C. Breast support and protection in the female athlete. *AAHPER Research Consortium Symposium Papers*, I:2, 1978.
Kretzler, H.H. Jr., Richardson, A.B. Rupture of the pectoralis major muscle. *Am J Sports Med* 17(4):453-458, 1989.
Leffert, R.D., Rowe C.R. Tendon Ruptures, in Rowe, C.R. (Ed). *The Shoulder*. New York, NY, Churchill Livingston Publishers, pgs. 152-153, 1988.
Levit, F. Jogger's nipple. *JAMA* 297:1127, 1977.
Martinez, J., McNulty, P.A. et al. Trauma rounds: a fractured sternum. *EmergMed* 51(3):30, 1984.
Mattox, K.L. Management of penetrating chest trauma. *Hospital Med* 8:6, 1977.
McMaster, P.E. Tendon and muscle ruptures: clinical and experimental studies on the courses and locations of subcutaneous ruptures. *J of Bone Joint Surgery* 1933, 50:705-722, 1933.
Otis, C.L. The female athlete-special concerns. *Sports Med Digest* 8(10):2, 1986.
Park, J.Y., Aespiniella, J.L. Rupture of pectoralis major muscle: a case report and review of the literature. *J Bone Joint Surgery* (AM), 53:577-581, 1970.
Richardson, A.B. Overview of soft tissue injuries of the shoulder, in Nicholas, J.A., Hershman, E.D., Posner, M.A. (Eds) *The Upper Extremity in Sports Medicine*. St. Louis, MO:C.V. Mosby Company, pgs. 228, 1990.
Rutherford, G.W. and Miles, R.B. Overview of sports related injuries to persons 5-14 years of age. *Report of U.S. Consumer Products Safety Commission*, pp. 17-20, 1981.
Ryan, A.J. *Medical Care of the Athlete*. New York: The Blakeston Division of McGraw-Hill Book Co., 1962.
Shangold, M., Mirkin, T. Women and Exercise. Philadelphia, PA:F.A. Davis Company, 1988. Smyth, B.T. Chest trauma in children. *J Ped Surg* 14:41, 1982.
Thomas, C. Factors important to women participants in vigorous athletics. *Sports Medicine Physiology*. Philadelphia: W.B. Saunders & Co, 1979.
Zeman, S.C. et al. Tears of the pectoralis major muscle. *AmJSportsMed* 7:343, 1979.

*Section B. Cardiovascular*

16th Bethesda Conference — Cardiovascular Abnormalities in the Athlete: Recommendations Regarding Eligibility for Competition. Journal of American College of Cardiology, 6:1189-1192, 1985.
Allen, C.J., Carvensy, M.A., Rosenbloom, D., Sutton, J.R. Beta-blockade and exercise in normal subjects and patients with coronary artery disease. *Phys and Sportsmed* 12:51-74, 1984.
American College of Sports Medicine Guidelines for Exercise Testing and Prescription, 3rd Edition, Eta and Fiber, 1986.
Amsterdam E.A., Wilmore, J.H. and Demaria, A.N. Exercise and Cardiovascular Health and Disease. Disturbance of Cardiac Rhythm and Conduction Induced by Exercise; Diagnostic, Prognostic and Therapeutic Implications, p. 209-217, 1977.
Arbogast, R.C. and White, R.S. Idiopathic hypertrophic subaortic stenosis. *American Family Physician* 24:97, 1981.
Blackburn, H. Physical activity and hypertension. *J Clinical Hypertension* 2(2):154-162, 1986.
Blackburn, H. Coronary disease prevention: Practical Approaches to Risk Factor Changes. *ADV Cardiology* 20:1, 1977.
Blackburn, H. Non-pharmacologic treatment of hypertension. *Annals of New York Academy of Science* 304:236, 1978.
Blair, S.N., Kolh, H.W., Paffenbarger, R.S. et al. Physical fitness and all-cause mortality: a prospective study of healthy men and women. *JAMA* 262(17):2395-2401, 1989.
Blair, S.M., Jacobs, D.R. Jr., Powell, K.E. Relationships between exercise for physical activity and other health behaviors. *Public Health Rep* 100(2):172-180, 1985.
Boyer, J.L. and Kasch, F.W. Exercise therapy in hypertensive men. *JAMA* 211:1668, 1970.
Bruce, R.A., Hossack, K.F. Rationale of physical training in patients with angina pectoris. *Advances in Cardiology* 31:186-190, 1982.
Choquette, G. and Ferguson, R.J. Blood pressure reduction in "borderline" hypertensives following physical training. *Canadian Medical Association Journal* 108:699, 1973.
Coberg, L., Elliot, D.L. The effect of exercise on lipid metabolism in men and women. *Sports Medicine* 4(5):307-321, 1987.
Cook, T.C., LaPorte, R.E., Washburn, R.A. et al. Chronic low level physical activity as a determinant of high density lipoprotein, cholesterol and subfractions. *Med Sci Sports Exer* 18(6):653-657, 1986.
Daniels, J. and Schweitzer, P. Unusual causes of sudden unexplained death. *Primary Cardiology* pgs. 75-84, July 1984.
Dibianco, R., Estes, N.A., Horowitz, L.N. Non-drug treatment for arrhythmias. *Patient Care* 525, pgs. 24-56, Feb. 15, 1991.
Duren, D.R., Becker, A.E., Dunning, A.J. Exercise during follow-up of idiopathic mitral valve prolapse in 300 patients: a prospective study. *J Am Col Cardiology* 11:42-47, 1988.
Eichner, E.R. Sickle cell trait and risk of exercise-induced death. *Phys and Sportsmed* 15(12):41-43, 1987.
Fisher, J.D., Kim, S.G, Mercando, A.D. Electrical devices for treatment of arrhythmias. *Am J Cardiology* 61:45a-57a, 1988.
Fraser, G.E. Can exercise prevent or reduce hypertension? *Primary Cardiology* 159-174, March 1985.
Froelicher, V.F. and McHenry, P.L. A symposium: Future Directions in Exercise Testing and Exercise Electrocardiography, Part I and II, *Am J of Cardiology* 47:1141, 1981.
Ghilarducci, L.E., Holly, R.G., Amsterdam, E.A. Effects of high resistance training in coronary artery disease. *Am J Cardiology* 67(14):866-870, 1989.
Gibbons, L.W., Cooper K.H. and Meyer B.M. Acute risk of strenuous exercise. *JAMA* 244:1799, 1980.
Goldberg, L., Elliott, D.L. The effects of exercise on lipid metabolism in men and women. *Sports Medicine*, 4(5):307-321, 1987.
Goldfin, E.H., Ward, A., Taylor, P. et al. Exercising to health: what's really in it for your patients. *Phys and SportsMed* 19(6):81-91, 1991.
Graboys, P.D. and Posser, R. Can sudden cardiac death be prevented? *Drug Therapy* pgs. 181-186, December 1982.
Halpern, B.C. et. al. Exercise in the hypertensive athlete. *J Am Board Fam Prac* pg. 17, April-June 1988.
Herley, D.F., Kokkinos, B.F. Effects of weight-training on risk factors for coronary artery disease. *Sports Medicine* 4(4):231-238, 1987.
Herley, D.F., Hagberg, J.M., Goldberg, A.P. et al. Resistive training can re-

duce coronary risk factors without altering VO₂max or percent body fat. *Med Sci Sports Exer* 20(2):150-154, 1988.

Hinkle, L.E. Precipitating factors in sudden death. *Cardiology Consultation* 3:182, 1982.

Huston, T.P., Puffer, J.C., Rodney, W.M. The athletic heart syndrome. *NEJM* 313:24, 1985.

Itskovitz, H.D. Alpha1 blockers. *Postgraduate Med* 89(8):89-110, 1989.

Jennings, G., Nelson, L., Nestel, P. et al. The effects of changes in physical activity on major cardiovascular risk factors, hemodynamics, sympathetic function, and glucose utilization in man: a controlled study of four levels of activity. *Circulation* 73(1):30-40, 1986.

Jeresaty, R.M. MVP definition and implication in athletes. *JACC* 7(1):231, 1986.

Kannel, W.B. Cardiovascular consequences of physical inactivity. *Primary Cardiology* pp. 74-90, April, 1984.

Kannel, W.B., Sorlie, P.D. Some health benefits of physical activity: the Framingham Study. *Archives Internal Medicine* 139:857-861, 1979.

Kark, J.A., Posey, D.M., Schumacher, H.R. et al. Sickle cell trait as a risk factor for sudden death in physical training. *NEJM* 317:781-787, 1987.

Kepowell, K.E., Thompson, P.D., Caspersen, C.G., et al. Physical activity and the incidence of coronary heart disease. *Annual Review of Public Health* 1987;8:253-287.

Kuller, L. Lilienfield, A. and Fisher, R. Epidemiologic study of sudden and unexpected death due to arterial stenotic heart disease. *Circulation* 34:1056, 1966.

Laslett, J., Paumer, L., Scott-Baier, P., et al. Efficacy of exercise training in patients with coronary artery disease who are taking propranolol. *Circulation*. 68:1029, 1983.

MacMahon, S.W., Wilcen, D.E., McDonald, G.J. The effect of weight reduction on left ventricular mass: a randomized control trial in young, overweight hypertensive patients. *NEJM* 314(16):334-339, 1986.

Malacoff, R.F. Sudden cardiac death. *Postgraduate Medicine* 75:69, 1984.

Marron, B.J., Roberts, W.C., McAllister, H.A. Jr., Rosing, D.R., Epstein, S.E. Sudden deaths in young athletes. *Circulation* 62:218, 1980.

Marron, B.J., Gaffney, F.A., Jeresaty, R.M., McKenna, W.J., Miller, W.W. Task force III: hypertrophic cardiomyopathy, other myopericardial diseases and MVP. *Journal American College of Cardiology*. 6:1215, 1985.

Martin, J.E., Dubbert, D.M., Cushman, W.C. Controlled trial of aerobic exercise in hypertension. *Circulation*, 81(5):1560-1567, 1990.

O'Hare, J.A., Murnaghan, D.J. Failure of anti-hypertensive drugs to control blood pressure rise with isometric exercise in hypertension. *Postgrad Med* 57(671):552-555, 1981.

Orenstein, D.M. Exercise in the Young. *Comprehensive Therapy*, 11(1):38-47, 1985.

Paffenbarger, S., Hyde, R.T., et al. Physical activity, all cause mortality, and longevity of college alumni. *NEJM* 314(10):605-613, 1986.

Podalsky, M.L. Don't rule out sports for hypertensive children. *Phys and Sports Med* 76(9):164-170, 1989.

Powles, A. The effect of drugs on the cardiovascular response to exercise. *Medical Science Sports and Exercise*. 13:252, 1981.

Reet, R.C., Bach, E.L., Johnson, C. Pectoralis major rupture: diagnosing and treating a weight-training injury. *Phys and SportsMed* 19(3):89-96, 1991.

Report of the 2nd Task Force on Blood Pressure Control in Children, 1987. National Heart, Lung and Blood Institute, Bethesda, MD, 79(1):1-25, 1987.

Ressel, J., Chrastek, J. and Jandova, R. Hemodynamic effects of physical training in essential hypertension. *Acta Cardiology* 32:121, 1977.

Rocchini, A.P. Childhood hypertension:etiology, diagnosis and treatment. *Ped Clinics North Am* 81(6):1259-1273, 1989.

Roeske, W.R., O'Rourke, R.A., Klein, A., Leopold, G. and Karlier, J.S. Non-invasive evaluation of ventricular hypertrophy in professional athletes. *Circulation* 53:286, 1976.

Ryan, A.J. Heart size in sports. *Phys and Sportsmed* 8:30, 1980.

Seals, D.R., Hagber, J.M. The effects of exercise training on human hypertension: a review. *Med Sci Sports Exer* 16(3):207-215, 1984.

Shepard, R.J. Exercise therapy in patients with angina pectoris. *Advances in Cardiology* 31:191-198, 1982.

Siscovick, D.S., Weiss, N.S., Hallstrom, A.P., Inui, T.S. and Peterson, D.R. Physical activity in primary cardiac arrest. *JAMA* 248:3113, 1982.

Siscovick, D.S., Weiss, M.S., Fletcher, R.H., Lasky, T. The incidence of primary cardiac arrest during vigorous exercise. *NEJM* 311:874, 1984.

Spain, D.N., Barades V.A., and Mohr, C. Coronary atherosclerosis as a cause of unexpected and unexplained death. *JAMA* 174:384, 1960.

Storer, T.W. and Ruhing, R.O. Essential hypertension in exercise. *Phys and Sportsmed* 9:59, 1981.

Teare, D. A symetrical hypertrophy of the heart in young adults. British Heart Journal 20:1, 1958.

The recommended quantity and quality of exercise for developing and maintaining cardiorespiratory and muscular fitness in healthy adults. *Med Sci Sports Exer* 22:2, 1990.

Theine, G., Nava, A., Corrado, D. et al. Right ventricular cardiomyopathy in sudden death in young people. *NEJM* 318:129-133, 1988.

Thompson, P.D., Funk, E.J., Carleton, R.A., et. al. Incidence of death during jogging in Rhode Island from 1975-1980. *JAMA* 247:2535, 1982.

Thompson, P.D., Stern, M.P., Williams, P. et al. Death during jogging or running: a study of 18 cases. *JAMA*, 242:1265-1267, 1979.

Topaz, O., Edwards, J.E. Pathologic features of sudden death in children, adolescents and young adults. *Chest* 87:476-482, 1985.

Tunstall-Pedo D: Exercise and Sudden Death. *British Journal of Sports Medicine* 12:215, 1979.

VanCamp, S.P. Exercise-related sudden death: risk and causes. *Phys and Sportsmed* 16(5):97-110, 1988.

VanCamp, S.P. Exercise-related sudden death: cardiovascular evaluation of exercise (Part 2). *Phys and Sportsmed* 16(6):47-53, 1988.

Virmani, R., Robinowitz, M., McAllister, H. Non-traumatic death in joggers. A series of thirty patients at autopsy. *Am J Med* 72:874-882, 1982.

Virmani, R. Jogging, marathon running and death. *Primary Cardiology* Vol 96, 1982.

Virmani, R., Robinowitz, M. and McAllister, H.A. Jr. Exercise and the heart. A review of cardiac pathology associated with physical activity. *Pathological Annual* 20:431, 1985.

Waller, B.F. Exercise-related sudden death in young (age < 30 yrs) and old (age > 30 yrs) conditioned subjects. In Wenger, N.K. (ed.) *Exercise and the Heart* 2nd Edition, Philadelphia, PA, F.A. Davis Company, pgs. 9-73, 1985.

Waller, B.F., Roberts, W.C. Sudden death while running in conditioned runners aged 40 years or older. *Am J Cardiology* 45:1292-1300, 1980.

Williams, R.S., Logue, E., Lewis, J.G., et al. Physical conditioning augments the fibrinolytic response to venous occlusion in healthy adults. *NEJM* 1980 302(18):1987-1991, 1980.

Wolfel, E., Hiatt, W., Brammel, H., et al. Effects of selective and non-selective beta-adrenergic blockaid on mechanisms of exercise conditioning. *Circulation*. 74:664, 1986.

Wood, D.L. Potentially lethal ventricular arrhythmias. *Postgrad Med* 88(6):65-74, 1990.

Zabetakis, P.M. Exercise and mild hypertension. *Primary Cardiology* 47-63, August 1984.

Zimmer, S.H., Martin, L.F., Sacks, F. et al. A longitudinal study of blood pressure and childhood. *Am J Epidemiology* 100(6):4367-442, 1975.

### Section C. Pulmonary

Anderson, S.D. EIA: New thinking and current management. *J of Respiratory Diseases*. p. 48, November 1986.

Anderson, S.D. Issues in exercise-induced asthma. *J Allergy and Clinical Immunology*.

Barnes, P.J., Wilson, M., Brown, M. A calcium antagonist, nifedipine, modifier in exercise-induced asthma. *Thorax* 36:726-730, 1981.

Barnes, P.J., Brown, J.J., Silverman, M. et al. Circulating catecholamines in exercise and hyperventilation-induced asthma. *Thorax* 36:435-440, 1981.

DiPalma, J.R. Beta2 agonists for acute asthma. *Am Fam Phys* 31(5):184, 1986. Gropp, J.A. Exercise-induced asthma. *Pediatric Clinics of North America*. 22:63, 1975.

Karofsky, P.S. Hyperventilation syndrome in adolescent athletes. *Phys and Sportsmed* 15(2):133, 1987.

Lee, T.H., Assoufi, B., Kay, A. The link between exercise, respiratory heat exchange, and the mast cell and bronchial asthma. *Lancet* 1:520-522, 1983.

Lewis, B.L. The hyperventilation syndrome. *Annals Int Med* 38:918, 1983.

McFadden, E.R. Jr, Ingram, R.H. Jr. Exercise-induced asthma: observations on the initiating stimulus. *NEJM* 301:763, 1979.

Pfeiffer, R.P., Young, T.R. Case report. Spontaneous pneumothorax in a jogger. *Phys and Sportsmed* 8:65, 1980.

Prenner, B.M. When asthma is induced by exercise. *Diagnosis* p.71, May 1986.

Smith, C.M., Anderson, S.D. Hyperosmolarity as the stimulus to asthma induced by hyperventilation. *J of Allergy and Clinical Immuniology* 77:729-736, 1986.

### Section D. Abdomen

Bergqvist, H., et al. Abdominal injury from sporting activities. *Br J SportsMed* 16:76, 1982.

Cantwell, J.D. and King, J.T. Karate chops and liver lacerations. *JAMA* 224:1424, 1973.

Fischer, R.P., Beverlin, B.C., Engrav, L.H., et al. Diagnostic peritoneal lavage, 14 years and 2,586 patients later. *AmJSurg* 136:701, 1978.

Frelinger, D.P. The ruptured spleen in college athletes: a preliminary report. *J Am Health Assoc* 26:217, 1978.

Soballe, P.W. Peritoneal lavage in blunt abdominal trauma. *AFP* 29(3):193, 1983.

### Section E. Back

Babcock, J.L. Spinal injuires in children. *Pediatric Clinics of North Am* 22:487, 1975.

Borenstein, D., Weisel, S. *Low Back Pain — Medical Diagnosis and Comprehensive Management*, Philadelphia, PA:W.B. Saunders Co., 1989.

Bundenf, D.A., Rechdine, G.R. Lumbar nerve root injection as an adjunct of sciatica diagnosis. *Orthopedic Review* 14:64-68, 1985.

Cailliet, R. *Soft Tissue Pain and Disability*. Philadelphia:F.A. Davis Co. pp. 41-106, 1977.

Calin, A. Back pain: mechanical or inflammatory? *AmFamPhys* 20:97, 1979.

Ciullo, J.V., Jackson, D.W. Pars interarticular stress reaction, spondylolysis and spondlyolesthesis. *Clinics in Sports Medicine* 4:95-109, 1985.

Cousins, M.J., Bridenbough, D.O. (eds.) *Neuroblockaid and Clinical Anesthesia and Management of Pain* 2nd Edition, New York, NY, Lippincott and Company, 1988.

DeOrio, J.K. and Bianco, A.J. Lumbar disk excision in children and adolescents. *J Bone Joint Surg* 64:991, 1982.

Destouet, J.M., Murphy, W.A. Lumbar facet block indications and technique. *Orthopedic Review* 14:280-285, 1985.

Ferguson, R.H. McMaster, J.H. and Stanitski, C.L. Low back pain in college football linemen. *AmJSportsMed* 2:63, 1974.

Foster, D.N., Fulton, M.N. Pain in the exercise prescription. *Clinics in Sports Med* 10(1):197-209, 1991.

Fredrickson, B.S. Natural history of spondylolysis and spondylolesthesis. *J Bone Joint Surg* 66-A(5):699, 1983.

Frymoyer, J. Back pain and sciatica. *NEJM* 313:291, 1988.

Frymoyer, J.W., Pope, M.H., Clements, J.H., et al. Risk factors in low back pain: an epidemiologic survey. *J Bone Joint Surg* 65-A:213, 1983.

Gelabert, R. Dancer's spinal syndrome. *JOSPT* 7:180, 1986.

Gibson, M. et al. Magnetic resonance imaging of adolescent discherniation. *J Bone Joint Surg* 69B:699, 1987.

Halpern, B.C, Smith, A.D. Catching the cause of low back pain. *Phys and Sportsmed* 19(6):71-79, 1991.

Ippolito, E. and Ponseti, I.V. Juvenile kyphosis: histological and histochemical studies. *J Bone Joint Surg* 63:175, 1981.

Jackson, D.W. and Wiltse, L.L. Stress reaction involving the pars interarticulars in young athletes. *Phys and Sportsmed* 9:304, 1981.

Jackson, D.W. and Wiltse, L.L. Low back pain in young athletes. *Phys and Sportsmed* 53, 1974.

Jackson, D.W. Low back pain in young athletes: evaluation of stress reaction and discogenic problems. *Am J Sports Med* 7:364, 1979.

Jacobs, B. Low back pain: the orthopedists' views. *Drug Therapy*, pp. 77-86, Dec. 1982.

Keene, J.S. Goletz, T.H. and Benson, R.C. Undetected genitourinary dysfunction in vertebral fractures. *J Bone Joint Surg* 62:997, 1980.

Keene, J.S. Low back pain in the athlete from spondylogenic injury during recreation and competition. *PostgradMed* 74:209, 1983.

Kirkady-Willis, W. (ed.) *Managing Low Back Pain* (2nd ed.) New York, NY: Churchill Livingstone, 1988.

Kulund, D.W. *The Injured Athlete*. Philadelphia, J.P. Lippincott Co, 1982:345-6.

Libson, E. Oblique lumbar spine radiographs: importance in young patients. *Radiology* 151:89, 1984.

McKenzie, R. A lumbar spine mechanical diagnosis and therapy. Waikanae, New Zealand, Spinal Publications, 1985.

Micheli, L.J. et al. Use of modified Boston brace for back injuries in athletes. *Am J Sports Med* 8:351, 1980.

Nicol, R.O., Scott, J.H. Lytic spondylolysis: repair by wiring. *Spine* 11(10): 1027-1030, 1986.

Oudenhoven, R. The role of laminectomy, facet rhizotomy and epidural steroids. *Spine* 4:145, 1979.

Pacelli, L.C. Straight talk on posture. *Phys Sportsmed* 19(2):124-127, 1991.

Rosenthal, D.I. CT scanning for disc disease. *J Fam Pract* 7-10, March 1984.

Rowlingson, J.C. The evaluation and management of acute low back pain. *Current Concepts in Pain* 1:3, 1983.

Sheehan, N.J. and Mathews, J.A. Options for treating low back pain. *Drug Therapy* 153-169, March 1984.

Stanitski, C.L. Low back pain in young athletes. *Phys and Sportsmed* 10:77, 1982.

VanHoesen, L. Mobilization of manipulation techniques for the lumbar spine. In Grieve, G.P. (ed.) *Modern Manual Therapy of the Vertebral Column*. New York, NY: Churchill Livingstone, 1986.

Wilson, F.D. and Lindseth, R.E. The adolescent swimmer's back. *Am J Sports Med* 10:174, 1982.

Wiltse, L.L. Widell, E.H. and Jackson, D.W. Fatigue fracture: the basic lesion in isthmic spondylolithesis. *J Bone Joint Surg* 57-A:17, 1975.

Wiltse, L.L. and Levine D.B. Spondylolithesis. *Aches & Pains* pp. 8-16, March, 1984.

### Section F. Genital Urinary

Blacklock, M.J. Bladder trauma in the long-distance runner (10,000 meters hematuria). *British J Urology* 1977 49(2):129-132.

Castenfors, J. Renal clearance of urinary sodium and potassium excretion and supine exercise in normal subjects. *ACTA Physiologika Scandanavia* 70:204-214, 1967.

Castenfors, J. Renal function during prolonged exercise. *Annals of New York Academy of Science* 301:151, 1978.

Eichner, E.R. Hematuria — a diagnostic challenge. *Phys and Sportsmed* 18(11):53-63, 1990.

Finney, J., Baum, N. Evaluation of hematuria. *Postgrad Med* 1989 85(8): 44-47, 51-53.

Gardner, K.D. Jr. Athletic pseudonephritis — alteration of urine sediment by athletic competition. *JAMA* 161:1613-1617, 1956.

Goldszer, Parsee, and Siegel. Renal abnormalities during exercise. *Your Patient and Fitness* 1(3):6-9, 1987.

Hoover, D.L., Cromie, W.J. Theory and management of exercise-related hematuria. *Phys and Sportsmed* 9:91, 1981.

Johnson, P.J. Nephrotoxicity associated with the use of nonsteroidal anti-inflammatory drugs. *JAMA* 251(23):3123, 1984.

Kraus, S.E., Siroky, M.B., Babayan, R.K. et al. Hematuria and the use of non-steroidal anti-inflammatory drugs. *Urol* 132(2):288-290, 1984.

Mandell, J. et al. Sports-related genitourinary injuries in children. *Clinics in Sports Med* 1:483-492, 1982.

Mariani, A.J., Mariani, M.C., Macchioni, C. et al. The significance of adult hematuria: 1000 hematuria dilations including a risk/benefit and cost/effective analysis. *J of Urology* 141(2):350-355, 1989.

Mohr, D.N., Offord, K.T., Owen, R.A., et al. Asymptomatic microhematuria and neurologic disease. A population-based study. *JAMA* 256(2): 224-229, 1986.

Morehouse, D.D. Delayed management of external urethral injuries. In Cass, A. (ed.) *Genital Urethral Trauma* Oxford, England, Blackwell Scientific Publications, pgs. 209-222, 1988.

O'Brien, K. Biker's bladder. *NEJM* 304(22):1367:1981.

Peggs, J.F. et al. Proteinuria in adolescent sports physical examinations. *JFP* 22:80-81, 1986.

Raghavan, D., Shipley, W.U., Garnick, M.B. et at. Biology and management of bladder cancer. *NEJM* 322(16):1129-1138, 1990.

Restepo, M.C., Carey, P.O. Evaluating hematuria in adults. *Am Fam Phys* 40:149-156, 1989.

Siegel, A.J. Urinary abnormalities in athletes. *Your Patient and Fitness* 1(3):6-9, 1987.

Skoglund, R.W., McRoberts, J.W., Ragde, H. Torsion of the spermatic cord: a review of the literature and an analysis of 17 cases. *J of Urology* 104(4):604-607, 1970.

Strauss, R.H. (ed.) *Sports Medicine* Philadelphia: W.B. Saunders, 130-139, 1984.

Sutton, J.M. Evaluation of hematuria in adults. *JAMA*, 263(18):2475-2480, 1990.

Vehaskari, V.M., Rapola, J., Koskimies, O., et al. Microscopic hematuria in school children: epidemiology and clinicalpathologic evaluation. *J Peds* 95(5 Part I):676-684, 1979.

West, C.D., Shapiro, F.L., Swartz, C.D. Proteinuria in the athlete. *Phys and Sportsmed* 9:45, 1981.

York, J.P. Sports and the male genital-urinary system. *Phys and Sportsmed* 18(10):92-100, 1990.

York, J.P., Drago, J.R. Torsion and the contralateral testicle. *J Urol* 133(2): 294-297, 1985.

## SUGGESTED READINGS

### Section A. Chest

Kulund, D.M. *The Injured Athlete*. Philadelphia: J.B. Lippincott Co. 332, 1982.

O'Donoghue, D.H. *Treatment of Athletic Injuries* (3rd Ed). Philadelphia: W.B. Saunders & Co. 394-395, 1976.

O'Donoghue, D.H. *Treatment of Athletic Injuries* (3rd Ed). Philadelphia: W.B. Saunders & Co. 384-385, 1976.

Schuster, K. Equipment update: jogging bras hit the streets. *Phys and Sportsmed* 7:125, 1979.

### Section B. Pulmonary

Carleton, R., et al. Statement on exercise — A.H.A. subcommittee on exercise/cardiac rehabilitation. *Circulation* 64:1302A, 1981.

Eliot, R. Role of emotions and stress in genesis of sudden death. *American College of Cardiology J* 5(6), 1985.

Epstein, S.E. et al. *Asymmetric septal hypertrophy*. Ann Intern Med 81:650-680, 1974.

Froelicher, V. *Exercise Testing and Training*. New York: Lejacq Publishing Co., 1983.

Gaughan, L.E., Lown, B., Lanigan, J., et al. Acute oral testing for determining antiarrhythmic drug efficacy: I.Quinidine. *Am J Cardiol* 38:677-682, 1976.

Graboys, T.B., Lown, B. Podrid, P.J., et al. Long-term survival of patients with malignant ventricular arrhythmia treated with antiarrhythmic drugs. *Am J Cardiol* 50:437-443, 1982.

Hagberg, J.M., Goldring, D., Ehsani, A.A. et al. Effect of exercise training on the blood pressure and hemodynamic features of hypertensive adolescents. *Am J Cardiol* 52:763, 1983.

Hearst, J.W. *The Heart*. Philadelphia: McGraw Hill Inc., pgs. 250-251, 1986.

Hirsowitz, G.S., Podrid, P., Lambert, S., et al. The use of beta blocking agents as adjunct therapy in the treatment of malignant ventricular arrhythmia. *J Am Coll Cardiol* 3:618, 1984.

Hossack, K.J., et al. Influence of propranolol on exercise prescription of training heart rates. *Cardiology* 65:47, 1980.

Kaplan, N. Psychosocial and behavioral factors. In Jenkins, C.D. (ed) *Prevention of Coronary Heart Disease* Philadelphia PA:W.B. Saunder Co, 1983.

Kulund, D.N. *The Injured Athlete*. Philadelphia: J.B. Lippincott, pgs 120-133, 1982.

Lambert, E.C., Menon, V.A., Wagner, H.R., et al. Sudden unexpected death from cardiovascular disease in children, a cooperative international study. *Am J Cardiol* 34:189-196, 1974.

Lown, B., Podrid, P.J., DeSilva, R.A., et al Sudden cardiac death: management of the patient at risk. *Curr Probl Cardiol* 4:1-62, March 1980.

Marcus, F.I., Fontaine, G.H., Guiaudon, G., et al. Right ventricular dysplasia: a report of 24 adult cases. *Circulation* 65:384-398, February 1982.

Markis, J.E., et al. Sustained effect of orally administered isosorbide dinitrate on exercise performance on patients with angina pectoris. *Am J Cardiol* 43:265, 1979.

Maron, B.J., Roberts, W.C., McAllister, H.A., et al. Sudden death in young athletes. *Circulation* 62:218-229, 1980.

Maurice, J.N., Polland, R., Evirtt, M.G., Chavez, P.W. Vigorous activity and leisure time in protection against coronary heart disease. *Lancet* 1207-1210, 1980.

Pollock, M., Foster, C. Exercise prescription for participants on propranolol. *Journal Americal College of Cardiology*. 2:624, 1983.

Moskowitz, R.M., et al. Hemodynamic and metabolic responses to upright exercise in patients with congestive heart failure. *Chest*. 76:640, 1979.

Rankin, A.C., McGovern, B.A. Adenosine or verapamil for the acute treatment of supraventricular tachycardia? *Annals of Int Med* 114(6):513, 1991.

Rose, K.D. Which cardiovascular problems should disqualify athletes? *Phys and Sportsmed* 62-68, June 1975.

Teare, D. Asymmetrical hypertrophy of the heart in young adults. *Br Heart J* 20:1-18, 1958.

Topaz, O., Edwards, J.E. Pathologic features of sudden death in children, adolescents, and young adults. *Chest* 87:476, 1985.

Wenger, N.K. The coronary patient: interactions of cardiovascular drugs and exercise. *Drug Therapy* 59-63, March 1982.

Whiting, R.B. et al. Idiopathic hypertrophic subaortic stenosis in the elderly. *NEJM* 285:196-200, 1971.

Wynne, J. Braunwald, E. The cardiomyopathies and myocarditides. In: Braunwald E., ed. *Heart Disease; A Textbook of Cardiovascular Medicine*. Philadelphia: WB Saunders, 1980.

### Section C. Abdomen

Anderson, S.D. Current concepts of exercise-induced asthma. A review. *Allergy* 38:289-302, 1983.

Anderson, S.D. Issues in exercise-induced asthma. *J Allergy Clin Immunol* 76:763-772, 1985.

Blanco, G. Spontaneous pneumothorax. *Hospital Medicine* 40-61, 1975.

Davies, S.E. The effect of disodium cromoglycate on exercise-induced asthma. *British Medical Journal* 3:593, 1968.

Deal, E.C., McFadden, E.R., Ingram, R.H., Strauss, R.H., Jaeger, J.J. Role of respiratory heat exchange in production of exercise-induced asthma. *J Appl Physiol* 46:467-475, 1979.

Fitch, K.D., Godrey, S. Asthma and athletic performance. *JAMA* 236:152, 1976.

Gerhard, H. and Schacter, E.N. Exercise-induced asthma. *Post-Graduate Medicine* 67:91, 1980.

Grossman, P., DeSwart, J.C., DeFares, P.B. A controlled study of a breathing therapy for treatment of hyperventilation syndrome. *J Psychosom Res* 29(1):49-58, 1985.

Hahn, A., Anderson, S.D., Morton, A.R. et al. A reinterpretation of the effect of temperature and water content of the inspired air in exercise-induced asthma. *Am Rev Respir Dis* 130:575-579, 1984.

Joorabchi, B. Expressions of the hyperventilation syndrome in childhood: studies in management, including an evaluation of the effectiveness of propranolol. *Clin Pediatr* 16:1110-1115, December 1977.

Pantell, R.H., Goodman, B.W. Jr. Adolescent chest pain: a prospective study. *Pediatrics* 71:881-887, June 1983.

Pearson, R.B. Exercise-incuded asthma. In Proceedings of the British Associated Allergists. *Acta Allerg.* (KbH) 5:310, 1952.

Schachter, E.N. Prevention of exercise-induced asthma. *NEJM* 299:1193, 1978.

Siegel, A.J. Exercise-induced antiphylaxis. *Phys and Sportsmed* 8(1):95, 1980.

Strauss, R.H. *Sports Medicine*. Philadelphia, W.B. Saunders, 1984.

### Section D. Genital Urinary

O'Donoghue, D.H. *Treatment of Injuries to Athletes* (3rd Ed). Philadelphia: W.B. Saunders and Co., 405-415, 1976.

Redman, H.C. Thoracic, abdominal, and peripheral trauma — evaluation with angiography. *JAMA* 237:2415, 1977.

Rutkow, I.M. Rupture of the spleen in infectious mononucleosis. *Arch Surg* 113:718, 1978.

### Section E. Back

Dickson, J.H. and Erwin, W.D. Scoliosis: Early detection crucial for successful treatment. *Modern Medicine*, 41-43, 4/30/79.

Frymoyer, J.W., Helping your patients avoid low back pain. *J Musucloskeletal Med* 65, 1984.

Frymoyer, J.W., Pope, M.H., Costanza, M.C. et al. Epidemiologic studies of Low back pain. *Spine* 5:419, 1980.

Hoshino, H. Spondylolysis in athletes. *Phys and Sportsmed* 8:75, 1980.

Hungerford, D.S. and Dawson, E.G. Scoliosis shows itself when you look for it. *Patient Care* 98-111, 7/1/76.

Jackson, D.W., Retting, A. and Wiltse, L.L. Epidural cortisone in the young athletic adult. *AmJSportsMed* 8:239, 1980.

Javid, M.J. Treatment of herniated lumbar disk syndrome with chymopapain. *JAMA* 243:2043, 1980.

Keim, H.A., Kirkaldy-Willis, W.H. *Low Back Pain*. Ciba Clinical Symposia. Summit, NJ: Ciba Pharamaceutical Co., 1980.

Kelsey, J.L. An epidemiological study of acute herniated lumbar disks. *Rheumatol Rehab* 14:144, 1975.

Micheli, L.J. Low back pain in the adolescent: differential diagnosis. *AmJSportsMed* 7:362, 1979.

### Section F. Genital-Urinary

Blacklock, N.J. Bladder trauma in the long distance runner. *Am J Sportsmed* 7:239-241, 1979.

Boileau, M., Fuchs, E., Barry, J.M., Hodges, C.V. Stress hematuria: athletic pseudonephritis in marathon runners. *Urology* 15:471, 1980.

Hershkowitz, M. Penile frostbite, an unforseen hazard of jogging. *NEJM* 296:178, 1977.

Hoover, D.L., and Cromie, W.J. Theory and management of exercise-related hematuria. *Phys and Sportsmed* 9:91, 1981.

Knochel, J.P. *Rhabdomyolysis and myoglobinuria*. Seminars in Nephrology. 1:75, 1981.

Kulund, D.N. *The Injured Athlete*. Philadelphia, J.P. Lippincott Co, 1982: 338-343.

Melvin, N. Trainer's corner: Protecting the kidney. *Phys and Sportsmed* 7(3):161, 1979.

Ryan, A.J. (moderator). Roundtable: diagnosing kidney injuries in athlete. *Phys and Sportsmed* 3(1):48-49, 1975.

Siegel, A.J. et al. Exercise-related hematuria. Findings in a group of marathon runners. *JAMA* 241:391-392, 1979.

# 14

# Common Sports-Related Injuries and Illnesses — Pelvis and Lower Extremity

## SECTION A: HIP AND PELVIS

The pelvis is designed to transfer body weight from the upper trunk to the lower extremity and provide protection to underlying internal organs. The hip joint is imbedded deeply within the acetabulum, forming a ball-and-socket joint whose functional stability is dependent on surrounding strong muscles and three capsular ligaments. The muscles of the pelvis and hip support the erect trunk and work in concert with the muscles of the lower extremity to propel the athlete's body.

Readily palpable landmarks of the pelvis region include the iliac crest with the anterior superior iliac spine (ASIS) and the posterior superior iliac spine (PSIS). Four to six inches below this, the ischial tuberosity is palpable. The greater trochanter of the femur forms a bony landmark about four inches lateral and superior to the ischial tuberosity.

A number of major muscles are located in the hip and pelvis region. The gluteus maximus originates in the sacroiliac region and runs laterally and downward to insert into the iliotibial band (ITB). The ITB is a longitudinal thickening in the fascia lata that extends from the iliac crest to the tibial condyle (Gerdy's tubercle). This muscle acts as an extensor and external rotator of the hip. Prominent and clinically significant bursae are located over the ischial tuberosity and greater trochanter of the femur. The gluteus medius and minimus run from the lateral ilium to the greater trochanter and aid in internal rotation of the hip, but primarily help hip abduction. The tensor fascia lata is a weak flexor and internal rotator at the hip and provides major stabilization of the lateral knee. The pyriformis, obturator internus, gemelli, and quadratus femoris are lateral rotators at the hip.

Finally, the iliopsoas muscle arises from the ilium and lumbar vertebrae and inserts on the lesser trochanter and is the most powerful flexor of the hip (Figure 14A-1). The quadriceps and hamstring muscles and their actions are described elsewhere (see upper leg injuries). Three nerves innervate the hip — the sciatic, femoral and obturator nerves, which lie posteriorly, anteriorly, and medially, respectively. Knowledge of the muscle actions and their innervation and vascular supply will aid in the diagnosis of most problems of the hip and pelvis.

### Hip Pointer (Iliac Crest Contusion)

Hip pointers often are caused by a fall onto the iliac crest or by direct contact with another player. It is a common injury in football, basketball, gymnastics, and volleyball (Clancy, 1980). There may be an avulsion of muscle fibers attaching to the iliac crest from the abdomen or back. Improper padding of the iliac crest contributes to the high incidence of hip pointers.

Immediately after injury, the athlete may have localized pain over the iliac crest, but relatively normal range of motion. As bleeding continues, the pain worsens and there is an increase in swelling and loss of function. Therefore, early treatment is important. Painful flexion of the hip toward the injured iliac crest could indicate a fracture and x-rays should be obtained, especially in high school athletes who may avulse the iliac crest apophysis.

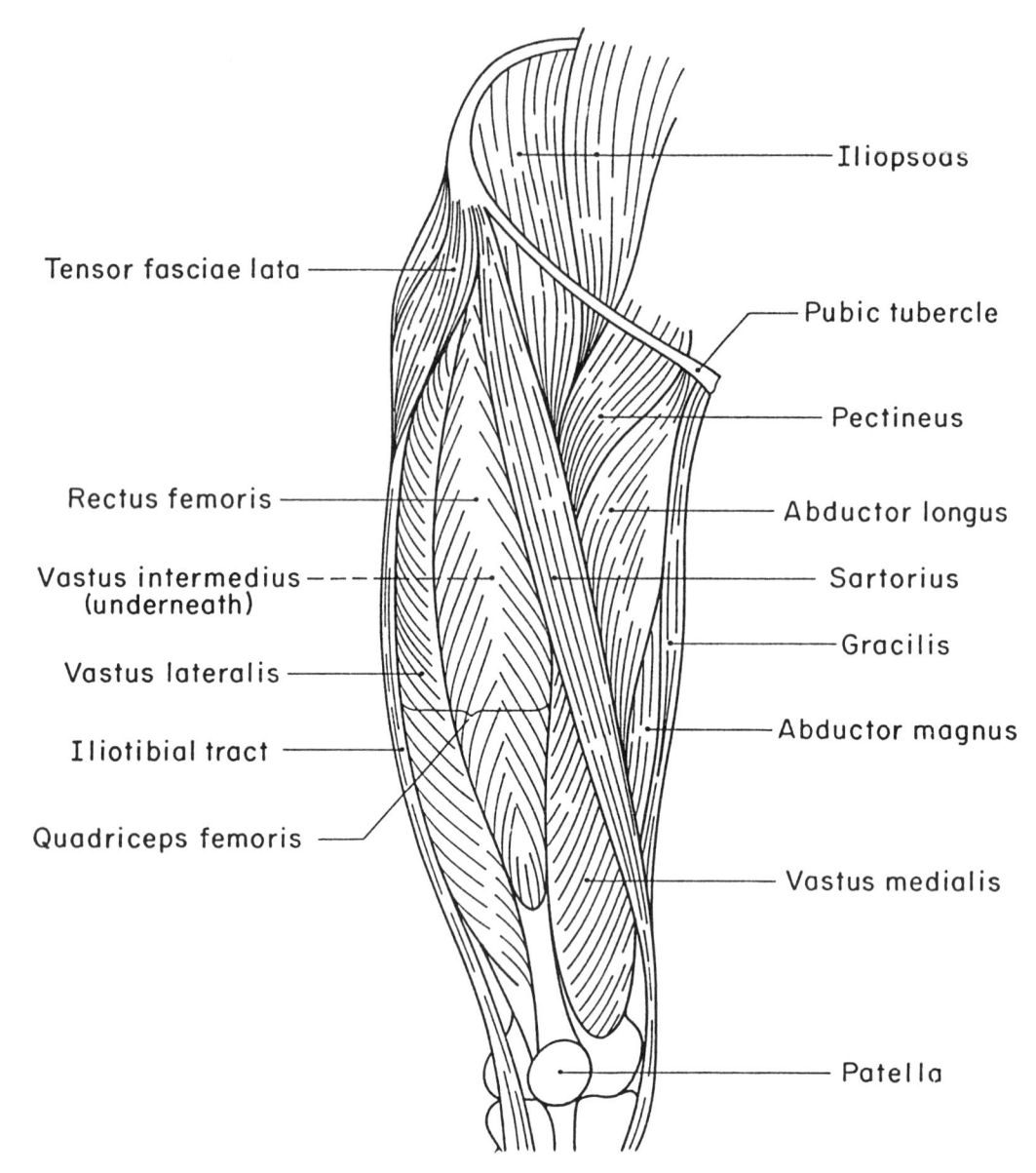

**Fig. 14A-1.** Muscular System of the Anterior Thigh

If there is a fluctuant hematoma, it should be aspirated. The athlete may experience pain with coughing or have persistent paraesthesia over the crest because of the many muscle attachments and nerves that pass over the iliac crest. Evaluate all abdominal or thigh muscle functions to rule out a rare complete avulsion of the muscular attachments.

Treatment consists of initial application of ice to the iliac crest with an elastic wrap. Localize the point of maximal tenderness and inject 1% Xylocaine® or 0.25% Marcaine® and a long acting corticosteroid into the iliac crest. This will reduce the time lost from the injury. Ice compression is continued for 48 hours. The use of non-steroidal anti-inflammatory medications (NSAID) may be warranted later. Once iliac crest soreness, swelling, and ecchymosis subside, begin hot-cold contrast treatments and ultrasound therapy. Hip range of motion exercises for thigh, gluteal, and lumbar muscles also should be started.

The athlete may return to practice or competition when there is pain-free range of motion of the hip and the athlete can run, change directions sharply, and turn and twist with minimal or no swelling or pain (usually within seven to ten days).

Wearing a protective lightweight football hip pad will help prevent reinjury. Hip pads are mandatory in college football and should protect the iliac crest, greater trochanter, and coccyx. They are available in several styles. Proper fitting of pads and educating the athlete are important; many athletes modify this equipment and increase their risk of injury.

## Iliac Apophysitis

Stress fracture and apophysitis of the anterior iliac crest happens most often to young runners who swing their arms across their body (Friermood, 1984; Lloyd-Smith, 1985). This overuse injury is caused by repetitive contractions of the oblique abdominal muscles, gluteus medius, and tensor fascia latae on the apophysis, and probably represents microscopic stress fractures within the growth center. The iliac crest ossification center begins anteriorly and advances posteriorly to the posterior iliac crest, closing at age 16-20 years in boys and 14-18 years in girls. The anterior half of the iliac crest is the most common site of involvement.

Muscular pain and localized tenderness develops over the anterior-lateral iliac crest and usually is present only with running. Hip abduction against resistance will increase the pain. X-ray of the pelvis often is normal but some displacement of the iliac apophysis may be seen. Posterior iliac crest apophysitis is less common and is diagnosed by reproducing the pain during abduction of the flexed hip while the patient is lying down. Rule out a fracture with x-rays.

Treatment consists of four to six weeks of rest and the use of ice and NSAID. After returning to running, do less mileage and avoid hills. Improved running form, with less arm swinging, aids recovery. Other forms of aerobic conditioning must be substituted for running (bike or swim) and recurrence is unusual.

## Osteitis Pubis

Osteitis pubis is more common in adults but may occasionally be seen in the older teenager in a high mileage training program. Osteitis pubis is common in running and jumping sports, race walkers, and soccer. Running, jumping, and kicking cause the pubic symphysis to move in all planes. Shear forces are transmitted to the symphysis, especially in running and soccer. Direct trauma may cause periosteal or subperiosteal damage, or it could be due to an increase in mileage or interval training with speed work. Small avulsion fractures may occur at the attachments of the hip adductor tendons to the pubic bone and medial portion of the descending ramus.

The characteristic history consists of prolonged suprapubic lower abdominal, medial inguinal, or proximal medial thigh pain that is unilateral or bilateral. Onset often is gradual and is exacerbated by activity and relieved by rest. The pain is located over the pubic symphysis on abduction or adduction of the hip against resistance. Serial x-rays will often show evidence of sclerosis. Radiographic changes often lag four to six weeks behind clinical findings. Long-term running programs may lead to asymptomatic osteitis pubis or osteitis condensans ilii. A bone scan may be necessary to detect early inflammatory changes (Koch & Jackson, 1981; Lloyd-Smith, 1985).

Occasionally an athlete may develop an unstable symphysis pubis and present with abdominal pain and tenderness over the symphysis. An x-ray of the pelvis with "flamingo views" (AP view while standing on one leg and then the other), looking for a shift in the symphysis, is helpful. The physician should differentiate osteitis pubis from adductor tendonitis, groin strain, inguinal hernia, prostatitis, traumatic vaginal delivery, femoral neck fracture, kidney stone, orchitis, and anklylosing spondylitis.

Rest is the most important therapy, along with a NSAID. Heat and adductor stretching exercises should be instituted. Corticosteroid injections are not recommended. Swimming (crawl or using arms only) is a good alternative exercise whereas biking may reproduce the athlete's symptoms. An adductor stretching program helps prevent these injuries but overstretching should be avoided. After the athlete is pain free, a gradual return to running over a six to twelve week period is indicated. This problem can take as long as two years to resolve.

## Avulsion Fractures of the Pelvis

An avulsion fracture of the pelvis may occur where the sartorius, rectus femoris, and hamstrings attach to the pelvis, and is caused by a sudden overloading of the muscle. Large bony fragments or major separation of the fragment from the pelvis may require surgical intervention. Otherwise, treatment should consist of ice therapy, rest, and conservative treatment. Return to exercise is dictated by a lack of pain and normal functional ability.

A complete discussion of various types of pelvic fractures pertinent to sports is beyond the scope of this text and may be found in the literature.

### Tensor Fascia Latae Syndrome (Iliotibial Band Friction)

The iliotibial tract (ITB) repeatedly rubs over the lateral femoral condyle as the knee flexes and extends during running (Figure 14A-2). Overuse can cause an inflammatory response, especially in novice runners with tibia vara and hyperpronation of the feet or in runners with worn shoes who run excessively or on banked surfaces (down-side leg). The syndrome is aggravated by smooth, even-paced running or extensive striding (Noble, 1980; Noble, Hajek and Porter, 1982).

ITB syndrome presents as stinging pain over the lateral femoral epicondyle (3 cm proximal to lateral joint line), which may radiate down the iliotibial band to its tibial attachment. The pain is most intense when the leg contacts the surface in deceleration. Ober's test is usually positive. Treatment involves cessation of running and ice massage for 20 min, two to four times daily. Exercises to stretch the ITB are helpful and should be continued until symptoms subside. NSAID agents and corticosteroid injection into the area of maximal tenderness may be necessary. Proper footwear or orthotics to control the forces at the knee during heel strike or the internal rotation of the hip are

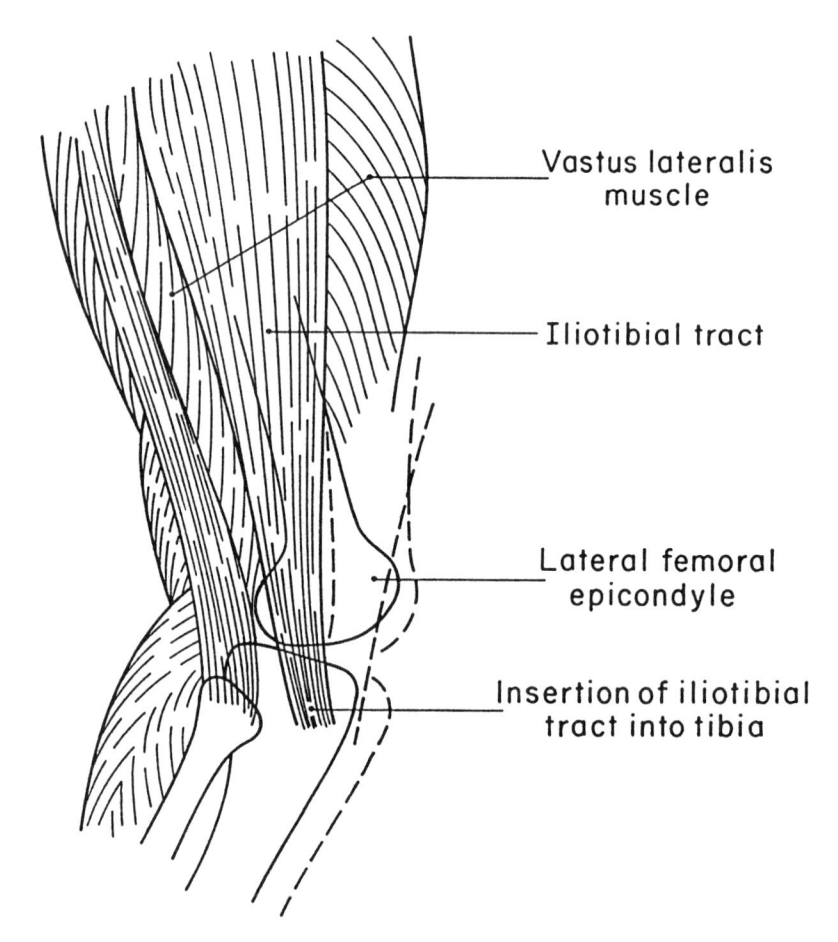

As knee flexes and extends, iliotibial tract glides back and forth over lateral femoral condyle which results in friction.

Fig. 14A-2. Iliotibial Tract Friction Syndrome

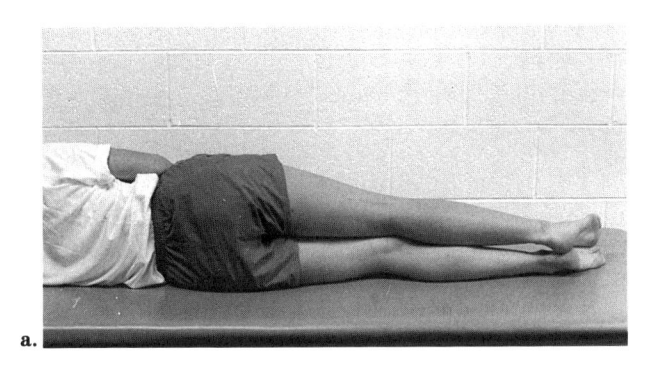

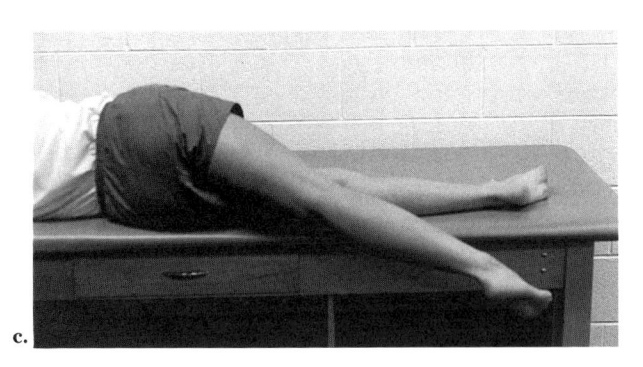

**14A-3.** A. The patient lies on side with the affected leg on top. B. Affected knee is held in extension. C. The leg is extended at the hip so it hangs over the table edge. Gravity passively adducts the leg as far as possible and stretches the iliotibial band.

necessary. Replace or repair all worn shoes that have excessive lateral sole wear. Static stretching exercises outlined in Figure 14A-3 & 4 are helpful in the treatment and prevention of ITB syndrome (Brody, 1980; Sutker, Jackson, 1981).

## Greater Trochanteric Bursitis

Several factors may lead to inflammation of the bursa overlying the greater trochanter: (1) muscle imbalance between hip abductors (gluteus medius) and adductor muscles in a runner with a broad pelvis; (2) novice runners, most often women,

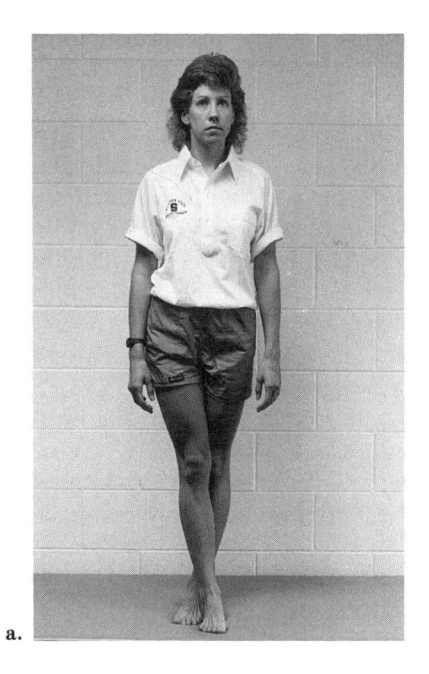

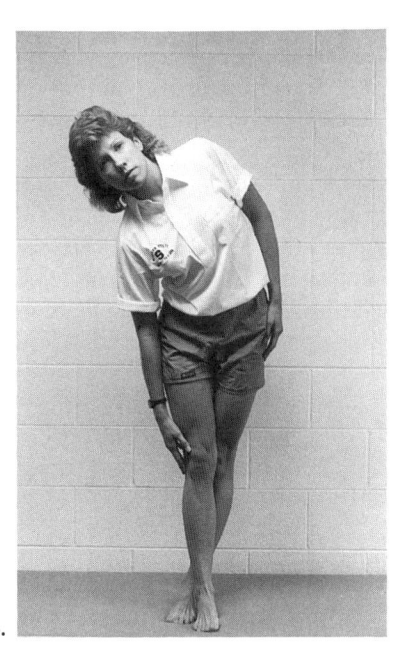

**Fig. 14A-4.** Iliotibial Band Stretching. (a) Athlete stands with both knees in full extension and extends and adducts the affected leg as far as possible. (b) Trunk is then flexed laterally as far as possible toward the unaffected side.

whose feet cross over the midline while running; (3) leg-length discrepancy, and (4) running on uneven or banked surfaces. The condition is caused by overuse and may occur in any sport involving running. The end result is that the iliotibial band moves over the greater trochanter and irritates the underlying bursa.

PELVIC AND LOWER EXTREMITY INJURIES/ILLNESSES

Localized, exquisite tenderness directly over the greater trochanter on the lateral aspect of the proximal thigh is common finding (Figure 14A-5). Clinically, the pain is reproduced by placing the patient on his/her side with the affected hip upwards and having him/her move the lower leg and hip from full extension to 30° of flexion while the examiner places the palm of his hand on the greater trochanter. Pain will be felt as the hip goes from flexion to extension. The examiner may feel a pop or snap as the leg goes into flexion. The snap is due to the ITB passing over the prominence of the greater trochanter. Poor flexibility of the tensor fascia lata and gluteus maximus muscles produce a tight ITB which leads to friction over the greater trochanter. Patients frequently have a positive Ober test. Often there is no history of trauma, the patient is afebrile, and the x-ray is normal. A sedimentation rate may be slightly increased.

Treatment consists of no running or activities that place the hip in extension. Rest, ice massage, and NSAIDs are helpful. Contrast baths may help after the first 48 hours post injury. Local injection of 2 cc of 1% Xylocaine and long-acting corticosteroid into the point of maximal tenderness often is of great benefit and may permit an earlier return to running when conservative measures fail. Institute a program of stretching the abductor muscles and ITB when ROM is pain free. Correct any leg length discrepancy with a lift in the shoe. Proper training techniques and running shoes, combined with a well-designed flexibility and strengthening program of the abductor and adductor muscles, help prevent this common injury. Surgery to release a tight ITB or remove a chronically inflamed bursa is rarely indicated (Clancy, 1991).

### Ischial Bursitis

Ischial bursitis is rare in runners but can be seen in a variety of other recreational athletes. This entity must be distinguished from tendinitis of the proximal hamstrings as they insert into the ischium (Figure 14A-5). The problem can be resolved by refraining from prolonged sitting, using a seat cushion, initiating flexibility training, and treating with NSAID.

### Pyriformis Syndrome

The pyriformis muscle may compress the sciatic nerve where the nerve exits the pelvis, causing localized tenderness in the buttock area between the ischium and greater trochanter (Figure 14A-6). This cause of buttock pain is less common than sciatic nerve involvement from a herniated disk, but it should be considered in athletes who have posterior hip and pelvic pain. Ice application, rest, and stretching by touching the toes with the legs crossed help alleviate the symptoms. Fluromethane spray and stretching techniques can be combined with regular ice applications. A gradual return to athletics is allowed once full, painless ROM returns.

### Groin Strain

Groin strains are common in football, ice hockey, soccer, bowling, baseball, and track, and may be due to acute trauma or repeated microtrauma (overuse). Strains can be caused by a sudden, powerful overstretching of the leg and thigh in abduction and external rotation, often against an opponent, ball, or the ground. They occur early in the season when the athlete has not properly stretched or warmed-up or if the athlete slips or stops suddenly. A groin strain most often affects the pubic symphysis and ramus or the adductor, gracilis, and rectus muscles at their insertion or origin.

Strains are painful when the thigh is adducted against resistance. Psoas muscle strains result in deep groin tenderness and pain radiating to the lower abdomen which is worsened by external rotation of the extended hip. A severe psoas strain

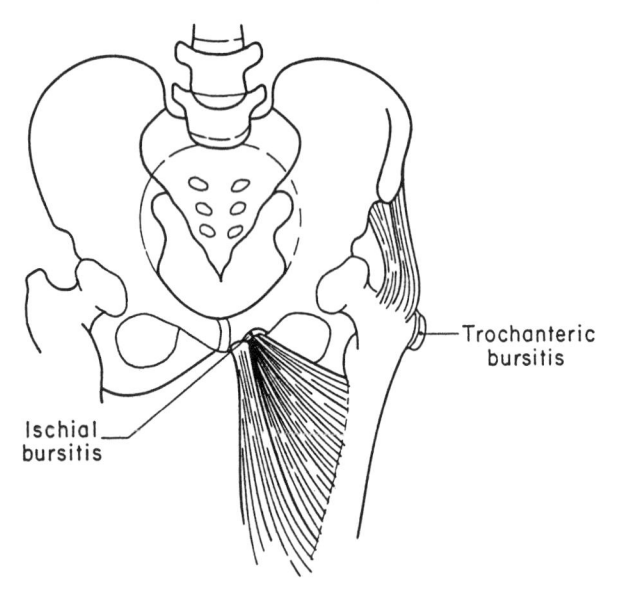

**Fig. 14A-5.** Trochanteric Bursitis and Ischial Bursitis

may be associated with avulsion of the lesser trochanter, and an x-ray should be obtained. The associated groin pain may be dull, sharp, localized, or diffuse, with radiation to the testicles, scrotum, hip, sacrum, or bladder through the obturator nerve. The examiner must rule out a direct or indirect inguinal hernia, femoral hernia, hip, back, or sacral problems, and genito-urinary causes of groin pain (urethritis, prostatitis, stone in the ureter, and testicular torsion). X-ray of the pubis and symphysis (AP, lateral and oblique views) looking for evidence of chronic overuse or fracture should be obtained.

Rest, physical therapy, NSAID, and rehabilitation are the main components of the treatment program for all groin strains. Initially, ice and compression for 30-60 minutes four to six times a day and rest are used. NSAIDs are instituted early to reduce pain and swelling. Injection of corticosteroids is not recommended.

After 36 hours, apply heat with warm compresses, hydrocollator packs, sitz baths, whirlpool, diathermy, or underwater ultrasound. Heat application for 10-15 minutes three or four times a day for 10-14 days often is required. Follow the heat treatment with massage of the affected muscles every other day. Encourage the patient to do other exercises like swimming or riding a stationary bike for endurance training. Rehabilitation starts with assisted range of motion exercises after heat application. Proceed gradually with stretching and active P.R.E., moving to weight bearing and light jogging as tolerated. Follow all treatment sessions with ice massage for 15-20 minutes. Return to competition is possible when there is pain free range of motion and normal function and strength, and often requires two to six weeks of therapy. A felt pad placed over the region and wrapped with a long elastic wrap helps support the strain during activity.

Strengthening of the adductors, iliopsoas, and rectus femoris muscles may be done by squeezing and lifting a medicine ball with the legs. Hip flexion is strengthened by lifting weight with the hip musculature. Perform all strength work against resistance through the full range of motion, with multiple repetitions to develop endurance. Finally, to prevent reinjury, the athlete should work on flexibility of the thigh, hip, low back, and abdominal muscles.

### Dislocated Hip

Dislocation of the hip can occur at any age but it usually is due to major trauma or a high-velocity collision (football) (Schottenfeld, 1979). A youngster's hip may dislocate with less force. The

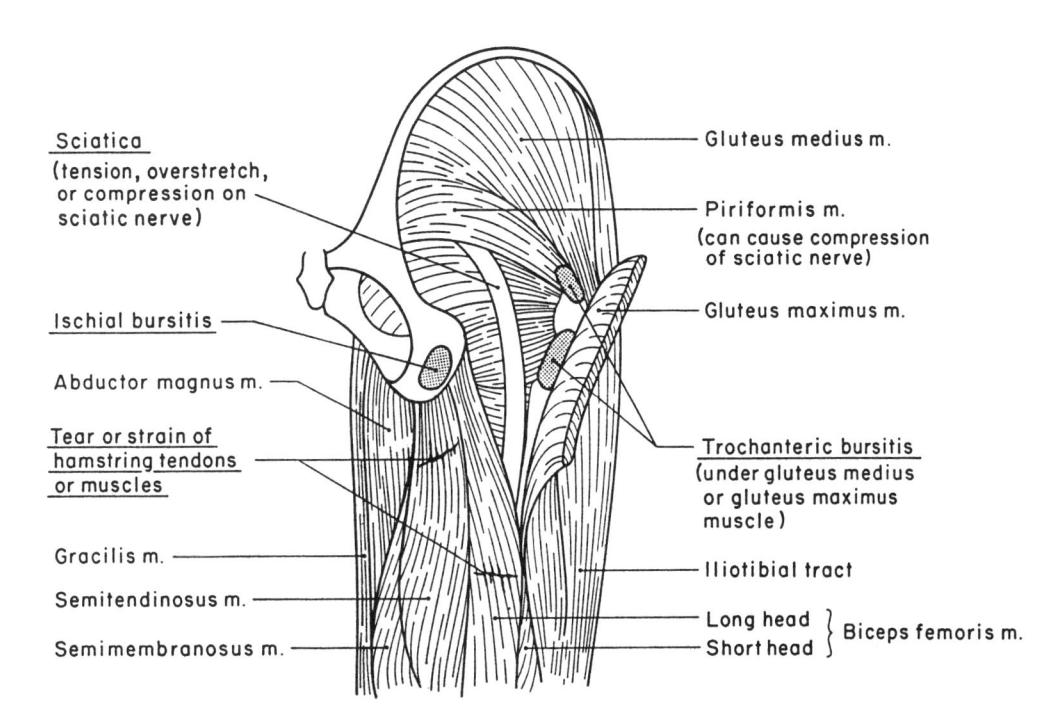

**Fig. 14A-6.** Common Causes of Pain in the Hip

most common dislocation is posterior in direction. The athlete lies with the hip flexed, adducted, and internally rotated. Hip dislocations cause complications, including early sciatic nerve injury, and late avascular necrosis of the femoral head from interruption of the vascular supply or myositis ossificans. Obtain an oblique x-ray of the hip to check for an avulsion fracture of the posterior lip of the acetabulum or of the femoral head. Strong muscles around the hip go into spasm and make closed reduction difficult without general anesthesia. Immobilize the hip after checking neurovascular function, and transport the athlete to the nearest hospital for definitive treatment by an orthopedic surgeon. Long-term crutch walking after reduction and a gradual return to activity is the usual course.

## Avascular Necrosis of the Femoral Head (Legg-Calve'-Perthes Disease)

Hip pain in a young athlete aged 5-12 years may be due to inflammation (synovitis) of the hip joint. As the joint fills with reactive synovial fluid, the fluid may interfere with the vascular supply and lead to ischemic necrosis of the femoral capital ossification center (Deluca, 1983). Any youngster complaining of chronic hip pain should be thoroughly evaluated. The disease affects boys five times more often than girls and most commonly develops between age 6-7; it is rare under the age of three. It is bilateral in 10% of patients and rarely affects blacks.

The athlete often presents with regional hip pain radiating to the knee, associated muscular spasm, limited internal rotation and abduction, and a limp. There are four stages of the disease with radiographs revealing necrosis of the ossification center, flattening of the femoral head, and widening of the femoral neck at advanced stages. The prognosis for this disease depends on how early it is detected and the degree of femoral head involvement. Early consultation by an orthopedic surgeon and strict bedrest are mandated. Depending on the patient's age and the severity of the disease, application of a special brace or surgery may be required.

The most common cause of a painful hip in children under 10 years of age is acute transient synovitis which usually is non-specific and self-limited. The patient has hip pain on walking, a low grade fever (<101°), and a normal CBC and sedimentation rate. Trauma and viral or bacterial infections cause the problem. Bed rest eases the pain almost immediately, but return to full range of motion may take several days. Legg-Calve'-Perthes disease may develop several months later. Acute septic arthritis may occur in children as young as one or two years old. *Staphylococcus aureus* is the organism most likely to cause this problem. Joint aspiration should be performed in all suspected cases of septic arthritis, and orthopedic consultation and treatment should be obtained.

## Slipped Capital Femoral Epiphysis

Slipped capital femoral epiphysis may occur in any sport involving even a minor injury. However, it occurs more often in obese youngsters aged 9-15 years, often during their growth spurt or in youths with an endocrine imbalance. Early history reveals aching around the hip or knee for several weeks and a limp (preslip phase). AP and lateral radiographs show widening of the epiphysis and early rarefaction of the metaphysis. All youngsters with hip pain should be evaluated although knee pain may be the presenting complaint because of referred pain from the hip via the obturator nerve. X-ray evidence of "pre-slip" and hip pain indicate a need for bedrest and possible pinning. Consult an orthopedic surgeon early. The unaffected hip should be x-rayed since 25% of cases involve both hips (Garrett, 1991).

Minor slips of the epiphysis may lead to hip osteoarthritis as an adult. Prevention can occur only when there is thorough evaluation of all youngsters with hip pain. Major slippage of the epiphysis may happen during activity and be followed by hip or knee pain. The athlete often presents with the hip externally rotated as he tries to flex the hip. Carefully transport the athlete to the hospital and obtain a frog-leg lateral view before allowing the athlete to move the hip. This procedure lessens the chance of a full slip. On x-ray, the slipped femoral head is tilted or in a drooped position, and is eccentrically placed on the femoral neck.

Usually the femoral head slips posteromedially on the neck. Major slips should be treated with traction and stabilization or with pinning by an orthopedic surgeon. Attempts to manipulate the head back onto the femoral neck may lead to avascular necrosis and should not be performed on the field or in the emergency room. This situation is a true orthopedic emergency and requires the expertise of a surgeon (Schottenfeld, 1979; Garrett, 1991).

# SECTION B.
# UPPER LEG

## Anatomical Considerations

The upper leg consists of the femur, which is completely surrounded by heavy muscles in two compartments. The anterior compartment (see Figure 14A-1) contains the quadriceps femoris and sartorius muscles. The quadriceps femoris has four portions: the rectus femoris arises from the anterior iliac spine and is a flexor at the hip; the vasti lateralis, medialis, and intermedius arise from the femur, join the rectus femoris, and insert through the patella into the tibial tuberosity, acting as a knee extensor. These muscles can be tested by the knee jerk reflex and knee extension against resistance in the recumbent or sitting position. The sartorius muscle runs from the anterior superior iliac spine downward and medially behind the knee and attaches to the anterior medial tibia. The sartorius acts as a flexor, extensor rotator, and abductor at the hip and flexor and internal rotator at the knee.

The posterior compartment includes the three hamstring muscles (see Figure 14A-6). The biceps femoris inserts on the fibular head and acts as a knee flexor and external rotator of the flexed knee. The semimembranosus and semitendinosus insert, respectively, on the postero-medial and antero-medial aspects of the upper tibia. They are primarily extensors of the hip and aid knee flexion and medial rotation when the knee is flexed.

## Thigh Contusion

A common cause of contusion of the anterior or anteriolateral thigh muscle is a direct blow by a helmet or shoulder pad in football, but it may occur in any contact sport. The severity of this injury often is underestimated, as the athlete may continue to play with this injury and then develop pain, stiffness, and swelling within hours. If this injury is untreated, myositis ossificans could develop and cause partial disability for up to a year post injury.

The athlete usually presents with severe pain in the anterior thigh and may or may not be able to walk, or walk with a limp. There may be considerable swelling present with limited range of motion and effusion of the knee. Resistance to knee extension may be present. Quadricep contusions vary in severity from mild (Grade I), with minimal pain or swelling and a normal range of motion, to severe (Grade III), with marked pain, effusion, muscle spasm, limited range of motion, and marked hematoma formation. Muscle rupture and herniation also may occur. Attempts to aspirate a fluctuant hematoma usually are unsuccessful and may introduce infection. The practice of injecting local anesthetics, corticosteroids, and enzymes should be discouraged.

Initial treatment consists of wrapping the thigh with ice for 30-40 minutes, four to six times a day during the first 72 hours after injury, and then twice daily thereafter, with the athlete's knee flexed as much as possible during icing. Crutches are suggested for easier ambulation. An athlete with a severe contusion should remain at bed rest with the thigh wrapped and iced. Serial measurements of thigh circumference should be made. The athlete should be fitted with a thigh pad and wrapped with an elastic thigh support or ace wrap except during ice therapy. A foam rubber or air pad can be covered with a football thigh pad for added compression and protection.

The athlete may do anything that does not cause pain, including walking. Do not allow the athlete to "run the injury out," as further bleeding may occur and lead to myositis ossificans. Active exercises are allowed only within a pain free range of motion. Avoid massage, heat, or whirlpool, or ultrasound treatments which could potentiate further bleeding. The athlete may shower as long as ice bags are kept over the area.

Once range of motion is normal, isometric quadriceps strengthening exercises should be started. Running may be started once range of motion and strength are normal and there is no pain. The athlete may gradually increase the speed of running and once he is able to run and cut at a normal speed without pain, may return to competition with full protective padding. This usually requires three to six weeks. Pain free motion and activity must be stressed to avoid the late complications and long-term disability associated with myositis ossificans.

## Myositis Ossificans Traumatica

The thigh is particularly prone to myositis ossificans secondary to a direct blow from a helmet, another player, or from a severe quadriceps muscle strain that caused significant bleeding. Heterotrophic bone may form adjacent to or attached to the femur and may be large (Figure 14B-1). The initial injury usually is aggravated by early use of heat, ultrasound, massage treatments, or by repeated unprotected thigh contusions.

Initial x-rays show a soft tissue mass that develops into one of three types of bone formation within two to four weeks after trauma: (1) a stalk-type connected to bone; (2) a broad-based type connected to bone, or (3) one with no connection to bone (Lipscomb et al, 1976)(see Figure 14B-1). These bony growths may be mistaken for tumors (osteogenic sarcoma) and are often incorrectly excised. Myositis ossificans follows muscle trauma within two to four weeks. It usually is painless and typically is anterior to the midshaft of the femur. The mass gradually decreases in size and becomes more compact. After three to six months the mass stabilizes and may shrink in size. It is less likely to reabsorb if it is near the muscle insertion or origin. Early surgical excision (before one year) should be avoided to prevent recurrence and enlargement of the lesion.

Prevention is important in reducing the incidence of myositis ossificans. It involves using proper protective equipment, early recognition, and aggressive treatment of quadriceps contusions.

## Quadriceps and Hamstring Muscle Strains

The mechanism of injury to these muscles often involves a sudden stop or start, or an increase in muscular exertion, especially in a fatigued or tight muscle of a running athlete. The hamstring muscles are injured most often but there can be a strain to the rectus femoris portion of the quadricep muscle. Strains may happen when there is an imbalance between quadriceps and hamstring strength. The normal hamstring should have 60%-70% of the strength of the quadriceps. Quick starts may tear the athlete's hamstring (a sprinter leaving the starting blocks, hurdles, or long jumps). Athletes who improperly stretch either of these antagonistic muscle groups can develop muscle strains. They occur most often during eccentric contractions (Garrett, 1990). The short-head of the biceps femoris, however, is strained most frequently in sports.

The athlete usually presents with tenderness over the area of muscle strain, and there may be evidence of hemorrhage and swelling. The strain may be at either end of the muscle-tendon unit or within the muscle belly itself. A complete tear (Grade III) may cause a defect that can be seen on initial examination or it may not be seen until later because of the organization of the hematoma. Pain on motion and limited range of movement usually are associated. Ecchymosis often migrates down the course of the muscle.

The four muscles of the quadriceps attach to the tibia by a conjoined tendon that passes over the patella (Figure 14A-1). Partial to complete ruptures of the quadriceps tendon do occur in sports but are rare. The diagnosis is made on findings of localized pain, tenderness, swelling, and pain with stress of the knee extensor mechanism. Treatment is the same for quadriceps and hamstring muscle strains.

Strains range in severity from Grade I (stretch of the muscle) to a Grade III strain (complete tear). A thigh or hamstring strain usually does not hurt until the athlete cools down or ends competition; however, the athlete may feel a pop or a snap in

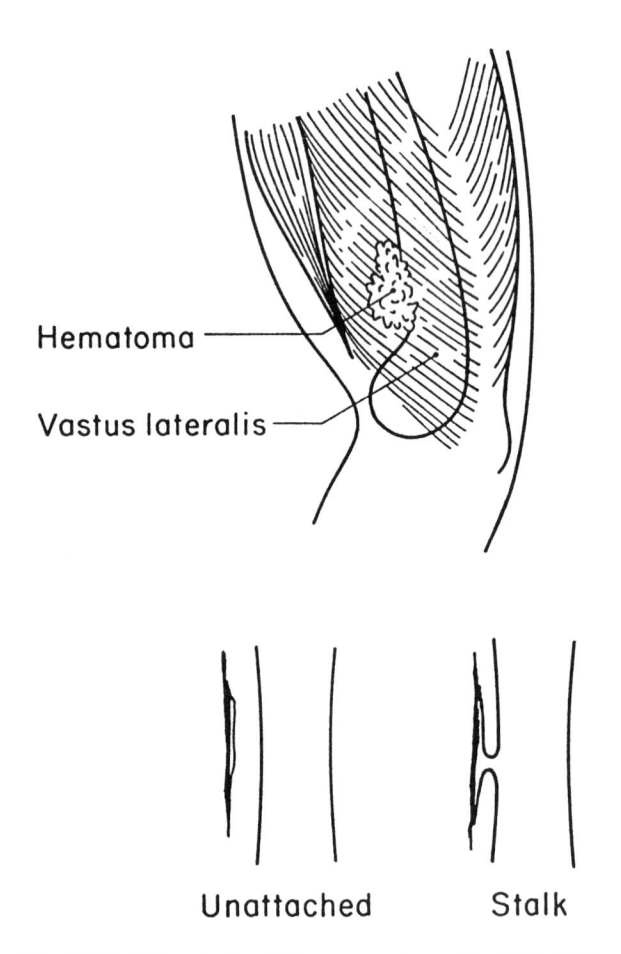

**Fig. 14B-1.** A blow to the thigh may produce a hematoma that ossifies. It may take many forms as it matures and may need to be excised.

the muscle along with immediate pain and loss of function in most Grade II and Grade III strains.

The athlete should not try to run out a hamstring or quadriceps strain. A compression dressing, combined with icing and immobilization with crutches, is appropriate therapy. Crushed ice will conform to the shape of the thigh and should be applied overnight, with a felt or foam rubber pad secured over the injured area by elastic wrap. Oral enzyme medications or corticosteroid injections have not been useful in treating this injury.

When muscle soreness is gone, the athlete may begin knee extension and flexion exercises and high speed cycling. Light jogging may be started as soon as the athlete is capable of walking without difficulty. Active range of motion exercises within the limits of pain may be started at this time. When the range of motion is normal and the athlete is capable of jogging lightly, light stretching exercises and isometric progressive resistance exercises (P.R.E.) of both the hamstrings and quadriceps should begin. A return to full activity is allowed when the athlete is capable of running at full speed with good range of motion and normal muscle, strength.

Mild strains heal within a few days to a week, while most Grade II strains take one to three weeks for recovery. Complete muscle ruptures may require an entire season. Complete muscle tears that occur at the musculo-tendonous junction often need surgical repair. Athletes who have had previous hamstring strains should be cautioned about returning to sports activity without proper stretching because recurrence is common. Since healing of strains occur with scar tissue formation, the muscle does not have the same inherent flexibility as normal muscle. When the athlete returns to practice, he should wear an elastic support around the thigh that is fitted to the tapering circumference of the upper leg. Athletic tape is too restricting and elastic wraps loosen too easily to be effective. Elasticized biker shorts may help support the upper thigh muscles and inguinal area and they may be useful in the rehabilitation of pulled hamstring muscles that are difficult to support with elastic wraps (Cooper, 1976).

## Fracture of the Femur

Fracture of the femoral shaft is infrequent in sports. The athlete usually presents with swelling, obvious deformity, and tenderness on palpation over the fracture site. Crepitation on motion as well as significant disability and inability to bear weight are common findings. The fracture is the result of excessive force, often rotary in nature, applied to the lower extremities. The ankle, leg, or knee usually give way before the femur. An athlete with a suspected femoral fracture should be taken to the hospital by stretcher and a traction splint applied. The Thomas splint commonly is used for proximal femoral fractures. It has a half ring that rests against the ischial tuberosity while traction is applied to the foot. Midshaft and distal femoral fractures can be splinted with airsplints or plaster splints. Airsplints should not be applied when a gross deformity cannot be brought into general anatomic shape.

After checking for normal neurovascular function, the patient should be taken to the nearest medical facility for definitive care from an orthopedic surgeon. The surgeon may elect to perform an open reduction of the fracture or may treat conservatively with traction for six to eight weeks. Rehabilitation is extremely important with this type of fracture. The athlete should be carefully instructed about exercises for other extremities and in the use of uninjured muscles of the involved extremity. Active competition cannot be permitted until the fractured femur is solidly united. Muscular strength and full range of motion of the thigh and calf should be present before a return to activity is allowed.

Stress fractures of the proximal femur are more common in endurance athletes. They present with groin pain or hip tenderness. Examination reveals decreased ROM of the hip and pain with passive ROM. X-rays may not be positive but a bone scan will demonstrate the fracture. Two types of stress fracture occur (Garrett, 1991):

- The transverse stress fracture across the superior portion of the femoral neck is prone to a complete break and displacement. It is treated with pinning to protect the fracture site.
- The more common compression stress fracture is along the inferior neck of the femur and located in an area of compressive load. It rarely displaces or causes major difficulty.

Of further note, distal physeal fractures of the femur may be mistaken for a knee ligament injury. These injuries in young adolescents and children require surgery for proper healing but are often misinterpreted without stress x-rays.

## SECTION C. KNEE

### Introduction

The knee is the joint most often injured in sports participation (DeHaven, 1985). This is because of its unique structure and the types of forces to which it is subjected. The keys to correct diagnosis and management are knowledge of the functional anatomy, understanding the mechanisms of injury, and familiarity with the more common knee injuries in sports.

### Epidemiology

A. Diagnosis of Acute and Chronic Knee Pathology by Gender (see Table 14C-1)
B. Diagnosis of Knee Pathology by Age (see Table 14C-2)
C. Most Common Acute Knee Injuries by Sports (see Table 14C-3)

### Anatomy

The following abbreviations are used throughout this chapter:

ACL — anterior cruciate ligament
ITB — Iliotibial band
LCL — lateral collateral ligament
MCL — medial collateral ligament
PCL — posterior cruciate ligament
VMO — vastus medialis obliquis — originates over distal medial femur and inserts into medial aspect of patella; responsible for stabilizing the patella in the femoral groove during terminal extension.
ALRI — anterolateral rotary instability
AMRI — anteromedial rotary instability
ASIS — anterior superior iliac spine
PFD — patellofemoral dysfunction

The knee anatomy relevant to the sports medicine physician is presented in Figure 14C-1. The patella articulates in the femoral groove as the knee goes from complete extension into flexion.

**Table 14C-1. Diagnosis of Acute and Chronic Knee Pathology by Gender (DeHaven, 1985)**

| Male Diagnosis (42% of all injuries) | | Female Diagnosis (59% of all injuries) | |
|---|---|---|---|
| Torn Menicus | 33.5% | PFD, Chondromalacia | 33.2% |
| PFD, Chondromalacia | 18.1% | Torn Meniscus | 20.4% |
| MCL Sprain | 16.9% | MCL Sprain | 12.7% |
| ACL Sprain | 9.6% | Subluxation (patella) | 7.7% |
| Chronic Instability | 5.3% | ACL Sprain | 6.7% |
| Reactive Synovitis (Inflammatory Knee) | 4.9% | Reactive Synovitis | 5.2% |
| LCL Sprain | 3.6% | Dislocation (patella) | 4.5% |
| Subluxation (patella) | 1.7% | Chronic Instability | 4.2% |
| Osgood-Schlatter | 1.7% | | |
| Dislocation (patella) | 1.7% | | |

**Table 14C-2. Diagnosis of Knee Injuries by Age (Adapted from DeHaven, 1985)**

| Diagnosis | % of Age Groups Diagnosis |
|---|---|
| Under 13 years (N=90) | |
|   Torn Meniscus | 9.0% |
|   PFD | 6.7% |
|   MCL Sprain | 5.6% |
| 13-15 years (N=514) | |
|   PFD | 14.2% |
|   Torn Meniscus | 11.7% |
|   MCL Sprain | 5.8% |
| 16-19 years (N=1408) | |
|   Torn Meniscus | 12.5% |
|   PFD | 8.1% |
|   MCL Sprain | 7.8% |
|   ACL Sprain | 4.2% |
| 20-24 years (N=769) | |
|   Torn Meniscus | 14.4% |
|   PFD | 7.3% |
|   MCL Sprain | 6.6% |
|   ACL Sprain | 5.5% |
| 25-30 years (N=198) | |
|   PFD | 15.2% |
|   Torn Meniscus | 13.6% |
|   ACL Sprain | 7.1% |
|   MCL Sprain | 5.1% |
| 31-40 years (N=232) | |
|   PFD | 16.4% |
|   Torn Meniscus | 15.9% |
|   MCL Sprain | 6.9% |
| 41-50 years (N=110) | |
|   Torn Meniscus | 20.0% |
|   PFD | 110.0% |
|   MCL Sprain | 10.0% |
| 51-60 years (N=43) | |
|   Torn Meniscus | 25.6% |
|   MCL Sprain | 11.6% |
|   PFD | 9.3% |

Inappropriate tracking in the groove due to muscle weakness of the VMO or other anatomical factors is a frequent source of anterior knee pain in sports.

The knee is supported by a muscular tripod, the quadriceps anteriorly and the hamstrings (semitendenosis, semimembranosis and biceps femoris) posteriorly. The primary support is provided by a fibrous capsule and strong thick ligaments that prevent anterior (ACL), posterior (PCL), medial (MCL), and lateral (LCL) displacement. The capsule surrounds the joint, extends superior to the patella, and becomes obvious with a major knee effusion. The cruciate ligaments are intracapsular and cross over from their point of origin on the femur to the point of insertion on the tibial plateau. The MCL is a broad, long ligament extending from the femoral condyle to the medial tibia at the level of the tibia tubercle. The short, narrow LCL originates from the lateral femoral condyle and goes to the head of the fibula. Significant injury to any of these ligaments will result in instability.

The ITB acts both to stabilize the patella as it moves in the femoral groove and to provide lateral stability as a portion of the band crosses the joint line and inserts into Gerdy's tubercle. A group of three muscles, the semitendenosis, gracilis, and sartorius insert below and medial to the MCL, and are collectively known as the pes anserine. Both the ITB and the pes anserine are common sites of overuse injury. The popliteus muscle originates from the posterior tibia and inserts onto the lateral femoral condyle just anterior to the LCL. This tendon is a less common site of overuse injury.

There are many bursae around the knee. The *prepatellar* bursa located directly over the patella and the *suprapatella* bursa located superior to the suprapatellar pouch of the capsule are frequent sites of direct trauma. Bursae associated with the ITB, pes anserine, patellar tendon, and other muscle groups are prone to overuse injuries.

The menisci are made of cartilage and act to distribute body weight evenly through the femoral condyle onto the articular surface of the tibia. Total removal of a meniscus will result in degenerative arthritis secondary to a redistribution of forces (Baratz, 1986). The medial meniscus is attached to the MCL and joint capsule and is sometimes involved in knee injury involving a valgus force. The lateral meniscus is not attached to the LCL and is less frequently torn.

## History

An accurate history is required to form a differential diagnosis quickly and efficiently. The knee evaluation sheet used in the Michigan State University Sports Medicine Clinic is shown in Appendix 14C-1. The different sections of this form will be discussed below.

The mechanism of injury provides insight into the anatomical structures likely to be involved in a traumatic injury, whereas the physical exam helps confirm the extent of involvement of these structures. Table 14C-4 identifies the type of force and the relative order of involvement of the supporting structures. Most overuse injuries result from

Table 14C-3. Common Knee Injuries by Sport

| Sport | % of all Knee Injuries | % of Sports Injuries or Most Common Injuries |
|---|---|---|
| **Ballet** | | |
| Beginner (Teitz) | | MCL, PFD, patellar tendinitis, subluxation |
| Professional | 10% | PFD, patellar tendinitis, torn meniscus (17% of total dance injuries — Quirk) |
| **Baseball** (DeHaven) | 2.3% | Torn meniscus (27%); PFD (20%); MCL (17%); Chronic medial instability (10%) |
| **Basketball** (DeHaven) | 7.9% | Torn meniscus (29%); ACL (17%); PFD (13%); MCL (11%); Subluxation (10%); also patellar tendinitis |
| **Cycling** (Dickson) | | PFD, patellar tendinitis, overuse |
| **Football** (DeHaven) | 60% | Torn meniscus (36%); PFD (26%); MCL (9%); ACL (7.5%); reactive synovitis (6%) |
| **Gymnastics** (Andrish) | | PFD, patellar tendinitis, subluxation, torn meniscus, ACL, MCL |
| **Ski** | | |
| Downhill (Howe) | | MCL, ACL, PCL |
| Cross Country (Clancy) | | PFD, serious ligament injury rare |
| **Soccer** | | |
| Youth (Maehlum) | | Injury rate very low |
| Adolescent, adult (DeHaven) | | Torn meniscus (34%); PFD (17%); ACL (9%); MCL (8%); subluxation (8%) |
| **Swimming** (Fowler) | | MCL (1st degree), PFD, reactive synovitis, plica |
| **Track/Running** (DeHaven, Lutter) | | PFD, MCL, ITB, reactive synovitis, torn meniscus (field events) |
| **Wrestling** (Estwanik) | | Prepatellar bursitis, torn meniscus (50% lateral), MCL, capsular sprain |

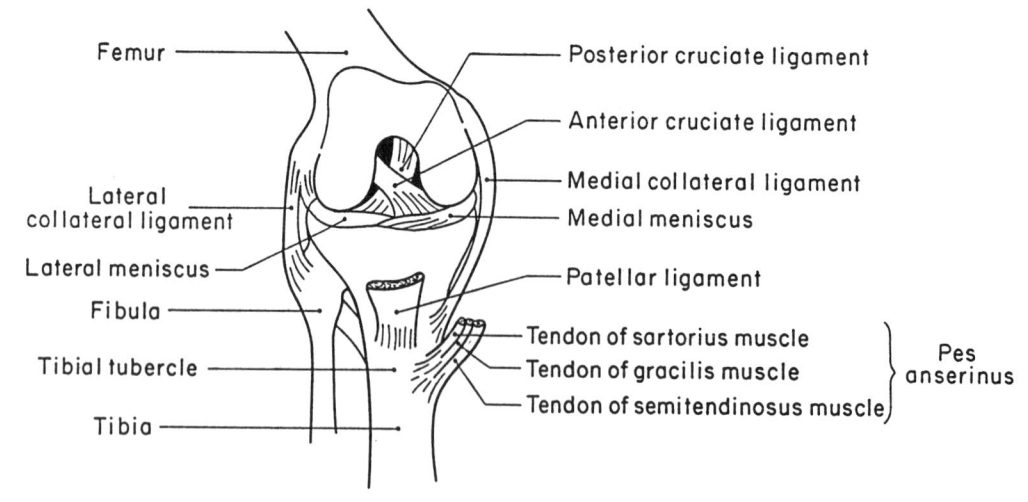

**a.** Anterior Aspect

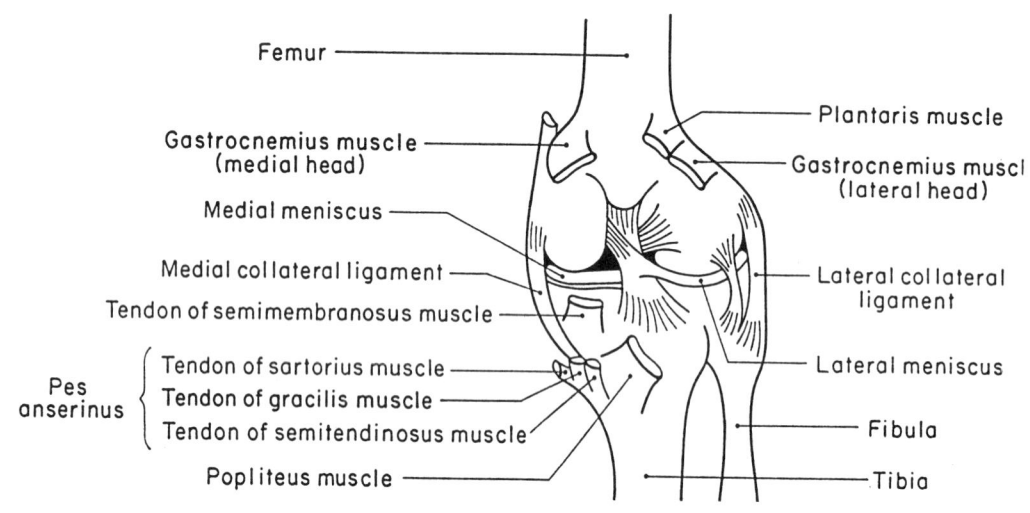

**b.** Posterior Aspect

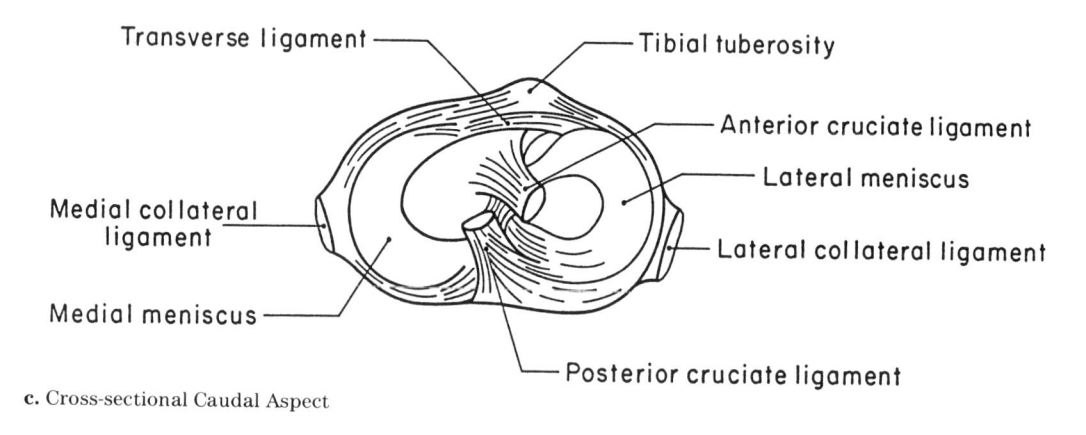

**c.** Cross-sectional Caudal Aspect

**Fig. 14C-1.** Anatomy of the Knee

**Table 14C-4. History Mechanism of Injury**

| Direction of Force | Knee Position | Relative Order of Involvement Supporting Structures | Examples |
|---|---|---|---|
| Valgus (medial side) | Extension | 1) superficial MCL, 2) ACL, postcapsule, 3) deep MCL (medial capsule), 4) PCL (rule out medial meniscus involvement) | 1) clip in football; 2) baserunner rolls into second baseman with foot planted while trying to break up double play. |
|  | Flexion | 1) superficial MCL, 2) ACL, 3) PCL |  |
| Varus (lateral side) | Extension | 1) LCL, ACL, popliteus, 2) PCL | Ball carrier hit on inside of knee by opponents shoulder pad while making a tackle. |
|  | Flexion | 1) LCL |  |
| Hyperextension (may be noncontact) |  | 1) posterior capsule, 2) ACL, 3) PCL | Gymnast landing from dismount. |
| Anterior against fixed tibia | Flexion | 1) isolated PCL | Catcher blocking plate and runner sliding into the tibia. |
| Posterior against fixed tibia | Flexion | 1) isolated ACL | Football linebacker has opponent fall onto posterior calf as he is attempting to make a tackle. |
| Anterior against patella |  | 1) patellar fracture, 2) osteochondral fracture (batter being struck with fastball) | 1) Batter being struck with a fastball directly over patella; 2) soccer player kicked in knee by overzealous opponent trying to steal the ball. |

Direct contact to the knee may cause an osteochondral fracture by a shearing mechanism.

*Non-Contact-Rotation: Tibia on Femur*
Differential Diagnosis: 1) torn menicus, 2) subluxation of patella, 3) osteochondral fracture.

| | | | |
|---|---|---|---|
| Internal Rotation | Extension | 1) ACL; 2) LCL, popliteus, ITB; 3) PCL | 1) Defensive back plants foot and suddenly pivots to stay with wide receiver that broke to outside; 2) Basketball player pivots and extends knee as he jumps to block the shot. |
|  | Flexion | 1) ACL, PCL; 2) LCL; 3) popliteus, ITB |  |
| External Rotation | Extension | 1) ACL, MCL | Football player plants foot and suddenly turns to avoid the tackle. |
|  | Flexion | 1) MCL; 2) ACL, LCL, popliteus; 3) posterior medial capsule |  |

To date prophylactic knee bracing in football to protect against the valgus force seems to be ineffective (Zemper, 1989), but may be advantageous for a subset of the team (i.e., interior lineman or linebackers).

---

training errors that must be identified in order to be corrected. These training and/or biomechanical errors should be listed under the mechanism of injury.

### Important Symptoms Utilized in Diagnosis of Knee Injuries

**History** (Jensen et al, 1985)

1. Effusion (intra-articular)
   a. Immediate (2-6 hours)
      (1) ACL
      (2) subluxation/dislocation of patella
      (3) osteochondral fracture
   b. Gradual over 24 hours (may also be recurrent)
      (1) torn meniscus
      (2) reactive synovitis
      (3) chondromalacia
   c. Absence of trauma
      (1) septic (GC)
      (2) osteoarthritis
      (3) arthritis (gout, pseudogout, RA)
2. Swelling (extra-articular) — often localized
   a. Tendinitis

b. Bursitis
   c. Sprain
   d. Contusion
3. Audible "pop"
   a. ACL
   b. Subluxation of patella
   c. Meniscal tear
   d. Osteochondral fracture
4. Locking
   a. Meniscal Tear
   b. Loose body
   c. Plica (pseudolocking)
5. "Giving way"
   a. Rotary instability
   b. ACL deficient knee
   c. Torn meniscus
   d. Nonspecific pain
6. Pain
   a. Constant (infection, fracture — chondral or osteochondral, DJD)
   b. Intermittant (mechanical dysfunction, overuse injury)
   c. Immediate (capsular or ligament injury, torn meniscus, subluxation)
   d. Delayed (overuse, reactive synovitis, torn meniscus)
   e. Exacerbated by up and down stairs (extensor mechanism, popliteus tendinitis)
   f. Location — see soft tissue palpation
7. Immediate Disability — Indicative of serious injury: ligament injury, cartilage injury; or subluxation of patella
8. Treatment to Date
   a. Ice, heat or other modalities
   b. Medication
   c. Results of prior aspiration
9. Past Medical History
   a. Significant previous injury, surgery
   b. Rehabilitation to date
10. Family History — arthritis, gout, RA, etc.

## Physical Exam (Jensen et al, 1985)

**Inspection.** Note effusion or swelling, deformity, ecchymosis or erythema, and abrasion.

## Biomechanical Alignment

- Genu varum or valgus, tibia varum, femoral anteversion, tibial rotation
- Q angle — angle formed by bisecting the midpatella from the ASIS and from the tibial tubercle is less than 10° in men and 15° in women
- Leg length — ASIS to medial malleolus measurement
- Thigh circumfrence 4 and 15 cm above superior pole of patella with muscle contracted to estimate VMO and quadriceps atrophy. Dramatic change will take place in even two weeks time if one leg is favored.

**Knee Range of Motion** — limited secondary to pain, mechanical locking, or effusion.

**Bony and Soft Tissue Palpation**

A diagram is a tool to identify sites. Many overuse syndromes affect very localized structures which emphasizes the necessity of knowing the anatomy and of doing a precise exam. The knee exam can be modified depending on the patient's clinical presentation. For an acute severe injury, the exam should be carried out with the patient in the supine position; otherwise, a sitting position is comfortable for the patient and facilitates identification of relevant landmarks for the examiner.

**Exam in Sitting Position**

Table 14C-5 lists the differential diagnosis that should be considered when examining the patient in the sitting position.

---

**Table 14C-5. Exam in Sitting Position on Exam Table (Differential Diagnosis)**

1. Tibial tubercle (Osgood Schlatter's disease, patellar tendinitis)
2. Patellar tendon (patellar tendinitis, infrapatellar bursitis)
3. Inferior pole of patella (patella tendinitis, Sinding-Larsen-Johansson Syndrome)
4. Medial joint line (medial meniscus, reactive synovitis, MCL sprain)
5. MCL — origin to insertion (contusion, sprain)
6. Lateral joint line (lateral meniscus, LCL sprain, ITB, popliteus)
7. LCL can be isolated by placing patient's foot on opposite knee and palpating ligament (sprain)
8. Gerdy's tubercle — (ITB syndrome — overuse, contusion)
9. Lateral femoral condyle (ITB syndrome — overuse, osteochondral fracture)
10. Pes Anserine — (overuse — tendinitis, bursitis)
11. Posterior knee — (capsular sprain, Bakers cyst)
12. Peripatellar — (PRD, subluxation, retinacular sprain plica)
13. Superior pole of patella — (bipartate patella — overuse, quadriceps, tendinitis)
14. Patella — (prepatellar bursitis, contusion)

**Exam in Supine Position**

This portion of the exam is carried out with the patient in the supine position. Placing a pillow under the head will make the patient more comfortable and relaxed.

1. *Effusion* — Graded on a scale from 0 — 4+.
   4+ = tense effusion of entire capsule
   3+ = nontense but effusion of entire capsule
   2+ = obvious medial bulge with compression of supra-patellar pouch (see Figure 14C-2 for procedure to detect minor effusion)
   1+ = less obvious but distinct medial bulge with compression of supra-patellar pouch
   0 = Normal (no effusion)
2. *Patellar Stability* — To test for lateral excursion of the patella, place both thumbs over the medial patellar border, with the hands around the quadriceps and proximal tibia, respectively. The knee is flexed from 0° to 30° while applying a lateral force. Movement greater than 1.5-2.0 cm will bring on the positive apprehension sign in which the patient will sense subluxation is imminent, contract the quadriceps, sit up immediately, and grasp the knee. Excessive lateral excursion in the absense of a positive apprehension sign is an indication of potential subluxation of the patella, and the VMO should be strengthened. Medial stability can be tested in the same way using a medial force. Decreased medial stability indicates a tight lateral retinaculum.
3. *Ligament-Cartilage Testing*
   a. *Medial Stability* (see Figure 14C-3a, b)

   Valgus stress is applied to the knee at *full extension* to test the integrity of the MCL, capsule, and cruciate ligaments. Significant laxity ($> 0.5-1$ cm) compared to the opposite knee indicates major ligament and capsular damage.

   Valgus stress applied to the knee at 30° flexion tends to isolate the MCL as other structures are relaxed. Laxity greater than the control knee indicates tearing or complete rupture of the MCL.

   It is important to identify the quality of the end point when stressing the knee. A solid, abrupt end point indicates at least a partially intact MCL, while a soft, mushy end point and 3+ laxity indicates a complete rupture of the MCL. It also is important to note the presence of pain during the exam. Ab-

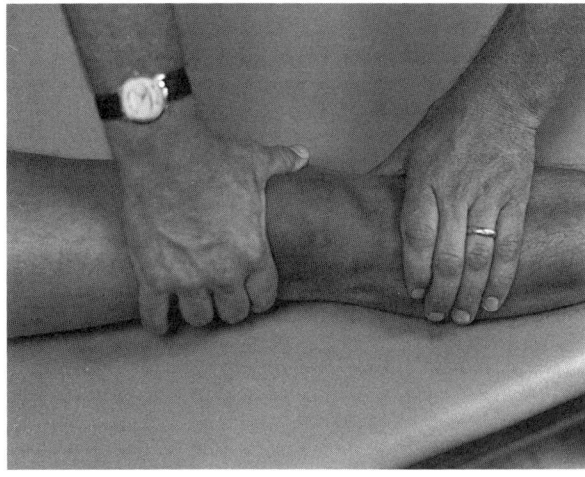

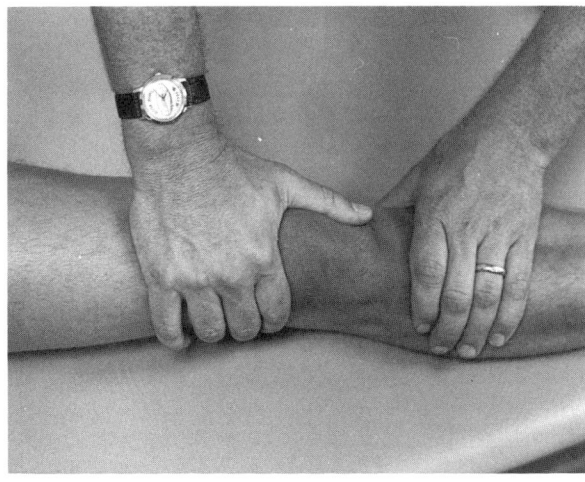

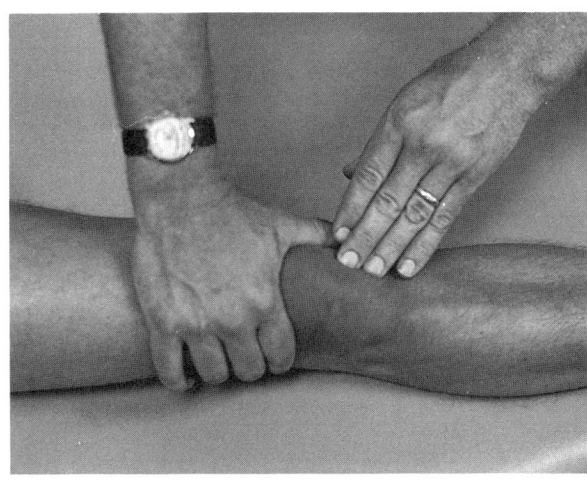

**Fig. 14C-2.** (A) Patella ballottement test for major effusion. (B, C) Tests for minor effusion.

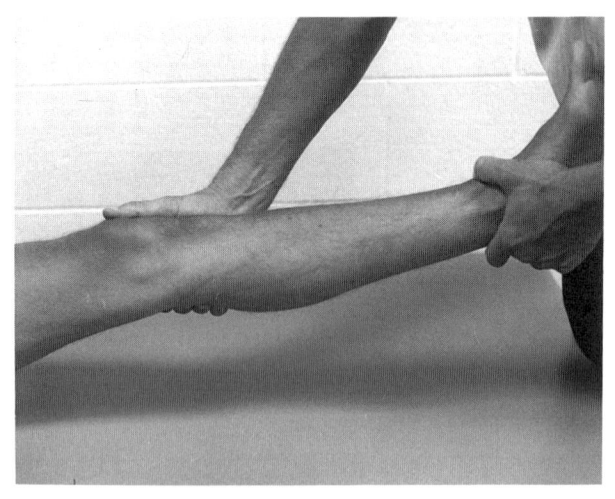

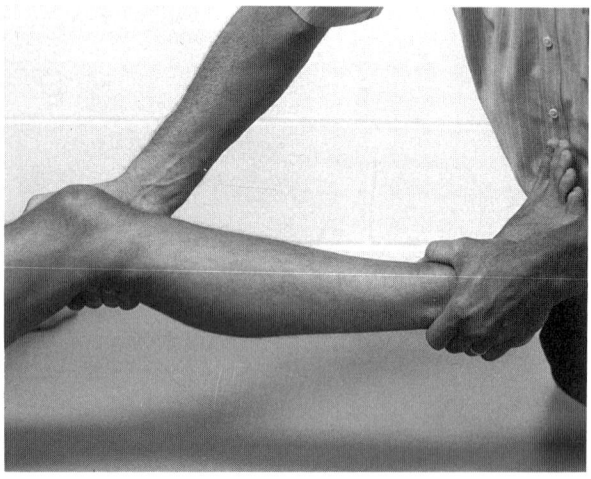

**Fig. 14C-3.** Medial Stability Testing. a) 0° varus stress; b) 30° varus stress

sence of pain could indicate laxity from previous injury or complete rupture of the MCL, since a patient with a complete MCL tear has less discomfort than one with a partial tear.

b. *Lateral Stability*

Varus stress is applied to the knee at full extension to test the integrity of the LCL, ITB, popliteus, lateral capsule, and cruciate ligament. As above, significant laxity indicates major injury.

Varus stress applied to the knee at 30° flexion tends to isolate the LCL and ITB. It is important to note that most people have a degree of physiological laxity in this position. By placing the lateral ankle of the affected leg onto the contralateral knee, the LCL can be readily palpated.

c. *Anterior/Posterior Stability*
1. *Lachman* — the most reliable test for isolated cruciate tears (Katz, 1986; Donaldson, 1985) is performed by placing the hands on the anterior distal femur and posterior proximal tibia (see Figure 14C-4). With the knee in 15-20° flexion (to relax hamstring muscles), a gentle anterior force is applied to the tibia while stabilizing the femur. The amount of anterior excursion, as well as the quality of the end point, should be noted. It can be difficult to distinguish between PCL and ACL involvement. In both cases, there is a significant amount of anterior excursion. The PCL-deficient knee begins its excursion from an abnormally posterior position and moves forward to the normal position. The mechanism of injury is an indication of the particular cruciate ligament involved, but a careful physical exam is the key to diagnosis. PCL rupture will produce a positive sag sign. When the hips are flexed to 45°, and knees flexed to 90° in the supine position, there is a sagging of the tibial tubercle on the affected side.
2. *Drawer Test* — Performed with the patient in the supine position, with the hip flexed to 45° and the knee to 90° and the examiner sitting on the patient's foot to stabilize the tibia (see Figure 14C-5). The hands are placed behind the proximal tibia and the tibia is pulled toward the examiner. It is important to check for relaxation of the hamstring muscle, as the examination is difficult to perform in the presence of tight hamstrings. The test is performed with the foot straight ahead and then in full internal and external rotation.

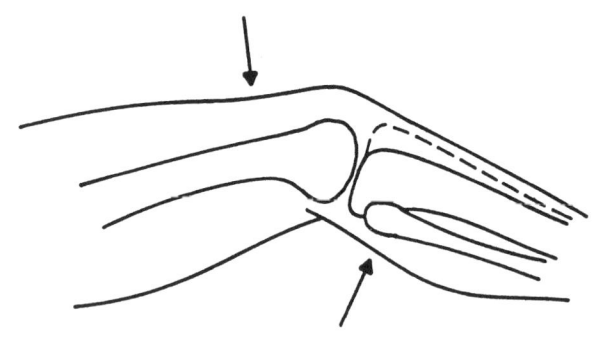

**Fig. 14C-4.** Lachman Test for ACL Deficiency

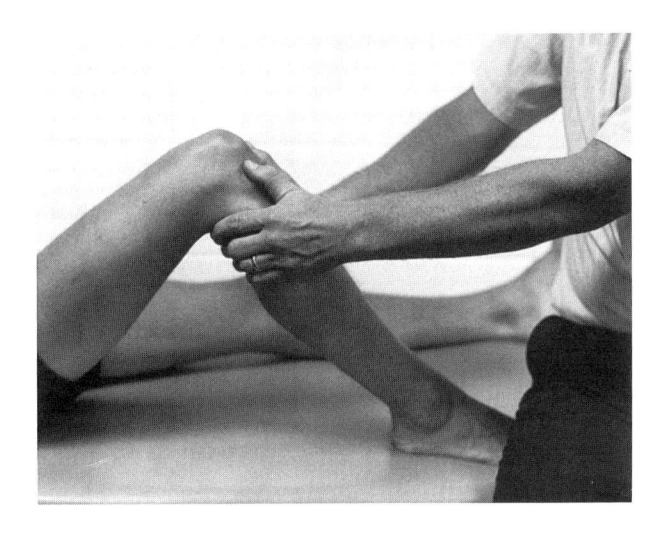

**Fig. 14C-5.** Anterior Drawer Stress Test

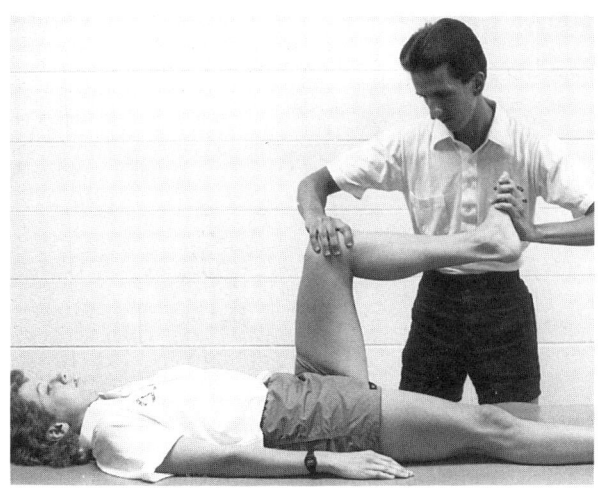

   a. Forward movement with foot straight ahead implies ACL laxity or rupture.
   b. Backward movement with foot straight ahead implies PCL laxity or rupture.
   c. Forward movement with foot turned out implies AMRI (a laxity of the ACL and the posterior medial capsule).
   d. Forward movement with foot turned in implies ALRI (laxity of the ACL and the posterior lateral capsule).
   e. Excessive and equal excursion of the tibia in the neutral, external rotation, and internal rotation position implies deficiency of the PCL and also likely deficiency of the ACL.
3. *Meniscus Evaluation*
   a. *McMurray Test* (see Figure 14C-6) — Performed with the patient in the supine position and the knee completely flexed. (Full flexion of the knee will often produces pain if the meniscus is torn.) The tibia is then externally rotated and the knee is extended with a valgus force exerted on the knee. Thumb and index or middle finger are held over the joint line to feel for a click as the knee is extended. Repeated but with a varus force on the knee. Then the tibia is internally rotated and the knee extended with a valgus followed by a varus force as above. By doing the test in this manner, pressure is exerted on different portions of the medial and lateral meniscus. A positive test results when a painful click or pain alone is felt. A painless click is not significant.
   b. *Apley* (see Figure 14C-7a) — Performed in

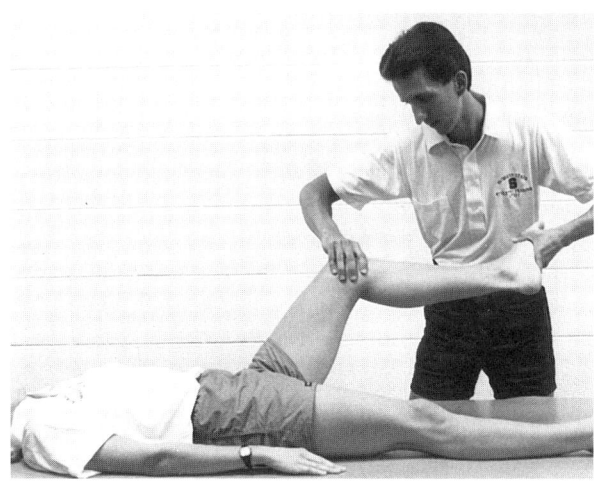

a.

b.

**Fig. 14C-6.** McMurray Test
A. Knee in flexed position. B. Test is performed by externally rotating the tibia and extending the knee.

the prone position with the knee flexed while axial force is applied to the heel while rotating the tibia. The test is positive when there is pain with the above procedure *but absence of pain* with simple rotation of the tibia without axial loading, and absence of pain with distraction of the tibia away from the femur (see Figure 14C-7b). The latter procedure is performed by pulling up on the ankle while the opposite hand stabilizes the femur. Pain with the latter two procedures indicates a source of pain other than the meniscus (e.g., ligament sprain).
4. *Anteriolateral Rotary Instability (ALRI)* — Many exams have been devised to test for ALRI. The Losee test seems most appropriate because it reproduces the exact mechanism of instabil-

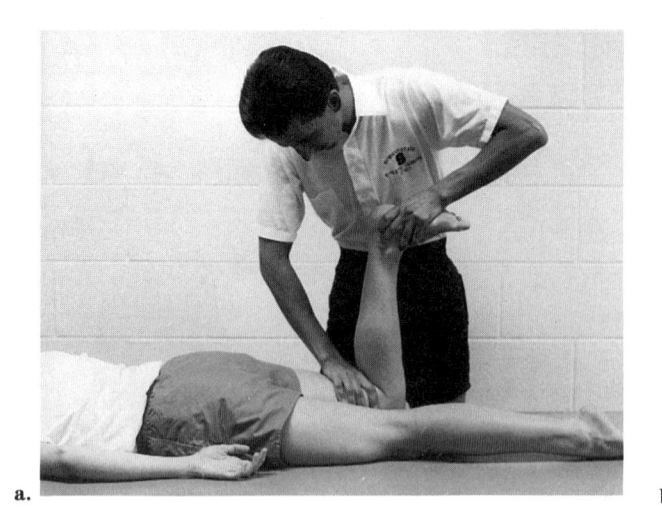

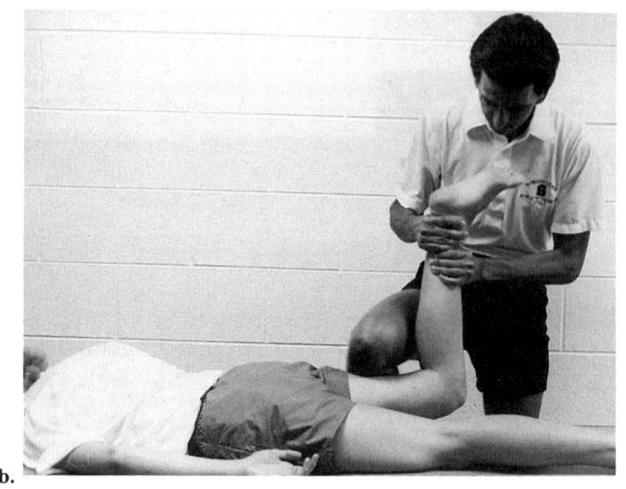

**Fig. 14C-7.** Apley Test
A. Apley Test performed in prone position with knee flexed while applying axial force to the heel while rotating the tibia. B. Distraction of the tibia away from the femur by holding the femur with the examiner's knee and pulling upward on the patient's knee.

ity that the patient experiences and gives minimal discomfort. Other tests demonstrate a "different" instability and also often cause pain. The Losee test is performed by externally rotating the tibia (to keep the tibia in a reduced position), placing a valgus stress on the knee (to accentuate subluxation), and slowly extending the knee. Anterior subluxation of the lateral tibial plateau, recognized by the patient as similar to his instability makes the test positive. See the knee exam sheet for the rating scales that relate to the above tests.

5. *Ober Test for ITB* (see Figure 14C-8a-c) — This test is performed with the individual lying on his side with the painful knee in the superior position. The examiner grasps the ankle with one hand and places the opposite hand on the patient's hip. The hip is fully extended by pulling on the ankle with the knee in 45° flexion. With a tight iliotibial band, the knee will remain in the same plane instead of falling into the adducted position that would result if good flexibility of the iliotibial band existed. Lateral knee pain is reproduced when the tight iliotibial band is forced into an adducted position.

6. *Related Areas* — It is important to realize that knee pain may originate from a number of different sources:
    1. *Hip* — A completely painless ROM of the hips eliminates the possibility of a slipped femoral epiphysis, Legg-Calve-Perthes disease, or significant degenerative joint disease as sources of pain. An abnormal hip exam should have further work-up.
    2. *Lower Back* — A negative SLR makes sciatic pain unlikely but not impossible.
    3. *Feet* — Biomechanical analysis to identify overpronation is important, as PFD and MCL pain can result from this biomechanical problem.

**Joint Fluid Aspiration**

A patient with significant ligamentous damage should be referred to an orthopedic surgeon who may perform joint aspiration. However, knee injuries where there is a questionable history and no audible pop on examination, no immediate effusion, or positive test should undergo a diagnostic aspiration if an effusion eventually develops. A bloody, as opposed to a serosanguinous, tap indicates a need for more immediate orthopedic referral. The details of performing a proper joint aspiration are not presented in this text, but strict aseptic technique is mandatory.

**Radiographic Studies.** Routine x-rays consist of AP and lateral views. "Sunrise and "tunnel" views also help differentiate certain knee complaints. Weight-bearing views are used to detect significant osteoarthritis and joint narrowing. MRI will show ligamentous (especially ACL and PCL) and meniscus tears. Kinematic MRI is used to evaluate patellar tracking. CT scanning also has a role in the workup of specific knee complaints. Detailed eval-

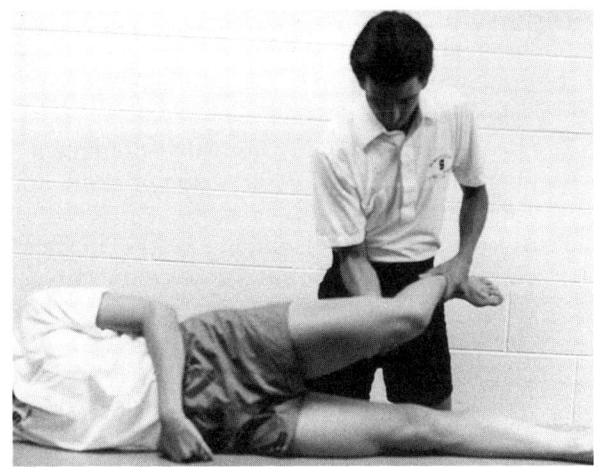

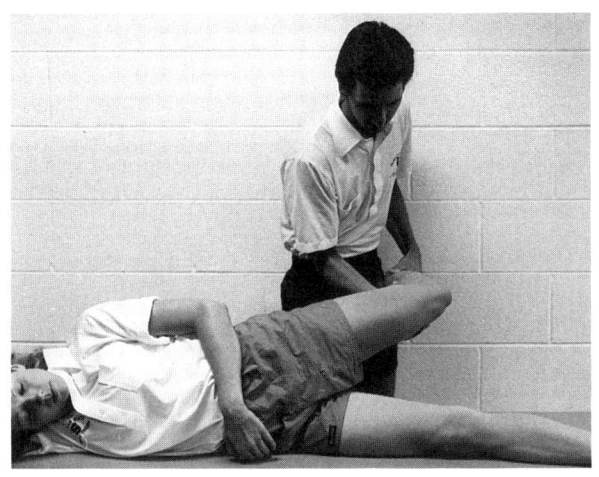

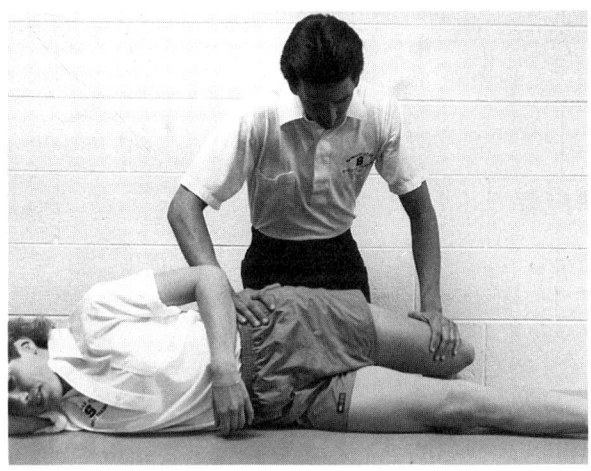

**Fig. 14C-8.** Ober Test for ITB Tightness
A. Ober Test performed with patient on his/her side with painful knee superior. B. Hip is fully extended with the knee in 45° flexion. C. Illiciting pain by abducting the hip.

uation of patients has led to more accurate diagnosis and specific treatment programs for common knee injuries discussed below (Jacobson, 1989).

## MOST COMMON INJURIES TO THE KNEE

### Knee Extensor Mechanism

1. **Prepatellar Bursitis** (Housemaid's Knee)
    *Mechanism of Injury* — direct trauma, or friction, as in kneeling position in wrestling.
    *Most Common Sports* — Wrestling, basketball, baseball/softball (sliding)
    *Presenting Complaint* — Anterior knee pain and/or swelling
    *Physical Findings* — Prepatellar swelling, often crepitation, tenderness, pain-free ROM except in terminal flexion
    *Differential Diagnosis* — PFD, contusion
    *Treatment*
    - Aspiration of bursa (may be hemorrhagic) using sterile technique; examine fluid for infection.
    - Compression bandage or knee pad is helpful.
    - An Iowa study done over a three year period (Mysnyk, 1986) had 6 cases out of 15 that were septic bursitis; 50% were asymptomatic. Gram stain and culture should be done on all aspirates.
    - Injection of corticosteroids is controversial (King, 1990).
    - Recurrent episodes are likely after the initial occurence.
    - No activities are allowed which place the knee in contact with the ground (kneeling, etc.).

2. **Subluxating or Dislocating Patella**
    *Mechanism of Injury* — Extending and externally rotating (tibia on femur) the weight bearing knee such as a football player suddenly changing direction. It often occurs as an acute injury and the patient feels as if the leg is giving way. Usually occurs with the knee in a slightly flexed position. Spontaneous reduction usually follows dislocation.
    *Most Common Sports* — Football, basketball, ballet, gymnastics
    *Presenting Complaint* — Rapid onset of effusion, often audible "pop," inability to continue playing, and history of giving way. Less

swelling and disability are noted if the condition is chronic.

*Presenting Findings* — Moderate effusion, diffuse tenderness, point tenderness over the VMO and medial retinaculum, positive apprehension test, negative Lachman. Most of the muscle and retinacular attachments to the medial patella are torn.

*Differential Diagnosis* — ACL sprain, MCL sprain

*X-ray* — The Laurin view (Laurin, 1978) of the lateral patellofemoral angle is very useful in diagnosing subluxation. A parallel angle or one that opens medially is present in patellar subluxation. Occasionally, a fracture of the patella or lateral femoral condyle occurs and results in loose body (Eisele, 1991).

*Treatment* — RICE, knee immobilized 4-6 weeks. Consider orthopedic consult for arthroscopy if there is severe pain (rule out osteochondral fracture), or if unsure of the diagnosis. Rehabilitation is done with VMO exercises to stabilize lateral excursion and therapy for hamstrings and ITB stretching and strengthening. With recurrent subluxation or dislocation, use immobilization until symptoms resolve, then make a referral to an orthopedic surgeon to assess need for surgery (lateral release or realignment procedures) (Henry, 1986; Eisele, 1991). A dynamic patellar brace or NSAID may be appropriate. Conservative treatment may take four to six months with 80%-90% of patients improving (Henry, 1989; Whitelaw, 1989; Steiner, 1988).

3. **Osteochondral Fracture** (Hopkinson, 1985)

*Mechanism of Injury* — Associated with subluxation or dislocation of the patella, direct trauma over patella, medial, or lateral condyles, or rotation on flexed weight bearing knee. Severe trauma not necessary to produce an osteochondral fracture.

*Most Common Sports* — Football, basketball.

*Presenting Complaint* — Often audible "pop," pain at specific joint angle, swelling; pain often is out of proportion to the known injury. Locking is possible if there are loose bony fragments and causes an inability to move the knee.

*Presenting Findings* — Moderate effusion (bloody effusion with fat globules), point tender at site of fracture, negative Lachman, ligaments intact.

*Differential Diagnosis* — ACL, patellar subluxation, meniscus tear.

*X-ray* — Standard AP, lateral plus tangential views, such as the merchant or skyline, may be needed to identify bony defect. Remember that chondral defects do not show up on x-ray.

*Treatment* — 1) RICE — immobilization in knee immobilizer; 2) special x-rays as indicated, 3) orthopedic referral for arthroscopy and possible removal or reattachment of fragments. Note that the larger the fracture fragment, the poorer the prognosis (Cahill, 1985; Eisele, 1991).

4. **Patellofemoral Dysfunction Versus Chondromalacia Patella** (see Overuse)
5. **Patellar Tendinitis** (see Miscellaneous and Overuse)
6. **Patellar Fracture.** This is an uncommon sports injury caused by severe trauma directly to the patella. This type of force could be produced in a snowmobiling accident. There is limited ROM, pain, and swelling over the anterior knee. X-rays will reveal the fracture which is often comminuted. Orthopedic referral is necessary for repair. Initial treatment includes RICE, immobilization, and crutches.
7. **Osgood-Schlatter's Disease** (see Miscellaneous)
8. **Suprapatellar Bursitis**

*Mechanism of Injury* — Direct trauma over suprapatellar bursa

*Most Common Sports* — Football, wrestling

*Presenting Complaint* — Pain over distal, anterior quadricep muscle

*Physical Findings* — Point tenderness over suprapatellar bursa, may have crepitus; will often have pain with resistance to extension. Chronic swelling may persist despite treatment.

*Differential Diagnosis* — Quadriceps strain, contusion

*Treatment* — 1) NSAID, Butazolidin® 100 mg QID (short 6 day course); 2) activity as tolerated, 3) use of knee pads for protection, 4) avoid aggravating activities.

## Ligaments/Capsule Injury

1. **MCL Sprains**

*Mechanism of Injury* — 1) Valgus force applied to the knee. Limited force can result in isolated MCL involvement, while greater force can result in capsular as well as ACL rupture; 2) external rotation (femur on tibia), 3) overuse.

*Most Common Sports* — Football, wrestling, gymnastics, swimming, running, ballet.

**Grade I MCL Sprain** — Stretching of MCL fibers without an increase in joint laxity.

*Presenting Complaint* — Pain over medial aspect of knee.

*Physical Findings* — Point tenderness at any site along MCL, often at proximal or distal attachments. No swelling. No joint instability, but often pain with valgus stressing.

*Differential Diagnosis* — Meniscus tear, contusion, or pes anserine tendinitis.

*Treatment* — Ice, NSAID; use a knee immobilizer for three or four days. Activity — relative rest, substitute cycling (for aerobic endurance) until resumption of full activity is possible; three to four min VMO protocol (to maintain strength). See Wisconsin program for rehabilitation of isolated 1st and 2nd degree MCL sprains (Table 14C-6).

**Grade II MCL Sprain** — Partial tearing of MCL fibers with increased laxity on valgus stressing. Grade II can involve anything from 5% to 95% of the fibers.

*Presenting Complaint* — Pain and swelling over medial aspect of knee so that the athlete often is unable to continue playing.

*Physical Findings* — Swelling localized to medial aspect of knee, point tenderness at site of injury along MCL. Pain and increased laxity with valgus stressing (1-2+) at 30° but with distinct end point. Rule out ACL sprain or capular injury that would make orthopedic referral necessary.

*Treatment* — 1) Rest, immobilizer from 1-3 weeks to allow MCL fibers to reapproximate, ice initial 2-3 days, 3-4 times a day; 2) while wearing splint, encourage patient to do 4 min VMO; 3) as soon as pain has started to subside, discontinue immobilizer and follow Wisconsin program for rehabilitation of isolated Grade II MCL injury (see Table 14C-6).

---

Table 14C-6. Wisconsin Program

REHABILITATION OF 1° and 2° MEDIAL and LATERAL COLLATERAL LIGAMENT INJURIES

*Day 1 to Day 3:*
1. Crutches with partial weight bearing
2. Compression dressing — loosen if ankle becomes swollen
3. Ice 3 to 4 times a day for 10 minutes
4. Quad sets — 3 sets of 20; 3 times per day
5. Straight leg lifts — 3 sets of 20; 3 times per day
6. Wear knee immobilizer at night

*Day 3 to Approximately Day 7:*
1. Whirlpool for range of motion (biking motion), cold water for first 3 to 4 days then warm water.
2. May utilize swimming pool instead, 30-45 minutes straight ahead flutter kick trying to bend knee.
3. Straight leg raises with maximum weight that can be done 12 times. Do 3 sets of 12:
   a. hip extension
   b. hip flexion
   c. hip abduction
      1. knee must be kept straight
      2. no hip adduction
4. Continue with crutches and may use the knee immobilizer only while sleeping.
5. Continue with quad set exercises

*Day 7 to Day 14 (if 90° knee flexion present):*
1. Whirlpool or swimming for range of motion
2. Exercise bike for 15 minutes; if Fitron 60 RPM
3. Quad sets
4. Orthotron, speed 5; 3 sets of 10, or Universal or Nautilus weight program. Quad, 3 sets of 12 with maximum weight; hamstrings, 3 sets of 12 with maximum weight

**Table 14C-6. Wisconsin Program (*Continued*)**

*Day 14 to Completion (if full range of flexion and extension):*
1. Whirlpool
2. Bike 15 minutes
3. Orthotron, 3 sets of 10 at speed 3; 3 sets of 10 at speed 5 when equal to opposite side; then 3 sets of 10 at speed 7. Nautilus or Universal, 3 sets of 12 of maximum weight for quads and hamstrings.
4. Start Running Program. See additional sheet.

*To Return to Practice you must have:*
1. Full range of motion
2. No pain
3. Quad and hamstring strength must be within 40% of the normal leg
4. Must be able to complete the entire running program
5. Athlete should be rechecked by a physician when he completes the entire program if there has been a 2° or 3° ligament injury.

RUNNING PROGRAM

The following running program should be used as a measure of an athlete's progress as he/she returns from an injury to a lower extremity. When an athlete has completed the *ENTIRE* program, he/she is ready to return to competition.

The athlete may begin the running program when he/she can hop up and down on the toes of the injured extremity without bearing weight on the other leg, 5 times.

*Outdoors*
1. Jog one mile; stop immediately when limping is noticed or when there is mild pain. When the athlete can jog one mile pain free;*
2. Do six eighty yard sprints at 1/2 speed. If no pain or limp;
3. Do six eighty yard sprints at 3/4 speed. If no pain or limp;
4. Do six eighty yard sprints at full speed. If no pain;
5. Do six eighty yards cutting at 3/4 speed. If no pain;
6. Do six eighty yards cutting at full speed. Always plant on outside foot to cut. If no pain; 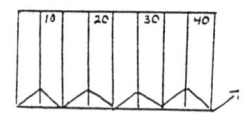
7. Do ten minutes of running and/or jumping drills related to your sport. When the athlete has completed the entire running program, he/she is ready to return to competition.**

*Indoors*
1. Jog eighteen laps around the basketball court. Stop immediately when limping is noticed or when there is mild pain. If pain free;
2. Do fifteen lengths of the gym at 1/2 speed. If no pain;
3. Do fifteen lengths of the gym at 3/4 speed. If no pain;
4. Do fifteen lengths of the gym at full speed. If no pain;
5. Do 15 lengths cutting at 3/4 speed. Be sure to plant the outside foot with each cut. If no pain; 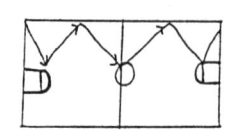
6. Do fifteen lengths cutting at full speed. If no pain;
7. Do ten minutes of running or jumping drills related to your sport. When the athlete has completed the entire program, he/she is ready to return to competition.**

Adapted from the University of Wisconsin Division of Orthopedic Surgery.
*If the athlete does not complete the entire program on a particular day, he/she should start at the beginning the following day.
**Each running workout must be followed by a fifteen minute application of ice.

---

**Grade III MCL Sprain** — Complete disruption of superficial MCL fibers
*Presenting Complaint* — Same as second degree, often less pain as complete nerve fibers are torn.
*Physical Findings* — Swelling over medial aspect, point tender over MCL, increased laxity (3+) with soft end point at 30° flexion and valgus stress. Any increased laxity at 0° and valgus stressing represents ACL and capsular injury. Rule out ACL or meniscus injury.
*Treatment* — 1) Orthopedic referral 2) Isolated third degree MCL sprains are treated conser-

vatively with longer period of knee immobilization, use of ice, NSAID and a rehabilitation period lasting 6-10 weeks (Indelicato, 1983). Most isolated MCL sprains allow complete return to activities.

**2. ACL Sprain**

*Mechanism of Injury* — 1) Noncontact — running down field with sudden change of direction toward planted foot; 2) hyperextension injury, or 3) part of multiple ligament injury (severe valgus, varus, or rotational stress).

*Most Common Sports* — Football, basketball, gymnastics — All sports are possible.

**Partial Tears**

*Presenting Complaint* — May have audible "pop" associated with immediate effusion (usually within two hours after injury).

*Physical Findings* — Effusion 2-3+ (less if seen immediately), Apprehension — negative, Lachman-positive (1-2+) with abrupt end point. The Lachman, anterior drawer, and lateral pivot shift have been the traditional tests for ACL instability. Recent research has shown the Lachman to be the superior test for isolated ACL injury; other tests become positive as additional ligamentous and capsular damage occurs. See Lachman test under physical exam. It is important to do the Losee test for ALRI.

*Differential Diagnosis* — Capsular strain.

*Treatment* — 1) Knee immobilizer, ice, crutches; 2) orthopedic consultation to confirm partial versus complete tear with arthroscopic exam (golden period for ACL operation is 12-48 hrs and certainly no longer than 10 days after injury), and 3) aggressive rehabilitation has yielded very good results for partial ACL tears (Odensten, 1985). A full discussion of indications for surgery and rehabilitation techniques are discussed in orthopedic and rehabilitation textbooks; therapy is constantly being reevaluated and changed.

**Complete Rupture ACL**

*Presenting Complaint* — Most often audible "pop" and immediate effusion.

*Physical Findings* — Effusion 2-4+, apprehension negative, Lachman positive (3+) with soft end point. Patient often feels little pain.

*Treatment* — Knee immobilizer, ice, crutches, immediate orthopedic referral if there is any reason to consider reconstructive surgery. This decision is based on the age, activity level, and sports of the patient (Cabaud, 1985). Conservative treatment of the older or non-athletic individual is appropriate but they do need careful follow-up. The knee should be 1) immobilized to let any injured ligamentous tissue heal; 2) transferred to cast brace for return of motion, and 3) functionally rehabilitated with emphasis on hamstring strength. Free weights or isokinetic devices may be used. *Immediate surgical repair* is appropriate for athletic individuals who want the best knee function possible. The rehabilitation period may take up to 12 months. Derotation braces are readily available for the later stages of rehabilitation and for activity.

Chronic ACL laxity will result in the development of ALRI, a predisposition for meniscal tearing and recurrent giving way of the knee joint and osteoarthritis. Activity restrictions for ACL deficient knees include no participation in long court sports such as tennis or basketball, or in sports involving sprinting and sudden changes of direction. Short court sports such as racquetball, swimming, cycling, and down hill skiing are well tolerated. Derotation braces will not completely protect the ACL deficient knee.

**3. PCL Sprain** (Parolie, 1986)

*Mechanism of Injury* — Direct force against anterior tibia, [such as having a baseball catcher block the plate before an oncoming player slides into the anterior tibia.] It is associated with multiple ligamentous injuries, severe varus, valgus, or rotational forces.

*Most Common Sports* — Football, skiing.

*Presenting Complaint* — Audible "pop" and immediate effusion not as classic as in ACL sprain.

*Physical Findings* — Effusion 2-4+, positive Lachman associated with positive sag sign. Partial tears will have 1-2+ Lachman and abrupt end point. Complete ruptures will have 3+ Lachman with soft end point with more instability in the posterior plane on testing.

*Differential Diagnosis* — Meniscus tear, MCL sprain, or capsular tears.

*Treatment* — 1) Orthopedic referral. Isolated PCL tears (both partial and complete) do very well with aggressive rehabilitation. If there is 3+ Lachman that does not decrease with internal rotation on drawer testing, surgical repair is likely to be required. 2) Rehabilitation of injured knee to equal or greater strength of unaffected knee should be confirmed by isokinetic testing. This has a very strong correlation with a good result, independent of the degree of laxity. Most isolated low grade PCL sprains do not require surgical repair. The rehabilitation phase often takes a minimum of three to four months with emphasis on all supporting knee musculature.

4. **LCL** — Uncommon injury — less than 1% of acute knee injuries (Jensen, 1985)

   *Mechanism of Injury* — Varus force, or severe rotational force

   *Most Common Sports* — Football, wrestling, gymnastics

   **Grade I LCL Sprain**

   *Presenting Complaint* — Lateral knee pain, able to continue playing. May hear sound at time of injury.

   *Physical Findings* — No swelling but point tenderness over LCL (see Physical Exam). No increase in varus instability at 30° of knee flexion.

   *Differential Diagnosis* — popliteus tendinitis, ITB syndrome, or lateral meniscus tear

   *Treatment* — Same as Grade I MCL sprain

   **Grade II LCL Sprain**

   *Presenting Complaint* — Lateral knee pain; usually not able to continue playing.

   *Physical Findings* — Mild swelling over lateral aspect of the knee, point tenderness over LCL, 1-2+ varus instability with distinct end point.

   *Differential Diagnosis* — Same as Grade I.

   *Treatment* — Same as Grade II MCL sprain. Orthopedic referral needed if conservative measures fail.

   **Grade III LCL Sprain**

   *Presenting Complaint* — Lateral knee pain; unable to continue playing.

   *Physical Findings* — Mild to moderate swelling over lateral aspect of the knee, point tenderness over LCL, 3+ varus instability with soft end point

   *Treatment* — Knee immobilizer, ice, and immediate orthopedic referral for surgical repair.

5. **ALRI** — The most common form of disabling instability for the athlete

   *Mechanism of Injury* — May occur as acute injury involving ACL and posteriolateral capsule. Most often, ALRI is a late development of progressive laxity of other capsular and ligamentous supports in the ACL-deficient knee.

   *Most Common Sports* — Football, skiing, wrestling, gymnastics

   *Presenting Complaint* — 1) Acute — see ACL sprain; 2) chronic - recurrent giving way of the knee.

   *Physical Findings* — Positive Lachman (2-3+), positive Losee (2-3+).

   *Treatment* — The conservative method is aggressive rehabilitation emphasizing the hamstring, abductor, and external rotator muscle groups using free weights or isokinetic devices (Walla, 1985). A derotation brace may be helpful. The second method is orthopedic referral for possible surgical repair (Andrews, 1985) if giving way persists after an attempt at aggressive rehabilitation.

6. **AMRI**

   *Mechanism of Injury* — 1) May occur as an acute injury involving ACL, MCL, and posteromedial capsule (valgus force, rotational force); 2) late development of ACL-deficient knee.

   *Most Common Sports* — Football, skiing, gymnastics.

   *Presenting Complaint* — Recurrent giving way.

   *Physical Findings* — Positive anterior drawer with foot externally rotated; Lachman often positive with increased valgus laxity.

   *Treatment* — Conservative treatment involves aggressive rehabilitation emphasizing the hamstring and internal rotator muscles. A derotation brace may be helpful. A second method is orthopedic referral for possible surgical repair involving tightening of the capsule, transfer of the patellar tendon, and possible ACL reconstruction.

### Intra-Articular Injury

1. **Meniscus** — Tears may be at the periphery or within the body of the meniscus and they may be complete or partial, longitudinal or horizontal. Medial tears are more common than lateral tears.

   *Mechanism of Injury* — 1) Weight bearing; noncontact; internal or external rotation; 2) associated with major ligament injury (valgus force causing "Terrible Triad").

*Most Common Sports* — Football, basketball, skiing, wrestling (50% lateral), baseball, gymnastics (Baker, 1985)

*Presenting Complaint* — Locking, pain, giving way, mild to moderate swelling developing over 24 hours. Symptoms may be recurrent.

*Physical Findings* — Effusion 1-2+, joint line tenderness, pain with extreme flexion, locking or block preventing terminal extension, positive McMurray and or positive Apley sign, may have VMO atrophy if there is a history of one to two week old injury. All ligament and Lachman tests intact.

*Differential Diagnosis* — Coronary ligament sprain (attaches anterior horns of meniscus), reactive synovitis, MCL sprain, LCL sprain, capsular sprain, popliteus tendinitis, or ITB Syndrome Contusion.

*Treatment* — 1) Rest, ice, knee immobilizer, NSAID; 2) if locked, attempt to manipulate and unlock; 3) during immobilization —4 min VMO exercises; 4) orthopedic referral for acute locked knee, combined major ligamentous and meniscus injury or for giving way, recurrent pain, effusion, and locking. Orthopedic options include allowing the torn meniscus to heal (5%); surgical repair (20%); partial menisectomy (75%), and rarely, complete menisectomy (DeHaven, 1985). OD of patella is rare (Eisele, 1991).

2. **Osteochondritis Dessicans** (OD) — Juvenile OD begins before adult OD and after the closure of the epiphysis. A stress fracture of the subchondral bone may be the cause of juvenile OD. It is not an osteochondral fracture or an accessary ossification center. If the fracture heals before closure of the epiphysis, the prognosis is good; if not, there will be a high incidence of nonunion, joint deterioration, and pain (Cahill, 1985). OD of the patella is rare (Eisele, 1991).

*Presenting Complaint* — Nonspecific diffuse knee pain, giving way (locking if loose body).

*Physical Findings* — Tender to palpation over affected condyle; may have specific arc in ROM that is painful.

*Differential Diagnosis* — Meniscus tear, osteochondral fracture, or subluxation of patella.

*X-ray* — Most common site of fracture is the posterolateral aspect of the medial condyle; positive Wilson sign (foot internally rotated while the valgus force is applied as the knee is extended from 30° of flexion, causing pain).

*Treatment* — 1) Orthopedic referral, as arthroscopic evaluation to remove fragment and curretage of the patella may be indicated; 2) follow-up with bone scans; the larger the lesion, the poorer the prognosis; 3) cast immobilization may be required, and 4) lateral release may be necessary for coexisting conditions (Steiner, 1988; Schwarz, 1988).

3. **Plica** — The medial patellar plica represents a redundancy in the synovial fold found in 18.5-55% of the population (Patel, 1986). Approximately 4% incidence of all knee injuries seen in a large sports medicine clinic (Broom, 1986).

*Mechanism of Injury* — 1) Direct trauma (60%) (Broom, 1986) which may cause hemmorhage, effusion, and intermittant synovitis that can lead to fibrosis and thickening of the plica; 2) overuse in 40% of cases.

*Most Common Sports* — Running sports, soccer, basketball.

*Presenting Complaint* — Pain (65-100%), snapping or clicking (50-64%), giving way (42-59%), pseudolocking (45%) (Broom, 1986; Nottage, 1983; Patel, 1986).

*Physical Findings* — Medial plica tenderness (one finger breadth above medial joint line beside the patella); positive Apley test (37%); pain with resistance to extension; medial joint line tenderness (19%) (Nottage, 1986); pseudolocking (plica impinges on medial femoral condyle during knee extension causing clicking).

*Differential Diagnosis* — PFD, meniscus tear, reactive synovitis

*Treatment* — 1) Ice, NSAID, relative rest for two to four weeks; 2) hamstring stretches, quadriceps strengthening (4 min VMO); 3) orthopedic referral for excision of medial patellar plica.

4. **Reactive Synovitis**

*Mechanism of Injury* — Nonspecific synovitis, most often after activity without specific incidence of trauma.

*Presenting Complaint* — Pain free to mild discomfort, gradual onset of effusion.

*Physical Findings* — Mild effusion (trace-2+); may have anterior joint-line tenderness.

*Differential Diagnosis* — Meniscus tear, plica.

*Treatment* — 1) rest one to two days; NSAID if pain present; 2) as effusion resolves over two to five days, normal activity can be resumed, but symptoms may recur periodically; 3) slow, gradual return to activity, especially running, 4) ice after all activity.

## Miscellaneous Knee Injuries

1. **Epiphyseal Fracture** — The epiphysis is the weakest link in the young knee, and major trauma could result in a fractured epiphysis rather than a Grade III ligament sprain.
   *Mechanism of Injury* — Severe varus or valgus force or severe rotational force.
   *Presenting Complaint* — Severe knee pain.
   *Physical Findings* — Marked effusion and swelling, severe tenderness over distal femoral epiphysis, limited ROM.
   *Differential Diagnosis* — Ligament injury or contusion.
   *Treatment* — 1) Ice, immobilization, crutches; 2) immediate orthopedic referral for repair, 3) may require x-ray stress views to demonstrate opening of epiphysis.

2. **Discoid Meniscus** — Uncommon abnormality resulting from failure of the meniscal tissue to reabsorb in infancy.
   *Presenting Complaint* — Chronic instability with movement
   *Physical Findings* — Painless snap and jerking with flexion and extension of knee; no effusion; nontender to palpation
   *Differential Diagnosis* — Meniscal cyst (Seger, 1986)
   *Treatment* — 1) Orthopedic referral for arthroscopic menisectomy; 2) once there is absence of pain and swelling, full ROM and full strength are required prior to return to sports. Patient commonly has recurrent symptoms, and high intensity sports often require modification.

3. **Osgood Schlatters Disease** (Kujahn, 1985) — Osteochondrosis at the tibial tubercle, possibly associated with repetitive microtrauma in preadolescents (Eisele, 1991). The most common form of traction apophysitis represents inflammation of the patellar tendon at its insertion. Cartilage fragments and bony ossicles may form in the tendon (Schmidt, 1989).
   *Mechanism of Injury* — Genetic but can be exacerbated by overuse.
   *Most Common Sports* — Track, basketball, jumping, running sports.
   *Presenting Complaint* — Enlarged and painful tibial tubercle.
   *Physical Findings* — Swelling and point tenderness over tibial tubercle.
   *Differential Diagnosis* — X-ray needed to rule out fracture of the tibial tubercle.
   *Treatment* — 1) Relative rest, restrict activity (especially jumping) as needed to control pain until self-limited problem resolves by early to mid-adolescence; 2) persistent pain unresponsive to rest necessitates x-ray to check for bony ossicles within tendon sheath; 3) orthopedic referral for possible excision of ossicles; 4) occasionally, long-leg casting is necessary but it should be avoided if possible; 5) NSAID may be attempted, and 6) regular ice application daily when symptomatic.

4. **Bipartite Patella** — .05%-2% incidence; males than females; condition related to inflammation of the synchondrosis (cartilage between bones). Occurs when superior lateral quadrant and patella fails to unite with the rest of patella. This results in a separate bony fragment which is attached to the rest of the patella by a fibrocartilaginous tissue which can become tender with direct trauma (Bourne, 1990).
   *Mechanism of Injury* — Overuse and direct trauma.
   *Presenting Complaint* — Anterior knee pain, mild to severe.
   *Physical Findings* — Point tenderness at the superolateral border of patella, often has palpable ridge.
   *Differential Diagnosis* — Quadriceps strain or quadriceps tendinitis
   *X-ray* — Houghston view demonstrates defect.
   *Treatment* — 1) Modify activity as tolerated; 2) NSAID or aspirin; 3) symptoms resolve in three to six weeks after which participation in active sports is allowed if protective padding is worn, and 4) rarely, conservative treatment fails and surgical excision of the fragment is required, with return to active sports in two to three months (Singer, 1985).

5. **Patellar Tendinitis** (Sinding-Larsen-Johansson Syndrome)

True apophysitis of inferior pole of patella seen in 8-13 year olds. Inflammation at the superior pole of patella where the quadriceps tendon is attached is less commonly seen (Schmidt, 1989).
   *Mechanism of Injury* — Overuse.

*Presenting Complaint* — Gradual onset of anterior knee pain, exacerbated by running and jumping sports.

*Physical Findings* — Point tenderness over inferior pole of patella, pain with resistance to extension.

*X-ray* — May see elongated inferior pole of patella in chronic cases.

*Treatment* — 1) Restrict activity to become symptom-free; 2) reassurance; 3) severe cases require cast immobilization for three weeks, then a slow return to activity over one or two weeks; 4) complete radiographic healing six to eight weeks after onset, and 5) may use NSAID.

6. **Ligament and Meniscal Injury** — This is uncommon in children, but the injury pattern becomes more similar to that of adults as adolescents approach adulthood. In the case of a severe ACL injury in adolescense, consider timing of augmentation or reconstruction procedures prior to epiphyseal closure.

## Overuse Injuries

1. **ITB Syndrome**

    *Mechanism of Injury* — Fatigue of tensor fascia lata (TFL) muscle results in tightening of the ITB. As the band tightens, it tends to rub against the lateral femoral condyle.

    *Presenting Complaint* — Delayed lateral knee pain usually beginning midway through a run (3 miles into a 6 mile run); may be associated with an audible snap at the lateral femoral condyle or over the greater trochanter.

    *Physical Findings* — Most often tender over lateral femoral condyle, but may be tender over insertion at Gerdy's tubercle and may involve bursa. Positive Ober's test that reproduces the pain felt by the patient.

    *Treatment* — 1) Relative rest — exercise is kept below pain threshold; 2) NSAID, ice massage; 3) stretching of ITB (see Figure 14C-9); 4) strengthening of TFL muscle by doing abduction on side with ankle weights; 3 sets of 20 repetitions, three to four times a week; symptoms usually subside in three weeks but may take as long as six months (Lindenburg, 1984), and 5) corticosteroid injection and surgery are reserved for resistant cases.

2. **Patellar Tendinitis** (Jumper's Knee) — Inflammation of patellar tendon at inferior pole of patella or at insertion of tendon on the tibial tubercle. May also involve infrapatellar bursa.

    *Mechanism of Injury* — Overuse — Grade I-IV.

    *Most Common Sports* — Running, basketball, volleyball, track and field.

    *Presenting Complaint* — Anterior knee pain with loading of patellofemoral joint; giving way of knee possible.

    *Physical Findings* — May have mild swelling over patellar tendon; tender to palpation over tendon; may have crepitus if the infrapatellar bursa is involved; pain with resistance to knee extension.

    *Differential Diagnosis* — PFD, Osgood-Schlatter's Disease, pes anserine tendinitis.

    *Treatment* — 1) Activity — as tolerated; for severe continuous pain (Grade IV), very restricted activity for one to two weeks; 2) ice massage before and after activity 5-10 minutes — may ice up to six to eight times per day; 3) NSAID 7-10 days; 4) patellar band or sleeve beneficial for some people; 5) 4 min VMO exercises; 6) stretching of quadriceps and hamstrings; 7) orthotics are beneficial in runner with excessive pronation, and 8) gradual return to activity.

3. **Patello-Femoral Dysfunction** (PFD) — Pain coming from the patellofemoral articulation can be caused from a minor abrasion of the patellar cartilage or a severe fibrillation of the undersurface of the patella. Chondromalacia patella represents the severe form and is an arthroscopic diagnosis.

    *Mechanism of Injury* — Overuse, especially in preadolescent and adolescent athletes; females more common than males; there is an uneven gliding of the patella in the femoral groove when the knee is flexed. The VMO portion of the quadriceps is responsible for locking the knee into extension and for keeping the patella in the femoral groove. Increased physical activity with a relatively weak VMO predisposes to PFD. Also, a female athlete with her wider pelvis tends to increase the Q angle > 15°, predisposing her to abnormal patellofemoral tracking.

    *Presenting Complaint* — Anterior knee pain, exacerbated after sitting for hours and then getting up (positive "theater sign") and going up or down stairs. May have intermittant effusion (caused by shredded particles of the patellar cartilage — chondromalacia).

*Physical Findings* — May have mild effusion, tender to palpation on under-surface of patella (exam performed by testing for medial and lateral excursion of the patella as described under physical exam, with direct palpation of the under surface of the patella with the thumb and index finger. Test for decreased medial excursion (indication of tight lateral retinaculum).

*Differential Diagnosis* — patellar tendinitis, plica.

*Treatment* — 1) Relative rest — substituting pain-free activity; 2) ice 5-10 min before and after activity (Antichm, 1986) or use contrast baths (heat 3 min then ice 2 min for three cycles); 3) NSAID; 4) 4 min VMO program; 5) patellar neoprene sleeve has been beneficial for some patients, and 6) if there is no response after six months of conservative treatment, surgical options, including patellar shaving or lateral release can be considered (Fulkerson, 1986; Eisele, 1991; Johnson, 1989).

4. **Pes Anserine Tendinitis/Bursitis** — Inflammation of gracilis, semitendonosis, and sartorius muscle insertion on the anteriomedial tibia.

*Mechanism of Injury* — Overuse-Grade I-IV.

*Most Common Sports* — Running, dancing, soccer.

*Presenting Complaint* — Anterior knee pain; mild swelling; pain with knee flexion, adduction, internal or external rotation.

*Physical Findings* — Mild swelling over pes anserine insertion; point tenderness over pes; crepitus indicates involvement of bursa; pain with resistance to flexion, adduction, internal or external rotation.

*Differential Diagnosis* — PFD, MCL sprain, plica, contusion

*Treatment* — 1) Relative rest — substitute cycling or swimming to maintain fitness; 2) ice 5-10 min before and after activity; 3) NSAID, and 4) four min VMO program.

# SECTION D.
# LOWER LEG

The lower leg, that portion of the body between the knee and ankle but not inclusive of those two joints, is the site of frequent, usually minor, injury. Injuries to the lower leg make up 3%-5% of all reported sports injuries (NEISS, 1981). More importantly, if those sports in which running is a major component are counted, the injury rate increases to 30% of all injuries seen for these sports (Brody, 1987).

## Anatomy

The proximal lower leg serves as the insertion for muscles originating from the thigh. The distal portion of the lower leg is intimately involved in the function of the ankle joint. The cortical surfaces of the tibia and fibula are the origin of muscles that move the ankle, foot, and toes (Figure 14D-1). Functionally, the fibula is considered a non-weight bearing bone although there is argument to the contrary in the literature. The tibia is the main weight bearing bone. It is triangular in shape, with its anterior border and anterior medial surface primarily subcutaneous. The fibula is situated posterio-laterally on the lower leg. While not directly involved with the knee joint, it does form the distal attachment of the lateral collateral ligament (LCL). In addition, it forms the vital lateral border of the ankle mortise. Connecting the tibia and fibula is an interosseous membrane that serves as the floor of the anterior compartment of the leg.

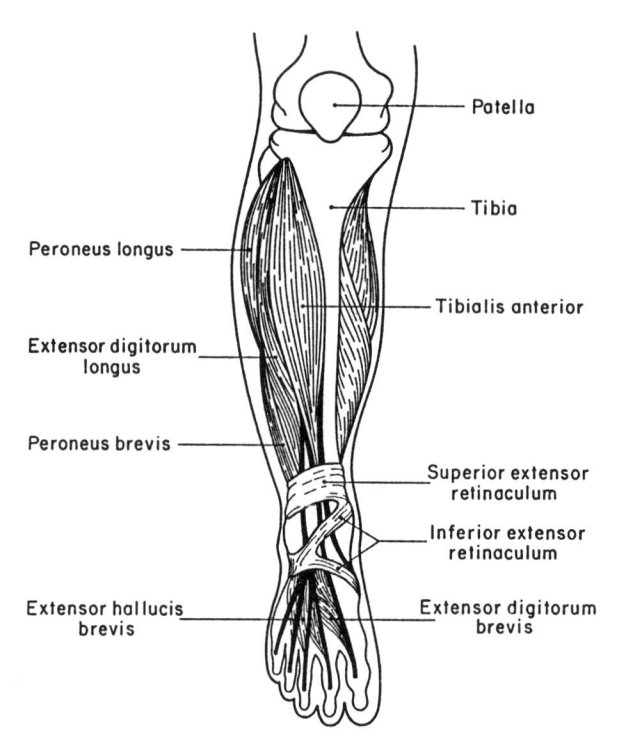

**Fig. 14D-1.** Lower Leg Muscle Origins and Attachments

On cross-section, the lower leg (Figure 14D-2) consists of five muscular compartments separated by intermuscular septa or fascial sheaths (Rorabeck and Armstrong, 1985). The anterior and lateral compartments permit little flexibility or expansion of the muscles contained within. Conversely, the posterior compartment is a loosely contained space not subject to the same constriction that might result from expansion due to injury. The muscles and neuromuscular bundles of the various compartments are:

*Anterior Compartment* — anterior tibial, extensor digitorum longus, extensor hallicus longus muscles, and peroneus tertius muscles. Also contained within the compartment is the anterior tibial neurovascular bundle.

*Lateral Compartment* — Peroneus longus and peroneus brevis muscles.

*Posterior Compartment* — subdivided into:

   a. superficial posterior — gastrocnemius, soleus, plantaris muscles, and lesser saphenous nerve
   b. posterior tibial — posterior tibial muscle
   c. deep posterior — flexor digitorum longus, flexor hallicus longus muscle, and posterior tibial vessels and nerves (including the peroneal vessels)

## Contusions

Contusions of the lower leg are extremely common because of the exposed anatomy of the lower leg. Sports in which contusions occur regularly include:

- Soccer, rugby, football — blow from an opponent's kick, usually to anterior lower leg
- Field hockey — blow from an opponent's stick to the anterior or posterior lower leg
- Baseball — two common mechanisms are a blow from a batted ball or laceration and contusion resulting from being "spiked" by a sliding opponent

*Biomechanics*— Acute trauma to the exposed lower leg usually occurs anteriorly and results in a contusion and/or hematoma of the underlying structures. These injuries are treated as bruises.

*Signs and Symptoms* — Classically, pain at impact, disability secondary to guarding, and swelling are associated with most soft tissue trauma. Swelling comes from extravasation of blood. Subsequent discoloration of the skin progresses within hours after injury. Assessment should include evaluation of the neurovascular bundles examined distally, as well as muscle group testing using active and passive resistance.

*Differential Diagnosis* — While a contusion to the lower leg is considered a straightforward injury, several complications can develop. Consider these specific injuries in the differential diagnosis:

1. *Subperiosteal hematoma* — The infamous "bone bruise" so commonly seen in the lower

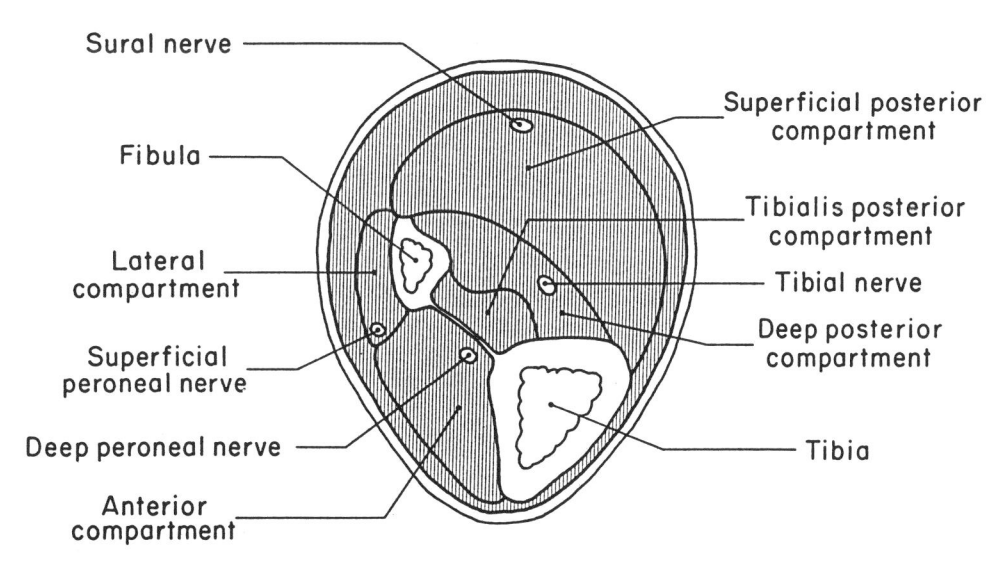

**Fig. 14D-2.** Cross Section of Lower Leg Showing Five Fascial Compartments

leg because of the subcutaneous nature of the tibia. This injury can be suspected when the degree of debilitation and pain is severe and out of proportion to the relatively negative physical examination. Diagnosis of such an injury calls for x-rays. Additional treatment includes close observation and continued ice therapy long past the normal contusion treatment guidelines.

2. *Tibial or Fibular Fracture* — The full blown extension of direct trauma to the lower leg is fracture of one or both of its bony elements. Fractures as a result of blunt trauma are unusual, but should be suspected when considering a diagnosis of a subperiosteal hematoma (see above). Pain is elicited on palpation over the fracture. In addition, percussion at the ankle can produce pain over the fracture site. Most of these fractures involve the weight-bearing tibia and usually prevent the athlete from walking. If the history of trauma is to the lateral side of the leg, fracture to the fibula should be suspected. Examination of the fibula is difficult except at its most proximal and distal margins, so a fracture should be considered if palpation at these margins produces pain anywhere along the fibula. Remember, as a nonweight-bearing bone, the fractured fibula will allow ambulation without much pain. If pain is present, the fibular fracture usually is more proximal in nature, and the result of muscle spasm along the insertion of the upper leg muscles. Special note — a proximal fibular fracture also can mimic laxity in the LCL.

3. *Peroneal Nerve Palsy* — This injury is secondary to direct trauma of the peroneal nerve as it courses superficially over the proximal lateral surface of the lower leg, usually at the point of the head of the fibula. The injury will vary greatly according to its severity, but usually results in a transient period of pain, numbness, and paresthesia in the distribution of the common peroneal nerve. The patient usually describes a sharp shock-like pain that shoots to the lateral side of the leg and foot. Most of these cases need no specific treatment except for control of the resultant contusion. The presence of continued neuropraxia should eliminate the athlete from competition. Presence of a foot drop should be indication for further investigation and/or referral.

4. *Hematomas* — These usually occur in the anterior and lateral compartments and are present in most contusions of the lower leg. A severe hematoma in the anterior or lateral compartment may lead to a compartment syndrome and eventual ischemia or necrosis of muscles if not watched and controlled. While uncommon, a hematoma to the posterior calf can cause damage to the venous outflow system and cause stasis of blood flow and possible deep vein thrombophlebitis. Suspect such a complication 36-48 hours following an injury if an athlete complains of increasing dull ache in the posterior calf aggravated by ambulation or attempted exercise. Signs include observation of a red streak proximal to the tender calf (lymphangitis), palpation of a tender "cord" (thrombosed vein) and/or a positive Homan's sign. Treatment includes bedrest, elevation, heat, and anticoagulation in a hospital. If the condition is undiagnosed, it can become lifethreatening with emboli "seeding" to the heart and lungs via the inferior vena cava.

*Treatment* — Most minor contusions and/or hematomas are treated with ice, elevation, and judicious use of NSAIDs to control inflammation and prevent serious complications. Rest and nonweight-bearing should be advised if the contusion limits or affects function of the leg. This will prevent further injury or extension of injury.

*Return to Play* — With the return of full function of the leg, an athlete can return to play so long as there is protective padding over the injured area. Aspiration of fluid from the hematoma can be considered acutely, but becomes a needless risk to the patient if coagulation of blood already has occurred after the passage of several hours. Laceration, hematoma, and contusion (such as seen in baseball) should be appropriately cleaned, repaired, and treated with prophylactic antibiotics for a one-week period. A wide spectrum antibiotic (cephalothin) is indicated. Any breakage of skin should be accompanied by tetanus prophylaxis unless immunization is up-to-date (within 10 years — adult; 5 years — child).

*Prevention* — Sports where lower leg injury is a

common threat have adopted standard equipment for their prevention (baseball catcher's shinguards, ice hockey shinguards). A patient with a past history of serious injury should be protected by a rigid shinguard.

## Shinsplints

The term "shinsplints" is a general, relatively useless term referring to anterior pain between but not involving the knee and ankle. It should not be used to describe all pain below the knee and above the ankle. In particular, the clinician should never use a *diagnosis* of shinsplints, opting instead for more specificity. Diagnoses may include chronic compartment syndrome, acute exertional compartment syndrome, posterior tibial tendinitis, periostitis, or stress fracture. Shinsplints are basically an overuse syndrome that can be diagnosed and treated according to guidelines given earlier in this chapter. Running generates many of these injuries. In one study by Brody (1987), shinsplints made up 15% of all running injuries, while stress fractures of the lower leg accounted for another 15%.

*Biomechanics and Etiology* — Shinsplints result from any number of the following factors: poor conditioning, inappropriate training, improper footwear, running on inconsistent surfaces, running on sloped or banked surfaces, running on unbanked tracks, or any situation that allow for excessive pronation, excessive external rotation of the hip, or malalignment, putting undue stress on the posterior tibial tendon. This stress takes place at midstance with the foot pronated.

*Diagnostic Aids* — After three weeks to a month, x-rays show irregularity of the bony cortex and new bone formation along a portion of the wide attachment of the posterior tibial tendon to the proximal midshaft of the fibula and tibia (see Chapter 17, Figure 5B). Bone scans will reveal increased uptake in a longitudinal pattern in the same area (Brody, 1987) (as compared with the localized, usually transverse, uptake seen in a stress fracture).

*Treatment* — In addition to treatment in accordance with grades 2 and 3 of the overuse guidelines (Chapter 10, Table 2) proper support and possible orthotic devices should be considered to prevent hyperpronation and excessive tibial rotation.

## Stress Fractures

*Epidemiology* — Stress fractures occur most often in the lower leg, usually from running or jumping too much, too fast, or because other factors are overloading the tibia and fibula. Location varies but most occur in the distal third of the tibia or the midshaft of the fibula. Prognostically, stress fractures occurring proximally are a greater cause for concern.

*Signs and Symptoms* — Consistent with Grade 4 overuse (Chapter 10, Table 2).

*Differential Diagnosis*

- Exertional compartment syndrome — pain worsens as exercise continues, but decreases with cessation of activity.
- Popliteal artery obstruction — immediate pain with exercise, followed by numbing and tingling.
- Shinsplint diagnosis — pain consistent with Grade 2 or 3 overuse.
- Tenosynovitis of the dorsiflexors of the foot —superficial pain located directly over the dorsal-anterior portion of the lower leg with elicitation of pain on dorsiflexion.
- Cellulitis — usually the result of an infectious process involving the skin, accompanied by swelling, erythema.

*Diagnostic Aids* — A complete tibia/fibula x-ray can be helpful but is effective only after at least three to four weeks of symptoms. Typical stress fractures showing cortical defects and bony repair are seen in Chapter 17, Figure 7 and 8. Bone scans can be ordered but are not necessary if the overuse protocol is used. In cases where the diagnosis is in question, compliance is a concern, and the cost of testing is justified, a bone scan is appropriate.

*Initial Treatment* — Complete rest from weight bearing exercise is necessary. In most cases, the patient can ambulate with the concomitant use of NSAIDs. A cast is rarely necessary; the exception may be a stress fracture of the proximal tibia or calcaneus. To maintain conditioning, alternative nonweight-bearing sports such as swimming, running in water, or bicycling are appropriate. Once the individual is able to walk without pain, low intensity training (LIT) guidelines are applied (Chapter 10).

*Prevention* — While it would seem that certain people are prone to develop stress fractures, such a hypothesis has not been proven. Repeated stress fractures are certainly a cause of concern and should be worked up for a possible calcium phosphate metabolic error, although this is highly unlikely. Prolonged amenorrhea secondary to hypo-estrogenism may be a factor. Most importantly, the patient's training regimen should be thoroughly examined with an educated look at both environment, equipment, and psychological status of the athlete.

## Compartment Syndrome

*Epidemiology* — Theoretically, the signs and symptoms that make up a compartment syndrome could happen in any of the five major muscle compartments located in the lower leg. The most common are the anterior or tibial compartment syndromes. Next in order of frequency are the lateral or peroneal compartment syndromes.

*Biomechanics* — These syndromes can be either acute (trauma) or chronic (overuse), and are the result of intrinsic swelling followed by compression of vascular and muscular structures. The initial swelling is the result of overload on the muscles comprising the compartment.

*Symptoms* — The onset of pain over the compartment begins with the start of exercise. This differentiates compartment involvement from that of generalized overuse (shinsplints), where pain usually begins late in or after exercise. Numbing or tingling of the distal lower extremity may be present and reflect involvement of the neurovascular bundle. Differentiation of specific compartment involvement is summarized in Figure 14D-3. There clearly is controversy surrounding the deep posterior compartment incorporating the flexor muscles of the foot and the posterior tibial neurovascular bundle. Melberg (1989) rejects the existence of compartment syndrome in this area. There is some concern about the method used for measuring intracompartmental pressures.

*Signs* — In the ambulatory setting, swelling and possible edema of the compartment may be noted. Compartment muscle will be painful to touch, possibly weak, but seldom is neurovascular compromise clinically evident.

*Differential Diagnosis* — In addition to shinsplint overuse and tibial/fibular stress fracture, consider thrombophlebitis, osteomyelitis, cellulitis, tumor, and intermittent claudication.

*Treatment* — Correction of biomechanics, especially those mechanics that isolate the muscle group. Rest, stretching exercises in the case of a chronic injury, and fasciotomy may be required if conservative measures fail. The decision to intervene surgically should be based on compartmental pressure measurements that are at least 25-30 mmHg (Rorabeck, 1985).

## Superficial Posterior Compartment Strain

*Anatomy* — The three muscles of the superficial posterior compartment — gastrocnemius, soleus, and plantaris are frequently acutely strained or torn in their muscle belly. The gastrocnemius is injured most often in its medial belly when the foot is dorsiflexed and the knees are forcibly extended. When this happens, the medial head of the gastrocnemius near its musculotendinous junction can strain or tear. The gastrocnemius is vulnerable because it works across two joints and is a muscle of short action.

*Epidemiology* — The middle-aged athlete (usually between 35-45 years of age) appears most at risk. Racket sports are most commonly implicated and this condition is sometimes termed "tennis leg".

*Treatment* — Following the standard RICE regimen for two to three days, passive stretching exercises are done. Ultrasound can be used. Active stretching and strengthening exercises can be started within a week. If a partial tear has taken plac( casting and immobilization in a long leg cast for approximately three weeks is recommended. This cast can then be removed and replaced with an ankle-foot orthosis for an additional three weeks. The prognosis is quite good so long as the injury is adequately rehabilitated.

## Achilles Tendon

*Anatomy* — The Achilles tendon represents the conjointed tendon of the gastrocnemius and soleus muscles, the latter a major contributor to the plantar flexion strength of the foot. The extreme distal portion of the Achilles tendon appears to have a poor blood supply, especially in the region 2-6 cm above the insertion on the calcaneus. A normal tendon is extremely

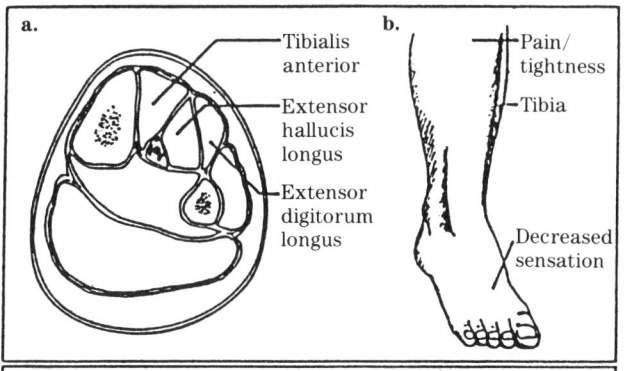

*Muscles of the anterior compartment (a) and complaints of patients with anterior chronic compartment syndrome (b).*

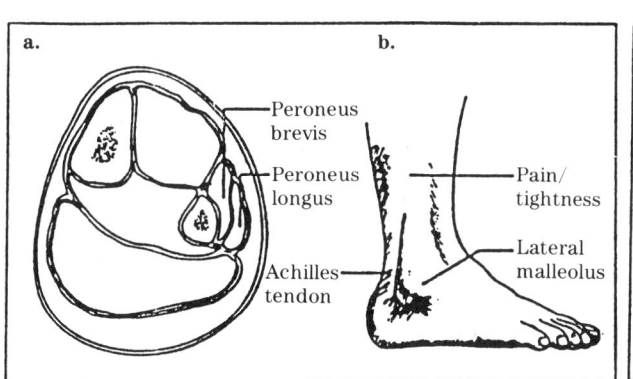

*Muscles of the lateral compartment (a) and complaints of patients with lateral chronic compartment syndrome (b).*

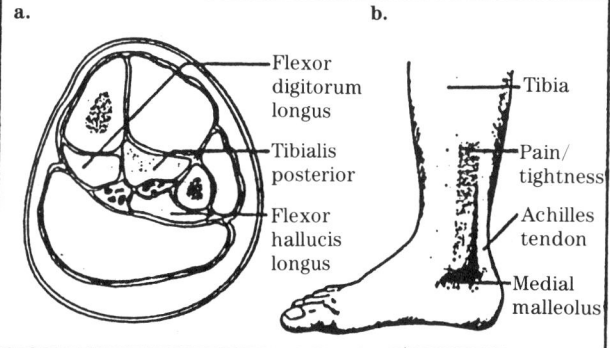

*Muscles of the deep posterior compartment (a) and complaints of patients with deep posterior chronic compartment syndrome (b).*

**Fig. 14D-3.** Muscles of the Anterior Compartment (From Wiley, 1987)

strong and able to withstand forces up to 2000 pounds during fast running.

*Epidemiology* — Three clinical entities will be discussed here:

- Achilles tendinitis — usually seen in repetitive overload overuse, common in running.
- Complete tear or Achilles tendon rupture — seen in sports such as basketball, tennis, or skiing that involve sudden maximal contraction of the musculotendinous unit.
- Partial tear — represents a crossover variant, with etiology representing either overuse and/or acute overload.

**Achilles Tendinitis**

This can be divided into two clinical presentations:

- *Acute* — involving just the peritenon (tendon sheath), not the tendon itself. The peritenon is

not a true synovial sheath as are with other tendons in the body.
- *Chronic* — the result of prolonged mucoid degeneration of the tendon substance itself.

*Biomechanics* — The usual mechanism of injury is chronic, repetitive overload on the musculotendinous unit (Figure 14D-4). Biomechanical causes include tibia varus, functional talipes, equinus, tight hamstring muscles, tight calf muscles, and cavus foot. In addition, several training errors can cause this injury: constant hill running, shoes with rigid soles or soft heel counter, shifting from high heel dress shoes to low heel training shoes, changing from cross country running on uneven surfaces to more consistent elastic track surfaces, "ankling" too much in cycling. Each of these situations results in increased pull and tension on the Achilles unit. Furthermore, other injuries present, such as plantar fascitis, can cause the foot to land in excessive supination and cause the ankle to dorsiflex to avoid pronating the foot. The Achilles tendon can move laterally or medially in response to such running biomechanics.

*Signs and Symptoms* — As with any soft tissue overuse injury, signs and symptoms are consistent with those outlined in the earlier discussion of overuse syndromes.

*Differential Diagnosis* — While rarely a problem in running, partial rupture of the Achilles tendon should be ruled out.

*Diagnostic Aids* — The work-up of severe or chronic tendinitis, especially if the examination has been accompanied by palpation and thickening of the Achilles tendon, should include x-ray evaluation of Kager's triangle seen in the lateral view of the affected ankle. This triangle is bounded anteriorly by the flexor tendons of the foot, posteriorly by the Achilles tendon unit, and inferiorly by the os calcis. The radiolucent area will become more dense and less radiolucent in cases of severe tendinitis or partial rupture (Ljungqvist and Erikkson, 1982).

*Treatment* — Initial treatment should consist of ice, initial stretching prior to exercise, use of NSAIDs, decreasing mileage, avoiding banked roads and hills, and reassessing shoes, making sure that the following exist: flexible sole, molded heel pad, a heel wedge at least 1.5 cm high, and a rigid heel counter. Ultrasound has been of use in these injuries.

*Rehabilitation* — Should consist of stretching and strengthening exercises for the Achilles tendon.

*Prevention* — Address any preexisting injury or deformity and attempt to correct before resuming exercise.

*Special Considerations* — At no point in the therapy of Achilles tendinitis should steroid injections be used. The potential compromise to the vascular system of the Achilles tendon, as well as the weakening and possible necrosis stimulated by such an injection, precludes this form of therapy for this injury.

**Achilles Tendon Rupture**

*Epidemiology* — Rupture occurs predominantly in male athletes, in their third to fifth decade of life, in sports of sudden extreme movement, such as basketball, tennis, long jumping, and skiing. Most ruptures occur 2-6 cm above the insertion of the Achilles tendon on the os calcis in the area of decreased vascularity. The left tendon is ruptured significantly more often than the right. Predisposing factors: 1) nonspecific degeneration, perhaps secondary to vascular impairment produced by the particular repetitious form of exercise; 2) history of

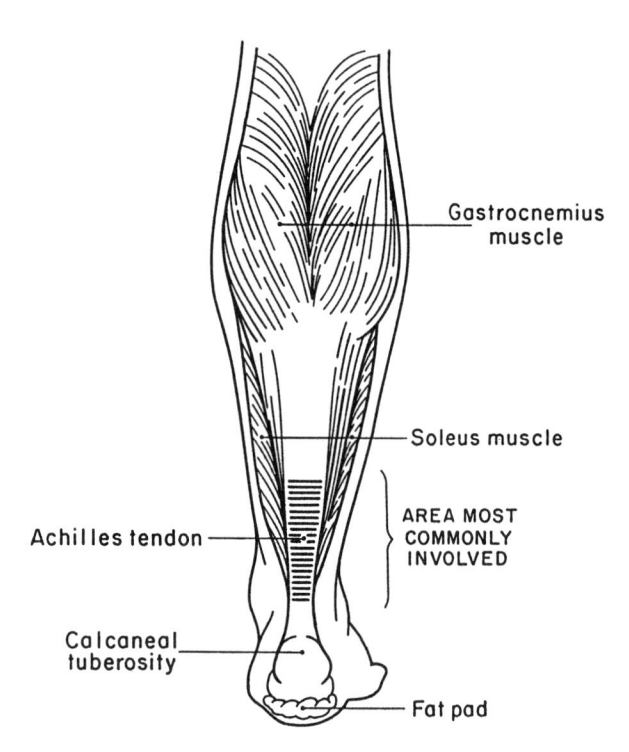

**Fig. 14D-4.** Achilles Tendinitis

corticosteroid injections; 3) repeated subclinical injury leading to necrosis and weakening of the unit, or 4) normal tendon physiology that has undergone extreme pathomechanical stress.

*Symptoms* — Most published theories on acute tendon rupture include the statement that misdiagnoses can be as high as 20%-25%. Usual symptoms include a sudden forced movement followed by a loud audible snap. Many times, the initial pain will diminish and walking is possible. There is a weakness of the foot while in plantar flexion and, at times, a feeling of the foot penetrating through the floor as if in plantar flexion.

*Signs* — The affected tendon may be thicker and a palpable gap may be felt. However, blood in the form of a hematoma often may collect underneath the peritenon and fill the gap, making it difficult to palpate the defect. The patient demonstrates a notable weakness in plantar flexion and an inability to stand on tiptoe. Whether this inability is due to pain or actual loss of function must be determined. Careful palpation usually can show a difference between an entrapped hematoma and an intact tendon. On occasion there may be a slight increase in dorsiflexion in the position of rest. The Thompson Test should be done with the athlete prone, knee bent, and foot hanging. The calf should be squeezed with the examiner's hand distal to the apex of the soleus muscle. If plantar flexion cannot be elicited, it is strong (but not absolute) evidence for complete tendon rupture and the test is positive.

*Diagnostic Aids* — Lateral x-ray of the ankle usually shows two changes after acute tendon rupture: a loss of radiolucence in the Kager's triangle, and a distortion of the triangle (Arner, 1959). Kuland (1982) advocates using fluoroscopy with contrast media to determine the juxtaposition of the ruptured ends of the tendon. Magnetic resonance imaging (MRI) can depict rupture and partial rupture of the achilles tendon in excellent detail and is now being advocated as a diagnostic aid (Marcus, 1989). The authors feel that the merits of MR imaging with regard to the decision-making process are not cost effective and therefore do not recommend this as part of the work-up.

*Initial Treatment* — Immediate ice, immobilization in slight plantar flexion, crutches, pain relief, if necessary.

*Definitive Treatment* — There appear to be three options: open surgery, percutaneous repair, and closed repair. A good deal of controversy exists about which is the most appropriate treatment. Ingles (1976) examined two groups of athletes with Achilles tendon rupture. The non-surgical group achieved only 72% normal strength, 70% normal power and endurance, and experienced nine re-ruptures. The surgical group was able to achieve full strength and power with no occurrence of repeated rupture. Some surgeons advocate surgery for the athlete and closed repair for the non-athlete (Stein and Leukens, 1976). Others (Nistor, 1981; Hattrup, 1985) favor conservative closed treatment which allows for adequate plantar flexion strength and avoids the complications inherent to surgery. Surgery probably is mandated where the rupture site is close to insertion. It likely is not needed if the rupture is at or above the musculotendinous junction (greater than 10 cm from os calcis attachment). From the primary care standpoint, clinical evidence of a ruptured Achilles tendon should be followed by referral to an orthopedic surgeon.

*Rehabilitation* — While recommendations vary somewhat, the affected leg should be placed in plantar flexion in a long leg cast with slight knee flexion for three weeks. Note: to prevent atrophy of the soleus muscle, place the foot in as much dorsi flexion as possible without straining the integrity of the tendon repair. Then a short leg cast or ankle-foot orthosis should be used for three more weeks. After immobilization, both legs should be fitted with an elevated heel and weight bearing begun until there is normal heel to toe gait. Heel elevation can then be decreased and stretching exercises begun. Strengthening should take place beginning with simple plantar flexion and gradually increasing the resistance until toe stands can be done without pain. Achilles tendon stretching using an incline board should follow. The prognosis is guarded and seems to be dependent upon how delayed initial treatment is. A tendon graft may be necessary if there is a significant delay or misdiagnosis. Quite often, elite athletes are unable to return to full performance levels. In a five-year follow-up study on surgery for Achilles tendon rupture or partial rupture, 76% of the top athletes returned to their competitive sports and 90% of joggers returned to full activity (Gillström and Ljungqvist, 1978).

### Partial Rupture of Achilles Tendon

*Epidemiology* — Partial rupture usually occurs in the young athlete (20-30 years of age) at his or her highest level of performance.

*Biomechanics* — Biomechanics are similar to those seen with tendon rupture as well as tendinitis.

*Symptoms* — Symptoms can present either as a tendinitis-like picture except that symptoms do not clear with standard tendinitis treatment, or there can be a sudden onset, but with a negative Thompson test.

*Signs* — Classic signs include nodular or fusiform swelling (Clancy, 1980), pain with motion, decreased function, possible crepitus, localized tenderness on palpation, pain on forced passive dorsiflexion, as well as resistance to active plantar flexion. A partial rupture can become chronic and result in calf muscle atrophy, as well as possible passive dorsiflexion of the ankle. A "hop" test (patient hops on bended affected leg) can help identify this complication.

*Diagnostic Aids* — A soft tissue x-ray of the lateral aspect of the ankle will show a loss of radiolucence of Kagar's triangle, but no distortion. In the case of a complex presentation of a possible partial tear, electromyography (EMG) can be helpful later in the course. If the partial tear is in the soleus, contraction time will be shortened. If the partial tear is in either head of the gastrocnemius muscle, the contraction time will be prolonged. Of course, if the partial rupture is close to the insertion of the tendon unit, no abnormality will be present.

*Treatment* — Initial treatment consists of ice, strapping, heel lift, NSAIDs, and short-term immobilization. Steroid injections are discouraged for the reasons stated previously. If conservative treatment is not effective, the patient should be referred to an orthopedic surgeon.

### Retrocalcaneal Bursitis

*Epidemiology* — Running or any sport involving the possibility of an ill-fitting shoe. Commonly referred to as a "pump bump".

*Biomechanics* — Irritation of the posterior calcaneal prominence by the heel counter causing swelling of the retrocalcaneal bursa.

*Symptoms* — Localized pain.

*Signs* — Palpation of the tendon elicits tenderness anterior to the attachment of the tendon on the os calcis (Figures 14D-5 and 6).

*Diagnostic Aids* — X-rays may reveal increased bony deposition on the calcaneus.

*Treatment* — Correction of ill-fitting shoe with a higher (or lower) heel counter or pad, ice, injection of steroids with care taken not to involve the tendon.

### Acute Fracture

In the lower leg, athletes can fracture the tibia, fibula or both. Mid-shaft and proximal tibial fractures must be immobilized with a long leg cast following reduction. Fibular fractures (because the bone is essentially non-weight bearing) can be treated with a short leg cast or ankle-foot ortho-

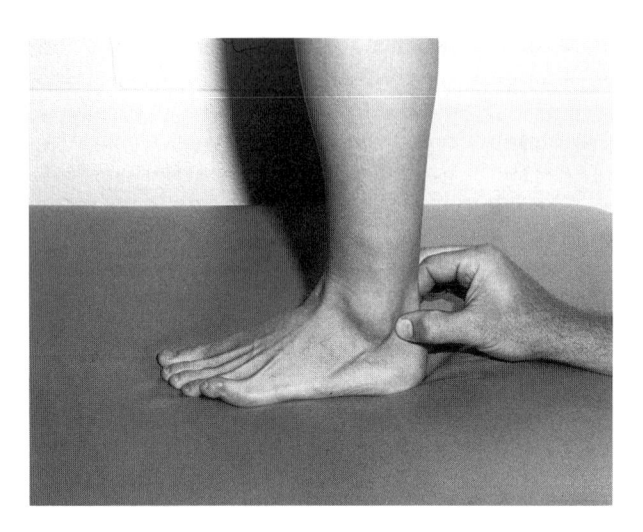

**Fig. 14D-5.** Retrocalcaneal Bursitis

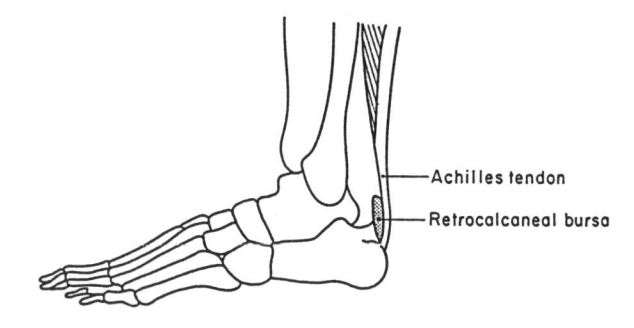

**Fig. 14D-6.** Retrocalcaneal Bursitis

sis. A combination tibia/fibula fracture, or the common "boot top" fracture of skiing, must be reduced and immobilized in a long leg cast. This serious fracture should be referred to an orthopedic surgeon for possible open reduction and internal fixation.

## SECTION E. ANKLE

The ankle is the most vulnerable and therefore the most frequently injured joint in the body. It accounts for 30%-50% of all reported athletic injuries and 20%-25% of all time-loss athletic injuries (Mack, 1982). While some believe it is a relatively simple joint to understand, ankle injury often is misdiagnosed and inadequately treated. Unfortunately, longstanding sequellae from inappropriate treatment are considerable. The chronically unstable painful ankle accounts for significant disability, as well as premature osteoarthritis in the older athlete.

### Anatomy

The ankle is a synovial hinge joint that functions basically in flexion and extension (Figure 14E-1). The ankle mortise has the shape of an inverted U with the lateral border formed by the distal fibula and the dorsal — medial border by the distal tibia. The talus, upon which these long bones sit, is a trapezoid shaped, thick bone with flat lateral and dorsal surfaces for stability.

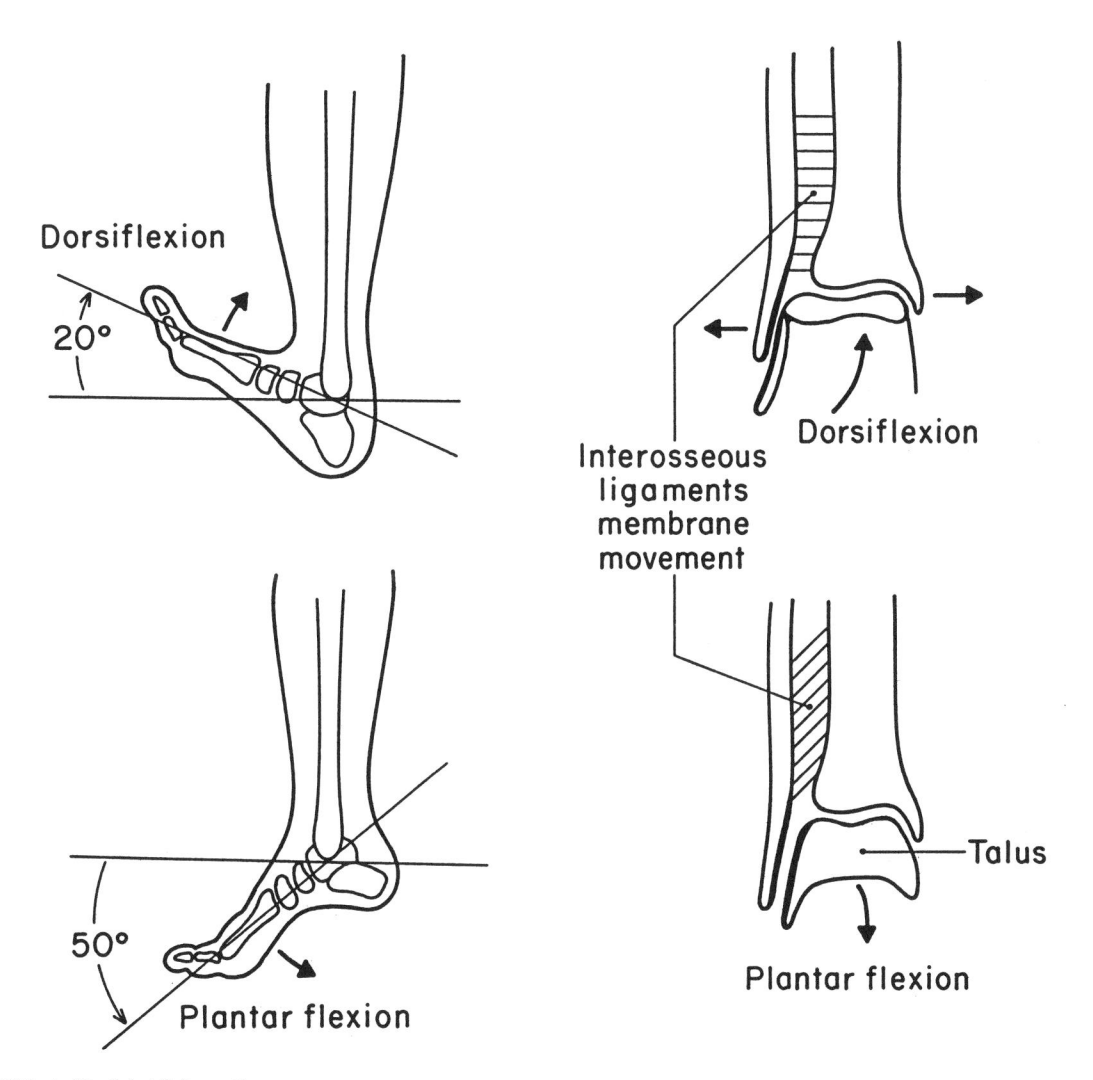

**Fig. 14E-1.** Ankle Joint Schematic

### Ligaments

A protective shield of ligaments and tendons lies over the joint capsule (Figure 14E-2). The main ligaments involved in ankle stability include:

- *Internal Stability* — the distal tibiofibular ligament, a thickened extension of the interosseus membrane maintains the anatomical relationship between the tibia and fibula.
- *Medial Stability* — the thick deltoid ligament, made up of three or four major bands, prevents eversion.
- *Lateral Stability* — achieved by three major ligaments (anterior to posterior): a) anterior talofibular; b) calcaneofibular; c) posterior talofibular. A special function of the latter is stabilizing the mid and hind foot by means of an insertion on the tarsal cuboid and base of the fifth metatarsal.

### Muscles

Overlying the ligament are the tendons of muscles further stabilizing the joint (Figure 14E-2):

- *Anterior and Medial Stability* — extensor tendons of the toes; anterior tibial tendon.
- *Lateral Stability* — peroneal longus and brevis muscles, evertors of the foot.
- *Posterior Stability* — flexor tendons of the toes; posterior tibial muscle; gastrocnemius, and soleus muscles (Achilles complex).

### Special Notes

The anterior and posterior tibial muscles coordinate to cause inversion, balancing the effect of the peroneal muscles.

Joint forces generated in the ankle are a function of externally applied forces and the internal forces from muscles and ligaments around the joint (Scheller, 1980).

The common pathophysiological insult in soft tissue ankle injuries is an applied force that exceeds soft tissue strength. Thus, more injuries are seen in areas where there are relatively weak bony interrelationships and soft tissue stabilizing structures (Hume, 1984).

### Ankle Evaluation

#### History

There are six important facets of the history involved in any ankle injury (please consult Appendix 14E-1 for suggested examination form):

1. *Biomechanics* — an understanding of the biomechanical action that produce the injury is the most important part of the history with an ankle injury.
2. *Weight-bearing* — was the athlete able to bear weight upon the injured extremity after injury?
3. *Sounds* — were any sounds (pop, snap) heard at the time of injury? While perhaps not as sen-

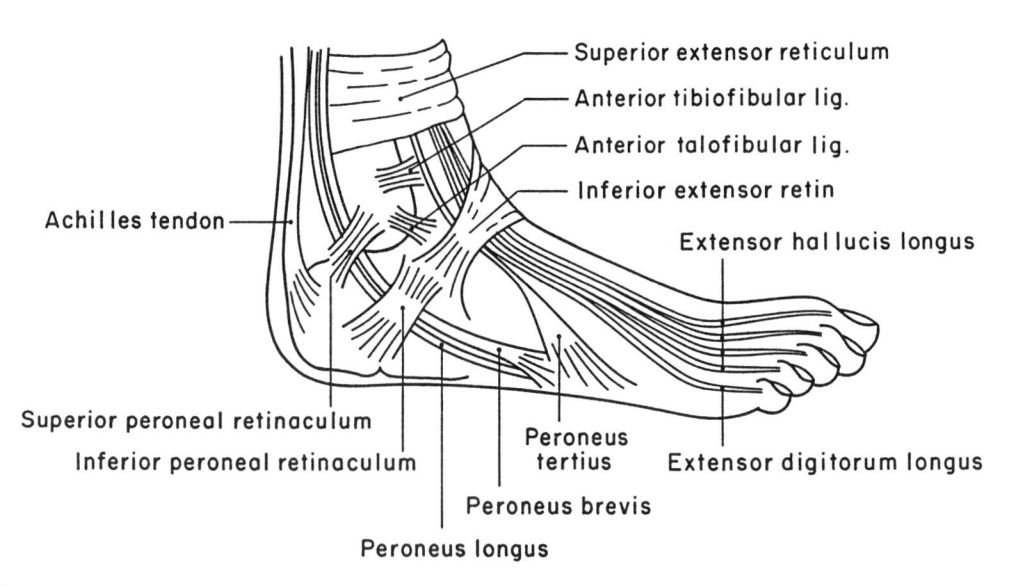

**Fig. 14E-2.** Tendons and Ligaments of the Foot

sitive a measurement as similar sounds with knee injuries, their presence may help the physician in his differential diagnosis.
4. *Onset of Swelling* — the timing of swelling after injury is also not as sensitive as it is with knee injuries, but it gives a general idea of the seriousness of an ankle injury.

*Special Note* — recurrent ankle soft tissue injury is common and it appears that scar tissue may actually serve to impede ankle swelling. Relatively mild swelling should not mislead the examiner into considering a diagnosis of minor ankle injury.
5. *Treatment* — has any treatment been given for the injury before the examination? The misguided application of heat instead of ice can significantly change the presentation of ankle injuries.
6. *Past Medical History* — Many people have recurrent ankle injuries. This must be taken into account in assessing the current signs and symptoms.

**Physical Examination**

As with any other impaired extremity, always use the uninjured ankle as a reference and examine it first. Important points in the approach to the examination of an injured ankle are:

- *Observation* — The authors find that simply examining the ankle while it dangles over an examination table is an accurate way of observing bruising, swelling, or deformity that may be present.
- *Palpation* — It is important to begin proximal to the injury, and both the dorsal pedal and posterior tibial pulse should be assessed for possible bony tenderness and its location.
- *Range of Motion* — Both passive and active range of motion surrounding the four major movements of the ankle (dorsiflexion, plantar flexion, inversion, and eversion) should be assessed. While doing ROM, crepitation signaling tenosynovitis and tendinitis can be noticed.
- *Stress Testing* — The following five tests are in order (see Figure 14E-3 and 4):
  a. Thompson Test — for patency of the Achilles tendon.
  b. Eversion Stress Test — for stability of the medial compartment of the ankle. Any give at all, especially a tilt of up more than 5°, should be considered abnormal.
  c. Inversion Stress Test — because of relatively weaker stabilizing structures, the lateral compartment is looser so that a talor tilt of up to 10° can be accepted as normal.
  d. Anterior Drawer — depending upon comparison with the other side, the anterior drawer may have a normal shift of up to 3 mm.
  e. Side-to-Side Test — this maneuver assesses widening of the ankle mortise caused by instability of the tibial-fibular ligament. If the examiner hears a "thud" or elicits pain on a side-to-side test, it is considered positive.

**X-ray**

Not everyone needs ankle x-rays. As many as 75%-85% of all ankle injuries involve no fractures and are essentially soft tissue trauma. A reasonable way to predict whether x-rays are necessary is to consider whether the individual can bear weight without pain and if ankle tenderness is non-bony in nature. Where both of these conditions are true, up to 97% will involve only soft tissue. Early x-rays should be obtained for serious deformity, abnormal swelling, or where there is a high index of suspicion based on historical information. Stress films can be done but should serve only to document the degree of laxity found on a clinical exam. This is not a comfortable test for an injured athlete.

Routine x-ray views for assessing ankle injuries should include: AP, lateral, and oblique (this view is most informative when assessing tibiofibular joint problems) (see Chapter 17, Figure 17-42).

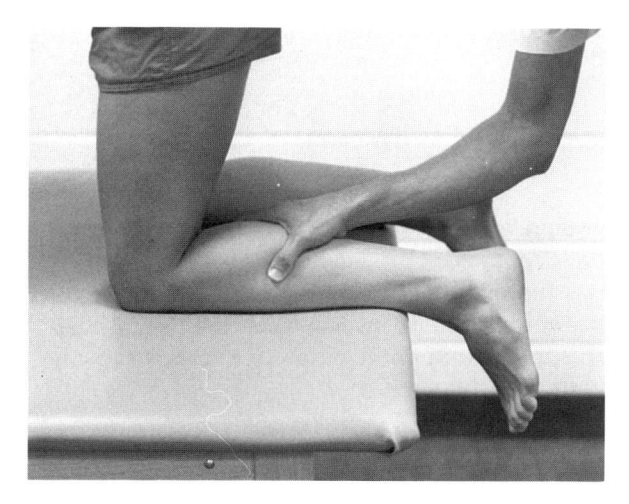

**Fig. 14E-3.** Thompson Test

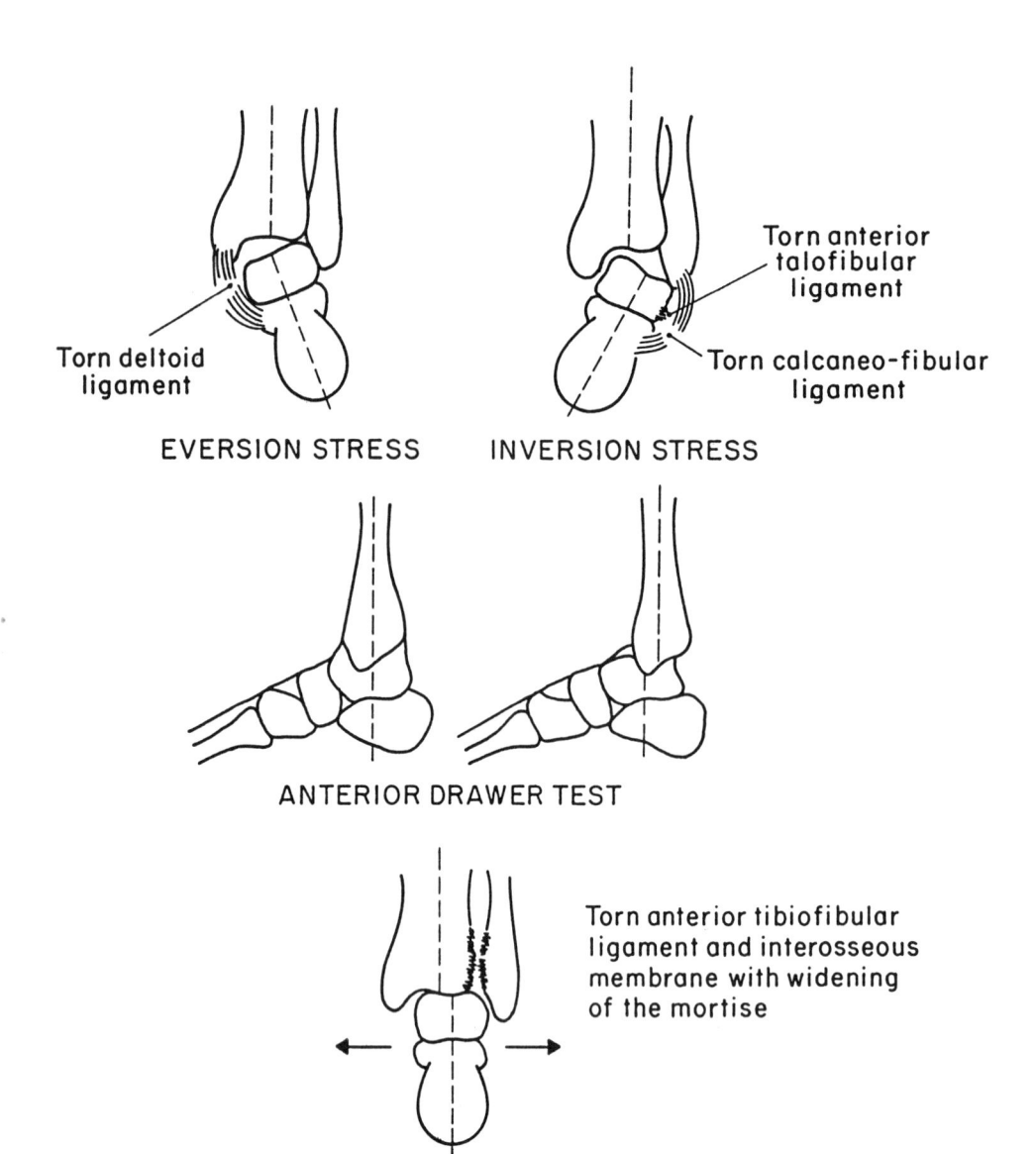

**Fig. 14E-4.** Stress Tests

## COMMON INJURIES

### Sprains

There are three major biomechanical types of ankle sprains: lateral inversion sprains, medial eversion sprains, and dorsiflexion or anterior capsule sprain.

#### Lateral Inversion Sprain

The lateral inversion sprains account for 80%-85% of all ankle sprains (O'Donoghue, 1984).

*Biomechanics* — Plantar flexion, inversion, and internal rotation of the ankle results in isolation and stretching (followed by tearing) of the three lateral stabilizing ligaments of the ankle. These ligaments usually are torn in the same order. As stress is placed on the lateral compartment, the medial malleolus acts as a fulcrum for the talus so that the anterior talofibular ligament is injured. If the stress is enough, the calcaneofibular ligament and, finally the posterior talofibular ligament will give way. Occasionally, with the torque forces of rotation, the calcaneofibular ligament can be isolated and injured. Associated with the lateral inversion sprain is compression of the medial malleolar tip or evulsion of the distal fibula. Additional etiologic factors that contribute to inversion injury include a tight Achilles tendon and an irregular playing surface.

*Epidemiology* — Eighty-five percent of all inversion injuries involve an isolated tear of the anterior talofibular ligament (Birrer, 1984). This injury is most frequently seen in sports such as football, basketball, baseball, and soccer.

*Symptoms* — Sudden onset of lateral ankle pain as a result of misstep and/or "turning-over" of ankle.

*Signs* — Ankle sprains usually begin with immediate swelling, localized tenderness, signs of hemorrhage, varying degrees of weight-bearing intolerance, and joint laxity. Joint laxity is easily assessed by stress tests (Figure 14E-4) and it is important as the basis of a grading system to specify injury severity: Grade 1 — no significant loss in ligament continuity or laxity (mild symptoms and signs); Grade 2 — definite partial tear with laxity but also endpoint present (moderate ankle injury); and Grade 3 — complete rupture of ligament with subsequent laxity and no endpoint (severe ankle injury). The degree of swelling does not correlate well with the severity of the injury. Swelling can be pronounced in a "virgin" uninjured ankle with a minimal injury and be almost non-existent in a recurrent serious ankle sprain.

*Treatment* — A major purpose in developing a grading system for injuries is to define the prognosis and establish different treatment protocols for various injuries. Recent studies indicate there is little difference in the treatment protocols for the three grades (Smith, 1986; Evans, 1984; Niedermann, 1981). There is only a difference in severity, requiring different healing times. What appears to be important clinically is whether an ankle sprain is considered significant or insignificant. If it seems to be insignificant (signs of minimal or no edema, absence of laxity, the ability to weight-bear and walk without a limp), the treatment should consist of ice, compression, and elevation followed by a gradual resumption of activity with prophylactic taping or bracing. On the other hand, if grading indicates a significant injury (swelling and clinical or radiographic instability preventing normal ambulation) most physicians immobilize using the RICE regimen. After 24-36 hours when swelling has stabilized begin range of motion exercises, contrast baths, and possible electrogalvanic stimulation. When 50% of normal range of motion is achieved, resistance exercises are begun, as well as weight-bearing using a functional semi-rigid support (Figure 14E-5) to prevent inversion and eversion of the foot but allow plantar and dorsiflexion (Stover, 1980). Ankle proprioception should be reinforced by means of a balance board (Figure 14E-6). It is uncommon to surgically repair any grade of lateral inversion ankle injury unless it is chronic.

There has been a battle concerning which ankle brace should be used after injury or for

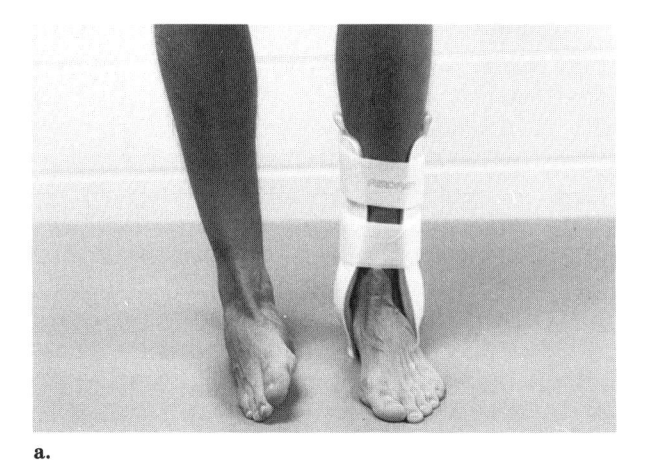

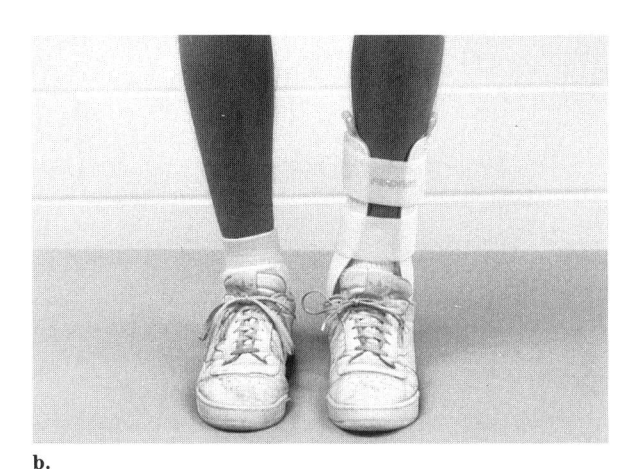

**Fig. 14E-5.** Functional Semirigid Bracing
A. Brace permits dorsi and plantar flexion but prevents excessive inversion. B. Brace can be readily accommodated by an ordinary athletic shoe.

Fig. 14E-6. Proprioceptive Balance Board

prophylaxis but no clear winner. The use of ankle braces as part of the rehabilitation program is indicated to give the injured athlete some degree of protection. Assessment of the various protective devices involves their comfort to the athlete and how restricted the ankle range of motion will be after exercise.

- *Taping* — In the hands of a knowledgeable athletic trainer, ankle taping remains an effective means of restricting range of motion. It takes knowledge and time and does have undesirable aspects such as skin and soft tissue irritations.
- *Semirigid-orthosis* (Aircast™) — This brace can maintain restricted range of motion longer (Gross, 1987).
- *Ankle Ligament Protector* (ALP) — Consists of a single posterior strut riding on top of the heel cup and topped with a moveable tibial cuff. This brace is not particularly comfortable but is effective in protecting the ankle against chronic reinjury (Greene, 1990).
- *Swede-O*™ Ankle Brace — A laceable, cloth brace reinforced by medial and lateral plastic inserts. This brace is comfortable and functional and also holds restricted range of motion as well as the above braces.

The authors believe that any bracing mechanism used to prevent further ankle injuries in a person with chronic, recurrent ankle sprains is appropriate. Economics and convenience, as well as comfort and functional performance, are factors to consider in choosing an appropriate brace. The primary care physician may present information on all braces, with the eventual decision being made by the athlete.

*Special Note* — The most convenient and economical way to present the sometimes overwhelming intricacies of ankle rehabilitation is through the use of an all inclusive packet. One such patient-oriented kit is the Ankle REPAC™, generated by one of us (D.B. McKeag). It has worked well guiding patients with many different ankle injuries.

**Medial Eversion Sprains**

*Epidemiology* — This injury is commonly seen in wrestlers who push off the inside or medial component of their ankle. The mechanism represents less than 10% of all ankle sprains, but more than 75% of all ankle fractures (Kleizer, 1974).

*Biomechanics* — External rotation of the leg, dorsiflexion, and pronation lead to isolation of and injury to the deltoid ligament. Medial compartment injury is more likely to cause bony damage than lateral compartment injury. The deltoid ligament is such a strong support structure that the medial malleolar bony substance will often avulse before a tear occurs in the deltoid ligament. Common extensions of this injury include (Figure 14E-7): 1) deltoid ligament tear and/or medial malleolar avulsion fracture; 2) extension to the tibiofibular ligament (usually anterior); 3) further extension to involve fracture of the distal fibular shaft, or 4) extension to the interosseous membrane.

*Signs and Symptoms* — Similar to those seen in the lateral ankle sprain.

*Diagnostic Aids* — X-rays (possibly augmented by stress views) are indicated in medial compartment injuries. They may show a medial malleolar fracture creating an unstable joint, or a widening of the ankle mortise between the talus and medial malleolus. This often is not appreciated unless an oblique view is taken, giving a clear view of the ankle mortise, because the tibia and fibula frequently overlap in the straight AP view.

*Treatment* — Similar treatment protocols are outlined for the lateral ankle sprains (including home rehabilitation programs such as Ankle Repac™). Surgery may be indicated if any of

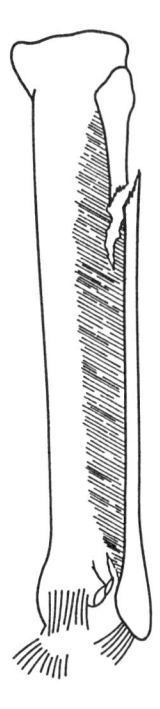

Fig. 14E-7. Injury to the Distal Tibiofibular Ligament

the four extensions outlined above have occurred, primarily because of side-to-side instability which does not respond well to rehabilitation.

**Dorsiflexion Injuries (ATFL)**

*Epidemiology* — This injury is caused by trauma or forced dorsiflexion to the anterior capsule such as seen in soccer, gymnastics, tennis, skiing, basketball, running backs in football, or sliding in baseball.

Anterior-inferior tibial-fibular ligament (ATFL) injury has been considered rare but the medical literature is reporting more of them (Briner, 1989).

*Biomechanics* — Extreme dorsiflexion past the normal ROM causes tearing of the extensor retinaculum and anterior tibiofibular ligament. The trapezoid-shaped talar dome, wider-anteriorly, may account for much of the insult. Partial tears of this ligament commonly are seen after a forward fall or rupture of the Achilles tendon. The gastrocnemius and soleus muscles of the Achilles tendon usually exert a protective effect in prevention.

An alternate biomechanical explanation is external rotation of the foot and ankle followed by an ATFL sprain. The injured player will relate a history of severe pain.

*Diagnosis* — Physical examination of an athlete with ATFL injury differs significantly from the normal findings of lateral ankle sprain.

- Significant swelling is rarely seen initially.
- Tenderness can be elicited above the anterior talofibular ligament lateral to the distal fibular head in the tibial fibular syndesmosis.
- Radiation of the pain may occur proximally along syndesmosis.
- There is less tenderness over the lateral and medial compartments.
- Pain can be reproduced either by passively rotating the foot externally or dorsiflexing the foot.
- Walking on toes may be uncomfortable and ambulation difficult because of pain with "toe-off".

*X-ray* — X-rays of patients with ATFL injuries are usually negative. Sometimes small fragments of the fibula may be avulsed and incorporated near the syndesmosis. Widening of the ankle mortise may be seen. A "ragged" lateral border of the tibia or medial border of the fibula may represent injury to the interosseous ligament.

*Treatment* — These injuries take much longer to heal than the more common lateral inversion injury. Return to a normal level of activity may take from 5-10 weeks, depending on the severity of the injury (Briner, 1989). Fortunately, chronic instability or recurrent sprains do not appear to be problems with the ATFL injury. Note - Suspect a missed dorsiflexion ankle injury if an athlete is making slower than normal rehabilitation progress.

It is advisable — especially if pain persists for several months — to obtain a follow-up x-ray (once again in the oblique view) to discover whether ossification of the interosseous membrane or ATFL ligament have occurred. Such a development may need surgical intervention.

**Achilles Tendon**

The Achilles tendon is the true conjoined tendon of the gastrocnemius and soleus muscles, the latter being the major contributor to plantar flexion. The major blood supply for this conjoined tendon comes from its own anterior mesentery and is pushed into a region 2-6 cm above the os calcis

(Thompson, 1962). The normal Achilles tendon is very strong and can withstand forces up to 2000 lbs during running. It can be overused, inflamed, partially torn, or completely ruptured, usually as a result of some sports or exercise activity. Achilles tendon injury accounted for 6.5% of all overuse running injuries in one study (Clement, 1984). The tendon is prone to degeneration, primarily because of poor blood supply and vessel blanching. It often does not heal well or rapidly. Sports injuries to the Achilles tendon generally follow the same spectrum found in any soft tissue unit of the body. Because it is prone to rupture, treatment of its various maladies has come under some discussion. We will look at three different points on the spectrum: Tendinitis — both acute and chronic degenerative; partial rupture, and complete rupture.

**Tendinitis**

*Biomechanics* — Any mechanism that causes an athlete's Achilles tendon to overstretch, thus preloading the unit during the push-off phase, will predispose the individual to Achilles tendon overuse and tendinitis. Running appears to be the most affected sport (Clement, 1984).

Some predisposing factors include:

- Change from padded heeled training shoes to competition shoes without heels.
- Varus knee alignments with functional overpronation.
- Plantar fasciitis (compensation with ankle dorsiflexion to avoid pronation of the athlete's foot and subsequent pain).
- Rigid cavus deformity of the foot.
- Uphill running.
- Soft running shoe heel counter causing twisting of the tendon
- Cyclists emphasizing dorsiflexion at the ankle while pedaling.

*Symptoms* — Symptoms are shooting or cutting pain, often sudden in onset, after increased activity, and many times associated with one of the above factors.

*Signs* — Signs include pain, usually focal in nature, along the course of the Achilles proximal to the os calcis (usually 2-6 cm above the os calcis). If the tendinitis has been chronic, there usually is an intensely painful area of thickening or induration irregular in contour (Ljungqvist, 1982).

*Treatment* — Because the tendon's blood supply reaches it from its sheath, injection of a steroid into the sheath and peritenon area can cause several complications: adhesions between the peritenon and tendon, causing constricting bands that restrict movement of the tendon through the sheath; depression of collagen synthesis and eventual necrosis encouraged by the action of the corticosteroid within the sheath, and/or increased pressure from the injected substance within the peritenon can embarrass/blanch the blood supply and lead to ischemic necrosis.

Appropriate therapy includes:

- A heel pad — to lessen the stretching of the Achilles tendon.
- A better heel counter on the athletic shoe to limit side to side shifting and irritation of the Achilles tendon (what Clement, 1984, calls "the whipping action").
- Proper treatment of plantar fasciitis where it exists.
- Cryotherapy.
- Removal or correction of all detrimental environmental factors.
- NSAIDS.

Most cases of Achilles tendinitis can and should be treated according to the protocols found in Chapter 10.

**Partial Rupture**

*Biomechanics* — Essentially the same biomechanics hold for partial rupture of the Achilles tendon as outlined above. A partial rupture involves a more serious process over a longer period of time. Clancy (1976) demonstrated that many patients thought to have tendinitis actually had partial rupture and focal degeneration of their Achilles tendon.

*Signs and Symptoms* — Signs and symptoms are basically the same as those with Achilles tendinitis, but more debilitating and of longer duration.

*Diagnosis* — Soft tissue x-rays usually show pronounced thickening of the tendon, confirming what already is known clinically. Electromyography (EMG) can be helpful in diagnosing a partial Achilles tendon tear (Persson, 1971). EMG often shows a reduction in motor unit activity of the specific muscle within the Achilles tendon at the site of the partial rupture. If the rupture occurs in the soleus portion, the time of contraction is shortened but the contraction time is prolonged if the rupture occurs in the gastrocnemius portion.

*Treatment* — Treatment guidelines are the same as those listed above. Similar warnings exist for steroid injections. If this conservative program, in addition to complete rest of the tendon does not produce positive results within two to three weeks, surgery may be indicated.

**Complete Rupture**

*Biomechanics* — The usual tearing mechanism is stress applied to an already contracting musculotendinous unit, usually the push-off foot which most often is the left foot. Other mechanics may come into play when an individual falls forward over fixed or anchored feet (cross-country skiing), causing forced dorsiflexion of the ankle, or when an individual who is pushing against someone has another individual fall onto an already loaded Achilles tendon, snapping it. Monroe (1991) feels that previous injury or trauma that causes inactivity over a prolonged period of time may predispose the young elite athlete to a subsequent Achilles tendon rupture. An Achilles tendon may rupture secondary to corticosteroid injections and subsequent degeneration. Most often the tendon tears in the area of poor circulation (2-6 cm above the os calcis).

*Epidemiology* — Achilles tendon rupture is most likely in men between the ages of 30 and 50 years. Older runners appear to be more susceptible. Most tendon ruptures occur 2-5 cm above the insertion into the os calcis in the area of decreasing vascularity. Surprisingly, Achilles tendon rupture is missed in approximately 20%-25% of cases. They are most apt to occur in basketball, volleyball, cross-country skiing, football, and racket sports.

*Signs and Symptoms* — Patients do not always have as much pain as expected from a major musculoskeletal tear like the Achilles tendon. They hear a loud pop and have sudden pain that gradually subsides. Patients say that the sensation with weight-bearing is that their foot is "falling through the floor." Blood and swelling accumulate in the tendon sheath, the patient is unable to stand on tiptoe, and there often is marked weakness in the posterior calf muscle group. The Thompson test (Thompson, 1962) which involves squeezing the relaxed posterior calf muscles on the affected and unaffected side (Figure 14E-8) usually is positive. If plantar flexion of the foot occurs, the Achilles tendon should be intact. If it does not, the Achilles tendon may be ruptured.

*Treatment* — Many recent studies suggest that operative and nonoperative treatment produce similar clinical results. Several excellent articles review these options (Inglis, 1981; Nistor, 1981; Beskin, 1987). Some points to be considered in treatment are:

- The more proximal the rupture site, the more appropriate conservative, nonsurgical treatment becomes.
- The potential rerupture rate is slightly higher with nonoperative vs operative treatment.
- Operative complications such as infection, skin necrosis, or sensory loss must be considered. Strength and endurance of the posterior calf unit appear to be slightly greater in those surgically treated.

After a decision is reached regarding surgery, the following care should be outlined to the patient:

- Long leg cast with ankle at 20° plantar flexion or less for three weeks. Important note

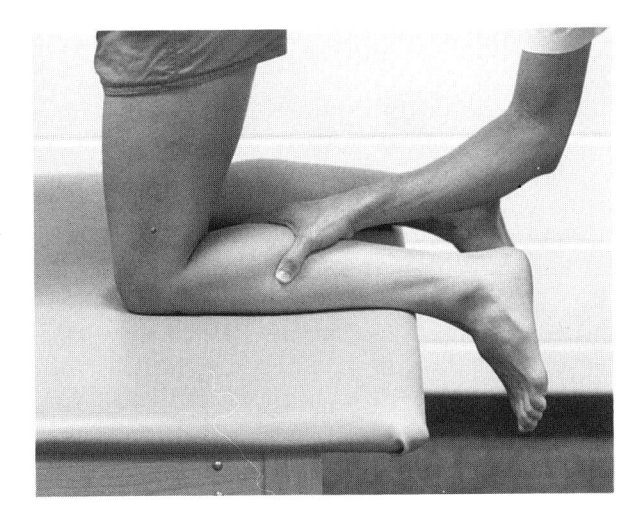

**Fig. 14E-8.** Thompson Test. A test for continuity of the gastrocsoleus muscles' common tendon. Absence of foot-plantar flexion motion indicates a ruptured Achilles tendon.

— Hägmark (1979) recommends that the foot be placed in as much dorsiflexion as possible up to neutral to minimize the selective atrophy in the posterior calf muscles as repair takes place.
- Change to short leg, non-walking cast with less plantar flexion for three weeks.
- Change to short leg, walking cast or ankle-foot orthosis for three additional weeks.
- Once out of immobilization, the patient should wear an elevated heel on both feet for two to three weeks, and walk with crutches until he/she can do a normal heel-toe gait. Stretching, heel lifts, proprioceptive neural facilitation, and range of motion is vital throughout the entire rehabilitation process.

## Fractures

There are two types of ankle fractures:

1. *Stable* — fractures that do not involve the articular surface or disrupt the stability of the joint. Treatment is closed reduction and casting. Immobilize the ankle at neutral (90°) in most cases. Post-reduction x-ray may help establish the correct position.
2. *Unstable* — fractures that involve much of the articular surface and cause significant instability in the ankle joint. The primary care physician must be able to recognize these fractures and refer appropriately.

Differentiating between stable and unstable ankle fractures is difficult but crucial for the team physician. For the purpose of discussion, consider the ankle as a horizontal ring comprised of the deltoid ligament and medial malleolus on the medial side, the lateral malleolus and lateral supporting ligaments on the lateral side, and the anterior and posterior lips of the tibia. This ring encloses and supports the talus. The talus bears more weight per unit area than any other bone in the body and a lateral shift of as little as 1 mm can reduce the contact area of the talus by 40% (Yablon, 1984). Such a reduction in contact area greatly increases the force per unit area on the talus and enhances the development of osteoarthritis. Consult Table 14E-1 for complete delineation of stable and unstable ankle fractures.

**Table 14E-1. Stable and Unstable Ankle Fractures**

| Stable | Unstable |
|---|---|
| Isolated fracture of the lateral malleolus | Fracture of the lateral malleolus combined with a tear of the deltoid ligament |
| Isolated fracture of the medial malleolus | Fracture of the medial malleolus and fibular shaft |
|  | Bimalleolar fracture |
| Fracture of the anterior or posterior lip of the tibia (less than 25% of the articular surface) | Fracture of the anterior or posterior lip of the tibia (greater than 25% of the articular surface) |

(Adapted from Yablon, 1984)

### Epiphyseal Fractures

Epiphyseal fractures in the adolescent athlete that break through the distal epiphyses of the fibula and tibia are of some concern. Consult Figure 14E-9 for examples of the Salter-Harris classification. Without stress films, both Salter I (separation along the epiphysis) and Salter V (crush injury) can be missed. However, Salter I fractures through the epiphysis can be routinely diagnosed with stress films. These injuries should be suspected in young individuals. Careful clinical examination of the lateral or medial compartment will show tenderness over the substance of the malleoli and not at its distal border, the common site of ligamentous pain. Treatment involves immobilization, with a longer period of non-weightbearing than normally would be done for a typical ankle fracture. Salter II, III, and IV, by definition, have bony fragments that stabilize the fracture site and they can be treated just as any other stable ankle fracture. Salter V crush injuries should be suspected in individuals jumping from heights (playground equipment, skiing, cliffs). They also should be suspected when no fracture is found on x-ray, pain continues on weightbearing, and symptoms do not resolve over the normal recovery time for ankle sprains or strains. Once again, non-weightbearing immobilization becomes an important part of the treatment.

### Osteochondral Fracture

Osteochondral fracture of the dome of the talus may follow a compression injury to the subchondral bone. Lesions are often small and difficult

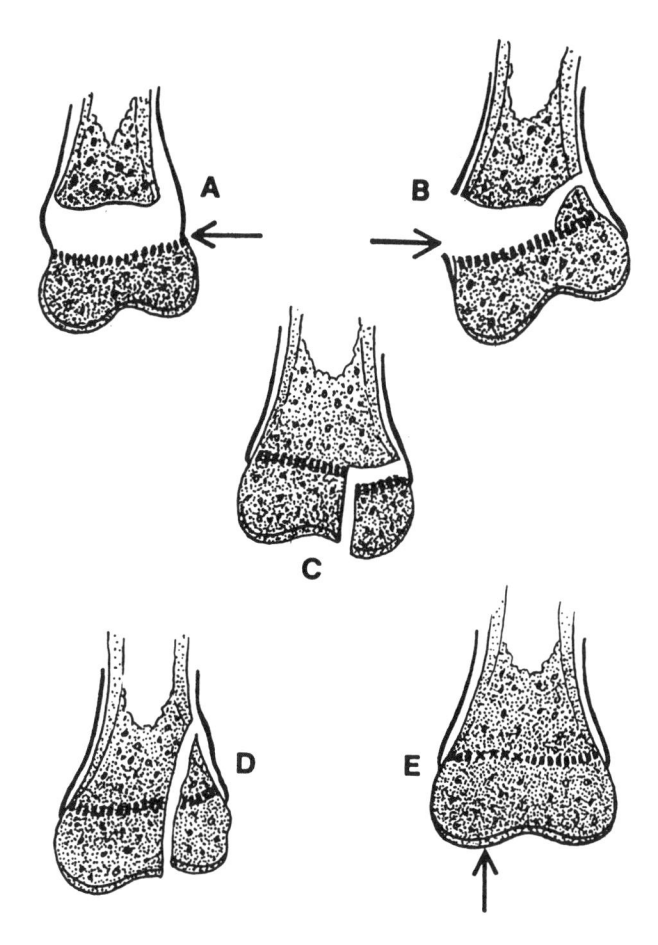

**Fig. 14E-9.** Salter-Harris classification of epiphyseal injury. A. Type I — separation of epiphysis. B. Type II — fracture-separation of epiphysis. C. Type III — fracture of part of epiphysis. D. Type IV — fracture of epiphysis and epiphyseal plate. E. Type V — crush injury to epiphyseal plate.

A. Type I — Separation of Epiphysis
B. Type II — Fracture-Separation of Epiphysis
C. Type III — Fracture of Part of Epiphysis
D. Type IV — Fracture of Epiphysis and Epiphyseal Plate
E. Type V — Crush Injury to Epiphyseal Plate

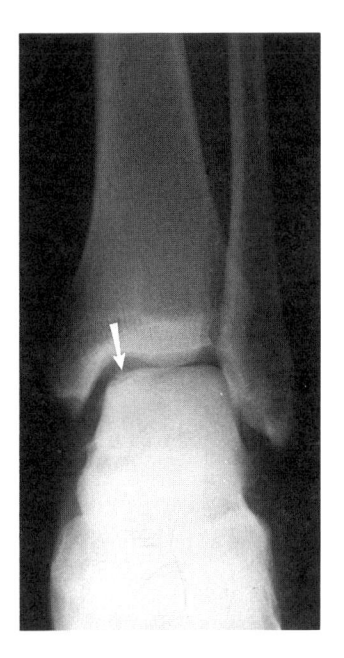

**Fig. 14E-10.** Osteochondral Fracture

| STAGE | DESCRIPTION | TREATMENT |
|-------|-------------|-----------|
| Stage 1 | Compression of subchondral bone and articular cartilage | Cast 12 weeks |
| Stage 2 | Osteochondral fragment is partially detached | Cast 18 weeks |
| Stage 3 | Fragment is completely avulsed but undisplaced | Medial lesion — cast 18 weeks (if symptoms persist-surgery); Lateral lesion — surgery |
| Stage 4 | Fragment is displaced and rotated away from rest of talus | Surgery |

(Flick, 1985; Berndt, 1959)

to appreciate clinically. This fracture might be seen in a runner who missteps and later develops a weak ankle with deep pain, recurrent swelling, and crepitation. The lesion usually is found on the lateral dome of the talus and is caused by shearing forces produced by the accompanying inversion injury (Figure 14E-10) when the foot is dorsiflexed. Less common medial talar dome fractures occur with the foot plantar flexed.

*Diagnostic Aids* — Tomograms (or CAT scan) are needed if the lesions cannot be detected on a straight AP plantar-flexed view. MRI also can be used. Treatment depends on the stage of the lesion (Figure 14E-11) as follows:

Occult fracture (Figure 14E-12), unusual and often undetected fractures, can mimic the tenderness of the lateral ankle sprain. Many can be seen on standard x-ray views of the ankle, especially in the oblique position. However, tomograms, CT scan, and MRI can augment a questionable ankle x-ray. Below are some of the occult fractures to keep in mind: (Amis, 1987)

- Anterior process of the calcaneus.
- Lateral tubacle (posterior process of the talus — Shepherd's fracture)
- Lateral aspect of the cuboid
- Lateral process of the talus
- Base of the fifth metatarsal

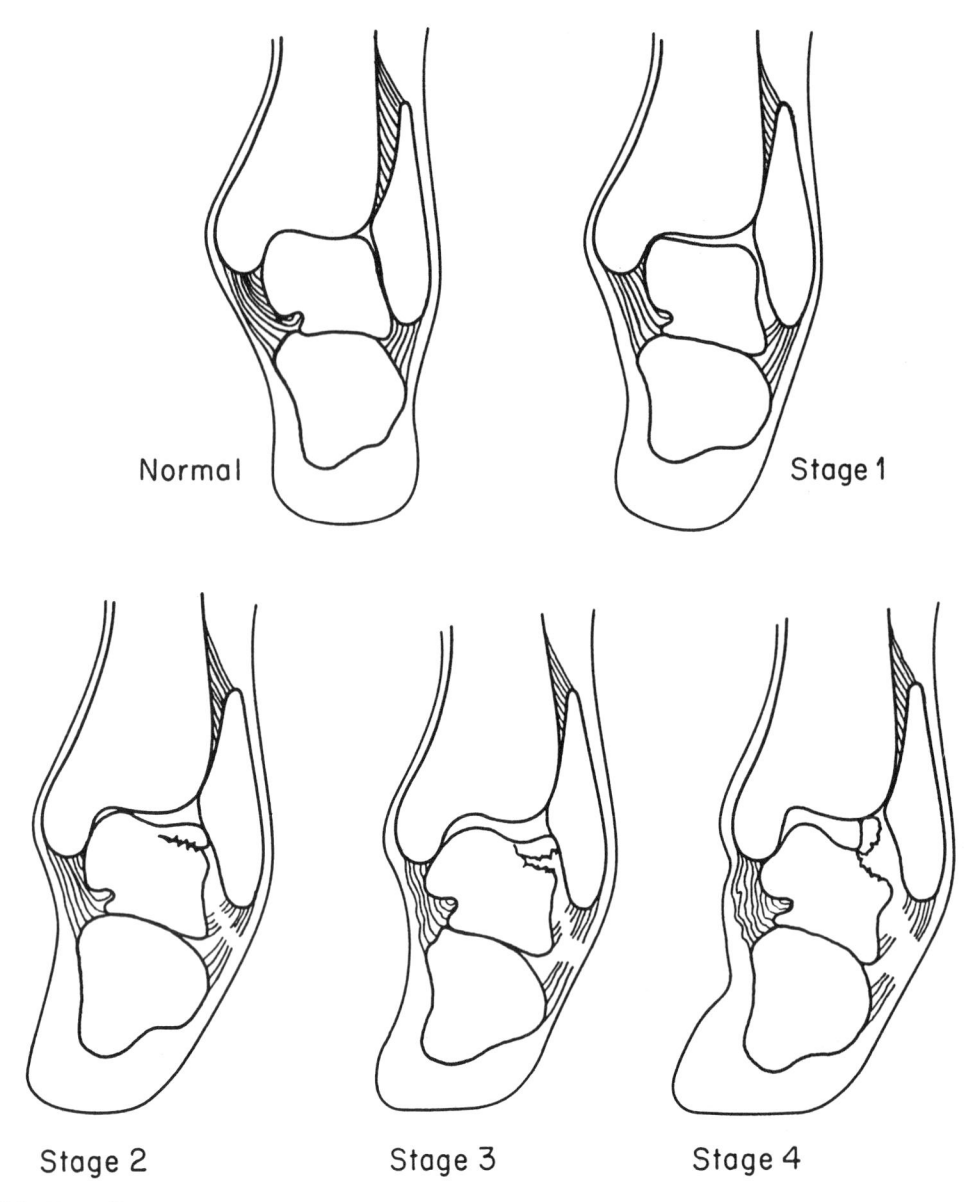

**Fig. 14E-11.** Talar Dome Fractures

### Tendon Injury

#### Peroneal Tendons

Laterally, the peroneal tendons pass around the posterior distal aspect of the lateral malleolus in a shallow grove covered by a retinacular "roof". The peroneus longus is the major lateral tendon of the ankle. It is a strong everter and weak plantar flexor. Injuries of these structures include:

- tendinitis secondary to overuse — related to the pulley action of the tendon and analogous to the avascularity and blanching induced by the supraspinatus tendon of the shoulder (impingement syndrome).
- subluxation/dislocation.
- rupture.

*Epidemiology* — Sports most frequently involved are skiing and ballet dancing (Arrowsmith, 1983). However, Hamilton (1988) argues that diagnosed perineal tendon injuries (tendinitis) are not nearly as common in dancers as they are in athletes. Tenderness found behind the lateral malleolus is really a posterior impingement syndrome involving chronic irritation of

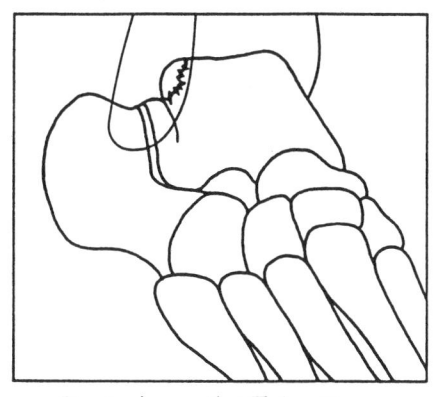

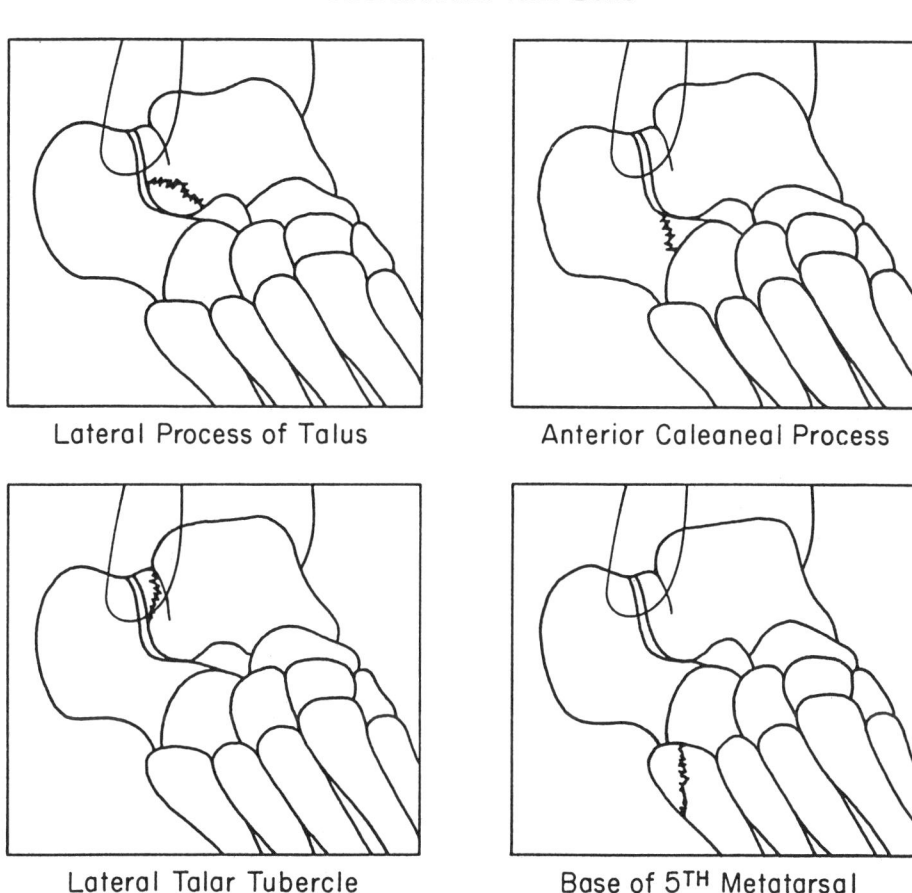

**Fig. 14E-12.** Occult Fracture Producing Lateral Compartment Ankle Tenderness

an os trigonum or Steida's Process (trigonal process).

**Peroneal Tendinitis**

*Biomechanics* — Injuries to the peroneal tendons are often incorrectly diagnosed and treated as sprains. These tendons are subject both to overuse and acute/chronic dislocation. Injury is caused by acute dorsiflexion coupled with internal rotation that isolates the tendons and produces stress, resulting in either strain of the musculotendinous unit or dislocation across the lateral malleolus.

*Signs and Symptoms* — There is increased pain with passive plantar flexion and inversion as well as active resistance to dorsiflexion and eversion (Figure 14E-13). Careful clinical exam-

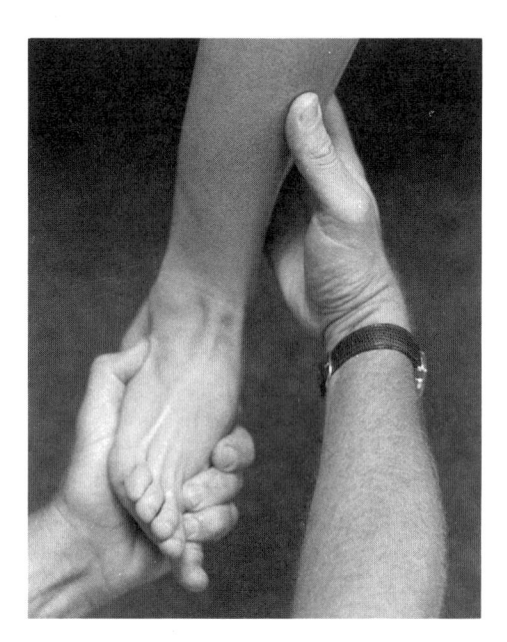

**Fig. 14E-13.** Testing the Peroneal Muscles

ination will show the point of pain located posteriorly and laterally to the malleolus. Swelling may be present. This injury should be differentiated from a lateral ligament injury which is most often anterior and/or inferior to the malleolus.

*Treatment* — Decreasing the causal biomechanics (acute dorsiflexion) must be recommended. Refer to the protocol for overuse injuries and for other ankle injuries (Ankle Repac™). Steroid injection into the sheath of the peroneal tendons is acceptable in recalcitrant cases. Lateral ankle strapping may decrease the strain on the unit.

### Subluxation/Dislocation of Peroneal Tendon

*Biomechanics* — Forceful passive dorsiflexion with the ankle in slight eversion, which creates a violent reflex contracture of the tendons and disruption of the peroneal retinaculum or "roof". Injury to the lateral compartment of the ankle is normally associated with inversion stress. A history of lateral pain with eversion should raise suspicion about a perineal tendon subluxation/dislocation (Grana, 1990). Some believe that the depth of the groove may be a factor.

*Signs* — This condition can be demonstrated by performing a stress test with active dorsiflexion and eversion of the foot and ankle that will reproduce the pain over the peroneal tendons and possibly subluxation.

*Treatment* — Use of a U-shaped felt pad incorporated into ankle taping to discourage dislocation is recommended for a primary dislocation. Severe cases may require immobilization in a cast for 10-12 days, then use of an air cast for four weeks. With elite athletes, a case can be made for surgical repair, if only to prevent chronic dislocation, eventual rupture, ankle instability, and chronic pain (Abraham, 1979).

### Rupture

This is rare, and may be caused by iatrogenic injections of corticosteroids into the tendon substance. Classic absence of ability to evert the foot should lead the physician to the diagnosis. It requires immediate referral and surgical reconstruction.

### Anterior Tibial Tendon

The anterior tibial tendon accounts for 80% of the dorsiflexion power of the ankle (Figure 14E-14). Three injuries should be considered:

- Tendinitis — This is rare but may occur in people running long periods of time, hiking, or running downhill. Inappropriate shoelace pressure may be a contributing factor. The resulting inflammation may lead to swelling and the development of an anterior compartment syndrome. Such swelling usually is short-lived because the

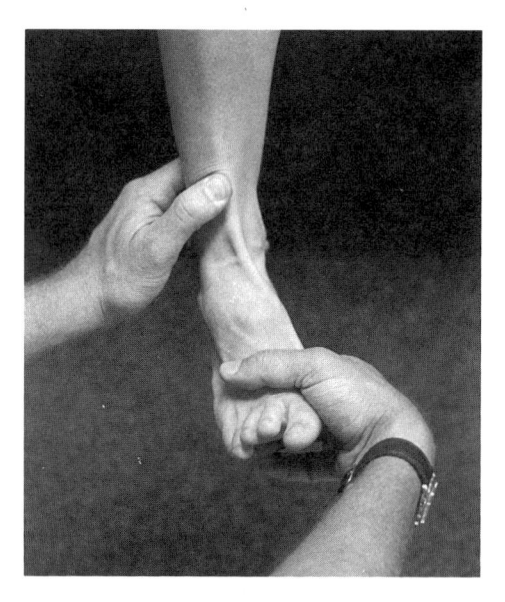

**Fig. 14E-14.** Anterior Tibial Muscle Testing

tendon has no bony fulcrum or pulley-like action and has an excellent vascular supply.
- Rupture — Rupture may present with minimal pain but a "foot-drop" gait. It usually is an injury of the non-athlete.
- Avulsion Fracture of Navicular Bone — If the anterior tibial tendon comes under enough stress, it may actually pull or fracture its insertion on the navicular bone. However, this is extremely rare.

### Posterior Tibial Tendon

The medial malleolus serves as a fulcrum for this tendon, predisposing it to tendinitis and tenosynovitis. Inflammation of this tendon is seen mostly in the 40-60 year old individual. Active inversion will reproduce the symptoms. For treatment refer to overuse guidelines.

## Chronic Ankle Injury

Over a period of time, perhaps as long as decades, the margins of the ankle joint tend to react to increased stress with heterotopic calcification and exostosis. Impingements upon the architecture of the joint can cause involvement of synovium. This normally occurs on the anterior medial margin and frequently is seen in gymnasts, secondary to dismounting. In ballet dancers, the movements referred to as grand plie and en pointe, create forced plantar flexion that contributes to an increase in this problem (Bergfeld, 1982). Ankles that were injured in the past, treated inadequately, or post-surgical ankles are prone not only to bony exostosis, but also avascular necrosis of the talus, premature osteoarthritis, and Sudeck's atrophy (nerve damage resulting in post-traumatic osteoporosis and reflex sympathetic dystrophy).

## Tarsal Tunnel Syndrome

*Epidemiology* — This is seen infrequently but occurs in jogging, walking, tennis, and basketball.
*Biomechanics* — The jarring action of these sports causes nerve compression, specifically to the posterior tibial nerve as it passes through the tarsal tunnel with the flexor tendons of the foot on the medial side of the foot. Improperly fitted shoes are a major contributing factor (Mandel, 1987). The biomechanics of tarsal tunnel syndrome are similar to those of the carpal tunnel, with edema secondary to repeated trauma and tendinitis of those tendons coursing through the "tunnel".
*Anatomy* — The tarsal tunnel is bordered across its roof by the lacunate ligament coursing from the medial malleolus to the calcaneus. The plantar surfaces of the tarsal bones and the proximal metatarsals form the floor of the tunnel. The tunnel contents include: posterior tibial tendon, flexor digitorum longus tendon, flexor hallicus longus tendon, and the posterior tibial neurovascular bundle. After emerging through the tunnel, the posterial tibial nerve splits into three branches: the medial calcaneal sensory to the heel, the medial plantar motor and sensory to the medial foot, and the lateral plantar motor and sensory to the lateral foot.
*Symptoms* — Medial posterior foot pain accompanied by burning and tingling characterizes the syndrome. The foot may become numb over the plantar innervation with toe flexors becoming weak. Pain is increased by standing and may be exacerbated at night, similar to that of carpal tunnel syndrome.
*Signs* — Tinel's sign (percussion over the posterior tibial nerve recreating the pain) should be positive.
*Differential Diagnosis* — Tendinitis of any of the tendons coursing through this area; sprain of some of the underlying medial ligaments.
*Diagnostic Aids* — EMG shows a prolonged nerve conduction of the medial plantar nerve (branch of the posterior tibial nerve).
*Treatment* — Correctly fitting arch supports, local injection of corticosteroids in severe cases, immobilization (cast) for three weeks, prevention of eversion using a medial heel wedge, and surgical decompression if conservative treatment fails.
*Sequelae* — Atrophy of the intrinsic foot muscles and the development of hammer toe deformities can develop.

## Other Entities

Because ankle sprains are so common and diagnosis potentially so evasive, the primary care physician should consider the following when *conservative treatment of routine ankle sprains has failed:*

- Osteochondral fracture of the talar dome — usually occurs on the medial dome as a result of

impaction associated with a lateral eversion sprain. This entity was discussed earlier.
- Synovial pinch syndrome — this develops when a piece of hypertrophic synovium (the result of recurrent ankle sprains) becomes entrapped in the anterior aspect of the talo-fibular articulation. Arthroscopy can demonstrate the problem definitively but manual realignment of the synovium is usually all that is needed. Occasionally a trial injection of local anesthestic is helpful. Rarely, surgery may be needed to correct the entrapment.
- Traction Neuropraxia of the Peroneal Nerve — overstretching of the lateral compartment and the peroneal nerve can result from an initial ankle sprain.
- Posterior Impingement Syndrome — a small bony prominence (os trigonum), located posterior to the talus, can be fractured or pinched off during plantar flexion injuries to the ankle (seen frequently in ballet dancers). Discussed earlier and outlined later in this chapter.

## SECTION F.
## FEET AND TOES

### Introduction

While national studies of injuries treated in emergency rooms put the number of foot injuries at only 7% (NEISS, 1983), all that this indicates is that most foot and toe injuries may be major to the athlete but not serious enough to be seen in an emergency room setting. Most foot injuries are either self-treated or seen in an ambulatory care setting. In this particular anatomical area of the body, injury treatment and advice is administered by both medical and paramedical providers. A whole discipline (podiatry) has been devoted to the care and prevention of foot injuries.

The foot forms the base of support for the entire body in any gravity-controlled induced situation. Standing, walking, running, or cycling require the foot to transfer the mechanical power of the legs to the ground for locomotion and to dissipate the forces generated by ground-body interaction (Figure 14F-1). Forces dissipate at three sites with three different actions: knee flexion, ankle dorsiflexion, and subtalar pronation. The foot is adaptable, being both rigid and flexible in different parts of the same motion. It is rigid with the transfer of power from the lower extremity to the surface, and flexible when responding to changing surface characteristics. There are many demands upon the foot. It must absorb sudden stops and starts, the act of jumping up and the impact load of landing, sustained loads while lifting and standing, and repetitive loads when walking or running. The foot can be totally encased in a rigid or semi-rigid ski-boot "cast" or it may be devoid of all extrinsic protection when barefoot. Waller (1982) has proposed that the foot and structures deep within it are

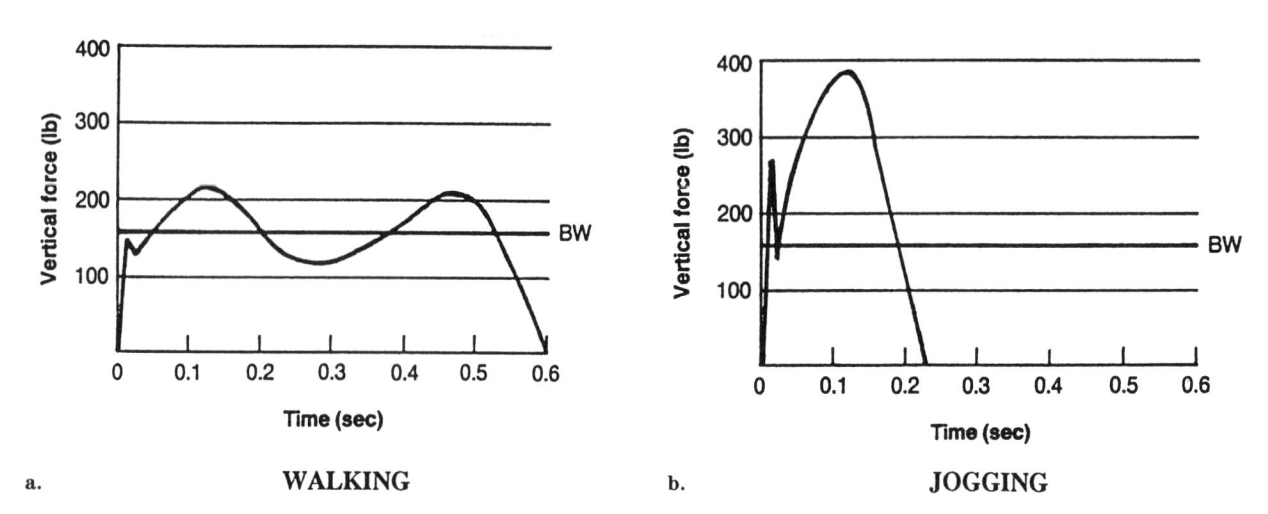

a. WALKING      b. JOGGING

**Fig. 14F-1.** Vertical force measured by force plate in a 160 lb. athlete
A. At time of initial ground contact, vertical force is equal to about 90% of body weight (BW). Force then drops slightly before rising above BW. During midportion of stance phase, force decreases to less than BW as center of gravity reaches peak elevation. This is followed by second period in which ground reaction is greater than BW as center of gravity falls. Force then goes to zero as foot is lifted off ground. B. In jogging, foot is on ground 0.25 second, compared with 0.6 second in walking. Force has increased significantly over that recorded during walking.

merely part of a chain linkage system and that a problem with any "link" in the system can cause imbalance in another segment. The secondarily affected system may actually be more symptomatic than the primary site of involvement. Because the sport of running demands so much of the foot (depending on stride, there are 400-800 heel strikes per mile), this sport generates most of the foot injuries seen in sports medicine. Most sports require running of one sort or another, but it is jogging and running that generate the most stress on the foot (Nuber, 1988). Garrick (1988) has given us a good epidemiologic look at foot injuries by sport, differentiating acute vs. overuse type (see Figure 14F-2).

## Anatomy

The foot is made up of 26 bones located in three segments (Figure 14F-3): 1) hind foot or heel — talus and calcaneus; 2) midfoot — navicular, cuboid and cuneiform bones, and 3) forefoot — metatarsals and phalangeal bones of the toes.

*Physical Examination* — Important aspects of the history and physical exam can be found in the protocol (Appendix 14F-1). They will be summarized here:

*History*
- What sport and specific activity produces the pain.

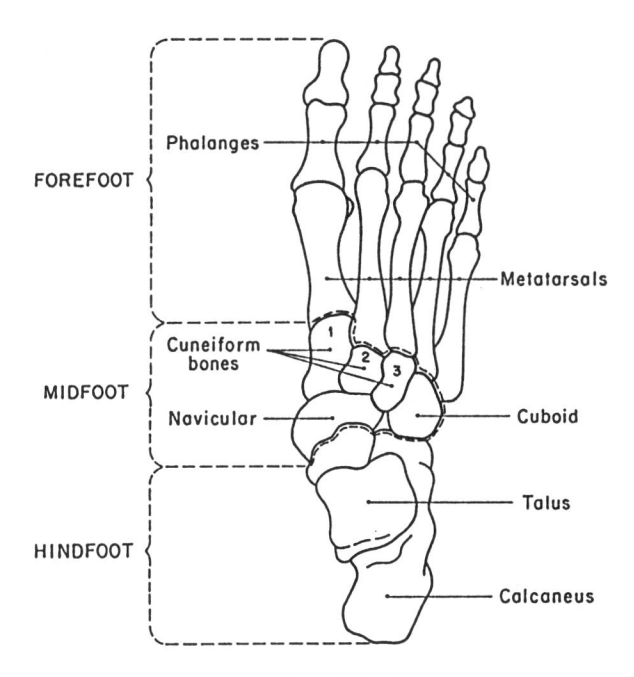

**Fig. 14F-3.** Foot Anatomy (Dorsal View)

- Specific location of the pain.
- Previous treatment.
- Training schedule.
- Past medical history and family history — most important to determine here is the possible presence of a history of rheumatoid arthritis, gout, or past foot surgery.
- Training schedule including surface interfaced and intensity of activity.

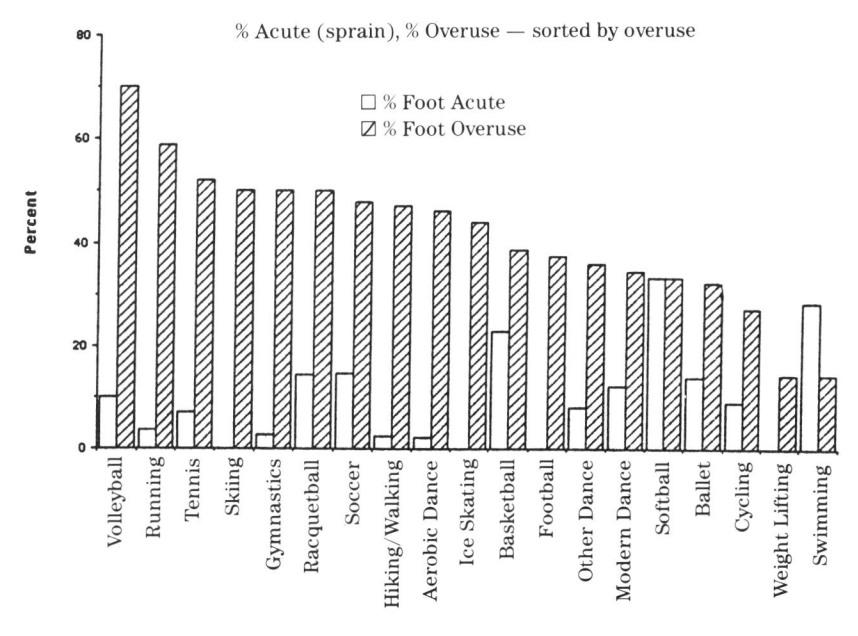

**Fig. 14F-2.** Percentage of foot injuries by sport: acute versus overuse

PELVIC AND LOWER EXTREMITY INJURIES/ILLNESSES

- Equipment — specifically what footwear is worn.
- Proximal pain — the presence of discomfort above the foot in the ankle, knee, leg, hip, and lower back.

*Physical Examination*
- Inspection — for effusion, ecchymosis, deformity.
- Gait pattern.
- Examination of shoe wear pattern.
- Pelvic/spinal abnormalities — done with the patient standing.
- Lower extremity abnormalities.
- Leg length measurement.
- Skin — examine for corn, callus, wart, blisters.
- Heel exam.
- Range of Motion — First MTP joint, forefoot, and ankle.
- Midfoot exam — arch.
- Forefoot exam.

Biomechanics and anatomy play an important part in foot pain and/or injury. Please refer to Figures 14F-4 and 5 for an understanding of functional muscle involvement during walking and running that should help understanding foot injuries described in the remaining chapter.

## Hindfoot

The talus sits on top of the calcaneus and forms the subtalar joint. This joint contributes to the range of motion in the hind foot. Range of motion of the hind foot is 5° pronation and 20° supination. This joint is stabilized by the extrinsic lower leg muscles and intrinsic foot muscles. Anteriorly, the border between the hindfoot and midfoot is the transverse tarsal joint. This joint allows the midfoot to rotate for terrain adaptation. The subtalar joint is flexible in pronation but rigid in supination. Note: The biomechanics may explain why

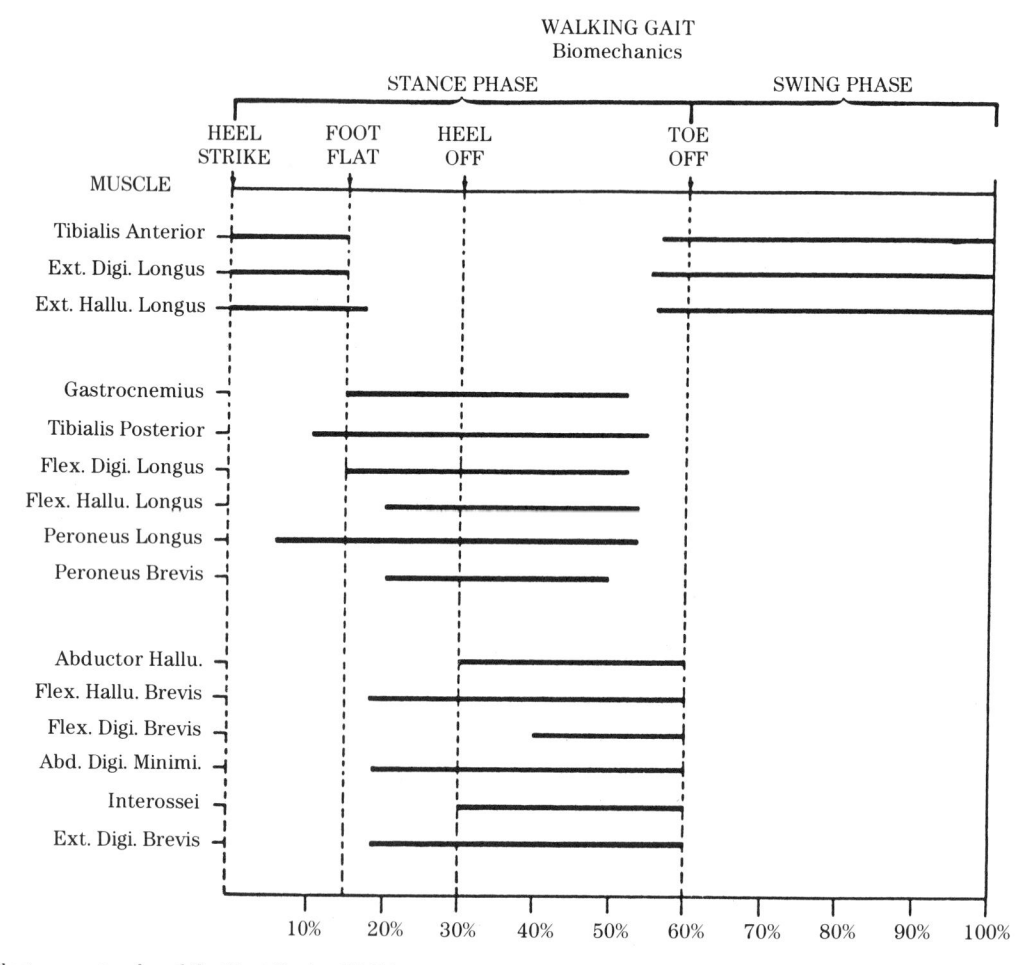

**Fig. 14F-4.** Electromyography of the Foot During Walking

Fig. 14F-5. Electromyography of the Foot During Running. (Adapted from Mann R.A., Moran G.T., Daugherty S.E.: Comparative electromyography of the lower extremities in jogging, running and sprinting. *Am J Sports Med* 14:501, 1986.)

a pronated foot is better tolerated in running than a supinated one. Posteriorly, the Achilles tendon inserts on the posterior aspect of the calcaneus, at which point it becomes thinner, with its fibers sweeping underneath the posterior inferior aspect of the heel, then continuing forward as the plantar fascia to insert on the metatarsal heads and proximal toes. Two bursae are found at the insertion of the Achilles tendon, one in front of the tendon (subcutaneous, retro-Achilles bursa) and one between the tendon and the calcaneus (retro-calcaneal bursa).

*Biomechanics* — As might be expected, most foot problems are caused by overuse or repeated microtrauma. Granted, congenital defects may predispose a foot to injury, but the initial etiologic factor is almost always overuse (Figure 14F-6).

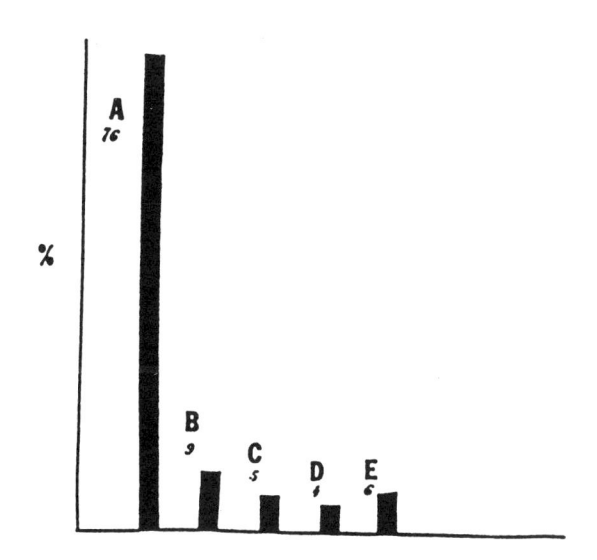

Fig. 14F-6. Various Sports Contributing to Heel Pain. A. Running/jogging, 76%; B. racquet sports, 9%; C. basketball, 5%; D. soccer, 4%; and E. miscellaneous, 6%. (Lutter, 1986)

## Painful Heel

A painful heel can be caused by any one of the following (depending upon location of pain and structure involved): bone bruise, bursitis, plantar fasciitis, plantar tear, heel spur, apophysitis, exostosis, Achilles tenosynovitis, calcaneal stress fracture, calcaneal fracture, os trigonum pain, black-dot heel, bruised or torn fat pad.

### Plantar Calcaneal Pain

*Plantar Fasciitis* — Heel Spur Syndrome.
*Epidemiology* — This is the most common cause

of heel pain in sports medicine. Graham (1986) contends that most of the pathology is seen around the calcaneal attachment of the plantar fascia and flexor digitorum brevis muscle. In fact, these two structures attach inferior to calcaneal spur and not at its leading edge. Inflammation and/or microtearing near the origin of the plantar fascia is usually involved. The mechanics of the plantar fascia are illustrated in Figure 14F-7.

*Predisposing Factors* — Pronated foot with high longitudinal arch or a tight Achilles tendon mechanism. Associated conditions include: cavus foot, pronated foot with forefoot varus, or hypermobile pes planus.

*Signs* — Pain on palpation of the anterior medial calcaneus.

*Symptoms* — Gradual onset of pain, usually located in the medial heel radiating toward the longitudinal arch of the foot. Pain on first few steps in the morning (secondary to relaxation and shortening of the fascia during sleep) and then a second episode, usually following exercise.

*Diagnostic Aids* — X-ray is negative unless there is a traction spur — which is present 60% of the time but is not responsible for the patient's pain (Leach, 1985). Test passive dorsiflexion of the ankles. The patient should have 10-15° dorsiflexion. If dorsiflexion is less, a tight Achilles mechanism is presumed.

*Differential Diagnosis*
1. Microfracture (stress) or evulsion of the calcaneus.
2. Entrapment of the medial calcaneal branch of the posterior tibial nerve.
3. Tarsal tunnel syndrome.

*Treatment* — Taping (see Figure 14F-8) arch support, ¼ inch heel lifts, correction of underlying

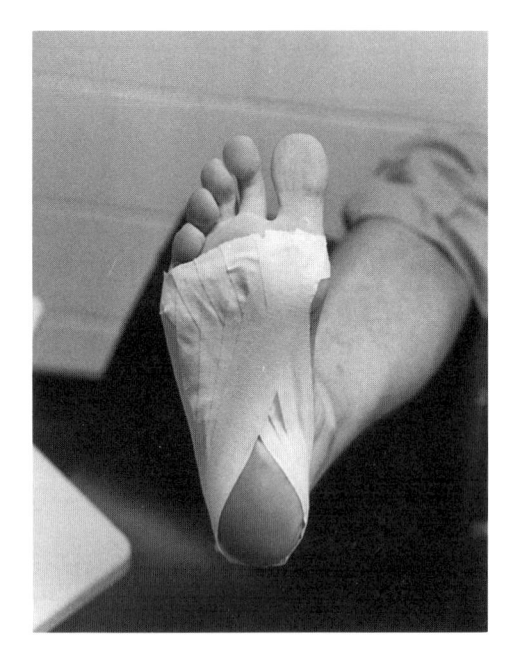

**Fig. 14F-8.** Taping for Plantar Fasciitis

imbalance with orthotics, and stretching in the bent leg position. A word about orthotics — The authors suggest using soft, inexpensive orthotics which will frequently alleviate the symptoms. The more expensive hard orthotics often are no more effective a treatment.

Surgical intervention for any type of calcaneal/hindfoot pain is to be avoided and used only as a last resort. Surgical removal of calcaneal spurs has been less than satisfactory in the non-athletic population. It should be avoided in an injured athlete. Because the heel pain syndrome is self-limited, patience may be the most important aspect of any treatment. Also, Achilles and gastrocnemius tendon stretch-

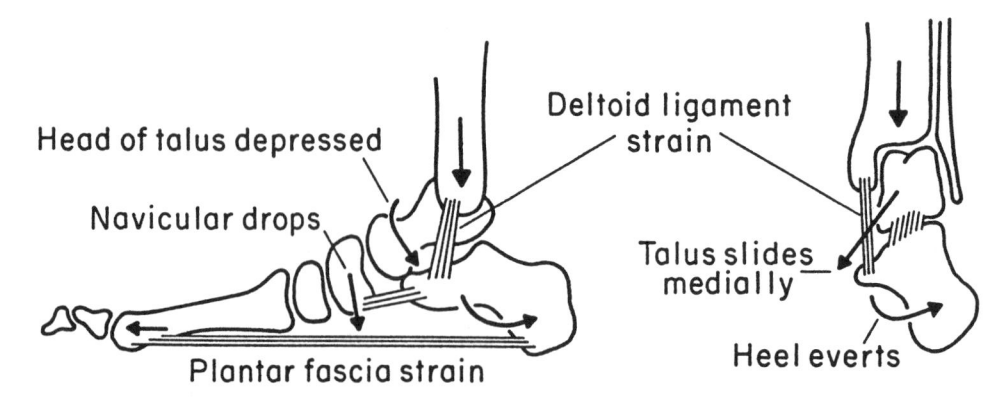

**Fig. 14F-7.** Biomechanics of the Plantar Fascia

ing are appropriate. Overuse protocols should be followed. Steroid injection as well as arch taping may be indicated if conservative treatment fails.

**Calcaneal Stress Fracture**

*Epidemiology* — Most commonly seen in beginning runners, runners who train on asphalt or concrete, or where there is a sudden increase in exercise time. The most likely sports are running and ballet.

*Symptoms* — A sudden onset of constant pain is seen here with this injury.

*Signs* — Percussion tenderness over the calcaneus, compression of the medial and lateral calcaneal tuberosities which creates extreme pain.

*Differential Diagnosis* — 1) Acute calcaneal fracture — usually the result of trauma such as a fall from height; 2) Plantar fasciitis — pain not as constant nor onset as sudden in this condition.

*Diagnostic Aids* — X-ray — usually negative because of the usual lack of sensitivity of x-rays to pick up stress fractures earlier than three weeks, and an extremely thin calcaneal cortex. It takes between four to six weeks before any sclerotic line or cortical change can be seen on x-ray (see Chapter 17, Figure 48). A bone scan can be helpful.

*Treatment* — Similar to any stress fracture. Ambulation should be encouraged as comfort permits. Alternate non-gravity dependent sports like swimming can be pursued to keep up cardiovascular fitness.

*Return To Competition* — Consult overuse guidelines.

**Posterior Calcaneal Pain**

*Os Trigonum Syndrome (posterior impingement syndrome)*

*Anatomy* — An os trigonum is found in approximately 10% of the general population (Kuland, 1982). The most common sports involved are jumping and ballet — especially in young female dancers (Hamilton, 1988). The os trigonum is an accessory ossicle sometimes attached to the posterior talus (then it is referred to Stieda's process) (Figure 14F-9).

*Symptoms* — Pain in the back of the ankle that occurs during extreme plantar flexion. A runner will find it exacerbated by downhill running; a dancer by positioning en pointe.

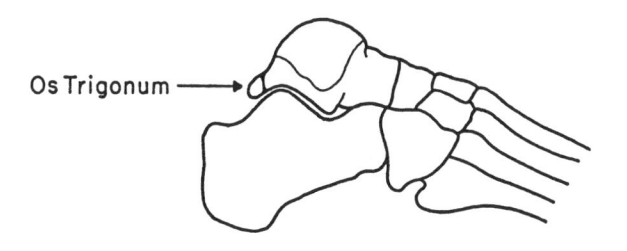

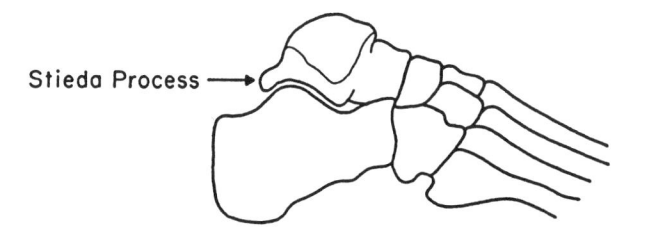

Fig. 14F-9. Os Trigonum and Stieda's Process (Lateral View)

*Differential Diagnosis* — This syndrome is a result of one of several injuries: 1) acute os trigonum fracture; 2) irritation of a previous os trigonum fracture, or 3) congenital os trigonum non-union with irritation. Diagnosis is very difficult because an x-ray may reveal an os trigonum separated from the talus, but the physician does not know if it is a pseudarthrosis, chronic pseudarthrosis, or acute fracture of its bony attachment (synostosis). Comparison x-rays of the opposite ankle help differentiate fracture versus os trigonum. Ancillary lateral views of the ankle in maximum plantar flexion also may help. The diagnosis can be confirmed, if necessary by a Xylocaine injection into the posterior capsule (Hamilton, 1988).

*Treatment* — Ice, rest, and NSAIDs. Surgery may be required for recalcitrant pain usually only in a dancer at least 16 years of age.

**Calcaneo Apophysitis (Seiver's Disease)**

*Epidemiology* — Found most often in males between the ages of 8 and 13. With increased participation in youth sports, this problem has become more common and is also seen more in girls.

*Biomechanics* — Considered a traction injury eliciting stress from the Achilles tendon on a not yet fused posterior calcaneoapophysis.

*Symptoms* — Pain usually occurs bilaterally with increased sensitivity to the back of the heel.

Walking is usually painless but wearing shoes causes pain.
- *Diagnostic Aids* — X-ray is usually of little help, especially if the condition appears to be bilateral. At best, some cortical hypertrophy may be present.
- *Treatment* — Symptomatic since the problem is self-limiting. Activities should be decreased to the point of comfort. Quarter inch heel lifts may take some pressure off of the Achilles tendon attachment.

### "Black-Dot" Heel

- *Epidemiology* — Seen primarily in runners and athletes in walking casts where cotton padding has balled-up (Kuland, 1982).
- *Biomechanics* — Caused by pinching of skin at the bottom of heel between the heel counter and the sole of the shoe.
- *Symptoms* — Painless black or blue plaque on the posterior or posterio-lateral heel.
- *Signs* — Oval or circular lesion(s) lying just above thickened plantar skin. These lesions are not raised, but represent microhemorrhages of capillaries secondary to repetitive trauma.
- *Treatment* — Self-limiting if insult is removed.
- *Prevention* — Felt inside shoe to smooth out heel counter-sole junction, change shoe, or replace cast.

### Heel Bruise

- *Biomechanics* — The calcaneal fat pad normally cushions the heel on impact. However, the quality of the fat pad changes with age and softens, offering less protection. This predisposes the heel of the older athlete, usually a runner, to bone bruising and subperiosteal bleeding. Runners with short overstrides or who run downhill a great deal are predisposed to this condition.
- *Treatment* — Firm heel counter or heel cup (should be worn in everyday shoes as well). A donut pad initially to relieve inflammation, and correction in training technique.

### Bursitis

#### Subcutaneous (Retro-Achilles; "Pump Bump")

- *Biomechanics* — Secondary to a thin heel pad like those used in competitive sprint or cycling shoes.
- *Signs and Symptoms* — Redness, swelling, and pain localized to the area of the bursa overlying the Achilles tendon (Figure 14F-10).

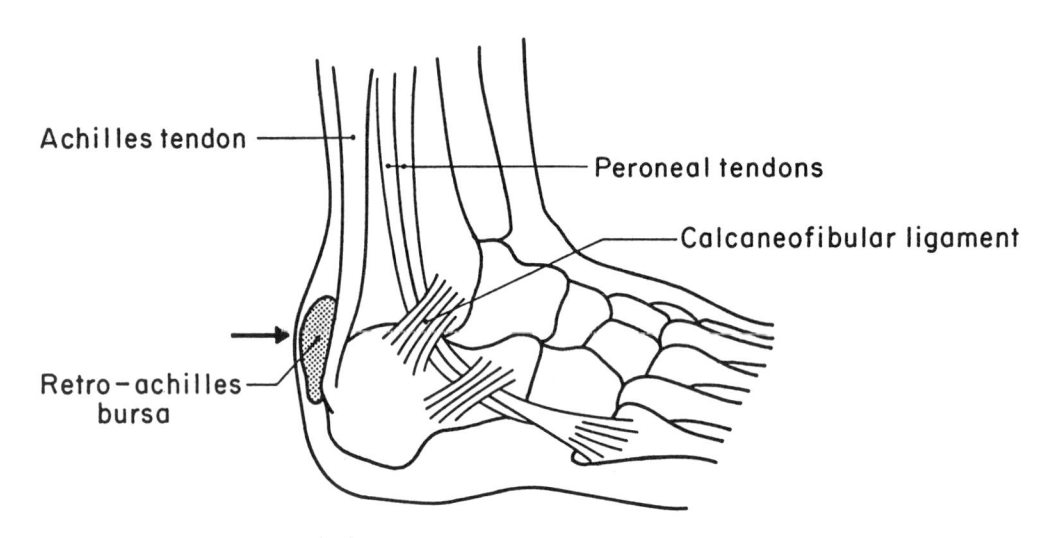

**Fig. 14F-10.** Retro-Achilles (subcutaneous) Bursitis

Location of pain: The superior calcaneal tuberosity.
Characteristics: Tenderness located between the posterior part of the calcaneus and the Achilles tendon.
Offending activities: Wearing shoes with closely fitting heel counters, skiing, ice hockey.
Examination:
*Look for swelling superficial to the Achilles tendon and a bony prominence (pump bump) directly beneath the position of the heel counter.
*If the bursa is thickened or enlarged, you should be able to palpate it.
*Squeezing the area between the posterior part of the calcaneus and the Achilles tendon should elicit pain.
*Check for evidence of decreased passive dorsiflexion.

*Treatment* — Change shoe or apply padding; ice; aspiration and subsequent steroid injection. Note: a pump bump may result from a chronically inflamed subcutaneous bursitis — small bony flakes or evulsions from the os calcis can form a hardened, thickened bony prominence in longtime running athletes. To treat this, increase padding. Surgery is not indicated because of the close proximity of Achilles tendon.

### Retrocalcaneal

*Biomechanics* — Pain located in the posterior superior and usually lateral prominence of the calcaneus (Figure 14F-11). Note: This is one of the few entities where marked inflammation can lead to complete degeneration of the bursae.

*Treatment* — Reduce pressure by lowering the heel counter, wear clogs without heel support, add a heel lift or cup, or use padding or a latex shield. Aspiration and steroid injection is appropriate for recalcitrant cases. Surgery is rare.

### Flexor Hallucis Longus Tendinitis

*Biomechanics* — Flexor hallucis longus (FHL) tendon is considered the achilles tendon of the foot for the dancer (Hamilton, 1988). It passes through the tarsal tunnel which acts as a pulley on it.

*Signs and Symptoms* — Pain and tenderness are present behind the medial malleolus of the ankle, especially in dancers. There is pain on resisted plantar flexion of the great toe. While often misdiagnosed as posterior tibial or achilles tendinitis, pain is deeper than the achilles tendon (Figure 14F-12).

*Treatment* — Ice, ultrasound, range of motion stretching. This injury typically responds to conservative measures. NSAIDs can help. Please refer to Table 2, Chapter 10 for treatment of generic overuse problems. Steroid injections into the tendon should be avoided.

### Midfoot

*Anatomy* — The longitudinal arch is located across this portion of the foot. The roof of that arch is formed by the bones of the midfoot, the floor by the plantar fascia and medial plantaris muscles. The joint motion between the bones, of the midfoot is restricted both by the shape of the bones, the taut ligaments between the bones and the relatively constant contrac-

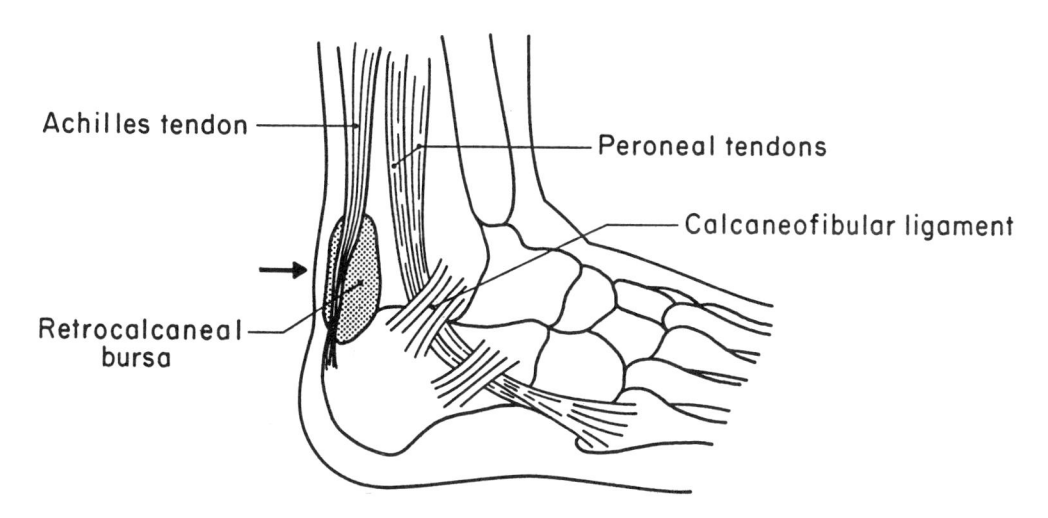

**Fig. 14F-11.** Retrocalcaneal Bursitis

Location of pain: Either at the insertion of the Achilles tendon just distal to the tip of the tuberosity of several centimeters proximal to that.
Characteristics: Pain is accentuated by activity; frequently, athletes report that the pain is worse at the beginning of activity and decreases as they warm up. Ultimately, the pain may become so severe that they even have trouble walking.
Offending activities: Running.
Examination:
*Look for tenderness, swelling, and fullness in an area directly in front of the Achilles tendon and behind the calcaneus (this can be detected by applying pressure medially and laterally just anterior to the tendon and above its insertion into the calcaneus).
*Check for evidence of decrease passive dorsiflexion.

tion of intrinsic as well as extrinsic foot muscles. While the motion between any two bones is small, the total motion of the midfoot can vary from a few degrees dorsiflexion to 15° plantar flexion. The transitional area (border) between the midfoot and forefoot is located across the tarsal metatarsal (T-MT) joints. The second T-MT joint is recessed and therefore more stable, allowing a greater transfer and dissipation of force coming from the first metatarsal during running. A major factor in shaping the arch of the midfoot is the truss of plantar fascia that spans the midfoot. This truss acts as a mild shock absorber.

*Epidemiology* — Midfoot pain is common among athletes who wear lightweight shoes. This is especially true in gymnastics and competitive running. These shoes cause excessive pronation because the lack of support causes midtarsal joint synovitis.

**Medial Midfoot Pain**

**Spring Ligament Sprain.** This entity usually is seen in a runner wearing light shoes and running for the first time on hard, frozen, uneven ground in the spring. The lesion is a sprain of the calcaneal navicular ligament and creates deep midfoot aching and pain in the medial side.

**Posterior Tibial Tendinitis.** This condition creates pain at the insertion of the navicular bone and usually is found after a twisting injury to the foot in which the other symptoms of a medial ankle sprain resolve but pain over the medial midfoot persists (Figure 14F-13). It can be confused with FHL tendinitis.

*Treatment* — 1/8 inch inner heel wedge; NSAIDs using the protocol for overuse; stretching for posterior calf muscles.

**Tarsal Tunnel Syndrome.** Pain may be pres-

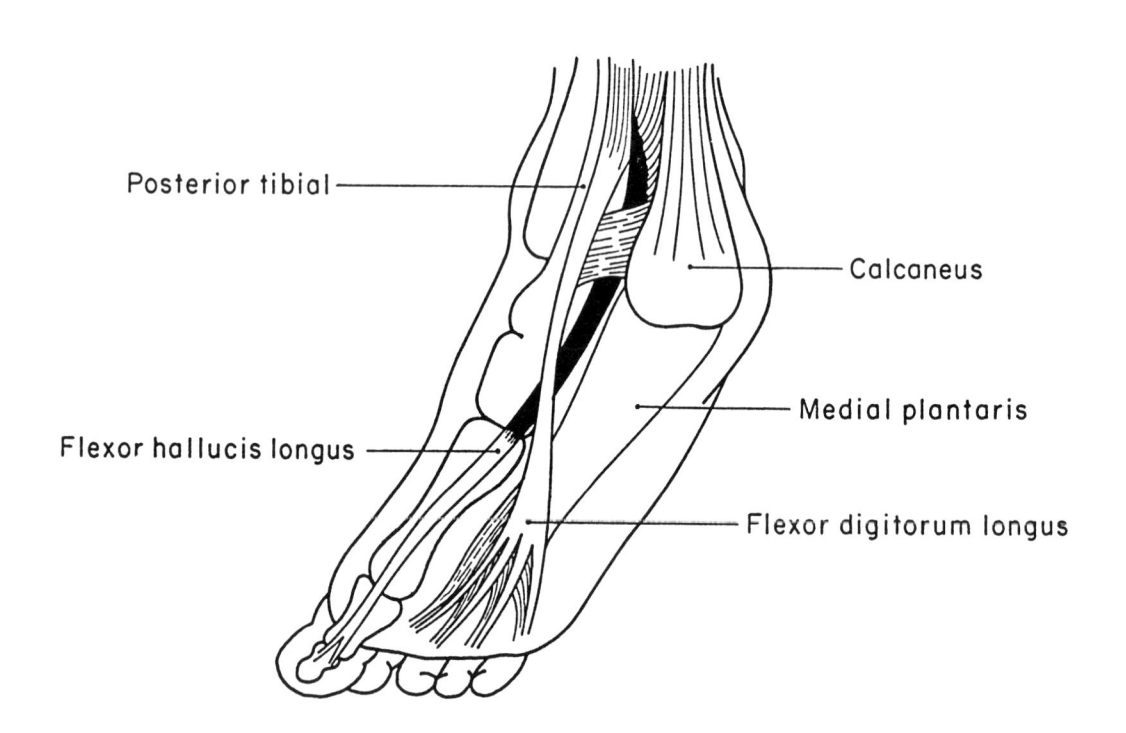

**Fig. 14F-12.** Flexor Hallucis Longus Tendinitis

Location of pain: The medial side of the hindfoot.
Characteristics: Pain is brought on by activity and relieved by rest.
Offending activities: Dancing "sur les pointes."
Examination:
*Look for tenderness along the path of the flexor hallucis longus tendon (particularly tenderness that radiates beneath the medial-arch and under the sustentaculum tali).
*Active plantar flexion and passive dorsiflexion of the ankle will aggravate the patient's syndrome.

ent in the midfoot, depending upon the branch of the posterior tibial nerve.

### Anterior Lateral Midfoot Pain

**Synovial Pinch Syndrome** (Anterior Lateral Corner Compression Syndrome) — Presentation of pain at the anterior inferior border of the fibula and anterior lateral surface of the talus.

*Biomechanics* — This syndrome most likely represents compression of hypertrophied synovium or possibly a chondromalacia of the lateral talar dome (Waller, 1982).
*Symptoms* — History of numerous inversion injuries of a chronic nature in the past. Patient achieves a position of comfort by holding the feet in the inverted position.
*Signs* — Pain on deep palpation of the areas outlined above. A valgus heel is present.
*Diagnostic Aids* — X-ray is not useful.
*Treatment* — ⅛-¼ inch inner heel wedge.

### Anatomical Variants (Midfoot)

The following are the more common anatomical variants of the foot, either presenting primarily or caused by previous surgery or injury (Figure 14F-14). All are predisposing factors to some of the midfoot pain mentioned above and they depend, to a great extent, on the ligamentous integrity of the subtalar and midtarsal joints.

**Pronated Foot.** Accompanied by the following: heel valgus, descended or depressed arch, abducted forefoot.

*Biomechanics* — This clinical picture is a reflection of ligament laxity and sometimes termed a "flexible flat foot." While not necessarily pathologic, this syndrome may be adaptive to accommodate the runner allowing for spring and to cushion the heel. The hyperpronation seen may be compensating for genu varus or a tight gastroc-soleus complex (the most common coexisting problem).

**Pes Planus (Flat Foot).** This is a condition in which the height of the longitudinal arch is reduced considerably.

*Etiology* — 1) congenital; 2) intrinsic muscle weakness; 3) neurologic deficit.
*Biomechanics* — Excessive pronation and outward rotation of the foot resulting in loss of shock absorption (Figure 14F-15). Note: all infants

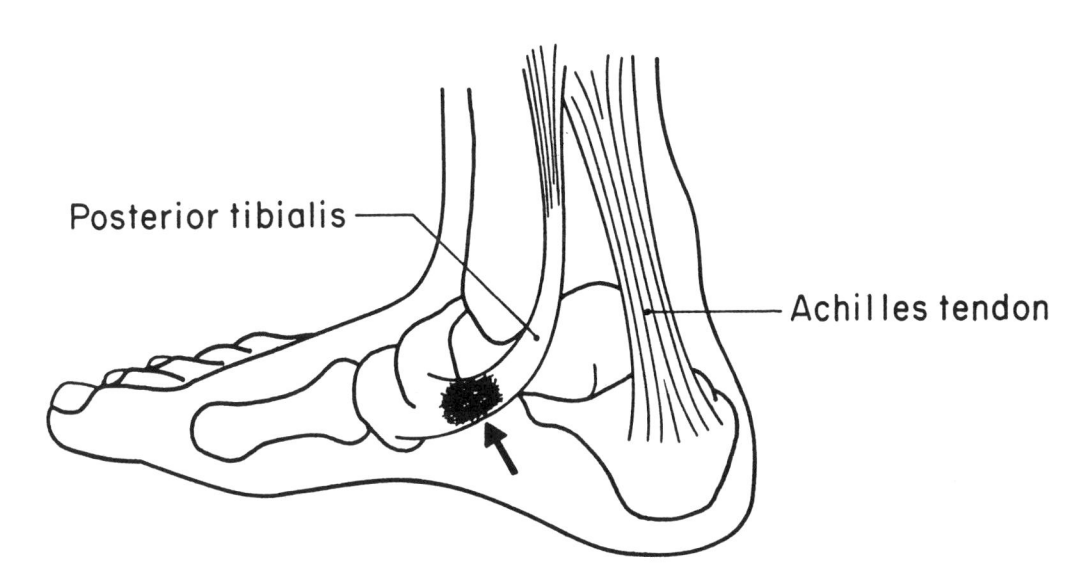

**Fig. 14F-13.** Posterior Tibial Tendinitis

Location of pain: The medial side of the hindfoot.
Characteristics: Pain is brought on by activity and relieved by rest.
Offending activities: Running, sports that require eversion of the hindfoot (for example, ice hockey).
Examination:
*Look for tenderness along the path of the posterior tibial tendon (discomfort may be particularly evident at the insertion of the tendon on the navicular tuberosity).
*Both passive pronation and active supination of the foot will aggravate the patient's pain.

**NORMAL**   **PES PLANUS**   **PES CAVUS**

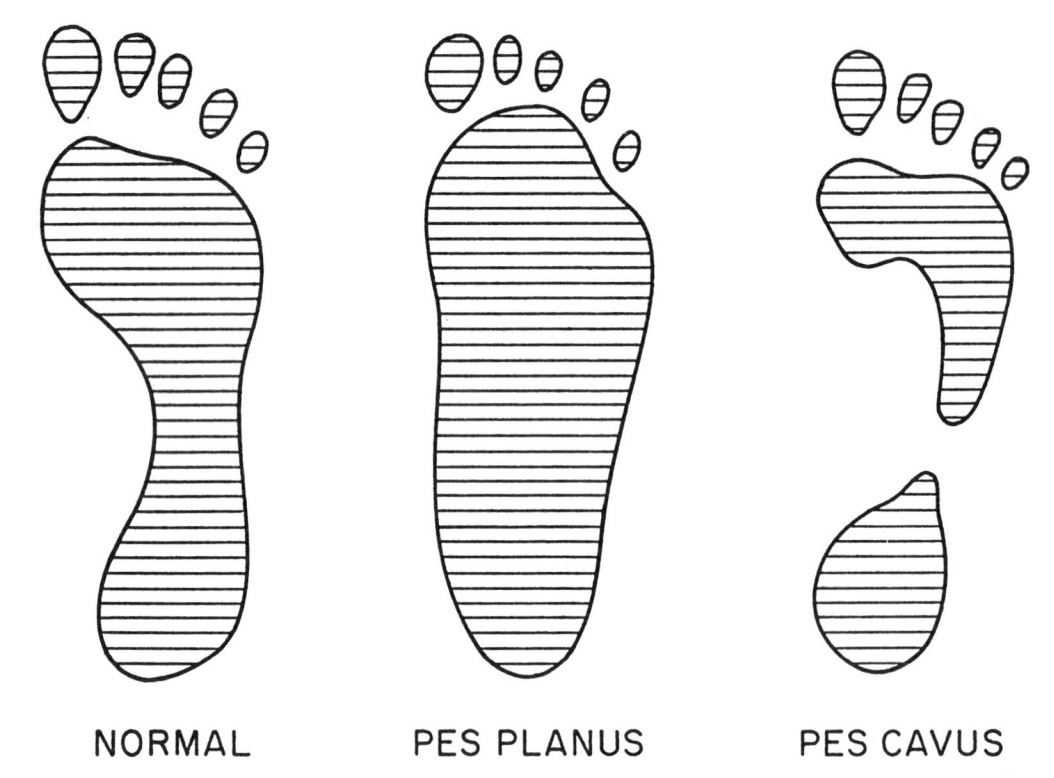

**Fig. 14F-14.** Anatomical Variant Footprints
A comparison of a normal footprint with A. one with pes planus, or flatfoot, and B. one with pes cavus, or high arch.

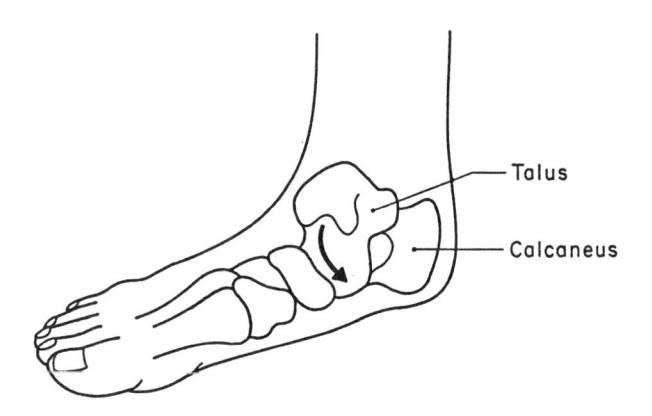

**Fig. 14F-15.** Pes Planus — the talar head displaces medially and plantarward.

up to two years of age are flat-footed after they have begun to stand.

*Treatment* — Arch support with medial heel wedge; strengthening of the intrinsic muscles of the foot and extrinsic muscles of the lower leg.

**Pes Cavus.** Clinically, a higher than normal inflexible longitudinal arch is present (Figure 14F-16).

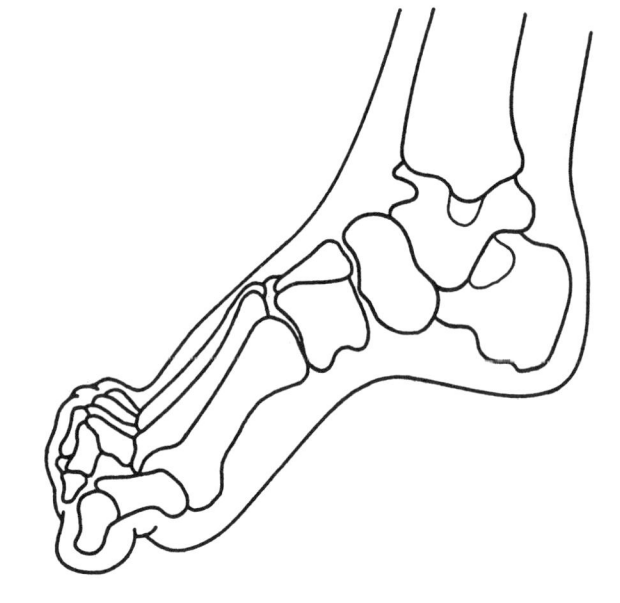

**Fig. 14F-16.** Pes Cavus

*Etiology* — Usually congenital, rarely neurologic deficit can be the cause.

*Biomechanics* — This inflexible anatomical variation of the foot structure causes poor shock absorption, with an inability of the individual to tolerate much repetitive loading. Pain radiates from the proximal arch distally, as well as causing lateral knee and lateral lower leg problems. The patient is at high risk for fascial rupture, creating great disability because healing of plantar fasciitis usually is associated with scar tissue which many times is more painful than the original problem.

*Treatment* — Lightweight padding to be inserted to take pressure off the plantar fascial truss; increase flexion in the heel cords and strength in the flexor hallicus longus.

## Morton's Foot

*Anatomy* — This condition is the result of a short, highly mobile first metatarsal unit (1st MT), with the second toe longer than the first.

*Biomechanics* — Hypermobility of the first metatarsal unit leads to overpronation with a shift of load dissipation from first to second metatarsal. Usual result is a painful callus under the second metatarsal head.

*Treatment* — Foot insert with Morton's extension (extra padding proximal to second MT head) allowing first metatarsal to assume weight bearing in its normal sequence.

## DORSUM OF THE FOOT — MEDIAL TO LATERAL

### Instep Bruise

*Biomechanics* — Trauma from a ball or other equipment used in sport (e.g. field hockey stick) hitting the instep.

*Treatment* — Treated as a soft tissue injury once fracture has been ruled out.

*Prevention* — Felt pad, molded plastic shield instep guard is used in baseball (umpires).

### OS Supranaviculare

*Anatomy* — The navicular bone of the midfoot is located at the apex of the arch of the foot. In some people, an accessory ossification center of the navicular bone is located in the posterior superior aspect of the forefoot over the navicular bone.

*Biomechanics* — Athletic shoes without arch support and ill fitting shoes will cause increased pronation and irritation of the accessory bone at the top of the shoe. Additionally, irritation of the bone can occur because shoe laces are too tight.

*Signs* — Swelling and pain over the os prominence.

*Treatment* — Ice and steroid injection, rarely surgery.

### Fracture of the Fifth Metatarsal

This condition is secondary to lateral inversion sprain of the ankle. If there is involvement of the proximal fifth metatarsal, one of three injuries can occur:

- Strain of the insertion of the peroneus brevis muscle — many times caused by stepping on an uneven, unexpected surface. Usually seen in running athletes (cross country or road runners).
- Avulsion fracture of the base of the 5th metatarsal — this is the more serious injury relating to the same biomechanics mentioned above.
- Jones fracture — a frank fracture through the diaphysis of the 5th metatarsal (Figure 14F-17). This may have originated as a stress fracture commonly seen in jumping sports such as basketball and, occasionally, volleyball (Lehman, 1987).

*Treatment* — 1) Peroneus brevis strain — eversion strapping, ice, no cast necessary; 2) Avulsion fracture — immobilization and casting is necessary to prevent nonunion (a common occurrence); 3) Jones fracture - if only stress fracture present, immobilization by casting for four weeks in a short leg cast, followed by reassessment. If the fracture is complete, then surgery

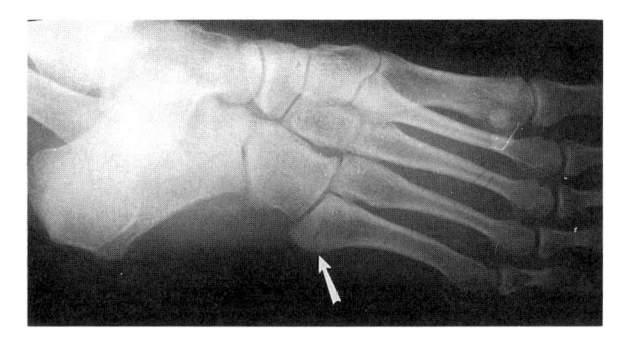

**Fig. 14F-17.** Jones' Fracture

usually is indicated, with compression screw fixation. If surgery is delayed, a bone graft may be needed.

## Dorsal Compression Neuropathy

*Epidemiology* — Most often seen in skiers and hunters. This condition is a neuritis of the deep peroneal nerve as well as a synovitis of the extensor tendons.

*Biomechanics* — Compression between bone and shoe/boot lead to the inflammatory neuritis and synovitis mentioned above.

*Symptoms* — Numbness and tingling, mimicking a compartment syndrome.

*Treatment* — Ice, elevation, and NSAIDs.

## FOREFOOT, TOES

*Anatomy* — Practically all of the motion of the forefoot is located in the metatarsal phalangeal (MTP) joints. These joints adapt to uneven surfaces. Range of motion of the first MTP joint is 30° plantar flexion, 90° dorsi-flexion. With dorsiflexion, the MTP joints (because they are sliding joints) can become jammed and compressed. These joints can be actively or passively extended by external force past the normal dorsiflexion.

## Metatarsalgia

This vague term has been clarified by Scranton (1980) into three categories: 1) primary metatarsalgia — pain across the articulation secondary to imbalance in the weight distribution between the metatarsals and toes (calluses, halux valgus, wearing high-heeled shoes); 2) secondary metarsalgia — joint imbalance caused by other than the MTP joint (metatarsal stress fracture, sesamoiditis); 3) forefoot pain caused by disorders of weight distribution unrelated to the MTP joint (Morton's Foot, plantar fasciitis).

## Metatarsal Area

### Metatarsal Stress Fracture

*Epidemiology* — Most commonly occurs in the second metatarsal secondary to loading on push-off during running. This bone hypertrophies with long term running and has been hypertrophied in swimmers who push off walls on turns.

Many times hypertrophy of the distal metatarsals, especially the metatarsal heads, is a result of bone remodeling (response to Wolff's Law). In activities like dancing or long distance running, this radiographic change is common. Its use should be considered adaptive to the stresses involved. Amenorrheic dancers with persistent pain and tenderness in a metatarsal shaft should be considered to have a metatarsal stress fracture until proven otherwise (Warren, 1986). Predisposing factors to a second metatarsal fracture include: Amenorrhea/delayed menarche, Morton's foot, rigid cavus foot, anterior ankle impingement.

*Biomechanics* — May be caused not only by overuse, but also by biomechanical adjustments for other foot injuries (blisters). If that happens, the third to fifth metatarsals can be subject to stress fracture. Drez (1980) showed that the commonly held belief that a shorter than normal first metatarsal is not a contributing factor to metatarsal stress injury. In this area, the nerve is covered only by plantar skin. Morton's Neuroma is truly not a neuroma but rather a thickening of the tissues surrounding the nerve, probably due to chronic trauma (Mann, 1984). This disorder is more common in women in men (ratio — 8:1).

*Signs* — Pain on plantar and dorsiflexion of the specific metatarsal in question.

*Diagnostic Aids* — X-ray after three weeks; bone scan is diagnostic although not usually necessary.

*Treatment* — Follow protocol for overuse/stress fracture management (Table 2, Chapter 10). See Figure 14F-18 for MT pad placement.

### Intermetatarsal Neuroma (Morton's)

*Biomechanics* — Metatarsals roll during hyperpronation, occasionally pinching a intermetatarsal nerve, usually the one between the third and fourth toes (Figure 14F-19).

*Symptoms* — Patient complains of sharp, burning pain on impact with any uneven surface. The pain is well localized and sometimes radiates to the involved web space. It is aggravated by wearing snug, thin soled shoes. There is sharp burning pain on impact.

*Signs* — Reproduction of pain by squeezing fore-

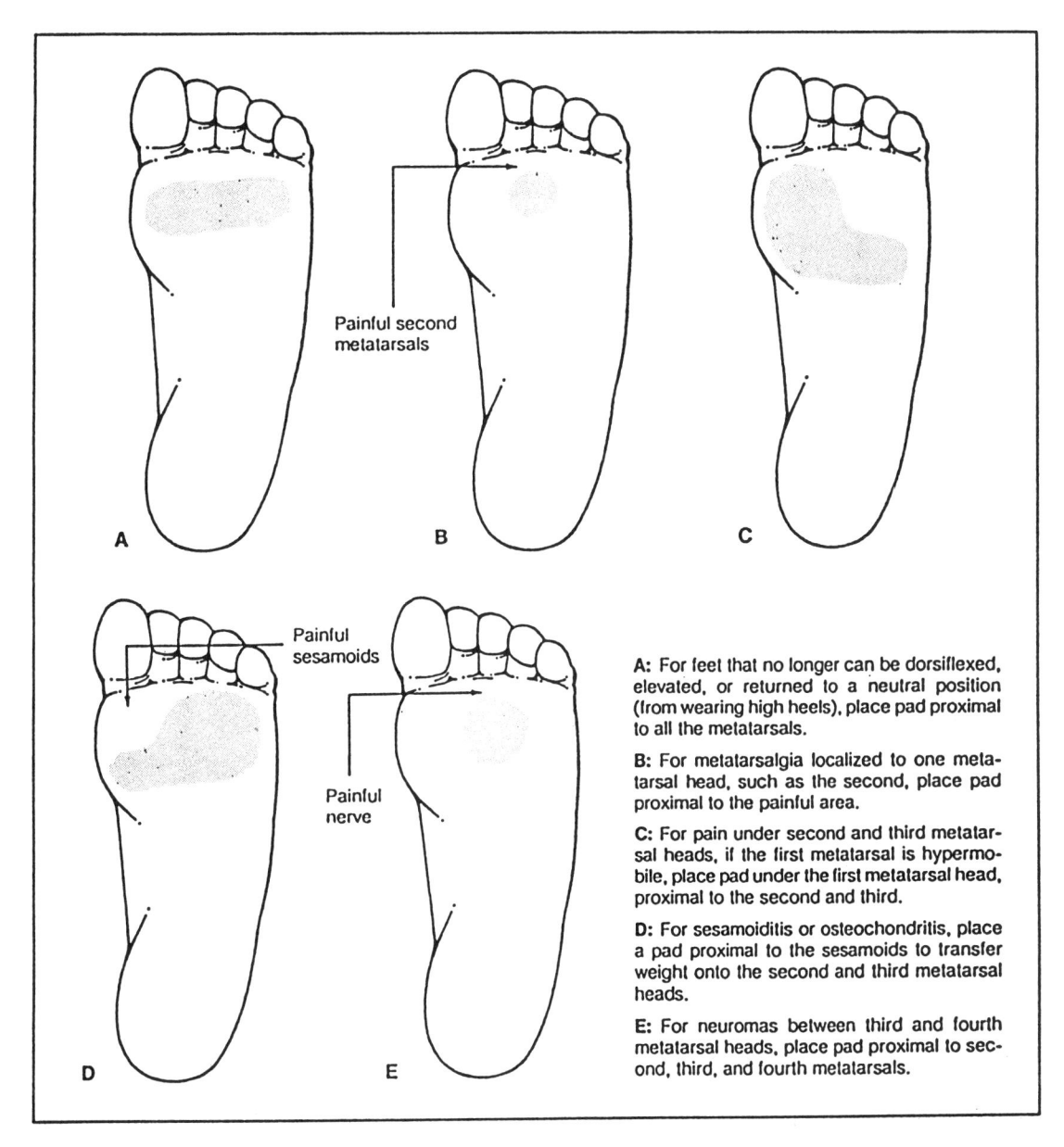

**Fig. 14F-18.** Metatarsal Pad Placement

**A:** For feet that no longer can be dorsiflexed, elevated, or returned to a neutral position (from wearing high heels), place pad proximal to all the metatarsals.

**B:** For metatarsalgia localized to one metatarsal head, such as the second, place pad proximal to the painful area.

**C:** For pain under second and third metatarsal heads, if the first metatarsal is hypermobile, place pad under the first metatarsal head, proximal to the second and third.

**D:** For sesamoiditis or osteochondritis, place a pad proximal to the sesamoids to transfer weight onto the second and third metatarsal heads.

**E:** For neuromas between third and fourth metatarsal heads, place pad proximal to second, third, and fourth metatarsals.

foot together. A good clinical test is to inject a local anesthetic into the area to see if the pain dissipates.

*Treatment* — Procedures to decrease pronation, shoe with wider forefoot, steroid injection, metatarsal bar to relieve and dissipate force. If the patient fails to respond to conservative management, excision of the thickened nerve gives satisfactory relief in about 80% of patients. Usually the metatarsal head heals by "creeping substitution" with only minimal deformity (Hamilton, 1988). Occasionally, if the MTP joint becomes involved, surgical intervention may be necessary.

### Osteochondrosis Metatarsal Head (Freberg's Infarction)

*Biomechanics* — This condition is the result of a vascular insult to the primary growth center. It usually is located in the second metatarsal head and occurs during the second decade of life.

*Signs and Symptoms* — Localized tenderness.

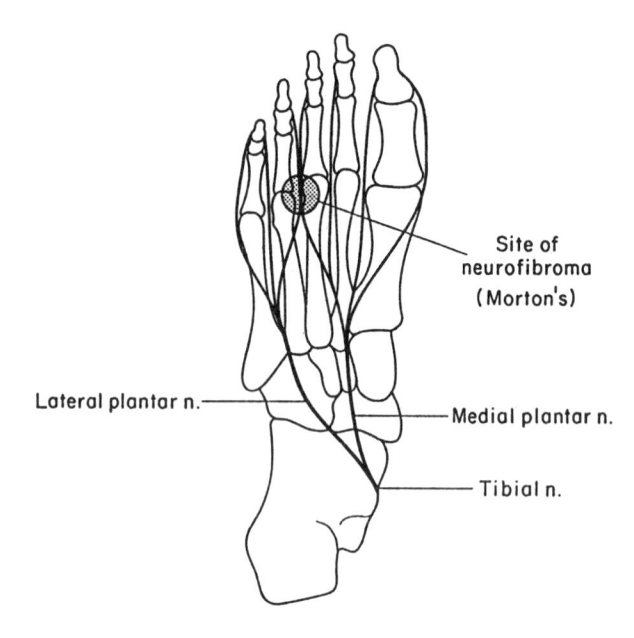

**Fig. 14F-19.** Morton's Neuroma

*Treatment* — Pads to relieve pressure (Figure 14F-18).

## Sesamoid Disorders

**Sesamoiditis.** The two sesamoid bones found in the tendon of the flexor hallicus longus can become inflamed secondary to cleat placement in such sports as football, baseball, or soccer.

*Treatment* — Pad to unburden the first metatarsal head (Figure 14F-18).

**Fracture of the Sesamoid.** Hyperextension of the first MTP joint can result in a fracture of the sesamoid (Figure 14F-20). This is seen in dancers.

*Treatment* — Treated like a turf toe.

**Stress Fracture.** Has been seen in runners, basketball and tennis players, and dancers. Bone

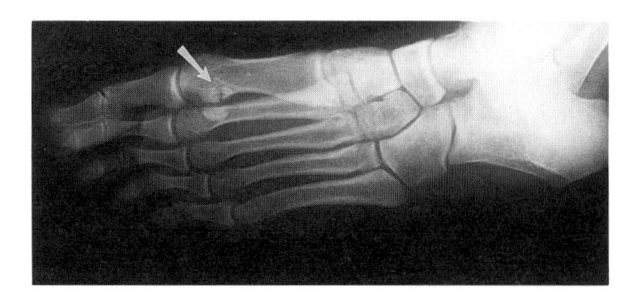

**Fig. 14F-20.** Sesamoid Fracture

scan is positive. Treatment involves prolonged casting (6 weeks) (McBryde, 1988).

**Bipartate/Tripartate Sesamoid.** A normal variant that becomes clinically important only in differentiating between pathology and normality.

*Surgical Intervention* — Controversy surrounds the option of surgical intervention for sesamoid pain. This controversy is based upon the unpredictable results and complications seen after sesamoidectomy. While conservative treatment may take longer, the option is no better. The one exception to the recommendation not to intervene involves osteonecrosis of the sesamoids. This condition occurs most often in the lateral sesamoid; its cause is unknown and its prognosis is often poor. This may be the one true indication for surgical intervention in sesamoid pain (Hamilton, 1988).

## Skin Lesions of the Forefoot
(Figure 14F-21)

**Callus.** Reactive keratotic skin usually found in the feet of runners.

*Differential Diagnosis* — Must differentiate from plantar warts. Calluses lack "seeds" (thrombosed capillaries) seen in warts.

*Treatment* — Free distribution of weight bearing forces by cushioning shoes on ball of foot or in heel. Frequent shaving of skin layers to prevent skin build-up is necessary to keep condition from getting worse. Skin lotion should be applied to soften skin. Note: A pinch callus on the great toe is associated with Morton's foot.

### Blisters

*Biomechanics* — Friction between shoe and skin as a result of sudden stopping, creates a shearing force between the epidermis and dermis into which fluid accumulates and creates a blister.

*Epidemiology* — Blisters usually occur early in a season when the skin is soft or new equipment (shoes) is worn.

*Treatment* — Felt padding (donut); if necessary, aspiration followed by the application of Silvadene, to control and prevent infection. If contamination of a blister does occur, it should be unroofed, thoroughly debrided, and aseptic soap (Betadine) applied.

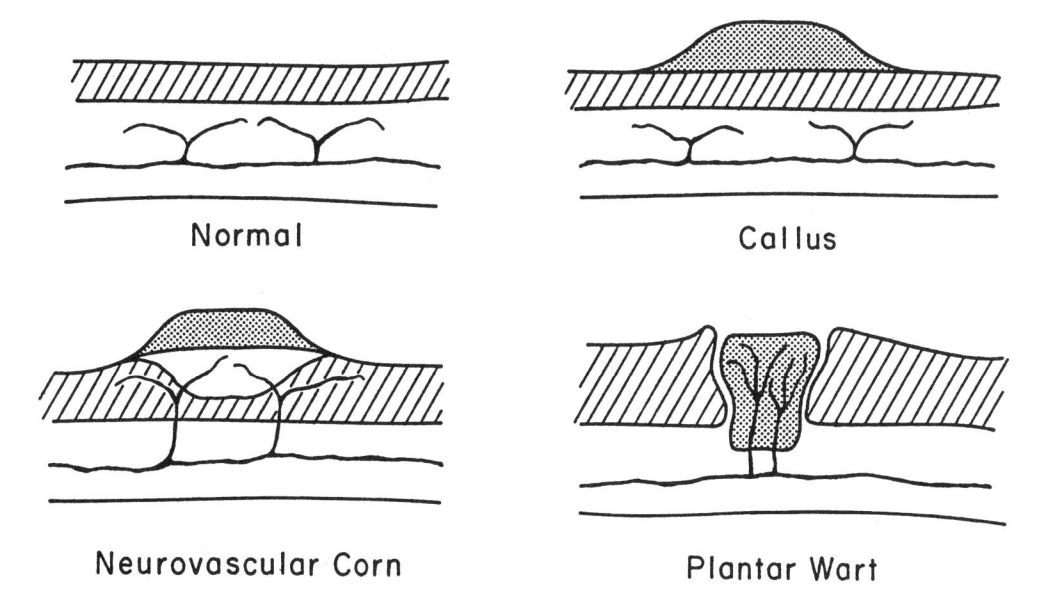

**Fig. 14F-21. Dermatological Conditions of the Foot**
The callus is merely a hyperkeratotic area that forms at the point of persistent pressure or friction. The neurovascular corn is a hyperkeratotic area with an avascular translucent base that may have a blood vessel lying parallel to the surface. Plantar wart is a papilloma, cone shaped, with a cleft between it and the surrounding skin. Blood vessels in the wart are vertical and the ends are visible when pared.

### Warts

*Etiology* — Caused by the virus, *Verruca vulgaris*. This usually enters the skin through damaged areas.

*Biomechanics* — Because of pressure, warts tend to move inward as opposed to warts on nonweight bearing surfaces like the hand which grow outward.

*Signs* — "Seeds" (thrombosed capillaries).

*Treatment* — Shaving plus application of 40% salicylate plaster every day; liquid nitrogen applied every two weeks.

## Toes

### Hallux Deformity

- *Limitus* — limited painful motion of the first MTP joint. This becomes a chronic problem when the athlete pushes off to run. Stretching and firm shoe soles can help as can a metatarsal bar pad (Figure 14F-18).
- *Rigidus* — completely rigid first MTP joint.
  *Treatment* — Firm soled shoes; steroids should not be injected into the joint.
- *Valgus* — condition creating a bunion irritated by push off of the foot. It can create medial knee pain.

*Treatment* — Taping to hold great toe in position; orthotic bunion splint at night to decrease the progression of hallux valgus; shoes with a wider forefoot, and surgery.

**Turf Toe.** This is a sprain of the first MTP joint capsule because flexible shoes cause the great toe to undergo forced hyperextension.

*Epidemiology* — Most commonly seen in football offensive lineman, receivers, and defensive backs. It usually is more prevalent on unyielding playing surfaces like artificial turf.

*Signs* — Pain can be reproduced by passive extension of first MTP, specifically around the plantar joint capsule.

*Treatment* — Firmer shoe; taping; immobilization using steel or orthoplast insert for forefoot; first metatarsal splint (Figure 14F-22) (restricting extension of 1st MTP).

### Claw Toe (Figure 14F-23)

*Anatomy* — MTP joint extended, PIP joint flexed.

*Treatment* — Strengthening of the intrinsic muscles of the foot with the use of towel pulls, marble pick-up exercise.

### Hammer Toe (Figure 14F-24)

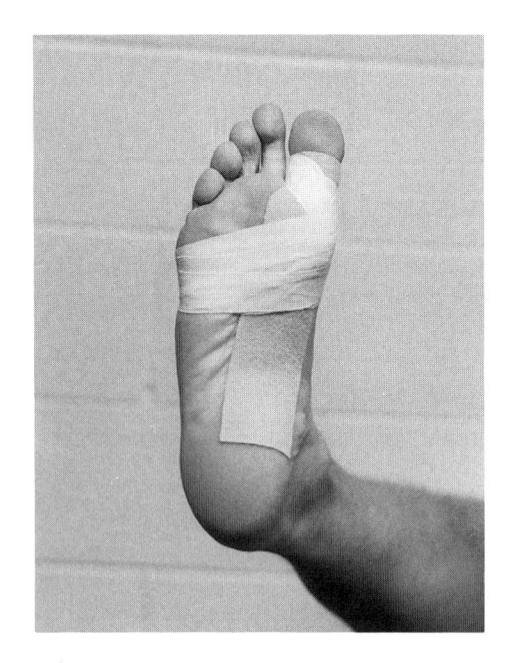

**Fig. 14F-22.** Turf Toe

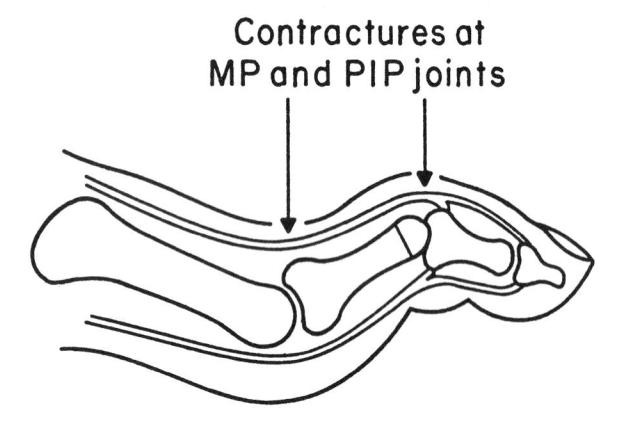

**Fig. 14F-23.** Claw Toe Deformity

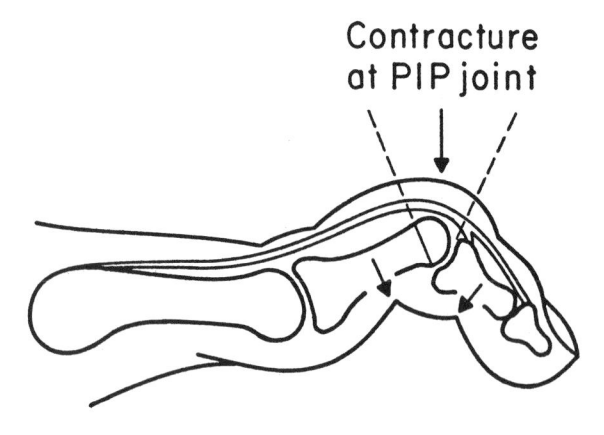

**Fig. 14F-24.** Hammer Toe Deformity

*Anatomy* — Flexion of both PIP and DIP joints.
*Biomechanics* — Result of ill-fitting shoes.
*Signs* — Corns or calluses form on the dorsum of the PIP joints.

**Subungual Hematoma** — "Tennis Toe" or "Black Toe."

*Epidemiology* — Seen commonly in running and tennis and caused by ill-fitting shoes.
*Treatment* — Hematoma can be relieved (if painful) by use of a sterile hot paper clip penetrating the distal nail.

**Onchonychia.** Ingrown Toenail — usually the result of ill-fitting or dirty shoes.

*Note:* High school students often grow during a season and shoewear that was appropriately fitted at the start of the season may become too small.
*Treatment* — Hot soaks, lift edge of nail with cotton and pull back skin. If condition is chronic, a portion or an entire nail may need to be removed with in-office surgery.

**Ganglion Cyst** — Presents as a dorsal mass in the web space between the toes that increases in size during activity and decreases with rest. Usually the result of evagination of the flexor tendon sheaths. Aspiration and steroid injection are indicated and surgery may be necessary.

**REFERENCES**

*Section A. Hip & Pelvis*

Brody, D.M. Running Injuries. *Clinical Symposia*, Summit, N.J., CIBA Pharmaceutical Co., 32(4):28-29, 1980.
Clancy, W.G. Runner's injuries, Part 2. Evaluation and treatment of specific injuries. *Am J Sports Med* 8:287-289, 1980.
Clancy, W.G. Injuries in school-aged runners. *ACSM Team Physician Course Notes*, Orlando, FL, March 1991.
Deluca, S.A and Rhea, J.T. Legg-Calve'-Perthes disease. *Am Fam Phys* 28:147, 1983.
Friermood, T.G. Hip and thigh injuries on field and track. *Consultant* p.157-167, May 1984.
Garrett, W.E. Hip injuries. *ACSM Team Physician Course Notes*, Orlando, FL, March 1991.
Koch, R.A. and Jackson, D.W. Pubic symphysitis in runners — report of two cases. *Am J Sports Med* 9:62, 1981.
Lloyd-Smith, R., Clement, D.B., McKenzie, D.C. and Taunton, J.E. A survey of overuse and traumatic hip and pelvic injuires in athletes. *Phys and Sportsmed* 13(10):131, 1985.
Noble, C.A., Iliotibial band friction syndrome in runners. *Am J Sports Med* 8:232, 1980.
Noble, H.B, Hajek, M.R. and Porter, M. Diagnosis and treatment of iliotibial band tightness in runners. *Phys and Sportsmed* 10:61, 1982.
Schottenfeld, M. Primary care guide to diagnosing and treating the painful hip. *Modern Medicine*, pp 33-39, April/May 1979.
Sutker, A.N., Jackson, D.W. and Pagliano, J.W. Iliotibial band syndrome in distance runners. *Phys and Sportsmed* 9:69, 1981.

*Section B. Upper Leg*

Cooper, D.L, Fair, J. Trainer's Corner: Girdle may stir giggles, but it helps. *Phys and Sportsmed* January 1976:113.

Garrett, W.E. Muscle strain injuries: clinical and basic aspects. *Med Sc Sports Exer* 22(4):436-443, 1990.

Lipscomb, A.B. et al. Treatment of myositis ossificans traumatica in athletes. *Am J Sports Med* 4:111, 1976.

*Section C. Knee*

Andrews, J.R., Sanders, R.A., Morin, B. Surgical treatment of ALRI. *AJSM* 13(2):112-119, 1985.

Antich, T.J., Randall, C.C., Westbrook, R.A. et al. Physical therapy treatment of knee extensor mechanism disorders: comparison of four treatment modalities. *J of Orthopedic and Sports Physical Therapy* 8(5):255-259, 1986.

Baker, B.E., Peckham, A.C., Pupparo, F., et al. Review of meniscal injury and associated sports. *AJSM* 13(1):1-4, 1985.

Baratz, M.E., Fu, F.M., Mengato, R. Meniscal tears: the effect of meniscalectomy and of repair on intra-articular contact areas and stress in the human knee. *AJSM* 14(4):270-275, 1986.

Bourne, M.H., Bianco, A.J. Jr. Bipartite patella in the adolescent: results of surgical excision. *J Pediatr Orthop* 10(1):69-73, 1990.

Broom, M.J., Fulkerson, J.P. The plica syndrome: a new perspective. *Orthopedic Clinics of North America* 17(2):279-281, April 1986.

Cabaud, H.E., Rodkey, W.G. Philosophy and rationale for the management of anterior cruciate injuries and the resultant deficiencies. *Clinics in Sports Medicine* 4(2):313-324, April 1985.

Cahill, B. Treatment of juvenile osteochondritis dessicans and osteochondritis dessicans of the knee. *Clinics in Sports Medicine* 4(2):367-380, April 1985.

DeHaven, K.E. Rationale for meniscus repair or excision. *Clinics in Sports Medicine* 4(2):267-74, April 1985.

Donaldson, W.F., Warren, R.F., Wickiewicz, T. A comparison of acute anterior cruciate ligament examination. *AJSM* 13(1):5-10, 1985.

Eisele, S.A. A precise approach to anterior knee pain. *Phys and Sportsmed* 19(6):127-139, 1991.

Fulkerson, J.P., Schutzer, S.F. After failure of conservative treatment for painful patellofemoral malalignment: lateral release or realignment? *Orthopedic Clinics of North America* 17(2):283-288, April 1986.

Henry, J.M., Goletz, T.M., Williamson, B. Lateral retinacular release in patellofemoral subluxation. *AJSM* 14(2):121-129, 1986.

Henry, J.H. Conservative treatment of patellofemoral subluxation. *Clini Sports Med* 8(2):261-278, 1989.

Hewson, G.F., Mendini, R.A., Wang, J.B. Prophylactic knee bracing in college football. *AJSM* 114(4):262-266, 1986.

Hopkinson, W.J., Mitchell, W.A., Curl, W.W. Chondral fractures of the knee -cause for confusion. *AJSM* 13(5):309-312, 1985.

Indelicato, P.A. Non-operative treatment of complete tears of the medial collateral ligament of the knee. *JBJS* 64-A(3):313-323, 329, March 1983.

Jacobson, K.E., Flandry, F.C. Diagnosis of anterior knee pain. *Clin Sports Med* 8(2):179-195, 1989.

Jensen, J.E., Conn, R.R., Hazelrigg, G., et al. Systematic evaluation of acute knee injuries. *Clinics in Sports Medicine* 4(2):306, April 1985.

Johnson, R.P. Lateral facet syndrome of the patella: lateral restrain analysis and use of lateral resection. *Clin Orthop* 238(Jan):148-158, 1989.

Katz, J.W., Fingeroth, R.J. The diagnostic accuracy of ruptures of the ACL comparing Lachman, anterior drawer and pivot ship test in acute and chronic knee injuries. *AJSM* 14(1):88-91, 1986.

King, J.B., Perry, D.J., Mourad K. et al. Lesions of the ligament. *J Bone Joint Surg (Br)* 72(1):46-48, 1990.

Kujala, U.M., Kvist, M., Heinonen, O. Osgood-Schlatter's disease in adolescent athletes. *AJSM* 13(4):236-241, 1985.

Laurin C.A., Levesque, M.P., Dussault, R. et al. The abnormal lateral patellofemoral angle. *JBJS* 60-A(1):55-60, January 1978.

Lindenburg, B.S., Pinshaw, R., Noakes, T.D. Iliotibial band friction syndrome in runners. *Phys and Sportsmed* 12(5):118-130, May 1984.

Mysnyk, M.C., Wroble, R.R., Foster, M.A., et al. Prepatellar bursitis in wrestlers. *AJSM* 14(1):46-54, 1986.

Nottage, W.M., Sprague, N.F., Auerbach, B.J., et al. The medial patellar plica syndrome. *AJSM* 11(4):211-214, 1983.

Odensten, M., Lysholm, J., Gillquist, J. The course of partial ACL ruptures. *AJSM* 13(3):183-6, 1985.

Parolie, J.M., Bergfeld, J.A. Long-term results of nonoperative treatment of isolated posterior cruciate ligament injuries in the athlete. *AJSM* 14(1):35-38, 1986.

Patel, D. Plica as a cause of anterior knee pain. *Orthop Clin North Am* 17(2):273-277, April 1986.

Schmidt, D.R., Henry J.H. Stress injuries of the adolescent extensor mechanism. *Clin Sports Med* 8(2):343-355, 1989.

Schwartz, C., Blazina, M.E., Sisto, D.J. et al. The results of operative treatment of osteochondritis dessicans of the patella. *Am J Sports Med* 16(5):522-529, 1988.

Seger, B.M., Woods, G.W. Arthroscopic management of lateral meniscus cysts. *AJSM* 14(2):105-108, 1986.

Singer, K.M., Henry, J. Knee problems in children and adolescents. *Clinics in Sports Med* 4(2):385-398, April 1985.

Steiner, M.E., Grana, W.A. The young athlete's knee: recent advances. *Clin Sports Med* 7(3):527-546, 1988.

Walla, D.J., Albright, J.P., McAuley, E., et al. Hamstring control and the unstable anterior cruciate ligament — deficient knee. *AJSM* 13(1):34-39, 1985.

Whitelaw, G.P. Jr., Rullo, D.J. Markowitz, H.D. et al. A conservative approach to anterior knee pain. *Clin Orthop* 246(SepZ):234-237, 1989.

*Section D. Lower Leg*

Arner, O., et al. Roentgen changes in subcutaneous rupture of the Achilles tendon. *Acta Chir Scand* 116:496-511, 1958/1959.

Brody, D.M. Running injuries — prevention and management. *Clinical Symposia*, Ciba-Geigy Corp., 39(3), 1987.

Clancy, W.G. Runners' injuries. *Am J Sports Med* 8(4):287-289, 1980.

Gillström, P., Ljungqvist, R. Long-term results after operation for subcutaneous partial rupture of the Achilles tendon. *Act Chir Scand* 482 (suppl):78, 1978.

Hattrup, S.J., Johnson, K.A. Recognizing ruptures of the Achilles tendon. *J Musculoskel Med* 2(7):65-69, 1985.

Inglis, A.E., Scott, W.N., Sculco, T.P., Patterson, A.H. Ruptures of the tendo Achilles. *J Bone Joint Surg* 58A:990, 1976.

Ljungqvist, R., Eriksson, E. Partial tears of the patellar tendon and the Achilles tendon. In *Symposium on the Foot and Leg in Running Sports*, R.P. Mack (ed.), C.V. Mosby, St. Louis, 92-98, 1982.

Marcus, D.S., Reicher, M.A., Kellerhouse, L.E. Achilles tendon injuries: the role of MR imaging. *J Compt Assist Tomog* 13:480-486, 1989.

Melberg, P.E., Styf, J. Posteriomedial pain in the lower leg. *Am J Sports Med* 17:747-750, 1989.

National Electronic Injury Surveillance System, U.S. Consumer Product Safety Commission, Washington, D.C., 1981.

Nistor, L. Surgical and nonsurgical treatment of Achilles tendon rupture. *J Bone Joint Surg* 63A:394, 1981.

Rorabeck, C.H., Armstrong, R.D. Compartment syndromes: how to avert uncorrectable deformities. *J. Musculoskeletal Med* 2(9):54-61, 1985.

Stein, S.R., Luekens, C.A. Methods and rationale for closed treatment of Achilles tendon ruptures. *Am J Sports Med* 4:162-169, 1976.

Wiley, J.P., Clement, D.B., Doyle, D.L., Taunton, J.E. A primary care perspective of chronic compartment syndrome of the leg. *Phys Sportsmed* 15(3):111-120, 1987.

*Section E. Ankle*

Abraham, E. Neglected rupture of the peroneal tendons and recurrent ankle sprains. *J Bone Joint Surg* 61A:1247, 1979.

Amis, J.A., Gangl, P.M. When inversion injury is more than a "sprained ankle". *J Musculoskel Med* 4(9):68-87, 1987.

Arrowsmith, S.R., Fleming, L.L., Allman, F.L. Traumatic dislocation of the peroneal tendons. *Am J Sports Med* 11:142, 1983.

Bergfeld, J.A. Medical problems in ballet: A round table. *Phys Sportsmed* 10(3):98-112, 1982.

Berndt, A.L., Harty, M. Transchondral fractures (osteochondritis dissecans) of the talus. *J Bone Joint Surg* 41A:988, 1959.

Beskin, J.L., Sanders, R.A., Hunter, S.C., Hughston, J.C. Surgical repair of Achilles tendon ruptures. *Am J Sports Med* 15(1):1-8, 1987.

Birrer, R.B. Ankle trauma: looking beyond the sprain. *Diagnosis* 6(1):32-46, 1984.

Briner, W.W., Carr, D.E., Lavery, K.M. Anterioinferior tibiofibular ligament injury: not just another ankle sprain. *Phys Sportsmed* 17(11):63-69, 1989.

Clancy, W.G., Neidhart, D., Brand, R.L. Achilles tendinitis in runners: a report of five cases. *Am J Sports Med* 4:45, 1976.

Clement, D.B., Taunton, J.E., Smart, G.W. Achilles tendinitis and peritendinitis: etiology and treatment. *Am J Sports Med* 12(3):179-184, 1984.

Evans, G.A., Hardcastle, P., Frenyo, A.D. Acute rupture of the lateral ligament of the ankle — to suture or not to suture? *J. Bone Joint Surg.* 66B:209-212, 1984.

Flick, A.B., Gould, N. Osteochondritis dissecans of the talus: review of the literature and new surgical approach for medial dome lesions. *Foot Ankle* 5:165, 1985.

Grana, W.A., Chronic pain persisting after ankle sprain. *J Musculoskel Med* 7(6):35-49, 1990.

Greene, T.A., Wright, C.R. A comparative support evaluation of three ankle orthosis before, during and after exercise. *J Orthop Sports Phys Ther* 11(10):453-466, 1990.

Gross, M.T., Bradshaw, M.K., Ventry, L.C. Weller, K.H., Comparison of support provided by ankle taping and semirigid orthosis. *J Orthop Sports Phys Ther* 9(1):33-39, 1987.

Häggmark, T., Eriksson, E. Hypotrophy of the soleus muscle in man after Achilles tendon rupture. *Am J Sports Med* 7:121, 1979.

Hamilton, W.G. Foot and ankle injuries in dancers. *Clinics in Sports Med* 7(1):143-173, 1988.

Hume, E.L., McKeag, D.B. Soft-tissue ankle injuries: the need for compulsive assessment and therapy. *Emergency Medicine Report* 5(7):45-52, 1984.

Inglis, A., Sculco, T.P. Surgical repair of ruptures of the tendo Achillis. *Clin Orthop* 156:160-169, 1981.

Kleizer, B. Mechanisms of ankle injury. *Orthop Clinics North Am* 5(1), 1974.

Ljungqvist, R., Eriksson, E. Partial tears of the patellar tendon and the Achilles tendon. In *Symposium on the Foot and Leg in Running Sports*, ed.: R.P. Mack, AOS, C.V. Mosby, St. Louis, 92-98, 1982.

Mack, R.P. Ankle injuries in athletics. *Clinics in Sports Med* 1(1):71-84, 1982.

Mandel, S. Neurologic syndromes from repetitive trauma at work. *Postgraduate Med* 82(6):87-92, 1987.

Monroe, J.S., Nogle, S.E. A retrospective study of achilles tendon rupture and their relationship to previous trauma to the lower extremity (personal communication), 1991.

Niedermann, B., Andersen, A., Andersen, S.B. Rupture of the lateral ligaments of the ankle — operation or plaster cast? A prospective study. *Acta Orthop Scand* 52:579-587, 1981.

Nistor, L. Surgical and nonsurgical treatment of Achilles tendon rupture. *J Bone Joint Surg* 63A:394-399, 1981.

O'Donoghue, D.H. *Treatment of Injuries to Athletes*, 4th ed., Philadelphia, W.B. Saunders, Co., 1984.

Persson, A., Ljunggvist, R. Electrophysioloical observations in cases of partial and total ruptures of the Achilles tendon. *Clinic Neurophysiol* 31:239, 1971.

Scheller, A.D., Kasser, J.R., Quigley, T.B. Tendon injuries about the ankle. *Orthop Clin North Am* 11:801, 1980.

Smith, R.W., Reischl, S.F. Treatment of ankle sprains in young athletes. *Am J Sports Med* 14(6):465-471, 1986.

Stover, C.N. Airstirrup management of ankle injuries in the athlete. *Am J Sports Med* 8(5):360-365, 1980.

Thompson, T.C., Doherty, J.H. Spontaneous rupture of tendon of Achilles: a new clinical diagnostic test. *J Trauma* 2:126-129, 1962.

Whitelow, G.P., Getelman, M.H., Corbett, M. Painful ankle: differential diagnosis. *Hosp Med* pp. 47-58, June, 1991.

Yablon, I.G. Which ankle fractures can be managed conservatively? *J Musculoskeletal Med* 1(13):19-26, 1984.

### Section F. Feet

Drez, D., Young, J.C., Johnston, R.D., Parker, W.D. Metatarsal stress fractures. *Am J Sports Med* 8(2):123-125, 1980.

Garrick, J.G., Requa, R.K. The epidemiology of foot and ankle injuries in sports. *Clinics in Sports Med* 7(1):29-36, 1988.

Graham, C.E. Painful heel syndrome. *J of Musculoskeletal Med*, 3(10):42-47, 1986.

Kuland, D.M. *The Injured Athlete*. J.B. Lippincott, Philadelphia, 1982, p. 450.

Leach, R.E., Schepsis, A. Hindfoot pain in athletes: why, and what can be done? *J Musculoskel Med* 2(10):16-25, 1985.

Lehman, R., Torg, J., Pavlov, H., DeLee J. Fractures of the base of the fifth metatarsal distal to the tuberosity: a review. *Foot Ankle* 7(4):242-252, 1987.

Lutter, L.D. Surgical decisions in athletes' subcalcaneal pain. *Am J Sports Med* 14(6):481-485, 1986.

Mann, R.A., Moran, G.T., Daugherty, S.E. Comparative electromyography of the lower extremities in jogging, running and sprinting. *Am J Sports Med* 14:501, 1986.

Mann, R.A. Foot disorders symposium — Introduction. *Postgrad Med* 75(5):146-149, 1984.

McBryde, A.M., Anderson, R.B. Sesamoid foot problems in the athlete. *Clinics in Sports Med* 7(1):51-60, 1988.

Movant, R., Baxter, D.E. Management strategies for common foot problems. *Consultant* pp. 146-157, August 1984.

Rose, G.K. Pes planus. In Jahss, M.H. *Disorders of the Foot* Vol. 1, W.B. Saunders Company, Philadelphia, PA, 1982.

National Electronic Injury Surveillance Survey, U.S. Consumer Protection Agency, 1983.

Nuber, G.W. Biomechanics of the foot and ankle during gait. *Clinics in Sports Med* 7(1):1-13, 1988.

Scranton, P.E., Jr. Metatarsalgia: diagnosis and treatment. *J Bone Joint Surg* 62A:723, 1980.

Waller, J.F. Hindfoot and midfoot problems of the runner. In *The Foot and Leg in Running Sports*, Mack, R.P., (ed.), AAOS, C.V. Mosbly, St. Louis, MO, pp 64-72, 1982.

Warren, M.P., Brooks-Gunn, J., Hamilton, L.H. et al. Scoliosis and fractures in young ballet dancers: relation to delayed menarche and secondary amenorrhea. *N Eng J Med* 314:1348-1353, 1986.

## SUGGESTED READINGS

Andrish, J.T. Knee injuries in gymnastics. *Clinics in SM* 4(1):111-122, January 1985.

Clancy, W.G. Cross-country ski injuries. *Clinics in Sports Medicine* 1(2): 333-338, July 1982.

Clancy, W. G. Runners' injuries, pt 2, Evaluation and treatment of specific injuries. *Am J Sports Med* 8:287-289, 1980.

Clancy, W.G. and Foltz, A.S. Iliac apophysitis and stress fractures in adolescent runners. *AmJSportsMed* 4:214, 1976.

Cooper, D.L., Fair, J. Trainer's Corner: Hamstring strains. *Phys and Sportsmed* 6:104, 1978.

Cooper, D.L., Fair, J. Trainer's corner: Treating the charleyhorse. *Phys and Sportsmed* 7:157, 1979.

Craig, C.L. Hip injuries in children and adolescents. *Orthop Clin North Am* 11:743-754, 1980.

D'Ambrosia, R.D., Drez, D. Jr. *Prevention and Treatment of Running Injuries* Thorofare, NJ: Charles B. Slack, 1982.

Dickson, T.B. Preventing overuse cycling injuries. *Phys and Sportsmed* 13(10):116-124, October 1985.

Ekstrand, J., Gillquist, J. Soccer injuries and their mechanisms: a prospective study. *Medicine and Science in Sports and Exercise* 15(3): 267-270, 1983.

Estwanik, J.J., Bergfeld, J.A., Collins, M.R., et al. Injuries in interscholastic wrestling. *Phys and Sportsmed* 8(3):111-121, March 1980.

Fowler, P.J., Regan, W.D. Swimming injuries of the knee. *Clinics in Sports Medicine* 5(1):139-148, January 1986.

Halvorsen, J. Tips from the training room: Hip pointer padding for women. *Phys and Sportsmed* 11:123, 1983.

Hanson, P.G., et al. Osteitis pubis in sports activities. *Phys and Sportsmed* 7:111, 1978.

Hawkins, R.J., Misamore, G.W., Merrett, T.R. Followup of acute nonoperated isolated ACL tear. *AJSM* 14(3):205-210, 1986.

Howe, J., Johnson, R.J. Knee injuries in skiing. *Clinics in Sports Medicine* 1(2):227-288, July 1982.

Jackson, D.W. Managing myositis ossificans in the young athlete. *Phys and Sportsmed* 3:56, 1975.

Kalenak, A. Medlar, C.E. et al. Treating thigh contusions with ice. *Phys and Sportsmed* 3:65, 1975.

Lutter, L.D. The knee and running. *Clinics in Sports Medicine* 4(4):685-698, October 1985.

Maehlum, S., Dahl, E., Daljord, O.A. Frequency of injuries in a youth soccer tournament. *Phys and Sportsmed* 14(7):73-80, July 1986.

Mandelbaum, B.R., Finerman, G.A., Reicher, M.A., et al. Magnetic resonance imaging as a tool for evaluation of traumatic knee injuries. *AJSM* 14(5):361-371, 1986.

Marshall, J.L., Rubin, R.M. Knee ligament injuries — a diagnostic and therapeutic approach. *Orthopedic Clinics of North America* 8(3): 641-668, July 1977.

O'Donoghue, D.H. *Treatment of Athletic Injuries* (3rd Ed). Philadelphia: W.B. Saunders & Co. 1976:505-521.

Ogden, J.A. *Skeletal Injury in the Child*. Philadelphia: Lea & Febiger, 1982.

Quirk, R. Ballet injuries: the Ausrailian experience. *Clinics in Sports Med* 2(3):507-514, November 1983.

Schottenfeld, M. What's causing the hip pain? *Consultant* pp 47-59, Aug. 1981.

Smodlaka, V.N. Groin pain in soccer players. *Phys and Sportsmed* 8:57, 1980.

Teitz, C.L. Sports medicine concerns in dance and gymnastics. *Clinics in Sports Med* 2(3):571-593, November 1983.

# Appendix 14C-1.
## Knee Examination

**Knee Exam Sheet**

Date: _____
B ____ R ____ L ____
S: Present History/Complaints/Treatments: _____
_____
_____

Allergies: _____ Medications: _____ PMH: _____

Swelling: ____ Yes ____ No                              Snap or Pop: _____
Within: minutes ____ hours ____ days ____              Locking: _____
Pain Location: _____                          Giving Way: _____

O: Leg Alignment: _____ Q Angle: _____ PATELLA:
   Foot Exam: NL: _____
                                                                    R | L
   QUADRICEPS:         R | L              NL ☐ Crepitis: ____|____
   Circumferences: ____|____                   Stability: ____|____
   CM Above Patella: ____|____                 Position:  ____|____
   Atrophy:        ____|____                   Tenderness:____|____
   JOINT:                                      Apprehension:__|____
   Effusion: _____                   Distal Push: __|____

                         R                           L
   ROM: ____ (Flexion +135°) ____ Pain | ____ (Extension -10°) ____ Pain
        ____ (Extension -10°) ____ Pain | ____ (Flexion +135°) ____ Pain
Bounce Home: _____
Palpation of Tenderness: R ____ L ____

| Ligament Tests | R | L |                     |         |              | R | L |
|---|---|---|---|---|---|---|---|
| Medial:  0° | | |                            | NL ☐    | Anterior Drawer: | | |
|         30° | | |                            |         | Lachman's:       | | |
| Lateral: 0° | | |                            |         | Posterior Drawer:| | |
|         30° | | |                            |         | Pivot Shift:     | | |

Meniscal Tests:        R | L      Comments:
Joint Line Tenderness: ____|____
McMurray:              ____|____
Apley:
  Compression:         ____|____
  Distraction:         ____|____

X-Ray: _____ Date: _____ Results: _____

P: DX: _____ Referral: _____
   TX: _____
   PT. ED: _____
   FU: _____ Signature _____

*PELVIC AND LOWER EXTREMITY INJURIES/ILLNESSES*

Appendix 14E-1.
# Ankle Examination

**Ankle Examination**

Date: _____

## HISTORY

1. Acute _____ Chronic _____ 2. Date of injury _____
3. Biomechanics: _____
_____

|  | N | Y | Comments |
|---|---|---|---|
| 4. Weight-bearing after injury? | | | |
| 5. Sounds heard at injury? | | | |
| 6. Treatment since injury? | | | |
| 7. PMH of any ankle injuries? | | | |

## PHYSICAL EXAMINATION

1. Observation:

| | N | Y | Comments |
|---|---|---|---|
| Bruising | | | |
| Swelling | | | |
| Deformity | | | |

2. Palpation:

Pulses DP _____
PT _____
Bony Tenderness  N____ Y____
Where? _____

3. Restricted ROM:

| | Active | Passive |
|---|---|---|
| Dorsi-flexion | | |
| Plantar flexion | | |
| Inversion | | |
| Eversion | | |

| | N | Y |
|---|---|---|
| 4. Thompson test | | |
| 5. Crepitation | | |
| 6. Eversion stress | | |
| 7. Inversion stress | | |
| 8. Anterior drawer | | |
| 9. Side-to-side | | |

## X-RAY

1. Routine _____ Reading _____
2. Stress Films _____ Reading _____

## ASSESSMENT

## PLAN

Signature _____

# Appendix 14F-1.
# Foot Examination

**Foot Examination**

NAME _____  DATE _____/_____/_____
AGE _____                    SPORT _____

1. History (onset, course, treatment to date): _____
   _____
   _____
2. Date of injury _____
3. Training schedule (footwear, surface, intensity): _____
   _____
4. Pain location _____
5. Swelling and location _____
6. Pertinent medical history (RA, gout, surgery, previous injury): _____
   _____
   _____
7. Family history (gout, RA, other) _____

### Exam
1. Inspection (effusion, erythema, ecchymosis) _____
   _____
2. Gait _____
3. Shoe wear pattern                          4. Pelvis/spine:
                                                    lordosis           _____
                                                    scoliosis          _____
                                                    malalignment       _____
                                                    other:             _____
5. Knees                                      6. Tibia
       valgus              _____                   varus              _____
       varus               _____                   internal torsion   _____
       neutral             _____                   external torsion   _____
7. Ankle                                      8. Feet
       varus               _____                   pronated           _____
       valgus              _____                   cavus              _____
       neutral             _____                   planus             _____
9. Leg length                                 10. Pulses: DP       PT
       R _____ cm                                  R _____   _____
       L _____ cm                                  L _____   _____
11. Heel                          _____     12. DTR's: Knee  Achilles
       plantar fascia             _____           R _____   _____
       pump bump                  _____           L _____   _____
       tendonitis                 _____

13. Skin
    blister _____
    callus _____
    corn _____
    ingrown toenail _____
    subungual hematoma _____
    wart _____

15. Range of Motion
    Ankle

|  | R | L |
|---|---|---|
| dorsiflex (20°) | ___ | ___ |
| plantarflex (50°) | ___ | ___ |
| heel invers (5°) | ___ | ___ |
| heel evers. (5°) | ___ | ___ |

16. Midfoot
    spring ligaments _____
    acces. navicular _____

14. Foot
    bunion _____
    exostosis _____
    ganglion _____
    hallus valgus _____
    metatarsus adductus _____
    Morton's foot _____

Forefoot (heel neutral position)

|  | R | L |
|---|---|---|
| adduction (20°) | ___ | ___ |
| abduction (10°) | ___ | ___ |

1st MTP joint

|  | R | L |
|---|---|---|
| plantarflex (30°) | ___ | ___ |
| dorsiflex (80°) | ___ | ___ |

17. Forefoot
    metatars. jts. _____
    1st MTP _____
    sesamoid _____
    Morton's neuroma _____
    metatars. head _____

17. X-ray: _____

18. Assessment: _____
_____

19. Plan: _____
_____

Examiner _____

# 15

# Common Sports-Related Injuries and Illnesses — Skin

## SKIN PROBLEMS IN ATHLETICS

Skin problems in athletes are affected by several factors - age, sex, skin type, hereditary, the sport, and the playing environment. Most problems are benign unless infection is present. The most common skin problems will be discussed in this chapter. Pictures of all lesions can be found in most dermatological texts. Conditions that exclude an individual from further athletic participation, especially in contact sports, include infectious disorders such as herpes simplex, molluscum contagiosum, herpes zoster, impetigo, furunculosis, skin infestation, and secondary syphilis. Proper recognition and treatment is important. Athletes should be protected from recurrence and epidemic spread of skin disease among team members and opponents. An athlete with contagious skin lesions should not be in contact with healthy individuals until the skin disorder has been satisfactorily treated (Bergfeld, 1982; Snook, 1984). Prevention will be aided by maintaining clean locker rooms, uniforms, and equipment.

Some problems that affect an athlete's skin that may be aggravated by existing skin conditions such as Raynaud's disease, atopic dermatitis or excema, recurrent urticaria, or psychological problems. These conditions should be kept in mind in evaluating an athlete with skin problems.

## ABRASIONS AND FRICTION BLISTERS

Abrasions sustained on natural or artificial turf or wrestling mats are seen frequently and can occur wherever skin comes in contact with the surface. Abrasions may be secondary to frictional rubbing of the skin against the playing field or equipment. This friction may cause callus formation or a frank blister. The primary aim of treatment is to prevent lesser injuries from becoming infected.

Abrasions appears as erythematous, crusted weeping lesions, whereas blister formations often start with a burning sensation before developing into the common elevated lesion that usually fills with fluid within an hour. First-aid measures include soaking or washing the lesion with soap and water and application of an appropriate corticosteroid or antibiotic cream. Friction blisters have been treated in several ways (Levine, 1982). A common treatment is draining the intact blister through a small hole made with a #11 blade and injecting the blister with Silvadene® cream. The area is protected with a donut bandage and the skin is trimmed away three to four days later. Some physicians and trainers will trim away the injured skin immediately and then cover with Silvadene and a donut pad.

Prevention of abrasions includes the use of

protective padding and proper equipment, especially on artificial surfaces. Blisters can be prevented by gradually increasing "load" on the skin and by proper shoe wear. A number of commercial skin tougheners are available but they make the skin sticky and can lead to more severe blistering. Ice massage or application to the friction hot spot may prevent the development of blisters (Brown & Childers, 1966).

## COLD-INDUCED INJURIES

### Frostbite

Frostbite may occur in athletes exposed to the cold in alpine and nordic skiing, snowshoeing, tobogganing, ice skating, ice sailing, snowmobiling, or mountain climbing. Cold exposure initially causes mild blanching of the skin, commonly known as "frost nip." Frostbite may involve the superficial or deep layers of the skin. Superficial frostbite of the external skin and subcutaneous tissue results in an initial white appearance of the skin. Blisters may appear within 24-36 hours.

Frostbite to the deep layers of the skin affects not only the skin and subcutaneous tissue but may involve the neurovascular supply and bone. Progressive skin cooling results initially in erythema, burning, and hypothesia followed by numbness, redness, and occasional white patchy areas if the skin temperature drops below 10°C. As the skin temperature increases during rewarming, the blood vessels dilate and cause increased permeability of capillaries and tissues which leads to swelling and further impairment of the circulation.

Skin areas most frequently affected by frostbite are the ears, nose, cheeks, hands, feet, and penis. Frostbite can be recognized by hypothesia of the skin or discomfort of the injured part, followed by a pleasant warm feeling. However, deep layer frostbite can occur without these symptoms. Wind, wetness next to the skin, and exercise increase the likelihood of frostbite.

Clothing protects the skin, but its insulating properties are reduced or lost when wet. Skin temperature is lowered when wind speed is increased (wind chill index). This effect is slightly less at high altitudes because of a reduction in air density. Exercise in a cold environment may increase the chances of frostbite of unprotected skin surfaces. Instant frostbite can be induced by touching extremely cold metal, especially if the skin is wet. The skin sticks to metal and is pulled off as the body part moves away from the metal surface. Frostbite also can happen if skin comes in contact with gasoline or with frozen synthetic jell packs that are placed in the freezer. Jell packs should not be applied to the skin until after they have been slightly warmed (Basler, 1983).

Superficial frostbite may be treated by gently rewarming the skin with steady pressure from a warm hand, but rubbing the affected area can cause further damage and should be discouraged. The best treatment is rewarming next to unaffected skin, making sure that adequate circulation is present, and then being covered with warm dry clothing.

Refreezing of affected skin results in more tissue loss so that a frozen extremity should not be thawed if it will be followed by refreezing. Do not rub the area with snow or give alcohol to frostbite victims. Alcohol may provide a warm feeling but it causes peripheral vasodilation and results in increased heat loss from the skin. The patient should refrain from smoking. Be cautious about exposing the patient to an open fire because of the possibility of a skin burn that is unnoticed by the patient who has a loss of normal sensory function.

Once the patient is brought to a hospital or treatment area, gently warm the skin with a warm water bath kept at a temperature between 40-42°C. Do not allow the temperature to rise above 44°C. (The water should feel warm but not hot to the normal touch.) Even brief exposure to high temperatures can cause serious damage to a frostbitten extremity. Dry heat is difficult to regulate and does not give even rewarming. For this reason, never expose a frostbitten extremity to an open fire or engine exhaust as a rewarming method. Continue the rewarming process until normal sensation returns to the distal tip of the thawed part, usually within 20-30 minutes. During rewarming, the patient will not experience much initial discomfort, but pain will increase as rewarming continues. Analgesics such as aspirin may be necessary.

Heavy doses of narcotic analgesics should be avoided, especially at high altitudes where they may lead to respiratory depression. After rapid rewarming, the injured part should be soaked in a whirlpool of 37°C for 20-30 minutes twice a day until healing is complete. An iodine solution may be added to the bath and active motion of the part in the bath usually is allowed. After thawing, the frostbitten area usually resembles burned tissue and has blister formation. This tissue is susceptible to infection and should be treated as an open burn with appropriate debridement and antibiotics. Further cold exposure and weight bearing should be avoided.

The patient should be kept warm at normal body temperature with the frostbitten area uncovered. If the area must be covered, use a dry dressing that is changed frequently and avoid wet or greasy dressings. Sterile cotton gauze may be applied between affected fingers or toes. Keep the limb well supported and horizontal; a foot cradle may be necessary.

A complication of any frostbite injury can be the development of gangrene. Debridement and/or amputation are best postponed to allow for either spontaneous debridement of the dead tissue, or appropriate care in a medical facility. Most gangrenous tissue secondary to frostbite will debride on its own if treated properly.

There are reports that horseback riders who ride long hours in cold temperatures may develop cold injury to the lateral thigh, especially if they are wearing uninsulated riding pants. A person who must ride in the winter should be advised to do it for shorter periods of time and to wear insulated pants.

## Prevention

A layer of cream should be applied to the face and exposed skin for added protection in cold environments. The athlete should attempt to stay warm enough to ensure adequate circulation to the peripheral extremities and skin. Heavy perspiring in cold temperatures should be avoided. Multiple clothing layers provide the best insulation for the skin. Several layers of socks and mittens are advised for cold weather athletes or mountain climbers. If the athlete needs to use fingers, a glove can be worn on one hand and a mitten on the other. Silk or rayon gloves can be worn for work on cold metal or the metal can be covered with adhesive tape. Extra mittens, removable wool mitten inserts, or glove linings should always be carried by an athlete who exercises in cold weather. The lips also need adequate protection to avoid sustaining cold injury (chilitis). A commercial lip balm should be adequate (Savin, 1975).

## Cold Urticaria

Cold urticaria may be caused by exposure to extreme cold or by jumping into cold water. Cold exposure triggers a histamine release that may result in the development of hives and possible anaphylaxis. The diagnosis is made by the history. When ice cubes are applied to the flexor surface of the forearm for two minutes and urticaria develops within 15 minutes, the presence of cold urticaria is demonstrated.

This problem is difficult to treat, as desensitization with cold carries the danger of anaphylaxis. Limited use of histamine blocking agents such as cromolyn sodium have been utilized with minimal success. Any athlete with this problem should be advised about the seriousness of cold exposure and the importance of being adequately protected.

## HEAT-INDUCED INJURIES

Ultraviolet radiation affects human skin continuously throughout life. In addition to acute adverse effects such as sunburn, chronic exposure may cause premature aging of the skin, actinic, keratoses, and basal and squamous cell carcinoma. Now that the perfect tan can be maintained all year by visiting tanning booths, the potential for trouble is greater. Equipment in tanning salons emits five times more ultraviolet radiation per unit of time than solar radiation measured at the equator (NIH, 1989).

Heat exposure and excessive sweating may cause many problems for athletes, the most common being sunburn, miliaria, and solar urticaria. Some may also develop conditions related to inappropriate or excessive sweating such as hyperhydrosis or anhydrosis. Individuals with hyperhydrosis are especially prone to excessive peeling of the skin of the palms and soles and are best treated with topical corticosteroids.

## Sunburn

Sunburn is the result of excessive exposure to sunlight, sunlamps, or occupational light sources. It is a common dermatitis that damages and ages skin. Sunburn is a hazard for athletes involved in water sports or skiing on bright sunny days when reflection of the sun's rays is extremely high. Sun exposure at higher altitudes is more likely to cause significant sunburn. Athletes with less melanin pigment withstand sun exposure poorly, burn easier, and may suffer the chronic effects of sun exposure earlier in life. Gradual exposure to the sun may be achieved by applying a sun screen containing PABA (para-amino benzoic acid) to partly absorb ultraviolet rays and permit slow tanning. A sun screen with an alcohol base should be used by athletes in water sports.

## Phototrauma

A mild sunburn will be tender to touch and cause a hot, drawn feeling. Severe burns cause intense pain and an inability to tolerate contact with clothing and sheets. Biochemically, phototrauma is a manifestation that 1) damages the membranes and DNA; 2) produces transient disturbances in protein synthesis; and 3) causes elevation of cytokines and inflammatory mediators (Taylor, 1991). Nausea, tachycardia, chills, and fever also are possible. The earliest sign of a sunburn is a pink hue and mild edema, which may then progress to intense erythema, edema, and pruritus. Evidence of sunburn is delayed, usually becoming evident two to six hours after exposure, and reaching maximum intensity after 15-24 hours. It is less severe in patients over age 60 than in those under age 30. However, redness lasts longer in older patients (Taylor, 1990, Soter, 1990).

Treatment includes applying a soothing solution or cool tap water for 20 minutes Q.I.D and the use of corticosteroid sprays, lotions, or creams to reduce inflammation and pain. Emollients (Ecerin®) may soothe and relieve dryness. Severe sunburns will require topical application of continuous cool compresses, topical steroids and emollients, a cradle for bed linens, and appropriate analgesics. If there is severe blistering, observe for bacterial superinfection and treat appropriately. Analgesic agents likely will be required, and some patients are given systemic corticosteroids for potentially severe sunburns (initially, 40-60 mg of prednisone tapered over seven to ten days). Topical anesthetics should be avoided because of the potential for allergic reactions.

## Photosensitivity

Photosensitivity refers to an abnormal response of the skin to sun exposure (Taylor, 1990). It includes phototoxic and photoallergic reactions and polymorphous light eruptions. A phototoxic reaction presents as an exaggerated sunburn and is far more severe than would be expected from the length of solar exposure. It also can occur after ingestion of or contact with a photosensitizer (Gilchrest, 1990). Many drugs can cause phototoxic reactions. A photoallergic reaction is a normal response of chemically exposed skin to sunlight and occurs when the immune system is involved. Reactions appear more as a rash than as a sunburn. All phototoxins are also photoallergins (Gilchrest, 1990). The polymorphous light eruption is the most common abnormal response seen after sunlight exposure and may affect up to 10% of the population. This response is triggered by intense sun exposure and is often called "sun poisoning." Within hours after exposure, pruritic papules and plaques cover exposed areas. These lesions subside in one to two weeks if the patient avoids further sun exposure (Gilchrest, 1990).

## Photo Protection

Avoiding long exposure to the sun will decrease the likelihood of severe sunburn. Sunscreens and sunblockers with PABA are available; the most effective formulations contain 5% PABA and 50%-70% alcohol. Benzophenone-containing products (Uval®) also are useful, but they are less effective than PABA, wash off the skin more easily, and must be reapplied more frequently. Use of a minimum SPF 15 up to age 18 is recommended. Products that are "water-resistant" and "waterproof" are protective for up to 40 or 80 minutes respectively of continuous water exposure (Nicol, 1989; Prawer, 1991). Proper education of athletes about sun exposure should be helpful in preventing sunburns.

## Miliaria

Miliaria, or heat rash, may affect a well-tanned individual who is sweating. Sweat gets trapped under layers of thick stratum corneum, resulting in crystalline miliaria. There is a symptomatic eruption of small, superficial, clear non-inflammatory vesicles. These lesions resolve with cooling and a reduction in sweating. A second type of lesion is miliaria rubra — a pruritic, discrete, papular-vascular eruption surrounded by erythema. There is no danger of contagious spread of miliaria to others, but continued contact can result in the development of secondary bacterial infection.

These conditions may be difficult to correct during active sports participation but the incidence of miliaria can be reduced by preventing sweating and overheating. A more severe form of miliaria involves the formation of sterile pustules in the deep layers of the skin, and should be differentiated from Staphylococcal folliculitis. Cooling the athlete in a shaded area with adequate ventilation or cold-bath immersion is effective in treating miliaria. Topical steroids are recommended for more difficult cases.

## Solar Urticaria

Solar urticaria is associated with light-induced hives characterized by redness and welts on the exposed skin that fade over a period of hours. It is a common finding among skiers, and may be due to overheating and excessive sweating. Some athletes may develop a true allergy to sunlight as a result of delayed hypersensitivity to light. The appearance of a polymorphic rash in light exposed areas is common. It will persist for one or two weeks and resolve spontaneously, even with continuous sun exposure. Treatment involves avoidance of sun exposure, sustained use of sun screens, and topical and/or systemic corticosteroids.

## ACNE

Acne is a heritable disease of the hair follicle and sebaceous gland. Abnormal hair follicle keratinization results in blackheads and whiteheads. These are the primary lesions of acne, whereas inflammatory papules, pustules, and cysts are the secondary lesions. Acne commonly appears on the face, trunk, and upper extremities and may affect individuals of any age.

Multiple factors lead to acne formation, including abnormal keratinization of hair follicles, increased sebum production, bacterial and yeast growth, enzymatic release of irritating short-chain prefatty acids, and an inflammatory dermal response. Acne may be precipitated by friction, heat, perspiration, application of occlusive topical agents, stress and anxiety, hormonal dysfunction, and medications. Friction from shoulder pads or helmet straps may inflame the skin and lead to inflammatory papules, which then may rupture and form a pustule or small abcess. Control of precipitating factors can reduce the severity of acne.

Acne treatment includes frequent washing of the affected skin with soap and warm water, especially after practice or a game and at bedtime. Many topical and parenteral agents are available (Bergfeld, 1982) (see Table 15-1). A topical cleansing or drying agent containing benzoyl peroxide (5% or 10%) promotes healing. The use of comedolytic agents (Retin-A), astringent lotions, or lipolytic agents may be useful. Mechanical or surgical removal of blackheads and whiteheads is helpful, but the athlete should be discouraged from squeezing a pustule which may increase the spread of infection. Topical and systemic antibiotics are recommended to reduce the activity of inflammatory acne. This includes tetracycline or erythromycin given in divided doses of 1 gm/day for six weeks. Topical antibiotics applied once or twice a day can have a similar effect and include such agents as clindamycin (Cleocin-T®) or Erythromycin. These agents are not as effective as benzoyl/peroxide, tretinoin, or salicylic acid (Taylor, 1991). Intralesional injections of corticosteroids may be indicated.

Topical Vitamin A preparations have been used to reduce blackheads and pustules. The athlete should be cautioned about possible sensitivity to sun exposure secondary to use of this drug. More recent developments include an oral vitamin A analog, (Accutane®), which is helpful in patients with cystic acne. Patients are treated for four months with Accutane in doses of 0.5 to 1 mg/kg with 90% clearing of cystic lesions in most cases.

---

Table 15-1. Treatment for Acne Vulgaris

Astringent lotions or salicylic acid
Benzoyl peroxide 5%-10% applied twice daily to inflammatory lesions
Topical Retin-A (tretinoin) Gel or Cream applied to blackheads at bedtime
Systemic antibiotics
• Tetracycline 500 mg twice a day for 6 weeks, then 500 mg/day taken on an empty stomach
• Erythromycin 500 mg twice a day for 6 weeks, then 500 mg/day
• Bactrim®, Minocin, Doxycycline
Topical antibiotic lotions or creams twice a day — 1% clindamycin or 2% Erythromycin
Physical Agents — UV light, liquid $N_2$ (for superficial acne)
Intralesional injection of triamcinolone acetonide (Kenalog)
Accutane® (isotretinoin) 0.5-1 mg/kg daily for 4 to 5 months
Dermabrasion, acne surgery

Toxicity of the drug is dose related and includes extreme dryness of the skin, blepharitis, bone pain, and hypertriglyceridemia. This drug should not be used more than four months without a rest period between treatments. Patients receiving oral Vitamin A should have periodic measurements of CBC, liver function tests, serum triglycerides, and sedimentation rate. Pre-treatment screening and contraceptive counseling are mandatory in sexually active patients of childbearing age. The cost of the drug and its side effects must be considered carefully (Taylor, 1991; Lever, 1990).

## SKIN INFECTIONS IN ATHLETES

Common skin infections in sports may result in contagious spread to opponents or participants. Infectious spread throughout an entire team is possible, especially in sports like wrestling. The infection may be bacterial, fungal, or viral.

### Bacterial Infections in Athletes

**Impetigo** is common in swimming and wrestling and is caused by a streptococcal or staphylococcal infection. Younger athletes often develop single or multiple blisters on normal skin, whereas older patients develop small vesicular lesions covered with a heavy, yellowish, serosanguinous crust. The diagnosis can be made from clinical appearance but cultures should be obtained.

Treatment includes local cleansing agents and debridment with soap and water. Astringent or alcohol-containing solutions are added to dry the lesions. A seven to ten-day course of oral antibiotics, primarily erythromycin or penicillin derivatives, may be necessary but topical antimicrobial agents usually are not helpful.

**Furunculosis** is caused primarily by staphylococcal organisms and presents as a red, tender area of swelling that evolves into a fluctuant abcess. Diagnosis is confirmed by culture. Treat with topical warm compresses with a 5%-10% solution of benzoyl peroxide four times a day. Oral antibiotics for 10-14 days are indicated. Incision and drainage of the lesions usually is unnecessary. All athletes with furunculosis should be disqualified from contact sports or swimming.

**Pseudofolliculitis** is a common disorder of bearded men, especially black males. It presents as an inflammatory papule secondary to curled hair that reenters the skin. Active folliculitis should be treated topically with acne preparations. Systemic erythromycin or penicillin derivatives occasionally are necessary. Prevention includes shaving the skin closely, use of a topical depilatory, or allowing longer growth of the beard.

**Erythrasma** is a chronic infection caused by a diphteroid, *Corynebacterium minutissimus*, which may be part of the normal skin flora. The organism survives in a warm and humid environment and usually is associated with a skin laceration. Clinically, the lesion appears as a diffuse, uniform, reddish-brown eruption with fine, dry, scaling and slightly wrinkled skin. Examination of the skin with a Wood's light will show the coral red floresence that confirms the diagnosis. Bacterial cultures usually are unnecessary. Treatment consists of systemic erythromycin, 1 gm per day for 7-10 days, and the use of topical cleansing or germicidal agents.

**Other Skin Infections** may develop secondary to inflammatory diseases, traumatic abrasions, or friction blisters.

Another common infection known as "fishtank granuloma," is caused by *Mycobacterium marinum* and is acquired from freshwater or fishtanks. This condition presents as a small, red nodule or pustule that forms on the skin and later develops of induration and crusting. The lesion may remain solitary or give way to more proximal lesions due to lymphatic spread. Treatment with anti-tuberculosis drugs is successful, but spontaneous regression after many months is the rule.

### Fungal Infections

Fungal infections of the skin are prevalent in athletics, and are common to participants in football and wrestling or those who exercise in a hot, humid environment. Microscopic organisms are capable of growing within the hair follicle and underneath its membranes. The most common fungal infections include tinea versicolor, tinea corporis, tinea cruris, tinea pedes, or Candidiasis.

**Tinea Versicolor** is caused by *Pityrosporon furfur*, a yeast organism. It appears as a salmon pink, finely scaling macule that fails to tan with repeated sun exposure. These areas are lightly tanned or white after prolonged tanning. The diagnosis is made by KOH examination that demonstrates short hyphae and grape-like spores. Cultures often are difficult to obtain.

It is treated with 2% selenium sulphide, a common agent in antidandruff shampoos. There are two treatment protocols: 1) an overnight application for 6-12 hours followed by rinsing and reapplication one week later, or 2) daily application of 15 minutes duration for 7-14 days, which often is curative. Pigment changes will remain until the pigment is naturally restored. A complete cure may be difficult to achieve because the spores are found deep within the hair follicles and are inaccessible to topical agents.

**Tinea Corporis, Cruris or Pedes (Ringworm).** These fungal organisms are found in the keratin of the skin, hair, and nails and are named according to the site of involvement: tinea corporis (body), tinea cruris (groin), or tinea pedes (feet). Several organisms are responsible for these infections: *Trichophyton rubrum*, *T. mentagrophytes*, *T. tonsurans*, *Candida albicans* and *Epidermophyton floccosum* (Brodin, 1979).

The infection appears as a raised border of activity with a clearing central area (sometimes hyperpigmented), forming the angular morphology of ringworm. The raised border often is scaly and sharply demarcates the peripheral normal skin from the eruption. Multiple lesions can coalesce and become arcuate in shape. On occasion, the inflammatory response will become erythematous with vesicle formation and pronounced induration. Fungal infections of the nails may act as a reservoir for reinfection of the skin so that the condition is difficult to eradicate without prolonged systemic griseofulvin therapy. These cases should be referred to a dermatologist for proper treatment. Diagnosis is made by the presence of hyphae upon KOH examination of the scale or vesical top, or by specific fungal cultures.

Treatment consists of topical antifungal agents applied once or twice daily for one to two months (see Table 15-2). Dryer lesions are treated with a variety of agents: Tinactin® (tolnastate), 2% Micatin (miconazole nitrate), 1% Lotrimin (clotrimazole), Mycelex (clotrimaze), or 1% Loprox (ciclopiroxolamine). Inflammatory infections with vesicles are treated with oral griseofulvin in doses of 125 mg to one gram per day for approximately one month.

Treatment of onychomycosis must be spaced over a 6-12 month period (Bergfeld, 1982; Brodin, 1979). Ketoconazole, a newer parenteral antifungal agent, is effective against dermatophytes, Candida organisms, and deep fungal infections. This agent is toxic to the liver toxcity so that liver en-

Table 15-2. Treatment for Cutaneous Fungal Infections

| Dry Lesions | Wet Lesions |
| --- | --- |
| •Soap and water cleansing<br>•Topical keratolytic agents (acne soap)<br>•Topical antifungal agents, applied twice a day for at least 1 month (Tinactin, 2% Micatin, Lotrimin, Mycelex, 1% Loprox) | •Soap and water cleansing<br>•Wet dressing (Domeboro Solution)<br>•Topical antifungal agents<br>•Phenolic dyes or antifungal creams or lotions |

zyme tests should be done during therapy. Infections of the intertrigonous areas or groin may be caused by Candida, other dermatophytes, erythrasma, or contact dermatitis. Each should be considered in the differential diagnosis.

**Candidiasis** is caused by *Candida albicans*, an opportunistic yeast organism, commonly found in the genital area. The organism becomes pathogenic in patients with altered immune status or diabetes mellitus. Characteristic lesions include satellite papules or pustules. The rash often is partially eroded, foul smelling, and has a cheesy exudate that may involve any area of the body.

Diagnosis is confirmed by a KOH preparation that demonstrates pseudohyphae (non-septate, non-branching, elongated growth) and budding yeast cells. Fungal cultures usually are unnecessary. Most infections are inflammatory and necessitate a topical drying antifungal agent such as Mycostatin® (Nystatin), 2% Micatin,® Lotrimin,® Mycelex, or 1% Loprox® cream. Resistant cases may require oral Nystatin. Acutely inflamed eruptions may require treatment with tap water or Burrow's Solution (1:20 dilution) compresses for 20 minutes T.I.D. until the acute phase subsides. This treatment is followed by antifungal topical agents.

## VIRAL INFECTIONS

### Herpes Simplex

This common viral infection is caused by *Herpes hominis* Type I and Type II viruses, which are extremely contagious and frequently affect wrestlers. The lesions start as a small crop of blisters that increase in size and rupture to form small crested lesions which usually last about two weeks. The infection starts with erythema and commonly is associated with malaise and local neuralgia. The vesicles may be tender and painful. In the late stages, small pinpoint painful ulcerations are noted on an erythematous base. Lesions are self-limited and appear to resolve without therapy. Therapy is to alleviate pain or promote early healing. Chronic and recurring infections occur.

The diagnosis is made by the clinical appearance of the lesions and by obtaining a positive smear of the vesicle base. Viral tissue cultures and serum antibody tests can be performed but are more costly. Clinically, Type I infections generally represent extragenital lesions, whereas the Type II virus is found in genital lesions and has been associated with cervical carcinoma.

The condition usually is self-limited. Drying agents have been used to hasten healing and limit the spread of infection (see Table 15-3). Useful preparations include 5% or 10% benzoyl peroxide, tincture of Benzoin, CamphoPhenique, or a 4% zinc solution. Topical anti-inflammatory agents may be used in late lesions that are dry and scaly. Frequent washing of the affected area with Dombro® solution may be helpful. Other treatments include: Oral L-lysine, 1 gm per day, and topical 4% zinc solution, which are thought to interfere with DNA systhesis of the virus. Zovirax® (Acyclovir) and Vira-A® (Vidarabine) are helpful in the treatment of early lesions (Bergfeld, 1978).

To prevent herpes infections, athletes participating in sports that require close contact should shower before and after practice, use only a personal towel, and have towels and clothes washed daily. All open wounds should be reported to the team physician and athletes with any lesions should be removed from competition immediately.

Team physicians and trainers for wrestling should check all wrestlers before practices or meets for active lesions and stop any infected participants from competition. Scrubbing wrestling mats with germicidal agents has not been proven to be helpful but it does maintain cleanliness. Athletes with atopic dermatitis or eczema may have rapid dissemination of herpes simplex virus after infection. Immediate consultation with a dermatologist and appropriate therapy is usually necessary.

### Herpes Zoster

Herpes zoster is a viral infection characterized by vesicles situated on an inflammatory base and arranged along the course of a sensory nerve. After the appearance of vesicles the lesions are contagious, and any athlete with lesions should be removed from contact sports to avoid giving herpes zoster or chicken pox to athletes not previously infected. Treatment consists of cool soaks and drying agents. Steroids are not indicated for uncomplicated cases and do not reduce the incidence of the post-herpetic neuralgia commonly seen in older patients.

### Molluscum Contagiosum

Molluscum contagiosum is a viral disorder caused by a large pox virus. It may present as a solitary lesion but more often appears in groups. These lesions are characterized by flesh-colored papules with a central umbilication that is filled by keratogenous debris and virons. The surrounding skin is not inflamed. Common sites of infection include the trunk, axilla, face, perineum, and thighs. This is a contagious viral infection that can be transmitted.

The diagnosis is established by clinical characteristics, skin biopsy, or viral smear. Several treatments that are similar to the therapy for warts have been instituted, in addition to using curettage under local anesthesia, dermabrasion with an abrasive pad, or topical Retin-A® gel or cream.

Early recognition and proper treatment of these lesions is important. Infected athletes should not participate in close contact sports such as wrestling until all the lesions have cleared.

### Verrucae (Warts)

The common wart is a benign epithelial tumor caused by several different papilloma viruses. Clinical lesions occur in the skin and mucous mem-

---

**Table 15-3. Treatment for Herpes Simplex Infections**

- Soap and water cleansing or use of germicidal agents
- Topical drying agents for viral blisters
    Benzoyl peroxide 5-10%
    Tincture of benzoin
    Camphor agent (Campho-Phenique)
    Zinc solution, 4%
    Antiviral agents for early lesions

branes and range in size from 1-2 mm to large tumors that are well circumscribed, firm, and elevated. The incubation period for the wart virus from contact to development of a tumor is about six months. The wart virus is not as contagious as other viral infections. These lesions should be differentiated from plantar keratoses.

Pain from the wart may hinder physical activity so that electrodessication and curettage to remove the tissue is indicated. Otherwise, lesions can be treated with liquid nitrogen. Chemical cautery with bichloroacetic acid or 25% Podophyllin has also been used. Other treatments are 40% salicylic acid plasters applied daily for one to three months, topical Retin-A gel, 0.025%, applied twice a day for two to three months, or topical 5-Fluorouracil, 2%-5% applied in a similar fashion. Excision and radiotherapy of warts are not recommended because there may be further development of the warts or scar tissue. During the active athletic season, wart treatment requires the physician to use whatever treatment will interfere least with participation. Their increasing presence and potential relationship to cervical cancer require thorough treatment.

Viral warts should be distinguished from condyloma accuminata which present as moist, pinpoint projections in the skin that may multiply to form large, clustered vegetating papillomas. These lesions may be found on the penis, mucous membranes of the vulva, or perianal area. They should be distinguished from the syphillitic wart. Treatment of condyloma accuminata involves destruction of warts by electrosurgery, cryocautery, 25% podophyllin, or a combination of the above. Five-flurururacil or Vitamin A cream or gel has been used and appears to be somewhat effective. These lesions present no contraindications for sports participation. However, their increasing presence and potential relationship to cervical cancer require thorough treatment of all lesions.

## INFESTATIONS

The most common infestations in athletes are caused by the crab louse and scabetic mite. These are transmitted by intimate contact and, in that regard, are contagious. Transmission can take place through sexual contact or be spread by frictional contact. In addition to the infected individual, all personal contacts such as teammates and household members should be treated.

### Scabies

Scabies is caused by the mite *Sarcoptes scabiei*. It presents as severe pruritus which often is the primary complaint. Early lesions appear as erythematous burrows under the skin and may be found on the hands or site of contact. Lesions are inflammatory papules or nodules on the hands, wrist, flexure areas, arms, axillae, nipples, or umbilicus. Eczematous dermatitis may occur late in the disease, but folliculitis and furunculosis are rare.

The diagnosis is made by demonstrating mite eggs or fecal material in skin scrapings under a microscope. Treatment includes the use of Kwell® lotion or shampoo applied over the entire affected area for 6-24 hours, followed by a warm water rinse. Clothing and bedding should be washed but not used again for seven to ten days. The treatment should be repeated if viable mites remain. Overuse of Kwell® may lead to neurological toxicity.

### Pediculosis Pubis (Crab Louse)

The crab louse is transmitted by intimate contact and is limited to certain areas of the body — perineum, abdominal wall, axillary areas, and eye lashes, but is rarely found on the scalp. The head louse will be found on the scalp. Pediculosis presents as severe pruritus, and skin scrapings may reveal the presence of nits (eggs), louse, or louse excretion under the microscope. Treatment is the same as for scabies.

## OTHER SKIN PROBLEMS IN ATHLETICS

### Contact Dermatitis

Contact dermatitis may present either as an acute or chronic inflammatory condition of the skin, and may be secondary to a skin irritation or allergy (see Tables 15-4 and 15-5). Contact irritant dermatitis is a nonallergic reaction of the skin from exposure to an irritating substance or physical agent that produces skin damage, ulceration, or pain. Contact allergies are skin disorders resulting from acquired hypersensitivity to a specific allergen such as poison ivy and are Type IV (delayed hypersensitivity) immune reactions (Whittington, 1989).

**Table 15-4. Primary Causes of Contact Allergic Reactions**

1. Plants of the genus Rhus (poison ivy, oak and sumac)
2. Paraphenyl diamine (blue and black dyes)
3. Nickel compounds (jewelry, metal protective gear)
4. Rubber compounds
5. Chromates (tanned leather and metal parts)
6. Topical medications (Benzocaine, antihistamines, antibiotics, tincture of benzoin)

**Table 15-5. Causes of Irritant Skin Reactions in Athletes**

1. Dry ice burns
2. Abrasions from synthethic turf
3. Poorly fitting gear (football helmet)
4. Callous formation in gymnasts and bicyclists
5. Stria in weight lifters
6. Increased sweating and eczematous dermatitis in hockey players
7. Loss of skin secondary to application of old adhesive tape or direct impact

Contact dermatitis may also occur after application of topical or over-the-counter medications or taping. Materials that can cause contact dermatitis include tape, especially the rubberbacked adhesive tape; sprays that help tape stick; topical medications; athletic shoes; iodine preparations; rubber materials used in sports equipment, and handles on exercise equipment. Irritant (nonallergic) reactions occur more commonly with commercially washed uniforms, chalk dust, and various first aid treatment products.

The clinical appearance of both types of contact dermatitis include either dry, thickened skin or an acute vesicular dermatitis. Both may cause pruritus and pain. The history is very important in isolating causative agents and in identifying the distribution and pattern of the rash. Patch testing, skin biopsy, or Tzanck smear based on these clues may be valuable diagnostic aids.

Therapy for contact dermatitis includes avoiding the agent responsible for the reaction. Particular reactions are treated with cool compresses or soaks and topical corticosteroid preparations. These should be combined with vehicles to promote drying such as aerosol sprays, gels, lotions, solutions, or creams. These traditional adjunctive treatments improve symptoms only mildly (Pariser, 1991). Systemic antihistamines and aspirin will reduce pruritus, and a limited course of systemic steroids may reduce the severity of the inflammation. The premeasured dose form of corticosteroids which tapers over one week is often insufficient for adequate treatment. Whether the athlete can participate in sports is totally dependent upon the degree of skin involvement and severity of the symptoms.

Chronic forms of contact dermatitis may be managed by avoiding contact with the agent or by establishing a protective barrier between the skin and inducing agent. Chronic contact dermatitis is treated with topical corticosteroids and emolient bases. After the agent is identified, a thorough check should be made of all materials used by the trainer or physician with that athlete.

## Dyshydrosis

Dyshydrosis may flare from what the athlete wears on his feet and must be differentiated from contact dermatitis. The diagnosis is made by observing small vesicles along the lateral aspects of the toes. Negative patch testing will eliminate other causes of contact dermatitis. An absorbent powder to reduce the moisture content on the skin, drying solutions (Burrows), and topical steroid creams are helpful. Frequent changing of white socks and shoes helps reduce moisture retention and this form of eczema.

## Intertrigo

Intertrigo is a noninfectious inflammatory response of the skin to friction and maceration that may be caused by tight fitting garments, athletic supporters, and obesity. An overgrowth of bacteria or yeast will be present in the inflamed area. Redness and thickening or lichenification of the skin is seen at friction points. The diagnosis is based on exclusion of other eruptions previously described.

Treatment consists of eliminating skin irritation and chaffing. Use talcum powder or Zeasorb® on the involved areas, especially in the groin, and avoid tight fitting garments. Mild topical corticosteroids such as 1% hydrocortisone cream will alleviate symptoms although stronger topical corticosteroid preparations may be required. A secondary bacterial infection could develop and lead to cellulitis. The athlete should be treated with appropriate systemic antibiotics.

## Plantar Keratoses

Many athletes have painful plantar callouses or keratoses that often are confused with plantar warts. This condition is unresponsive to the typical treatment procedures for plantar warts (Cangialosi, 1977).

Plantar keratoses present as a painful, hornified lesion of the sole that closely resembles a callous or wart. There is a well demarcated hypertrophy of the stratum corneum. Gentle debridment will reveal a pale, waxy, haloed center that may occur singularly or in multiple numbers. These lesions usually are associated with structural and functional abnormalities of the foot. The most common structural problems are abnormally long or short metatarsals, enlarged metatarsal heads, or degenerative changes in the tarsals, and this should be confirmed by x-rays. Plantar keratoses also may be associated with excessive pronation of the foot, a short Achilles or hamstring tendon, and pes planus (flat feet).

Gentle debridment with a #10 blade and application of a ⅛" or ¼" horseshoe-shaped adhesive felt pad over the keratosis provides immediate but temporary relief. The lesion will return but treatment can be administered monthly. Simple wedge excision of the lesion under local anesthesia, electrocautery, intralesional steroid injection, and topical acid preparations should be avoided because they generate painful plantar scars and may cause further pain and disability. Keratoses that do not respond to these methods should be referred to a qualified specialist or podiatrist for management.

## INSECT ALLERGIES AND SPORTS

Many athletes are allergic to biting and stinging insects, especially Hymenoptera (bees, wasps, hornets and ants), spiders, fleas, and scorpions (Frazier, 1980). Stinging marine animals such as jellyfish, corals, and man-o-wars, plus other marine life, may be hazardous to swimmers and divers (Halstead, 1976). Many individuals with allergies are unaware of their hypersensitivity so that severe or fatal anaphylactic reactions to insect or marine bites or stings may occur.

Mild symptoms of systemic reactions include itching around the eyes, flushing, urticaria, and a feeling of faintness and with anxiety. Symptoms may proceed to a more severe generalized systemic reaction that can intensify. Fatal anaphylactic shock may occur within a half hour after the sting or bite.

Insect sting kits are available and contain epinephrine 1:1000 in sterile syringes, along with tourniquets, alcohol pads, and complete instructions. Antihistamine tablets also are included. Patients with insect allergies should be instructed how to use the kit. Desensitization therapy for Hymenoptera allergies should be considered as a preventive measure. Anyone with an insect allergy should wear a medical identification bracelet.

Awareness and prevention of potentially severe allergic reactions to insects is important. The athlete should wear proper footgear and avoid brightly colored clothing or perfumed lotions and shampoos. Prompt treatment of an insect sting or bite is most important to avoid severe anaphylactic reactions.

### REFERENCES

Basler, R.S.W. Skin lesions related to sports activity. *Primary Care* 10(3): 479, 1983.
Bergfeld, W. Nonvenereal Sexually-Transmitted Disease in Athletes. *Phys and Sportsmed* pgs. 124-129, March 1978.
Bergfeld, W.F. Dermatologic problems in athletes. *Clin Sports Med*, 1:419, 1982.
Brodin, M.B. Jock itch. *Phys and Sportsmed* 8:102, 1980.
Brodin, M.B. Athlete's foot. *Phys and Sportsmed* 7:95, 1979.
Brown, J. and Childers, P. Blister prevention: an experimental method. *Research Quarterly*, 37:183, 1966.
Cangialosi, C.P.: Plantar Keratoses. *Postgraduate Medicine* 75:128, 1984.
Frazier, C.A. Insect allergy and the sportsman. *Phys and Sportsmed* 8:124, 1980.
Freeman, M.J. and Bergfeld, W.F. Skin diseases of football and wrestling participants. *Cutis* 20:330, 1977.
Gilchrest, B.A. Actinic injury. *Annal Review Medicine* 41:199-210, 1990.
Halstead, B.W. *Hazardous Marine Life*. In RH Strauss (Ed.) Diving Medicine, New York: Grune and Stratton, 1976.
Lever, L., Marks, R. Current views on the etiology, pathogenesis and treatment of acne vulgaris. *Drugs* 93(5):681-692, 1990.
Levine, N. Friction blisters. *Phys and Sportsmed* 10:84, 1982.
Mithailov, P., Berova, N. and Andreev, V.C. Physical urticaria and sport. *Cutis* 20:381, 1977.
Nicol, N.H. Actinic keratosis: preventable and treatable like other precancerous and cancerous skin lesions. *Plastic Surgical Nursing* 9(2):49-55, 1989.
Pariser, R.J. Allergic and reactive dermatoses. *PostGrad Med* 89(8):75-85, 1991.
Prawer, S. Sun-related skin diseases. *Post-Graduate Med* 89(8):51-66, 1991.
Savin, R.C. Keeping a healthy skin on skis-how to do it. *Phys and Sportsmed* pgs. 49-52, November 1975.
Snook, G.A. How I managed skin problems in wrestling. *Phys and Sportsmed* 12:97, 1984.
Soter, M.A. Acute effects of ultraviolet radiation on the skin. *SEMIN Dermatological* 9(1):11-15, 1990.
Sunlight, ultraviolet radiation and the skin. National Institute of Health, Conference, Consensus Statement, 7(8):1-10, 1989.
Taylor, C., Stein, R.S., Ryden, J. et al. Photo-aging photo-image and photo-protection. *J Am Academy Dermatology* 22(1):1-15, 1990.
Tayor, M.B. Treatment of acne vulgaris. *PostGrad Med* 89(8):40-47, 1991.
Whittington, C. Clinical aspects of contact dermatitis. *Primary Care* 16(3):729-738, 1989.

## ADDITIONAL READINGS

### Acne

Frank, S.B. (ed) *Acne: Update for the Practitioner.* New York: Yorke Medical Books, 1979.
Thomsen, R.R., Stanieri, A., Knutson, D., and Strauss, J.S. Topical clindamycin treatment of acne. *Arch. Dermatol* 116:1031, 1980.

### Bacterial Infection

*Impetigo*

Dillon, H.C., Jr. Topical and systemic therapy for pyoderma. *Int J Dermatol* 19:443, 1980.
Ferrieri, P., Dajoni, A. et al. Natural history of impetigo. *J Clin Infest* 51:2851, 1972.
Leyden, J. Experimental infection with Group A Streptococci in humans. *J Infest Dermatol* 75:196, 1980.

*Furuculosis*

Dillon, H.C. Jr. Topical and systemic therapy for pyoderma, *Int J Dermatol* 19:443, 1980.
Leyden, J. Experimental infection with Group A Streptococci in humans. *J Infest Dermatol* 75:196, 1980.
Steele, R. Recurrent staphylococcal infections in families. *Arch Dermatol* 116:189, 1980.

### Viral Infection

*Herpes*

Jones, B.R., Fisan, P.N., Cobo, L.M., et al. Efficacy of acycloquanosine against herpes simplex corneal ulcer. *Lancet* 1:243, 1979.
Spruance, S.L., Overall, J.C., Kern, E.R. et al. The natural history of recurrent herpes simplex labialis: implications for antiviral therapy. *NEJM* 297:69, 1977.

*Warts/Molluscum Contagiosum*

Bender, M.E., and Pass, F. Anogenital warts. In Maddin, A. (ed). *Current Dermatologic Therapy.* Philadelphia: W.B. Saunders Company, 1982.
Henaco, M. and Freeman, R.C. Inflammatory molluscum contagiosum. *Arch Dermatol* 90:479, 1964.
Massing, A.M. and Epstein, W.L. Natural history of warts: a two-year study. *Arch Dermatol* 87:306, 1963.

### Fungal Infection

*Tinea Versicolor*

Catterall, M.D. Tinea versicolor. In Maddin, A. (ed). *Current Dermatologic Therapy.* Philadelphia: W.B. Saunders Company, 1982.

*Tinea Corporis and Pedis*

Borgers, M. Mechanism of actions of antifungal drugs with special reference to the imidazole derivative. *rev Infect Dis* 2:520, 1980.
Eaglestein, W.H. and Pariser, D.M. *Office Techniques for Diagnosing Skin Diseases.* Chicago: Year Book Medical Publishers, 1978.
Smith, E.B. New topical agents for dermatophytosis. *Cutis* 17:54, 1976.

*Erythrasma*

Schlapper, O.L.A., et al. Concomitant erythrasma and dermatophytosis of the groin. *Br J Dermatol* 100:147, 1979.

### Contact Dermatitis

Arndt, K.A. *Manual of Dematologic Therapeutics.* Boston: Little, Brown, 1974. Fisher, A.A. *Contact Dermatitis* 2nd ed. Philadelphia, Lea & Febiger, 1973.
Peystowski, S.B. et al. Allergic contact hypersensitivity of nickel, neomycin, ethylenediamine and benzocaine: relationships between age, sex history of exposure and reactivity standard patch tests and use tests in general populations. *Arch Dermatol* 115:950, 1979.

*Sunburn*

Epstein, J.H. Polymorphous light eruption. *Ann Allergy* 24:397, 1966.
Lorencz, A.L. Physiological and pathological changes in skin from sunburn and sun tan. *JAMA* 173:1227, 1960.

*Blisters*

Sedar, J.L. Treatment of blisters in the running athlete. *Arch Podiatric Med and Foot Surgery.* Sports Medicine (Supplement 1), 1978, pp. 29-34.

*Infestations*

Rasmussen, J.E. The problem of lindane. *J Am Acad Dermatol* 5:507, 1981.
Schacter, B. Treatment of scabies and pediculosis with lindane preparations: evaluation. *J am Acad Dermatol* 5:517, 1981.

# 16

# Common Sports-Related Injuries and Illnesses — Hematology, Endocrine & Environment

## SECTION A. HEMATOLOGY

### Anemia

Sports medicine literature indicates a certain amount of confusion about athletic anemia. Four different terms have evolved referring to clinical states that overlap — sports anemia, pseudoanemia, iron deficiency anemia, and iron deficiency. Iron deficiency decreases performance capacity because of the vital role iron plays in energy production (Buskirk, 1981). We know that iron deficiency is a consequence of exercise; strenuous conditioning and training are associated with decreased hemoglobin concentrations and capacity. When serum ferritin levels were determined randomly, athletes were more prone to the iron deficient state than their non-exercising peers (Clement, 1984). Mechanical destruction of older red blood cells ("heel-strike" hemolysis in long distance runners (Eichner, 1985)) causes an increased release of iron into the plasma, creating myoglobin — a stimulus to produce new red blood cells. Erythrocyte fragility increases with training, and iron also is lost in sweat.

About 22% to 25% of female athletes but less than 10% of male athletes will have decreased plasma iron levels (Haymes, 1980), and 3% will suffer from iron deficiency anemia. Black women athletes especially are prone to iron deficiency anemia.

Summarized below are the hematologic alterations of aerobic exercise to give the primary care physician a basis for diagnosing and treating sports anemias.

- In sedentary individuals, hemoglobin is reduced during strenuous exercise (Yoshimura, 1980).
- Endurance athletes show evidence of acute hemolysis and greater RBC fragility after vigorous exercise (Falsetti, 1983).
- Depressed, suboptimal hemoglobin levels are common among male runners (Hunding, 1981).
- Exercise-induced increases in plasma volume secondary to water and electrolyte conservation, produce a dilutional anemia and improve performance by increasing stroke volume (Eichner, 1986).
- An increase in red blood cell mass by 16%-18% is present in elite athletes (Eichner, 1985).
- Three possible mechanisms for sports anemias are:
  a. hemodilution — the most common cause of suboptimal hemoglobin in athletes.
  b. hemolysis — secondary to destruction of senescent RBCs interacting with contracting muscles or heel strike. The extent of this hemolysis is affected by the hardness of running surface, running distance, heaviness of stride, adequacy of footwear, and temperature increase in soles of feet (Tate, 1983).
  c. Decrease in erythropoeisis (hemoglobin synthesis) with iron deficiency anemia being the most common cause.

### Signs and Symptoms

All four conditions present in the same basic manner, with symptoms of premature fatigue and tiredness. Signs may include skin pallor or tachycardia relative to the individual's normal resting heart rate. Past this point, the clinical picture varies and laboratory results become important (Risser, 1990). Refer to Table 16A-1.

### Iron Deficiency

Elevated serum ferritin levels, no change in hemoglobin/hematocrit or number of red blood cells; decreased iron stores. Secondary to decreased iron intake or the effect of exercise on iron metabolism.

### Iron Deficiency Anemia

Increased serum ferritin, hemoglobin/hematocrit below normal levels, lowered red blood cell count, decreased iron stores, and microcytosis. It is secondary to a decreased iron intake either from poor nutrition or a voluntary decrease intake of meat, an increase in training, GI blood loss secondary to training, weight loss for any reason, or resumption of menses after amenorrhea.

### Sports Anemia (Yoshimura, 1970)

Normocytic, normochromic anemia — a splenic secretion (lysolecithin) released during exercise may initiate sports anemia. Training often produces significant decreases in RBC, hemoglobin count, and packed cell volume, but rarely clinical anemia (Frederickson, 1983). Protein nutritional status appears to be important in preventing sports anemia because the severity of the anemia appears to be related to protein intake (Yoshimura, 1980). This is a self-limited condition.

Table 16A-1. Laboratory Test Profiles of Exercise-Induced Anemias

|  | H/H | RBC# | RBC Size | Serum Ferritin | Serum Iron |
|---|---|---|---|---|---|
| Iron Deficiency | — | — | — | ↑ | ↓ |
| Iron Deficiency Anemia | ↓ | ↓ | ↓ | ↑ | ↓ |
| Sports Anemia | ↓ | ↓ | — | — | — |
| Pseudoanemia | ↑ | ↓ | — | — | ↑ |

### Pseudoanemia

This has been described in marathon runners with no clinical evidence (Dressendorfer, 1981). Decreased red blood cell count, decreased hemoglobin, increased plasma iron, increased RBC distruction are present, however.

*Treatment*

- Regular monitoring of serum ferritin, hemoglobin, and diet.
- Replacement of dietary iron: a) hemiron (liver, heart, lean red meat, poultry, fish); b) non-hemiron (peas, beans, nuts, cereals, leafy vegetables, eggs, fruits, wine); and c) occasional supplementation with elemental iron.

### G6PD Deficiency in Athletes

There is no specific evidence that individuals with heredity hemolytic disorders are adversely affected by exercise; it is certainly appropriate to be aware of drugs that can elicit hemolysis in G6PD deficient athletes. Please examine and use Table 16A-2.

## Bleeding Disorders

Exercise often unmasks borderline disorders or deficiencies.

### Aplastic Anemia

This condition has been described in a marathon runner who used rubber cement containing benzene to keep adhesive tape on his feet in place (Roodman, 1980). The use of NSAIDs, especially phenylbutazone, has been implicated. This classic side effect of the anti-inflammatory, antipyretic drug phenylbutazone (Butazolidin®) is a time-related, not dose related side effect. Thus, using NSAIDs such as phenylbutazone over a brief and appropriate period of time like one or two weeks to treat soft tissue injury does not carry with it the same concern about bone marrow effects as described in the literature. However, prophylactic use of NSAIDs, even aspirin, over a protracted period of time is cause for concern and should be discouraged.

### Thrombocytopenia

Occasionally, quinine has been used effectively to treat muscle cramps. College and professional

**Table 16A-2. Drugs Causing Hemolysis in G6PD Deficient Subjects**

**Clinically significant hemolysis**
  Acetanilid
  Disphenylsulphon (Dapsone)
  Furazolidone
  Naphthalene
  Neoarsphenamine
  Pentaquine
  Pamaquine
  Primaquine
  Napofurazone (Furacin)
  Napofurantoin (Furadantin)
  Phenylbydrazine
  Quinocide
  Sulphanilamide
  N-Acerylsulphanilamide
  Sulphapyridine
  Sulphamethoxypyridazine (Kynex)
  Salicylazosulphapyridine (Azulfidine)
  2-Amino-5-sulphanylthiazole (Thiazolsulfone)

**Drugs which may cause hemolysis in presence of infection**
  Acetophenetidin
  Acetylsalicylic acid
  Chloramphenicol (Chloromycetin)
  Chloroquine
  Dimercaprol
  Sulphlsoxazole (Gantrisin)
  Sulphoxone
  Quinadrine (Atabrine)

athletes have used it for symptomatic relief of muscle cramps associated with rigorous training. Quinine-induced thrombocytopenia is an uncommon but potentially fatal complication of such use by athletes and has been reported (Barnes, personal communication). Primary care physicians need to be aware of this possibility.

### Hemophilia

The most important concern with potential athletes who have some type of hemophilia is whether the individual should have restrictions on physical activity and what the risk factors are for injury. Before making a decision, primary care physicians must assess the type and severity of the hemophilia.

Someone with hemophilia likely will have one of the following four clotting deficiencies:

- Hemophilia A — decreased factor VIII. Sex linked. Males.
- Hemophilia B — decreased factor IX. Sex linked recessive trait. Males.
- Hemophilia C — decreased factor XI. Autosomal trait. Males and females.
- VonWillebrand's Disease — deficiency in factor VIII and dysfunction in platelet adhesiveness. Autosomal trait. Males and females.

Two laboratory tests are sufficient for screening in most patients, partial thromboplacin time (PTT), and bleeding time.

McClain (1990) has summarized disease severity and recommended types of sports participation for athletes with hemophilia. Refer to Tables 16A-3 and 16A-4 for this information.

### Sickle Cell Anemia

Black and some Oriental athletes may be prone to this problem which may present initially with joint pain, swelling, hematuria, or abdominal pain. All are common symptoms that could easily be overlooked on the basis of sports activity. It is important to identify athletes with sickle cell trait (through screening) to prevent complications and to give proper treatment. We know that exercise causes ischemic electrocardiographic responses in children with sickle cell anemia (Alpert, 1981). Athletes with sickle cell anemia do not need restrictions provided they are never allowed to dehydrate significantly. Moderate fluid loss will precipitate a crisis.

### Creatine Phosphokinase Alterations

There are many reports in the literature describing alarming elevations of CPK levels in athletes (LaPorta, 1978; Kielblock, 1979). The authors have seen and heard of 25-fold elevations of CPK isoenzyme bands MM and MB and it has been reported by Siegel (1983). Exertional rhabdomyolysis appears to be responsible for much of the elevation. There are three isoenzyme fractions identified for CPK — MM, MB and BB. The MM band is associated with skeletal muscle, MB with heart, and BB with brain or shock. Elevation secondary to rhabdomyolysis results in primary elevations of MM and MB isoenzyme bands. This is an important consideration in treating the many post-cardiac patients now exercising. Care must be taken not to over-diagnose or treat patients complaining of chest pain without first correlating clinical EKG and other enzyme changes. Additionally, an elevation in the BB CPK

Table 16A-3. Factor Levels, Disease Severity and Causes of Bleeding in Patients with Hemophilia

| Deficiency Level of Factor VIII or IX (%) | Severity of Hemophilia | Cause of Bleeding |
|---|---|---|
| 5-20 | Mild | Severe trauma |
| 1-5 | Moderate | Mild to moderate trauma |
| <1 | Severe | Spontaneous |

From McLain, 1990.

Table 16A-4. Recommended Sports Participation for Athletes with Hemophilia*

| May Participate | Participation not Recommended |
|---|---|
| **Limited contact/impact** | **Collision/contact** |
| Track-and-field | Field hockey |
|   High jump** | Football |
|   Pole vault** | Ice hockey |
| Cross-country skiing | Lacrosse |
|  | Martial arts |
| **Noncontact** | Rugby |
| Archery | Soccer |
| Badminton | Water polo |
| Bowling | Wrestling |
| Crew (rowing) |  |
| Field | **Limited contact/impact** |
|   Discus | Baseball |
|   Javelin | Basketball |
|   Shotput | Cycling |
| Cross-country running | Diving |
| Golf | Gymnastics |
| Swimming** | Skiing (downhill) |
| Tennis** |  |

From McLain, 1990.
*Participation can vary depending on the individual's age, emotional and physical maturity, and severity of the disease.
**Participation may be appropriate if the disease is mild.

isoenzyme band has been described in boxers following competition (Brayne, 1982). Given the probability that such boxing bouts do produce minor head trauma, such an elevation is significant. Also, see previous discussion on head injuries (Chapter 11).

### Infectious Mononucleosis (Chapter 10)

### Acquired Immune Deficiency Syndrome (AIDS)

Acquired Immune Deficiency Syndrome (AIDS) is our nation's number one health priority. It is no longer viewed as a condition exclusive to homosexuals and IV drug users. Consideration of AIDS is an important issue for the athlete and the primary care team physician because it is a sexually transmitted disease. All sexually active individuals taking part in competitive or recreational sports are at risk. Athletes can be at greater risk when they compete in sports requiring close physical contact such as wrestling, football, or boxing. In addition, athletes may be at risk because of homosexual behavior or because of IV or IM drug use. AIDS has been reported in a bodybuilder who injected himself with anabolic steroids with a contaminated needle (Sklarek, 1984). The human immunoefficiency virus (HIV) is not readily transmitted other than by sexual routes or IV inoculation. There is no evidence of transmission by touching, rubbing, or casual contact. An HIV infection has never been identified in swimming (Calabrese, 1989). While the risks of injury — even death — on the playing field far outweigh the risk of contracting AIDS, there are some situations of concern. Facial lacerations secondary to boxing can expose significant portions of mucus membranes to blood. Wrestlers who sustain cuts or abrasions and then come into close contact with other wrestlers pose another health hazard. Sharing blood-stained towels with team members could spread AIDS as well as hepatitis, herpes, and other viral infections. The primary care physician may well be the only source of health information for an athlete and must assume the role of a resource person and caregiver who is up-to-date about this devastating illness and will know where to obtain additional information. The only preventive measures in addition to what has been outlined already is covering open wounds prior to participation.

### Viral Influenza (Colds)

Viral Influenza or colds appear to be influenced by exercise (Fitzgerald, 1988). The normal immune system keeps an athlete free of infection but too much exercise can have a damaging effect on the immune system. Does intensive training decrease resistance? There presently are no definitive studies to answer this question. Several clinical reports indicate that intensive training does increase susceptibility to illness. Athletes who seem to be at risk are those who participate in winter sports in northern climates. The college setting, where athletes travel from one campus to another to compete and then travel home for the holidays to different parts of the country allows maximum exposure to influenza, viral illness, and other epidemic infections. The authors believe that optional yearly influenza immunizations are simply good preventive medicine for college athletes at risk. Athletes work too hard for too long to jeopardize their performance because of a preventable illness (Johnson, 1990).

### Oncology

It has been suggested that exercise may alter the response to cancer but exactly how that happens is as yet undetermined. Polednak (1976) looked at the prevalence of neoplasms in a large cohort of college men and discovered that major athletes (football and basketball) died significantly more often from neoplasms than nonathletes. This is an interesting study, but explanations of the findings are tenuous:

- Athletes tend to gain more weight after college than their nonathlete classmates (not well documented in the literature).
- The relationship between body size and cancer risk suggests some positive associations.
- Chronic exercise may be viewed as stress that profoundly affects the adrenocortical function, leading to possible carcinogenic effects.
- Differences in lifestyle and psychological traits between athletes and nonathletes may contribute.

In our experience, we have seen young athletes compete with various forms of cancer in remission. From a clinical standpoint, the major differences in these athletes deal not so much with their cancer as with the treatment for it. The effects of chemotherapy and radiation are wide-ranging in the body. Our experience with radiation therapy for Hodgkin's Disease is that respiratory function is decreased after treatment but gradually improves. Host (1973) showed that vital capacity was reduced on an average of 10% shortly after treatment. When dealing with athletes undergoing cancer therapy, it is imperative that limitations on cardio-respiratory performance be anticipated and expected by the athlete and physician and understood by coaches and parents.

## SECTION B.
## ENDOCRINE

Endocrine abnormalities and their relationship to exercise have become better understood over the past several years. The following list of endocrinologic abnormalities are discussed elsewhere in the book: 1) diabetes mellitus, Chap. 6, Sect. A; 2) amenorrhea (primary and secondary), Chap. 5, Sect. C; 3) eating disorders (anorexia nervosa, anorexia athletica, bulimia, bulimorexia), Chap. 2, Sect. D; 4) dysmenorrhea, Chap. 5, Sect. C, and 5) drug-induced abnormalities; Chap. 2, Sect. E.

### Fatigue

Persistent fatigue in an athlete poses an extremely difficult diagnostic challenge for the primary care physician because there are so many possible causes, even more than might be found in a sedentary individual. Fatigue may be due to something as innocuous as being "out of shape," or as life-threatening as a cardiomyopathy. An appropriate work-up takes information from the history, considers the most likely factors, and directs the physical exam to allow the primary physician to focus on a short differential diagnostic list of causes. Rowland (1986) has summarized a differential diagnosis of fatigue in adolescent athletes (see Table 16B-1).

## SECTION C.
## ENVIRONMENTAL INDUCED INJURY

### Heat Stress/Hyperthermia

#### Temperature, Humidity and Exercise

The body's ability to thermoregulate during exercise depends upon ambient temperature, humidity, wind velocity, radiant heat from the sun, and the intensity and duration of exercise. Measurement of environmental factors is a means of assessing environmental heat stress, an important factor in any outdoor event. This is most efficiently accomplished by the *wet bulb globe temperature* (WBGT) using several instruments: 1) a dry bulb thermometer which measures ambient temperature, 2) a wet bulb thermometer which measures humidity, and 3) a black globe thermometer which measures radiant heat. If the WBGT Index (Figure 16C-1) and wind speed are both measured, an effective temperature can be calculated. Table 16C-1 correlates WBGT measurements and exercise safety.

Warm season events and practices are best scheduled during the early morning and evening hours. If the WBGT index is moderate at the start

Table 16B-1. Diagnosis of Fatigue in Adolescent Athletes*

| Diagnosis | Best Screening Method | Therapy | Reversibility of Symptoms |
|---|---|---|---|
| Anemia | Serum hemoglobin | Etiology-specific | Etiology-dependent |
| Nonanemic iron deficiency | Serum ferritin | Oral iron supplement | Reversible |
| Exercise-induced asthma | Pulmonary function assessment with testing | Prophylactic bronchodilators | Reversible |
| Medication | History | Discontinue or decrease dose | Reversible |
| Abnormal weight | History, physical exam | Nutrition counseling | Reversible |
| Psychosocial state | History | Psychological counseling | Often reversible |
| Insufficient training | History, exercise testing | Aerobic training program | Reversible |
| Cardiac disease | Physical exam, chest x-ray, ECG | Etiology-specific | Etiology-dependent |
| Neuromuscular | History, physical exam | Usually supportive | Rarely reversible |
| Overtraining | History, morning pulse | Rest | Potentially reversible |

*From Rowland, 1986.

$$WBGT = 0.70\, T_{wb} + 0.2\, t_g + 0.1\, T_{db}$$

where $T_{wb}$ = wet bulb temp

$T_g$ = black globe temp

$T_{db}$ = dry bulb temp

**Fig. 16C-1.** Wet Globe Temperature (WBGT) Index

Table 16C-1. ACSM Position Stand For Race Risk

| WBGT | Risk | Flag Color |
|---|---|---|
| <10°C | Hypothermic Risk | White |
| <18°C >10°C | Low risk of heat illness | Green |
| 18-23°C | Moderate | Amber |
| 23-28°C | High | Red |
| >28°C | *CANCEL EVENT* | |

(Based on average runner in T-shirt and shorts)
(Adapted from ACSM Position Stand, 1985)

of a morning event or race, it can be assumed that the risk will be high before the end of the race or competition. Light loose-fitting clothing is recommended for any sport where practice or conditioning is done in the warm season.

Several factors affect the likelihood of developing heat illness (Table 16C-2). Acclimatization to heat and/or humidity requires continuous or repeated exposure to the new environmental conditions. If acclimatization is desired before an athletic event, practice should take place during the acclimatization period. Improvement in heat tolerance occurs as a result of increased sweating and decreased blood flow to the skin. Increased sweating lowers the skin temperature so that there is less vasodilation in the skin and better cooling of blood flowing through the skin.

During the first four to seven days of acclimatization, the plasma volume expands, the heart rate increases, and stroke volume is reduced. Gradually, heart rate decreases and stroke volume approaches normal. Cardiac output and arterial blood pressure remain stable during this time. Sweat losses can increase by 100% above normal during acclimatization so it is very important to replace fluid and electrolyte losses during this period.

### Clinical Condition

Heat illness covers a spectrum from heat cramps, nausea, headache, and other minor symptoms to heat exhaustion or heat stroke. Lines of division between these conditions are not always clear during exertional heat illness.

Heat illness occurs when the body is unable to dissipate heat generated or absorbed. It occurs most often where the temperature approaches or exceeds normal core temperature and where the humidity is high enough to decrease or prevent evaporative cooling. The sports most often linked with heat illness are distance running, football, and wrestling (Table 16C-3).

Recognition of heat illness, especially in its severe forms, can be life-saving. Too often, the absence of sweating is used to distinguish between heat exhaustion and heat stroke. However, absence of sweating is rare in athletes participating in highly exertional activities. Unfortunately, severe, life-

**Table 16C-2. Factors Affecting Response to Exercise in the Heat**

*DIET*
1. High protein requires increased $H_2O$ and therefore can predispose to heat illness.
2. Metabolism of protein generates more heat than that of either fat or carbohydrates — predisposes to heat illness.

*DRUGS*
1. Amphetamines increase core body temperature faster than normal.
2. Diuretics precipitate water loss and heat illness.

*ILLNESS*
1. Increases resting pulse, therefore decreases the ability to produce adequate cardiovascular response to increase temperature.

*OBESITY*
1. Increases insulation — prevents efficient cooling.

*STATE OF HYDRATION*
1. 2%-3% dehydration →rectal temperature of approximately 101°F.
2. 6% dehydration →rectal temperature 105-106°F.
3. Dehydration also predisposes to hypothermia in cold weather.

*ACCLIMATIZATION*
1. Requires 10-15 days for complete acclimatization to increase heat or humidity.
2. Insufficient acclimatization increases likelihood of heat illness.

*LEVEL OF TRAINING*
1. Highly trained athlete is more heat tolerant than less trained athlete.
2. Acclimatizes faster.
3. Sweats sooner.

*EXERCISE DURATION AND INTENSITY*
1. Faster athletes generate more metabolic heat but are exposed to environmental stress for less time. Higher risk for *heat* illness.
2. Slower athletes may dissipate more heat than is generated. Higher risk for hypothermia.

*WBGT INDEX*
1. The closer to normal body temperature the WBGT, the higher the risk of hyperthermia.
2. High WBGT index diminishes the body's ability to lose heat by radiation and convection.

*EXTREMES OF AGE*
1. Young have a greater surface area to mass ratio and produce less sweat.
2. Young generate more metabolic heat and are less efficient in transferring heat energy to the skin.
3. Children acclimatize more slowly.
4. Elders sweat less, have lower total body water and decreasing aerobic capacity.

*PREVIOUS HEAT STROKE*
1. Definite predisposition to recurrence of hyperthermia.
2. Uncertain whether genetically predisposed or predisposed as a result of damage to thermoregulatory system.

(Adapted from Cummings, 1983; Beyer, 1984; Mangi, 1981; Smith, G., 1981; O'Donnell, 1980; Johnson, 1982; Sutton, Bar-Or, 1980; N. Smith, 1983)

threatening heat stroke is not as rare. Heat production can outstrip body heat dissipating abilities (Tables 16C-4 and 5).

The best treatment for heat illness is, of course, prevention. Table 16C-6 outlines prevention measures which supplement the ACSM Position Paper guidelines for event and practice scheduling.

## Malignant Hyperthermia

Malignant hyperthermia is a variably expressed inherited condition transmitted by a single autosomal dominant gene affecting 50% of offspring. It has been known and feared as a complication of anesthesia for many years. Exercise and increased physical stress recently have been implicated as causes of malignant hyperthermia (Faust, 1985).

Stanec and Steffano (1984) have promising results from their study of the use of plasma cyclic-AMP concentrations during peak exercise as a predictor of malignant hyperthermia in susceptible individuals. A family history of malignant hyperthermia in response to anesthesia or stress is extremely important when screening athletes who may be at risk.

The introduction of Dantrolene (Faust, 1985),

**Table 16C-3. Sports Activities with High Risk for Heat Illness**

1. RUNNING
   a. Fun runs (usually shorts) attract many marginally fit, obese, and poorly acclimatized persons.
   b. Marathon — highly trained athletes generate increased metabolic heat and, in attempting to improve times, may not rehydrate adequately during the race.
2. FOOTBALL
   a. Many players arrive at the first practice unfit and overweight.
   b. Full pads and uniforms lessen the ability to dissipate heat.
3. WRESTLING
   a. Attempts to "make weight" contribute to dehydration.
      (1) fluid restriction
      (2) wearing of plastic sweat suits during exercise
      (3) starvation leads to use of body proteins for calories necessitating increased water use for metabolism

**Table 16C-4. High Risk Activities**

*HEAT CRAMPS*
1. 60% in gastrocs, 30% in thigh.
2. Painful cramps associated with fluid depletion and elevated core temperature.

*HEAT SYNCOPE*
1. Postural hypotension secondary lower extremity pooling.
2. Typically seen at the end of a fun run or marathon.

*HEAT EXHAUSTION*
1. Altered level of consciousness.
2. Elevated core temperature > 102°F.
3. Postural or supine hypotension.

*HEAT STROKE*
1. Confusion, delirium, coma.
2. Core temperature > 102°F and as high as 108°F (e.g., Salazar, Boston Marathon).
3. Hypotension.
4. Decreased urine output.

(Adapted from Murphy, 1984; Johnson, 1982; O'Donnell, 1980; Smith, G., 1981; Mangi, 1981)

**Table 16C-5. Factors Affecting Recovery From Heat Illness**

*RECOVERY*
1. Adequacy of rehydration.
2. Renal function prior to heat illness.
3. Presence/absence of rhabdomyolysis (1/3 of cases develop renal failure)
4. Pre-event health/fitness.
5. Development of disseminated intravascular coagulation.

*SEQUELLAE*
1. 10% of patients with heat stroke develop renal failure.
2. Disseminated intravascular coagulation is common.
3. Cerebellar dysfunction.
4. Ischemic damage secondary to decreased blood volume.

(Adapted from Cummings, 1983; Mangi, 1981; O'Donnell, 1980)

**Table 16C-6. Measures to Prevent Heat Illness**

1. Adequacy of rehydration.
2. Renal function prior to heat illness.
3. Presence/absence of rhabdomyolysis — 1/3 of cases develop renal failure.
4. Pre-event health/fitness.
5. Development of disseminated intravascular coagulation.

---

a drug that is effective in reversing the hypermetabolic process of malignant hyperthermia, has greatly reduced the mortality from this condition.

## Cold Injury/Hypothermia

Man is basically a tropical animal and has few significant adaptive capabilities to cold. Adaptive behaviors related to intelligence are more effective in increasing survival ability in a cold environment (clothing, shelter, artificial heating). Man must carry his tropical microclimate with him to survive in the cold. However, extreme cold requires education in methods for preserving body heat and for protecting skin and the extremities.

Skin, the thermoregulatory organ, is *always* losing heat. Adaptation to cold requires *losing less heat*. Heat is lost through conduction, convection, radiation, and evaporation. The body generates heat by *shivering* and controls heat loss by *vasomotor adjustment*. Individuals who exercise sweat and consequently lose heat even in a cold environment (Table 16C-7).

- *Conduction* heat loss occurs when the skin comes into contact with something cold and heat is transferred to the cold object. This is usually insignificant except where there is cold water immersion or prolonged contact with snow or ice.
- *Convection* occurs when heat is transferred from the skin by movement of air and there is actually a continual conductive heat loss. Air contacts the skin, is warmed, then moves away.
- *Radiation* from the body causes the loss of as

Table 16C-7. Heat Loss and Heat Gain

| | HEAT LOSS |
|---|---|
| Conduction | Water conducts heat away from the body 25-30 times faster than air. |
| Convection | Losses depend on running speed and wind speed. |
| Radiation | 65% of heat produced by the body is lost by infrared radiation of heat. |
| Evaporation | 1. 20% of all heat loss in humans.<br>2. Dependent upon humidity.<br>3. 1/3 from lungs.<br>4. 2/3 from skin.<br>5. Wet clothing increases evaporation heat loss and decreases insulation.<br>6. Continues to occur even in extreme cold. |

| | HEAT GAIN |
|---|---|
| Shivering | 1. Increases heat production by as much as 5 times resting value.<br>2. Capable of compensating for a change of 25°C in ambient temperature (Matz 1986). |
| Vasomotor Adjustments | Compensates for only 4°C change in environmental temperatures at most. |

much as 65% of the heat produced by the body (Bang, 1984) — even more if the skin is completely exposed. Much of the radiant heat loss comes from the highly vascular and usually uncovered head and neck.

- *Evaporation* causes heat loss of 0.58 kilocalories per ml of water. Since adults produce approximately one liter of sweat every six hours, this accounts for a loss of 580 kilocalories of heat every six hours. Twenty percent of all heat loss in resting humans occurs by evaporation (Bang, 1984). Of this, 33% is lost through the lungs and 33% through the skin. Wet clothing increases evaporative heat loss and decreases insulation, producing even greater heat loss.
- *Shivering* is the essential ingredient of cold adaptation. It can increase heat production to five times resting levels. Shivering can increase heat loss as well, but is capable of compensating for a change of about 25°C ambient temperature (Matz, 1986).
- *Vasomotor Adjustments* alone can compensate for an environmental temperature change of only 4°C at most. However, repeated exposure of the hands to cold temperature causes a local adaptation to cold, an increase in blood flow to the hands, providing greater dexterity for the performance of work in cold environments (LeBlanc, 1975).
- *Sweating* continues even in extremely cold environments; it may be decreased in extreme cold but does not disappear. There is also a loss of heat and moisture from the lungs. Although sweat losses are decreased in extreme cold, they do not disappear.

### Clinical Condition

Hypothermia can be either acute or chronic but in either case, core body temperature drops to at least 35°C (95°F). Acute hypothermia is most frequently encountered in accidental exposures to cold such as immersion. It also can be a result of athletic activity with excessive sweating in a cool or cold environment.

Accidental immersion in cold water can cause death by three different mechanisms:

- Death by asphyxiation. The *gasp reflex*, triggered when the face is immersed in cold water, causes sudden aspiration of water and severe laryngospasm.
- Arrhythmic death. The *dive reflex*, triggered by cold water coming into contact with the face, is associated with severe bradycardia and apnea.
- Death from hypothermia. Severe conductive heat losses from the skin to cold water result in rapid cooling of the body core whose temperature declines at a rate that is linearly related to the temperature of the water (e.g., the lower the

water temperature, the more rapid the body heat loss). *Cooling occurs more rapidly with active swimming.*

Recovery from cold water immersion is determined by: 1) age — the younger the better the chances of recovery; 2) duration of immersion; 3) temperature of the water — the colder the better, if removed in time for resuscitation; 4) quality of resuscitation efforts; 5) quality of water, and 6) presence of predisposing risk factors (Table 16C-8).

Acute hypothermia is also seen in alpine climbers and trekkers. Runners in distance events who maintain a slow pace are at risk because evaporative and radiant heat loss may outstrip heat production. Dehydration from inadequate fluid replacement inhibits normal hypothermic temperature regulation. Sports activities associated with hypothermia are listed in Table 16C-9.

Chronic hypothermia can occur in athletes exposed to cold temperatures on successive days who have not opportunity to recover normal core temperature. This is especially true of individuals taking multiple day kayak, canoe, or rafting trips where repeated cold water immersion is the rule, not the exception. In these cases, shivering may decrease or even cease over time and allow even more core cooling. This type of exposure also occurs in climbers and trekkers at high altitude (see Table 16C-10).

*Prevention* — Hypothermia is preventable by means of intelligent planning and sensible reaction to unexpected occurrences. Preventive measures are listed in Table 16C-11.

*Signs and Symptoms* — Clinical signs and symptoms of hypothermia are listed in order of their occurrence in Table 16C-12. Severe hypothermia, requiring sophisticated resuscitation and rewarming techniques, occurs at a core temperature of 33°C (91.4°F) or less. It may not be possible to obtain a rectal temperature in the field so that relying on clinical symptoms is necessary. In this event, anyone displaying im-

---

**Table 16C-8. Predisposing Contributions to Hypothermia**

*ELDERLY*
decreased perception of cold
decreased function of ANS (decrease in shivering, decrease in peripheral blood flow, decreases in vasomotor tone)
decreased BMR
decreased body water

*DRUGS*
anesthetics and narcotics
phenothiazines
barbiturates
benzodiazipines
ethanol
reserpine

*METABOLIC*
hypothyroidism
hypopituitarism
hypoadrenalism
protein — calorie malnutrition (e.g., anorexia nervosa)
diabetic ketoacidosis
hypoglycemia

*IMPAIRED THERMOREGULATION*
10 CNS pathology (CVA, hemorrhage, trauma, Wernickes encephalopathy, poliomyelitis, sarcoidosis, cord transection, seizure, spontaneous periodic hypothermia, sepsis)
systemic diseases influencing the hypothalamus (uremia, hepatic failure, CO poisoning)

*INCREASED HEAT LOSS*
dermal dysfunction (exfoliative conditions or burns)
Paget's disease
arteriovenous shunts

(Adapted from Matz, 1986; Dembert, 1982; Reed, 1984)

---

**Table 16C-9. Sports Activities Predisposing to Hypothermia**

1. Alpine climbing and trekking.
2. Cold water swimming or diving.
3. Cold water/cold weather kayaking, canoeing, or rafting.
4. Cold weather running with inadequate insulation (i.e., no insulation or wet clothing).
5. Distance running at a slow pace (e.g., over 5 hour marathoners).
6. Spelunking.
7. Cross country skiing.

---

**Table 16C-10. Predisposing Factors to Hypothermia in Athletes**

1. Immersion in water 21 degrees Celsius (70 degrees Fahrenheit) or less for more than 15-20 minutes.
2. Extremes of age.
3. Serious injuries and shock.
4. Alcohol and drug use.
5. Lack of protective insulation, often from wet clothing.
6. Leanness.
7. Wind chill.
8. Use of ice or snow to relieve thirst.
9. Immobilization due to injury, drugs, getting lost.

**Table 16C-11. Prevention of Hypothermia**

1. Be *prepared* for inclement weather.
2. Train properly prior to event.
3. Stay *dry* and avoid sweating and overexertion in cold environments.
4. Cover head, neck, hands, and feet as well as trunk (heat loss from uncovered head can be as much as *50%* of the body's total heat production).
5. If lost at altitude or cold weather, make camp and *stay* there. *Protect self* from wind, moisture, and ground temperature/damp.
6. Do not swim alone in cold weather.
7. Do not run alone in cold weather.
8. Maintain adequate nutrition.
9. Inform someone of plans and destination prior to leaving for trip or workout in cold weather.

(Adapted from Matz, 1986; Bang, 1984; Dembert, 1982)

pairment of mental capacity should be treated as a severely hypothermic individual. Pronouncement of death should be withheld until core temperature is normal and resuscitation efforts have failed (Bang, 1984).

*Treatment* — Treatment of hypothermia has been outlined in Appendix 16C-1.

## Frostbite

Table 16C-13 lists factors which predispose individual to frostbite. Frostbite injury is categorized from first degree through the fourth. The depth of injury corresponds to in burns of the same degree. These are listed in Table 16C-14. The risk of frostbite rises with trauma — damaged tissue freezes readily. This victim may be immobilized by pain and unable to exercise to produce heat. Both clinical shock and emotional shock hasten frostbite (Steele, 1989).

Christenson and Stewart (1984) describe a rewarming procedure adapted from the U.S. Army (see Appendix 16C-2) that should be undertaken only when there is certainty that refreezing is not a possibility. During and after rewarming, the affected parts must be handled very gently. Persons with frostbite of the lower extremities must *not* be allowed to ambulate. All frostbite victims should

**Table 16C-12. Clinical Signs of Hypothermia**

| °F | °C | Signs and Symptoms | |
|---|---|---|---|
| Core Temp | | | |
| 98.6 | 37 | None | |
| 96.8 | 36 | Sensation of cold, confusion, stumbling, disorientation | |
| 95 | 35 | Skin cold to touch, slurred speech, decreased coordination, introversion | |
| | 34 | Amnesia | |
| Hypothermia | | | |
| 91.4 | 33 | Cardiac arrhythmias esp. atrial fibrillation, bradycardia *unresponsive to atropine* | Shivering |
| | 32 | Cyanosis, respiratory alkalosis, muscular rigidity; BP difficult to obtain, failure to protect oneself | |
| | 31 | Pupils dilated, paradoxical undressing | |
| 86 | 30 | Hypoventilation (3-4 min), lactic acidosis | |
| | 29 | Decreased renal blood flow, cold diuresis, DTR's absent | |
| | 28 | Ventricular fibrillation if hearing is irritated | Semiconscious |
| 80.6 | 27 | Clinically dead appearance, flaccid, pupils fixed and dilated | |
| | 26 | | |
| | 25 | Decrease BP, spontaneous V-fib | |
| | 24 | | Unconscious |
| | 23 | Apnea | |
| | 22 | | |
| | 21 | Cardiac standstill | |
| | 18 | Lowest accidental hypothermia associated with survival | |

(Adapted from Dembert, 1982; Matz, 1986; Bang, 1984)

#### Table 16C-13. Predisposing Factors to Frostbite

1. Poor nutritional status — decreased cellular metabolic reserves
2. Amount of exposed tissue — the larger the surface exposed — the greater the thermal loss
3. Temperature, wind humidity
4. Wet clothing or skin
5. Previous cold injury
6. Constricting clothing
7. Trauma, shock, blood loss
8. Drugs impairing peripheral circulation, mental capacity, or altering thermal reflex arcs (e.g., vasodilation in the face of extreme cold)
9. High altitude and decreased ambient oxygen tension
10. Smoking
11. Race — Black

be hospitalized for one to two days to determine the depth of injury — which may not be obvious at first.

Treatment and rewarming regimens can be found in Appendices 16C-1 to 4. Significant sequellae (Table 16C-15) can be slow to evolve in frostbite.

## Drowning — Freshwater and Salt

### Epidemiology

Drowning is the second leading cause of accidental death up to age 44 (Smith, 1984). Some 6,000-7,000 people drown each year and 60%-70% can't swim nor did they intend to enter the water in the first place (Smith, 1980). Males account for 80% of deaths; it may be that women drown less often because they float naturally and tend to conserve body heat better. Cold water is an important factor in the progress of drowning. Fifty three percent of those who drown are under the age of 25 years and alcohol and other drugs are a major factor in 67% (PHS, 1981).

### Drowning Pathophysiology

The major insult and most devastating aspect of drowning is hypoxemia to the tissues. The sequence of events in drowning is panic, violent struggle, automatic swimming movements, apnea and breath holding, swallowing water, vomiting, aspiration, and convulsion, coma, and death.

#### Table 16C-14. Frostbite

*Degrees of Injury*

1°  hyperemia, edema
    rewarming → mottling, cyanosis, pain, intense pruritus or burning sensation
    superficial desquamation after 5-10 days

2°  hyperemia, vesicle formation
    rewarming — deep red color, hot and dry to touch; after two to three hours swelling begins; after 6-12 hours → blebs with clear fluid

3°  necrosis of skin and underlying tissue, violaceous or hemorrhagic bullae
    rewarming → after six days entire region is edematous; early anesthesia followed in one to two weeks by severe aching or throbbing

4°  complete necrosis and tissue loss — even bone
    rewarming →deep red, cyanotic or mottled, anesthesia, swelling of proximal area after 6-12 hours. Injured area does *not* swell.
    dry gangrene and mummification rapidly develop

(Christenson and Stewart, 1984)

#### Table 16C-15. Sequellae of Frostbite

Small muscle atrophy
Scarring with possible stricture formation
Cold sensitivity
Phantom pain
Growth plate abnormalities
Arthritic changes
Tissue loss

(Christenson and Stewart, 1984)

## Drowning Classification

### Dry Drowning

Dry drowning accounts for only 10% of drowning (Podolsky, 1981). Laryngospasm continues until breathing stops so that no water is aspirated into the lungs. If these individuals are rescued in time, they recover with few pulmonary problems.

### Wet Drowning

Wet drowning accounts for most cases of aspiration of water and vomitus that causes extensive pulmonary and alveolar damage and which results in greater hypoxia and in extensive tissue and brain damage.

- *Freshwater* — The aspiration of freshwater into the lungs inactivates pulmonary surfactant causing alveolar instability and collapse. Hypertonic water in alveoli cross into the blood creating a hyponatremic environment leading to cellular and cerebral edema (Figure 16C-2a).
- *Salt Water* — The aspiration of 3.5% hypertonic saline solution of salt water into the lungs causes an increased volume of fluids in the alveoli drawing fluid from blood and resulting in pulmonary edema and hypernatremia (Figure 16C-2b).

### Secondary Drowning

This term refers to the fulminating, pulmonary edema that occurs after successful initial resuscitation and apparent clinical improvement (Poldosky, 1981). It also can be caused by the initial therapy (oxygen).

### Immersion Syndrome

This occurs when an individual is suddenly immersed in cold water causing hyperventilation followed by loss of consciousness and creating a drowning situation (also see hyperventilation section).

### Hyperventilation Syndrome

Hyperventilation is practiced by swimmers trying to swim underwater as far as possible (breath-holding)(Craig, 1976). Physiologically, the level of $pCO_2$ in the lungs is the major stimulus to breathe. Hyperventilation decreases or "blows off" $pCO_2$ while not significantly increasing $pO_2$. In addition, it causes vasoconstriction of the cerebral blood flow. After hyperventilation and during breath holding, a valsalva maneuver is performed causing a decrease in venus return and cardiac output. If exercise is added to this equation, the athlete increases oxygen utilization. The combination of hyperventilation, breath holding, and exercise predisposes an athlete to severe hypoxemia and artificial hypercapnia, decreasing cerebral blood flow and cardiac output and resulting in syncope with no prodromal symptoms.

### Typical Drowning Situations (Smith, 1984)

Common and very typical factors in most drownings are *cold water*, *alcohol consumption*, and *nonswimmers*. In near drowning situations, the colder the water, the younger the patient, the quicker CPR is started, and the shorter the time of submission, the better the prognosis. The following situations are typical:

- *Immediate Disappearance* — The individual usually has been diving into the water from a

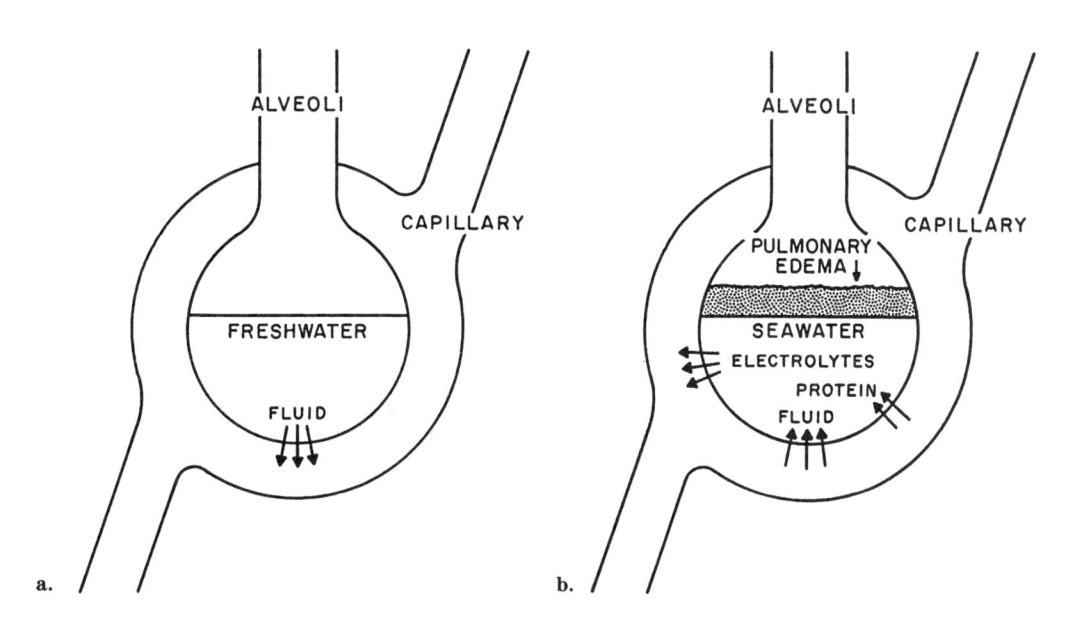

**Fig. 16C-2a and 2b.** Effects of Near Drowning on Lungs at Alveolar Level

height and may have struck his head resulting in injury or unconsciousness.
- *Hyperventilation Syndrome* — Discussed previously.
- *Distressed Non-Swimmer* — Represents the most frequent drowning situation.
  a. The non-swimmer is on the surface for 20-60 sec before sinking (children sink more rapidly).
  b. Typical signs include the victim doing a vertical breaststroke with hands out of the water, the head is thrown back and the mouth is open but no vocalization takes place.
- *Sudden Disappearance* — The victim is usually a swimmer and the situation often is a result of fatigue or cold. The best advice for a tired or cold swimmer is to float on his/her back.
- *Hyperthermia-Induced Debility* — This situation occurs after approximately 15 minutes of exposure to cold water but the victim can conserve body heat and lessen the effect by minimizing movement, assuming the individual has some form of a personal floatation device (PFD).

### Treatment

- CPR must be started immediately (in the water if possible) and the Heimlich maneuver should be attempted to evacuate water from the lungs. Some suggest doing the maneuver before the actual start of CPR (Heimlich, 1988).
- Manually clear the airway.
- Administer $O_2$ as high a percentage as possible.
- If there is a respiratory impairment, pass an endotracheal or nasoltracheal tube.
- Pass a nasogastric tube to decompress the stomach and lessen the hazard of aspiration. Also, a decompression will release the check on diafragmatic excursion that may have taken place and help to expand the lungs.
- During and after transport:
  a. maintain ventilation
  b. sodium bicarbonate should be infused
     -one meg/kg — adult
     -two meg/kg — children
  c. positive and expiratory pressure (PEEP) should be administered if more than 60% oxygen is required to maintain a $PAO_2$ at 60 ml of Hg
  d. monitor vital signs, pupillary reflex, and urinary output frequently
  e. get a chest x-ray and laboratory tests including serum electrolyte, CBC, and urinalysis.

An x-ray of the neck or other areas that may have been injured should be obtained if suggested by the history.

### Delayed Death (Secondary Drowning)

There are two types of delayed death secondary to drowning: those who sustain severe pulmonary injury and never regain autonomic control, and those whose vital signs normalize but who succumb to secondary damage of $O_2$ toxicity or the pressures required to treat the original hypoxemia (Podolsky, 1981).

## Underwater Sports Concerns

### Intrinsic Factors — Hyperventilation Syndrome

Voluntary HV for the purpose of breath holding in swimming underwater is a major concern for the water sport athlete. The HV syndrome was discussed in the previous section.

### Extrinsic Factors — Barotrauma

The major extrinsic concern of underwater sport athletes is injury secondary to increased atmospheric pressure created by the depth of water. Barotrauma can occur during descent and ascent.

- *Barotrauma of Descent "Squeeze Syndromes"* — These are due to compression of the body's gas filled spaces as depth and ambient atmospheric pressure are increased (Table 16C-16). Ears and paranasal sinuses are the organs most commonly affected by barotrauma of descent.
  a. *Ear Canal Squeeze* — This injury is usually secondary to exostosis, ear infection, a tight fitting wet hood, or ear plugs and is the result of lack of equilibration of the external auditory canal with the ambient atmosphere. It causes erythema, petechiae, and blebs in the canal wall. It is found most prominently in springboard divers or swimmers diving under the surface. The athlete needs to go only 6-8 feet under the surface of the water for this phenomenon to take place.

     *Treatment* — Keep the external auditory canal dry, use analgesics as needed, and prescribe antibiotics if a secondary infection develops.

Table 16C-16. Pressure-Volume Relationships According to Boyle's Law

|  | Depth (fsw) | Gauge pressure (atmos) | Absolute pressure (atmos) | Gas volume (%) | Bubble-diameter (%) |
|---|---|---|---|---|---|
| air | 0 | 0 | 1 | 100 | 100 |
| sea water | 33 | 1 | 2 | 50 | 79 |
|  | 66 | 0 | 3 | 33 | 69 |
|  | 99 | 3 | 4 | 25 | 63 |
|  | 132 | 4 | 5 | 20 | 58 |
|  | 165 | 5 | 6 | 17 | 54 |

b. *Middle Ear Squeeze (Barotitis media)* — This is the most common of the squeeze syndromes and is secondary to occlusion and/or dysfunction of the eustachian tube (Figure 16C-3). The symptoms have been graded in severity from 0 (symptoms present but no signs) to 5 (ruptured tympanic membrane) (Kizer, 1984). Grades 2 or 3 involving erythema or hemorrhage of the tympanic membrane are seen most often.

*Treatment* — Discontinuation of diving for 7-10 days and use of a decongestant as recommended. No antibiotics are needed unless the tympanic membrane has ruptured (stage 5 cases).

c. *Inner Ear Barotrauma* — This is most often the result of a forceful valsalva maneuver attempted to clear the ears and it usually results in the rupture of the round window at the junction of the middle and inner ear. Unfortunately, a perilymph fistula can result which is a true medical emergency. The symptoms of inner ear barotrauma are a classic triad (sensorineural hearing loss, roaring tinnitus, and vertigo). The major symptom seen most often in practice is vertigo. This injury is common in diving sports and also in such sports as weightlifting.

*Signs* — The patient is usually pale and diaphoretic and has nystagmus but this may be absent if both labyrinths are injured.

*Treatment* — Prompt surgical repair is necessary. It is not advisable under most circumstances to treat by decompression.

- *Perinasal Sinuses* (Barosinusitis) — The most common sinuses effected are the maxillary and frontal sinuses.

*Symptoms* — Pain, epistaxis, and a full feel-

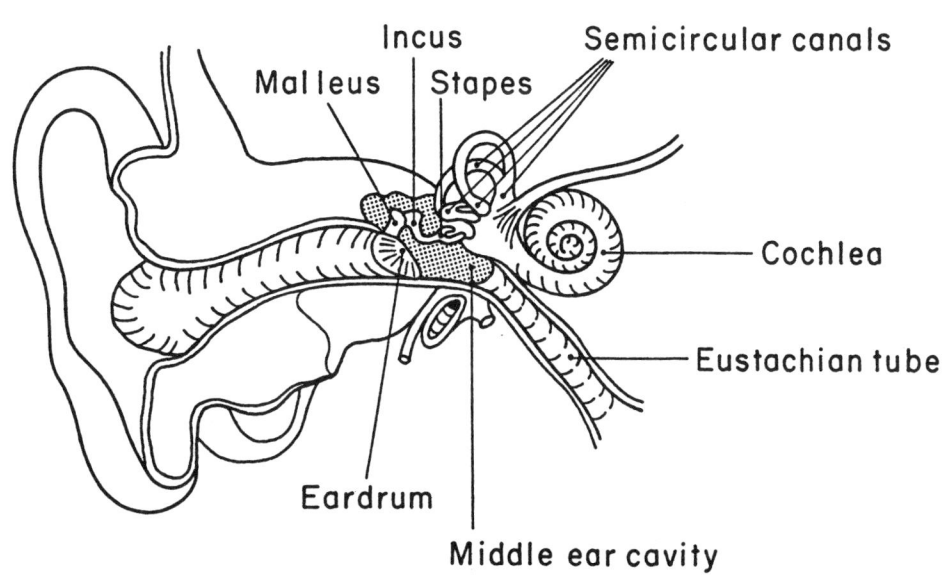

Fig. 16C-3. External Ear

ing in the injured sinus are the usual symptoms. Occasionally, pain in the upper teeth as a result of maxillary sinusitis is present.

*Signs* — Tenderness over the affected sinus, blood in the nose, mouth, or pharynx. Half of those with barosinusitis have concomitant barotititis media. X-rays are helpful and can show either cloudiness or air fluid levels present in the affected sinuses.

*Treatment* — Decongestants and antibiotics if there is purulent drainage, fever, or a possibility of secondary infections.

Other organs that are occasionally affected include the lungs, teeth (especially if a pocket of air has remained following any dental work), and the face — usually the result of failure to exhale into the mask through the nose.

**Barotrauma of Ascent**

The problem with barotrauma of ascent is that gases in the body's airfilled spaces expand (see Table 16C-16). Normally these are vented off slowly without producing signs or symptoms. However, abnormal elimination can be blocked or prevented by some medical conditions (Table 16C-17). Commonly affected organs include:

- *Ears* — Middle ear barotrauma can occur on ascent, especially when divers use short acting decongestants that wear off during a dive. In addition, a condition known as alternobaric vertigo takes place when an individual has unequal pressure between the two inner ears, creating vertigo during ascent.
- *Gastrointestinal* (aerogastralgia) — "Gas in the gut" is the result of expansion of interluminal bowel gas and can cause distension if not naturally eliminated.
- *Pulmonary Overpressurization* — Can occur during ascent and result in the "burst lung" syndrome leading to alveolar rupture. Other forms of this syndrome include pneumomediastinum (the most common), subcutaneous emphysema, pneumoperitoneum, pneumothorax, and air emboli to the brain or abdominal viscera (emboli to the viscera is the commonest cause of abdominal free air found in man, not related to ruptured viscus) (Kizer, 1984).

*Symptoms* of the pulmonary overpressurization syndrome include hoarseness, substernal chest pain, a feeling of throat fullness, cough, dyspnea, and dysphagia.

*Signs* — Often subcutaneous air is in the neck or superclavicular fossa area. Upright x-rays have been helpful in making the diagnosis.

*Treatment* — This is a mostly benign condition that can be treated with oxygen if dyspnea is present and bedrest with close follow-up.

*Prevention* — Divers and athletes should be instructed not to hold their breath upon descending. Diving is definitely contraindicated with a history of spontaneous pneumothorax (Table 16C-17).

*Complications* — Air embolism is a major cause of death in underwater sports (Strauss, 1984). Pathophysiologically — air from a rupture alveoli → entrance into the pulmonary venous circulation → thru the left heart → into the systemic circulation → embolism. Symptoms of an air embolism appear within the first few minutes after surfacing. The brain is the organ most often affected and the clinical picture depends upon where the embolism has taken place. Any localizing neurologic sign can be present. There usually is altered mental status ranging from loss of consciousness to simple personality changes.

*Complications* — Hemoptysis once thought to be a pathopneumonic sign of air embolism is rarer than once thought (Kizer, 1984). Treatment involves stabilizing the patient and then referral to a decompression chamber. Radiographic imaging techniques such as CT scans and MRI have been helpful.

---

**Table 16C-17. Medical Conditions That Contraindicate Scuba Diving**

Acute or chronic ear infection
Tympanic membrane perforation
Glaucoma (unless under satisfactory control)
Asthma that is active or under suboptimal control
Any chronic pulmonary disease (including tuberculosis)
History of spontaneous pneumothorax
History of thoracotomy for any reason
Any significant cardiac or peripheral vascular disease
Uncontrolled hypertension
Any symptomatic acute or chronic gastrointestinal disease
Diabetes mellitus requiring insulin therapy (risk of hypoglycemic reaction)
Any organic central nervous system disease, a history of head injury with sequelae, or a history of syncope, epilepsy, or convulsion
Neuropsychiatric disturbances that might compromise safety in the diving environment
Pregnancy at any stage

### Nitrogen Necrosis

Nitrogen necrosis is caused by breathing air under high pressure which pushes nitrogen into the blood. This is referred to as rapture of the deep and generally results in impaired judgment, sometimes loss of consciousness, and occasionally panic. It does not usually happen in less than 100 feet of water.

### Decompression Sickness "Bends"

Decompression sickness is simply a multisystem disorder caused by a too rapid ascent. Nitrogen is liberated from solution in the blood into gas bubbles, which are seen as foreign bodies so that an immune response is activated. There are many types of decompression sickness, depending upon which systems are involved (Table 16C-18). There are two patterns of involvement, *Pattern I* — affecting the cutaneous, lymphatic, and musculoskeletal systems, and *Pattern II* — affecting the neurologic system.

Generally speaking, Pattern I is much more common, with the most frequent presenting symptom (50%-75% of all patients with decompression sickness) being joint pain, usually the upper extremities in divers (shoulders, elbows). Other symptoms include itching skin, scarlatiniform rashes, and neurologic signs such as tingling and numbness of the lower extremity, and an inability to urinate. The brain is usually not affected. More than half of all "bends" patients manifest some neurologic signs (Kizer, 1984).

Table 16C-18. Types of Decompression Sickness and Common Symptoms

| Type | Symptoms |
| --- | --- |
| Cutaneous | Paresthesia |
| Lymphatic | Swelling |
| Musculoskeletal | Joint stiffness and pain |
| Neurologic | Headache, dizziness, seizures |
| Spinal Cord | Lower extremity weakness, bowel and bladder dysfunction |
| Cerebral | Lethargy, confusion, coma |
| Cerebellar | Gait disturbance |
| Inner Ear | Vertigo |
| Peripheral Nerve | Numbness and weakness (handgrip weakness or foot drop) |
| Pulmonary | Cough, shortness of breath |
| Cardiovascular | Chest pain and syncope |
| Visceral | Abdominal distension and pain |

*Important aspects of the history*

- *Timing* — Suspect air embolis if symptoms appear less than 10 minutes after resurfacing; if symptoms appear more than 10 minutes after resurfacing, other etiologies should be suspect.
- *What kind of diving?* — Snorkeling, scuba, surface diving.
- *How many dives and at what intervals?*
- *Where was the patient diving?*
- *Any predisposing factors?* Look at the amount of activity while diving, age, cardiovascular condition of the patient, temperature of the water, and history of application of heat after diving.

*Diagnostic Tests* — A blood pressure cuff can be placed around a painful joint and expanded to 200-300 mg of mercury. If pain decreases and then increased with deflation, decompression sickness is definitely present. Other laboratory tests are of little use.

*Treatment* — The primary treatment of decompression sickness is hyperbaric oxygen therapy. That requires special facilities and transportation is almost always necessary so the following measures should be taken to stabilize the patient:

- Oxygen should be given by mask at a rate of 6-8 liters per minute.
- Fluids should be replaced either orally or by IV.
- Start corticosteroid therapy — 125 mg methylprednisolone along with 4 mg of dexamethasone to combat edema, followed by dexamethasone 4 mg 4 times a day for three days.
- The patient should be transported with the head down in the left lateral position.

### Hazardous Marine Stings/Bites

There are hazardous marine animals, primarily ones that sting, that can cause a great deal of injury to underwater sport divers.

- *Coelenterates (Portuguese man-of-war, thyacoral, hydroids, jelly fish, sea anemones)* — all sting via a nematocyst.

  *Signs and Symptoms* — The victim experiences an immediate stinging, pyrites, and burning or throbbing pain radiating from the trauma site. The stung area generally becomes discolored in a linear pattern, followed by blistering, local edema, and petechial hemorrhages.

*Treatment* — If central systems are involved, management is primarily supportive and depends upon the patient's signs and symptoms (Auerbach, 1989). Treatment of the skin lesions should begin by rinsing the injured area with sea water. Do not use fresh water or abrasion techniques since this encourages further release of toxic substances. Larger tentacles should be removed from the skin with forceps. Inactivate the toxin by soaking the stung area with 5% acetic acid (vinegar) for 30 minutes. An alternative is rubbing alcohol. The next step is to remove remaining nematocysts by shaving them off with a razor blade or piece of wood. Antibiotics are never indicated or used unless there is secondary infection. Tetanus prophylactic should be checked.

- *Echinodermata* (Sea Lilies, brittle stars, sea urchins, star fish, sea cucumbers) — Most envenomations occur when recreational divers step on or handle a sea urchin and it frequently happens when individuals are exploring tide pools.

  *Signs and Symptoms* — Immediate intense burning pain followed by erythremia, edema and deep muscle aches. Systemic symptoms, usually the result of multiple puncture wounds, occur frequently. Secondary infection and skin ulceration also occur frequently.

  *Treatment* — Immerse the part with venom in hot water to tolerance for 30-90 minutes. Next, remove all accessible spines and shave off the rest. Infection is common after such a sting so prophylactic antibiotics like Trimethoprim-sulfamethoxazole or ciprofloxacin should be used.

- *Vertebrates* (Sting rays, scorpion fish, catfish) — These animals generally come into contact with divers as a result of effective camouflage and being stepped on or mishandled. The commonest site of injury are the lower extremities.

  *Signs and Symptoms* — Envenomations cause immediate and intense local pain, edema, and bleeding.

  *Treatment* — The wound or laceration should be irrigated first with cold saline. Explore the wound and remove any fragments. This should be followed by immersion in hot water for 30-90 minutes. Thorough wound exploration and debridement is important.

## Acute Mountain Sickness (AMS) — (Altitude Sickness)

As more and more people seek high altitude for recreational climbing, acute mountain sickness and its more serious associated syndromes naturally have become more prevalent. Presenting signs and symptoms of acute mountain sickness include headache, lassitude, insomnia, nausea, dyspnea, chest tightness, and dizziness (Comp, 1985).

Sutton (1991) has identified several high risk activities for the primary care physicians:

- Skiing — it is common for skiers to spend four to eight hours in flight before reaching their destination. They may then drink alcohol and go to bed later than usual. Their subsequent sleep is restless and coincides with headache and dyspnea.
- Trekking — once again, quick arrival at a high altitude instead of a slow ascent makes tourists in mountain areas vulnerable to high altitude sickness.

### Natural History

AMS usually occurs above 8,000 feet. It is a relatively benign condition and subsides in three or four days. Its severity is greatest when the ascent to higher altitudes is rapid (Hackett, 1976). From 50%-75% of those climbing Mount Rainer get AMS within six to eight hours after reaching the 8,000 ft. altitude.

Of concern are the associated syndromes referred to as high-altitude pulmonary edema (HAPE), high-altitude cerebral edema (HACE), and high-altitude retinal hemorrhage (HARH). The first two syndromes are lifethreatening and are at the severe end of the AMS spectrum.

### Etiology

AMS is believe to be the result of a vascular response to relative hypoxemia in predisposed individuals. Being in good physical condition does not prevent AMS.

### Prophylactic

Slow ascent remains the major method or prevention. Guidelines include staying 24 hours at an intermediate altitude (4000-6000 ft), then minimizing exertion in the first 24-48 hours at higher altitudes (Mountain, 1983).

Some pharmacologic help is available — acetezolamide. 250 mg of acetazolamide (Diamox®) should be taken every eight hours for a period beginning 32 hours before and 48 hours after a climb (Larson, 1982).

### Treatment

Descent as above. Since altitude sickness is usually self-limited and symptoms improve over 24 hours, symptomatic treatment is usually all that is needed. Treatment for high-altitude cerebral edema (HACE) is oxygen at 2 liters/minute, betamethasone 4 mg every six hours. Treatment of high-altitude pulmonary edema (HAPE) again involves the administration of oxygen at 2 liters/minute and the judicious use of diuretics (if the patient isn't already dehydrated).

A summary of manifestations and treatment can be found in Table 16C-19.

## Air Pollution

One of the environmental insults that can affect athletes and sports performance is air pollution, defined as the presence of small amounts of gases and particulates not normally found in ambient air. One term used for air pollution is smog of which there are three types (Raven, 1985).

- Reductive — carbon monoxide (CO), sulfuroxides (SO), particulates (high humidity, high or lower temperature)
- Oxidant/photochemical — carbon monoxide (CO), ozone ($O_3$), nitric oxides ($NO_x$), and peroxyacyl nitrates (PANs)
- Particulates (low humidity; high temperatures)

Smog occurs in urban environments during periods of air stagnation created by thermal inversion (warm air trapped below cool air). All of the following can affect exercise performance.

- *Carbon Monoxide (CO)* — The major effect of CO is to combine with hemoglobin to interfere with tissue oxygenation. Studies suggest that the $VO_2$max levels of healthy males are decreased in inverse proportion to blood levels of COHB in the range from 5%-35% COHB (Vogel, 1972). Even levels less than 5% COHB decrease maximum performance time in exercise testing. Especially important is the fact the exercising recreational athlete with cardiovascular impairment (rehabilitating post-MI, post-CABG patients) appears to be at increased risk for further coronary events if ambient levels of carbon monoxide cause blood COHB to increase.
- *Ozone* — Ozone is the major oxidant in the air that affects man. It causes eye irritation, conjunctivitis, dyspnea, cough, chest tightness in resting people, and certainly has an effect on athletics because ozone is responsible for significant changes in lung function. These changes are directly associated with the level of ventilation and the time of exposure, both of which magnify the initial effect.
- *Sulfur Oxides* — In the sulfur oxides, sulfur dioxide ($SO_2$) is the major problem causing upper airway and bronchial irritation and decreasing

Table 16C-19. Manifestations and Treatment of Altitude Illness*

| Illness | Manifestations | Treatment |
| --- | --- | --- |
| Acute mountain sickness | Headache, excessive fatigue, nausea and/or vomiting, sleep disturbances | Symptomatic therapy (condition usually self-limited) |
|  |  | Acetazolamide (Diamox) or dexamethasone (Decadron, Dexone, Hexadrol) |
| High altitude pulmonary edema | Severe dyspnea, cough (often productive), exhaustion | Descent, oxygen, pressure bag |
|  | Coma and death, if not treated | Acetazolamide or dexamethasone |
| High altitude cerebral edema | Severe headache, ataxia, confusion, hallucinations | Descent mandatory |
|  | Coma and death, if not treated | Dexamethasone |

*The various forms of altitude illness are a continuous spectrum in which no one manifestation dominates, and one form may lead to another. High altitude retinal hemorrhages are frequent above 14,000 ft. Chronic mountain sickness also affects some long-time residents above 12,000 ft.
(From Houston, 1990)

airway resistance, especially in athletes with chronic pulmonary disease (asthmatics).
- *Nitric Oxide* — Nitrogen dioxide is the most prevalent of these compounds with exposure coming mainly from automobile exhaust and cigarette smoke.

**Potentially Hazardous Situations**

- Any urban environment with a high probability of reductive or oxidant pollution.
- Any urban environment that is prone to thermal inversion.
- Any indoor environment where a combustion engine is used (e.g., an ice resurfacing machine on a hockey rink) (CDC, 1984).

**Prevention**

Athletes at greatest risk for being affected by pollution are cardiac and pulmonary patients and they must be encouraged to consider indoor exercise when the outside environment outside becomes hazardous. At present, there is considerable question about whether a human can adapt or acclimatize to urban pollution.

**Recommendations**

- If competition is scheduled where pollutant levels are high, participants should prepare in a nonpolluted environment and minimize their exposure.
- During a smog alert or under other hazardous conditions, replace outdoor with indoor activity whenever possible (this is especially true for athletes at risk).
- Athletes should train in the early morning when pollution is low whenever possible.

## Lightning Injuries

Lightning is responsible for more deaths in the United States than any other natural phenomena. The overall mortality rate in patients with lightning injuries is 38%. The morbidity rate in survivors approaches 70% (Ghezzi, 1989). There are three types of injuries:

- Minor injuries — Patients are conscious but confused. Most common symptoms are muscle pain and paresthesia, but no burns or paralysis. Complete recovery can be expected.
- Moderate Injury — Signs of disorientation are present. Mottled extremities and an absence of peripheral pulses along with first and second degree burns that appear over several hours are common. The tympanic membrane of the ear is often ruptured. These patients may have an incomplete recovery accompanied by chronic sleep problems and coordination difficulties.
- Severe Injury — Patients may present with ventricular fibrillation or systole. Prognosis in this group is uniformly poor unless CPR is immediate. Treatment of these patients should follow the basic advanced life support guidelines. Cervical spine injuries secondary to the initial lightning strike are possible and should be suspected so that excessive movement of the cervical spine is avoided.

**Prevention.** Prevention of lightning injuries should first take into account which athletes are most likely to be hit. Golfers, fishermen, and baseball players often are caught in open areas when there is lightning. Play should be halted and athletes should take cover with the approach of a storm but the shelter should not be under a high standing structure or tree. If suitable shelter cannot be found, individuals should lie prone on the ground until the storm has passed.

## Inhalations

### Smoking

Chronic inhalation of tobacco smoke impairs sports performance. The decrease in physical capacity is especially prevalent at high work loads (FINS, 1980). The use of smokeless tobacco, a habit common among football and baseball players, should be discouraged, not so much for fear of a decrease in physical performance but because of the significant health risk.

### Chlorine

Incidental exposure to chlorine gas fumes secondary to exercise in a pool can cause significant side effects in some athletes. The systems usually affected and their treatments are:

*Pulmonary* — coughing and dyspnea → oxygen
*Cardiovascular* — tachycardia → see above
*Eye* — conjunctivitis → irrigation with water
*Skin* — occasional rashes → soap and water

# REFERENCES

## Section A. Hematology

Alpert, B.S., Gilman, P.A., Strong, W.B., Ellison, M.F., Miller, M.D., McFarlane, J., Hayashidera, T. Hemodynamic and ECG responses to exercise in children with sickle cell anemia. *Am J Dis Child* 135:362-366, 1981.

Barnes, R. Quinine-induced thrombocytopenia in a professional football player. Personal communication, 1990.

Brayne, C.E.G., Calloway, S.P., Thompson, R.J. Blood creatine kinose isoenzyme BB in boxers. *Lancet* 2:1308-1309, 1982.

Buskirk, E.R. Some nutritional considerations in the conditioning of athlete. *Ann. Rev. Nutri* 1:319-350, 1981.

Calabrese, L.H., Kelley, D. AIDS and athletes. *Phys Sportsmed* 17(1):127-132, 1989.

Clement, D.B., Sawchuk, L.L. Iron status and sports performance. *Sports Medicine*, 1(1):65-74, 1984.

Dressendorfer, R.H., Wade, C.E., Amsterdam, E.A. Development of pseudoanemia in marathon runners during a 20-day road race. *JAMA* 246(11):1215-1218, 1981.

Eichner, E.R The anemias of athletics. *Phys Sportsmed* 14(9):123-130, 1986.

Eichner, E.R. Runner's macrocytosis: a clue to footstrike hemolysis. *Am J Med* 78:321-325, 1985.

Falsett, H.L., Burker, E.R., Feld, R.D., Frederick, E.C., Ratering, C. Hematological variations after endurance running with hard and soft-soled running shoes. *Phys Sportsmed* 8:118-127, 1983.

Fitzgerald, L. Exercise and the immune system. *Immunology Today* 9(11):337-339, 1988.

Frederickson, L.A., Puhl, J.L., Runyan, W.S. Effects of training on indices of iron status of young female cross-country runners. *Med Sci Sports Exer* 15:871-876, 1983.

Haymes, E.M. Iron supplementation. In *Encyclopedia of Physical Education, Fitness and Sports*, ed. G.A. Stull, T.K. Cureton, Jr., Brighton Publ., Salt Lake City, 1980, pp 335-344.

Host, H., Vale, J.R. Lung function after mantle field irradiation in Hodgkin's disease. *Cancer* 32:328-332, 1973.

Hunding, A., Jordeal, R., Paulav, P.E. Runner's anemia and iron deficiency. *Acta Med Scan* 209(4):315-318, 1981.

Johnson, C.C. Do athletes need influenza vaccines? *Phys Sportsmed* 18(9):81-84, 1990.

Kielblock, A.J., Manjoo, M., Booyens, J., Katzeff, I.E. Creatine phosphokinase and lactate dehydrogenase levels after ultra-long-distance running. *S Afr Med J* 55:1061-1064, 1979.

LaPorta, M.A., Linde, H.W., Bruce, D.L., Fitzsimmons, E.J. Elevation of creatine phosphokinase in young men after recreational exercise. *JAMA* 239:2685-2686, 1978.

McLain, L.G., Heldrich, F.T. Hemophilia and sports. *Phys Sportsmed* 18(11):73-80, 1990.

Pate, R.R. Sports anemia: a review of the current literature. *Phys Sportsmed* 11(2):115-126, 1983.

Polednak, A.P. College athletics, body size, and cancer mortality. *Cancer* 38:382-387, 1976.

Risser, W.L., Risser, J.M.H. Iron deficiency in adolescents and young athletes. *Phys Sportsmed* 18(12):87-101, 1990.

Roodman, G.D., Reese, E.P. Jr., Cardamone, J.M. Aplastic anemia associated with rubber cement used by a marathon runner. *Arch Intern Med* 140:703, 1980.

Rowland, T.W. Exercise fatigue in adolescents: diagnosis of athlete burnout. *Phys Sportsmed* 14(9):69-77, 1986.

Siegel, A.J., Silverman, L.M., Evans, W.J. Elevated skeletal muscle creatine kinose MB isoenzyme levels in marathon runners. *JAMA* 250(20):2835-2837, 1983.

Sklarek, H.M., Mantovani, R.P., Erens, E. AIDs in a bodybuilder using anabolic steroids. *N. Engl J Med* 311:1701, 1984.

Yoshimura, H. Anemia during physical training (sports anemia). *Nutr. Rev.* 28:251-253, 1970.

Yoshimura, H., Inoue, T., Yamada, T., Shiraki, K. Anemia during hard physical training (sports anemia) and its causal mechanism with special reference to protein nutrition. *World Rev. Nutr. Diet* 35:1-86, 1980.

## Section C. Environmental

Astrand, P.O. *Textbook of Work Physiology: Physiological Basis of Exercise*. 2nd edition, McGraw-Hill, New York, 1977.

Auerbach, P.S. Stings of the deep. *Emer Med*, p. 26-41, June 30, 1989.

Bang, C. "Cold injuries", *Sports Medicine*. Strauss (ed.), W.B. Saunders Co. 1984.

Beyer, C. Heat stress and the young athlete. *Postgrad Med* 76(1):109-112.

Center for Disease Control (CDC): Carbon Monoxide Intoxication Associated with Use of a Resurfacing Machine at an Ice-Skating Rink. *Morbidity and Mortality Weekly Report* 33(4):1984.

Christenson, C., Stewart, C. Frostbites. *Am Fam Prac* 30(6):111-122, 1984.

Comp, R.A., Levine, B.E. Acute high altitude illness. *Continuing Education*, 107-114, 1985.

Craig, A.B. Summary of 58 cases of loss of consciousness during underwater swimming and diving. *Med Sci Sports* 8(3):171-175, 1976.

Cummings, P. Felled by the heat. *Emer Med*, pgs. 94-110, 1983.

Dembert, M.L. Medica problems from cold exposure. *Am Fam Prac* 25(1):99-106, 1982.

Faust, D.K. Malignant hyperthermia. *Alaskan Medicine* 28(1):1-2, 1985.

Ghezz, K.T. Lightning injuries. *Postgrad Med* 85(8):197-208, 1989.

Hackett, P.H., Rennie, D., Levine, H.D. The incidence, importance and prophylaxis of acute mountain sickness. *Lancet* 2:1149-1154, 1976.

Heimlich, H.J., Patrick, E.A. Using the Heimlich maneuver to save near-drowning victims. *Postgrad Med* 84(2):62-73, 1988.

Houston, C.S. Trekking at high altitudes. *Postgrad Med* 88(1):56-71, 1990.

Johnson, L.W. Preventing heat stroke. *American Family Practitioner* 26(1), 1982.

Kizer, K.W. Disorders of the deep. *Emer Med*, 6:18-58, 1984.

Larson, E.B., Roach, R.C., Schoene, R.B., Hornbein, T.F. Acute mountain sickness and acetazolamide. *JAMA* 248(3):328-332, 1982.

LeBlanc, J., Dulat, S., Co'te', J., Girard, B. Autonomic nervous system and adaptation to cold in man. *J of Applied Physiology* 30(181), 1975.

Mangi, R. Runners in the sun. *Emer Med*, pgs. 135-144, 1981.

Matz, R. Hypothermia: mechanisms and countermeasures. *Hospital Practice*, January 30, 1986.

Mountain, R.D. Treatment of acute mountain sickness (letter). *JAMA* 250(11):1392, 1983.

Murphy, R.J. Heat illness in the athlete. *Am J Sports Med* 12(4):258-261, 1984.

O'Donnell, T.F. Management of heat stressed injuries in the athlete. *Orthopaedic Clinics of North American* 11(4):841-855, 1980.

Oelz, O. A case of high-altitude pulmonary edema treated with nifedipine (letter). *JAMA*, 1987.

Podolsky, M.L. Action plan for near drowning. *Phys and Sportsmed* 9(7):45-51, 1981.

Public Health Service, National Institute on Alcohol Abuse and Alcoholism: Alcohol and Health. Washington, D.C., 1981.

Raven, P.B. Environmental factors in injury. Given at 1985 Sports Medicine Congress and Exposition, Indianapolis, 1985.

Reed, G. Emergency: accidental hypothermia. *Topics in Acute Care Medicine*, pgs. 13-42, February 1984.

Smith, D.S. Notes on drowning: the misunderstood, preventable tragedy. *Phys Sportsmed* 12(7):66-73, 1984.

Smith, G.K. Heat injuries in athletics. *Sideline View* 2(10):1-4, 1981.

Smith, N.J. Weight control and heat disorders in youth sports. *J of Adolescent Health Care*, Vol. 3, pgs. 231-236, 1983.

Smith, D.S. Sudden drowning syndrome. *Phys and Sportsmed* 8(6):76-83, 1980.

Stanec, A. and G. Steffano. Cyclic AMP in normal and malignant hyperpyrexia susceptible individuals following exercise. *British J of Anaesthesia* Vol. 56, pgs. 1243-1246, 1984.

Statement on Smoking and Health, International Federation of Sports Medicine (FINS), 1980.

Steele, P. Management of frostbite. *Phys Sportsmed* 17(1):135-144, 1989.

Strauss, R.H. Medical aspects of scuba and breath-hold diving. In *Sports Medicine*, R.H. Strauss, ed., W.B. Saunders, Philadelphia, 1984.

Sutton, J.R. and O. Bar-Or. Thermal illness in fun running Part 1. *Am Heart J* 100(6):778-781, 1980.

Sutton, J.R. Helping your patient avoid high-altitude sickness. *J Resp Dis* 12(2):125-134, 1991.

Vogel, J.A., Gleser, M.A. Effect of carbon monoxide an oxygen transport during exercise. *J Appl Physiol* 32:234-239, 1972.

# Appendix 16C-1.
# Treatment of Hypothermia

**Mild** > 33°C and No Alteration in Mentation

1. Rapid rewarming
2. Seek other causes for hypothermia
3. Document risk factors

**Severe** < 33°C or Altered Mental Status — Field Management

1. Rapid assessment of ABC and level of consciousness (LOC)
2. Look for and *treat* correctable causes of change of LOC (i.e. hypoglycemia, hypoxia, arrhythmia, drug overdose)
3. Consider any confused or unconscious person in a cold environment a victim of hypothermia
4. Prevent further heat loss — remove wet clothing, provide shelter and insulation
5. Begin external rewarming *only* if *volume replacement* therapy is possible
6. Move carefully to prevent sudden jolts which could cause ventricular fibrillation
7. Do not attempt CPR just because BP and pulse are not palpable
8. Avoid intubation if possible since it may cause ventricular fibrillation
9. Do *not* overventillate — respiratory alkalosis can cause ventricular fibrillation
10. Hypotension should be treated with *volume expansion. Not* pressors.
11. Bretylium rather than lidocaine should be used for ventricular arrhythmias — for *prevention* and *treatment*
12. IV — large bore
13. Cardiac monitor
14. $O_2$ not >50% — watch for depression of ventilation

**Severe** < 33°C or Altered Mental Status — Hospital Management

1. Manage in critical care area — ABC's first
2. Handle gently, minimal initial lab (ABG's, CBC, electrolytes, glucose)
3. Large bore IV line and *fluid replacement* — 1st L over 30-60 minutes. Do not delay fluid resuscitation to wait for warm fluids
4. Cardiac monitor
5. Treat the life-threatening causes of LOC — hypoglycemia, narcotic overdose, shock, arrhythmia, airway obstruction
6. Use low-reading thermometer or thermocouple — obtain rectal or esophageal temperature
7. Prevent further heat loss
8. Begin rewarming — acute hypothermia can cause death in one or two hours
9. Assess whether acute or chronic onset
10. Acutely hypothermic patients should be rapidly rewarmed *after* volume expansion is begun
11. CPR and ACLS measures should be continued until the patient is resuscitated or clearly warm and not able to be resuscitated
12. Treatment of chronic hypothermia depends upon precipitating factors and core temperature
    a. If temperature > 33°C — passive, slow rewarming or rapid external rewarming will suffice
    b. Treat underlying disease — its severity significantly affects outcome
    c. If coma present and core temp > 28°C — look for another cause of coma and treat
    d. Spontaneous V-fib does not usually occur above 26°C. It may respond to bretylium.
    e. Correct hypoglycemia and hypoxia; give naloxone; give thiamine (if any suspicion of alcohol intoxication)
    f. If hyperglycemic — remember that insulin is ineffective below 30°C, administering it will cause precipitous drop in blood sugar on rewarming
    g. Cautiously restore volume to avoid overloading the heart and causing pulmonary edema
    h. If stable rhythm is present on monitor and ABG's are acceptable do *not* institute vigorous CPR
    i. Do *not* hyperventillate — correct pH, $pO_2$, $pCO_2$ for temperature
    j. Rewarm appropriately — *after* volume expansion begun

(1) extracorporeal support for patient with unstable or life-threatening arrhythmia
(2) warm hemo — or peritoneal dialysis if patient has taken a dialyzable drug
(3) warm gastric lavage
(4) warmed IV fluids, humidified oxygen
(5) external rewarming — immersion or warmed blanket

k. Acidosis will usually correct itself with rewarming; use bicarb only if pH, corrected for temperature, is less than 7.2
l. Blood glucose levels of 400 or less will usually correct with rewarming

# Appendix 16C-2.
# Rewarming Procedure

**Before Thawing**

- Protect the affected part
- Do not massage or rub area
- Take core temperature with hypothermia thermometer

**Thawing**

- Rewarm extremities in 37.8 to 42.2°C (100-108°F) water
- The only safe method of rewarming is a water bath with thermometer control
- Whirlpool is the best form of water bath
- Leave blisters and blebs intact
- Administer morphine or meperidine (Demerol[R]) for pain
- Do not debride the injury
- All patients with cold injuries of lower extremities should be treated as litter patients

**After Thawing**

- See routine orders
- Do not allow area to refreeze
- Protect area from mechanical damage

(Christenson and Stewart, 1984)

# Appendix 16C-3.
# Routine Frostbite Treatment

### Diet

- High-calorie, high-protein diet
- High intake of fluids
- May have two or three beers per day with meals after initial thaw and rewarming phase

### Vital Sign

- Every two hours for 24 hours, every four hours for 24 hours
- Pulse and capillary fill of involved extremities using Doppler ultrasonography as indicated

### Isolation

- "Reverse" isolation for one week with caps, gowns, and masks

### Smoking

- Smoking prohibited; causes peripheral vasoconstriction that hampers healing

### Activity

- Bathroom and shower privileges
- In hall, to and from tub only
- Whirlpool immediately following shower
- For lower extremity injuries:
  -use of wheelchair or litter
  -protection of feet with stockinette
  -shower in sitting position only (no standing)
- For upper extremity injuries:
  -use of plastic bags over mitts for bowel care, oral hygiene, and shaving
  -whirlpool after shaving
  -assistance with shower, if needed

### Wound Care

- Whirlpool twice a day with poviodone-iodine (Betadine[R]) solution at 35°C (95°F), followed by clear rinse and air dry
- For lower extremity injuries:
  -feet to air under sheet cradle
  -insertion of cotton between digits
  -protection of feet with stockinette
  -elevation of foot of bed
  -Berger's exercises, 20 minutes four times a day, with two sessions just before whirlpool
- For upper extremity injuries:
  -elevation of hands with pillows
  -continuous use of stockinette mitt
  -constant digital exercises while awake
  -use of plastic bags over mitts for bowel care, oral hygiene, and shaving

### Consultation

- Physical therapy for whirlpool and exercise program

### Laboratory Studies

- Complete blood count, urinalysis, electrolytes, blood sugars and smooth muscle antibodies
- Culture of any purulent drainage

### X-Ray Evaluation

- Chest x-ray
- X-ray of all affected extremities

### Medications

- Phenoxybenzamine (Dibenzyline[R]), 10 mg orally, on admission and daily for 10 days
- Tetanus booster as indicated
- Propoxyphene napsylate (Darvocet-N 100[R]), one tablet every 3-4 hours as need for pain
- Diazepam (Valium[R]), 5 mg orally, every six hours as needed for anxiety, for three days
- Temazepam (Restoril[R]), 15 to 30 mg at bedtime as needed for sleep

(Christenson and Stewart, 1984)

# Appendix 16C-4.
# Stay Warm . . . And Alive

Every year you can read accounts of hikers freezing to death in the mountains. They die of hypothermia, the No. 1 killer of outdoor recreationists. Hypothermia is subnormal body temperature, which is caused outdoors by exposure to cold, usually aggravated by wetness, wind and exhaustion. The moment your body begins to lose heat faster than it produces it, your body makes involuntary adjustments to preserve the normal temperature in its vital organs. *If you've begun uncontrolled shivering, you have hypothermia and must act accordingly; seek shelter, insulation and warmth.*

### Your First Line of Defense: Avoid Exposure.

1. *Stay dry.* Wet clothes can lose 90% of their insulation value. Wear synthetics and wool. Avoid cotton and down.
2. *Beware of the wind.* A slight breeze carries heat away from bare skin much faster than still air does.
3. *Understand cold.* Most hypothermia cases develop in air temperatures between 30 and 50 degrees. Don't underestimate your danger.

### Your Second Line of Defense: Terminate Exposure.

1. *Be brave enough* to give up reaching your destination.
2. *Get out of the wind and rain.*
3. *Never ignore shivering.*
4. *Forestall exhaustion.* Make camp while you still have a reserve of energy.
5. *Appoint a foul-weather leader.* Make the best-protected member of your party responsible for calling a halt before the least-protected member becomes exhausted.

### Your Third Line of Defense: Detect Hypothermia.

Watch yourself and others for hypothermia's symptoms:

1. Uncontrollable fits of shivering.
2. Vague, slow, slurred speech.
3. Memory lapses; incoherence.
4. Immobile, fumbling hands.
5. Frequent stumbling; lurching gait.
6. Drowsiness — to sleep is to die.
7. Apparent exhaustion, such as inability to get up after a rest.

### Your Fourth and Last Line of Defense: Treatment.

The victim may deny he's in trouble. Believe the symptoms, not the patient.

1. Get the victim out of the wind and rain.
2. Strip off all wet clothes.
3. If the patient is only mildly impaired:
   a. Give him warm drinks.
   b. Get him into dry clothes and a warm sleeping bag.
4. If the patient is semiconscious or worse:
   a. Try to keep him awake. Do not give him warm drinks.
   b. Put him in a sleeping bag with another person (also stripped). Never leave the victim as long as he is alive. To do so is to kill him — it's that simple.
5. Build a fire to warm the camp.

### Other Notes on Avoiding Hypothermia.

1. Choose rainclothes that are effective against wind-driven rain and cover head, neck, body and legs.
2. Cotton clothing is worse than useless when wet; one stays warmer in cold rain stark naked than bundled up in wet clothes of natural materials.
3. Carry a stormproof tent with a good rain fly and set it up before you need it.
4. Carry trail food rich in calories, and keep nibbling during hypothermia weather.
5. Take a gas stove or a plumber's candle, flammable paste, or other reliable fire starter.
6. Never abandon survival gear under any circumstances.

Excerpted and modified from *The Pacific Crest Trail* published by the Wilderness Press.

# 17

# Radiology of Sports Injuries

Radiology is essential in evaluating most sports injuries. The number of available radiologic diagnostic methods has increased significantly over the past few years, the most recent addition being Magnetic Resonance Imaging (MRI). However, the primary diagnostic tool continues to be the standard plain-film radiograph. Radionuclide scanning, computed x-ray tomography (CT), ultrasound imaging, and MRI are available for further assessment of a specific problem. The appropriate use of each modality in evaluating the injured athlete will be defined.

## PLAIN FILM X-RAY

This is the basic way to assess any musculoskeletal injury. It best defines bony anatomy and the relationship and integrity of bony structures. The equipment is inexpensive, relatively easy to operate, and in some instances, portable. Linear tomography lets us evaluate a specific area of bone, such as an initially occult tibial plateau fracture, by blurring out overlying bony structures. Accurate positioning is always extremely important in producing reliable radiographs because pathology may be easily hidden when inadequate views are obtained (1, 2).

## RADIONUCLIDE SCANNING

Technetium 99m labelled phosphate compounds are used to image bones (3). Following IV injection, these compounds identify radiographically occult fractures by localizing in areas of active bone deposition. Most fractures in young patients, even those not detected by plain x-rays, may be demonstrated by radionuclide bone scanning within 24 hours of the injury. In older, debilitated individuals, visualizing a fracture may not be possible for 72 hours after the initial trauma. Abnormal uptake will persist for a long time, up to two years in some weight bearing bones. Subtle breaks like stress fractures are often difficult to demonstrate on plain x-rays. It may take as long as 7 to 10 days before there is enough bone resorption for the x-ray to detect the pathology. However, radionuclide imaging may readily define these lesions when the patient first has symptoms. The radionuclide scan is a more sensitive examination for demonstrating osteomyelitis earlier than the plain-film x-ray.

## COMPUTED X-RAY TOMOGRAPHY (CT)

Musculoskeletal computed x-ray tomography (CT) is most useful in examining the spine. Subtle or complicated fractures of the vertebral bodies and posterior elements can be accurately portrayed. Three dimensional reformatting of the CT images can be done. These images provide very detailed evaluation of the spinal canal and can demonstrate impingement on neural structures from bone fragments. Herniation of disc material that causes nerve compression also can be seen. In the cranial vault, intracerebral collections of blood (contusions and hematomas), extracerebral pathologic fluid collections (epidural and subdural hemorrhages), and subtle calvarial fractures can be identified. Outside of the central nervous system, the CT scan is used to evaluate areas that are not well delineated on plain films. An example is in diagnosing sternoclavicular dislocation or fracture. Joint spaces usually are poorly evaluated with CT because of its limitation to acquire images only in the axial plane. Magnetic resonance imaging (MRI), on the other hand, is very good in evaluating joint pathology because multiple planes can be imaged. In addition to the axial plain, both the sagittal and coronal aspects of a joint can be evaluated. CT examination, using intravenous contrast material, is used to evaluate the chest and abdominal areas in such injuries as thoracic aortic transections and in blunt trauma (4).

## MAGNETIC RESONANCE IMAGING (MRI)

MRI is the newest of the radiographic modalities. Instead of radiation, a strong magnetic field and radiofrequent energy are used to produce an image. Excellent soft tissue contrast and the ability to directly image in any plane give us a unique opportunity to evaluate joints without using intra-articular contrast injection (5, 6, 7). In the knee, for example, MRI is very sensitive in detecting meniscal tears. The cruciate ligaments can be seen throughout their course and a disruption readily demonstrated. Following plain film x-rays, MRI should be considered the imaging modality of choice for joint pathology if it is available. Cine magnetic resonance imaging (the ability to evaluate a joint in motion) also can be done. This technique may soon become useful in evaluating joint dysfunction in the athlete. Within the central nervous system, magnetic resonance is the preferred imaging method because its unique acquisition of images allows us to visualize the brain and associated structures in a manner not previously available (17).

## ULTRASOUND

Ultrasound uses transmitted and reflected sound waves to visualize soft tissues. Its utility in imaging abdominal organs and in obstetrics is well established. However, its use in the musculoskeletal system is not generally appreciated. Ultrasound can be used in the injured athlete to evaluate soft tissue masses such as hematomas, popliteal cysts, hip effusions, and even rotator cuff tears. Its non invasive nature and lack of ionizing radiation make it a good exam for serial follow up of these lesions (8, 9, 10).

## FRACTURES

A fracture is the result of an overload of stress applied to a bone. The fracture may be microscopic and involve only a part of the cortex as in the stress or "fatigue" fractures, or it can be a complete fracture with frank discontinuity between the two bone segments. The terms "open" or "closed" refer to whether or not a fracture fragment has penetrated the overlying skin. A fracture can further be described a transverse, oblique, or spiral depending on its orientation to the long axis of the bone involved. A comminuted fracture has more than two fragments. Avulsion fractures are fragments of bone that are pulled from the site of a ligamentous attachment. Displacement and angulation of fracture segments are described by giving the relation of the distal segment to that of the proximal.

Fractures in growing bones may involve the epiphyseal plate. The Salter-Harris classification is used to describe these fractures because it has prognostic and therapeutic implications (Figure 17-1 to 4). The most frequent type of fracture in this classification is the Type II injury identified as an epiphyseal fracture which has an associated metaphyseal fragment. The prognosis is generally favorable. The Type V injury, a growth plate crush injury, is the most ominous because it is difficult to see on the x-ray initially. This injury can result in later shortening of the bone because of growth plate dysfunction (1).

Stress fractures, a specific type of bone trauma, were first described in 1855 by Breithaupt, a Prussian military surgeon. These fractures are usually found in unconditioned individuals who begin stressful physical activity like walking (march fractures sustained by new recruits in the military) (11) or in trained athletes who start a new activity without proper conditioning. Clinically, these patients present with pain but no specific single traumatic event in the history. Routine radiographs may not detect stress fracture pathology in the first 10 to 20 days after the onset of pain. Radionuclide bone scanning, however, can detect stress fractures early while x-rays are negative (12). The radionuclide scan is usually positive within 24 hours of onset of the injury (Figure 17-5 A & B). After a stress frac-

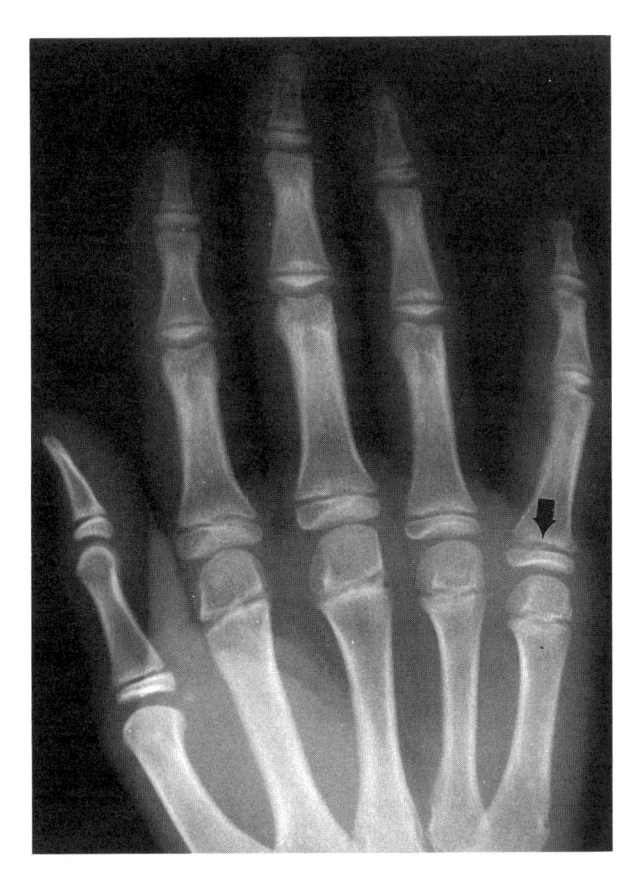

**Fig. 17-1.** Salter I fracture of the little finger at the base of the proximal phalanx. These are often very subtle. Note the epiphyseal plate widening (arrow) compared to other phalanges.

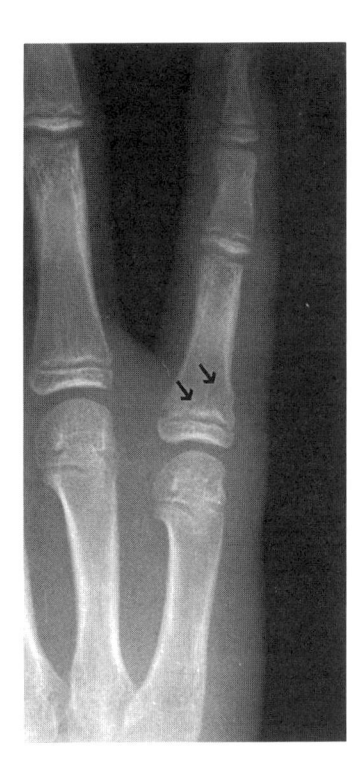

**Fig. 17-2.** Salter II fracture of the little finger at the proximal phalanx base (arrows).

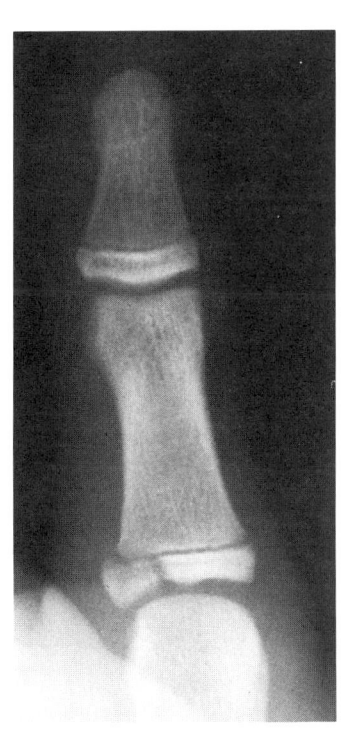

**Fig. 17-3.** Salter III fracture through the epiphysis of the thumb at the proximal phalanx.

ture is demonstrated, therapy consists of abstinence from the precipitating activity. When exercise is stopped early, the recovery time is markedly shortened. The earliest stress fracture plain-film finding may be a thin corticle lucency accompanied by a fluffy periosteal callus formation (see Figure 17-7), which can mimic a primary bone malignancy. Biopsy results often reveal histologic similarity between a healing stress fracture and an osteosarcoma. An erroneous diagnosis can have a devastating effect. It is prudent to follow the radiographic findings over a four to six week period to be certain of the diagnosis. If healing occurs, obviously no biopsy is needed and inappropriate therapy can avoided. In some bones such as the calcaneus (see Figure 17-10), the tibia at its plateau, and the first metatarsal, an endosteal line of sclerosis may be seen at the healing site.

Certain locations are classic for stress fractures. Knowing these sites may help identify the lesions. The most common sites are the distal shafts

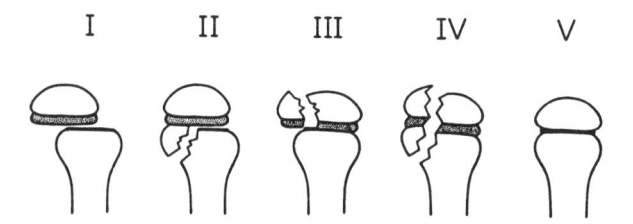

**Fig. 17-4.** The Salter-Harris fracture classification.

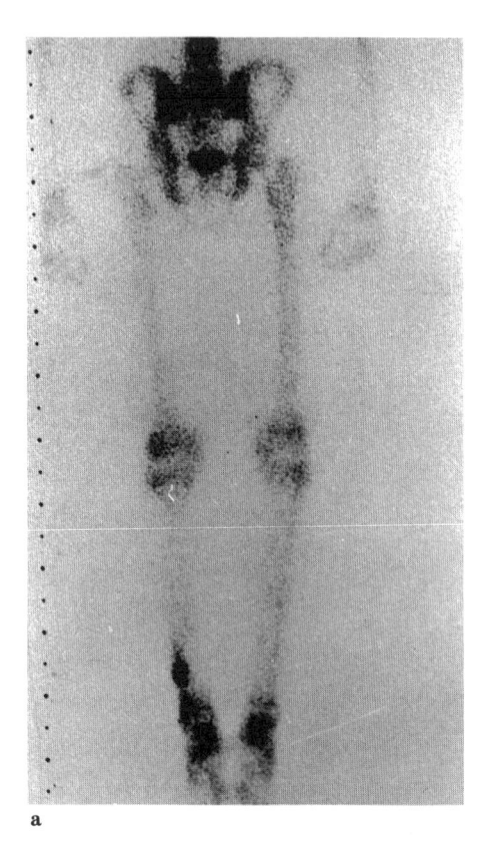

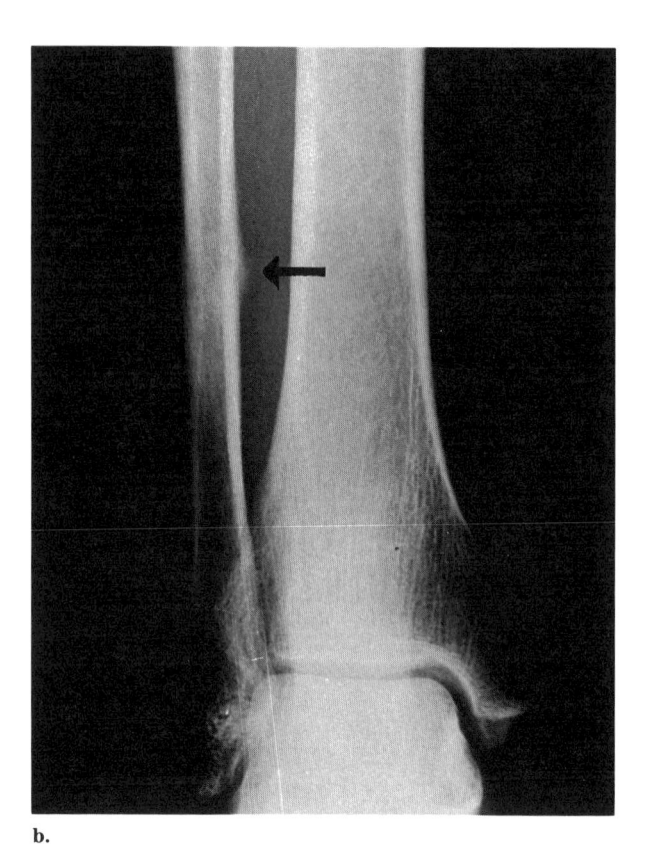

**Fig. 17-5.** Stress fracture distal fibula. Initial radiographs (not shown) were negative in this 17-year-old with pain in the distal leg. A. Bone scan showed increased activity in the distal fibula. B. Follow-up radiographs demonstrate callus formation indicative of healing. (Case courtesy of Dr. C. Roseland, Lansing General Hospital.)

of the second and third metatarsal (Figure 17-6), the calcaneus, the proximal and distal shafts of the tibia and fibula (Figure 17-7 & 8), the femoral shaft and neck, and the ischial and pubic rami. Other less common sites are the clavicle, first rib, the scapula on its lateral margin, and the distal aspect of the radius and ulna.

## HEAD

The most frequent cause of head injuries are motor vehicle accidents although head and face trauma do occur in sports activities. Skull radiographs are too often routinely obtained with little clinical discretion, especially in cases of closed head injury. The routine skull examination usually is of little or no help in treating the patient. If significant trauma has occurred and the patient has objective clinical findings such as focal neurological deficit or change in sensorium, immediate computed tomography study of the head is indicated. This exam evaluates epidural, subdural, and intracerebral blood collections. Intracerebral injuries can occur with or without an associated skull fracture. Small subdural hematoma, however, may not

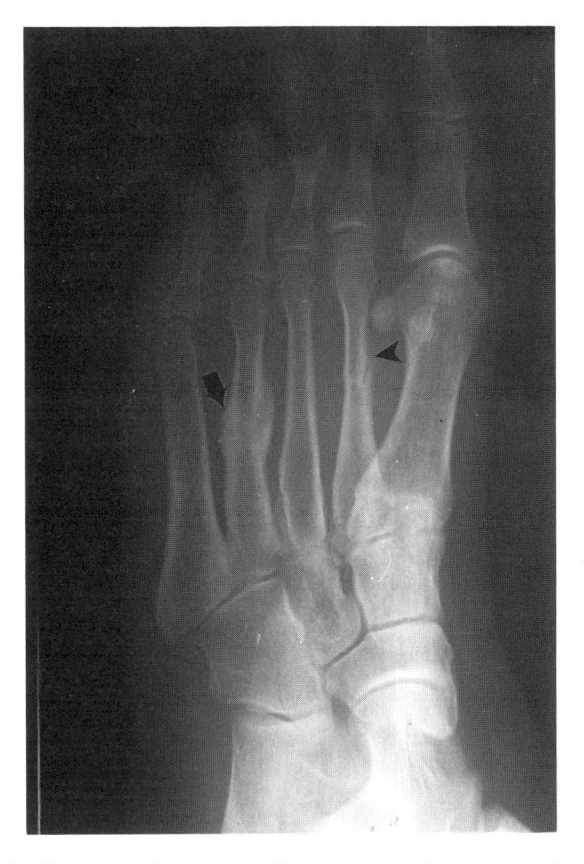

**Fig. 17-6.** Stress fractures in 20-year-old female runner. In the fourth metatarsal, marked callus formation is seen (arrow). In the second metatarsal there is a complete fracture (arrowhead).

be detected with CT, especially in the subacute setting, but MRI is able to demonstrate this entity (Figure 17-9). MRI also is more sensitive than CT in showing intrinsic brain injury. Where MRI is available, it should be the primary choice for examining patients with significant head injury. This is especially true if a CT examination has been performed and is essentially negative for pathology, yet the patient's clinical condition is unimproved.

## FACE

Plain film x-rays are useful in evaluating suspected facial fractures but these injuries can be difficult to evaluate and classify, even in the most experienced hands. In addition to routine facial radiographs, CT examination may be necessary. Certain secondary signs may lead the observer to the proper diagnosis on the plain films. The most important of these is opacification or air fluid levels in the maxillary sinuses (Figure 17-10 A & B).

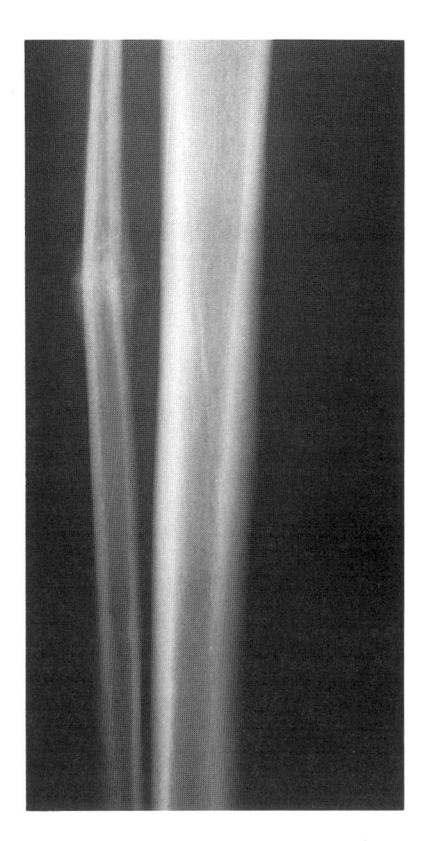

**Fig. 17-7.** Stress fracture in the mid-fibula which has progressed to frank fracture with continued use.

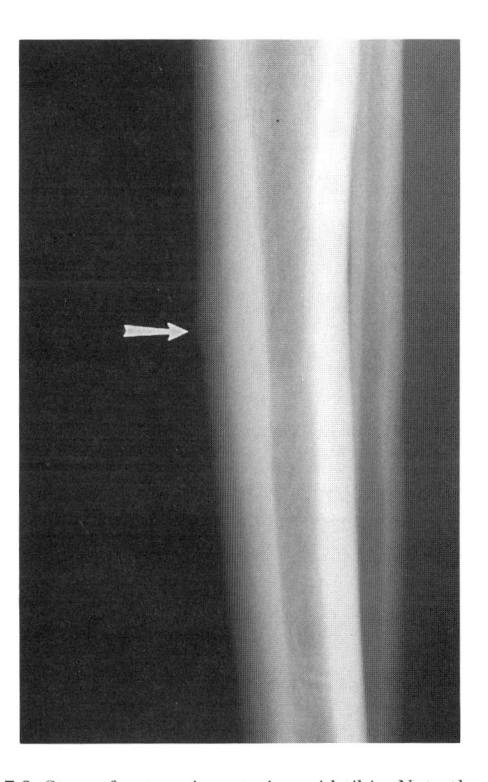

**Fig. 17-8.** Stress fracture in anterior mid-tibia. Note the thin cortical lucency and mild cortical thickening (arrow).

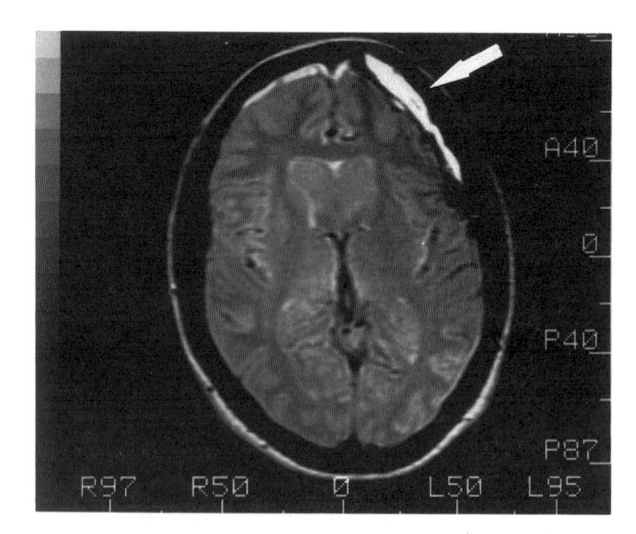

**Fig. 17-9.** Bilateral anterior subdural hematomas, larger on the left. The bright intensity (arrow) of the blood indicates subacute bleed.

This usually is indicative of fracture of one of the walls of this sinus area. A "blow-out" fracture of the facial area involves the orbital floor, with entrapment of the inferior rectus muscle in the superior aspect of the maxillary sinus. This is usually caused by a direct blow to the eye from a ball or some other hard object. The condition of entrapment is difficult to evaluate clinically because the eye lid usually is swollen shut and eye movements cannot be examined. Radiographically, this injury demonstrates a soft tissue density in the superior maxillary sinus, indicating a possible defect of the orbital floor at the fracture site. Frequently, there is intra-orbital emphysema from an associated fracture of the medial wall of the orbit into the ethmoid sinuses.

Zygomatic arch fractures are best seen on the submental vertex view; indeed, if injury here is suspected, this specific view must be obtained (Figure 17-11). Nasal bone fractures, the most frequent facial bone break, are seen best on the lateral x-ray. Specific soft tissue technique for this area allows clear visualization of both bony and soft tissue structures (Figure 17-12).

## NECK

The cervical spine is the most common spinal area involved in athletic injury. A great amount of stress is generated on the cervical spine by a blow to the head. Plain film examination must be performed with as little manipulation of the head and neck as possible. The first radiographic projection obtained should be the cross-table lateral view of the cervical spine (Figure 17-13) because it is the most useful for immediate assessment and diagnosis. With patients who have sustained significant neck trauma, this film must be reviewed before proceeding with any additional views that may require neck movement. The film must include all seven cervical vertebrae and their posterior ele-

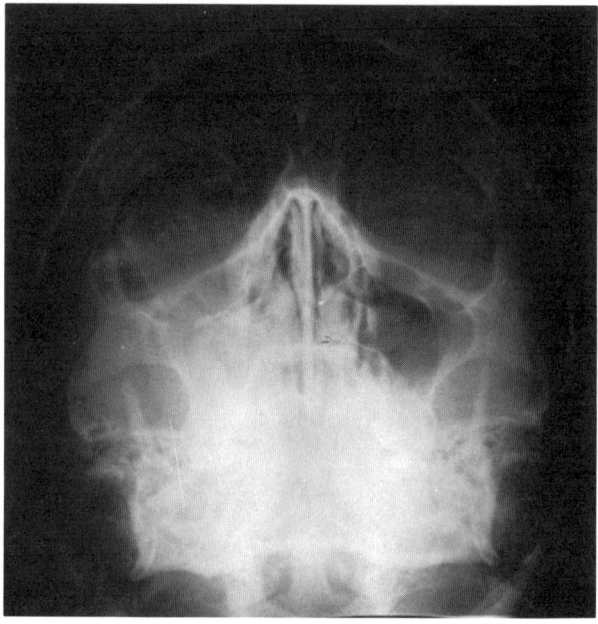

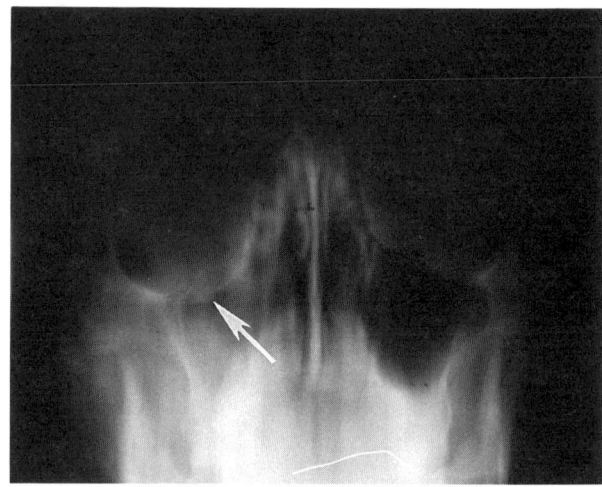

**Fig. 17-10.** Right orbital floor ("blowout") fracture. A. The initial "Water's" view shows clouding of the right maxillary sinus, a common finding secondary to hemorrhage. B. Subsequent tomograms better demonstrate the actual fracture (arrow).

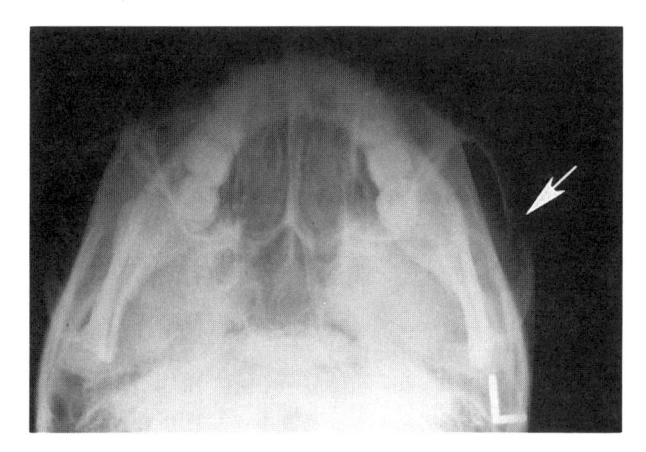

Fig. 17-11. Left zygoma fracture. These may be isolated or associated with other facial bone fractures (arrow).

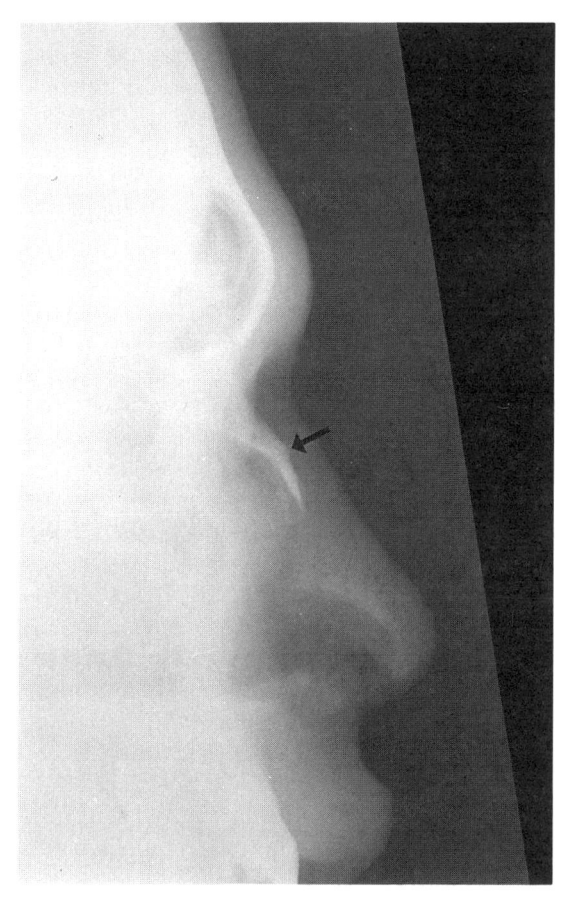

Fig. 17-12. Nasal fracture (arrow). These are best seen in this projection using the lighter, "soft-tissue" technique.

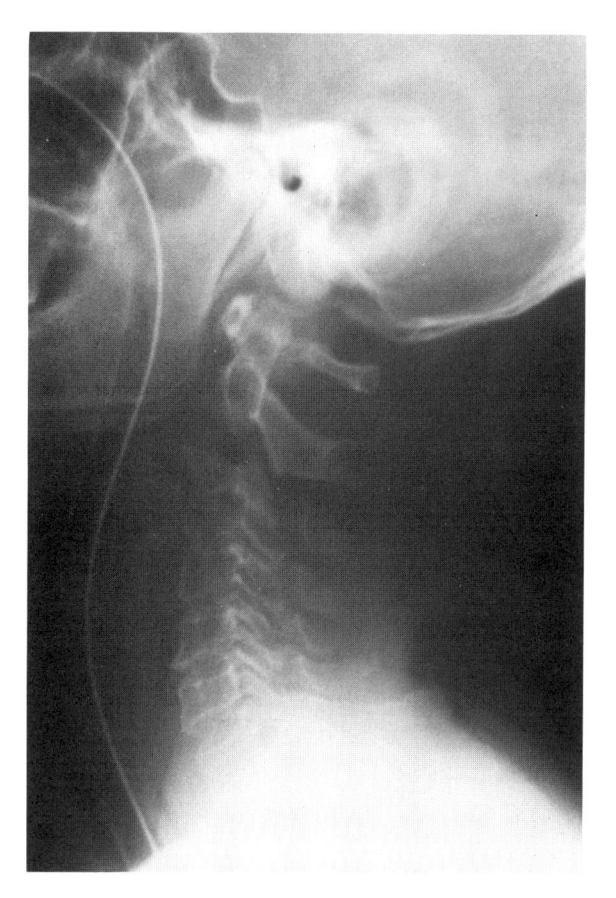

Fig. 17-13. Fracture through the body of C2, with distraction.

ments (Figure 17-14). The pre-vertebral soft tissues should be no greater than 5 millimeters thick at the C-3 level. The alignment of the vertebral bodies and posterior elements must be evaluated. An imaginary line connecting the pre-vertebral, post-vertebral, spinolaminal, and posterior spinous processes should appear to be smoothly curving, with no sharp angulations. The vertebral bodies must all be of similar height with a somewhat square to rectangular configuration. If there are questionable findings, further radiographic evaluation must be done by an expert in spinal examination. Unnecessary movement where there is an unstable fracture could precipitate permanent spinal cord injury. Anteroposterior and bilateral oblique views should be obtained only after a normal cross-table lateral projection. Flexion and extension views of the cervical spine are obtained to demonstrate the integrity of the supporting ligamentous structures. Flexion and extension stress views may also be obtained in non-acute cases to rule out chronic instability from ligamentous disruption. Specific open-mouth views of the C-1 and C-2 spine area are required if pathology is suspected. The odontoid process or the lateral masses of C-1 cannot be adequately demonstrated by routine anteroposterior and lateral projections alone.

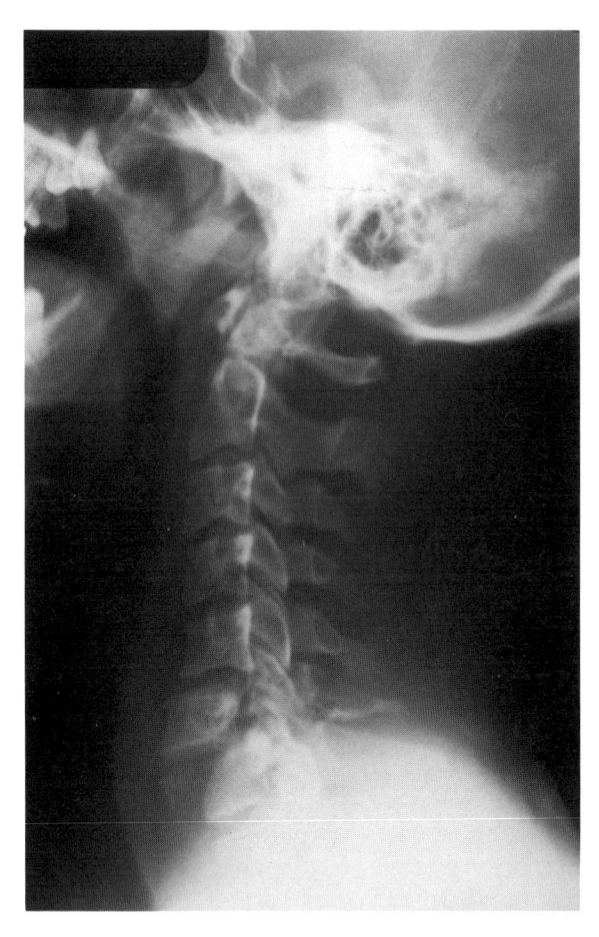

**Fig. 17-14.** Anterior fracture of C7 vertebral body with dislocation of the C6-7 area.

## SHOULDER

The bony portion of the shoulder girdle is comprised of the humeral head, scapula, glenohumeral joint, acromion and acromio-clavicular joints, the clavicle, and sterno-clavicular joints. Some portion of the shoulder girdle is moving in nearly every sport activity. The humeral head is much longer than the glenoid labrum, giving this joint range of motion but making it more susceptible to injury.

Medially, sternal-clavicular joint disruption may be caused by rupture of the sterno-clavicular and costo-clavicular ligaments, an injury that occurs when there is a significant direct blow to the area. An associated fracture of the clavicle makes rupture of these ligaments more likely. However, a normal plain-film clavicle examination does not preclude the possibility of significant ligamentous injury. CT examination is indispensable in evaluating the sterno-clavicular relationship, with the axial projection being most important. Use of CT easily demonstrates anterior and posterior dislocation of the clavicle to the sternum (12). Posterior dislocation is quite ominous because of the close proximity of major vessels in this area. A pitfall in evaluating the medial aspect of the clavicle is its secondary ossification center. Because this is the last center in the body to close, care must be taken not to mistake it for an avulsion fracture caused by trauma.

Clavicles are prone to fracture and radiographic evaluation is usually sufficient to demonstrate pathology. Two projections should be obtained. A routine anteroposterior and an anteroposterior projection with a 15 degree cephalad tilt of the x-ray tube is required to locate fracture fragments. If there has been major trauma to the clavicular area, a chest x-ray also should be obtained to check for associated rib fractures or a pneumothorax.

The acromio-clavicular and coraco-clavicular areas are routinely involved in athletic injuries. This area should be examined with a 15 degree cephalad angled view, centered at the acromio-clavicular joint. Sprains of these ligaments allow the distal clavicle to move away from the acromion and coracoid processes of the scapula. The clavicle can displace anteriorly or posteriorly when these is disruption of the acromio-clavicular ligaments. When the involvement includes the coraco-clavicular ligaments, the clavicle may be displaced superiorly. Stress views, with 15 pound weights passively suspended from the patient's wrist or forearm, help define the integrity of these ligaments better. If the patient holds the weights used for stress views, he may overcome an occurring separation by the contraction of the muscles of the shoulder girdle (Figure 17-15 A & B). The tendons of the rotator cuff muscles fuse around the shoulder and form a fibrous capsule which separates inferior to the shoulder joint from the subacromian and subdeltoid bursa, located above. Most experts think that rotator cuff tears are secondary to degenerative changes with superimposed trauma. They are usually seen in older individuals but may be found in athletes who have sustained acute trauma.

If complete rupture of the rotator cuff is suspected, do arthrography with contrast material injected into the joint space to demonstrate extravasation into the subacromian and subdeltoid bursa. Because there is no communication between the joint capsule and the bursa, incomplete tears may be considered normal on arthrography.

Plain film x-rays of an acute injury may be

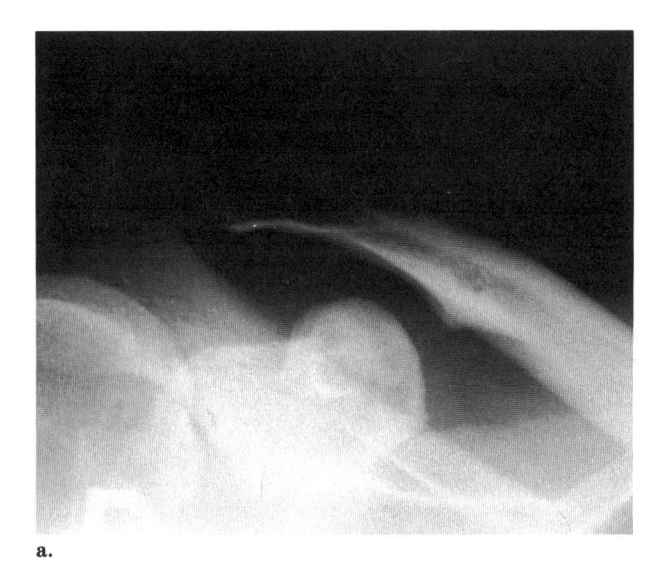

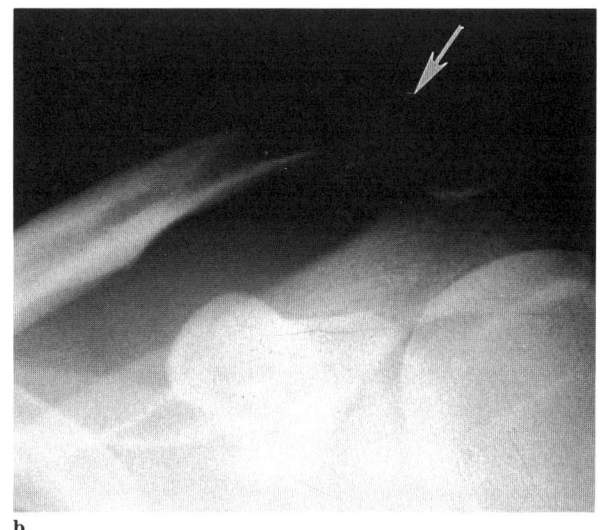

**Fig. 17-15.** Acromioclavicular (AC) joint separation. With weights attached to the wrists, views of the AC joints show widening on the left (B. arrow) compared with the normal right side (A).

normal but, over time, a patient can develop sclerosis, irregularity, or cystic changes at the greater tuberosity and neck of the humerus. The most common abnormality is narrowing of the distance between the inferior edge of the acromion process and the humeral head to less than 6 millimeters. MRI is now used to evaluate the shoulder joint and rotator cuff (Figure 17-16) and will likely become the primary imaging modality to rule out rotator cuff pathology (5).

The glenohumeral joint is the most frequently dislocated joint in the body. If the initial dislocation occurs before the age of 20, recurrent dislocations are more likely to happen. Approximately 95% of all shoulder dislocations are anterior dislocations. In these cases, the x-ray study usually will show the head of the humerus anterior to and below the coracoid process. Anteroposterior projection radiographs will demonstrate this abnormal position (Figure 17-17). Approximately 15% of these dislocations have associated fractures of the greater tuberosity, so that open reduction surgery and fixation may be required. A smaller number will have fractures of the anterior glenoid rim.

Chronic anterior shoulder dislocations can have associated fractures called the Hill-Sachs defect in the posterolateral aspect of the humeral head. A fracture of the inferior rim of the glenoid, or Bankart fracture, is an associated fracture of the scapula. These defects probably occur as the head of the humerus slips below the inferior rim of the glenoid labrum and causes impaction of the humeral head on the inferior glenoid. These types of fractures can happen with a single dislocation; however, they are more likely with recurring dislocations. Posterior dislocations are less frequent but are important because they may be difficult to diagnose clinically and radiographically. Approximately 50% of these dislocations are not initially identified on the anteroposterior radiograph of the shoulder (16). An axillary view is helpful in showing the location of the humeral head in relation to the glenoid fossa. It is obtained with the patient lying supine and the injured arm extended laterally.

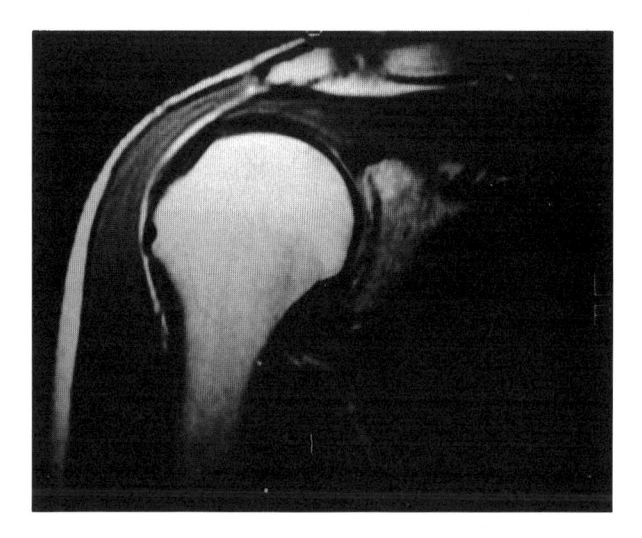

**Fig. 17-16.** Normal coronal shoulder MR image. There is excellent visualization of the rotator cuff as well as other soft tissue structures.

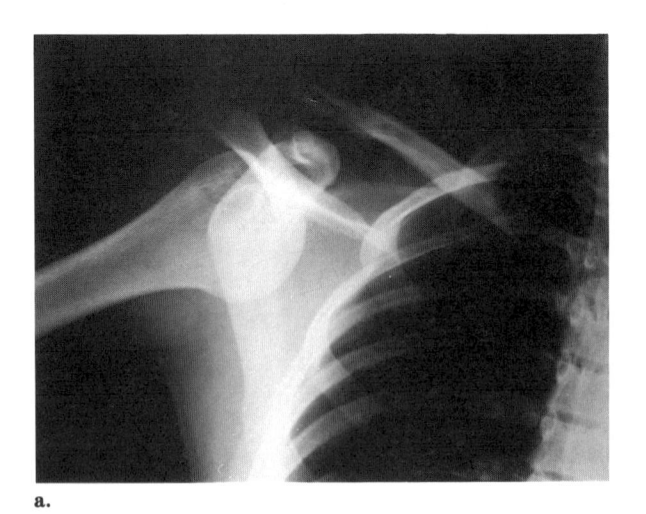

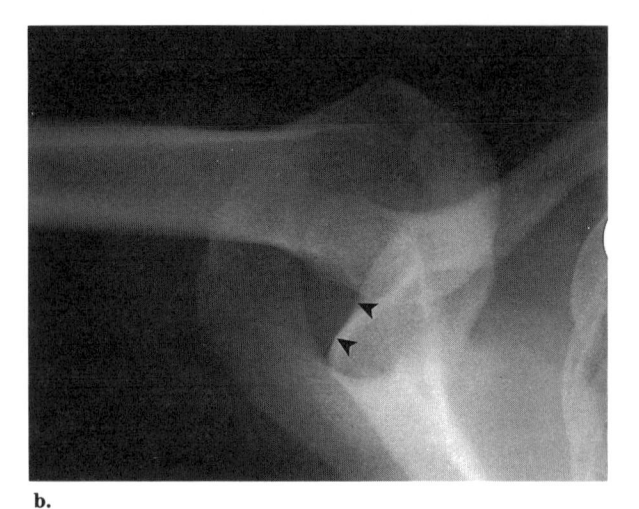

**Fig. 17-17.** A. AP shoulder view demonstrates anterior, inferior humeral dislocation. B. Axillary shoulder view also demonstrates anterior humeral dislocation with respect to the glenoid fossa (arrowheads).

The film cassette is positioned above the patient's shoulder and the x-ray beam is projected through the axilla.

## ELBOW

Radiographic evaluation of the elbow includes views in anteroposterior, "true" lateral, and oblique positions. The lateral view, obtained by flexing the arm 90 degrees, is especially useful. Two radiographically visible fat pads can be present at the elbow. The anterior fat pad normally is seen in the flexed lateral view but the posterior fat pad is located within the olecranon fossa and normally is not visible with elbow flexion (Figure 17-18). However, when the joint capsule is distended, this fat pad becomes displaced posteriorly and does become visible. With an acute injury, the identification of this posterior fat pad may be the only sign of an occult fracture. If the lateral view is not obtained with 90 degree flexion, the posterior fat pad is visible even in a normal elbow.

Supracondylar fractures are located outside the joint space of the elbow and are seen most often in children and the elderly. Careful radiographic assessment is necessary before reduction because neurovascular injury can be caused by fracture fragments. Significant displacement warrants open reduction repair because of this potential complication. Transcondylar, intracondylar, and oblique fractures of a single condyle can occur. These are located within the elbow joint so that there should be a positive fat pad sign.

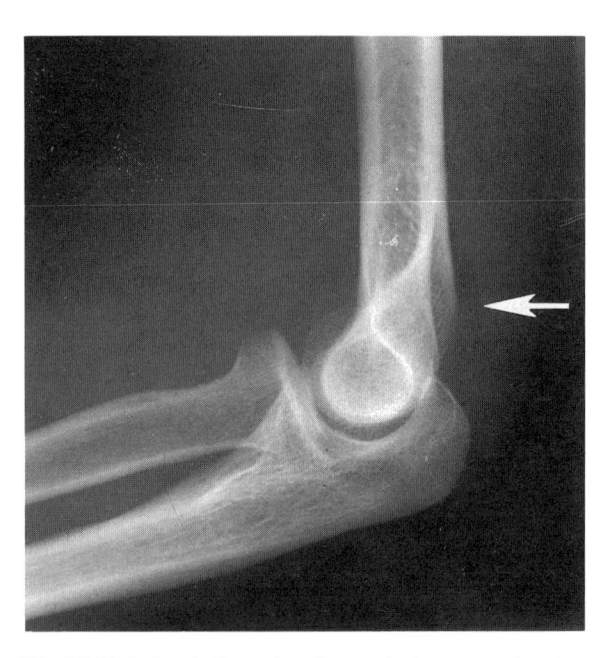

**Fig. 17-18.** Lateral elbow view demonstrates a prominent posterior fat pad (arrow), indicative of joint effusion which in this case was due to an occult radial head fracture.

The ossification centers in the distal humerus of children are complex so that liberal use of comparison views of the opposite side are indicated. The medial epicondyle usually ossifies by the age of four or five years and does not unite with the humerus until age 18 or 19. Avulsions of this epicondyle may occur with displacement of fragments within the elbow joint. Adolescents incur this injury by violent contraction of the flexor pronator muscles during throwing activities. The term "little league elbow" was coined by Brogden and Crow to describe this injury (15).

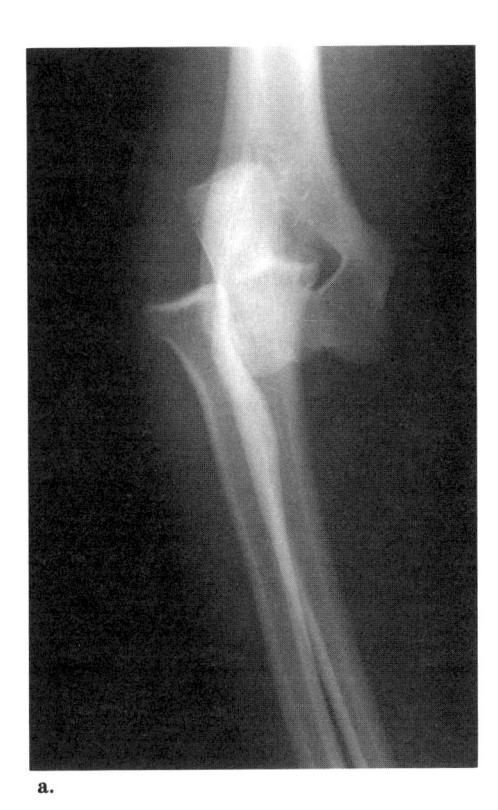

Elbow dislocations usually present with posterior displacement of the radius and ulna (Figure 17-19 A, B & C). Post-reduction films must be obtained routinely to evaluate potential radial head, coronoid process, or medial humeral epicondyle fractures. The capitellum is not connected to muscle but may be displaced from its normal location when it is fractured. When this occurs, it can be located anterior to the radial head and coronoid process and can be seen well on the lateral x-ray view. Radial head fractures occur most frequently in adults and can be quite difficult to identify. Aids to identification are the posterior fat pad sign, the use of angled oblique x-ray projections of the area, and follow-up examinations within 7-10 days after the initial injury.

## WRIST, HAND AND FINGERS

The distal forearm is a frequent site of injury in the adult and adolescent. There are many common terms to describe fractures of this area but the terms are occasionally misused so that it is important to be certain of the anatomical disruption caused by these fractures. Memorizing eponyms

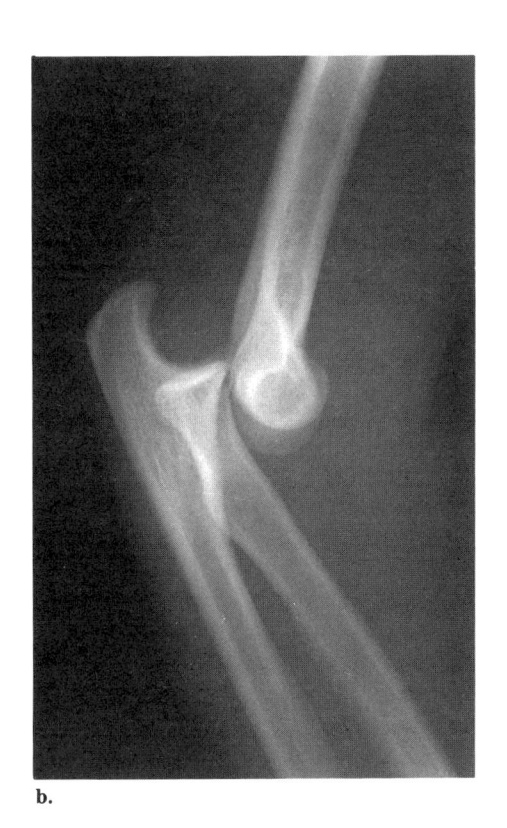

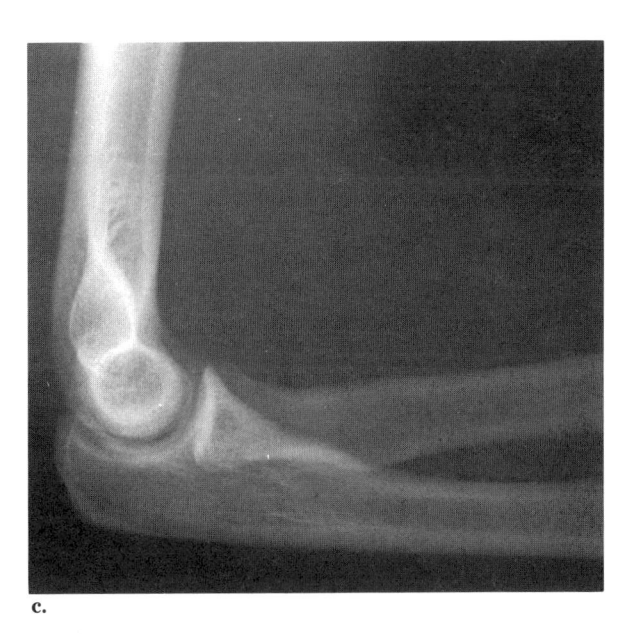

**Fig. 17-19.** A. AP elbow shows radial and ulnar dislocation. B. Lateral elbow view better demonstrates this. C. Post reduction lateral view demonstrating good position of the bone.

RADIOLOGY OF SPORTS INJURIES 519

and applying them incorrectly causes confusion. Common use of the terms requires knowledge of both the term and its implications. A "Colles" fracture refers to a fracture of the distal radius with dorsal angulation of the distal segment. The ulna may or may not be involved. A reverse Colles' or Smith's fracture, however, involves the distal radius with volar angulation of the distal segment. Barton's fracture is one that involves the posterior rim of the radius with posterior radiocarpal dislocation. A reverse Barton's fracture involves the anterior rim of the radius with anterior, or volar, radiocarpal dislocation. Fracture of the radial styloid is referred to as a chauffeur's fracture and usually is caused by a direct blow. This was first described in drivers of early automobile models with a crank stick. The crank stick would recoil on starting and strike the driver's wrist, breaking it.

A torus fracture of the distal radius happens often in children between the ages of six and ten years of age. This usually occurs as an incomplete fracture with "buckling" of the cortex, causing focal irregularity (Figure 17-20). This type of fracture is seen on the dorsal aspect of the distal radius and is best demonstrated on the lateral x-ray projection. The Salter-Harris classification criteria are used to grade epiphyseal fractures of the radial and ulnar epiphyseal plates. Epiphysis fractures are routinely managed through closed reduction technique and rarely cause growth disturbance.

The bones of the wrist are supported by a complex set of ligamentous attachments. Certain abnormalities may be difficult to see because of the multi-faceted configuration and overlapping of the wrists's carpal bones. Obtain specific radiographic views of the wrist area when there has been trauma to the carpal bones. It is not adequate to merely include the "wrist area" on routine views of a hand examination. A detailed discussion of wrist injuries is beyond the scope of this chapter although certain conditions must be mentioned. The carpal navicular, or scaphoid bone, is a frequent site of injury and it is difficult to evaluate with just routine anteroposterior and lateral projection. An oblique projection of the wrist is necessary to evaluate the scaphoid bone. Fractures occur in the "waist" of this bone and if they are not detected and adequately stabilized (Figure 17-21), complications occur secondary to ischemic necrosis.

On a normal lateral projection, the lunate bone is positioned immediately above the distal radius and the capitate bone directly above the lunate. When there is a lunate dislocation, the bone is projected to the volar aspect of the wrist, with the radius and capitate remaining in relatively normal orientation. With perilunate dislocation, the lunate bone usually retains its normal alignment to the radius, with the capitate bone dislocated in either a volar or dorsal direction. Unfortunately, aseptic necrosis of the lunate bone can occur with relatively minor trauma to the wrist. Radiographically, aseptic necrosis of the lunate is characterized as a

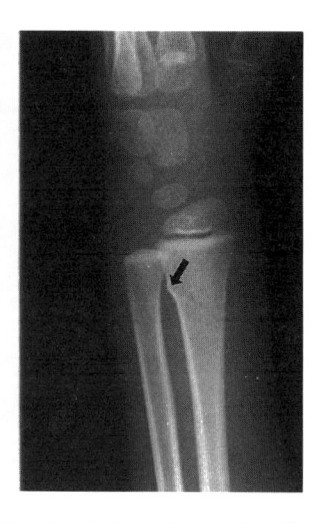

**Fig. 17-20.** "Torus" or "buckle" fracture is typically seen in children and represents an incomplete type of fracture. Note it is best seen on the oblique view in this example (arrow).

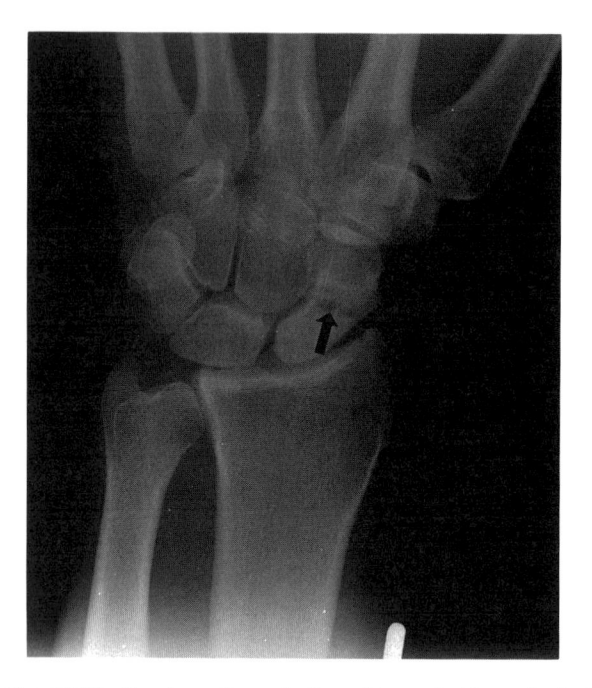

**Fig. 17-21.** Fracture through the mid-scaphoid, or "waist" (arrow).

dense bone on the film (Figure 17-22 A & B). Surgical removal of the bone will be necessary and occasionally a prosthesis is required.

The skeletal areas most prone to injury in the athlete are the phalanges and metacarpals. Many acute injuries are self-treated and are usually assessed as a "jammed" finger. However, if they are not properly evaluated and treated, they can cause long term instability. In radiographing them, it is important to obtain focused views of the area of interest to define subtle abnormalities. Once again, a single projection is not adequate; anteroposterior, oblique, and lateral projections are required. The anteroposterior view should include the entire metacarpal row to rule out unsuspected associated injuries.

Disruption of the ulnar collateral ligament is known as the "gamekeepers" thumb. This name originated when hunters used to break the necks of small game by snapping them between their thumb and the metacarpal of the index finger (Figure 17-23 A & B). The snapping action sometimes caused an avulsion fracture. Consequently, when there is a small avulsion fracture of the ulnar aspect of the proximal phalanx, a ligamentous disruption should be suspected. If a purely ligamentous injury is sustained, stress views may be required to demonstrate the disruption (Figure 17-24 A & B). This condition causes chronic instability and pain. It is seen most often in skiing mishaps where the jamming force of the ski pole against hands held secure by the ski pole strap causes the snapping trauma.

A boxer's fracture involves the distal metacarpal of the little finger. Besides the fracture, there is palmar angulation and displacement of the distal segment. It is usually caused by a dorsal blow to the head of the metacarpal area such as might occur if someone hit a wall or other relatively immovable object with a closed fist. This injury is best demonstrated with lateral and oblique hand views.

Interphalangeal and metacarpal-phalangeal dislocations are common injuries and are usually secondary to volar impact to the hand. Post-reduction films are mandatory to rule out small associated peri-articular fractures that may have been occult initially. This is particularly important in an injury such as the Salter-Harris type that involves the epiphyseal plate, and must be classified to properly monitor and treat them.

Volar plate fractures and avulsions may be difficult to see in the inter-phalangeal area of the hand. A true lateral projection is helpful in demonstrating small avulsions of attached bony cortex. The lateral radiographic projection must be done routinely in cases of phalangeal injuries. "Baseball" or "mallet finger" describes a condition caused

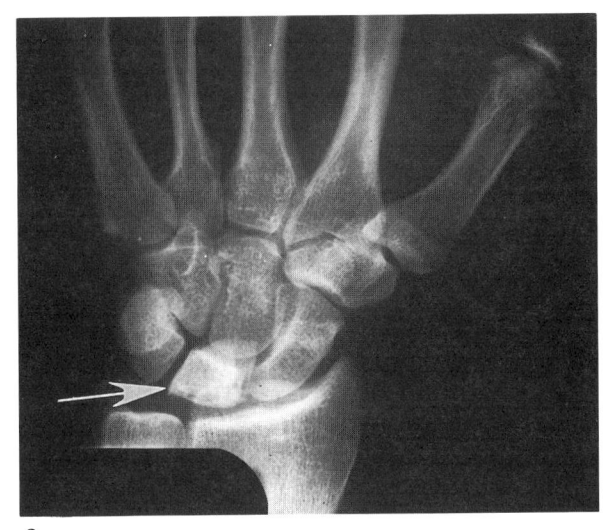

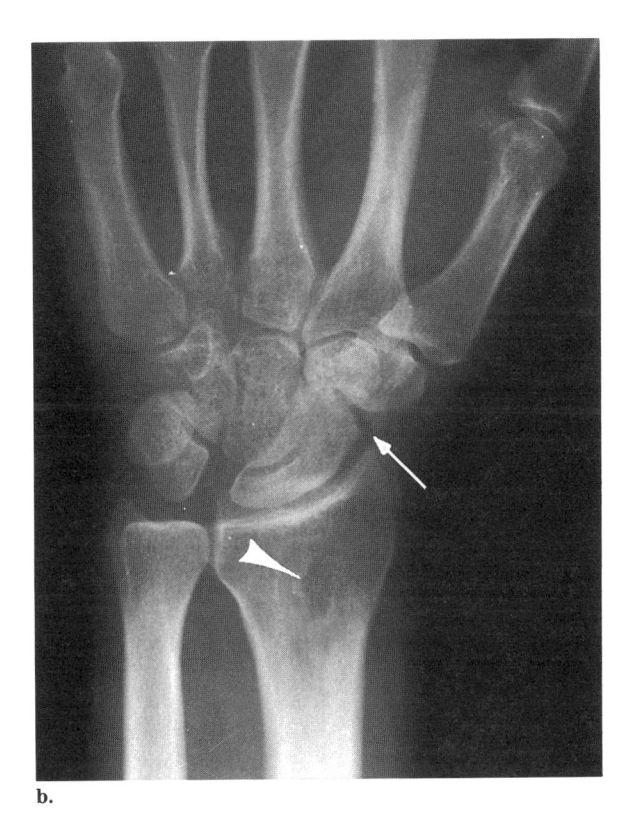

**Fig. 17-22.** A. Aseptic necrosis of the lunate, with sclerosis (arrow). B. Post-operative film following lunate resection. Note the internal development of a small scaphoid fracture (arrow) and an incidental bone cyst in the distal radius (arrowhead).

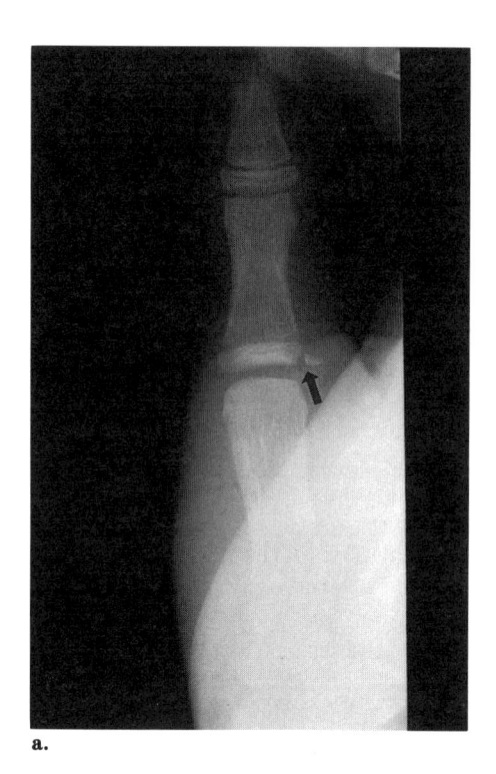

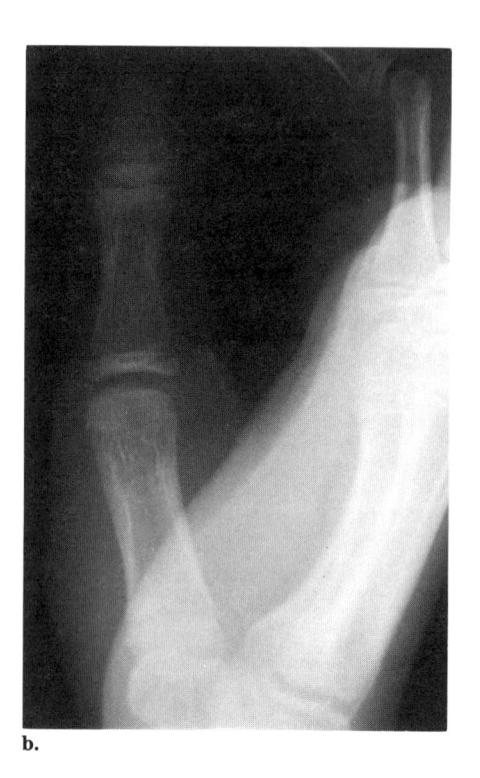

**Fig. 17-23.** Small avulsion fracture of proximal phalanx, thumb. It is seen only on one view (arrow).

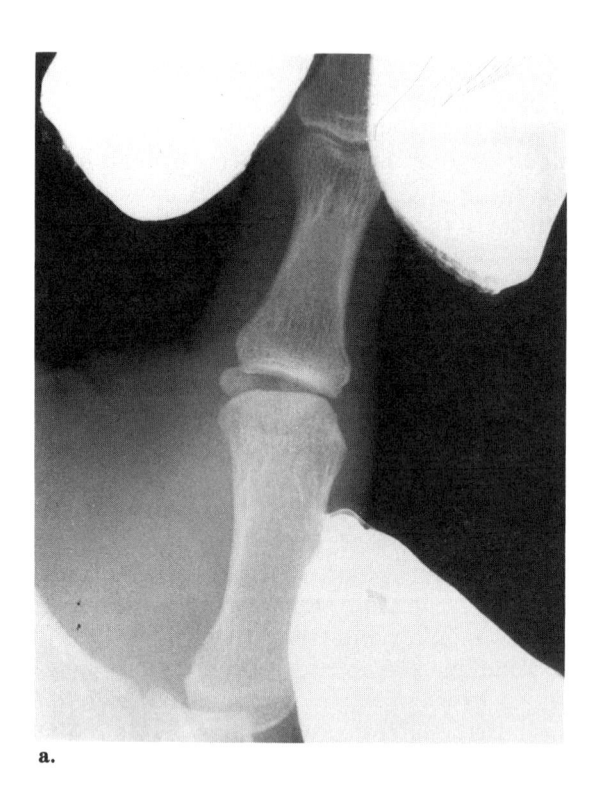

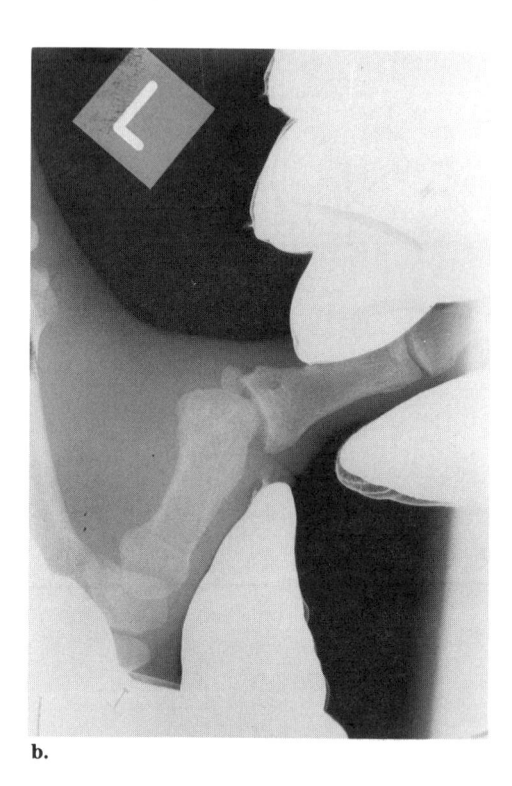

**Fig. 17-24.** A. Stress views of the normal thumb. B. The same amount of stress causes a much greater joint widening in a patient with ligamentous injury.

by a direct blow to the dorsal tip of the distal phalanx that causes sudden, severe flexion at the extensor tendon. This results in disruption or avulsion of this tendon at the dorsal base of the distal phalanx. There is a loss of function of this tendon so that the distal interphalangeal joint is maintained in a flexed position. Direct trauma from a crush injury to the subungual area of the phalanges may cause a comminuted fracture of the distal phalanx that is often referred to as a "tuft fracture" (Figure 17-25).

## CHEST

Bony injuries of the thorax often can be seen in routine posteroanterior and lateral chest films. If not shown with these views, specific rib views may be warranted to evaluate the injured areas. Rib fractures can cause a prominent hematoma in the chest wall which protrudes into the chest cavity. This can simulate a pleural mass to an inexperienced observer. Old rib fractures that have prominent callus formation may give a similar appearance. Posteroanterior and lateral chest x-rays are used to examine for a pneumothorax. If it is not apparent on the routine chest films but still clinically suspected, a chest examination obtained with the patient in full expiration may demonstrate a small free air collection. Severe trauma like that cause by deceleration injuries or direct blows to the chest may cause pulmonary contusion, cardiac injury, or even aortic dissection. These injuries should be treated at a major trauma unit and their radiographic presentation is beyond the scope of this chapter.

## ABDOMEN

The visceral organs, the liver, spleen, and kidneys are most apt to be injured. Here, CT evaluation is the imaging modality of choice to demonstrate pathology. Contusions, lacerations, intra-capsular blood collections, and free intraperitoneal bleeding are detectable with CT (Figure 17-26). Angiography is sometimes necessary to show vascular injury. The bowel usually is immune to blunt abdominal trauma because it floats freely in the peritoneal cavity. However, the third portion of the duodenum is located in the retroperitoneum and is fixed in place and crosses over the vertebral column. Direct trauma can create a vise-like compression that causes a rupture or hematoma of this portion of bowel. The pancreas can be transected by this type of injury. Within the pelvis, an intravenous pyelogram with contrast can demonstrate the bladder and ureters well. If urethral trauma is suspected, a retrograde urethrogram should be done before a catheter is inserted into the bladder.

## BACK

Acute injuries to the thoracic and lumbar spine may affect the vertebral bodies, the transverse processes, or the spinous processes. Again, the overall alignment and contour of these structures must be evaluated at each level, as well as at the intervertebral disc spaces. Paravertebral soft tissue swelling may contribute a specific sign and help localize the exact area of injury. Look carefully also for adjacent soft tissue injury in the abdomen or chest whenever a spinal fracture is demonstrated.

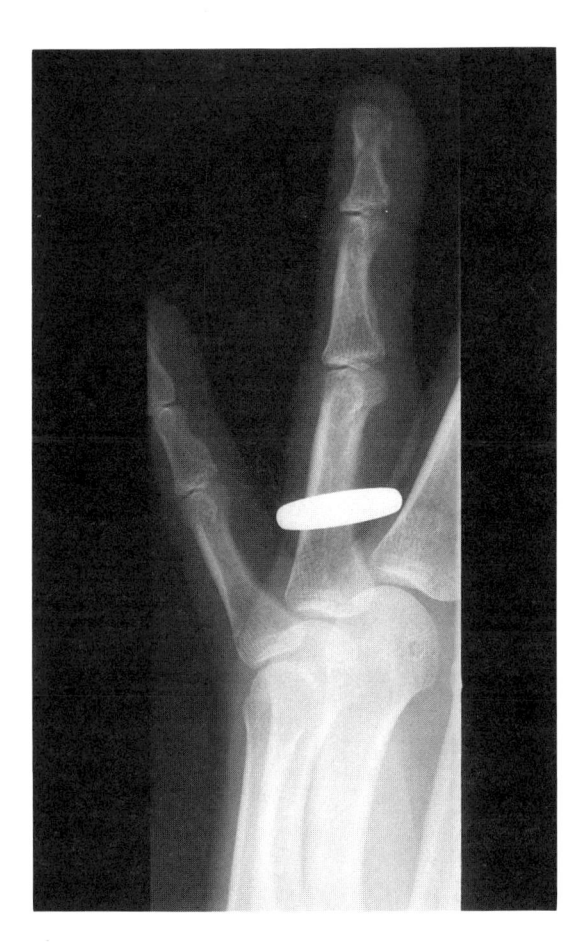

**Fig. 17-25.** Comminuted fracture of the distal phalanx, ring finger. These are usually caused by a crushing mechanism.

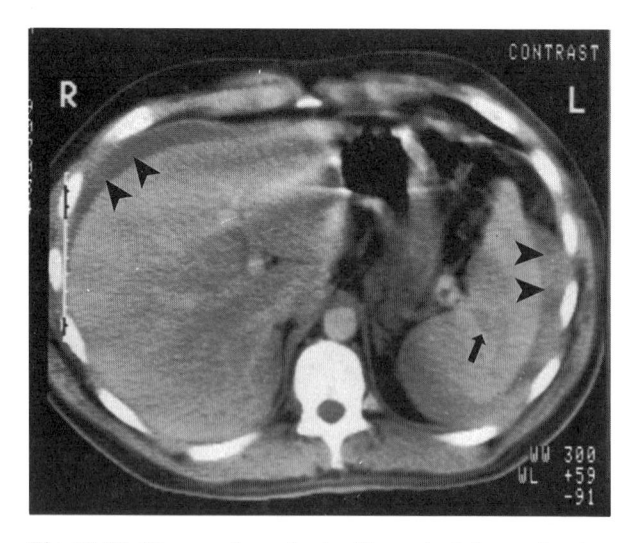

**Fig. 17-26.** CT scan of a patient with a splenic laceration (arrow) causing free blood in the peritoneal cavity (arrowheads).

## HIP AND PELVIS

Fractures and dislocations in the pelvic girdle are usually secondary to major trauma. Fractures of the iliac wing, coccyx, and pubes are caused by direct blows and these fractures are readily visible on routine x-rays. Pelvic strains happen frequently and if only muscle or tendon involvement is present, there will be no specific radiographic observation. If there is an avulsion of the apophysis, it usually is at the ischial tuberosity as a result of a pull of the hamstrings (Figure 17-27) and this condition can be radiographically observed. These injuries are most often seen in sprinters, cheerleaders, and hurdlers, but also occur in someone who has a sharp flexion movement of the hip while the knee is extended. Other hip and pelvic areas involved in this type of injury are the anterosuperior iliac spine (Figure 17-28), the iliac crest, and the lesser trochanter of the femur (14). Correct assessment is important because exuberant bone formation that can be mistaken for malignancy occurs during healing. A thorough medical history and follow-up examinations will prevent this error. If a biopsy is performed, a healing fracture can be histologically indistinguishable from a malignant bone tumor so that biopsy results alone can be misleading if they are not properly correlated with all elements of the presenting condition.

Subluxation of the symphysis pubis occurs in athletes, most often in soccer players (Figure 17-29). The subluxation is radiographically demon-

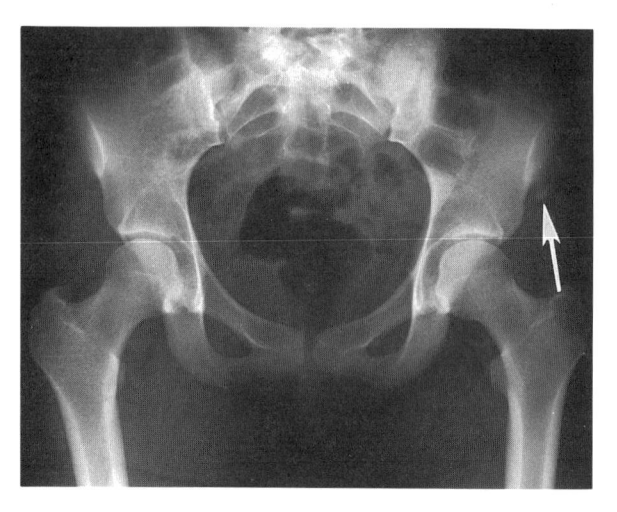

**Fig. 17-28.** Avulsion of the anterior superior iliac spine (arrow).

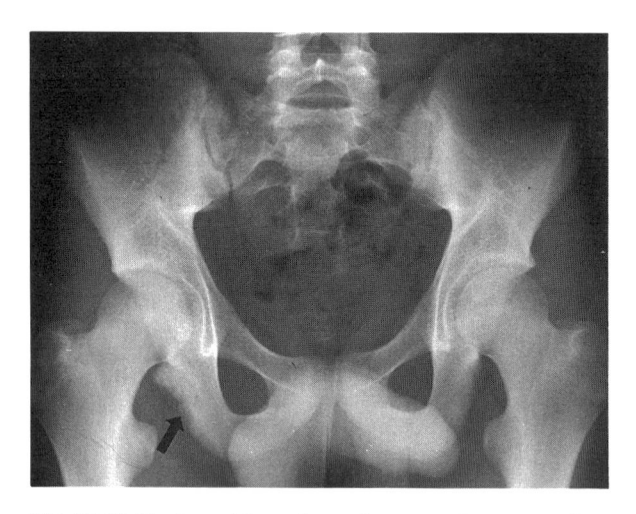

**Fig. 17-27.** Exuberant bone formation secondary to previous avulsion of the right ischmal tuberosity (arrow).

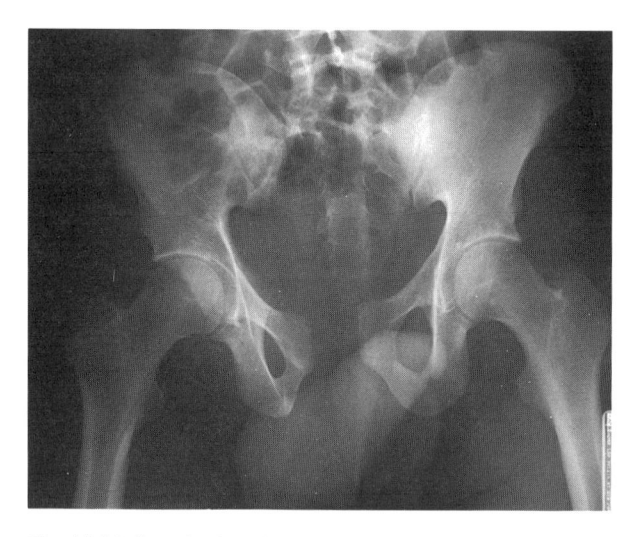

**Fig. 17-29.** Symphysis pubis diastasis.

strated in the anteroposterior projection of the pelvis, taken with the patient standing. Obtain two projections, with the patient first on one foot and then the other to demonstrate movement between the symphysis pubis that occurs with the shift in weight between the two projections.

Hip fracture is uncommon in the adolescent and young adult patient. In this age group, the bones are quite resistant to fracture. Dislocation is more likely but this too is uncommon. When there is a dislocation, it is clinically obvious that a major injury has been sustained. Reduction should never be attempted on the athletic field. The patient must be transferred immediately to an emergency medical facility and plain-film x-rays obtained. If the condition is confirmed, reduction is usually done under anesthesia. If reduction is attempted without anesthesia, additional trauma from this painful maneuver could further damage the fragile articulating cartilage of the hip joint. There is a direct relationship between the amount of time a hip remains dislocated and the likelihood of developing an avascular necrosis of the femoral head. Avascular necrosis is a major complication of this type of injury so that the need to quickly address the hip dislocation should be apparent.

Routine radiographic evaluation of the hip includes anteroposterior views in the straight-leg and frog-leg positions. Fluoroscopy, simple linear tomography, and computed axial tomography examinations help identify subtle hip fractures and posterior dislocations. If posterior hip dislocation is superiorly displaced, it usually is not difficult to visualize. However, that is not the case if the dislocation is directly posterior. After reduction, an associated fragment from the acetabular portion of the injured hip can impinge in the joint space and cause a nonconcentric fit of the femoral head into the acetabulum. On post-reduction films, the joint space must be examined closely for evidence of retained fragments. Osteochondral fractures can occur in the hip joint and these fractures are difficult to demonstrate because of overlying bones. Osteochondral fractures are radiographically similar to fractures described in the knee and ankle, where there is central sclerotic area surrounded by a radiolucent ring. Computed axial tomography and MRI examination may be needed when this complication is suspected.

In evaluating an injured or painful adolescent hip, always give consideration to a slipped capital femoral epiphysis (Figure 17-30 A & B). This condition is usually associated with violent trauma in

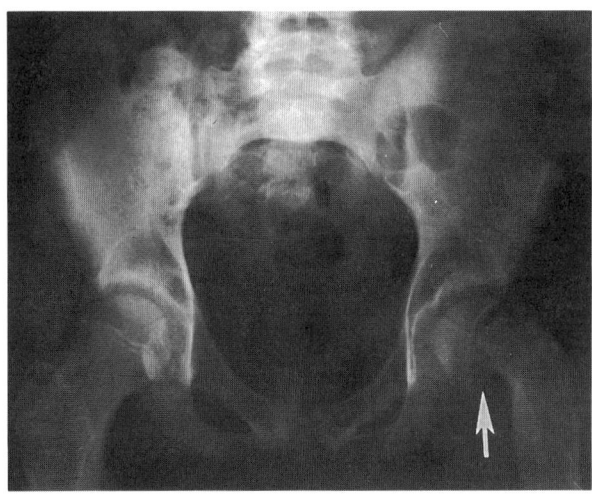

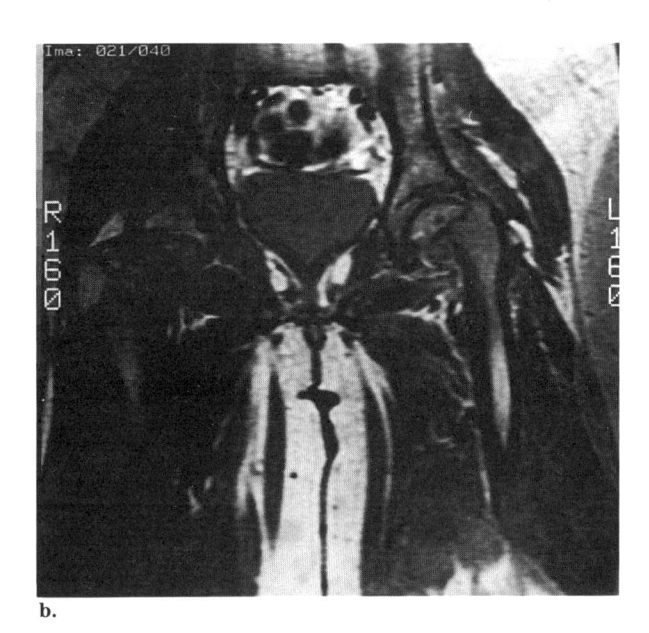

**Fig. 17-30.** A. Slipped capital femoral epiphysis (arrow). B. Slipped capital femoral epiphysis can best be demonstrated by using MRI in the early stages.

children from infancy to 10 years of age. In early adolescence it is found in individuals who are mildly obese and have delayed secondary sexual characteristics. Usually, there is no single specific traumatic event to blame in this group. Clinically, pain may be referred to the knee. Radiographically, an oblique or frog-leg projection best demonstrates the pathology. The anteroposterior projection may appear normal but the frog-leg projection will show the classic appearance, with the epiphysis displaced posteriorly and medially. If not properly diagnosed and treated, complications can be devastating and include premature fusion, avascular necrosis, nonunion, and early degenerative changes. Avascular necrosis can be diagnosed on plain-films in its later stages after some healing has taken place; however, MRI consistently identifies this pathology at an earlier stage than any other existing imaging modality. It should be the imaging technique of choice when avascular necrosis is suspected (6).

Occult fractures of the femoral neck occur and are usually secondary to stress fractures in the athlete (Figure 17-31 A & B). Plain-film radiographs often appear unremarkable but isotope bone scan, linear tomography, and MRI help define this pathology.

## KNEE

The knee is extremely vulnerable to athletic injury. Extensive ligamentous injuries can occur without being obviously discernable on plain film x-ray. Also, primary hip pathology in the pediatric age group may present with referred pain to the knee. Radiographic evaluation should include anteroposterior, lateral, and externally and internally rotated oblique views. The "sunrise" or axial view may help evaluate the patella. To assess the intercondylar eminence, the "notch" or "tunnel" view is recommended to show the cruciate ligament attachments or to locate loose calcified bodies in the joint.

Soft tissue signs can indicate significant injury and must be carefully reviewed on x-ray examination of any bone. In a lateral view of the knee joint, distention of the suprapatellar bursae causes anterior displacement of the quadriceps tendon (Figure 17-32). This displacement is caused by blood or synovial effusion that fills the joint and distends the bursae. The specific character of the fluid may be defined by aspiration. In acute fractures where intracapsular bone surfaces are involved, a fat-fluid line may be formed in the distended bursae. The fat-fluid configuration is caused by extravasation of intramedullary fat into the joint space through the fracture and can be seen only on a cross-table lateral view. If this fat-fluid line is present, suspect an occult fracture in this area. Further investigation is warranted even when no obvious fracture is seen (Figure 17-33 A & B).

Pellegrini-Stieda disease refers to calcification of the medial collateral knee ligament at its insertion on the medial femoral condyle. It is thought to be secondary to an old sprain but it is not clear whether a small bony avulsion occurs with the original injury or whether subsequent calcification is formed from hematoma in the injured area. It must be differentiated from an acute avulsion of the medial collateral ligament.

Dislocation of the knee is rare but dislocation of the patella occurs, and this condition is usually clinically obvious. It occurs more often laterally and, at the time radiographs are obtained, has

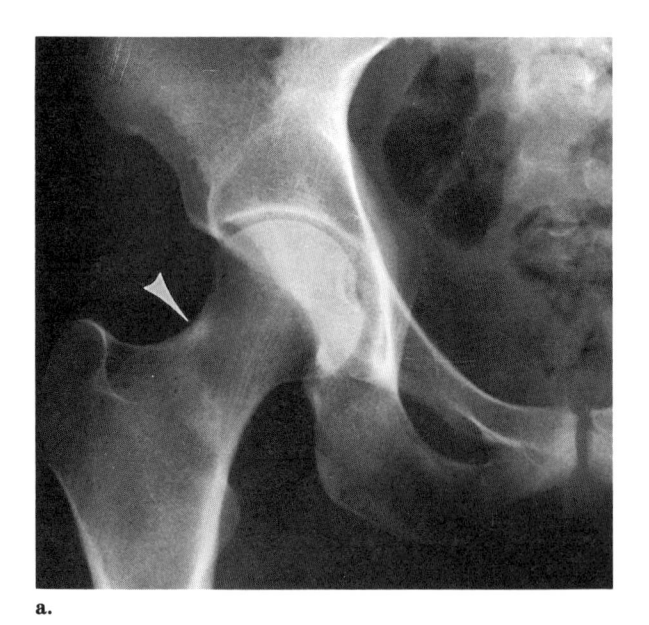

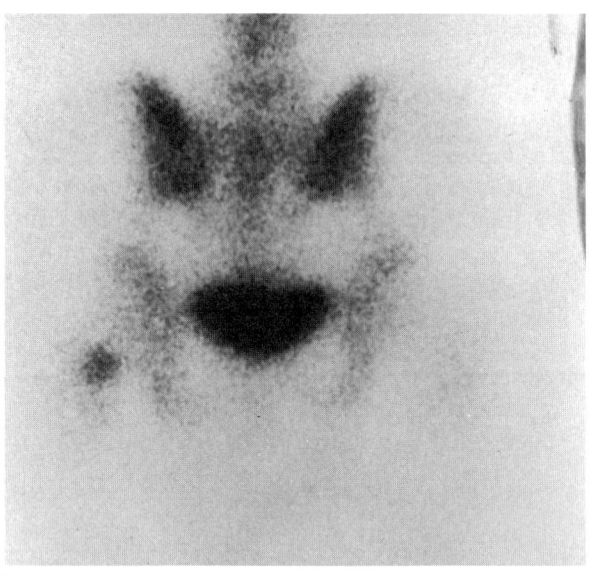

**Fig. 17-31.** A. Subtle femoral neck stress fracture; note the tiny radio-opaque region (arrowhead). B. Subsequent bone scan shows increased activity at the same sight.

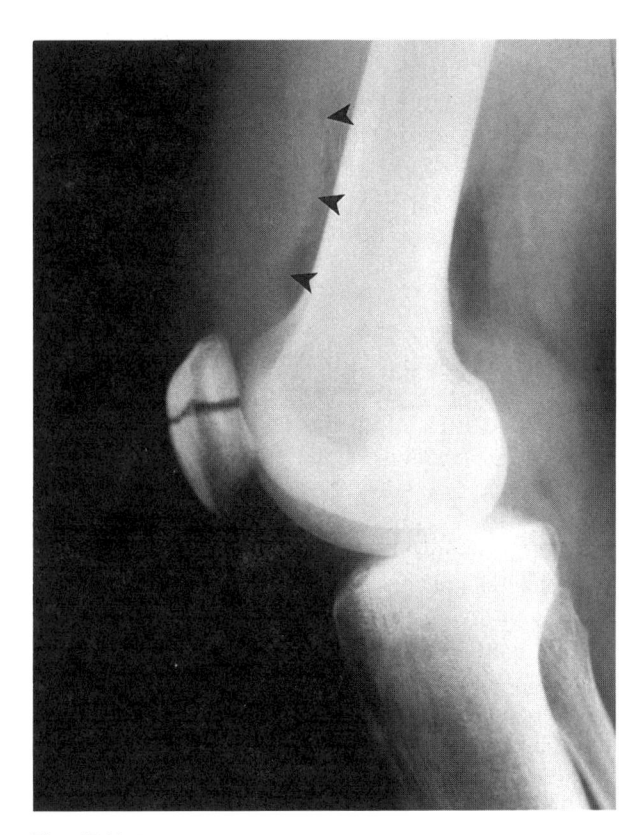

**Fig. 17-32.** Horizontal patellar fracture (arrowheads) with associated joint effusion.

often been self-reduced (Figure 17-34). Osteochondral fracture of the medial patellar surface or of the lateral femoral condyle can occur with reduction. This thin sliver of bone is best seen on an axial view of the patella. The significance of osteochondral fracture is that bone slivers may remain as loose bodies within the knee joint where they will cause impaired motion and lead to early knee degeneration. Surgical removal of these fragments may be necessary when they are demonstrated to be freely moving in the joint.

The patella routinely develops from a single ossification center but may occasionally develop from multiple centers. This most typically occurs in the upper outer quadrant of the knee and may be difficult to differentiate from a fracture. Comparison views of the opposite side that show a similar appearance or smooth, well rounded, sclerotic parallel borders are characteristic of a bipartite patella. Clinical evaluation is helpful because a fracture will cause local tenderness.

Tibial plateau fractures can be occult and usually involve the lateral plateau. If suspected they should be pursued aggressively. Linear tomography is the technique of choice. Osgood-Schlatter dis-

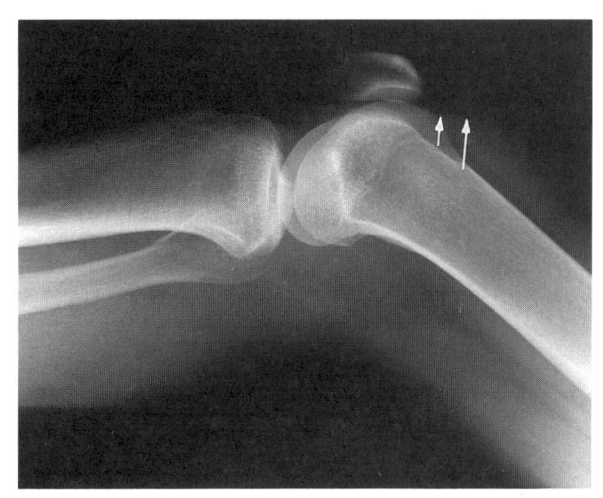

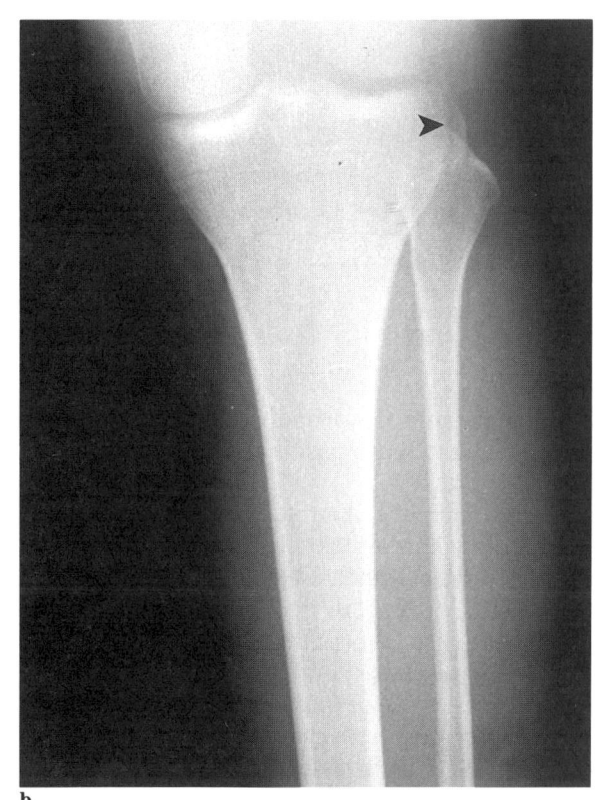

**Fig. 17-33.** A. Lipohemarthrosis of the knee joint, with a horizontal fluid — fluid (fat-blood) level (shown by arrows). This indicates a nearby fracture with marrow fat extrusion, in this case the fracture is in the lateral proximal tibia (B. arrowhead).

ease is typically found in children undergoing a growth spurt in their early teens. Radiographically, it is seen as elevation and fragmentation of the tibial tubercle, with local soft tissue swelling. However, these findings are not specific and may also

RADIOLOGY OF SPORTS INJURIES 527

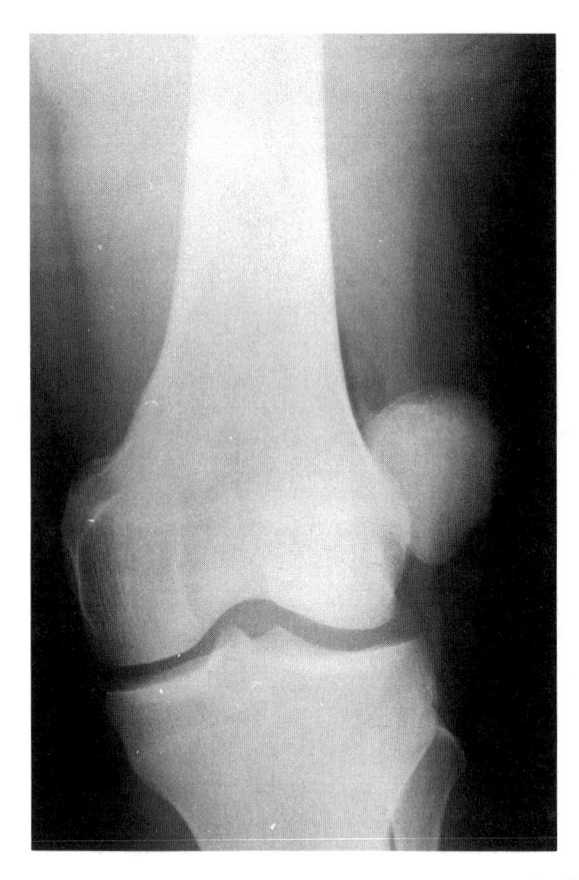

**Fig. 17-34.** Patella dislocation. These are typically lateral in location. Compare to normal patella location in Figure 17-23.

be seen in asymptomatic individuals so that diagnosis of Osgood-Schlatter's is confirmed primarily by clinical evaluation.

Osteochondritis dissecans is an osteochondral fracture that causes defects in the articulating surface of the affected bone. In the knee, this condition is usually found in the lateral aspect of the medial condyle of the femur (Figure 17-35 A, B & C). Rarely, other locations in the knee, such as the articulating surface of the lateral femoral condyle, may be affected. Osteochondritis dissecans may be associated with a calcified loose body within the knee joint and the significance of this finding must be determined through clinical examination. Where there is limitation of motion or persistent pain, surgical removal of a loose body may be warranted.

The meniscus of the knee has been evaluated best by arthrography in the past but MRI now is more accurate in showing these structures and associated pathology, without the need for contrast injection (Figure 17-36). In addition, the cruciate ligaments, the articulating cartilages, and the surrounding structures are clearly delineated (Figure 17-37 A & B, Figure 17-38) with MRI and it is certain to emerge as the method of choice to evaluate the knee joint (7).

## ANKLE

The ankle is the most frequently injured joint in the athlete. Musculotendinous strains and sprains that cause ligamentous disruption are the most most ankle injuries. Soft tissue swelling is the usual radiographic manifestation (Figure 17-39). If a ligamentous tear is suspected, stress views may help to establish the diagnosis (Figure 17-40). With applied stress, the normal talus may tilt 10 to 12 degrees from the base of the tibial plafond. If the degree of movement is questionable, do comparison views of the unaffected side while applying the same amount of stress. Where the talar tilt exceeds 25 degrees, a pathologic joint is present. Arthrography of the ankle joint may demonstrate integrity of the joint capsule and further identify ligamentous injury.

Fractures of the ankle joint require assessment of the joint's stability (13). Fractures at or above the plafond of the tibia generally are unstable (Figure 17-41). However, disruption of one or more of the major ligaments of the ankle, in conjunction with a fracture below the plafond, can also cause an unstable fracture. Since the major movement of the ankle is dorsal and plantar flexion, most ankle injuries are due to eversion, inversion, or rotational force. Knowing the mechanism of injury can direct attention to the structure most likely injured. Clinically, subtle fracture of the calcaneus and avulsion fracture of the base of the fifth metatarsal present as ankle injuries. These areas should be examined closely on each ankle x-ray exam. Multiple views should be obtained for full evaluation (Figure 17-42 A, B & C).

## FOOT AND TOES

Fractures of the toes are usually quite obvious radiographically but may be missed if only a single radiographic view is obtained. If the site of injury can be localized to one toe, a "coned-down" radiograph of that specific area should be obtained. This coning-down affords a better examination of bone, with increased resolution in areas that might

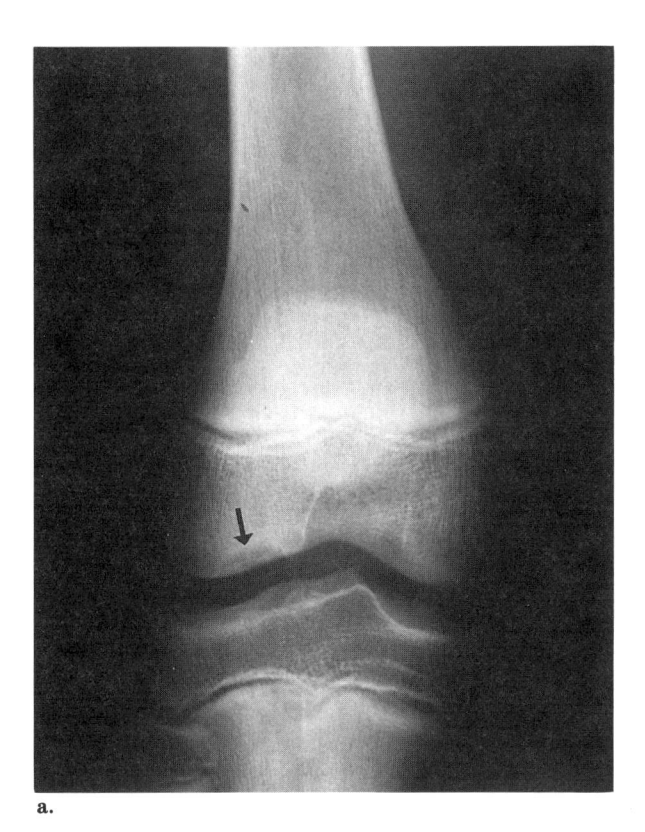

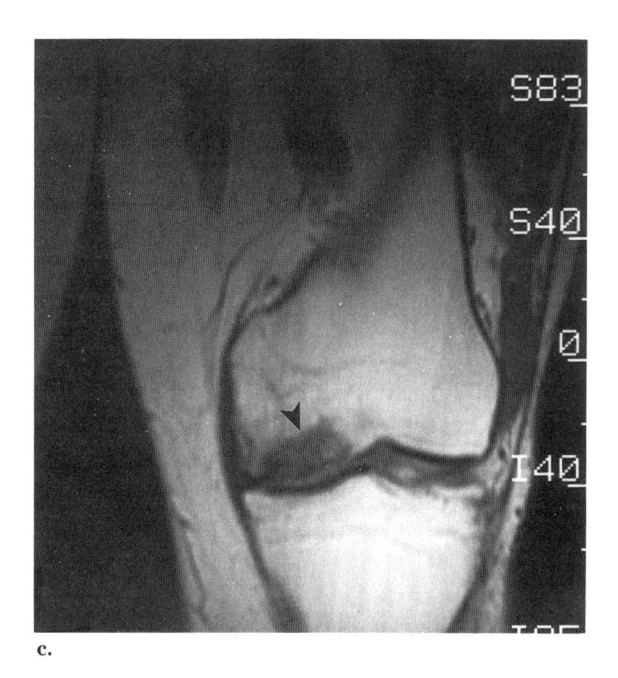

**Fig. 17-35.** A. & B. Osteochondritis dissecans of the lateral femoral condyle (arrows). C. This may also be demonstrated with MR (arrowhead).

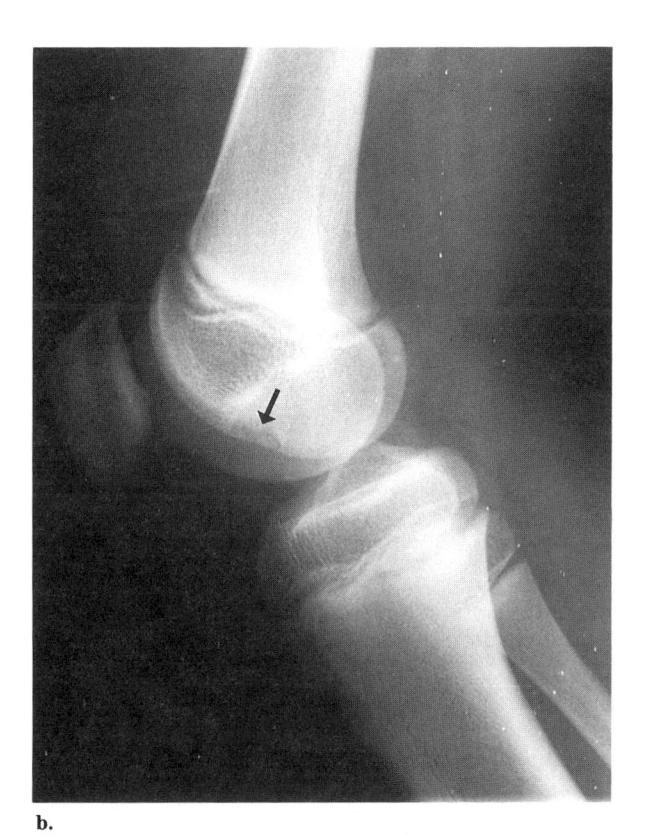

**Fig. 17-36.** Torn medial meniscus on MR demonstrated as high signal in the inferior aspect of the black normal meniscus (arrowhead).

RADIOLOGY OF SPORTS INJURIES 529

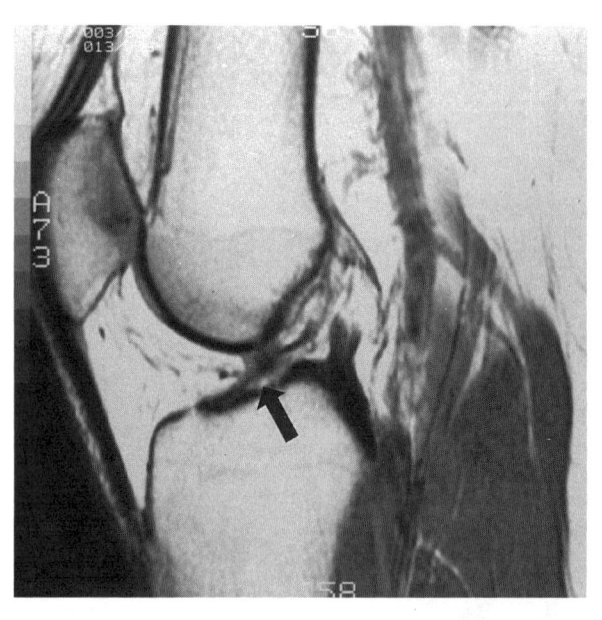

**Fig. 17-38.** Torn anterior cruciate ligament on MR. Note irregularity (arrow) and compare with Figure 37A.

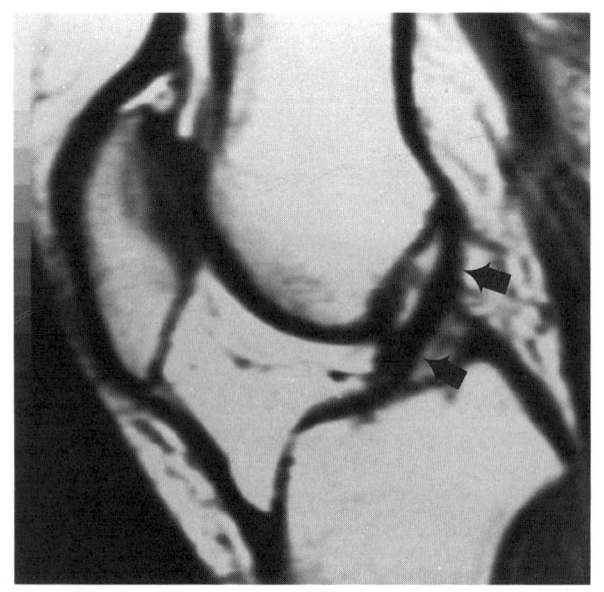

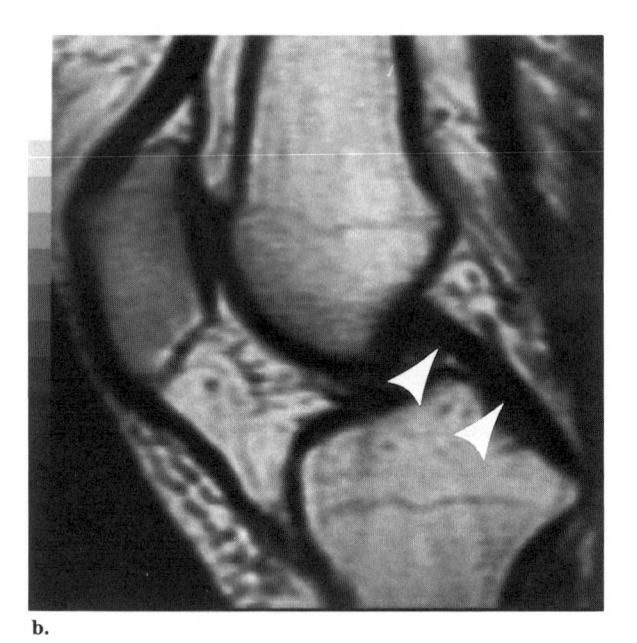

**Fig. 17-37.** Normal anterior (A. arrow) and the posterior (B. arrowhead) cruciate ligaments on sagittal MR images.

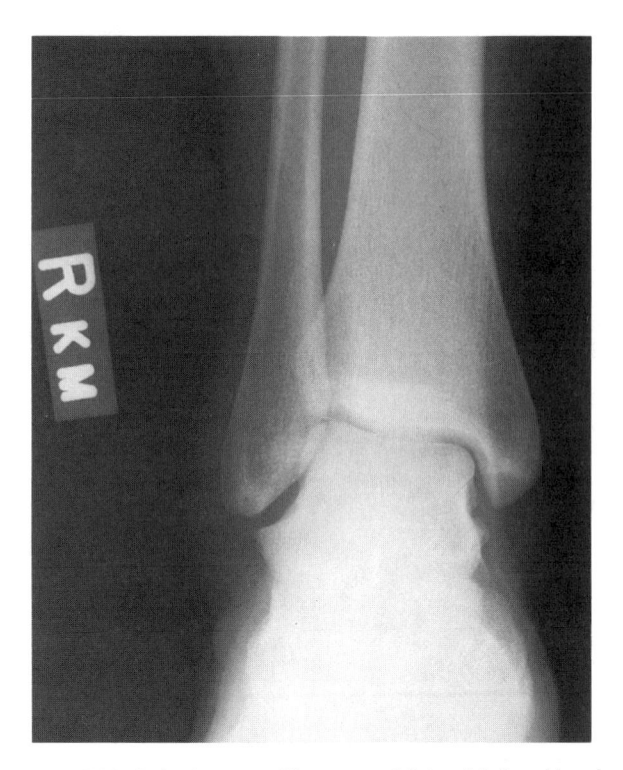

**Fig. 17-39.** Soft tissue swelling around lateral left ankle, although no bony fracture is seen. Compare the medial ankles soft tissues, which are relatively normal.

have occult fractures. Where there is a subtle but questionable area of bony lucency, magnification views may give additional information.

Avascular necrosis of the metatarsal heads, or Freiberg's disease, is initially seen as a lucency in the metatarsal head. Later, there may be significant distortion of the architecture leading to a degenerative change. Bony destruction may advance to a point where a surgical prosthesis is required (Figure 17-43 A & B). The most common site of destruction is the second metatarsal head,

530    *CLINICAL SPORTS MEDICINE*

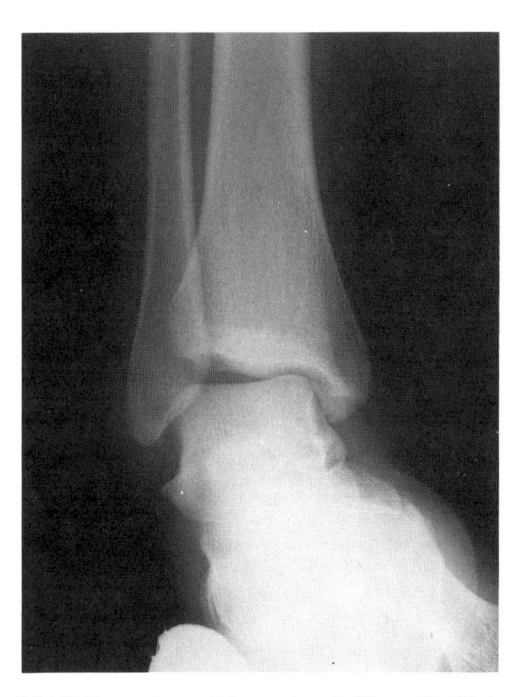

**Fig. 17-40.** Stress views of the patient in Figure 17-16 show noticeable widening of the joint, indicating significant ligamentous injury.

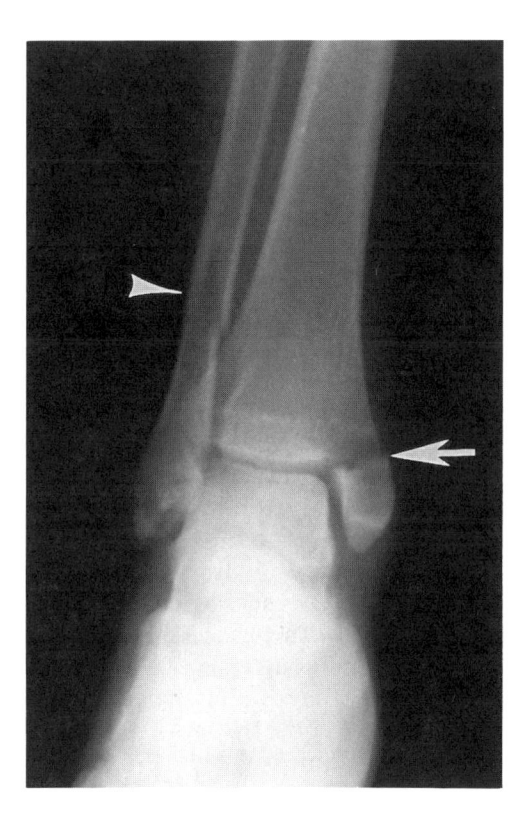

**Fig. 17-41.** Combination medial malleolar fracture (arrow) and distal fibular shaft fracture (arrowhead), with associated soft tissue swelling.

but the third and fourth may also be involved. This localization is believed to be related to the weight bearing focus of these structures. Shaft fractures may occur in any of the metatarsal bones and do not usually present a diagnostic dilemma (Figure 17-44 A & B). Stress fractures are commonly seen in the metatarsal shafts.

Sesamoid bones, accessory bones within tendons of the foot, may fracture, usually as a result of direct trauma either from a fall or dropping a heavy object on the bone. A bipartite sesamoid bone, usually seen at the base of the great toe, must be distinguished from a fracture (Figure 17-45). Comparison views of the uninjured toe or a radionuclide bone scan of the injured toe may be needed to establish whether a fracture is present.

Tarsal-metatarsal injuries are relatively rare because of the support given by footwear. Radiographically, a fracture-dislocation of this region is difficult to demonstrate due to overlap and complex bony relationships. Anteroposterior, lateral, and oblique views are required. In some instances, comparison views of the opposite foot may be helpful. Midtarsal dislocation, also called Chopart's joint, involve the talonavicular and calcaneocuboid joints.

Fracture of the navicular bone of the foot is not common and usually is an avulsion fracture on the dorsal surface at the talonavicular joint. A true lateral view is necessary to appropriately demonstrate this pathology. A secondary center of ossification os supranavicular is frequently found and must be distinguished from an avulsion fracture. Comparison views of the other foot may help differentiate this normal variant.

Both talar fractures and dislocation occur. This bone is especially susceptible to osteochondral fractures because 60% of its surface consists of articular cartilage. Obtain radiographs in the anteroposterior, oblique, and lateral positions. A frequent subtle fracture is an avulsion of the superoanterior aspect of the talus, adjacent to the navicular bone at the insertion of the joint capsule. Because the associated bone fragment may be minute, a high index of suspicion is necessary to confirm the existence of this injury. It also is necessary to differentiate a secondary center of ossification from frank pathology. The most posterior aspect of the talus is a relatively frequent site of fracture when the mechanism of injury occurs with the foot in severe plantar flexion. This injury happens when the posterior tubercle becomes caught beneath the inferior aspect of the tibia and the fracture must

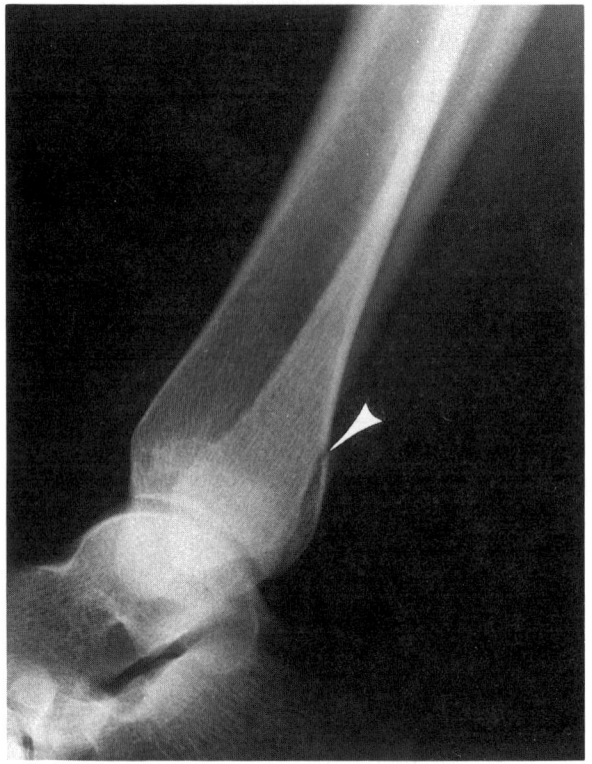

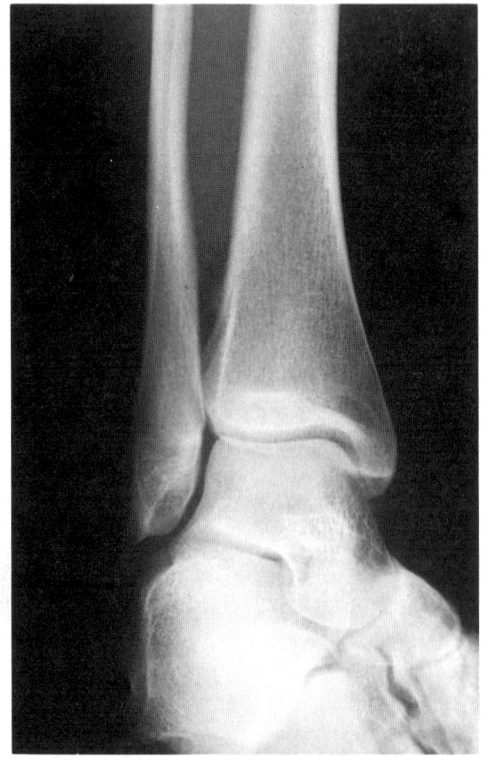

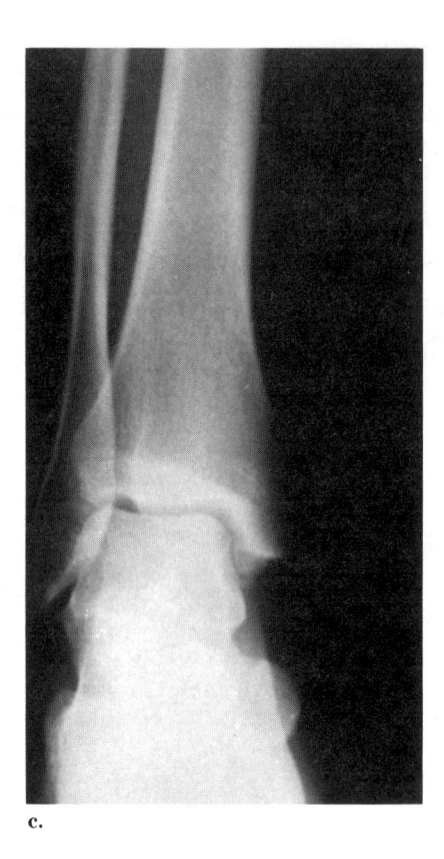

**Fig. 17-42A, B, C.** Subtle posterior malleolar fracture, seen only on the lateral view (arrowhead).

be differentiated from the normal accessory ossification center, the os trigonum.

The calcaneus, the largest tarsal bone of the foot, is frequently fractured and it is best evaluated with the lateral view (Figure 17-46 A & B). An axial view of this bone can be helpful in diagnosing existing pathology (Figure 17-47). Place the foot in maximal dorsal flexion with the x-ray tube positioned in a steep angle and the x-ray beam directed through the talocalcaneal joint. This view will show a fracture of the sustentaculum tali that may not be seen on the lateral view.

Avascular necrosis of the apophysis of the calcaneus is called Siever's disease and is radiographically manifested as sclerosis and fragmentation of the apophysis. This condition is difficult to identity because the apophysis of the calcaneus may normally have multiple ossification centers and be relatively sclerotic, the same configuration as Siever's disease. Clinical correlation is obviously necessary.

The mechanism of injury for stress fractures of the calcaneus is similar to those of other bones in the foot. On x-ray examination there is a scle-

a.

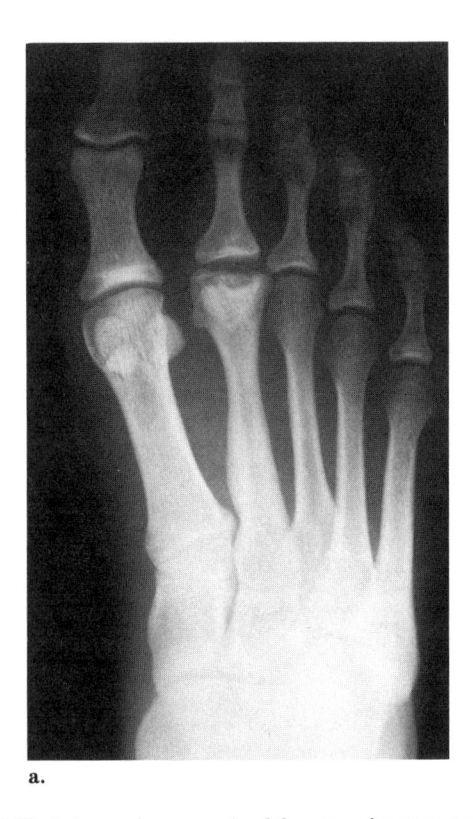

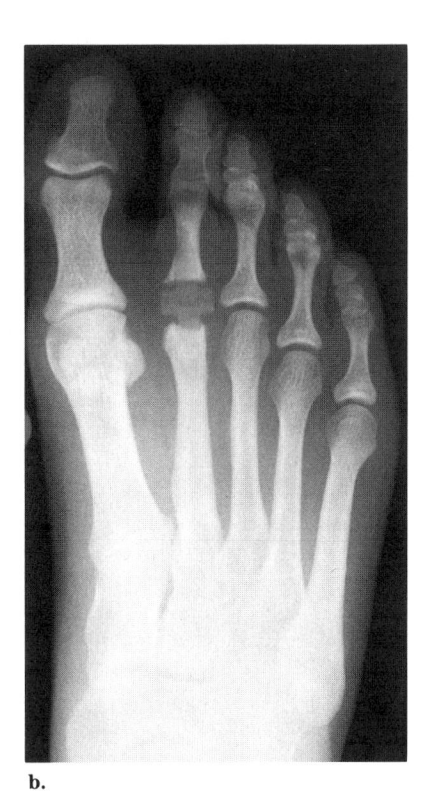

b.

**Fig. 17-43.** A. Avascular necrosis of the second metatarsal head (Freiberg's disease) with joint distortion and bony deformity. B. Postoperative film on the same patient demonstrating synthetic joint prosthesis.

a.

b.

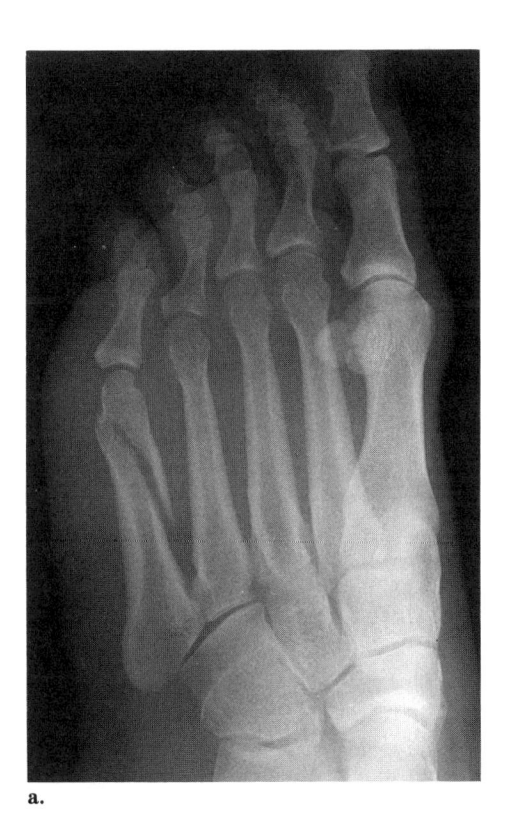

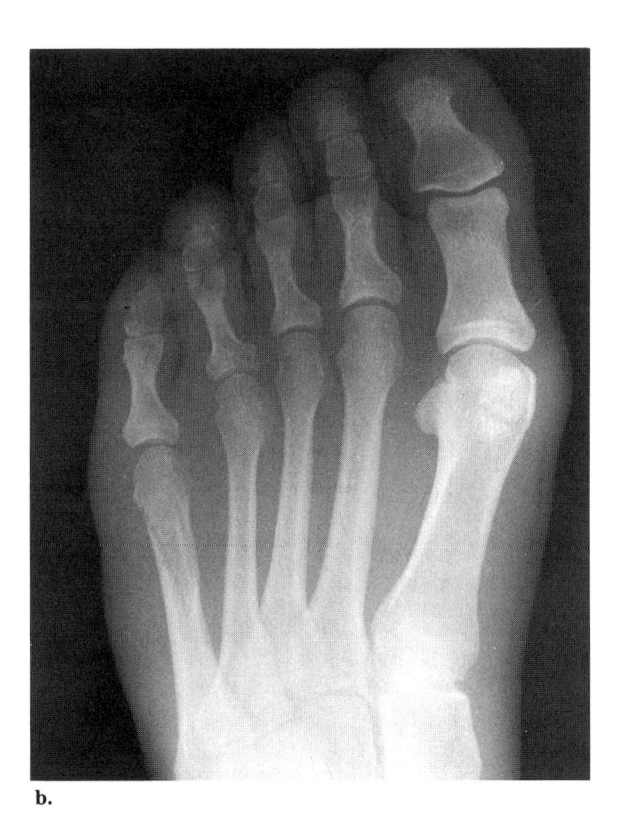

**Fig. 17-44.** Fifth metatarsal fracture. AP view (A) does not demonstrate the fracture, whereas the oblique view (B) does.

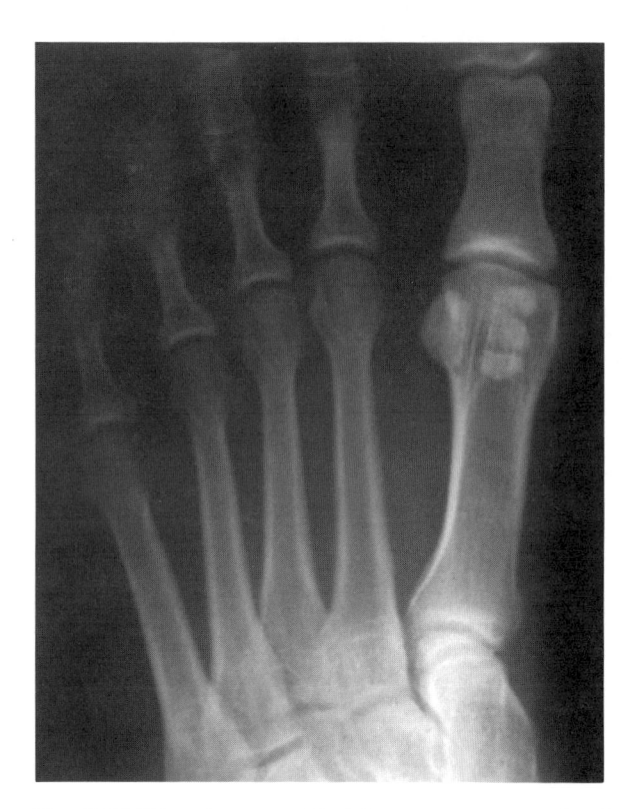

**Fig. 17-45.** Tripartite sesamoid of the great toe, a normal variant. At times it may be difficult to exclude fracture; sesamoids usually have round, well defined cortical margins, while fractures have sharp edges. Comparison views of the opposite side or nuclear medicine bone scan may be used in questionable cases.

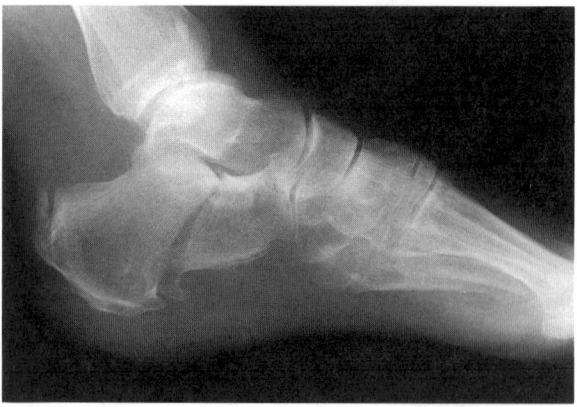

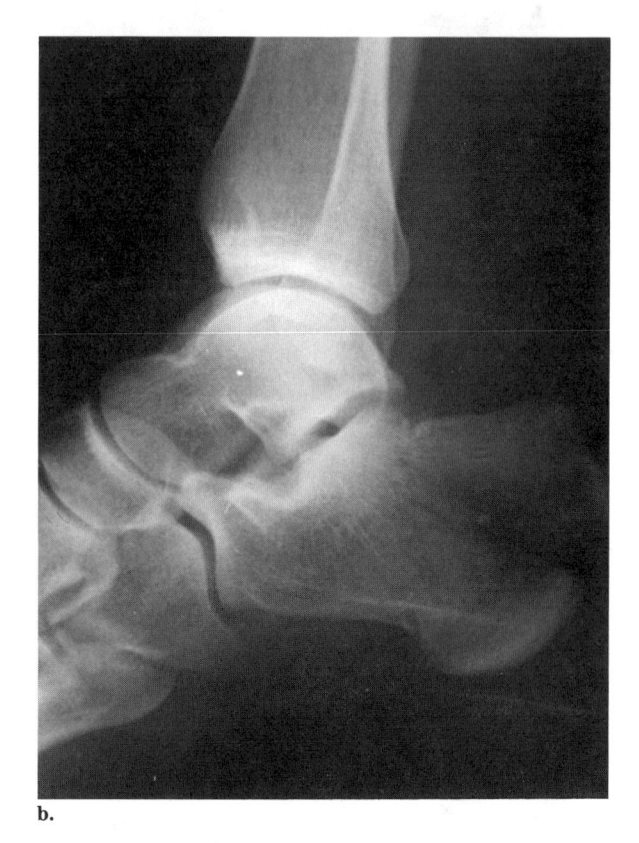

**Fig. 17-46A, B.** Calcaneal fractures in two different people.

rotic band parallel to the posterior aspect of the bone (Figure 17-48). A quarter of these fractures may be bilaterally symmetrical so that comparison views may be misleading. Nuclear medicine studies are useful with mature patients whose growth plates have closed.

Avulsion fracture of the posterosuperior calcaneus, a Beak fracture, can occur with traction from the powerful achilles tendon or the achilles tendon itself may become disrupted. This is best imaged by MRI (Figure 17-49). Compression fractures of this bone can be caused by a fall from a significant height. Compression fractures may be radiographically occult initially. Plain-film tomography in the lateral view, or nuclear medicine studies may be needed for diagnosis.

## SUMMARY

The primary evaluation for common athletic injuries is clinical examination. Radiology is used to objectively demonstrate the exact site of involvement and extent of injury. Follow-up evaluation may be performed to demonstrate healing or progression of an abnormality. Many techniques are now available and new imaging procedures are introduced regularly. Those responsible for the medical care of athletes must be familiar with the techniques that are available to identify injuries and follow-up the healing process. Plain film x-ray is still the first line approach in radiographic evalua-

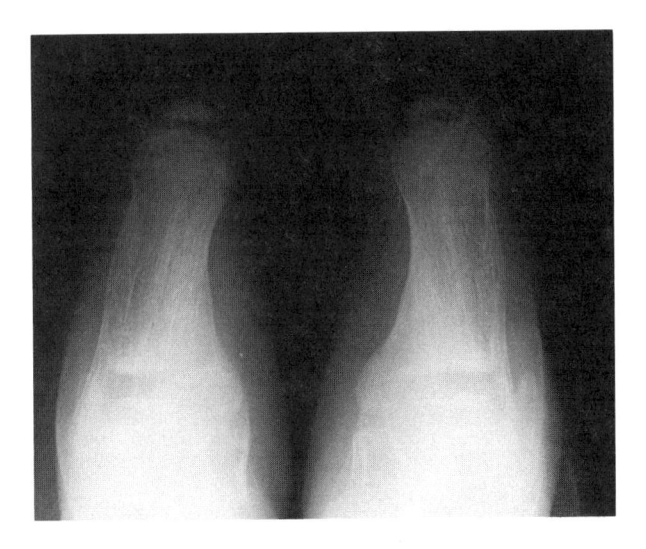

**Fig. 17-47.** Normal axial or tangential views of the calcaneus. This is sometimes helpful to demonstrate subtle lesions.

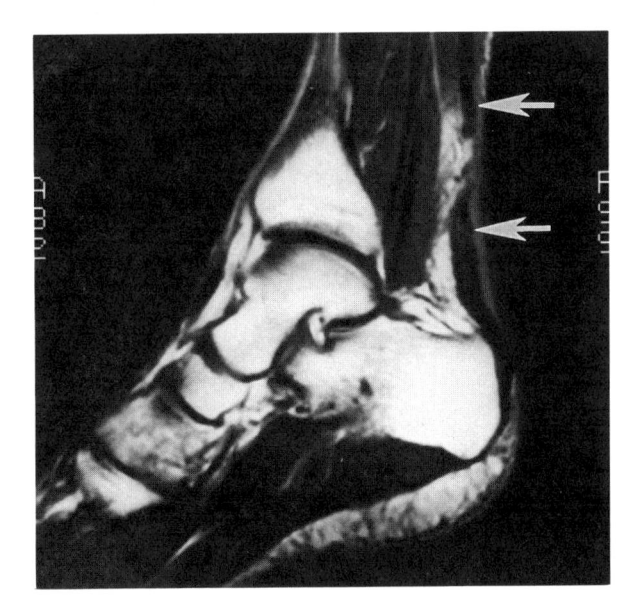

**Fig. 17-49.** Achilles tendon rupture. On these sagittal MR views, the irregular disruption of the achilles tendon (arrows) is obvious.

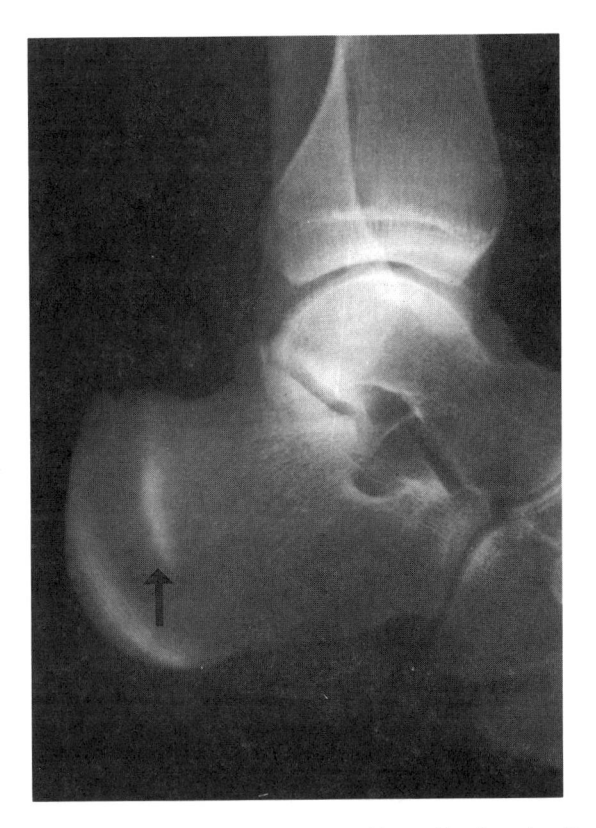

**Fig. 17-48.** Calcaneal stress fracture evidenced by the sclerotic region (arrow).

tion but other techniques must be used in specific instances. In addition to knowledge of techniques for assessing injury, correlation of pertinent information is imperative to provide the best approach to address the medical concern.

### REFERENCES

1. Rogers, L.F. *Radiology of skeletal trauma*. New York. Churchill Livingston 1982.
2. Weissmann, B.N.W. and Sledge, C.B. *Orthopedic radiology*. Philadelphia, W.B. Saunders 1986.
3. Mettler, F.A. Jr. and Guiberteau, M.J. *Essentials of nuclear medicine imaging*. 2nd edition, Philadelphia, W.B. Saunders, 1986.
4. Lee, J.K.T., Sagel, S.S. and Stanley, R.S. *Computed body tomography*. New York. Raven Press 1983.
5. Kneeland, J.B., Middleton, W.D., Carrera, G.F., Zeuge, R.C., Jesmanowicz, A., Froncisz, W., and Hyde, J.S. MR imaging of the shoulder: diagnosis of rotator cuff tears. *AJR* 149:333,1987.
6. Mitchell, M.D., Kundel, H.L. and Steinberg M.E. Avascular necrosis of the hip: comparison of MR, CT, and scintigraphy. *Radiology* 161:739, 1986.
7. Reicher, M.A., Hartzman, S., Bassett, L.W., Mandelbaum, B., Duckwiler, G.R. and Gold, R.H. MR imaging of the knee, part 1, traumatic disorders. *Radiology* 162:547,1987.
8. Berman, L. and Hollingdale, J. Ultrasound appearance of positive hip instability tests. *Clin Radiol* 38:117,1987.
9. Berman, L., Catterall, A., and Meire H.B. Ultrasound of the hip; review of the applications of a new technique. *BR J Radiol* 59:13,1986.
10. Mack, L.A., Matsen, F.A. III, Kilcoyne, R.F., Davies, P.K. and Sickler, M.E. US evaluation of the rotator cuff. *Radiology* 157:205,1976.
11. Hallel, T., Amit, S. and Segal, D., Fatigue fractures of tibial and femoral shaft in soldiers. *Clin Orthop* 118:35,1976.
12. Zwas, S.T., Elkanovitch, R. and Frank, G. Interpretation and classification of bone scintigraphic findings in stress fractures. *J Nucl Med* 28:452,1987.
13. Sclafani, S.J.A. Ligamentous injury of the lower tibiofibular syndesmosis: radiographic evidence. *Radiology* 156:21,1985.
14. Fernbach, S.K. and Wilkinson, R.H. Avulsion injuries of the pelvis and proximal femur. *AJR* 137:581-584,1981.
15. Brogdon, B.G. and Crow, N.E. Little leaguer's elbow. *AJR* 83:671,1960.
16. Cisternino, S.J., Rogers, L.F., Stufflebaum, B.C. and Kruglik, G.D., The trough line: a radiographic sign of posterior shoulder dislocation. *AJR* 130:951,1978.
17. Stark, D. and Bradley, W. *Magnetic Resonance Imaging*, St. Louis, Mosby 1987.

# 18

# Rehabilitation

## INTRODUCTION

"Doc, when do you think I will be ready to play again?" I am asked this question on a daily basis. Once athletes are injured, they typically have only one thing on their minds: how long it will be before they can return to competition? Highly motivated athletes have tunnel vision after an injury. Very often they are willing to risk re-injury (and perhaps even more serious injury) in order to return to their sport as soon as possible. Once the correct diagnosis is made, the team physician's role is largely devoted to answering this basic question.

This chapter is written for primary care physicians who may be serving as team doctors for their community schools and/or caring for recreational athletes as part of their office practice. The purpose of this chapter is to help the physician answer questions about when an athlete is ready to return to competition.

The time it takes to *safely* return to competition is often critical. Factors that influence the length of the recovery phase and ultimate return to activity include the specific injury, level of competition, age and sex of the athlete, and the ability to carefully monitor the rehabilitation process. When the question about returning to competition is asked, it is tempting to respond, "You should be ready by next Tuesday at 3:15!" Obviously, the situation is not that clear-cut. The appropriate response is to outline a progressive, functional, rehabilitation (P.F.R.) protocol. When certain objective, functional goals are met, the athlete can expect to safely return to competition. Before the injured athlete leaves the training room or your office, make it clear that most of the responsibility for reaching these objectives is on his shoulders. An injured athlete who stops by the training room infrequently, forgets to take medications, or neglects to follow the rehabilitation protocol, must understand the consequences. The recovery time is prolonged each time there is a variation from the prescribed plan of action.

Without a good understanding of the importance of the team approach to athletic injuries, it may be difficult to exercise common sense and good judgment. Consequently, deciding when an athlete is ready to play again becomes even harder. An injured athlete may attempt to get one member of the sports medicine staff to allow him to return to competition before it is safe so that it is paramount that everyone involved understands the concept of *progressive functional rehabilitation*.

The author recommends that physicians who take care of athletes have regular athletic pursuits of their own. When challenged with the responsibility of outlining and supervising the rehabilitation of an injured athlete, personal insight and experience can be very helpful.

It is also important to understand the psychology of athletic competition and the impact that even minor injuries have on performance. For example, I recently heard a physician tell a marathon runner with a soft-tissue overuse injury that he should give up running and try swimming "if exercise is that important to you." Obviously, a little insight could have gone a long way toward helping this man safely return to an activity that was more than just a form of "exercise" for him. In addition, personal experience as an athlete will make you aware that most injured athletes prefer to avoid treatment of minor injuries. Often, injuries that are brought to the attention of the trainer or physician have progressed to a point where more intense action must be taken. As a rule, athletes prefer to have as little intervention as possible. Complications and disabilities that result from "minor injuries" can be minimized or even eliminated with timely intervention. This concept should be familiar to athletes and coaches alike, since it is truly a false economy if an athlete attempts to play with a minor injury that ultimately may lead to a more serious problem. Finally, regular participation in athletic and fitness activities gives team physicians insight into sports specific injuries. It is beneficial to be a sports participant in order to understand the training requirements, equipment needs, and biomechanical aspects of specific athletic endeavors. However, participation and enthusiasm are not substitutes for medical expertise. The rehabilitation of any athletic injury is predicated on an accurate diagnosis.

Before discussing when an injured athlete is ready to return to play, one should be familiar with the principles of sports medicine rehabilitation (Table 18-1). After these principles are covered, several rehabilitation protocols for common athletic injuries are outlined. Because 80%-90% of these injuries are due to disruption of soft tissue structures, the primary focus of this chapter will be on restoring the integrity of soft tissue and preventing reinjury.

## PRINCIPLES OF REHABILITATION

### Prevention of Injuries

It has been said that "an ounce of prevention is worth a pound of cure" and this is very appropriate with regard to athletic injuries. Injury prevention is extremely important to any team or individual. As team physicians, we attempt to minimize the overall impact that injuries may have during a season and one of the best ways is to prevent them from occurring. Prevention is the fundamental axiom of sports medicine rehabilitation. All other guidelines stem from this primary concept. Table 18-2 gives the basic principles of injury prevention and a more thorough discussion is presented in Chapter 7.

### P.R.I.C.E.

One of the most important concepts in managing acute athletic injuries is prompt intervention in order to mitigate the inflammatory response and resulting edema that follows soft tissue trauma. The inflammatory response to soft tissue damage is a cascade of chemical, metabolic, and vascular events that lead to increased capillary permeability. (41, 46, 90, 94) Initially, these events serve a necessary and useful purpose in promoting soft tissue healing. However, excessive swelling within or around a joint leads to pain, decreased range of motion, joint laxity, and diminished proprioception. (8, 116) Therefore, prompt, aggressive action to minimize the inflammatory response can reduce recovery time and permit an earlier safe return to activity. The basic treatment of these injuries consists of protection, rest, ice, compression, and elevation (P.R.I.C.E.). The rationale is to minimize soft

---

Table 18-1. Principles of Sports Medicine Rehabilitation

---

Prevention of Injuries
P.R.I.C.E.
Early Mobilization and Restoration of R.O.M.
Modalities
Medications
Restoration of Balanced Muscle Strength and Endurance
Maintaining Cardiovascular Fitness
Proprioception, Balance and Agility
Flexibility
Protective Taping and Bracing
Psychological Support
Functional Progressive Rehabilitation

---

Table 18-2. Principles of Injury Prevention

---

Preparticipation Evaluations
Complete Rehabilitation of Previous Injuries
Balanced Muscle Strength and Flexibility
Proper Body Mechanics
In Season and Off Season Conditioning
Aerobic and Anaerobic Fitness
Proper Nutrition and Hydration
Avoidance of Overtraining and Burnout
Appropriate Warm-ups and Cool-downs
Safe and Appropriate Equipment
Safe and Appropriate Field and Court Conditions
Protective Equipment, Taping and Bracing
Proper Coaching Techniques
Understanding the Rules of Various Sports
Community Education
Sports Medicine Network
Understanding the Ethical Dilemmas in Sports Medicine

tissue swelling and hasten healing. The first few hours of treatment often determine how quickly an injury will heal.

Protection may involve several of strategies. Temporary immobilization with a cast or splint is sometimes indicated or the athlete might use crutches to prevent weight bearing on an injured lower extremity or a sling to support the upper extremity. Bracing across an injured joint may be indicated. Prevention further injury to a joint or extremity is paramount. Placing an athlete with a Grade I or Grade II ankle sprain on crutches for three to five days after injury may seem a bit extreme. However, depending upon how much walking the athlete must do, the condition of the walking surfaces, and the reliability of the athlete, this protective step may be warranted. If there are any suspicions about the potential for further injury, always err on the side of safety and protect the injured joint or extremity as much as possible.

Rest is probably the most difficult thing to convince an athlete to do but it is very important early in the course of acute injury. In some situations, *relative* rest is indicated as opposed to absolute rest. Some key points must be made about the type and amount of rest needed. First, repeated microtrauma to already injured tissue can cause further injury and prolong healing. However, immobilization can lead to soft tissue contracture, loss of range of motion, muscle atrophy, and deconditioning. There is a fine line between rest and activity in any rehabilitation protocol. You can be assured that you are on the correct side of the line so long as progression through functional stages continues in the *absence* of increased pain, progressive joint stability, and/or swelling.

Ice probably is the single most important part of any sports medicine staff's armamentarium. It is cheap, easy to use, readily available, and has few contraindications (53). Ice therapy causes vasoconstriction, thus decreasing edema and the metabolic demands of injured tissues. It also decreases muscle spasticity and has a local analgesic effect. Ice helps limit the inflammatory response, and thus the extent of injury. The controversy about cold therapy versus heat therapy will be discussed below. The important thing to remember is that ice is the modality of choice for the initial treatment of acute soft tissue injuries.

Compression is very useful in minimizing the extent of soft tissue swelling (115-116). In fact, several authors believe that it is the single most effective deterrent (61, 115). Again, the rationale is to control edema so as to reduce the recovery time. Figure 18-1a-f demonstrates how compression is used after an ankle injury. A foam pad is taped to the lateral side of the ankle to prevent capillary leakage and enhance lymphatic drainage. A U-shaped foam pad (Figure 18-2) tailored to fit around the malleolus is probably more effective. Once the pad is applied, it is imperative to keep it in position. Ice packs can be placed on top of the pad but the pad itself should not be removed until the ecchymosis begins to turn yellowish. The change in skin coloration represents the breakdown of hemoglobin and rebound swelling is unlikely at this stage.

This technique is much more effective in controlling edema than using standard elastic wrapping. Elastic wraps may actually be counter-productive. If wrapped too tightly and left on for prolonged periods, they can have a tourniquet effect. Once the appropriate compression wrap is placed, regular monitoring is essential to assure that the edema is not increasing. A pneumatic compression device may also be very helpful for controlling edema (Figure 18-3).

Elevation plays an obvious role in minimizing swelling but it is often forgotten. Rather that telling an athlete to go home and soak his/her newly sprained ankle in a bucket of ice water, explain that it would be more effective to wrap an ice pack around the ankle and elevate it. This is particularly true within the first 24 hours when keeping the injured extremity elevated higher than the heart is essential.

The P.R.I.C.E. protocol is aimed at minimizing the swelling that accompanies acute trauma. Taken individually, each step may seem insignificant but the summation of each intervention can be dramatic (8, 53, 59, 61, 94-95, 115-116).

## Early Mobilization and Restoration of Range of Motion

Early mobilization after soft tissue injuries, fractures, and surgery is a topic that warrants considerable attention. The reader should be aware that not everyone supports this concept. For instance, there is considerable controversy about the non-operative management of ankle sprains (18, 86, 95, 116). As noted earlier, temporary immobilization may be indicated depending upon the athlete and the circumstances. However, long term immobilization should be avoided whenever possible.

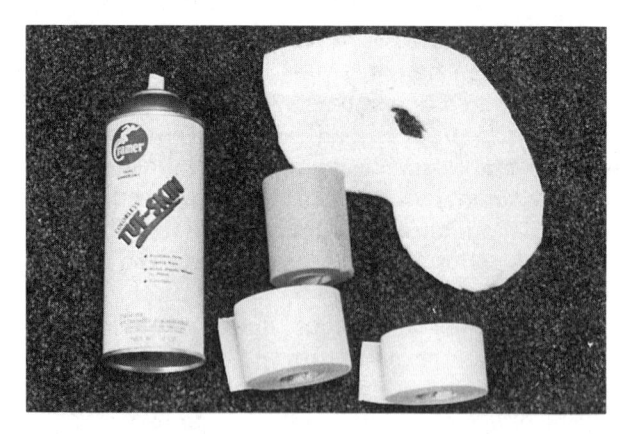

**Fig. 18.1a.** Materials needed: 1½" adhesive tape, 1" adhesive tape, prewrap, tape adherent spray, pressure padding.

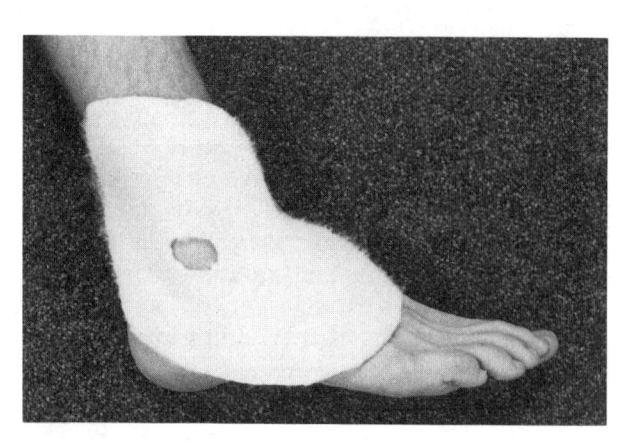

**Fig. 18-1b.** Spray ankle with adherent, then apply pressure pad(s).

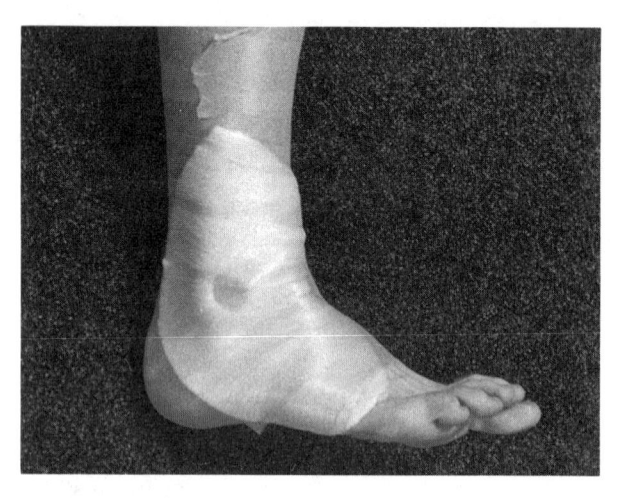

**Fig. 18-1c.** Apply prewrap beginning distally at the head of metatarsals continuing proximally to midcalf.

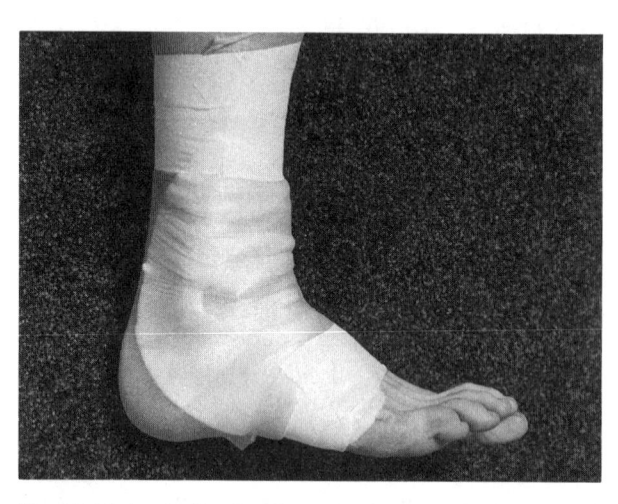

**Fig. 18-1d.** Apply distal and proximal tape anchors.

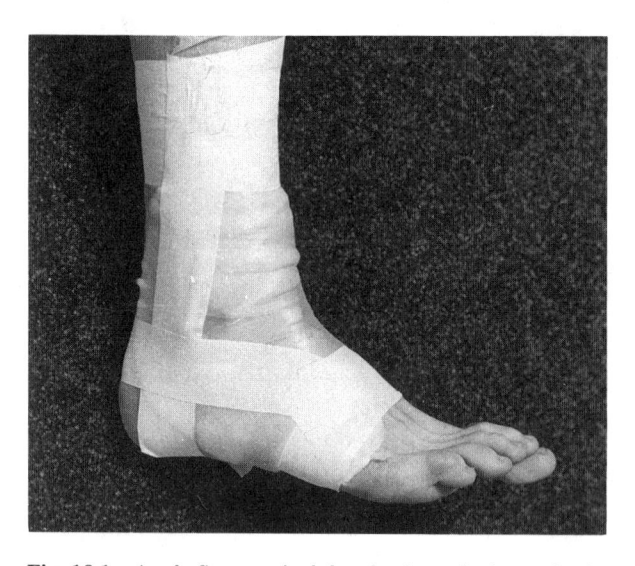

**Fig. 18-1e.** Apply first *vertical* then horizontal stirrups beginning slightly behind and below malleoli.

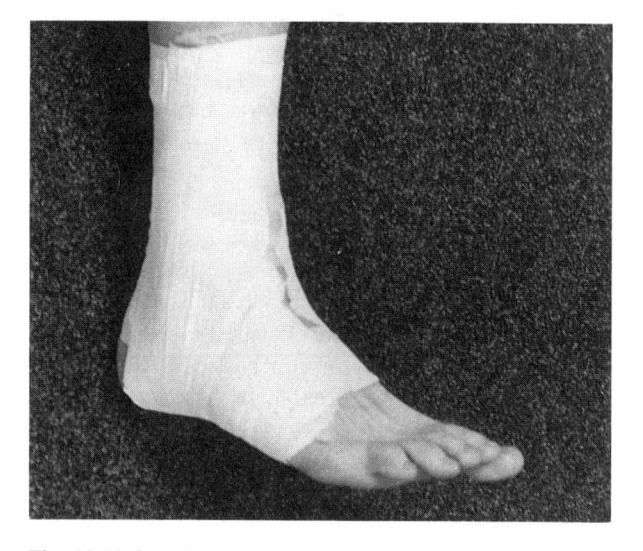

**Fig. 18-1f.** Completed ankle taping should be tight enough for support and protection and loose enough to allow for swelling.

**Fig. 18-1.** Ankle Taping

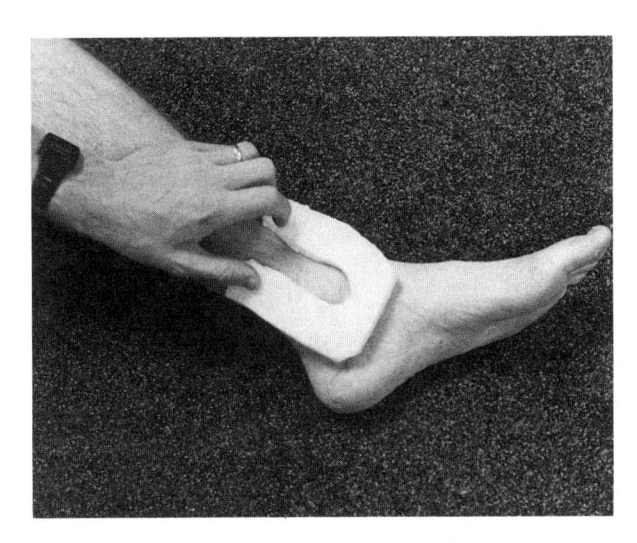

**Fig. 18-2.** A U-shaped foam pad tailored to fit around the malleolus is applied to the injured ankle.

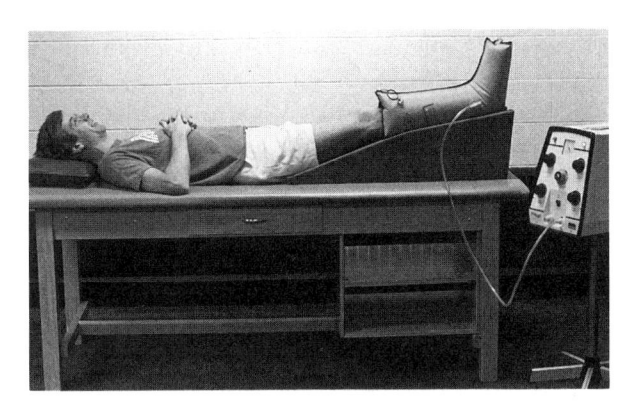

**Fig. 18-3.** Pneumatic compression device for controlling edema.

There are several reasons to begin gentle range of motion exercises soon after an injury. Early motion enhances lymphatic drainage and clearing of necrotic debris and also helps maintain joint proprioception and muscle strength (18, 86, 95). Significant increases in the strength and thickness of ligamentous tissue as a result of early motion and endurance exercises has been well-documented (11, 15, 25, 76-77, 81, 106). Finally, and probably most important, early mobilization minimizes joint stiffness and inhibits the development of soft tissue contractures due to excessive scar formation. Collagen proliferation is part of the inflammatory response. Appropriate stressing of this new tissue promotes optimal organization of collagen fibrils and limits randomized scar tissue from impending joint motion (3). Recovery time can be prolonged for several days or even weeks if an injured joint develops stiffness and a significant loss of range of motion. Immobilization may be needed initially for protection but some movement can usually begin shortly after injury. Always work within the "pain-free" range of motion. Joint stability should always be monitored because an unstable joint should not be subjected to excessive range of motion exercises. As rehabilitation advances, flexibility exercises can be escalated. However, if there is prolonged post-exercise pain, the range of motion exercises should be backed-off to previous pain-free levels.

## Therapeutic Modalities

Detailed discussions about the technical application of different modalities often seem boring and pointless. Many physicians have little knowledge of the principles behind the various modalities and the application, partly because this work generally falls under the domain of athletic trainers and therapists. Even so, a fundamental understanding of each is important. Every time one of the modalities is used, a *specific, objective goal* should be kept in mind, including the timing and sequence of their use. The intensity, duration, and frequency of application can be critical in expediting recovery.

Finally, the reader should be reminded that many treatment regimes become popular without adequate evidence of their efficacy. One comprehensive review article highlights how little we actually know about the physiological principles and efficacy of many modalities.

### Cryotherapy

Cold therapy used immediately after injury limits the overall degree of injury. Cooling an injured joint or extremity raises the threshold of pain, reduces muscle spasm, causes vasocontriction, and may provide a relative anesthesia (31, 53-54). A sensation of coldness occurs in an immersed extremity within the first two to three minutes. There may be a burning or aching feeling next. It takes seven to ten minutes to get local numbness and anesthesia. At this stage, greater pain-free motion is possible. The concept of cooling to break the cycle of pain and spasm and establish greater range of motion is called cryokinetics.

There are several ways to apply cold therapy, including ice massage, ice water immersion in a whirlpool bath, an ice blanket or pack, or immersion in an ice water slush. Coolant sprays in the forms of ethychloride or fluromethane are used for topical anesthesia and in the techniques of spray and stretch.

The therapeutic temperature range of cold applications ranges for 0°C to 4°C (32°F to 39.2°F). Ice massage means local application of an ice cup in a circular motion for a period of five to ten minutes. Ice water immersion, either in a whirlpool or ice water slush, is good for treating a larger area of injury or one involving bony or irregular surfaces (e.g. lateral malleolus). After analgesia occurs, the athlete can begin gentle range of motion exercises while the injured part is immersed. This therapy should usually last 20 to 30 minutes and can be repeated every one and a half to two hours. Ice packs are applied in a similar way. Remember that the application of any form of cryotherapy for extended periods of time may cause temporary or even permanent injury to nervous tissue (16, 85). The therapeutic effects of cold therapy are listed in Table 18-3 and the contraindications are given in Table 18-4.

A physician often reads that ice should be used for the first 24-48 hours after acute, soft tissue injury and then followed by heat. We caution against using any set period of time. So long as there is evidence that swelling is increasing, do not start heat therapy. Edema can easily continue after the first 48 hours in an injured joint that is not treated appropriately. Heat in this situation would only make it worse. Use ice until you are convinced the swelling has stopped. This may take several days, depending upon the type and extent of injury. Ice application after activity may also be indicated after an athlete begins progressive functional rehabilitation. Too often the use of ice is neglected after athletes are allowed to return to activity. When that happens, a small amount of edema may recur and prolong the recovery time.

### Heat Therapy

The application of heat can also bring about analgesia and decreased muscle spasms. However, if applied too soon, heat may actually increase pain because it increases edema. Therefore, it should *not* be considered for initial treatment of an acute injury. The desirable therapeutic effects of heat include reducing pain, relieving muscle spasm, increasing blood flow, decreasing joint stiffness, and increasing the elasticity of collagen fibers (53, 54). The effective therapeutic temperature range is very narrow, 40°C to 45.5°C (104°F to 113.9°F) and it is essential to remember that there is a narrow margin between the therapeutic range and the tissue damage range, which begins at 46°C (114.8°F) The therapeutic effects are determined by the duration of heating, the total area treated, the tissue temperature, and the rate of temperature rise in the tissues. The most effective duration is three to 30 minutes, depending upon the modality of application. Heat can be applied by convection (moist air cabinet, hydrotherapy), conduction (hot packs, paraffin), radiation (infrared), or conversion (diathermy, ultrasound). It can be applied in either superficial or deep form. The most common modalities for superficial heat are whirlpool baths and hydroculator packs. The most common modality for deep heat is ultrasound.

Superficial heat produces the highest temperature at the body surface but penetrates only a few millimeters into the tissue. (53, 54). Because the penetration of heat is minimal, superficial heat often is chosen for reflex muscle relaxation and its sedative effect. It may be chosen for its cleansing action and buoyancy. Immersing the trunk and all four extremities in a hubbard tank will induce a mild fever in most people. Consequently, the maximum water temperature should not exceed 38°C (100.4°F). Immersion of a single extremity can be done safely up to 41°C (105.8°F). Remember that heating increases the metabolic demand of tissues. If ischemia is a problem (ischemic ulcer), keep the temperature at 35°C to 37°C (95°F to 98.6°F). Heat application by hydrotherapy should be done in 20

---

**Table 18-3. Therapeutic Effects of Cold**

1. Vasoconstriction
2. Decrease muscle spasm
3. Increase threshold of pain
4. Relative anesthesia

---

**Table 18-4. Contraindications to Cold Therapy**

1. Raynaud's phenomenon
2. Raynaud's disease
3. Cold allergy
4. Cryoglobulinemia
5. Paraxysmal Hemoglobinuria
6. Cold presser response positive

to 30 minute periods because longer immersion may cause local tissue damage.

Hydroculator packs contain dried silica gel capable of absorbing and retaining water and heat. They are usually heated to a temperature of 76.4°C to 82.2°C (170°F to 180°F) and then wrapped in several towels before being placed on the athlete. This helps control the transfer of heat by conduction. Treatment periods usually are 20 to 30 minutes long.

Another form of superficial heat is paraffin wax baths. The wax mixture usually consists of four to eight parts paraffin mixed with one part mineral oil. The mixture is heated and maintained at 51.8°C to 52.7°C (125°F to 127°F) and can be applied by dipping or continuous immersion. The total treatment time usually is 20 to 30 minutes. This is a very effective method of treating injured joints of the hands and feet.

Radiant heat from infrared lamps has limited application in sports medicine; they are used mostly for dermatological conditions.

Deep heating modalities include short wave, microwave, and ultrasound. Ultrasound is the one most often used to apply deep heat for sports injuries.

Short wave diathermy is the therapeutic application of an electric current with a very high frequency that is converted to heat within the tissues. The two techniques of application are the condenser method and induction coil applicators. Treatment usually lasts 20 to 30 minutes and the highest temperature is obtained in the deep subcutaneous tissues of superficial muscles. It does not penetrate into deep joint structures.

A big disadvantage of short wave diathermy is that it cannot be accurately dosed nor can the amount of energy transferred to the patient be monitored. The only safeguard against excessive heating is the athlete's perception of warmth and pain. In addition, the patient must be kept dry because perspiration, which contains electrolytes, can serve as an electrical conductor and cause burning of the skin.

Microwave diathermy is a deep heating modality using high frequency electromagnetic waves. As with short wave diathermy, there is no accurate way to monitor the dose. Because microwave applicators are small and cannot be used to treat very large areas, their effectiveness is limited at present.

Ultrasound is a form of acoustic energy produced by mechanical vibrations. Ultrasound waves are at frequencies which are inaudible to the human ear (above 2,000 cycles per second). To produce ultrasonic energy for therapeutic purposes, a machine requires a generator of high frequency current and an applicator sound head with a transducer that receives electrical currents of sufficient frequency to cause it to vibrate and produce sound waves.

Ultrasound energy is transmitted to the tissues by this applicator. The waves do not pass easily through air so that an air-free medium must be interposed between the applicator and the skin. Mineral oil or a gel is the usual coupling medium. Ultrasound has the *deepest* penetration of any deep heating modalities. It is the only one that can directly increase deep tissue (muscle and bone interfaces) temperature to a therapeutic level (53-54). That makes it very useful for treating joint contractures. Deep heat can increase the elastic properties of collagen tissue. When ultrasound is used with a gentle stretching and strengthening program, range of motion often is returned to stiff and contracted joints. Ultrasound can be more accurately dosed than short wave and microwave diathermy. The therapeutic range is 0.5 to 4 watts per cm and usually is applied for a period of four to eight minutes. It may cause a feeling of local warmth and tingling but if pain occurs, too much energy is being used. Another advantage of ultrasound is that it can be used with whirlpool baths to deliver deep heat over irregular bony surfaces such as the lateral malleolus.

The therapeutic effects of heat are summarized in Table 18-5. Table 18-6 list the contraindications to heat.

### Contrast Baths

Contrast baths produce a maximum increase in blood flow to an injured limb. This technique produces hyperemia by alternating vasoconstriction and vasodilation of superficial blood vessels.

---

**Table 18-5. Therapeutic Effects of Heat**

1. Increased blood flow
2. Increased visco elastic properties of collagen
3. Sedation
4. Analgesia
5. Muscle relaxation and decreased muscle spasm
6. Increased metabolic rate
7. Increases the suppurative process

**Table 18-6. Contraindications to Heat Therapy**

1. Impaired sensation or an anesthetic area
2. Non-inflammatory edema
3. Ischemia in the area being treated
4. Malignancy in the area being treated
5. Metallic implants (except in ultrasound diathermy)
6. Application over the gonads
7. Exposure to a developing fetus
8. Skin disorders that are aggravated by heat
9. Altered level of consciousness
10. Hemorrhagic diathesis
11. Very young or very old patient

It often is used several days after acute injury when the beneficial effects of cold therapy alone have declined. Contrast baths also are used to treat chronic injuries.

Typically, the injured extremity is immersed for ten minutes in hot water, 40.0°C to 43.3°C (104°F to 110°F). Then the injured part is placed in cold water between 10°C to 15.5°C (50°F to 60°F) for one minute. The total treatment time of 30 minutes is an alternating process with hot water immersion for four minutes followed by cold water immersion for one minute after the initial 10 minute period of heat. A second method calls for submerging the limb in an ice slush bath for two minutes and then in tepid water at 33.9°C to 37.7°C (93°F to 98°F) for 30 seconds. The baths are alternated for 15 minutes beginning and ending with cold immersion (17).

## Electric Stimulation

Electrotherapy has recently become very popular in sports medicine (10, 35, 39, 68, 103). It is used to increase the strength of healing ligaments and tendons (103), prevent muscle atrophy (68), and control swelling and edema (10, 35). In addition, electrotherapy is being used to introduce medications into subcutaneous tissues after they have been applied to overlying skin, ionophoresis (6). Even so, there is considerable debate about the effectiveness of electrotherapy and its usefulness should *not* be oversold. Claims that electrical stimulation can actually reduce body fat, increase cardiorespiratory endurance, and build strength in muscle mass should be received with caution. A very good understanding of the applications and limitations of electrotherapy obviously is important.

### Tens

Perhaps the most widespread use of electrotherapy has been for pain control. Transcutaneous nerve stimulation (TENS) is the application of low or high frequency electrical currents through skin electrodes. TENS is based on the "gate" theory by Melzack and Wall (64). The endogenous opiate system of the central nervous system may also have a role in explaining how TENS therapy actually reduces pain (119). The effectiveness of TENS is controversial, including the correlation between the appropriate frequency, pulse, output intensity, and wave form of use. TENS can be applied for brief periods with very intense stimulation or for longer periods at lower intensity. In acute situations, TENS may be applied alone or with ice for 30-minute periods. This can be repeated every two to three hours. For chronic pain, TENS may be used on a more regular basis throughout the day. It should *never* be used to mask pain during competition. TENS has been used to control post-operative pain (39) and reduce post-operative muscular atrophy (103). Controlling pain after an injury and during the earlier phases of rehabilitation is essential to expediting recovery. Pain does play a protective role so that masking it in uncontrolled activities can lead to further and perhaps more serious injury.

### HVGMS

Another popular concept with purported effectiveness is high voltage galvanic muscle stimulation (HVGMS) to reduce edema after soft tissue injuries. HVGMS is an electrical stimulator that uses a voltage greater that 150 volts. It is supposed to have advantages over low voltage stimulators because it creates less caustic sensation due to the specific wave form and depth of penetration. However, there is very little research to support the claims. There have been many anecdotal reports of effectiveness. One study did show an increase in blood flow in healthy volunteers when HVGMS was used at the highest frequency and with negative polarity for 20-30 minutes (35).

### Ionophoresis

Ionophoresis is a method by which ionized medication is driven through the skin by an electrical current. Corticosteriod preparations, local anesthetics, and salicylates are the most common medications used. The indications for ionophoresis are to treat inflammatory soft tissue injuries. The recommendation is that the current intensity be no greater than five mA, and that the duration of treatment not exceed 15 to 20 minutes. This form of therapy reportedly has several advantages over injections of anti-inflammatory medications, including more consistent drug delivery and a lower overall dose. Because the treatment is not invasive, it is supposed to be painless. Again, there is very little research to substantiate these claims. Some authors have found that the initial depth of penetration is less than one cm with this method (33). There is considerable disagreement about its efficaciousness and if it proves to be useful, the question is whether the beneficial results are due to local responses or to systemic effects of the medications.

### Phonophoresis

Phonophoresis is similar to ionophoresis. Whole molecules of medications are driven through the skin into the subcutaneous tissues by means of ultrasound. As with any other application of ultrasound, a coupling medium must be used in addition to the medicated cream preparations. As with ionophoresis, phonophoresis may be used to treat inflammatory soft tissue injuries. The treatment period usually lasts about ten minutes. Two authors have found that the depth of penetration with this modality is anywhere from five to six cm (33, 87).

Many anecdotal reports that phonophoresis is very effective in treating a variety of soft tissue injuries exist. However, there have been no control studies to substantiate these clinical observations. The author has used phonophoresis with a 10% preparation of hydrocotisone cream to treat both acute and chronic inflammatory conditions such as tendinitis and bursitis and it seems to be very effective. This is particularly true for large musculotendon units (Achilles tendon) where the risk of tendon damage secondary to local steroid injection must be weighed against the benefits. Lidocaine, available in 5% preparations, also can be used with the hydrocortisone preparation. In addition, aspirin creams are available on an over-the-counter basis.

### Massage, Tissue Mobilization, and Manipulation

Manual therapy such as soft tissue mobilization and massage are used to reduce swelling and alleviate pain. Common forms of massage are stroking, compression, and percussion and these may produce sensations of pleasure, relaxation of muscle, and sedation. It also may be helpful in decreasing edema by increasing lymphatic drainage, stretching adhesions, and mobilizing accumulative fluids. Contraindications to massage include infection, deep vein thrombosis, skin disease, hemorrhagic diastases, and malignancy. Soft tissue mobilization requires keen palpatory skills and a good understanding of manual techniques. It should be done only by someone who has knowledge of the fundamental concepts and experience in its use.

Manipulation is defined as the abrupt, passive movement of a joint beyond its physiological range but within its anatomical range. Most studies have focused on vertebral manipulation. A few studies have shown temporary relief of pain, versus other modalities, but there are no controlled studies that support many of the popular benefits ascribed to manipulation (52).

### Traction

Traction is a technique in which a distracting force is applied to a particular part of the body to promote stretching of soft tissue and separation of joint surfaces. Traction may be intermittent or continuous and may be directed at any angle. Indications for traction include stretching muscles and ligaments, opening up vertebral foramina, and the distraction of vertabral bodies (50). Contraindications include spinal cord compression, extreme osteoporosis, atherosclerotic disease of the vertebral and/or carotid system, malignancy involving the vertebra, infectious diseases of the intervertebral disk or vertebral body, and rheumatoid arthritis with odontoid disease.

Clinically, the most effective application of traction is in the cervical spine to relieve pressure on cervical nerve roots. The patient sits on a chair with the neck at approximately 25° of forward flexion. The weight of the head, approximately 10 lbs, must be overcome before effective cervical traction occurs. Distraction of the cervical vertebra usually happens when the weight reaches 20 to 35 lbs. (50). If this treatment relieves the athlete's symptoms, a home program can be used several times a day.

The overall effectiveness of lumbosacral traction is controversial. It has been reported that traction forces exceeding 300 lbs. are necessary to achieve a significant degree of lumbar vertabra distraction (91). Therefore, lumbosacral traction has limited practical use in a clinical setting. Using 20 to 30 lbs. of pelvic traction while a person is lying in bed serves only to keep him still. Higher distraction forces that are tolerated can be achieved with intermittent traction. However, there is still considerable debate about whether significant distraction occurs.

Gravity inversion to achieve lumbar distraction has become popular even though there are serious potential complications such as hypertensive responses and increased intraocular pressure (45). Despite anecdotal reports of its effectiveness, the author believes that this form of therapy generally should be avoided.

### Summary

In summary, the use of therapeutic physical modalities is widespread in sports medicine. Specific objective goals (decrease swelling, increase ROM, or decrease pain) should guide each individual's therapy program.

The timing and sequence of heat and cold therapy are outlined in the protocols at the end of the chapter. It is worth noting that considerable research has been done on the general use and effects of heat and cold therapy but very little of it has been on specific applications of particular modalities and their comparative effects. We are left with many anecdotal claims. The very nature of athletic competition makes sports medicine providers anxious to come up with an edge in treatment. Couple this general mind-set with today's advancing technology and enterprising marketing pressures and it is easy to see how difficult it is to make rational decisions about the use of these modalities. Resist being oversold.

Finally, there is the placebo effect. As long as common sense prevails, we know we will see improvement in soft tissue injuries regardless of which modality is used. Keep an open mind about trying different ways. Avoid cook-book routines; do not treat every sprained ankle alike. Also, if one combination is not working, do not be afraid to try a different approach.

### Medications

Anti-inflammatory medications have become very popular in sports medicine settings (12, 57). Since the mid-70s, the number of non-steriodal anti-inflammatory drugs (NSAIDs) available for use in the United States has tripled (98-99). A detailed discussion of NSAIDs and other medications is in Chapter 2.

A few points about anti-inflammatory drugs are worth emphasizing. As mentioned previously, the initial focus of rehabilitation for most athletic injuries involves controlling inflammation and pain. Anti-inflammatories are effective agents, with aspirin still the most commonly used. Its relatively low toxicity, low cost, and efficacy make aspirin the standard against which all other NSAIDs are compared. Its value in treating rheumatoid arthritis has been well established. Aspirin has been shown to be an irreversible inhibitor of the enzyme cyclooxygenase. This enzyme is the key enzyme in the biochemical pathway where arachidonic acid is converted into prostaglandins, thromboxane, and prostacyclin. These end-products are mediators of the inflammatory response. NSAIDs are irreversible inhibitors of cyclooxygenase. The mechanism by which corticosteriod mitigate the inflammatory response is less well understood. Presumably they act at the membrane level by inhibiting release of phospholipase from the phospholipids in membranes. It is likely that aspirin, NSAIDs, and corticosteriods act through other biochemical pathways to interrupt the inflammatory process (98-99).

None of these medications can be used without some risk. NSAIDs are believed to be more effective than aspirin for treating many inflammatory conditions, and there are fewer adverse symptoms (12, 46, 98-99). Cost effectiveness aside, another advantage is that fewer pills are taken and compliance is improved. When NSAIDs are used for athletic injuries, mistakes about dosage are common. Use them to maximize their benefits. Rather than prescribing small doses over a prolonged period of time (as often is the case when treating arthritis), use maximum doses for short periods of time (three-seven days) if there are no contraindications.

Corticosteriods for treating athletic injuries are somewhat controversial. However, if used judiciously and with proper techniques, they can be very effective in reducing inflammation and hastening recover. While injectable corticosteriods reduce soft tissue inflammation, they may cause significant weakening or even rupture of tendons if introduced directly into the tendon (43-112).

The use of short term *oral* corticosteriods is even more controversial. The side effects of oral corticosteriods are well documented (1-2, 34, 65, 70). However, there have been no clinical trials to study short term (seven to ten days) use of oral corticosteroids in healthy young adults. They do seem to be of particular value in treating peripheral nerve injuries. A 10-day, tapering course of oral steroid may be very dramatic in relieving pain and restoring function with injuries following blunt trauma to nerves, overuse entrapments, and for nerve root lesions (radiculopathy). There are many anecdotal reports of their effectiveness, presumably without side effects. We need more randomized, double-blind clinical trials to investigate these issues. There may be times when the normal first-line approaches are not as successful nor as expedient for acute inflammatory disorders. If used judiciously and within appropriate guidelines, corticosteriods can be a valuable part of the sports medicine physician's armamentarium.

## Restoring Muscle Strength and Endurance

After an injury or surgery, restoring muscle strength and muscle endurance becomes a primary focus of rehabilitation. Strength can be defined as the maximum force exerted against an immovable object (isotonic strength), the heaviest weight lifted against gravity (isotonic strength), or the maximum torque developed against an accommodating resistance at a constant velocity of joint motion (isokinetic strength). Muscle power is defined as the amount of force generated times the distance through which that force is generated per unit of time. Muscular endurance is the ability of a muscle to generate force repetitively.

The principles of strength training for conditioning or for rehabilitation are similar, except for the *intensity* of training. Some athletes are accustomed to spending time in weight training rooms for conditioning. However, strength training after an injury must be done in a controlled, supervised manner with much less intensity. If the strengthening program is started too early or improperly done, the potential for reinjury is significant and the rehabilitation course may be prolonged.

In designing any strengthening program for rehabilitation, keep in mind five basic principles:

- The need to overload muscle in order to increase strength
- The concept of progressive resistant exercises (PREs)
- Methods of strength training
- Specificity of training
- Achieving balanced strength while maintaining flexibility

The need to work muscle against greater than normal resistance to produce strength gains was popularized in the 1940s by DeLorme (19-20). Strength gains in human muscle fibers are primarily the result of hypertrophy of individual muscle fibers (22, 56). With animal models, researchers have shown that the actual number of muscle cells increases as a result of training (56). Whether this is true for humans has yet to be shown.

DeLorme also popularized the concept of progressive resistant exercises (PREs) which is an extension of the overload principle. As strength increases, the initial resistance is no longer effective in providing a stimulus for overload. Therefore, resistance must be progressively increased. Based on this principle, a format was designed using three sets of 10 repetitions for weight training workouts. This format uses a repetitive maximum (RM) which is the maximum load of muscle or group of muscle can lift a given number of times prior to fatigue. For instance, the 10-RM is the amount of weight an athlete can lift ten times before fatigue. A common format for weight training used in training rooms across the country consist of 10 repetitions at one-half of the 10-RM, followed by 10 repetitions at three-quarters of the 10-RM, and a final set of 10 repetitions at the 10-RM. The technique of PREs is a practical application of the overload principle and forms the basis of most weight training programs.

Methods of strength training are summarized in Table 18-7. There is considerable debate about the best method for increasing strength and no one technique really can be considered superior to another (22, 56). Isometrically trained muscles are stronger when *measured* isometrically. Similarly,

**Table 18-7. Methods of Strength Training**

1. Static
   a. Isometric
2. Dynamic
   a. Constant resistance or isotonic
      (Universal Gym or Free Weights)
   b. Variable resistance
      (DeLand Sports Medical Industries, David, Eagle, or Nautilus Equipment)
   c. Accommodating resistance at fixed speeds or isokinetic
      (Cybex, Kin-Com, Lido, and Orthotron Machines)

isotonically trained muscles are stronger when *measured* isotonically. In deciding which strength training method to use, take into account the status of the athlete's injury, overall physical condition, and intended purpose of the strength training. Static or isometric strengthening is often useful when joint movements must be restricted or when movement still causes pain. Muller showed that strength decreases at approximately 5% per day in the absence of contraction, but one contraction a day at half the maximum strength is enough to prevent this loss (69). If isometric training is used to develop greater strength for a particular movement, these exercises must be done at several points throughout the range of motion. In view of the availability of dynamic methods of strength training, this particular form of training may be extremely time consuming and compliance may be a problem. Also, there is a certain lack of carryover to specific motor skills (69). Despite these disadvantages, it is important to start isometric strength training as early as possible after an injury. This form of exercise can help prevent muscle atrophy in an injured extremity. As noted earlier, high voltage galvanic muscular stimulation may be useful by inducing isometric contraction of muscles to prevent atrophy and maintain strength.

Once swelling subsides and motion is almost pain-free, dynamic strengthening can begin. Isotonic strengthening is a dynamic exercise involving changes in muscle length as tension develops against a constant resistance. A concentric isotonic contraction is the type of muscular contraction that occurs when a muscle shortens as it develops tension (e.g. a barbell curl). An eccentric muscle contraction occurs when a muscle actually lengthens as it develops tension (e.g. lowering a weight to the floor with the arms). There are limitations to isotonic exercises. The amount of weight or resistance is fixed and is a function of the *weakest* part of the range of motion of a particular lift. Simply stated, the muscles moving the weight are working at below maximum intensities throughout most of the range of motion. Examples of this type of training include free weights and the Universal weight lifting system. Despite these limitations, free weights are the most affordable strength training equipment available to most high schools. Free weights have the advantage of allowing the user to *isolate* a specific muscle or muscles for strength training.

Methods of strength training using variable resistance are an attempt to increase the intensity of work for a group of muscles *throughout* the full range of motion. Hydraulic or cam-shaped machines have been developed for this purpose (Nautilus, David Systems). Surgical tubing and elastic bands are simpler forms of this method. The resistance of the hydraulic or cam-shaped machines attempts to match the angle-specific strength of specific muscle groups. Advantages to this type of training include the ability to work muscles at a higher maximal rate, and to provide strengthening in both eccentric and concentric fashion (remember, many athletic movements involve eccentric contractions). The principles of overload and PREs apply to the variable resistance methods of strength training as well as the constant resistance method.

Isokinetic strength training involves accommodating resistance (or "weight") at fixed speeds. The amount of resistance encountered accommodates to match the force applied. Therefore, one advantage of this method is that an appropriate amount of resistance is encountered throughout the entire range of motion. If there is pain, or a muscle becomes fatigued at any point in the range of motion, the amount of resistance encountered decreases proportionally as the force applied decreases. That makes this mode of strength training very helpful early in the course of rehabilitation when safety is a concern. Examples of isokinetic equipment include Cybex, Kim-Com, and Lido.

Another advantage of isokinetic strengthening is that direct measurements of muscle power, torque, and endurance can be made. Serial measurements can be used to document the progress an athlete is making in rehabilitation. In addition, strength training can be done at speed settings ranging from 0 per second to 300 per second. Many functional activities in athletics involve very fast joint ranges of motion (the elbow and shoulder may reach speeds up to 5000-8000/sec. during the acceleration phase of pitching). Therefore, this method of strength training has the advantage of being able to develop strength at joint speeds that cannot be developed by other methods. In addition, once a particular amount of muscle strength is achieved, work can begin on muscle power and endurance. Muscle power is usually developed at slower speeds (180/sec.) and with fewer repetitions. Muscle endurance is developed at faster speeds (300/sec.) with multiple repetitions, often to the point of exhausting the muscle (69).

To summarize the advantages of isokinetic exercise: (1) It is the only way to load a contracting muscle to its maximum capacity through the full range of motion. (2) More resistance than can be withstood is never given since the equipment accommodates resistance. (3) It allows accommodation to pain and fatigue throughout the range of motion. (4) Exercise can occur at faster, more functional joint velocities. (5) There are decreased joint compressive forces at faster speeds which helps people with articular cartilage problems. There is ongoing debate about the reproducibility, specificity, and accuracy of isokinetic testing but this method comes closer to measuring muscle performance at functional speeds than any other method currently available. After an athlete undergoes a complete rehabilitation program, the injured extremity should be compared to the non-injured side and to pre-injury measurements if they were made.

**Specificity of Training**

This principle is simply that there are very specific motor skill requirements for different sports. Athletes develop particular movement patterns that are characteristic of gross and fine motor skills needed to perform different athletic activities. Specificity of training should also be recognized when incorporating strengthening programs into rehabilitation activities. This is based on the fact that all voluntary movements are a function not only of the strength of the muscles used in the movement but on a finely regulated series of neuromuscular events. These include central and peripheral nervous system factors that cause the recruitment and coordination of firing of appropriate motor units. To illustrate this concept, note that strengthening activities for leg muscles, like squats or deep knee bends, typically do not demonstrate the same increased ability to generate force when used in other movements such as jumping. Similarly, the strength and fine motor skills needed to swing a bat at a baseball are far different from the ones needed to swing a golf club.

The need for exercise protocols that re-educate muscles and joints in sports specific patterns is illustrated by the concept of proprioceptive neuromusclar facilitation (PNF). PNF is a form of exercise in which accommodating resistance is manually applied to various patterns of movement to strengthen and retrain the muscles that guide joint motion (48, 93). PNF is based on stimulation of proprioceptors within the skin, muscle, and tendons to promote the reeducation of muscles through rotational and diagonal patterns specific to the athlete's sport. This technique uses a contraction and relaxation phase that increases the flexibility of tight muscle groups. In addition to the isometric contraction, relaxation, and stretch sequence, rotational and diagonal patterns are used with appropriate manual resistance to maintain facilitory sensory inputs and to recruit appropriate muscles throughout the sport specific pattern. Increasingly heavier gauges of surgical tubing or elastic band material can be used to raise the resistance level of specific functional patterns of movement (Figure 18-4a & b).

Strengthening programs are frequently used *after* injury or surgery. However, consider placing injured athletes scheduled for surgery on a pre-operative strengthening program to hasten recovery and mitigate the invariable loss of strength.

Sports specific strength training can be extremely helpful in preventing injury. For example, football players should be encouraged to strengthen their neck muscles, quads, and hamstrings in order to protect their necks and knees from serious injury. Swimmers, throwers, and tennis players should concentrate on achieving a balance of strength and flexibility in their shoulders.

**Sequence of Exercises**

In designing rehabilitation protocols, keep in mind not only the type and number of exercises to be done, but also their order. Take care to avoid exercising the same set of muscles without planned rest periods. Larger groups of muscles should be exercised first to avoid fatigue in smaller muscle groups. Exercising smaller muscle groups first may limit the subsequent effectiveness of exercise intended to overload larger groups. The concept of circuit training illustrates sequencing. Circuit training is a series of strengthening exercises done in sequence to maximize strength gains and avoid muscle fatigue. As an injured athlete progresses through the rehabilitation program, the intensity and the number of repetitions per unit time can be increased.

**Achieving Balanced Strength and Maintaining Flexibility**

It is very easy for the athlete and the sports medicine staff to focus on strengthening one set of muscles after an injury but it is very important that balanced strength be regained, not just in the

**Fig. 18-4a-b.** Demonstration of functional patterns of movement using varying gauges of elastic bands to increase resistance.

injured group of muscles, but also in the agonists and antagonists of the muscle group.

Reaching balanced strength is not enough. Regular stretching to increase and maintain full flexibility and range of motion is paramount. Normal strength without complete joint motion can lead to reinjury or to new injuries. This is particularly true for injuries to the shoulder of throwing athletes and in spinal injury.

### Summary

In summary, the post-injury program calls for improving muscle strength, endurance, and power beginning with static or isometric strengthening at multiple joint angles. Dynamic resistive exercises should start when swelling has been controlled and 60%-70% of pain-free range of motion has been reestablished. During later stages of rehabilitation, there should be progressive increases in the intensity of the workout. Specificity of strength training should be incorporated into the program which should be individualized to the athlete's particular sports specific movements. Isokinetic exercise is helpful initially to protect a joint from further damage secondary to pain or fatigue. In later stages, it can increase muscular power and endurance.

Progression through these stages in restoring normal muscle function should be monitored carefully. So long as the athlete is not experiencing increased pain, loss of (or excessive) range of motion, or significant swelling, progression through the early, intermediate, and final stages of rehabilitation may safely continue. Remember that balanced strength and flexibility must be achieved before the final phases of rehabilitation can safely begin.

## Maintaining Cardiovascular Fitness

Once an athlete is injured, every effort should be made to maintain the pre-injury aerobic fitness level. If an injury has been managed successfully, it is unfortunate when the return to competition must be delayed because the athlete has a diminished cardiopulmonary fitness level. The potential for reinjury or new injury secondary to premature fatigue is considerable.

If an athlete has an upper extremity injury, fitness levels can be maintained by stationary bicycling, jogging, or swimming. With lower extremity injuries, alternatives include one-legged bicycling, arm ergometry, or swimming. Remember that the benefits of aerobic conditioning are a function of training frequency, duration, and intensity. Regardless of the type of exercise, the target heart rate must be maintained for 30 to 45 minutes at least three times a week to prevent a significant loss of aerobic fitness.

## Restoration of Balance and Agility

It stands to reason that an athlete who possesses good balance and agility will be less prone to injury. During the intermediate and later phases of rehabilitation, it is important to incorporate drills that increase balance and agility. Agility is a function of coordination, strength, power, endurance, reaction time, and speed of movement. Taken together, these variables determine how quickly the body is able to change direction. Balance is the maintenance of body position in relation to the forces of gravity. Balanced human movement is a finely regulated but complex mechanism involving end organ feedback to the central nervous system from muscle spindles, golgi tendon organs, skin receptors, and proprioceptive receptors in the joints. The cerebellum is the primary integrating center that controls feedback from the peripheral receptors and cortex.

Immobilization, surgery, or an injury may compromise both balance and agility due to interruption of this feedback mechanism (42). Balance and agility drills can be included in the functional progressive exercises discussed below (see engram programming). Balance activities include walking on a beam and hopping (one-legged, two-legged, and back and forth across a string, six to ten inches off the ground). Jumping rope is also a good activity for improving balance. Drills that improve reaction time, the rate of acceleration, and maximum speed should also be included. Proprioception and reaction time can be improved in athletes who have recurring ankle sprains by using a balance or tilt board (Figure 18-5).

### Flexibility

There are no well-designed, controlled studies to support the principles most sports staffs use as

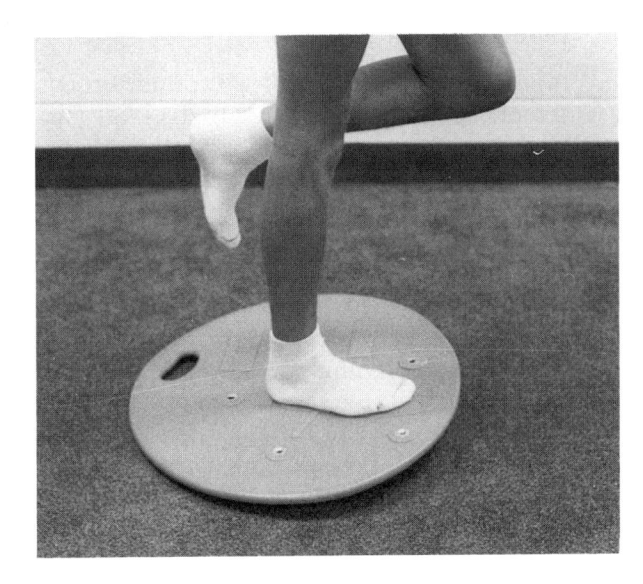

**Fig. 18-5.** Use of a balance or tilt board to improve proprioception and reaction time.

guides to promote increased flexibility for performance enhancement or to prevent and rehabilitate athletic injuries. Flexibility is a function of structural properties of muscotendinous units and joint capsules, and the neurophysiological principles of feedback and adjustment. Thus, much of what we "know" about flexibility is intuitive and anecdotal. Theoretically, a lack of flexibility in tendons, muscles, and joint capsules predisposes athletes to injury. For example, tightness of the gastrocsoleus group can cause an athlete to excessively pronate the foot. Decreased flexibility in the hamstrings, quadriceps, tensor fascia lata, or gastrocsoleus group may interfere with reaction time in the knee joint and predispose it to injury. Thus, maintenance of *general* flexibility is important both as a preventive measure and for injury rehabilitation. It is difficult to determine an optimal state of flexibility for any given athlete.

Flexibility exercises can be done individually or with a partner. Stretching should always involve warm-up and cool-down periods and may be more effective after an activity is completed, while the soft tissues are more distensible. Static stretching, which involves prolonged, gentle stretching at moderate tension, is believed to be safer and more effective than short term intermittent or ballistic stretching (4, 49). In spite of the paucity of controlled data supporting the benefits of stretching and maintaining a state of flexibility, this concept warrants considerable attention, both for prevention and rehabilitation.

## Taping and Bracing

Taping is one of the athletic trainer's most useful tools. It can be considered both an art and a science. Questions about the effectiveness of taping, either prophylactically or after injuries, have not been settled. The reader should be aware that there is considerable controversy on this subject. Proponents for regular taping claim that statistics show it actually prevents new injuries (28, 63, 89). One article compared strapping, taping, and no support on unstable ankle joints of 51 athletes (113). The author stated that taping provided the greatest decrease in talor tilt angle, even after 30 minutes of activity. However, others argue against routine taping (51, 88, 97). These authors claim that the actual support from taping is reduced by 40% to 70% after 10 to 15 minutes of exercise, and that taping may actually give an athlete a false sense of security. It is important to recognize that taping is very important to some athletes from psychological point of view and that it often reaches level of superstition and ritual.

There is no consensus about the effectiveness of taping but this author believes that preventative taping of ankles and supportive taping after ankle injuries is indicated. As an athlete progresses through the stages of rehabilitation, enough range of motion, agility, and strength may be restored to make further taping unwarranted. However, the recommendation after an ankle injury is that the athlete be taped prior to any practice or competition for the rest of the season. Taping of other joints following complete rehabilitation is usually unnecessary.

The use of braces, particularly knee braces, also has received a considerable amount of attention in the last few years and, like taping, their use is controversial (84). Braces currently available can be divided into three categories. First are braces used prophylactically to prevent knee injuries (McDavid, Don Joy, Iowa, and Anderson). After an injury or surgery, there are knee braces used during rehabilitation (Bledsoe, Watco, OSI). Finally, there is a whole group of braces designed to protect unstable knees during athletic competition. These functional braces include the Lenox Hill, C.T.I., Lerman, Can-Am, and Pro-Am.

As stronger, lighter weight materials are developed that provide functional stability without interfering with reaction time, speed of joint movement, and coordination, we find that athletes are more inclined to use them. Further clinical investigation needs to be done to substantiate their effectiveness. In spite of this lack of research data, bracing the knee after medial collateral, lateral collateral, and anterior cruciate ligament injuries is strongly advised.

## Psychological Support

The need to attend to the overall psychological well-being of athletes was discussed in Chapter 3. The entire sports medicine staff must be aware of the potential psychological impact of surgery and/or injuries on an athlete. The athlete's level of confidence and self-esteem may suffer tremendously. This may be the first time the athlete has been in a situation where he is not totally in control of factors affecting him. This may have a profound effect not only on the athlete but also on the relationships he or she has with family, coaches, and members of the sports medicine staff (24, 58, 74, 100). This may be particularly true with high caliber young athletes.

There are at least two important factors to keep in mind during rehabilitation. First, injured athletes need to feel they are still a part of the team so that everything within reason should be done to allow them to attend practices and do their rehabilitation as part of the team. The athlete will want to attend team meetings and social functions. Second, every team physician should be aware of the athlete who is looking for a way out of competition. Frequent reoccurring or new injuries should alert the physician to the possibility that a particular athlete may not want to continue. These situations must be handled very delicately as there may be many complicating factors (social and family situations). Finally, during the later phases of rehabilitation, it is important for the athlete to have psychologically adjusted to the injury and feel ready to return to full competition before actually being allowed to do so. Any hesitation on the part of the athlete to return to competition should be recognized and addressed.

## Functional Progressive Rehabilitation

We started this chapter with the basic question: "Doc, when do you think I'll be ready to play again?" We see there is no easy answer. Reviewing the principles of rehabilitation should shed some light on the basic requirements of any rehabilitation protocol. Functional progressive rehabilitation is nothing more than the integration of these general principles we have been discussing into an organized, progressively more difficult sequence of exercises designed to meet the specific needs of an injured athlete's particular sport. These principles are outlined in Table 18-8.

---

**Table 18-8. Phases of Sports Medicine Rehabilitation**

A. Early Phase (one to three days)
 1. P.R.I.C.E.
 2. Early Active R.O.M. in an Ice Slush
 3. Anti-inflammatories
 4. Static (Isometric) Strengthening
 5. Consider Electrotherapy and Pneumatic Compression
 6. Possible Immobilization and Non-Weight Bearing Status

B. Intermediate Phase (two to seven days)
 1. Progressive Weight Bearing with Protection
 2. Continue Ice Until Swelling Stops
 3. Consider Contrast Baths, Electrotherapy and/or Heat
 4. Work Toward Full R.O.M.
 5. Continue Anti-Inflammatories
 6. Begin Dynamic Strengthening When 60% to 70% of Pain-Free Motion is Present
 7. Begin Proprioceptive Training
 8. Begin Exercises to Maintain Cardiopulmonary Endurance
 9. Once Comfortable Weight Bearing Has Been Achieved, Begin Functional Progressions with Protective Taping and/or Bracing
 10. Engram Programming Begins
 11. Continue Ice After Workouts

C. Late Phase (five days to several weeks or even months)
 1. Heat Before Workouts, Ice Afterwards
 2. Establish Full R.O.M. (Heating May Be Very Helpful to Increase R.O.M.)
 3. Possibly Discontinue Anti-Inflammatories
 4. Advance Muscle Strengthening and Include Power and Endurance Training
 5. Isokinetic Testing
 6. Advance Proprioceptive Training, Include Balance and Agility Drills
 7. Advance Aerobic Fitness Activities
 8. Advance Engram Programming
 9. Advance Functional Progressions to Competitive Levels, Testing Strength, Mobility, Agility, Speed, and Balance

D. Final Phase (When an athlete is ready to return to competition)
 1. Normal R.O.M.
 2. Symmetric, Balanced Muscle Strength and Endurance
 3. Pain-Free Activity at Functional Levels
 4. Successful Completion of Functional Progressions
 5. Appropriate Fitness Level
 6. Has Returned to a Non-Competitive Setting Without Difficulty (Has Practiced With the Team)
 7. Mentally and Emotionally Prepared to Return to Competition

---

After injury, the basic principles of early rehabilitation treatment should be followed. However, at some point, the injured extremity or joint must be put to a functional test. Functional tasks should begin during the intermediate phases of rehabilitation after comfortable weight bearing and/or pain-free range of motion have been established.

**Engrams**

In addition, engram programming should begin. This is a process of retraining the neuromusculoskeletal system to invoke desired, complex sports-specific, motor movements in an "automatic" fashion. Skilled movement patterns involve balance, feedback, and agility. Care must be taken to develop the desired motion slowly with supervised repetition to ensure that substitutional patterns do not develop. It is indicative of inadequate rehabilitation if they do. In that situation, look for subtle weakness of muscles, soft tissue contractions causing restriction, joint motion, and/or other possible causes for pain with movement.

As functional progressive exercises are advanced, it is imperative to see that the specific motor skill in question remains "pure". Remember that proper form and motion are important to establish before adding speed to the protocol. Each task begins at half speed, is advanced to three-quarter speed, and then to full speed as intensity and frequency are also increased. A task is not considered complete until it can be done with sufficient repetitions at full speed *without* subsequent swelling, loss of range of motion, pain, increased joint laxity, substitutional patterns, or hesitation on the part of the athlete. Progression along this continuum of increasingly more difficult tasks continues only as the criteria are met. Do not permit the athlete to advance to a new, more difficult task until the previous task is successfully completed.

Developing functional progressive exercise protocols is not difficult so long as there is an understanding of the principles of rehabilitation, the extent and subsequent constraints of the injury, and the demands of the athlete's particular sport. This type of exercise protocol allows the final phases of rehabilitation to be carefully monitored. If it appears the athlete is being pushed too quickly, previous activity levels should be resumed and the intensity and frequency of the workout decreased. With this protocol, the athlete can psychologically adjust to the recovery phase and it makes him more aware of the timetable for returning to competition.

A number of articles have been published outlining rehabilitation programs for both upper and lower extremity injuries (5, 23, 27, 32, 36, 40, 47, 60, 67, 80, 82, 104-105, 117-118). In addition, several protocols are outlined below. Where it is appropriate, these include functional progressions that can be made a part of the overall rehabilitation. The reader is cautioned not to follow a cookbook approach because any protocol is, at best, only a guideline.

In the final stages of rehabilitation, observation of the athlete in practice situations is necessary to decide when to allow full participation under game conditions. The rule: "No practice by Thursday, no play on Saturday" is a good one. If the athlete is a football player, he is allowed to practice for a few days with a red jersey to remind his teammates not to hit him with full contact. After successfully completing this stage, he participates in full contact team practices before being released to play in the next game.

Using this type of graduated program takes much of the burden of answering that ultimate question off the shoulders of the physician. The answer to the question about a return to competition is usually readily apparent to the athlete, the sports medicine staff, and the physician.

Once an athlete does resume competition, it is imperative that rehabilitation continue for the duration of the competitive season. Soft tissue, particularly ligamentous structures, may take several months to heal completely (76, 77). Strengthening, conditioning, agility drills, and protective bracing or taping will continue to be important.

## REHABILITATION PROTOCOLS FOR SPECIFIC ATHLETIC INJURIES

The last section of this chapter contains several protocols outlining the rehabilitation of a few of the more common athletic injuries. Complete discussion of the rehabilitation of many of these injuries is beyond the scope of this chapter. Therefore, guidelines and general principles have been offered. More detailed references for specific injuries have been included. Keep in mind that each of these protocols is based upon the four fundamental phases of rehabilitation outlined in Table 18-8.

## Protocols for Rehabilitation

### I. *Knee Injuries*

Athletes frequently injure their knees. It is a complex joint and many of the biochemical factors relating to structure and function remain a mystery. Although clinical diagnosis of specific injuries may be difficult, the use of arthroscopy and MRI scanning has greatly enhanced the precision of diagnosis. Treatment must be based upon an accurate diagnosis.

The treatment and rehabilitation of knee injuries has changed significantly in the past decade. Surgical philosophies about ligament tears and injuries to the meniscus have been reevaluated and there is a trend toward non-surgical treatment. The role of the meniscus in knee joint stability and in maintaining proper biomechanics has received considerable attention (75). Noyes reported that patients with anterior cruciate-deficient knees, who also had had a meniscectomy, demonstrated a two to fourfold increase in swelling and pain with activity (78). Therefore, preserving the meniscus or as much of it as possible is very important.

In general, the evolution of knee injury rehabilitation has gone from prolonged immobilization to early, protected mobilization. The disadvantages of long term immobilization have been well documented (76). A functionally progressive sequence is the cornerstone for the rehabilitation of knee injuries (see Table 18-9).

The approach to collateral ligament injuries also has changed dramatically. If the anterior cruciate ligament is intact and the menisci are undamaged, then collateral ligament injuries often can be managed non-surgically (37). Outlined below is a protocol for Grade I and II medial and lateral collateral ligament sprains.

A. *Rehabilitation Guidelines following 1 and 2 Medial and Lateral Collateral Ligament Sprains*

*Day 1 through 5*:

1. P.R.I.C.E.
   - Knee immobilizer (especially at night).
   - Crutches with partial weight bearing.
   - Ice 20 to 30 minutes every three to four hours.
   - Compression dressing; loosen if ankle begins to swell.

**Table 18-9. Knee Rehabilitation**

1. Walking
2. Running at 1/2 speed
3. Advance to full speed
4. Changes of direction
5. Quick stops and starts
6. Protective bracing
7. Engram assembly and functional progressions
8. Practice in a controlled environment, simulating game conditions
9. Return to full activity

2. Protected Range of Motion (R.O.M.) to pain tolerance (30 of flexion to 90 of flexion).
3. Isometric Quadriceps Exercises; 15-20, three sets per day.
4. Straight leg lifts; three sets of 20, three to five times per day.
5. Anti-inflammatories.
6. Arm ergometry for cardiovascular conditioning.

*Day 3 through 12:*

1. Progression from cryotherapy to contrast baths to heat therapy once swelling has stopped.
2. Continue with crutches and immobilizer until swelling stops, and complete pain-free range of motion and weight bearing are established.
3. Whirlpool bath with biking motion for range of motion.
4. Swimming with kickboard doing gentle flutter kicks for 20 to 30 minutes.
5. Continue isometrics.
6. Continue anti-inflammatories.
7. Straight leg raises with knee held straight.
   - Work up to 10 R.M. three sets of ten per day.
   - Incorporate hip flexion, extension and abduction exercises.
8. Advance arm ergometry.

*Day 10 through 20:*

1. Heat prior to workout, ice afterwards.
2. Wean off crutches; knee immobilizer may need to be worn at night.
3. Continue whirlpool and/or swimming range of motion exercises.
4. If 90° of comfortable knee flexion is present, begin stationary bicycling with toe clips (for hamstring work) 15 to 20 minutes per day.
5. Running straight ahead in waist-deep water with good footing can begin for 15 to 20 minutes per day.
6. Anti-inflammatories may be discontinued depending upon pain and swelling.
7. Begin hamstring curls; three sets of ten R.M.
8. Advance quadriceps exercises or begin isokinetic work.

*Day 16 to Completion:*

1. Continue advancing strengthening program.
2. Continue cardiovascular conditioning on the bicycle or running in the pool.
3. Begin functional progressions.
   - Walk/jog intervals (walk ¼ mile, jog ⅛ mile, three sets per day for one to three days).
   - Jog/run intervals (jog ¼ mile, run ⅛ mile, three sets per day from one to three days).
   - Hop/jump intervals (jump rope with both feet for three minutes; then left foot for one minute followed by the right foot for one minute. Three sets, increasing the times, for one to three days).
   - Sprint intervals (straight-ahead sprints beginning at half speed advancing to full speed over 20 to 50 yards).
   - Cutting/agility drills (large figure 8s, advance to smaller figure 8s, zigzag patterns, lateral shuffles, cariocas, tire drills, running pass routes, and dummy drills). (See Figure 18-6)
   - Careful attention to slow, repetitions of sports-specific patterns is necessary to ensure proper engram assembly.
4. Continue ice after workouts.
5. Isokinetic strength testing (the athlete can return to practice once 90%-100% strength is obtained).
6. Strengthening and agility must continue throughout the remainder of the season.

B. *Rehabilitation Guidelines for Patello-Femoral Dysfunction (Chondromalacia)*

**Fig. 18-6a-b.** Use of cutting or agility drills such as cross-overs or cariocas are useful in the rehabilitation of knee injuries.

Patello-femoral dysfunction or knee extensor mechanism disorders are often incorrectly called chondromalacia. These disorders can be divided into three subsets:

1. Malalignment of the spine, hip, and/or lower extremity which results in altered knee biomechanics;
2. Abnormalities of the patello-femoral joint articulation;
3. An imbalance of strength and/or flexibility of the surrounding muscles, tendons, retinaculum, and ligaments (67).

This problem is often seen in runners and cyclists. A few of the more obvious predispositions include increased Q angle of the knee, excessive pronation of the foot, genu recurvation, pelvic obliquity, scoliosis, femoral anteversion, iliotibial band tightness, "squinting" patellae, and relative weakness of the vastus medialis oblique muscle. There are many more subtle biochemical factors to be considered.

Non-surgical treatment often is successful. The focus of treatment should not be on V.M.O. strengthening alone. Increasing flexibility in tightness antagonists (hamstrings) and the vastus lateralis is very important. Also, make sure there is no concomitant injury to these musculotendinous units which may be causing reflex-inhibition. Manual patellar retraction is helpful in the early phases. Finally, slow repetitive practice of V.M.O. contraction in sports-specific settings is important for proper engram coding. These functional steps should be undertaken once proper techniques have passed critical evaluation.

1. P.R.I.C.E.
   - Avoid compression around the knee; this may actually make the condition worse.
   - Avoid deep knee bends, climbing stairs, squatting, and getting out of low chairs.
   - If the condition is severe, the athlete may need to use crutches and be non-weight bearing for several days.
   - Avoid wearing high heeled shoes.
   - Rest is extremely important. (Relative

or absolute rest may be indicated. See chapter on Overuse Syndromes.)
- Ice should be used frequently during the initial and intermediate phases of rehabilitation. (Consider TENS and deep friction massage.)
2. Anti-inflammatories (these are usually very helpful for this condition).
3. Isometric Quadriceps (with manual patellar retraction placing force on the lateral side of the patellar and pushing medially with each contraction).
4. Consider electrotherapy to the V.O.M.
5. Increase flexibility of hamstrings, vastus lateralis, and ilio-tibial band.
6. Short arc quads to selectively strengthen the vastus medialis obliques muscle.
   - Short arc quads should be done in the last 15° to 20° of extension.
   - Begin with one to two lb. weight boots or ankle weights and progress to 100 R.M.; three sets of 100 q. day.
   - Bent knee leg presses and partial squats may be done instead of short arc quads. This may cause less compressive force on the patellae.
7. Slow, repetitive contractions of V.M.O. to begin engram coding. (Figure 18-7)
8. Advance, skilled coordinated movements using proprioceptive, neuromuscular techniques.
9. Cardiovascular conditioning (arm ergometry, one-legged bicycling, or running in waist-deep water may begin in the initial phases of rehabilitation).
10. Once functional progressions begin, a patellar knee sleeve may be helpful.

    A slowly progressive return to running may begin when the athlete is pain-free, has good range of motion, and good strength.
    - Begin running in the pool.
    - Advance by running on consistent indoor or outdoor surfaces.
    - Avoid hill and speed work until the athlete's previous weekly mileage is obtained.
11. Continue quadriceps strengthening and maintain hamstring flexibility after full activity has resumed.

C. *Rehabilitation Following Anterior Cruciate Ligament Injury*

The treatment and subsequent rehabilitation of anterior cruciate ligament injuries varies. These injuries may be treated nonoperatively or they may require surgery. Consideration must be on an individual basis. The athlete's level of competition or recreational pursuits, future demands, job requirements, and ability to maintain compliance with a long-term rehabilitation program must be assessed and integrated into treatment decisions. If surgery is required, there are several different procedures including a number of intra articular and/or extra articular repairs. The reader may wish to read some of the articles that have been written on this topic (25, 27, 38, 40, 60, 67, 76-78, 81-82). Although there are many variable to any protocol for A.C.L. rehabilitation, all contain certain key points. Also, regardless of the protocol, the total recovery time may be 4-12 months, depending upon the exact nature of the injury and the subsequent treatment. The therapist or trainer must understand the surgical procedure that was performed so as to individualize the program for each athlete.

As mentioned previously, early, protected mobilization is the current standard of care for many knee injuries. This also is true for A.C.L. reconstructions, whereas a decade ago an athlete might have been immobilized in a cast for several weeks or months. Now, complete casting is often avoided and range of motion exercises may begin in the recovery room, using continuous passive range of mo-

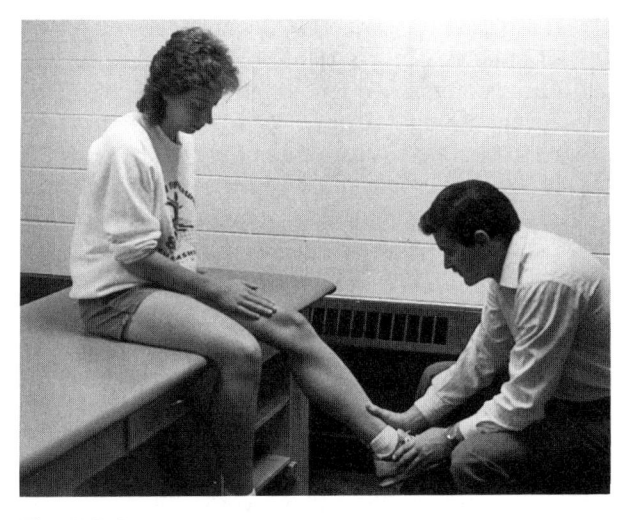

**Fig. 18-7.** Slow, repetitive contractions of the V.M.O.

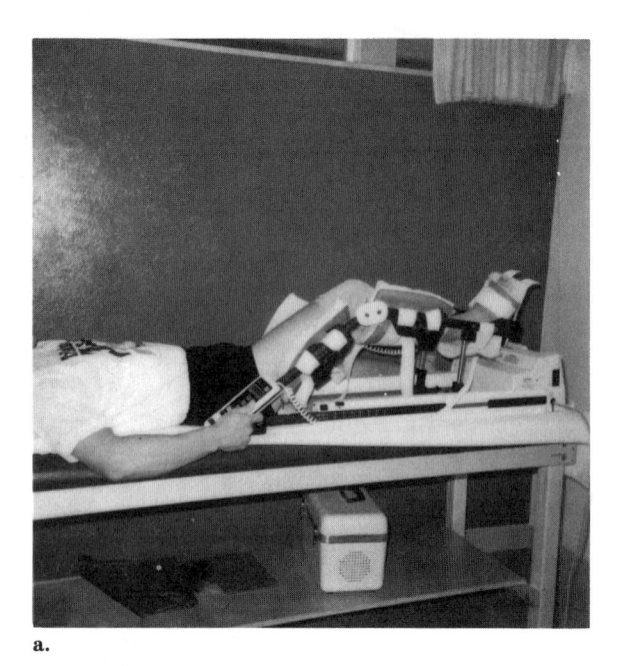

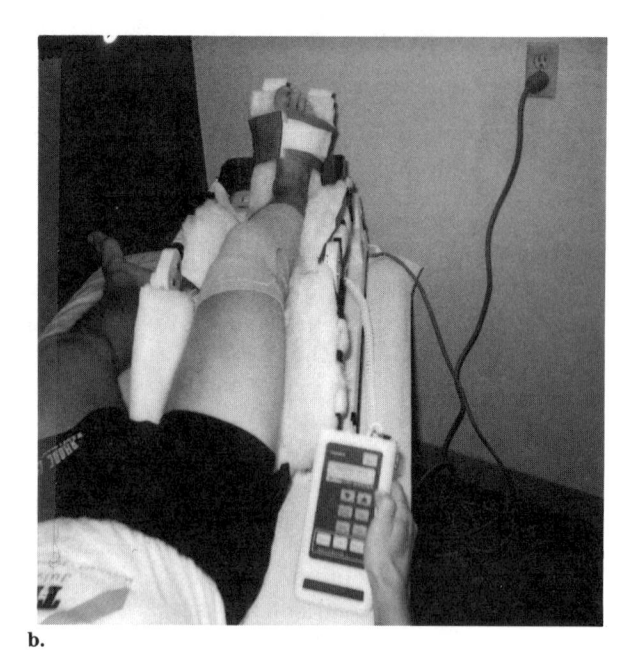

**Fig. 18-8a-b.** Use of a continuous passive range of motion machine in early post-operative period.

tion machines (Figure 18-8). Salter has shown C.P.M. reduces adhesions, decreases the incidence of post-operative hemathrosis, facilitates regeneration of articular cartilage, and increases joint nutrition (96). Paulo and Noyes have also studied early motion and documented the promotion of organized collagen healing as a result (82).

The basic premise behind A.C.L. rehabilitation focuses on our evolving concept of ligamentous healing. The appropriate amount of stress is a matter of considerable debate. The result is that a reader can find several published "protocols" for A.C.L. rehab that contain conflicting information. Paulos and Noyes divided their protocol into five phases (82). They recommend complete immobilization for the first six weeks of controlled motion. Steadman claims that the immobilization period should be eight weeks and that terminal knee extension should be avoided for at least six months (104). However, Steadman also has stated that earlier terminal knee extension may be done safely if the exercise involves a "closed kinetic chain". For example, an athlete with a repaired ACL may be encouraged to do half-squats to full standing exercises (and thus achieving terminal extension of the knee) so long as the injured-side foot is on the ground, creating a *closed*, kinetic chain. Presumably due to the coactivation of the hamstrings, less torque is placed across the autograph than when the chain is "open" (i.e., when the knee is brought to full extension without the foot being on the ground).

The major source of controversy in A.C.L. rehab is about the timing of terminal knee extension. It is hard to reconcile promoting patello-femoral joint motion and strength around the joint and protecting the newly repaired graft from undue stress. Jackson and Drez have shown that the anterior drawer forces placed upon the A.C.L. increase dramatically after 40° of knee flexion, as the knee is brought to full extension in an "open" kinetic chain (38). Also, recent animal studies have convinced many that the A.C.L. in humans may take up to 24 months to reach full maturity and that without some augmentive repair, A.C.L. strength probably never returns completely (38).

So it is easy to see that designing a universally accepted A.C.L. protocol is not easy. Regardless of which protocol the reader follows, bear in mind the general principles of rehabilitation outlined in Table 18-1. Also remember that prolonged immobility should be avoided and that healing tissues have stress limits and should not be overloaded.

*Guidelines for A.C.L. Rehabilitation Following Surgery*

1. Explain the rehabilitation protocol and its timetable to the athlete before surgery. Depending upon the injury and the subsequent surgical repair, rehab may take 4-12 months.
2. Immobilization should be minimized. If there are no concomitant ligament or meniscus repairs continuous *passive* range of motion often can begin in the perioperative period.
3. Isometric strengthening can usually begin in the immediate post-operative phase. These should be done several times throughout the day. Electrical stimulation may be effective during the immobilization phase.
4. Immobilization should not exceed six to eight weeks.
5. Immobilization with a knee brace (instead of cast) permits controlled changes for eventual active range of motion, wound inspection, and early patellar mobilization.
6. In the early phases of rehab, *active* knee extension is often controlled between 40°-70° of flexion to avoid excessive anterior drawer forces across the patella.
7. Terminal knee extension may be allowed early in the course of rehabilitation as long as it involves a "closed" kinetic chain.
8. In two to four months, the majority of R.O.M. should be established.
9. At four to six weeks, partial weight bearing and light strengthening and endurance can begin.
10. Progressive resistive exercises (P.R.E.s) can begin at six to eight weeks and should not be advanced too aggressively in the first six months.
11. Eccentric and concentric strength gains occur independently. Therefore, include exercises for both.
12. Isokinetic exercises may begin at 10 to 12 weeks as long as isotonic progressions have been pain-free without substituted patterns or recurrent effusions. Don't overload healing tissues.
13. Monitoring patello-femoral joint reaction forces during isokinetic exercise is difficult; thus, care must be taken not to create patello-femoral pain or abnormal tracking that will prolong rehab.
14. An extension block may be needed with all forms of strengthening until the latter phases of rehab.
15. Running straight ahead may usually begin at four to six months, depending upon progression thru the previous phases. Quadriceps strength should be 75% of total body weight (peak torques on isokinetic testing) or a minimum of 80% of the uninjured quad, before running is allowed.
16. Progressive, functional tasks with cariocas, soft cutting, and backwards running can begin after successful completion of full speed straight ahead running. All running should be done in a protective brace.
17. Remember the final phases of all rehabilitation (Table 18-8). These steps must be accomplished before full sports participation is allowed.

## II. Rehabilitation Guidelines Following 1 and 2 Lateral Ligament Sprains of the Ankle

This is the most common injury in sports medicine. Please refer to the discussions of Principles of Rehabilitation for further details.

*Day 1 through 3:*

1. P.R.I.C.E.
   - Compression wrap with U-shaped pads (consider pneumatic compression with a JOBST pump - See Figures 18-1 through 18-3).
   - Air splint.
   - Possible use of crutches for temporary non-weight bearing.
   - Early range of motion in an ice slush.
   - Elevate as much as possible.
2. Anti-Inflammatories.
3. Consider electrotherapy
4. Cardiovascular conditioning with arm ergometry, one-legged bicycling, or swimming.

*Days 3 through 7:*

1. Continue ice until swelling stops then consider contrast baths and heating modalities.

2. Increase range of motion both passively and actively (theraband or towel stretches).
3. Continue anti-inflammatories.
4. Progressive weight bearing (continue to wear air splint).
5. Begin isometric strengthening of inverters, eveters, plantar, and dorsi flexors.
6. Begin strengthening istrinsic foot muscles (pulling a weight on a towel toward the athlete with the toes, as in Figure 18-9; picking up marbles with the toes).
7. Achilles tendon stretching.
8. Advanced cardiovascular conditioning with stationary bicycling or swimming.
9. Proprioceptive exercises with a tilt board when pain-free range of motion is present.

*Days 5 through 14:*
1. Heat before activities (whirlpool or ultrasound) and ice after activities.
2. Consider discontinuing anti-inflammatories.
3. Consider discontinuing air splint.
4. Continue stretching and flexibility.
5. Continue tilt board activities.
6. Begin lower extremity functional progression and engram assembly. (Hopping, jumping rope, gentle cutting activities.)
7. Continue strengthening and flexibility exercises after return to competition.
8. Protective taping prior to practice and competition.

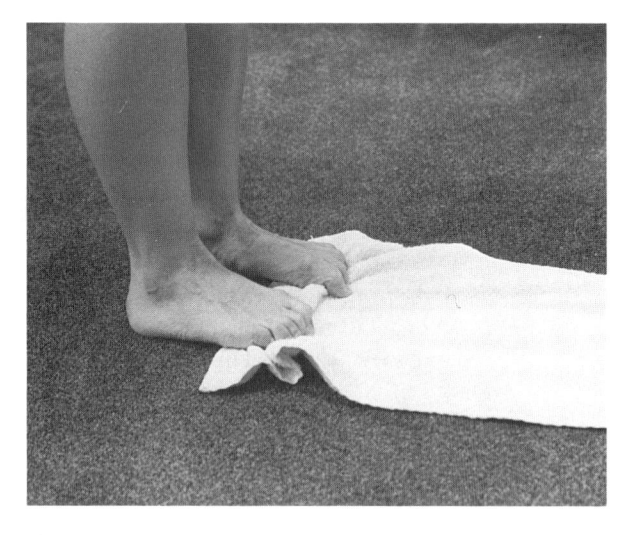

**Fig. 18-9.** Strengthening of intrinsic foot musculature by pulling a weight on a towel with the toes.

## III. Rehabilitation Guidelines after Injuries to the Shoulder

The shoulder joint is unique. Because it is designed to allow maximum mobility, it has an inherent degree of structural instability. There is only one point where the shoulder girdle is attached to the axial skeleton: the sternoclavicular joint. Thus, the stability of the shoulder is maintained primarily by the surrounding muscles. That means that rehabilitation of an injured shoulder directly or indirectly involves increasing the strength and flexibility of the muscles surrounding the shoulder joint. Regardless of the injury, the important thing to remember is that a balance between strength and flexibility is necessary to prevent re-injury.

The shoulder is frequently injured by throwing athletes, swimmers, gymnasts, tennis players, and wrestlers. Direct trauma to the shoulder causing glenohumeral dislocation or acromialclavicular separation is a common mechanism for injury. However, overuse injuries resulting from repetitive microtrauma are far more common and often more difficult to treat.

Repetitive, efficient motion of the shoulder in carrying out sports-specific tasks is a finely orchestrated event that involves more than glenohumeral biomechanics. This is particularly true when all five phases of throwing are considered: wind-up, cocking, acceleration, release and deceleration, and follow-through (117). Throwing is a delicately balanced interplay of strength, flexibility, and neuromusculoskeletal engrams which coordinate lower extremity, trunk, and arm motion while maintaining a very small center of glenohumeral joint rotation.

Injuries frequently occur when one small part of this finely orchestrated event breaks down. For instance, if a pitcher has a knee injury and loses quad strength, he may substitute a whipping motion of his arm in an attempt to make up for the loss of one of this primary accelerators (his quads) during the acceleration phase of throwing.

As with the knee, shoulder rehabilitation requires a working knowledge of fundamental biomechanical principles which govern normal shoulder motion. Perry has addressed the biomechanics of the shoulder during sports-specific tasks (83).

Regardless of the type of shoulder injury, there are several key points to be kept in mind. If a setback occurs, it often can be traced to one or more of the following points:

- The rotator cuff muscles act primarily to maintain the center of rotation of the glenohumeral joint. An injury to one of the cuff muscles may allow repetitive, subtle subluxation.
- Acceleration of the throwing arm is primarily a function of trunk rotation, hip and knee extension, and conversion of stored energy in the glenohumeral capsule. The rotator cuff muscles are *not* accelerators.
- The posterior shoulder muscles, including the rotator cuff muscles, the biceps, brachialis, and brachioradialis are the primary decelerators of the arm.
- Proper scapulothoracic motion is critical for fluid glenohumeral motion. Always evaluate scapulothoracic motion and look for substitutional patterns, decreased mobility, and myofascial pain syndromes of this joint as a cause of abnormal shoulder biomechanics.
- The deltoid and other large muscles surrounding the shoulder often create substantial, subluxing shear forces across the glenohumeral joint in addition to their purposeful actions. This is a common cause of impingement syndromes.
- The supraspinatus and infraspinatus are the two key muscles which counter the shear force of the deltoid by maintaining joint compressions, and thus the center of rotation.
- Along with the infraspinatus, the teres minor acts to offset the upward displacement caused by initial deltoid action. Therefore, selective strengthening of these muscles may significantly increase a downward pulling force of the humerus and reduce impingement forces in the subacromial space.
- Injuries to the cervical spine, nerve roots, brachial plexus, and peripheral nerves of the upper extremity are often overlooked in shoulder injuries. Nerve entrapment or a chronic radiculopathy can cause weakness in any one of the key muscles of the shoulder and alter joint biomechanics and performance. Undiagnosed nerve injuries frequently cause delayed or unsuccessful rehabilitation. Electromyography (E.M.G.) can be helpful in delineating these problems.
- Always ensure that proper form and motion are encoded engrams before working on increasing speed and delivery. This requires paying attention to strength, flexibility, and timely motion of the trunk and lower extremities.
- Conditioning should continue throughout the competitive season, including strengthening and flexibility.

Below are protocols for treating anterior dislocations of the glenohumeral joint and injuries to the rotator cuff.

A. *Rehabilitation Guidelines Following Anterior Dislocation of the Glenohumeral Joint*

1. Immediately after an acute anterior dislocation of the shoulder, the joint should be reduced.
2. Place ice over the entire shoulder for 30 minutes every two to three hours while awake for the first 48 hours.
3. Anti-inflammatory medications may be helpful and should be started immediately if there are no contraindications.
4. The arm should be placed in a sling in an internally rotated position with the elbow flexed at 90°. It can be further immobilized by placing an ace wrap or swathe around the arm and trunk (Figure 18-10).
5. The injured extremity should remain immobilized in a sling for a minimum of three weeks.
6. One week post-injury, while still in a sling, begin:
   - isometric hand grips or squeezing of a tennis ball.
   - forearm range of motion.
   - isometric adduction and internal rotation.
   - EXTERNAL ROTATION AND ABDUCTION ARE TO BE AVOIDED.
   - begin aerobic conditioning with stationary bicycling.
7. Three weeks post-injury, while out of the sling:
   - Codman's pendulum exercises.
   - isometric internal rotation.
   - finger climbing.
   - shoulder shrugs and retraction.
8. Four weeks post-injury:
   - evaluation of shoulder muscle weakness

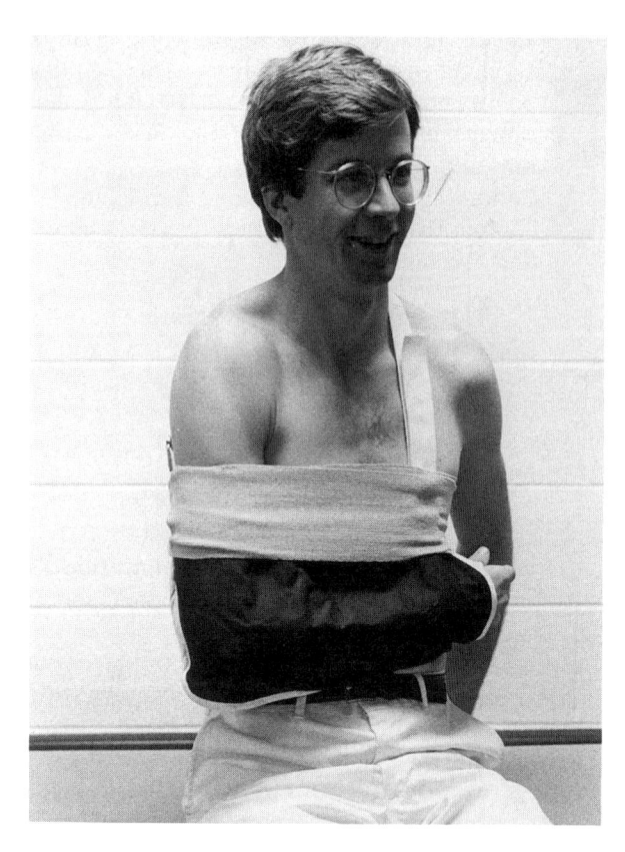

**Fig. 18-10.** Immobilization of the acutely injured shoulder using an ace wrap.

and prescription for home strengthening exercises using surgical tubing (Figure 18-11a-c).

9. Four to five weeks post-injury:
   - external rotation exercises may begin with light resistant surgical tubing.
   - a complete isokinetic program should be started to include strengthening of all muscles about the shoulder, particularly muscles of *internal rotation* and *adduction*.
   - if an isokinetic machine is unavailable, simply advance the surgical tubing program by using heavier material, and increase the intensity and frequency of workouts.
   - PNF should begin as long as there is pain-free range of motion. This is the beginning of engram assembly.

10. Nine to twelve weeks post-injury:
    - isokinetic testing comparing the uninjured shoulder to the injured shoulder.
    - if 75% of strength is obtained, begin functional progressions which could include progressive workouts on a swim bench, light throwing activities beginning with mirror throwing, then throwing a tennis ball at 10 feet, 20 feet, 30 feet, etc., or in the case of hockey, an athlete might begin practicing wrist and slap shots at half speed. In addition, functional progressions may include medium and half speed workouts on an isokinetic machine. Make sure that substantial patterns do not occur and "contaminate" the encoded engram.
    - advance functional progressions slowly until at least 90% strength is obtained in the injured shoulder compared to the uninjured side or pre-injury data on the injured side. Advance throwing program to include light throwing at larger distances (100 ft. or more), short tosses at one half to three quarters speed.
    - advance aerobic conditioning.
    - return to competition once the final criteria of rehabilitation have been met.
    - continue an active strengthening and stretching program after returning to competition.

B. *Rehabilitation Guidelines Following Rotator Cuff Injuries*

The "pitchers" or "swimmers" shoulder often involves some type of injury to the rotator cuff. This could include either a tear of the rotator cuff, tendinitis of one of the cuff tendons, a glenoid labrum tear, bursitis, or an impingement syndrome. Specific treatment depends upon the exact nature and extent of the injury. Following the healing phase, rehabilitation should focus on balancing both strength and flexibility of the muscles around the shoulder girdle. An imbalance between these factors often leads to improper biomechanics and reinjury (100). A good understanding of the biomechanics of throwing is helpful in designing a rehabilitation protocol (117). Remember, the rotator cuff impingement syndrome may represent a spectrum of pathology ranging from rotator tears to bursitis and tendinitis.

Therefore, timetables for recovery may vary significantly depending upon the ex-

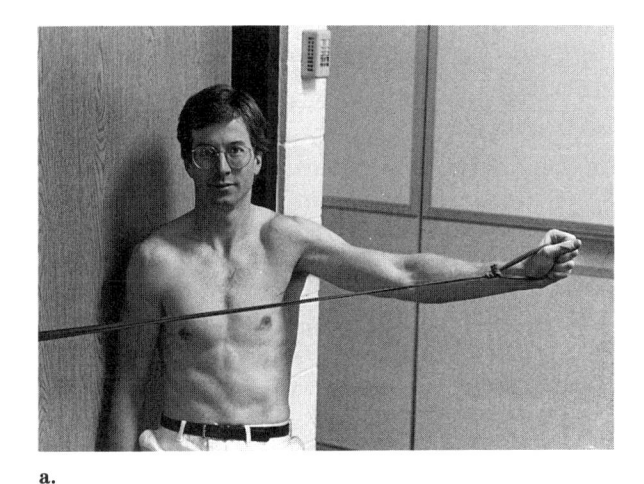

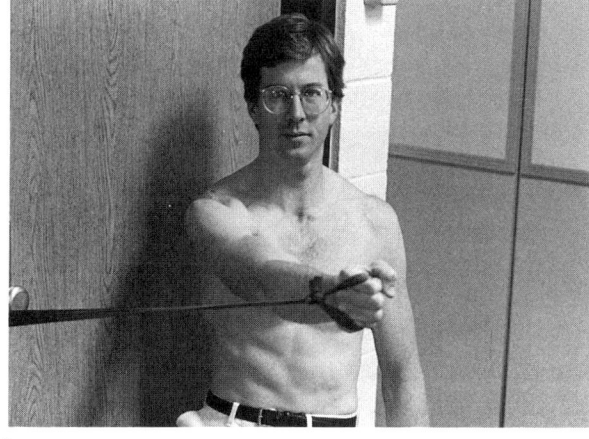

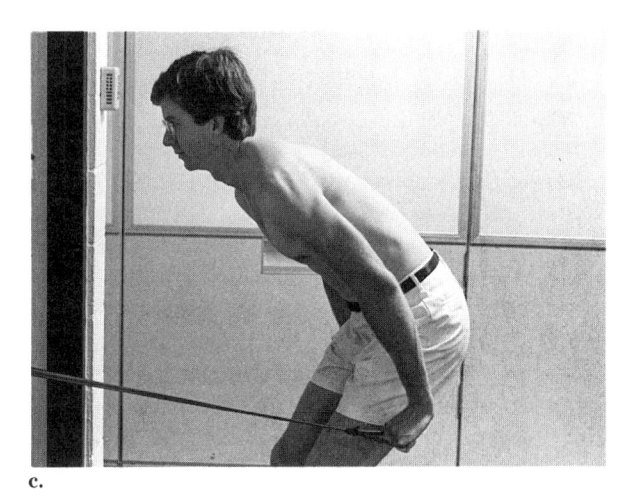

**Fig. 18-11a, b, c.** Shoulder strengthening exercises using surgical tubing attached to a door.

tent of the injury. Be sure your diagnosis is accurate and reassess it if recovery is prolonged or reinjury occurs.

The following highlight some key points in the rehabilitation of rotator cuff injuries:

1. Sufficient rest while tissue healing occurs.
2. Gentle range of motion exercises.
3. Anti-inflammatory medications to reduce swelling and to control pain.
4. Begin *isometric* strengthening within the first week, avoid excessive abduction, and external rotation.
5. Once pain-free range of motion is established, begin PNF with emphasis on static stretching and diagonal movements of the shoulder.
6. Maximum flexibility in horizontal flexion, combined abduction and external rotation should be established.
7. Dynamic strengthening should not begin until maximum flexibility and synchrony of motion is established. Dynamic strengthening can include physical tubing exercises, one to five lb. weights or an isokinetic program. Frequent repetition with low weights or resistance are recommended initially. Particular attention should be directed toward the infraspinatus, teres minor and subscapularis muscles (Figure 18-12, 18-13). These muscles act to create a downward pull on the humeral head, thus increasing the suprahumeral space.
8. Improving muscle *endurance*, especially of the rotator cuff muscles, is critical. Therefore, high speed isokinetic with low resistance should begin once the acute inflammatory stage is controlled.
9. Light throwing or swimming exercises can begin once a balanced of strength and flexibility has been achieved.
10. Functional progression and initial engram encoding for throwing includes mirror throwing (slowly performing the act of throwing with a 1 lb. weight in the hand while standing in front of a mirror). Advance to short distance throwing (starting with a tennis ball at 10 to 15 feet throwing no more than 10 minutes daily initially); long distance throwing can begin for 15 to 20 minutes at a time and distances should increase up to 120 feet.

**Fig. 18-12.** Strengthening of the infraspinatus, teres minor and subscapularis muscles using free weights.

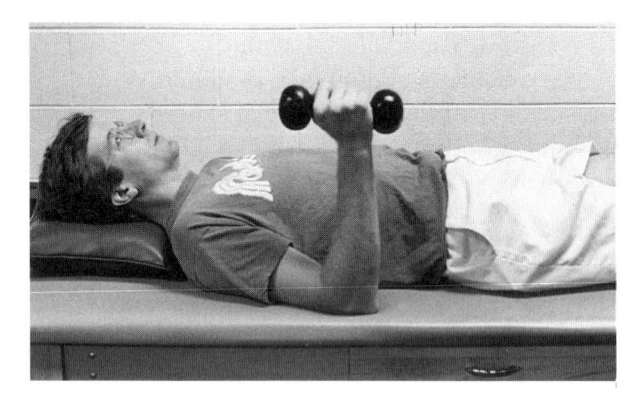

**Fig. 18-13.** Strengthening of the infraspinatus, teres minor and subscapularis muscles using free weights.

11. Six to eight weeks post-injury, forearm pitching may begin allowing the athlete to begin throwing from the mound. Only the fast ball should be thrown at first and it should begin at half speed. Workouts should not last longer than 30 minutes initially. Functional progression should be done in stages with maximum velocity and breaking balls gradually introduced toward the end of this phase.
12. Once the criteria for return to competition have been met, conditioning must continue with emphasis on maintaining flexibility and balanced strength of the rotator cuff muscles. Additionally, all throwing athletes should be on a regular off-season program to avoid injury or reinjury.
13. For swimmers, functional progressions are designed using the swim bench, beginning short distance swimming with a variety of strokes, progressing to use hand paddles for increased resistance, and finally increasing the duration and intensity of the workouts. As with throwing athletes, swimmers must maintain a balance of strength and flexibility in the shoulder both during the season and in the off-season. Excessive buildup of strength at the expense of flexibility may actually predispose swimmers and throwing athletes to rotator cuff injuries.

## IV. Guidelines for Rehabilitation of Spine Injuries

Injuries to the spine are among the most difficult problems encountered by physicians. A central theme that has been emphasized here is that successful treatment is contingent upon accurate diagnosis.

Several articles have discussed *traumatic* injuries in athletic settings which result in vertebral fractures and dislocations (92, 101, 107-110). Torg's pioneering work has set out the biomechanical factors associated with traumatic cervical spine injuries and subsequent spinal cord damage (107-110). Because of studies, the N.C.A.A. and American High School Athletic Association adopted rule changes in 1976, that outlawed spearing or using the head as a weapon during tackling. The result was that incidence of quadriplegia from football injuries dropped from 28 in 1975 to five in 1984 (107-110). These data are based upon approximately 1.75 million high school and college athletes participating in football on an annual basis.

Most spine injuries do not involve vertebral fractures or dislocations. Most fall into a broad, nebulous diagnostic subset of soft-tissue injuries. Establishing a specific diagnosis based upon clear-cut pathological entities that cause pain and spinal dysfunction is a very difficult task.

Everyday static and dynamic functions of the spine are still somewhat mysterious and some of the basic principles of spine biomechanics are not fully understood (30, 92, 101, 107-110). Thus, injuries to the spine, particularly where repetitive motion is involved in sports-specific tasks, can be difficult to diagnose. A detailed discussion of spine anatomy biomechanics, differential diagnosis, diagnostic testing, and subsequent treatment is beyond the scope of this chapter but there are many excellent sources (7, 9, 13, 21, 30, 44, 55, 62, 66, 71-73, 79, 92, 101, 107-110, 114).

Because lumbar spine soft-tissue injuries are so common in athletes participating in football, wrestling, shooting sports, gymnastics, and dance, a brief discussion of the general approach to these injuries is in order. First, it is important to use a methodical diagnostic approach to establish a precise diagnosis so that the rationale for subsequent treatment plans is optimal. Table 18-10 lists diagnostic categories that provide a framework for handling complaints of low back pain. It is important to obtain a history of the onset, timing, mechanism of injury, and response to previous treatment.

"Shot-gunning" work-ups for spine injuries can be very costly. CT Scans, MRI Scans, EMGs, SSEPs, myelograms, and diagnostic blocks may be needed to pinpoint the diagnosis but it is important to approach the diagnostic work-up methodically. Decide which tests are cost-effective and appropriate given the circumstances.

In my experience, most lumbar spine injuries in sports settings involve acute and chronic overloading of the facet joints, acute and chronic stress injuries to the pars interarticulars resulting in spondylolosis and spondylolisthesis, and malalignment problems. These injuries are the most common because athletes are often in a hyperlordotic position with an increased lumbosacral angle. This causes significantly increased axial and torsional loads to be placed upon the facets and other posterior elements (13, 55).

Rehabilitation of lumbar spine injuries often requires retraining the athlete to obtain a more neutral spine both in static and dynamic posturing, and correcting imbalances of strength and flexibility in the soft-tissue associated with lumbar spine and pelvic support. Much of what we know about these two principles is the result of research on low back injuries in industrial settings (7, 13, 21, 44, 55, 62, 66, 71-73, 79, 114). They are worth emphasizing from both the standpoint of prevention and rehabilitation. With all of our college and high school athletes, we have included an exercise protocol specifically to address these two principles, both in season and in off-season training programs.

The concept of obtaining a more neutral spine addresses the issue of decreasing hyperlordosis and thus mitigating the increased loads placed on the posterior elements of the spine. It also addresses many of the malalignment issues and the critical interplay between the lumbar spine and pelvis in both static and dynamic posturing. The muscles and soft tissues that interact to provide support for the spine and pelvis can dramatically alter the posture of both the spine and its base of support, the pelvis. The goal is not to eliminate all of lumbosacral lordosis; "neutral" spine is a relative term which must be determined on an individual basis.

An athlete with relatively tight hip flexors could have an increased lumbosacral angle (LSA), subsequent hyperlordosis, and in-

---

**Table 18-10. Diagnostic Categories of Traumatic and Overuse Lumbar Spine Injuries in Sports**

1. Vertebral fractures and/or dislocations
   a. With spinal cord injury
   b. Without spinal cord injury
2. Facet joint syndromes
3. Spondylolysis and Spondylolethesis
4. Malalignment syndromes
   a. Pelvic and S.I. joint dysfunction due to an imbalance of muscle strength and flexibility
   b. Scoliosis, hyperlordosis
   c. Leg length discrepancies
   d. Scheuermann's disease
5. Disogenic: with and without nerve root irritation
   a. Herniation
   b. Annular tear
   c. Internal disc disruption syndrome
6. Segmental instabilities:
   a. With nerve root irritation
   b. Without nerve root irritation
7. Soft-tissue
   a. Acute and chronic myofascial pain syndromes
   b. Interspinous ligament disruption with and without segmental instability
8. Stenosis: Central and lateral
   a. Congenital vs. acquired
   b. Dynamic vs. static lesion

creased loading of his facet joints, resulting in low back pain. In this example, a primary goal would be to correct this malalignment through proper strengthening of his antagonists (hip extensor muscles), and increase the flexibility of the hip flexors. This decreases both the LSA and the lordosis and achieves a more neutral spine. This approach us a bit oversimplified, but it illustrates the concept of "neutral" spine. Several other supporting structures also would need to be assessed and included in the treatment plan.

Using the example above, once a more neutral posture was determined for the individual in a static setting, the concept of maintaining a neutral spine would be carried over to his dynamic sports movements during functional progressions and engram assembly. This would be accomplished by carefully monitoring slow repetitions of the movement and reinforcing proper techniques as his progressions advanced.

This is the principle of engram programming. For example, let's assume that the athlete is a pitcher. Once he obtains a more neutral spine, he is taught to pitch using these same principles. By lowering his center of gravity during his delivery (which requires quadriceps strengthening), using his abdominal muscles, hip extensors, and muscles of the back, he is taught to concentrate on maintaining balance and proper posture throughout the five phases of pitching. This type of training continues after the athlete returns to full competition and also in the off-season to prevent recurrent back injury.

A finely orchestrated interplay among several key muscles and soft tissue supports helps achieve a more neutral spine. Outlined below and illustrated in Figure 18-14 is the basic protocol we use for our athletes to prevent and treat back injuries.

Remember that successful treatment depends upon an accurate diagnosis. "Soft-tissue strain" is a broad and nebulous diagnostic category. Avoid using this protocol in a cookbook fashion for all athletic back injuries. Young, healthy appearing athletes can have significant underlying disease. A methodical approach, with judicious use of diagnostic testing procedures, will lead to a precise diagnosis and help establish a rational approach to rehabilitation. Finally, all of the general principles of rehabilitation for controlling inflammation and pain, establishing relative rest but maintaining cardiovascular fitness, etc., are a part of this protocol.

## Guidelines for Rehabilitation of Lumbar Spine Injuries

A. *Static Phase of Neutral Spine Training*

1. Pelvic tilts (used as a part of all the following exercise whenever possible) (Figure 18-14A)
2. Knee to chest (Figure 18-14B & C)
3. Partial and rotational sit-ups (Figure 18-14D & E)
4. Cat and camel (Figure 18-14F & G)
5. Trunk flexion, prone and seated (Figure 18-14H, I, J)
6. Prone extension (Figure 18-14K)
7. Hamstring stretching (Figure 18-14L, M)
8. Quadriceps stretching (Figure 18-14N)
9. Hip flexor stretching (Figure 18-14O)
10. Gastroc-soleus stretching (Figure 18-14P)
11. Bridging (Figure 18-14Q)
12. Bridging with stepping (Figure 18-14Q)
13. Incline sit-ups, partial and rotational (Figure 18-14R)
14. Wall leg raises with pelvic tilt (Figure 18-14S)
15. Spine extensor strengthening (Figure 18-14T)
16. Latisimus Dorsi strengthening (Figure 18-14U)
17. Hip extensor strengthening (Figure 18-14V)
18. Quadriceps strengthening (Figure 18-14W)

B. *Dynamic Phase of Neutral Spine Training*

1. Balance and agility training with neutral spine positioning (engram reinforcement)
2. Swimming (breaststroke and backstroke)
3. Stationary bicycling
4. Slow motion, sports-specific tasks once proper form has been achieved in slow motion
5. Advanced speed of sports-specific tasks once proper form has been achieved in slow motion

**Fig. 18-14a.** Pelvic tilt exercises for neutral spine training.

**Fig. 18-14b.** Knee to chest exercises with one leg at a time.

**Fig. 18-14c.** Knee to chest exercises with both knees flexed simultaneously.

**Fig. 18-14d.** Partial sit-up position.

**Fig. 18-14e.** Rotational sit-up position.

**Fig. 18-14f.** Cat position of neutral spine training.

**Fig. 18-14g.** Camel position.

**Fig. 18-14h.** Trunk flexion in prone position.

*REHABILITATION* 567

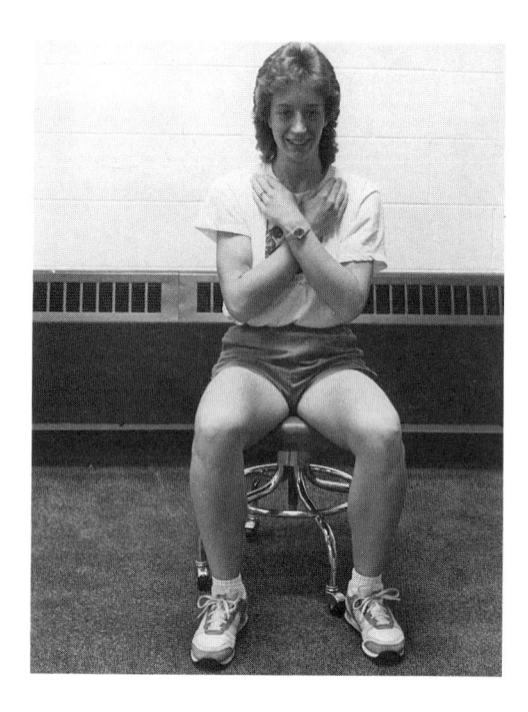

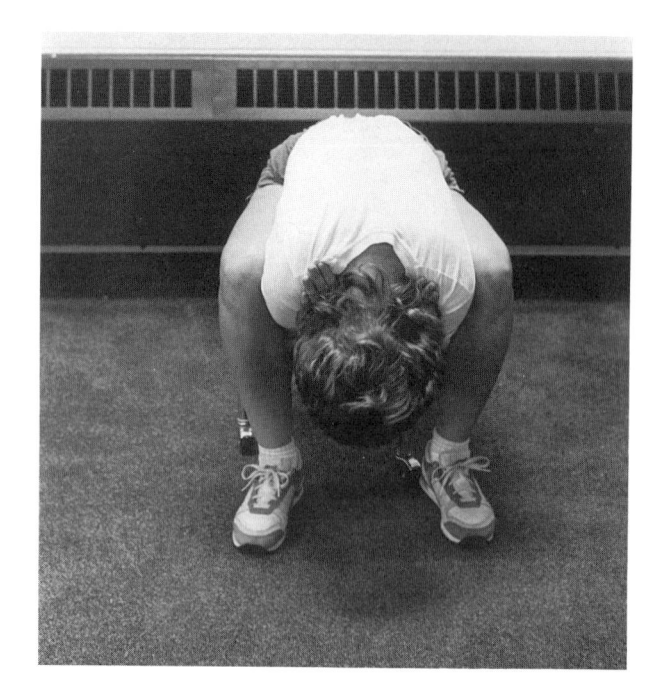

**Fig. 18-14i & j.** Trunk flexion in seated position.

**Fig. 18-14k.** Prone extension position.

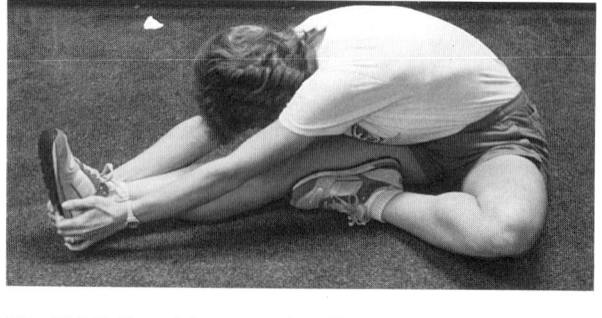

**Fig. 18-14l.** Hamstring extension (Hurdler's position)

**Fig. 18-14m.** Hamstring extension with knee extended.

**Fig. 18-14n.** Quadricep stretching which promotes balance.

**Fig. 18-14o.** Hip flexor stretching position.

**Fig. 18-14p.** Stretching of gastroc-soleus muscles.

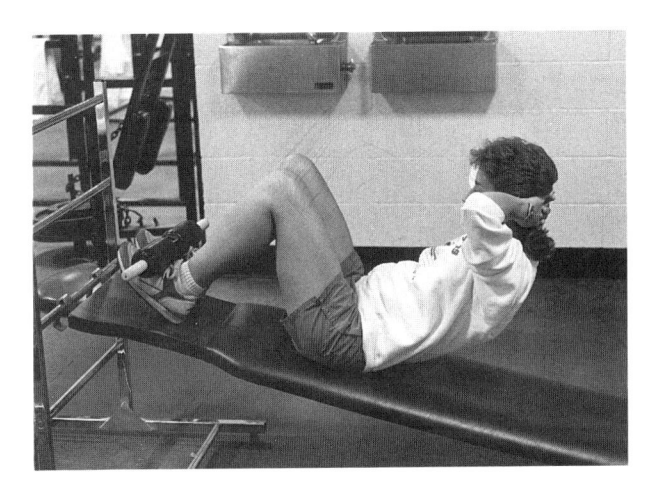

**Fig. 18-14q.** Bridging exercise.

**Fig. 18-14r.** Partial incline sit-ups with knees bent.

**Fig. 18-14s.** Leg raises which can be performed while hanging from elbows.

**Fig. 18-14t.** Spine extensor strengthening exercise.

**Fig. 18-14u.** Strengthening of the latisimus dorsi using weight machine.

**Fig. 18-14v.** Hip extensor strengthening using weight machine.

6. Full speed analysis of sports-specific tasks; videotape as necessary

## SUMMARY

We began this chapter with the question: "When will I be ready to play again?" We hope you are ready now to answer this question on a case by case basis. The key to successful rehabilitation is contingent upon a precise diagnosis. Once an accurate diagnosis is established, refer to a checklist of items (see Table 18-1) to review the principles of rehabilitation and to set up realistic guidelines for a given athlete.

Part of the job as a sports medicine physician is rehabilitation supervision and it often becomes a difficult task. Even after a fine balance between relative rest and reconditioning is achieved, there may be outside pressures from the coaching staff, trainers, athletes, and parents to shorten the recovery period. A good working relationship among the sports staff is important and a key ingredient in such a relationship is a consistent rehabilitation protocol that has measurable, progressive, functional outcomes. Having this framework lets everyone involved in the athlete's care observe progress or setbacks daily. A structured rehabilitation protocol takes the guesswork out of the formula so that the athlete can answer his question about rehabilitation himself.

**Fig. 18-14w.** Quadriceps strengthening using knee extension machine.

### BIBLIOGRAPHY

1. Abeles, M., Urman, J., Rothfield N. Aseptic necrosis of bone in systemic lupus erythematosus. *Arch Intern Med*; 138 5:750-754, 1978.
2. Ackerman, G., Nolan, C. Adrenocortical responsiveness after alter-

nate-day corticosteroid therapy. *New England J Med*; 278:8, 405-409, 1968.
3. Akeson, W.H., Wo, S., Amiel, D., et al. Connective tissue response to immobility. *Clin Orthop*; 93:356-362, 1973.
4. Anderson, B. *Stretching*. Shelter Publications, 1980.
5. Aronen, J. Shoulder rehabilitation. *Clin Sport Med*; 4(3):447-494, 1985.
6. Bertolucci, L. Introduction of anti-inflammatory drugs by iontophoresis: double-blind study. *J Orthop Sports Phys Therapy*; 103-108, 1982.
7. Bettencourt, C.M., Calstrom, P., Brown, S.H., et al. Using work simulation to treat adults with back injuries. *Am J Occup Therapy*; 40(1):12-18, 1986.
8. Brand, R.L., Black, H.M., Cox, J.S. The natural history of inadequately treated ankle sprains. *Am J Sports* 5:248-249, 1977.
9. Brown, F.W. (ed). *Symposium of the Lumbar Spine*. American Academy of Orthopedic Surgeons. St Louis: Mosby, 1979.
10. Brown, S. Ankle edema and galvanic muscle stimulation. *Phys Sports Med*; 8:79-86, 1980.
11. Cabaud, H., et al. Exercise effects on the strength of the rat anterior cruciate ligament. *Am J Sports Med*; 8:79-86, 1980.
12. Calabrese, L., Rooney, T. The use of nonsteroidal anti-inflammatory drugs in sports. *Phys Sports Med*; 14 2:89-87, 1986.
13. Calliet, R. *Low Back Pain Syndrome*. 3rd edition. Philadelphia: FA Davis, 1981.
14. Carson, W.G. Diagnosis of extensor mechanism disorders. *Clinics in Sports Med*; 4:2, 231-245, 1985.
15. Clayton, M., Miles, J., Abdulla, M. Experimental investigations of ligamentous healing. *Clin Orthop*; 61:146-153, 1968.
16. Collins, K., Storey, M., Peterson, K. Peroneal nerve palsy after cryotherapy. *Phys Sports Med*; 14:105-108, 1986.
17. Cooper, D., Fair, J. Contrast baths and pressure treatment of ankle sprains. *Phys Sports Med*; 14:105-108, 1986.
18. Cox, J., Brand, R. Evaluation and treatment of lateral ankle sprains. *Phys Sports Med*; 5 6:51-55, 1977.
19. DeLorme, T. Restoration of muscle power by heavy resistance exercises. *J Bone Joint Surg*; 27-645, 1945.
20. DeLorme, T., Watkins A. Techniques of progressive resistant exercise. *Arch Phys Med Rehabil*; 29:263, 1948.
21. Deyo, R.A. (ed). Occupational Back Pain. *Spine: State of the Art Reviews*; 2(1), 1987.
22. Downey, J., Darling, R. *Physiological Basis of Rehabilitation Medicine*. Saunders, 1971.
23. Duda, N. Prevention and treatment of throwing-arm injuries. *Phys Sport Med*; 13 6:181-185, 1985.
24. Eldridge, W. The importance of psychotherapy for athletic-related orthopedic injuries among adults. *Comprehensive Psychiatry*; 24 3:271-277.
25. Frank, K. Clincal experience in 130 anterior cruciate ligament reconstructions. *Orthop Clin North Am*; 7:191-193, 1976.
26. Franklin, B., Rubenfire, M. Cardiac rehabilitation. *Clin Sport Med*; 3:2, 1984.
27. Giove, T., Sayer, J., Kent, G., et al. Non-operative treatment of the torn anterior cruciate ligament. *J Bone Joint Surg*; 65A:184-192, 1983
28. Glick, J. The prevention and treatment of ankle injuries. *Am J Sports Med*; 4:4, 1976.
29. Goodfellow, J., Hyngerford, D.S., Zindel, M. Patellofemoral joint mechanics and pathology: functional anatomy of the patellofemoral joint. *J Bone Joint Surg*; 58:B, 287, 1976.
30. Gracovetsky, S., Farhan, H. The optimum spine. *Spine*; 11(6):543-573, 1986.
31. Grant, A. Massage with ice and treatment of painful conditions of the musculoskeletal system. *Arch Phys Med Rehab*; 45:233-8, 1964.
32. Greipp, J. Swimmer's shoulder: The influence of flexibility and weight training. *Sports Med*; 13 8:92-105, 1985.
33. Griffin, J., Karsellis, T. *Physical agents for physical therapists*. Springfield, Illinois, Charles C. Thomas, Publisher, 1978.
34. Hahn, T. Corticosteriod-induced osteopenia. *Arch Intern Med*; 138 (May): 882-885, 1978.
35. Hecker, B., Carron, H., Schwartz, D. Pulsed galvanic stimulation: effects of current frequency and polarity on blood flow in healthy subjects. *Arch Phys Med Rehabil*; 66 6:369-371, 1985.
36. Holden, D., Eggert, A., Butler, J. The non-opeative treatment of grade I and II medial collateral ligament injuries to the knee. *Am J Sport Med*; 11(5):340-344, 1983.
37. Holden, D.L., Eggert, A.W., Butler, J.E. The non-operative treatment of Grade I and II medical collateral ligament injuries to the knee. *Am J Sports Med*; 11:340, 1983.
38. Jackson, D.W., Drez, D., Jr. (eds). *The Anterior Cruciate Deficient Knee: New Concepts in Ligament Repair*. St. Louis: CV Mosby Co., 1987.
39. Jensen, J., Conn, R., Hazelrigg, G., et al. The use of transcutaneous neurostimulation and isokinetic testing in arthroscopic knee surgery. *Am J Sports Med*; 13:27-32, 1985.
40. Jokl, P., Kaplan, N., Stovell, P., et al. Non-opeative treatment of severe injuries to the medial and anterior cruciate ligaments of the knee. *J Bone Joint Surg*; 66A(5):741-744, 1984.
41. Kelley, W. *Text Book of Rheumatology*. 2nd Edition. Saunder, 1985.
42. Kennedy, J., Alexander, I., Hayes, K. Nerve supply of the human knee and its functional importance. *Am J Sports Med*; 10:329-335, 1982.
43. Kennedy, J.C., Baxter, W.R. The effects of local steroid injections on tendons. A biomechanical and microscopic correlative study. *Am J Sports Med*; 4:11-21, 1976.
44. Kirkaldy-Willis, W.H. *Managing Low Back Pain*. New York: Churchill Livingstone, 1983.
45. Klatz, R.M., Goldman, P.M., Pinchunk, B.G., et al. The effects of gravity inversion procedures on systemic blood pressure, intraocular pressure, and cental retinal asterial pressure. *J Am Osteopath Assoc*; 82:853-857, 1983.
46. Knight, K. Guidelines for rehabilitation of sports injuries. *Athletic Training*; 11(1):7, Spring 1976.
47. Knight, K. The effects of hypothermia on inflammation and swelling. *Clin Sports Med*; 4 3:405-416, 1985.
48. Knott, M., Voss, D. *Proprioceptive Neuromuscular Facilitation: Patterns and Techniques*. Harper and Row, 1985.
49. Kottke, F., Pauley, D., Ptak, R. The rationale for prolonged stretching for correction of shortening of connective tissue. *Arch Phys Med Rehabil*; 47:345-352, 1966.
50. Kottke, F., Stillwell, K., Lehmann, J. *Krusen's Handbood of Physical Medicine and Rehabilitation*. 3rd Edition. Saunders, 1982.
51. Kozar, B. Effects of ankle taping upon dynamic balance. *Athletic Training*; 9:04, 1974.
52. LaRocca, H. (ed). Scientific approach to the assessment and management of activity-related spinal disorders — a monograph for physicians. *Spine*; 12:75, 1987.
53. Lehmann, J. *Therapeutic Heat and Cold*. Williams and Wilkins. 3rd Edition, 1982.
54. Lehmann, J., Warren, C., Scham, S. Therapeutic heat and cold. *Clin Orthop*; 99:207-45, 1974.
55. Lippitt, A.B. The facet joint and its role in spine pain. *Spine*; 9(7), 1984.
56. McArdle, W., Katch, F., Katch, V. *Exercise Physiology: Energy Nutrition, and Human Performance*. (Chapter 21) Lea and Febiger, 1981.
57. McKeag, D. The primary care aspects of overuse syndromes in sports. *Primary Care*; 11 3:43-59, 1984.
58. McKeag, D., Brody, H., Hough, D. Medical ethics in sports. *Phys Sports*; 12 8:8, 145-150, 1984.
59. McMaster, W. Cryotherapy. *Phys Sports Med*; 10 11:112-119, 1982.
60. Markey, K. Rehabilitation of the anterior cruciate deficient knee. *Clin Sports Med*; 4 3:513-526, 1985.
61. Matsen, S., Krugmire, R. The effect of externally applied pressure on post fracture swelling. *Clin Sports Med*; 4 3:513-526, 1985.
62. Mayer, T.G. Orthopedic conservation care: The functional restoration approach. *Spine: State of the Arts Review*; 1(1), 1986.
63. Mayhew, J., Riner, W. Effects of ankle wrapping on motor performance. *Athletic Training*; 9:27, 1974.
64. Melzack, R., Wall, P. Pain mechanisms: A new theory. *Science*; 150: 971, 1965.
65. Messer, J., Reitman, D., Sack, H., et al. Association of adrenocorticosteroid therapy and peptic ulcer disease. *New England J Med*; 309:1, 41-47, 1983.
66. Moffett, J.A., Chase, S.M., Porteck, B.S., Ennis, J.R. A controlled prospective study to evaluate the effectiveness of a back scholl in the relief of chronic low back pain. *Spine*; 11(2), 1986.
67. Montgomery, J.B., Steadman, J.R. Rehabilitation of the injured knee. *Clinics in Sports Med*; 4:2, 333-343, 1985.
68. Morrissey, M., Brewster, C., Shields, C., et al. The effects of electrical stimulation on the quadriceps during post-operative knee immobilization. *Am J Sports Med*; 13:1, 40-48, 1985.
69. Muller, A. Influence of Training and Inactivity on Muscle Strength. *Arch Phys Med Rehab*; 51:449-462, 1970.
70. Murphy, R. The use and abuse of drugs in athletics. *Sports Injuries Mechanisms, Prevention and Treatment*. Editor: Scheider R. Williams and Wilkins, Chapter 33, 1985.
71. Nachemson, A. The influence of spinal movements on the lumbar intradiscal pressure and on the tensile stresses in the annulus fibrosis. *Acta Orthop Scand*; 33:183-207, 1963.

72. Nachemson, A. Lumbar intradiscal pressure. *Acta Orthop Scand*; (Supp 143):1 1-104, 1960.
73. Nachemson, A.L. The lumbar spine: An orthopedic challanged. *Spine*; 1:59, 1976.
74. Nideffer, R. The injured athlete: Psychological factors and treatment. *Orthop Clinic North Am*; 14 2:373-385, 1983.
75. Noble, J., Erat, K. In defense of the meniscus. A prospective study of 200 menisectomy patients. *J Bone Joint Surg*; 620-7, 1980.
76. Noyes, F. Functional properties of knee ligaments and alterations induced by immobilization. A correlative biochemical and histological study in primates. *Clin Orthop*; 123:210-242, 1977.
77. Noyes, F., et al. Biomechanics of ligament failure II. An analysis of immobilization, exercise and reconditioning effects in primates. *J Bone Joint Surg*; 56A:1406-1418, 1974.
78. Noyes, F.R., Moar, P.A., Mathews, D.S., et al. The symptomatic anterior cruciate-deficient knee. *J Bone Joint Surg*; 65A:154, 1983.
79. Owen, B.D. Posture, exercise can help prevent low back injuries. *Occup Health and Safety*; 55(6):33-37, 1986.
80. Pappas, A., Zawacki, R., McCarthy, C. Rehabilitation of the pitching shoulder. *Am J Sports Med*; 13(4):223-232, 1985.
81. Paulos, L., et al. Knee rehabilitation after anterior cruciate ligament reconstruction and repair. *Am J Sports Med*; 9:140-149, 1981.
82. Paulos, L., Noyes, F.R., Grood, E., et al. Knee rehabilitation after anterior cruciate ligament reconstruction and repair. *Am J Sports Med*; 9:140-149, 1981.
83. Perry, J. Anatomy and biomechanics of the shoulder in throwing, swimming, gymnastics and tennis. *Clin Sports Med*; 2:247-270, 1983.
84. Potera, C. Knee braces: Questions raised about performance. *Phys Sports Med*; 13(9), 1985.
85. Prez, D., Faust, D.C., Evans, J.P. Cyrotherapy and nerve palsy. *Am J Sports Med*; 9:256-257, 1981.
86. Quillen, W. An alternative management protocol for lateral ankle sprains. *Orthop Sports Phys Ther*; 2(4):187-190, 1981.
87. Quillen, W. Phonophoresis: a review of the literature and technique. *Athletic Training*; 15:109-110, 1980.
88. Rarick, L. The measurable support of ankle joint by conventional methods of taping. *JBone Joint Surg*; 44A:1183, 1962.
89. Reid, D. Ankle injuries in sports *Am J Sports Med*; 1:3, 1973.
90. Rodnan, G.P., Schumacher, H.R., Zvaifler, N.S. (eds). *Primer on the Rheumatic Diseases*. Arthritis Foundation: 8th Edition, 1983.
91. Rogoff, J. *Manipulation, Traction and Massages*. 2nd Edition, Williams & Williams, 1980.
92. Rovere, G.D. Low back pain in athletes. *Phys and Sports Med*; 15(1):105-117, 1987.
93. Roy, S., Irvin, R. *Sports Medicine Prevention, Evaluation, Management and Rehabilitation*. (Chapter 8) Prentice-Hall, 1983.
94. Roy, S., Irvin, R. *Sports Medicine Prevention, Evaluation, Management and Rehabilitation*. Prentice-Hall, 1983.
95. Ryan, A. Ankle sprains, a roundtable. *Phys Sports Med*; 14 2:101-118, 1986.
96. Salter, R.B., et al. Clinical application of basic research on continuous passive motions for disorders of and injuries to syovial joints: a preliminary report. *J Ortho Res*; 1:325, 1984.
97. Sammarco, J. Biocmechanics of the ankle: surface velocity and instant center of rotation in the sagittal plane. *Am J Sports Med*; 5:6, 1977.
98. Simon, L, Mills, J. Nonsteroidal anti-inflammatory drugs Part I. *New Eng J Med*; 302-21, 1179-1185, 1980.
99. Simon, L., Mills, J. Nonsteroidal anti-inflammatory drugs Part II. *New Eng J Med*; 302:22, 1327-1343, 1980.
100. Smith, R. The dynamics in prevention of stress-induced burnout in athletics. *Primary Care*; 11 1:115-124, 1984.
101. Spencer, C.W. (ed). Injuries to the spine. *Clinics in Sports Med*; 5:2, 1986.
102. Stanford, B. The myth of electrical exercise. *Phys Sports Med*; 11 12:144, 1983.
103. Stanish, W., Rubinovich, M., Kozey, J., et al. The use of electricity of ligament and tendon repair. *Phys Sport Med*; 13 8:109-116, 1985.
104. Steadman, J.R. Rehabilitation of acute injuries in the anterior cruciate ligament. *Clin Orthop Rel Research*; 172:129-132, 1983.
105. Sutter, J. Rehabilitation of the knee following arthroscopic surgery. *Contemporary Orthopedics*; 11(3):29-41, 1985.
106. Tipton, C., Matthes, R., Maynar, J., et al. The influence of physical activity on ligaments and tendons. *Med Sci Sport*; 7(3):165-175, 1975.
107. Torg, J.S. (ed). Head and neck injuries. *Clinics in Sports Med*; 6:1, 1987.
108. Torg, J.S., Quendenfeld, T.C., Burnstein, A., et al. National Football Head and Neck Injury Registry report on cervical quadraplegia: 1971-1975. *Am J Sports Med*; 7:127-132, 1977.
109. Torg, J.S., Quendenfeld, T.C., Theiler, E.R., Lignelli, G.J. Collision with spring-loaded football tackeling and blocking dummies. *JAMA*; 236:1270-1271, 1976.
110. Torg, J.S., Truex, R.C., Marshall, J., et al. Spinal injury at the third and fourth cervical vertebrae from football. *J Bone Joint Surg*; 59A:1015-1019, 1977.
111. Travel, J., Simons, D. Myofascial Pain and Dysfunction. *The Trigger Point Manual*; Williams & Williams, 1983.
112. Unverferth, L.J., Olix, M.L. The effect of local steroid injection on tendons. *J Sports Med*; 1:31-37, 1973.
113. Vaes, P., DeBoeck, H., Handleberg, S., et al. Comparative radiologic study of the influence of ankle joint bandages on ankle stability. *Am J Sports Med*; 13:46-49, 1983.
114. White, A.H. (ed). Failed Back Surgery Syndrome. *Spine: State of the Art Reviews*; 1(1), 1986.
115. Wilkerson, G. External compression for controlling traumatic edema. *Phys Sports Med*; 13 6:97-104, 1985.
116. Wilkerson, G. Treatment of ankle sprains with external compressions and early mobilization. *Phys Sports Med*; 13 6:83-90, 1985.
117. Zarins, B., Andrews, J., Carson, W. (eds). *Injuries to the Throwing Arm*. Philadelphia: WB Saunders Co., 1985.
118. Zarins, B., Boyle, J., Harris, B. Knee rehabilitation following arthroscopic meniscectomy. *Clinical Orthop and Related Res*; 198: 36-42, 1985.
119. Zimmerman, M. Peripheral and central nervous mechanics of nociception, pain, and pain therapy: facts and hypotheses. In Bonica J. Editor: Advances in Pain Research and Therapy; New York: Raven Press, 1979.

# 19

# Establishing A Local Sports Medicine Network

Previous chapters dealt primarily with clinical aspects of sports medicine. Other topics are important in supporting these clinical activities, including education and information sources, suggested equipment and record keeping forms, assessing the sports medicine literature, community resources, and working with the community to promote physical fitness. Information on national resources for information and educational materials, local resources for developing a sports medicine network, and suggestions for reviewing research literature are given in this chapter.

## RESOURCES FOR THE PRIMARY CARE SPORTS MEDICINE PRACTITIONER

### National Resources

Because sports medicine is changing and progressing rapidly, it is essential that the primary care physician keep up with the literature and communicate with others in the field. Procedures that are faster, more reliable, more precise, or which allow your patients to return to their activities sooner will be in the literature. Review it and be willing to incorporate new ideas and procedures into your practice. Using the simple literature assessment skills given later in this chapter, you can develop a broader perspective and avoid choosing poorly conceived procedures to incorporate into your practice.

Keeping current with new developments in medicine demands initiative and specific planning by the practicing physician. Journals are often used as a means of "self-directed learning." Set aside time daily, or weekly at a minimum, for reading to maintain awareness of current medical progress. Some physicians may believe themselves too busy, but they should heed the advice often given patients. Physicians tell patients to make regular exercise and relaxation an inviolate part of their daily routine. Physicians should do the same for relaxing and reading books and journals.

It is recommended that the family practice physician develop a small library of sports medicine reference books and journals for quick reference when presented with a problem that may be outside the usual range of experience. The resources of a major library or an area university hospital or medical school library may be needed for some more extensive literature reviews. These libraries will have literature searching tools such as *Index Medicus* or computer data bases such as *Medline* or *Excerpta Medica*. Staff at these libraries will provide assistance in using the available information retrieval systems.

Many national organizations deal wholly or in part with sports medicine and provide publications, position statements, public and professional education materials, and national or regional meetings where there are many opportunities for information exchange on a formal and informal basis. Membership in one or more of these organizations will provide access to many valuable resources. Many make their services and publications available to nonmembers at slightly higher costs. Appendix 19-1 is a list of organizations that deal with sports medicine. Appendix 19-2 is a list of journals devoted primarily to sports medicine, and the addresses for subscriptions.

## Local Resources for the Sports Medicine Team

Most communities have school athletic programs, sports programs for younger children and adults, and individuals who are interested in attaining or maintaining a certain measure of physical fitness. The entire community could benefit from having a well-established sports medicine team or network involved in injury prevention, recognition, treatment, rehabilitation, follow-up and proper referral. Farmer (4) and Bloomberg (2) have described examples of such networks. However, most communities do not have a local sports medicine network and the medical care of athletes is often haphazard (9). A primary care physician in the community who is interested in sports medicine could be a focal point for starting a network.

A local sports medicine network can be conceived of as having primary and secondary levels. At the primary level, those involved are concerned with on the field coverage of contests and practices, injury recognition and screening, initial diagnosis and treatment of injuries, and referral to the proper medical professional, either the athlete's family physician or a specialist. This primary group could include other primary care physicians, osteopathic physicians, emergency physicians, nurses, certified athletic trainers, registered physical therapists, and student athletic trainers. The secondary level consists of individuals involved in long-term treatment, rehabilitation, and follow-up. Some of the primary level people would be joined by additional specialists such as orthopaedists, dentists, surgeons, gynecologists, psychiatrists, psychologists, nutritionists, and podiatrists. Some of these specialists could serve at the primary level if they wish and if they have a broad enough experience in athletic injuries beyond their specialized training.

The development of a local network likely will have to be accomplished on a voluntary basis with little or no monetary support. While schools and other organizations will benefit directly, they usually will not have extra funding for an activity such as this. (On the other hand, beyond the altruistic contribution to fulfilling a community need, the members of the network gain considerable exposure that often translates into new patients.) School administrators, coaches, parents, and athletes themselves are becoming increasingly aware of the need for well-organized medical support. In this situation the primary care physician can and should serve as the catalyst.

Establishing a local sports medicine network begins with contacting other medical professionals in the community. In smaller communities, there may be no more than one or two primary level individuals available to provide initial coverage of community athletes. In larger communities, more individuals may be available but they will have more schools and activities to cover. In any case, it is advisable to develop a training program for school administrators, coaches, and interested individuals like parents to teach the fundamentals of emergency care and injury recognition. Rarely can a medical professional attend every contest and practice, so it is useful to have administrators and coaches who are capable of recognizing when an injury or other problem should be seen by a physician or handled by other members of the local sports medicine network. However, it has been demonstrated that most school staff (coaches and administrators) responsible for the health care of athletes are not competent for such responsibilities (13). We also know that high school coaches who receive specific training in injury recognition report injuries at a rate equivalent to that of a certified athletic trainer (6, 11). Coaches who do not have training report less than half the injuries. Trained coaches are much more confident in their ability to handle injuries and their athletes miss significantly less time after injury. Untrained coaches recognize less than half of the referable injuries and do not ensure proper rehabilitation before athletes return to participation (11).

Most coaches who are truly concerned about the health and welfare of their athletes are willing to learn about injury recognition. There is a trend for school systems and local sports organizations to require coaches to have some minimal training in emergency medical care and injury recognition. Medical professionals should actively encourage this trend and offer to help provide the training in their communities.

Once a core of individuals is available to serve as the primary level of the local sports medicine network, the group should develop plans for coverage of local athletic activities. It also should plan for its own continuing education. There always will be some individuals who are inexperienced or weak in certain areas. A regular series of team training sessions to share knowledge, experience, or expertise, and to bring everyone up to speed on the fundamentals of athletic injury care will be helpful.

Planning coverage for all the athletic activities in a community can be exasperating because it seems there are never enough team members to cover everything adequately and still leave time for regular professional duties and family and social activities. This is yet another reason why it is useful to train coaches and administrators in injury recognition. They can give minimal coverage during practices and contests that cannot be covered by network members. Another approach is to encourage one or two interested high school students to become student athletic trainers. Many states have a college or university that conducts summer training sessions in this field for high school students. Student trainers can be given further training from members of the local sports medicine network during the school year and can become an integral part of the network. Their schools would benefit by having individuals with a higher level of medical training than most coaches normally have available to cover practices and contests.

In the organization stages, members of the network also should contact administrators for the local school systems and local athletic leagues to inform them about the activities and personnel of the network, and to request a formal working relationship with the school or league. These administrators will have to give permission to have athletic activities under their jurisdiction covered by members of the network, but this normally will not be a problem. Referring to articles such as the one by Rice (10) in the professional publications for education administrators could be helpful in boosting the interest and support of local school administrators in the services of the sports medicine network, as well as in training their coaches and staff. Most administrators usually appreciate having better medical coverage for their athletes.

It is important to consider the legal aspects of these arrangements at the outset. Refer to Chapter 1 for a brief review of the legal ramifications of providing on-site care of athletic injuries. If the school system has a team physician, that person presumably will already be a part of the network. If this is not the case, make an effort to include the physician in the primary level of the network or, at a minimum, set up a good working relationship with the person, who already is established as having primary responsibility for the medical care of the school's athletes. This working relationship could include assistance in covering events, training school staff, or providing access to the network's referral system.

As members of the primary network are recruited and organized, begin developing a set of written procedures to be followed by network members. These procedures should spell out the duties and responsibilities of the various categories of medical professionals in the network. Having written procedures is important because each individual then has a clear understanding of his duties and how he fits into the total operation. A vital element in establishing and maintaining the credibility and success of the network is an agreement by all primary level members and secondary level specialists to see an athlete immediately upon referral by another network member. Without that agreement by all parties, it is difficult to provide timely care, particularly for athletes on school teams who often are under pressure to return to activity as soon as possible.

A primary emphasis for the network should be prevention of injuries. This includes providing appropriate pre-season physical examination and screening. Other important elements include ensuring proper fit of protective equipment, seeing that adequate fluids are available during practices and contests, and educating coaches and athletes about proper pre-season preparation, proper warm-up and stretching (remember "warm-up" and "stretching" are *not* interchangeable terms; they refer to two distinctly different activities), and proper cool-down after exercise.

Much of the burden of preventing injuries, initial care of injuries, rehabilitation, referral and follow-up that falls on physicians in the sports medicine network could be alleviated if each high school in the community had a certified athletic trainer on staff. Recent research (8) has shown that having an athletic trainer on a high school staff is associated with lower athletic injury rates and a shorter time away from activity for those who are injured. Most school administrators say they cannot afford a full-time staff position for an athletic trainer even though they agree it would be desirable. This argument assumes that the individual would be hired only as an athletic trainer, but many certified athletic trainers also have degrees in education and hold teaching certificates in academic subject areas. Such an individual could be hired as a teacher and assigned extra-curricular duties as a trainer, with a supplemental pay scale equivalent to that of a head coach. Many high schools have found this approach works very well. An alternative is the "teacher-athletic trainer," a teacher on staff who becomes certified in first aid, CPR, and completes a basic and advanced course in athletic training. This person will not qualify for national certification, but they can meet state guidelines and are paid a stipend for their extra-curricular duties as an athletic trainer. This concept has been tried successfully by North Carolina high schools under a 1979 state law requiring all high schools to have nationally certified athletic trainers or state certified teacher-athletic trainers by the 1984-85 academic year (7, 8). Another option in larger school districts is to hire an athletic trainer for the district, who spends a specified amount of time at each school. The costs are distributed across all the schools in the district (14). The members of the local sports medicine network can actively encourage consideration of these approaches by discussing their merits with parents, coaches, administrators, and school board members.

As the network becomes organized and reaches a stage of readiness to cover athletic events, specific plans must be in place for emergency care and transportation. All network members, coaches, and administrators must know how to obtain emergency transportation during practices and contests. In most cases, this means knowing the phone number of the local ambulance service. (The phone number should be taped to the back of a coach's clipboard, along with other reminders of what to do in emergencies.) At every practice and contest, coaches and any network members present must know specifically where the nearest *accessible* telephone is located. Accessibility is important; it does no good to know that the nearest telephone is in the principal's office if the building or office is locked and no one on the field has the key. When an ambulance is called, the caller should give specific instructions on the quickest route to reach the patient. The fastest access to the playing field or gymnasium may not always be readily apparent to the ambulance driver. It is wise to discuss access routes with ambulance staffs before an emergency occurs. Cover both practice and game situations because different access routes may be required because of time of day, traffic patterns, and presence of spectators and parked cars.

It is highly recommended that an ambulance be present at all football games, and preferably at all basketball games. Arranging and paying for ambulance coverage should be the responsibility of the host school. In most communities, ambulance service is available through local fire or police departments, hospitals, or private companies. Bear in mind that having an ambulance at events is not only for the welfare of the athletes, but also for the welfare of the spectators. The excitement generated by football and basketball games and the relatively large crowds make it commomplace to have an emergency situation develop that requires care and transportation of a spectator. Members of the network must also be trained and prepared to handle spectator emergencies. Work out agreements with the local ambulance service concerning specific responsibilities of various network members who may be present to provide emergency care, and how these responsibilities should mesh with those of the ambulance staff. Have a clear understanding of where authority and responsibility begin and end for everyone. Having agreements in place prevents conflict and confusion when an ambulance or paramedic crew arrives to transport a stricken individual at an athletic event being covered by a network member, particularly if that network member is a non-physician.

During the initial meetings and subsequent training sessions, discuss and agree upon the specific materials and equipment to be carried by team members when they cover contests and practices. Suggestions for equipment are presented in Chapter 8 and listed in Appendices. Another matter of agreement is what record keeping forms will be used. All team members should use a common set of forms and all members should know how to use them. With a volunteer sports medicine team providing medical coverage for local athletes and sports events, it is important to maintain clear and concise records of every service provided by every team member. This becomes vital in the event of public inquiry into the treatment of an individual athlete or if a lawsuit arises from an athletic injury. See Chapter 4 for suggestions about record keeping forms.

We suggest using a four part form with space to describe the injury and initial treatment by the primary network team member, and to indicate whether the athlete should be seen by a physician before returning to activity. The first copy (original) should be signed by the network team member and retained in a central network file. (This central network file can be useful for research on community athletic injury rates.) The remaining three copies are taken by the athlete to his or her parents or guardians who sign them before they are taken to the family or team physician or to a secondary level network specialist. This physician notes the complete diagnosis and treatment/rehabilitation plan on the form, signs it, and keeps the second copy for office files. The remaining two copies are returned to the athlete. The third copy is kept by the athlete's parents or guardians and the fourth copy (again signed by the parent or guardian) is given to the team coach. Everyone then will be aware of the diagnosis, treatment, and rehabilitation recommendations. The fourth copy, signed by all parties, should be kept in the school files. Figure 19-1 illustrates this sequence.

Once a local sports medicine network is operational, team members should take advantage of any locally available continuing education activities dealing with sports medicine. Even if there is no local network, a primary care physician interested in sports medicine likely will be able to find locally available continuing education activities such as symposia and workshops on sports medicine. If there is no sports medicine committee in the state or local medical society, there probably are enough interested physicians to form a committee if someone takes the initiative to raise the issue.

A primary care physician interested in sports medicine should be aware of the growing number

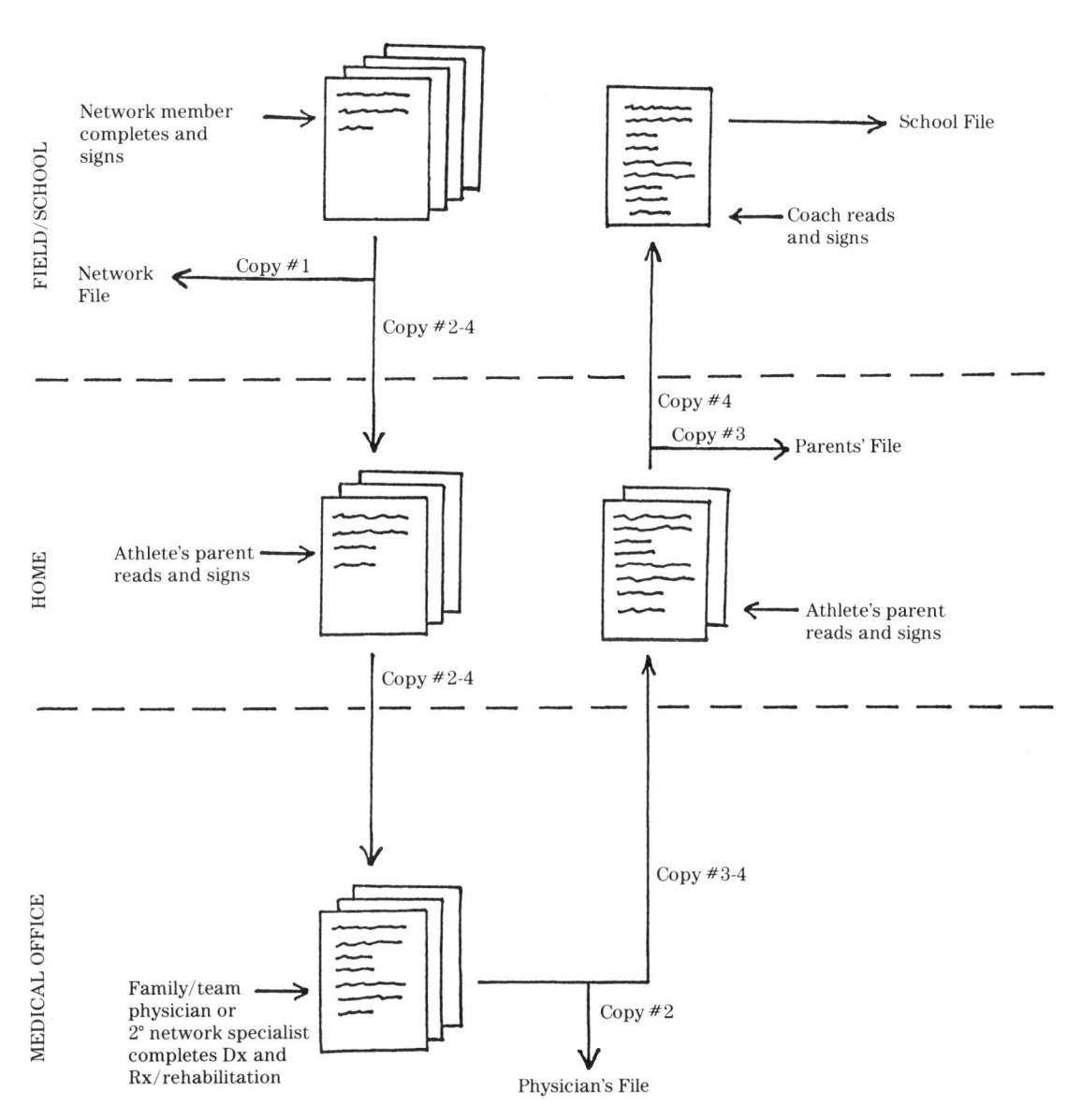

Fig. 19-1. Use of a four-part form in record-keeping for the community sports medicine network.

of training programs available. Many are associated with residency programs but some, like the successful program that has been available since 1979 at Michigan State University, are available to practicing physicians, residents, and medical students. The program consists of one month of intensive exposure to sports medicine through daily clinical practice with a variety of university athletic teams and a community sports medicine clinic, as well as didactic presentations. Some programs also accept allied health personnel like nurses and athletic trainers. This book serves as an example of a sports medicine curriculum for family practice residency programs, and Appendix 19-3 contains a list of training programs available across the country.

In addition to training programs for the medical professional, the primary care physician working to establish a local sports medicine network also should be aware of new programs to train local coaches and school administrators in health care of students participating in athletic programs. These are so new that coaches and school administrators are barely aware of them and very few have received any training. The athletic programs of most schools reveal four major areas of weakness with regard to medical care (12): 1) inadequate knowledge about sports medicine and athletic training on the part of coaches and other athletic staff; 2) no established standards for athletic medical care (e.g., criteria for return to participation after injury), no written guidelines, and no protocols for action; 3) lack of an organized record-keeping system for athletic medical care, and 4) often poor communication with the medical community. The establishment of a local sports medicine network will go a long way toward correcting these areas of weakness. An excellent example of successful athletic care program training materials that are available for use by schools (and by medical professionals) is the Athletic Health Care System, developed by Stephen G. Rice, M.D., Ph.D., and his colleagues at the University of Washington (12). These materials show how a school and community can develop an optimal athletic health care program to fit local needs and meet established standards in seven important areas: staff training, athletic facilities, athletic equipment, emergency preparedness, central training room, provision of athletic health care and training services, and record keeping. Using tested materials like those of the Athletic Health Care System will aid considerably in implementing the local sports medicine network.

## SUGGESTIONS FOR ASSESSING SPORTS MEDICINE LITERATURE

As we said earlier, a physician can maintain awareness of current developments in sports medicine or any other branch of medicine by reading professional journals. Journals naturally make every effort to publish only research that meets professional standards of quality. Despite these efforts, some research does get published that is not well done, or that contains subtle design or analysis flaws that make the study less relevant than it might appear at first. It falls to the physician-reader to pick out the well done studies from those that are questionable. Following is a brief introduction to the skills and information needed to make such distinctions.

### Seven Basic Steps to Check When Assessing Research Literature

The process of assessing research literature can be divided into seven steps. They may be expressed or organized differently by other authors, but the basic ideas will be similar, if not identical, to those presented here. The seven basic steps are:

- Definition of the problem.
- Definition of the variables.
- Specification of the research question.
- Selection of the subjects.
- Selection of an appropriate research design.
- Analysis of the data.
- Interpretation of the results.

These steps are a checklist against which a research article can be measured. Each step will be discussed in this chapter. Keep in mind that not every step applies to every journal article. For example, theoretical proposals do not contain an analysis of results because there are no results to analyze. Other types of articles that may not contain all the steps are literature reviews, criticisms of research, and opinion essays.

There are a few other sources of information on assessing research literature that go into more detail and are written specifically for the physician, such as the book by Gehlbach (5). Other resources that provide a more extensive treatment of each of the topics presented here are listed in the Suggested Readings at the end of this chapter.

**Definition of the Problem and the Variables.** The first two steps in reviewing research articles are defining the basic problem addressed in the research and defining the variables related to the problem. Clear definitions are vital to good research. Indeed, the solution to a problem often flows naturally from a clear definition of it. A definition should explicitly specify the parameters and boundary conditions of the problem. Parameters are properties whose values determine the characteristics or behaviors of the system under study. Examples of parameters are a patient's nutritional status, exposure to athletic injury, social pressure to behave in certain ways, how irritating cigarette smoke is to the lungs, or the patient's ability to obtain medical care. Boundary conditions are characteristics that distinguish this problem from other problems or that specify the context in which the problem is found. Boundary conditions include descriptions of the extent of the problem and the population at risk. Examples are a problem found only in distance runners, in white males, in the spring, where influenza has broken out, or where fresh water is in short supply. Together, the parameters and the boundary conditions define the population of interest and suggest relevant variables for study. In most research articles, the parameters and boundary conditions are stated in the first section of the article where a review of any previous research on the problem is presented, as well as a general overview of the problem addressed in the study.

The boundary conditions of the problem identify the appropriate population to study. The parameters of the problem identify the appropriate variables to use. Variables are properties, behaviors, or characteristics a researcher manipulates or uses to measure various aspects of the problem. The variable manipulated by the researcher is called the *independent* variable. The variable used as a measurement of outcome is called the *dependent* variable, because its value depends on what occurs in the study. Take as an example a study of weight loss in individuals on different types of diets. The dependent (outcome) variable is the amount of weight lost and the independent variable is the type of diet. Besides the independent and dependent variables, the researcher should be aware of a third type of variable, the confounding variable or nuisance variable. A confounding variable is one that is likely to interfere with obtaining accurate results. In the study of weight loss, a confounding variable could be the amount of clothing worn by the subjects. Because this could vary from subject to subject, differences in weight loss might be hidden or exaggerated by wearing different amounts of clothing. This particular confounding variable can be controlled by weighing all subjects nude. When a variable is "controlled," its influence upon the results is eliminated. Another confounding variable in this study could be the amount and type of exercise the subjects did during the study. This variable could be controlled by making sure the subjects did not exercise during the study or that they all engage in the same amount and type. Another approach would be to make exercise a second independent variable that is manipulated by "crossing" with the type of diet. In other words, half the control group and half of each diet group would engage in a specified amount of exercise, while the other half of each group would not exercise. This approach naturally requires a larger number of subjects.

Sometimes the effect of a confounding variable cannot be eliminated. Nonetheless, the impact of confounding variables should be minimized as much as possible so as to enhance the interpretability of results. A full treatment of how to control confounding variables is found in standard statistics and experimental design textbooks. The basic principle underlying these methods is the effort to design the study in such a way that the results can be attributed only to the variable considered in the study, and not to other variables not evaluated whose impact is therefore unknowable.

**Specification of the Research Question.** After defining the problem and identifying the relevant variables, the investigator develops the research question. The research question specifies the particular aspects of the problem to be investigated in a given study. There are two common categories for research questions and they are listed here with examples:

- The relationship between variables.
  - How is amount of exercise related to post-MI recovery?
  - What is the relationship between the type of football playing surface (artificial or natural grass) and football injury rates?

- The value or status of variables.
  - How many surgical knee injuries occurred in college football last year?
  - Do obese patients have a high rate of surgical complications?

You can see that the formulation of research questions depends upon knowledge of the variables that are relevant to the problem under study.

The research question usually is found at the beginning of the study and often is labeled the research question, the target question, or "the question this study seeks to answer." If not explicitly labeled, it often can be identified by determining which variables were manipulated or measured. The usual focus of the research question is the effect of manipulating the independent variable upon the variable that is measured (the dependent variable).

**Selection of the Subjects.** Most research is done to find out something about a population. In most cases, the conclusion about the population is generalized from the results obtained from a sample of that population. In order to make valid generalizations, the sample should be representative of the total population. A sample is representative when it does not differ from the population it represents in any systematic way. The only differences between the sample and the population are due to chance. Typically, this is achieved by a procedure known as random sampling where subjects are chosen at random from the population to increase the probability that the only differences between the sample and the population are due to chance. A full treatment of random sampling can be found in any standard statistics textbook.

An important aspect of evaluating a research article is determining the adequacy of the subjects selected for study. The principal goal of subject selection procedures is to use subjects that are representative of the population. If they are not representative, the generalizability of the results is jeopardized and the information gained will not necessarily apply to the total population. For example, think about a study of skin cancer incidence intended to give information about black and Caucasian people that has a sample of two black subjects and 48 Caucasian subjects. The results likely will not apply to black people. There are many shades of black and brown skin tones in the black population so it is highly unlikely that these two people represent all or even most of the black population. It is more likely that the results apply to Caucasian people, but there could be difficulty if the Caucasians in the study all are very pale Scandinavians and the results are applied to persons of Mediterranean descent. The subjects must be described more fully before we would know to which population the results would actually apply.

Returning to our example of the weight loss study involving different types of diets, the selection of subjects is important not only to ensure that the results can be generalized to the population of interest, but also because of the potential impact on results. If the study is intended to help practitioners select an appropriate diet plan for their average patients, a study sample comprised of college basketball players would not be representative of the general population. Such a sample also would have an impact on the results of the study because college basketball players tend to be fairly lean and probably do not have much weight to lose in the first place. An article describing a research study should contain a sufficiently detailed description of the subjects to allow the reader to decide whether they are representative of the population of interest and appropriate for the purposes of the study.

Another important aspect of sample selection is the number of subjects selected. This topic is beyond the scope of a brief presentation, and the reader is referred to the texts listed in the Suggested Readings. However, as a rule, the larger the number of subjects in the sample, the more you can trust the results (assuming the sample is representative). The ultimate, of course, is to include the entire population of interest in the study, in which case no statistical tests of significance would be necessary and the results would be an absolute representation of the true situation in that population. Unfortunately, it seldom is practical to include the entire population of interest in a study. At the other extreme, public opinion research like the Gallup Poll are able to represent the entire U.S. population on the basis of answers from only twelve- to fourteen-hundred individuals. These very small samples are selected with extreme care, based on many years of experience, to be representative of all segments of our society. In most cases, a good rule of thumb for the non-researcher to follow is the smaller the sample, the less faith should be put in the results.

**Selection of an Appropriate Research Design.** The design of a study has a powerful effect upon the conclusions. For conclusions on causality, the usual requirement is that the study be designed as a true experiment. However, not all studies seek to find causal connections between variables; the researcher sometimes is looking for associations between variables or descriptions of the status or value of a variable. In cases where the researcher is not seeking to establish a causal connection, a true experimental design is not always necessary.

There are two basic types of research designs, experimental and non-experimental. In experimental designs, one or more independent variables are manipulated and the effects on the dependent variables are measured. In non-experimental studies, no variables are manipulated by the researcher, but the status of selected variables are measured. Most epidemiological studies are examples of non-experimental studies.

Designs also can be sorted into those requiring only one sample and those requiring two samples. When a researcher is seeking initial information about a population, only one sample may be drawn to test the sampling procedures or measuring instrument before doing a full-scale comparison study. An initial study like this sometimes is called a pilot study. Non-experimental studies very often are one-sample studies.

A common example of a two-sample study is a true experimental design in which two separate samples are randomly drawn from the population. The experimental treatment then is applied to only one of the samples, with the untreated group acting as a control. In all other respects, the two samples are treated identically. In some cases, when two different treatments are compared, each sample receives a different treatment. (A third untreated sample could be added to the study as a control group.) If the only difference between the two groups is in the treatment of interest they receive, the researcher can be fairly confident in ascribing any resulting large difference in the measured dependent variables to the difference in treatment. If the samples have been appropriately selected and are of sufficient size, the researcher can be fairly confident in generalizing the results to the total population. Further details on this subject are available in the publications listed in the Suggested Readings, but we can say that, in most cases, it is not appropriate to generalize the results of a study to a larger population if the sample is not representative of that population (representativeness is usually assured by some means of random selection of subjects from the larger population), or if the sample size is very small. In most cases, sample sizes of at least 50 are needed to demonstrate anything but the largest differences between groups or to ensure adequate generalizability.

A further way of classifying research is into prospective and retrospective studies. This classification is based on the time perspective of the study design. A prospective study starts with a defined population sample and follows it into the future, continuing to observe the status or values of variables of interest in non-experimental studies, or observing the results of manipulating variables in experimental studies. A retrospective study, on the other hand, begins with a sample with certain characteristics as they are measured today and traces the past history of the individuals in the sample, through questionnaires or medical records, to try to discover antecedent factors that might be related to the current status of the variables of interest in the study. Most studies of smoking and lung cancer are retrospective. More prospective studies of this relationship would provide useful evidence, but unfortunately they are more difficult to do and, in the case of following the development of lung cancer, it takes a relatively long time to complete such a study.

**Analysis of the Data.** The sixth step in evaluating research articles is checking the analysis of the data. After the researcher collects data, it must be analyzed and the results interpreted. This can be the most difficult and also the most rewarding part. It is also the part of a research article that is the most difficult and most important to understand. No matter how elegant the design and how voluminous and accurate the data, nothing will be gained if the analysis and interpretation are not appropriate to the type of study.

One of the most common statistical tests seen in research studies that are looking for cause-effect relationships is the *t-test*. Basically, this test indicates the significance of the difference between *two sample means*. There are different forms of the t-test that are used in different situations, depending on whether one sample mean is being compared to a known or assumed population mean, or two means from independent samples are being compared, or two means from dependent samples are being compared.

Another commonly seen statistical test in the literature is the *chi-square test*. The chi-square test is commonly used to test the significance of the *differences between the observed and the expected frequencies of an event*. An important point to remember in deciding whether a t-test or chi-square test should be used is that the t-test is used when the values of the variables being sampled can have any value, such as lab test values, whereas the chi-square test must be used when the values are integers only, such as counts of the numbers of people or cases. Such data is usually presented in tabular form. Both the t-test and chi-square test are appropriate when a single causative variable is being studied. If more than one causative factor is involved, a multivariate procedure must be used, such as multivariate analysis or analysis of variance (ANOVA). A very readable explanation of the t-test and several other statistical tests and their uses in causal-comparative research is presented on pages 421-470 of Borg and Gall (3), listed in the Suggested Readings.

Many research articles do not involve searches for causality, and instead report observations of data that do not necessarily require using statistical tests. In such cases, descriptive analysis procedures are used and results usually are presented in the form of various types of rates. A rate is simply the number of events or cases of a medical condition of interest in a given number of people exposed, or the "population at risk." The most common way of presenting case rates is:

$$\frac{\# \text{ of cases or events}}{\text{Total \# of people at risk}} \times 1{,}000 = \text{case rate per 1,000}$$

The "numerator data" is the total number of cases or events occurring in a given period of time, which is divided by the "denominator data" comprised of all those at risk during that period. To make comparisons easier, this ratio is multiplied by some convenient multiple of 10 to translate the rate into a common metric, such as a rate per 1,000 or 10,000. However, one of the major weaknesses of many research articles in sports medicine that purport to present rate data, particularly injury data, is that they do not include information on the population at risk, or "denominator data." Very often they only present data on the number of cases, or the "numerator data." For example, many articles present a compilation of cases seen at a particular event or in a specific clinic. Often the "rates" these articles present are only percentages of the total number of cases seen. No attempt has been made to determine the size of the population from which the series of cases was drawn. While a case series may be of some use in determining the relative proportion of various types of injuries in a particular situation, such articles are of little value from an epidemiological perspective because of the lack of denominator data ("population at risk") that prevents generalizing the data to other situations.

Another commonly seen form of presenting rates in the sports injury literature is the rate per 100 participants, usually with the implicit assumption that the time frame is one season or one year. While this is an improvement over the type of presentation mentioned above, it still poses problems in interpretation and in comparing rates across studies and across different sports. The use of simple rates per 100 participants assumes that all participants take part in all practices and in all games or contests, and that all teams and sports have the same number of practices and contests each season or year. Anyone familiar with the sports scene should have no trouble realizing that these assumptions are not valid. Not all athletes participate in every practice and many do not get to participate in every contest. Different teams have different numbers of practices and games during a season, especially if different sports are being compared. Therefore, using a simple rate per 100 participants can cause some very misleading conclusions when there is an effort to compare across different sports or different studies. This is the reason for the recommendation in Chapter 2 that a rate based on athlete-exposures to the possibility of being injured should be used. Ideally, a rate based on time of exposure would be the most nearly accurate for comparative purposes but this often is impractical, particularly in larger studies involving many teams. Rates based on athlete-exposures is a reasonable compromise that allows much more accurate comparisons than rates per 100 participants. In reading an article utilizing case rates, always determine the specific type of rate being used, and decide whether the denominator or the population at risk has been identified and used in the rate calculation and whether this "population at risk" is appropriate to the situation being studied.

**Interpretation of Results.** The final step in judging the worth of a research article is to assess the interpretation of the results. This is easier when you have adequately completed the first six steps of this seven-step process. Assuming the author has stated a researchable problem, has developed an appropriate hypothesis or hypotheses, concisely defined the variables to be measured, properly selected the subjects, developed an adequate research design, and used the appropriate statistical procedures to analyze the data, the reader must now ask if the conclusions drawn are warranted by the data. Are the conclusions and interpretations consistent with the statistical data? Authors sometimes draw conclusions that go beyond the data actually presented. Has the experimental hypothesis been supported by the data or, if no hypothesis was stated, was the general problem clarified further? Finally, are the results generalizable to other places, times, or situations? The adequacy of the sampling procedure is the key element in answering this latter question.

If the article presents new information relevant to your patients or your practice — say a conclusion that immediate application of ice to sprained ankles results in more rapid recovery than application of heat — you must evaluate the study to decide whether the conclusion is well-conceived and whether it is of sufficient importance to cause you to change some aspect of your practice or advice you give your patients. Not all research is perfectly done. Whether the imperfections in a particular article are sufficient in number or magnitude to cause the reader to discount the article is strictly a value judgement. We hope this will give you some basic criteria on which to base these judgments. If a reader is still uncertain after reading and analyzing an article, the best bet is to wait and see if the author receives support from other researchers in the future. If there are major flaws in the design, analysis, or interpretation, you can be certain they will be forcefully pointed out in letters to the journal or in follow-up articles during succeeding months.

**Summary.** In summary, the seven basic steps for assessing a journal article are:

- Look for the definition of the problem.
- Find an explicit statement of the research question or hypothesis.
- Pick out the variables being measured.
- Assess the selection of the subjects.
- Evaluate the appropriateness of the research design.
- Decide whether the data have been properly analyzed.
- Decide whether the conclusions are warranted by the information presented.

Although not stated in the same manner, these are the same steps suggested earlier in this chapter, but phrased in more operational terms. If any of these aspects of evaluating a research article, particularly the last four, are not satisfactory, it is best to wait for further published research on the topic before incorporating the ideas presented in an article into your practice.

## Validity

Several related topics are of importance in assessing research. The first is validity. Validity often is invoked in discussions and critiques of research literature. In some academic fields, like educational test and measurement theory, there are several distinct types of validity, some with precise mathematical definitions. For assessing medical literature, the reader needs to be concerned only with two global types of validity. The first of these is internal validity. As the name implies, this refers to the internal structure of the study. If the results appear to have been adequately and accurately obtained, appropriately analyzed, and the authors have drawn supportable conclusions based on their results, the study then may be considered internally valid. Most of the seven steps in assessing research literature deal with the issue of internal validity.

The second type of validity is called external validity and is what has been referred to in this chapter as the generalizability of study results. It is primarily an assessment of whether the results apply beyond the sample used in the study to the total population of interest or to other populations. As you recall, the adequacy of the selection of a truly representative sample is critical to the generalizability (or external validity) of the study. More will be said about this later.

## Statistical Significance

The term "significant" often is applied to results of research. However, many people confuse results labeled significant with an evaluation of how important or meaningful a result is. A statistician uses the term "significant" in a special way with a specific meaning. A result is significant to a statistician when it is improbable under the given set of conditions. Suppose an outcome showing a relationship between two variables is obtained under a specified set of conditions and suppose that a t-test shows that outcome is significant at the five percent level ($p<.05$). This means there is only a five percent chance that this outcome could have occurred by chance alone when there is truly no relationship between the variables. The significance level is sometimes expressed as the p-value or the alpha level of a study.

It is important to remember that significant does not necessarily mean important. Significant results arise for many reasons, including by accident. The laws of chance say that a result indicating a relationship between variables where there is no true relationship occurs only a certain percent of the time. This means that there are times when apparently significant results occur by chance alone. In designing statistical analyses, a researcher will set an upper limit to the acceptable level of chance of a false indication of a relationship. Usually this acceptable limit is five percent, but sometimes it is set higher or lower, depending on the experimenter's purposes. The significance level gives the probability of a false "significant" result if the circumstances specified were to be repeated over many trials. Since the given experiment is only one trial, there is a possibility that it is significant by chance.

Other important facts to keep in mind about significant results are that a result significant at $p<.0001$ really is not any more "important" in a well-designed study than a result that is significant at $p<.05$ or $p<.01$. Also, a result that is statistically significant may have no real practical significance. For instance, in a study with a large sample, a difference of four or five percent between two treatment groups could be statistically significant. However, the physician may find such a small difference meaningless in deciding between the two treatments. The small difference was statistically significant because smaller differences tend to become mathematically significant as the sample gets larger. On the other hand, a statistically non-significant result in a study with a small sample size could still have a great deal of practical significance. A small sample size could cause a difference between treatment groups of 15% or 20% to be statistically non-significant. Yet, if the study were repeated with a larger sample, and the difference was still 15% or 20%, the results would be statistically significant and the difference between treatments clearly of practical importance. You may be wondering what good are statistical tests? The thing to remember is that statistics are a useful tool but they must be used appropriately and wisely. A thorough reading of a straightforward explanation, such as that by Gehlbach (5), is advisable to help guide the reader through the statistics jungle.

**Common Design Flaws**

Design flaws are aspects of the design that interfere with the interpretation of the results of the study. A list of specific flaws is not possible because every study has its unique problems, depending upon the nature of the research and the circumstances under which it was conducted. There are common types of flaws, however. These do not, in general, have to do with statistical inference per se, but with the logical inferences that may be drawn from the data.

The idea of logical versus statistical inference brings us to a very important design flaw: the use of inappropriate statistics. When the logic of the design and the logic of the statistical test used do not agree, the wrong statistical test has been used. This is the reason it is important to understand the logic of statistical tests. For example, chi-square is a test of significant differences between observed and expected frequencies of an event. If a study is not designed to compare frequencies, the chi-square test is inappropriate.

Further, most statistical tests are based upon the assumption of independent observations. This is the assumption that the result of each observation in the study is independent of the result of conducting any other observation in the study. Sometimes this problem is posed as whether one has obtained independent responses on the dependent variable.

> Example: It is the object of this study to evaluate the efficacy of family therapy with respect to individual family members.

This is a study question that has the violation of independent responses built right into it. The response of a given individual to the therapy is not independent of the responses of other family members. What can be evaluated as an independent response is the response of each family as a whole compared to other families, if each family receives therapy as a unit separate from other families.

The example given not only is an example of a design that violates an assumption necessary to conduct a statistical test, it is also an example of the inappropriate choice of variables. Families should be used as the unit to study family therapy. After all, family therapy is directed at families, not at individuals. It is the assumption of family therapy that an illness in one member is a symptom that the family is ill, not the individual. A problem related to the choice of inappropriate variables is the choice of an inappropriate sample. An extreme example would be the study of child rearing practices in women over the age of 80 years. Very few women in this age group are still rearing children. This sample would only be appropriate to study *former* child rearing practices. Even then, it might be better to choose somewhat younger women whose memories are more recent and, thus, more likely to be reliable. A sample can be inappropriate because it is not representative of the population of interest, perhaps because it is too small. When a small sample is used, the impact of choosing an unrepresentative subject is greatly magnified.

If the sample is inappropriate because it is too narrowly defined, not representative, or too small, the difficulty of generalization of results becomes a serious problem. This is sometimes referred to as a problem of external validity. The generalizability of results rests largely on the appropriateness of the sample and the conditions under which research is conducted. For example, a drug trial conducted on tissue cultures might be valuable, but it would not be as generalizable as a drug trial conducted with people. A study of exercise habits in 45-year-old men would not necessarily be generalizable to 18-year-old women. If the sample were intended to give information about exercise habits of Americans in general, a sample of only 45-year-old men would be inappropriate because it would be too narrowly defined and unrepresentative, and thus would introduce considerable bias into the study.

Generalizability is a problem of interpreting the results of a study. The problem of ascribing a cause and effect relationship also is a problem of interpreting the results of a study. Cause and effect relationships between variables can be logically ascribed only in the context of an experiment. If a study meets the criteria of an experiment, causal statements can be made. The criteria for an experiment are:

- A pool of homogeneous subjects, randomly assigned to treatment and control groups.
- The absence of confounding variables.
- No systematic variance between groups other than the treatment administered by the experimenter.

The second condition is redundant with the first and third, but important enough to be mentioned specifically. If the first and third conditions are met, there will be no confounding variables, of course. To repeat, a confounding variable is any variable not included in the study that could plausibly be advanced as the cause of the observed effect. In the presence of a confounding variable, a cause and effect relationship between the variables studied cannot be postulated.

This discussion on evaluating research literature is intended to give the reader exposure to the variety of factors that must be considered in assessing a research article. For detailed reading on design flaws and the other topics presented on assessing research, please refer to the Suggested Readings that follow.

## REFERENCES

1. Alles, W.F., et al. The National Athletic Injury/Illness Reporting System: 3-Year Findings of High School and College Football Injuries. *J Orthop Sports Phys Ther* 1:103, 1979.
2. Bloomberg, R. Trainers for High School Athletes: Seattle Develops a Model Program. *Phys Sportsmed* 9(11):113, 1981.
3. Borg, W.R., and Gall, M.D. *Educational Research: An Introduction* (Third Edition). New York: Longman, Inc., 1979.
4. Farmer, M. Forming a Sport Health Team to Meet Community Needs. *Interschol Athl Administrator* 10(3):22, 1984.
5. Gehlbach, S.H. *Interpreting the Medical Literature: Practical Epidemiology for Clinicians* (Second Edition) New York: Macmillan, 1988.
6. Hage, P. Courses Help Coaches Identify Sports Injuries. *Phys Sportsmed* 10(10):32, 1982.
7. Hage, P. Program at Northwestern Trains Faculty Members During Summer. *Phys Sportsmed* 10(4):85, 1982.
8. Hage, P. Injury Rate Lowered By High School Trainers. *Phys Sportsmed* 11(11):35, 1983
9. Redfearn, R.W. Are High School Athletes Getting Good Health Care? *Phys Sportsmed* 3(9):34, 1975.
10. Rice, S.G. Heads Up: Keep Sports Safe *The Executive Educator* p. 19, August 1984.
11. Rice, S.G., Schlotfeldt, J.D., and Foley, W.E. The Athletic Health Care and Training Program. *West J Med* 142:352, 1985.
12. Rice, S.G. (Ed.) *Athletic Health Care System* Seattle, WA: HMS Publishing Services, 1988
13. Rowe, P.J., and Miller, L.K. Treating High School Sports Injuries — Are Coaches/Trainers Competent? *JOPERD* 62(1):49, 1991.
14. Stopka, C., and Kaiser, D. Certified Athletic Trainers in Our Secondary Schools: The Need and the Solution *Athletic Training* 23:322, 1988

## SUGGESTED READINGS

### Statistics and Research Methodology

Austin, D.F. and Werner, S.B. *Epidemiology for the Health Sciences: A Primer on Epidemiologic Concepts and Their Uses* Springfield, IL.: Charles C. Thomas, 1979.

Borg, W.R. and Gall, M.D. *Educational Research: An Introduction* (Third Edition). New York: Longman Inc., pp. 420-472, 1979.

Cox, D.R. *Planning Experiments* New York: Wiley, 1957.

Gehlbach, S.H. *Interpreting the Medical Literature: Practical Epidemiology for Clinicians* (Second Edition). New York: Macmillan, 1988

Hayes, W.L. *Statistics for the Social Sciences* New York: Holt, Rinehart and Winston, 1973.

Kilpatrick, S.J., Jr. *Statistical Principles in Health Care Information* Baltimore: University Park Press, 1977.

# Appendix 19-1.
# Sports Medicine-Related Organizations

American Academy of Physical Medicine and Rehabilitation
30 N. Michigan Avenue, Chicago, IL 60602

American Academy of Podiatric Sports Medicine (AAPSM)
P.O. Box 31331, San Francisco, CA 94131

American Academy of Sports Physicians
7535 Laurel Canyon Blvd.,
North Hollywood, CA 91605

American Alliance for Health, Physical Education, Recreation & Dance (AAHPERD)
1900 Association Dr., Reston, VA 22091

American Athletic Trainers Association & Certification Board, Inc.
638 W. Duarte Rd., Arcadia, CA 91006

American College of Sports Medicine (ACSM)
P.O. Box 1440, Indianapolis, IN 46206

American Medical Society for Sports Medicine (AMSSM)
P.O. Box 623, Middleton, WI 53562

American Orthopaedic Society for Sports Medicine (AOSSM)
70 W. Hubbard, Suite 202, Chicago, IL 60610

American Osteopathic Academy of Sports Medicine
P.O. Box 623, Middleton, WI 53562

American Physical Therapy Association — Sports Medicine Section
University of Wisconsin at Lacrosse,
2036 Cowley Hall, Lacrosse, WI 54601

American Society for Biomechanics
c/o Dr. Malcom H. Pope,
Department of Orthopaedics and Rehabilitation,
University of Vermont, Burlington, VT 05405

Canadian Association for Sports Medicine (CASM)
1600 James Naismith Dr., Gloucester, ON K1B 5N4

Institute for Aerobics Research
12200 Preston Rd., Dallas, TX 75230

National Association for Disabled Athletes
1 Executive Dr., Ft. Lee, NJ 07024

National Athletic Trainers Association (NATA)
2952 Stemmons (Inwood Exit), Dallas, TX 75247

National Handicapped Sports and Recreation Association
P.O. Box 18664, Capitol Hills Station,
Denver, CO 80218

National Strength and Conditioning Association
P.O. Box 81410, Lincoln, NE 68501

North American Society for the Psychology of Sport and Physical Activity
Department of HPRE, Louisiana State University,
Baton Rouge, LA 70803

President's Council on Physical Fitness and Sports
450 5th St., NW, Washington, D.C. 20015

Special Olympics
1701 K St., NW, Suite 203, Washington, D.C. 20006

United States Olympic Committee (USOC)
1750 E. Boulder St., Colorado Springs, CO 80909

United States Sports Academy
124 University Blvd., P.O. Box 8650,
Mobile, AL 36608

Women's Sports Foundation
195 Moulton St., San Francisco, CA 94123

# Appendix 19-2.
# Sports Medicine Journals

American Journal of Sports Medicine
Williams & Wilkins Co.,
428 E. Preston St., Baltimore, MD 21202

Archives of Physical Medicine and Rehabilitation
30 N. Michigan Ave., Chicago, IL 60602

Athletic Training (NATA Journal)
2952 Stemmons (Inwood Exit), Dallas, TX 75247

Australian Journal of Sports Medicine
AJSM, Department of Human Movement Studies,
University of Queensland
St. Lucia, Queensland, Australia 4067

British Journal of Sports Medicine
Journals Fulfilment Department, Butterworth's,
80 Montvale Ave., Stoneham, MA 02180

Clinical Journal of Sports Medicine
2500 University Dr., NW.
Calgary, Alb, Canada T2N 1N4

Clinical Sports Medicine
B-100 Clinical Center, MSU
East Lansing, MI 48824

Clinics in Sports Medicine
W.B. Saunders Co.,
West Washington Square, Philadelphia, PA 19105

Exercise and Sport Sciences Reviews (Annual)
Williams & Wilkins Co.,
428 E. Preston St., Baltimore, MD 21202

International Journal of Sport Psychology
Via Della Camilluccia 195, 1-00135 Roma, Italy

International Journal of Sports Medicine
Georg Thieme Verlag, Rudigerstaze 14,
P.O. Box 732, D-7000, Stuttgart 1, Germany

Journal of Applied Physiology: Respiratory,
Environmental and Exercise Physiology
American Physiological Society,
9650 Rockville Pike, Bethesda, MD 20814

Journal of Cardiac Rehabilitation
c/o Jacq Publishing Co.,
130 John St., New York, NY 10038

Journal of Orthopaedic and
Sports Physical Therapy
Williams & Wilkins Co.,
428 E. Preston St., Baltimore, MD 21202

Journal of Sport Psychology
Human Kinetics Publishers, Box 5076,
Champaign, IL 61820

Journal of Sports Medicine and Physical Fitness
Minerva Medica, Torino, Italy

Medicine and Science in Sports and Exercise
ACSM, P.O. Box 1440, Indianapolis, IN 46206

New Zealand Journal of Sports Medicine
Dr. Noel Roydhouse, P.O. Box 26-179M,
Auckland, New Zealand

The Physician and Sportsmedicine
McGraw-Hill Inc., 4530 W. 77th St.,
Minneapolis, MN 55435

Research Quarterly for Exercise and Sport
AAHPERD Circulation Department,
1900 Association Dr., Reston, Va 22091

Scandinavian Journal of Sports Sciences
Finnish Society for Research in
Sport & Physical Education,
Annankatu 4B, SF-00120 Helsinki 12, Finland

Soviet Sports Review
P.O. Box 2878, Escondido, CA 92025

Sports Medicine: An International Journal of
Applied Medicine and Science
in Sport and Exercise
ADIS Press International Inc.,
401 S. State St., Newton, PA 18940

Sports Medicine, Training and Rehabilitation
Harwood Academic Publishers GMBH,
P.O. Box 786 Cooper Station, New York, NY 10276

Year Book of Sports Medicine (Annual)
Year Book Medical Publishers,
35 E. Wacker Dr., Chicago, IL 60601

# Appendix 19-3.
## Partial List of Institutions With Sports Medicine Fellowship Programs

Alabama Sports Medicine and Orthopedic Center, Birmingham, AL

Bell Memorial Hospital, Muncie, IN

Center for Sports Medicine and Orthopedics, Phoenix, AZ

Chicago College of Osteopathic Medicine — Division of Sports Medicine, Chicago, IL

Childrens Hospital Medical Center — Sports Medicine Center, Akron, OH

Cleveland Clinic Foundation, Cleveland, OH

Deaconess Sports Medicine, St. Louis, MO

Eastern Oklahoma Orthopedic Center
Tulsa, OK

Grant Medical Center, Columbus, OH

Hughston Sports Medicine Center
Columbus, GA

Indiana University — Long Hospital
Indianapolis, IN

Johnson Medical School/UMNDJ — Department of Family Medicine
New Brunswick, NJ

Kaiser-Fontana Department of Family Medicine
Fontana, CA

Kaiser Permanente Medical Center
Santa Clara, CA

Lutheran General Hospital — Sports Medicine
Park Ridge, IL

Marshall University School of Medicine — Division of Sports Medicine and Adult Fitness
Huntington, WV

Mayo Clinic — Sports Medicine Center
Rochester, MN

Methodist Hospital — Sports Medicine
Indianapolis, IN

Michigan State University — Sports Medicine Clinic
East Lansing, MI

North Carolina Baptist Hospital/ Wake Forest University
Winston-Salem, NC

Ohio Physical Therapy and Sports Medicine
Chesterland, OH

Ohio State University Sports Medicine
Columbus, OH

Orthopedic Specialty Hospital
Salt Lake City, UT

St. Elizabeth Sports Medicine Center
Dayton, OH

San Diego State University — UCSD/SDSU Preventive Medicine Residency
San Diego, CA

Scripps Clinic, San Diego, CA

Stanford University — San Jose Medical Center
San Jose, Ca

Steingard Orthopedics and Sports Medicine
Phoenix, AZ

Union Hospital —
Sports Medicine Advanced Training, Union, NJ

University of British Columbia — McGavin Sports Medicine Centre
Vancouver, BC Canada

UCLA Medical School — Department of Family Medicine
Los Angeles, CA

University of California — San Diego Department of Community and Family Medicine
La Jolla, CA

University of Hawaii, Honolulu, HI

University of Michigan Medical School — Department of Family Practice, Ann Arbor, MI

University of Oklahoma — OKC
Oklahoma City, OK

University of Western Ontario — Kennedy Athletic Injury Clinic
University Hospital, London, Ontario, Canada

University of Wisconsin — Department of Pediatrics, Madison, WI

Virginia Sports Medicine Institute — Arlington Hospital
Arlington, VA

# 20

# Patient and Community Education on Physical Fitness

The emphasis of this final chapter is on patient and community education. It is important for the primary care physician to be involved in educating people about the need for physical fitness activities, to raise patient and public awareness, and to motivate people to act on this information.

## IMPORTANCE OF BEING INVOLVED IN PATIENT AND COMMUNITY EDUCATION

During the first half of this century there was a shift in the morbidity and mortality rates of Americans away from acute infectious diseases to a predominance of chronic illnesses related to lifestyle. Of the approximately two million deaths in the U.S. in 1988, 35% were due to cardiovascular disease, 22% due to cancer, and about 10% were due to cerebrovascular disease. There is good evidence that personal lifestyle (what and how much we eat and drink, amount and type of exercise we engage in, whether we smoke, and how we deal with daily stress) is strongly related to these three leading causes of death.

Some still hope that the way to reduce the amount of chronic disease lies in improved medical technology, but an increasingly prevalent view is that technology can play only a limited role. While there have been several spectacular technological successes (e.g., organ transplants), these achievements generally affect a relatively small number of people. Despite these advances and despite increases in our knowledge about chronic diseases, there has been little change in the last 30 to 40 years in the rates of these major diseases (40). Many physicians now believe that advances in medical technology will have little impact on the overall health of Americans, and that control of present major health problems depends directly on modification of individual behavior and lifestyle habits (12).

Therefore, primary care physicians who want to have a long-term impact on the health of their patients must become involved in educating them and helping them change their behavior. You may wonder why primary care physicians have not been more involved in prevention efforts against the major lifestyle-related diseases. The answer is complex, but some reasons are clear. Few medical schools include the necessary training for young physicians to assume these roles. Emphasis historically has been on treating sick patients, and the rewards in terms of money, prestige, and a sense of accomplishment act as powerful reinforcement for physicians to maintain their focus almost exclusively on these aspects of medical practice. Despite the shift from acute to chronic diseases and the obvious logic inherent in prevention, it will be quite difficult to change the situation very rapidly because the reward system in medicine is so heavily geared toward waiting until people are ill to treat them. For now, the impetus for change will have to come from individual physicians who decide to put their emphasis on preventing diseases.

Most physicians do not realize that their every word and action can be regarded as a form of health education, not just by patients and their families but by the whole community. It is not a question of whether primary care physicians are providing health education for their community but whether they are doing it well or poorly. Primary care physicians should speak out about the benefits of physical activity and other aspects of a healthy lifestyle. They should be a major community resource for health education, and they should be involved in coordinating access to other community health resources and organizations.

The call for changing destructive lifestyle habits comes from many sources, but primary care physicians have one of the best opportunities to help people initiate positive change or prevent the formation of negative habits because of their respected role in our culture and their potential to influence the health practices of families. New attitudes and skills will be required of physicians who choose this path. They will need the ability to be confrontive without being judgmental. They must recognize that old, unhealthy habits are hard to change and there are numerous social inducements and pressures to maintain or start these habits and discourage adoption of healthier ones. Dealing with discouragement by both the patient and physician will be a necessary part of the effort. However, it has been demonstrated repeatedly that patients *can* change habits and lifestyles with the help of their physicians and the support of their families.

A recent study of access to health care (25) indicates that 90% of the American population has a usual source of health care and that 80% had seen a physician within the previous 12 months. Another study (24) indicated that 54% of all patient encounters involved primary care physicians (family practice, general practice, pediatrics, or internal medicine). The average encounter is sufficiently long to allow counseling on fitness and activity, even if such counseling is not directly related to the reason the patient is seeing the physician. Even so, the physicians did this in less than 10% of these encounters. Several studies have shown that patients expect their physicians to be concerned about health habits and to actively encourage appropriate lifestyle changes, including recommending fitness activities (c.f., 6, 10). Given the number of people that have contact with and can be influenced by primary care physicians, the potential impact on the total health picture of our society is enormous.

Much work must be done to define the impact of habitual physical activity and exercise on various chronic diseases, but a fairly clear and consistent picture is beginning to emerge with regard to several major diseases (34). The relationship of physical activity to coronary heart disease (CHD) has received the most attention so far. Many studies have shown that physical inactivity and lack of exercise are associated with increased risk of CHD, whereas habitually active individuals have reduced risk of CHD and sudden cardiac death (c.f., 8, 17, 18, 19, 30, 35). These associations hold even when other risk factors such as age, smoking, hypertension, family history, and obesity are taken into account. "Selection" (i.e., sick or unfit persons are less active) was shown in a variety of ways *not* to be an explanation for these findings. There is a transient rise in the risk of a cardiac event during vigorous exercise, but it is outweighed by an overall reduction of risk during non-exercise periods (36). Paffenbarger et al. (20) report that mortality rates from all causes are reduced by one quarter to one third in individuals who expend 2000 or more kcal during exercise per week as compared with those who are less active. A major conclusion of this study is that regular exercise does increase life expectancy.

Other chronic diseases for which exercise appears to have an ameliorating effect include hypertension, diabetes, and osteoporosis. Several studies indicate that habitual activity is associated with decreased risk of hypertension (c.f., 3, 27), and these studies also suggest that exercise may improve hypertension control. Other studies have shown that exercise helps noninsulin-dependent diabetics by reducing blood glucose levels, increasing sensitivity of insulin receptors, and increasing the effectiveness of insulin (22). Although few controlled studies have been completed on whether exercise may prevent or postpone development of noninsulin-dependent diabetes, such a possibility is strongly implied by the metabolic and hormonal effects produced by regular exercise. There is a lack of research data on the effects of exercise in insulin-dependent diabetics, but physical activity is generally recommended as an important part of an overall treatment program. There is evidence that exercise and physical activity are inversely related to the development of osteoporosis (1, 4, 5, 14). These studies do indicate that the protective effect of exercise holds true only for weight-bearing activities; nonweight-bearing activities like swimming apparently do not reduce bone loss.

Regular exercise also appears to have an effect on mental health. Taylor, Sallis, and Needle (39) reviewed a number of studies and concluded that physical activity and exercise are associated with improved self-concept and confidence, alleviation of symptoms of mild-to-moderate depression, reduction of anxiety, and that it may alter some aspects of the stress response and coronary-prone (Type A) behavior.

Regular aerobic exercise has been increasingly recognized as an important factor in the prevention and control of obesity. Aerobic exercise is a vital element in conjunction with dietary measures in the weight loss programs that are most likely to achieve long term success. It is becoming more apparent that neither exercise nor diet alone are as likely to produce long term weight loss as is an appropriate combination of the two.

There is still room for debate on some of the specifics related to the impact of habitual activity and exercise on various chronic diseases, but evidence from longer term studies such as Paffenbarger et al. (20) indicates it is a reasonable assumption that physical activity and exercise have a positive effect on health, longevity, and prevention of chronic illnesses. At the very least, an appropriate exercise program will not shorten life and likely will improve the quality of it through positive effects on psychological and physical factors. Moreover, current research indicates that it is not necessary to have been exercising all your life to reap the benefits. Many positive effects can be gained from beginning a moderate program at any age. However, it is only logical that more benefits will be gained and fewer negative effects of being sedentary will accrue if good exercise habits are developed early in life.

The intensity of exercise does not have to be great to gain benefits (9). Many have recommended doing exercise at 60% or more of aerobic capacity. This figure was based on earlier short-term studies on young men, but came to be regarded as a *minimal* standard for everyone. Now it is apparent that exercise at less than 60% of aerobic capacity produces beneficial effects, although it may take longer (9). This is an important point when a physician is trying to achieve a permanent change to a more active lifestyle, because exercises at a lower intensity are more acceptable and any associated medical risk will be much less. It also is important to note that the overall impact of adopting an exercise program will be much greater for sedentary individuals who successfully adopt a lower intensity program than for reasonably active individuals who adopt a more intensive exercise program (9).

Given the evidence that regular physical activity is an important part of a healthy lifestyle and will reduce the occurrence or severity of some chronic illnesses (see Table 20-1), it should be apparent that primary care physicians need to be aware of basic approaches to educating individual patients and the general community about the desirability of being physically active.

## RAISING PATIENT AND PUBLIC AWARENESS

The primary care physician can work at two levels to raise public awareness about the need for a healthy, active lifestyle: with individual patients as they are seen by the physician, and with the community at large. While the emphasis here is on the value of being physically active, the same principles apply to promoting other aspects of a healthy lifestyle, such as proper nutrition, smoking cessation, and other factors that reduce the risk of cardiovascular disease, cancer, and cerebrovascular disease. All these elements should be covered in a prevention-oriented medical practice.

The primary care physician should initiate a systematic program of health risk assessment for all patients (26). This involves completing a thorough patient history that includes questions about

Table 20-1. Effects of Exercise on Various Diseases and Conditions

|  | Source | Citation # |
|---|---|---|
| Obesity | Blair, Jacobs and Powell (1985) | 2 |
| BP/Hypertension | Blair, et al. (1984) | 3 |
|  | Roman, et al. (1981) | 27 |
| CHD risk | Garcia-Palmeri, et al. (1982) | 8 |
|  | Morris, et al. (1980) | 17 |
|  | Paffenbarger and Hale (1975) | 18 |
|  | Paffenbarger, Wing and Hyde (1978) | 19 |
|  | Salonen, Puska and Tuomilehto (1982) | 30 |
|  | Siscovick, et al. (1982) | 35 |
| Blood glucose levels (Diabetes) | Richter and Schneider (1981) | 22 |
| Osteoporosis | Aloia (1981) | 1 |
|  | Chalmers and Ho (1980) | 4 |
|  | Dalen and Olsson (1974) | 5 |
|  | Krolner, et al. (1983) | 14 |
| Mental health status | Taylor, Sallis and Needle (1985) | 39 |

diet, genetic background, prior physical condition, and attitudes toward health and fitness. Several health risk assessment packages, such as the Health Hazard Appraisal (23), are available commercially or in the medical literature. Another interesting approach to health risk appraisal is available from The Carter Center of Emory University. The Carter Center's health risk appraisal form estimates total risk from 42 causes of death and compares that total risk with individuals of the same age and gender. The results are measured in "years of potential life lost." A thorough health risk appraisal will produce a wealth of data that must not be just filed away. The risk assessment should be used as an educational tool as well as a data gathering tool. The results of the health risk assessment are the first step in educating the patient and guiding him or her to a realization of the options available. The guidance and support of the physician will be crucial in the early stages of lifestyle adjustment.

The beginning stages of the patient education process generally take place on a one-to-one basis, but the patient's family should be involved as soon as possible when major changes are being contemplated. Spousal support has a major influence on adherence to exercise programs (7). The need for family support is most evident in smoking cessation or alcoholism, but it is no less important in adopting a physically active lifestyle. In fact, it is likely that one or more other family members should be making similar changes. Once change is under way, many of the continuing elements of patient education can be handled by office staff, but the physician should continue to monitor progress. The patient education process and encouragement of necessary behavioral changes involve more information than can be presented here. Such information is available from a number of sources, including articles by Shapiro (32), Tapp et al. (38), and in *Patient Education: A Handbook for Teachers*, available from the Society of Teachers of Family Medicine (37). Chapters 5 and 6 of this book also contains information on prescribing appropriate exercise for patients.

The primary care physician also should be involved with making the entire community aware of the impact of lifestyle on health and longevity. The physician can work individually or act as a catalyst in promoting action. It might mean speaking to local civic, social, or church groups, providing brochures and using slides, movies, or videotapes. If used appropriately, the mass media can be quite effective in informing and motivating the community to act on health maintenance (15). The physician's role is to ensure that what is presented is accurate and will not be misinterpreted by those it is supposed to inform and motivate.

Other approaches include participating in local health fairs or contests, either as a separate activity through a local hospital or in conjunction with yearly county or state fairs. Videotapes and slides can be used in displays and brochures provided. Various attention-getting activities such as doing blood pressures or demonstrating health and cancer self-screens or how to take a heart rate in monitoring exercise levels can be used to raise awareness.

The physician should become involved with local school programs. Health education and physical education in the schools are important factors in long-term improvement of health in the general population (13). Unfortunately, the recent trend is for local schools to be cutting back on these programs. The physician should take a leading role in seeing that school health and physical education programs are improved and strengthened. Physical education should not consist of just playing games, but should have a specified teaching curriculum with emphasis on the importance of lifetime physical activity and fitness habits, and basic instruction in individual sports that can be pursued and enjoyed beyond the school years to provide necessary aerobic fitness. The availability of adult fitness and activity courses through the local school district or other community education organizations also should be encouraged.

## MOTIVATING PEOPLE TO ACT ON INFORMATION

Possession of knowledge is a necessary factor, but it is not always sufficient to induce action on matters of personal health. There are several current theories to explain individual health behavior, such as the Health Belief Model (28). According to this model, a person will take action to avoid disease if they believe: 1) they are personally susceptible to the disease; 2) having the disease will have at least a moderately severe impact on some component of their life; and 3) taking a particular action will be beneficial by reducing their personal susceptibility or the severity of the disease. A corollary to the third condition is that the action taken does not require overcoming one or more psychological barriers like cost, inconvenience, pain, or embarrassment.

Based on this theory, the physician who is trying to encourage a patient to adopt an active lifestyle must address all three conditions. The second condition is relatively easy; few would deny that having cardiovascular disease would have a major impact on their life. The first condition is a little more difficult. People tend to deny that they are susceptible to cardiovascular disease or any other lifestyle-related disease. It may be true that a particular individual is less susceptible, but no one can be positive they are immune. The physician should point out the incidence of the disease using national statistics and, if possible, local statistics. A health risk assessment can be used to great effect. The third condition is the most difficult. The physician must convince the patient that a physically active lifestyle and regular exercise will reduce the risk of cardiovascular and other diseases and contribute to a longer, healthier life. Using research results may help with some individuals, although it seems that those who would benefit most are often the most resistant. Interventions may be more successful if they focus on helping patients feel good about themselves rather than focusing entirely on the health benefits of exercise (7).

The physician should help the patient decide the type and amount of exercise, being careful to minimize the previously mentioned psychological barriers (16). The most popular fitness activities are done alone or in groups without special classes or facilities. Of the approximately 20% of the adult population that is active at a minimal level to maintain cardiovascular fitness, only a small percentage are in organized formal exercise programs (11). However, some patients may need the support offered in a group setting. The physician's knowledge of the patient and of the results of the health risk assessment regarding the patient's attitudes toward health and fitness may help in making these decisions.

The ultimate responsibility for managing a patient's behavior is in the hands of the patient, but this does not preclude a role for the physician (and the office staff) in evaluating the progress and success of a behavior change. After a change is instituted, both patient and physician will be involved with monitoring, recording, and reinforcing efforts over a period of time. Three levels of outcome can be measured in efforts to change behavior to prevent disease (21). First are changes in the target behavior; for example, how many days during the past week did the patient go for a brisk walk or take part in other aerobic exercise? How many total minutes were spent? Second are short-term and medium-term physiological changes such as lowered resting heart rate, improved work capacity, or lowered blood pressure. Finally, there are long-term changes in morbidity and mortality, such as prevention or delay of onset of cardiovascular disease as a result of regular exercise and its physiological adaptations. The first level of outcomes, changes in target behavior, usually is monitored and recorded by the patient (an activity or exercise log) and reviewed with the physician periodically. Short-term physiological changes normally will be monitored in the physician's office. Time and history will record third level changes in morbidity and mortality. The physician-recorded outcome measures of short-term and medium-term physiological changes provide the patient with important reinforcement and feedback on the success (or failure) of his or her efforts. Failures exposed by first or second level evaluations should not be used as an accusatory tool against a noncomplying patient. Rather, it should signal a need for the physician to review the goals, strategies, support, and rewards for the lifestyle change being attempted. Shelton and Rosen (33) have outlined a number of techniques and considerations in using patient self-monitoring.

An important tool that should be developed and maintained in the office of a primary care physician is a community resource file. This file, on 3x5 cards or in a notebook or in computer memory, should contain listings of resources available within the community that can be mobilized to help patients make lifestyle changes, whether it be maintaining a regular exercise program, changing nutrition and eating patterns, or practicing regular self-screens for various forms of cancer. The resource file should list the resources, their location within the community, their cost (and if they are cheaper in volume), and how to gain access. In addition to sources of information, the file should contain educational materials, information on groups like Weight Watchers or Alcoholics Anonymous, screening labs, and exercise groups, to name a few examples. A review of this community resource file may reveal gaps and, if any of the missing resources are important enough, the physician may want to work for their establishment. A thorough listing of suggested resources on local, state, and national levels is contained in *Patient Education: A Handbook for Teachers*, mentioned earlier.

There will be times when the physician has done all that normally would be necessary to induce a patient to adopt a healthier lifestyle, including reviewing a health risk assessment with the patient, educating the patient about susceptibility to cardiovascular or other diseases, developing an acceptable fitness program and encouraging family support, and yet the patient does not take that final step and actually implement the change. It may take an additional cue or catalyst to prompt these patients to make the effort. This can be as simple as an occasional telephone call from the physician or office staff to see how the plan is going. Another effective catalyst or "trigger" is using examples of famous people or local people who have successfully adopted a physically active lifestyle. These examples can show that the barriers to regular exercise are not insurmountable. An example of the impact of a trigger on adoption of a healthy habit is the increase in requests for instruction in breast self-examination after the publicity surrounding the breast cancers of Betty Ford and Happy Rockefeller some years ago.

## IMPORTANCE OF THE PHYSICIAN, STAFF AND OFFICE ENVIRONMENT IN PROMOTING HEALTHY LIFESTYLES

In some instances it may not be the absence of an appropriate cue that causes a patient to fail to make lifestyle improvements, but rather the presence of negative cues from the physician, office staff or even the office environment. This happens not because of a planned, systematic learning effort, but rather through unplanned, unknowing instruction given patients by the daily health behaviors of the physician and office staff members. Patients pick up the behavioral lessons being taught by an overweight physician or the receptionist who smokes.

Whether they intend to be or not, the physician and other health care professionals are role models for their patients and other members of the community who know them as "doctor" or "nurse". A conscientious commitment to good health practices by the physician and staff members is necessary. The staff must show concern for their own health if patients are to see them as credible sources of preventive health information. A physician or other health professional who has health habits that run counter to recommendations given to patients should attempt to correct them and be ready to answer patient questions, sometimes unspoken, about those habits.

The environment in the medical office is an extension of the health practices modeled by physician and staff. A prohibition against smoking in the waiting room or reception area is a must. Posters and signs encouraging healthful practices extend the educational strategies and reinforce the role modeling. Apparently insignificant aspects of the office environment contribute or detract from the preventive health messages. For example, the choice of magazines for the public areas of the office can have an impact. *Reader's Digest* is a good choice because its editorial board stopped carrying cigarette advertisements in the 1950s when smoking was correlated with major health problems. Magazines that contain many tobacco and alcohol product advertisements would be poor choices. Subtle aspects of the office environment such as these may not be obvious to the patient but they can be mentioned in a patient brochure to help highlight the commitment to maintenance of a healthy lifestyle. However, the physician remains the key individual in promoting appropriate health habits and must be cognizant of that role in dealing with patients. Even though medicine can be a stressful profession, a physician should not maintain poor health habits nor use self-destructive coping behaviors (29, 31)

We have briefly touched upon a very extensive topic that is very important in the primary care setting. The primary care physician must be able to care for the acute medical needs of physically active patients, and this has been the focus of the clinical chapters that comprise most of this book, but the physician must also meet long-term needs of all patients by encouraging adoption of healthier, more active lifestyles. The primary care physician must be concerned not only with his or her own patients, but take an active part in encouraging and providing proper sports medicine care for all members of the community. In essence, because of his or her special knowledge and expertise, the primary care physician has an obligation to get involved with the community.

**REFERENCES**

1. Aloia, J.F. Exercised skeletal health. *J Amer Geriatr Soc* 29:104, 1981.

2. Blair, S.N., Jacobs, D.R., and Powell, K.E. Relationships between exercise or physical activity and other health behaviors. *Publ Health Rep* 100(2):172-180, 1985.
3. Blair, S.N., et al. Physical activity and incidence of hypertension in health normotensive men and women. *JAMA* 252:487, 1984.
4. Chalmers, J., and Ho, K.C. Geographical variations in senile osteoporosis: The association of physical activity. *J Bone Joint Surg* 52:667, 1980.
5. Dalen, N., and Olsson, K.E. Bone mineral content and physical activity. *Acta Orthop Scand* 45:170, 1974.
6. David, A.K., and Boldt, J.F. A study of preventive health attitudes and behaviors in a family practice setting. *J Fam Pract* 11:77, 1980.
7. Dishman, R.K., Sallis, J.F., and Orenstein, D.R. The determinants of physical activity and exercise. *Publ Health Rep* 100(2):158, 1985.
8. Garcia-Palmeri, M.R., et al. Increased physical activity: A protective factor against heart attacks in Puerto Rico. *Am J Cardiol* 50:749, 1982.
9. Haskell, W.L., Montoye, H.J., and Orenstein, D. Physical activity and exercise to achieve health-related physical fitness components. *Publ Health Rep* 100(2):202, 1985.
10. Hyatt, J.D. Perception of the family physician by patients and family physicians. *J Fam Pract* 10:295, 1980.
11. Iverson, D.C., et al. The promotion of physical activity in the United States population: The status of programs in medical, worksite, community, and school settings. *Publ Health Rep* 100(2):212, 1985.
12. Knowles, J.H. The responsibility of the individual. In: Knowles, J.H. (Ed.), *Doing Better and Feeling Worse*, New York: W.W. Norton & Co., 1977.
13. Kolbe, L.J., and Gilbert, G.G. Involving the schools in the national strategy to improve the health of Americans. In: *Proceedings of Prospects for a Healthier America: Achieving the Nation's Health Promotion Objectives*, Washington, D.C.: U.S. Dept. of Health and Human Services/Public Health Service, 1984.
14. Krolner, B., et al. Physical exercise as a prophylaxis against involuntary bone loss. *Clin Sci* 64:541, 1983.
15. Marshall, C.L. *Toward an Educated Health Consumer: Mass Communication and Quality in Medical Care*, DHEW Publication No. (NIH) 77-81. Washington, D.C.: U.S. Government Printing Office, 1977.
16. Martin, J.E., and Dubbert, P.M. Behavioral management strategies for improving health and fitness. *J Card Rehab* 4(May):200, 1984.
17. Morris, J.N., et al. Vigorous exercise in leisure-time: Protection against coronary heart disease. *Lancet* No. 8206:1207, 1980.
18. Paffenbarger, R.S., and Hale, W.E. Work activity and coronary heart mortality. *NEJM* 292:545, 1975.
19. Paffenbarger, R.S., Wing, A.L., and Hyde, R.T. Physical activity as an index of heart attack risk in college alumni. *Am J Epidemiol* 108:161, 1978.
20. Paffenbarger, R.S., et al. Physical activity, all-cause mortality, and longevity of college alumni. *NEJM* 314:605, 1986.
21. Pomerleau, O., Bass, F., and Crown, V. Role of behavior modification in preventive medicine. *NEJM* 292:1277, 1975.
22. Richter, E.A., and Schneider, S.H. Diabetes and exercise. *Am J Med* 70:201, 1981.
23. Robbins, L.C. A system for indications for preventive medicine: Health hazard appraisal. In: Kane, R.L. (Ed.), *The Behavioral Sciences and Preventive Medicine*, DHEW Publ. No. NIH 76-878. Washington, D.C.: U.S. Government Printing Office, 1974.
24. Robert Wood Johnson Foundation. America's health care system: A comprehensive portrait. Princeton, NJ, 1978.
25. Robert Wood Johnson Foundation. Updated report on access to health care for the American people. Princeton, NJ, 1983.
26. Rodnick, J. Health screening: What should you do? *Fam Pract Recertif* 2:45, 1980.
27. Roman, O., et al. Physical training program in arterial hypertension: A long-term prospective follow-up. *Cardiology* 67:230, 1981.
28. Rosenstock, I.M. The health belief model and preventive health behavior. In: Becker, M.H. (Ed.), *The Health Belief Model and Personal Health Behavior*, Thorofare, NJ: Charles B. Slack, Inc., 1976.
29. Sach, R.L., Weingarten, R., and Freeman, A.M., Sach, R.L., and Berger, P.A. *Psychiatry for the Primary Care Physician*, Baltimore: Williams & Wilkins, 1979.
30. Salonen, J.T., Puska, P., and Tuomilehto, J. Physical activity and risk of myocardial infarction, cerebral stroke and death: A longitudinal study in Eastern Finland. *Am J Epidemiol* 115:526, 1982.
31. Shangold, M.M. The health care of physicians: 'Do as I say and not as I do'. *J Med Educ* 54:668, 1979.
32. Shapiro, J. Development of family self-control skills. *J Fam Pract* 12(1):67,1981.
33. Shelton, J.L., and Rosen, G.M. Self-monitoring by patients. In: Rosen, G.M., Geyman, J.P., and Layton, R.H. (Eds.), *Behavioral Science in Family Practice*, New York: Appleton-Century-Crofts, 1980.
34. Siscovick, D.S., LaPorte, R.E., and Newman, J.M. The disease-specific benefits and risks of physical activity and exercise. *Publ Health Rep* 100(2):180, 1985
35. Siscovick, D.S., et al. Physical activity and primary cardiac arrest. *JAMA* 243:3113, 1982.
36. Siscovick, D.S., et al. The incidence of primary cardiac arrest during vigorous exercise. *NEJM* 311:874, 1984.
37. Society of Teachers of Family Medicine. *Patient Education: A Handbook for Teachers*, Kansas City, MO: STFM, 1979.
38. Tapp, J.T., et al. The application of behavior modification to behavior management: Guidelines for the family physician. *J Fam Pract* 6(2):293, 1978.
39. Taylor, C.B., Sallis, J.F., and Needle, R. The relation of physical activity and exercise to mental health. *Publ Health Rep* 100(2):195, 1985.
40. Thomas, L. On the science and technology of medicine. In: Knowles, J.H. (Ed.), *Doing Better and Feeling Worse*, New York: W.W. Norton & Co., 1977.

# Index

Abdomen injury, 343-394
  radiology, 523
Abdominal wall injuries, 367-368
  blows to solar plexus, 368
  hernia, 368
  hip pointer, 368
  illiopsoas muscle rupture, 368
  muscle contusion, 368
  muscle cramp, 368
  rectus muscle strain, 367-368
Abrasions, 471-472
  facial, 246
  nose, 267-268
Achilles tendon, 428-432, 439-442
  complete rupture, 441-442
  partial rupture, 440-441
  rupture, 430-432
  tendinitis, 429-430, 440
Acne, 475-476
Acquired Immune Deficiency Syndrome (AIDS), 486
Acromioclavicular
  joint, 282-283
  separation, 289-290
Acute fracture, lower leg, 432-433
Acute infections, 232-233
  mononucleosis, 232-233
  myocarditis, 232
  non-traumatic skin, 233
  wounds, 233
Acute injury, 223-228
  contusions, 227
  fractures, 227
  inflammation, 227
  lacerations, 227-228
  myostis ossificans, 227
  sprains, 226-227
  strains, 226-227
  treatment, competition, 224-226
  types of, 226-228
Acute mountain sickness (AMS), 500-501
  etiology, 500
  history, 500
  manifestations/treatment, 501
  prophylactic, 500-501
Adenosine triphosphate (ATP), 113

Adhesive capsulitis (frozen shoulder), 297
Administration, scholastic athletic programs, 84
Adrenal corticosteroids, 45
Aerobic capacity, 15
Aerobic power, female athletes, 123-124
Aerobics,
  pregnancy training recommendations, 131
  sedentary adults, 138-140
Age, blood pressure, 351
Agility, rehabilitation, 551
Aid stations, distance running, 188-189
Air pollution, 501-502
  carbon monoxide (CO), 501
  hazardous situations, 502
  nitric oxide, 502
  ozone, 501
  prevention, 502
  recommendations, 502
  sulfur oxides, 501-502
Air sickness, 500-501
Airway occlusion, 210
Allergies, 234-235
  insect, 481
Alpha blockers, sports, 352
American Academy of Family Physicians, 3
American Academy of Pediatrics, 84
American College of Sports Medicine, 3, 37
  position stand, 185-189
  position statement, 143-149
American Orthopaedic Society for Sports Medicine, 3, 65
Anabolic steroids, 45-46
Anaerobic capacity, 15
Anemia, 483-484
  aplastic, 484
  G6PD deficiency, 484-485
  iron deficiency, 484
  sickle cell, 485
  signs/symptoms, 484
  sports, 484
Ankle injuries

  achilles tendon, 439-442
  anterior tibial tendon, 446-447
  chronic, 447
  dorsiflexion (ATFL), 439
  epiphyseal fracture, 442
  fractures, 442-444
  history, 434-435
  lateral inversion sprain, 436-438
  medial eversion sprain, 438-439
  osteochondral fracture, 442-443
  peroneal tendinitis, 445-446
  peroneal tendon rupture, 446
  peroneal tendon subluxation/dislocation, 446
  peroneal tendons, 444-445
  physical examination, 435
  posterior tibial tendon, 447
  radiology, 528
  sprains, 436-439
  tarsal tunnel syndrome, 447
  tendinitis, 440
  tendons, 444-447
  x-ray, 435
Ankles
  anatomy, 433-434
  examination form, 468
  ligaments, 434
  muscles, 434
Ankylosing spondylitis, 375-376
Anorexia nervosa, 38
Anterior cruciate ligament
  injury, rehabilitation, 557-559
  sprain, 419
Anterior dislocations, 291-292
Anterior tibial tendon injury, 446-447
Anti-depressants, 46-47
Anti-inflammatory medications, 232
Aplastic anemia, 484
Archery, elbow injury, 303
Arm ergometry, 166
Arrhythmias, 161
  athletes, managing, 355-360
  atrial fibrillation, 357
  atrial flutter, 357
  congenital long QT syndrome, 358
  exercise induced, 356
  heart blocks, 358

597

Holter monitoring, 357
premature ventricular contractions (PVC), 356, 358
sinus node functions, 357
supraventricular tachycardia, 357
ventricular pre-excitation, 357-358
ventricular tachycardia, 358
Articular fracture, 335
Aseptic meningitis, 233
Aspiration, 210
Assessment, preparticipation screening, 103-105
Assumption of risk, 7
Asthma, 156-158, 233-234, 363, 367
Athletes
arrhythmias, 355-360
breastfeeding, 40-42
conditioning/training programs, 113-149
handicapped, 165-168
heart, 348
injury rehabilitation, 182-184
injury responsibility, 181-182
low back pain, 372
pregnant, 40-42
psychological aspects, 80-81
skin problems in, 471
vegetarian, 42
Athletic programs, scholastic considerations, 84-86
Athletic training, 5
Atrial fibrillation, 357
Atrial flutter, 357
Avascular necrosis of the femoral head, 402
Axillary nerve injury, 300

Back injuries, 369-380
anatomical considerations, 370-371
ankylosing spondylitis, 375-376
intervertebral disc, 373-375
low back pain, 370-374
major disorders, 370
mechanical back pain, 377
radiological evaluation, 379, 523
Scheuermann's disease, 372
spondylolisthesis, 371-372, 378-379
spondylolysis, 377-378
treatment, 379-380
vertebral fractures, 372-373
Backpackers, low back pain, 371
Back pain
disorders, 370
mechanical, 377
spondylolisthesis, 371-372, 378-379
Bacterial infections, 476
Balance, rehabilitation, 551
Ballet
knee injury, 407
medial collateral ligament sprain, 416
patella dislocation, 415
peroneal tendon injury, 444-445
Barosinusitis, 497-498
Barotrauma, 267
of ascent, 498
underwater sports, 496-498
Barton's fracture, 323

Baseball
contusions, 425-427
decreased vascular perfusion, 329
elbow injury, 303
eye injury, 257-258
face injury prevention, 249
groin strain, 400-401
knee injury, 407
lateral inversion sprain, 436-437
mandatory equipment, 178
meniscus tear, 421
prepatellar bursitis, 415
rotator cuff injury, 294
shoulder injury, 281
Basketball
achilles tendon rupture, 441
anterior cruciate ligament sprain, 419
elbow injury, 303
eye injury, 257-258
hip pointer, 395
knee injury, 407
lateral inversion sprain, 436-437
meniscus tear, 421
mens, mandatory equipment, 178
osteochondral fracture, 416
patella dislocation, 415
patellar tendinitis, 423
plica injury, 421
prepatellar bursitis, 415
shoulder injury, 281
women, mandatory equipment, 178
Bends (decompression sickness), 499
Bennett's fracture, 331-332
Beta blockers, 47
hypertension, 352
sports, 352
Biceps tendinitis injury, 296-297
Biceps tendon injury, 296-301
dislocation, 297
rupture, 297
Biker's bladder, 383
Bill of Rights for athletes, 86, 121
Bioelectrical impedance, 29
Biologic mechanisms, exercise, 355
Bipartate/tripartate sesamoid, 462
Bipartite patella, 422
Bites, marine, 499-500
Black-dot heel, 454
Bladder injuries, 382-383
biker's bladder, 383
hematuria, 383-385
hemoglobinuria, 387
myoglobinuria, 387
NSAID associated nephrotoxicity, 387
proteinuria, 385-387
urinary incontinence, 383
Bleeding disorders, 484-486
aplastic anemia, 484
creatine phosphokinase alterations, 485-486
hemophilia, 485-486
sickle cell anemia, 485
thrombocytopenia, 484-485
Blisters, foot, 462
Blocker's (tackler's) exostosis, upper arm, 302
Blood borne viruses, 233
Blood doping, 47-48, 58-60

applications, 58
ergogenic effect, 58-59
ethical considerations, 60
medical implications, 60
physiological mechanism, 58
storage/reinfusion, 59-60
Blood pressure
by age, 351
drug treatment, 351-352
exercise, 350-353
hypertension treatment, 352
Blunt trauma chest injury, 347
Body composition, 27-29, 182
estimating, 28-29
female athletes, 125
Body fat tests, handicapped athletes, 166
Body mass index table, 54
Boutonniere deformity, 334
Bowling
bowler's thumb, 327
elbow injury, 303
groin strain, 400-401
Boyle's law, pressure-volume relationships, 497
Brachial plexus, 254-255
testing nerves, 209
treatment, 255-256
vs nerve root impingement, 254
x-ray, 255
Brachial plexus injuries, 298-300
axillary nerve, 300
clinical classification, 299
long thoracic nerve, 300
musculocutaneous nerve, 300
spinal accessory nerve, 300-301
superscapular nerve, 300
Bracing, rehabilitation, 552
Brain injury, 239-244
Breast injuries, 343-344
contusions, 343-344
women, 344
Breastfeeding athletes, 40-42
Burner, 208-209, 298
Bursitis
greater trochanteric, 399-400
heel, 454-455
ischial, 400
prepatellar (housemaid's knee), 415
retrocalcaneal, 432
shoulder, 283
suprapatellar, 416


Calcaneal stress fracture, 453
Calcaneo apophysitis (Seiver's disease), 453-454
Calcium, 34-36
Calisthenics, proteinuria, 385
Callus, foot, 462
Candidiasis, 477
Canoeing
elbow injury, 303
hypothermia, 492
Capsule injury, 416-420
Carbohydrate, 33
Carbon monoxide (CO), air pollution, 501
Cardiac

*see also* Cardiovascular, Heart
arrhythmias, exercise induced, 356
death, 358-360
defects, 161-162
Cardiology, 5
Cardiomyopathies, 360-362
    treatment, 361-362
Cardiopulmonary equipment, 197
Cardiorespiratory fitness, exercise prescription, 144-147
Cardiovascular
    *see also* Cardiac, Heart
    fitness, rehabilitation, 550-551
    illness, 348-362
    system, pregnancy effects, 128
Carpal bones, wrist injury, 325
Carpal joint, 330-331
Carpal tunnel syndrome, 327-328
Cataracts, 262
Certificates of Added Qualifications (CAQ), 3
Cervical fractures, 209-210
Cervical nerves
    nerve root evaluation, 255
    peripheral nerve evaluation, 255
Cervical spine injuries, 206-210, 253-256
    brachial plexus, 254-255
    contusion, 253-254
    dislocation, 256
    fracture, 256
    nerve root impingement, 254-255
    neurapraxia w/transient quadriplegia, 256
    physical complaints, 254
    physical exam, 254
    sprains, 254
    strains, 254
    treatment, 254
    x-rays, 254
Cervical vertebra subluxation w/o fracture, 254
Checklist, sports events physician, 279
Chest injuries
    contusions, 343
    radiology, 523
Chest wall injuries
    blunt trauma, 347
    costochondral separation, 346
    muscular strain, 344-346
    pectoralis major, rupture, 345-346
    protective equipment, 347
    rib fractures, 346-347
Children, hypertension, 352-353
Chlorine, 502
Chondromalacia, rehabilitation protocol, 555-557
Chronic ankle injury, 447
Chronic
    epidermal hemorrhage, 243
    illness, 233-234
    musculoskeletal problems, 162-164
    obstructive pulmonary disease, 158-159
Chronic injuries, 228-232
    anti-inflammatory medications, 232
    electrical impulse therapy, 232
    return to activity, 231-232
    surgery, 232
    treatment modalities, 232
    types of, 229-231
Clap test, pectoralis major rupture, 345
Clavicular fractures, 287-289
Claw toe, 463
Clearance/recommendations form, 107
Climbing, hypothermia, 492
Clubs, equipment responsibilities, 199-200
Coach, injury responsibility, 191-192
Coaching techniques, injury prevention, 180-181
Cold-induced injury, 472-473
Cold injury, 490-493
Cold urticaria, 473
Colds (viral influenza), 486-487
Collateral ligament injury, 334
Colles' fracture, 322-323, 342
Common digital extensor (CDE) avulsion, 336-337
Communications, distance running, 189
Community-oriented medicine, 3
Community, physical fitness education, 589-595
Compartment syndrome, 428
Competencies, primary care residents, 11-13
Competition site
    acute injury management, 194-195
    injury prevention, 180, 191-200
    physician responsibilities, 193-195
Competitor education, distance running, 186
Compulsive
    dieters, 38
    runner, 38
Computed x-ray tomography (CT), 509-510
Concussion, 204-206, 240-244
    classification, 243-244
    return to play, 206
Conditioning
    athletes responsibility, 181-182
    programs, athletes/non-athletes, 113-149
Conduction defect arrhythmias, 356
Conduction, heat loss, 490
Congenital heart disease, 161-162
Congenital long QT syndrome, 358
Conjunctivitis, 262
Contact allergic reactions, primary causes, 480
Contact dermatitis, 479-480
Contact lenses, 263
Contact sports, pregnancy training recommendations, 131
Contrast baths, therapeutic modality, 543-544
Contributory negligence, 7
Contusions, 227, 242, 253-254
    abdominal muscles, 368
    breast, 343-344
    chest, 343
    facial, 246
    lower leg, 425-427
    nose, 267-268
    thigh, 403
    upper arm, 302
Convection, heat loss, 490
Corneal abrasion, 261
Coronary artery disease (CAD), 353-355
    biologic mechanisms, 355
Costochondral separation, 346
Cranial nerve function, evaluation, 279-280
Creatine phosphokinase alterations, 485-486
Cross country skiing, pregnancy training recommendations, 131
Cryotherapy, therapeutic modality, 541-542
Cutaneous fungal infections, treatment, 477
Cybex testing, 181-182
Cycling
    handlebar palsy, 327
    knee injury, 407
    pregnancy training recommendations, 131
Cystic fibrosis, 234

Death
    cardiac, 358-360
    joggers, 359
    marathon runners, 359
    young athletes, 359
Decision-making, 8-9
Decompression sickness (bends), 499
    diagnostic tests, 499
    treatment, 499
Deep digital flexor (DDF) avulsion, 336
Deltoid muscle, 283
Diabetes mellitus, 151-156, 233-234
    exercise response, 152
    insulin dependent, 152-153
    non-insulin dependent, 154-156
Dieters, compulsive, 38
Dimethylsulfoxide (DMSO), 47
Discoid meniscus, 422
Disease, exercise effects, 591
Dislocations, 209-210
    elbow, 309-312
    finger, 335
    glenohumeral joint, 561-562
    hand, 330-331
    hip, 401-402
    peroneal tendon, 446
    shoulder, 290-291
    wrist, 324-325
Distal forearm injuries, 322-324
    Barton's fracture, 323
    Colles' fracture, 322-323
    radial epiphyseal separation, 323
    radial styloid fracture, 323
    Smith's fracture, 323-324
    ulnar styloid fracture, 324
Distal interphalangeal joint (DIP), 336
Distal phalanx fracture, 337
Distal radial epiphyseal fracture, 323
Distance running
    communications/surveillance, 189
    competitor education, 186
    environmental heat stress measurement, 187-188
    hyperthermia, 187
    injury prevention, 185-189

medical director, 185
medical facilities, 186, 188-189
race organization, 185-186
road race checklist, 188-189
thermal stress color-coded flags, 188
thermoregulation, 187
Diuretics, 46
  abuse, 55
  blood pressure, 351-352
Dorsal compression neuropathy, 460
Dorsiflexion (ATFL) injury, 439
Downs syndrome, 165
Downhill skiing, pregnancy training recommendations, 131
Drowning, 494-496
  classifications, 494-496
  delayed death, 496
  distressed non-swimmer, 496
  dry, 494
  epidemiology, 494
  freshwater, 495
  hyperthermia-induced debility, 496
  hyperventilation syndrome, 495-496
  immediate disappearance, 495-496
  immersion syndrome, 495
  pathophysiology, 494
  salt water, 495
  secondary, 495
  sudden disappearance, 496
  treatment, 496
  typical situations, 495-496
  wet, 494-495
Drug use, epidemiology of, 43-44
Drugs
  blood pressure, 351-352
  cardiopulmonary, 197
Dry drowning, 494
Dshydrosis, 480
Dysfunctions, patella-femoral, 555-557

Ear canal squeeze, 497
Ear injuries, 264-267
  barotrauma, 267
  laceration, 264
  middle ear, 267
  otitis externa (swimmer's ear), 265-267
  otitis media, 267
  otosclerosis, 267
  tympanic membrane rupture, 267
Education, scholastic athletic programs, 85-86
EKG, athlete's heart, 348
Elbow injuries, 303-314
  anatomy, 303-304
  dislocation assessment/treatment, 309-312
  extensor overload, 306
  fractures, 312-314
  hyperextension, 308
  lateral compression, 305
  lateral epicondylitis (tennis elbow), 306-307
  medial epicondyle fracture, 314
  medial epicondylitis, 307-308
  medial tendon overload, 304-305
  olecranon bursitis, 308-309
  osteochondritis dessicans, 308
  posterior compartment, 308
  radial head dislocation, 311-312
  radiology, 518-519
  subluxation/dislocation, 309
  supracondylar fracture, 312
Electric stimulation, 544
  HVGMS, 544
  ionophoresis, 544-545
  phonophoresis, 545
  TENS, 544
Electrolytes, 29-31
Emergency, on-site, 203-222
Endocrine illnesses, 487
Endurance exercise, coronary artery disease, 353-355
Endurance, exercise prescription, 147-149
Endurance training, heart, 348
Energy, rate of supply, 113
Energy systems, overloading/testing, 21-27
Engrams, rehabilitation, 553-554
Environment
  induced injury, 487-508
  injury prevention, 175-181
Environmental heat stress, measurement, 187-188
Epidemiologic, rates, 63-64
Epidemiology, 63-73
  drug use, 43-44
  injuries, 173-175
Epididymitis, 389
Epidural hematoma, 206
Epidural hemorrhage, 243
Epilepsy, 159-161, 233-234
Epiphyseal fracture, 422, 442
Epiphyseal injury, 297-298
Epistaxis, nasal passage, 269-270
Equipment
  cardiopulmonary, 197
  competition site medical, 192-193
  injury prevention, 175-177
  protective, 347
  provided by schools/clubs, 199-200
  scholastic athletic programs, 85
  trainer, 198-200
Ergogenic aids, 39-40
  blood doping as, 58-60
Erythrasma, 476
Ethics, 8-9
Evaporation, heat loss, 491
Event coverage, scholastic athletic programs, 85
Exercise guidelines
  light intensity training (LIT), 231
  pediatric, 219-220
  runners, 221-222
Exercise-induced asthma (EIA), 363-367
  alpha adrenergic drugs, 363-367
  medications approved, 365
  parents, 367
  pharmacologic agents, 366
  treatment, 365-367
Exercise prescription
  concepts, 117-118
  detraining, 117-118
  duration, 115-117
  endurance, 147-149
  energy equivalents, 118
  epidemiologic studies, 118
  frequency, 115, 117
  intensity, 115, 117
  mode of activity, 116-117
  progression, 116-117
  training programs, 115-118
Exercises
  chronic illness effects, 151-169
  effects on disease, 591
  hypertension, 350-353
  induced arrhythmias, 356-357
  intensity, sedentary adults, 135-136
  physiology, 15-27
  renal changes, 382
  sequence, 549
  warm-up, 48
Eye injuries, 256-264
  anatomy, 257
  blow-out fracture of the orbit, 262
  conjunctivitis, 262
  contact lenses, 263
  corneal abrasion, 261
  epidemiology, 257-258
  etiology, 258
  glasses, 263
  globe, 261
  hyphema, 261
  intraocular foreign bodies, 261
  lacerations, 259
  ophthalmic examination, 258-259
  orbital, 259-261
  penetrating, 262
  perspective, 256-257
  prevention, 263-265
  retinal detachment, 262
  snow blindness, 261
  traumatic cataract, 262
  traumatic optic neuritis, 262
  vision evaluation, 263
Eye protectors, 263-265

Face injuries, 245-249
  abrasions, 246
  common factors, 245-246
  contusions, 246
  fractures, 246-249
  lacerations, 246
  prevention, 249
  radiology, 513-514
Facilities, scholastic athletic programs, 85
Fast Glycolytic (FT), 26
Fast Oxidative Glycolytic (FOG), 26
Fat, 32
Fatfolds, 29
Fatigue, 487
  adolescent athletes diagnosis, 488
Felon infection, 338
Female athlete training program, 123-132
  aerobic power, 123-124
  body composition, 125
  exercise during pregnancy, 127-132
  heat intolerance, 125
  menstrual cycle effects, 125-127
  osteoporosis, 127
  post-pactum exercises, 132
  pregnancy recommendations, 129-132
  strength, 124-125
Female genitalia, injuries, 390

Femur fracture, 405
Fencing, mandatory equipment, 178
Fetal hypoxia, 129
Fetal weight, 129
Field hockey, contusions, 425-427
Fifth metatarsal fracture, 459-460
Finger injuries, 333-338
    articular fracture, 335
    boutonniere deformity, 334
    collateral ligament, 334
    common digital extensor (CDE) avulsion, 336-337
    decreased vascular perfusion, 329
    deep digital flexor (DDF) avulsion, 336
    diagnostic imaging, 320-321
    dislocations, 335
    distal interphalangeal joint (DIP), 336
    distal phalanx fracture, 337
    epidemiology, 314-315
    felon infection, 338
    fracture dislocations, 335
    human bite infection, 338
    infections, 338
    mallet finger pathology, 336-337
    middle phalanx fracture, 335-336
    paronychia infection, 338
    perspective, 321-322
    proximal interphalangeal joint (PIP), 333-334
    proximal phalanx, 333
    pseudo-boutonniere deformity, 334-335
    radiology, 519-523
    subungual hematoma, 337
    tendon sheath tenosynovitis infection, 338
    volar plate, 335
Fingers
    anatomy, 315-317
    motor test, 320
    neurologic test, 319
    palpation, 318
    range of motion test, 318-319
    sensory test, 319
First rib fractures, 346-347
Fishtank granuloma, 476
Fitness
    cardiovascular, 550-551
    patient/community education, 589-595
    specificity of, 16-17
Flexibility, rehabilitation, 551
Flexion exercises, intervertebral disc injuries, 373-375
Flexor hallucis longus tendinitis, 455
Flu, 233
Fluids, 29-31
    replacement, 30
Foot, anatomy, 449-450
Foot examination form, 469-470
Foot injuries
    bipartate/tripartate sesmoid, 462
    "black-dot" heel, 454
    blisters, 462
    bursitis, 454-455
    calcaneal stress fracture, 453
    calcaneo apophysitis (Seiver's disease), 453-454
    callus, 462

claw toe, 463
dorsal compression neuropathy, 460
fifth metatarsal fracture, 459-460
flexor hallucis longus tendinitis, 455
ganglion cyst, 464
hallus deformity, 563
hammer toe, 463
heel bruise, 454
instep bruise, 459
intermetatarsal neuroma, 460-461
medial midfoot pain, 456-457
metatarsal stress fracture, 460
metatarsalgia, 460
Morton's foot, 459
onchonychia, 464
OS supranaviculare, 459
osteochondrosis metatarsal head, 461-462
painful heel, 451-455
pes cavus, 458-459
pes planus (flat foot), 457-458
plantar calcaneal pain, 451-453
posterior calcaneal pain, 453
posterior tibial tendinitis, 456
radiology, 528-534
retrocalcaneal, 455
sesamoid 462
sesamoiditis, 462
spring ligament sprain, 456
subungual hematoma, 464
tarsal tunnel syndrome, 456-457
toes, 463-464
turf toe, 463
warts, 463
Football
    achilles tendon rupture, 441
    anterior cruciate ligament sprain, 419
    cervical spine injuries, 250, 254
    contusions, 425-427
    dislocated hip, 401-402
    elbow injury, 303
    eye injury, 257-258
    face injury prevention, 249
    groin strain, 400-401
    heat illness risk, 490
    hematuria, 383
    hip pointer, 395-397
    knee injury, 407
    lateral collateral ligament sprain, 420
    lateral inversion sprain, 436-437
    low back pain, 371
    mandatory equipment, 178
    medial collateral ligament sprain, 416
    meniscus tear, 421
    mouth protectors, 271
    neck injury, 250
    osteochondral fracture, 416
    patella dislocation, 415
    posterior cruciate ligament sprain, 419
    proteinuria, 385
    rotator cuff injury, 294
    shoulder injury, 281
    suprapatellar bursitis, 416
    thigh contusion, 403
Forefoot, 460-463
Forefoot injuries
    metatarsalgia, 460

skin lesions, 462-463
Foreign body aspiration, 363
Forms
    ankle examination, 468
    clearance/recommendations, 107
    foot examination, 469-470
    initial PPPE form, 108-109
    intercurrent PPPE, 111-112
    knee examination, 467
    medical history, 106
    physical examination, 107, 110
Fractures, 227
    acute, 432-433
    ankle, 442-444
    articular, 335
    Barton's, 323
    Bennett's, 331-332
    calcaneal stress, 453
    clavicular, 287-289
    Colles', 322-323, 342
    distal phalanx, 337
    distal radial epiphyseal, 323
    elbow, 312-314
    epiphyseal, 422, 442
    facial, 246-249
    femur, 405
    fifth metatarsal, 459-460
    lateral condyle, 313-314
    LeFort, 248
    mandibular, 248-249
    maxillary trauma, 247
    medial epicondyle, 314
    metatarsal, 460
    middle phalanx, 335-336
    nasal, 268-269
    navicular, 325-326
    orbital blowout, 247-248
    osteochondral, 416, 442-443
    patellar, 416
    pelvis avulsion, 397-398
    radial styloid, 323
    radiology, 510-512
    rib, 346-347
    Rolando's, 332
    scaphoid, 325-326
    sesamoid, 462
    sinus, 248
    Smith's, 323-324
    sternum, 347
    stress, 427-428
    supracondylar, 312-314
    ulnar styloid, 324
    vertebral, 372-373
    wrist, 325-326
Friction blisters, 471-472
Frostbite, 472-473, 493-494
    degrees of injury, 494
    penile, 389
    predisposing factors, 494
    prevention, 473
    treatment, 507
Fungal infections, 476-477
Furunculosis, 476


G6PD deficiency, 484-485
Ganglion cyst, 464
Gastrointestinal (aerogastralgia), 498
Gatekeeper, 5

INDEX  601

General Adaptation Syndrome (GAS), 20-21
Genital injuries, 387-390
   epididymitis, 389
   penile, 389-390
   scrotal masses, 389
   spermatic cord torsion, 388-389
   testicle, 387-388
   urethral, 389-390
Genital-Urinary injuries, 380-390
Genitourinary infections, 390
   herpes simplex, 390-391
   prostatitis, 390
   urethritis, 390
   venereal warts, 390
Genitourinary system, anatomy, 381
Glasgow Coma Scale, 240
Glasses, 263
Glenohumeral joint, 282
   dislocation, rehabilitation protocol, 561-562
   subluxation/dislocation, 290-291
Glucose, 30-31
Golf
   elbow injury, 303
   low back pain, 371
Greater trochanteric bursitis, 399-400
Groin strain, 400-401
Growth hormone, 46
Gymnastics
   anterior cruciate ligament sprain, 419
   hip pointer, 395
   knee injury, 407
   lateral collateral ligament sprain, 420
   mandatory equipment, 179
   medial collateral ligament sprain, 416
   meniscus tear, 421
   neck injury, 251
   patella dislocation, 415
Gymnasts, female, low back pain, 371

Hammer toe, 463
Hand injuries, 329-332
   Bennett's fracture, 331-332
   carpal/metacarpal joint, 330-332
   diagnostic imaging, 320-321
   dislocations, 330-331
   epidemiology, 314-315
   perspective, 321-322
   radiology, 519-523
   Rolando's fracture, 332
   sprains, 329
   strains, 329
   thumb, 329-330
Hands
   anatomy, 315-317
   motor test, 320
   neurologic test, 319
   palpation, 318
   sensory test, 319
Handicapped athletes, 165-168
   body fat test, 166
   classifying, 166
   paraplegic/wheelchair, 165-166
   participation characteristics, 166-168
   sensory deficiencies, 168
Head injuries, 237-280
   anatomy, 237-238
   biomechanics, 238
   brain, 239-244
   chronic epidermal hemorrhage, 243
   concussion, 240-244
   differential diagnosis, 242
   epidural hemorrhage, 243
   intracranial lesions, 242-243
   long-term minor disability, 245
   mechanisms, 283
   post-concussion syndrome, 244-245
   post-traumatic problems, 244-245
   post-traumatic seizures, 245
   radiology, 512-513
   scalp layers, 237-238
   skull fractures, 238-239
   skull tissue layers, 238
   subdural hematoma, 243-244
   subdural hemorrhage, 243-244
   treatment protocol, 205, 210, 241, 278
   trend of consciousness, 244
Health care maintenance, 182
Heart
   see also Cardiac, Cardiovascular
   athlete, 348
   blocks, 358
   EKG, 348
Heart disease, 161-162, 234
   arrhythmias, 355-360
   cardiomyopathy, 360-362
   coronary artery disease, 353-355
   Marfan's syndrome, 349
   mitral valve prolapse, 349-350
   rheumatic mitral stenosis, 348
   septal defects, 350
   sports participation, 362
   valvular, 38-350
Heat cramps, 490
Heat disorders, prevention, 219-220
Heat exhaustion, 215, 490
Heat illness
   prevention methods, 490
   recovery factors, 490
Heat-induced injury, 473-475
Heat injuries, 211-215
Heat intolerance, female athletes, 125
Heat loss, types of, 490-491
Heat rash, 474-475
Heat stress, 487-490
   clinical condition, 488-489
   event scheduling considerations, 487-488
   response factors, 489
Heat stroke, 215, 490
Heat syncope, 214, 490
Heat therapy, 542-543
   contraindications, 544
   therapeutic modality, 543-544
Heel bruise, 454
Hematology illness, 483-509
   AIDS, 486
   anemia, 483-484
   bleeding disorders, 484-486
   oncology, 487
   viral influenza, 486-487
Hematuria, 383-385
Hemoglobinuria, 387
Hemophilia, 485-486
   disease severity, 486
   sports participation levels, 486
Hemothorax, 212
Hepatitis B, 233
Hernia, abdominal wall injury, 368
Herpes gladiatorum, 233
Herpes rugbeiorum, 233
Herpes simplex, 233, 390-391, 477-478
   treatment, 478
Herpes zoster, 478
High altitude training, 48
High voltage galvanic muscle stimulation (HVGMS), 544
Hindfoot, anatomy, 450-451
Hip injury, radiology, 524-526
Hip/pelvis injuries, 395-402
   avascular necrosis of the femoral head, 402
   avulsion fractures, 397-398
   dislocation, 401-402
   greater trochanteric bursitis, 399-400
   groin strain, 400-401
   iliac apophysitis, 397
   iliac crest contusion (hip pointer), 395-397
   ischial bursitis, 400
   Legg-Calve'-Perthes disease, 402
   osteitis pubis, 397
   pyriformis syndrome, 400
   slipped capital femoral epiphysis, 402
   staphylococcus aureus, 402
   tensor fascia latae syndrome (ITB), 398-399
Hip pointer (iliac crest contusion), 368, 395-397
HIV, 233
Hollow viscus, ruptured, 369
Holter monitoring, 357
Housemaid's knee (prepatellar bursitis), 415
Humerus, lateral condyle fracture, 313-314
Hydrostatic weighing, 28-29
Hyperabduction (Wright's syndrome), 301-302
Hypertension, 234
   children, 352-353
   exercise, 350-353
Hyperthermia, 129, 487-490
   clinical condition, 488-489
   distance running, 187
   event scheduling considerations, 487-488
   malignant, 489-490
   response factors, 489
Hypertrophic cardiomyopathy (HCM), 360
   murmur, 361
Hyperventilation syndrome, 362-363, 495
Hyphema, 261
Hypoglycemia
   exercise effects, 153-154
   prevention of, 155
Hypothermia, 215-218, 490-493
   clinical condition, 491-493
   death mechanisms, 491-492
   predisposing contributions, 492
   prevention, 218, 492-493

prevention measures, 508
recovery from, 492
rewarming procedure, 506
symptoms, 492-493
treatment, 216-218, 493, 504-505

Ice hockey
  cervical spine injuries, 250, 254
  eye injury, 257-258
  face injury prevention, 249
  groin strain, 400-401
  mandatory equipment, 179
  mouth protectors, 271
  neck injury, 250-251
Ice skating, pregnancy training recommendations, 131-132
Iliac apophysitis injury, 397
Iliac crest contusion (hip pointer), 395-397
Iliotibial band friction (ITB), 398-399
Iliotibial band syndrome, 423
Illiopsoas muscle, rupture, 368
Illnesses
  abdomen, 343-394
  hematology, 483-487
  lower extremity, 395-470
  pulmonary, 362-367
  skin, 471-482
  thorax, 343-394
  upper extremity, 281-342
Immersion syndrome, 495
Impetigo, 476
Individual differences, training/conditioning programs, 114
Infections
  acute, 232-233
  bacterial, 476
  felon, 338
  finger injury, 338
  fungal, 476-477
  genitourinary, 390
  human bites, 338
  paronychia, 338
  skin, 476-477
  tendon sheath tenosynovitis, 338
  viral, 477-479
Infestations, 479
Informed consent, 7-8
Infraspinatus muscle, 284, 294
Inhalations, 502
Initial PPPE form, 108-109
Injuries
  abdomen, 343-394, 523
  abdominal wall, 367-368
  acute, 223-228
  ankle, 528
  anterior cruciate ligament, rehabilitation, 557-559
  anterior dislocations, 291-292
  anterior tibial tendon, 446-447
  athletes responsibility, 181-182
  axillary nerve, 300
  back, 369-380, 523
  biceps tendinitis, 296-297
  biceps tendon, 296-301
  bladder, 382-383
  brachial plexus, 298-300
  capsule, 416-420
  cervical fractures, 209-210

cervical spine, 206-210, 253-256
chest, 343-347, 523
chronic, 228-232
chronic ankle, 447
clavicular fractures, 287-289
coaching responsibilities, 191-192
collateral ligament, 334
concussions, 204-206
dislocations, 209-210
distal forearm, 322-324
distance running, 185-189
dorsiflexion (ATFL), 439
ear, 264-267
elbow, 303-314, 518-519
epidemiology, 63-73, 173-175
epidural hematoma, 206
epiphyseal, 297-298
eye, 256-264
face, 245-249, 513-514
female genitalia, 390
finger, 333-338, 519-523
foot, 528-534
fractures, 510-512
generic conditions, 223-235
genital, 387-390
genital-urinary, 380-390
glenohumeral joint, 561-562
glenohumeral subluxation/dislocation, 290-291
hamstring muscle, 404-405
hand, 329-332, 519-523
head, 205, 210, 237-280, 512-513
heat, 211-215
hip, 524-526
hip/pelvis, 395-402
hypothermia, 215-218
iliac apophysitis, 397
Intra-abdominal organs, 368-369
intra-articular, 420-422
intracranial, 204-206
knee, 526-528
ligament, 416-420
lightning, 502
long thoracic nerve, 300
lower extremity, 395-470
lumbar spine, 566-570
maxillofacial, 245-249
median nerve, 327-329
mouth, 270-272
musculocutaneous nerve, 300
musculoskeletal, 6
musculoskeletal overuse, 230
myositis ossificans traumatic, 403-404
neck, 210, 237-280, 514-516
nerve, 326-328
neurapraxia, 208-209
orthopedic, 203-204
osteitis pubis, 397
pelvis, 524-526
plica, 421
posterior compartment, 308
posterior tibial tendon, 447
precluding participation, 224
predicting, 105
prevention, 171-189
preventive impact areas, 175-181
proximal interphalangeal joint (PIP), 333-334
proximal phalanx, 333
psychological treatment, 77-78

quadriceps muscle, 404-405
radiology, 509-563
rate data, 64-68
reasons for increase, 3-4
rehabilitation, 182-184, 537-572
rotator cuff, 293-296, 562-564
scalp, 238
shoulder, 281-302, 516-518
skin, 471-482
spinal accessor nerve, 300-301
spine, 564-566
sternoclavicular, 286-287
subdural hematoma, 206
superscapular nerve, 300
thorax, 343-394
throat, 272-274
throwing, 304-312
thumb, 329-330
toe, 528-534
trainer responsibilities, 191-192
ulnar nerve, 327
upper arm, 302
upper extremity, 281-342
upper leg, 403-405
ureter, 382-383
volar plate, 335
wrist, 314-329, 519-523
Injury rates, 3-4
Inner ear barotrauma, 497
Insect allergies, 481
Instep bruise, 459
Institutions, sports medicine fellowship programs, 588
Intercurrent PPPE form, 111-112
Interdisciplinary approach, 5-6
Intermetatarsal neuroma injury, 460-461
International Olympic Committee, (IOC), 43, 60
  approved medication, EIA, 365
Intertrigo, 480
Intervertebral disc injuries, 373-375
Intra-abdominal organ injuries, 368-369
  kidney, 369
  liver, 369
  mesentary, 369
  pancreas, 368-369
  ruptured hollow viscus, 369
  spleen, 368
Intra-articular injury, 420-422
Intracranial injury, 204-206
Intracranial lesions, 242-243
Intraocular foreign bodies, 261
Ionophoresis, 544-545
Iron, 36
Iron deficiency anemia, 484
Irritant skin reactions, causes, 480
Ischial bursitis, 400
Isometric exercises, blood pressure, 351


Javelin
  low back pain, 371
  shoulder injury, 281
Jogging
  death, 359
  low back pain, 371

pregnancy training recommendations, 131
Joint capsule injury, 292
Joints
    carpal, 330-331
    Distal interphalangeal (DIP), 336
    distal radio-ulnar, 324-325
    glenohumeral, 561-562
    metacarpal, 330-332
Justification for study, 3-5

Kayaking
    elbow injury, 303
    hypothermia, 492
Kidney injuries, 369, 381-382
    heavy lifting, 382
    traumatic, 381-382
Knee
    anatomy, 406-407
    epidemiology, 406
    examination form, 467
Knee injuries
    acute/chronic knee pathology diagnosis, 406
    age/injury diagnosis, 406
    anterior cruciate ligament, 419
    biomechanical alignment, 410
    bipartite patella, 422
    bony tissue palpation, 410
    capsule, 416-420
    discoid meniscus, 422
    epiphyseal fracture, 422
    history, 407-409
    iliotibial band syndrome, 423
    intra-articular, 420-422
    joint fluid aspiration, 414
    knee extensor mechanism, 415-416
    lateral collateral ligament, 420
    ligament, 416, 420, 423
    medial collateral ligament sprain, 416-417
    meniscal, 423
    meniscus, 420-421
    Osgood Schlatters disease, 422
    osteochondral fracture, 416
    osteochondritis dessicans, 421-422
    overuse, 423
    partial tears, 419
    patella-femoral dysfunction, 423
    patellar fracture, 416
    patellar tendinitis, 422-423
    pes anserine tendinitis/bursitis, 424
    physical exam, 410-415
    plica, 421
    posterior cruciate ligament, 419-420
    prepatellar bursitis (housemaid's knee), 415
    radiographic studies, 414-415
    radiology, 526-528
    range of motion, 410
    reactive synovitis, 421-422
    rehabilitation protocol, 554-559
    sitting position exam, 410
    soft tissue palpation, 410
    subluxating/dislocating patella, 415-416
    supine position exam, 411-414
    suprapatellar bursitis, 416

symptoms, 409-410
Wisconsin program, 417-418

Lacerations, 227-228
    ear, 264
    eyelid, 259
    facial, 246
    nose, 268
    scalp, 238
    tongue, 270-271
Lacrosse
    hematuria, 383
    mandatory equipment, 179
Laryngeal fracture, 210-211
Laryngeo-tracheal injury, 272-274
Laryngospasm, 274
Lateral collateral ligament sprain, 420
    rehabilitation, 554-555
Lateral condyle fracture, 313-314
Lateral epicondylitis (tennis elbow), 306-307
Lateral inversion sprain, 436-438
Lateral ligament ankle sprain, rehabilitation protocol, 559-560
Lawsuits, avoiding, 7-8
Laxative abuse, 55
LeFort fracture, 248
Legal aspects, 6-8
Legg-Calve'-Perthes disease, 402
Ligament injury, 416-420, 423
Ligaments, ankle, 434
Light Intensity Training (LIT), 231
    program, 119-120
Lightning injuries, 502
Literature, sports medicine, 578-585
Liver injury, 369
Local anesthesia, 46
Local sports medicine network, 573-588
Long thoracic nerve injury, 300
Low back pain (LBP), 370-374
    athletics, 372
    disorders, 370
    prevention, 380
    treatment, 376-377
Lower extremity injury, 395-470
Lower leg, anatomy, 424-425
Lower leg injuries
    achilles tendon, 428-432
    acute fracture, 432-433
    compartment syndrome, 428
    contusions, 425-427
    retrocalcaneal bursitis, 432
    shinsplints, 427
    stress fractures, 427-428
    superficial posterior compartment strain, 428
Lumbar spine injury, rehabilitation protocol, 566-570

Macrotrauma, 224
Magnetic resonance imaging (MRI), 510
Malignant hyperthermia, 489-490
Mandibular
    dislocation, 249

fracture, 248-249
Manipulation, 545
Marathon runners, death, 359
Marfan's syndrome, 349
Martial arts athletes, low back pain, 371
Massage, 545
Maxillofacial injuries, 245-249
Meals, pregame, 38
Measles, 233
Mechanical back pain, 377
Medial collateral ligament sprain, 416-417
Medial epicondyle fracture, 314
Medial epicondylitis, 307-308
Medial lateral ligament sprain, rehabilitation protocol, 554-555
Medial midfoot pain, 456-457
Median nerve injury, 327-329
    carpal tunnel syndrome, 327
Medical director, distance running, 185
Medical equipment, competition site, 192-193
Medical facilities, distance running, 186, 188-189
Medical history
    form, 106
    preparticipation screening, 96-97
Medical student, 3
Medical support, distance running, 186
Medications, 44-47
    adrenal corticosteroids, 45
    anabolic steroids, 45-46
    anti-depressants, 46-47
    anti-inflammatory, 232
    beta blockers, 47, 352, 357
    cardiopulmonary, 197
    dimethylsulfoxide, 47
    diuretics, 46
    growth hormone, 46
    local anesthesia, 46
    nonsteroidal anti-inflammatory, 47
    pain, 46
    recreational drugs, 47
    rehabilitation, 546-547
    sedatives, 46-47
    stimulants, 46
    sunscreens/sunblockers, 474
    tranquilizers, 46-47
    vitamins, 47
Meniscus injury, 420-421
Menstrual cycle effects, 125-127
Mental retardation, 164-165, 234
Mesentery injury, 369
Metabolic specificity, 113-115
Metacarpal joint, 330-332
Metatarsal stress fracture, 460
Metropolitan Life Insurance tables, 28
Microtrauma, 224
Middle phalanx fracture, 335-336
Midfoot
    anatomical variants, 457-459
    anatomy, 455-456
Midfoot injuries
    medial pain, 456-457
    Morton's foot, 459
    pes cavus, 458-459
    pes planus (flat foot), 457-458
    spring ligament sprain, 456
    tarsal tunnel syndrome, 456-457

Migraine seizures, 242
Miliaria, 474-475
Minerals, 33-34
Miscarriage, 129
Mitral valve prolapse (MVP), 349-350
Molluscum contagiosum, 478
Mononucleosis, 232-233
Morton's foot, 459
Mouth injuries, 270-272
  abscessed tooth, 271
  jaw, 271
  laryngospasm, 274
  mouth protectors, 271-272
  prevention, 271-272
  teeth, 270
  temporo-mandibular joint, 271
  tongue laceration, 270-271
  Vincent's stomatitis, 271
  wisdom tooth, 271
Mouth protectors, 271-272
Muscle building myths, 56
Muscle cramp, abdominal wall injuries, 368
Muscle fatigue, chest wall, 345
Muscle strength/endurance, rehabilitation, 547-548
Muscle strength tests, handicapped athletes, 166
Muscles
  ankle, 434
  deltoid, 283
  hamstring, 404-405
  infraspinatus, 284, 294
  quadriceps, 404-405
  shoulder, 283-284
  subscapularis, 284, 294
  supraspinatus, 283, 294
  teres minor, 284, 294
Muscular strain, chest wall, 344-346
Muscular strength, exercise prescription, 147-149
Musculocutaneous nerve injury, 300
Musculoskeletal
  disorders, 233-234
  injury, 6
  overuse injuries, 230
  problems, 162-164
  pregnancy effects, 128
Myocarditis, 232
Myoglobinuria, 387
Myostis ossificans, 227
  traumatic, 403-404
  upper arm, 302

National Association for Intercollegiate Athletics (NAIA), 65
National Athletic Injury/Illness Reporting System (NAIRS), 64, 67
National Collegiate Athletic Association (NCAA), 65
  Injury Surveillance System (ISS), 67
National Electronic Injury Surveillance System (NEISS), 174
National Federation of State High School Associations (NFSHSA), 65
National Junior College Athletic Association (NJCAA), 65
Navicular fracture, 325-326

Neck injuries, 237-280, 249-253
  anatomy, 251
  cervical spine assessment, 252
  conscious athlete assessment, 252
  epidemiology, 250-251
  history/physical exam, 251
  prevention, 251
  radiology, 514-516
  strengthening program, 251-253
  treatment protocol, 210
  unconscious athlete assessment, 252
Neck sprain, 298
Negligence, 6-7
Nerve injury, 326-328
Nerve root impingement, 254-255
  treatment, 256
Neurapraxia, 208-209
Neurological exam, 208
Nitric oxide, air pollution, 502
Nitrogen necrosis, 499
Non-athletes, conditioning/training programs, 113-149
Non-pharmacologic performance aids, 47-48
Non-steroidal anti-inflammatory drugs (NSAID), 47, 308, 345, 396-397
  associated nephrotoxicity, 387
Normal stress/abnormal tissue, 228
Nose injuries, 267-270
  abrasions, 267-268
  contusions, 267-268
  epistaxis, 269-270
  fracture, 268-269
  lacerations, 268
Nutrition, 6, 31-42
  energy needs, 31
  myths, 38-40, 56-57

Oarsmen, low back pain, 371
Obligatory athletes, 38
Officiating, injury prevention, 180
Older athlete training program, 132-134
Olecranon bursitis
  elbow injury, 308-309
  treatment, 309
On-site emergencies
  airway occlusion, 210
  aspiration, 210
  cervical fractures, 209-210
  cervical spine injury, 206-210
  concussions, 204-206
  dislocations, 209-210
  epidural hematoma, 206
  heat exhaustion, 215
  heat injuries, 211-215
  heat stroke, 215
  heat syncope, 214
  hypothermia, 215-218
  intracranial injury, 204-206
  laryngeal fracture, 210-211
  management of, 203-222
  neurapraxia, 208-209
  orthopedic, 203-204
  respiratory obstruction, 210-211
  subdural hematoma, 206
Onchonychia, 464
Oncology, 487

Optic neuritis, 262
Orbital blowout fracture, 247-248
Organization, scholastic athletic programs, 84
OS supranaviculare, 459
Osgood Schlatters disease, 422
Osteitis pubis injury, 397
Osteochondral fracture, 416, 442-443
Osteochondritis dessicans, 308, 421-422
Osteochondrosis metatarsal head (Freberg's Infarction), 461
Osteoporosis, female athletes, 127
Otitis externa (swimmer's ear), 265-267
Otitis media, 267
Otosclerosis, 267
Overload, training/conditioning programs, 114
Ozone, air pollution, 501


P.R.I.C.E. (protection, rest, ice, compression, elevation), 538
Pain medications, 46
Pain, psychological treatment, 77-78
Painful heel, 451-455
Pancreas injury, 368-369
Paraplegic athletes, 165-166
Parental selection guide, youth sports programs, 87
Paronychia infection, 338
Patella-femoral dysfunction, 423
  rehabilitation protocol, 555-557
Patella, subluxating/dislocating, 415-416
Patellar fracture, 416
Patellar tendinitis, 422-423
Patient, physical fitness education, 589-595
Pectoralis major, rupture, 345-346
Pediatric exercise guidelines, 219-220
Pediculosis pubis (crab louse), 479
Pelvis injury, radiology, 524-526
Penile injuries, 389-390
Percent of fat tables, 50-53
Performance aids, non-pharmacologic, 47-48
Performance myths, 56-57
Perinasal sinuses, 497-498
Peroneal tendinitis, 445-446
Peroneal tendon
  rupture, 446
  subluxation/dislocation, 446
Pes anserine tendinitis/bursitis, 424
Pes cavus, 458-459
Pes planus (flat foot), 457-458
Pharmacologic agents, exercise-induced asthma (EIA), 366
Pharmacology, 43-48
Philosophy, scholastic athletic programs, 84
Phonophoresis, 545
Photo protection, 474
Photosensitivity, 474
Phototrauma, 474
Physical examinations
  contents of, 98-102
  form, 107, 110

preparticipation screening, 91
Physical fitness, patient/ community education, 589-595
Physical rehabilitation, 5
Physician, sports event checklist, 279
Physiology, 5-6
  exercise, 15-27
Plain film x-ray, 509
Plantar calcaneal pain, 451-453
Plantar keratoses, 481
Playing conditions, injury prevention, 177-181
Plica injury, 421
Pneumothorax, 212-213, 363
Post-concussion syndrome, 244-245
Post-pactum exercises, 132
Post-pubescent athlete training program, 122-123
Post-traumatic seizures, 245
Posterior calcaneal pain, 453
Posterior compartment injury, 308
Posterior cruciate ligament sprain, 419-420
Posterior tibial tendon injury, 447
Pregame meal, 38
Pregnancy
  athlete, 40-42
  cardiovascular system, 128
  exercise during, 127-132
  fetal hypoxia, 129
  fetal weight, 129
  hyperthermia, 129
  musculoskeletal changes, 128
  physiological changes, 128
  potential risks, 128-129
  premature delivery/miscarriage, 129
  respiratory system, 128
  training recommendations, 129-132
  weight gain effects, 128
Premature atrial complexes (PAC) 357
Premature delivery, 129
Premature ventricular contractions (PVC), 356, 358
Preparticipation screening, 91-112
  assessment, 103-105
  clearance/recommendations form, 107
  contemplated exercise program, 93
  content, 96-103
  disqualifying conditions, 104
  essentials, 91-92
  frequency, 94-96
  implementation, 94
  initial PPPE form, 108-109
  injury prediction, 105
  intercurrent PPPE form, 111-112
  medical history, 96-97
  medical history form, 106
  motivation, 93-94
  objectives, 92
  physical examination form, 107, 110
  physical examinations, 91, 98-102
  prospective athletes, 92-93
  timing, 96
Prepatellar bursitis (housemaid's knee), 415
Prepubescent athlete training program, 120-122
Primary care physician, 3
  competition responsibilities, 193-195
  field protocol, 193-194

fitness education, 589-591
lifestyle influences, 594-595
national resources, 573-574
patient motivation, 592-594
preparticipation physical examinations, 91
public awareness, 591-592
sports psychology, 75-87
sportsmedicine bag, 197
Primary care residents, minimal competencies, 11-13
Primary care sports medicine, 3-6
Principles, scholastic athletic programs, 84
Progressive functional rehabilitation, 537
Progressive Resistance Exercises (P.R.E.), 345
Prostatitis, 390
Protein, 31-32
Proteinuria, 385-387
Protocols, injury rehabilitation, 554-570
Proximal interphalangeal joint (PIP) injury, 333-334
Proximal phalanx injury, 333
Pseudo-boutonniere deformity, 334-335
Pseudoanemia, 484
Pseudofolliculitis, 476
Psychological assessment, 80
Psychological support, rehabilitation, 552
Psychologist, role of, 79-80
Psychology, sports, 6, 75-87
Pulmonary disease, 158-159
  exercise-induced asthma (EIA), 363-367
  foreign body aspiration, 363
  hyperventilation syndrome, 362-363
  illnesses, 362-367
  medical treatment, 158-159
  pneumothorax, 363
  testing protocols, 159
  training protocols, 159
Pyriformis syndrome, 400


QRS pattern, 357
Quick energy myths, 56


R.I.C.E. regimen (rest, ice, compression, elevate), 227, 416
Race organization, distance running, 185-186
Race walking, osteitis pubis, 397
Racket sports
  achilles tendon rupture, 441
  elbow injury, 303
  eye injury, 257-258
  face injury prevention, 249
  rotator cuff injury, 294
  shoulder injury, 281
Racquetball, carpal tunnel syndrome, 327-328
Radial styloid fracture, 323
Radiation, heat loss, 490-491

Radiological evaluation, back injuries, 379
Radiology, 509-536
  abdomen, 523
  ankle, 528
  back, 523
  chest, 523
  computed x-ray tomography (CT), 509-510
  elbow injury, 518-519
  face injury, 513-514
  finger injury, 519-523
  foot, 528-534
  fractures, 510-512
  hand injury, 519-523
  head injury, 512-513
  hip, 524-526
  knee, 526-528
  magnetic resonance imaging (MRI), 510
  neck injury, 514-516
  pelvis, 524-526
  radionuclide scanning, 509
  shoulder injury, 516-518
  toe, 528-534
  ultrasound, 510
  wrist injury, 519-523
Radionuclide scanning, 509
Rafting, hypothermia, 492
Rating for perceived exertion (RPE), 146
Reactive synovitis, 421-422
Recommended Dietary Allowances (RDA), 33-36
Rectus muscle strain, 367-368
Recurrent uri/tonsillitis, 272
Rehabilitation, 537-572
  balance/agility, 551
  balanced strength, 549-550
  bracing, 552
  cardiovascular fitness, 550-551
  contrast baths, 543-544
  cryotherapy, 541-542
  early mobilization, 539-541
  engrams, 553-554
  exercise sequence, 549
  flexibility, 551
  functional progressive, 552-554
  heat therapy, 542-543
  injury, 182-184
  injury prevention principles, 538
  manipulation, 545
  massage, 545
  medications, 546-547
  muscle flexibility maintenance, 549-550
  muscle strength/endurance, 547-550
  P.R.I.C.E. protocol, 538-539
  phases, 553
  prevention, 538
  principles, 538
  progressive functional, 537
  protocols, 554-570
  psychological support, 552
  range of motion restoration, 539-541
  taping, 552
  therapeutic modalities, 541-544
  tissue mobilization, 545
  traction, 545-546
  training specificity, 549
Renal abnormalities, 385

Respiratory obstruction, 210-211
Respiratory system, pregnancy effects, 128
Retinal detachment, 262
Retrocalcaneal, 455
Retrocalcaneal bursitis, 432
Reversibility, training/conditioning programs, 114
Rheumatic mitral stenosis, 348
Rheumatoid arthritis, 162-163
Rib fractures, 346-347
   treatment, 347
Rifle, mandatory equipment, 179
Ringworm, 477
Rolando's fracture, 332
Role of team physician vs role of fan, 8
Rotator cuff, functional anatomy, 294
Rotator cuff injuries, 293-296
   classification, 295
   history, 294-296
   impingement, 294
   physical exam, 294-296
   rehabilitation protocol, 562-564
Rowing
   hematuria, 383
   proteinuria, 385
Rugby
   contusions, 425-427
   neck injury, 250
Rule enforcement, injury prevention, 180
Runner's nipple, 343
Runners, compulsive, 38
Running
   heat illness risk, 490
   hamstring muscle strain, 404-405
   hematuria, 383
   hot weather guidelines, 221-222
   hypothermia, 492
   iliac apophysitis injury, 397
   knee injury, 407
   medial collateral ligament sprain, 416
   osteitis pubis injury, 397
   patellar tendinitis, 423
   proteinuria, 385
   quadriceps muscle strain, 404-405
Ruptures
   hollow viscus, 369
   Illiopsoas muscle, 368
   pectoralis major, 345-346

Scabies, 479
Scalp injury, 238
Scapulothoracic joint, 282
Scheuermann's disease, 372
Scholastic athletic programs
   administration, 84
   considerations, 84-86
   education, 85-86
   equipment, 85
   event coverage, 85
   facilities, 85
   organization, 84
   philosophy, 84
   principles, 84
   staff, 84-85
Schools, equipment responsibilities, 199-200

Scoliosis, 163-164
Screening, preparticipation, 91-112
Scrotal masses, 389
Scuba diving, pregnancy training recommendations, 131
Secondary drowning, 495
Sedatives, 46-47
Sedentary adults
   aerobic activities, 138-140
   duration, 136
   exercise intensity, 135-136
   exercise mode, 137-138
   frequency, 136-137
   monitoring exercise, 140
   progression, 140
   training programs, 134-141
Seizures, post-traumatic, 245
Sensory handicapped athletes, 168
Septal defects, 350
Sesamoid disorders, 462
Sesamoid fracture, 462
Sesamoiditis, 462
Shinsplints, 427
Shivering, heat gain, 491
Shoulder injuries
   acceleration phase, 293
   acromioclavicular separation, 289-290
   adhesive capsulitis, 297
   adolescent, 297-298
   anatomy, 281-283
   anterior dislocations, 291-292
   biceps tendon, 296-301
   biomechanics, 281-283
   brachial plexus, 298-300
   burner/stinger phenomenon, 298
   clavicular fractures, 287-289
   cocking/recovery phase, 293
   diagnostic injections, 286
   epidemiology, 281
   epiphyseal, 297-298
   etiology, 290-291
   follow-through phase, 293
   fracture, 292
   generic examination, 284
   glenohumeral subluxation/ dislocation, 290-291
   hyperabduction (Wright's syndrome), 301-302
   joint capsule, 292
   neck sprain, 298
   neurovascular, 292
   on-field examination, 288
   overuse, 292-293
   physical examination, 284-285
   radiologic evaluation, 291
   radiology, 516-518
   reduction, 291-292
   rehabilitation, 292
   rehabilitation protocol, 560-564
   rotator cuff, 293-296
   rotator cuff tear, 292
   signs, 291
   sternoclavicular, 286-287
   symptoms, 291
   tests, 285-286
   treatment, 291-292
   types of, 286-290
Shoulders
   articulations, 282-283
   bursae, 283

   instability classifications, 290
   muscle actions, 287
   muscles, 283-284
   muscular function testing, 340-341
   planes of motion, 282
Sickle cell anemia, 485
Sinus fracture, 248
Sinus node functions, disturbances, 357
Skiing
   achilles tendon rupture, 441
   acute mountain sickness (AMS), 500-501
   hypothermia, 492
   knee injury, 407
   low back pain, 371
   meniscus tear, 421
   peroneal tendon injury, 444-445
   posterior cruciate ligament sprain, 419
   shoulder injury, 281
Skin illness, 471-482
   acne, 475-476
Skin infections, 233
   bacterial, 476
   fungal, 476-477
Skin injuries, 471-482
   abrasions, 471-472
   cold-induced, 472-473
   cold urticaria, 473
   friction blisters, 471-472
   frostbite, 472-473
   heat-induced, 473-475
   miliaria, 474-475
   photo protection, 474
   photosensitivity, 474
   phototrauma, 474
   solar urticaria, 475
   sunburn, 473-474
Skull fractures, 238-239
Slipped capital femoral epiphysis (SCFE), 164, 402
Smoking, 502
Snow blindness, 261
Soccer
   contusions, 425-427
   groin strain, 400-401
   knee injury, 407
   lateral inversion sprain, 436-437
   mandatory equipment, 179
   osteitis pubis injury, 397
   plica injury, 421
Softball, face injury prevention, 249
Solar plexus, blows to, 368
Solar urticaria, 475
Spelunking, hypothermia, 492
Spermatic cord torsion, 388-389
Spinal accessory nerve injury, 300-301
Spine injuries
   overuse diagnostic categories, 565
   rehabilitation protocol, 564-566
Spleen injury, 368
Spondylolisthesis, 378-379
   back injuries, 371-372
Spondylolysis, 377-378
Sports anemia, 484
Sports brassiere, 344
Sports environment
   balancing competition, 180
   coaching techniques, 180-181
   equipment, 175-177

playing conditions, 177-181
  rule enforcement/officiating, 180
  spectator initiated obstacles, 177-180
Sports injuries, radiology, 509-536
Sports injury rate data, 64-68
  applications of, 70-71
  collection systems, 67-72
  literature on, 66-67
  uses of, 64-66
Sports medicine fellowship programs, 588
Sports medicine literature
  assessing, 578-585
  chi-square test, 581
  data analysis, 581
  design flaws, 584-585
  journals, 587
  question specification, 579-580
  reasearch design, 580-581
  results interpretation, 582-583
  statistical significance, 583-584
  subject selection, 580
  validity, 583
  variables, 579
Sports medicine physician's bag, 197
Sports medicine related organizations, 586
Sports medicne rotation, 10-11
Sports medicine team, local resources, 574-578
Sports physician, performance facilitating, 78-79
Sports psychologist, 79-80
Sports psychology, 75-87
  future of, 80
  importance of, 75-76
  injury treatment, 77-78
  performance factors, 76-77
Sports, violence in, 82
Sprains, 226-227
  ankle, 436-439
  anterior cruciate ligament, 419
  hand injury, 329
  lateral collateral ligament, 420, 554-555
  lateral inversion, 436-438
  lateral ligament, 559-560
  medial collateral ligament, 416-417
  medial eversion, 438-439
  medial lateral ligament, 554-555
  neck, 298
  posterior cruciate ligament, 419-420
  spring ligament, 456
  wrist, 324
Staff, scholastic athletic programs, 84-85
Staphylococcus aureus, 402
Sternoclavicular injury, 286-287
Sternoclavicular joint, 383
Sternum fractures, 347
Stimulants, 46
Stinger, shoulder injury, 298
Stings, marine, 499-500
Strains, 226-227
  groin, 400-401
  hamstring muscle, 404-405
  hand injury, 329
  quadriceps muscle, 404-405
  superficial posterior compartment, 428

Strength, female athletes, 124-125
Strength training, methods, 547
Stress fractures, lower leg, 427-428
Subdural hematoma, 206, 243-244
Subdural hemorrhage, 243-244
Subglial hematoma, 238
Subscapularis muscle, 284, 294
Substrate phosphocreatine (PC), 113
Subungual hematoma, 337, 464
Sudden unexpected death (SUD), 359-360
  causes, 360, 362
  etiology, 359-360
Sulfur oxides, air pollution, 501-502
Sunburn, 473-474
Sunscreens, 474
Superficial posterior compartment strain, 428
Superscapular nerve injury, 300
Supracondylar fracture
  biomechanics, 312
  diagnostic aids, 312-313
  elbow injury, 312
  return to competition, 313
  signs/symptoms, 312
  treatment, 312-313
Suprahumeral joint, 282
Suprapatellar bursitis, 416
Supraspinatus muscle, 283, 294
Supraventricular arrhythmias, 356
Supraventricular tachycardia, 357
Surgery, chronic injury, 232
Surveillance, distance running, 189
Sweating, heat loss, 491
Swimming
  hypothermia, 492
  knee injury, 407
  mandatory equipment, 179
  medial collateral ligament sprain, 416
  pregnancy training recommendations, 131
  rotator cuff injury, 294


Taping, rehabilitation, 552
Tarsal tunnel syndrome, 447
Teeth, injuries, 270
Temperature
  wet-bulb, 217
  wet bulb globe, 487
Temporo-mandibular joint injury, 271
Tendon injury, ankle, 444-447
Tendon sheath tenosynovitis infection, 338
Tennis elbow, 306-307
Tennis
  lateral epicondylitis, 306-307
  low back pain, 371
  medial epicondylitis, 307-308
Tension pneumothorax, 213
Tensor fascia latae syndrome (ITB), 398-399
Teres minor muscle, 284, 294
Testicle injuries, 387-388
Testing, cybex, 181-182
Testing programs, handicapped athletes, 166
Therapeutic modalities
  contrast baths, 543-544

  cryotherapy, 541-542
  heat therapy, 542-543
Therapy, electrical impulse, 232
Thermoregulation, distance running, 187
Thigh contusion, 403
Thorax, injury, 343-394
Throat injuries, 272-274
  laryngeo-tracheal, 272-274
  recurrent uri/tonsillitis, 272
Thrombocytopenia, 484-485
Throwing, biomechanics, 304
Throwing injuries, 304-312
  extensor overload, 306
  hyperextension, 308
  lateral compression, 305
  lateral epicondylitis (tennis elbow), 306-307
  medial epicondylitis, 307-308
  medial tendon overload, 304-305
  olecranon bursitis, 308-309
  osteochondritis dessicans, 308
Thumb injury, 329-330
Tinea corporis, 477
Tinea cruris, 477
Tinea pedes, 477
Tinea versicolor, 476-477
Tissue mobilization, 545
Toe injury, radiology, 528-534
Toes, 463-464
Tongue, lacerations, 270-271
Track
  groin strain, 400-401
  knee injury, 407
  mandatory equipment, 179
  proteinuria, 385
Traction, 545-546
Trainer
  equipment, 198-200
  injury responsibility, 191-192
Training, 19-27
  chronic obstructive pulmonary disease protocols, 159
  energy systems, 21-27
  high altitude, 48
  principles of, 20
  specificity, 549
  strength, 547
  theoretical basis, 20-21
  visual-motor behavior rehearsal (VMBR), 78
  weight gain, 37-38
  weight loss, 37
Training programs
  athletes/non-athletes, 113-149
  components of, 118-120
  cool-down, 119
  exercise prescription, 115-118
  female athletes, 123-132
  handicapped athletes, 166
  light intensity training (LIT), 119-120
  older athletes, 132-134
  preconditioning, 118
  principles of, 114
  progression, 119
  return from injury, 119
  sedentary adults, 134-141
  warm-up, 118-119
  young athletes, 120-123
Tranquilizers, 46-47

Transcutaneous nerve stimulation (TENS), 544
Trekking, acute mountain sickness (AMS), 500-501
Turf toe, 463
Tympanic membrane rupture, 267

Ulnar nerve injuries, 327
  blunt trauma, 327
  bowler's thumb, 327
  handlebar palsy, 327
Ulnar styloid fracture, 324
Ultrasound, 28, 510
Underwater sports
  barotrauma, 496-498
  decompression sickness (bends), 499
  ear canal squeeze, 496
  extrinsic factors, 496-498
  gastrointestinal (aerogastralgia), 498
  hazardous marine stings/bites, 499-500
  hyperventilation syndrome, 496
  inner ear barotrauma, 497
  intrinsic factors, 496
  middle ear squeeze, 497
  nitrogen necrosis, 499
  perinasal sinuses, 497-498
  pulmonary overpressurization, 498
  squeeze syndromes, 496
Upper arm injuries, 302
  blocker's (tackler's) exostosis, 302
  contusion, 302
  hematoma, 302
  myositis ossificans, 302
Upper extremity injury, 281-342
  motor testing, 320
Upper leg injuries, 403-405
  anatomical considerations, 403
  femur fracture, 405
  hamstring muscle strains, 404-405
  myositis ossificans traumatica, 403-404
  quadriceps muscle strains, 404-405
  thigh contusion, 403
Ureter injuries, 382-383
Urethral injuries, 389-390
Urethritis, 390
Urinary incontinence, 383


Valvular abnormalities, 349
Valvular heart disease, 348-350
Vasomotor adjustment, controlling heat loss, 490-491
Vasovagal syncope, 242
Venereal warts, 390
Ventricular arrhythmias, 356
  exercise induced, 356-357
Ventricular pre-excitation, 357-358
Ventricular tachycardia, 358
Verrucae (warts), 478-479
Vertebral fractures, 372-373
Vincent's stomatitis, 271
Viral infections, 477-479
Viral influenza (Colds), 486-487
Viscus, ruptured hollow, 369
Vision, evaluation, 263
Visual-motor behavior rehearsal (VMBR) training, 78
Vitamins, 33-34, 47
Volar plate injury, 335
Volleyball
  achilles tendon rupture, 441
  elbow injury, 303
  hip pointer, 395
  patellar tendinitis, 423
  shoulder injury, 281
Vomiting, 55


Warm-up exercises, 48
Warts, 463, 478-479
Water, 29-30, 37
Water intoxication, 31
Water polo, mandatory equipment, 179
Water sports
  neck injury, 251
  shoulder injury, 281
Waterskiing, elbow injury, 303
Weight gain, pregnancy effects, 128
Weight-lifting
  low back pain, 371
  pregnancy training recommendations, 131
  ruptures, 345
Weight loss, hazardous complications, 55
Weight training, elbow injury, 303
Welfare of the athlete
  vs welfare of the family, 8
  vs welfare of the team, 8
  vs wishes of the athlete, 8
Wet bulb globe temperature (WBGT), 487
Wet bulb temperature, 217
Wet drowning, 494-495
Wheelchair athletes, 165-166
Wheelchair tests, 166
Winter flu, 233
Wisconsin program, 417-418
Wolff-Parkinson White Syndrome (WPW), 357-358
Wounds, 233
Wrestling
  cervical spine injury, 254
  heat illness risk, 490
  knee injury, 407
  lateral collateral ligament sprain, 420
  mandatory equipment, 180
  medial collateral ligament sprain, 416
  meniscus tear, 421
  neck injury, 251
  prepatellar bursitis, 415
  shoulder injury, 281
  suprapatellar bursitis, 416
Wrist injuries, 314-329
  carpal bones, 325
  diagnostic imaging, 320-321
  dislocations, 324-325
  distal radio-ulnar joint, 324-325
  epidemiology, 314-315
  fractures, 325-326
  hook of the hamate and pisiform, 326
  navicular fracture, 325-326
  perspective, 321-322
  physical examination, 317-321
  radiology, 519-523
  scaphoid dislocation, 325
  scaphoid fracture, 325-326
  sprains, 324
Wrists
  anatomy, 315-317
  motor test, 320
  neurologic test, 319
  palpation, 317
  range of motion test, 318-319
  sensory test, 319
  tests, 317-318


X-rays, plain film, 509


Youth sports programs, parental selection guide, 87


Zygoma fracture, 247